$49.50

2002 NATIONAL RENOVATION & INSURANCE REPAIR ESTIMATOR

with data from the Rutlidge Institute

Ri RUTLIDGE institute

edited by Jonathan Russell

Includes inside the back cover:

- An estimating CD with all the costs in this book, plus,
- An estimating program that makes it easy to use these costs,
- An interactive video guide to the National Estimator program,
- A program that converts your estimates into invoices,
- A program that exports your estimates to QuickBooks Pro.

The Show Me video guide to National Estimator starts a few seconds after you insert the CD in your CD-ROM drive.

Craftsman Book Company
6058 Corte del Cedro / P.O. Box 6500 / Carlsbad, CA 92018

 ISBN 1-57218-112-5 Published October 2001 for the year 2002.

contents

about this book

NEW IN 2002

Fluctuating energy prices threaten to have an increasing impact on the cost of supplies, but at least some of the additional costs will be absorbed by manufactureres, who—at least in some cases—are struggling to stay competitive.

As was true in 1999 and 2001, contractors still report difficulty finding skilled workers and spot material shortages still occur, especially during busy times of the year.

A TOOL

This book is a tool and like all tools it can be misused. It is an excellent tool for the renovation and repair professional. It is not a substitute for experience, skill, and knowledge.

Prices in this book are based on research of actual jobs and successful estimates. They represent an average of the typical conditions.

Estimators should compare the conditions described in this book with actual conditions on site and adjust the price accordingly.

UNIQUE TO RENOVATION AND REPAIR WORK

This book is compiled specifically for the unique problems and conditions found in renovation and repair work. *It is not a new construction cost book.*

Renovation and repair work involve different circumstances than those found in new construction.

For example, the renovation or repair professional must work around existing conditions including home contents, access problems, out-of-plumb or out-of-square buildings, outdated materials, and existing conditions that violate current building codes.

New-construction professionals have the luxury of placing items in a logical order, but the renovation, remodel, or repair professional must deal with conditions as they find them.

This means that joists have to be replaced in an existing floor system, paint has to be applied in a room where stain-grade base and carpeting are already installed, structures may have to be braced, contents have to be moved or worked around, and materials and installation techniques must be matched.

DETERMINING COSTS

All costs in this book are based on typical conditions and typical problems found when remodeling or repairing a structure.

This means a door takes 10 to 15 minutes longer to install than it would in the ideal circumstances found in new construction.

Stairs are more difficult to install around pre-existing walls, wall framing takes longer when walls are typically splicing into existing work, and so on.

Some prices in this book will closely match prices used in new construction. Other prices will reflect the complex conditions found in renovation and repair and will be dramatically different.

rounding

This book rounds hourly wage rates and the material, labor, and equipment components of a unit price.

These prices are rounded to "three significant digits." This means that prices under three digits (including two to the right of the decimal) are not rounded. Prices four digits and larger are rounded to the third digit from the left.

For example:

.23 is not rounded
2.33 is not rounded
23.33 is rounded to **23.30**
233.33 is rounded to **233.00**
2,333.33 is rounded to **2,330.00**
23,333.33 is rounded to **23,300.00**

For example, using this book's stair building prices to estimate stair work in a series of 150 tract homes will result in an estimate that is far too high.

THE ART OF ESTIMATING

Estimating is part art, part science. Estimators must consider many factors, including access, crew productivity, special techniques, special abilities, temperament of the owner, and how busy the company is.

A contractor who is desperate for work will estimate much lower than a contractor who is swamped with work.

All of these factors—and many other similar ones—cannot be included in this or any other price book. They are part of the art of estimating.

The science of estimating, which includes prices, typical techniques, and materials, *is* included in this book.

This book is designed to make the *science* of estimating easier, which allows you to spend much more time focusing on the *art* of estimating, where your skill is crucial to the success of your company.

GENERAL vs. SPECIFIC

It is important to note that the more specific the estimator is, the more accurate the final estimate will be.

For example, when an estimator calculates all electrical costs for a typical home using a square foot cost, it may not be as accurate as if the estimator priced each fixture, outlet, and appliance hook-up.

Since the square foot price is based on a typical installation, it will not be exact for a home that is atypical in any way–for example, one with special outdoor lighting or with an expensive crystal fixture in the entry.

The more specific the item, the more exact the prices. The more general an item, the more assumptions must be made.

To help ensure the accuracy of your estimates we describe any assumptions made when determining general items.

For example, the *Rough Carpentry* chapter contains a square foot price for estimating 2" by 4" wall framing. To help you make sure that this price will work for you, we describe our assumptions: the stud centers, the number of openings, headers, corners, plates, and so forth, that would typically be found in a wall.

In most cases the square foot price will apply, but you will always want to carefully consider items that are more general, and if needed, adjust them to fit the conditions.

In the case above, the estimator may want to use the square-foot price for average fixtures, then add an allowance for the crystal fixture and the outdoor lighting.

TIME AND MATERIAL CHARTS

Almost all chapters include time and material charts at the end. These time and material charts are designed to show you the materials used, waste, labor rates, labor burden costs, and labor productivity.

When materials with a range of sizes appear, only the small and large size are usually listed.

When materials with a range of qualities appear, often only the low and high prices are listed.

These charts are designed to give you accurate detail on the exact prices used.When prices change, this book does not become obsolete. Compare current prices with those used and factor accordingly.

MATERIAL COSTS

National average material costs are compiled from surveys of suppliers throughout the country.

Costs for some materials, such as clay tile, building stone and hardwood, will vary a great deal from region to region.

For example, clay tile plants are located near naturally occurring clay sources. Because clay tiles are heavy, the further the tiles have to be shipped, the more expensive the tiles will be. The user of this book must be aware of local price variations.

Materials commonly found in every city are priced based on local delivery. In most cases this will be delivery no greater than 20 miles away from a local source. However, many rural areas have lumber yards that will deliver to a wider area at no additional charge.

Materials that are not commonly available locally, like hand-carved moldings or historical wallpaper, include shipping costs anywhere in North America. Estimators in Hawaii, Alaska and remote areas of Canada should add for additional shipping costs when applicable.

Material waste is often indicated with the items, but it's always a good idea to check the time and material charts for the exact waste calculated for all the components of an item.

Waste indicates material that is discarded during installation. It does not include waste that occurs when materials are taken to storage and ruined, run over at the job site, spilled, improperly cut, or damaged due to mishandling.

These types of occurrences are kept to a minimum by every good contractor, but will still occur on any job site.

Another common waste issue in renovation and repair is when a contractor must buy a minimum quantity for a small repair. For example, to replace a six-inch section of base, it is necessary to buy a piece of base that is eight-feet long or longer. In these cases, use the minimum price.

Material prices may not be listed with the time and material charts in some chapters. In these chapters little new information would be provided by the materials chart so the space is saved for other information.

For example, a materials chart in the *Appliance* chapter will not provide an estimator with any new information.

The materials component of the unit price for an oven as listed in the main body of the chapter will tell the estimator how much the oven and connections cost.

Relisting these appliances in a materials chart wastes valuable space.

LABOR COSTS

Labor costs are national average rates that usually are consistent with union labor wages.

See the time and material charts for specific costs and labor rates.

Crew labor rates are an average hourly rate for each member of the crew. For example, a masonry crew might consist of a mason, a mason's helper, and a hod carrier.

The hourly rate for this crew is the average cost of all three. In other words, the hourly rate is for 20 minutes work by the mason, 20 minutes work by the mason's helper, and 20 minutes work by the hod carrier.

Separation of labor in renovation and insurance repair work is much more difficult than is separation of labor on large commercial construction projects.

On a typical repair or renovation job a carpenter may participate in demolition, frame walls, set doors, set toilets, install electrical outlets and fixtures, and do a little painting.

In the jobs analyzed for this cost book, well over 40 percent of the demolition work was done by skilled workers. This is because demolition is often selective, requiring a skilled worker to ensure that additional damage does not occur.

Many renovation and repair companies are also relatively small, so skilled workers participate in all phases of construction.

These realities are reflected in the labor costs used in this book. This means that a demolition laborer's hourly rate may seem higher than is normal for an unskilled worker.

The time and material charts show all items that are built into each labor rate.

Some contractors may not provide health insurance or retirement plans to some or all of their workers. Estimators can "back-out" these expenses from the labor costs.

It is critical that estimators examine the Worker's Compensation costs calculated in the wage rates. Some states have Worker's Compensation rates that are double, triple, or even quadruple the national average rates used in this book.

Worker's Compensation rates should be adjusted to match local conditions.

Labor productivity is based on observation of work performed in renovation and repair conditions.

These conditions differ from new construction in many ways, but a few of the most common are:

❶ difficulty matching existing work, ❷ access problems, ❸ materials that must be more carefully shaped and attached than is typical in new construction, ❹ out-of-plumb or out-of-square structures, ❺ reinforcing, ❻ more trips and effort are required to find materials, ❼ much more travel time is required because most jobs will have a relatively small amount of work in some trades, ❽ more vehicles are required by the renovation or repair contractor because many tradespeople are often traveling between jobs, compared to new construction where crews may spend weeks or months on one job, and because crews tend to be smaller and each crew may need a vehicle, ❾ more unexpected problems, and ❿ more restrictions in established neighborhoods.

Labor productivity is based on a clean job site where tools are put away and secured at the end of each day.

Depending on the trade, 20 to 30 minutes per eight hours is allowed for cleanup and putting away tools. Normally skilled workers spend half as much time cleaning up as do unskilled workers.

As is typical in new construction, labor includes unpacking and in some cases unloading materials from a truck on site, some travel to pick up minor materials (e.g. a forgotten tube of caulk, or a forgotten tool), typical breaks, lay-out, planning, discussion, coordination, mobilization (many companies meet at a central location each morning to receive instructions), recording hours (including specific information needed for job costing), occasional correction of mistakes in installation, and so forth.

Supervision is not included in these costs but should not generally be required. This is because each crew includes a skilled tradesperson who normally would not require supervision beyond the normal dispatch and mobilization discussed previously.

EQUIPMENT COSTS

Equipment costs are included only when equipment will be used that is not typically a part of the tools used by the majority of renovation or repair contractors.

For example, each carpenter should have a worm-drive saw, miter box, compressor, nail guns, and so forth. These types of tools are not included in the equipment costs.

However, equipment like cranes, backhoes, concrete saws, and jack hammers are not assumed to be part of the equipment and tools owned by a typical renovation or repair contractor. When these are needed, equipment rates are included in the unit price.

Equipment costs include the typical cost to rent the equipment from a local equipment rental shop. When applicable, they also include fuel or blade costs.

Check each item to determine if it includes delivery to the job site or operator labor. Also be careful to note minimum costs for work where rented equipment is needed.

MARKUP

Prices in this book do not include markup. Insurance repair markup is almost always 20 percent: 10 percent for overhead and 10 percent for profit.

In renovation work on historical structures, markup may be as high as 30 percent, although markup over 20 percent may be "hidden" inside the unit cost. Typical remodeling work markup varies from 15 percent to 25 percent. The most common markup for all types of work is 20 percent.

REGIONAL DIFFERENCES

Construction techniques vary from region to region. Different climates and local customs provide a variety of unique regional methods.

For example, in southern Florida it is common to build the first floor of a home from concrete block capped with a grade beam. This method won't be found in Colorado.

Similarly, coral stone walls aren't common in Denver, although they are often seen in Miami.

Slate roofs are common on historical homes and newer custom homes in Philadelphia but are virtually nonexistent in Rapid City.

Homes in the south often include screened porches which aren't nearly so common in the west.

A Georgia home is much more likely to include a series of architecturally-correct columns with Corinthian capitals than is a home in Minnesota.

A Hawaii home may be built entirely from treated wood, when an Arizona home only uses treated lumber when it contacts dirt or concrete.

Many regional materials and techniques are priced in this book. Keep in mind that you should not use these prices if the item is not common to your area.

WE WANT TO HEAR FROM YOU

If you have questions or concerns about this cost book, let us hear from you. Send letters to:

Craftsman Book Company
NRI Editor
P.O. Box 6500
Carlsbad, CA 92018-9974
or send e-mail to:
j_russell@mindspring.com

abbreviations

ABS	Acrylonitrile butadiene styrene
ac	alternating current
bf	board foot
btu	British thermal units
CEC	California Earthquake Code (also see page 83)
cf	cubic foot
cfm	cubic foot per minute
ci	cubic inch
cy	cubic yard
ea	each
FUTA	Federal Unemployment Compensation Act tax
gal	gallon
GFCI	ground fault circuit interrupter
gph	gallon(s) per hour
gpm	gallon(s) per minute
hp	horsepower
hr(s)	hour(s)
IMC	intermediate metal conduit
kd	kiln dried
kv	kilovolt(s)
kva	1,000 volt amps
kw	kilowatt(s)
lb(s)	pound(s)
lf	lineal foot
li	lineal inch
m	one thousand
mbf	1,000 board feet
mBtu	1,000 British thermal units
mh	man hour
mi	mile
mlf	1,000 lineal feet
mm	millimeter(s)
mo	month
mph	miles per hour
msf	1,000 square feet
no.	number
oc	on center
oz	ounce
pr	pair
psi	pounds per square inch
PVC	polyvinyl chloride
qt	quart
R/L	random length(s)
R/W/L	random widths and lengths
RSC	rigid steel conduit
S1S2E	surfaced 1 side, 2 edges
S2S	surfaced 2 sides
S4S	surfaced 4 sides
SBS	styrene butyl styrene
sf	square foot
sh	sheet
si	square inch
sq	100 square feet
st	step
sy	square yard
t&g	tongue-&-groove edge
TV	television
UBC	Uniform Building Code
UL	Underwriters' Laboratory
vlf	vertical lineal foot
wk	week
w/	with
x	by or times

SYMBOLS

/	per
-	through or to
@	at
%	percent
$	U.S. dollars
'	feet
"	inches
#	pound or number

acknowledgements

The editor wishes to gratefully acknowledge the contribution of the following: 18th Century Hardware Co., Inc. • A-Ball Plumbing Supply • A&Y Lumber • American Building Restoration Chemicals, Inc. • American Custom Millwork, Inc. • American Society for Testing and Materials (ASTM) • Anderson Windows • Anthony Lombardo Architectural Paneling Inc. • Anthony Wood Products Incorporated • The Antique Hardware Store • Architectural Components, Inc. • Architectural Woodwork Institute • The Balmer Architectural Art Studios • Bathroom Hardware, Inc. • Bathroom Machineries • Bendix Mouldings, Inc. • Brass Reproductions • Brick Institute of America • C & H Roofing, Inc. • C. G. Girolami & Sons • Caradco • Cataumet Sawmills • CertainTeed • Chadsworth Incorporated • Chelsea Decorative Metal Company • Classic Accents, Inc. • Classic Ceilings • CMW, Inc. • Conant Custom Brass • Conklin Metal Industries • Craftsman Lumber Company • Crown City Hardware Co. • Cumberland General Stores • Cumberland Woodcraft Co. Inc. • Designs in Tile • Dimension Hardwood • Donnell's Clapboard Mill • Driwood Moulding • Eisenhart Wallcoverings • Empire Wood Works • Raymond Enkeboll Designs • James Facenelli, *CGR #28* • Focal Point Architectural Products • Four Seasons Sun Rooms • Futurbilt • Garland • Gates Moore • General Electric Company • George Taylor Specialties Co. • Goodwin Heart Pine Company • Gougeon Brothers, Inc. • Grand Era, Inc. • Granville Manufacturing Company • Groff & Hearne Lumber • Hampton Decor • Harris-Tarkett, Inc. • Heatway • Heritage Vinyl Products • Michael Higuera • Italian Tile Center • J. G. Braun Company • Jeffries Wood Works, Inc. • Jennifer's Glass Works • JGR Enterprises • Johnson Paint Company, Inc. • Joseph Biunno Ltd • Kenmore Industries • King's Chandelier Company • Kraftmaid Cabinetry, Inc. • David Lawrence, illustrator • Lasting Impression Doors • Lehman's • Linoleum City, Inc. • Ludowici-Celadon, Inc. • MCA, Inc. • Millwork Specialties • The Millworks, Inc. • Mountain Lumber Co. • National Oak Flooring Manufacturers Association (NOFMA) • National Wood Flooring Association • Northwest Energy, Inc. • Oak Flooring Institute • The Old Fashioned Milk Paint Company, Inc. • Ole Fashion Things • Omega Too • Pagliacco Turning & Milling • Pella Corporation • Permaglaze • Piedmont Home Products, Inc. • Piedmont Mantel & Millwork Ltd • Pinecrest • Radiantec • The Readybuilt Products Company • Rejuvenation Lamp & Fixture, Co. • Runtal Radiators • The Saltbox • Salvage One Architectural Artifacts • Silverton Victorian Millworks • Stairways Inc. • Steptoe and Wife Antiques Ltd • Stromberg's Architectural Stone • The Structural Slate Co. • Sunbilt • Supradur Manufacturing Corporation • Taylor Door • Touchstone Woodworks • Turncraft • USG Company • Vande Hey's Roofing Tile Co., Inc. • Velux-America Inc. • Vixen Hill Manufacturing Co. • W. F. Norman Corporation • Watercolors, Inc. • WELco • Western Wood Products Association • Williamsburg Blacksmiths • Windy Hill Forge • Wolverine Technologies • The Wood Factory • Worthington Group Ltd •

area modification factors

Construction costs are higher in some cities than in other cities. Use the factors on this and the following page to adapt the costs listed in this book to your job site. Increase or decrease your estimated total project cost by the percentage listed for the appropriate city in this table to find your estimated building cost.

These factors were compiled by comparing the actual construction cost of residential, institutional and commercial buildings in 740 communities throughout the United States. Because these factors are based on completed project costs, they consider all construction cost variables, including labor, equipment and material costs, labor productivity, climate, job conditions and markup.

Use the factor for the nearest or most comparable city. If the city you need is not listed in the table, use the factor for the appropriate state. Note that these location factors are composites of many costs and will not necessarily be accurate when estimating the cost of any particular part of a building. But when used to modify all estimated costs on a job, they should improve the accuracy of your estimates.

Location	Factor
ALABAMA	**-1%**
Anniston	-1%
Birmingham	0%
Coosa	0%
Dothan	-4%
Huntsville	0%
Jasper	0%
Mobile	2%
Montgomery	0%
Sheffield	-4%
Troy	-2%
ALASKA	**74%**
Aleutian Islands	90%
Anchorage	70%
Barrow	77%
Clear	76%
Delta Junction	73%
Fairbanks	75%
Galena	73%
Gambel	73%
Goodnews Bay	75%
Haines	74%
Huslia	74%
King Salmon	86%
Nome	73%
Whittier	73%
ARIZONA	**2%**
Douglas	0%
Flagstaff	5%
Gila Bend	6%
Holbrook	0%
Mesa	0%
Phoenix	0%
Sierra Vista	2%
Tuba City	5%
Tucson	0%
Yuma	1%
ARKANSAS	**-2%**
Arkadelphia	-2%
Blytheville	-2%
Camden	-2%
Conway	-2%
El Dorado	-2%
Fayetteville	0%
Fort Smith	-1%
Harrison	-2%
Hot Springs	-2%
Jonesboro	-2%
Little Rock	2%
Pine Bluff	-1%
CALIFORNIA	**17%**
Alameda	19%
Bakersfield	18%
Barstow	12%
Centerville	15%
Concord	24%
Coronado	13%
Desert Area	13%
El Centro	12%
El Monte	18%
El Toro	13%
Forestville	25%
Fresno	18%
Hanford	18%
Herlong	19%
Jolon	15%
Lathrop	13%
Lawndale	17%
Lompoc	15%
Long Beach	22%
Los Alamitos	22%
Los Angeles	26%
Marysville	12%
Modesto	13%
Mojave	13%
CALIFORNIA *continued*	
Monterey	16%
Novato	25%
Oakland	27%
Oceanside	14%
Oxnard	14%
Paso Robles	18%
Rancho Cordova	13%
Ridgecrest	13%
Rio Vista	20%
Riverbank	13%
Riverside	16%
Sacramento	11%
Salinas	17%
San Bernardino	15%
San Bruno	27%
San Diego	17%
San Francisco	88%
San Jose	24%
San Leandro	25%
San Mateo	25%
San Pablo	25%
Santa Rosa	25%
Seal Beach	18%
Stockton	13%
Sunnyvale	19%
Tracy	20%
Tustin	18%
Twentynine Palms	13%
Ukiah	20%
Upland	18%
Vallejo	19%
Victorville	18%
COLORADO	**3%**
Colorado Springs	7%
Denver	5%
Fort Carson	4%
Grand Junction	2%
COLORADO *continued*	
La Junta	2%
Lakewood	2%
Pueblo	-5%
Ski resorts	32%
CONNECTICUT	**12%**
Bridgeport	13%
Cromwell	12%
Fairfield	12%
Hartford	12%
Milford	11%
New London	11%
Stratford	11%
West Hartford	12%
DELAWARE	**5%**
Dover	4%
Kirkwood	6%
Lewes	6%
Milford	4%
Wilmington	7%
DISTRICT OF COLUMBIA	**4%**
Washington	4%
FLORIDA	**4%**
Baldwin	9%
Jacksonville	9%
Key West	22%
Lakeland	2%
Lynn Haven	0%
Melbourne	10%
Miami	6%
Milton	0%
Ocala	2%
Ocean City	-4%
Orlando	10%
Palatka	2%
FLORIDA *continued*	
Panama City	2%
Pensacola	0%
St Petersburg	1%
Tampa	1%
GEORGIA	**3%**
Albany	-1%
Athens	2%
Atlanta	12%
Augusta	-5%
Chamblee	2%
Columbus	-3%
Dublin	2%
East Point	2%
Forest Park	13%
Fort Valley	2%
Hinesville	0%
Kings Bay	2%
Macon	2%
Marietta	2%
Rome	2%
Savannah	0%
Tifton	12%
Valdosta	2%
HAWAII	**82%**
Alimanu	82%
Ewa	82%
Halawa Heights	82%
Hilo	82%
Honolulu	82%
Kailua	90%
Lualualei	82%
Mililani Town	82%
Pearl City	82%
Wahiawa	82%
Waianae	82%
Wailuku (Maui)	82%

IDAHO **0%**
Boise 4%
Coeur d'Alene 2%
Idaho Falls .... -1%
Mountain Home .... -1%
Twin Falls .... -2%

ILLINOIS **5%**
Addison 5%
Arlington Heights 5%
Aurora 5%
Belleville 3%
Bloomington 5%
Champaign 5%
Chicago 16%
Decatur 5%
Forest Park 9%
Galesburg 5%
Gibson City 5%
Granite City 5%
Green River 5%
Hanover 1%
Harvey 5%
Highland Park 5%
Homewood 5%
Joliet 5%
Kankakee 5%
Mascoutah 3%
North Chicago 9%
North Park 5%
Northfield 5%
Orland Park 5%
Peoria 5%
Peru 5%
Rantoul 5%
Rock Island 4%
Rockford 5%
Springfield 5%
Urbana 5%

INDIANA **0%**
Bloomington 1%
Crane .... -2%
Fort Wayne 1%
Gary 1%
Indianapolis .... -1%
Jeffersonville 1%
Kokomo 1%
Lafayette 1%

INDIANA .... *continued*
Lawrence .... -1%
Logansport 1%
New Albany 1%
North Judson 1%
Peru 1%
Porter 1%
Richmond 1%
Rushville 1%
South Bend 1%

IOWA .... **-1%**
Ames 3%
Burlington .... -2%
Cedar Rapids .... -2%
Cherokee .... -2%
Council Bluffs .... -2%
Davenport 0%
Decorah .... -2%
Des Moines .... -3%
Keokuk .... -2%
Mason City .... -2%
Pocahontas .... -2%
Sac City .... -2%
Sioux City .... -2%
Washington .... -2%
Waterloo .... -2%

KANSAS .... **-1%**
Atchison .... -1%
Emporia .... -1%
Hays .... -1%
Independence .... -1%
Junction City .... -1%
Kansas City .... -1%
Lawrence .... -1%
Leavenworth 7%
Manhattan .... -4%
Olathe .... -1%
Osage City .... -1%
Parsons .... -1%
Pittsburg .... -1%
Topeka .... -1%
Wichita 3%

KENTUCKY .... **-3%**
Ashland .... -3%
Bardstown .... -3%
Bowling Green .... -3%

KENTUCKY .... *continued*
Fort Thomas .... -3%
Hopkinsville .... -1%
Lexington .... -5%
Louisville .... -1%
Madisonville .... -3%
Paducah .... -3%
Radcliff .... -1%
Richmond .... -3%
Russell .... -3%

LOUISIANA .... **-4%**
Alexandria .... -4%
Baton Rouge .... -4%
Bogalusa .... -4%
Bossier Base .... -8%
Hammond .... -4%
Leesville .... -7%
Monroe .... -4%
New Orleans 11%
Shreveport .... -4%

MAINE **2%**
Auburn 1%
Bangor .... -1%
Brunswick 4%
Caribou 1%
Cutler 1%
Dexter 1%
Northern Area 1%
Portland 3%
Winter Harbor 1%

MARYLAND **2%**
Aberdeen 0%
Annapolis 2%
Baltimore 1%
Bel Air, Hartford 1%
Bethesda 3%
Cascade 0%
College Park 1%
Cumberland 1%
Curtis Bay 1%
Edgewood 1%
Frederick 1%
Hagerstown 1%
Hyattsville 3%
Indian Head 3%
Lexington Park 3%

MARYLAND .... *continued*
Olney 1%
Patuxent River Area 3%
Prince Georges 3%
Westminster 1%
White Oak 1%

MASSACHUSETTS **15%**
Ayer 15%
Bedford 15%
Boston 15%
Brockton 15%
Chicopee 15%
Fitchburg 15%
Hingham 15%
Lawrence 15%
Natick 15%
Pittsfield 15%
Quincy 15%
Roslindale 15%
South Weymouth 15%
Springfield 15%
Taunton 15%
Watertown 15%

MICHIGAN **4%**
Ann Arbor 5%
Bad Axe 5%
Battle Creek 5%
Bay City 5%
Carleton 5%
Detroit 16%
Flint 5%
Grand Rapids 5%
Grayling 5%
Inkster 5%
Ishpeming .... -1%
Lansing 5%
Livonia 5%
Marquette .... -1%
Muskegon 5%
Newport 15%
Northern Area 5%
Oscoda .... -1%
Pontiac 5%
Republic .... -1%
Saginaw 5%
Southfield 5%
Traverse City .... -6%

MICHIGAN .... *continued*
Warren 5%

MINNESOTA **5%**
Brainerd 5%
Buffalo 5%
Duluth 2%
Fairbault 5%
Fergus Falls 5%
Fort Ripley 5%
International Falls 5%
Mankato 5%
Minneapolis 8%
New Brighton 8%
Rochester 5%
St Cloud 5%
St Paul 8%
Walker 5%
Willmar 5%

MISSISSIPPI .... **-4%**
Bay St Louis .... -5%
Biloxi .... -5%
Clarksdale .... -5%
Columbus .... -7%
Greenville 4%
Greenwood .... -5%
Gulfport Area .... -3%
Jackson .... -5%
Laurel .... -5%
Meridian .... -5%
Pascagoula .... -3%
Tupelo .... -5%
Vicksburg .... -5%

MISSOURI **1%**
Belton 0%
Bolivar 0%
Caruthersville 0%
Farmington 0%
Independence 0%
Kansas City 2%
Kirksville 0%
Knob Noster .... -1%
Lebanon 2%
Portageville 0%
St Louis 4%
Washington 4%
Weldon Springs 4%

MONTANA	**-1%**
Billings	-1%
Butte	-1%
Cut Bank	-1%
Fairview	-1%
Glasgow	-1%
Great Falls	-1%
Havre	-1%
Helena	-1%
Kalispell	-1%
Lewistown	-1%
Miles City	-1%
Missoula	-1%

NEBRASKA	**-1%**
Ashland	0%
Bellevue	0%
Fremont	0%
Grand Island	-4%
Lincoln	-4%
Omaha	1%

NEVADA	**4%**
Carson City	5%
Fallon	7%
Hawthorne	6%
Las Vegas	14%
North Las Vegas	14%
Reno	12%
Yerington	5%

NEW HAMPSHIRE	**1%**
Claremont	1%
Concord	1%
Dover	1%
Manchester	1%
New Boston	1%
Portsmouth	1%

NEW JERSEY	**11%**
Bayonne	11%
Browns Mills	11%
Burlington	11%
Camden	11%
Earle	11%
Edison	11%
Freehold	11%
Highlands	11%
Lakehurst	11%
Lodi	11%
Long Branch	11%
Middletown	11%
Mount Hope	12%
Newark	12%
Pedricktown	11%
Red Bank	11%
Trenton	11%
Wallington	11%
Wrightstown	11%

NEW MEXICO	**2%**
Alamogordo	2%
Albuquerque	4%
Clovis	1%
Fort Sumner	3%
Gallup	3%
Las Cruces	2%
Sandia Base	3%
Santa Fe	3%

NEW YORK	**17%**
Albany	7%
Amherst	12%
Amityville	12%
Auburn	12%
Batavia	12%
Bellmore	12%
Brooklyn	12%
Buffalo	12%
Canandaigua	11%
Canton	12%
Corning	12%
Lockport	12%
Long Island	76%
Malone	12%
Manhattan Beach	32%
Massena	12%
Mattydale	12%
Montauk	12%
New York City	84%
New York City (Manhattan)	84%
Newark-Arcadia	11%
Newburgh	11%
Niagara Falls	10%
Niskayuna	11%
Penn Yan	11%
Plattsburgh	4%
Rochester	10%
Rockaway	12%
Rome	12%
Schenectady	11%
Seneca Falls	5%
Staten Island	77%
Stewart	11%
Syracuse	12%
Utica	12%
Watertown	4%
Wayland	10%
West Point	12%

NORTH CAROLINA	**-3%**
Albemarle	-4%
Asheville	-4%
Burlington	-4%
Camp Mackall	-4%
Charlotte	-4%
Cherry Point	-3%
Durham	-4%
Fayetteville	-4%
Goldsboro	-4%
Greensboro	-4%
Jacksonville	-4%
Kinston	-4%
New Bern	-4%
Raleigh	-4%
Salisbury	-4%
Southport	-4%
Wilmington	-4%
Wilson	-4%
Winston-Salem	-4%

NORTH DAKOTA	**-3%**
Bismarck	-3%
Grand Forks	-4%
Minot	-1%
Nekoma	-2%
Williston	-2%

OHIO	**3%**
Akron	3%
Chillicothe	3%
Cincinnati	3%
Cleveland	4%
Columbus	3%
Dayton	2%
Fairborn	2%
Fremont	4%
Lima	4%
Marietta	3%
Newark	3%
Sandusky	4%
Springfield	3%
Steubenville	2%
Toledo	4%
Warren	3%
Wooster	3%
Youngstown	3%
Zanesville	3%

OKLAHOMA	**-2%**
Ada	-2%
Altus	-4%
Ardmore	-2%
Bartlesville	-2%
Chickasha	-2%
Clinton	-2%
Durant	-2%
El Reno	-2%
Enid	-2%
Lawton	-2%
McAlester	-6%
Miami	-2%
Midwest City	-2%
Muskogee	0%
Norman	-2%
Oklahoma City	0%
Okmulgee	-2%
Ponca City	-2%
Shawnee	-2%
Stillwater	-1%
Tulsa	-1%

OREGON	**6%**
Coos Bay	6%
Pendleton	6%
Portland	5%
Salem	6%
Umatilla	7%

PENNSYLVANIA	**3%**
Allentown	4%
Altoona	4%
Annville	4%
Bristol	4%
Brookville	4%
Butler	4%
Carlisle	-2%
Chambersburg	-3%
Clearfield	4%
Erie	4%
Frankfort	4%

PENNSYLVANIA ..*continued*

City	%
Gettysburg	4%
Johnstown	4%
Kittanning	4%
Lancaster	4%
Meadville	4%
Mechanicsburg Area	4%
New Castle	4%
New Cumberland	-2%
Oakdale	1%
Philadelphia	7%
Pittsburgh	1%
Punxsutawney	4%
Scranton	4%
Tobyhanna	3%
Valley Forge	4%
Warminster Area	7%
Wilkes Barre	4%
Willow Grove	4%

RHODE ISLAND 9%

City	%
Bristol	9%
Coventry	9%
Cranston	9%
Davisville	9%
Narragansett	9%
Newport	9%
Providence	9%
Warwick	9%

SOUTH CAROLINA ... -1%

City	%
Anderson	-12%
Beaufort Area	5%
Charleston	1%
Clemson	-2%
Columbia	-2%
Greenville	-2%
Myrtle Beach	1%
Rock Hill	-2%
Spartanburg	-2%
Sumter	-2%

SOUTH DAKOTA -2%

City	%
Aberdeen	-3%
Box Elder	1%
Hot Springs	-3%
Mitchell	-3%
Rapid City	1%
Sioux Falls	-4%

TENNESSEE 2%

City	%
Chattanooga	2%
Greeneville	2%
Kingsport	2%
Manchester	0%
Memphis	4%
Milan	2%
Oak Ridge	2%

TEXAS 2%

City	%
Abilene	1%
Alice	1%
Amarillo	1%
Austin	1%
Bay City	1%
Beaumont	1%
Beeville	1%
Brownsville	1%
Bryan	1%
Corpus Chrsti	1%
Dallas	8%
Del Rio	12%
Del Valle	1%
El Paso	1%
Ft Worth	8%
Harlingen	1%
Houston	1%
Huntsville	1%
Killeen	1%
Kingsville	1%
Laredo	1%
Longview	1%
Lubbock	4%

TEXAS ....*continued*

City	%
Marshall	1%
McAllen	1%
Mineral Wells	1%
Paris	1%
Pasadena	1%
Port Arthur	1%
Rio Grande City	1%
San Angelo	-1%
San Antonio	4%
San Marcos	1%
Sinton	1%
Texarkana	6%
Victoria	1%
Wichita Falls	1%
Yoakum	2%

UTAH 4%

City	%
Brigham City	5%
Clearfield	-6%
Green River	-6%
Logan (Cache Valley)	5%
Ogden	5%
Price	-4%
Provo	5%
Salt Lake City	5%
St. George	5%
Tooele	4%

VERMONT .... -1%

City	%
Burlington	0%
Chester	-1%
Montpelier	-1%
Rutland	-1%

VIRGINA 2%

City	%
Abingdon	1%
Alexandria	15%
Arlington	15%
Berryville (Winchester)	1%
Blackstone	3%

VIRGINA ....*continued*

City	%
Bowling Green	4%
Charlottesville	1%
Chesapeake	1%
Chincoteague	1%
Churchland	1%
Dahlgren	-3%
Dam Neck	1%
Dublin (Radford)	1%
Galax	1%
Hampton	3%
Herndon	1%
Marion	1%
Newport News	3%
Norfolk	3%
Petersburg	2%
Quantico	-1%
Richmond	1%
Vint Hill Farms	-1%
Virginia Beach	3%
Warrenton	1%
Williamsburg	3%
Woodbridge	1%
Yorktown	1%

WASHINGTON 7%

City	%
Bangor	7%
Bremerton	10%
Keyport	6%
Lakewood	6%
Olympia	6%
Pacific Beach	6%
Pasco	6%
Puget Sound Area	6%
Seattle	6%
Spokane	9%
Tacoma	6%
Trentwood	7%
Vancouver	6%
Whidbey Island	6%
Yakima	1%

WEST VIRGINIA .. -3%

City	%
Bluefield	-5%
Charleston	-1%
Dawson	-3%
Fairmont	-3%
Grafton	-3%
Huntington	-3%
Martinsburg	-3%
New Martinsville	-3%
Parkersburg	-3%
Ripley	-3%
Romney	-3%
Sugar Grove	-5%
Weirton	-3%
Wheeling	-3%

WISCONSIN 1%

City	%
Clam Lake	1%
Cornell	1%
Dodgeville	1%
Fond du Lac	1%
Junction City	1%
Kewaunee	1%
La Crosse	1%
Ladysmith	1%
Madison	-5%
Milwaukee	6%
Oshkosh	1%
Wausau	1%

WYOMING .... -8%

City	%
Casper	-4%
Cheyenne	-4%
Cody	0%
Evanston	-6%
Gillette	-8%
Jackson	6%
Laramie	-8%
Powell	-9%
Sheridan	0%
Star Valley	4%

unit price pages

The unit price pages have six columns. ❶ The column in the outside margin is the QuickFinder column. It contains headings and information designed to help you quickly find the item you need. ❷ The second column contains the item description along with applicable material, labor, and equipment prices and any necessary item information. ❸ The third column contains a two-letter abbreviation that indicates the unit of measure. ❹ The fourth column contains the price to tear out the item and place the debris in a dumpster on site. ❺ The fifth column contains the price to install the new item. ❻ The sixth column gives the total remove and replace cost.

Use the *QuickFinder* headings to quickly find items within a trade.

Use the *QuickFinder* sub-headings to quickly find items within a group.

Text below *QuickFinder* headings describe the item including installation techniques and waste.

Illustrated descriptions of an item are often most useful to determine if the item is the one you are looking for.

When needed, information about a specific item appears in the description column.

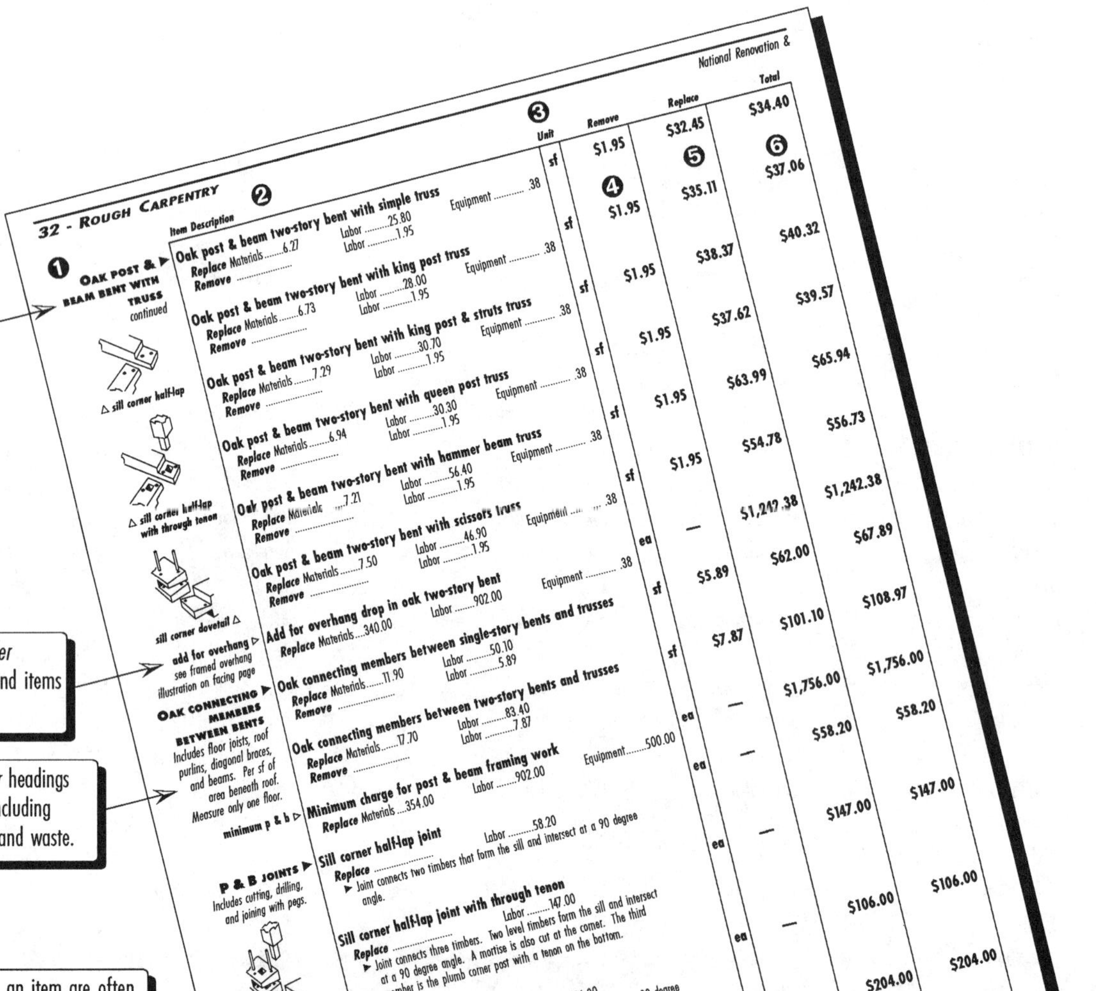

National Renovation &

32 - Rough Carpentry

❶ Oak post & beam bent with truss continued

Item Description ❷	Unit ❸	Remove ❹	Replace ❺	Total ❻
Oak post & beam two-story bent with simple truss. Replace Materials...6.27 Labor...25.80 Equipment...38; Remove Labor...1.95	sf	$1.95	$32.45	$34.40
Oak post & beam two-story bent with king post truss. Replace Materials...6.73 Labor...28.00 Equipment...38; Remove Labor...1.95	sf	$1.95	$35.11	$37.06
Oak post & beam two-story bent with king post & struts truss. Replace Materials...7.29 Labor...30.70 Equipment...38; Remove Labor...1.95	sf	$1.95	$38.37	$40.32
Oak post & beam two-story bent with queen post truss. Replace Materials...6.94 Labor...30.30 Equipment...38; Remove Labor...1.95	sf	$1.95	$37.62	$39.57
Oak post & beam two-story bent with hammer beam truss. Replace Materials...7.21 Labor...56.40 Equipment...38; Remove Labor...1.95	sf	$1.95	$63.99	$65.94
Oak post & beam two-story bent with scissors truss. Replace Materials...7.50 Labor...46.90 Equipment...38; Remove Labor...1.95	sf	$1.95	$54.78	$56.73
add for overhang (see framed overhang illustration on facing page) — Add for overhang drop in oak two-story bent. Replace Materials...340.00 Labor...902.00 Equipment...38	ea	—	$1,242.38	$1,242.38
Oak connecting members between bents (Includes floor joists, roof purlins, diagonal braces, and beams. Per sf of area beneath roof. Measure only one floor.) — Oak connecting members between single-story bents and trusses. Replace Materials...11.90 Labor...50.10; Remove Labor...5.89	sf	$5.89	$62.00	$67.89
Oak connecting members between two-story bents and trusses. Replace Materials...17.70 Labor...83.40; Remove Labor...7.87	sf	$7.87	$101.10	$108.97
minimum p & b — Minimum charge for post & beam framing work. Replace Materials...354.00 Labor...902.00 Equipment...500.00	ea	—	$1,756.00	$1,756.00
P & B joints (Includes cutting, drilling, and joining with pegs.) — Sill corner half-lap joint. Replace Labor...58.20. Joint connects two timbers that form the sill and intersect at a 90 degree angle.	ea	—	$58.20	$58.20
Sill corner half-lap joint with through tenon. Replace Labor...147.00. Joint connects three timbers. Two level timbers form the sill and intersect at a 90 degree angle. A mortise is also cut at the corner. The third member is the plumb corner post with a tenon on the bottom.	ea	—	$147.00	$147.00
Sill corner dovetail joint. Replace Labor...106.00. Joint connects two timbers that form the sill and intersect at a 90 degree angle.	ea	—	$106.00	$106.00
Sill corner dovetail joint with through tenon. Replace Labor...204.00. Joint connects three timbers. Two level timbers form the sill and intersect at a 90 degree angle. A mortise is also cut at the corner. The third member is the plumb corner post with a tenon on the bottom.	ea	—	$204.00	$204.00
Sill corner tongue & fork joint. Replace Labor...94.70. Joint connects two timbers that form the sill and intersect at a 90 degree angle.	ea	—	$94.70	$94.70

sill corner half-lap; sill corner half-lap with through tenon; sill corner dovetail; sill corner dovetail with through tenon; sill corner tongue & fork; sill corner tongue & fork with through tenon

426

time & material charts

Material charts show the material description, the material cost priced per typical unit purchased, the gross coverage, the typical waste, the net coverage after waste has been subtracted, and the resulting materials price including waste and often converted to a different unit of measure.

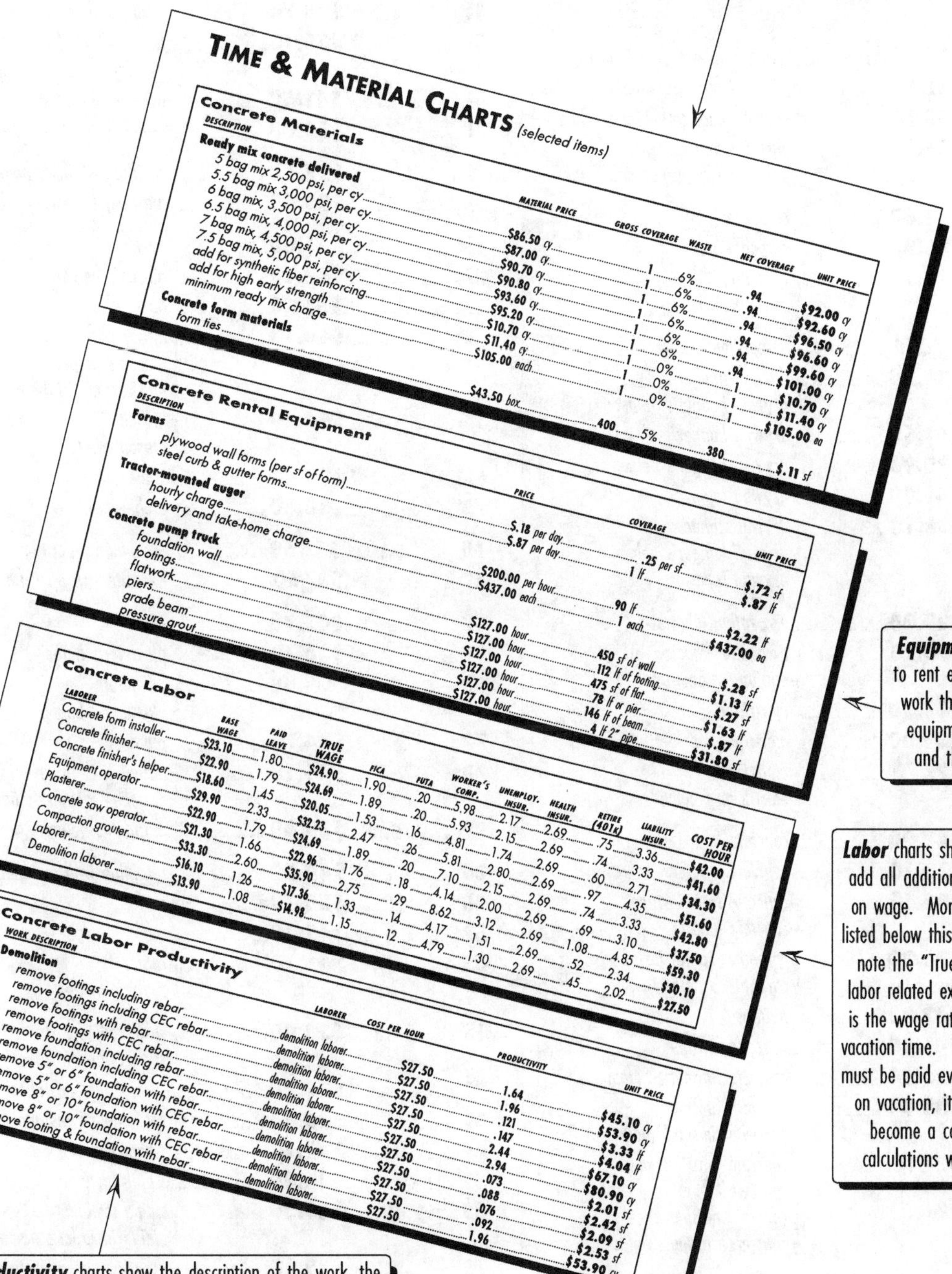

Equipment charts show the cost to rent equipment, the amount of work that can be done with the equipment per period of time, and the resulting unit price.

Labor charts show the base wage, then add all additional costs that are based on wage. More information is always listed below this chart. It's important to note the "True" wage before adding labor related expenses. The true wage is the wage rate plus an allowance for vacation time. Since all the other costs must be paid even when an employee is on vacation, it is important that they become a component in the cost calculations when estimating work.

Labor productivity charts show the description of the work, the laborer or crew who will do the work, the average cost per man hour, the productivity and the resulting cost per unit.

crews

Craft Code	Avg. Cost per Hour	Crew Composition
1A	$32.70	acoustic ceiling installer
2A	$37.10	appliance installer
3A	$45.80	appliance refinisher
4A	$44.00	awning installer
5A	$30.50	awning installer's helper
6A	$37.30	awning installer awning installer's helper
1B	$24.60	cleaning laborer
2B	$52.90	post & beam carpenter
3B	$37.20	post & beam carpenter's helper
4B	$45.10	post & beam carpenter post & beam carpenter's helper
1C	$41.60	carpenter
5C	$30.80	carpenter's helper
6C	$36.20	carpenter carpenter's helper
1D	$27.50	demolition laborer
2D	$36.20	drywall hanger drywall hanger's helper
3D	$41.50	drywall hanger
4D	$30.90	drywall hanger's helper
5D	$41.90	drywall taper
6D	$38.10	drywall hanger drywall hanger's helper drywall taper
5E	$29.80	excavation laborer
6E	$40.70	excavation laborer equipment operator
7E	$43.30	electrician
8E	$32.00	electrician's helper
9E	$37.70	electrician electrician's helper
1F	$42.00	concrete form installer
2F	$30.10	concrete laborer
3F	$36.10	concrete form installer concrete laborer
4F	$36.20	carpenter (fence installer) carpenter's helper
5F	$42.80	painter
6F	$41.60	concrete finisher
7F	$34.30	concrete finisher's helper
8F	$38.00	concrete finisher concrete finisher's helper
9F	$37.10	concrete form installer concrete laborer concrete finisher concrete finisher's helper
1G	$59.30	compaction grouting specialist
2G	$44.70	compaction grouting specialist concrete laborer
1H	$43.10	hazardous materials laborer
2H	$46.40	HVAC installer
3H	$35.30	wallpaper hanger
1I	$30.40	insulation installer
2I	$34.40	cabinet installer laborer
3I	$41.50	flooring installer
4I	$30.70	flooring installer's helper
5I	$36.10	flooring installer flooring installer's helper
6I	$41.50	paneling installer
7I	$30.60	paneling installer's helper
2L	$27.10	cabinet installer's helper
3L	$26.40	masking & moving laborer
1M	$46.00	mason
2M	$42.10	mason's helper
3M	$32.20	hod carrier
4M	$40.10	mason mason's helper hod carrier / laborer
5M	$44.10	mason mason's helper
6M	$108.00	stone carver
7M	$30.60	mobile home repair specialist
1O	$51.60	equipment operator
2O	$37.50	concrete saw operator
4P	$42.80	plasterer
5P	$36.70	plasterer's helper
6P	$39.80	plasterer plasterer's helper
7P	$44.70	plumber
8P	$36.10	paneling installer paneling installer's helper
9P	$38.00	plumber's helper
3R	$40.50	retaining wall installer
4R	$50.10	roofer
5R	$42.10	roofer's helper
6R	$46.10	roofer roofer's helper
1S	$33.90	susp. ceiling installer susp. ceiling installer's helper
2S	$38.90	susp. ceiling installer
3S	$28.80	susp. ceiling installer's helper
4S	$41.10	siding installer
5S	$30.40	siding installer's helper
6S	$35.80	siding installer siding installer's helper
7S	$38.10	security system installer
8S	$50.80	swimming pool installer
9S	$35.50	water extractor
1T	$38.90	tile layer

1 .... Acoustic Ceilings

Item Description	Unit	Remove	Replace	Total
Minimum charge for acoustic ceiling tile work ***Replace*** Materials......16.70 Labor..........40.90	ea	—	$57.60	$57.60
1/2" ceiling tiles on furring strips, smooth face ***Replace*** Materials...... 1.07 Labor............. .82 ***Remove*** .... Labor............. .33	sf	$.33	$1.89	$2.22
1/2" ceiling tiles on furring strips, fissured face ***Replace*** Materials........1.27 Labor............. .82 ***Remove*** .... Labor............. .33	sf	$.33	$2.09	$2.42
1/2" ceiling tiles on furring strips, textured face ***Replace*** Materials........1.48 Labor............. .82 ***Remove*** .... Labor............. .33	sf	$.33	$2.30	$2.63
1/2" ceiling tiles on furring strips, patterned face ***Replace*** Materials........1.58 Labor............. .82 ***Remove*** .... Labor............. .33	sf	$.33	$2.40	$2.73
1/2" ceiling tiles on flat ceiling, smooth face ***Replace*** Materials...... 1.07 Labor............. .95 ***Remove*** .... Labor............. .44	sf	$.44	$2.02	$2.46
1/2" ceiling tiles on flat ceiling, fissured face ***Replace*** Materials........1.27 Labor............. .95 ***Remove*** .... Labor............. .44	sf	$.44	$2.22	$2.66
1/2" ceiling tiles on flat ceiling, textured face ***Replace*** Materials........1.48 Labor............. .95 ***Remove*** .... Labor............. .44	sf	$.44	$2.43	$2.87
1/2" ceiling tiles on flat ceiling, patterned face ***Replace*** Materials........1.58 Labor............. .95 ***Remove*** .... Labor............. .44	sf	$.44	$2.53	$2.97
5/8" ceiling tiles on furring strips, smooth face ***Replace*** Materials........1.27 Labor............. .82 ***Remove*** .... Labor............. .33	sf	$.33	$2.09	$2.42
5/8" ceiling tiles on furring strips, fissured face ***Replace*** Materials........1.48 Labor............. .82 ***Remove*** .... Labor............. .33	sf	$.33	$2.30	$2.63
5/8" ceiling tiles on furring strips, textured face ***Replace*** Materials........1.69 Labor............. .82 ***Remove*** .... Labor............. .33	sf	$.33	$2.51	$2.84
5/8" ceiling tiles on furring strips, patterned face ***Replace*** Materials........1.79 Labor............. .82 ***Remove*** .... Labor............. .33	sf	$.33	$2.61	$2.94
5/8" ceiling tiles on flat ceiling, smooth face ***Replace*** Materials........1.27 Labor............. .95 ***Remove*** .... Labor............. .44	sf	$.44	$2.22	$2.66

◄ **MINIMUM**

◄ **1/2" ON STRIPS**
12" x 12" tiles stapled in place. Does not include furring strips. Includes 3% waste.

◄ **1/2" ON FLAT**
12" x 12" tiles glued in place. Includes 3% waste.

◄ **5/8" ON STRIPS**
12" x 12" tiles stapled in place. Does not include furring strips. Includes 3% waste.

RELATED ITEMS

Cleaning 55
Painting 333
Suspended Ceilings......483

◄ **5/8" ON FLAT**
12" x 12" tiles glued in place. Includes 3% waste.

	Item Description	Unit	Remove	Replace	Total
5/8" ON FLAT ▶ *continued*	**5/8" ceiling tiles on flat ceiling, fissured face** ***Replace*** Materials........1.48 Labor............ .95 ***Remove*** .... Labor............ .44	sf	$.44	$2.43	$2.87
	5/8" ceiling tiles on flat ceiling, textured face ***Replace*** Materials........1.69 Labor............ .95 ***Remove*** .... Labor............ .44	sf	$.44	$2.64	$3.08
	5/8" ceiling tiles on flat ceiling, patterned face ***Replace*** Materials........1.79 Labor............ .95 ***Remove*** .... Labor............ .44	sf	$.44	$2.74	$3.18
3/4" ON STRIPS ▶ *12" x 12" tiles stapled in place. Does not include furring strips. Includes 3% waste.*	**3/4" ceiling tiles on furring strips, smooth face** ***Replace*** Materials........1.48 Labor............ .82 ***Remove*** .... Labor............ .33	sf	$.33	$2.30	$2.63
	3/4" ceiling tiles on furring strips, fissured face ***Replace*** Materials........1.58 Labor............ .82 ***Remove*** .... Labor............ .33	sf	$.33	$2.40	$2.73
	3/4" ceiling tiles on furring strips, textured face ***Replace*** Materials........1.76 Labor............ .82 ***Remove*** .... Labor............ .33	sf	$.33	$2.58	$2.91
	3/4" ceiling tiles on furring strips, patterned face ***Replace*** Materials........1.90 Labor............ .82 ***Remove*** .... Labor............ .33	sf	$.33	$2.72	$3.05
3/4" ON FLAT ▶ *12" x 12" tiles glued in place. Includes 3% waste.*	**3/4" ceiling tiles on flat ceiling, smooth face** ***Replace*** Materials........1.48 Labor............ .95 ***Remove*** .... Labor............ .44	sf	$.44	$2.43	$2.87
	3/4" ceiling tiles on flat ceiling, fissured face ***Replace*** Materials........1.58 Labor............ .95 ***Remove*** .... Labor............ .44	sf	$.44	$2.53	$2.97
	3/4" ceiling tiles on flat ceiling, textured face ***Replace*** Materials........1.76 Labor............ .95 ***Remove*** .... Labor............ .44	sf	$.44	$2.71	$3.15
	3/4" ceiling tiles on flat ceiling, patterned face ***Replace*** Materials........1.90 Labor............ .95 ***Remove*** .... Labor............ .44	sf	$.44	$2.85	$3.29
ADDITIONAL COSTS ▶	**Add for 3/4" tiles with fire rating** ***Replace*** Materials........ .28	sf	—	$.28	$.28
	Add for aluminum-coated tiles ***Replace*** Materials........ .41	sf	—	$.41	$.41
FURRING STRIPS ▶ *Nailed and glued to joists or flat ceiling. Includes 4% waste.*	**1" x 2" furring strips 12" on center** ***Replace*** Materials........ .23 Labor............ .23 ***Remove*** .... Labor............ .25	sf	$.25	$.46	$.71
REPAIR LOOSE TILE ▶	**Repair loose acoustic tile** ***Replace*** Materials........ .13 Labor...........8.27	ea	—	$8.40	$8.40
ANGLED INSTALL ▶	**Add 24% for diagonal install**				
	Add 31% for chevron install				
	Add 40% for herringbone install				

TIME & MATERIAL CHARTS *(selected items)*

Acoustic Ceiling Materials

DESCRIPTION	MATERIAL PRICE	GROSS COVERAGE	WASTE	NET COVERAGE	UNIT PRICE
1/2" thick acoustic tile (per 12" x 12" tile)					
smooth face	**$.90** *each*	1	3%	.97	**$.93** *sf*
fissured face	**$1.10** *each*	1	3%	.97	**$1.13** *sf*
textured face	**$1.30** *each*	1	3%	.97	**$1.34** *sf*
patterned face	**$1.40** *each*	1	3%	.97	**$1.44** *sf*
5/8" thick acoustic tile (per 12" x 12" tile)					
smooth face	**$1.10** *each*	1	3%	.97	**$1.13** *sf*
fissured face	**$1.30** *each*	1	3%	.97	**$1.34** *sf*
textured face	**$1.50** *each*	1	3%	.97	**$1.55** *sf*
patterned face	**$1.60** *each*	1	3%	.97	**$1.65** *sf*
3/4" thick acoustic tile (per 12" x 12" tile)					
smooth face	**$1.30** *each*	1	3%	.97	**$1.34** *sf*
fissured face	**$1.40** *each*	1	3%	.97	**$1.44** *sf*
textured face	**$1.57** *each*	1	3%	.97	**$1.62** *sf*
patterned face	**$1.71** *each*	1	3%	.97	**$1.76** *sf*
Additional material costs					
add for fire rating	**$.27** *per sf*	1	3%	.97	**$.29** *sf*
add for aluminum-coated face	**$.40** *per sf*	1	3%	.97	**$.43** *sf*
*add **5%** for diagonal installation*					
*add **10%** for chevron installation*					
*add **15%** for herringbone installation*					
Tile adhesion					
adhesive	**$13.20** *per gallon*	102	2%	99.96	**$.13** *sf*
staples	**$8.20** *per box*	1,200	4%	1,152	**$.01** *sf*
1" x 2" furring strips 12" on center	**$.70** *per 8' strip*	6.77	4%	6.5	**$.11** *sf*
construction adhesive (for furring strips)	**$5.20** *per cartridge*	87	4%	83.52	**$.06** *sf*
nails (for furring strips)	**$51.00** *per box*	3,212	4%	3,083.52	**$.02** *sf*

Acoustic Ceiling Labor

LABORER	BASE WAGE	PAID LEAVE	TRUE WAGE	FICA	FUTA	WORKER'S COMP.	UNEMPLOY. INSUR.	HEALTH INSUR.	RETIRE (401K)	LIABILITY INSUR.	COST PER HOUR
Acoustic ceiling installer	**$19.20**	1.50	**$20.70**	1.58	.17	2.38	1.80	2.69	.62	2.79	**$32.70**
Demolition laborer	**$13.90**	1.08	**$14.98**	1.15	.12	4.79	1.30	2.69	.45	2.02	**$27.50**

Paid Leave is calculated based on two weeks paid vacation, one week sick leave, and seven paid holidays. Employer's matching portion of **FICA** is 7.65 percent. **FUTA** (Federal Unemployment) is .8 percent. **Worker's compensation** for the acoustic ceiling trade was calculated using a national average of 11.49 percent. **Unemployment insurance** was calculated using a national average of 8.7 percent. **Health insurance** was calculated based on a projected national average for 2002 of $535 per employee (and family when applicable) per month. Employer pays 80 percent for a per month cost of $428 per employee. **Retirement** is based on a 401(k) retirement program with employer matching of 50 percent. Employee contributions to the 401(k) plan are an average of 6 percent of the true wage. **Liability insurance** is based on a national average of 13.2 percent.

Acoustic Ceiling Labor Productivity

WORK DESCRIPTION	LABORER	COST PER HOUR	PRODUCTIVITY	UNIT PRICE
Demolition				
tiles attached with adhesive	demolition laborer	$27.50	.016	**$.44** sf
tiles attached with fasteners	demolition laborer	$27.50	.012	**$.33** sf
ceiling furring strips	demolition laborer	$27.50	.009	**$.25** sf
Repair				
repair loose tile	installer	$32.70	.253	**$8.27** ea
Installation				
tiles on furring strips	installer	$32.70	.025	**$.82** sf
tiles on flat ceiling	installer	$32.70	.029	**$.95** sf
furring strips	installer	$32.70	.007	**$.23** sf
Additional labor costs				
minimum labor charge	installer	$32.70	1.25	**$40.90** ea
*add **55%** for diagonal installation*				
*add **65%** for chevron installation*				
*add **85%** for herringbone installation*				

NOTES:

end

2 Appliances

Item Description	Unit	Remove	Replace	Total
Minimum charge for appliance work ***Replace*** Materials......33.00 Labor...........72.30	ea	—	$105.30	$105.30
Gas cook top, standard grade ***Replace*** Materials.....410.00 Labor..........89.00 ***Remove*** .... Labor...........26.80 ► Baked enamel finish, standard burners, pilotless ignition.	ea	$26.80	$499.00	$525.80
Gas cook top, high grade ***Replace*** Materials....530.00 Labor..........89.00 ***Remove*** .... Labor...........26.80 ► Tempered glass or brushed chrome finish, sealed burners, pilotless ignition, automatic reignition. May have retractable downdraft unit.	ea	$26.80	$619.00	$645.80
Gas cook top with grill / griddle ***Replace*** Materials....720.00 Labor..........89.00 ***Remove*** .... Labor...........26.80 ► Tempered glass or brushed chrome finish, two sealed burners, downdraft exhaust unit, gas grill with griddle attachment, pilotless ignition, automatic reignition.	ea	$26.80	$809.00	$835.80
Remove gas cook top for work, then reinstall ***Replace*** Materials........3.00 Labor.........164.00	ea	—	$167.00	$167.00
Gas range, economy grade ***Replace*** Materials....480.00 Labor...........91.60 ***Remove*** .... Labor...........28.30 ► Free-standing with standard-clean oven, chrome drip pans, analog clock and timer.	ea	$28.30	$571.60	$599.90
Gas range, standard grade ***Replace*** Materials....640.00 Labor...........91.60 ***Remove*** .... Labor..........28.30 ► Free-standing with continuous-clean oven, chrome drip pans, digital clock and timer.	ea	$28.30	$731.60	$759.90
Gas range, high grade ***Replace*** Materials ....870.00 Labor...........91.60 ***Remove*** .... Labor..........28.30 ► Free-standing with self-clean oven, sealed burners, digital clock and timer.	ea	$28.30	$961.60	$989.90
Gas range with grill / griddle ***Replace*** Materials ...1160.00 Labor..........93.90 ***Remove*** .... Labor..........28.30 ► Free-standing with self-clean oven, two sealed burners, grill, digital clock and timer.	ea	$28.30	$1,253.90	$1,282.20
Space-saver gas range, standard grade ***Replace*** Materials ....620.00 Labor..........89.00 ***Remove*** .... Labor..........28.30 ► 20" free-standing with continuous-clean oven, chrome drip pans, digital clock and timer.	ea	$28.30	$709.00	$737.30
Space-saver gas range, high grade ***Replace*** Materials.....810.00 Labor..........89.00 ***Remove*** .... Labor..........28.30 ► 20" free-standing with self-clean oven, sealed burners, digital clock and timer.	ea	$28.30	$899.00	$927.30

◄ **MINIMUM**

◄ **GAS COOK TOP**

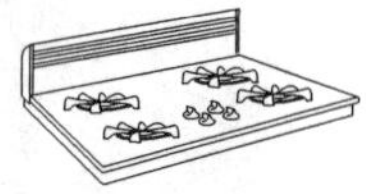

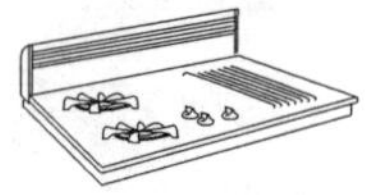

◄ **GAS RANGE**

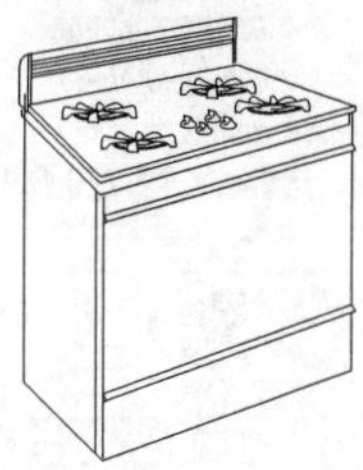

◄ **SPACE SAVER GAS RANGE**

RELATED ITEMS

Electrical *(wiring)*
gas oven or range..........143

HIGH-LOW GAS RANGE ▶

RESTAURANT GAS RANGE ▶

*Some common manufacturers are Viking, Thermador and Garland. Many of these manufacturers also deliver economy models starting at around **$1,310**. Also beware of "mimicked" restaurant styles from prominent manufacturers of standard ranges that sell from **$840** to **$2,130**.*

GAS WALL OVEN ▶

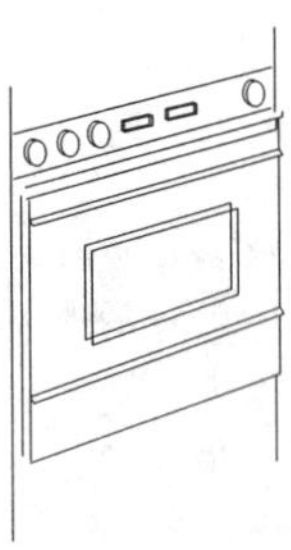

Item Description	Unit	Remove	Replace	Total
High-low gas range with microwave high, standard grade ***Replace*** Materials..1900.00 Labor..........94.80 ***Remove*** .... Labor..........32.50 ▶ 1.4 cf microwave with touch-pad controls. Range with continuous-clean oven, chrome drip pans, digital clock and timer.	ea	$32.50	$1,994.80	$2,027.30
High-low gas range with microwave high, high grade ***Replace*** Materials..2090.00 Labor..........94.80 ***Remove*** .... Labor..........32.50 ▶ 1.4 cf microwave with touch-pad controls. Range with self-clean oven, chrome drip pans, digital clock and timer.	ea	$32.50	$2,184.80	$2,217.30
High-low gas range with microwave high, deluxe grade ***Replace*** Materials..2360.00 Labor..........94.80 ***Remove*** .... Labor..........32.50 ▶ 1.4 cf microwave with touch-pad controls. Range with self-clean oven, chrome drip pans, digital clock and timer, integrated hood and venting system.	ea	$32.50	$2,454.80	$2,487.30
Remove gas range for work, then reinstall ***Replace*** Materials........3.00 Labor.........181.00	ea	—	$184.00	$184.00
Restaurant-style gas range, standard grade ***Replace*** Materials...2610.00 Labor.........198.00 ***Remove*** .... Labor..........82.50 ▶ Stainless-steel or black epoxy finish, zero clearance, insulated handles, stainless-steel upper shelf, electronic ignition, push-to-turn controls, six burners, single oven with in-oven infrared gas broiler.	ea	$82.50	$2,808.00	$2,890.50
Restaurant-style gas range, high grade ***Replace*** Materials...5710.00 Labor.........198.00 ***Remove*** .... Labor..........82.50 ▶ Stainless-steel or colored epoxy finish, zero clearance, insulated handles, stainless-steel upper shelf, electronic ignition, push-to-turn controls, four burners with griddle, and single oven.	ea	$82.50	$5,908.00	$5,990.50
Restaurant-style gas range, deluxe grade ***Replace*** Materials..9000.00 Labor.........198.00 ***Remove*** .... Labor..........82.50 ▶ Stainless-steel or colored epoxy finish, zero clearance, insulated handles, stainless-steel upper shelf, electronic ignition, push-to-turn controls, six burners with griddle, and convection oven.	ea	$82.50	$9,198.00	$9,280.50
Remove restaurant-style gas range for work, then reinstall ***Replace*** Materials........5.00 Labor.........257.00	ea	—	$262.00	$262.00
Gas wall oven, economy grade ***Replace*** Materials....532.00 Labor..........80.50 ***Remove*** .... Labor..........36.90 ▶ Standard-clean oven, pilotless ignition.	ea	$36.90	$612.50	$649.40
Gas wall oven, standard grade ***Replace*** Materials.....613.00 Labor..........80.50 ***Remove*** .... Labor..........36.90 ▶ Standard-clean oven, pilotless ignition, electronic pad controls.	ea	$36.90	$693.50	$730.40
Gas wall oven, high grade ***Replace*** Materials....781.00 Labor..........80.50 ***Remove*** .... Labor..........36.90 ▶ Continuous-clean oven, pilotless ignition, electronic pad controls with clock.	ea	$36.90	$861.50	$898.40

Item Description	Unit	Remove	Replace	Total
Gas wall oven, deluxe grade ***Replace*** Materials....965.00 Labor..........80.50 ***Remove*** .... Labor..........36.90 ► One self-clean oven, pilotless ignition, electronic pad controls with clock.	ea	$36.90	$1,045.50	$1,082.40
Remove gas wall oven for work, then reinstall ***Replace*** Materials........5.00 Labor.........148.00	ea	—	$153.00	$153.00
Gas double wall oven, economy grade ***Replace*** Materials..1040.00 Labor.........148.00 ***Remove*** .... Labor..........53.60 ► Two standard-clean ovens with pilotless ignition.	ea	$53.60	$1,188.00	$1,241.60
Gas double wall oven, standard grade ***Replace*** Materials...1190.00 Labor.........148.00 ***Remove*** .... Labor..........53.60 ► One standard-clean oven, one continuous-clean oven, pilotless ignition, electronic pad controls with clock.	ea	$53.60	$1,338.00	$1,391.60
Gas double wall oven, high grade ***Replace*** Materials...1520.00 Labor.........148.00 ***Remove*** .... Labor..........53.60 ► One continuous-clean oven, one self-clean oven, pilotless ignition, electronic pad controls with clock.	ea	$53.60	$1,668.00	$1,721.60
Gas double wall oven, deluxe grade ***Replace*** Materials..1880.00 Labor.........148.00 ***Remove*** .... Labor..........53.60 ► Two self-clean ovens, pilotless ignition, electronic pad controls with clock.	ea	$53.60	$2,028.00	$2,081.60
Remove gas double wall oven for work, then reinstall ***Replace*** Materials........5.00 Labor.........268.00	ea	—	$273.00	$273.00
Electric cook top, standard grade ***Replace*** Materials....360.00 Labor...........76.60 ***Remove*** .... Labor..........28.30 ► Baked enamel finish with Calrod coil burners.	ea	$28.30	$436.60	$464.90
Electric cook top, high grade ***Replace*** Materials....460.00 Labor...........76.60 ***Remove*** .... Labor..........28.30 ► Brushed chrome finish with Calrod coil burners.	ea	$28.30	$536.60	$564.90
Electric cook top with grill / griddle ***Replace*** Materials....540.00 Labor...........76.60 ***Remove*** .... Labor..........28.30 ► Tempered glass or brushed chrome finish, downdraft exhaust unit, two Calrod burners, grill with griddle attachment.	ea	$28.30	$616.60	$644.90
Solid-disk electric cook top, standard grade ***Replace*** Materials....570.00 Labor...........76.60 ***Remove*** .... Labor..........28.30 ► Solid cast-iron burners, rotary heat controls.	ea	$28.30	$646.60	$674.90
Solid-disk electric cook top, high grade ***Replace*** Materials....640.00 Labor...........76.60 ***Remove*** .... Labor..........28.30 ► Solid cast-iron burners, rotary heat controls, low profile, brushed chrome finish.	ea	$28.30	$716.60	$744.90

RELATED ITEMS

Electrical *(wiring)*
gas oven or range..........143
electric appliance...........142
cook top......................144
Cleaning........................55

◄ **GAS DOUBLE WALL OVEN**

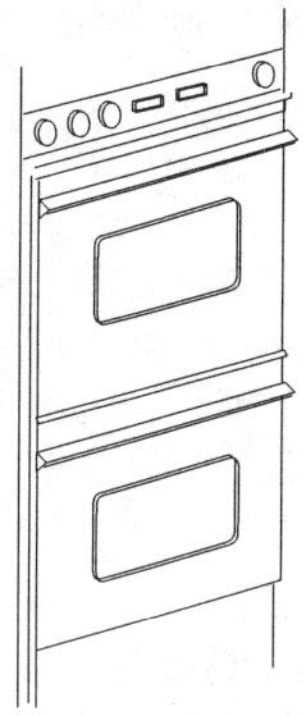

◄ **ELECTRIC COOK TOP**

◄ **SOLID-DISK ELECTRIC COOK TOP**

Solid-disk ▶ electric cook top *continued*

Item Description	Unit	Remove	Replace	Total
Solid-disk electric cook top with grill / griddle ***Replace*** Materials....700.00 Labor...........76.60 ***Remove*** .... Labor..........28.30 ▶ Downdraft exhaust unit, two solid cast-iron burners, grill with griddle attachment.	ea	$28.30	$776.60	$804.90

Flat-surface ▶ electric cook top

*For halogen instant-heat burners instead of radiant heat burners add **$130** per burner.*

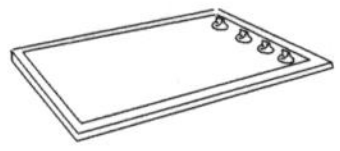

Item Description	Unit	Remove	Replace	Total
Flat-surface radiant electric cook top, standard grade ***Replace*** Materials....680.00 Labor...........76.60 ***Remove*** .... Labor..........28.30 ▶ White on white or almond on almond, 30" smooth surface, fingerprint and scratch resistant.	ea	$28.30	$756.60	$784.90
Flat-surface radiant electric cook top, high grade ***Replace*** Materials....780.00 Labor...........76.60 ***Remove*** .... Labor..........28.30 ▶ Black on black radiant cook top, 30" smooth surface, fingerprint and scratch resistant.	ea	$28.30	$856.60	$884.90
Flat-surface radiant cook top with grill / griddle ***Replace*** Materials....830.00 Labor...........76.60 ***Remove*** .... Labor..........28.30 ▶ Two flat radiant burners, center down draft unit, grill with griddle attachment.	ea	$28.30	$906.60	$934.90

Modular ▶ electric cook top unit

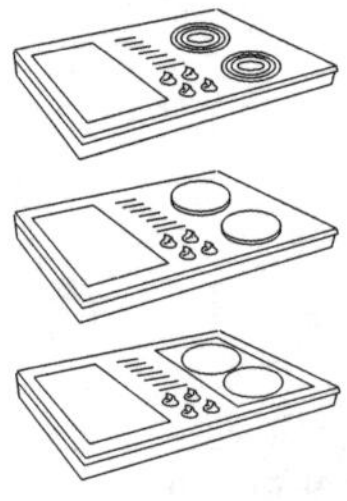

Item Description	Unit	Remove	Replace	Total
Modular electric cook top, two coil (Calrod) burners ***Replace*** Materials....280.00 Labor...........27.20 ***Remove*** .... Labor...........14.00 ▶ Two Calrod coil burners module.	ea	$14.00	$307.20	$321.20
Modular electric cook top, two solid-disk burners ***Replace*** Materials....330.00 Labor...........27.20 ***Remove*** .... Labor...........14.00 ▶ Two solid-disk cast-iron burners module.	ea	$14.00	$357.20	$371.20
Modular electric cook top, two flat-surface radiant burners ***Replace*** Materials....380.00 Labor...........27.20 ***Remove*** .... Labor...........14.00 ▶ Two smooth-surface radiant heat burners module. For halogen instant-heat burners instead of radiant heat burners add **$130** per burner.	ea	$14.00	$407.20	$421.20
Modular electric cook top, griddle ***Replace*** Materials....390.00 Labor...........27.20 ***Remove*** .... Labor...........14.00 ▶ Griddle module. (See grill for units with a griddle attachment that fits on top of the grill module.)	ea	$14.00	$417.20	$431.20
Modular electric cook top, grill ***Replace*** Materials....430.00 Labor...........27.20 ***Remove*** .... Labor...........14.00 ▶ Grill module with one-piece grill and removable porcelain enamel reflector pan. Includes griddle accessory.	ea	$14.00	$457.20	$471.20
Modular electric cook top, downdraft unit ***Replace*** Materials....200.00 Labor...........21.10 ***Remove*** .... Labor...........14.00 ▶ Two- to three-speed fan, 350 to 500 cfm. Add **$140** for telescopic downdraft unit.	ea	$14.00	$221.10	$235.10

Remove & ▶ reinstall cook top

Item Description	Unit	Remove	Replace	Total
Remove modular cooking unit for work, then reinstall ***Replace*** .... Labor...........51.10	ea	—	$51.10	$51.10
Remove modular downdraft unit for work, then reinstall ***Replace*** Materials........2.00 Labor..........38.20	ea	—	$40.20	$40.20

Item Description	Unit	Remove	Replace	Total
Remove electric cook top for work, then reinstall ***Replace*** Materials........2.00 Labor.........141.00	ea	—	$143.00	$143.00
Electric range, standard grade ***Replace*** Materials....540.00 Labor...........75.30 ***Remove*** .... Labor...........26.80 ► Free-standing range with standard-clean oven, four Calrod coil burners, chrome drip pans, analog clock and timer.	ea	$26.80	$615.30	$642.10
Electric range, high grade ***Replace*** Materials....730.00 Labor...........75.30 ***Remove*** .... Labor...........26.80 ► Free-standing range with continuous-clean oven, four Calrod coil burners, chrome drip pans, digital clock and timer.	ea	$26.80	$805.30	$832.10
Electric range, deluxe grade ***Replace*** Materials....940.00 Labor...........75.30 ***Remove*** .... Labor...........26.80 ► Free-standing range with self-clean oven, four Calrod coil burners, chrome drip pans, digital clock and timer.	ea	$26.80	$1,015.30	$1,042.10
Electric range with grill / griddle ***Replace*** Materials...1160.00 Labor...........75.30 ***Remove*** .... Labor...........26.80 ► Free-standing range with self-clean oven, two Calrod coil burners, grill with griddle accessory and cover, digital clock and timer.	ea	$26.80	$1,235.30	$1,262.10
Solid-disk electric range, standard grade ***Replace*** Materials....750.00 Labor...........75.30 ***Remove*** .... Labor...........26.80 ► Free-standing range with standard-clean oven, four cast-iron solid-disk burners, chrome drip pans, analog clock and timer.	ea	$26.80	$825.30	$852.10
Solid-disk electric range, high grade ***Replace*** Materials....800.00 Labor...........75.30 ***Remove*** .... Labor...........26.80 ► Free-standing range with continuous-clean oven, four cast-iron solid-disk burners, chrome drip pans, digital clock and timer.	ea	$26.80	$875.30	$902.10
Solid-disk electric range, deluxe grade ***Replace*** Materials....980.00 Labor...........75.30 ***Remove*** .... Labor...........26.80 ► Free-standing range with self-clean oven, four cast-iron solid-disk burners, digital clock and timer.	ea	$26.80	$1,055.30	$1,082.10
Solid-disk electric range with grill / griddle ***Replace*** Materials...1210.00 Labor...........75.30 ***Remove*** .... Labor...........26.80 ► Free-standing range with self-clean oven, two cast-iron solid-disk burners, grill with griddle accessory and cover, digital clock and timer.	ea	$26.80	$1,285.30	$1,312.10
Flat-surface radiant electric range, standard grade ***Replace*** Materials.....910.00 Labor...........75.30 ***Remove*** .... Labor...........26.80 ► Free-standing range with standard-clean oven, four smooth-surface burners, chrome drip pans, analog clock and timer.	ea	$26.80	$985.30	$1,012.10
Flat-surface radiant electric range, high grade ***Replace*** Materials..1040.00 Labor...........75.30 ***Remove*** .... Labor...........26.80 ► Free-standing range with continuous-clean oven, four smooth-surface burners, chrome drip pans, digital clock and timer.	ea	$26.80	$1,115.30	$1,142.10

◄ **ELECTRIC RANGE**

◄ **SOLID-DISK ELECTRIC RANGE**

◄ **FLAT-SURFACE ELECTRIC RANGE**
*For halogen instant-heat burners instead of radiant heat burners add **$130** per burner.*

RELATED ITEMS

Electrical *(wiring)*
electric appliance............142
cook top......................144
electric oven or range......144

FLAT-SURFACE ► ELECTRIC RANGE *continued*

Item Description	Unit	Remove	Replace	Total
Flat-surface radiant electric range, deluxe grade ***Replace*** Materials..1280.00 Labor...........75.30 ***Remove*** .... Labor...........26.80 ► Free-standing range with self-clean oven, four smooth-surface burners, digital clock and timer.	ea	$26.80	$1,355.30	$1,382.10
Flat-surface radiant electric range with grill / griddle ***Replace*** Materials..1880.00 Labor...........75.30 ***Remove*** .... Labor...........26.80 ► Free-standing range with self-cleaning oven, two smooth-surface burners, grill with griddle accessory and cover, digital clock and timer.	ea	$26.80	$1,955.30	$1,982.10
Remove electric range for work, then reinstall ***Replace*** Materials........4.00 Labor.........157.00	ea	—	$161.00	$161.00

DROP-IN OR ► SLIDE-IN ELECTRIC RANGE

Item Description	Unit	Remove	Replace	Total
Drop-in or slide-in electric range, standard grade ***Replace*** Materials....680.00 Labor..........90.50 ***Remove*** .... Labor..........33.60 ► Drop-in or slide-in range with standard-clean oven, four Calrod coil burners, chrome drip pans, analog clock and timer.	ea	$33.60	$770.50	$804.10
Drop-in or slide-in electric range, high grade ***Replace*** Materials.....910.00 Labor..........90.50 ***Remove*** .... Labor..........33.60 ► Drop-in or slide-in range with continuous-clean oven, four solid-disk cast-iron burners, chrome drip pans, digital clock and timer.	ea	$33.60	$1,000.50	$1,034.10
Drop-in or slide-in electric range, deluxe grade ***Replace*** Materials...1070.00 Labor..........90.50 ***Remove*** .... Labor..........33.60 ► Drop-in or slide-in range with self-clean oven, four smooth-surface burners, digital clock and timer.	ea	$33.60	$1,160.50	$1,194.10
Drop-in or slide-in electric range with grill / griddle ***Replace*** Materials...1310.00 Labor..........90.50 ***Remove*** .... Labor..........33.60 ► Drop-in or slide-in range with self-clean oven, two smooth-surface burners, grill with griddle accessory and cover, digital clock and timer.	ea	$33.60	$1,400.50	$1,434.10
Remove drop-in or slide-in electric range, for work, then reinstall ***Replace*** Materials........5.00 Labor.........172.00	ea	—	$177.00	$177.00

SPACE-SAVER ► ELECTRIC RANGE

Item Description	Unit	Remove	Replace	Total
Space-saver electric range, standard grade ***Replace*** Materials.....910.00 Labor...........73.10 ***Remove*** .... Labor...........26.80 ► 20" free-standing range with standard-clean oven, four Calrod coil burners, and chrome drip pans.	ea	$26.80	$983.10	$1,009.90
Space-saver electric range, high grade ***Replace*** Materials ....970.00 Labor...........73.10 ***Remove*** .... Labor...........26.80 ► 20" free-standing range with continuous-clean oven, four Calrod coil burners, and chrome drip pans.	ea	$26.80	$1,043.10	$1,069.90

HIGH-LOW ► ELECTRIC RANGE

Item Description	Unit	Remove	Replace	Total
High-low electric range with microwave high, standard grade ***Replace*** Materials...1760.00 Labor..........77.90 ***Remove*** .... Labor..........28.30 ► 1.4 cf microwave with touch-pad controls. Range with continuous-clean oven, four Calrod burners, chrome drip pans, digital clock and timer.	ea	$28.30	$1,837.90	$1,866.20

Item Description	Unit	Remove	Replace	Total
High-low electric range with microwave high, high grade ***Replace*** Materials...1950.00 Labor..........77.90 ***Remove*** .... Labor..........28.30 ► 1.4 cf microwave with touch-pad controls. Range with self-clean oven, four Calrod burners, chrome drip pans, digital clock and timer.	ea	$28.30	$2,027.90	$2,056.20
High-low electric range with microwave high, deluxe grade ***Replace*** Materials...2170.00 Labor..........77.90 ***Remove*** .... Labor..........28.30 ► 1.4 cf microwave with touch-pad controls. Range with self-clean oven, four Calrod burners, chrome drip pans, digital clock and timer, integrated hood and venting system.	ea	$28.30	$2,247.90	$2,276.20
Electric wall oven, economy grade ***Replace*** Materials....506.00 Labor...........72.30 ***Remove*** .... Labor..........32.50 ► Standard-clean oven.	ea	$32.50	$578.30	$610.80
Electric wall oven, standard grade ***Replace*** Materials....584.00 Labor...........72.30 ***Remove*** .... Labor..........32.50 ► Continuous-clean oven, electronic pad controls with clock.	ea	$32.50	$656.30	$688.80
Electric wall oven, high grade ***Replace*** Materials.....742.00 Labor...........72.30 ***Remove*** .... Labor..........32.50 ► Self-clean oven, electronic pad controls with clock.	ea	$32.50	$814.30	$846.80
Electric wall oven, deluxe grade ***Replace*** Materials.....919.00 Labor...........72.30 ***Remove*** .... Labor..........32.50 ► Convection oven, electronic pad controls with clock.	ea	$32.50	$991.30	$1,023.80
Remove electric wall oven for work, then reinstall ***Replace*** Materials........2.00 Labor.........134.00	ea	—	$136.00	$136.00
Electric double wall oven, economy grade ***Replace*** Materials....985.00 Labor.........134.00 ***Remove*** .... Labor..........44.80 ► Two standard-clean ovens.	ea	$44.80	$1,119.00	$1,163.80
Electric double wall oven, standard grade ***Replace*** Materials...1140.00 Labor.........134.00 ***Remove*** .... Labor..........44.80 ► One continuous-clean oven, one self-clean oven, electronic pad controls with clock.	ea	$44.80	$1,274.00	$1,318.80
Electric double wall oven, high grade ***Replace*** Materials..1440.00 Labor.........134.00 ***Remove*** .... Labor..........44.80 ► Two self-clean ovens, electronic pad controls with clock.	ea	$44.80	$1,574.00	$1,618.80
Electric double wall oven, deluxe grade ***Replace*** Materials...1790.00 Labor.........134.00 ***Remove*** .... Labor..........44.80 ► One self-clean oven, one convection oven, electronic pad controls with clock.	ea	$44.80	$1,924.00	$1,968.80
Remove electric double wall oven for work, then reinstall ***Replace*** Materials........3.00 Labor.........226.00	ea	—	$229.00	$229.00

◄ **ELECTRIC WALL OVEN**

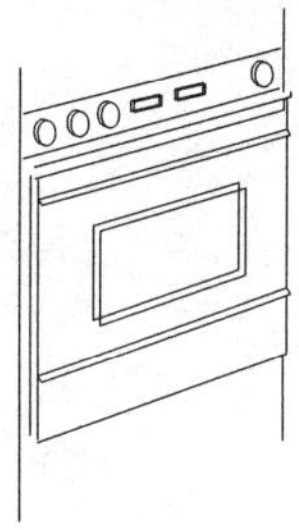

◄ **ELECTRIC DOUBLE WALL OVEN**

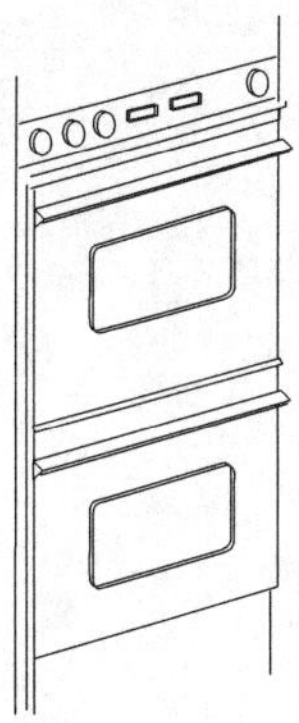

RELATED ITEMS

Cleaning........................55
Electrical *(wiring)*
electric oven or range......144

	Item Description	Unit	Remove	Replace	Total
RANGE HOOD ▶ 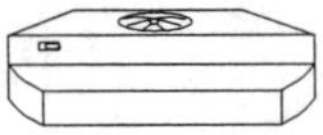	**Range hood, economy grade** ***Replace*** Materials......59.00 Labor...........61.20 ***Remove*** .... Labor..........20.20 ▶ 30" wide, two-speed fan, light, non-vented with disposable charcoal filter, baked enamel finish.	ea	$20.20	$120.20	$140.40
	Range hood, standard grade ***Replace*** Materials......98.00 Labor...........61.20 ***Remove*** .... Labor..........20.20 ▶ 30" or 36" wide, two-speed fan, light with night setting, vented with up to 16 lf duct, baked enamel finish.	ea	$20.20	$159.20	$179.40
	Range hood, high grade ***Replace*** Materials.....118.00 Labor...........61.20 ***Remove*** .... Labor..........20.20 ▶ 30" or 36" wide, variable-speed fan, two lights, vented with up to 16 lf duct, baked enamel finish.	ea	$20.20	$179.20	$199.40
	Range hood, deluxe grade ***Replace*** Materials....144.00 Labor...........61.20 ***Remove*** .... Labor..........20.20 ▶ 30" or 36" wide, variable-speed fan, two lights, vented with up to 16 lf duct, brushed chrome finish.	ea	$20.20	$205.20	$225.40
	Range hood, custom grade ***Replace*** Materials.....190.00 Labor...........61.20 ***Remove*** .... Labor..........20.20 ▶ 30" or 36" wide, variable-speed fan, two lights, vented with up to 16 lf duct, specialty deep design, copper finish.	ea	$20.20	$251.20	$271.40
OVERSIZED ▶ RANGE HOOD 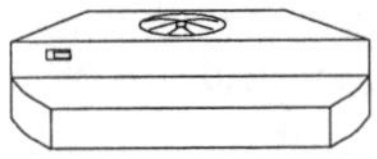	**Oversized range hood, standard grade** ***Replace*** Materials....284.00 Labor...........76.10 ***Remove*** .... Labor...........24.40 ▶ 42" wide, two-speed fan, light with night setting, vented with up to 16 lf duct, baked enamel finish.	ea	$24.40	$360.10	$384.50
	Oversized range hood, high grade ***Replace*** Materials....342.00 Labor...........76.10 ***Remove*** .... Labor...........24.40 ▶ 42" wide, variable-speed fan, two lights, vented with up to 16 lf duct, baked enamel finish.	ea	$24.40	$418.10	$442.50
	Oversized range hood, deluxe grade ***Replace*** Materials.....418.00 Labor...........76.10 ***Remove*** .... Labor...........24.40 ▶ 42" wide, variable-speed fan, two lights, vented with up to 16 lf duct, brushed chrome finish.	ea	$24.40	$494.10	$518.50
	Oversized range hood, custom grade ***Replace*** Materials ....551.00 Labor...........76.10 ***Remove*** .... Labor...........24.40 ▶ 42" wide, variable-speed fan, two lights, vented with up to 16 lf duct, specialty deep design, copper finish.	ea	$24.40	$627.10	$651.50
	Remove range hood for work, then reinstall ***Replace*** Materials........2.00 Labor.........129.00	ea	—	$131.00	$131.00
PUSH-BUTTON ▶ DISHWASHER	**Push-button dishwasher, economy grade** ***Replace*** Materials....390.00 Labor...........72.30 ***Remove*** .... Labor..........38.20 ▶ Three cycles, five options, standard insulation package.	ea	$38.20	$462.30	$500.50

Item Description	Unit	Remove	Replace	Total
Push-button dishwasher, standard grade ***Replace*** Materials.....510.00 Labor...........72.30 ***Remove*** .... Labor..........38.20 ► Five cycles, eight options, standard insulation package.	ea	$38.20	$582.30	$620.50
Push-button dishwasher, high grade ***Replace*** Materials....640.00 Labor...........72.30 ***Remove*** .... Labor..........38.20 ► Five cycles, fourteen options, deluxe insulation package.	ea	$38.20	$712.30	$750.50
Push-button dishwasher, deluxe grade ***Replace*** Materials....740.00 Labor...........72.30 ***Remove*** .... Labor..........38.20 ► Six cycles, eighteen options, deluxe insulation package.	ea	$38.20	$812.30	$850.50
Electronic dishwasher, economy grade ***Replace*** Materials....780.00 Labor...........72.30 ***Remove*** .... Labor..........38.20 ► Electronic touch-pad control, six cycles, twelve options, deluxe insulation package, specialty racks.	ea	$38.20	$852.30	$890.50
Electronic dishwasher, standard grade ***Replace*** Materials....870.00 Labor...........72.30 ***Remove*** .... Labor..........38.20 ► Electronic touch-pad control, seven cycles, twenty-three options, deluxe "quiet" insulation package, water saver cycle, delayed start option, specialty racks.	ea	$38.20	$942.30	$980.50
Electronic dishwasher, high grade ***Replace*** Materials..1030.00 Labor...........72.30 ***Remove*** .... Labor..........38.20 ► Electronic touch-pad control, seven cycles, twenty-three options, deluxe "quiet" insulation package, water saver cycle, delayed start option, specialty racks, self-cleaning filter system.	ea	$38.20	$1,102.30	$1,140.50
Electronic dishwasher, deluxe grade ***Replace*** Materials...1100.00 Labor...........72.30 ***Remove*** .... Labor..........38.20 ► Electronic touch-pad control, seven cycles, twenty-three options, deluxe "quiet" insulation package, water saver cycle, delayed start option, specialty racks, self-cleaning filter system, smooth-surface exterior panels that can integrate with cabinet design.	ea	$38.20	$1,172.30	$1,210.50
Convertible (portable) dishwasher, standard grade ***Replace*** Materials.....410.00 Labor..........43.80 ***Remove*** .... Labor..........38.20 ► Push-button control, four cycles, seven options, standard insulation package, plastic laminate top.	ea	$38.20	$453.80	$492.00
Convertible (portable) dishwasher, high grade ***Replace*** Materials....520.00 Labor..........43.80 ***Remove*** .... Labor..........38.20 ► Push-button control, four cycles, thirteen options, deluxe insulation package, specialty racks, wood veneer top.	ea	$38.20	$563.80	$602.00
Convertible (portable) dishwasher, deluxe grade ***Replace*** Materials.....610.00 Labor..........43.80 ***Remove*** .... Labor..........38.20 ► Push-button control, four cycles, fourteen options, deluxe insulation package, specialty racks, solid wood top (often butcher block), delay start option.	ea	$38.20	$653.80	$692.00

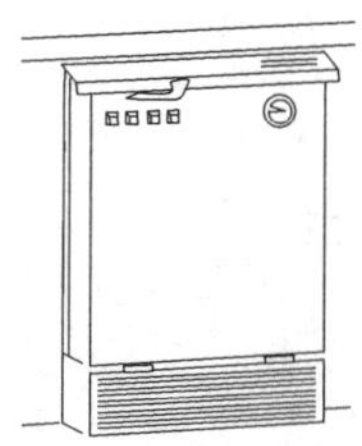

◄ **ELECTRONIC DISHWASHER**

◄ **CONVERTIBLE DISHWASHER**

RELATED ITEMS

Cleaning........................55
Electrical *(wiring)*
range hood..................143
dishwasher....................142
Plumbing
dishwasher..................368

	Item Description	Unit	Remove	Replace	Total
SPACE-SAVER UNDER-SINK DISHWASHER ▶	**Space-saver under-sink dishwasher, standard grade** *Replace* Materials....570.00 Labor..........111.00 *Remove* .... Labor..........38.20 ▶ Push-button control, four cycles, seven options, standard insulation package.	ea	$38.20	$681.00	$719.20
	Space-saver under-sink dishwasher, high grade *Replace* Materials.....670.00 Labor..........111.00 *Remove* .... Labor..........38.20 ▶ Push-button control, five cycles, eight options, deluxe insulation package.	ea	$38.20	$781.00	$819.20
	Remove dishwasher for work, then reinstall *Replace* Materials........5.00 Labor.........137.00	ea	—	$142.00	$142.00
GARBAGE DISPOSAL ▶	**1/3 hp garbage disposal** *Replace* Materials.....116.00 Labor...........71.50 *Remove* .... Labor...........35.80 ▶ Continuous feed.	ea	$35.80	$187.50	$223.30
	1/2 hp garbage disposal *Replace* Materials.....138.00 Labor...........71.50 *Remove* .... Labor...........35.80 ▶ Continuous feed, sound shield.	ea	$35.80	$209.50	$245.30
	1/2 hp stainless steel garbage disposal with auto-reverse *Replace* Materials....322.00 Labor...........71.50 *Remove* .... Labor...........35.80 ▶ Continuous feed, sound shield, auto-reverse.	ea	$35.80	$393.50	$429.30
	3/4 hp garbage disposal *Replace* Materials....387.00 Labor...........71.50 *Remove* .... Labor...........35.80 ▶ Batch feed, deluxe "quiet" sound shield, non-corroding, glass-filled polyester drain housing and hopper.	ea	$35.80	$458.50	$494.30
	3/4 hp stainless steel garbage disposal with auto-reverse *Replace* Materials....460.00 Labor...........71.50 *Remove* .... Labor...........35.80 ▶ Batch feed, deluxe "quiet" sound shield, non-corroding, glass-filled polyester drain housing and hopper, with auto-reverse.	ea	$35.80	$531.50	$567.30
	1 hp garbage disposal *Replace* Materials.....670.00 Labor...........71.50 *Remove* .... Labor...........35.80 ▶ Batch feed, deluxe "quiet" sound shield, non-corroding, glass-filled polyester drain housing and hopper.	ea	$35.80	$741.50	$777.30
	1 hp stainless steel garbage disposal with auto-reverse *Replace* Materials....729.00 Labor...........71.50 *Remove* .... Labor...........35.80 ▶ Batch feed, deluxe "quiet" sound shield, non-corroding, glass-filled polyester drain housing and hopper, with auto-reverse.	ea	$35.80	$800.50	$836.30
	Remove garbage disposal for work, then reinstall *Replace* Materials........5.00 Labor.........134.00	ea	—	$139.00	$139.00
MICROWAVE ▶	**Microwave oven, standard grade** *Replace* Materials....278.00 Labor...........14.50 *Remove* .... Labor...........13.80 ▶ To 800 watts, defrost, multiple power levels, time cook.	ea	$13.80	$292.50	$306.30

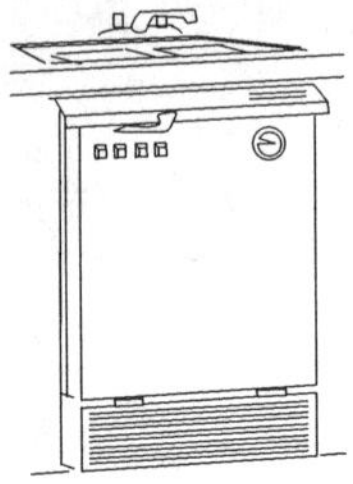

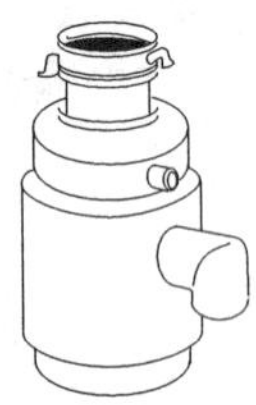

Item Description	*Unit*	*Remove*	*Replace*	*Total*
Microwave oven, high grade ***Replace*** Materials....387.00 Labor...........14.50 ***Remove*** .... Labor...........13.80 ► To 800 watts, defrost, popcorn pad, 10 power levels, time cook, reheat pad.	ea	$13.80	$401.50	$415.30
Microwave oven, deluxe grade ***Replace*** Materials....532.00 Labor...........14.50 ***Remove*** .... Labor...........13.80 ► To 800 watts, defrost, popcorn pad, 10 power levels, time cook, reheat pad, roasting and defrost automatic sensing controls.	ea	$13.80	$546.50	$560.30
Microwave oven, custom grade ***Replace*** Materials....657.00 Labor...........14.50 ***Remove*** .... Labor...........13.80 ► To 800 watts with convection heating, defrost, popcorn pad, 10 power levels, time cook, reheat pad, baking, defrost sensing controls.	ea	$13.80	$671.50	$685.30
Microwave oven, under cabinet, standard grade ***Replace*** Materials.....611.00 Labor...........72.30 ***Remove*** .... Labor...........13.80 ► To 750 watts (many models around 550 to 600 watts), defrost, popcorn pad, 10 power levels, time cook, reheat pad, baking, defrost sensing controls, with high-capacity exhaust vent fan (includes up to 16 lf of duct).	ea	$13.80	$683.30	$697.10
Microwave oven, under cabinet, high grade ***Replace*** Materials.....916.00 Labor...........72.30 ***Remove*** .... Labor...........13.80 ► To 750 watts (many models around 550 to 600 watts) with convection, defrost, popcorn pad, 10 power levels, time cook, reheat pad, baking, defrost sensing controls, with high-capacity exhaust vent fan (includes up to 16 lf of duct).	ea	$13.80	$988.30	$1,002.10
Side-by-side refrigerator / freezer, 24 to 27 cf capacity, standard grade ***Replace*** Materials...1720.00 Labor ....30.20 ***Remove*** .... Labor...........26.80 ► Standard-style shelves, energy efficient.	ea	$26.80	$1,750.20	$1,777.00
Side-by-side refrigerator / freezer, 24 to 27 cf capacity, high grade ***Replace*** Materials...2170.00 Labor ....30.20 ***Remove*** .... Labor...........26.80 ► Specialty-style shelves, deep doors, energy efficient.	ea	$26.80	$2,200.20	$2,227.00
Side-by-side refrigerator / freezer, 24 to 27 cf capacity, deluxe grade ***Replace*** Materials..2600.00 Labor ....30.20 ***Remove*** .... Labor...........26.80 ► Specialty-style shelves and doors, deep doors, highly energy efficient.	ea	$26.80	$2,630.20	$2,657.00
Side-by-side refrigerator / freezer, 20 to 23 cf capacity, standard grade ***Replace*** Materials ...1120.00 Labor ....30.20 ***Remove*** .... Labor...........26.80 ► Standard-style shelves, energy efficient.	ea	$26.80	$1,150.20	$1,177.00
Side-by-side refrigerator / freezer, 20 to 23 cf capacity, high grade ***Replace*** Materials ...1610.00 Labor ....30.20 ***Remove*** .... Labor...........26.80 ► Specialty-style shelves, deep doors, energy efficient.	ea	$26.80	$1,640.20	$1,667.00
Side-by-side refrigerator / freezer, 20 to 23 cf capacity, deluxe grade ***Replace*** Materials ..1880.00 Labor ....30.20 ***Remove*** .... Labor...........26.80 ► Specialty-style shelves and doors, deep doors, highly energy efficient.	ea	$26.80	$1,910.20	$1,937.00

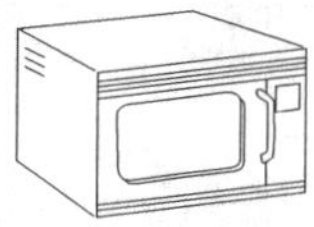

◄ **UNDER CABINET MICROWAVE**

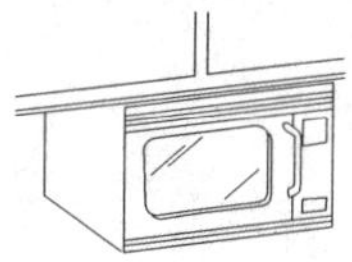

◄ **SIDE-BY-SIDE REFRIGERATOR / FREEZER**

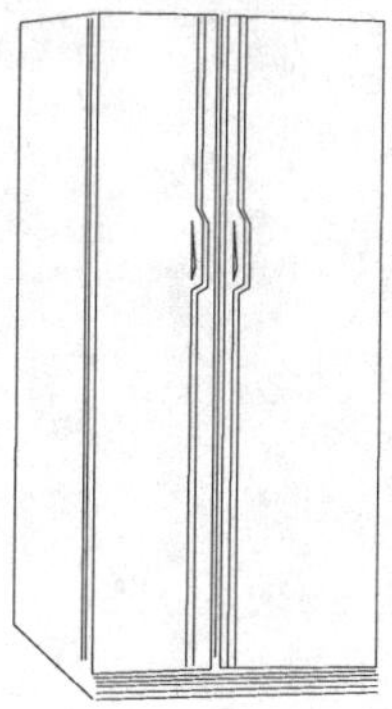

RELATED ITEMS

Cleaning........................55
Electrical *(wiring)*
dishwasher.........................142
garbage disposal............143
electric appliance............142
Plumbing
dishwasher...................368

	Item Description	Unit	Remove	Replace	Total
SIDE-BY-SIDE ► CABINET MATCH	**Add for side-by-side refrigerator / freezer with cabinet-matching doors** *Replace* Materials....341.00	ea	—	$341.00	$341.00
OVER-UNDER ► REFRIGERATOR / FREEZER 	**Over-under refrigerator / freezer, 21 to 25 cf capacity, standard grade** *Replace* Materials...1180.00 Labor...........26.80 *Remove* .... Labor ....23.30 ► Standard-style shelves, energy efficient.	ea	$23.30	$1,206.80	$1,230.10
	Over-under refrigerator / freezer, 21 to 25 cf capacity, high grade *Replace* Materials...1350.00 Labor...........26.80 *Remove* .... Labor ....23.30 ► Specialty-style shelves, deep doors, energy efficient.	ea	$23.30	$1,376.80	$1,400.10
	Over-under refrigerator / freezer, 21 to 25 cf capacity, deluxe grade *Replace* Materials..1680.00 Labor...........26.80 *Remove* .... Labor ....23.30 ► Specialty-style shelves and doors, deep doors, highly energy efficient.	ea	$23.30	$1,706.80	$1,730.10
	Over-under refrigerator / freezer, 17 to 20 cf capacity, standard grade *Replace* Materials..1040.00 Labor...........26.80 *Remove* .... Labor ....23.30 ► Standard-style shelves, energy efficient.	ea	$23.30	$1,066.80	$1,090.10
	Over-under refrigerator / freezer, 17 to 20 cf capacity, high grade *Replace* Materials...1180.00 Labor...........26.80 *Remove* .... Labor ....23.30 ► Specialty-style shelves, deep doors, energy efficient.	ea	$23.30	$1,206.80	$1,230.10
	Over-under refrigerator / freezer, 17 to 20 cf capacity, deluxe grade *Replace* Materials..1430.00 Labor...........26.80 *Remove* .... Labor ....23.30 ► Specialty-style shelves and doors, deep doors, highly energy efficient.	ea	$23.30	$1,456.80	$1,480.10
	Over-under refrigerator / freezer, 13 to 16 cf capacity, standard grade *Replace* Materials....886.00 Labor...........26.80 *Remove* .... Labor ....23.30 ► Standard-style shelves, energy efficient.	ea	$23.30	$912.80	$936.10
	Over-under refrigerator / freezer, 13 to 16 cf capacity, high grade *Replace* Materials..1040.00 Labor...........26.80 *Remove* .... Labor ....23.30 ► Specialty-style shelves, deep doors, energy efficient.	ea	$23.30	$1,066.80	$1,090.10
	Over-under refrigerator / freezer, 13 to 16 cf capacity, deluxe grade *Replace* Materials...1210.00 Labor...........26.80 *Remove* .... Labor ....23.30 ► Specialty-style shelves and doors, deep doors, highly energy efficient.	ea	$23.30	$1,236.80	$1,260.10
	Over-under refrigerator / freezer, 10 to 12 cf capacity, standard grade *Replace* Materials....735.00 Labor...........26.80 *Remove* .... Labor ....23.30 ► Standard-style shelves, energy efficient.	ea	$23.30	$761.80	$785.10
	Over-under refrigerator / freezer, 10 to 12 cf capacity, high grade *Replace* Materials....899.00 Labor...........26.80 *Remove* .... Labor ....23.30 ► Specialty-style shelves, deep doors, energy efficient.	ea	$23.30	$925.80	$949.10

RELATED ITEMS

Cleaning........................55
Electrical *(wiring)*
trash compactor..............143
clothes washer...............142
Plumbing
clothes washer..............368
ice maker.....................368

Item Description	*Unit*	*Remove*	*Replace*	*Total*
Over-under refrigerator / freezer, 10 to 12 cf capacity, deluxe grade	ea	$23.30	$1,056.80	$1,080.10
Replace Materials..1030.00 Labor..........26.80 ***Remove*** .... Labor..........23.30 ► Specialty-style shelves and doors, deep doors, highly energy efficient.				
Remove refrigerator for work, then reinstall	ea	—	$55.90	$55.90
Replace .... Labor..........55.90				
Add for refreshment center in refrigerator / freezer	ea	—	$485.00	$485.00
Replace Materials.....374.00 Labor..........111.00				
Disconnect refrigerator water line for work, then re-connect	ea	—	$13.40	$13.40
Replace Materials........ .70 Labor..........12.70				
Refreshment center plumbing hook-up in existing building	ea	—	$317.00	$317.00
Replace Materials......26.00 Labor.........291.00				
Refreshment center plumbing hook-up, new construction	ea	—	$169.00	$169.00
Replace Materials......24.00 Labor.........145.00				
Refinish refrigerator	ea	—	$390.00	$390.00
Replace Materials......39.00 Labor.........351.00				
Refinish and recondition refrigerator	ea	—	$462.00	$462.00
Replace Materials......59.00 Labor........403.00				
Trash compactor, economy grade	ea	$23.30	$530.60	$553.90
Replace Materials....479.00 Labor..........51.60 ***Remove*** .... Labor..........23.30 ► Convertible or built-in, 12".				
Trash compactor, standard grade	ea	$23.30	$662.60	$685.90
Replace Materials.....611.00 Labor..........51.60 ***Remove*** .... Labor..........23.30 ► Convertible or built-in, 12" to 15", key lock, automatic anti-jam, reversible panel.				
Trash compactor, high grade	ea	$23.30	$740.60	$763.90
Replace Materials....689.00 Labor..........51.60 ***Remove*** .... Labor..........23.30 ► Convertible or built-in, 12" to 15", key lock, automatic anti-jam, heavy gauge construction, reversible panel.				
Remove trash compactor for work, then reinstall	ea	—	$108.70	$108.70
Replace Materials........ .70 Labor.........108.00				
Clothes washing machine, economy grade	ea	$14.90	$423.10	$438.00
Replace Materials....407.00 Labor..........16.10 ***Remove*** .... Labor..........14.90 ► Large capacity, five cycles, three water levels, bleach dispenser.				
Clothes washing machine, standard grade	ea	$14.90	$522.10	$537.00
Replace Materials....506.00 Labor..........16.10 ***Remove*** .... Labor..........14.90 ► Large capacity, six cycles, two speeds, two wash / spin combinations, three water levels, bleach dispenser.				
Clothes washing machine, high grade	ea	$14.90	$600.10	$615.00
Replace Materials....584.00 Labor..........16.10 ***Remove*** .... Labor..........14.90 ► Extra large capacity, nine cycles with pre-wash, three speeds, four wash / spin combinations, three water levels, bleach dispenser.				

◄ **REFRESHMENT CENTER**

◄ **REFRESHMENT CENTER PLUMBING**
With supply lines and hookup to appliances. For installation of supply lines only see Plumbing on page 368.

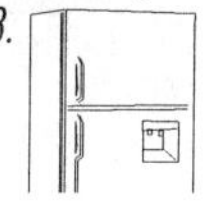

◄ **REFINISH REFRIGERATOR**

◄ **TRASH COMPACTOR**

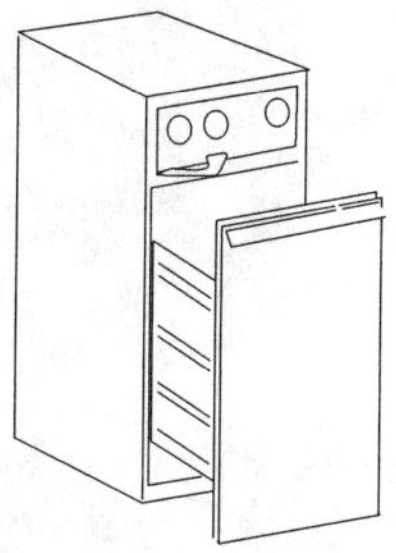

◄ **WASHING MACHINE**

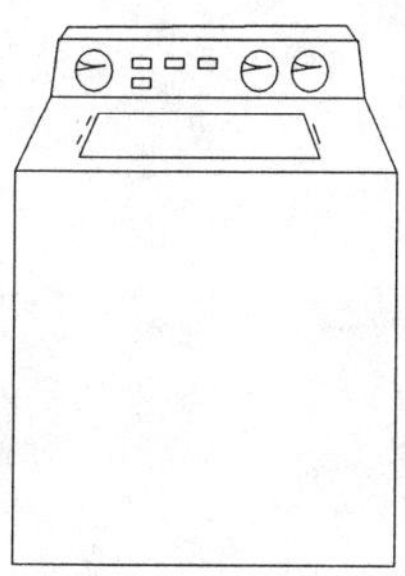

WASHING MACHINE ▶ *continued*

CLOTHES DRYER ▶ *Electric dryers with up to 20' of vent pipe. Add* ***$125*** *for gas dryer (includes additional cost of dryer and additional cost to install).*

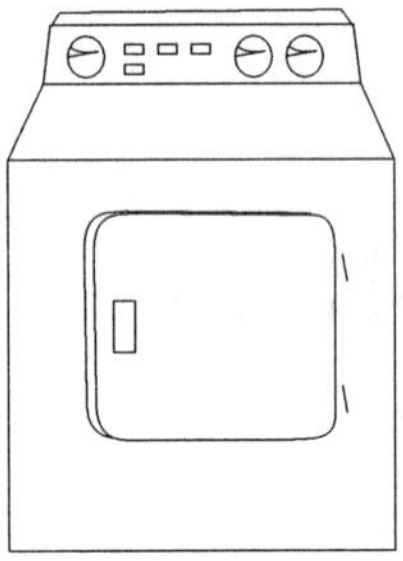

Item Description	Unit	Remove	Replace	Total
Clothes washing machine, deluxe grade ***Replace*** Materials....775.00 Labor...........16.10 ***Remove*** .... Labor...........14.90 ▶ Extra large capacity, programmable, ten cycles with pre-wash, four programmable speeds, four programmable wash / spin combinations, variable water levels, bleach / fabric softener dispenser.	ea	$14.90	$791.10	$806.00
Remove washing machine for work, then reinstall ***Replace*** .... Labor..........30.20	ea	—	$30.20	$30.20
Clothes dryer, electric, economy grade ***Replace*** Materials....328.00 Labor...........14.50 ***Remove*** .... Labor...........13.80 ▶ Large capacity, two cycles, three heat selections.	ea	$13.80	$342.50	$356.30
Clothes dryer, electric, standard grade ***Replace*** Materials....407.00 Labor...........14.50 ***Remove*** .... Labor...........13.80 ▶ Large capacity with automatic drying control, six cycles, four heat selections.	ea	$13.80	$421.50	$435.30
Clothes dryer, high grade ***Replace*** Materials....525.00 Labor...........14.50 ***Remove*** .... Labor...........13.80 ▶ Extra large capacity with electronic drying control, five cycles with delicate fabrics option, four heat selections, drum lamp.	ea	$13.80	$539.50	$553.30
Clothes dryer, deluxe grade ***Replace*** Materials....663.00 Labor...........14.50 ***Remove*** .... Labor...........13.80 ▶ Extra large capacity with electronic drying control, six cycles with delicate fabrics option, four heat selections, drum lamp.	ea	$13.80	$677.50	$691.30
Remove clothes dryer for work, then reinstall ***Replace*** .... Labor...........26.80	ea	—	$26.80	$26.80

✍ NOTES:

end

TIME & MATERIAL CHARTS (selected items)

Appliance Materials

See **Appliance** material prices with the line items and other information in the **QuickFinder** column.

Appliance Labor

LABORER	BASE WAGE	PAID LEAVE	TRUE WAGE	FICA	FUTA	WORKER'S COMP.	UNEMPLOY. INSUR.	HEALTH INSUR.	RETIRE (401K)	LIABILITY INSUR.	COST PER HOUR
Appliance installer	$21.80	1.70	$23.50	1.80	.19	2.97	2.04	2.69	.71	3.17	$37.10
Appliance refinisher	$24.80	1.93	$26.73	2.04	.21	7.43	2.33	2.69	.80	3.61	$45.80
Electrician	$26.10	2.04	$28.14	2.15	.23	3.03	2.45	2.69	.84	3.80	$43.30
Plumber	$25.90	2.02	$27.92	2.14	.22	4.66	2.43	2.69	.84	3.77	$44.70
Demolition laborer	$13.90	1.08	$14.98	1.15	.12	4.79	1.30	2.69	.45	2.02	$27.50

Paid Leave is calculated based on two weeks paid vacation, one week sick leave, and seven paid holidays. Employer's matching portion of **FICA** is 7.65 percent. **FUTA** (Federal Unemployment) is .8 percent. **Worker's compensation** was calculated using a national average of 12.63 percent for the appliance installer; 27.79 percent for the appliance refinisher; 10.78 percent for the electrician; 16.69 percent for the plumber; and 31.99 percent for the demolition laborer. **Unemployment insurance** was calculated using a national average of 8.7 percent. **Health insurance** was calculated based on a projected national average for 2002 of $535 per employee (and family when applicable) per month. Employer pays 80 percent for a per month cost of $428 per employee. **Retirement** is based on a 401(k) retirement program with employer matching of 50 percent. Employee contributions to the 401(k) plan are an average of 6 percent of the true wage. **Liability insurance** is based on a national average of 13.2 percent.

Appliances Labor Productivity

WORK DESCRIPTION	LABORER	COST PER HOUR	PRODUCTIVITY	UNIT PRICE
Demolition				
remove gas cook top	demolition laborer	$27.50	.975	$26.80 ea
remove gas range	demolition laborer	$27.50	1.03	$28.30 ea
remove high-low gas range	demolition laborer	$27.50	1.18	$32.50 ea
remove restaurant-style gas range	demolition laborer	$27.50	3.00	$82.50 ea
remove gas wall oven	demolition laborer	$27.50	1.34	$36.90 ea
remove gas double wall oven	demolition laborer	$27.50	1.95	$53.60 ea
remove electric cook top	demolition laborer	$27.50	1.03	$28.30 ea
remove modular electric cook-top unit	demolition laborer	$27.50	.510	$14.00 ea
remove electric range	demolition laborer	$27.50	.975	$26.80 ea
remove drop-in or slide-in electric range	demolition laborer	$27.50	1.22	$33.60 ea
remove high-low electric range	demolition laborer	$27.50	1.03	$28.30 ea
remove electric wall oven	demolition laborer	$27.50	1.18	$32.50 ea
remove electric double wall oven	demolition laborer	$27.50	1.63	$44.80 ea
remove range hood	demolition laborer	$27.50	.736	$20.20 ea
remove over-sized range hood	demolition laborer	$27.50	.886	$24.40 ea
remove dishwasher	demolition laborer	$27.50	1.39	$38.20 ea
remove garbage disposal	demolition laborer	$27.50	1.30	$35.80 ea
remove microwave oven	demolition laborer	$27.50	.500	$13.80 ea
remove side-by-side refrigerator / freezer	demolition laborer	$27.50	.975	$26.80 ea
remove over-under refrigerator / freezer	demolition laborer	$27.50	.848	$23.30 ea
remove trash compactor	demolition laborer	$27.50	.848	$23.30 ea
remove clothes washing machine	demolition laborer	$27.50	.542	$14.90 ea
remove clothes dryer	demolition laborer	$27.50	.500	$13.80 ea

. . . More >

Appliances Labor Productivity *continued*

WORK DESCRIPTION	LABORER	COST PER HOUR	PRODUCTIVITY	UNIT PRICE
Install appliances				
gas cook top	plumber	$44.70	1.99	**$89.00** ea
gas range	plumber	$44.70	2.05	**$91.60** ea
gas range with grill / griddle	plumber	$44.70	2.10	**$93.90** ea
space-saver gas range	plumber	$44.70	1.99	**$89.00** ea
high-low gas range with microwave high	plumber	$44.70	2.12	**$94.80** ea
restaurant-style gas range	plumber	$44.70	4.43	**$198.00** ea
gas wall oven	installer	$37.10	2.17	**$80.50** ea
gas double wall oven	installer	$37.10	3.98	**$148.00** ea
electric cook top	electrician	$43.30	1.77	**$76.60** ea
modular cooking unit	electrician	$43.30	.629	**$27.20** ea
modular electric cook top downdraft unit	electrician	$43.30	.488	**$21.10** ea
electric range	installer	$37.10	2.03	**$75.30** ea
drop-in or slide-in electric range	installer	$37.10	2.44	**$90.50** ea
space-saver electric range	installer	$37.10	1.97	**$73.10** ea
high-low electric range with microwave high	installer	$37.10	2.10	**$77.90** ea
electric wall oven	installer	$37.10	1.95	**$72.30** ea
electric double wall oven	installer	$37.10	3.61	**$134.00** ea
range hood	installer	$37.10	1.65	**$61.20** ea
oversized range hood	installer	$37.10	2.05	**$76.10** ea
dishwasher	installer	$37.10	1.95	**$72.30** ea
convertible (portable) dishwasher	installer	$37.10	1.18	**$43.80** ea
space-saver under-sink dishwasher	installer	$37.10	3.00	**$111.00** ea
garbage disposal	plumber	$44.70	1.60	**$71.50** ea
microwave oven	installer	$37.10	.390	**$14.50** ea
microwave oven under cabinet	installer	$37.10	1.95	**$72.30** ea
side-by-side refrigerator / freezer	installer	$37.10	.813	**$30.20** ea
refreshment center in side-by-side refrigerator / freezer	installer	$37.10	3.00	**$111.00** ea
over-under refrigerator / freezer	installer	$37.10	.722	**$26.80** ea
refreshment center in over-under refrigerator / freezer	installer	$37.10	3.00	**$111.00** ea
refreshment center plumbing hook-up in existing building	plumber	$44.70	6.50	**$291.00** ea
refreshment center plumbing hook-up, new construction	plumber	$44.70	3.25	**$145.00** ea
trash compactor	installer	$37.10	1.39	**$51.60** ea
clothes washing machine	installer	$37.10	.433	**$16.10** ea
clothes dryer	installer	$37.10	.390	**$14.50** ea

NOTES:

end

3 .... Awnings

Item Description	Unit	Remove	Replace	Total
Free-standing aluminum carport, 150 sf or less ***Replace*** Materials.......15.90 Labor............2.87 ***Remove*.........................** Labor............1.38	sf	$1.38	$18.77	$20.15
Free-standing aluminum carport, 151 to 250 sf ***Replace*** Materials.......13.80 Labor............2.87 ***Remove*.........................** Labor............1.38	sf	$1.38	$16.67	$18.05
Free-standing aluminum carport, 251 to 480 sf ***Replace*** Materials.......13.20 Labor............2.87 ***Remove*.........................** Labor............1.38	sf	$1.38	$16.07	$17.45
Remove free-standing aluminum carport for work, then reinstall ***Replace*** Materials........ .40 Labor............6.01	sf	—	$6.41	$6.41
Attached aluminum carport or patio cover, 150 sf or less ***Replace*** Materials ......14.50 Labor............2.65 ***Remove*.........................** Labor............1.49	sf	$1.49	$17.15	$18.64
Attached aluminum carport or patio cover, 151 to 250 sf ***Replace*** Materials ......12.60 Labor............2.65 ***Remove*.........................** Labor............1.49	sf	$1.49	$15.25	$16.74
Attached aluminum carport or patio cover, 251 to 480 sf ***Replace*** Materials ......12.10 Labor............2.65 ***Remove*.........................** Labor............1.49	sf	$1.49	$14.75	$16.24
Remove attached aluminum carport or patio cover for work, then reinstall ***Replace*** Materials........ .40 Labor............5.60	sf	—	$6.00	$6.00
Minimum charge for carport or patio cover work ***Replace*** Materials......47.00 Labor...........69.00	ea	—	$116.00	$116.00
Add for heavy gauge aluminum carport or patio cover ***Replace*** Materials........3.50	sf	—	$3.50	$3.50
Carport or patio cover post ***Replace*** Materials......52.40 Labor..........38.90 ***Remove*.........................** Labor............7.60	ea	$7.60	$91.30	$98.90
Remove carport or patio cover post for work, then reinstall ***Replace*** Materials........2.10 Labor..........63.00	ea	—	$65.10	$65.10
Carport or patio cover post scroll ***Replace*** Materials......63.00 Labor...........14.60 ***Remove*.........................** Labor............2.61	ea	$2.61	$77.60	$80.21
Remove carport or patio cover post scroll for work, then reinstall ***Replace*** Materials........1.00 Labor..........23.70	ea	—	$24.70	$24.70
Carport or patio cover aluminum fascia ***Replace*** Materials.......13.00 Labor............4.40 ***Remove*.........................** Labor............ .75	lf	$.75	$17.40	$18.15

◀ **FREE-STANDING CARPORT** *40 psf. Aluminum with baked enamel finish. With 4 posts under 200 sf. With 6 posts over 200 sf.*

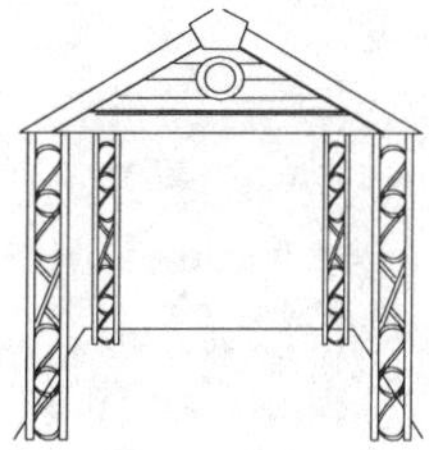

◀ **ATTACHED CARPORT** *40 psf. Aluminum with baked enamel finish. With 3 posts under 200 sf. With 4 to 5 posts over 200 sf.*

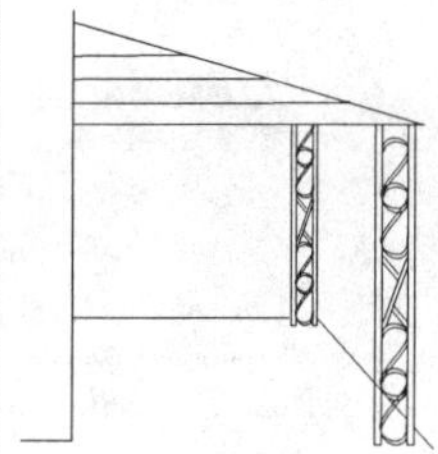

◁ **minimum**

◁ **add for heavy gauge**

◁ **post**

◁ **scroll**

◁ **fascia**

	Item Description	Unit	Remove	Replace	Total
	Remove carport or patio cover aluminum fascia for work, then reinstall *Replace* Materials.......... Labor............7.40	lf	—	$7.40	$7.40
roof panel ▷	**Carport or patio cover roof panel** *Replace* Materials......79.00 Labor...........27.20 *Remove*......................... Labor...........13.20	ea	$13.20	$106.20	$119.40
	Remove carport or patio cover roof panel for work, then reinstall *Replace* Materials........4.00 Labor..........43.50	ea	—	$47.50	$47.50
downspout ▷	**Carport or patio cover downspout** *Replace* Materials......52.00 Labor............3.90 *Remove*......................... Labor............2.64	ea	$2.64	$55.90	$58.54
	Remove carport or patio cover downspout for work, then reinstall *Replace* Materials.......... Labor............5.80	ea	—	$5.80	$5.80
42″ ALUMINUM DOOR AWNING ▶ *25 to 40 psf. Aluminum with baked enamel finish. Includes all hardware and adjustable supports.*	**Aluminum door awning with 42″ projection, 2 to 4 lf** *Replace* Materials.....165.00 Labor...........17.30 *Remove*......................... Labor...........13.20	lf	$13.20	$182.30	$195.50
	Aluminum door awning with 42″ projection, 5 to 8 lf *Replace* Materials....140.00 Labor...........17.30 *Remove*......................... Labor...........13.20	lf	$13.20	$157.30	$170.50
	Aluminum door awning with 42″ projection, 9 to 12 lf *Replace* Materials.....126.00 Labor...........17.30 *Remove*......................... Labor...........13.20	lf	$13.20	$143.30	$156.50
54″ ALUMINUM DOOR AWNING ▶ *25 to 40 psf. Aluminum with baked enamel finish. Includes all hardware and adjustable supports.*	**Aluminum door awning with 54″ projection, 2 to 4 lf** *Replace* Materials....221.00 Labor...........18.10 *Remove*......................... Labor...........13.80	lf	$13.80	$239.10	$252.90
	Aluminum door awning with 54″ projection, 5 to 8 lf *Replace* Materials.....185.00 Labor...........18.10 *Remove*......................... Labor...........13.80	lf	$13.80	$203.10	$216.90
	Aluminum door awning with 54″ projection, 9 to 12 lf *Replace* Materials.....165.00 Labor...........18.10 *Remove*......................... Labor...........13.80	lf	$13.80	$183.10	$196.90
	Remove aluminum door awning for work, then reinstall *Replace* Materials........6.00 Labor...........35.80	lf	—	$41.80	$41.80
3′ HIGH WINDOW AWNING ▶ *25 to 40 psf. Aluminum with baked enamel finish. Includes all hardware and adjustable supports.*	**3′ high aluminum window awning, 2 to 4 lf** *Replace* Materials......53.40 Labor...........12.90 *Remove*......................... Labor...........11.10	lf	$11.10	$66.30	$77.40
	3′ high aluminum window awning, 5 to 8 lf *Replace* Materials......41.80 Labor...........12.90 *Remove*......................... Labor...........11.10	lf	$11.10	$54.70	$65.80
	3′ high aluminum window awning, 9 to 12 lf *Replace* Materials......39.10 Labor...........12.90 *Remove*......................... Labor...........11.10	lf	$11.10	$52.00	$63.10
	Remove 3′ high aluminum window awning for work, then reinstall *Replace* Materials........6.00 Labor...........31.00	lf	—	$37.00	$37.00

Item Description	Unit	Remove	Replace	Total	
4′ high aluminum window awning, 2 to 4 lf ***Replace*** Materials......62.50 Labor..........13.20 ***Remove*** .... Labor..........11.40	lf	$11.40	$75.70	$87.10	◀ **4′ HIGH WINDOW AWNING** *25 to 40 psf. Aluminum with baked enamel finish. Includes all hardware and adjustable supports.*
4′ high aluminum window awning, 5 to 8 lf ***Replace*** Materials......51.70 Labor..........13.20 ***Remove*** .... Labor..........11.40	lf	$11.40	$64.90	$76.30	
4′ high aluminum window awning, 9 to 12 lf ***Replace*** Materials......48.10 Labor..........13.20 ***Remove*** .... Labor..........11.40	lf	$11.40	$61.30	$72.70	
Remove 4′ high aluminum window awning for work, then reinstall ***Replace*** Materials........6.00 Labor..........31.50	lf	—	$37.50	$37.50	
5′ high aluminum window awning, 2 to 4 lf ***Replace*** Materials......83.10 Labor..........13.50 ***Remove*** .... Labor..........11.60	lf	$11.60	$96.60	$108.20	◀ **5′ HIGH WINDOW AWNING** *25 to 40 psf. Aluminum with baked enamel finish. Includes all hardware and adjustable supports.*
5′ high aluminum window awning, 5 to 8 lf ***Replace*** Materials......75.30 Labor..........13.50 ***Remove*** .... Labor..........11.60	lf	$11.60	$88.80	$100.40	
5′ high aluminum window awning, 9 to 12 lf ***Replace*** Materials......59.70 Labor..........13.50 ***Remove*** .... Labor..........11.60	lf	$11.60	$73.20	$84.80	
Remove 5′ high aluminum window awning for work, then reinstall ***Replace*** Materials........6.00 Labor..........32.10	lf	—	$38.10	$38.10	
6′ high aluminum window awning, 2 to 4 lf ***Replace*** Materials......96.10 Labor..........13.70 ***Remove*** .... Labor..........11.80	lf	$11.80	$109.80	$121.60	◀ **6′ HIGH WINDOW AWNING** *25 to 40 psf. Aluminum with baked enamel finish. Includes all hardware and adjustable supports.*
6′ high aluminum window awning, 5 to 8 lf ***Replace*** Materials......91.40 Labor..........13.70 ***Remove*** .... Labor..........11.80	lf	$11.80	$105.10	$116.90	
6′ high aluminum window awning, 9 to 12 lf ***Replace*** Materials......70.20 Labor..........13.70 ***Remove*** .... Labor..........11.80	lf	$11.80	$83.90	$95.70	
Remove 6′ high aluminum window awning for work, then reinstall ***Replace*** Materials........6.00 Labor..........32.70	lf	—	$38.70	$38.70	
Minimum charge for door or window awning work ***Replace*** Materials......47.00 Labor..........69.00	ea	—	$116.00	$116.00	◁ **minimum**
Door or window awning slat ***Replace*** Materials......20.00 Labor..........13.40 ***Remove*** .... Labor..........6.30	ea	$6.30	$33.40	$39.70	
Roll-up aluminum awning, 2 to 5 lf ***Replace*** Materials......59.90 Labor..........10.20 ***Remove*** .... Labor..........11.50	lf	$11.50	$70.10	$81.60	◀ **ROLL-UP AWNING** *Security awning that covers window. Aluminum with baked enamel finish. Includes all hardware and adjustable supports.*
Roll-up aluminum awning, 6 to 12 lf ***Replace*** Materials......45.80 Labor..........10.20 ***Remove*** .... Labor..........11.50	lf	$11.50	$56.00	$67.50	

Item Description	Unit	Remove	Replace	Total
Remove roll-up aluminum window awning for work, then reinstall *Replace* Materials........4.60 Labor..........22.70	lf	—	$27.30	$27.30
CANVAS AWNING ▶ *Waterproof acrylic duck colorfast fabric with retractable metal frame and hardware.*				
Canvas awning with 24" drop, 2 to 3 lf *Replace* Materials......84.60 Labor...........18.40 *Remove*......................... Labor............8.91	lf	$8.91	$103.00	$111.91
Canvas awning with 24" drop, 4 to 5 lf *Replace* Materials......78.80 Labor...........18.40 *Remove*......................... Labor............8.91	lf	$8.91	$97.20	$106.11
Canvas awning with 30" drop, 2 to 3 lf *Replace* Materials......99.10 Labor...........19.60 *Remove*......................... Labor............8.91	lf	$8.91	$118.70	$127.61
Canvas awning with 30" drop, 4 to 5 lf *Replace* Materials......87.00 Labor...........19.60 *Remove*......................... Labor............8.91	lf	$8.91	$106.60	$115.51
Canvas awning with 30" drop, 5 to 6 lf *Replace* Materials......78.30 Labor...........19.60 *Remove*......................... Labor............8.91	lf	$8.91	$97.90	$106.81
Canvas awning with 30" drop, 7 to 8 lf *Replace* Materials......69.70 Labor...........19.60 *Remove*......................... Labor............8.91	lf	$8.91	$89.30	$98.21
Canvas awning with 30" drop, 9 to 10 lf *Replace* Materials......57.20 Labor...........19.60 *Remove*......................... Labor............8.91	lf	$8.91	$76.80	$85.71
Canvas awning with 30" drop, 11 to 12 lf *Replace* Materials......53.00 Labor...........19.60 *Remove*......................... Labor............8.91	lf	$8.91	$72.60	$81.51
Remove canvas awning for work, then reinstall *Replace* Materials........4.90 Labor...........42.90	lf	—	$47.80	$47.80
minimum ▷ **Minimum charge for canvas awning work** *Replace* Materials......41.00 Labor...........61.50	ea	—	$102.50	$102.50
VINYL AWNING ▶ *Vinyl awning with acrylic coating. Includes metal frame and all hardware.*				
Vinyl awning with 24" drop, 2 to 3 lf *Replace* Materials......50.10 Labor...........18.30 *Remove*......................... Labor............8.91	lf	$8.91	$68.40	$77.31
Vinyl awning with 24" drop, 4 to 5 lf *Replace* Materials......46.00 Labor...........18.30 *Remove*......................... Labor............8.91	lf	$8.91	$64.30	$73.21
Vinyl awning with 30" drop, 2 to 3 lf *Replace* Materials......58.60 Labor...........19.40 *Remove*......................... Labor............8.91	lf	$8.91	$78.00	$86.91
Vinyl awning with 30" drop, 4 to 5 lf *Replace* Materials......51.40 Labor...........19.40 *Remove*......................... Labor............8.91	lf	$8.91	$70.80	$79.71
Vinyl awning with 30" drop, 5 to 6 lf *Replace* Materials......46.80 Labor...........19.40 *Remove*......................... Labor............8.91	lf	$8.91	$66.20	$75.11

Item Description	Unit	Remove	Replace	Total	
Vinyl awning with 30" drop, 7 to 8 lf ***Replace*** Materials......37.40 Labor...........19.40 ***Remove***......................... Labor 8.91	**lf**	**$8.91**	**$56.80**	**$65.71**	
Vinyl awning with 30" drop, 9 to 10 lf ***Replace*** Materials......34.20 Labor...........19.40 ***Remove***......................... Labor 8.91	**lf**	**$8.91**	**$53.60**	**$62.51**	
Vinyl awning with 30" drop, 11 to 12 lf ***Replace*** Materials......33.30 Labor...........19.40 ***Remove***......................... Labor 8.91	**lf**	**$8.91**	**$52.70**	**$61.61**	
Remove vinyl awning for work, then reinstall ***Replace*** Materials........4.90 Labor...........42.10	**lf**	**—**	**$47.00**	**$47.00**	
Minimum charge for vinyl awning work ***Replace*** Materials......28.00 Labor..........54.80	**ea**	**—**	**$82.80**	**$82.80**	◁ **minimum**

NOTES: ____

____

____ end

TIME & MATERIAL CHARTS *(selected items)*

Awning Materials

DESCRIPTION	UNIT PRICE
Aluminum carport	
free-standing, 151 to 250 sf	**$13.80** *sf*
attached, 151 to 250 sf	**$12.60** *sf*
Aluminum door awning	
with 42" projection, 5 to 8 lf	**$140.00** *lf*
with 54" projection, 5 to 8 lf	**$185.00** *lf*
Aluminum window awning	
3' high, 5 to 8 lf	**$41.80** *lf*
4' high, 5 to 8 lf	**$51.70** *lf*
5' high, 5 to 8 lf	**$75.30** *lf*
6' high, 5 to 8 lf	**$91.40** *lf*
Roll-up aluminum awning	
2 to 5 lf	**$59.90** *lf*
6 to 12 lf	**$45.80** *lf*
Canvas awning	
24" drop, 2 to 3 lf	**$84.60** *lf*
24" drop, 4 to 5 lf	**$78.80** *lf*
30" drop, 2 to 3 lf	**$99.10** *lf*
30" drop, 7 to 8 lf	**$69.70** *lf*
30" drop, 11 to 12 lf	**$53.00** *lf*
Vinyl awning	
24" drop, 2 to 3 lf	**$50.10** *lf*
24" drop, 4 to 5 lf	**$46.00** *lf*
30" drop, 2 to 3 lf	**$58.60** *lf*
30" drop, 7 to 8 lf	**$37.40** *lf*
30" drop, 11 to 12 lf	**$33.30** *lf*

Awning Labor

LABORER	BASE WAGE	PAID LEAVE	TRUE WAGE	FICA	FUTA	WORKER'S COMP.	UNEMPLOY. INSUR.	HEALTH INSUR.	RETIRE (401K)	LIABILITY INSUR.	COST PER HOUR
Awning installer	$24.90	1.94	$26.84	2.05	.21	5.39	2.34	2.69	.81	3.62	$44.00
Awning installer's helper	$16.80	1.31	$18.11	1.39	.14	3.64	1.58	2.69	.54	2.44	$30.50
Demolition laborer	$13.90	1.08	$14.98	1.15	.12	4.79	1.30	2.69	.45	2.02	$27.50

Paid Leave is calculated based on two weeks paid vacation, one week sick leave, and seven paid holidays. Employer's matching portion of **FICA** is 7.65 percent. **FUTA** (Federal Unemployment) is .8 percent. **Worker's Compensation** for the awning trade was calculated using a national average of 20.09 percent. **Unemployment insurance** was calculated using a national average of 8.7 percent. **Health insurance** was calculated based on a projected national average for 2002 of $535 per employee (and family when applicable) per month. Employer pays 80 percent for a per month cost of $428 per employee. **Retirement** is based on a 401(k) retirement program with employer matching of 50 percent. Employee contributions to the 401(k) plan are an average of 6 percent of the true wage. **Liability insurance** is based on a national average of 13.2 percent.

Awning Labor Productivity

WORK DESCRIPTION	LABORER	COST PER HOUR	PRODUCTIVITY	UNIT PRICE
Demolition				
remove free-standing aluminum carport	demolition laborer	$27.50	.050	$1.38 sf
remove attached aluminum carport or patio cover	demolition laborer	$27.50	.054	$1.49 sf
remove 42" projection aluminum door awning	demolition laborer	$27.50	.481	$13.20 sf
remove 54" projection aluminum door awning	demolition laborer	$27.50	.500	$13.80 sf
remove 3' high aluminum window awning	demolition laborer	$27.50	.403	$11.10 lf
remove 4' high aluminum window awning	demolition laborer	$27.50	.415	$11.40 lf
remove 5' high aluminum window awning	demolition laborer	$27.50	.423	$11.60 lf
remove 6' high aluminum window awning	demolition laborer	$27.50	.429	$11.80 lf
remove roll-up aluminum window awning	demolition laborer	$27.50	.417	$11.50 lf
remove canvas or vinyl window awning	demolition laborer	$27.50	.324	$8.91 lf
Awning Installation Crew				
install, awnings and patio covers	awning installer	$44.00		
install, awnings and patio covers	awning installer's helper	$30.50		
awning installation crew	awning installation crew	$37.30		
Install aluminum carport or patio cover				
free-standing carport	awning installation crew	$37.30	.077	$2.87 sf
attached carport or patio cover	awning installation crew	$37.30	.071	$2.65 sf
Install aluminum door awning				
42" projection	awning installation crew	$37.30	.463	$17.30 lf
54" projection	awning installation crew	$37.30	.484	$18.10 lf
Install aluminum window awning				
3' high	awning installation crew	$37.30	.346	$12.90 lf
4' high	awning installation crew	$37.30	.354	$13.20 lf
5' high	awning installation crew	$37.30	.361	$13.50 lf
6' high	awning installation crew	$37.30	.368	$13.70 lf
Install roll-up aluminum awning				
per lf	awning installation crew	$37.30	.274	$10.20 lf
Install canvas awning				
24" drop	awning installation crew	$37.30	.493	$18.40 lf
30" drop	awning installation crew	$37.30	.526	$19.60 lf
Install vinyl awning				
24" drop	awning installation crew	$37.30	.491	$18.30 lf
30" drop	awning installation crew	$37.30	.520	$19.40 lf

NOTES:

end

4 Bathroom Hardware

Item Description	Unit	Remove	Replace	Total
Minimum charge for bathroom hardware work *Replace* Materials......21.00 Labor..........23.40	ea	—	$44.40	$44.40
Bath hardware for complete bathroom, economy grade *Replace* Materials.....107.00 Labor.........167.00 *Remove* .... Labor...........61.10	ea	$61.10	$274.00	$335.10
Bath hardware for complete bathroom, standard grade *Replace* Materials....200.00 Labor.........167.00 *Remove* .... Labor...........61.10	ea	$61.10	$367.00	$428.10
Bath hardware for complete bathroom, high grade *Replace* Materials....290.00 Labor.........167.00 *Remove* .... Labor...........61.10	ea	$61.10	$457.00	$518.10
Bath hardware for complete bathroom, deluxe grade *Replace* Materials....392.00 Labor.........167.00 *Remove* .... Labor...........61.10	ea	$61.10	$559.00	$620.10
Bath hardware for complete bathroom, custom grade *Replace* Materials....448.00 Labor.........167.00 *Remove* .... Labor...........61.10	ea	$61.10	$615.00	$676.10
Bath hardware for complete bathroom, antique reproduction *Replace* Materials....733.00 Labor.........167.00 *Remove* .... Labor...........61.10	ea	$61.10	$900.00	$961.10
1/2 bath hardware for complete bathroom, economy grade *Replace* Materials......35.00 Labor..........90.30 *Remove* .... Labor..........44.00	ea	$44.00	$125.30	$169.30
1/2 bath hardware for complete bathroom, standard grade *Replace* Materials......68.00 Labor..........90.30 *Remove* .... Labor..........44.00	ea	$44.00	$158.30	$202.30
1/2 bath hardware for complete bathroom, high grade *Replace* Materials......98.00 Labor..........90.30 *Remove* .... Labor..........44.00	ea	$44.00	$188.30	$232.30
1/2 bath hardware for complete bathroom, deluxe grade *Replace* Materials.....133.00 Labor..........90.30 *Remove* .... Labor..........44.00	ea	$44.00	$223.30	$267.30
1/2 bath hardware for complete bathroom, custom grade *Replace* Materials.....152.00 Labor..........90.30 *Remove* .... Labor..........44.00	ea	$44.00	$242.30	$286.30
1/2 bath hardware for complete bathroom, antique reproduction *Replace* Materials....259.00 Labor..........90.30 *Remove* .... Labor..........44.00	ea	$44.00	$349.30	$393.30
Glass bathroom shelf *Replace* Materials......75.00 Labor...........11.70 *Remove* .... Labor............8.94 ► With plated chrome hardware.	ea	$8.94	$86.70	$95.64

◄ **MINIMUM**

◄ **COMPLETE BATH**
Bathroom with toilet, sink, and bathtub / shower. Includes towel bar, wash cloth bar, door-mount robe hook, toilet paper dispenser, and cup / toothbrush holder.

HARDWARE QUALITY

Some "rules of thumb" for determining bathroom hardware quality:

Economy: Light-gauge metal, chrome plated. May have some plastic components. Little or no pattern.

Standard: Heavier gauge metal, chrome or brass plated with little or no pattern or wood hardware made of ash or oak.

◄ **1/2 BATH**
Bathroom with toilet, and sink. Includes wash cloth bar, towel ring, and toilet paper dispenser.

QUALITY *continued*

High: Brass, chrome over brass, or nickel over brass with minimal detail, or plated hardware with ornate detail, or European style curved plastic, or hardware with porcelain components, or wood hardware made of walnut, cherry, or similar wood.

Deluxe: Brass, chrome over brass, or nickel over brass with ornate detail.

Antique Reproduction / Custom: Brass, chrome over brass, or nickel over brass with ornate and/or antique style detail.

◄ **GLASS SHELF**
21" x 5-1/2" glass shelf.

	Item Description	Unit	Remove	Replace	Total
Glass shelf ▶ *continued*	**Glass & brass bathroom shelf** ***Replace*** Materials....108.00 Labor...........11.70 ***Remove*** .... Labor...........8.94 ▶ With solid brass or chrome-plated brass hardware.	ea	$8.94	$119.70	$128.64
	Remove glass bathroom shelf for work, then reinstall ***Replace*** .... Labor...........13.80	ea	—	$13.80	$13.80
Cup & tooth-brush holder ▶ *For quality indicators see page 41.*	**Cup & toothbrush holder, standard grade** ***Replace*** Materials......10.00 Labor...........7.03 ***Remove*** .... Labor...........4.48	ea	$4.48	$17.03	$21.51
	Cup & toothbrush holder, high grade ***Replace*** Materials......16.70 Labor...........7.03 ***Remove*** .... Labor...........4.48	ea	$4.48	$23.73	$28.21
	Remove cup & toothbrush holder for work, then reinstall ***Replace*** .... Labor...........9.03	ea	—	$9.03	$9.03
Door clothes hanger ▶ *For quality indicators see page 41.*	**Door-mounted clothes hanger, standard grade** ***Replace*** Materials........9.00 Labor...........5.87 ***Remove*** .... Labor...........3.82	ea	$3.82	$14.87	$18.69
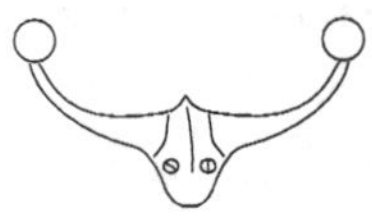	**Door-mounted clothes hanger, high grade** ***Replace*** Materials.......15.10 Labor...........5.87 ***Remove*** .... Labor...........3.82	ea	$3.82	$20.97	$24.79
	Remove door-mounted clothes hanger for work, then reinstall ***Replace*** .... Labor...........7.28	ea	—	$7.28	$7.28
Robe hook ▶ *For quality indicators see page 41.*	**Robe hook, standard grade** ***Replace*** Materials......10.00 Labor...........5.87 ***Remove*** .... Labor...........3.82	ea	$3.82	$15.87	$19.69
	**Robe hook, high grade** ***Replace*** Materials.......17.00 Labor...........5.87 ***Remove*** .... Labor...........3.82	ea	$3.82	$22.87	$26.69
	Remove robe hook for work, then reinstall ***Replace*** .... Labor...........7.28	ea	—	$7.28	$7.28
Soap holder ▶ *For quality indicators see page 41.*	**Soap holder, standard grade** ***Replace*** Materials......37.00 Labor...........7.03 ***Remove*** .... Labor...........4.48	ea	$4.48	$44.03	$48.51
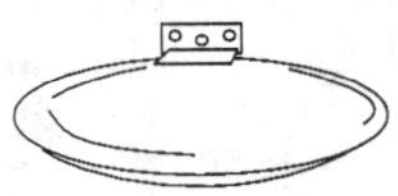	**Soap holder, high grade** ***Replace*** Materials......60.00 Labor...........7.03 ***Remove*** .... Labor...........4.48	ea	$4.48	$67.03	$71.51
	Remove soap holder for work, then reinstall ***Replace*** .... Labor...........9.03	ea	—	$9.03	$9.03
Recessed soap holder ▶ *For quality indicators see page 41.*	**Recessed soap holder, standard grade** ***Replace*** Materials......20.00 Labor...........8.36 ***Remove*** .... Labor...........4.48	ea	$4.48	$28.36	$32.84
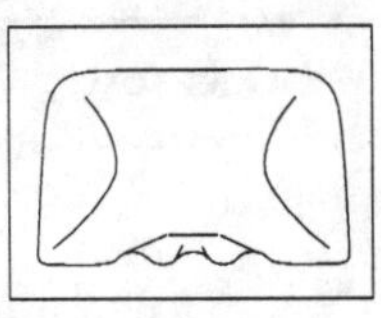	**Recessed soap holder, high grade** ***Replace*** Materials......50.00 Labor...........8.36 ***Remove*** .... Labor...........4.48	ea	$4.48	$58.36	$62.84

Item Description	Unit	Remove	Replace	Total
Remove recessed soap holder for work, then reinstall *Replace* .... Labor...........11.10	ea	—	$11.10	$11.10
Soap dispenser, standard grade *Replace* Materials.......17.00 Labor............7.57 *Remove* .... Labor............4.48	ea	$4.48	$24.57	$29.05
Soap dispenser, high grade *Replace* Materials......38.00 Labor............7.57 *Remove* .... Labor............4.48	ea	$4.48	$45.57	$50.05
Remove soap dispenser for work, then reinstall *Replace* .... Labor............9.32	ea	—	$9.32	$9.32
Recessed tissue holder, standard grade *Replace* Materials......38.00 Labor............7.11 *Remove* .... Labor............3.82	ea	$3.82	$45.11	$48.93
Recessed tissue holder, high grade *Replace* Materials......60.00 Labor............7.11 *Remove* .... Labor............3.82	ea	$3.82	$67.11	$70.93
Remove recessed tissue holder for work, then reinstall *Replace* .... Labor...........10.40	ea	—	$10.40	$10.40
Shower curtain rod *Replace* Materials......38.00 Labor............4.70 *Remove* .... Labor............2.45	ea	$2.45	$42.70	$45.15
Remove shower curtain rod for work, then reinstall *Replace* .... Labor............5.41	ea	—	$5.41	$5.41
Towel bar, economy grade *Replace* Materials......16.00 Labor...........16.30 *Remove* .... Labor............8.94	ea	$8.94	$32.30	$41.24
Towel bar, standard grade *Replace* Materials......23.00 Labor...........16.30 *Remove* .... Labor............8.94	ea	$8.94	$39.30	$48.24
Towel bar, high grade *Replace* Materials......37.00 Labor...........16.30 *Remove* .... Labor............8.94	ea	$8.94	$53.30	$62.24
Towel bar, deluxe grade *Replace* Materials......55.00 Labor...........16.30 *Remove* .... Labor............8.94	ea	$8.94	$71.30	$80.24
Remove towel bar for work, then reinstall *Replace* .... Labor..........23.40	ea	—	$23.40	$23.40
Toilet paper dispenser, economy grade *Replace* Materials......29.00 Labor............7.82 *Remove* .... Labor............8.94	ea	$8.94	$36.82	$45.76
Toilet paper dispenser, standard grade *Replace* Materials......37.00 Labor............7.82 *Remove* .... Labor............8.94	ea	$8.94	$44.82	$53.76

◀ **SOAP DISPENSER**
For quality indicators see page 41.

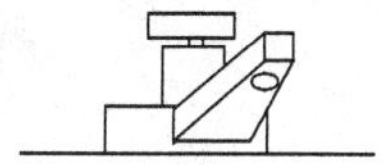

◀ **RECESSED TISSUE HOLDER**
For quality indicators see page 41.

◀ **SHOWER ROD**
For quality indicators see page 41.

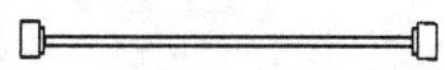

◀ **TOWEL BAR**
For quality indicators see page 41.

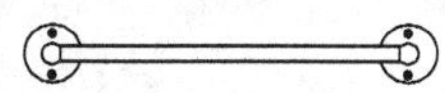

◀ **TOILET PAPER DISPENSER**
For quality indicators see page 41.

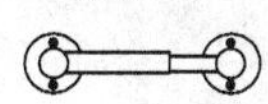

RELATED ITEMS

Cleaning........................56

	Item Description	Unit	Remove	Replace	Total
Toilet paper dispenser *continued*	**Toilet paper dispenser, high grade** ***Replace*** Materials......51.00 Labor............7.82 ***Remove*** .... Labor............8.94	ea	$8.94	$58.82	$67.76
	Toilet paper dispenser, deluxe grade ***Replace*** Materials......59.00 Labor............7.82 ***Remove*** .... Labor............8.94	ea	$8.94	$66.82	$75.76
	Remove toilet paper dispenser for work, then reinstall ***Replace*** .... Labor..........10.20	ea	—	$10.20	$10.20
Towel ring *For quality indicators see page 41.* 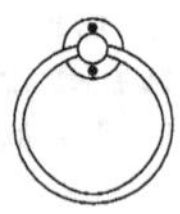	**Towel ring, economy grade** ***Replace*** Materials......16.00 Labor............9.90 ***Remove*** .... Labor............8.94	ea	$8.94	$25.90	$34.84
	Towel ring, standard grade ***Replace*** Materials......20.00 Labor............9.90 ***Remove*** .... Labor............8.94	ea	$8.94	$29.90	$38.84
	Towel ring, high grade ***Replace*** Materials......22.00 Labor............9.90 ***Remove*** .... Labor............8.94	ea	$8.94	$31.90	$40.84
	Towel ring, deluxe grade ***Replace*** Materials......26.00 Labor............9.90 ***Remove*** .... Labor............8.94	ea	$8.94	$35.90	$44.84
	Remove towel ring for work, then reinstall ***Replace*** .... Labor..........12.40	ea	—	$12.40	$12.40
Wash cloth bar *For quality indicators see page 41.* 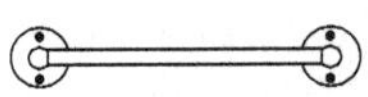	**Wash cloth bar, economy grade** ***Replace*** Materials.......13.00 Labor..........16.30 ***Remove*** .... Labor............8.94	ea	$8.94	$29.30	$38.24
	Wash cloth bar, standard grade ***Replace*** Materials.......17.00 Labor..........16.30 ***Remove*** .... Labor.............	ea	$8.94	$33.30	$42.24
	Wash cloth bar, high grade ***Replace*** Materials......23.00 Labor..........16.30 ***Remove*** .... Labor............8.94	ea	$8.94	$39.30	$48.24
	Wash cloth bar, deluxe grade ***Replace*** Materials......31.00 Labor..........16.30 ***Remove*** .... Labor............8.94	ea	$8.94	$47.30	$56.24
	Remove wash cloth bar for work, then reinstall ***Replace*** .... Labor..........23.40	ea	—	$23.40	$23.40
Recessed medicine cabinet 	**Recessed medicine cabinet, economy grade** ***Replace*** Materials......50.00 Labor..........54.50 ***Remove*** .... Labor..........16.70 ► Plastic or polystyrene box with two to three shelves. Up to 16" wide and up to 25" tall. Mirror doors with chrome-plated trim.	ea	$16.70	$104.50	$121.20
	Recessed medicine cabinet, standard grade ***Replace*** Materials......62.00 Labor..........54.50 ***Remove*** .... Labor..........16.70 ► Plastic or polystyrene box with two to three shelves. Up to 16" wide and up to 25" tall. Mirror door with brass-plated or wood trim or vinyl shutter door.	ea	$16.70	$116.50	$133.20

Item Description	Unit	Remove	Replace	Total
Recessed medicine cabinet, high grade ***Replace*** Materials......88.00 Labor..........54.50 ***Remove*** .... Labor...........16.70 ► Steel box with adjustable shelves. Up to 16" wide and up to 25" tall. Mirror door with chrome-plated or wood trim; or real wood door (includes stain & varnish). May have beveled mirror with no trim.	ea	$16.70	$142.50	$159.20
Recessed medicine cabinet, deluxe grade ***Replace*** Materials....104.00 Labor..........54.50 ***Remove*** .... Labor...........16.70 ► Steel box with adjustable shelves. Up to 20" wide and up to 32" tall. Arched mirror door with brass or wood trim; or real wood door (includes stain & varnish). May have beveled mirror with no trim.	ea	$16.70	$158.50	$175.20
Recessed medicine cabinet, custom grade ***Replace*** Materials....129.00 Labor..........54.50 ***Remove*** .... Labor...........16.70 ► Steel box with adjustable shelves. Up to 20" wide and up to 32" tall. Arched or oval mirror door brass or wood trim; or real wood door (includes stain & varnish). May have beveled mirror with no trim.	ea	$16.70	$183.50	$200.20
Remove recessed medicine cabinet for work, then reinstall ***Replace*** .... Labor...........78.20	ea	—	$78.20	$78.20
Surface-mounted medicine cabinet, economy grade ***Replace*** Materials......62.00 Labor...........62.80 ***Remove*** .... Labor...........17.90 ► Plastic or polystyrene box with two to three shelves. Up to 16" wide and up to 25" tall. Hinged mirror doors with chrome-plated trim; or vinyl shutter door. Also larger mirror styles with small sliding door cabinet below mirror.	ea	$17.90	$124.80	$142.70
Surface-mounted medicine cabinet, standard grade ***Replace*** Materials......89.00 Labor...........62.80 ***Remove*** .... Labor...........17.90 ► Metal box with adjustable shelves. Up to 16" wide and up to 25" tall. Hinged mirror doors with chrome-plated trim or wood trim; or wood shutter door (includes stain & varnish).	ea	$17.90	$151.80	$169.70
Surface-mounted medicine cabinet, high grade ***Replace*** Materials.....151.00 Labor...........62.80 ***Remove*** .... Labor...........17.90 ► Metal box with two to three shelves. Up to 16" wide and up to 25" tall. Hinged mirror doors with chrome-plated trim or wood trim; or wood shutter door (includes stain & varnish). Also up to 30" by 30" cabinets with bypassing mirror doors.	ea	$17.90	$213.80	$231.70
Surface-mounted medicine cabinet, deluxe grade ***Replace*** Materials....256.00 Labor...........62.80 ***Remove*** .... Labor...........17.90 ► Wood plastic laminate coated box with two to three shelves. Up to 30" wide and up to 30" tall. 3 door hinged doors usually with oak trim.	ea	$17.90	$318.80	$336.70
Surface-mounted medicine cabinet, custom grade ***Replace*** Materials....366.00 Labor...........62.80 ***Remove*** .... Labor...........17.90 ► Metal box (may be chrome) with two to three shelves. Up to 38" wide and up to 32" tall. 3 hinged doors usually with oak trim.	ea	$17.90	$428.80	$446.70
Remove surface-mounted medicine cabinet for work, then reinstall ***Replace*** .... Labor..........82.00	ea	—	$82.00	$82.00
Bathroom mirror with stainless-steel trim ***Replace*** Materials.......17.00 Labor............4.41 ***Remove*** .... Labor............1.13	sf	$1.13	$21.41	$22.54

◄ **SURFACE-MOUNT MEDICINE CABINET**

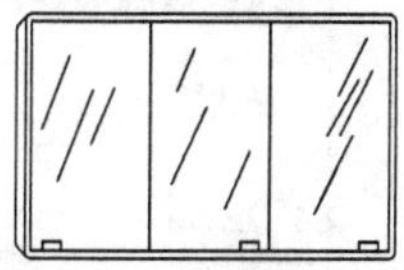

RELATED ITEMS

Cleaning......................56

◄ **BATHROOM MIRROR**

Bathroom Mirror continued

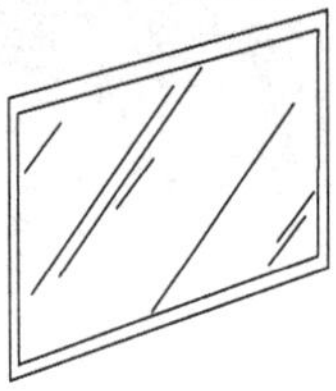

Item Description	Unit	Remove	Replace	Total
Bathroom mirror with brass-finished trim *Replace* Materials......18.00 Labor............4.41 *Remove* .... Labor............1.13	sf	$1.13	$22.41	$23.54
Bathroom mirror with wood frame *Replace* Materials......18.00 Labor............4.41 *Remove* .... Labor............1.13	sf	$1.13	$22.41	$23.54
Bathroom mirror beveled glass *Replace* Materials.......19.00 Labor............4.41 *Remove* .... Labor............1.13	sf	$1.13	$23.41	$24.54
Remove bathroom mirror for work, then reinstall *Replace* .... Labor............7.03	sf	—	$7.03	$7.03

Time & Material Charts *(selected items)*

Bathroom Hardware Materials

*See **Bathroom Hardware** material prices with the line items and other information in the **QuickFinder** column.*

Bathroom Hardware Labor

Laborer	Base Wage	Paid Leave	True Wage	FICA	FUTA	Worker's Comp.	Unemploy. Insur.	Health Insur.	Retire (401k)	Liability Insur.	Cost per Hour
Carpenter (installer)	$23.60	1.84	$25.44	1.95	.20	4.96	2.21	2.69	.76	3.43	$41.60
Demolition laborer	$13.90	1.08	$14.98	1.15	.12	4.79	1.30	2.69	.45	2.02	$27.50

Paid Leave is calculated based on two weeks paid vacation, one week sick leave, and seven paid holidays. Employer's matching portion of **FICA** is 7.65 percent. **FUTA** (Federal Unemployment) is .8 percent. **Worker's compensation** for the bathroom hardware trade was calculated using a national average of 19.50 percent. **Unemployment insurance** was calculated using a national average of 8.7 percent. **Health insurance** was calculated based on a projected national average for 2002 of $535 per employee (and family when applicable) per month. Employer pays 80 percent for a per month cost of $428 per employee. **Retirement** is based on a 401(k) retirement program with employer matching of 50 percent. Employee contributions to the 401(k) plan are an average of 6 percent of the true wage. **Liability insurance** is based on a national average of 13.2 percent.

Bathroom Hardware Labor Productivity

Work Description	Laborer	Cost per Hour	Productivity	Unit Price
Demolition				
hardware for complete bathroom	demolition laborer	$27.50	2.22	$61.10 ea
hardware for complete 1/2 bathroom	demolition laborer	$27.50	1.60	$44.00 ea
recessed medicine cabinet	demolition laborer	$27.50	.609	$16.70 ea
surface-mounted medicine cabinet	demolition laborer	$27.50	.650	$17.90 ea
bathroom mirror attached with glue	demolition laborer	$27.50	.041	$1.13 sf
Install complete bathroom hardware				
full bathroom	carpenter	$41.60	4.02	$167.00 ea
1/2 bathroom	carpenter	$41.60	2.17	$90.30 ea
Install hardware				
soap holder	carpenter	$41.60	.169	$7.03 ea
recessed tissue holder	carpenter	$41.60	.171	$7.11 ea
towel bar	carpenter	$41.60	.393	$16.30 ea
toilet paper dispenser	carpenter	$41.60	.188	$7.82 ea
towel ring	carpenter	$41.60	.238	$9.90 ea
wash cloth bar	carpenter	$41.60	.393	$16.30 ea
recessed medicine cabinet	carpenter	$41.60	1.31	$54.50 ea
surface-mounted medicine cabinet	carpenter	$41.60	1.51	$62.80 ea
bathroom mirror	carpenter	$41.60	.106	$4.41 sf

5 Cabinets

Item Description	Unit	Remove	Replace	Total
Minimum charge for cabinet work *Replace* Materials......43.00 Labor...........91.80	ea	—	$134.80	$134.80
Lower kitchen cabinets, standard grade *Replace* Materials......85.00 Labor...........12.40 *Remove* .... Labor 7.21	lf	$7.21	$97.40	$104.61
Lower kitchen cabinets, high grade *Replace* Materials....109.00 Labor...........12.40 *Remove* .... Labor 7.21	lf	$7.21	$121.40	$128.61
Lower kitchen cabinets, deluxe grade *Replace* Materials....154.00 Labor...........12.40 *Remove* .... Labor 7.21	lf	$7.21	$166.40	$173.61
Lower kitchen cabinets, custom grade *Replace* Materials....220.00 Labor...........12.40 *Remove* .... Labor 7.21	lf	$7.21	$232.40	$239.61
Lower kitchen cabinets, custom deluxe grade *Replace* Materials....285.00 Labor...........12.40 *Remove* .... Labor 7.21	lf	$7.21	$297.40	$304.61
Remove lower kitchen cabinets for work, then reinstall *Replace* .... Labor...........21.80	lf	—	$21.80	$21.80
Upper kitchen cabinets, economy grade *Replace* Materials......59.00 Labor...........12.00 *Remove* .... Labor 6.49	lf	$6.49	$71.00	$77.49
Upper kitchen cabinets, standard grade *Replace* Materials......79.00 Labor...........12.00 *Remove* .... Labor 6.49	lf	$6.49	$91.00	$97.49
Upper kitchen cabinets, high grade *Replace* Materials......98.00 Labor...........12.00 *Remove* .... Labor 6.49	lf	$6.49	$110.00	$116.49
Upper kitchen cabinets, deluxe grade *Replace* Materials.....142.00 Labor...........12.00 *Remove* .... Labor 6.49	lf	$6.49	$154.00	$160.49
Upper kitchen cabinets, custom grade *Replace* Materials....205.00 Labor...........12.00 *Remove* .... Labor 6.49	lf	$6.49	$217.00	$223.49
Upper kitchen cabinets, custom deluxe grade *Replace* Materials.....261.00 Labor...........12.00 *Remove* .... Labor 6.49	lf	$6.49	$273.00	$279.49
Remove upper kitchen cabinets for work, then reinstall *Replace* .... Labor...........21.10	lf	—	$21.10	$21.10

◄ **MINIMUM**

◄ **LOWER CABINETS**

CABINET CONSTRUCTION

STOCK CABINETS Stock-grade cabinets are manufactured in standard sizes and warehoused until sold.

SEMI-CUSTOM CABINETS Semi-custom grade cabinets are available in a wide variety of styles and shapes. Within limits, the manufacturer builds the cabinets to match the kitchen.

CUSTOM CABINETS Custom-grade cabinets are built specifically for the kitchen and include specialty doors, woods and construction.

◄ **UPPER CABINETS**

CABINET GRADES

ECONOMY GRADE Stock-grade cabinets with flush-face doors. Doors made from veneered particle board.

STANDARD GRADE Stock-grade cabinets with raised panel or cathedral doors. Interior panel may be plywood. Lower grade plastic-laminate face cabinets.

HIGH GRADE Semi-custom cabinets with raised panel or cathedral doors. Higher grade plastic-laminate face and foil-face cabinets.

continued on next page

RELATED ITEMS

Cleaning.......................56

Lower Island ▶ cabinets

Item Description	Unit	Remove	Replace	Total
Lower kitchen island cabinets, economy grade *Replace* Materials......70.00 Labor..........12.80 *Remove* .... Labor...........6.96	lf	$6.96	$82.80	$89.76
Lower kitchen island cabinets, standard grade *Replace* Materials......88.00 Labor..........12.80 *Remove* .... Labor...........6.96	lf	$6.96	$100.80	$107.76
Lower kitchen island cabinets, high grade *Replace* Materials.....113.00 Labor..........12.80 *Remove* .... Labor...........6.96	lf	$6.96	$125.80	$132.76
Lower kitchen island cabinets, deluxe grade *Replace* Materials.....160.00 Labor..........12.80 *Remove* .... Labor...........6.96	lf	$6.96	$172.80	$179.76
Lower kitchen island cabinets, custom grade *Replace* Materials....229.00 Labor..........12.80 *Remove* .... Labor...........6.96	lf	$6.96	$241.80	$248.76
Lower kitchen island cabinets, custom deluxe grade *Replace* Materials....296.00 Labor..........12.80 *Remove* .... Labor...........6.96	lf	$6.96	$308.80	$315.76
Remove lower kitchen island cabinets for work, then reinstall *Replace* .... Labor..........22.50	lf	—	$22.50	$22.50

Cabinet Grades

continued from prior page

Deluxe grade Semi-custom cabinets with raised panel or cathedral doors. May include special slide-out drawers, pull-out baskets, glass doors, foil-face, cherry, pecan, or Shaker style maple or pine.

Custom grade Custom cabinets with raised panel or cathedral doors. May include specialty slide-out drawers, pull-out baskets, glass mullion or leaded glass doors, cherry, pecan, or Shaker style maple or pine.

Custom Deluxe grade Same as Custom Grade may have some curved wood cabinets and more custom features.

Upper Island ▶ cabinets

Item Description	Unit	Remove	Replace	Total
Upper kitchen island cabinets, economy grade *Replace* Materials.......61.00 Labor..........12.30 *Remove* .... Labor...........6.55	lf	$6.55	$73.30	$79.85
Upper kitchen island cabinets, standard grade *Replace* Materials......82.00 Labor..........12.30 *Remove* .... Labor...........6.55	lf	$6.55	$94.30	$100.85
Upper kitchen island cabinets, high grade *Replace* Materials....102.00 Labor..........12.30 *Remove* .... Labor...........6.55	lf	$6.55	$114.30	$120.85
Upper kitchen island cabinets, deluxe grade *Replace* Materials....148.00 Labor..........12.30 *Remove* .... Labor...........6.55	lf	$6.55	$160.30	$166.85
Upper kitchen island cabinets, custom grade *Replace* Materials.....213.00 Labor..........12.30 *Remove* .... Labor...........6.55	lf	$6.55	$225.30	$231.85
Upper kitchen island cabinets, custom deluxe grade *Replace* Materials....271.00 Labor..........12.30 *Remove* .... Labor...........6.55	lf	$6.55	$283.30	$289.85
Remove upper kitchen island cabinets for work, then reinstall *Replace* .... Labor..........21.70	lf	—	$21.70	$21.70

Full-height ▶ utility cabinet

Item Description	Unit	Remove	Replace	Total
Full-height utility cabinet, economy grade *Replace* Materials.....162.00 Labor..........20.40 *Remove* .... Labor...........9.10	lf	$9.10	$182.40	$191.50
Full-height utility cabinet, standard grade *Replace* Materials....204.00 Labor..........20.40 *Remove* .... Labor...........9.10	lf	$9.10	$224.40	$233.50

Item Description	Unit	Remove	Replace	Total
Full-height utility cabinet, high grade	lf	$9.10	$269.40	$278.50
Replace Materials.....249.00 Labor..........20.40				
Remove .... Labor............9.10				
Full-height utility cabinet, deluxe grade	lf	$9.10	$338.40	$347.50
Replace Materials.....318.00 Labor..........20.40				
Remove .... Labor............9.10				
Full-height utility cabinet, custom grade	lf	$9.10	$368.40	$377.50
Replace Materials....348.00 Labor..........20.40				
Remove .... Labor............9.10				
Full-height utility cabinet custom, deluxe grade	lf	$9.10	$410.40	$419.50
Replace Materials....390.00 Labor..........20.40				
Remove .... Labor............9.10				
Remove full-height kitchen cabinets for work, then reinstall	lf	—	$24.30	$24.30
Replace .... Labor...........24.30				
Full-height built-in oven cabinet, economy grade	lf	$9.10	$174.40	$183.50
Replace Materials....154.00 Labor..........20.40				
Remove .... Labor............9.10				
Full-height built-in oven cabinet, standard grade	lf	$9.10	$214.40	$223.50
Replace Materials.....194.00 Labor..........20.40				
Remove .... Labor............9.10				
Full-height built-in oven cabinet, high grade	lf	$9.10	$257.40	$266.50
Replace Materials....237.00 Labor..........20.40				
Remove .... Labor............9.10				
Full-height built-in oven cabinet, deluxe grade	lf	$9.10	$322.40	$331.50
Replace Materials....302.00 Labor..........20.40				
Remove .... Labor............9.10				
Full-height built-in oven cabinet, custom grade	lf	$9.10	$351.40	$360.50
Replace Materials....331.00 Labor..........20.40				
Remove .... Labor............9.10				
Full-height built-in oven cabinet, custom deluxe grade	lf	$9.10	$391.40	$400.50
Replace Materials....371.00 Labor..........20.40				
Remove .... Labor............9.10				
Remove full-height built-in oven cabinets for work, then reinstall	lf	—	$24.30	$24.30
Replace .... Labor...........24.30				
Full-height built-in double oven cabinet, economy grade	lf	$9.10	$169.40	$178.50
Replace Materials.....149.00 Labor..........20.40				
Remove .... Labor............9.10				
Full-height built-in double oven cabinet, standard grade	lf	$9.10	$208.40	$217.50
Replace Materials....188.00 Labor..........20.40				
Remove .... Labor............9.10				
Full-height built-in double oven cabinet, high grade	lf	$9.10	$249.40	$258.50
Replace Materials....229.00 Labor..........20.40				
Remove .... Labor............9.10				
Full-height built-in double oven cabinet, deluxe grade	lf	$9.10	$313.40	$322.50
Replace Materials....293.00 Labor..........20.40				
Remove .... Labor............9.10				

◄ **FULL-HEIGHT OVEN CABINET**

FOIL-FACE CABINETS

Foil-faced cabinets (also called thermo foil) are coated with rigid polyvinyl chloride (PVC) that has been heated and pressed. The interior core is usually medium density particle board.

Currently, there is no good way to repair scratched or dented foil-face cabinets. Although colors do not fade from foil-faces, it is almost impossible to replace doors or other parts with colors that will match.

Foil-face cabinets are high to custom deluxe quality depending on the interior features and the complexity of the design.

◄ **FULL-HEIGHT DOUBLE OVEN CABINET**

RELATED ITEMS

Cleaning 56

FULL-HEIGHT DOUBLE OVEN CABINET *continued*

Item Description	Unit	Remove	Replace	Total
Full-height built-in double oven cabinet, custom grade *Replace* Materials....320.00 Labor..........20.40 *Remove* .... Labor............9.10	lf	$9.10	$340.40	$349.50
Full-height built-in double oven cabinet, custom deluxe grade *Replace* Materials....359.00 Labor..........20.40 *Remove* .... Labor............9.10	lf	$9.10	$379.40	$388.50
Remove full-height built-in double oven cabinets for work, then reinstall *Replace* .... Labor...........24.30	lf	—	$24.30	$24.30

CABINET DRAWER FRONT

Item Description	Unit	Remove	Replace	Total
Cabinet drawer front *Replace* Materials.......13.00 Labor............4.06 *Remove* .... Labor............3.96	ea	$3.96	$17.06	$21.02

CABINET DOOR

flat panel

raised panel

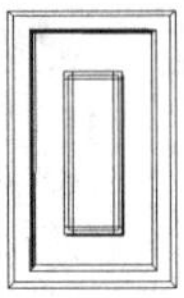

raised panel cathedral

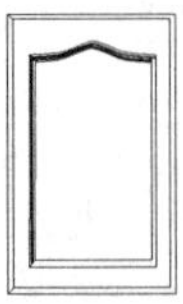

with leaded glass

Item Description	Unit	Remove	Replace	Total
Flush-face cabinet door *Replace* Materials.......17.00 Labor............8.67 *Remove* .... Labor............7.34	ea	$7.34	$25.67	$33.01
Flat panel cabinet door *Replace* Materials......23.00 Labor............8.67 *Remove* .... Labor............7.34	ea	$7.34	$31.67	$39.01
Raised panel cabinet door *Replace* Materials......34.00 Labor............8.67 *Remove* .... Labor............7.34	ea	$7.34	$42.67	$50.01
Raised panel cathedral cabinet door *Replace* Materials......43.00 Labor............8.67 *Remove* .... Labor............7.34	ea	$7.34	$51.67	$59.01
Cabinet door with glass *Replace* Materials......53.00 Labor............8.67 *Remove* .... Labor............7.34	ea	$7.34	$61.67	$69.01
Cabinet door with leaded glass per door *Replace* Materials....105.00 Labor............8.67 *Remove* .... Labor............7.34	ea	$7.34	$113.67	$121.01

REFINISH CABINET

Cabinets are stripped and restained. Edge surfaces that are finished with 1/4" hardwood plywood are replaced.

Item Description	Unit	Remove	Replace	Total
Refinish cabinet drawer front *Replace* Materials........1.50 Labor............9.37	ea	—	$10.87	$10.87
Refinish cabinet door *Replace* Materials........3.40 Labor..........22.00	ea	—	$25.40	$25.40
Refinish cabinet door with glass *Replace* Materials........1.60 Labor..........22.00	ea	—	$23.60	$23.60
Refinish cabinets & doors, re-face plywood ends *Replace* Materials.......13.00 Labor..........48.40	lf	—	$61.40	$61.40
Refinish island cabinets & doors, re-face plywood ends & faces *Replace* Materials......14.00 Labor...........62.90	lf	—	$76.90	$76.90

repair gouge or hole ▷

Item Description	Unit	Remove	Replace	Total
Repair gouge or hole in cabinet, grain patch to match finish *Replace* Materials........7.00 Labor..........50.90 ► Gouge or hole is filled, then "grained" by the painter to look like natural wood grain, matched to the finish of the cabinets.	ea	—	$57.90	$57.90

Item Description	Unit	Remove	Replace	Total
Post-formed plastic laminate countertop ***Replace*** Materials........3.70 Labor............9.84 ***Remove*** .... Labor............3.63 ► Backsplash is integrated into countertop with a rounded cove transition.	sf	$3.63	$13.54	$17.17
Flat-laid plastic laminate countertop ***Replace*** Materials........3.60 Labor...........10.60 ***Remove*** .... Labor............3.63 ► Countertop butts into wall with flat edge.	sf	$3.63	$14.20	$17.83
Cultured marble countertop ***Replace*** Materials.......17.00 Labor...........10.80 ***Remove*** .... Labor............3.63	sf	$3.63	$27.80	$31.43
Add for integrated sink in cultured marble countertop ***Replace*** Materials....148.00	ea	—	$148.00	$148.00
Cultured granite countertop ***Replace*** Materials......23.00 Labor...........10.80 ***Remove*** .... Labor............3.63	sf	$3.63	$33.80	$37.43
Add for integrated sink in cultured granite countertop ***Replace*** Materials....186.00	ea	—	$186.00	$186.00
Onyx countertop ***Replace*** Materials......22.00 Labor...........10.80 ***Remove*** .... Labor............3.63	sf	$3.63	$32.80	$36.43
Add for integrated sink in onyx countertop ***Replace*** Materials.....181.00	ea	—	$181.00	$181.00
Solid-surface countertop, economy grade ***Replace*** Materials....103.00 Labor...........11.40 ***Remove*** .... Labor............3.63 ► Off-white colors, bull-nose edge.	sf	$3.63	$114.40	$118.03
Solid-surface countertop, standard grade ***Replace*** Materials....148.00 Labor...........11.40 ***Remove*** .... Labor............3.63 ► All standard colors, patterned edge detail, with thin strip inlay.	sf	$3.63	$159.40	$163.03
Solid-surface countertop, high grade ***Replace*** Materials....206.00 Labor...........11.40 ***Remove*** .... Labor............3.63 ► All standard colors, patterned edge detail, with wood or strip inlay.	sf	$3.63	$217.40	$221.03
Solid-surface countertop, deluxe grade ***Replace*** Materials.....249.00 Labor...........11.40 ***Remove*** .... Labor............3.63 ► Layered with alternating colored layers, wood strip inlays, custom edge detailing.	sf	$3.63	$260.40	$264.03
Solid-surface countertop, custom grade ***Replace*** Materials....278.00 Labor...........11.40 ***Remove*** .... Labor............3.63 ► Layered with alternating colored layers, wood strip inlays, custom edge detailing, inlaid patterns in countertop.	sf	$3.63	$289.40	$293.03
Granite countertop ***Replace*** Materials.....157.00 Labor...........14.30 ***Remove*** .... Labor............3.63	sf	$3.63	$171.30	$174.93

◄ **PLASTIC LAMINATE COUNTERTOP**
*Most commonly known by the trade name "Formica." Add **6%** for installation on bathroom vanity.*

◄ **CULTURED MARBLE COUNTERTOP**
*Add **6%** for installation on bathroom vanity.*

◄ **CULTURED GRANITE COUNTERTOP**
*Add **6%** for installation on bathroom vanity.*

◄ **CULTURED ONYX COUNTERTOP**
*Add **6%** for installation on bathroom vanity.*

◄ **SOLID-SURFACE COUNTERTOP**
*Commonly known by the trade name Corian. Other trade names include Avonite, Surell, Gibraltar, and Fountainhead. Add **9%** for installation on bathroom vanity.*

◄ **GRANITE COUNTERTOP**
*Add **6%** for installation on bathroom vanity.*

	Item Description	Unit	Remove	Replace	Total
Stainless steel countertop	**Stainless steel countertop** *Replace* Materials......24.00 Labor..........13.00 *Remove* .... Labor...........3.63	sf	$3.63	$37.00	$40.63
Butcher-block countertop Add **6%** for installation on bathroom vanity.	**Butcher-block countertop** *Replace* Materials......22.00 Labor..........10.80 *Remove* .... Labor...........3.63	sf	$3.63	$32.80	$36.43
Solid wood countertop Add **6%** for installation on bathroom vanity.	**Solid wood countertop** *Replace* Materials........7.60 Labor..........10.00 *Remove* .... Labor...........3.63 ► Maple or oak.	sf	$3.63	$17.60	$21.23
	Remove countertop for work, then reinstall *Replace* .... Labor..........15.40	sf	—	$15.40	$15.40
Tile countertop Add **6%** for installation on bathroom vanity.	**Tile countertop, economy grade tile** *Replace* Materials......12.00 Labor...........8.63 *Remove* .... Labor...........6.30 ► Average priced tile set in thinset mortar bed over cement backer board.	sf	$6.30	$20.63	$26.93
	Tile countertop, standard grade tile *Replace* Materials......18.00 Labor...........8.63 *Remove* .... Labor...........6.30 ► Average priced tile set in mortar bed or higher priced tile set in thinset mortar over cement backer board.	sf	$6.30	$26.63	$32.93
	Tile countertop, high grade tile *Replace* Materials......22.00 Labor...........8.63 *Remove* .... Labor...........6.30 ► Higher priced tile set in mortar bed or deluxe priced tile set in thinset mortar over cement backer board.	sf	$6.30	$30.63	$36.93
	Tile countertop, deluxe grade tile *Replace* Materials......35.00 Labor...........8.63 *Remove* .... Labor...........6.30 ► Deluxe priced tile set in mortar bed.	sf	$6.30	$43.63	$49.93
Repair tile countertop	**Replace tile in tile countertop to match** *Replace* Materials......29.00 Labor..........31.60	ea	—	$60.60	$60.60
	Re-affix loose tile in tile countertop *Replace* Materials.......19.00 Labor..........21.50	ea	—	$40.50	$40.50
	Minimum charge for tile countertop work *Replace* Materials......20.00 Labor..........76.40	ea	—	$96.40	$96.40
Bathroom vanity cabinet	**Bathroom vanity cabinet, economy grade** *Replace* Materials......69.00 Labor..........12.80 *Remove* .... Labor...........7.43	lf	$7.43	$81.80	$89.23
	Bathroom vanity cabinets, standard grade *Replace* Materials......88.00 Labor..........12.80 *Remove* .... Labor...........7.43	lf	$7.43	$100.80	$108.23
	Bathroom vanity cabinets, high grade *Replace* Materials.....112.00 Labor..........12.80 *Remove* .... Labor...........7.43	lf	$7.43	$124.80	$132.23
	Bathroom vanity cabinets, deluxe grade *Replace* Materials.....159.00 Labor..........12.80 *Remove* .... Labor...........7.43	lf	$7.43	$171.80	$179.23

Item Description	Unit	Remove	Replace	Total
Bathroom vanity cabinets, custom grade	lf	$7.43	$239.80	$247.23
Replace Materials....227.00 Labor..........12.80				
Remove Labor............7.43				
Bathroom vanity cabinets, custom deluxe grade	lf	$7.43	$306.80	$314.23
Replace Materials....294.00 Labor..........12.80				
Remove Labor............7.43				
Remove bathroom vanity cabinet for work, then reinstall	lf	—	$22.50	$22.50
Replace Labor..........22.50				

RELATED ITEMS

Cleaning......................56

NOTES:

end

TIME & MATERIAL CHARTS *(selected items)*

Cabinets Materials

See **Cabinets** material prices with the line items and other information in the **QuickFinder** column.

Cabinets Labor

LABORER	BASE WAGE	PAID LEAVE	TRUE WAGE	FICA	FUTA	WORKER'S COMP.	UNEMPLOY. INSUR.	HEALTH INSUR.	RETIRE (401K)	LIABILITY INSUR.	COST PER HOUR
Cabinet installer	$23.60	1.84	$25.44	1.95	.20	4.96	2.21	2.69	.76	3.43	$41.60
Painter	$23.20	1.81	$25.01	1.91	.20	6.65	2.18	2.69	.75	3.38	$42.80
Tile layer	$22.10	1.72	$23.82	1.82	.19	4.32	2.07	2.69	.71	3.22	$38.80
Laborer	$14.80	1.15	$15.95	1.22	.13	3.11	1.39	2.69	.48	2.15	$27.10
Demolition laborer	$13.90	1.08	$14.98	1.15	.12	4.79	1.30	2.69	.45	2.02	$27.50

Paid Leave is calculated based on two weeks paid vacation, one week sick leave, and seven paid holidays. Employer's matching portion of **FICA** is 7.65 percent. **FUTA** (Federal Unemployment) is .8 percent. **Worker's Compensation** was calculated using a national average of 19.50 percent for the cabinet installer and helper; 26.59 percent for the painter; and 18.14 percent for the tile layer. **Unemployment insurance** was calculated using a national average of 8.7 percent. **Health insurance** was calculated based on a projected national average for 2002 of $535 per employee (and family when applicable) per month. Employer pays 80 percent for a per month cost of $428 per employee. **Retirement** is based on a 401(k) retirement program with employer matching of 50 percent. Employee contributions to the 401(k) plan are an average of 6 percent of the true wage. **Liability insurance** is based on a national average of 13.2 percent.

Cabinets Labor Productivity

WORK DESCRIPTION	LABORER	COST PER HOUR	PRODUCTIVITY	UNIT PRICE
Demolition				
remove lower kitchen cabinets	demolition laborer	$27.50	.262	$7.21 lf
remove lower island kitchen cabinets	demolition laborer	$27.50	.253	$6.96 lf
remove upper kitchen cabinets	demolition laborer	$27.50	.236	$6.49 lf
remove upper island kitchen cabinets	demolition laborer	$27.50	.238	$6.55 lf
remove full-height kitchen cabinets	demolition laborer	$27.50	.331	$9.10 lf
remove bathroom vanity cabinet	demolition laborer	$27.50	.270	$7.43 lf

. . . More ➢

Cabinets Labor Productivity *continued*

WORK DESCRIPTION	LABORER	COST PER HOUR	PRODUCTIVITY	UNIT PRICE
remove countertop	demolition laborer	$27.50	.132	**$3.63** sf
remove tile countertop	demolition laborer	$27.50	.229	**$6.30** sf
remove cabinet door	demolition laborer	$27.50	.267	**$7.34** ea
remove cabinet drawer front	demolition laborer	$27.50	.144	**$3.96** ea
Cabinet crew				
install cabinets & countertop	cabinet installer	$41.60		
install cabinets & countertop	laborer	$27.10		
cabinet installation	**installation crew**	$34.40		
Install kitchen cabinets				
lower kitchen cabinets	installation crew	$34.40	.360	**$12.40** lf
upper kitchen cabinets	installation crew	$34.40	.349	**$12.00** lf
lower kitchen island cabinets	installation crew	$34.40	.371	**$12.80** lf
upper kitchen island cabinets	installation crew	$34.40	.359	**$12.30** lf
full-height cabinet	installation crew	$34.40	.593	**$20.40** lf
Install cabinet drawer fronts & doors				
drawer front	installation crew	$34.40	.118	**$4.06** ea
door	installation crew	$34.40	.252	**$8.67** ea
Refinish cabinets				
cabinet drawer front	painter	$42.80	.219	**$9.37** ea
cabinet door	painter	$42.80	.513	**$22.00** ea
cabinet door with glass	painter	$42.80	.515	**$22.00** ea
cabinets & doors, re-face plywood ends	painter	$42.80	1.13	**$48.40** lf
island cabinets & doors, re-face plywood ends & faces	painter	$42.80	1.47	**$62.90** lf
Cabinet repair				
repair gouge or hole in cabinet, grain to match	painter	$42.80	1.19	**$50.90** ea
Install countertop				
post-formed plastic laminate	installation crew	$34.40	.286	**$9.84** sf
flat-laid plastic laminate	installation crew	$34.40	.309	**$10.60** sf
cultured material	installation crew	$34.40	.314	**$10.80** sf
solid-surface	installation crew	$34.40	.330	**$11.40** sf
granite	installation crew	$34.40	.415	**$14.30** sf
stainless steel	installation crew	$34.40	.377	**$13.00** sf
butcher block	installation crew	$34.40	.314	**$10.80** sf
solid wood	installation crew	$34.40	.292	**$10.00** sf
tile	installation crew	$34.40	.251	**$8.63** sf
Install bathroom vanity cabinet				
bathroom vanity cabinet	installation crew	$34.40	.371	**$12.80** lf

NOTES:

end

6 Cleaning

Item Description	Unit			Total	
Minimum charge for cleaning work *Clean* Materials............2.00 Labor..........44.30	ea	—	—	$46.30	◄ **Minimum**
Clean acoustic ceiling tiles *Clean* Materials............ .02 Labor............. .34	sf	—	—	$.36	◄ **Acoustic tile**
Clean cook top *Clean* Materials............ .90 Labor...........21.50	ea	—	—	$22.40	◄ **Appliances**
Clean range *Clean* Materials............1.50 Labor...........37.90	ea	—	—	$39.40	
Clean space-saver range *Clean* Materials............1.40 Labor...........35.70	ea	—	—	$37.10	
Clean high-low range *Clean* Materials............2.00 Labor...........49.70	ea	—	—	$51.70	
Clean restaurant-style gas range *Clean* Materials............2.10 Labor...........51.90	ea	—	—	$54.00	
Clean wall oven *Clean* Materials............1.20 Labor...........31.20	ea	—	—	$32.40	
Clean double wall oven *Clean* Materials............2.10 Labor...........51.90	ea	—	—	$54.00	
Clean modular electric cook top unit *Clean* Materials............ .40 Labor...........10.80	ea	—	—	$11.20	
Clean drop-in or slide-in range *Clean* Materials............1.40 Labor..........34.40	ea	—	—	$35.80	
Clean range hood *Clean* Materials............ .40 Labor...........10.53	ea	—	—	$10.93	
Clean oversize range hood *Clean* Materials............ .40 Labor...........11.20	ea	—	—	$11.60	
Clean dishwasher *Clean* Materials.......... 1.00 Labor...........24.60	ea	—	—	$25.60	
Clean microwave *Clean* Materials............ .50 Labor...........12.00	ea	—	—	$12.50	
Clean side-by-side refrigerator *Clean* Materials............1.80 Labor..........44.30	ea	—	—	$46.10	
Clean over-under refrigerator *Clean* Materials............1.60 Labor..........39.90	ea	—	—	$41.50	
Clean trash compactor *Clean* Materials............ .60 Labor...........13.80	ea	—	—	$14.40	

Cleaning

Unless otherwise noted, all cleaning prices are for items typically smoke stained. For lightly stained items deduct **10%**.

For heavily stained items add **15%**.

RELATED ITEMS

	Item Description	Unit			Total
APPLIANCES ► *continued*	**Clean clothes washing machine** ***Clean*** Materials............ .60 Labor...........15.80	ea	—	—	$16.40
	Clean clothes dryer ***Clean*** Materials............ .50 Labor...........11.60	ea	—	—	$12.10
AWNINGS ►	**Clean aluminum or steel carport or patio** ***Clean*** Materials............ .02 Labor............. .47	sf	—	—	$.49
	Clean aluminum or steel door or window awning ***Clean*** Materials............ .19 Labor............4.75	lf	—	—	$4.94
BATHROOM ► HARDWARE	**Clean complete bathroom fixtures and hardware** ***Clean*** Materials...........3.90 Labor...........98.20	ea	—	—	$102.10
	Clean complete 1/2 bathroom fixtures and hardware ***Clean*** Materials...........2.50 Labor 63.20	ea	—	—	$65.70
	Clean bathroom hardware (per piece) ***Clean*** Materials............ .24 Labor 6.05	ea	—	—	$6.29
	Clean medicine cabinet ***Clean*** Materials............ .56 Labor...........14.00	ea	—	—	$14.56
	Clean bathroom mirror ***Clean*** Materials............ .03 Labor............. .64	sf	—	—	$.67
CABINETS ►	**Clean lower cabinets** ***Clean*** Materials............ .44 Labor...........11.00	lf	—	—	$11.44
	Clean upper cabinets ***Clean*** Materials............ .41 Labor...........10.30	lf	—	—	$10.71
	Clean lower island cabinets ***Clean*** Materials............ .45 Labor...........11.20	lf	—	—	$11.65
	Clean upper island cabinets ***Clean*** Materials............ .50 Labor...........12.60	lf	—	—	$13.10
	Clean full-height cabinets ***Clean*** Materials............ .74 Labor...........18.40	lf	—	—	$19.14
countertop ▷	**Clean plastic laminate countertop** ***Clean*** Materials............ .03 Labor............. .86	sf	—	—	$.89
	Clean cultured stone countertop ***Clean*** Materials............ .04 Labor............. .93	sf	—	—	$.97
	Clean solid-surface countertop ***Clean*** Materials............ .04 Labor............. .96	sf	—	—	$1.00
	Clean granite countertop ***Clean*** Materials............ .04 Labor........... 1.06	sf	—	—	$1.10
	Clean stainless steel countertop ***Clean*** Materials............ .04 Labor............. .98	sf	—	—	$1.02
	Clean wood countertop (butcher block or solid wood) ***Clean*** Materials............ .04 Labor............1.11	sf	—	—	$1.15

Item Description	Unit			Total	
Clean tile countertop *Clean* Materials .... .06 Labor 1.53	sf	—	—	$1.59	
Clean bathroom vanity cabinet *Clean* Materials .... .34 Labor 8.51	lf	—	—	$8.85	
Clean column *Clean* Materials .... .16 Labor 3.89	lf	—	—	$4.05	◄ COLUMNS
Clean pilaster *Clean* Materials .... .09 Labor 2.14	lf	—	—	$2.23	
Clean capital *Clean* Materials............1.36 Labor 33.90	ea	—	—	$35.26	
Clean ornate capital (Corinthian) *Clean* Materials............2.42 Labor 60.50	ea	—	—	$62.92	
Clean column base *Clean* Materials .... .84 Labor...........21.10	ea	—	—	$21.94	
Clean pilaster base *Clean* Materials .... .45 Labor...........11.30	ea	—	—	$11.75	
Clean concrete wall *Clean* Materials .... .02 Labor............ .34	sf	—	—	$.36	◄ CONCRETE
Clean concrete floor *Clean* Materials .... .02 Labor............ .30	sf	—	—	$.32	
Clean concrete step (per step) *Clean* Materials .... .22 Labor 5.46	lf	—	—	$5.68	
Clean door jamb and casing (per lf) *Clean* Materials .... .02 Labor............ .49	lf	—	—	$.51	◄ DOORS
Clean door jamb and casing (per door) *Clean* Materials .... .34 Labor 8.59	ea	—	—	$8.93	
Clean folding door *Clean* Materials .... .26 Labor 6.40	ea	—	—	$6.66	
Clean louvered folding door *Clean* Materials .... .43 Labor...........10.80	ea	—	—	$11.23	
Clean bypassing door *Clean* Materials .... .46 Labor...........11.40	ea	—	—	$11.86	
Clean louvered bypassing door *Clean* Materials .... .62 Labor...........15.40	ea	—	—	$16.02	
Clean French door *Clean* Materials .... .80 Labor 20.10	ea	—	—	$20.90	
Clean standard flush door *Clean* Materials .... .43 Labor...........10.80	ea	—	—	$11.23	
Clean pocket door *Clean* Materials .... .44 Labor...........11.00	ea	—	—	$11.44	

RELATED ITEMS

Bathroom Hardware......41
Cabinets.........................47
Columns.........................71
Concrete.........................83
Doors............................101

	Item Description	Unit			Total
DOORS ▶ *continued*	**Clean panel door** *Clean* Materials............ .45 Labor...........11.30	ea	—	—	$11.75
	Clean transom *Clean* Materials............ .23 Labor............5.66	ea	—	—	$5.89
	Clean batten door *Clean* Materials............ .47 Labor...........11.80	ea	—	—	$12.27
	Clean storm door *Clean* Materials............ .45 Labor...........11.20	ea	—	—	$11.65
	Clean exterior door side lite *Clean* Materials............ .36 Labor............9.10	ea	—	—	$9.46
	Clean Dutch door *Clean* Materials............ .46 Labor...........11.40	ea	—	—	$11.86
	Clean fan lite *Clean* Materials............ .33 Labor............8.34	ea	—	—	$8.67
	Clean cafe doors *Clean* Materials............ .35 Labor............8.66	ea	—	—	$9.01
sliding patio door ▷	**Clean 6′ wide sliding patio door** *Clean* Materials.......... 1.00 Labor...........26.10	ea	—	—	$27.10
	Clean 8′ wide sliding patio door *Clean* Materials............1.20 Labor..........29.50	ea	—	—	$30.70
	Clean 12′ wide sliding patio door *Clean* Materials............1.40 Labor..........33.90	ea	—	—	$35.30
garage door ▷	**Clean 8′ wide garage door** *Clean* Materials............1.50 Labor..........38.40	ea	—	—	$39.90
	Clean 9′ wide garage door *Clean* Materials............1.60 Labor..........40.60	ea	—	—	$42.20
	Clean 10′ wide garage door *Clean* Materials............1.70 Labor...........42.80	ea	—	—	$44.50
	Clean 12′ wide garage door *Clean* Materials............1.80 Labor...........45.00	ea	—	—	$46.80
	Clean 14′ wide garage door *Clean* Materials............1.90 Labor...........47.50	ea	—	—	$49.40
	Clean 16′ wide garage door *Clean* Materials............2.00 Labor..........50.20	ea	—	—	$52.20
	Clean 18′ wide garage door *Clean* Materials............2.10 Labor..........53.10	ea	—	—	$55.20
	Clean garage door opener *Clean* Materials............ .95 Labor..........23.80	ea	—	—	$24.75
DRYWALL OR ▶ PLASTER	**Clean wall** *Clean* Materials............ .02 Labor............. .32	sf	—	—	$.34

Item Description	Unit			Total	
Clean ceiling *Clean* Materials............ .01 Labor............ .34	sf	—	—	$.35	
Clean ceiling acoustic texture *Clean* Materials............ .02 Labor............ .42	sf	—	—	$.44	
Clean outlet or switch *Clean* Materials............ .08 Labor............2.07	ea	—	—	$2.15	◀ ELECTRICAL
Clean breaker panel *Clean* Materials............ .68 Labor...........17.00	ea	—	—	$17.68	
Clean circuit breaker *Clean* Materials............ .22 Labor............5.58	ea	—	—	$5.80	
Clean door bell or chime button *Clean* Materials............ .03 Labor............ .84	ea	—	—	$.87	
Clean bathroom exhaust fan *Clean* Materials............ .29 Labor............7.13	ea	—	—	$7.42	
Clean bathroom exhaust fan with heat lamp *Clean* Materials............ .32 Labor............7.90	ea	—	—	$8.22	
Clean kitchen exhaust fan *Clean* Materials............ .29 Labor............7.36	ea	—	—	$7.65	
Clean whole-house exhaust fan *Clean* Materials............ .35 Labor............8.66	ea	—	—	$9.01	
Clean intercom system station *Clean* Materials............ .19 Labor............4.75	ea	—	—	$4.94	
Clean detector *Clean* Materials............ .18 Labor............4.55	ea	—	—	$4.73	
Clean thermostat *Clean* Materials............ .21 Labor............5.19	ea	—	—	$5.40	
Clean light fixture *Clean* Materials............ .44 Labor...........11.00	ea	—	—	$11.44	◁ light fixtures
Clean bathroom light bar (per light) *Clean* Materials............ .16 Labor............3.94	ea	—	—	$4.10	
Clean chandelier, typical detail *Clean* Materials............1.25 Labor...........31.50	ea	—	—	$32.75	
Clean chandelier, ornate detail *Clean* Materials............1.95 Labor...........49.20	ea	—	—	$51.15	
Clean chandelier, very ornate detail *Clean* Materials............2.95 Labor...........73.60	ea	—	—	$76.55	
Clean crystal chandelier, typical detail *Clean* Materials............4.40 Labor.........110.00	ea	—	—	$114.40	
Clean crystal chandelier, ornate detail *Clean* Materials............5.70 Labor.........143.00	ea	—	—	$148.70	

RELATED ITEMS

	Item Description	Unit			Total
ELECTRICAL ▶ (light fixtures) *continued*	**Clean crystal chandelier, very ornate detail** *Clean* Materials..........7.70 Labor.........192.00	ea	—	—	$199.70
	Clean fluorescent light fixture *Clean* Materials........... .50 Labor..........12.80	ea	—	—	$13.30
	Clean ceiling fan *Clean* Materials........... .55 Labor..........14.30	ea	—	—	$14.85
	Clean ceiling fan with light *Clean* Materials........... .70 Labor..........16.90	ea	—	—	$17.60
	Clean recessed spot light fixture *Clean* Materials........... .40 Labor...........9.64	ea	—	—	$10.04
	Clean strip light (per spot) *Clean* Materials........... .19 Labor...........4.80	ea	—	—	$4.99
	Clean exterior flood light fixture (per spot) *Clean* Materials........... .20 Labor...........5.09	ea	—	—	$5.29
	Clean exterior light fixture *Clean* Materials........... .48 Labor..........12.00	ea	—	—	$12.48
	Clean exterior post light fixture *Clean* Materials........... .57 Labor..........14.30	ea	—	—	$14.87
FENCES ▶	**Clean 4′ high wood fence** *Clean* Materials........... .06 Labor...........1.57	lf	—	—	$1.63
	Clean 6′ high wood fence *Clean* Materials........... .08 Labor...........1.92	lf	—	—	$2.00
	Clean 8′ high wood fence *Clean* Materials........... .10 Labor...........2.46	lf	—	—	$2.56
	Clean 4′ high chain-link fence *Clean* Materials........... .04 Labor.......... 1.08	lf	—	—	$1.12
	Clean 6′ high chain-link fence *Clean* Materials........... .05 Labor...........1.23	lf	—	—	$1.28
	Clean 8′ high chain-link fence *Clean* Materials........... .06 Labor...........1.43	lf	—	—	$1.49
	Clean 4′ high vinyl fence *Clean* Materials........... .06 Labor...........1.38	lf	—	—	$1.44
	Clean 6′ high vinyl fence *Clean* Materials........... .07 Labor...........1.65	lf	—	—	$1.72
	Clean 8′ high vinyl fence *Clean* Materials........... .08 Labor...........2.02	lf	—	—	$2.10
	Clean 60″ high ornamental iron fence *Clean* Materials........... .08 Labor...........1.92	lf	—	—	$2.00
	Clean 72″ high ornamental iron fence *Clean* Materials........... .07 Labor...........1.70	lf	—	—	$1.77

Item Description	Unit			Total
Clean molding *Clean* Materials............ .01 Labor............. .37	lf	—	—	$.38
Clean interior wood architrave *Clean* Materials............ .04 Labor............. .91	lf	—	—	$.95
Clean exterior wood architrave *Clean* Materials............ .04 Labor........... 1.03	lf	—	—	$1.07
Clean exterior door surround *Clean* Materials............ .08 Labor 2.02	lf	—	—	$2.10
Clean exterior window surround *Clean* Materials............ .07 Labor 1.77	lf	—	—	$1.84
Clean closet shelf and brackets *Clean* Materials............ .04 Labor............. .93	lf	—	—	$.97
Clean closet organizer *Clean* Materials............ .03 Labor............. .74	sf	—	—	$.77
Clean linen closet shelves *Clean* Materials............ .04 Labor............. .89	sf	—	—	$.93
Clean closet rod *Clean* Materials............ .02 Labor............. .49	lf	—	—	$.51
Clean bookcase *Clean* Materials............ .03 Labor............. .71	sf	—	—	$.74
Clean fireplace mantel *Clean* Materials............ .96 Labor...........24.00	ea	—	—	$24.96
Clean ceiling with exposed beams *Clean* Materials............ .03 Labor............. .69	sf	—	—	$.72
Clean coffered ceiling *Clean* Materials............ .04 Labor............. .91	sf	—	—	$.95
Clean wall niche *Clean* Materials............ .22 Labor 5.58	ea	—	—	$5.80
Clean gingerbread trim *Clean* Materials............ .02 Labor............. .62	lf	—	—	$.64
Clean gingerbread bracket *Clean* Materials............ .19 Labor 4.75	ea	—	—	$4.94
Clean gingerbread corbel *Clean* Materials............ .21 Labor 5.26	ea	—	—	$5.47
Clean gingerbread spandrel *Clean* Materials............ .19 Labor 4.75	lf	—	—	$4.94
Clean gingerbread cornice *Clean* Materials............ .17 Labor 4.21	lf	—	—	$4.38
Clean gingerbread gable ornament *Clean* Materials............ .43 Labor...........10.80	ea	—	—	$11.23

◄ FINISH CARPENTRY

RELATED ITEMS

	Item Description	Unit			Total
FINISH CARPENTRY ▶ *continued*	**Clean gingerbread finial** *Clean* Materials............ .35 Labor............8.83	ea	—	—	$9.18
	Clean porch post *Clean* Materials............ .04 Labor........... 1.03	lf	—	—	$1.07
FIREPLACES ▶	**Clean fireplace screen** *Clean* Materials............1.10 Labor...........27.60	ea	—	—	$28.70
	Clean fireplace door *Clean* Materials.......... 1.04 Labor...........26.10	ea	—	—	$27.14
	Clean marble fireplace face *Clean* Materials............ .05 Labor............1.16	sf	—	—	$1.21
	Clean brick fireplace face *Clean* Materials............ .05 Labor............1.33	sf	—	—	$1.38
	Clean stone fireplace face *Clean* Materials............ .06 Labor............1.43	sf	—	—	$1.49
	Clean tile fireplace face *Clean* Materials............ .06 Labor............1.38	sf	—	—	$1.44
	Clean marble fireplace hearth *Clean* Materials............ .09 Labor............2.34	lf	—	—	$2.43
	Clean brick fireplace hearth *Clean* Materials............ .10 Labor............2.61	lf	—	—	$2.71
	Clean stone fireplace hearth *Clean* Materials............ .11 Labor............2.76	lf	—	—	$2.87
	Clean tile fireplace hearth *Clean* Materials............ .10 Labor............2.61	lf	—	—	$2.71
FLOORING ▶	**Clean carpet** *Clean* Materials............ .02 Labor............. .57	sf	—	—	$.59
	Clean wool carpet *Clean* Materials............ .03 Labor............. .81	sf	—	—	$.84
	Clean carpet cove *Clean* Materials............ .02 Labor............. .52	lf	—	—	$.54
	Add per step for carpet cleaning *Clean* Materials............ .15 Labor............3.81	ea	—	—	$3.96
	Clean stone floor *Clean* Materials............ .02 Labor............. .62	sf	—	—	$.64
	Clean tile floor *Clean* Materials............ .03 Labor............. .84	sf	—	—	$.87
	Clean tile base *Clean* Materials............ .02 Labor............. .39	lf	—	—	$.41
	Clean and wax vinyl floor *Clean* Materials............ .03 Labor............. .69	sf	—	—	$.72

Item Description	Unit			Total	
Clean vinyl cove *Clean* Materials .... .02 Labor .... .39	lf	—	—	$.41	
Clean and wax wood floor *Clean* Materials .... .03 Labor .... .86	sf	—	—	$.89	
Clean and deodorize ducts (per lf of duct) *Clean* Materials .... .15 Labor 3.84	lf	—	—	$3.99	◄ HVAC
Clean furnace *Clean* Materials............2.90 Labor...........72.60	ea	—	—	$75.50	
Clean heat pump *Clean* Materials............1.25 Labor...........31.50	ea	—	—	$32.75	
Clean humidifier *Clean* Materials .... .95 Labor 23.30	ea	—	—	$24.25	
Clean through-wall AC unit *Clean* Materials............1.10 Labor...........27.60	ea	—	—	$28.70	
Clean evaporative cooler *Clean* Materials............1.35 Labor 33.90	ea	—	—	$35.25	
Clean evaporative cooler grille *Clean* Materials .... .25 Labor 6.15	ea	—	—	$6.40	
Clean heat register *Clean* Materials .... .24 Labor 5.90	ea	—	—	$6.14	
Clean cold-air return cover *Clean* Materials .... .24 Labor 5.98	ea	—	—	$6.22	
Clean brick wall *Clean* Materials .... .02 Labor............ .62	sf	—	—	$.64	◄ MASONRY
Clean block wall *Clean* Materials .... .02 Labor............ .57	sf	—	—	$.59	
Clean slump block wall *Clean* Materials .... .02 Labor............ .62	sf	—	—	$.64	
Clean fluted block wall *Clean* Materials .... .03 Labor............ .71	sf	—	—	$.74	
Clean glazed block wall *Clean* Materials .... .03 Labor............ .69	sf	—	—	$.72	
Clean split-face block wall *Clean* Materials .... .03 Labor............ .79	sf	—	—	$.82	
Clean split-rib block wall *Clean* Materials .... .03 Labor............ .74	sf	—	—	$.77	
Clean stone wall *Clean* Materials .... .03 Labor............ .81	sf	—	—	$.84	
Clean glazed structural tile wall *Clean* Materials .... .02 Labor............ .59	sf	—	—	$.61	

RELATED ITEMS

	Item Description	Unit			Total
MASONRY ▶ *continued*	**Clean glass block wall** *Clean* Materials............ .02 Labor............ .59	sf	—	—	$.61
	Clean pavers *Clean* Materials............ .02 Labor............ .62	sf	—	—	$.64
	Clean stone veneer panels *Clean* Materials............ .02 Labor............ .62	sf	—	—	$.64
	Clean cultured stone veneer panels *Clean* Materials............ .02 Labor............ .62	sf	—	—	$.64
	Clean stone architrave *Clean* Materials............ .04 Labor............1.11	lf	—	—	$1.15
	Clean stone trim stones *Clean* Materials............ .04 Labor............ .98	lf	—	—	$1.02
PANELING ▶	**Clean wood paneling** *Clean* Materials............ .02 Labor............ .42	sf	—	—	$.44
	Clean wood paneling with moldings or onlays *Clean* Materials............ .02 Labor............ .52	sf	—	—	$.54
	Clean panel wall *Clean* Materials............ .03 Labor............ .86	sf	—	—	$.89
	Clean pegboard *Clean* Materials............ .02 Labor............ .44	sf	—	—	$.46
	Clean rough-sawn wood paneling *Clean* Materials............ .02 Labor............ .57	sf	—	—	$.59
	Clean tongue-and-groove paneling *Clean* Materials............ .02 Labor............ .49	sf	—	—	$.51
STUCCO ▶	**Clean stucco** *Clean* Materials............ .02 Labor............ .59	sf	—	—	$.61
	Clean stucco architrave *Clean* Materials............ .05 Labor............1.13	lf	—	—	$1.18
PLASTER ▶ See **Drywall** heading in this chapter for prices to clean interior plaster walls.	**Clean plaster molding** *Clean* Materials............ .03 Labor............ .86	lf	—	—	$.89
	Clean plaster architrave *Clean* Materials............ .04 Labor........... 1.03	lf	—	—	$1.07
	Clean ceiling medallion *Clean* Materials............ .55 Labor...........13.70	ea	—	—	$14.25
	Clean ceiling rose *Clean* Materials............ .93 Labor...........23.30	ea	—	—	$24.23
PLUMBING ▶	**Clean sink faucet** *Clean* Materials............ .46 Labor...........11.60	ea	—	—	$12.06
	Clean shower faucet and head *Clean* Materials............ .57 Labor...........14.30	ea	—	—	$14.87

Item Description	Unit			Total
Clean tub faucet ***Clean*** Materials............ .49 Labor...........12.30	ea	—	—	$12.79
Clean tub faucet and shower head ***Clean*** Materials............ .61 Labor...........15.30	ea	—	—	$15.91
Clean wet bar sink ***Clean*** Materials............ .38 Labor............9.62	ea	—	—	$10.00
Clean bathroom sink ***Clean*** Materials............ .41 Labor...........10.30	ea	—	—	$10.71
Clean kitchen sink, per bowl ***Clean*** Materials............ .42 Labor...........10.50	ea	—	—	$10.92
Clean laundry sink, per bowl ***Clean*** Materials............ .44 Labor...........11.00	ea	—	—	$11.44
Clean visible sink supply lines ***Clean*** Materials............ .25 Labor............6.32	ea	—	—	$6.57
Clean toilet ***Clean*** Materials............ .66 Labor...........16.40	ea	—	—	$17.06
Clean bidet ***Clean*** Materials............ .68 Labor...........17.00	ea	—	—	$17.68
Clean toilet seat ***Clean*** Materials............ .18 Labor............4.43	ea	—	—	$4.61
Clean porcelain enamel finish tub ***Clean*** Materials............ .98 Labor...........24.60	ea	—	—	$25.58
Clean porcelain enamel finish tub with whirlpool jets ***Clean*** Materials............1.25 Labor...........31.50	ea	—	—	$32.75
Clean fiberglass finish tub ***Clean*** Materials............1.20 Labor..........29.50	ea	—	—	$30.70
Clean fiberglass finish tub with whirlpool jets ***Clean*** Materials............1.60 Labor..........40.10	ea	—	—	$41.70
Clean tub and shower combination ***Clean*** Materials............1.60 Labor..........40.10	ea	—	—	$41.70
Clean fiberglass or metal shower stall ***Clean*** Materials............1.15 Labor..........28.80	ea	—	—	$29.95
Clean glass shower stall ***Clean*** Materials............1.45 Labor..........36.20	ea	—	—	$37.65
Clean tub surround ***Clean*** Materials............ .55 Labor...........13.40	ea	—	—	$13.95
Clean shower door ***Clean*** Materials............ .85 Labor...........21.70	ea	—	—	$22.55
Clean sliding glass tub door ***Clean*** Materials............1.15 Labor..........29.00	ea	—	—	$30.15

RELATED ITEMS

Masonry......................287
clean masonry...........321
Paneling......................347
Plaster & Stucco.........353
Plumbing......................361

	Item Description	Unit			Total
PLUMBING ► *continued*	**Clean folding plastic tub door** *Clean* Materials............1.20 Labor..........29.50	ea	—	—	$30.70
	Clean water heater *Clean* Materials............ .95 Labor..........23.30	ea	—	—	$24.25
	Clean claw-foot tub faucet *Clean* Materials............ .50 Labor...........12.30	ea	—	—	$12.80
	Clean claw-foot tub faucet and shower conversion *Clean* Materials............ .65 Labor...........16.80	ea	—	—	$17.45
	Clean freestanding water feeds *Clean* Materials............ .30 Labor............7.00	ea	—	—	$7.30
	Clean pedestal sink *Clean* Materials............ .50 Labor...........12.60	ea	—	—	$13.10
	Clean pill-box toilet *Clean* Materials............ .80 Labor..........20.10	ea	—	—	$20.90
	Clean low-tank toilet *Clean* Materials.......... 1.05 Labor...........26.10	ea	—	—	$27.15
	Clean high-tank toilet *Clean* Materials............1.35 Labor..........33.90	ea	—	—	$35.25
	Clean antique tub *Clean* Materials............1.15 Labor..........28.80	ea	—	—	$29.95
SIDING ►	**Clean fiberglass corrugated siding** *Clean* Materials............ .02 Labor............. .34	sf	—	—	$.36
	Clean metal or vinyl siding *Clean* Materials............ .01 Labor............. .37	sf	—	—	$.38
	Clean wood lap siding *Clean* Materials............ .01 Labor............. .37	sf	—	—	$.38
	Clean vertical wood siding (board on board, etc.) *Clean* Materials............ .01 Labor............. .37	sf	—	—	$.38
	Clean cement fiber shingle siding *Clean* Materials............ .02 Labor............. .42	sf	—	—	$.44
	Clean shake or wood shingle siding *Clean* Materials............ .02 Labor............. .47	sf	—	—	$.49
	Clean hardboard or plywood siding *Clean* Materials............ .37 Labor............. .37	sf	—	—	$.38
	Clean tongue-and-groove siding *Clean* Materials............ .02 Labor............. .39	sf	—	—	$.41
	Clean metal or vinyl fascia *Clean* Materials............ .02 Labor............. .39	sf	—	—	$.41
	Clean wood fascia *Clean* Materials............ .02 Labor............. .39	sf	—	—	$.41

Item Description	Unit			Total	
Clean metal or vinyl soffit ***Clean*** Materials............ .01 Labor............ .34	sf	—	—	$.35	
Clean wood soffit ***Clean*** Materials............ .01 Labor............ .37	sf	—	—	$.38	
Clean rough-sawn wood soffit ***Clean*** Materials............ .02 Labor............ .44	sf	—	—	$.46	
Clean shutter ***Clean*** Materials............ .35 Labor............8.83	ea	—	—	$9.18	
Clean wood stair tread ***Clean*** Materials............ .16 Labor............4.01	ea	—	—	$4.17	◄ **STAIRS**
Clean spiral stair balustrade ***Clean*** Materials............ .11 Labor............2.78	lf	—	—	$2.89	
Clean stair balustrade ***Clean*** Materials............ .11 Labor............2.80	lf	—	—	$2.91	
Clean disappearing attic stair ***Clean*** Materials............2.35 Labor...........59.00	ea	—	—	$61.35	
Clean stair bracket ***Clean*** Materials............ .31 Labor............7.63	ea	—	—	$7.94	
Clean suspended ceiling grid ***Clean*** Materials............ .02 Labor............ .25	sf	—	—	$.27	◄ **SUSPENDED CEILING**
Clean tile shower ***Clean*** Materials............1.35 Labor...........33.90	ea	—	—	$35.25	◄ **TILE** *See **Cabinet** heading in this chapter for prices to clean tile countertops and **Flooring** for prices to clean tile floors and base.*
Clean tile tub surround ***Clean*** Materials............1.75 Labor...........44.30	ea	—	—	$46.05	
Clean vinyl wallpaper ***Clean*** Materials............ .01 Labor............ .37	sf	—	—	$.38	◄ **WALLPAPER**
Clean paper wallpaper ***Clean*** Materials............ .02 Labor............ .42	sf	—	—	$.44	
Clean grass or rice cloth wallpaper ***Clean*** Materials............ .02 Labor............ .62	sf	—	—	$.64	
Clean window up to 8 sf ***Clean*** Materials............ .40 Labor...........10.04	ea	—	—	$10.44	◄ **WINDOWS**
Clean window 9 to 14 sf ***Clean*** Materials............ .46 Labor...........11.60	ea	—	—	$12.06	
Clean window 15 to 20 sf ***Clean*** Materials............ .57 Labor...........14.30	ea	—	—	$14.87	
Clean window 21 to 30 sf ***Clean*** Materials............ .84 Labor...........21.10	ea	—	—	$21.94	
Clean window, per sf ***Clean*** Materials............ .03 Labor............ .74	sf	—	—	$.77	

RELATED ITEMS

Bathroom Hardware......41
mirrors..........................45
Siding..........................455
Stairs..........................465
Wall Coverings............495
Windows.....................501

	Item Description	Unit			Total
WINDOWS *continued*	**Clean skylight up to 8 sf** ***Clean*** Materials............ .42 Labor...........10.50	ea	—	—	$10.92
	Clean skylight 9 to 14 sf ***Clean*** Materials............ .49 Labor...........12.30	ea	—	—	$12.79
	Clean skylight 15 to 20 sf ***Clean*** Materials............ .61 Labor...........15.30	ea	—	—	$15.91
	Clean skylight 21 to 30 sf ***Clean*** Materials............ .88 Labor 22.10	ea	—	—	$22.98
	Clean skylight per sf ***Clean*** Materials............ .03 Labor............ .79	sf	—	—	$.82
	Add 15% to clean windows with multiple, small panes				
MIRROR ▶ *Also see **Bathroom Hardware** heading.*	**Clean wall mirror** ***Clean*** Materials............ .03 Labor............ .66	sf	—	—	$.69
FINAL CLEAN ▶	**Final construction clean-up to broom clean** ***Clean*** Materials............ .02 Labor............ .30	sf	—	—	$.32

✍ NOTES: ______________________________

______________________________ end

TIME & MATERIAL CHARTS *(selected items)*

Cleaning Materials

*See **Cleaning** material prices with the line items and other information in the **QuickFinder** column.*

Cleaning Labor

LABORER	BASE WAGE	PAID LEAVE	TRUE WAGE	FICA	FUTA	WORKER'S COMP.	UNEMPLOY. INSUR.	HEALTH INSUR.	RETIRE (401K)	LIABILITY INSUR.	COST PER HOUR
Cleaning laborer	$13.80	1.08	$14.88	1.14	.121	2.01	1.29	2.69	.45	2.01	**$24.60**

Paid Leave is calculated based on two weeks paid vacation, one week sick leave, and seven paid holidays. Employer's matching portion of **FICA** is 7.65 percent. **FUTA** (Federal Unemployment) is .8 percent. **Worker's compensation** for the cleaning trade was calculated using a national average of 13.53 percent. **Unemployment insurance** was calculated using a national average of 8.7 percent. **Health insurance** was calculated based on a projected national average for 2002 of $535 per employee (and family when applicable) per month. Employer pays 80 percent for a per month cost of $428 per employee. **Retirement** is based on a 401(k) retirement program with employer matching of 50 percent. Employee contributions to the 401(k) plan are an average of 6 percent of the true wage. **Liability insurance** is based on a national average of 13.2 percent.

Cleaning Labor Productivity

WORK DESCRIPTION	LABORER	COST PER HOUR	PRODUCTIVITY	UNIT PRICE
Clean appliances				
cook top	*cleaning laborer*	$24.60	.876	$21.50 *ea*
range	*cleaning laborer*	$24.60	1.54	$37.90 *ea*
wall oven	*cleaning laborer*	$24.60	1.27	$31.20 *ea*

. . . More ➢

Cleaning Labor Productivity *continued*

WORK DESCRIPTION	LABORER	COST PER HOUR	PRODUCTIVITY	UNIT PRICE
Clean appliances *continued*				
range hood	cleaning laborer	$24.60	.428	$10.53 ea
dishwasher	cleaning laborer	$24.60	1.00	$24.60 ea
microwave	cleaning laborer	$24.60	.486	$12.00 ea
side-by-side refrigerator	cleaning laborer	$24.60	1.80	$44.30 ea
over-under refrigerator	cleaning laborer	$24.60	1.62	$39.90 ea
trash compactor	cleaning laborer	$24.60	.561	$13.80 ea
Clean awnings				
aluminum or steel carport or patio	cleaning laborer	$24.60	.019	$.47 sf
aluminum or steel door or window awning	cleaning laborer	$24.60	.193	$4.75 lf
Clean bathroom hardware				
bathroom hardware (per piece)	cleaning laborer	$24.60	.246	$6.05 ea
medicine cabinet	cleaning laborer	$24.60	.570	$14.00 ea
Clean cabinets				
lower cabinets	cleaning laborer	$24.60	.446	$11.00 lf
upper cabinets	cleaning laborer	$24.60	.418	$10.30 lf
full-height cabinets	cleaning laborer	$24.60	.749	$18.40 lf
plastic laminate countertop	cleaning laborer	$24.60	.035	$.86 sf
tile countertop	cleaning laborer	$24.60	.062	$1.53 sf
Clean concrete				
wall	cleaning laborer	$24.60	.014	$.34 sf
floor	cleaning laborer	$24.60	.012	$.30 sf
Clean door				
folding door (per section)	cleaning laborer	$24.60	.260	$6.40 ea
bypassing door	cleaning laborer	$24.60	.462	$11.40 ea
door	cleaning laborer	$24.60	.438	$10.80 ea
storm door	cleaning laborer	$24.60	.454	$11.20 ea
Clean drywall or plaster				
wall	cleaning laborer	$24.60	.013	$.32 sf
ceiling	cleaning laborer	$24.60	.014	$.34 sf
ceiling acoustic texture	cleaning laborer	$24.60	.017	$.42 sf
Clean electrical				
light fixture	cleaning laborer	$24.60	.449	$11.00 ea
bathroom light bar (per light)	cleaning laborer	$24.60	.160	$3.94 ea
chandelier, typical detail	cleaning laborer	$24.60	1.28	$31.50 ea
fluorescent light fixture	cleaning laborer	$24.60	.519	$12.80 ea
ceiling fan	cleaning laborer	$24.60	.580	$14.30 ea
ceiling fan with light	cleaning laborer	$24.60	.686	$16.90 ea
Clean fence				
4' high wood	cleaning laborer	$24.60	.064	$1.57 lf
4' high chain-link	cleaning laborer	$24.60	.044	$1.08 lf
4' high vinyl	cleaning laborer	$24.60	.056	$1.38 lf
60" high ornamental iron	cleaning laborer	$24.60	.078	$1.92 lf
Clean finish carpentry				
molding	cleaning laborer	$24.60	.015	$.37 lf
Clean fireplace				
screen	cleaning laborer	$24.60	1.12	$27.60 ea
door	cleaning laborer	$24.60	1.06	$26.10 ea
Clean flooring				
carpet	cleaning laborer	$24.60	.023	$.57 sf
stone floor	cleaning laborer	$24.60	.025	$.62 sf
tile floor	cleaning laborer	$24.60	.034	$.84 sf
vinyl floor and wax	cleaning laborer	$24.60	.028	$.69 sf
wood floor and wax	cleaning laborer	$24.60	.035	$.86 sf
Clean HVAC				
furnace	cleaning laborer	$24.60	2.95	$72.60 ea
through-wall AC unit	cleaning laborer	$24.60	1.12	$27.60 ea
evaporative cooler	cleaning laborer	$24.60	1.38	$33.90 ea

... More ➢

Cleaning Labor Productivity *continued*

WORK DESCRIPTION	LABORER	COST PER HOUR	PRODUCTIVITY	UNIT PRICE
Clean masonry				
brick wall	cleaning laborer	$24.60	.025	$.62 sf
block wall	cleaning laborer	$24.60	.023	$.57 sf
stone wall	cleaning laborer	$24.60	.033	$.81 sf
glass block wall	cleaning laborer	$24.60	.024	$.59 sf
stone veneer panels	cleaning laborer	$24.60	.025	$.62 sf
Clean paneling				
wood paneling	cleaning laborer	$24.60	.017	$.42 sf
wood paneling with moldings or onlays	cleaning laborer	$24.60	.021	$.52 sf
panel wall	cleaning laborer	$24.60	.035	$.86 sf
rough-sawn wood paneling	cleaning laborer	$24.60	.023	$.57 sf
tongue-and-groove paneling	cleaning laborer	$24.60	.020	$.49 sf
Clean plaster *(also see clean drywall)*				
stucco	cleaning laborer	$24.60	.024	$.59 sf
Clean plumbing				
sink faucet	cleaning laborer	$24.60	.473	$11.60 ea
tub faucet	cleaning laborer	$24.60	.499	$12.30 ea
tub faucet and shower head	cleaning laborer	$24.60	.620	$15.30 ea
bathroom sink	cleaning laborer	$24.60	.418	$10.30 ea
kitchen sink, per bowl	cleaning laborer	$24.60	.428	$10.50 ea
laundry sink, per bowl	cleaning laborer	$24.60	.449	$11.00 ea
toilet	cleaning laborer	$24.60	.665	$16.40 ea
bidet	cleaning laborer	$24.60	.691	$17.00 ea
porcelain enamel finish tub	cleaning laborer	$24.60	1.00	$24.60 ea
fiberglass finish tub	cleaning laborer	$24.60	1.20	$29.50 ea
tub and shower combination	cleaning laborer	$24.60	1.63	$40.10 ea
fiberglass or metal shower stall	cleaning laborer	$24.60	1.17	$28.80 ea
glass shower stall	cleaning laborer	$24.60	1.47	$36.20 ea
tub surround	cleaning laborer	$24.60	.544	$13.40 ea
shower door	cleaning laborer	$24.60	.881	$21.70 ea
sliding glass tub door	cleaning laborer	$24.60	1.18	$29.00 ea
pedestal sink	cleaning laborer	$24.60	.513	$12.60 ea
pill-box toilet	cleaning laborer	$24.60	.817	$20.10 ea
Clean siding				
fiberglass corrugated	cleaning laborer	$24.60	.014	$.34 sf
metal or vinyl siding	cleaning laborer	$24.60	.015	$.37 sf
wood lap siding	cleaning laborer	$24.60	.015	$.37 sf
vertical wood siding (board on board, etc.)	cleaning laborer	$24.60	.015	$.37 sf
cement fiber shingle siding	cleaning laborer	$24.60	.017	$.42 sf
shake or wood shingle siding	cleaning laborer	$24.60	.019	$.47 sf
plywood siding	cleaning laborer	$24.60	.015	$.37 sf
tongue-and-groove siding	cleaning laborer	$24.60	.016	$.39 sf
Clean stairs				
wood stair tread	cleaning laborer	$24.60	.163	$4.01 ea
stair balustrade	cleaning laborer	$24.60	.114	$2.80 lf
disappearing attic stair	cleaning laborer	$24.60	2.40	$59.00 ea
Clean tile				
tile shower	cleaning laborer	$24.60	1.38	$33.90 ea
tile tub surround	cleaning laborer	$24.60	1.80	$44.30 ea
Clean wallpaper				
vinyl wallpaper	cleaning laborer	$24.60	.015	$.37 sf
paper wallpaper	cleaning laborer	$24.60	.017	$.42 sf
grass or rice cloth wallpaper	cleaning laborer	$24.60	.025	$.62 sf
Clean window				
window up to 8 sf	cleaning laborer	$24.60	.408	$10.00 ea
window 21 to 30 sf	cleaning laborer	$24.60	.856	$21.10 ea
window, per sf	cleaning laborer	$24.60	.030	$.74 ea
skylight up to 8 sf	cleaning laborer	$24.60	.428	$10.50 ea
skylight 21 to 30 sf	cleaning laborer	$24.60	.898	$22.10 ea
skylight per sf	cleaning laborer	$24.60	.032	$.79 ea

7 Columns

Item Description	Unit	Remove	Replace	Total
Minimum charge for column or pilaster work *Replace* Materials......30.00 Labor..........83.00	lf	—	$113.00	$113.00
12″ round column made from composite materials *Replace* Materials......39.00 Labor..........13.90 *Remove*........................ Labor............5.83	lf	$5.83	$52.90	$58.73
12″ round pine column *Replace* Materials......39.90 Labor..........13.90 *Remove*........................ Labor............5.83	lf	$5.83	$53.80	$59.63
12″ round redwood column *Replace* Materials......47.00 Labor..........13.90 *Remove*........................ Labor............5.83	lf	$5.83	$60.90	$66.73
12″ round oak column *Replace* Materials......52.10 Labor..........13.90 *Remove*........................ Labor............5.83	lf	$5.83	$66.00	$71.83
12″ round stone column *Replace* Materials......72.40 Labor..........13.90 *Remove*........................ Labor............5.83	lf	$5.83	$86.30	$92.13
12″ round synthetic stone column *Replace* Materials......68.30 Labor..........13.90 *Remove*........................ Labor............5.83	lf	$5.83	$82.20	$88.03
12″ round aluminum column *Replace* Materials......41.30 Labor..........13.90 *Remove*........................ Labor............5.83	lf	$5.83	$55.20	$61.03
12″ round interior plaster column *Replace* Materials......38.00 Labor..........13.90 *Remove*........................ Labor............5.83	lf	$5.83	$51.90	$57.73
12″ round exterior stucco column *Replace* Materials......37.10 Labor..........13.90 *Remove*........................ Labor............5.83	lf	$5.83	$51.00	$56.83
12″ round pilaster made from composite materials *Replace* Materials......24.90 Labor..........12.10 *Remove*........................ Labor............3.69	lf	$3.69	$37.00	$40.69
12″ round pine pilaster *Replace* Materials......25.50 Labor..........12.10 *Remove*........................ Labor............3.69	lf	$3.69	$37.60	$41.29
12″ round redwood pilaster *Replace* Materials......30.10 Labor..........12.10 *Remove*........................ Labor............3.69	lf	$3.69	$42.20	$45.89
12″ round oak pilaster *Replace* Materials......33.40 Labor..........12.10 *Remove*........................ Labor............3.69	lf	$3.69	$45.50	$49.19

◄ **MINIMUM**

◄ **12″ COLUMN**
Round columns with no taper. *See page 72 to add for taper, fluting, and architecturally correct taper.*

COLUMN MATERIALS

Composite materials: A combination of marble (or similar material) polymers, and fiberglass or columns made from high-density polyurethane.

Pine: Made from laminated staves of Douglas fir or Ponderosa pine.

Redwood: Made from laminated staves of redwood.

Oak: Made from laminated staves of red oak.

Stone: Crushed and reconstructed limestone reinforced with glass fibers.

Synthetic stone: Lightweight simulated stone which are either cement or gypsum-based fiberglass.

Aluminum: Cast aluminum.

continued on next page

◄ **12″ PILASTER**
Half-round pilaster with no taper. *See page 72 to add for taper, fluting, and architecturally correct taper.*

RELATED ITEMS

Cleaning........................57
Finish Carpentry..........199
Painting......................333

COLUMN MATERIALS

continued from prior page

Plaster: Made from fibrous plaster and gypsum products reinforced with fiberglass or jute, or steel or sisal for use on interior of structure.

Stucco: Made from fibrous plaster products reinforced with fiberglass or jute or steel or sisal for use on exterior of structure.

	Item Description	Unit	Remove	Replace	Total
12" PILASTER ► *continued*	**12" round stone pilaster** ***Replace*** Materials......46.30 Labor...........12.10 ***Remove***......................... Labor 3.69	lf	$3.69	$58.40	$62.09
	12" round synthetic stone pilaster ***Replace*** Materials......43.60 Labor...........12.10 ***Remove***......................... Labor 3.69	lf	$3.69	$55.70	$59.39
	12" round aluminum pilaster ***Replace*** Materials......26.40 Labor...........12.10 ***Remove***......................... Labor 3.69	lf	$3.69	$38.50	$42.19
	12" round interior plaster pilaster ***Replace*** Materials......24.10 Labor...........12.10 ***Remove***......................... Labor 3.69	lf	$3.69	$36.20	$39.89
	12" round exterior stucco pilaster ***Replace*** Materials......23.80 Labor...........12.10 ***Remove***......................... Labor 3.69	lf	$3.69	$35.90	$39.59
ADDITIONAL COLUMN COSTS ►	**Add 18% for round fluted column or pilaster**				
	Add 13% for tapered column or pilaster ► Consistent taper from bottom to top.				
	Add 65% for architecturally correct tapered column or pilaster ► Columns that taper according to the classic Greek or Roman styles.				
12" SQUARE COLUMN ►	**12" square column made from composite materials** ***Replace*** Materials......51.50 Labor...........12.80 ***Remove***......................... Labor 5.83	lf	$5.83	$64.30	$70.13
	12" square pine column ***Replace*** Materials......52.60 Labor...........12.80 ***Remove***......................... Labor 5.83	lf	$5.83	$65.40	$71.23
	12" square redwood column ***Replace*** Materials......62.00 Labor...........12.80 ***Remove***......................... Labor 5.83	lf	$5.83	$74.80	$80.63
	12" square oak column ***Replace*** Materials......68.90 Labor...........12.80 ***Remove***......................... Labor 5.83	lf	$5.83	$81.70	$87.53
	12" square stone column ***Replace*** Materials......95.60 Labor...........12.80 ***Remove***......................... Labor 5.83	lf	$5.83	$108.40	$114.23
	12" square synthetic stone column ***Replace*** Materials......90.00 Labor...........12.80 ***Remove***......................... Labor 5.83	lf	$5.83	$102.80	$108.63
	12" square aluminum column ***Replace*** Materials......54.60 Labor...........12.80 ***Remove***......................... Labor 5.83	lf	$5.83	$67.40	$73.23
	12" square interior plaster column ***Replace*** Materials......50.10 Labor...........12.80 ***Remove***......................... Labor 5.83	lf	$5.83	$62.90	$68.73

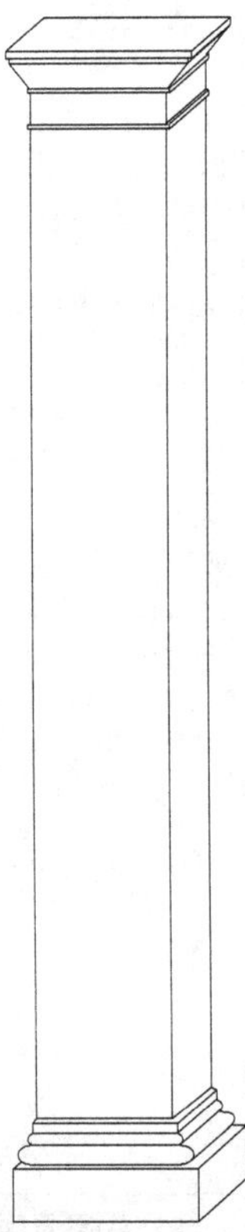

Item Description	Unit	Remove	Replace	Total
12″ square exterior stucco column ***Replace*** Materials......49.00 Labor..........12.80 ***Remove***........................ Labor...........5.83	lf	$5.83	$61.80	$67.63
12″ square pilaster made from composite materials ***Replace*** Materials......32.90 Labor..........11.20 ***Remove***........................ Labor...........3.69	lf	$3.69	$44.10	$47.79
12″ square pine pilaster ***Replace*** Materials......33.80 Labor..........11.20 ***Remove***........................ Labor...........3.69	lf	$3.69	$45.00	$48.69
12″ square redwood pilaster ***Replace*** Materials......39.80 Labor..........11.20 ***Remove***........................ Labor...........3.69	lf	$3.69	$51.00	$54.69
12″ square oak pilaster ***Replace*** Materials......44.00 Labor..........11.20 ***Remove***........................ Labor...........3.69	lf	$3.69	$55.20	$58.89
12″ square stone pilaster ***Replace*** Materials......61.00 Labor..........11.20 ***Remove***........................ Labor...........3.69	lf	$3.69	$72.20	$75.89
12″ square synthetic stone pilaster ***Replace*** Materials......57.80 Labor..........11.20 ***Remove***........................ Labor...........3.69	lf	$3.69	$69.00	$72.69
12″ square aluminum pilaster ***Replace*** Materials......34.90 Labor..........11.20 ***Remove***........................ Labor...........3.69	lf	$3.69	$46.10	$49.79
12″ square interior plaster pilaster ***Replace*** Materials......31.90 Labor..........11.20 ***Remove***........................ Labor...........3.69	lf	$3.69	$43.10	$46.79
12″ square exterior stucco pilaster ***Replace*** Materials......31.30 Labor..........11.20 ***Remove***........................ Labor...........3.69	lf	$3.69	$42.50	$46.19
Repair wood column or pilaster with wood patch ***Replace*** Materials........3.30 Labor..........26.90	ea	—	$30.20	$30.20
Repair fluted wood column or pilaster with wood patch ***Replace*** Materials........3.30 Labor..........33.40	ea	—	$36.70	$36.70
Repair wood column or pilaster by replacing section ***Replace*** Materials........5.90 Labor..........74.50	ea	—	$80.40	$80.40
Repair fluted wood column or pilaster by replacing section ***Replace*** Materials........7.40 Labor..........96.90	ea	—	$104.30	$104.30
Repair dry rot in column or pilaster with epoxy ***Replace*** Materials........5.90 Labor.........108.00	ea	—	$113.90	$113.90
Repair dry rot in fluted column or pilaster with epoxy ***Replace*** Materials........5.90 Labor.........121.00	ea	—	$126.90	$126.90
Add for column repair if column is removed from structure ***Replace*** Materials......59.00 Labor........388.00 ► Additional cost to build temporary brace wall and remove column from structure.	ea	—	$447.00	$447.00

◄ **12″ SQUARE PILASTER**

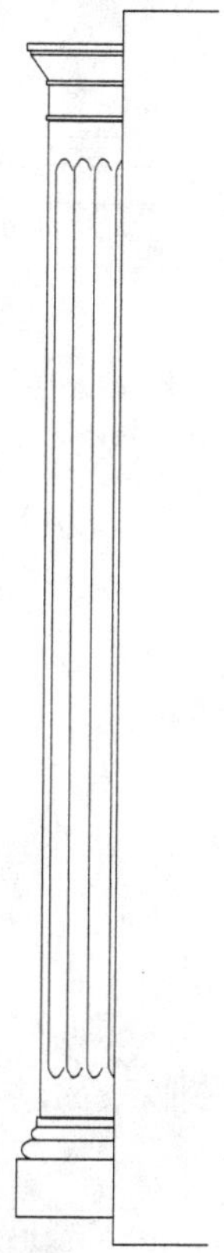

◄ **COLUMN REPAIR**

RELATED ITEMS

COLUMN REPAIR ▶ *continued*

Item Description	Unit	Remove	Replace	Total
Minimum charge for column or pilaster repair *Replace* Materials......16.00 Labor...........96.90	ea	—	$112.90	$112.90

CONTEMPORARY ▶ CAPITAL

Capital up to 4" high. Includes load-bearing plug.

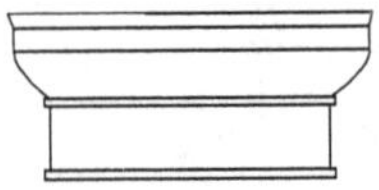

Item Description	Unit	Remove	Replace	Total
Contemporary capital made from composite materials *Replace* Materials.....149.00 Labor ....23.50 *Remove*......................... Labor 23.40	ea	$23.40	$172.50	$195.90
Contemporary capital made from pine *Replace* Materials.....166.00 Labor ....23.50 *Remove*......................... Labor 23.40	ea	$23.40	$189.50	$212.90
Contemporary capital made from redwood *Replace* Materials.....190.00 Labor ....23.50 *Remove*......................... Labor 23.40	ea	$23.40	$213.50	$236.90
Contemporary capital made from oak *Replace* Materials.....218.00 Labor ....23.50 *Remove*......................... Labor 23.40	ea	$23.40	$241.50	$264.90
Contemporary capital made from stone *Replace* Materials....301.00 Labor ....23.50 *Remove*......................... Labor 23.40	ea	$23.40	$324.50	$347.90
Contemporary capital made from synthetic stone *Replace* Materials....282.00 Labor ....23.50 *Remove*......................... Labor 23.40	ea	$23.40	$305.50	$328.90
Contemporary capital made from aluminum *Replace* Materials.....170.00 Labor ....23.50 *Remove*......................... Labor 23.40	ea	$23.40	$193.50	$216.90
Contemporary capital made from interior plaster *Replace* Materials.....156.00 Labor ....23.50 *Remove*......................... Labor 23.40	ea	$23.40	$179.50	$202.90
Contemporary capital made from exterior stucco *Replace* Materials ....154.00 Labor ....23.50 *Remove*......................... Labor 23.40	ea	$23.40	$177.50	$200.90

CORINTHIAN ▶ CAPITAL

Capital up to 14" high. Includes load-bearing plug.

Item Description	Unit	Remove	Replace	Total
Corinthian capital made from composite materials *Replace* Materials ....456.00 Labor ....23.50 *Remove*......................... Labor 23.40	ea	$23.40	$479.50	$502.90
Corinthian capital made from pine *Replace* Materials....786.00 Labor ....23.50 *Remove*......................... Labor 23.40	ea	$23.40	$809.50	$832.90
Corinthian capital made from redwood *Replace* Materials ....896.00 Labor ....23.50 *Remove*......................... Labor 23.40	ea	$23.40	$919.50	$942.90
Corinthian capital made from oak *Replace* Materials.1,030.00 Labor ....23.50 *Remove*......................... Labor 23.40	ea	$23.40	$1,053.50	$1,076.90
Corinthian capital made from stone *Replace* Materials....606.00 Labor ....23.50 *Remove*......................... Labor 23.40	ea	$23.40	$629.50	$652.90
Corinthian capital made from synthetic stone *Replace* Materials ....567.00 Labor ....23.50 *Remove*......................... Labor 23.40	ea	$23.40	$590.50	$613.90

Item Description	Unit	Remove	Replace	Total
Corinthian capital made from aluminum ***Replace*** Materials....342.00 Labor..........23.50 ***Remove***........................ Labor..........23.40	ea	$23.40	$365.50	$388.90
Corinthian capital made from interior plaster ***Replace*** Materials.....315.00 Labor..........23.50 ***Remove***........................ Labor..........23.40	ea	$23.40	$338.50	$361.90
Corinthian capital made from exterior stucco ***Replace*** Materials....309.00 Labor..........23.50 ***Remove***........................ Labor..........23.40	ea	$23.40	$332.50	$355.90
Doric or Tuscan capital made from composite materials ***Replace*** Materials.....156.00 Labor..........23.50 ***Remove***........................ Labor..........23.40	ea	$23.40	$179.50	$202.90
Doric or Tuscan capital made from pine ***Replace*** Materials.....173.00 Labor..........23.50 ***Remove***........................ Labor..........23.40	ea	$23.40	$196.50	$219.90
Doric or Tuscan capital made from redwood ***Replace*** Materials.....197.00 Labor..........23.50 ***Remove***........................ Labor..........23.40	ea	$23.40	$220.50	$243.90
Doric or Tuscan capital made from oak ***Replace*** Materials....226.00 Labor..........23.50 ***Remove***........................ Labor..........23.40	ea	$23.40	$249.50	$272.90
Doric or Tuscan capital made from stone ***Replace*** Materials.....313.00 Labor..........23.50 ***Remove***........................ Labor..........23.40	ea	$23.40	$336.50	$359.90
Doric or Tuscan capital made from synthetic stone ***Replace*** Materials....292.00 Labor..........23.50 ***Remove***........................ Labor..........23.40	ea	$23.40	$315.50	$338.90
Doric or Tuscan capital made from aluminum ***Replace*** Materials.....175.00 Labor..........23.50 ***Remove***........................ Labor..........23.40	ea	$23.40	$198.50	$221.90
Doric or Tuscan capital made from interior plaster ***Replace*** Materials.....161.00 Labor..........23.50 ***Remove***........................ Labor..........23.40	ea	$23.40	$184.50	$207.90
Doric or Tuscan capital made from exterior stucco ***Replace*** Materials.....158.00 Labor..........23.50 ***Remove***........................ Labor..........23.40	ea	$23.40	$181.50	$204.90
Empire capital made from composite materials ***Replace*** Materials....291.00 Labor..........23.50 ***Remove***........................ Labor..........23.40	ea	$23.40	$314.50	$337.90
Empire capital made from pine ***Replace*** Materials....501.00 Labor..........23.50 ***Remove***........................ Labor..........23.40	ea	$23.40	$524.50	$547.90
Empire capital made from redwood ***Replace*** Materials....572.00 Labor..........23.50 ***Remove***........................ Labor..........23.40	ea	$23.40	$595.50	$618.90

◄ **DORIC OR TUSCAN CAPITAL**
Capital up to 4" high. Includes load-bearing plug.

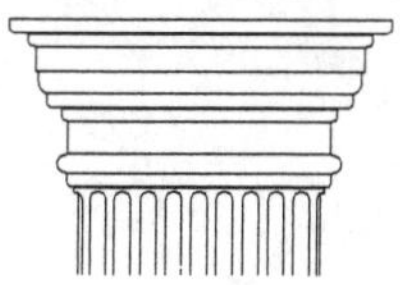

◄ **EMPIRE CAPITAL**
Capital up to 7" high. Includes load-bearing plug.

RELATED ITEMS

Cleaning........................57
Finish Carpentry..........199
Painting......................333

Empire capital ► *continued.*

Item Description	Unit	Remove	Replace	Total
Empire capital made from oak ***Replace*** Materials....657.00 Labor..........23.50 ***Remove***........................ Labor..........23.40	ea	$23.40	$680.50	$703.90
Empire capital made from stone ***Replace*** Materials....387.00 Labor..........23.50 ***Remove***........................ Labor..........23.40	ea	$23.40	$410.50	$433.90
Empire capital made from synthetic stone ***Replace*** Materials.....361.00 Labor..........23.50 ***Remove***........................ Labor..........23.40	ea	$23.40	$384.50	$407.90
Empire capital made from aluminum ***Replace*** Materials.....218.00 Labor..........23.50 ***Remove***........................ Labor..........23.40	ea	$23.40	$241.50	$264.90
Empire capital made from interior plaster ***Replace*** Materials....200.00 Labor..........23.50 ***Remove***........................ Labor..........23.40	ea	$23.40	$223.50	$246.90
Empire capital made from exterior stucco ***Replace*** Materials.....196.00 Labor..........23.50 ***Remove***........................ Labor..........23.40	ea	$23.40	$219.50	$242.90

Erechtheum capital ►

*Capital up to 7" high. Add **50%** for necking. Includes load-bearing plug.*

Item Description	Unit	Remove	Replace	Total
Erechtheum capital made from composite materials ***Replace*** Materials....282.00 Labor..........23.50 ***Remove***........................ Labor..........23.40	ea	$23.40	$305.50	$328.90
Erechtheum capital made from pine ***Replace*** Materials....486.00 Labor..........23.50 ***Remove***........................ Labor..........23.40	ea	$23.40	$509.50	$532.90
Erechtheum capital made from redwood ***Replace*** Materials....553.00 Labor..........23.50 ***Remove***........................ Labor..........23.40	ea	$23.40	$576.50	$599.90
Erechtheum capital made from oak ***Replace*** Materials....636.00 Labor..........23.50 ***Remove***........................ Labor..........23.40	ea	$23.40	$659.50	$682.90
Erechtheum capital made from stone ***Replace*** Materials.....374.00 Labor..........23.50 ***Remove***........................ Labor..........23.40	ea	$23.40	$397.50	$420.90
Erechtheum capital made from synthetic stone ***Replace*** Materials....351.00 Labor..........23.50 ***Remove***........................ Labor..........23.40	ea	$23.40	$374.50	$397.90
Erechtheum capital made from aluminum ***Replace*** Materials.....211.00 Labor..........23.50 ***Remove***........................ Labor..........23.40	ea	$23.40	$234.50	$257.90
Erechtheum capital made from interior plaster ***Replace*** Materials.....195.00 Labor..........23.50 ***Remove***........................ Labor..........23.40	ea	$23.40	$218.50	$241.90
Erechtheum capital made from exterior stucco ***Replace*** Materials.....191.00 Labor..........23.50 ***Remove***........................ Labor..........23.40	ea	$23.40	$214.50	$237.90

Item Description	Unit	Remove	Replace	Total
Roman Ionic capital made from composite materials *Replace* Materials....295.00 Labor..........23.50 *Remove*......................... Labor..........23.40	ea	$23.40	$318.50	$341.90
Roman Ionic capital made from pine *Replace* Materials....506.00 Labor..........23.50 *Remove*......................... Labor..........23.40	ea	$23.40	$529.50	$552.90
Roman Ionic capital made from redwood *Replace* Materials....577.00 Labor..........23.50 *Remove*......................... Labor..........23.40	ea	$23.40	$600.50	$623.90
Roman Ionic capital made from oak *Replace* Materials....663.00 Labor..........23.50 *Remove*......................... Labor..........23.40	ea	$23.40	$686.50	$709.90
Roman Ionic capital made from stone *Replace* Materials....391.00 Labor..........23.50 *Remove*......................... Labor..........23.40	ea	$23.40	$414.50	$437.90
Roman Ionic capital made from synthetic stone *Replace* Materials....365.00 Labor..........23.50 *Remove*......................... Labor..........23.40	ea	$23.40	$388.50	$411.90
Roman Ionic capital made from aluminum *Replace* Materials....220.00 Labor..........23.50 *Remove*......................... Labor..........23.40	ea	$23.40	$243.50	$266.90
Roman Ionic capital made from interior plaster *Replace* Materials....202.00 Labor..........23.50 *Remove*......................... Labor..........23.40	ea	$23.40	$225.50	$248.90
Roman Ionic capital made from exterior stucco *Replace* Materials.....199.00 Labor..........23.50 *Remove*......................... Labor..........23.40	ea	$23.40	$222.50	$245.90
Scamozzi capital made from composite materials *Replace* Materials....309.00 Labor..........23.50 *Remove*......................... Labor..........23.40	ea	$23.40	$332.50	$355.90
Scamozzi capital made from pine *Replace* Materials....531.00 Labor..........23.50 *Remove*......................... Labor..........23.40	ea	$23.40	$554.50	$577.90
Scamozzi capital made from redwood *Replace* Materials....605.00 Labor..........23.50 *Remove*......................... Labor..........23.40	ea	$23.40	$628.50	$651.90
Scamozzi capital made from oak *Replace* Materials.....696.00 Labor..........23.50 *Remove*......................... Labor..........23.40	ea	$23.40	$719.50	$742.90
Scamozzi capital made from stone *Replace* Materials.....410.00 Labor..........23.50 *Remove*......................... Labor..........23.40	ea	$23.40	$433.50	$456.90
Scamozzi capital made from synthetic stone *Replace* Materials....384.00 Labor..........23.50 *Remove*......................... Labor..........23.40	ea	$23.40	$407.50	$430.90

◄ **ROMAN IONIC CAPITAL**
Capital up to 5" high. Includes load-bearing plug.

◄ **SCAMOZZI CAPITAL**
Capital up to 5" high. Includes load-bearing plug.

RELATED ITEMS

Cleaning........................57
Finish Carpentry..........199
Painting.......................333

	Item Description	Unit	Remove	Replace	Total
Scamozzi capital *continued.*	**Scamozzi capital made from aluminum** *Replace* Materials....231.00 Labor..........23.50 *Remove*......................... Labor..........23.40	ea	$23.40	$254.50	$277.90
	Scamozzi capital made from interior plaster *Replace* Materials.....213.00 Labor..........23.50 *Remove*......................... Labor..........23.40	ea	$23.40	$236.50	$259.90
	Scamozzi capital made from exterior stucco *Replace* Materials....209.00 Labor..........23.50 *Remove*......................... Labor..........23.40	ea	$23.40	$232.50	$255.90
Temple-of-the-winds capital *Capital up to 12" high. Includes load-bearing plug.*	**Temple-of-the-Winds capital made from composite materials** *Replace* Materials....353.00 Labor..........23.50 *Remove*......................... Labor..........23.40	ea	$23.40	$376.50	$399.90
	Temple-of-the-Winds capital made from pine *Replace* Materials....608.00 Labor..........23.50 *Remove*......................... Labor..........23.40	ea	$23.40	$631.50	$654.90
	Temple-of-the-Winds capital made from redwood *Replace* Materials....693.00 Labor..........23.50 *Remove*......................... Labor..........23.40	ea	$23.40	$716.50	$739.90
	Temple-of-the-Winds capital made from oak *Replace* Materials....796.00 Labor..........23.50 *Remove*......................... Labor..........23.40	ea	$23.40	$819.50	$842.90
	Temple-of-the-Winds capital made from stone *Replace* Materials....468.00 Labor..........23.50 *Remove*......................... Labor..........23.40	ea	$23.40	$491.50	$514.90
	Temple-of-the-Winds capital made from synthetic stone *Replace* Materials....439.00 Labor..........23.50 *Remove*......................... Labor..........23.40	ea	$23.40	$462.50	$485.90
	Temple-of-the-Winds capital made from aluminum *Replace* Materials....264.00 Labor..........23.50 *Remove*......................... Labor..........23.40	ea	$23.40	$287.50	$310.90
	Temple-of-the-Winds capital made from interior plaster *Replace* Materials....243.00 Labor..........23.50 *Remove*......................... Labor..........23.40	ea	$23.40	$266.50	$289.90
	Temple-of-the-Winds capital made from exterior stucco *Replace* Materials....238.00 Labor..........23.50 *Remove*......................... Labor..........23.40	ea	$23.40	$261.50	$284.90
Capital repair	**Repair wood capital with wood patch (each patch)** *Replace* Materials........2.60 Labor..........44.10	ea	—	$46.70	$46.70
	Repair wood capital by replacing section *Replace* Materials......24.00 Labor.........161.00	ea	—	$185.00	$185.00
	Repair dry rot in capital with epoxy *Replace* Materials........2.60 Labor..........86.50	ea	—	$89.10	$89.10
	Minimum charge for capital repair *Replace* Materials......29.00 Labor.........121.00	ea	—	$150.00	$150.00

Item Description	Unit	Remove	Replace	Total
Add 78% for spiral column or pilaster				
Deduct 45% for 6″ column, pilaster, capital, or base				
Deduct 35% for 8″ column, pilaster, capital, or base				
Deduct 17% for 10″ column, pilaster, capital, or base				
Add 59% for 14″ column, pilaster, capital, or base				
Add 81% for 16″ column, pilaster, capital, or base				
Add 115% for 18″ column, pilaster, capital, or base				
Add 185% for 20″ column, pilaster, capital, or base				
Column base made from composite materials *Replace* Materials......46.00 Labor..........23.50 *Remove*........................ Labor...........21.60	ea	$21.60	$69.50	$91.10
Column base made from pine *Replace* Materials......47.00 Labor..........23.50 *Remove*........................ Labor...........21.60	ea	$21.60	$70.50	$92.10
Column base made from redwood *Replace* Materials......55.00 Labor..........23.50 *Remove*........................ Labor...........21.60	ea	$21.60	$78.50	$100.10
Column base made from oak *Replace* Materials......61.00 Labor..........23.50 *Remove*........................ Labor...........21.60	ea	$21.60	$84.50	$106.10
Column base made from stone *Replace* Materials......85.00 Labor..........23.50 *Remove*........................ Labor...........21.60	ea	$21.60	$108.50	$130.10
Column base made from synthetic stone *Replace* Materials......80.00 Labor..........23.50 *Remove*........................ Labor...........21.60	ea	$21.60	$103.50	$125.10
Column base made from aluminum *Replace* Materials......48.00 Labor..........23.50 *Remove*........................ Labor...........21.60	ea	$21.60	$71.50	$93.10
Column base made from interior plaster *Replace* Materials......44.00 Labor..........23.50 *Remove*........................ Labor...........21.60	ea	$21.60	$67.50	$89.10
Column base made from exterior stucco *Replace* Materials......43.00 Labor..........23.50 *Remove*........................ Labor...........21.60	ea	$21.60	$66.50	$88.10
Column pedestal, standard grade *Replace* Materials.....166.00 Labor.........353.00 *Remove*........................ Labor...........11.30 ► Pedestal framed with 2″ x 4″ up to 3′ high. Outside trimmed with paint-grade pine or poplar. Moldings around top of pedestal and bottom.	ea	$11.30	$519.00	$530.30

◄ **ADDITIONAL COLUMN SIZES**
Add or deduct from the costs for 12″ columns, pilasters, capitals and bases. (Bases are built to hold columns of the size indicated.)

◄ **COLUMN BASE**

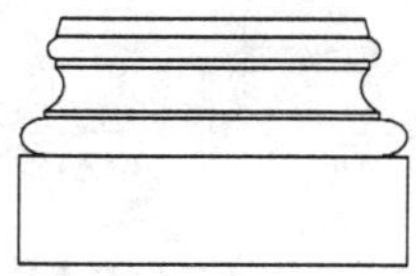

◄ **COLUMN PEDESTAL**

RELATED ITEMS

Cleaning........................57
Finish Carpentry..........199
Painting......................333

Column pedestal *continued*

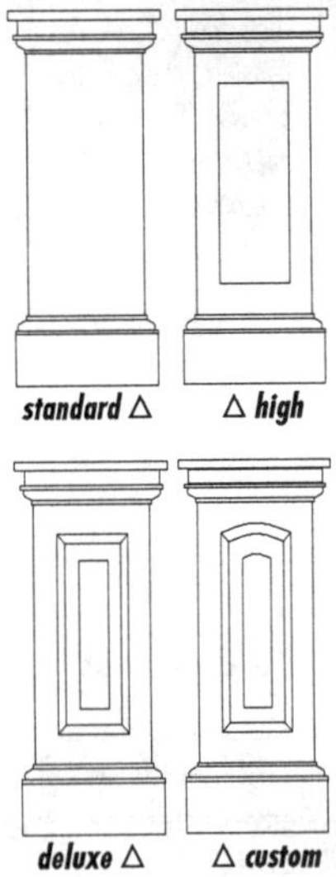

Item Description	Unit	Remove	Replace	Total
Column pedestal, high grade ***Replace*** Materials.....219.00 Labor.........391.00 ***Remove***......................... Labor...........11.30 ► Pedestal framed with 2" x 4" up to 3' high. Outside trimmed with paint-grade pine or poplar. Moldings around top of pedestal and bottom. Each of the four sides also includes panel molding. Or standard grade from stain-grade fir.	ea	$11.30	$610.00	$621.30
Column pedestal, deluxe grade ***Replace*** Materials....325.00 Labor.........441.00 ***Remove***......................... Labor...........11.30 ► Pedestal framed with 2" x 4" up to 3' high. Outside trimmed with paint-grade pine or poplar. Moldings around top of pedestal and bottom. Each of the four sides includes a recessed raised panel. Or standard grade from red oak or mahogany.	ea	$11.30	$766.00	$777.30
Column pedestal, custom grade ***Replace*** Materials....383.00 Labor.........487.00 ***Remove***......................... Labor...........11.30 ► Pedestal framed with 2" x 4" up to 3' high. Outside trimmed with paint-grade pine or poplar. Moldings around top of pedestal and bottom. Each of the four sides includes a recessed raised cathedral panel. Or deluxe grade from red oak or mahogany.	ea	$11.30	$870.00	$881.30

Pilaster pedestal

Item Description	Unit	Remove	Replace	Total
Pilaster pedestal, standard grade ***Replace*** Materials.....101.00 Labor........250.00 ***Remove***......................... Labor............9.19 ► Pedestal framed with 2" x 4" up to 3' high. Outside trimmed with paint-grade pine or poplar. Moldings around top of pedestal and bottom.	ea	$9.19	$351.00	$360.19
Pilaster pedestal, high grade ***Replace*** Materials.....133.00 Labor.........277.00 ***Remove***......................... Labor............9.19 ► Pedestal framed with 2" x 4" up to 3' high. Outside trimmed with paint-grade pine or poplar. Moldings around top of pedestal and bottom. Each of the three sides also includes panel molding. Or standard grade from stain-grade fir.	ea	$9.19	$410.00	$419.19
Pilaster pedestal, deluxe grade ***Replace*** Materials.....196.00 Labor.........311.00 ***Remove***......................... Labor............9.19 ► Pedestal framed with 2" x 4" up to 3' high. Outside trimmed with paint-grade pine or poplar. Moldings around top of pedestal and bottom. Each of the three sides includes a recessed raised panel. Or standard grade from red oak or mahogany.	ea	$9.19	$507.00	$516.19
Pilaster pedestal, custom grade ***Replace*** Materials....231.00 Labor.........347.00 ***Remove***......................... Labor............9.19 ► Pedestal framed with 2" x 4" up to 3' high. Outside trimmed with paint-grade pine or poplar. Moldings around top of pedestal and bottom. Each of the three sides includes a recessed raised cathedral panel. Or deluxe grade from red oak or mahogany.	ea	$9.19	$578.00	$587.19

Add for other wood species

Item Description	Unit	Remove	Replace	Total
Add 12% for stain-grade redwood materials ► Add to the cost of any redwood item listed above.				
Add 16% for mahogany materials ► Add to the cost of any redwood item listed above.				

NOTES:

end

TIME & MATERIAL CHARTS *(selected items)*

Columns Materials

DESCRIPTION	MATERIAL PRICE	GROSS COVERAGE	WASTE	NET COVERAGE	UNIT PRICE
Minimum materials charge for column or pilaster work					
minimum	$30.00 *ea*				$30.00 *ea*
12" round column					
composite materials	$312.00 *8'*	8	0%	8	$39.00 *lf*
pine	$319.00 *8'*	8	0%	8	$39.90 *lf*
12" round pilaster					
composite materials	$199.00 *8'*	8	0%	8	$24.90 *lf*
pine	$204.00 *8'*	8	0%	8	$25.50 *lf*
12" square column					
composite materials	$412.00 *8'*	8	0%	8	$51.50 *lf*
pine	$421.00 *8'*	8	0%	8	$52.60 *lf*
12" square pilaster					
composite materials	$263.00 *8'*	8	0%	8	$32.90 *lf*
pine pilaster	$270.00 *8'*	8	0%	8	$33.80 *lf*
Contemporary capital					
composite materials	$149.00 *ea*				$149.00 *ea*
pine	$166.00 *ea*				$166.00 *ea*
Corinthian capital					
composite materials	$456.00 *ea*				$456.00 *ea*
pine	$786.00 *ea*				$786.00 *ea*
Doric or Tuscan capital					
composite materials	$156.00 *ea*				$156.00 *ea*
pine	$173.00 *ea*				$173.00 *ea*
Empire capital					
composite materials	$291.00 *ea*				$291.00 *ea*
pine	$501.00 *ea*				$501.00 *ea*
Erechtheum capital					
composite materials	$282.00 *ea*				$282.00 *ea*
pine	$486.00 *ea*				$486.00 *ea*
Roman Ionic capital					
composite materials	$295.00 *ea*				$295.00 *ea*
pine	$506.00 *ea*				$506.00 *ea*
Scamozzi capital					
composite materials	$309.00 *ea*				$309.00 *ea*
pine	$531.00 *ea*				$531.00 *ea*
Temple-of-the-Winds capital					
composite materials	$353.00 *ea*				$353.00 *ea*
pine	$608.00 *ea*				$608.00 *ea*
Column base					
composite materials	$46.00 *ea*				$46.00 *ea*
pine	$47.00 *ea*				$47.00 *ea*
Column pedestal					
standard grade	$166.00 *ea*				$166.00 *ea*
custom grade	$383.00 *ea*				$383.00 *ea*
Pilaster pedestal					
standard grade	$101.00 *ea*				$101.00 *ea*
custom grade	$231.00 *ea*				$231.00 *ea*

Columns Labor

LABORER	BASE WAGE	PAID LEAVE	TRUE WAGE	FICA	FUTA	WORKER'S COMP.	UNEMPLOY. INSUR.	HEALTH INSUR.	RETIRE (401K)	LIABILITY INSUR.	COST PER HOUR
Carpenter	$23.60	1.84	$25.44	1.95	.20	4.96	2.21	2.69	.76	3.43	$41.60
Demolition laborer	$13.90	1.08	$14.98	1.15	.12	4.79	1.30	2.69	.45	2.02	$27.50

Paid Leave is calculated based on two weeks paid vacation, one week sick leave, and seven paid holidays. Employer's matching portion of **FICA** is 7.65 percent. **FUTA** (Federal Unemployment) is .8 percent. **Worker's compensation** for columns was calculated using a national average of 19.50 percent. **Unemployment insurance** was calculated using a national average of 8.7 percent. **Health insurance** was calculated based on a projected national average for 2002 of $535 per employee (and family when applicable) per month. Employer pays 80 percent for a per month cost of $428 per employee. **Retirement** is based on a 401(k) retirement program with employer matching of 50 percent. Employee contributions to the 401(k) plan are an average of 6 percent of the true wage. **Liability insurance** is based on a national average of 13.2 percent.

Columns Labor Productivity

WORK DESCRIPTION	LABORER	COST PER HOUR	PRODUCTIVITY	UNIT PRICE
Demolition				
remove column	demolition laborer	$27.50	.212	$5.83 lf
remove pilaster	demolition laborer	$27.50	.134	$3.69 lf
remove column or pilaster capital	demolition laborer	$27.50	.850	$23.40 ea
remove column or pilaster base	demolition laborer	$27.50	.785	$21.60 ea
remove column pedestal	demolition laborer	$27.50	.410	$11.30 ea
remove pilaster pedestal	demolition laborer	$27.50	.334	$9.19 ea
Install column				
round	finish carpenter	$41.60	.333	$13.90 lf
square	finish carpenter	$41.60	.308	$12.80 lf
Install pilaster				
round	finish carpenter	$41.60	.292	$12.10 lf
square	finish carpenter	$41.60	.270	$11.20 lf
Install capital				
column or pilaster capital	finish carpenter	$41.60	.566	$23.50 ea
Install column or pilaster base				
column or pilaster base	finish carpenter	$41.60	.566	$23.50 ea
Repair column or pilaster				
round with wood patch	finish carpenter	$41.60	.706	$29.40 ea
fluted with wood patch	finish carpenter	$41.60	.863	$35.90 ea
round by replacing section	finish carpenter	$41.60	1.94	$80.70 ea
fluted by replacing section	finish carpenter	$41.60	2.59	$108.00 ea
round dry rot with epoxy	finish carpenter	$41.60	2.74	$114.00 ea
fluted dry rot with epoxy	finish carpenter	$41.60	3.24	$135.00 ea
minimum charge	finish carpenter	$41.60	2.33	$96.90 ea
Repair wood capital				
with wood patch	finish carpenter	$41.60	1.06	$44.10 ea
by replacing section	finish carpenter	$41.60	3.88	$161.00 ea
dry rot with epoxy	finish carpenter	$41.60	2.08	$86.50 ea
minimum charge	finish carpenter	$41.60	2.91	$121.00 ea
Build and install column pedestal				
standard grade	finish carpenter	$41.60	8.49	$353.00 ea
custom grade	finish carpenter	$41.60	11.7	$487.00 ea
Build and install pilaster pedestal				
standard grade	finish carpenter	$41.60	6.01	$250.00 ea
custom grade	finish carpenter	$41.60	8.33	$347.00 ea

8 Concrete

Item Description	Unit	Remove	Replace	Total
Minimum charge for concrete repair ***Replace*** Materials......59.00 Labor........333.00	ea	—	$392.00	$392.00
Concrete crack repair with pressurized epoxy injection ***Replace*** Materials........ .70 Labor............4.62 Equipment............1.47 ► A pressure pot is used to inject pressurized epoxy into a concrete crack. Care is taken to fill and plug areas where the epoxy could escape.	lf	—	$6.79	$6.79
Minimum charge for pressurized epoxy injection concrete crack repair ***Replace*** Materials......66.00 Labor.........122.00 Equipment..........91.00	ea	—	$279.00	$279.00
Concrete hole repair with epoxy system per cubic inch of hole ***Replace*** Materials........ .03 Labor............2.20 ► Epoxy is poured or injected into a hole. Priced per cubic inch of the hole.	ci	—	$2.23	$2.23
Minimum charge for concrete hole repair with epoxy system ***Replace*** Materials......59.00 Labor..........20.80	ea	—	$79.80	$79.80
Concrete crack repair with caulking gun epoxy injection ***Replace*** Materials........ .40 Labor........... 1.04	lf	—	$1.44	$1.44
Minimum charge for concrete crack repair with epoxy injection ***Replace*** Materials......66.00 Labor..........20.80	ea	—	$86.80	$86.80
Repair spalled concrete with concrete resurfacer ***Replace*** Materials........ .81 Labor............ .37	sf	—	$1.18	$1.18
Minimum charge to repair spalled concrete ***Replace*** Materials......39.30 Labor...........41.60	ea	—	$80.90	$80.90
Concrete footings including rebar package & forming ***Replace*** Materials.....113.00 Labor..........90.50 ***Remove***........................ Labor...........45.10 Equipment..........55.60	cy	$100.70	$203.50	$304.20
Concrete footings including CEC rebar package & forming ***Replace*** Materials.....138.00 Labor.........109.00 ***Remove***........................ Labor..........53.90 Equipment..........92.80	cy	$146.70	$247.00	$393.70
16" wide by 10" deep concrete footings with rebar ***Replace*** Materials........4.92 Labor............5.57 ***Remove***........................ Labor............3.33 Equipment............2.86	lf	$6.19	$10.49	$16.68
16" wide by 10" deep concrete footings with CEC rebar ***Replace*** Materials........6.37 Labor............6.69 ***Remove***........................ Labor............4.04 Equipment............3.46	lf	$7.50	$13.06	$20.56
20" wide by 10" deep concrete footings with rebar ***Replace*** Materials........5.88 Labor............5.91 ***Remove***........................ Labor............3.33 Equipment............2.86	lf	$6.19	$11.79	$17.98
20" wide by 10" deep concrete footings with CEC rebar ***Replace*** Materials........7.47 Labor............7.03 ***Remove***........................ Labor............4.04 Equipment............3.46	lf	$7.50	$14.50	$22.00

CEC = California Earthquake Code.

◄ **MINIMUM**

◄ **EPOXY REPAIR**

CALIFORNIA EARTHQUAKE CODE

Items that include "CEC" in the description are priced according to California earthquake code requirements.

Although these *Universal Building Code* or similar standards are also required in other areas of the country, they are most commonly associated with efforts initiated in the State of California to improve the construction and engineering of structures in quake zones.

◄ **FOOTING**

Standard 16", 20", and 24" footings include 3 horizontal lengths of #4 rebar. Standard 32" footing includes 4 horizontal lengths of #4 rebar. CEC 16" and 20" footings include 3 horizontal lengths of #5 rebar. CEC 24" and 32" footings include 4 horizontal lengths of #5 rebar. Tie-in rebar from foundation wall bent continuously into the footing is included in the foundation wall prices.

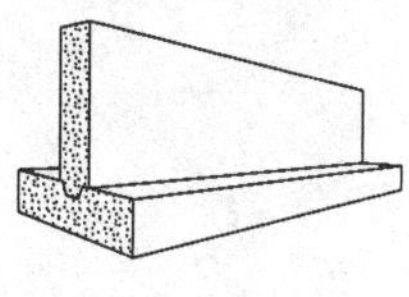

FOOTINGS ▶ *continued*

	Item Description	Unit	Remove	Replace	Total
	24″ wide by 12″ deep concrete footings with rebar ***Replace*** Materials........8.33 Labor ....6.18 ***Remove***......................... Labor ....3.33 Equipment............2.86	lf	$6.19	$14.51	$20.70
	24″ wide by 12″ deep concrete footings with CEC rebar ***Replace*** Materials......10.08 Labor ....7.30 ***Remove***......................... Labor ....4.04 Equipment............3.46	lf	$7.50	$17.38	$24.88
	32″ wide by 14″ deep concrete footings with rebar ***Replace*** Materials......12.30 Labor ....6.56 ***Remove***......................... Labor ....3.33 Equipment............2.86	lf	$6.19	$18.86	$25.05
	32″ wide by 14″ deep concrete footings with CEC rebar ***Replace*** Materials......14.00 Labor ....7.68 ***Remove***......................... Labor ....4.04 Equipment............3.46	lf	$7.50	$21.68	$29.18
minimum ▷	**Minimum charge for concrete footing work** ***Replace*** Materials......43.80 Labor 38.00	ea	—	$81.80	$81.80

FOUNDATION ▶

Standard foundation walls include horizontal and vertical lengths of #4 rebar 24″ on center. Vertical rebar is bent continuously into footing. CEC foundations include horizontal and vertical lengths of #5 rebar 12″ on center. Vertical rebar is bent continuously into footing.

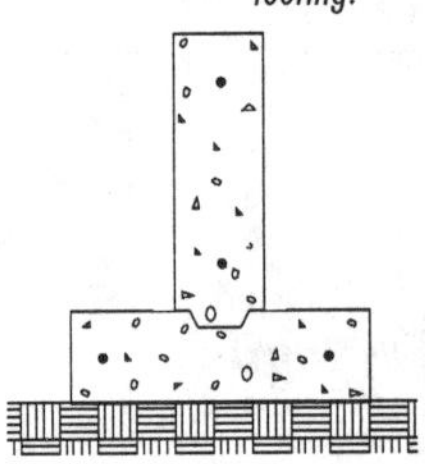

Item Description	Unit	Remove	Replace	Total
Concrete foundation wall including rebar package & forming ***Replace*** Materials....106.00 Labor.........100.00 Equipment..........29.20 ***Remove***......................... Labor...........67.10 Equipment..........69.70	cy	$136.80	$235.20	$372.00
Concrete foundation wall including CEC rebar package & forming ***Replace*** Materials.....128.00 Labor..........116.00 Equipment..........29.20 ***Remove***......................... Labor ....80.90 Equipment..........93.00	cy	$173.90	$273.20	$447.10
5″ wide concrete foundation wall ***Replace*** Materials........1.48 Labor ....2.18 Equipment .... .72 ***Remove***......................... Labor ....2.01 Equipment............1.72	sf	$3.73	$4.38	$8.11
Rebar package for 5″ wide concrete foundation wall ***Replace*** Materials .... .23 Labor 1.34	sf	—	$1.57	$1.57
CEC rebar package for 5″ wide concrete foundation wall ***Replace*** Materials .... .72 Labor 2.42	sf	—	$3.14	$3.14
6″ wide concrete foundation wall ***Replace*** Materials........1.79 Labor ....2.37 Equipment .... .72 ***Remove***......................... Labor ....2.01 Equipment............1.72	sf	$3.73	$4.88	$8.61
Rebar package for 6″ wide concrete foundation wall ***Replace*** Materials .... .23 Labor 1.34	sf	—	$1.57	$1.57
CEC rebar package for 6″ wide concrete foundation wall ***Replace*** Materials .... .72 Labor 2.42	sf	—	$3.14	$3.14
8″ wide concrete foundation wall ***Replace*** Materials........2.38 Labor ....2.75 Equipment .... .72 ***Remove***......................... Labor ....2.09 Equipment............1.98	sf	$4.07	$5.85	$9.92
Rebar package for 8″ wide concrete foundation wall ***Replace*** Materials .... .23 Labor 1.34	sf	—	$1.57	$1.57
CEC rebar package for 8″ wide concrete foundation wall ***Replace*** Materials .... .72 Labor 2.42	sf	—	$3.14	$3.14
10″ wide concrete foundation wall ***Replace*** Materials........2.98 Labor ....3.13 Equipment .... .72 ***Remove***......................... Labor ....2.09 Equipment............1.98	sf	$4.07	$6.83	$10.90

CEC = California Earthquake Code.

Item Description	Unit	Remove	Replace	Total
Rebar package for 10″ wide concrete foundation wall *Replace* Materials........ .23 Labor............1.34	sf	—	$1.57	$1.57
CEC rebar package for 10″ wide concrete foundation wall *Replace* Materials........ .72 Labor............2.42	sf	—	$3.14	$3.14
Add for insulating foam stay-in-place foundation wall forms *Replace* Materials...... 1.39 Labor............1.62	sf	—	$3.01	$3.01
Minimum charge for concrete foundation wall work *Replace* Materials......58.00 Labor.........148.00 Equipment..........98.00	ea	—	$304.00	$304.00
Single-pour footing and foundation wall with rebar package *Replace* Materials......98.20 Labor...........21.80 Equipment..........36.10 *Remove*........................ Labor..........53.90 Equipment..........62.50	cy	$116.40	$156.10	$272.50
Single-pour footing and foundation wall with CEC rebar package *Replace* Materials....100.50 Labor...........26.50 Equipment..........36.10 *Remove*........................ Labor..........64.10 Equipment..........67.30	cy	$131.40	$163.10	$294.50
Single-pour footing with 6″ wide by 3′ stem wall *Replace* Materials......10.30 Labor...........12.80 Equipment............4.32 *Remove*........................ Labor............9.52 Equipment............8.80	lf	$18.32	$27.42	$45.74
Single-pour footing with 8″ wide by 3′ stem wall *Replace* Materials......12.10 Labor...........12.80 Equipment............4.32 *Remove*........................ Labor............9.52 Equipment............8.80	lf	$18.32	$29.22	$47.54
Single-pour footing with 10″ wide by 3′ stem wall *Replace* Materials......12.40 Labor...........12.80 Equipment............4.32 *Remove*........................ Labor............9.52 Equipment............8.80	lf	$18.32	$29.52	$47.84
Rebar package for single-pour footing & 3′ stem wall *Replace* Materials........1.65 Labor............5.02	lf	—	$6.67	$6.67
CEC rebar package for single-pour footing & 3′ stem wall *Replace* Materials........3.96 Labor............8.77	lf	—	$12.73	$12.73
Single-pour footing with 6″ wide by 4′ stem wall *Replace* Materials......12.10 Labor...........16.30 Equipment............5.76 *Remove*........................ Labor...........11.60 Equipment............8.80	lf	$20.40	$34.16	$54.56
Single-pour footing with 8″ wide by 4′ stem wall *Replace* Materials......14.50 Labor...........16.30 Equipment............5.76 *Remove*........................ Labor...........11.60 Equipment............8.80	lf	$20.40	$36.56	$56.96
Single-pour footing with 10″ wide by 4′ stem wall *Replace* Materials......16.90 Labor...........16.30 Equipment............5.76 *Remove*........................ Labor...........11.60 Equipment............8.80	lf	$20.40	$38.96	$59.36
Rebar package for 6″ wide by 4′ single-pour footing & stem wall *Replace* Materials........1.90 Labor............5.49	lf	—	$7.39	$7.39
CEC rebar package for 6″ wide by 4′ single-pour footing & stem wall *Replace* Materials........4.42 Labor............9.21	lf	—	$13.63	$13.63
Minimum charge for single-pour footing & stem wall work *Replace* Materials......23.00 Labor.........148.00 Equipment..........98.00	ea	—	$269.00	$269.00

◁ **minimum** (concrete foundation wall work)

◀ **SINGLE-POUR FOOTING & FOUNDATION**
Single-pour footing and foundation wall. See footings on page 83 and foundations on 84 for explanations about the rebar included in each system.

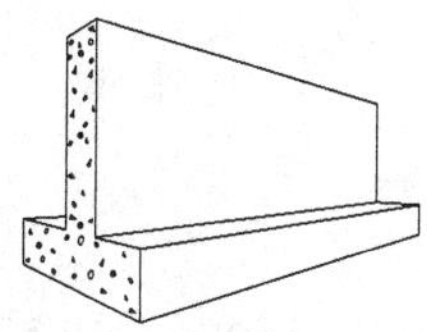

◁ **minimum** (single-pour footing & stem wall work)

RELATED ITEMS

Cleaning........................57
Painting......................333

CEC = California Earthquake Code.

Drill pier hole ► *Pier hole from 12″ to 24″ in diameter. (Most common sizes are 16″ and 18″.)*

Item Description	Unit	Remove	Replace	Total
Delivery & take home charge for tractor-mounted auger (mobilization) ***Replace*** .... Labor.........323.00 Equipment........437.00	ea	—	$760.00	$760.00
Drill concrete pier hole for hillside home construction ***Replace*** .... Labor ....4.28 Equipment............2.22	lf	—	$6.50	$6.50
Minimum charge to drill concrete pier ***Replace*** .... Labor.........257.00 Equipment........520.00	ea	—	$777.00	$777.00

Pier ► *Pier from 12″ to 24″ in diameter. (Most common sizes are 16″ and 18″.) In most cases piers are not removed. When removed they are pulled from the ground with a crane or trackhoe. An engineer should be consulted when piers are removed and a new structure will be built on the same site.*

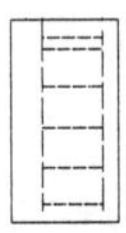

Item Description	Unit	Remove	Replace	Total
Concrete pier including rebar cage ***Replace*** Materials ....421.00 Labor.........553.00 ***Remove***........................ Labor...........19.20 Equipment..........52.60	cy	$71.80	$974.00	$1,045.80
Concrete pier with up to 36″ fiber tube wrapped cap ***Replace*** Materials.......15.40 Labor...........65.00 ***Remove***........................ Labor ....2.26 Equipment............6.12	lf	$8.38	$80.40	$88.78
Above-grade concrete pier with fiber tube wrap ***Replace*** Materials......39.00 Labor...........67.10 ***Remove***........................ Labor ....2.26 Equipment............6.12	lf	$8.38	$106.10	$114.48
Rebar cage for concrete pier (meets CEC requirements) ***Replace*** Materials......38.00 Labor 3.29	lf	—	$41.29	$41.29
Minimum charge for concrete pier work ***Replace*** Materials.....318.00 Labor.........457.00	ea	—	$775.00	$775.00

Jacket Pier ►

Item Description	Unit	Remove	Replace	Total
Jacket concrete pier with new concrete and rebar ties ***Replace*** Materials......36.10 Labor.........183.00 Equipment..........33.80 ► Existing pier is jackhammered. Holes are drilled for rebar. Rebar is secured with epoxy. Pier is formed and concrete jacket poured.	ea	—	$252.90	$252.90
minimum ▷ **Minimum charge to jacket a concrete pier with concrete and rebar** ***Replace*** Materials......89.00 Labor.........296.00 Equipment 117.00	ea	—	$502.00	$502.00

Shallow Pier ► *Usually poured in hand-dug holes for light structures or decks.*

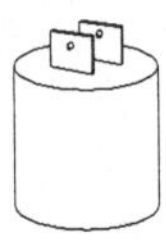

Item Description	Unit	Remove	Replace	Total
Shallow concrete pier (less than 3′ deep) for deck or light structure ***Replace*** Materials ......18.40 Labor.........109.10 ***Remove***........................ Labor...........31.40	ea	$31.40	$127.50	$158.90
Pre-cast concrete pier for deck or light structure ***Replace*** Materials......20.00 Labor ....9.66 ***Remove***........................ Labor 6.41	ea	$6.41	$29.66	$36.07

Grade Beam ► *Grade beams include pre-fabricated rebar cage. All rebar cages are to CEC standards. When removed, grade beams are detached from piers with a jackhammer or concrete saw. The beams are broken into manageable chunks and loaded by crane or back-hoe into a truck. (Does not include hauling or dump fees.)*

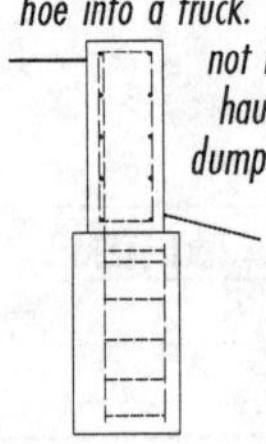

Item Description	Unit	Remove	Replace	Total
Grade beam with rebar cage per cy ***Replace*** Materials....604.00 Labor.........148.00 ***Remove***........................ Labor ....64.10 Equipment..........38.40	cy	$102.50	$752.00	$854.50
12″ wide by 18″ deep grade beam with rebar cage ***Replace*** Materials......43.40 Labor ....9.77 Equipment............2.88 ***Remove***........................ Labor ....4.79 Equipment............4.11	lf	$8.90	$56.05	$64.95
12″ wide by 20″ deep grade beam with rebar cage ***Replace*** Materials......44.00 Labor...........10.72 Equipment............2.88 ***Remove***........................ Labor ....4.79 Equipment............4.11	lf	$8.90	$57.60	$66.50
12″ wide by 22″ deep grade beam with rebar cage ***Replace*** Materials......44.60 Labor...........12.60 Equipment............2.88 ***Remove***........................ Labor ....5.36 Equipment............4.75	lf	$10.11	$60.08	$70.19

CEC = California Earthquake Code.

Item Description	Unit	Remove	Replace	Total
12″ wide by 24″ deep grade beam with rebar cage	lf	$10.11	$58.42	$68.53
Replace Materials......45.20 Labor..........10.34 Equipment............2.88				
Remove Labor............5.36 Equipment...........4.75				
14″ wide by 18″ deep grade beam with rebar cage	lf	$8.90	$58.68	$67.58
Replace Materials......44.30 Labor...........11.50 Equipment............2.88				
Remove Labor............4.79 Equipment...........4.11				
14″ wide by 20″ deep grade beam with rebar cage	lf	$8.90	$61.48	$70.38
Replace Materials......44.90 Labor...........13.70 Equipment............2.88				
Remove Labor............4.79 Equipment...........4.11				
14″ wide by 22″ deep grade beam with rebar cage	lf	$10.31	$62.28	$72.59
Replace Materials......45.70 Labor...........13.70 Equipment............2.88				
Remove Labor............5.47 Equipment...........4.84				
14″ wide by 24″ deep grade beam with rebar cage	lf	$10.31	$65.08	$75.39
Replace Materials......46.30 Labor...........15.90 Equipment............2.88				
Remove Labor............5.47 Equipment...........4.84				
16″ wide by 18″ deep grade beam with rebar cage	lf	$11.20	$68.48	$79.68
Replace Materials......45.20 Labor..........20.40 Equipment............2.88				
Remove Labor............5.94 Equipment...........5.26				
16″ wide by 20″ deep grade beam with rebar cage	lf	$11.20	$73.68	$84.88
Replace Materials......45.90 Labor...........24.90 Equipment............2.88				
Remove Labor............5.94 Equipment...........5.26				
16″ wide by 22″ deep grade beam with rebar cage	lf	$11.56	$69.98	$81.54
Replace Materials......46.70 Labor..........20.40 Equipment............2.88				
Remove Labor............6.13 Equipment...........5.43				
16″ wide by 24″ deep grade beam with rebar cage	lf	$11.56	$75.28	$86.84
Replace Materials......47.50 Labor...........24.90 Equipment............2.88				
Remove Labor............6.13 Equipment...........5.43				
18″ wide by 18″ deep grade beam with rebar cage	lf	$11.20	$60.38	$71.58
Replace Materials......46.00 Labor...........11.50 Equipment............2.88				
Remove Labor............5.94 Equipment...........5.26				
18″ wide by 20″ deep grade beam with rebar cage	lf	$11.20	$63.48	$74.68
Replace Materials......46.90 Labor...........13.70 Equipment............2.88				
Remove Labor............5.94 Equipment...........5.26				
18″ wide by 22″ deep grade beam with rebar cage	lf	$11.56	$64.38	$75.94
Replace Materials......47.80 Labor...........13.70 Equipment............2.88				
Remove Labor............6.13 Equipment...........5.43				
18″ wide by 24″ deep grade beam with rebar cage	lf	$11.56	$67.48	$79.04
Replace Materials......48.70 Labor...........15.90 Equipment............2.88				
Remove Labor............6.13 Equipment...........5.43				
Minimum charge for concrete grade beam work	ea	—	$443.00	$443.00
Replace Materials....307.00 Labor..........38.00 Equipment..........98.00				
Jacket concrete grade beam with new concrete and rebar ties	lf	—	$35.60	$35.60
Replace Materials.......11.10 Labor..........20.00 Equipment............4.50				
► Existing grade beam is jackhammered. Holes are drilled for rebar. Rebar is secured with epoxy. Grade beam is formed and concrete jacket poured.				

RELATED ITEMS

Cleaning........................57
Masonry
grade beam wall cap......303
Painting......................333

◁ **minimum**

◄ **JACKET GRADE BEAM**

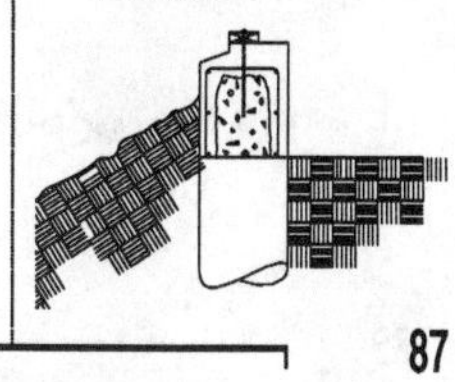

	Item Description	Unit	Remove	Replace	Total
JACKET ▶ GRADE BEAM *continued*	**Minimum charge to jacket grade beam with concrete and rebar** *Replace* Materials......52.00 Labor.........296.00 Equipment.........117.00	ea	—	$465.00	$465.00
LIGHTWEIGHT ▶ FLATWORK	**Lightweight concrete flatwork per cy (no rebar)** *Replace* Materials.....121.00 Labor...........75.70 *Remove*......................... Labor..........64.60 Equipment..........47.80	cy	$112.40	$196.70	$309.10
	2″ lightweight concrete slab *Replace* Materials........ .75 Labor............. .86 *Remove*......................... Labor............ .72 Equipment............ .64	sf	$1.36	$1.61	$2.97
	4″ lightweight concrete slab *Replace* Materials........1.50 Labor............. .89 *Remove*......................... Labor............ .72 Equipment............ .64	sf	$1.36	$2.39	$3.75
	6″ lightweight concrete slab *Replace* Materials........2.25 Labor............. .97 *Remove*......................... Labor............ .72 Equipment............ .64	sf	$1.36	$3.22	$4.58
minimum ▷	**Minimum charge for lightweight concrete slab work** *Replace* Materials......58.00 Labor.........148.00	ea	—	$206.00	$206.00
FLATWORK ▶	**Concrete flatwork by cy (no rebar)** *Replace* Materials......96.50 Labor...........75.70 *Remove*......................... Labor...........65.70 Equipment..........48.20	cy	$113.90	$172.20	$286.10
	4″ concrete slab *Replace* Materials........1.19 Labor............1.31 *Remove*......................... Labor............ .74 Equipment............ .64	sf	$1.38	$2.50	$3.88
	6″ concrete slab *Replace* Materials........1.79 Labor............1.77 *Remove*......................... Labor............ .74 Equipment............ .64	sf	$1.38	$3.56	$4.94
	8″ concrete slab *Replace* Materials........2.38 Labor............1.77 *Remove*......................... Labor............ .74 Equipment............ .64	sf	$1.38	$4.15	$5.53
minimum ▷	**Minimum charge for concrete slab work** *Replace* Materials......46.00 Labor.........148.00	ea	—	$194.00	$194.00
UTILITY ▶ FLATWORK	**Concrete footing for chimney** *Replace* Materials........2.61 Labor............1.64 *Remove*......................... Labor............ .83 Equipment............ .72	sf	$1.55	$4.25	$5.80
	Concrete slab for exterior heat pump, condenser, etc. *Replace* Materials........1.42 Labor............1.64 *Remove*......................... Labor............ .74 Equipment............ .64	sf	$1.38	$3.06	$4.44
REBAR FOR ▶ FLATWORK	**Rebar for concrete slab, #4 24″ on center** *Replace* Materials........ .51 Labor............1.30	sf	—	$1.81	$1.81
	**Rebar for concrete slab, #4 12″ on center** *Replace* Materials...... 1.06 Labor............2.89	sf	—	$3.95	$3.95
	Wire mesh for concrete slab, 6″ x 6″ #10 *Replace* Materials........ .16 Labor............. .54	sf	—	$.70	$.70
FLATWORK ▶ BASE	**2″ aggregate slab base** *Replace* Materials........ .04 Labor............. .49 Equipment............ .12	sf	—	$.65	$.65

Item Description	Unit	Remove	Replace	Total
4″ aggregate slab base ***Replace*** Materials .... .09 Labor .... .55 Equipment .... .12	sf	—	$.76	$.76
2″ sand slab base ***Replace*** Materials .... .04 Labor .... .41 Equipment .... .12	sf	—	$.57	$.57
4″ sand slab base ***Replace*** Materials .... .09 Labor .... .47 Equipment .... .12	sf	—	$.68	$.68
6 mil slab membrane ***Replace*** Materials .... .04 Labor .... .06	sf	—	$.10	$.10
5 mil slab membrane ***Replace*** Materials .... .04 Labor .... .06	sf	—	$.10	$.10
Concrete sidewalk per cy ***Replace*** Materials.....107.10 Labor.........155.00 ***Remove***........................ Labor...........65.70 Equipment..........48.20 ► Sidewalks 4″ to 6″ thick.	cy	$113.90	$262.10	$376.00
3″ concrete sidewalk ***Replace*** Materials .... .89 Labor ....1.55 ***Remove***........................ Labor............. .94 Equipment .... .64	sf	$1.58	$2.44	$4.02
4″ concrete sidewalk ***Replace*** Materials........1.19 Labor ....1.82 ***Remove***........................ Labor............. .94 Equipment .... .64	sf	$1.58	$3.01	$4.59
6″ concrete sidewalk ***Replace*** Materials........1.79 Labor ....2.31 ***Remove***........................ Labor............. .94 Equipment .... .64	sf	$1.58	$4.10	$5.68
Minimum charge for concrete sidewalk work ***Replace*** Materials.....110.00 Labor..........111.00	ea	—	$221.00	$221.00
Add for troweled-in concrete dye in flatwork ***Replace*** Materials........1.42 Labor............. .34	sf	—	$1.76	$1.76
Add for concrete dye in flatwork per 1″ deep layer, blacks and grays ***Replace*** Materials .... .08	sf	—	$.08	$.08
Add for concrete dye in flatwork per 1″ deep layer, blues ***Replace*** Materials .... .30	sf	—	$.30	$.30
Add for concrete dye in flatwork per 1″ deep layer, browns & terra cotta reds ***Replace*** Materials .... .30	sf	—	$.30	$.30
Add for concrete dye in flatwork per 1″ deep layer, bright reds ***Replace*** Materials .... .30	sf	—	$.30	$.30
Add for concrete dye in flatwork per 1″ deep layer, greens ***Replace*** Materials .... .63	sf	—	$.63	$.63
Add for concrete stamping of slab or sidewalk ***Replace*** .... Labor............2.01	sf	—	$2.01	$2.01
Add for paver-pattern concrete stamping of slab or sidewalk ***Replace*** .... Labor............1.71	sf	—	$1.71	$1.71

RELATED ITEMS
Cleaning........................57
Painting......................333

◄ **FLATWORK VAPOR BARRIER**

◄ **SIDEWALK**
Sidewalk to 3′ wide.

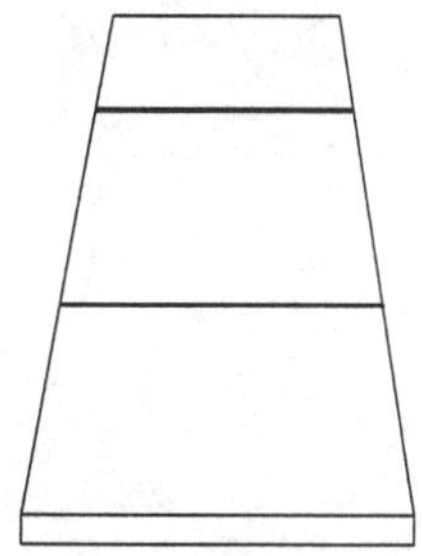

◁ **minimum**

◄ **CONCRETE DYE**
*For concrete quantities under 350 sf add **$29** per truck for wash-out. This charge does not apply to troweled-in dyes.*

◄ **STAMPING**

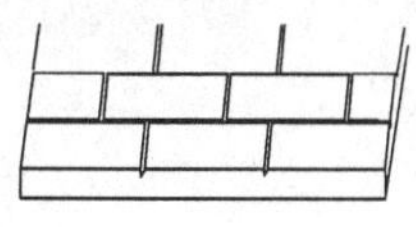

	Item Description	Unit	Remove	Replace	Total
STAMPING ▶ *continued*	**Add for paver stamped slab or sidewalk with grouted joints** *Replace* Materials .... .32 Labor 2.58	sf	—	$2.90	$2.90
EXPOSED AGGREGATE ▶	**Add for exposed aggregate finish on slab or sidewalk** *Replace* Materials .... .16 Labor............. .72 ▶ Where required, add for disposal of slurry.	sf	—	$.88	$.88
CURB & GUTTER ▶	**Concrete curb & gutter** *Replace* Materials........4.91 Labor...........10.14 Equipment .... .87 *Remove*......................... Labor ....3.99 Equipment............1.30	lf	$5.29	$15.92	$21.21
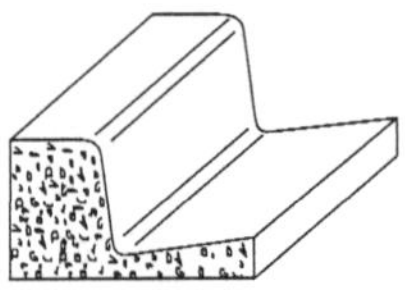	**Minimum charge for concrete curb & gutter work** *Replace* Materials ......37.00 Labor.........136.00 Equipment..........87.00	ea	—	$260.00	$260.00
CONCRETE STEP ▶ *Includes rebar reinforcement: 2 horizontal pieces on each step with vertical tie-ins.*	**Concrete step per cy** *Replace* Materials....266.00 Labor.........285.00 *Remove*......................... Labor..........85.80 Equipment..........53.20	cy	$139.30	$551.00	$690.30
	Concrete step per lf of step *Replace* Materials........2.95 Labor ....8.60 *Remove*......................... Labor ....1.29 Equipment .... .70	lf	$1.99	$11.55	$13.54
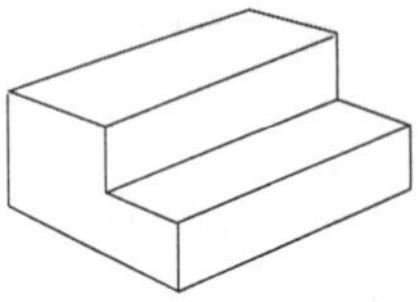	**Concrete step landing per sf of landing** *Replace* Materials........7.45 Labor ....2.53 *Remove*......................... Labor ....1.27 Equipment .... .84	sf	$2.11	$9.98	$12.09
minimum ▷	**Minimum charge for a concrete step** *Replace* Materials......70.00 Labor 222.00	ea	—	$292.00	$292.00
PARGETING ▶ *Break ties, prep, and plaster above grade exterior foundation wall.*	**Foundation wall pargeting (break ties if necessary)** *Replace* Materials .... .33 Labor............. .94	sf	—	$1.27	$1.27
	Minimum charge for foundation wall pargeting *Replace* Materials......23.00 Labor...........42.80	ea	—	$65.80	$65.80
CONCRETE SAWING ▶ *Includes blade wear.*	**Saw concrete wall with standard rebar package per lf of cut, 1″ deep** *Replace* .... Labor ....4.16 Equipment............1.64	lf	—	$5.80	$5.80
	Saw concrete wall with CEC rebar package per lf of cut, 1″ deep *Replace* .... Labor ....4.69 Equipment............2.38	lf	—	$7.07	$7.07
	Saw concrete floor (no rebar) per lf of cut, 1″ deep *Replace* .... Labor ....1.88 Equipment .... .62	lf	—	$2.50	$2.50
	Saw concrete floor with rebar package *Replace*......................... Labor ....2.03 Equipment .... .73	lf	—	$2.76	$2.76
	Saw concrete floor with wire mesh reinforcement *Replace*......................... Labor ....1.95 Equipment .... .86	lf	—	$2.81	$2.81
	Saw expansion joint in "green" concrete pad *Replace*......................... Labor ....7.09 Equipment............2.48	lf	—	$9.57	$9.57
minimum ▷	**Minimum charge for concrete wall sawing** *Replace*......................... Labor..........113.00 Equipment........104.70	ea	—	$217.70	$217.70
	Minimum charge for concrete slab sawing *Replace*......................... Labor ....84.40 Equipment..........91.00	ea	—	$175.40	$175.40

CEC = California Earthquake Code.

Item Description	Unit	Remove	Replace	Total
Core drill 2" concrete wall per inch of depth *Replace*........................ Labor ....2.48 Equipment .... .72	li	—	$3.20	$3.20
Core drill 4" concrete wall per inch of depth *Replace*........................ Labor ....2.74 Equipment .... .83	li	—	$3.57	$3.57
Core drill 2" concrete floor per inch of depth *Replace*........................ Labor ....2.40 Equipment .... .67	li	—	$3.07	$3.07
Core drill 4" concrete floor per inch of depth *Replace*........................ Labor ....2.51 Equipment .... .78	li	—	$3.29	$3.29
Add for pumping footing concrete with pump truck *Replace*........................ .... Equipment...........1.13	lf	—	$1.13	$1.13
Add for pumping foundation wall concrete with pump truck *Replace*........................ .... Equipment .... .28	sf	—	$.28	$.28
Add for pumping pier concrete with pump truck *Replace*........................ .... Equipment...........1.63	lf	—	$1.63	$1.63
Add for pumping grade-beam concrete with pump truck *Replace*........................ .... Equipment .... .87	lf	—	$.87	$.87
Add for pumping slab or sidewalk concrete with pump truck *Replace*........................ .... Equipment .... .27	sf	—	$.27	$.27
Minimum charge for pump truck *Replace*........................ .... Equipment........390.00	ea	—	$390.00	$390.00
#3 rebar (3/8") *Replace* Materials .... .18 Labor............. .51	lf	—	$ .69	$.69
#4 rebar (1/2") *Replace* Materials .... .23 Labor............. .51	lf	—	$.74	$.74
#5 rebar (5/8") *Replace* Materials .... .36 Labor............. .51	lf	—	$.87	$.87
#6 rebar (3/4") *Replace* Materials .... .54 Labor............. .51	lf	—	$1.05	$1.05
#7 rebar (7/8") *Replace* Materials .... .73 Labor............. .54	lf	—	$1.27	$1.27
#8 rebar (1") *Replace* Materials .... .96 Labor............. .54	lf	—	$1.50	$1.50
Foundation coating *Replace* Materials .... .05 Labor............. .49	sf	—	$.54	$.54
Excavate exterior of foundation *Replace* .... Labor ....6.24 Equipment...........1.45	sf	—	$7.69	$7.69
Hand excavate interior of foundation in crawl space *Replace* .... Labor..........13.80	sf	—	$13.80	$13.80
Hand excavate interior of footing in basement *Replace* .... Labor 6.14	sf	—	$6.14	$6.14

◀ **CONCRETE CORE DRILLING**
Includes drill bit wear.

RELATED ITEMS

Cleaning........................57
Excavation..................177
Painting......................333

◀ **PUMP TRUCK**
When pumping concrete 50 feet or less and no more than three stories high.

◁ **minimum**

◀ **REBAR**
Tied and bent into place.

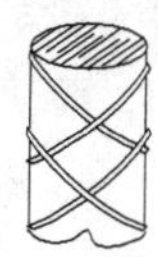

◀ **FOUNDATION COATING**

◀ **BUTTRESS FOUNDATION**
Excavation, forming, pouring, and finishing of concrete buttress over existing foundation. Does not include shoring.

	Item Description	Unit	Remove	Replace	Total
BUTTRESS ▶ FOUNDATION *continued*	**Backfill foundation when work is complete** *Replace* .... Labor ....1.44 Equipment .... .12	sf	—	$1.56	$1.56
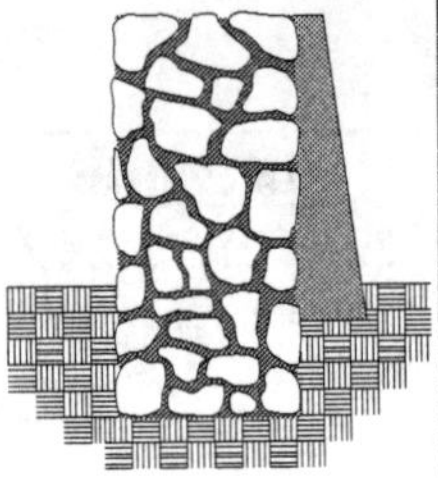	**Buttress exterior of existing foundation wall** *Replace* Materials........3.88 Labor 2.40	sf	—	$6.28	$6.28
	Buttress interior of existing foundation with crawl space *Replace* Materials........3.88 Labor 3.40	sf	—	$7.28	$7.28
	Buttress interior of existing foundation with basement *Replace* Materials........3.88 Labor 7.73	sf	—	$11.61	$11.61
	Minimum charge to buttress existing foundation with concrete *Replace* Materials.....162.00 Labor 506.00	ea	—	$668.00	$668.00
COMPACTION ▶ GROUTING *Does not include excavation. (See excavation under concrete buttress above.) The process can form a "pier" for the foundation and compacts the destabilized soil. An engineer is required to supervise and dictate specifications.*	**2" core drill through footings for compaction grouting** *Replace* .... Labor ....16.90 Equipment............8.64 ▶ When footings and foundation walls are exposed, 2" holes are core drilled through footings around all corners and approximately 10' on center.	ea	—	$25.54	$25.54
	Insert 2" compaction grouting pipes into ground beneath footings *Replace* .... Labor ....6.39 ▶ 2" pipes are inserted into the ground through holes in the footing (usually much deeper than is shown in the illustration to the left).	lf	—	$6.39	$6.39
	Pump pressurized concrete grout through pipes *Replace* Materials........4.08 Labor ....11.20 Equipment..........31.80 ▶ Pressurized grout is pumped into the ground as the pipe is slowly withdrawn.	lf	—	$47.08	$47.08
ASPHALT ▶ GRADED BASE	**4" graded base for asphalt** *Replace* Materials .... .04 Labor............ .04 Equipment .... .11	sf	—	$.19	$.19
	6" graded base for asphalt *Replace* Materials...........05 Labor ....04 Equipment...............13	sf	—	$.22	$.22
	Minimum grading charge *Replace* Materials......57.00 Labor...........74.20 Equipment........260.00	sf	—	$391.20	$391.20
ASPHALT ▶ DRIVEWAY	**2" asphalt driveway** *Replace* Materials .... .54 Labor............ .45 Equipment .... .45 *Remove*........................ Labor............ .22	sf	$.22	$1.44	$1.66
	3" asphalt driveway *Replace* Materials .... .81 Labor............ .52 Equipment .... .50 *Remove*........................ Labor............ .25	sf	$.25	$1.83	$2.08
	4" asphalt driveway *Replace* Materials ...... 1.08 Labor............ .59 Equipment .... .56 *Remove*........................ Labor............ .28	sf	$.28	$2.23	$2.51
ASPHALT ▶ OVERLAY	**1" asphalt overlay** *Replace* Materials .... .27 Labor............ .56 Equipment .... .47 *Remove*........................ Labor............ .25	sf	$.25	$1.30	$1.55
	2" asphalt overlay *Replace* Materials .... .54 Labor............ .63 Equipment .... .51 *Remove*........................ Labor............ .25	sf	$.25	$1.68	$1.93

Item Description	Unit	Remove	Replace	Total
3" asphalt overlay *Replace* Materials........ .81 Labor............ .70 Equipment............ .57 *Remove*........................ Labor............ .25	sf	$.25	$2.08	$2.33
Fill pothole in asphalt driveway *Replace* Materials........4.40 Labor...........17.00	ea	—	$21.40	$21.40
Seal crack in asphalt driveway *Replace* Materials........ .26 Labor............ .60	lf	—	$.86	$.86
Minimum charge for asphalt paving work *Replace* Materials....140.00 Labor.........445.00 Equipment........750.00	ea	—	$1,335.00	$1,335.00
Seal asphalt *Replace* Materials........ .05 Labor............ .07	sf	—	$.12	$.12
Seal and sand asphalt *Replace* Materials........ .08 Labor............ .11	sf	—	$.19	$.19

◄ **FILL ASPHALT POTHOLE**

◄ **SEAL ASPHALT CRACK**

◄ **MINIMUM ASPAHLT**

◄ **SEAL ASPAHLT**

NOTES: ____________________

____________________ end

TIME & MATERIAL CHARTS *(selected items)*

Concrete Materials

DESCRIPTION	MATERIAL PRICE	GROSS COVERAGE	WASTE	NET COVERAGE	UNIT PRICE
Ready mix concrete delivered					
5 bag mix 2,500 psi, per cy	$86.50 cy	1	6%	.94	**$92.00** cy
5.5 bag mix 3,000 psi, per cy	$87.00 cy	1	6%	.94	**$92.60** cy
6 bag mix, 3,500 psi, per cy	$90.70 cy	1	6%	.94	**$96.50** cy
6.5 bag mix, 4,000 psi, per cy	$90.80 cy	1	6%	.94	**$96.60** cy
7 bag mix, 4,500 psi, per cy	$93.60 cy	1	6%	.94	**$99.60** cy
7.5 bag mix, 5,000 psi, per cy	$95.20 cy	1	6%	.94	**$101.00** cy
add for synthetic fiber reinforcing	$10.70 cy	1	0%	1	**$10.70** cy
add for high early strength	$11.40 cy	1	0%	1	**$11.40** cy
minimum ready mix charge	$105.00 each	1	0%	1	**$105.00** ea
Concrete form materials					
form ties	$43.50 box	400	5%	380	**$.11** sf
footing forms (2 x lumber, use 6 times, use key 3 times)	$.40 lf	1	0%	1	**$.40** lf
Concrete footings					
with rebar per cy	$106.00 cy	1	6%	.94	**$113.00** cy
with CEC rebar per cy	$130.00 cy	1	6%	.94	**$138.00** cy
16" wide by 10" deep	$90.70 lf	24.3	6%	22.84	**$3.97** lf
rebar package for 16" by 10"	$.38 pound	.7	6%	.69	**$.55** lf
CEC rebar package for 16" by 10"	$.38 pound	.2	6%	.19	**$2.00** lf
20" wide by 10" deep	$90.70 lf	19.44	6%	18.27	**$4.96** lf
rebar package for 20" by 10"	$.38 pound	.74	2%	.73	**$.52** lf
CEC rebar package for 20" by 10"	$.38 pound	.19	4%	.18	**$2.11** lf
24" wide by 12" deep	$90.70 lf	13.5	6%	12.69	**$7.15** lf
rebar package for 24" by 12"	$.38 pound	.5	2%	.49	**$.78** lf
CEC rebar package for 24" by 10"	$.38 pound	.16	4%	.15	**$2.53** lf
32" wide by 14" deep	$90.70 lf	8.68	6%	8.16	**$11.10** lf
rebar package for 32" by 14"	$.38 pound	.5	2%	.49	**$.78** lf
CEC rebar package for 32" by 14"	$.38 pound	.16	4%	.15	**$2.53** lf

. . . More ➤

CEC = California Earthquake Code.

Concrete Materials *continued*

DESCRIPTION	MATERIAL PRICE	GROSS COVERAGE	WASTE	NET COVERAGE	UNIT PRICE
Foundation wall					
including rebar package per cy	$100.00 cy	1	6%	.94	**$106.00** cy
including CEC rebar package per cy	$120.00 cy	1	6%	.94	**$128.00** cy
5" wide wall	$90.70 cy	65.06	6%	61.16	**$1.48** ea
rebar package for 5" wide	$.38 pound	1.71	2%	1.68	**$.23** sf
CEC rebar package for 5" wide	$.38 pound	.55	4%	.53	**$.72** sf
6" wide wall	$90.70 cy	54	6%	50.76	**$1.79** ea
rebar package for 6" wide wall	$.38 pound	1.71	2%	1.68	**$.23** sf
CEC rebar package for 6" wide wall	$.38 pound	.55	4%	.53	**$.72** sf
concrete for 8" wide wall	$90.70 cy	40.5	6%	38.07	**$2.38** ea
rebar package for 8" wide wall	$.38 sf	1.71	2%	1.68	**$.23** sf
CEC rebar package for 8" wide wall	$.38 sf	.55	4%	.53	**$.72** sf
concrete for 10" wide wall	$90.70 cy	32.4	6%	30.46	**$2.98** ea
rebar package for 10" wide wall	$.38 sf	1.71	2%	1.68	**$.23** sf
CEC rebar package for 10" wide wall	$.38 sf	.55	4%	.53	**$.72** sf
insulating foam stay-in-place foundation wall forms	$1.39 sf	1	0%	1	**$1.39** sf
Pier					
concrete	$90.70 cy	8.6	6%	8.08	**$11.20** lf
fiber tube with bracing	$90.60 10' tube	3.33	2%	3.26	**$27.80** ea
prefabricated rebar cage	$.38 pound	.01	0%	.01	**$38.00** lf
Grade beam					
concrete for 12" by 18"	$90.70 cy	18	6%	16.92	**$5.36** lf
concrete for 12" by 24"	$90.70 cy	13.5	6%	12.69	**$7.15** lf
concrete for 14" by 18"	$90.70 cy	15.43	6%	14.50	**$6.26** lf
concrete for 14" by 24"	$90.70 cy	11.57	6%	10.88	**$8.34** lf
concrete for 16" by 18"	$90.70 cy	13.5	6%	12.69	**$7.15** lf
concrete for 16" by 24"	$90.70 cy	10.13	6%	9.52	**$9.53** lf
concrete for 18" by 18"	$90.70 cy	12	6%	11.28	**$8.04** lf
concrete for 18" by 24"	$90.70 cy	9	6%	8.46	**$10.70** lf
rebar cage	$.38 pound	.01	0%	.01	**$38.00** lf
Lightweight concrete flatwork					
per cy	$114.00 cy	1	6%	.94	**$121.00** cy
2" slab	$114.00 cy	162	6%	152.28	**$.75** sf
4" slab	$114.00 cy	81	6%	76.14	**$1.50** sf
6" slab	$114.00 cy	54	6%	50.76	**$2.25** sf
Concrete flatwork					
per cy	$90.70 cy	1	6%	.94	**$96.50** cy
4" slab	$90.70 cy	81	6%	76.14	**$1.19** sf
6" slab	$90.70 cy	54	6%	50.76	**$1.79** sf
8" slab	$90.70 cy	40.5	6%	38.07	**$2.38** sf
rebar #4, 24" on center	$.38 pound	.75	2%	.74	**$.51** sf
rebar #4, 12" on center	$.38 pound	.37	2%	.36	**$1.06** sf
wire mesh (6" x 6" #10)	$118.00 roll	750	2%	735	**$.16** sf
aggregate for 2" slab base	$6.90 cy	162	0%	162	**$.04** sf
aggregate for 4" slab base	$6.90 cy	81	0%	81	**$.09** sf
sand for 2" slab base	$6.90 cy	162	0%	162	**$.04** sf
sand for 4" slab base	$6.90 cy	81	0%	81	**$.09** sf
Sidewalk					
3" sidewalk	$90.70 cy	108	6%	101.52	**$.89** sf
4" sidewalk	$90.70 cy	81	6%	76.14	**$1.19** sf
6" sidewalk	$90.70 cy	54	6%	50.76	**$1.79** sf
Rebar					
#3 (3/8" .376 pound per lf)	$3.44 20' bar	20	4%	19.2	**$.18** lf
#4 (1/2" .668 pounds per lf)	$4.39 20' bar	20	4%	19.2	**$.23** lf
#5 (5/8" 1.043 pounds per lf)	$6.82 20' bar	20	4%	19.2	**$.36** lf
#6 (3/4" 1.502 pounds per lf)	$10.30 20' bar	20	4%	19.2	**$.54** lf
#7 (7/8" 2.044 pounds per lf)	$14.10 20' bar	20	4%	19.2	**$.73** lf
#8 (1" 2.670 pounds per lf)	$18.40 20' bar	20	4%	19.2	**$.96** lf

CEC = California Earthquake Code.

Concrete Rental Equipment

DESCRIPTION	PRICE	COVERAGE	UNIT PRICE
Forms			
plywood wall forms (per sf of form)	**$.18** per day	**.25** per sf	**$.72** sf
steel curb & gutter forms	**$.87** per day	**1** lf	**$.87** lf
Tractor-mounted auger			
hourly charge	**$200.00** per hour	**90** lf	**$2.22** lf
delivery and take-home charge	**$437.00** each	**1** each	**$437.00** ea
Concrete pump truck			
foundation wall	**$127.00** hour	**450** sf of wall	**$.28** sf
footings	**$127.00** hour	**112** lf of footing	**$1.13** lf
flatwork	**$127.00** hour	**475** sf of flat	**$.27** sf
piers	**$127.00** hour	**78** lf or pier	**$1.63** lf
grade beam	**$127.00** hour	**146** lf of beam	**$.87** lf
pressure grout	**$127.00** hour	**4** lf 2" pipe	**$31.80** sf
Dump truck			
5 cy, average aggregate base haul	**$63.00** day	**540** sf	**$.12** sf
Jackhammer with compressor			
foundation wall demo	**$189.00** day	**110** sf	**$1.72** sf
footing demo	**$189.00** day	**66** lf	**$2.86** lf
flatwork demo	**$189.00** day	**295** sf	**$.64** sf
grade beam demo	**$189.00** day	**46** lf	**$4.11** lf
jacket grade beam	**$189.00** day	**42** lf	**$4.50** lf
jacket pier	**$189.00** day	**5.6** each	**$33.80** ea
curb & gutter	**$189.00** day	**145** lf	**$1.30** lf
Portable concrete saw			
wall sawing	**$128.00** day	**78** 1" x 1'	**$1.64** lf
floor sawing	**$99.00** day	**160** 1" x 1'	**$.62** lf
Concrete core drill			
per day	**$90.00** day	**125** 1" x 1'	**$.72** lf
Crane			
concrete pier removal	**$600.00** day	**98** day	**$6.12** lf
Pressure pot			
for pressurized epoxy injection	**$176.00** day	**120** day	**$1.47** lf
Backhoe			
per day	**$467.00** day	**322** day	**$1.45** cy

Concrete Labor

LABORER	BASE WAGE	PAID LEAVE	TRUE WAGE	FICA	FUTA	WORKER'S COMP.	UNEMPLOY. INSUR.	HEALTH INSUR.	RETIRE (401K)	LIABILITY INSUR.	COST PER HOUR
Concrete form installer	**$23.10**	1.80	**$24.90**	1.90	.20	5.98	2.17	2.69	.75	3.36	**$42.00**
Concrete finisher	**$22.90**	1.79	**$24.69**	1.89	.20	5.93	2.15	2.69	.74	3.33	**$41.60**
Concrete finisher's helper	**$18.60**	1.45	**$20.05**	1.53	.16	4.81	1.74	2.69	.60	2.71	**$34.30**
Equipment operator	**$29.90**	2.33	**$32.23**	2.47	.26	5.81	2.80	2.69	.97	4.35	**$51.60**
Plasterer	**$22.90**	1.79	**$24.69**	1.89	.20	7.10	2.15	2.69	.74	3.33	**$42.80**
Concrete saw operator	**$21.30**	1.66	**$22.96**	1.76	.18	4.14	2.00	2.69	.69	3.10	**$37.50**
Compaction grouter	**$33.30**	2.60	**$35.90**	2.75	.29	8.62	3.12	2.69	1.08	4.85	**$59.30**
Laborer	**$16.10**	1.26	**$17.36**	1.33	.14	4.17	1.51	2.69	.52	2.34	**$30.10**
Demolition laborer	**$13.90**	1.08	**$14.98**	1.15	12	4.79	1.30	2.69	.45	2.02	**$27.50**

Paid Leave is calculated based on two weeks paid vacation, one week sick leave, and seven paid holidays. Employer's matching portion of **FICA** is 7.65 percent. **FUTA** (Federal Unemployment) is .8 percent. **Worker's Compensation** was calculated using a national average of 24.01 percent for the concrete trade; 18.04 percent for the equipment operator, 18.04 percent for the concrete saw operator; 28.74 percent for the plastering trade; 24.01 percent for the compaction grouting specialist; and 31.99 percent for the demolition laborer. **Unemployment insurance** was calculated using a national average of 8.7 percent. **Health insurance** was calculated based on a projected national average for 2002 of $535 per employee (and family when applicable) per month. Employer pays 80 percent for a per month cost of $428 per employee. **Retirement** is based on a 401(k) retirement program with employer matching of 50 percent. Employee contributions to the 401(k) plan are an average of 6 percent of the true wage. **Liability insurance** is based on a national average of 13.2 percent.

Concrete Labor Productivity

WORK DESCRIPTION	LABORER	COST PER HOUR	PRODUCTIVITY	UNIT PRICE
Demolition				
remove footings including rebar	demolition laborer	$27.50	1.64	**$45.10** cy
remove footings including CEC rebar	demolition laborer	$27.50	1.96	**$53.90** cy
remove footings with rebar	demolition laborer	$27.50	.121	**$3.33** lf
remove footings with CEC rebar	demolition laborer	$27.50	.147	**$4.04** lf
remove foundation including rebar	demolition laborer	$27.50	2.44	**$67.10** cy
remove foundation including CEC rebar	demolition laborer	$27.50	2.94	**$80.90** cy
remove 5" or 6" foundation with rebar	demolition laborer	$27.50	.073	**$2.01** sf
remove 5" or 6" foundation with CEC rebar	demolition laborer	$27.50	.088	**$2.42** sf
remove 8" or 10" foundation with rebar	demolition laborer	$27.50	.076	**$2.09** sf
remove 8" or 10" foundation with CEC rebar	demolition laborer	$27.50	.092	**$2.53** sf
remove footing & foundation with rebar	demolition laborer	$27.50	1.96	**$53.90** cy
remove footing & foundation with CEC rebar	demolition laborer	$27.50	2.33	**$64.10** cy
remove footing & 3' foundation	demolition laborer	$27.50	.346	**$9.52** lf
remove footing & 3' foundation with CEC rebar	demolition laborer	$27.50	.418	**$11.50** lf
remove footing & 4' foundation	demolition laborer	$27.50	.422	**$11.60** lf
remove footing & 4' foundation with CEC rebar	demolition laborer	$27.50	.510	**$14.00** lf
remove pier per cy	demolition laborer	$27.50	.699	**$19.20** cy
remove pier	demolition laborer	$27.50	.082	**$2.26** lf
remove grade beam per cy	demolition laborer	$27.50	2.33	**$64.10** cy
remove grade beam	demolition laborer	$27.50	.174	**$4.79** lf
remove lightweight slab	demolition laborer	$27.50	.026	**$.72** sf
remove lightweight slab with rebar	demolition laborer	$27.50	.029	**$.80** sf
remove lightweight slab with wire mesh	demolition laborer	$27.50	.031	**$.85** sf
remove slab	demolition laborer	$27.50	.027	**$.74** sf
remove slab with rebar	demolition laborer	$27.50	.030	**$.83** sf
remove slab with wire mesh	demolition laborer	$27.50	.033	**$.91** sf
remove sidewalk	demolition laborer	$27.50	.034	**$.94** sf
remove curb & gutter	demolition laborer	$27.50	.145	**$3.99** lf
remove step	demolition laborer	$27.50	.047	**$1.29** lf
remove step landing	demolition laborer	$27.50	.046	**$1.27** sf
Forming and rebar setting crew				
form and set rebar	concrete form installer	$42.00		
form and set rebar	laborer	$30.10		
form and set rebar	***forming crew***	$36.10		
Pouring and finishing crew				
pour & finish concrete	concrete finisher	$41.60		
pour & finish concrete	concrete finisher's helper	$34.30		
pour and finish concrete	***finishing crew***	$38.00		
Concrete footings				
form, set rebar, pour, & finish per cy	forming & finishing crews	$37.10	2.44	**$90.50** cy
form, set CEC rebar, pour, & finish per cy	forming & finishing crews	$37.10	2.94	**$109.00** cy
set forms for concrete footings	forming crew	$36.10	.041	**$1.48** lf
strip forms from concrete footings & clean	forming crew	$36.10	.009	**$.32** lf
set rebar in forms for concrete footings	forming crew	$36.10	.036	**$1.30** lf
set CEC rebar in forms for concrete footings	forming crew	$36.10	.067	**$2.42** lf
pour and finish 16" by 10" footings	finishing crew	$38.00	.065	**$2.47** lf
pour and finish 20" by 10" footings	finishing crew	$38.00	.074	**$2.81** lf
pour and finish 24" by 12" footings	finishing crew	$38.00	.081	**$3.08** lf
pour and finish 32" by 14" footings	finishing crew	$38.00	.091	**$3.46** lf
Concrete foundation wall				
form, set rebar, pour, & finish per cy	forming & finishing crews	$37.10	2.70	**$100.00** cy
form, set CEC rebar, pour, & finish per cy	forming & finishing crews	$37.10	3.13	**$116.00** cy
set forms	forming crew	$36.10	.029	**$1.05** sf
strip forms & clean	forming crew	$36.10	.006	**$.22** sf
set rebar package	forming crew	$36.10	.037	**$1.34** sf
set CEC rebar package	forming crew	$36.10	.067	**$2.42** sf
pour and finish 5" wide wall	finishing crew	$38.00	.024	**$.91** sf
pour and finish 6" wide wall	finishing crew	$38.00	.029	**$1.10** sf
pour and finish 8" wide wall	finishing crew	$38.00	.039	**$1.48** sf
pour and finish 10" wide wall	finishing crew	$38.00	.049	**$1.86** sf

. . . More >

CEC = California Earthquake Code.

Concrete Labor Productivity *continued*

WORK DESCRIPTION	LABORER	COST	PRODUCTIVITY	UNIT PRICE
Tractor-mounted auger (hole drilling for pier)				
delivery and take home charges (mobilization)	equipment operator	$51.60	6.25	$323.00 ea
drill pier hole	equipment operator	$51.60	.083	$4.28 sf
Concrete pier				
form, set rebar cage, pour and finish per cy	forming & finishing crews	$37.10	14.9	$553.00 cy
set and brace fiber tube cap	forming crew	$36.10	.125	$4.51 lf
pour concrete pier	finishing crew	$38.00	1.54	$58.50 lf
set and brace fiber tube for above-grade pier	forming crew	$36.10	.183	$6.61 lf
strip fiber tube	forming crew	$36.10	.056	$2.02 lf
pour above-grade concrete pier	finishing crew	$38.00	.185	$7.03 sf
set rebar cage for concrete pier	forming crew	$36.10	.091	$3.29 lf
Jacket pier				
jackhammer for jacket, drill for new rebar	demolition laborer	$27.50	2.32	$63.80 ea
set forms	forming crew	$36.10	1.09	$39.30 ea
set rebar, secure with epoxy	forming crew	$36.10	.833	$30.10 ea
pour concrete jacket	finishing crew	$38.00	1.30	$49.40 ea
Grade beam				
form, set rebar cage, pour, and finish per cy	forming & finishing crews	$37.10	4.00	$148.00 cy
set forms	forming crew	$36.10	.127	$4.58 lf
set rebar cage	forming crew	$36.10	.067	$2.42 lf
pour and finish 12" by 18"	finishing crew	$38.00	.073	$2.77 lf
pour and finish 12" by 24"	finishing crew	$38.00	.088	$3.34 lf
pour and finish 14" by 18"	finishing crew	$38.00	.118	$4.48 lf
pour and finish 14" by 24"	finishing crew	$38.00	.235	$8.93 lf
pour and finish 16" by 18"	finishing crew	$38.00	.353	$13.40 lf
pour and finish 16" by 24"	finishing crew	$38.00	.470	$17.90 lf
pour and finish 18" by 18"	finishing crew	$38.00	.118	$4.48 lf
pour and finish 18" by 24"	finishing crew	$38.00	.235	$8.93 lf
Jacket grade beam				
jackhammer for jacket	demolition laborer	$27.50	.088	$2.42 lf
set forms	forming crew	$36.10	.150	$5.42 lf
set rebar, secure with epoxy	forming crew	$36.10	.083	$3.00 lf
pour concrete	finishing crew	$38.00	.240	$9.12 lf
Lightweight concrete flatwork				
form, pour, and finish per cy	forming & finishing crews	$37.10	2.04	$75.70 cy
pour and finish 2" slab	finishing crew	$38.00	.012	$.46 sf
pour and finish 4" slab	finishing crew	$38.00	.013	$.49 sf
pour and finish 6" slab	finishing crew	$38.00	.015	$.57 sf
Concrete flatwork				
form, pour, and finish per cy	forming & finishing crews	$37.10	2.04	$75.70 cy
set forms for concrete slab	forming crew	$36.10	.011	$.40 sf
set rebar 24" on center	forming crew	$36.10	.036	$1.30 sf
set rebar 12" on center	forming crew	$36.10	.080	$2.89 sf
set wire mesh	forming crew	$36.10	.015	$.54 sf
pour and finish 4" slab	finishing crew	$38.00	.024	$.91 sf
pour and finish 6" slab	finishing crew	$38.00	.036	$1.37 sf
pour and finish 8" slab	finishing crew	$38.00	.036	$1.37 sf
haul aggregate for slab base to job site	equipment operator	$51.60	.002	$.10 sf
spread 2" aggregate slab base	laborer	$30.10	.013	$.39 sf
spread 4" aggregate slab base	laborer	$30.10	.015	$.45 sf
haul sand for slab base to job site	equipment operator	$51.60	.001	$.05 sf
spread 2" sand slab base	laborer	$30.10	.012	$.36 sf
spread 4" sand slab base	laborer	$30.10	.014	$.42 sf
Sidewalk				
form, pour, and finish per cy	forming & finishing crews	$37.10	4.17	$155.00 cy
set forms	forming crew	$36.10	.023	$.83 sf
pour and finish 3" sidewalk	finishing crew	$38.00	.019	$.72 sf
pour and finish 4" sidewalk	finishing crew	$38.00	.026	$.99 sf
pour and finish 6" sidewalk	finishing crew	$38.00	.039	$1.48 sf

. . . More ➢

CEC = California Earthquake Code.

Concrete Labor Productivity *continued*

WORK DESCRIPTION	LABORER	COST	PRODUCTIVITY	UNIT PRICE
Concrete dye				
trowel into wet concrete	finishing crew	$38.00	.009	**$.34** sf
Stamp concrete				
slab or sidewalk	finishing crew	$38.00	.053	**$2.01** sf
with paver pattern	finishing crew	$38.00	.045	**$1.71** sf
grout stamped paver pattern joints	finishing crew	$38.00	.023	**$.87** sf
Exposed aggregate				
Finish with exposed aggregate finish	finishing crew	$38.00	.019	**$.72** sf
Curb & gutter				
set forms	forming crew	$36.10	.123	**$4.44** lf
pour and finish	finishing crew	$38.00	.150	**$5.70** lf
Concrete step				
form, set rebar, pour, and finish per cy	forming & finishing crews	$37.10	7.69	**$285.00** cy
set forms and rebar per lf of step	forming crew	$36.10	.133	**$4.80** lf
pour and finish per lf of step	finishing crew	$38.00	.100	**$3.80** lf
set forms and rebar for landing per cubic foot	forming crew	$36.10	.011	**$.40** cf
pour and finish landing per cubic foot	finishing crew	$38.00	.056	**$2.13** cf
Saw concrete				
wall with rebar per lf, 1" deep	saw operator	$37.50	.111	**$4.16** lf
wall with CEC rebar per lf, 1" deep	saw operator	$37.50	.125	**$4.69** lf
floor per lf, 1" deep	saw operator	$37.50	.050	**$1.88** lf
floor with rebar per lf, 1" deep	saw operator	$37.50	.054	**$2.03** lf
floor with wire mesh per lf, 1" deep	saw operator	$37.50	.052	**$1.95** lf
expansion joint in "green" slab	saw operator	$37.50	.189	**$7.09** lf
Core drill concrete				
2" wall per inch of depth	saw operator	$37.50	.066	**$2.48** li
4" wall per inch of depth	saw operator	$37.50	.073	**$2.74** li
2" floor per inch of depth	saw operator	$37.50	.064	**$2.40** li
4" floor per inch of depth	saw operator	$37.50	.067	**$2.51** li
Set rebar				
#3 (3/8")	forming crew	$36.10	.014	**$.51** lf
#4 (1/2")	forming crew	$36.10	.014	**$.51** lf
#5 (5/8")	forming crew	$36.10	.014	**$.51** lf
#6 (3/4")	forming crew	$36.10	.014	**$.51** lf
#7 (7/8")	forming crew	$36.10	.015	**$.54** lf
#8 (1")	forming crew	$36.10	.015	**$.54** lf
Buttress foundation				
machine excavate to 12" to 24" of ext. foundation	equipment operator	$51.60	.027	**$1.39** sf
hand excavate exterior of foundation	laborer	$30.10	.161	**$4.85** sf
backfill buttressed foundation	laborer	$30.10	.048	**$1.44** sf
set forms for exterior buttress	forming crew	$36.10	.021	**$.76** sf
set rebar for exterior buttress	forming crew	$36.10	.017	**$.61** sf
pour and finish exterior buttress	finishing crew	$38.00	.027	**$1.03** sf
hand excavate interior crawl space for buttress	laborer	$30.10	.457	**$13.80** sf
set forms for interior buttress in crawl space	forming crew	$36.10	.032	**$1.16** sf
set rebar for interior buttress in crawl space	forming crew	$36.10	.023	**$.83** sf
pour and finish interior buttress in crawl space	finishing crew	$38.00	.037	**$1.41** sf
hand excavate interior foundation in basement	laborer	$30.10	.204	**$6.14** sf
set forms for interior buttress in basement	forming crew	$36.10	.025	**$.90** sf
set rebar for interior buttress in basement	forming crew	$36.10	.019	**$.69** sf
pour and finish interior buttress in basement	finishing crew	$38.00	.032	**$1.22** sf
Compaction grouting crew				
core drill, insert pipes, pump grout	compaction grouting specialist	$59.30		
core drill, insert pipes, pump grout	laborer	$30.10		
core drill, insert pipes, pump grout	**compaction grouting crew**	$44.70		
Foundation & footing stabilization with pressurized grout				
2" core drill through footings	compaction grouting crew	$44.70	.379	**$16.90** ea
insert 2" pipes into ground beneath footings	compaction grouting crew	$44.70	.143	**$6.39** lf
pump pressurized grout through pipes	compaction grouting crew	$44.70	.250	**$11.20** lf

CEC = California Earthquake Code.

9 Demolition & Hauling

Item Description			Unit			Total	
Minimum demolition charge			ea	—	—	$182.50	◄ **Minimum**
Demo	Labor 82.50	Equipment........100.00					
Dump charge per cy			cy	—	—	$43.10	◄ **Dump fee** *Typical metro area landfill fees. Will be up to 60% higher in major metro areas and 30% to 60% lower in rural areas.*
Demo Fee.................43.10							
Dump charge per ton			tn	—	—	$81.00	
Demo Fee.................81.00							
3 cy dumpster rental per week			ea	—	—	$110.00	◄ **Dumpster** *Includes up to two dumps per week.*
Demo		Equipment.........110.00					
5 cy dumpster rental per week			ea	—	—	$180.00	
Demo		Equipment........180.00					
10 cy dumpster rental per week			ea	—	—	$230.00	
Demo		Equipment........230.00					
30 cy dumpster rental per week			ea	—	—	$330.00	
Demo		Equipment........330.00					
Minimum dumpster charge			ea	—	—	$150.00	
Demo		Equipment........150.00					
Plywood refuse chute			lf	—	—	$57.10	◄ **Refuse chute**
Demo Materials..........12.30	Labor..........44.80						
Minimum charge for plywood refuse chute			ea	—	—	$166.00	
Demo Materials..........65.00	Labor.........101.00						
18" prefabricated circular steel refuse chute			lf	—	—	$46.40	
Demo Materials..........13.90	Labor..........32.50						
36" prefabricated circular steel refuse chute			lf	—	—	$69.30	
Demo Materials..........25.30	Labor..........44.00						
Minimum charge for circular steel refuse chute			ea	—	—	$163.80	
Demo Materials..........73.00	Labor..........90.80						
Debris hauling (by trailer or dump truck) per cy			cy	—	—	$20.50	◄ **Debris hauling**
Demo		Equipment..........20.50					
Debris hauling (by trailer or dump truck) per ton			tn	—	—	$55.70	
Demo		Equipment..........55.70					
Debris hauling per pick-up truck load			ea	—	—	$19.40	
Demo		Equipment..........19.40					
Strip typical room to bare walls and sub-floor			sf	—	—	$2.04	◄ **Strip room** *Remove all wall and floor coverings, doors, trim, and underlayment. Stud walls and plywood subfloor remain. Per sf of floor.*
Demo	Labor............2.04						
Strip bathroom to bare walls and sub-floor			sf	—	—	$4.13	
Demo	Labor............4.13						

STRIP ROOM ▶ *continued*

For rooms with contents add 4%.

Item Description	Unit			Total
Strip kitchen to bare walls and sub-floor	sf	—	—	**$3.16**
Demo .... Labor 3.16				
Strip utility room to bare walls and sub-floor	sf	—	—	**$2.37**
Demo .... Labor 2.37				
Strip laundry room to bare walls and sub-floor	sf	—	—	**$2.61**
Demo .... Labor 2.61				

TIME & MATERIAL CHARTS *(selected items)*

Demolition & Hauling Materials

DESCRIPTION	MATERIAL PRICE	GROSS COVERAGE	WASTE	NET COVERAGE	UNIT PRICE
Refuse chute					
plywood					**$12.30** *lf*
18" prefabricated circular steel					**$13.90** *lf*
36" prefabricated circular steel					**$25.30** *lf*

Demolition & Hauling Rental Equipment

DESCRIPTION	PRICE	COVERAGE	UNIT PRICE
Dumpster rental per week			
3 cy	$100.00 *week*		**$100.00** *ea*
5 cy	$180.00 *week*		**$180.00** *ea*
10 cy	$230.00 *week*		**$230.00** *ea*
30 cy	$330.00 *week*		**$330.00** *ea*
Truck rental with driver			
3 cy dump truck	$450.00 *day*	22 *cy*	**$20.50** *cy*
3 cy dump truck	$450.00 *day*	8.08 *ton*	**$55.70** *ton*
pick-up truck	$175.00 *day*	9 *load*	**$19.40** *ea*

Demolition & Hauling Labor

LABORER	BASE WAGE	PAID LEAVE	TRUE WAGE	FICA	FUTA	WORKER'S COMP.	UNEMPLOY. INSUR.	HEALTH INSUR.	RETIRE (401K)	LIABILITY INSUR.	COST PER HOUR
Demolition laborer	$13.90	1.08	$14.98	1.15	.12	4.79	1.30	2.69	.45	2.02	**$27.50**

Paid Leave is calculated based on two weeks paid vacation, one week sick leave, and seven paid holidays. Employer's matching portion of **FICA** is 7.65 percent. **FUTA** (Federal Unemployment) is .8 percent. **Worker's Compensation** for Demolition was calculated using a national average of 32.0 percent. **Unemployment insurance** was calculated using a national average of 8.7 percent. **Health insurance** was calculated based on a projected national average for 2002 of $535 per employee (and family when applicable) per month. Employer pays 80 percent for a per month cost of $428 per employee. **Retirement** is based on a 401(k) retirement program with employer matching of 50 percent. Employee contributions to the 401(k) plan are an average of 6 percent of the true wage. **Liability insurance** is based on a national average of 13.2 percent.

Demolition & Hauling Labor Productivity

WORK DESCRIPTION	LABORER	COST PER HOUR	PRODUCTIVITY	UNIT PRICE
Build / install refuse chute				
plywood	*demolition laborer*	$27.50	1.63	**$44.80** *lf*
18" prefabricated circular steel	*demolition laborer*	$27.50	1.18	**$32.50** *lf*
36" prefabricated circular steel	*demolition laborer*	$27.50	1.60	**$44.00** *lf*
Strip room to bare walls and sub-floor				
typical	*demolition laborer*	$27.50	.074	**$2.04** *sf*
bathroom	*demolition laborer*	$27.50	.150	**$4.13** *sf*
kitchen	*demolition laborer*	$27.50	.115	**$3.16** *sf*
utility	*demolition laborer*	$27.50	.086	**$2.37** *sf*
laundry	*demolition laborer*	$27.50	.095	**$2.61** *sf*

10 .... Doors

Item Description	Unit	Remove	Replace	Total
Minimum charge for door work *Replace* Materials......33.00 Labor.........104.00	ea	—	$137.00	$137.00
Hardboard smooth or wood-textured folding door (per section) *Replace* Materials......27.40 Labor...........16.40 *Remove*......................... Labor............3.14	ea	$3.14	$43.80	$46.94
Hardboard wood-textured & embossed folding door (per section) *Replace* Materials......31.40 Labor...........16.40 *Remove*......................... Labor............3.14 ► Referred to by the brand name "Colonist" in many areas of the country.	ea	$3.14	$47.80	$50.94
Mahogany (lauan) or birch veneer folding door (per section) *Replace* Materials......29.40 Labor...........16.40 *Remove*......................... Labor............3.14	ea	$3.142	$45.80	$48.94
Ash or oak veneer folding door (per section) *Replace* Materials......32.00 Labor...........16.40 *Remove*......................... Labor............3.14	ea	$3.14	$48.40	$51.54
Walnut or cherry veneer folding door (per section) *Replace* Materials......36.60 Labor...........16.40 *Remove*......................... Labor............3.14	ea	$3.14	$53.00	$56.14
Paint-grade pine panel folding door (per section) *Replace* Materials......47.70 Labor...........16.40 *Remove*......................... Labor............3.14	ea	$3.14	$64.10	$67.24
Stain-grade pine panel folding door (per section) *Replace* Materials......58.80 Labor...........16.40 *Remove*......................... Labor............3.14	ea	$3.14	$75.20	$78.34
Paint-grade pine full-louvered folding door (per section) *Replace* Materials......56.20 Labor...........16.40 *Remove*......................... Labor............3.14	ea	$3.14	$72.60	$75.74
Stain-grade pine full-louvered folding door (per section) *Replace* Materials......65.30 Labor...........16.40 *Remove*......................... Labor............3.14	ea	$3.14	$81.70	$84.84
Paint-grade pine half-louvered folding door (per section) *Replace* Materials......53.60 Labor...........16.40 *Remove*......................... Labor............3.14	ea	$3.14	$70.00	$73.14
Stain-grade pine half-louvered folding door (per section) *Replace* Materials......62.10 Labor...........16.40 *Remove*......................... Labor............3.14	ea	$3.14	$78.50	$81.64
Red oak folding panel door (per section) *Replace* Materials......71.90 Labor...........16.40 *Remove*......................... Labor............3.14	ea	$3.14	$88.30	$91.44
Folding mirrored door (per section) *Replace* Materials......82.30 Labor...........16.40 *Remove*......................... Labor............3.14	ea	$3.14	$98.70	$101.84

◄ **MINIMUM**

◄ **FOLDING DOOR**
Folding doors usually used in closets. ***Priced per section.*** *For jamb & casing see page 102.*

USING DOOR ITEMS

When replacing a door, select the door type, then the jamb type, and add the two together.

Door prices are for the door slab only and include routing and drilling for standard hardware and hinges. Door tear-out is for the door slab only. Use this tear-out price when removing the slab and leaving the jamb and casing intact.

Jamb & casing prices include the cost to pre-hang the door in the jamb and the cost of hinges (but not the door lockset). Tear-out includes removal of the entire door. Use this tear-out price when removing the door, jamb and casing.

standard △ △ *full-louver*

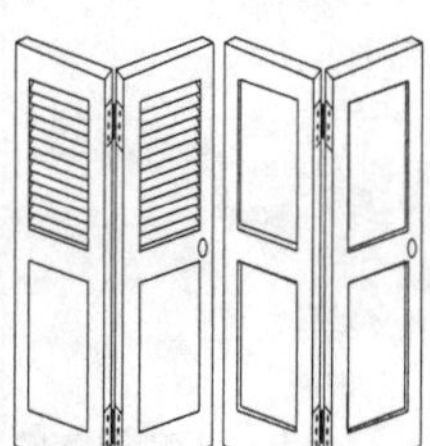

half-louver △ △ *panel*

Folding door ▶ *continued*

Item Description	Unit	Remove	Replace	Total
Remove folding doors for work, then reinstall (per section) *Replace* .... Labor 6.16	ea	—	$6.16	$6.16

Bypassing door ▶

Usually used in closets. ***Priced per door section.*** *Includes track and hardware. For jamb & casing see below.*

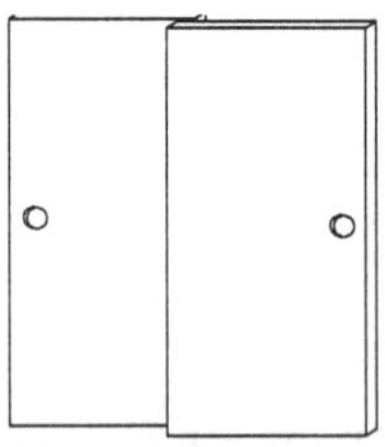

△ *standard*

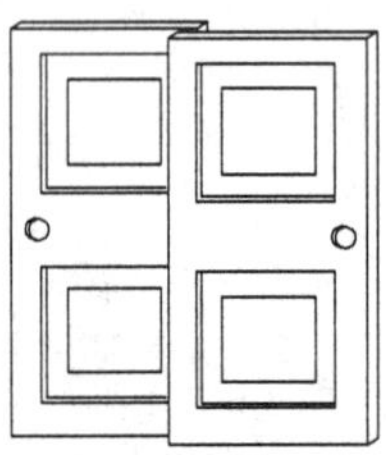

△ *panel*

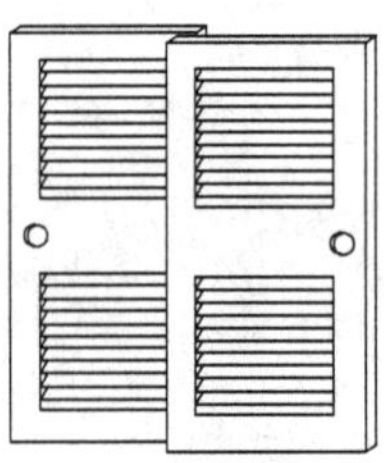

△ *full-louver*

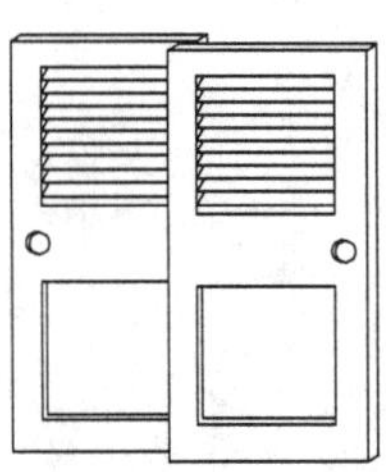

△ *half-louver*

Item Description	Unit	Remove	Replace	Total
Hardboard smooth or wood-textured bypassing door (per section) *Replace* Materials......54.20 Labor...........31.40 *Remove*........................ Labor 3.82	ea	$3.82	$85.60	$89.42
Hardboard wood-textured & embossed bypassing door (per section) *Replace* Materials......60.80 Labor...........31.40 *Remove*........................ Labor ....3.82 ▶ Referred to by the brand name "Colonist" in many areas of the country.	ea	$3.82	$92.20	$96.02
Mahogany (lauan) or birch veneer bypassing door (per section) *Replace* Materials......58.80 Labor...........31.40 *Remove*........................ Labor 3.82	ea	$3.82	$90.20	$94.02
Ash or oak veneer bypassing door (per section) *Replace* Materials.......61.40 Labor...........31.40 *Remove*........................ Labor 3.82	ea	$3.82	$92.80	$96.62
Walnut or cherry veneer bypassing door (per section) *Replace* Materials ......76.40 Labor...........31.40 *Remove*........................ Labor 3.82	ea	$3.82	$107.80	$111.62
Paint-grade pine panel bypassing door (per section) *Replace* Materials ......94.70 Labor...........31.40 *Remove*........................ Labor 3.82	ea	$3.82	$126.10	$129.92
Stain-grade pine panel bypassing door (per section) *Replace* Materials .....113.00 Labor...........31.40 *Remove*........................ Labor 3.82	ea	$3.82	$144.40	$148.22
Red oak bypassing panel door (per section) *Replace* Materials.....145.00 Labor...........31.40 *Remove*........................ Labor 3.82	ea	$3.82	$176.40	$180.22
Paint-grade pine full-louvered bypassing door (per section) *Replace* Materials.....110.00 Labor...........31.40 *Remove*........................ Labor 3.82	ea	$3.82	$141.40	$145.22
Stain-grade pine full-louvered bypassing door (per section) *Replace* Materials ....129.00 Labor...........31.40 *Remove*........................ Labor 3.82	ea	$3.82	$160.40	$164.22
Paint-grade pine half-louvered bypassing door (per section) *Replace* Materials....104.50 Labor...........31.40 *Remove*........................ Labor 3.82	ea	$3.82	$135.90	$139.72
Stain-grade pine half-louvered bypassing door (per section) *Replace* Materials ....122.00 Labor...........31.40 *Remove*........................ Labor 3.82	ea	$3.82	$153.40	$157.22
Mirrored bypassing door (per section) *Replace* Materials.....160.00 Labor...........31.40 *Remove*........................ Labor 3.82	ea	$3.82	$191.40	$195.22
Remove bypassing sliding doors for work, then reinstall (per section) *Replace* .... Labor 9.15	ea	—	$9.15	$9.15

Jamb & casing for closet door ▶

Per lf around opening.

Item Description	Unit	Remove	Replace	Total
Paint-grade jamb & casing for folding or bypassing door opening *Replace* Materials .... .97 Labor ....4.53 *Remove*........................ Labor............ .72	lf	$.72	$5.50	$6.22

Item Description	Unit	Remove	Replace	Total
Stain-grade pine jamb & casing for folding or bypassing door opening ***Replace*** Materials...... 1.07 Labor............4.53 ***Remove***........................ Labor............ .72	lf	$.72	$5.60	$6.32
Birch jamb & casing for folding or bypassing door opening ***Replace*** Materials...... 1.05 Labor............4.53 ***Remove***........................ Labor............ .72	lf	$.72	$5.58	$6.30
Mahogany jamb & casing for folding or bypassing door opening ***Replace*** Materials........1.49 Labor............4.53 ***Remove***........................ Labor............ .72 ► Deduct **$.17** for mahogany veneer jamb & casing.	lf	$.72	$6.02	$6.74
Ash or oak jamb & casing for folding or bypassing door opening ***Replace*** Materials........1.62 Labor............4.53 ***Remove***........................ Labor............ .72 ► Deduct **$.14** for ash or oak veneer jamb & casing.	lf	$.72	$6.15	$6.87
Walnut or cherry jamb & casing for folding or bypassing door opening ***Replace*** Materials........2.16 Labor............4.53 ***Remove***........................ Labor............ .72 ► Deduct **$.12** for walnut or cherry veneer jamb & casing.	lf	$.72	$6.69	$7.41
Hardboard smooth or wood-textured interior door ***Replace*** Materials......73.200 Labor............8.94 ***Remove*** .... Labor............5.97	ea	$5.97	$82.14	$88.11
Hardboard wood-textured and embossed interior door ***Replace*** Materials....102.00 Labor............8.94 ***Remove*** .... Labor............5.97 ► Called "colonist" style in many areas of the country.	ea	$5.97	$110.94	$116.91
Mahogany or birch veneer interior door ***Replace*** Materials......81.00 Labor............8.94 ***Remove*** .... Labor............5.97	ea	$5.97	$89.94	$95.91
Ash or oak veneer interior door ***Replace*** Materials......88.20 Labor............8.94 ***Remove*** .... Labor............5.97	ea	$5.97	$97.14	$103.11
Walnut or cherry veneer interior door ***Replace*** Materials.....115.00 Labor............8.94 ***Remove*** .... Labor............5.97	ea	$5.97	$123.94	$129.91
Mirrored interior door ***Replace*** Materials....189.00 Labor............8.94 ***Remove*** .... Labor............5.97	ea	$5.97	$197.94	$203.91
Plastic laminate faced interior door ***Replace*** Materials....294.00 Labor............8.94 ***Remove*** .... Labor............5.97	ea	$5.97	$302.94	$308.91
Add for solid-core, fire-rated interior door ***Replace*** Materials....104.50 ► 1 hour fire rating.	ea	—	$104.50	$104.50
Paint-grade wood French door ***Replace*** Materials....189.00 Labor............8.94 ***Remove*** .... Labor............5.97	ea	$5.97	$197.94	$203.91

RELATED ITEMS

Cleaning........................57
Door Hardware...........127
Finish Carpentry..........201
Painting......................334

◄ **Interior door**
Hollow-core interior doors. Pre-drilled and routed for hardware and hinges. *For jamb & casing see page 104.*

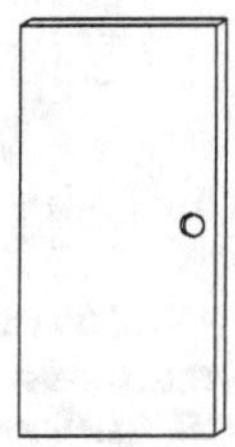

◁ **add for fire-rated**

◄ **French door**
For interior French doors Pre-drilled and routed for hardware and hinges. *For jamb & casing see page 104.*

	Item Description	Unit	Remove	Replace	Total
French door ▶ *continued* 	**Stain-grade fir French door** *Replace* Materials....229.00 Labor ....8.94 *Remove* .... Labor 5.97	ea	$5.97	$237.94	$243.91
	Metal French door *Replace* Materials.....196.00 Labor ....8.94 *Remove* .... Labor 5.97	ea	$5.97	$204.94	$210.91
	Full-lite door with simulated French door grid *Replace* Materials.....170.00 Labor ....8.94 *Remove* .... Labor 5.97	ea	$5.97	$178.94	$184.91
add for double-glazed ▷	**Add for double-glazed insulated glass in French door** *Replace* Materials......73.80	ea	—	$73.80	$73.80
add for fire-rated ▷	**Add for fire-rated glass in French door** *Replace* Materials......84.90 ▶ 1 hour fire rating.	ea	—	$84.90	$84.90
Full-louvered ▶ door 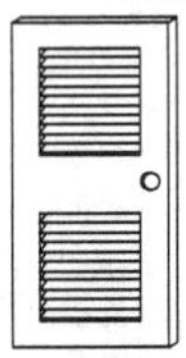	**Paint-grade full-louvered door** *Replace* Materials.....159.00 Labor ....8.94 *Remove* .... Labor 5.97	ea	$5.97	$167.94	$173.91
	Stain-grade pine full-louvered door *Replace* Materials.....196.00 Labor ....8.94 *Remove* .... Labor 5.97	ea	$5.97	$204.94	$210.91
Half-louvered ▶ door 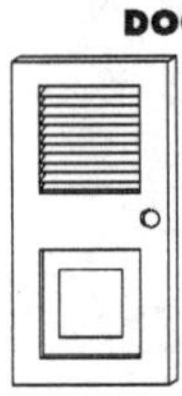	**Paint-grade pine half-louvered door** *Replace* Materials ....144.00 Labor ....8.94 *Remove* .... Labor 5.97	ea	$5.97	$152.94	$158.91
	Stain-grade pine half-louvered door *Replace* Materials ....188.00 Labor ....8.94 *Remove* .... Labor 5.97	ea	$5.97	$196.94	$202.91
Remove ▶ interior door & reinstall	**Remove door slab for work, then reinstall** *Replace* .... Labor 6.28	ea	—	$6.28	$6.28
	Remove door, jamb & casing for work, then reinstall *Replace* .... Labor...........67.80	ea	—	$67.80	$67.80
	Remove double door slabs for work, then reinstall *Replace* .... Labor...........12.20	ea	—	$12.20	$12.20
	Remove double doors, jamb & casing for work, then reinstall *Replace* .... Labor..........111.00	ea	—	$111.00	$111.00
Jamb & casing ▶ for interior door *Per door.*	**Paint-grade jamb & casing for interior door** *Replace* Materials.......17.20 Labor...........59.50 *Remove*......................... Labor...........10.70	ea	$10.70	$76.70	$87.40
	Paint-grade jamb & casing for double interior door *Replace* Materials......32.20 Labor...........59.50 *Remove*......................... Labor...........10.70	ea	$10.70	$91.70	$102.40
	Stain-grade pine jamb & casing for interior door *Replace* Materials.......19.70 Labor...........59.50 *Remove*......................... Labor...........10.70	ea	$10.70	$79.20	$89.90

Item Description	Unit	Remove	Replace	Total
Stain-grade pine jamb & casing for double interior door ***Replace*** Materials......36.10 Labor...........59.50 ***Remove*** .... Labor...........10.70	ea	$10.70	$95.60	$106.30
Birch jamb & casing for interior door ***Replace*** Materials......21.30 Labor...........59.50 ***Remove*** .... Labor...........10.70	ea	$10.70	$80.80	$91.50
Birch jamb & casing for double interior door ***Replace*** Materials......39.00 Labor...........59.50 ***Remove*** .... Labor...........10.70	ea	$10.70	$98.50	$109.20
Mahogany jamb & casing for interior door ***Replace*** Materials......25.50 Labor...........59.50 ***Remove*** .... Labor...........10.70 ► Deduct **$1.60** for mahogany veneer jamb & casing.	ea	$10.70	$85.00	$95.70
Mahogany jamb & casing for double interior door ***Replace*** Materials......49.20 Labor...........59.50 ***Remove*** .... Labor...........10.70 ► Deduct **$.72** for mahogany veneer jamb & casing.	ea	$10.70	$108.70	$119.40
Ash or oak jamb & casing for interior door ***Replace*** Materials......30.70 Labor...........59.50 ***Remove*** .... Labor...........10.70 ► Deduct **$2.90** for ash or oak veneer jamb & casing.	ea	$10.70	$90.20	$100.90
Ash or oak jamb & casing for double interior door ***Replace*** Materials......54.90 Labor...........59.50 ***Remove*** .... Labor...........10.70 ► Deduct **$2.40** for ash or oak veneer jamb & casing.	ea	$10.70	$114.40	$125.10
Walnut or cherry jamb & casing for interior door ***Replace*** Materials......44.40 Labor...........59.50 ***Remove*** .... Labor...........10.70 ► Deduct **$2.30** for walnut or cherry veneer jamb & casing.	ea	$10.70	$103.90	$114.60
Walnut or cherry jamb & casing for double interior door ***Replace*** Materials......82.30 Labor...........59.50 ***Remove*** .... Labor...........10.70 ► Deduct **$4.10** for walnut or cherry veneer jamb & casing.	ea	$10.70	$141.80	$152.50
Steel jamb & casing for interior door ***Replace*** Materials.....118.00 Labor...........59.50 ***Remove*** .... Labor...........10.70	ea	$10.70	$177.50	$188.20
Steel jamb & casing for double interior door ***Replace*** Materials....229.00 Labor...........59.50 ***Remove*** .... Labor...........13.30	ea	$13.30	$288.50	$301.80
Add for jamb & casing installed for pocket door ***Replace*** Materials......14.70 Labor...........13.40 ► Add to price above when jamb is installed for a pocket door.	ea	—	$28.10	$28.10
Add for jamb & casing installed for double pocket door ***Replace*** Materials......24.80 Labor..........36.20 ► Add to price above when jamb is installed for a double pocket door.	ea	—	$61.00	$61.00
Rough framing package for pocket door in 2" x 4" wall ***Replace*** Materials......24.20 Labor...........62.40	ea	—	$86.60	$86.60

RELATED ITEMS

◁ steel jamb & casing

◁ add for pocket door

◀ **ROUGH FRAMING FOR POCKET DOOR**

continued on next page

	Item Description	Unit	Remove	Replace	Total
Rough framing for pocket door *continued*	**Rough framing package for double pocket doors in 2" x 4" wall** *Replace* Materials......38.70 Labor.........120.00	ea	—	$158.70	$158.70
Includes track, hardware, and side framing kit. Antique systems include framing for walls on each side of the pocket door.	**Rough framing package for pocket door in 2" x 6" wall** *Replace* Materials......26.10 Labor..........63.20	ea	—	$89.30	$89.30
	Rough framing package for double pocket doors in 2" x 6" wall *Replace* Materials......46.60 Labor.........123.00	ea	—	$169.60	$169.60
	Rough framing package for pocket door in 2" x 8" wall *Replace* Materials......28.10 Labor..........64.10	ea	—	$92.20	$92.20
	Rough framing package for double pocket doors in 2" x 8" wall *Replace* Materials......49.60 Labor.........126.00	ea	—	$175.60	$175.60
	Rough framing package for antique pocket door *Replace* Materials......84.90 Labor.........102.00	ea	—	$186.90	$186.90
	Rough framing package for antique double pocket doors *Replace* Materials.....152.00 Labor.........213.00	ea	—	$365.00	$365.00
Pocket door track	**Overhead pocket door track for antique pocket door system** *Replace* Materials......49.60 Labor..........54.10 *Remove*........................ Labor..........20.70	ea	$20.70	$103.70	$124.40
	Overhead pocket door track for antique double pocket door system *Replace* Materials......67.90 Labor...........97.30 *Remove*........................ Labor...........35.20	ea	$35.20	$165.20	$200.40
	Clean and realign overhead pocket door track *Replace* .... Labor...........81.50	ea	—	$81.50	$81.50
	Floor track for antique pocket door system *Replace* Materials......54.90 Labor..........50.30 *Remove*........................ Labor..........20.70	ea	$20.70	$105.20	$125.90
	Floor track for antique double pocket door system *Replace* Materials......73.80 Labor...........91.50 *Remove*........................ Labor...........35.20	ea	$35.20	$165.30	$200.50
	Clean and realign pocket door floor track *Replace* .... Labor.........110.00	ea	—	$110.00	$110.00
Remove pocket door & reinstall	**Remove pocket door and trim for work, then reinstall** *Replace* .... Labor...........47.80	ea	—	$47.80	$47.80
	Remove pocket door, jamb & casing for work, then reinstall *Replace* .... Labor.........134.00	ea	—	$134.00	$134.00
	Remove double pocket doors & trim for work, then reinstall *Replace* .... Labor...........65.70	ea	—	$65.70	$65.70
	Remove double pocket doors, jamb & casing for work, then reinstall *Replace* .... Labor.........141.00	ea	—	$141.00	$141.00
Panel door *continued on next page*	**Paint-grade panel door** *Replace* Materials....503.00 Labor............7.40 *Remove* .... Labor............5.97 ► Add **67%** for panel door custom milled to match.	ea	$5.97	$510.40	$516.37

Item Description	Unit	Remove	Replace	Total
Reconditioned painted antique panel door ***Replace*** Materials....405.00 Labor............7.40 ***Remove*** .... Labor............5.97	ea	$5.97	$412.40	$418.37
Reconditioned grained antique panel door ***Replace*** Materials....588.00 Labor............7.40 ***Remove*** .... Labor............5.97 ► "Graining" is a method of painting wood to make it look like the grain of another wood. This process was used extensively in the 19th century, most often to paint pine to appear like quartersawn oak.	ea	$5.97	$595.40	$601.37
Stain-grade fir panel door ***Replace*** Materials....666.00 Labor............7.40 ***Remove*** .... Labor............5.97 ► Add **35%** for panel door custom milled to match.	ea	$5.97	$673.40	$679.37
Reconditioned stained fir antique panel door ***Replace*** Materials.....610.00 Labor............7.40 ***Remove*** .... Labor............5.97	ea	$5.97	$617.40	$623.37
Redwood panel door ***Replace*** Materials.....719.00 Labor............7.40 ***Remove*** .... Labor............5.97 ► Add **26%** for panel door custom milled to match.	ea	$5.97	$726.40	$732.37
Reconditioned redwood antique panel door ***Replace*** Materials....692.00 Labor............7.40 ***Remove*** .... Labor............5.97	ea	$5.97	$699.40	$705.37
Cypress panel door ***Replace*** Materials....682.00 Labor............7.40 ***Remove*** .... Labor............5.97 ► Add **17%** for panel door custom milled to match.	ea	$5.97	$689.40	$695.37
Reconditioned cypress antique panel door ***Replace*** Materials....634.00 Labor............7.40 ***Remove*** .... Labor............5.97	ea	$5.97	$641.40	$647.37
Oak panel door ***Replace*** Materials....608.00 Labor............7.40 ***Remove*** .... Labor............5.97 ► Add **35%** for panel door custom milled to match.	ea	$5.97	$615.40	$621.37
Reconditioned painted oak antique panel door ***Replace*** Materials.....451.00 Labor............7.40 ***Remove*** .... Labor............5.97	ea	$5.97	$458.40	$464.37
Reconditioned stained oak antique panel door ***Replace*** Materials....523.00 Labor............7.40 ***Remove*** .... Labor............5.97	ea	$5.97	$530.40	$536.37
Mahogany panel door ***Replace*** Materials....699.00 Labor............7.40 ***Remove*** .... Labor............5.97 ► Add **29%** for panel door custom milled to match.	ea	$5.97	$706.40	$712.37
Reconditioned mahogany antique panel door ***Replace*** Materials....647.00 Labor............7.40 ***Remove*** .... Labor............5.97	ea	$5.97	$654.40	$660.37

◄ **PANEL DOOR**
continued

6 to 9 panels. Each wood species includes line items for a new door, a reconditioned door, and a door that is custom milled to match a specific pattern. For more see below.

For interior jamb & casing see page 104. For exterior jamb and casing see page 116.

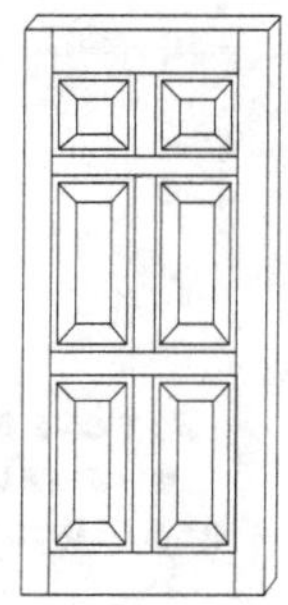

RECONDITIONED DOOR

Reconditioned panel doors have been removed from a historical structure and reconditioned by an architectural salvage company.

These doors will have some scratches, dents, patching and may have been stripped of paint.

CUSTOM-MILLED DOOR

Custom-milled doors include the additional costs for panel doors that are milled to match an existing door pattern.

For these doors it is necessary to cut custom shaper knives for the panels and custom molder (or shaper) knives for the stiles and rails. Add **60%** if milling two or less doors.

RELATED ITEMS

Cleaning........................57
Door Hardware...........127
Finish Carpentry..........201
Painting......................334

	Item Description	Unit	Remove	Replace	Total
Panel door ► *continued*	**Walnut panel door** ***Replace*** Materials..1060.00 Labor............7.40 ***Remove*** .... Labor............5.97 ► Add **17%** for panel door custom milled to match.	ea	$5.97	$1,067.40	$1,073.37
	Reconditioned walnut antique panel door ***Replace*** Materials....934.00 Labor............7.40 ***Remove*** .... Labor............5.97	ea	$5.97	$941.40	$947.37
Additional panel door costs ►	**Add for panel door with tempered glass lite** ***Replace*** Materials....248.00	ea	—	$248.00	$248.00
	Add for panel door with beveled or edged glass lite ***Replace*** Materials....465.00	ea	—	$465.00	$465.00
	Add for panel door with leaded or colored glass lite ***Replace*** Materials....538.00	ea	—	$538.00	$538.00
	Add for panel door with round or elliptical top ***Replace*** Materials....608.00 Labor.........189.00	ea	—	$797.00	$797.00
Remove & reinstall panel door ►	**Remove panel door slab only for work, then reinstall** ***Replace*** .... Labor............6.32	ea	—	$6.32	$6.32
	Remove panel door, jamb, & casing for work, then reinstall ***Replace*** .... Labor...........67.80	ea	—	$67.80	$67.80
Panel door repair ►	**Replace antique panel door panel (not including custom knife charges)** ***Replace*** Materials....102.00 Labor..........114.00	ea	—	$216.00	$216.00
	Replace antique panel door stile (not including custom knife charges) ***Replace*** Materials......74.00 Labor.........104.00	ea	—	$178.00	$178.00
	Minimum charge to repair antique panel door (no custom milling) ***Replace*** Materials.....118.00 Labor.........104.00	ea	—	$222.00	$222.00
	Minimum charge to repair antique panel door (custom milling) ***Replace*** Materials....405.00 Labor.........146.00	ea	—	$551.00	$551.00
	Custom work shaper or molder knife charge ***Replace*** Materials....320.00	ea	—	$320.00	$320.00
	Custom work shaper or molder setup charge ***Replace*** Materials....150.00	ea	—	$150.00	$150.00
	Minimum custom work shaper or molder charge ***Replace*** Materials.....614.00	ea	—	$614.00	$614.00
	Repair cracks & dry rot in antique door with epoxy, tighten stiles ***Replace*** Materials....146.00 Labor.........187.00	ea	—	$333.00	$333.00
	Repair cracks & dry rot in antique door jamb with epoxy ***Replace*** Materials......84.90 Labor.........141.00	ea	—	$225.90	$225.90
	Repair cracks & dry rot in antique door casing with epoxy ***Replace*** Materials......65.30 Labor.........141.00	ea	—	$206.30	$206.30
	Remove antique door casing, re-plumb door, & reinstall casing ***Replace*** .... Labor.........123.00	ea	—	$123.00	$123.00

Batten Doors

(on facing page)

Batten doors are built from vertical boards (usually tongue and groove) held in place by horizontal battens and diagonal braces.

Standard grade Boards held in place by horizontal battens that are braced diagonally. (Sometimes called ledged-and-braced doors.)

High grade Boards held in place by a stile frame and a single horizontal batten. Frame is joined with mortise and tenon joints. Also includes diagonal braces. (Sometimes called framed ledged-and-braced doors.)

Item Description	Unit	Remove	Replace	Total
Add 38% for antique panel door transom ► Includes hinges, jamb, casing and brass opening hardware. For newer style transoms see page 118.				
Paint-grade batten door, standard grade *Replace* Materials....379.00 Labor............7.40 *Remove* .... Labor............5.97	ea	$5.97	$386.40	$392.37
Paint-grade batten door, high grade *Replace* Materials....549.00 Labor............7.40 *Remove* .... Labor............5.97	ea	$5.97	$556.40	$562.37
Stain-grade batten door, standard grade *Replace* Materials....692.00 Labor............7.40 *Remove* .... Labor............5.97	ea	$5.97	$699.40	$705.37
Stain-grade batten door, high grade *Replace* Materials.....967.00 Labor............7.40 *Remove* .... Labor............5.97	ea	$5.97	$974.40	$980.37
Metal storm/screen door, economy grade *Replace* Materials.....128.00 Labor..........50.30 *Remove* .... Labor............6.24	ea	$6.24	$178.30	$184.54
Metal storm/screen door, standard grade *Replace* Materials....188.00 Labor..........50.30 *Remove* .... Labor............6.24	ea	$6.24	$238.30	$244.54
Metal storm/screen door, high grade *Replace* Materials....273.00 Labor..........50.30 *Remove* .... Labor............6.24	ea	$6.24	$323.30	$329.54
Metal storm/screen door, deluxe grade *Replace* Materials....346.00 Labor..........50.30 *Remove* .... Labor............6.24	ea	$6.24	$396.30	$402.54
Wood storm/screen door, economy grade *Replace* Materials.....145.00 Labor..........50.30 *Remove* .... Labor............6.24	ea	$6.24	$195.30	$201.54
Wood storm/screen door, standard grade *Replace* Materials....235.00 Labor..........50.30 *Remove* .... Labor............6.24	ea	$6.24	$285.30	$291.54
Wood storm/screen door, high grade *Replace* Materials....280.00 Labor..........50.30 *Remove* .... Labor............6.24	ea	$6.24	$330.30	$336.54
Wood storm/screen door, deluxe grade *Replace* Materials....346.00 Labor..........50.30 *Remove* .... Labor............6.24	ea	$6.24	$396.30	$402.54
Victorian style wood storm/screen door, standard grade *Replace* Materials....379.00 Labor..........50.30 *Remove* .... Labor............6.24	ea	$6.24	$429.30	$435.54
Victorian style wood storm/screen door, high grade *Replace* Materials.....451.00 Labor..........50.30 *Remove* .... Labor............6.24	ea	$6.24	$501.30	$507.54
Victorian style wood storm/screen door, deluxe grade *Replace* Materials....634.00 Labor..........50.30 *Remove* .... Labor............6.24	ea	$6.24	$684.30	$690.54

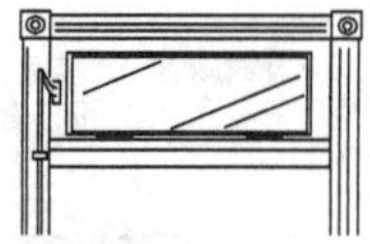

◄ **Batten door**

For interior jamb & casing see page 104. For exterior jamb and casing see page 116. See "Batten Doors" on facing page.

△ *standard* △ *high*

◄ **Storm door**

METAL . . .

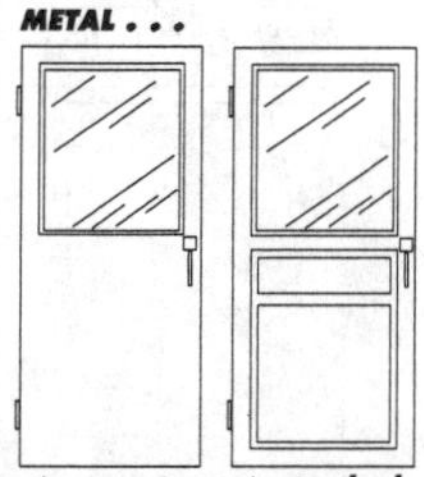

△ *economy* △ *standard*

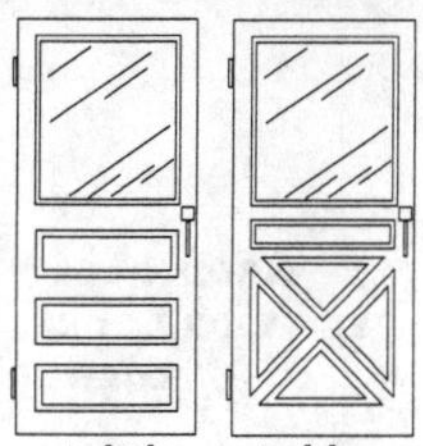

△ *high* △ *deluxe*

VICTORIAN WOOD . . .

△ *standard* △ *standard*

△ *high* △ *deluxe*

Storm door ► *continued*

Item Description	Unit	Remove	Replace	Total
Remove storm/screen door for work, then reinstall *Replace* .... Labor.........70.70	ea	—	$70.70	$70.70

Exterior French door ►

For exterior jamb & casing see page 116.

Item Description	Unit	Remove	Replace	Total
Exterior paint-grade wood French door *Replace* Materials....379.00 Labor..........8.82 *Remove* .... Labor..........7.78	ea	$7.78	$387.82	$395.60
Exterior stain-grade fir French door *Replace* Materials....431.00 Labor..........8.82 *Remove* .... Labor..........7.78	ea	$7.78	$439.82	$447.60
Exterior metal French door *Replace* Materials....421.00 Labor..........8.82 *Remove* .... Labor..........7.78	ea	$7.78	$429.82	$437.60
Exterior full-lite insulated door with simulated French door grid *Replace* Materials.....361.00 Labor..........8.82 *Remove* .... Labor..........7.78	ea	$7.78	$369.82	$377.60

Exterior veneer door ►

For exterior jamb & casing see page 116.

Item Description	Unit	Remove	Replace	Total
Mahogany (lauan) or birch veneer exterior door *Replace* Materials....180.00 Labor..........8.82 *Remove* .... Labor..........7.78	ea	$7.78	$188.82	$196.60
Ash or red oak veneer exterior door *Replace* Materials.....196.00 Labor..........8.82 *Remove* .... Labor..........7.78	ea	$7.78	$204.82	$212.60
Walnut or cherry veneer exterior door *Replace* Materials.....216.00 Labor..........8.82 *Remove* .... Labor..........7.78	ea	$7.78	$224.82	$232.60
Insulated steel exterior door *Replace* Materials....180.00 Labor..........8.82 *Remove* .... Labor..........7.78	ea	$7.78	$188.82	$196.60

Additional exterior door costs ►

Item Description	Unit	Remove	Replace	Total
Add for full-lite in exterior door *Replace* Materials.....242.00	ea	—	$242.00	$242.00
Add for leaded or colored glass full-lite in exterior door *Replace* Materials....538.00	ea	—	$538.00	$538.00
Add for half-lite in exterior door *Replace* Materials....105.00	ea	—	$105.00	$105.00
Add for leaded or colored glass half-lite in exterior wood door *Replace* Materials....300.00	ea	—	$300.00	$300.00
Add for 1′ by 1′ lite in exterior door *Replace* Materials......32.00	ea	—	$32.00	$32.00

Dutch door ►

See jambs and casing for Dutch doors on pages 116 and 117.

Bottom . . .

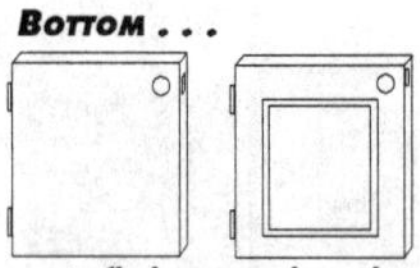

△ *flush* *raised panel* △

Item Description	Unit	Remove	Replace	Total
Bottom Dutch door section, flush *Replace* Materials.....178.00 Labor..........13.50 *Remove* .... Labor..........10.70	ea	$10.70	$191.50	$202.20
Bottom Dutch door section, raised panel *Replace* Materials....267.00 Labor..........13.50 *Remove* .... Labor..........10.70	ea	$10.70	$280.50	$291.20
Bottom Dutch door section, cross buck *Replace* Materials....345.00 Labor..........13.50 *Remove* .... Labor..........10.70	ea	$10.70	$358.50	$369.20

Item Description	Unit	Remove	Replace	Total
Add for shelf on bottom Dutch door section *Replace* Materials......57.50	ea	—	$57.50	$57.50
Top Dutch door section with full lite *Replace* Materials....235.00 Labor...........13.50 *Remove* .... Labor...........10.70	ea	$10.70	$248.50	$259.20
Top Dutch door section with four lites *Replace* Materials....282.00 Labor...........13.50 *Remove* .... Labor...........10.70	ea	$10.70	$295.50	$306.20
Top Dutch door section with six lites *Replace* Materials....300.00 Labor...........13.50 *Remove* .... Labor...........10.70	ea	$10.70	$313.50	$324.20
Top Dutch door section with nine lites *Replace* Materials....325.00 Labor...........13.50 *Remove* .... Labor...........10.70	ea	$10.70	$338.50	$349.20
Remove exterior Dutch door, jamb, & casing for work, then reinstall *Replace* .... Labor..........114.00	ea	—	$114.00	$114.00
Remove exterior Dutch door slabs for work, then reinstall *Replace* .... Labor...........16.40	ea	—	$16.40	$16.40
Steel entry door, standard grade *Replace* Materials.....216.00 Labor............8.82 *Remove* .... Labor............7.78	ea	$7.78	$224.82	$232.60
Steel entry door, high grade *Replace* Materials....289.00 Labor............8.82 *Remove* .... Labor............7.78	ea	$7.78	$297.82	$305.60
Steel entry door side-lite, standard grade *Replace* Materials.....111.00 Labor...........47.40 *Remove* .... Labor...........14.00	ea	$14.00	$158.40	$172.40
Steel entry door side-lite, high grade *Replace* Materials....144.00 Labor...........47.40 *Remove* .... Labor...........14.00	ea	$14.00	$191.40	$205.40
Paint-grade wood entry door, standard grade *Replace* Materials....233.00 Labor............8.82 *Remove* .... Labor............7.78	ea	$7.78	$241.82	$249.60
Paint-grade wood entry door, high grade *Replace* Materials....332.00 Labor............8.82 *Remove* .... Labor............7.78	ea	$7.78	$340.82	$348.60
Paint-grade wood entry door, deluxe grade *Replace* Materials....448.00 Labor............8.82 *Remove* .... Labor............7.78	ea	$7.78	$456.82	$464.60
Paint-grade wood entry door, custom grade *Replace* Materials....647.00 Labor............8.82 *Remove* .... Labor............7.78	ea	$7.78	$655.82	$663.60
Paint-grade wood entry door, custom deluxe grade *Replace* Materials.....751.00 Labor............8.82 *Remove* .... Labor............7.78	ea	$7.78	$759.82	$767.60

Bottom . . .

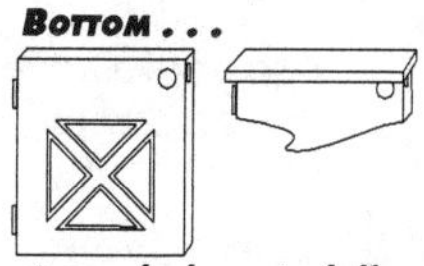

△ *crossbuck* △ *shelf*

Top . . .

◄ **Steel entry door**
For exterior jamb & casing see page 116. Standard grade is flush face and high grade is embossed.

◄ **Steel entry door side-lite**
Includes jamb & casing.

◄ **Paint-grade wood entry door**
For exterior jamb & casing see page 116. Also see quality indicators on page 112.

Entry Doors

All entry doors are solid wood with occasional veneered wood components in the lower grades.

Entry door prices do not include jamb & casing. See page 116 for exterior jambs.

See quality indicators on page 112.

Paint-grade wood entry door side-lite ▶
Includes jamb & casing. Also see quality grades below.

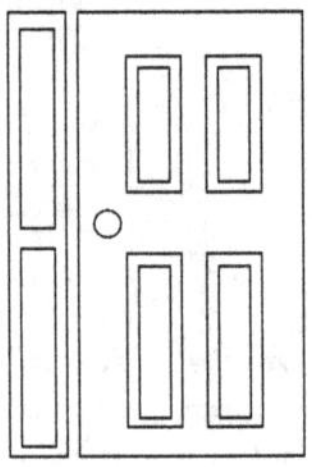

Item Description	Unit	Remove	Replace	Total
Paint-grade wood entry door side-lite, standard grade *Replace* Materials.....158.00 Labor...........47.40 *Remove* .... Labor...........14.00	ea	$14.00	$205.40	$219.40
Paint-grade wood entry door side-lite, high grade *Replace* Materials.....217.00 Labor...........47.40 *Remove* .... Labor...........14.00	ea	$14.00	$264.40	$278.40
Paint-grade wood entry door side-lite, deluxe grade *Replace* Materials.....315.00 Labor...........47.40 *Remove* .... Labor...........14.00	ea	$14.00	$362.40	$376.40
Paint-grade wood entry door side-lite, custom grade *Replace* Materials....435.00 Labor...........47.40 *Remove* .... Labor...........14.00	ea	$14.00	$482.40	$496.40
Paint-grade wood entry door side-lite, custom deluxe grade *Replace* Materials....525.00 Labor...........47.40 *Remove* .... Labor...........14.00	ea	$14.00	$572.40	$586.40

Fir entry door ▶
For exterior jamb & casing see page 116. Also see quality grades below.

Item Description	Unit	Remove	Replace	Total
Stain-grade fir entry door, standard grade *Replace* Materials.....516.00 Labor ....8.82 *Remove* .... Labor 7.78	ea	$7.78	$524.82	$532.60
Stain-grade fir entry door, high grade *Replace* Materials....627.00 Labor ....8.82 *Remove* .... Labor 7.78	ea	$7.78	$635.82	$643.60
Stain-grade fir entry door, deluxe grade *Replace* Materials....803.00 Labor ....8.82 *Remove* .... Labor 7.78	ea	$7.78	$811.82	$819.60
Stain-grade fir entry door, custom grade *Replace* Materials...1180.00 Labor ....8.82 *Remove* .... Labor 7.78	ea	$7.78	$1,188.82	$1,196.60
Stain-grade fir entry door, custom deluxe grade *Replace* Materials...1570.00 Labor ....8.82 *Remove* .... Labor 7.78	ea	$7.78	$1,578.82	$1,586.60

Entry Door Grades

Standard grade Multiple panel doors (nine and more) with some embossed components. May have lites in place of panels.

High grade Same as Standard grade with some embossed and carved components. Also may have carved on-lays.

Fir entry door side-lite ▶
Includes jamb & casing. Also see quality grades above and below.

Item Description	Unit	Remove	Replace	Total
Stain-grade fir entry door side-lite, standard grade *Replace* Materials....334.00 Labor...........47.40 *Remove* .... Labor...........14.00	ea	$14.00	$381.40	$395.40
Stain-grade fir entry door side-lite, high grade *Replace* Materials....431.00 Labor...........47.40 *Remove* .... Labor...........14.00	ea	$14.00	$478.40	$492.40
Stain-grade fir entry door side-lite, deluxe grade *Replace* Materials....536.00 Labor...........47.40 *Remove* .... Labor...........14.00	ea	$14.00	$583.40	$597.40
Stain-grade fir entry door side-lite, custom grade *Replace* Materials.....819.00 Labor...........47.40 *Remove* .... Labor...........14.00	ea	$14.00	$866.40	$880.40
Stain-grade fir entry door side-lite, custom deluxe grade *Replace* Materials...1100.00 Labor...........47.40 *Remove* .... Labor...........14.00	ea	$14.00	$1,147.40	$1,161.40

Entry Door Grades

Deluxe grade Door components have moderate carvings. May have exotic wood components.

Custom grade Door components have extensive carvings. May have exotic wood components, leaded glass or beveled glass.

Custom Deluxe grade Same as Custom grade with oval or elliptical-top windows.

Item Description	Unit	Remove	Replace	Total
Mahogany entry door, standard grade *Replace* Materials....438.00 Labor...........17.10 *Remove* .... Labor............7.78	ea	$7.78	$455.10	$462.88
Mahogany entry door, high grade *Replace* Materials....666.00 Labor...........17.10 *Remove* .... Labor............7.78	ea	$7.78	$683.10	$690.88
Mahogany entry door, deluxe grade *Replace* Materials..1030.00 Labor...........17.10 *Remove* .... Labor............7.78	ea	$7.78	$1,047.10	$1,054.88
Mahogany entry door, custom grade *Replace* Materials...1370.00 Labor...........17.10 *Remove* .... Labor............7.78	ea	$7.78	$1,387.10	$1,394.88
Mahogany entry door, custom deluxe grade *Replace* Materials...1740.00 Labor...........17.10 *Remove* .... Labor............7.78	ea	$7.78	$1,757.10	$1,764.88
Mahogany entry door side-lite, standard grade *Replace* Materials....302.00 Labor...........47.40 *Remove* .... Labor...........14.00	ea	$14.00	$349.40	$363.40
Mahogany entry door side-lite, high grade *Replace* Materials.....455.00 Labor...........47.40 *Remove* .... Labor...........14.00	ea	$14.00	$502.40	$516.40
Mahogany entry door side-lite, deluxe grade *Replace* Materials....721.00 Labor...........47.40 *Remove* .... Labor...........14.00	ea	$14.00	$768.40	$782.40
Mahogany entry door side-lite, custom grade *Replace* Materials....963.00 Labor...........47.40 *Remove* .... Labor...........14.00	ea	$14.00	$1,010.40	$1,024.40
Mahogany entry door side-lite, custom deluxe grade *Replace* Materials...1240.00 Labor...........47.40 *Remove* .... Labor...........14.00	ea	$14.00	$1,287.40	$1,301.40
Ash or oak entry door, standard grade *Replace* Materials.....418.00 Labor...........17.10 *Remove* .... Labor............7.78	ea	$7.78	$435.10	$442.88
Ash or oak entry door, high grade *Replace* Materials....647.00 Labor...........17.10 *Remove* .... Labor............7.78	ea	$7.78	$664.10	$671.88
Ash or oak entry door, deluxe grade *Replace* Materials....862.00 Labor...........17.10 *Remove* .... Labor............7.78	ea	$7.78	$879.10	$886.88
Ash or oak entry door, custom grade *Replace* Materials...1450.00 Labor...........17.10 *Remove* .... Labor............7.78	ea	$7.78	$1,467.10	$1,474.88
Ash or red entry door, custom deluxe grade *Replace* Materials..1840.00 Labor...........17.10 *Remove* .... Labor............7.78	ea	$7.78	$1,857.10	$1,864.88

◄ **MAHOGANY ENTRY DOOR**
For exterior jamb & casing see page 116. Also see quality indicators on facing page.

WOOD EMBOSSING

Wood is often embossed to appear like it has been carved. Embossing stamps a pattern onto the wood.

Embossing is far less expensive than carving and can only be used for relatively shallow patterns.

◄ **MAHOGANY DOOR SIDE-LITE**
Includes jamb & casing. Also see quality indicators on facing page.

WOOD ONLAYS

Wood onlays are mass-produced carved wood components that are nailed and glued on doors to give a hand-carved look.

◄ **ASH OR OAK ENTRY DOOR**
See exterior jamb & casing on page 116. Also see quality indicators on facing page.

RELATED ITEMS

Cleaning........................57
Door Hardware..........127
Finish Carpentry..........201
Painting......................334

Ash or oak entry door side-lite

Includes jamb & casing. Also see quality indicators on page 112.

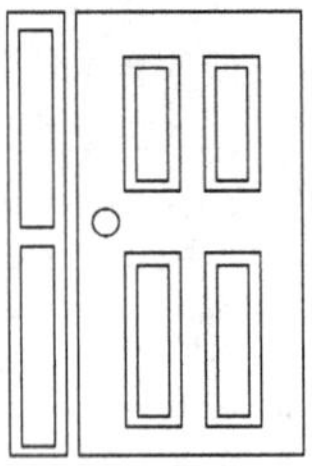

Item Description	Unit	Remove	Replace	Total
Ash or oak entry door side-lite, standard grade *Replace* Materials....282.00 Labor...........47.40 *Remove* .... Labor...........14.00	ea	$14.00	$329.40	$343.40
Ash or oak entry door side-lite, high grade *Replace* Materials ....457.00 Labor...........47.40 *Remove* .... Labor...........14.00	ea	$14.00	$504.40	$518.40
Ash or oak entry door side-lite, deluxe grade *Replace* Materials....564.00 Labor...........47.40 *Remove* .... Labor...........14.00	ea	$14.00	$611.40	$625.40
Ash or oak entry door side-lite, custom grade *Replace* Materials..1030.00 Labor...........47.40 *Remove* .... Labor...........14.00	ea	$14.00	$1,077.40	$1,091.40
Ash or oak entry door side-lite, custom deluxe grade *Replace* Materials..1300.00 Labor...........47.40 *Remove* .... Labor...........14.00	ea	$14.00	$1,347.40	$1,361.40

Redwood entry door

For exterior jamb & casing see page 116. Also see quality indicators on page 112.

Item Description	Unit	Remove	Replace	Total
Redwood entry door, standard grade *Replace* Materials....536.00 Labor...........17.10 *Remove* .... Labor...........7.78	ea	$7.78	$553.10	$560.88
Redwood entry door, high grade *Replace* Materials ....875.00 Labor...........17.10 *Remove* .... Labor...........7.78	ea	$7.78	$892.10	$899.88
Redwood entry door, deluxe grade *Replace* Materials....1110.00 Labor...........17.10 *Remove* .... Labor...........7.78	ea	$7.78	$1,127.10	$1,134.88
Redwood entry door, custom grade *Replace* Materials...1510.00 Labor...........17.10 *Remove* .... Labor...........7.78	ea	$7.78	$1,527.10	$1,534.88
Redwood entry door, custom deluxe grade *Replace* Materials...1730.00 Labor...........17.10 *Remove* .... Labor...........7.78	ea	$7.78	$1,747.10	$1,754.88

Redwood entry door side-lite

Includes jamb & casing. Also see quality indicators on page 112.

Item Description	Unit	Remove	Replace	Total
Redwood entry door side-lite, standard grade *Replace* Materials....353.00 Labor...........47.40 *Remove* .... Labor...........14.00	ea	$14.00	$400.40	$414.40
Redwood entry door side-lite, high grade *Replace* Materials....608.00 Labor...........47.40 *Remove* .... Labor...........14.00	ea	$14.00	$655.40	$669.40
Redwood entry door side-lite, deluxe grade *Replace* Materials ....785.00 Labor...........47.40 *Remove* .... Labor...........14.00	ea	$14.00	$832.40	$846.40
Redwood entry door side-lite, custom grade *Replace* Materials ..1060.00 Labor...........47.40 *Remove* .... Labor...........14.00	ea	$14.00	$1,107.40	$1,121.40
Redwood entry door side-lite, custom deluxe grade *Replace* Materials...1230.00 Labor...........47.40 *Remove* .... Labor...........14.00	ea	$14.00	$1,277.40	$1,291.40

Item Description	Unit	Remove	Replace	Total
Cypress entry door, standard grade ***Replace*** Materials....489.00 Labor...........17.10 ***Remove*** .... Labor 7.78	ea	$7.78	$506.10	$513.88
Cypress entry door, high grade ***Replace*** Materials....653.00 Labor...........17.10 ***Remove*** .... Labor 7.78	ea	$7.78	$670.10	$677.88
Cypress entry door, deluxe grade ***Replace*** Materials....827.00 Labor...........17.10 ***Remove*** .... Labor 7.78	ea	$7.78	$844.10	$851.88
Cypress entry door, custom grade ***Replace*** Materials...1190.00 Labor...........17.10 ***Remove*** .... Labor 7.78	ea	$7.78	$1,207.10	$1,214.88
Cypress entry door, custom deluxe grade ***Replace*** Materials...1550.00 Labor...........17.10 ***Remove*** .... Labor 7.78	ea	$7.78	$1,567.10	$1,574.88
Cypress entry door side-lite, standard grade ***Replace*** Materials....333.00 Labor...........47.40 ***Remove*** .... Labor...........14.00	ea	$14.00	$380.40	$394.40
Cypress entry door side-lite, high grade ***Replace*** Materials....447.00 Labor...........47.40 ***Remove*** .... Labor...........14.00	ea	$14.00	$494.40	$508.40
Cypress entry door side-lite, deluxe grade ***Replace*** Materials.....576.00 Labor...........47.40 ***Remove*** .... Labor...........14.00	ea	$14.00	$623.40	$637.40
Cypress entry door side-lite, custom grade ***Replace*** Materials....843.00 Labor...........47.40 ***Remove*** .... Labor...........14.00	ea	$14.00	$890.40	$904.40
Cypress entry door side-lite, custom deluxe grade ***Replace*** Materials...1100.00 Labor...........47.40 ***Remove*** .... Labor...........14.00	ea	$14.00	$1,147.40	$1,161.40
Walnut or cherry entry door, standard grade ***Replace*** Materials....686.00 Labor...........17.10 ***Remove*** .... Labor 7.78	ea	$7.78	$703.10	$710.88
Walnut or cherry entry door, high grade ***Replace*** Materials..1030.00 Labor...........17.10 ***Remove*** .... Labor 7.78	ea	$7.78	$1,047.10	$1,054.88
Walnut or cherry entry door, deluxe grade ***Replace*** Materials...1290.00 Labor...........17.10 ***Remove*** .... Labor 7.78	ea	$7.78	$1,307.10	$1,314.88
Walnut or cherry entry door, custom grade ***Replace*** Materials...1930.00 Labor...........17.10 ***Remove*** .... Labor 7.78	ea	$7.78	$1,947.10	$1,954.88
Walnut or cherry entry door, custom deluxe grade ***Replace*** Materials..2500.00 Labor...........17.10 ***Remove*** .... Labor 7.78	ea	$7.78	$2,517.10	$2,524.88

◄ **CYPRESS ENTRY DOOR**
For exterior jamb & casing see page 116. Also see quality indicators on page 112.

◄ **CYPRESS DOOR SIDE-LITE**
Includes jamb & casing. Also see quality indicators on page 112.

◄ **WALNUT OR CHERRY ENTRY DOOR**
For exterior jamb & casing see page 116. Also see quality indicators on page 112.

RELATED ITEMS

	Item Description	Unit	Remove	Replace	Total
Walnut or cherry entry door side-lite ► Includes jamb & casing. Also see quality indicators on page 112.	**Walnut or cherry entry door side-lite, standard grade** *Replace* Materials....446.00 Labor..........47.40 *Remove* .... Labor..........14.00	ea	$14.00	$493.40	$507.40
	Walnut or cherry entry door side-lite, high grade *Replace* Materials....704.00 Labor..........47.40 *Remove* .... Labor..........14.00	ea	$14.00	$751.40	$765.40
	Walnut or cherry entry door side-lite, deluxe grade *Replace* Materials....899.00 Labor..........47.40 *Remove* .... Labor..........14.00	ea	$14.00	$946.40	$960.40
	Walnut or cherry entry door side-lite, custom grade *Replace* Materials...1370.00 Labor..........47.40 *Remove* .... Labor..........14.00	ea	$14.00	$1,417.40	$1,431.40
	Walnut or cherry entry door side-lite, custom deluxe grade *Replace* Materials...1790.00 Labor..........47.40 *Remove* .... Labor..........14.00	ea	$14.00	$1,837.40	$1,851.40
Remove exterior door & reinstall ►	**Remove exterior door, jamb, & casing for work, then reinstall** *Replace* .... Labor..........91.50	ea	—	$91.50	$91.50
	Remove exterior door slab for work, then reinstall *Replace* .... Labor..........12.10	ea	—	$12.10	$12.10
	Remove exterior double door, jamb, & casing for work, then reinstall *Replace* .... Labor........130.00	ea	—	$130.00	$130.00
	Remove exterior double door slab for work, then reinstall *Replace* .... Labor..........15.20	ea	—	$15.20	$15.20
Exterior door jamb & casing ►	**Paint-grade jamb & casing for exterior door** *Replace* Materials......44.40 Labor..........72.80 *Remove* .... Labor..........13.60	ea	$13.60	$117.20	$130.80
	Paint-grade jamb & casing for double exterior door *Replace* Materials......79.70 Labor........129.00 *Remove* .... Labor..........13.60	ea	$13.60	$208.70	$222.30
	Stain-grade pine jamb & casing for exterior door *Replace* Materials......52.30 Labor..........72.80 *Remove* .... Labor..........13.60	ea	$13.60	$125.10	$138.70
	Stain-grade pine jamb & casing for double exterior door *Replace* Materials......95.40 Labor........129.00 *Remove* .... Labor..........13.60	ea	$13.60	$224.40	$238.00
	Birch jamb & casing for exterior door *Replace* Materials......49.60 Labor..........72.80 *Remove* .... Labor..........13.60	ea	$13.60	$122.40	$136.00
	Birch jamb & casing for double exterior door *Replace* Materials......88.20 Labor........129.00 *Remove* .... Labor..........13.60	ea	$13.60	$217.20	$230.80
	Mahogany jamb & casing for exterior door *Replace* Materials......58.80 Labor..........72.80 *Remove* .... Labor..........13.60 ► Deduct **$5.50** for mahogany veneer jamb and casing.	ea	$13.60	$131.60	$145.20

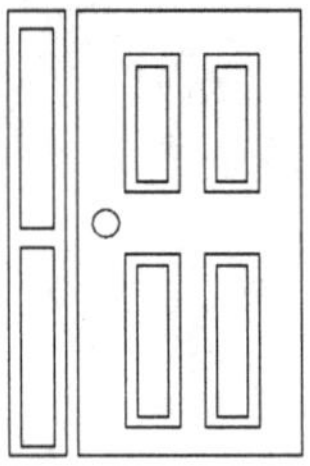

Item Description	Unit	Remove	Replace	Total
Mahogany jamb & casing for double exterior door ***Replace*** Materials....106.00 Labor.........129.00 ***Remove*** .... Labor...........13.60 ► Deduct **$8.20** for mahogany veneer jamb and casing.	ea	$13.60	$235.00	$248.60
Ash or oak jamb & casing for exterior door ***Replace*** Materials......62.10 Labor...........72.80 ***Remove*** .... Labor...........13.60 ► Deduct **$5.00** for ash or oak veneer jamb and casing.	ea	$13.60	$134.90	$148.50
Ash or oak jamb & casing for double exterior door ***Replace*** Materials.....111.00 Labor.........129.00 ***Remove*** .... Labor...........13.60 ► Deduct **$6.50** for ash or oak veneer jamb and casing.	ea	$13.60	$240.00	$253.60
Redwood jamb & casing for exterior door ***Replace*** Materials......55.50 Labor...........72.80 ***Remove*** .... Labor...........13.60	ea	$13.60	$128.30	$141.90
Redwood jamb & casing for double exterior door ***Replace*** Materials......99.30 Labor.........129.00 ***Remove*** .... Labor...........13.60	ea	$13.60	$228.30	$241.90
Cypress jamb & casing for exterior door ***Replace*** Materials......51.60 Labor...........72.80 ***Remove*** .... Labor...........13.60	ea	$13.60	$124.40	$138.00
Cypress jamb & casing for double exterior door ***Replace*** Materials......94.70 Labor.........129.00 ***Remove*** .... Labor...........13.60	ea	$13.60	$223.70	$237.30
Walnut or cherry jamb & casing for exterior door ***Replace*** Materials......73.20 Labor...........72.80 ***Remove*** .... Labor...........13.60 ► Deduct **$5.50** for walnut or cherry veneer jamb and casing.	ea	$13.60	$146.00	$159.60
Walnut or cherry jamb & casing for double exterior door ***Replace*** Materials.....125.00 Labor.........129.00 ***Remove*** .... Labor...........13.60 ► Deduct **$6.50** for walnut or cherry veneer jamb and casing.	ea	$13.60	$254.00	$267.60
Steel jamb & casing for exterior door ***Replace*** Materials......71.90 Labor...........72.80 ***Remove*** .... Labor...........13.60	ea	$13.60	$144.70	$158.30
Steel jamb & casing for double exterior door ***Replace*** Materials....105.00 Labor.........129.00 ***Remove*** .... Labor...........13.60	ea	$13.60	$234.00	$247.60
Add for hanging exterior Dutch door ***Replace*** .... Labor...........72.80	ea	—	$72.80	$72.80
Add for jamb & casing for a round- or elliptical-top door ***Replace*** Materials....150.00	ea	—	$150.00	$150.00
Fanlite for single entry door, standard grade ***Replace*** Materials....186.00 Labor..........77.00 ***Remove*** .... Labor..........20.60	ea	$20.60	$263.00	$283.60

RELATED ITEMS

◄ **ADDITIONAL EXTERIOR JAMB & CASING COSTS**

◄ **ENTRY DOOR FANLITE**

For more info about fanlites see the following page.

	Item Description	Unit	Remove	Replace	Total
Fanlite ► *continued*	**Fanlite for single entry door, high grade** *Replace* Materials.....314.00 Labor..........77.00 *Remove* .... Labor..........20.60	ea	$20.60	$391.00	$411.60
	Fanlite for single entry door, deluxe grade *Replace* Materials....435.00 Labor..........77.00 *Remove* .... Labor..........20.60	ea	$20.60	$512.00	$532.60
	Fanlite for single entry door, custom grade *Replace* Materials....602.00 Labor..........77.00 *Remove* .... Labor..........20.60	ea	$20.60	$679.00	$699.60
	Fanlite for single entry door, custom deluxe grade *Replace* Materials....792.00 Labor..........77.00 *Remove* .... Labor..........20.60	ea	$20.60	$869.00	$889.60
	Remove entry door fanlite & casing for work, then reinstall *Replace* .... Labor.........130.00	ea	—	$130.00	$130.00
Additional fanlite sizes ► *Includes jamb & casing.*	**Add 34% for fanlite for single door with side-lite**				
	Add 85% for fanlite for single door with two side-lites				
	Add 99% for fanlite for double doors				
	Add 147% for fanlite for double doors with two side-lites				
Entry door fixed transom ► *Includes jamb & casing.*	**Fixed transom for entry door, standard grade** *Replace* Materials.....124.00 Labor...........41.60 *Remove* .... Labor..........25.40	ea	$25.40	$165.60	$191.00
	Fixed transom for entry door, high grade *Replace* Materials....209.00 Labor...........41.60 *Remove* .... Labor..........25.40	ea	$25.40	$250.60	$276.00
	Fixed transom for entry door, deluxe grade *Replace* Materials....349.00 Labor...........41.60 *Remove* .... Labor..........25.40	ea	$25.40	$390.60	$416.00
	Fixed transom for entry door, custom grade *Replace* Materials....507.00 Labor...........41.60 *Remove* .... Labor..........25.40	ea	$25.40	$548.60	$574.00
	Fixed transom for entry door, custom deluxe grade *Replace* Materials....721.00 Labor...........41.60 *Remove* .... Labor..........25.40	ea	$25.40	$762.60	$788.00
	Remove fixed transom & casing for work, then reinstall *Replace* .... Labor.........114.00	ea	—	$114.00	$114.00
Additional transom sizes ► *Includes jamb & casing.*	**Add 42% for fixed transom for single door with side-lite**				
	Add 65% for fixed transom for single door with two side-lites				
	Add 89% for fixed transom for double doors				
	Add 106% for fixed transom for double doors with two side-lites				
Cafe doors ► *Includes hardware.*	**Cafe doors (bar doors) louvered paint-grade** *Replace* Materials......91.50 Labor..........28.30 *Remove* .... Labor............6.99	ea	$6.99	$119.80	$126.79

Fanlite Quality

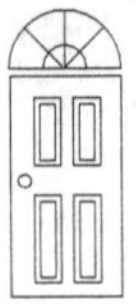

Fanlites are semi-circular or half-elliptical windows that appear above doors. True fanlites have mullions that fan out from the bottom center of the lite. Lower grades will have a simulated fan grid.

All fanlites include jamb and casing. Grades match entry door grades found on page 112.

Fixed Transoms

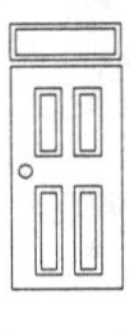

Fixed transoms are rectangular windows that appear above doors. Transoms may have circular, semi-circular, or elliptical components, but the unit fits in a rectangular jamb.

All transoms include jamb and casing. Grades match exterior door grades found on page 112.

Item Description	Unit	Remove	Replace	Total
Cafe doors (bar doors) louvered stain-grade	ea	$6.99	$143.30	$150.29
Replace Materials.....115.00 Labor..........28.30				
Remove .... Labor............6.99				
Cafe doors (bar doors) Victorian spindle & raised-panel paint-grade	ea	$6.99	$146.30	$153.29
Replace Materials.....118.00 Labor..........28.30				
Remove .... Labor............6.99				
Cafe doors (bar doors) Victorian spindle & raised-panel stain-grade	ea	$6.99	$174.30	$181.29
Replace Materials....146.00 Labor..........28.30				
Remove .... Labor............6.99				
Remove cafe doors for work, then reinstall	ea	—	$42.40	$42.40
Replace .... Labor...........42.40				
6′ wide by 6′8″ tall bronze finish sliding patio door single-glazed	ea	$51.40	$627.00	$678.40
Replace Materials....444.00 Labor.........183.00				
Remove .... Labor...........51.40				
6′ wide by 6′8″ tall mill finish sliding patio door double-glazed	ea	$51.40	$784.00	$835.40
Replace Materials....601.00 Labor.........183.00				
Remove .... Labor...........51.40				
8′ wide by 6′8″ tall bronze finish sliding patio door single-glazed	ea	$51.40	$721.00	$772.40
Replace Materials....538.00 Labor.........183.00				
Remove .... Labor...........51.40				
8′ wide by 6′8″ tall mill finish sliding patio door double-glazed	ea	$51.40	$889.00	$940.40
Replace Materials....706.00 Labor.........183.00				
Remove .... Labor...........51.40				
12′ wide by 6′8″ tall bronze finish sliding patio door single-glazed	ea	$77.30	$1,044.00	$1,121.30
Replace Materials....805.00 Labor.........239.00				
Remove .... Labor..........77.30				
► 3 lites				
12′ by 6′8″ mill finish sliding patio door double-glazed	ea	$77.30	$1,369.00	$1,446.30
Replace Materials...1130.00 Labor.........239.00				
Remove .... Labor..........77.30				
► 3 lites.				
6′ by 6′8″ wood sliding patio door single-glazed	ea	$51.40	$1,137.00	$1,188.40
Replace Materials....954.00 Labor.........183.00				
Remove .... Labor...........51.40				
6′ by 6′8″ wood sliding patio door double-glazed	ea	$51.40	$1,243.00	$1,294.40
Replace Materials..1060.00 Labor.........183.00				
Remove .... Labor...........51.40				
8′ by 6′8″ wood sliding patio door single-glazed	ea	$51.40	$1,323.00	$1,374.40
Replace Materials...1140.00 Labor.........183.00				
Remove .... Labor...........51.40				
8′ by 6′8″ wood sliding patio door double-glazed	ea	$51.40	$1,463.00	$1,514.40
Replace Materials..1280.00 Labor.........183.00				
Remove .... Labor...........51.40				
12′ by 6′8″ wood sliding patio door single-glazed (3 lites)	ea	$77.30	$1,959.00	$2,036.30
Replace Materials...1720.00 Labor.........239.00				
Remove .... Labor..........77.30				

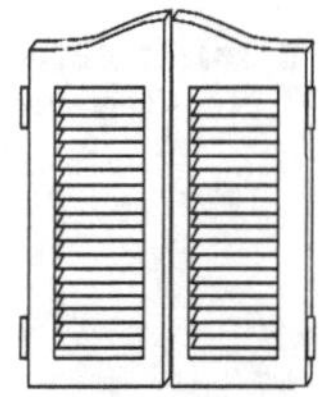

◄ SLIDING PATIO DOOR

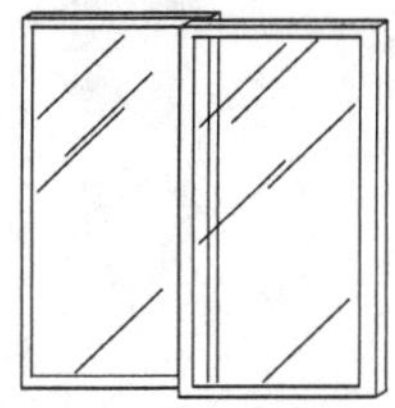

△ *two lite patio door*

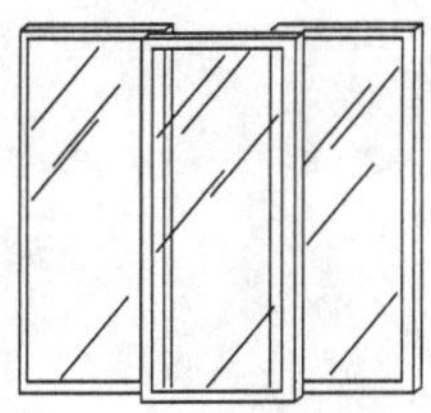

△ *three lite patio door*

RELATED ITEMS

Cleaning........................57
Door Hardware...........127
Finish Carpentry..........201
Painting.......................334

	Item Description	Unit	Remove	Replace	Total
Sliding patio ▸ door *continued*	**12′ by 6′8″ wood sliding patio door double-glazed (3 lites)** ***Replace*** Materials ..1890.00 Labor.........239.00 ***Remove*** .... Labor 77.30	ea	$77.30	$2,129.00	$2,206.30
	6′ by 6′8″ wood sliding patio door single-glazed clad exterior ***Replace*** Materials.....967.00 Labor.........183.00 ***Remove*** .... Labor...........51.40	ea	$51.40	$1,150.00	$1,201.40
	6′ by 6′8″ wood sliding patio door double-glazed clad exterior ***Replace*** Materials ...1180.00 Labor.........183.00 ***Remove*** .... Labor...........51.40	ea	$51.40	$1,363.00	$1,414.40
	8′ by 6′8″ wood sliding patio door single-glazed clad exterior ***Replace*** Materials ...1130.00 Labor.........239.00 ***Remove*** .... Labor...........51.40	ea	$51.40	$1,369.00	$1,420.40
	8′ by 6′8″ wood sliding patio door double-glazed clad exterior ***Replace*** Materials ..1380.00 Labor.........239.00 ***Remove*** .... Labor...........51.40	ea	$51.40	$1,619.00	$1,670.40
	12′ by 6′8″ wood sliding patio door single-glazed clad exterior ***Replace*** Materials ...1760.00 Labor.........239.00 ***Remove*** .... Labor ....77.30 ▸ 3 lites.	ea	$77.30	$1,999.00	$2,076.30
	12′ by 6′8″ wood sliding patio door double-glazed clad exterior ***Replace*** Materials..2300.00 Labor.........239.00 ***Remove*** .... Labor 77.30	ea	$77.30	$2,539.00	$2,616.30
Additional ▸ sliding patio door costs	**Add for sliding patio door tinted glass (per lite)** ***Replace*** Materials.....218.00	ea	—	$218.00	$218.00
	Remove sliding patio door, jamb, & casing for work, then reinstall ***Replace*** .... Labor.........231.00	ea	—	$231.00	$231.00
	Remove sliding patio door lites for work, then reinstall ***Replace*** .... Labor 68.60	ea	—	$68.60	$68.60
	Minimum charge for sliding glass patio door work ***Replace*** Materials ......26.00 Labor 135.00	ea	—	$161.00	$161.00
	Recondition sliding glass patio door, replace hardware ***Replace*** Materials ......59.00 Labor...........96.90	ea	—	$155.90	$155.90
Sliding patio ▸ door screen	**36″ sliding patio door screen** ***Replace*** Materials ......58.80 Labor ....5.20 ***Remove*** .... Labor 3.44	ea	$3.44	$64.00	$67.44
	48″ sliding patio door screen ***Replace*** Materials ......73.20 Labor ....5.20 ***Remove*** .... Labor 3.44	ea	$3.44	$78.40	$81.84
Pet door ▸ *Includes lock, aluminum frame, and PVC door.*	**Pet door for small dogs, cats** ***Replace*** Materials ......52.30 Labor...........35.10 ***Remove*** .... Labor 8.00	ea	$8.00	$87.40	$95.40
	Pet door for average size dogs ***Replace*** Materials ......91.50 Labor...........35.10 ***Remove*** .... Labor 8.00	ea	$8.00	$126.60	$134.60

Item Description	*Unit*	*Remove*	*Replace*	*Total*
Pet door for large dogs *Replace* Materials....144.00 Labor...........35.10 *Remove* .... Labor............8.00	ea	$8.00	$179.10	$187.10
Remove pet door for work, then reinstall *Replace* Materials........6.50 Labor..........53.70	ea	—	$60.20	$60.20
8′ garage door with hardware, economy grade *Replace* Materials....372.00 Labor.........260.00 *Remove* .... Labor.........100.00	ea	$100.00	$632.00	$732.00
8′ garage door with hardware, standard grade *Replace* Materials....431.00 Labor.........260.00 *Remove* .... Labor.........100.00	ea	$100.00	$691.00	$791.00
8′ garage door with hardware, high grade *Replace* Materials....594.00 Labor.........260.00 *Remove* .... Labor.........100.00	ea	$100.00	$854.00	$954.00
8′ garage door with hardware, deluxe grade *Replace* Materials....666.00 Labor.........260.00 *Remove* .... Labor.........100.00	ea	$100.00	$926.00	$1,026.00
9′ garage door with hardware, economy grade *Replace* Materials....405.00 Labor.........260.00 *Remove* .... Labor.........100.00	ea	$100.00	$665.00	$765.00
9′ garage door with hardware, standard grade *Replace* Materials....551.00 Labor.........260.00 *Remove* .... Labor.........100.00	ea	$100.00	$811.00	$911.00
9′ garage door with hardware, high grade *Replace* Materials....647.00 Labor.........260.00 *Remove* .... Labor.........100.00	ea	$100.00	$907.00	$1,007.00
9′ garage door with hardware, deluxe grade *Replace* Materials....732.00 Labor.........260.00 *Remove* .... Labor.........100.00	ea	$100.00	$992.00	$1,092.00
10′ garage door with hardware, economy grade *Replace* Materials....464.00 Labor.........260.00 *Remove* .... Labor.........100.00	ea	$100.00	$724.00	$824.00
10′ garage door with hardware, standard grade *Replace* Materials....575.00 Labor.........260.00 *Remove* .... Labor.........100.00	ea	$100.00	$835.00	$935.00
10′ garage door with hardware, high grade *Replace* Materials.....712.00 Labor.........260.00 *Remove* .... Labor.........100.00	ea	$100.00	$972.00	$1,072.00
10′ garage door with hardware, deluxe grade *Replace* Materials.....810.00 Labor.........260.00 *Remove* .... Labor.........100.00	ea	$100.00	$1,070.00	$1,170.00
12′ garage door with hardware, economy grade *Replace* Materials....523.00 Labor.........260.00 *Remove* .... Labor.........100.00	ea	$100.00	$783.00	$883.00
12′ garage door with hardware, standard grade *Replace* Materials....647.00 Labor.........260.00 *Remove* .... Labor.........100.00	ea	$100.00	$907.00	$1,007.00

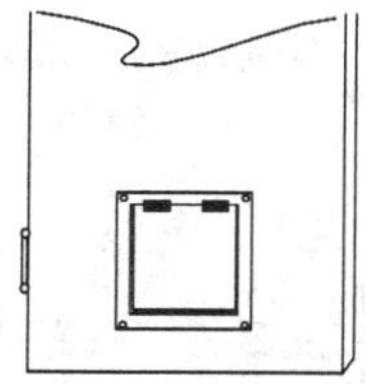

◄ **Garage door**

Garage Door Grades

Economy grade
Overhead doors that are plastic-faced polystyrene or flush steel or uninsulated fiberglass. Single-piece doors with flush surface or tongue-and-groove boards in herringbone or chevron patterns.

Standard grade
Overhead doors that are textured or embossed steel, aluminum or fiberglass, usually insulated. Single-piece doors same as economy grade with lites, and paneled patterns.

High grade
Overhead doors are same as standard grade with lites. Single-piece stain-grade wood doors with lites and carvings.

Deluxe grade
Overhead doors are stain-grade wood doors, specialty patterns, designed carvings or embossing, fan-tops, and so forth.

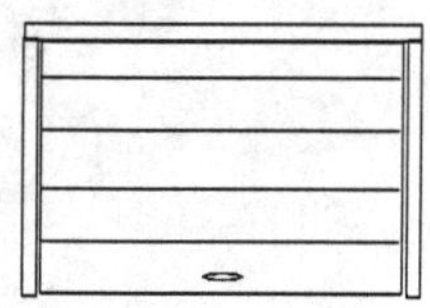

△ *economy*

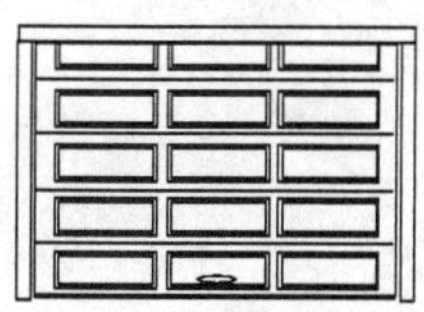

△ *standard*

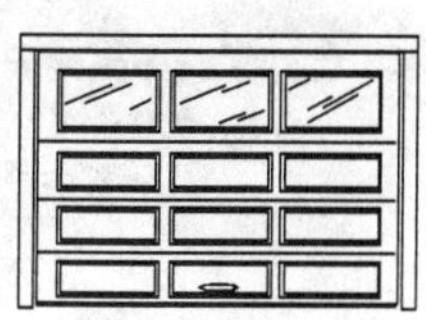

△ *high*

GARAGE DOOR ▶ *continued*

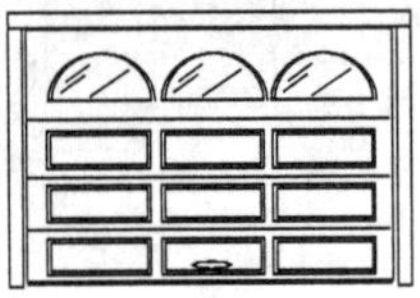

△ *deluxe*

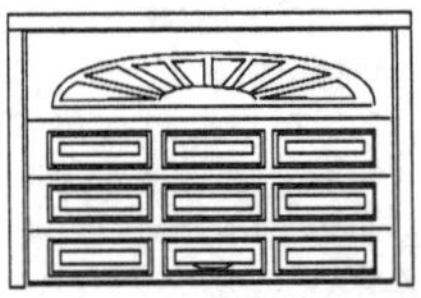

△ *deluxe (fanlite)*

Item Description	Unit	Remove	Replace	Total
12′ garage door with hardware, high grade ***Replace*** Materials.....817.00 Labor.........260.00 ***Remove*** .... Labor.........100.00	ea	$100.00	$1,077.00	$1,177.00
12′ garage door with hardware, deluxe grade ***Replace*** Materials....973.00 Labor.........260.00 ***Remove*** .... Labor.........100.00	ea	$100.00	$1,233.00	$1,333.00
14′ garage door with hardware, economy grade ***Replace*** Materials....559.00 Labor.........260.00 ***Remove*** .... Labor.........100.00	ea	$100.00	$819.00	$919.00
14′ garage door with hardware, standard grade ***Replace*** Materials....666.00 Labor.........260.00 ***Remove*** .... Labor.........100.00	ea	$100.00	$926.00	$1,026.00
14′ garage door with hardware, high grade ***Replace*** Materials.....817.00 Labor.........260.00 ***Remove*** .... Labor.........100.00	ea	$100.00	$1,077.00	$1,177.00
14′ garage door with hardware, deluxe grade ***Replace*** Materials....993.00 Labor.........260.00 ***Remove*** .... Labor.........100.00	ea	$100.00	$1,253.00	$1,353.00
16′ garage door with hardware, economy grade ***Replace*** Materials....608.00 Labor.........260.00 ***Remove*** .... Labor.........100.00	ea	$100.00	$868.00	$968.00
16′ garage door with hardware, standard grade ***Replace*** Materials....771.00 Labor.........260.00 ***Remove*** .... Labor.........100.00	ea	$100.00	$1,031.00	$1,131.00
16′ garage door with hardware, high grade ***Replace*** Materials.....915.00 Labor.........260.00 ***Remove*** .... Labor.........100.00	ea	$100.00	$1,175.00	$1,275.00
16′ garage door with hardware, deluxe grade ***Replace*** Materials..1060.00 Labor.........260.00 ***Remove*** .... Labor.........100.00	ea	$100.00	$1,320.00	$1,420.00
18′ garage door with hardware, economy grade ***Replace*** Materials....666.00 Labor.........260.00 ***Remove*** .... Labor.........100.00	ea	$100.00	$926.00	$1,026.00
18′ garage door with hardware, standard grade ***Replace*** Materials.....817.00 Labor.........260.00 ***Remove*** .... Labor.........100.00	ea	$100.00	$1,077.00	$1,177.00
18′ garage door with hardware, high grade ***Replace*** Materials....954.00 Labor.........260.00 ***Remove*** .... Labor.........100.00	ea	$100.00	$1,214.00	$1,314.00
18′ garage door with hardware, deluxe grade ***Replace*** Materials...1120.00 Labor.........260.00 ***Remove*** .... Labor.........100.00	ea	$100.00	$1,380.00	$1,480.00
GARAGE DOOR ▶ OPENER — **Garage door opener, standard grade** ***Replace*** Materials....300.00 Labor.........102.00 ***Remove*** .... Labor...........21.00	ea	$21.00	$402.00	$423.00

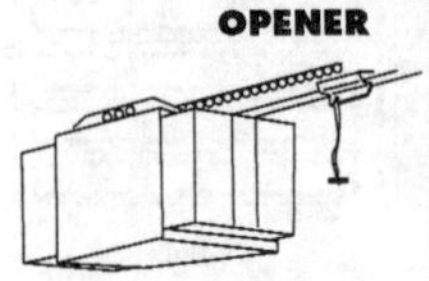

Item Description	Unit	Remove	Replace	Total
Garage door opener, high grade ***Replace*** Materials....327.00 Labor.........102.00 ***Remove*** .... Labor..........21.00	ea	$21.00	$429.00	$450.00
Garage door opener, deluxe grade ***Replace*** Materials....359.00 Labor.........102.00 ***Remove*** .... Labor..........21.00	ea	$21.00	$461.00	$482.00
Remote radio transmitter for overhead door opener ***Replace*** Materials......38.00	ea	—	$38.00	$38.00
Remove garage door opener for work, then reinstall ***Replace*** .... Labor.........146.00	ea	—	$146.00	$146.00
Replace garage door spring ***Replace*** Materials......54.00 Labor..........83.20	ea	—	$137.20	$137.20
Remove single-car garage door for work, then reinstall ***Replace*** .... Labor.........320.00	ea	—	$320.00	$320.00
Remove two-car garage door for work, then reinstall ***Replace*** .... Labor.........385.00	ea	—	$385.00	$385.00
Minimum charge for garage door work ***Replace*** Materials......33.00 Labor.........104.00	ea	—	$137.00	$137.00
Add 14% for 7′ tall doors				
Add 22% for 8′ tall doors				

RELATED ITEMS

Cleaning........................57
Door Hardware...........127
Finish Carpentry..........201
Painting.......................334

◁ **garage door spring**

◁ **remove and reinstall**

◀ **ADD FOR TALL DOOR**
All door types.

NOTES:

end

Time & Material Charts *(selected items)*

Doors Materials

See **Doors** material prices with the line items and other information in the **QuickFinder** column.

Doors Labor

Laborer	Base Wage	Paid Leave	True Wage	FICA	FUTA	Worker's Comp.	Unemploy. Insur.	Health Insur.	Retire (401k)	Liability Insur.	Cost per Hour
Finish carpenter	$23.60	1.84	$25.44	1.95	.20	4.96	2.21	2.69	.76	3.43	$41.60
Demolition laborer	$13.90	1.08	$14.98	1.15	.12	4.79	1.30	2.69	.45	2.02	$27.50

Paid Leave is calculated based on two weeks paid vacation, one week sick leave, and seven paid holidays. Employer's matching portion of **FICA** is 7.65 percent. **FUTA** (Federal Unemployment) is .8 percent. **Worker's compensation** for the doors trade was calculated using a national average of 19.50 percent. **Unemployment insurance** was calculated using a national average of 8.7 percent. **Health insurance** was calculated based on a projected national average for 2002 of $535 per employee (and family when applicable) per month. Employer pays 80 percent for a per month cost of $428 per employee. **Retirement** is based on a 401(k) retirement program with employer matching of 50 percent. Employee contributions to the 401(k) plan are an average of 6 percent of the true wage. **Liability insurance** is based on a national average of 13.2 percent.

Doors Labor Productivity

Work Description	Laborer	Cost per Hour	Productivity	Unit Price
Demolition				
folding door	demolition laborer	$27.50	.114	$3.14 ea
bypassing door	demolition laborer	$27.50	.139	$3.82 ea
bypassing or folding door jamb & casing	demolition laborer	$27.50	.026	$.72 lf
pre-hung interior door, jamb, & casing	demolition laborer	$27.50	.388	$10.70 ea
pre-hung interior door slab only	demolition laborer	$27.50	.217	$5.97 ea
double pre-hung interior door, jamb, & casing	demolition laborer	$27.50	.585	$16.10 ea
double pre-hung interior door slabs only	demolition laborer	$27.50	.321	$8.80 ea
garage door, overhead tracks, jamb, & casing	demolition laborer	$27.50	3.65	$100.00 ea
garage door, hardware, jamb, & casing	demolition laborer	$27.50	2.90	$80.00 ea
garage door only	demolition laborer	$27.50	1.82	$50.10 ea
garage door opener	demolition laborer	$27.50	.765	$21.00 ea
pocket door, jamb, & casing	demolition laborer	$27.50	1.02	$28.10 ea
pocket door slab only	demolition laborer	$27.50	.491	$13.50 ea
double pocket door, jamb, & casing	demolition laborer	$27.50	1.86	$51.20 ea
double pocket door slab only	demolition laborer	$27.50	.913	$25.10 ea
pocket door hardware	demolition laborer	$27.50	.496	$13.60 ea
double pocket door hardware	demolition laborer	$27.50	.733	$20.20 ea
panel door, jamb, & casing	demolition laborer	$27.50	.477	$13.10 ea
panel door slab only	demolition laborer	$27.50	.217	$5.97 ea
transom	demolition laborer	$27.50	.451	$12.40 ea
entry door fanlite & casing	demolition laborer	$27.50	.749	$20.60 ea
double entry door fanlite & casing	demolition laborer	$27.50	1.71	$47.00 ea
storm door	demolition laborer	$27.50	.227	$6.24 ea
entry door, jamb, casing, & threshold	demolition laborer	$27.50	.496	$13.60 ea
entry door slab only	demolition laborer	$27.50	.283	$7.78 ea
double entry door, jamb, casing, & threshold	demolition laborer	$27.50	.842	$23.20 ea
double entry door slabs only	demolition laborer	$27.50	.492	$13.50 ea
entry door side-lite	demolition laborer	$27.50	.508	$14.00 ea
Dutch door slabs, jamb, & casing	demolition laborer	$27.50	.883	$24.30 ea
Dutch door slabs only	demolition laborer	$27.50	.321	$8.80 ea
cafe door	demolition laborer	$27.50	.254	$6.99 ea
sliding glass patio door (per lite)	demolition laborer	$27.50	.427	$11.70 ea
pet door	demolition laborer	$27.50	.290	$8.00 ea

. . . More ➢

Doors Labor Productivity *continued*

WORK DESCRIPTION	LABORER	COST PER HOUR	PRODUCTIVITY	UNIT PRICE
Minimum labor charge for door work				
minimum charge	finish carpenter	$41.60	2.50	**$104.00** ea
Install interior doors				
folding door per section	finish carpenter	$41.60	.394	**$16.40** ea
bypassing door per section	finish carpenter	$41.60	.755	**$31.40** ea
bypassing or folding door jamb & casing	finish carpenter	$41.60	.109	**$4.53** lf
pre-hung interior door & casing	finish carpenter	$41.60	1.43	**$59.50** ea
pre-hung interior door slab only	finish carpenter	$41.60	.215	**$8.94** ea
double pre-hung interior door & casing	finish carpenter	$41.60	2.45	**$102.00** ea
double pre-hung interior door slabs only	finish carpenter	$41.60	.412	**$17.10** ea
Install garage door				
with overhead tracks, jamb, & casing	finish carpenter	$41.60	6.25	**$260.00** ea
with hardware, jamb, & casing	finish carpenter	$41.60	5.21	**$217.00** ea
door only	finish carpenter	$41.60	3.15	**$131.00** ea
opener	finish carpenter	$41.60	2.45	**$102.00** ea
Install pocket door				
door slabs	finish carpenter	$41.60	.850	**$35.40** ea
door, jamb, trim, & casing	finish carpenter	$41.60	1.35	**$56.20** ea
double doors	finish carpenter	$41.60	2.34	**$97.30** ea
double door, jamb, trim, & casing	finish carpenter	$41.60	3.12	**$130.00** ea
Install pocket door rough framing package including track and hardware				
single door in 2" x 4" wall	finish carpenter	$41.60	1.50	**$62.40** ea
double doors in 2" x 4" wall	finish carpenter	$41.60	2.88	**$120.00** ea
single door in 2" x 6" wall	finish carpenter	$41.60	1.52	**$63.20** ea
double doors in 2" x 6" wall	finish carpenter	$41.60	2.95	**$123.00** ea
single door in 2" x 8" wall	finish carpenter	$41.60	1.54	**$64.10** ea
double doors in 2" x 8" wall	finish carpenter	$41.60	3.03	**$126.00** ea
rough framing for antique door	finish carpenter	$41.60	2.45	**$102.00** ea
rough framing for antique double doors	finish carpenter	$41.60	5.12	**$213.00** ea
Install pocket door track				
overhead track for antique door	finish carpenter	$41.60	1.30	**$54.10** ea
overhead track for antique double door	finish carpenter	$41.60	2.34	**$97.30** ea
clean and realign overhead antique door track	finish carpenter	$41.60	1.96	**$81.50** ea
floor track for antique door	finish carpenter	$41.60	1.21	**$50.30** ea
floor track for antique double door	finish carpenter	$41.60	2.20	**$91.50** ea
clean and realign floor antique doors	finish carpenter	$41.60	2.64	**$110.00** ea
Install panel door				
hang door & install casing	finish carpenter	$41.60	1.23	**$51.20** ea
slab only	finish carpenter	$41.60	.178	**$7.40** ea
Install entry door, fanlite, transom				
fanlite & casing	finish carpenter	$41.60	1.85	**$77.00** ea
transom & casing	finish carpenter	$41.60	1.00	**$41.60** ea
hang entry door & install casing	finish carpenter	$41.60	1.75	**$72.80** ea
slab only	finish carpenter	$41.60	.212	**$8.82** ea
hang double-entry door & casing	finish carpenter	$41.60	3.11	**$129.00** ea
double door slabs only	finish carpenter	$41.60	.330	**$13.70** ea
side-lite	finish carpenter	$41.60	1.14	**$47.40** ea
Install Dutch door				
hang door & install casing	finish carpenter	$41.60	1.70	**$70.70** ea
slabs only	finish carpenter	$41.60	.325	**$13.50** ea
Install door lite				
cut hole in door and install	finish carpenter	$41.60	1.12	**$46.60** ea
Install cafe door				
per set	finish carpenter	$41.60	.681	**$28.30** ea
Install sliding glass patio doors				
with two lites	finish carpenter	$41.60	4.39	**$183.00** ea
Install pet door				
per door	finish carpenter	$41.60	.844	**$35.10** ea

. . . More ➢

Doors Labor Productivity *continued*

Work Description	Laborer	Cost per Hour	Productivity	Unit Price
Assemble & install storm door				
per door	finish carpenter	$41.60	1.70	$70.70 ea
Remove for work, then reinstall				
folding doors per section	finish carpenter	$41.60	.148	$6.16 ea
bypass sliding doors per section	finish carpenter	$41.60	.220	$9.15 ea
door slab	finish carpenter	$41.60	.151	$6.28 ea
door slab, jamb & casing	finish carpenter	$41.60	1.63	$67.80 ea
double door slabs	finish carpenter	$41.60	.293	$12.20 ea
double door slabs, jamb & casing	finish carpenter	$41.60	2.67	$111.00 ea
pocket door & casing	finish carpenter	$41.60	1.15	$47.80 ea
pocket door, jamb & casing	finish carpenter	$41.60	3.23	$134.00 ea
double pocket doors & casing	finish carpenter	$41.60	1.58	$65.70 ea
double pocket doors, jamb & casing	finish carpenter	$41.60	3.39	$141.00 ea
panel door slab	finish carpenter	$41.60	.152	$6.32 ea
panel door, jamb, & casing	finish carpenter	$41.60	1.63	$67.80 ea
antique door casing & re-plumb door	finish carpenter	$41.60	2.95	$123.00 ea
transom	finish carpenter	$41.60	1.12	$46.60 ea
storm door	finish carpenter	$41.60	1.70	$70.70 ea
Dutch door, jamb, & casing	finish carpenter	$41.60	2.74	$114.00 ea
Dutch door slabs	finish carpenter	$41.60	.394	$16.40 ea
exterior door, jamb, & casing	finish carpenter	$41.60	2.20	$91.50 ea
exterior door slab	finish carpenter	$41.60	.292	$12.10 ea
exterior double door, jamb, & casing	finish carpenter	$41.60	3.12	$130.00 ea
exterior double door slabs	finish carpenter	$41.60	.366	$15.20 ea
entry door fanlite & casing	finish carpenter	$41.60	3.12	$130.00 ea
entry door fixed transom & casing	finish carpenter	$41.60	2.74	$114.00 ea
cafe door	finish carpenter	$41.60	1.02	$42.40 ea
sliding patio door, jamb, & casing	finish carpenter	$41.60	5.55	$231.00 ea
sliding patio door lites	finish carpenter	$41.60	1.65	$68.60 ea
pet door	finish carpenter	$41.60	1.29	$53.70 ea
garage door opener	finish carpenter	$41.60	3.50	$146.00 ea
single-car garage door	finish carpenter	$41.60	7.70	$320.00 ea
two-car garage door	finish carpenter	$41.60	9.25	$385.00 ea
Door repair				
minimum labor to repair antique panel door (no custom milling)	finish carpenter	$41.60	2.49	$104.00 ea
minimum labor charge to repair antique panel door when custom milling is required	finish carpenter	$41.60	3.51	$146.00 ea
replace antique panel door panel (not including custom knife charges)	finish carpenter	$41.60	2.74	$114.00 ea
replace antique panel door stile (not including custom knife charges)	finish carpenter	$41.60	2.49	$104.00 ea
repair cracks & dry rot in antique door with epoxy, tighten stiles	finish carpenter	$41.60	4.49	$187.00 ea
repair cracks & dry rot in antique door jamb with epoxy	finish carpenter	$41.60	3.40	$141.00 ea
repair cracks & dry rot in antique door casing with epoxy	finish carpenter	$41.60	3.40	$141.00 ea
Additional door labor charges				
add for installation of full-lite in exterior door	finish carpenter	$41.60	1.39	$57.80 ea
add for installation of half-lite in exterior door	finish carpenter	$41.60	1.07	$44.50 ea
add for installation of 1′ by 1′ lite in exterior door	finish carpenter	$41.60	.594	$24.70 ea
recondition sliding glass door, replace hardware	finish carpenter	$41.60	2.33	$96.90 ea
minimum labor for garage door work	finish carpenter	$41.60	2.50	$104.00 ea
minimum labor for sliding glass door work	finish carpenter	$41.60	3.25	$135.00 ea

11 .... Door Hardware

Item Description	Unit	Remove	Replace	Total
Deadbolt, standard grade *Replace* Material ....22.00 Labor ....28.20 *Remove* .... Labor 7.59l;	ea	$7.59	$50.20	$57.79
Deadbolt, high grade *Replace* Material ....34.00 Labor ....28.20 *Remove* .... Labor 7.59	ea	$7.59	$62.20	$69.79
Deadbolt, deluxe grade *Replace* Material ....39.00 Labor ....28.20 *Remove* .... Labor 7.59	ea	$7.59	$70.20	$77.79
Remove deadbolt for work, then reinstall *Replace* .... Labor...........45.80	ea	—	$45.80	$45.80
Exterior door keyed lockset, standard grade *Replace* Material ....23.00 Labor...........19.20 *Remove* .... Labor 8.64	ea	$8.64	$42.20	$50.84
Exterior door keyed lockset, high grade *Replace* Material........37.00 Labor...........19.20 *Remove* .... Labor 8.64	ea	$8.64	$56.20	$64.84
Exterior door keyed lockset, deluxe grade *Replace* Material........49.00 Labor...........19.20 *Remove* .... Labor 8.64	ea	$8.64	$68.20	$76.84
Remove exterior lockset for work, then reinstall *Replace* .... Labor...........42.80	ea	—	$42.80	$42.80
Entry door keyed lockset, standard grade *Replace* Material ....83.00 Labor ....60.30 *Remove* .... Labor...........19.10	ea	$19.10	$143.30	$162.40
Entry door keyed lockset, high grade *Replace* Material ......217.00 Labor ....60.30 *Remove* .... Labor...........19.10	ea	$19.10	$277.30	$296.40
Entry door keyed lockset, deluxe grade *Replace* Material......365.00 Labor ....60.30 *Remove* .... Labor...........19.10	ea	$19.10	$425.30	$444.40
Entry door keyed lockset, custom grade *Replace* Material .....508.00 Labor ....60.30 *Remove* .... Labor...........19.10	ea	$19.10	$568.30	$587.40
Remove entry door lockset for work, then reinstall *Replace* .... Labor..........114.00	ea	—	$114.00	$114.00
Antique style door thumb latch, standard grade *Replace* Material......224.00 Labor...........72.00 *Remove* .... Labor...........14.20	ea	$14.20	$296.00	$310.20

◄ **Deadbolt**

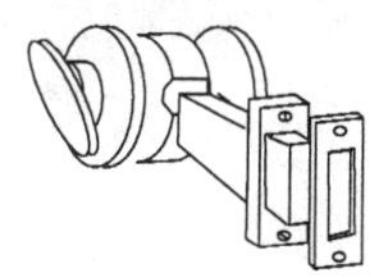

◄ **Exterior lockset**

◄ **Entry lockset**

Hardware Quality

Some rules of thumb:

Standard: Light gauge metal, chrome or brass plated with little or no pattern.

High: Brass, chrome over brass, or nickel over brass with minimal detail, or plated with ornate detail.

Deluxe: Brass, chrome over brass, or nickel over brass with moderate detail.

Custom: Brass, chrome over brass, or nickel over brass with ornate detail.

◄ **Thumb latch**

RELATED ITEMS

Bathroom Hardware......41
Doors..........................101

	Item Description	Unit	Remove	Replace	Total
Thumb latch ▶ *continued*	**Antique style door thumb latch, high grade** ***Replace*** Material......273.00 Labor..........72.00 ***Remove*** .... Labor..........14.20	ea	$14.20	$345.00	$359.20
Interior door lockset ▶ *See quality indicators on previous page.*	**Interior door lockset, standard grade** ***Replace*** Material........18.00 Labor..........16.80 ***Remove*** .... Labor...........7.73	ea	$7.73	$34.80	$42.53
	Interior door lockset, high grade ***Replace*** Material.......43.00 Labor..........16.80 ***Remove*** .... Labor...........7.73	ea	$7.73	$59.80	$67.53
	Interior door lockset, deluxe grade ***Replace*** Material........69.00 Labor..........16.80 ***Remove*** .... Labor...........7.73	ea	$7.73	$85.80	$93.53
	Remove interior door lockset for work, then reinstall ***Replace*** .... Labor..........29.50	ea	—	$29.50	$29.50
Door closer ▶ *See quality indicators on previous page.*	**Spring hinge door closer** ***Replace*** Material........17.00 Labor..........10.70 ***Remove*** .... Labor...........2.48	ea	$2.48	$27.70	$30.18
	Door closer, standard grade ***Replace*** Material.......43.00 Labor..........17.90 ***Remove*** .... Labor...........8.00	ea	$8.00	$60.90	$68.90
	Door closer, high grade ***Replace*** Material........76.00 Labor..........17.90 ***Remove*** .... Labor...........8.00	ea	$8.00	$93.90	$101.90
	Remove door closer for work, then reinstall ***Replace*** .... Labor..........30.90	ea	—	$30.90	$30.90
Security chain ▶ *See quality indicators on previous page.*	**Security chain** ***Replace*** Material........13.00 Labor..........10.90 ***Remove*** .... Labor...........7.10	ea	$7.10	$23.90	$31.00
	Remove security chain for work, then reinstall ***Replace*** .... Labor..........18.50	ea	—	$18.50	$18.50
Door hinges ▶ *See quality indicators on previous page. Deluxe grade hinges include embossed antique patterns.*	**Door hinges, standard grade** ***Replace*** Material........11.00 Labor..........18.20 ***Remove*** .... Labor..........13.30	ea	$13.30	$29.20	$42.50
	Door hinges, high grade ***Replace*** Material........24.00 Labor..........18.20 ***Remove*** .... Labor..........13.30	ea	$13.30	$42.20	$55.50
	Door hinges, deluxe grade ***Replace*** Material.......38.00 Labor..........18.20 ***Remove*** .... Labor..........13.30	ea	$13.30	$56.20	$69.50
	Batten door hinges ***Replace*** Material.......57.00 Labor..........20.60 ***Remove*** .... Labor..........13.30	ea	$13.30	$77.60	$90.90
	Remove door hinges for work, then reinstall ***Replace*** .... Labor..........32.70	ea	—	$32.70	$32.70

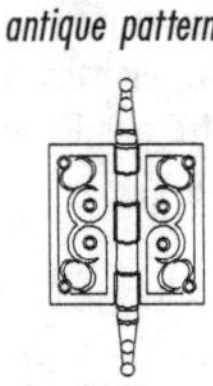

deluxe grade △

deluxe grade △

Item Description		Unit	Remove	Replace	Total
Door knocker, standard grade		ea	$6.88	$31.60	$38.48
Replace Material........17.00	Labor...........14.60				
Remove	Labor............6.88				
Door knocker, high grade		ea	$6.88	$53.60	$60.48
Replace Material.......39.00	Labor...........14.60				
Remove	Labor............6.88				
Door knocker, deluxe grade		ea	$6.88	$91.60	$98.48
Replace Material.......77.00	Labor...........14.60				
Remove	Labor............6.88				
Remove door knocker for work, then reinstall		ea	—	$26.50	$26.50
Replace	Labor...........26.50				
Storm door hinges		ea	$12.60	$33.20	$45.80
Replace Material........19.00	Labor...........14.20				
Remove	Labor...........12.60				
Remove storm door hinges for work, then reinstall		ea	—	$25.30	$25.30
Replace	Labor..........25.30				
Storm door lockset, standard grade		ea	$8.99	$40.10	$49.09
Replace Material........24.00	Labor...........16.10				
Remove	Labor............8.99				
Storm door lockset, high grade		ea	$8.99	$53.10	$62.09
Replace Material........37.00	Labor...........16.10				
Remove	Labor............8.99				
Remove storm door lockset for work, then reinstall		ea	—	$28.50	$28.50
Replace	Labor..........28.50				
Hinge door stop		ea	$2.31	$10.32	$12.63
Replace Material.........5.00	Labor............5.32				
Remove	Labor............2.31				
Flexible spring baseboard door stop		ea	$2.31	$11.74	$14.05
Replace Material.........6.00	Labor............5.74				
Remove	Labor............2.31				
Rigid baseboard door stop		ea	$2.31	$12.24	$14.55
Replace Material.........6.50	Labor............5.74				
Remove	Labor............2.31				
Remove door stop for work, then reinstall		ea	—	$10.50	$10.50
Replace	Labor...........10.50				
Door push plate, standard grade		ea	$4.40	$37.30	$41.70
Replace Material.......20.00	Labor...........17.30				
Remove	Labor............4.40				
Door push plate, high grade		ea	$4.40	$54.30	$58.70
Replace Material........37.00	Labor...........17.30				
Remove	Labor............4.40				
Remove door push plate for work, then reinstall		ea	—	$30.90	$30.90
Replace	Labor..........30.90				

◄ **DOOR KNOCKER**
See quality indicators on page 127.

◄ **STORM DOOR HINGES**

◄ **STORM DOOR LOCKSET**

◄ **DOOR STOP**
See quality indicators on page 127.

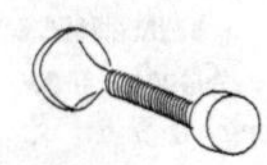

flexible spring △

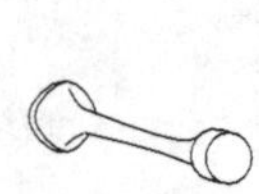

rigid △

◄ **PUSH PLATE**
See quality indicators on page 127.

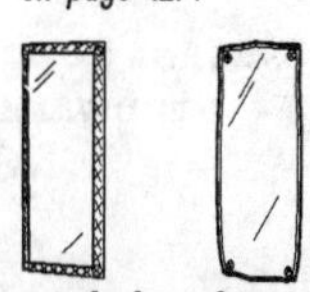

△ ***high grade*** △

RELATED ITEMS

	Item Description	Unit	Remove	Replace	Total
Kick plate ► See quality indicators on page 127.	**Door kick plate, standard grade** *Replace* Material.......34.00 Labor..........18.50 *Remove* .... Labor 5.86	ea	$5.86	$52.50	$58.36
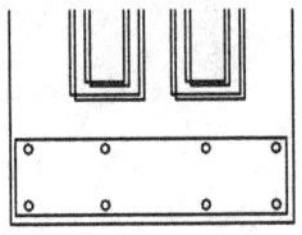	**Door kick plate, high grade** *Replace* Material.......50.00 Labor..........18.50 *Remove* .... Labor 5.86	ea	$5.86	$68.50	$74.36
	Remove door kick plate for work, then reinstall *Replace* .... Labor 33.70	ea	—	$33.70	$33.70
Letter plate ► See quality indicators on page 127.	**Letter plate, standard grade** *Replace* Material.......28.00 Labor ....20.80 *Remove* .... Labor 5.94	ea	$5.94	$48.80	$54.74
 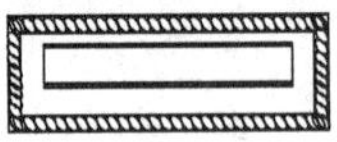	**Letter plate, high grade** *Replace* Material........55.00 Labor ....20.80 *Remove* .... Labor 5.94	ea	$5.94	$75.80	$81.74
	Remove letter plate for work, then reinstall *Replace* .... Labor..........37.50	ea	—	$37.50	$37.50
Peep hole ►	**Door peep hole** *Replace* Material........19.00 Labor ....20.10 *Remove* .... Labor 5.64	ea	$5.64	$39.10	$44.74
	Remove door peep hole for work, then reinstall *Replace* .... Labor 36.60	ea	—	$36.60	$36.60
Door sweep ►	**Door sweep** *Replace* Material ....28.00 Labor..........17.90 *Remove* .... Labor 6.57	ea	$6.57	$45.90	$52.47
	Remove door sweep for work, then reinstall *Replace* .... Labor..........31.70	ea	—	$31.70	$31.70
Threshold ► Standard grade is aluminum or flat wood.	**Door threshold, standard grade** *Replace* Material........16.00 Labor..........19.80 *Remove* .... Labor 7.21	ea	$7.21	$35.80	$43.01
	Door threshold, high grade *Replace* Material ....29.0000 Labor..........19.80 *Remove* .... Labor 7.21	ea	$7.21	$48.80	$56.01
	Remove door threshold for work, then reinstall *Replace* .... Labor..........35.90	ea	—	$35.90	$35.90
Weatherstrip ►	**Door weatherstripping** *Replace* Material........19.00 Labor..........17.30 *Remove* .... Labor 5.36	ea	$5.36	$36.30	$41.66
Garage door hardware ►	**Garage door hardware, standard grade** *Replace* Material........75.00 Labor..........95.70 *Remove* .... Labor..........21.00	ea	$21.00	$170.70	$191.70
	Garage door hardware, high grade *Replace* Material......102.00 Labor..........95.70 *Remove* .... Labor..........21.00	ea	$21.00	$197.70	$218.70
	Remove garage door hardware for work, then reinstall *Replace* .... Labor.........168.00	ea	—	$168.00	$168.00

Time & Material Charts *(selected items)*

Door Hardware Materials

*See **Door Hardware** material prices with the line items and other information in the **QuickFinder** column.*

Door Hardware Labor

LABORER	BASE WAGE	PAID LEAVE	TRUE WAGE	FICA	FUTA	WORKER'S COMP.	UNEMPLOY. INSUR.	HEALTH INSUR.	RETIRE (401K)	LIABILITY INSUR.	COST PER HOUR
Finish carpenter	$23.60	1.84	$25.44	1.95	.20	4.96	2.21	2.69	.76	3.43	$41.60
Demolition laborer	$13.90	1.08	$14.98	1.15	.12	4.79	1.30	2.69	.45	2.02	$27.50

Paid Leave is calculated based on two weeks paid vacation, one week sick leave, and seven paid holidays. Employer's matching portion of **FICA** is 7.65 percent. **FUTA** (Federal Unemployment) is .8 percent. **Worker's compensation** for the door hardware trade was calculated using a national average of 19.50 percent. **Unemployment insurance** was calculated using a national average of 8.7 percent. **Health insurance** was calculated based on a projected national average for 2002 of $535 per employee (and family when applicable) per month. Employer pays 80 percent for a per month cost of $428 per employee. **Retirement** is based on a 401(k) retirement program with employer matching of 50 percent. Employee contributions to the 401(k) plan are an average of 6 percent of the true wage. **Liability insurance** is based on a national average of 13.2 percent.

Door Hardware Labor Productivity

WORK DESCRIPTION	LABORER	COST PER HOUR	PRODUCTIVITY	UNIT PRICE
Demolition				
deadbolt	demolition laborer	$27.50	.276	$7.59 ea
exterior door keyed lockset	demolition laborer	$27.50	.314	$8.64 ea
entry door keyed lockset	demolition laborer	$27.50	.696	$19.10 ea
antique-style door thumb latch	demolition laborer	$27.50	.516	$14.20 ea
interior door lockset	demolition laborer	$27.50	.281	$7.73 ea
door closer	demolition laborer	$27.50	.291	$8.00 ea
security chain	demolition laborer	$27.50	.258	$7.10 ea
hinges	demolition laborer	$27.50	.485	$13.30 ea
door knocker	demolition laborer	$27.50	.250	$6.88 ea
storm door hinges	demolition laborer	$27.50	.457	$12.60 ea
storm door lockset	demolition laborer	$27.50	.327	$8.99 ea
door stop	demolition laborer	$27.50	.084	$2.31 ea
door push plate	demolition laborer	$27.50	.160	$4.40 ea
door kick plate	demolition laborer	$27.50	.213	$5.86 ea
door letter plate	demolition laborer	$27.50	.216	$5.94 ea
door peep hole	demolition laborer	$27.50	.205	$5.64 ea
door sweep	demolition laborer	$27.50	.239	$6.57 ea
door threshold	demolition laborer	$27.50	.262	$7.21 ea
door weatherstripping	demolition laborer	$27.50	.195	$5.36 ea
garage door hardware	demolition laborer	$27.50	.762	$21.00 ea
Install deadbolt				
install	finish carpenter	$41.60	.678	$28.20 ea
remove for work, then reinstall	finish carpenter	$41.60	1.10	$45.80 ea
Install exterior door keyed lockset				
install	finish carpenter	$41.60	.461	$19.20 ea
remove for work, then reinstall	finish carpenter	$41.60	1.03	$42.80 ea
Install entry door keyed lockset				
install	finish carpenter	$41.60	1.45	$60.30 ea
remove for work, then reinstall	finish carpenter	$41.60	2.73	$114.00 ea
Install antique style door thumb latch				
install	finish carpenter	$41.60	1.73	$72.00 ea

... More ➢

Door Hardware Labor Productivity *continued*

WORK DESCRIPTION	LABORER	COST PER HOUR	PRODUCTIVITY	UNIT PRICE
Install interior door lockset				
install	finish carpenter	$41.60	.405	$16.80 ea
remove for work, then reinstall	finish carpenter	$41.60	.710	$29.50 ea
Install door closer				
spring hinge	finish carpenter	$41.60	.257	$10.70 ea
typical	finish carpenter	$41.60	.431	$17.90 ea
remove for work, then reinstall	finish carpenter	$41.60	.742	$30.90 ea
Install security chain				
install	finish carpenter	$41.60	.262	$10.90 ea
remove for work, then reinstall	finish carpenter	$41.60	.445	$18.50 ea
Install door hinges				
typical	finish carpenter	$41.60	.438	$18.20 ea
for batten door	finish carpenter	$41.60	.495	$20.60 ea
remove for work, then reinstall	finish carpenter	$41.60	.786	$32.70 ea
Install door knocker				
install	finish carpenter	$41.60	.351	$14.60 ea
remove for work, then reinstall	finish carpenter	$41.60	.636	$26.50 ea
Install storm door hinges				
install	finish carpenter	$41.60	.342	$14.20 ea
remove for work, then reinstall	finish carpenter	$41.60	.607	$25.30 ea
Install storm door lockset				
install	finish carpenter	$41.60	.387	$16.10 ea
remove for work, then reinstall	finish carpenter	$41.60	.685	$28.50 ea
Install door stop				
hinge	finish carpenter	$41.60	.128	$5.32 ea
baseboard	finish carpenter	$41.60	.138	$5.74 ea
remove for work, then reinstall	finish carpenter	$41.60	.252	$10.50 ea
Install door push plate				
install	finish carpenter	$41.60	.417	$17.30 ea
remove for work, then reinstall	finish carpenter	$41.60	.742	$30.90 ea
Install door kick plate				
install	finish carpenter	$41.60	.445	$18.50 ea
remove for work, then reinstall	finish carpenter	$41.60	.809	$33.70 ea
Install letter plate				
install	finish carpenter	$41.60	.500	$20.80 ea
remove for work, then reinstall	finish carpenter	$41.60	.902	$37.50 ea
Install door peep hole				
install	finish carpenter	$41.60	.484	$20.10 ea
remove for work, then reinstall	finish carpenter	$41.60	.879	$36.60 ea
Install door sweep				
install	finish carpenter	$41.60	.431	$17.90 ea
remove for work, then reinstall	finish carpenter	$41.60	.763	$31.70 ea
Install door threshold				
install	finish carpenter	$41.60	.477	$19.80 ea
remove for work, then reinstall	finish carpenter	$41.60	.862	$35.90 ea
Install door weatherstripping				
install	finish carpenter	$41.60	.417	$17.30 ea
Install garage door hardware				
install	finish carpenter	$41.60	2.30	$95.70 ea
remove for work, then reinstall	finish carpenter	$41.60	4.05	$168.00 ea

NOTES:

end

12 .... Drywall

Item Description	Unit	Remove	Replace	Total
Remove drywall & prep walls for new installation *Remove*........ Labor........ .22	sf	$.22	—	$.22
Scrape (remove) acoustic ceiling texture *Remove*........ Labor........ .30	sf	$.30	—	$.30
Scrape (remove) painted acoustic ceiling texture *Remove*........ Labor........ .52	sf	$.52	—	$.52
Remove furring strips attached to wood, 16″ on center *Remove*........ Labor........ .28	sf	$.28	—	$.28
Remove furring strips attached to concrete or masonry, 16″ on center *Remove*........ Labor........ .30	sf	$.30	—	$.30
Remove furring strips attached to wood, 24″ on center *Remove*........ Labor........ .25	sf	$.25	—	$.25
Remove furring strips attached to concrete or masonry, 24″ on center *Remove*........ Labor........ .28	sf	$.28	—	$.28
3/8″ drywall installed with machine texture *Replace* Materials........ .47 Labor........1.20 *Remove*........ Labor........ .22	sf	$.22	$1.67	$1.89
3/8″ drywall installed with knock-down machine texture *Replace* Materials........ .47 Labor........1.24 *Remove*........ Labor........ .22	sf	$.22	$1.71	$1.93
3/8″ drywall installed with light texture *Replace* Materials........ .48 Labor........1.28 *Remove*........ Labor........ .22	sf	$.22	$1.76	$1.98
3/8″ drywall installed with medium texture *Replace* Materials........ .52 Labor........1.32 *Remove*........ Labor........ .22	sf	$.22	$1.84	$2.06
3/8″ drywall installed heavy texture *Replace* Materials........ .57 Labor........1.37 *Remove*........ Labor........ .22	sf	$.22	$1.94	$2.16
3/8″ drywall installed with smooth-wall finish *Replace* Materials........ .50 Labor........1.58 *Remove*........ Labor........ .22	sf	$.22	$2.08	$2.30
3/8″ drywall installed (all coats, no texture) *Replace* Materials........ .38 Labor........ 1.07 *Remove*........ Labor........ .22	sf	$.22	$1.45	$1.67
3/8″ drywall, hung & fire taped only *Replace* Materials........ .36 Labor........ .78 *Remove*........ Labor........ .22	sf	$.22	$1.14	$1.36

◄ **DEMOLITION**
Tear-out and debris removal to a truck or dumpster on site. Does not include hauling, dumpster, or dump fees. No salvage value is assumed.

◄ **3/8″ DRYWALL**

DRYWALL INSTALLATION

Drywall is hung and taped according to industry standards. Drywall is attached with nails when hung, then permanently affixed with screws. Perfatape and three coats of mud are applied plus texture.

One lf of corner bead is calculated for every 24 sf of installed drywall.

Productivity is based on repair installations.

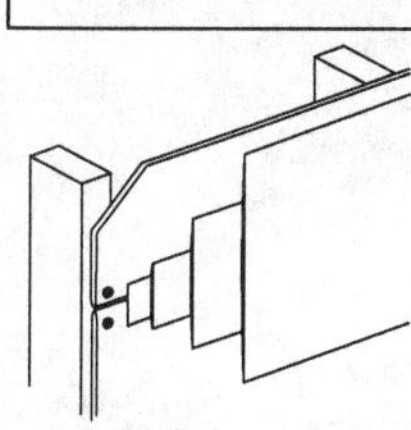

RELATED ITEMS

Cleaning........58
Painting........333
Paneling........347
Plaster........353
Wallpaper........495

	Item Description	Unit	Remove	Replace	Total
3/8" DRYWALL ▶ *continued*	**3/8" drywall, hung only (no tape, coating or texture)** *Replace* Materials........ .34 Labor............ .41 *Remove*........................ Labor............ .22	sf	$.22	$.75	$.97
	Add for installation of 3/8" drywall over existing plaster wall *Replace* .... Labor............ ..13	sf	—	$.13	$.13
	Add for 3/8" foil-backed drywall *Replace* Materials........ .11	sf	—	$.11	$.11
1/2" DRYWALL ▶	**1/2" drywall installed with machine texture** *Replace* Materials........ .46 Labor............1.20 *Remove*........................ Labor............ .22	sf	$.22	$1.66	$1.88
	1/2" drywall installed with knock-down machine texture *Replace* Materials........ .46 Labor............1.24 *Remove*........................ Labor............ .22	sf	$.22	$1.70	$1.92
	1/2" drywall installed with light texture *Replace* Materials........ .47 Labor............1.28 *Remove*........................ Labor............ .22	sf	$.22	$1.75	$1.97
	1/2" drywall installed with medium texture *Replace* Materials........ .51 Labor............1.32 *Remove*........................ Labor............ .22	sf	$.22	$1.83	$2.05
	1/2" drywall installed heavy texture *Replace* Materials........ .56 Labor............1.37 *Remove*........................ Labor............ .22	sf	$.22	$1.93	$2.15
	1/2" drywall installed with smooth-wall finish *Replace* Materials........ .49 Labor............1.58 *Remove*........................ Labor............ .22	sf	$.22	$2.07	$2.29
	1/2" drywall installed (all coats, no texture) *Replace* Materials........ .37 Labor........... 1.07 *Remove*........................ Labor............ .22	sf	$.22	$1.44	$1.66
	1/2" drywall, hung & fire taped only *Replace* Materials........ .35 Labor............ .78 *Remove*........................ Labor............ .22	sf	$.22	$1.13	$1.35
	1/2" drywall, hung only (no tape, coating or texture) *Replace* Materials........ .33 Labor............ .41 *Remove*........................ Labor............ .22	sf	$.22	$.74	$.96
	Add for installation of 1/2" drywall over existing plaster wall *Replace* .... Labor............ .13	sf	—	$.13	$.13
	Add for 1/2" moisture-resistant drywall *Replace* Materials........ .11	sf	—	$.11	$.11
	Add for 1/2" type X fire-rated drywall *Replace* Materials........ .09	sf	—	$.09	$.09
	Add for 1/2" foil-backed drywall *Replace* Materials........ .15	sf	—	$.15	$.15
	Add for 1/2" type X fire-rated, foil-backed drywall *Replace* Materials........ .22	sf	—	$.22	$.22

Item Description	Unit	Remove	Replace	Total
5/8″ drywall installed with machine texture *Replace* Materials........ .53 Labor............1.20 *Remove*........................ Labor............ .22	sf	$.22	$1.73	$1.95
5/8″ drywall installed with knock-down machine texture *Replace* Materials........ .53 Labor............1.24 *Remove*........................ Labor............ .22	sf	$.22	$1.77	$1.99
5/8″ drywall installed with light texture *Replace* Materials........ .54 Labor............1.28 *Remove*........................ Labor............ .22	sf	$.22	$1.82	$2.04
5/8″ drywall installed with medium texture *Replace* Materials........ .58 Labor............1.32 *Remove*........................ Labor............ .22	sf	$.22	$1.90	$2.12
5/8″ drywall installed heavy texture *Replace* Materials........ .63 Labor............1.37 *Remove*........................ Labor............ .22	sf	$.22	$2.00	$2.22
5/8″ drywall installed with smooth-wall finish *Replace* Materials........ .56 Labor............1.58 *Remove*........................ Labor............ .22	sf	$.22	$2.14	$2.36
5/8″ drywall installed (all coats, no texture) *Replace* Materials........ .44 Labor.......... 1.07 *Remove*........................ Labor............ .22	sf	$.22	$1.51	$1.73
5/8″ drywall, hung & fire taped only *Replace* Materials........ .42 Labor............ .78 *Remove*........................ Labor............ .22	sf	$.22	$1.20	$1.42
5/8″ drywall, hung only (no tape, coating or texture) *Replace* Materials........ .40 Labor............ .41 *Remove*........................ Labor............ .22	sf	$.22	$.81	$1.03
Add for installation of 5/8″ drywall over existing plaster wall *Replace* .... Labor............	sf	—	$.13	$.13
Add for 5/8″ moisture-resistant drywall *Replace* Materials........ .10	sf	—	$.10	$.10
Add for 5/8″ foil-backed drywall *Replace* Materials........ .18	sf	—	$.18	$.18
Acoustic ceiling (cottage cheese) texture, light coverage *Replace* Materials........ .14 Labor............ .34 *Remove*........................ Labor............ .30	sf	$.30	$.48	$.78
Acoustic ceiling (cottage cheese) texture, medium coverage *Replace* Materials........ .19 Labor............ .46 *Remove*........................ Labor............ .30	sf	$.30	$.65	$.95
Acoustic ceiling (cottage cheese) texture, heavy coverage *Replace* Materials........ .21 Labor............ .67 *Remove*........................ Labor............ .30	sf	$.30	$.88	$1.18
Glitter application to acoustic-ceiling texture *Replace* Materials........ .01 Labor............ .08	sf	—	$.09	$.09

◄ **5/8″ DRYWALL**

◄ **ACOUSTIC CEILING**

RELATED ITEMS

Cleaning........................58
Painting........................333
Paneling........................347
Plaster........................353
Wallpaper........................495

	Item Description	Unit	Remove	Replace	Total
MINIMUM ▶ **ACOUSTIC CHARGE**	**Minimum charge for acoustic-ceiling texture** *Replace* Materials....100.00 Labor..........66.20	ea	—	$166.20	$166.20
DRYWALL PATCH ▶	**Drywall patch (match existing texture or finish)** *Replace* Materials......25.00 Labor...........59.50	ea	—	$84.50	$84.50
MINIMUM ▶ **DRYWALL CHARGE**	**Minimum charge for drywall repair** *Replace* Materials......35.00 Labor.........243.00	ea	—	$278.00	$278.00
TEXTURE ▶	**Texture drywall with light hand texture** *Replace* Materials........ .100 Labor............. .21	sf	—	$.31	$.31
	Texture drywall with medium hand texture *Replace* Materials........ .140 Labor............. .25	sf	—	$.39	$.39
	Texture drywall with heavy hand texture *Replace* Materials........ .190 Labor............. .25	sf	—	$.44	$.44
	Texture drywall with thin-coat smooth-wall *Replace* Materials........ .120 Labor............. .50	sf	—	$.62	$.62
	Texture drywall, machine applied *Replace* Materials........ .090 Labor............. .17	sf	—	$.26	$.26
	Texture drywall, machine applied and knocked down with trowel *Replace* Materials........ .090 Labor............. .21	sf	—	$.30	$.30
METAL FURRING ▶ *See Rough Carpentry, page 430 for wood furring strips.*	**Metal hat-shaped furring channel, 16″ on center on wood** *Replace* Materials........ .170 Labor............. .40 *Remove*......................... Labor............. .28	sf	$.28	$.57	$.85
	Metal hat-shaped furring channel, 24″ on center on wood *Replace* Materials........ .130 Labor............. .29 *Remove*......................... Labor............. .25	sf	$.25	$.42	$.67
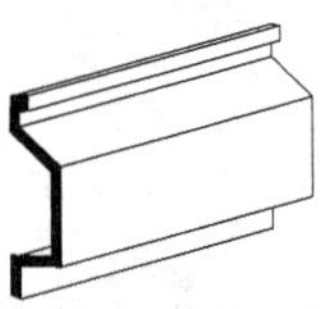 △ *hat-shaped channel*	**Metal sound-resistant furring channel, 16″ on center on wood** *Replace* Materials........ .190 Labor............. .40 *Remove*......................... Labor............. .28	sf	$.28	$.59	$.87
	Metal sound-resistant furring channel, 24″ on center on wood *Replace* Materials........ .140 Labor............. .29 *Remove*......................... Labor............. .25	sf	$.25	$.43	$.68
	Metal hat-shaped furring channel, 16″ on center on concrete or masonry *Replace* Materials........ .170 Labor............. .43 *Remove*......................... Labor............. .30	sf	$.30	$.60	$.90
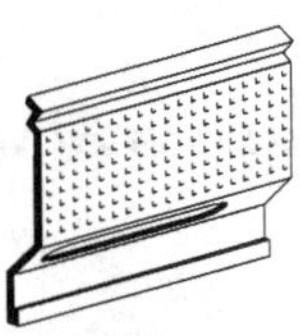 △ *sound-resistant channel*	**Metal hat-shaped furring channel, 24″ on center on concrete or masonry** *Replace* Materials........ .130 Labor............. .29 *Remove*......................... Labor............. .28	sf	$.28	$.42	$.70
	Metal sound-resistant furring channel, 16″ on center on concrete or masonry *Replace* Materials........ .190 Labor............. .43 *Remove*......................... Labor............. .30	sf	$.30	$.62	$.92
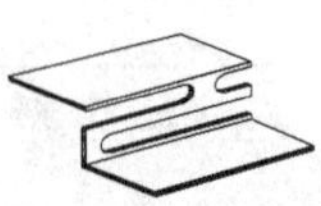 △ *Z channel*	**Metal sound-resistant furring channel, 24″ on center on concrete or masonry** *Replace* Materials........ .140 Labor............. .29 *Remove*......................... Labor............. .28	sf	$.28	$.43	$.71

Item Description	Unit	Remove	Replace	Total
Metal Z channel, 16″ on center on concrete or masonry *Replace* Materials........ .130 Labor............ .43 *Remove*........................ Labor............ .30	sf	$.30	$.56	$.86
Metal Z channel, 24″ on center on concrete or masonry *Replace* Materials........ .090 Labor............ .29 *Remove*........................ Labor............ .28	sf	$.28	$.38	$.66

RELATED ITEMS

Cleaning....................58
Painting....................333
Paneling....................347
Plaster....................353
Rough Carpentry
furring strips....................430
Wallpaper....................495

NOTES: ______________________

end

TIME & MATERIAL CHARTS *(selected items)*

Drywall Materials

DESCRIPTION	MATERIAL PRICE	GROSS COVERAGE	WASTE	NET COVERAGE	UNIT PRICE
3/8″ drywall board					
standard	$298.00 *per 1,000*	1,000	8%	920	$.32 *sf*
foil-backed	$396.00 *per 1,000*	1,000	8%	920	$.43 *sf*
1/2″ drywall board					
standard	$285.00 *per 1,000*	1,000	7%	930	$.31 *sf*
moisture-resistant	$392.00 *per 1,000*	1,000	7%	930	$.42 *sf*
foil-backed	$409.00 *per 1,000*	1,000	7%	930	$.44 *sf*
fire-rated type X	$351.00 *per 1,000*	1,000	7%	930	$.38 *sf*
fire-rated type X foil-backed	$496.00 *per 1,000*	1,000	7%	930	$.53 *sf*
5/8″ drywall board					
type X	$349.00 *per 1,000*	1,000	7%	930	$.38 *sf*
moisture-resistant	$449.00 *per 1,000*	1,000	7%	930	$.48 *sf*
Fasteners					
drywall nails, used to secure when hanging	$49.00 *per box*	32,000	4%	30,720	$.01 *sf*
drywall screws, used to attach after hung	$96.00 *per box*	8,534	3%	8,278	$.01 *sf*
Drywall taping materials					
perfatape (per 500′ roll)	$6.20 *per roll*	1,111	6%	1,044	$.01 *sf*
corner bead	$1.00 *per stick*	204	4%	196	$.01 *sf*
joint compound	$13.70 *per 50 lb box*	965	16%	811	$.02 *sf*
Drywall texture compound					
machine-sprayed	$14.90 *per 50 lb box*	190	13%	165	$.09 *sf*
light hand texture	$14.90 *per 50 lb box*	175	13%	152	$.10 *sf*
medium hand texture	$14.90 *per 50 lb box*	120	13%	104	$.14 *sf*
heavy hand texture	$14.90 *per 50 lb box*	93	14%	80	$.19 *sf*
heavy trowel texture	$14.90 *per 50 lb box*	77	15%	65	$.23 *sf*
smooth wall	$14.90 *per 50 lb box*	142	14%	122	$.12 *sf*
Acoustic ceiling (cottage cheese) texture compound					
light texture	$26.10 *per 50 lb bag*	220	17%	183	$.14 *sf*
medium texture	$26.10 *per 50 lb box*	170	17%	141	$.19 *sf*
heavy texture	$26.10 *per 50 lb box*	153	17%	127	$.21 *sf*
Acoustic ceiling glitter (per pound)					
light to heavy application	$3.20 *per pound*	2,350	22%	1,833	$.01 *sf*
Metal furring strips					
hat-shaped channel installed 24″ on center	$2.50 *per 12′ stick*	21	3%	20	$.13 *sf*
sound-resistant channel installed 24″ on center	$2.80 *per 12′ stick*	21	3%	20	$.14 *sf*
Z channel installed 24″ on center	$1.30 *per 8′ stick*	15	3%	15	$.09 *sf*

Drywall Rental Equipment

Description	Price	Coverage	Unit Price
Ames taping tools	**$10.00** per day	**416** per day	**$.02** sf
texture equipment (gun with hopper & compressor)	**$70.00** per day	**1,536** per day	**$.05** sf
glitter blower for acoustic ceilings	**$5.00** per day	**5,000** per day	**$.001** sf
drywall lifter (for one-person hanging)	**$15.00** per day	**102** per day	**$.15** sf
minimum charge	**$40.00** minimum	**1** minimum	**$40.00** each

Drywall Labor

Laborer	Base Wage	Paid Leave	True Wage	FICA	FUTA	Worker's Comp.	Unemploy. Insur.	Health Insur.	Retire (401k)	Liability Insur.	Cost per Hour
Drywall hanger	**$22.60**	1.76	**$24.36**	1.86	.19	6.26	2.12	2.69	.73	3.29	**$41.50**
Drywall hanger's helper	**$16.40**	1.28	**$17.68**	1.35	.14	4.54	1.54	2.69	.53	2.39	**$30.90**
Drywall taper	**$22.80**	1.78	**$24.58**	1.88	.20	6.32	2.14	2.69	.74	3.32	**$41.90**
Demolition laborer	**$13.90**	1.08	**$14.98**	1.15	12	4.79	1.30	2.69	.45	2.02	**$27.50**

Paid Leave is calculated based on two weeks paid vacation, one week sick leave, and seven paid holidays. Employer's matching portion of **FICA** is 7.65 percent. **FUTA** (Federal Unemployment) is .8 percent. **Worker's compensation** for the drywall trade was calculated using a national average of 25.70 percent. **Unemployment insurance** was calculated using a national average of 8.7 percent. **Health insurance** was calculated based on a projected national average for 2002 of $535 per employee (and family when applicable) per month. Employer pays 80 percent for a per month cost of $428 per employee. **Retirement** is based on a 401(k) retirement program with employer matching of 50 percent. Employee contributions to the 401(k) plan are an average of 6 percent of the true wage. **Liability insurance** is based on a national average of 13.2 percent.

Drywall Labor Productivity

Work Description	Laborer	Cost per Hour	Productivity	Unit Price
Demolition				
remove drywall and prep walls	demolition laborer	**$27.50**	**.008**	**$.22** sf
scrape and prep acoustical ceiling	demolition laborer	**$27.50**	**.011**	**$.30** sf
scrape and prep painted acoustical ceiling	demolition laborer	**$27.50**	**.019**	**$.52** sf
remove furring strips on wood, 16" oc	demolition laborer	**$27.50**	**.010**	**$.28** sf
remove furring strips on conc. or masonry, 16" oc	demolition laborer	**$27.50**	**.011**	**$.30** sf
remove furring strips on wood, 24" oc	demolition laborer	**$27.50**	**.009**	**$.25** sf
remove furring strips on conc. or masonry, 24" oc	demolition laborer	**$27.50**	**.010**	**$.28** sf
Hang drywall				
hang drywall	drywall hanger	**$41.50**		
hang drywall	drywall hanger's helper	**$30.90**		
hang drywall	**drywall hanging crew**	**$36.20**		
Tape and coat drywall				
to finish (no texture)	drywall taper	**$41.90**	**.017**	**$.71** sf
tape coat only	drywall taper	**$41.90**	**.010**	**$.42** sf
tape coat and one additional coat only	drywall taper	**$41.90**	**.012**	**$.50** sf
to finish, apply machine-sprayed texture	drywall taper	**$41.90**	**.020**	**$.84** sf
to finish, apply machine-sprayed, knock-down texture	drywall taper	**$41.90**	**.021**	**$.88** sf
to finish, apply light hand texture	drywall taper	**$41.90**	**.022**	**$.92** sf
to finish, apply heavy hand texture	drywall taper	**$41.90**	**.024**	**$1.01** sf
to finish, apply smooth-wall texture	drywall taper	**$41.90**	**.029**	**$1.22** sf
Apply texture				
with compressor and spray gun	drywall taper	**$41.90**	**.004**	**$.17** sf
with spray gun, then knock down with trowel	drywall taper	**$41.90**	**.005**	**$.21** sf
light hand texture	drywall taper	**$41.90**	**.005**	**$.21** sf
heavy hand texture	drywall taper	**$41.90**	**.006**	**$.25** sf
thin coat smooth-wall finish	drywall taper	**$41.90**	**.012**	**$.50** sf
Apply acoustical ceiling texture				
light	drywall taper	**$41.90**	**.008**	**$.34** sf
heavy	drywall taper	**$41.90**	**.016**	**$.67** sf
apply glitter to freshly sprayed ceiling	drywall taper	**$41.90**	**.002**	**$.08** sf

13 Electrical

Item Description	Unit	Remove	Replace	Total
Minimum charge for electrical work *Replace* Materials......20.00 Labor..........50.50	ea	—	$70.50	$70.50
Complete house wiring, outlets, switches & light fixtures, economy grade *Replace* Materials........1.57 Labor............2.00	sf	—	$3.57	$3.57
Complete house wiring, outlets, switches & light fixtures, standard grade *Replace* Materials........1.79 Labor............3.39	sf	—	$5.18	$5.18
Complete house wiring, outlets, switches & light fixtures, high grade *Replace* Materials........2.06 Labor............3.92	sf	—	$5.98	$5.98
Complete house wiring, outlets, switches & light fixtures, deluxe grade *Replace* Materials........2.18 Labor............4.11	sf	—	$6.29	$6.29
Complete house wiring, outlets, switches & light fixtures, low-voltage system *Replace* Materials........1.99 Labor............3.77	sf	—	$5.76	$5.76
Add for complete house electrical with wiring in conduit *Replace* Materials........1.99 Labor............2.07 ► EMT conduit with 4.4 terminations, 7 bends, and 4 clamps per 100 lf.	sf	—	$4.06	$4.06
Complete house rough electrical (no light fixtures), standard *Replace* Materials........ .92 Labor............2.64	sf	—	$3.56	$3.56
Complete house rough electrical (no light fixtures), in conduit *Replace* Materials........2.04 Labor............5.81 ► EMT conduit with 4.4 terminations, 7 bends, and 4 clamps per 100 lf.	sf	—	$7.85	$7.85
Complete house rough electrical (no light fixtures), low-voltage system *Replace* Materials...... 1.01 Labor............2.83	sf	—	$3.84	$3.84
Complete house light fixtures, economy grade *Replace* Materials...... 1.01 Labor............ .57	sf	—	$1.58	$1.58
Complete house light fixtures, standard grade *Replace* Materials........1.31 Labor............ .60	sf	—	$1.91	$1.91
Complete house light fixtures, high grade *Replace* Materials........1.84 Labor............ .60	sf	—	$2.44	$2.44
Complete house light fixtures, deluxe grade *Replace* Materials........2.41 Labor............ .64	sf	—	$3.05	$3.05
Complete house light fixtures for low-voltage system *Replace* Materials........1.74 Labor............ .64	sf	—	$2.38	$2.38
120 volt outlet with wiring run & box *Replace* Materials......15.00 Labor..........36.80 ► General-purpose use, average of 6 outlets per single-pole breaker (breaker not included). Includes up to 15 lf of #12/2 wire.	ea	—	$51.80	$51.80

◄ **MINIMUM**

◄ **COMPLETE HOUSE**
Complete house wiring, boxes, switches, outlets and fixtures to code for a house that is not electrically heated. (Electrical hookups for furnace, AC unit, and/or heat pump included.) Does not include breaker panel, main disconnect or service drop. Grades refer to quality of light fixtures (see pages 154-155).

◄ **COMPLETE HOUSE WIRING**
Same as above but does not include fixtures.

◄ **COMPLETE HOUSE FIXTURES**
See pages 154-155 for info about fixture grades.

VOLTAGE

Voltage listed as "120 volt" applies to 110, 115, 120, and 125 volt applications.

Voltage listed as "240 volt" applies to 220, 240, or 250 volt applications.

◄ **WIRE, OUTLETS & SWITCHES**
Unless otherwise indicated, includes outlet or switch, box, and up to 26 lf of wire.

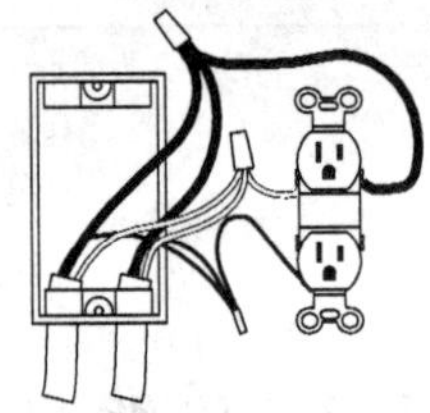

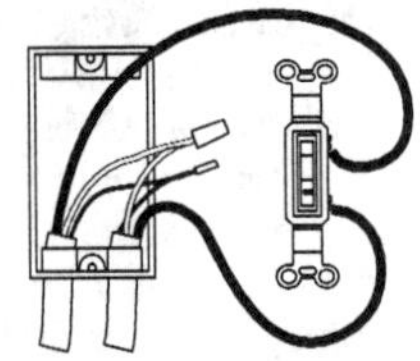

	Item Description	Unit	Remove	Replace	Total
WIRE, OUTLETS & SWITCHES *continued* ▶	**120 volt GFCI outlet with wiring run & box** ***Replace*** Materials......45.00 Labor..........36.80 ► Average of 3 outlets per single-pole breaker. Includes up to 26 lf of #12/2 wire.	ea	—	$81.80	$81.80
	120 volt exterior waterproof outlet with wiring run & box ***Replace*** Materials......20.00 Labor..........36.80 ► General-purpose use, average of 3 outlets per single-pole breaker (breaker not included). Includes up to 26 lf of #12/2 wire.	ea	—	$56.80	$56.80
	120 volt switch with wiring run & box ***Replace*** Materials......20.00 Labor..........36.80 ► Includes up to 15 lf of #12/2 wire.	ea	—	$56.80	$56.80
	120 volt 3-way switch with wiring run & box ***Replace*** Materials......30.00 Labor..........73.50 ► Includes up to 20 lf of #12/2 wire.	ea	—	$103.50	$103.50
	120 volt exterior waterproof switch with wiring run & box ***Replace*** Materials......20.00 Labor..........36.80 ► Includes up to 26 lf of #12/2 wire.	ea	—	$56.80	$56.80
240 volt ▷	**240 volt outlet with wiring run & box (30 amp)** ***Replace*** Materials......65.00 Labor..........50.50 ► Includes up to 30 lf of #10/3 wire and a 30 amp double-pole breaker. Common uses: small clothes dryers, through-wall AC / heat units, and baseboard heaters.	ea	—	$115.50	$115.50
	240 volt outlet with wiring run & box (40 amp) ***Replace*** Materials......75.00 Labor..........50.50 ► Includes up to 30 lf of #8/3 wire and a 40 amp double-pole breaker. Common uses: clothes dryers, kitchen ranges.	ea	—	$125.50	$125.50
	240 volt outlet with wiring run & box (50 amp) ***Replace*** Materials......85.00 Labor..........50.50 ► Includes up to 30 lf of #6/3 wire and a 50 amp double-pole breaker. Common use: air conditioning hookup.	ea	—	$135.50	$135.50
	240 volt switch with wiring run & box ***Replace*** Materials......70.00 Labor..........50.50 ► Includes up to 15 lf of #10/2 wire.	ea	—	$120.50	$120.50
low-voltage ▷	**Low-voltage switch wiring run & box** ***Replace*** Materials......20.00 Labor..........36.80 ► Includes up to 18 lf of #18/2 wire.	ea	—	$56.80	$56.80
OUTLETS & SWITCHES ▶ *Includes outlet or switch and cover only (no wire or box).*	**120 volt outlet with cover** ***Replace*** Materials........9.00 Labor............8.52 ***Remove*** .... Labor............4.13	ea	$4.13	$17.52	$21.65
	120 volt GFCI outlet with cover ***Replace*** Materials......29.00 Labor............8.52 ***Remove*** .... Labor............4.13	ea	$4.13	$37.52	$41.65
	120 volt exterior waterproof outlet with cover ***Replace*** Materials......14.50 Labor............8.52 ***Remove*** .... Labor............4.13	ea	$4.13	$23.02	$27.15
	120 volt switch with cover ***Replace*** Materials........6.00 Labor............8.52 ***Remove*** .... Labor............4.13	ea	$4.13	$14.52	$18.65

Item Description	Unit	Remove	Replace	Total	
120 volt lighted switch with cover ***Replace*** Materials........8.50 Labor............8.52 ***Remove*** .... Labor............4.13	ea	$4.13	$17.02	$21.15	
120 volt push-button switch with cover ***Replace*** Materials......18.50 Labor............8.52 ***Remove*** .... Labor............4.13 ► Antique reproduction style, also use this price when replacing an antique rotary snap switch (used between 1900 and 1925).	ea	$4.13	$27.02	$31.15	
120 volt rotary dimmer switch with cover ***Replace*** Materials......23.50 Labor............8.52 ***Remove*** .... Labor............4.13	ea	$4.13	$32.02	$36.15	
120 volt touch dimmer switch with cover ***Replace*** Materials......29.00 Labor............8.52 ***Remove*** .... Labor............4.13	ea	$4.13	$37.52	$41.65	
120 volt exterior waterproof switch with cover ***Replace*** Materials.......15.00 Labor............8.52 ***Remove*** .... Labor............4.13	ea	$4.13	$23.52	$27.65	
240 volt outlet with cover ***Replace*** Materials......14.00 Labor..........11.00 ***Remove*** .... Labor............5.50 ► 15, 30, or 50 amp style.	ea	$5.50	$25.00	$30.50	◁ **240 volt**
240 volt switch with cover ***Replace*** Materials.......15.00 Labor..........11.00 ***Remove*** .... Labor............5.50	ea	$5.50	$26.00	$31.50	
Low-voltage computer network outlet ***Replace*** Materials......29.00 Labor..........12.70 ***Remove*** .... Labor............4.13	ea	$4.13	$41.70	$45.83	◁ **low-voltage**
Low-voltage sound system speaker outlet ***Replace*** Materials........8.50 Labor............9.65 ► Use only when speaker wiring terminates at an outlet for connection to an external speaker. See page 145 for wiring speakers that are mounted in the wall.	ea	—	$18.15	$18.15	
Low-voltage TV outlet ***Replace*** Materials........8.00 Labor............9.65 ***Remove*** .... Labor............4.13	ea	$4.13	$17.65	$21.78	
Low-voltage phone outlet ***Replace*** Materials........5.50 Labor............9.65 ***Remove*** .... Labor............4.13	ea	$4.13	$15.15	$19.28	
Low-voltage switch with cover ***Replace*** Materials......10.50 Labor............8.52 ***Remove*** .... Labor............4.13	ea	$4.13	$19.02	$23.15	
Add for high grade outlet or switch cover ***Replace*** Materials........1.00 ► Decorative plastic, over-size plastic, and coated plastic covers.	ea	—	$1.00	$1.00	◁ **additional outlet covers**
Add for deluxe grade outlet or switch cover ***Replace*** Materials........3.00 ► Brass, chrome, hardwood, or porcelain covers.	ea	—	$3.00	$3.00	

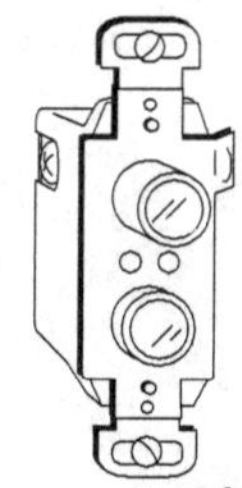

△ ***push-button switch***

RELATED ITEMS

Appliances......................19
Cleaning........................59

	Item Description	Unit	Remove	Replace	Total
OUTLET / SWITCH COVERS ►	**Outlet or switch cover, standard grade** *Replace* Materials........1.00 Labor............. .75 *Remove* .... Labor............. .96 ► Standard plastic cover style as is provided with typical switch.	ea	$.96	$1.75	$2.71
	Outlet or switch cover, high grade *Replace* Materials........3.00 Labor............. .75 *Remove* .... Labor............. .96 ► Decorative plastic, wide plastic, and coated plastic covers.	ea	$.96	$3.75	$4.71
	Outlet or switch cover, deluxe grade *Replace* Materials........7.00 Labor............. .79 *Remove* .... Labor............. .96 ► Brass, chrome, hardwood, or porcelain covers.	ea	$.96	$7.79	$8.75
WIRING RUN ►	**120 volt wiring for typical 120 volt appliance** *Replace* Materials......40.00 Labor..........38.50 ► One direct-wired run per appliance. Includes up to 26 lf of #12/2 wire and box. Does not include breaker or outlet.	ea	—	$78.50	$78.50
	120 volt wiring for through-wall air conditioner and/or heater *Replace* Materials......31.50 Labor...........47.10 ► One direct-wired run per unit. Includes up to 26 lf of #12/2 wire and box. Does not include breaker or outlet.	ea	—	$78.60	$78.60
	120 volt wiring for bathroom fan *Replace* Materials......16.50 Labor..........29.40 ► General-purpose circuit. Includes up to 20 lf of #12/2 wire. Does not include fan or vent hose.	ea	—	$45.90	$45.90
	120 volt wiring with GFCI for bathroom ceiling heater *Replace* Materials......44.50 Labor...........31.00 ► Includes up to 24 lf of #12/2 wire.	ea	—	$75.50	$75.50
	120 volt wiring for clothes washer *Replace* Materials......29.00 Labor..........29.40 ► Laundry room outlet includes up to 20 lf of #12/2 wire. 1 to 2 outlets per circuit. Does not include breaker.	ea	—	$58.40	$58.40
	120 volt wiring for dishwasher *Replace* Materials......18.50 Labor..........29.40 ► 1 direct-wired run. Includes up to 26 lf of #13/2 wire. Does not include breaker.	ea	—	$47.90	$47.90
	120 volt wiring for door bell or chime *Replace* Materials......28.00 Labor..........29.40 ► General-purpose circuit. Includes up to 15 lf of #12/2 wire, up to 30 lf of #18 low-voltage wiring, and box. Does not include breaker, transformer, or chime.	ea	—	$57.40	$57.40
	120 volt wiring for electric baseboard heater *Replace* Materials.......19.50 Labor...........31.00 ► 1 direct-wired run per 9 lf of baseboard heater or per location. Includes up to 30 lf of #12/2 wire. Does not include breaker. For 240 volt wiring see page 144.	ea	—	$50.50	$50.50
	120 volt wiring for electrical-resistance radiant heating system *Replace* Materials......27.50 Labor..........33.80 ► Direct-wired run. Includes up to 30 lf of #12/2 wire and single-pole breaker. Does not include electrical resistance wiring. For 240 volt wiring see page 144.	ea	—	$61.30	$61.30
	120 volt wiring for furnace *Replace* Materials.......11.00 Labor..........29.40 ► 1 direct-wired run. Includes up to 30 lf of #12/2 wire. Does not include breaker.	ea	—	$40.40	$40.40

Item Description	Unit	Remove	Replace	Total
120 volt wiring for garage door opener ***Replace*** Materials.......15.50 Labor...........31.00 ► Garage circuit. Includes up to 30 lf of #12/2 wire. Does not include breaker.	ea	—	$46.50	$46.50
120 volt wiring for garbage disposal ***Replace*** Materials......25.00 Labor...........37.70 ► 1 direct-wired run. Includes up to 30 lf of #12/2 wire, outlet with box, and switch with box. Does not include breaker.	ea	—	$62.70	$62.70
120 volt wiring for gas oven or range ***Replace*** Materials......16.50 Labor..........29.40 ► Light appliance circuit. 2 to 3 outlets per circuit. Includes up to 20 lf of #12/2 wire. Does not include breaker.	ea	—	$45.90	$45.90
120 volt wiring for humidifier ***Replace*** Materials.......15.50 Labor..........29.40 ► With no more than 1 to 3 fixtures or outlets per run. Includes up to 30 lf of #12/2 wire. Does not include breaker.	ea	—	$44.90	$44.90
120 volt wiring for in-sink hot water dispenser ***Replace*** Materials.......15.50 Labor..........29.40 ► Direct-wired run. Includes up to 30 lf of #12/2 wire. Does not include breaker.	ea	—	$44.90	$44.90
120 volt wiring for intercom master station ***Replace*** Materials......25.00 Labor..........33.70 ► Up to 20 lf of #12/2 wire. Does not include breaker.	ea	—	$58.70	$58.70
120 volt wiring for kitchen fan ***Replace*** Materials.......17.50 Labor..........29.40 ► Includes up to 20 lf of #12/2 wire. Does not include fan or breaker.	ea	—	$46.90	$46.90
120 volt wiring for light fixture ***Replace*** Materials......26.00 Labor..........29.40 ► General-purpose circuit, average of 6 outlets or lights per single-pole breaker. Includes up to 15 lf of #12/2 wire and box Does not include breaker or fixture.	ea	—	$55.40	$55.40
120 volt wiring for range hood fan and light ***Replace*** Materials.......17.00 Labor..........29.40 ► General-purpose circuit. Includes up to 20 lf of #12/2 wire. Does not include breaker.	ea	—	$46.40	$46.40
120 volt wiring for security system ***Replace*** Materials......29.00 Labor..........29.40 ► General-purpose circuit. Includes up to 15 lf of #12/2 wire and box. Does not include breaker or security system.	ea	—	$58.40	$58.40
120 volt wiring for smoke or carbon monoxide detector ***Replace*** Materials......23.50 Labor..........29.40 ► General-purpose circuit. Includes up to 15 lf of #12/2 wire and box. Does not include breaker or detector. (Also use for direct-wired radon and carbon monoxide detectors.)	ea	—	$52.90	$52.90
120 volt wiring for sump / water pump ***Replace*** Materials......18.50 Labor........203.00 ► Direct-wired run. Includes up to 50 lf of #12/2 wire, up to 13 lf liquid-tight flexible conduit, remote switch with box, and single-pole breaker.	ea	—	$221.50	$221.50
120 volt wiring for trash compactor ***Replace*** Materials......23.50 Labor..........36.80 ► On garbage disposal run. Includes up to 15 lf of #12/2 wire. Does not include breaker.	ea	—	$60.30	$60.30

WIRING RUN ▶ *continued*

Item Description	Unit	Remove	Replace	Total
120 volt wiring for built-in vacuum system *Replace* Materials.......15.50 Labor...........31.00 ▶ Up to 30 lf of #12/2 wire. Does not include breaker.	ea	—	$46.50	$46.50
120 volt wiring run for typical outlet *Replace* Materials......30.00 Labor..........30.20 ▶ General-purpose circuit, average of 6 outlets or lights per single-pole breaker. Includes up to 15 lf of #12/2 wire, box, and outlet. Does not include breaker.	ea	—	$60.20	$60.20
120 volt wiring for water heater *Replace* Materials......18.50 Labor...........79.50 ▶ Direct-wired run. Includes up to 30 lf of #12/2 wire and single-pole breaker.	ea	—	$98.00	$98.00
120 volt wiring for whole-house fan *Replace* Materials......21.00 Labor...........31.00 ▶ Up to 36 lf of #12/2 wire and remote switch with box. Does not include fan or breaker. For bathroom fan wiring see page 142. For kitchen fan wiring see page 143.	ea	—	$52.00	$52.00
240 volt ▷ **240 volt wiring for air conditioner** *Replace* Materials.....145.00 Labor..........113.00 ▶ Includes up to 36 lf of #6/3 wire, up to 32 lf of #3/2 wire, box, 60 amp disconnect switch, 40 amp 2 pole breaker, up to 6 lf of liquid-tight flexible conduit.	ea	—	$258.00	$258.00
240 volt wiring, box, & outlet for clothes dryer (30 amp) *Replace* Materials......65.50 Labor..........50.50 ▶ Includes up to 30 lf of #8/3 wire and a 30 amp double-pole breaker.	ea	—	$116.00	$116.00
240 volt wiring, box, & outlet for clothes dryer (40 amp) *Replace* Materials......73.50 Labor..........50.50 ▶ Includes up to 30 lf of #8/3 wire and a 40 amp double-pole breaker.	ea	—	$124.00	$124.00
240 volt wiring for electric cook top *Replace* Materials......78.50 Labor..........50.50 ▶ Includes up to 38 lf of #8/3 wire and a 40 amp double-pole breaker.	ea	—	$129.00	$129.00
240 volt wiring for electric baseboard heater *Replace* Materials......23.50 Labor..........50.50 ▶ 1 direct-wired run per 9 lf of baseboard heater or per location. Includes up to 30 lf of #10/2 wire. Does not include breaker. For 120 volt wiring see page 142.	ea	—	$74.00	$74.00
240 volt wiring for electrical-resistance radiant heating system *Replace* Materials....365.00 Labor..........46.00 ▶ Direct-wired run. Includes up to 30 lf of #8/2 wire and double-pole breaker. Does not include electrical resistance wiring. For 120 volt wiring see page 142.	ea	—	$411.00	$411.00
240 volt wiring, box & outlet for electric oven or range (40 amp) *Replace* Materials......65.50 Labor..........50.50 ▶ Includes up to 30 lf of #8/3 wire and a 40 amp double-pole breaker.	ea	—	$116.00	$116.00
240 volt wiring, box & outlet for electric oven or range (50 amp) *Replace* Materials......84.00 Labor..........50.50 ▶ Includes up to 30 lf of #6/3 wire and a 50 amp double-pole breaker.	ea	—	$134.50	$134.50
240 volt wiring for heat pump *Replace* Materials....320.00 Labor.........290.00 ▶ Includes up to 42 lf of #6/3 wire, up to 36 lf of #3/2 wire, box, 60 amp disconnect switch, 100 amp 2 pole breaker, 40 amp 2 pole breaker, up to 6 lf of liquid-tight flexible conduit.	ea	—	$610.00	$610.00

Item Description	Unit	Remove	Replace	Total
240 volt wiring for water heater *Replace* Materials......71.00 Labor..........50.50 ► Direct-wired run. Includes up to 30 lf of #10/2 wire and double-pole breaker.	ea	—	$121.50	$121.50
Low-voltage computer network wiring (per outlet) *Replace* Materials......25.00 Labor...........13.50 ► Up to 28 lf computer network cable.	ea	—	$38.50	$38.50
Low-voltage wiring for door bell or chime (per button) *Replace* Materials........3.30 Labor...........21.20 ► Up to 32 lf #18/2 wire.	ea	—	$24.50	$24.50
Low-voltage wiring for door or gate latch release *Replace* Materials......14.00 Labor...........27.00 ► Up to 40 lf of #18/2 low-voltage wire. Does not include transformer or breaker.	ea	—	$41.00	$41.00
Low-voltage wiring for intercom (per station) *Replace* Materials......12.50 Labor..........23.30 ► Up to 32 lf #18/2 wire.	ea	—	$35.80	$35.80
Low-voltage wiring for light fixture *Replace* Materials......29.00 Labor..........29.40 ► Average of 6 lights per circuit. Includes up to 24 lf of #18/2 wire and box. Also includes allowance for transformer. Does not include breaker or fixture.	ea	—	$58.40	$58.40
Low-voltage phone wiring (per outlet) *Replace* Materials........5.00 Labor...........13.50 ► Up to 30 lf of 4 or 8 wire bell wire.	ea	—	$18.50	$18.50
Low-voltage sound system speaker wiring (per speaker) *Replace* Materials........7.00 Labor...........13.50 ► Up to 30 lf of #20/2 wire.	ea	—	$20.50	$20.50
Low-voltage wiring for thermostat *Replace* Materials......12.00 Labor..........20.30 ► Up to 28 lf of #18/2 low-voltage wire.	ea	—	$32.30	$32.30
Low-voltage TV wiring (per outlet) *Replace* Materials........6.00 Labor...........13.50 ► Up to 30 lf shielded coaxial television cable.	ea	—	$19.50	$19.50
Electric metallic tubing (EMT) conduit, average installation *Replace* Materials........ .70 Labor............2.90 ► Typical house and light commercial installation per sf of floor, various diameters: 94% 1/2"; 3% 3/4"; 2% misc. flexible and larger IMC and RMC conduit.	sf	—	$3.60	$3.60
Flexible metal conduit, average installation *Replace* Materials........1.70 Labor............1.55 ► Typical house and light commercial installation per sf of floor, various diameters: 72% 1/2"; 13% 3/4"; 15% misc. EMT, IMC and RMC conduit.	sf	—	$3.25	$3.25
PVC conduit, average installation *Replace* Materials........ .50 Labor............1.70 ► Typical house and light commercial installation per sf of floor, various diameters: 94% 1/2"; 3% 3/4"; 2% misc. larger sizes.	sf	—	$2.20	$2.20
Intermediate conduit (IMC), average installation *Replace* Materials........1.60 Labor............4.26 ► Commercial and light industrial installation per sf of floor, various diameters: 44% 1/2"; 35% 3/4" or 1"; 22% misc. larger sizes.	sf	—	$5.86	$5.86

◁ **low-voltage**

◀ **CONDUIT**
Based on typical home or light commercial installation. Per sf of floor.

RELATED ITEMS

Cleaning........................57

	Item Description	Unit	Remove	Replace	Total
Conduit ► *continued*	**Rigid metal conduit (RMC), average installation** ***Replace*** Materials........5.10 Labor............2.53 ► Commercial, industrial and exposed installation per sf of floor, various diameters: 44% 1/2"; 35% 3/4" or 1"; 22% misc. larger sizes.	sf	—	$7.63	$7.63
Wire ► *Average installation and conditions for single family housing and light commercial construction. Per lf of installed wire.*	**#10 2 wire with ground non-metallic sheathed cable (Romex)** ***Replace*** Materials........ .57 Labor............1.92 ► Typical house or light commercial installation per lf of run.	lf	—	$2.49	$2.49
	#12 2 wire with ground non-metallic sheathed cable (Romex) ***Replace*** Materials........ .30 Labor............1.77 ► Typical house or light commercial installation per lf of run.	lf	—	$2.07	$2.07
	#14 2 wire with ground non-metallic sheathed cable (Romex) ***Replace*** Materials........ .20 Labor............1.51 ► Typical house installation per lf of run.	lf	—	$1.71	$1.71
Breaker panel ► 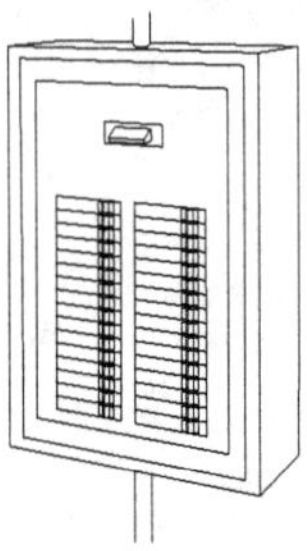	**100 amp exterior breaker panel** ***Replace*** Materials....335.00 Labor.........212.00 ***Remove*** .... Labor.........168.00 ► 20 breaker capacity, 5 breakers installed.	ea	$168.00	$547.00	$715.00
	100 amp interior breaker panel ***Replace*** Materials.....315.00 Labor.........186.00 ***Remove*** .... Labor.........168.00 ► 20 breaker capacity, 5 breakers installed.	ea	$168.00	$501.00	$669.00
	150 amp exterior breaker panel ***Replace*** Materials....430.00 Labor........333.00 ***Remove*** .... Labor.........168.00 ► 20 breaker capacity, 10 breakers installed.	ea	$168.00	$763.00	$931.00
	150 amp interior breaker panel ***Replace*** Materials.....410.00 Labor.........310.00 ***Remove*** .... Labor.........168.00 ► 20 breaker capacity, 10 breakers installed.	ea	$168.00	$720.00	$888.00
	200 amp exterior breaker panel ***Replace*** Materials....550.00 Labor........468.00 ***Remove*** .... Labor.........168.00 ► 40 breaker capacity, 15 breakers installed.	ea	$168.00	$1,018.00	$1,186.00
	200 amp interior breaker panel ***Replace*** Materials....520.00 Labor.........423.00 ***Remove*** .... Labor.........168.00 ► 40 breaker capacity, 15 breakers installed.	ea	$168.00	$943.00	$1,111.00
	300 amp exterior breaker panel ***Replace*** Materials....570.00 Labor..........619.00 ***Remove*** .... Labor.........168.00 ► 42 breaker capacity, 30 breakers installed.	ea	$168.00	$1,189.00	$1,357.00
	300 amp interior breaker panel ***Replace*** Materials....530.00 Labor........580.00 ***Remove*** .... Labor.........168.00 ► 42 breaker capacity, 30 breakers installed.	ea	$168.00	$1,110.00	$1,278.00
	40 amp interior breaker sub-panel ***Replace*** Materials.....145.00 Labor.........129.00 ***Remove*** .... Labor.........168.00 ► 10 breaker capacity, 2 breakers installed.	ea	$168.00	$274.00	$442.00

Item Description	Unit	Remove	Replace	Total
50 amp interior breaker sub-panel ***Replace*** Materials.....190.00 Labor.........137.00 ***Remove*** .... Labor.........168.00 ► 10 breaker capacity, 3 breakers installed.	ea	$168.00	$327.00	$495.00
70 amp interior breaker sub-panel ***Replace*** Materials....225.00 Labor.........150.00 ***Remove*** .... Labor.........168.00 ► 10 breaker capacity, 4 breakers installed.	ea	$168.00	$375.00	$543.00
Remove breaker panel for work, then reinstall ***Replace*** .... Labor.........358.00	ea	—	$358.00	$358.00
100 amp cable service ***Replace*** Materials....590.00 Labor.........515.00 ***Remove*** .... Labor.........289.00 ► Overhead installation. Up to 21 lf service entrance cable type SE, insulator, weather head, meter base, main disconnect breaker, up to 6 lf copper ground wire, grounding rod, clamps, fasteners, and waterproof connectors. (Does not include breaker panel.) Add **13%** for underground supply–includes excavation, trench shaping, sand bed, backfill, up to 38 lf USE cable, and underground materials.	ea	$289.00	$1,105.00	$1,394.00
150 amp cable service ***Replace*** Materials....785.00 Labor..........619.00 ***Remove*** .... Labor.........289.00 ► Overhead installation. Up to 21 lf service entrance cable type SE, insulator, weather head, meter base, main disconnect breaker, up to 6 lf copper ground wire, grounding rod, clamps, fasteners, and waterproof connectors. (Does not include breaker panel.) Add **13%** for underground supply–includes excavation, trench shaping, sand bed, backfill, up to 38 lf USE cable, and underground materials.	ea	$289.00	$1,404.00	$1,693.00
150 amp conduit service ***Replace*** Materials....830.00 Labor.........667.00 ***Remove*** .... Labor.........362.00 ► Overhead installation. Up to 21 lf service entrance cable type SE, insulator, weather head for conduit, EMT conduit with liquid-tight couplings, conduit straps, conduit entrance ell, meter base, main disconnect breaker, up to 6 lf copper ground wire, grounding rod, clamps, fasteners, and waterproof connectors. (Does not include breaker panel.) *Do not use this item if conduit extends through roof.* See rigid steel mast installations. Add **13%** for underground supply–includes excavation, trench shaping, sand bed, backfill, up to 38 lf USE cable, and underground materials.	ea	$362.00	$1,497.00	$1,859.00
150 amp rigid steel mast service ***Replace*** Materials....880.00 Labor.........667.00 ***Remove*** .... Labor.........425.00 ► Overhead installation. Rigid steel conduit extends through roof. Up to 21 lf service entrance cable type SE, insulator (clamps to mast), weather head for conduit, 2" galvanized rigid steel conduit with liquid-tight connections, roof flashing, conduit supports, conduit offset fittings, conduit entrance ell, meter base, main disconnect breaker, up to 6 lf copper ground wire, grounding rod, clamps, fasteners, and waterproof connectors. Add **$100** if guy wire is needed to support mast. (Does not include breaker panel.)	ea	$425.00	$1,547.00	$1,972.00
200 amp cable service ***Replace*** Materials..1030.00 Labor.........801.00 ***Remove*** .... Labor.........289.00 ► Overhead installation. Up to 21 lf service entrance cable type SE, insulator, weatherhead, meter base, main disconnect breaker, up to 6 lf copper ground wire, grounding rod, clamps, fasteners, and waterproof connectors. (Does not include breaker panel.) Add **13%** for underground supply–includes excavation, trench shaping, sand bed, backfill, up to 38 lf USE cable, and underground materials.	ea	$289.00	$1,831.00	$2,120.00

◁ **sub-panel**

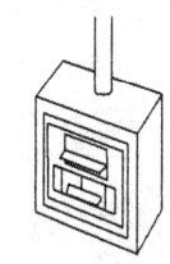

◁ **remove & reinstall**

◀ **ELECTRIC SERVICE**

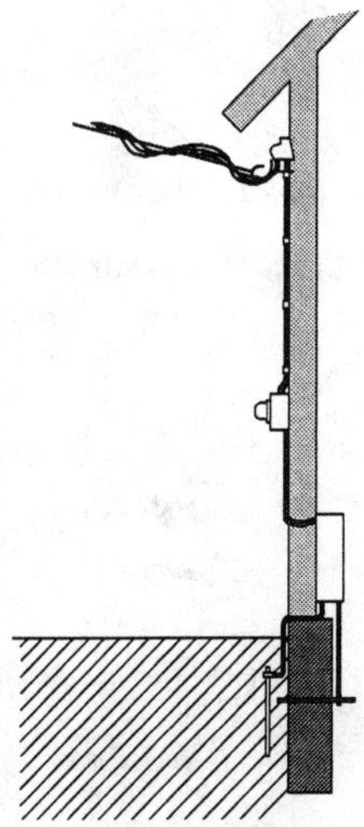

cable service △

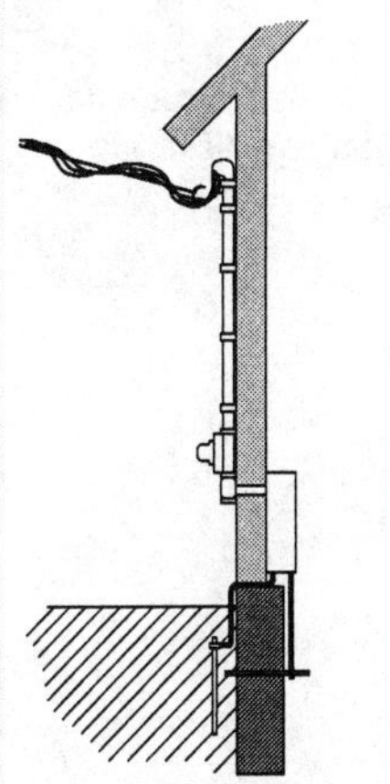

△ *conduit service*

RELATED ITEMS

Cleaning........................57

ELECTRIC SERVICE ► *continued*

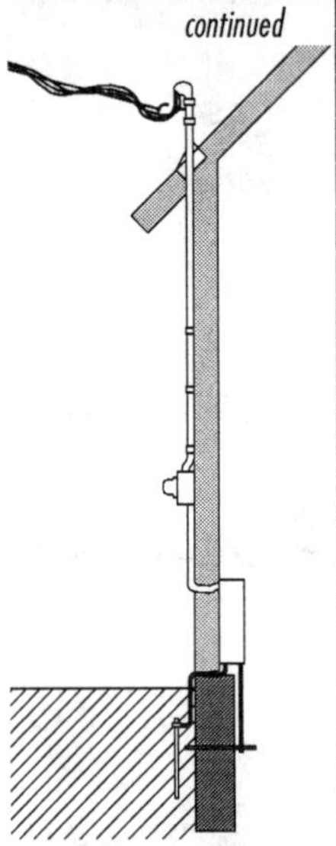

△ *rigid steel mast service*

Item Description	Unit	Remove	Replace	Total
200 amp conduit service ***Replace*** Materials..1090.00 Labor.........862.00 ***Remove*** .... Labor.........362.00 ► Overhead installation. Up to 21 lf service entrance cable type SE, insulator, weatherhead for conduit, EMT conduit with liquid-tight couplings, conduit straps, conduit entrance ell, meter base, main disconnect breaker, up to 6 lf copper ground wire, grounding rod, clamps, fasteners, and waterproof connectors. (Does not include breaker panel.) *Do not use this item if conduit extends through roof.* See rigid steel mast installations. Add **13%** for underground supply–includes excavation, trench shaping, sand bed, backfill, up to 38 lf USE cable, and underground materials.	ea	$362.00	$1,952.00	$2,314.00
200 amp rigid steel mast service ***Replace*** Materials...1150.00 Labor.........862.00 ***Remove*** .... Labor.........425.00 ► Overhead installation. Rigid steel conduit extends through roof. Up to 24 lf service entrance cable type SE, insulator (clamps to mast), weatherhead for conduit, 2" galvanized rigid steel conduit with liquid-tight connections, roof flashing, conduit supports, conduit offset fittings, conduit entrance ell, meter base, main disconnect breaker, up to 6 lf copper ground wire, grounding rod, clamps, fasteners, and waterproof connectors. Add **$100** if guy wire is needed to support mast. (Does not include breaker panel.)	ea	$425.00	$2,012.00	$2,437.00

CIRCUIT BREAKER ►

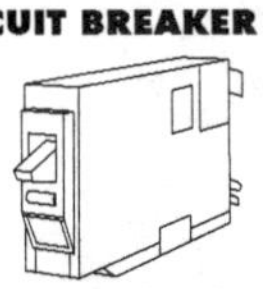

△ *single pole*

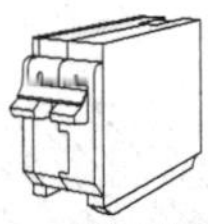

△ *double pole*

Item Description	Unit	Remove	Replace	Total
Single pole (120 volt) circuit breaker ***Replace*** Materials.......15.00 Labor...........27.50 ***Remove***......................... Labor 5.50	ea	$5.50	$42.50	$48.00
Double pole (240 volt) circuit breaker ***Replace*** Materials......35.00 Labor ....28.10 ***Remove***......................... Labor 5.50	ea	$5.50	$63.10	$68.60
Ground fault circuit interrupter breaker ***Replace*** Materials......58.00 Labor ....29.80 ***Remove***......................... Labor 5.50	ea	$5.50	$87.80	$93.30
main disconnect ▷ **Main disconnect circuit breaker** ***Replace*** Materials....340.00 Labor.........150.00 ***Remove***......................... Labor 5.50	ea	$5.50	$490.00	$495.50
remove & reinstall ▷ **Remove circuit breaker for work, then reinstall** ***Replace*** .... Labor 46.80	ea	—	$46.80	$46.80

DOOR BELL ► *See page 140 for wiring.*

Item Description	Unit	Remove	Replace	Total
Door bell or chime economy grade ***Replace*** Materials......53.00 Labor ....46.80 ***Remove*** .... Labor ....5.75 ► Single tone, entry door only.	ea	$5.75	$99.80	$105.55
Door bell or chime standard grade ***Replace*** Materials......95.00 Labor ....46.80 ***Remove*** .... Labor ....5.75 ► Separate tones for entry and secondary doors.	ea	$5.75	$141.80	$147.55
Door bell or chime high grade ***Replace*** Materials ....130.00 Labor ....46.80 ***Remove*** .... Labor ....5.75 ► Select from multiple tones.	ea	$5.75	$176.80	$182.55
Door bell or chime deluxe grade ***Replace*** Materials.....245.00 Labor ....46.80 ***Remove*** .... Labor ....5.75 ► Programmable, multiple tones.	ea	$5.75	$291.80	$297.55

Item Description	Unit	Remove	Replace	Total	
Door bell or chime button ***Replace*** Materials........5.90 Labor............5.15 ***Remove***......................... Labor............2.75 ► Button only, no wire.	ea	$2.75	$11.05	$13.80	◁ door bell button
Remove door chime for work, then reinstall ***Replace*** .... Labor..........71.40	ea	—	$71.40	$71.40	◁ remove & reinstall
Bathroom exhaust fan, economy grade ***Replace*** Materials......33.00 Labor..........25.90 ***Remove*** .... Labor..........13.90 ► 50 cfm. Includes up to 10 lf of 4" flexible vent duct, and wall outlet.	ea	$13.90	$58.90	$72.80	◄ BATH FAN 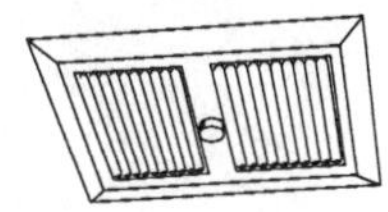
Bathroom exhaust fan, standard grade ***Replace*** Materials......55.00 Labor..........25.90 ***Remove*** .... Labor..........13.90 ► 65 cfm, low noise. Includes up to 10 lf of 4" flexible vent duct, and wall outlet.	ea	$13.90	$80.90	$94.80	
Bathroom exhaust fan, high grade ***Replace*** Materials......80.00 Labor..........25.90 ***Remove*** .... Labor..........13.90 ► 110 cfm, low noise. Includes up to 10 lf of 4" flexible vent duct, and wall outlet.	ea	$13.90	$105.90	$119.80	
Bathroom exhaust fan, deluxe grade ***Replace*** Materials.....125.00 Labor..........25.90 ***Remove*** .... Labor..........13.90 ► 110 cfm, low noise, variable speeds. Includes up to 10 lf of 4" flexible vent duct, and wall outlet.	ea	$13.90	$150.90	$164.80	
Remove bathroom exhaust fan for work, then reinstall ***Replace*** .... Labor..........42.30	ea	—	$42.30	$42.30	◁ remove & reinstall
Bathroom exhaust fan with heat lamp, standard grade ***Replace*** Materials......70.00 Labor..........33.30 ***Remove*** .... Labor..........20.00 ► 75 cfm, single heat lamp in center, single switch. Includes up to 10 lf of 4" flexible vent duct, and wall outlet.	ea	$20.00	$103.30	$123.30	◄ BATH FAN WITH HEAT LAMP 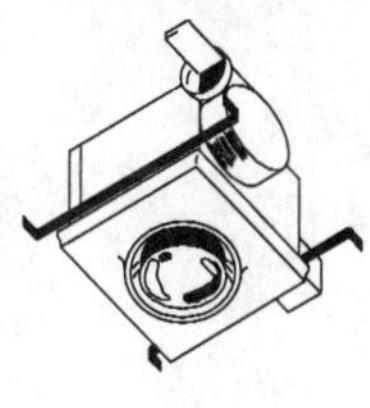
Bathroom exhaust fan with heat lamp, high grade ***Replace*** Materials....100.00 Labor..........33.30 ***Remove*** .... Labor..........20.00 ► 110 cfm, double heat lamp in center, separate timer switch for heat lamp. Includes up to 10 lf of 4" flexible vent duct, and wall outlet.	ea	$20.00	$133.30	$153.30	
Bathroom exhaust fan with heater, standard grade ***Replace*** Materials.....120.00 Labor..........35.80 ***Remove*** .... Labor..........20.00 ► 110 cfm, 200 watt heater, separate timer switch for heater. Includes up to 10 lf of 4" flexible vent duct, and wall outlet.	ea	$20.00	$155.80	$175.80	◄ BATH FAN WITH HEATER 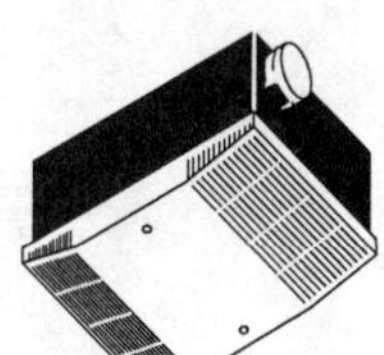
Bathroom exhaust fan with heater, high grade ***Replace*** Materials.....175.00 Labor..........35.80 ***Remove*** .... Labor..........20.00 ► 110 cfm, 450 watt heater, separate timer switch for heater. Includes up to 10 lf of 4" flexible vent duct, and wall outlet.	ea	$20.00	$210.80	$230.80	
Remove bathroom exhaust fan with heater for work, then reinstall ***Replace*** .... Labor..........54.10	ea	—	$54.10	$54.10	◁ remove & reinstall

	Item Description	Unit	Remove	Replace	Total
KITCHEN FAN ▶ *See page 26 for kitchen exhaust fans in range hoods.*	**Kitchen exhaust fan, economy grade** ***Replace*** Materials......70.00 Labor...........42.30 ***Remove*** .... Labor...........14.80 ▶ 110 cfm, no outside vent, charcoal filtration system.	ea	$14.80	$112.30	$127.10
	Kitchen exhaust fan, standard grade ***Replace*** Materials.....120.00 Labor...........42.30 ***Remove*** .... Labor...........14.80 ▶ 200 cfm. Includes up to 10 lf of 4" flexible vent duct, and wall outlet.	ea	$14.80	$162.30	$177.10
	Kitchen exhaust fan, high grade ***Replace*** Materials....225.00 Labor...........42.30 ***Remove*** .... Labor...........14.80 ▶ 300 cfm. Includes up to 10 lf of 4" flexible vent duct, and wall outlet.	ea	$14.80	$267.30	$282.10
remove & reinstall ▷	**Remove kitchen exhaust fan for work, then reinstall** ***Replace*** .... Labor..........60.60	ea	—	$60.60	$60.60
WHOLE-HOUSE ▶ FAN 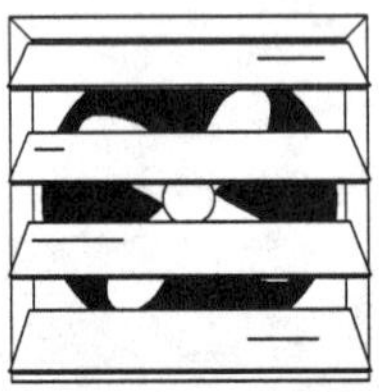	**Whole-house exhaust fan, standard grade** ***Replace*** Materials....565.00 Labor..........116.00 ***Remove*** .... Labor...........41.80 ▶ 4,500 cfm. Two-speed with automatic shutters.	ea	$41.80	$681.00	$722.80
	Whole-house exhaust fan, high grade ***Replace*** Materials....655.00 Labor..........116.00 ***Remove*** .... Labor...........41.80 ▶ 6,500 cfm. Variable speed with automatic shutters.	ea	$41.80	$771.00	$812.80
remove & reinstall ▷	**Remove whole-house exhaust fan for work, then reinstall** ***Replace*** .... Labor.........155.00	ea	—	$155.00	$155.00
INTERCOM ▶ MASTER STATION	**Intercom system master station, economy grade** ***Replace*** Materials....255.00 Labor..........93.10 ***Remove*** .... Labor..........20.60 ▶ Push to talk, release to listen.	ea	$20.60	$348.10	$368.70
	Intercom system master station, standard grade ***Replace*** Materials.....520.00 Labor..........93.10 ***Remove*** .... Labor..........20.60 ▶ AM/FM radio, room monitor, hands-free answer, privacy.	ea	$20.60	$613.10	$633.70
	Intercom system master station, high grade ***Replace*** Materials.....670.00 Labor..........93.10 ***Remove*** .... Labor..........20.60 ▶ AM/FM radio and cassette player, room monitor, hands-free answer, privacy.	ea	$20.60	$763.10	$783.70
	Intercom system master station, deluxe grade ***Replace*** Materials..1050.00 Labor..........93.10 ***Remove*** .... Labor..........20.60 ▶ AM/FM radio with cassette player, built-in telephone, telephone answering machine, room monitor, hands-free answer, privacy, gate or door latch release.	ea	$20.60	$1,143.10	$1,163.70
	Intercom system master station, custom grade ***Replace*** Materials..1600.00 Labor..........93.10 ***Remove*** .... Labor..........20.60 ▶ AM/FM radio with cassette player, built-in telephone, telephone answering machine, room monitor, hands-free answer, privacy, gate or door latch release, door video monitor.	ea	$20.60	$1,693.10	$1,713.70
remove & reinstall ▷	**Remove intercom master station for work, then reinstall** ***Replace*** .... Labor.........123.00	ea	—	$123.00	$123.00

Item Description	Unit	Remove	Replace	Total	
Intercom system remote station, economy grade ***Replace*** Materials......65.00 Labor..........25.90 ***Remove*** .... Labor............8.25 ► Push to talk, release to listen.	ea	$8.25	$90.90	$99.15	◄ **INTERCOM REMOTE STATION**
Intercom system remote station, standard grade ***Replace*** Materials....130.00 Labor..........25.90 ***Remove*** .... Labor............8.25 ► Hands-free answer, privacy.	ea	$8.25	$155.90	$164.15	
Intercom system remote station, high grade ***Replace*** Materials....250.00 Labor..........25.90 ***Remove*** .... Labor............8.25 ► Built-in telephone, hands-free answer, and privacy.	ea	$8.25	$275.90	$284.15	
Remove intercom remote station for work, then reinstall ***Replace*** .... Labor..........38.80	ea	—	$38.80	$38.80	◁ remove & reinstall
Sound system speaker with grille, economy grade ***Replace*** Materials......20.00 Labor............9.20 ***Remove*** .... Labor............6.46 ► 3" to 5" diameter speaker with plastic grille.	ea	$6.46	$29.20	$35.66	◄ **SOUND SYSTEM**
Sound system speaker with grille, standard grade ***Replace*** Materials......25.00 Labor............9.20 ***Remove*** .... Labor............6.46 ► 5" to 8" diameter elliptical speaker with wood-grain plastic grille.	ea	$6.46	$34.20	$40.66	
Sound system speaker with grille, high grade ***Replace*** Materials......35.00 Labor............9.20 ***Remove*** .... Labor............6.46 ► 5" to 8" diameter elliptical speaker with 1" to 2" "tweeter" speaker, wood-grain plastic grille.	ea	$6.46	$44.20	$50.66	
Sound system speaker with grille, deluxe grade ***Replace*** Materials......60.00 Labor............9.20 ***Remove*** .... Labor............6.46 ► Two 5" to 8" diameter speakers with two or three 1" to 2" "tweeter" speakers, wood-grain plastic grille.	ea	$6.46	$69.20	$75.66	
Check electrical circuits with megameter in small home ***Replace*** .... Labor.........169.00	ea	—	$169.00	$169.00	◄ **CHECK CIRCUITS**
Check electrical circuits with megameter in average size home ***Replace*** .... Labor.........245.00	ea	—	$245.00	$245.00	
Check electrical circuits with megameter in large home ***Replace*** .... Labor.........337.00	ea	—	$337.00	$337.00	
Smoke detector (battery operated) ***Replace*** Materials......30.00 Labor..........13.30 ***Remove*** .... Labor............5.50	ea	$5.50	$43.30	$48.80	◄ **SMOKE DETECTOR**
Smoke detector (direct wired) ***Replace*** Materials......40.00 Labor..........15.00 ***Remove*** .... Labor............5.50	ea	$5.50	$55.00	$60.50	
Remove smoke detector for work, then reinstall ***Replace*** .... Labor..........20.90	ea	—	$20.90	$20.90	◁ remove & reinstall

	Item Description	Unit	Remove	Replace	Total
CARBON MONOXIDE DETECTOR ▶	**Carbon monoxide detector (battery operated)** *Replace* Materials......35.00 Labor...........13.30 *Remove* .... Labor............5.50	ea	$5.50	$48.30	$53.80
	Carbon monoxide detector (direct wired) *Replace* Materials......45.00 Labor...........15.00 *Remove* .... Labor............5.50	ea	$5.50	$60.00	$65.50
remove & reinstall ▷	**Remove carbon monoxide detector for work, then reinstall** *Replace* .... Labor..........20.90	ea	—	$20.90	$20.90
RADON DETECTOR ▶	**Radon detector (battery operated)** *Replace* Materials......40.00 Labor...........13.30 *Remove* .... Labor............5.50	ea	$5.50	$53.30	$58.80
	Radon detector (direct wired) *Replace* Materials......50.00 Labor...........15.00 *Remove* .... Labor............5.50	ea	$5.50	$65.00	$70.50
remove & reinstall ▷	**Remove radon detector for work, then reinstall** *Replace* .... Labor..........20.90	ea	—	$20.90	$20.90
THERMOSTAT ▶ *Electrical line thermostat. See HVAC on page 278 for additional thermostats.*	**Thermostat for electric-resistance heating system** *Replace* Materials........8.00 Labor............6.90 *Remove* .... Labor............5.50	ea	$5.50	$14.90	$20.40
	Thermostat for electric heating system *Replace* Materials......16.50 Labor...........12.30 *Remove* .... Labor............5.50	ea	$5.50	$28.80	$34.30
ANTENNA ▶ *Includes up to 50 lf coaxial cable. Add **$175** for ground wire and grounding rod driven 8' deep into ground. (Required by many local codes.)*	**Television antenna, economy grade** *Replace* Materials....100.00 Labor..........46.80 *Remove* .... Labor..........23.00 ▶ 55" boom.	ea	$23.00	$146.80	$169.80
	Television antenna, standard grade *Replace* Materials.....175.00 Labor..........46.80 *Remove* .... Labor..........23.00 ▶ 100" boom.	ea	$23.00	$221.80	$244.80
	Television antenna, high grade *Replace* Materials....260.00 Labor..........46.80 *Remove* .... Labor..........23.00 ▶ 150" boom.	ea	$23.00	$306.80	$329.80
	Television antenna, deluxe grade *Replace* Materials....380.00 Labor..........46.80 *Remove* .... Labor..........23.00 ▶ 200" boom.	ea	$23.00	$426.80	$449.80
remove & reinstall ▷	**Remove television antenna for work, then reinstall** *Replace* .... Labor..........68.40	ea	—	$68.40	$68.40
WALL HEATER ▶	**Electric space heater recessed in wall, economy grade** *Replace* Materials....200.00 Labor..........93.10 *Remove* .... Labor...........13.90 ▶ 120 or 240 volt, 1,500 watt.	ea	$13.90	$293.10	$307.00

Item Description	Unit	Remove	Replace	Total	
Electric space heater recessed in wall, standard grade (240 volt) ***Replace*** Materials....230.00 Labor..........93.10 ***Remove*** .... Labor...........13.90 ► 2,250 watt.	ea	$13.90	$323.10	$337.00	
Electric space heater recessed in wall, high grade (240 volt) ***Replace*** Materials....275.00 Labor..........93.10 ***Remove*** .... Labor...........13.90 ► 4,000 watt.	ea	$13.90	$368.10	$382.00	
Remove electric space heater for work, then reinstall ***Replace*** .... Labor.........155.00	ea	—	$155.00	$155.00	◁ **remove & reinstall**
Electric-resistance heating cable, ceiling installation ***Replace*** Materials........2.40 Labor............1.36 ► Copper inner resistance wire embedded in gypsum.	sf	—	$3.76	$3.76	◄ **ELECTRIC-RESISTANCE HEATING CABLE** *For 120 volt wiring run see page 142. For 240 volt wiring run see page 144.*
Electric-resistance heating cable, floor installation ***Replace*** Materials........4.50 Labor............2.26 ► Wire contains copper inner resistance core and is sheathed with aluminum and a cross-linked polyethylene outer layer. Per sf of exposed floor space. Do not measure floor space underneath tubs, cabinets, or appliances.	sf	—	$6.76	$6.76	
Electric-resistance heating floor sensor ***Replace*** Materials......75.00 Labor..........23.80 ► For use with floor-installed electric-resistance heating that is not the only heat source. Floor sensors determine when floor is below desired temperature.	ea	—	$98.80	$98.80	
Electric baseboard heater, economy grade ***Replace*** Materials......16.50 Labor...........19.30 ***Remove*** .... Labor............4.54 ► 3 lf minimum. 165 watts per lf. Thermostat on heater.	lf	$4.54	$35.80	$40.34	◄ **BASEBOARD HEATER** *For 120 volt wiring run see page 142. For 240 volt wiring run see page 144.*
Electric baseboard heater, standard grade ***Replace*** Materials.......17.50 Labor...........19.30 ***Remove*** .... Labor............4.54 ► 3 lf minimum. 188 watts per lf. Includes up to 18 lf #18/2 thermostat wire, box and line thermostat.	lf	$4.54	$36.80	$41.34	
Remove electric baseboard heater for work, then reinstall ***Replace*** .... Labor...........27.00	lf	—	$27.00	$27.00	◁ **remove & reinstall**
Underground wiring for exterior post light fixture (to 30 lf) ***Replace*** Materials.....185.00 Labor..........46.00 ► Up to 36 lf #12/2 UF wire, sand bed in trench for wire, and up to 10 lf galvanized conduit. Does not include excavation, see page 178.	ea	—	$231.00	$231.00	◄ **POST FIXTURE WIRING**
Underground wiring for exterior post light fixture (to 50 feet) ***Replace*** Materials....290.00 Labor...........49.00 ► Up to 56 lf #12/2 UF wire, sand bed in trench for wire, and up to 10 lf galvanized conduit. Does not include excavation, see page 178.	ea	—	$339.00	$339.00	
Interior incandescent light fixture, economy grade ***Replace*** Materials.......15.00 Labor...........21.60 ***Remove*** .... Labor............8.25	ea	$8.25	$36.60	$44.85	◄ **LIGHT FIXTURE ALLOWANCE** *Contractor's allowance per light fixture in complete home.*
Interior incandescent light fixture, standard grade ***Replace*** Materials......35.00 Labor...........21.60 ***Remove*** .... Labor............8.25	ea	$8.25	$56.60	$64.85	

LIGHT FIXTURE ▶ *continued*

remove & reinstall ▷

LIGHT BAR ▶ *Standard grade light bars have decorative light bulbs. High grade light bars have decorative globe covers.*

CHANDELIER ▶ *To 28" in diameter. Suitable for installations on 8' and taller ceilings.*

Item Description	Unit	Remove	Replace	Total
Interior incandescent light fixture, high grade	ea	$8.25	$86.60	$94.85
Replace Materials......65.00 Labor..........21.60				
Remove .... Labor 8.25				
Interior incandescent light fixture, deluxe grade	ea	$8.25	$136.60	$144.85
Replace Materials.....115.00 Labor..........21.60				
Remove .... Labor 8.25				
Remove interior light fixture for work, then reinstall	ea	—	$38.50	$38.50
Replace .... Labor 38.50				
Bathroom light bar with 2 lights, standard grade	ea	$8.66	$68.10	$76.76
Replace Materials......45.00 Labor 23.10				
Remove .... Labor 8.66				
Bathroom light bar with 2 lights, high grade	ea	$8.66	$83.10	$91.76
Replace Materials......60.00 Labor 23.10				
Remove .... Labor 8.66				
Bathroom bar light with 3 to 4 lights, standard grade	ea	$8.66	$83.10	$91.76
Replace Materials......60.00 Labor 23.10				
Remove .... Labor 8.66				
Bathroom bar light with 3 to 4 lights, high grade	ea	$8.66	$93.10	$101.76
Replace Materials......70.00 Labor 23.10				
Remove .... Labor 8.66				
Bathroom bar light with 5 to 6 lights, standard grade	ea	$8.66	$108.10	$116.76
Replace Materials......85.00 Labor 23.10				
Remove .... Labor 8.66				
Bathroom bar light with 5 to 6 lights, high grade	ea	$8.66	$128.10	$136.76
Replace Materials....105.00 Labor 23.10				
Remove .... Labor 8.66				
Bathroom bar light with 7 to 8 lights, standard grade	ea	$8.66	$143.10	$151.76
Replace Materials.....120.00 Labor 23.10				
Remove .... Labor 8.66				
Bathroom bar light with 7 to 8 lights, high grade	ea	$8.66	$173.10	$181.76
Replace Materials ....150.00 Labor 23.10				
Remove .... Labor 8.66				
Remove bathroom bar light for work, then reinstall	ea	—	$40.70	$40.70
Replace .... Labor 40.70				
Chandelier, economy grade	ea	$15.30	$187.80	$203.10
Replace Materials.....125.00 Labor..........62.80				
Remove .... Labor..........15.30				
Chandelier, standard grade	ea	$15.30	$257.80	$273.10
Replace Materials.....195.00 Labor..........62.80				
Remove .... Labor..........15.30				
Chandelier, high grade	ea	$15.30	$337.80	$353.10
Replace Materials ....275.00 Labor..........62.80				
Remove .... Labor..........15.30				
Chandelier, deluxe grade	ea	$15.30	$457.80	$473.10
Replace Materials ....395.00 Labor..........62.80				
Remove .... Labor..........15.30				

LIGHT FIXTURE QUALITY

Economy Very light-gauge plated metal components, simple, thin glass shades. Chandeliers may contain 4 to 8 arms with turned wood center.

Standard Light-gauge plated metal components, simple glass shades. Chandeliers may contain 4 to 8 arms.

High Heavy-gauge plated metal components, glass shades with some intricate pattern or design, may have antique finish. Chandeliers may contain 4 to 8 arms.

Deluxe Heavy-gauge metal components, solid brass components, intricate glass shades, may have antique finish. Chandeliers may contain 6 to 12 arms.

FIXTURE QUALITY *continued*

Custom Heavy-gauge metal components, solid brass components, intricate glass shades, specialty antique finishes, polished brass, antiqued brass, polished nickel (or chrome) over brass. Chandeliers may contain 6 to 14 arms.

Item Description	Unit	Remove	Replace	Total
Chandelier, custom grade ***Replace*** Materials....505.00 Labor...........62.80 ***Remove*** .... Labor...........15.30	ea	$15.30	$567.80	$583.10
Chandelier, custom deluxe grade ***Replace*** Materials....645.00 Labor...........62.80 ***Remove*** .... Labor...........15.30	ea	$15.30	$707.80	$723.10
Entrance chandelier, economy grade ***Replace*** Materials....275.00 Labor.........126.00 ***Remove*** .... Labor...........15.30	ea	$15.30	$401.00	$416.30
Entrance chandelier, standard grade ***Replace*** Materials....395.00 Labor.........126.00 ***Remove*** .... Labor...........15.30	ea	$15.30	$521.00	$536.30
Entrance chandelier, high grade ***Replace*** Materials....520.00 Labor.........126.00 ***Remove*** .... Labor...........15.30	ea	$15.30	$646.00	$661.30
Entrance chandelier, deluxe grade ***Replace*** Materials....655.00 Labor.........126.00 ***Remove*** .... Labor...........15.30	ea	$15.30	$781.00	$796.30
Entrance chandelier, custom grade ***Replace*** Materials....845.00 Labor.........126.00 ***Remove*** .... Labor...........15.30	ea	$15.30	$971.00	$986.30
Entrance chandelier, custom deluxe grade ***Replace*** Materials..1050.00 Labor.........126.00 ***Remove*** .... Labor...........15.30	ea	$15.30	$1,176.00	$1,191.30
Grand entrance chandelier, economy grade ***Replace*** Materials....530.00 Labor.........173.00 ***Remove*** .... Labor...........15.30	ea	$15.30	$703.00	$718.30
Grand entrance chandelier, standard grade ***Replace*** Materials....870.00 Labor.........173.00 ***Remove*** .... Labor...........15.30	ea	$15.30	$1,043.00	$1,058.30
Grand entrance chandelier, high grade ***Replace*** Materials..1200.00 Labor.........173.00 ***Remove*** .... Labor...........15.30	ea	$15.30	$1,373.00	$1,388.30
Grand entrance chandelier, deluxe grade ***Replace*** Materials..1500.00 Labor.........173.00 ***Remove*** .... Labor...........15.30	ea	$15.30	$1,673.00	$1,688.30
Grand entrance chandelier, custom grade ***Replace*** Materials..1900.00 Labor.........173.00 ***Remove*** .... Labor...........15.30	ea	$15.30	$2,073.00	$2,088.30
Grand entrance chandelier, custom deluxe grade ***Replace*** Materials..3050.00 Labor.........173.00 ***Remove*** .... Labor...........15.30	ea	$15.30	$3,223.00	$3,238.30
Early American reproduction chandelier, economy grade ***Replace*** Materials....275.00 Labor...........62.80 ***Remove*** .... Labor...........15.30 ► Usually contains one or more of the following: hand-soldered brass, tin, or pewter, center wood turning, antique finishes, simulated candles (may be wax coated). 3 to 6 arms, curved metal & scalloped candle escutcheons. 12" to 20" diameter.	ea	$15.30	$337.80	$353.10

RELATED ITEMS

◄ **ENTRANCE CHANDELIER**
To 40" in diameter. Suitable for installations on 12' and taller ceilings.

FIXTURE QUALITY *continued*

Custom deluxe
Designed by prominent designer. Heavy-gauge metal components, solid brass components, intricate glass shades, specialty antique finishes, polished brass, antiqued brass, polished nickel (or chrome) over brass. Chandeliers usually contain 6 to 20 arms, often in two tiers.

◄ **GRAND ENTRANCE CHANDELIER**
To 60" in diameter. Suitable for installations on 18' and taller ceilings.

DESIGNER FIXTURES

The price of a light fixture can vary a great deal, often without any visible explanation.

For example, a light fixture that is designed by a prominent designer may be far more expensive than a light fixture with similar materials and design.

◄ **EARLY AMERICAN CHANDELIER**
Early American candle chandeliers converted to electrical.

continued on next page

EARLY AMERICAN CHANDELIER *continued*

These fixtures are antique reproductions and are hand tooled from tin, distressed tin, pewter, brass, or copper. Joints are hand soldered. The electric "candles" may be coated with bees wax. Although many modern fixtures use a candle style, they should not be confused with early American reproduction fixtures. Look for hand tooling inconsistencies and hand-soldered joints.

Item Description	Unit	Remove	Replace	Total
Early American reproduction chandelier, standard grade **Replace** Materials....375.00 Labor..........62.80 **Remove** .... Labor..........15.30 ► Same quality as economy grade with 4 to 8 arms. 21" to 30" diameter.	ea	$15.30	$437.80	$453.10
Early American reproduction chandelier, high grade **Replace** Materials....520.00 Labor..........62.80 **Remove** .... Labor..........15.30 ► Same quality as economy grade with 10 to 18 arms. 21" to 30" diameter.	ea	$15.30	$582.80	$598.10
Early American reproduction chandelier, deluxe grade **Replace** Materials....740.00 Labor..........62.80 **Remove** .... Labor..........15.30 ► Simulated candle-style light fixture. Same quality as economy grade with 10 to 18 arms. 21" to 30" diameter, two tiers.	ea	$15.30	$802.80	$818.10
Early American reproduction chandelier, custom grade **Replace** Materials....890.00 Labor..........62.80 **Remove** .... Labor..........15.30 ► Simulated candle-style light fixture. Same quality as economy grade with intricate metalwork. 10 to 18 arms. 21" to 30" diameter, two tiers.	ea	$15.30	$952.80	$968.10
Early American reproduction chandelier, custom deluxe grade **Replace** Materials...1150.00 Labor..........62.80 **Remove** .... Labor..........15.30 ► Simulated candle-style light fixture. Same quality as economy grade with intricate metalwork. 10 to 18 arms. 31" to 44" diameter, two tiers.	ea	$15.30	$1,212.80	$1,228.10

EARLY ELECTRIC CHANDELIER

Reproductions of chandeliers that were made when electricity was first introduced. Use these prices for true design reproductions. See quality indicators on pages 154-155.

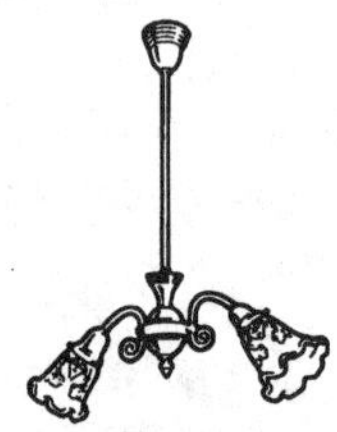

courtesy of **Rejuvenation Lamp & Fixture Co.**

Item Description	Unit	Remove	Replace	Total
Early electric reproduction chandelier, economy grade **Replace** Materials....320.00 Labor..........62.80 **Remove** .... Labor..........15.30	ea	$15.30	$382.80	$398.10
Early electric reproduction chandelier, standard grade **Replace** Materials.....410.00 Labor..........62.80 **Remove** .... Labor..........15.30	ea	$15.30	$472.80	$488.10
Early electric reproduction chandelier, high grade **Replace** Materials....550.00 Labor..........62.80 **Remove** .... Labor..........15.30	ea	$15.30	$612.80	$628.10
Early electric reproduction chandelier, deluxe grade **Replace** Materials....780.00 Labor..........62.80 **Remove** .... Labor..........15.30	ea	$15.30	$842.80	$858.10
Early electric reproduction chandelier, custom grade **Replace** Materials....930.00 Labor..........62.80 **Remove** .... Labor..........15.30	ea	$15.30	$992.80	$1,008.10
Early electric reproduction chandelier, custom deluxe grade **Replace** Materials ..1250.00 Labor..........62.80 **Remove** .... Labor..........15.30	ea	$15.30	$1,312.80	$1,328.10

EARLY GAS CHANDELIER

Electrified reproductions of chandeliers that were originally designed to burn coal gas. Can usually be identified by a fake gas valve on the arm.

Item Description	Unit	Remove	Replace	Total
Early gas reproduction chandelier, economy grade **Replace** Materials....335.00 Labor..........62.80 **Remove** .... Labor..........15.30	ea	$15.30	$397.80	$413.10
Early gas reproduction chandelier, standard grade **Replace** Materials....405.00 Labor..........62.80 **Remove** .... Labor..........15.30	ea	$15.30	$467.80	$483.10

continued on next page

Item Description	Unit	Remove	Replace	Total
Early gas reproduction chandelier, high grade ***Replace*** Materials....570.00 Labor..........62.80 ***Remove*** .... Labor..........15.30	ea	$15.30	$632.80	$648.10
Early gas reproduction chandelier, deluxe grade ***Replace*** Materials....775.00 Labor..........62.80 ***Remove*** .... Labor..........15.30	ea	$15.30	$837.80	$853.10
Early gas reproduction chandelier, custom grade ***Replace*** Materials.....915.00 Labor..........62.80 ***Remove*** .... Labor..........15.30	ea	$15.30	$977.80	$993.10
Early gas reproduction chandelier, custom deluxe grade ***Replace*** Materials..1300.00 Labor..........62.80 ***Remove*** .... Labor..........15.30	ea	$15.30	$1,362.80	$1,378.10
Early electric / gas combination reproduction chandelier, economy grade ***Replace*** Materials....350.00 Labor..........62.80 ***Remove*** .... Labor..........15.30	ea	$15.30	$412.80	$428.10
Early electric / gas combination reproduction chandelier, standard grade ***Replace*** Materials....420.00 Labor..........62.80 ***Remove*** .... Labor..........15.30	ea	$15.30	$482.80	$498.10
Early electric / gas combination reproduction chandelier, high grade ***Replace*** Materials....575.00 Labor..........62.80 ***Remove*** .... Labor..........15.30	ea	$15.30	$637.80	$653.10
Early electric / gas combination reproduction chandelier, deluxe grade ***Replace*** Materials....785.00 Labor..........62.80 ***Remove*** .... Labor..........15.30	ea	$15.30	$847.80	$863.10
Early electric / gas combination reproduction chandelier, custom grade ***Replace*** Materials....935.00 Labor..........62.80 ***Remove*** .... Labor..........15.30	ea	$15.30	$997.80	$1,013.10
Early electric / gas combination reproduction chandelier, custom deluxe grade ***Replace*** Materials..1250.00 Labor..........62.80 ***Remove*** .... Labor..........15.30	ea	$15.30	$1,312.80	$1,328.10
Imitation crystal chandelier, economy grade ***Replace*** Materials....205.00 Labor..........62.80 ***Remove*** .... Labor..........15.30 ► Cut glass imitation crystal. 4 to 8 arms.	ea	$15.30	$267.80	$283.10
Imitation crystal chandelier, standard grade ***Replace*** Materials....280.00 Labor..........62.80 ***Remove*** .... Labor..........15.30 ► Cut glass imitation crystal. 6 to 14 arms.	ea	$15.30	$342.80	$358.10
Crystal chandelier, standard grade ***Replace*** Materials.....670.00 Labor..........62.80 ***Remove*** .... Labor..........15.30 ► Lower quality crystal components, lightly festooned.	ea	$15.30	$732.80	$748.10
Crystal chandelier, high grade ***Replace*** Materials....855.00 Labor..........62.80 ***Remove*** .... Labor..........15.30 ► High quality crystal components, moderately festooned. Crystal fixture width is 65% to 80% of the fixture's height.	ea	$15.30	$917.80	$933.10

◄ **EARLY GAS CHANDELIER** *continued*

Because a flame burns upward, gas reproduction fixture shades always face upward. Also use these prices for electric reproductions of lantern style chandeliers. Modern designs of a gas or lantern style usually fall in the economy and standard grades. See quality indicators on pages 154-155.

◄ **EARLY ELECTRIC / GAS CHANDELIER**

When electricity was first introduced, builders were unsure whether it or gas was the wave of the future. Many builders played it safe by installing fixtures that used both. The original gas components can be identified by the fake valve on the arm. Gas components always face up. Electrical components often have a pull switch and usually, but not always, face down. See quality indicators on pages 154-155.

◄ **IMITATION CRYSTAL CHANDELIER**
Cut glass components.

◄ **CRYSTAL CHANDELIER**
*High-quality crystal components. Deduct **15%** for lower quality crystal. To 25" diameter. Suitable for installation on 8' or taller ceilings.*

RELATED ITEMS

Cleaning........................57

	Item Description	Unit	Remove	Replace	Total
CRYSTAL ▶ CHANDELIER *continued*	**Crystal chandelier, deluxe grade** ***Replace*** Materials..1000.00 Labor..........62.80 ***Remove*** .... Labor..........15.30 ▶ High quality crystal components, heavily festooned. Crystal fixture width is 65% to 80% of the fixture's height.	ea	$15.30	$1,062.80	$1,078.10
	Crystal chandelier, custom grade ***Replace*** Materials...1150.00 Labor..........62.80 ***Remove*** .... Labor..........15.30 ▶ High quality crystal components. Crystal fixture width is 50% to 60% of the fixture's height.	ea	$15.30	$1,212.80	$1,228.10
	Crystal chandelier, custom deluxe grade ***Replace*** Materials..1250.00 Labor..........62.80 ***Remove*** .... Labor..........15.30 ▶ High quality crystal components, heavily festooned. Crystal fixture width is 50% to 60% of the fixture's height.	ea	$15.30	$1,312.80	$1,328.10
ENTRANCE ▶ CRYSTAL CHANDELIER *High-quality crystal components. Deduct* **15%** *for lower quality crystal. To 32" diameter. Suitable for installation on 14' or taller ceilings.*	**Entrance crystal chandelier, standard grade** ***Replace*** Materials....985.00 Labor........126.00 ***Remove*** .... Labor..........15.30 ▶ Lower quality crystal components, lightly festooned.	ea	$15.30	$1,111.00	$1,126.30
	Entrance crystal chandelier, high grade ***Replace*** Materials...1150.00 Labor........126.00 ***Remove*** .... Labor..........15.30 ▶ High quality crystal components, moderately festooned. Crystal fixture width is 65% to 80% of the fixture's height.	ea	$15.30	$1,276.00	$1,291.30
	Entrance crystal chandelier, deluxe grade ***Replace*** Materials..1300.00 Labor........126.00 ***Remove*** .... Labor..........15.30 ▶ High quality crystal components, heavily festooned. Crystal fixture width is 65% to 80% of the fixture's height.	ea	$15.30	$1,426.00	$1,441.30
	Entrance crystal chandelier, custom grade ***Replace*** Materials...1750.00 Labor........126.00 ***Remove*** .... Labor..........15.30 ▶ High quality crystal components. Crystal fixture width is 50% to 60% of the fixture's height.	ea	$15.30	$1,876.00	$1,891.30
	Entrance crystal chandelier, custom deluxe grade ***Replace*** Materials..2500.00 Labor........126.00 ***Remove*** .... Labor..........15.30 ▶ High quality crystal components, heavily festooned. Crystal fixture width is 50% to 60% of the fixture's height.	ea	$15.30	$2,626.00	$2,641.30
GRAND ▶ ENTRANCE CRYSTAL CHANDELIER *High-quality crystal components. Deduct* **15%** *for lower quality crystal. To 52" diameter. Suitable for installation on 20' or taller ceilings.*	**Grand entrance crystal chandelier, standard grade** ***Replace*** Materials...1450.00 Labor........173.00 ***Remove*** .... Labor..........15.30 ▶ Lower quality crystal components, lightly festooned.	ea	$15.30	$1,623.00	$1,638.30
	Grand entrance crystal chandelier, high grade ***Replace*** Materials..3200.00 Labor........173.00 ***Remove*** .... Labor..........15.30 ▶ High quality crystal components, moderately festooned. Crystal fixture width is 65% to 80% of the fixture's height.	ea	$15.30	$3,373.00	$3,388.30
	Grand entrance crystal chandelier, deluxe grade ***Replace*** Materials..4350.00 Labor........173.00 ***Remove*** .... Labor..........15.30 ▶ High quality crystal components, heavily festooned. Crystal fixture width is 65% to 80% of the fixture's height.	ea	$15.30	$4,523.00	$4,538.30

Item Description	Unit	Remove	Replace	Total
Grand entrance crystal chandelier, custom grade ***Replace*** Materials..5900.00 Labor.........173.00 ***Remove*** .... Labor...........15.30 ► High quality crystal components. Crystal fixture width is 50% to 60% of the fixture's height.	**ea**	**$15.30**	**$6,073.00**	**$6,088.30**
Grand entrance crystal chandelier, custom deluxe grade ***Replace*** Materials..6900.00 Labor.........173.00 ***Remove*** .... Labor...........15.30 ► High quality crystal components, heavily festooned. Crystal fixture width is 50% to 60% of the fixture's height.	**ea**	**$15.30**	**$7,073.00**	**$7,088.30**
Crystal tier chandelier, standard grade ***Replace*** Materials....780.00 Labor...........62.80 ***Remove*** .... Labor...........15.30 ► 4 to 5 tiers, 6" to 10" diameter. Minimum 8' to 10' ceilings.	**ea**	**$15.30**	**$842.80**	**$858.10**
Crystal tier chandelier, high grade ***Replace*** Materials....855.00 Labor.........173.00 ***Remove*** .... Labor...........15.30 ► 4 to 5 tiers, 11" to 14" diameter. Minimum 8' to 10' ceilings.	**ea**	**$15.30**	**$1,028.00**	**$1,043.30**
Crystal tier chandelier, deluxe grade ***Replace*** Materials..1050.00 Labor.........173.00 ***Remove*** .... Labor...........15.30 ► 4 to 5 tiers, 15" to 20" diameter. Minimum 12' to 14' ceilings.	**ea**	**$15.30**	**$1,223.00**	**$1,238.30**
Crystal tier chandelier, custom grade ***Replace*** Materials...1150.00 Labor.........173.00 ***Remove*** .... Labor...........15.30 ► 4 to 5 tiers, 21" to 25" diameter. Minimum 15' to 18' ceilings.	**ea**	**$15.30**	**$1,323.00**	**$1,338.30**
Crystal tier chandelier, custom deluxe grade ***Replace*** Materials...1550.00 Labor.........173.00 ***Remove*** .... Labor...........15.30 ► 4 to 5 tiers, 26" to 34" diameter. Minimum 15' to 18' ceilings.	**ea**	**$15.30**	**$1,723.00**	**$1,738.30**
Crystal wall fixture, standard grade ***Replace*** Materials....235.00 Labor...........21.00 ***Remove*** .... Labor............8.25 ► Lower quality crystal components, lightly festooned.	**ea**	**$8.25**	**$256.00**	**$264.25**
Crystal wall fixture, high grade ***Replace*** Materials....365.00 Labor...........21.00 ***Remove*** .... Labor............8.25 ► High quality crystal components, moderately festooned. Crystal fixture width is 65% to 80% of the fixture's height.	**ea**	**$8.25**	**$386.00**	**$394.25**
Crystal wall fixture, deluxe grade ***Replace*** Materials....540.00 Labor...........21.00 ***Remove*** .... Labor............8.25 ► High quality crystal components, heavily festooned. Crystal fixture width is 65% to 80% of the fixture's height.	**ea**	**$8.25**	**$561.00**	**$569.25**
Crystal wall fixture, custom grade ***Replace*** Materials....785.00 Labor...........21.00 ***Remove*** .... Labor............8.25 ► High quality crystal components. Crystal fixture width is 50% to 60% of the fixture's height.	**ea**	**$8.25**	**$806.00**	**$814.25**
Remove crystal wall fixture for work, then reinstall ***Replace*** .... Labor..........38.50	**ea**	**—**	**$38.50**	**$38.50**

RELATED ITEMS

Cleaning........................57

◄ **CRYSTAL TIER CHANDELIER**
*High-quality crystal components. Deduct **15%** for lower quality crystal. Crystal tier chandeliers resemble an upside down wedding cake. They are usually 1.5 to 2 times taller than they are wide, so normally are installed on taller ceilings.*

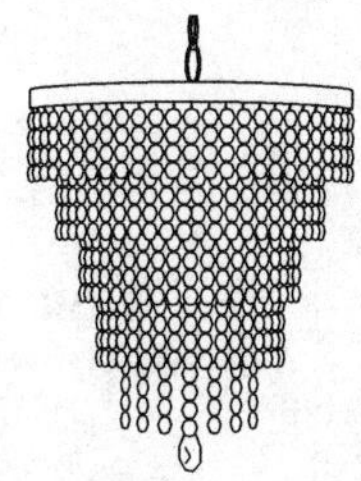

◄ **CRYSTAL WALL FIXTURE**
*High-quality crystal components. Deduct **15%** for lower quality crystal.*

◁ **remove & reinstall**

	Item Description	Unit	Remove	Replace	Total
CRYSTAL CHANDELIER REPAIR ►	**Repair crystal chandelier, minor repairs** *Replace* Materials......60.00 Labor...........69.30 ► Replace 2 to 4 components.	ea	—	$129.30	$129.30
	Repair crystal chandelier, significant repairs *Replace* Materials.....120.00 Labor.........139.00 ► Replace 5 to 10 components.	ea	—	$259.00	$259.00
	Repair crystal chandelier, major repairs *Replace* Materials....205.00 Labor.........277.00 ► Replace 11 to 16 components.	ea	—	$482.00	$482.00
	Repair crystal chandelier, rebuild *Replace* Materials....385.00 Labor.........576.00 ► Dismantle all or most of fixture, replace 25% to 35% of components.	ea	—	$961.00	$961.00
	Remove chandelier for work, then reinstall *Replace* .... Labor.........107.00	ea	—	$107.00	$107.00
	Remove vaulted ceiling chandelier for work, then reinstall *Replace* .... Labor.........231.00 ► For ceiling heights to 14'.	ea	—	$231.00	$231.00
	Remove high vaulted-ceiling chandelier for work, then reinstall *Replace* .... Labor.........314.00 ► For ceiling heights to 22'.	ea	—	$314.00	$314.00
TALL CEILING INSTALLATION ►	**Add for hanging chandelier on vaulted ceiling 12' to 14' tall** *Replace* .... Labor..........34.60	ea	—	$34.60	$34.60
	Add for hanging chandelier on vaulted ceiling 14' to 16' tall *Replace* .... Labor...........62.80	ea	—	$62.80	$62.80
	Add for hanging chandelier on vaulted ceiling 17' to 22' tall *Replace* .... Labor...........96.10	ea	—	$96.10	$96.10
SINGLE PENDANT FIXTURE ► *Pendant fixtures hang from a chain or rod and connect directly to an electrical box in the ceiling. (For hanging fixtures that connect to a switched outlet, see page 168.) See quality indicators on pages 154-155.*	**Single pendant light fixture, economy grade** *Replace* Materials......60.00 Labor...........21.60 *Remove* .... Labor............8.25	ea	$8.25	$81.60	$89.85
	Single pendant light fixture, standard grade *Replace* Materials......75.00 Labor...........21.60 *Remove* .... Labor............8.25	ea	$8.25	$96.60	$104.85
	Single pendant light fixture, high grade *Replace* Materials......90.00 Labor...........21.60 *Remove* .... Labor............8.25	ea	$8.25	$111.60	$119.85
	Single pendant light fixture, deluxe grade *Replace* Materials.....110.00 Labor...........21.60 *Remove* .... Labor............8.25	ea	$8.25	$131.60	$139.85
	Single pendant light fixture, custom grade *Replace* Materials....130.00 Labor...........21.60 *Remove* .... Labor............8.25	ea	$8.25	$151.60	$159.85
	Single pendant light fixture, custom deluxe grade *Replace* Materials.....145.00 Labor...........21.60 *Remove* .... Labor............8.25	ea	$8.25	$166.60	$174.85

Item Description	Unit	Remove	Replace	Total
Double pendant light fixture, economy grade ***Replace*** Materials....100.00 Labor...........21.60 ***Remove*** .... Labor 8.25	ea	$8.25	$121.60	$129.85
Double pendant light fixture, standard grade ***Replace*** Materials.....125.00 Labor...........21.60 ***Remove*** .... Labor 8.25	ea	$8.25	$146.60	$154.85
Double pendant light fixture, high grade ***Replace*** Materials ....150.00 Labor...........21.60 ***Remove*** .... Labor 8.25	ea	$8.25	$171.60	$179.85
Double pendant light fixture, deluxe grade ***Replace*** Materials.....170.00 Labor...........21.60 ***Remove*** .... Labor 8.25	ea	$8.25	$191.60	$199.85
Double pendant light fixture, custom grade ***Replace*** Materials.....190.00 Labor...........21.60 ***Remove*** .... Labor 8.25	ea	$8.25	$211.60	$219.85
Double pendant light fixture, custom deluxe grade ***Replace*** Materials....225.00 Labor...........21.60 ***Remove*** .... Labor 8.25	ea	$8.25	$246.60	$254.85
"Shower" style light fixture, economy grade ***Replace*** Materials.....145.00 Labor...........62.80 ***Remove*** .... Labor...........15.30	ea	$15.30	$207.80	$223.10
"Shower" style light fixture, standard grade ***Replace*** Materials.....190.00 Labor...........62.80 ***Remove*** .... Labor...........15.30	ea	$15.30	$252.80	$268.10
"Shower" style light fixture, high grade ***Replace*** Materials....250.00 Labor...........62.80 ***Remove*** .... Labor...........15.30	ea	$15.30	$312.80	$328.10
"Shower" style light fixture, deluxe grade ***Replace*** Materials....295.00 Labor...........62.80 ***Remove*** .... Labor...........15.30	ea	$15.30	$357.80	$373.10
"Shower" style light fixture, custom grade ***Replace*** Materials....380.00 Labor...........62.80 ***Remove*** .... Labor...........15.30	ea	$15.30	$442.80	$458.10
"Shower" style light fixture, custom deluxe grade ***Replace*** Materials.....410.00 Labor...........62.80 ***Remove*** .... Labor...........15.30	ea	$15.30	$472.80	$488.10
Small bowl-shade or globe light fixture, economy grade ***Replace*** Materials......30.00 Labor...........21.60 ***Remove*** .... Labor 8.25	ea	$8.25	$51.60	$59.85
Small bowl-shade or globe light fixture, standard grade ***Replace*** Materials......40.00 Labor...........21.60 ***Remove*** .... Labor 8.25	ea	$8.25	$61.60	$69.85
Small bowl-shade or globe light fixture, high grade ***Replace*** Materials......55.00 Labor...........21.60 ***Remove*** .... Labor 8.25	ea	$8.25	$76.60	$84.85

◀ **DOUBLE PENDANT FIXTURE**
Pendant fixtures hang from a chain or rod and connect directly to an electrical box in the ceiling. (For hanging fixtures that connect to a switched outlet, see page 168.) See quality indicators on pages 154-155.

◀ **"SHOWER" FIXTURE**
"Shower" style fixtures have a large base. Two to four (sometimes more) small lights with shades hang from the base on chains or rods. See quality indicators on pages 154-155.

◀ **SMALL BOWL-SHADE FIXTURE**
Fixture with a globe or bowl shade. Small sizes are typically found in halls. See quality indicators on pages 154-155.

RELATED ITEMS

Cleaning........................57

SMALL BOWL-SHADE FIXTURE *continued*

Item Description	Unit	Remove	Replace	Total
Small bowl-shade or globe light fixture, deluxe grade ***Replace*** Materials......75.00 Labor..........21.60 ***Remove*** .... Labor 8.25	ea	$8.25	$96.60	$104.85
Small bowl-shade or globe light fixture, custom grade ***Replace*** Materials......85.00 Labor..........21.60 ***Remove*** .... Labor 8.25	ea	$8.25	$106.60	$114.85
Small bowl-shade or globe light fixture, custom deluxe grade ***Replace*** Materials....105.00 Labor..........21.60 ***Remove*** .... Labor 8.25	ea	$8.25	$126.60	$134.85

BOWL-SHADE FIXTURE

Fixture with a globe or bowl shade. See quality indicators on pages 154-155.

Item Description	Unit	Remove	Replace	Total
Bowl-shade or globe light fixture, economy grade ***Replace*** Materials......45.00 Labor..........21.60 ***Remove*** .... Labor 8.25	ea	$8.25	$66.60	$74.85
Bowl-shade or globe light fixture, standard grade ***Replace*** Materials......80.00 Labor..........21.60 ***Remove*** .... Labor 8.25	ea	$8.25	$101.60	$109.85
Bowl-shade or globe light fixture, high grade ***Replace*** Materials....100.00 Labor..........21.60 ***Remove*** .... Labor 8.25	ea	$8.25	$121.60	$129.85
Bowl-shade or globe light fixture, deluxe grade ***Replace*** Materials....130.00 Labor..........21.60 ***Remove*** .... Labor 8.25	ea	$8.25	$151.60	$159.85
Bowl-shade or globe light fixture, custom grade ***Replace*** Materials.....160.00 Labor..........21.60 ***Remove*** .... Labor 8.25	ea	$8.25	$181.60	$189.85
Bowl-shade or globe light fixture, custom deluxe grade ***Replace*** Materials.....185.00 Labor..........21.60 ***Remove*** .... Labor 8.25	ea	$8.25	$206.60	$214.85

SUSPENDED BOWL-SHADE FIXTURE

Bowl-shade suspended on three rods or chains. See quality indicators on pages 154-155.

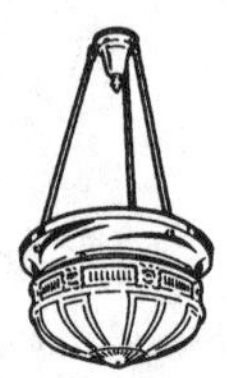

courtesy of ***Rejuvenation Lamp & Fixture Co.***

Item Description	Unit	Remove	Replace	Total
Suspended bowl-shade light fixture, economy grade ***Replace*** Materials.....175.00 Labor..........62.80 ***Remove*** .... Labor..........15.30	ea	$15.30	$237.80	$253.10
Suspended bowl-shade light fixture, standard grade ***Replace*** Materials....205.00 Labor..........62.80 ***Remove*** .... Labor..........15.30	ea	$15.30	$267.80	$283.10
Suspended bowl-shade light fixture, high grade ***Replace*** Materials....290.00 Labor..........62.80 ***Remove*** .... Labor..........15.30	ea	$15.30	$352.80	$368.10
Suspended bowl-shade light fixture, deluxe grade ***Replace*** Materials....365.00 Labor..........62.80 ***Remove*** .... Labor..........15.30	ea	$15.30	$427.80	$443.10
Suspended bowl-shade light fixture, custom grade ***Replace*** Materials....405.00 Labor..........62.80 ***Remove*** .... Labor..........15.30	ea	$15.30	$467.80	$483.10
Suspended bowl-shade light fixture, custom deluxe grade ***Replace*** Materials.....510.00 Labor..........62.80 ***Remove*** .... Labor..........15.30	ea	$15.30	$572.80	$588.10

Item Description	Unit	Remove	Replace	Total
Billiard-table style light fixture, economy grade ***Replace*** Materials.....190.00 Labor...........57.60 ***Remove*** .... Labor...........15.30 ► Single light on rod, with colored glass shade.	ea	$15.30	$247.60	$262.90
Billiard-table style light fixture, standard grade ***Replace*** Materials....420.00 Labor...........57.60 ***Remove*** .... Labor...........15.30 ► Single light on decorative rod, with ribbed glass shade.	ea	$15.30	$477.60	$492.90
Billiard-table style light fixture, high grade ***Replace*** Materials....645.00 Labor...........57.60 ***Remove*** .... Labor...........15.30 ► Double lights on decorative rods, with ribbed glass shades.	ea	$15.30	$702.60	$717.90
Billiard-table style light fixture, deluxe grade ***Replace*** Materials.....910.00 Labor...........57.60 ***Remove*** .... Labor...........15.30 ► Triple lights on decorative rods, with ribbed glass shades.	ea	$15.30	$967.60	$982.90
Billiard-table style light fixture, custom grade ***Replace*** Materials...1150.00 Labor...........57.60 ***Remove*** .... Labor...........15.30 ► Triple lights on decorative rods with brass scroll work above, ribbed glass shades with brass trim.	ea	$15.30	$1,207.60	$1,222.90
Billiard-table style light fixture, custom deluxe grade ***Replace*** Materials..1850.00 Labor...........57.60 ***Remove*** .... Labor...........15.30 ► Triple lights on decorative rods with elaborate brass scroll work above, ribbed glass shades with brass trim. May have copper shades.	ea	$15.30	$1,907.60	$1,922.90
Remove billiard-table style light fixture for work, then reinstall ***Replace*** .... Labor...........98.70	ea	—	$98.70	$98.70
Wall-mount light fixture, economy grade ***Replace*** Materials.......15.00 Labor...........21.00 ***Remove*** .... Labor............8.25	ea	$8.25	$36.00	$44.25
Wall-mount light fixture, standard grade ***Replace*** Materials......35.00 Labor...........21.00 ***Remove*** .... Labor............8.25	ea	$8.25	$56.00	$64.25
Wall-mount light fixture, high grade ***Replace*** Materials......90.00 Labor...........21.00 ***Remove*** .... Labor............8.25	ea	$8.25	$111.00	$119.25
Wall-mount light fixture, deluxe grade ***Replace*** Materials.....155.00 Labor...........21.00 ***Remove*** .... Labor............8.25	ea	$8.25	$176.00	$184.25
Wall-mount light fixture, custom grade ***Replace*** Materials.....175.00 Labor...........21.00 ***Remove*** .... Labor............8.25	ea	$8.25	$196.00	$204.25
Wall-mount light fixture, custom deluxe grade ***Replace*** Materials....255.00 Labor...........21.00 ***Remove*** .... Labor............8.25	ea	$8.25	$276.00	$284.25
Remove wall-mount light fixture for work, then reinstall ***Replace*** .... Labor..........38.50	ea	—	$38.50	$38.50

◄ **BILLIARD-TABLE STYLE FIXTURE**
See quality indicators on pages 154-155.

◄ **WALL-MOUNT FIXTURE**
See quality indicators on pages 154-155.

RELATED ITEMS

Cleaning........................57

◁ **remove & reinstall**

	Item Description	Unit	Remove	Replace	Total
FLUORESCENT FIXTURE ▶	**1′ one-tube surface-mounted fluorescent strip light** *Replace* Materials.......15.00 Labor..........39.50 *Remove* .... Labor...........13.80	ea	$13.80	$54.50	$68.30
	1-1/2′ one-tube surface-mounted fluorescent strip light *Replace* Materials......20.00 Labor..........39.50 *Remove* .... Labor...........13.80	ea	$13.80	$59.50	$73.30
	2′ one-tube surface-mounted fluorescent strip light *Replace* Materials......20.00 Labor..........39.50 *Remove* .... Labor...........13.80	ea	$13.80	$59.50	$73.30
	4′ one-tube surface-mounted fluorescent strip light *Replace* Materials......30.00 Labor..........39.50 *Remove* .... Labor...........13.80	ea	$13.80	$69.50	$83.30
	6′ one-tube surface-mounted fluorescent strip light *Replace* Materials......40.00 Labor..........39.50 *Remove* .... Labor...........13.80	ea	$13.80	$79.50	$93.30
	8′ one-tube surface-mounted fluorescent strip light *Replace* Materials......60.00 Labor..........39.50 *Remove* .... Labor...........13.80	ea	$13.80	$99.50	$113.30
	2′ one-tube surface-mounted fluorescent strip light with diffuser *Replace* Materials......30.00 Labor..........39.50 *Remove* .... Labor...........13.80	ea	$13.80	$69.50	$83.30
	4′ one-tube surface-mounted fluorescent strip light with diffuser *Replace* Materials......35.00 Labor..........39.50 *Remove* .... Labor...........13.80	ea	$13.80	$74.50	$88.30
	6′ one-tube surface-mounted fluorescent strip light with diffuser *Replace* Materials......45.00 Labor..........39.50 *Remove* .... Labor...........13.80	ea	$13.80	$84.50	$98.30
	8′ one-tube surface-mounted fluorescent strip light with diffuser *Replace* Materials......65.00 Labor..........39.50 *Remove* .... Labor...........13.80	ea	$13.80	$104.50	$118.30
two-tube ▷	**2′ two-tube surface-mounted fluorescent strip light** *Replace* Materials......35.00 Labor..........39.50 *Remove* .... Labor...........13.80	ea	$13.80	$74.50	$88.30
	2′ two-tube surface-mounted fluorescent strip light with diffuser *Replace* Materials......50.00 Labor..........39.50 *Remove* .... Labor...........13.80	ea	$13.80	$89.50	$103.30
	2′ two-tube surface-mounted fluorescent strip light with vinyl trim & diffuser *Replace* Materials......55.00 Labor..........39.50 *Remove* .... Labor...........13.80	ea	$13.80	$94.50	$108.30
	2′ two-tube surface-mounted fluorescent strip light with solid wood trim & diffuser *Replace* Materials......65.00 Labor..........39.50 *Remove* .... Labor...........13.80	ea	$13.80	$104.50	$118.30
	4′ two-tube surface-mounted fluorescent strip light *Replace* Materials......45.00 Labor..........39.50 *Remove* .... Labor...........13.80	ea	$13.80	$84.50	$98.30

Item Description	Unit	Remove	Replace	Total
4' two-tube surface-mounted fluorescent strip light with diffuser *Replace* Materials......60.00 Labor..........39.50 *Remove* .... Labor...........13.80	ea	$13.80	$99.50	$113.30
4' two-tube surface-mounted fluorescent strip light with vinyl trim & diffuser *Replace* Materials......65.00 Labor..........39.50 *Remove* .... Labor...........13.80	ea	$13.80	$104.50	$118.30
4' two-tube surface-mounted fluorescent strip light with solid wood trim & diffuser *Replace* Materials......85.00 Labor..........39.50 *Remove* .... Labor...........13.80	ea	$13.80	$124.50	$138.30
6' two-tube surface-mounted fluorescent strip light *Replace* Materials......50.00 Labor..........39.50 *Remove* .... Labor...........13.80	ea	$13.80	$89.50	$103.30
6' two-tube surface-mounted fluorescent strip light with diffuser *Replace* Materials......65.00 Labor..........39.50 *Remove* .... Labor...........13.80	ea	$13.80	$104.50	$118.30
6' two-tube surface-mounted fluorescent strip light with vinyl trim & diffuser *Replace* Materials......90.00 Labor..........39.50 *Remove* .... Labor...........13.80	ea	$13.80	$129.50	$143.30
6' two-tube surface-mounted fluorescent strip light with solid wood trim & diffuser *Replace* Materials......95.00 Labor..........39.50 *Remove* .... Labor...........13.80	ea	$13.80	$134.50	$148.30
8' two-tube surface-mounted fluorescent strip light *Replace* Materials......70.00 Labor..........39.50 *Remove* .... Labor...........13.80	ea	$13.80	$109.50	$123.30
8' two-tube surface-mounted fluorescent strip light with diffuser *Replace* Materials......85.00 Labor..........39.50 *Remove* .... Labor...........13.80	ea	$13.80	$124.50	$138.30
8' two-tube surface-mounted fluorescent strip light with vinyl trim & diffuser *Replace* Materials....105.00 Labor..........39.50 *Remove* .... Labor...........13.80	ea	$13.80	$144.50	$158.30
8' two-tube surface-mounted fluorescent strip light with solid wood trim & diffuser *Replace* Materials.....125.00 Labor..........39.50 *Remove* .... Labor...........13.80	ea	$13.80	$164.50	$178.30
4' four-tube surface-mounted fluorescent strip light *Replace* Materials......70.00 Labor..........39.50 *Remove* .... Labor...........13.80	ea	$13.80	$109.50	$123.30 ◁ **four-tube**
4' four-tube surface-mounted fluorescent strip light with diffuser *Replace* Materials.....110.00 Labor..........39.50 *Remove* .... Labor...........13.80	ea	$13.80	$149.50	$163.30
4' four-tube surface-mounted fluorescent strip light with vinyl trim & diffuser *Replace* Materials....130.00 Labor..........39.50 *Remove* .... Labor...........13.80	ea	$13.80	$169.50	$183.30
4' four-tube surface-mounted fluorescent strip light with solid wood trim & diffuser *Replace* Materials.....160.00 Labor..........39.50 *Remove* .... Labor...........13.80	ea	$13.80	$199.50	$213.30

RELATED ITEMS

Cleaning........................57

	Item Description	Unit	Remove	Replace	Total
Fluorescent fixture ▶ *continued* **for suspended ceilings** ▷ *add **$14** for boxed-in fixture for fire-rated ceiling.*	**2′ by 2′ drop-in two-tube fluorescent fixture for suspended ceiling** ***Replace*** Materials......75.00 Labor..........79.70 ***Remove*** .... Labor..........13.80	ea	$13.80	$154.70	$168.50
	2′ by 4′ drop-in two-tube fluorescent fixture for suspended ceiling ***Replace*** Materials......90.00 Labor..........79.70 ***Remove*** .... Labor..........13.80	ea	$13.80	$169.70	$183.50
	2′ by 4′ drop-in four-tube fluorescent fixture for suspended ceiling ***Replace*** Materials.....115.00 Labor..........79.70 ***Remove*** .... Labor..........13.80	ea	$13.80	$194.70	$208.50
remove & reinstall ▷	**Remove fluorescent light fixture for work, then reinstall** ***Replace*** .... Labor..........69.30	ea	—	$69.30	$69.30
replace ballast ▷	**Remove and replace fluorescent light fixture ballast** ***Replace*** Materials......60.00 Labor..........53.30	ea	—	$113.30	$113.30
Fluorescent circline fixture ▶	**Fluorescent circline fixture, economy grade** ***Replace*** Materials......35.00 Labor..........36.40 ***Remove*** .... Labor..........10.20 ▶ Single, exposed tube.	ea	$10.20	$71.40	$81.60
	Fluorescent circline fixture, standard grade ***Replace*** Materials......50.00 Labor..........36.40 ***Remove*** .... Labor..........10.20 ▶ Double, exposed tubes.	ea	$10.20	$86.40	$96.60
	Fluorescent circline fixture, high grade ***Replace*** Materials......80.00 Labor..........36.40 ***Remove*** .... Labor..........10.20 ▶ Double tubes with polystyrene diffuser.	ea	$10.20	$116.40	$126.60
	Fluorescent circline fixture, deluxe grade ***Replace*** Materials.....160.00 Labor..........36.40 ***Remove*** .... Labor..........10.20 ▶ Double tubes with polystyrene diffuser and wood or metal trim.	ea	$10.20	$196.40	$206.60
remove & reinstall ▷	**Remove fluorescent circline light fixture for work, then reinstall** ***Replace*** .... Labor..........62.80	ea	—	$62.80	$62.80
replace ballast ▷	**Remove and replace fluorescent circline light fixture ballast** ***Replace*** Materials......55.00 Labor..........53.30	ea	—	$108.30	$108.30
Ceiling fan ▶ *Fan only, no light.*	**Ceiling fan, economy grade** ***Replace*** Materials......60.00 Labor..........92.20 ***Remove*** .... Labor..........13.80 ▶ 4 blade fan up to 42″ diameter. Blades may have painted design. 3 speed pull-chain, reversible.	ea	$13.80	$152.20	$166.00
	Ceiling fan, standard grade ***Replace*** Materials......95.00 Labor..........92.20 ***Remove*** .... Labor..........13.80 ▶ 4 to 5 blade fan up to 52″ diameter. Plywood blades may have painted design or stained with cane inserts. 3 speed pull-chain, reversible.	ea	$13.80	$187.20	$201.00
	Ceiling fan, high grade ***Replace*** Materials.....155.00 Labor..........92.20 ***Remove*** .... Labor..........13.80 ▶ 4 to 5 blade fan up to 52″ diameter. Hardwood stained blades may have cane inserts. Variable speed wall controls, reversible.	ea	$13.80	$247.20	$261.00

Item Description	Unit	Remove	Replace	Total	
Ceiling fan, deluxe grade ***Replace*** Materials.....245.00 Labor..........92.20 ***Remove*** .... Labor...........13.80 ► 4 to 5 blade fan up to 52" diameter. Hardwood stained blades may have cane inserts. Brass motor housing contains intricate design. Variable speed wall controls, reversible.	ea	$13.80	$337.20	$351.00	
Remove ceiling fan for work, then reinstall ***Replace*** .... Labor.........103.00	ea	—	$103.00	$103.00	◁ remove and reinstall
Ceiling fan with light, economy grade ***Replace*** Materials.....155.00 Labor.........139.00 ***Remove*** .... Labor...........13.80 ► 4 blade fan up to 42" diameter. Blades may have painted design. 3 speed pull-chain, reversible. 2 to 3 lights with simple glass or metal shades, plated metal escutcheon.	ea	$13.80	$294.00	$307.80	◄ CEILING FAN WITH LIGHT
Ceiling fan with light, standard grade ***Replace*** Materials.....215.00 Labor.........139.00 ***Remove*** .... Labor...........13.80 ► 4 to 5 blade fan up to 52" diameter. Plywood blades may have painted design or stained with cane inserts. 3 speed pull-chain, reversible. 3 lights with detailed glass shades, plated metal escutcheon.	ea	$13.80	$354.00	$367.80	
Ceiling fan with light, high grade ***Replace*** Materials....260.00 Labor.........139.00 ***Remove*** .... Labor...........13.80 ► 4 to 5 blade fan up to 52" diameter. Hardwood stained blades may have cane inserts. Variable speed wall controls, reversible. 3 to 4 lights with intricately detailed glass shades, plated metal escutcheon.	ea	$13.80	$399.00	$412.80	
Ceiling fan with light, deluxe grade ***Replace*** Materials....375.00 Labor.........139.00 ***Remove*** .... Labor...........13.80 ► 4 to 5 blade fan up to 52" diameter. Hardwood blades may have cane inserts. Brass motor housing with intricate design. Variable speed wall control, reversible. 3 to 4 lights with intricate, detailed glass shades, solid brass escutcheon.	ea	$13.80	$514.00	$527.80	
Ceiling fan with light, custom grade ***Replace*** Materials....445.00 Labor.........139.00 ***Remove*** .... Labor...........13.80 ► 4 to 5 blade fan up to 52" diameter. Hardwood stained blades may have cane inserts. Brass motor housing contains intricate design. Variable speed wall controls, reversible. 3 to 4 lights with intricately detailed glass shades, solid brass escutcheon, detailed, curved arms.	ea	$13.80	$584.00	$597.80	
Remove ceiling fan with light for work, then reinstall ***Replace*** .... Labor.........107.00	ea	—	$107.00	$107.00	◁ remove and reinstall
Light for ceiling fan, economy grade ***Replace*** Materials......30.00 Labor...........19.80 ***Remove*** .... Labor............8.25 ► 2 to 3 lights with simple glass or metal shades, plated metal escutcheon.	ea	$8.25	$49.80	$58.05	◄ LIGHT FOR CEILING FAN
Light for ceiling fan, standard grade ***Replace*** Materials......65.00 Labor...........19.80 ***Remove*** .... Labor............8.25 ► 3 lights with detailed glass shades, plated metal escutcheon.	ea	$8.25	$84.80	$93.05	
Light for ceiling fan, high grade ***Replace*** Materials......90.00 Labor...........19.80 ***Remove*** .... Labor............8.25 ► 3 to 4 lights with intricately detailed glass shades, plated metal escutcheon.	ea	$8.25	$109.80	$118.05	

RELATED ITEMS

Cleaning........................57

	Item Description	Unit	Remove	Replace	Total
LIGHT FOR CEILING FAN *continued*	**Light for ceiling fan, deluxe grade** *Replace* Materials.....155.00 Labor...........19.80 *Remove* .... Labor............8.25 ► 3 to 4 lights with intricately detailed glass shades, solid brass escutcheon.	ea	$8.25	$174.80	$183.05
	Light for ceiling fan, custom grade *Replace* Materials.....245.00 Labor...........19.80 *Remove* .... Labor............8.25 ► 3 to 4 lights with intricately detailed glass shades, solid brass escutcheon, detailed, curved arms.	ea	$8.25	$264.80	$273.05
remove & reinstall ▷	**Remove light from ceiling fan for work, then reinstall** *Replace* .... Labor..........34.60	ea	—	$34.60	$34.60
HANGING FIXTURE *Hanging light fixtures usually hang from ceiling hooks and plug into a switched outlet. For hanging fixtures that connect into a ceiling box, see pendant fixtures on pages 160-161. See quality indicators on pages 154-155.*	**Hanging light fixture, economy grade** *Replace* Materials......35.00 Labor...........11.50 *Remove* .... Labor............2.75	ea	$2.75	$46.50	$49.25
	Hanging light fixture, standard grade *Replace* Materials......45.00 Labor...........11.50 *Remove* .... Labor............2.75	ea	$2.75	$56.50	$59.25
	Hanging light fixture, high grade *Replace* Materials......55.00 Labor...........11.50 *Remove* .... Labor............2.75	ea	$2.75	$66.50	$69.25
	Hanging light fixture, deluxe grade *Replace* Materials......85.00 Labor...........11.50 *Remove* .... Labor............2.75	ea	$2.75	$96.50	$99.25
DOUBLE HANGING FIXTURE *Hanging light fixtures usually hang from ceiling hooks and plug into a switched outlet. For hanging fixtures that connect into a ceiling box, see pendant fixtures on pages 160-161. See quality indicators on pages 154-155.*	**Double hanging light fixture, economy grade** *Replace* Materials......55.00 Labor...........11.50 *Remove* .... Labor............2.75	ea	$2.75	$66.50	$69.25
	Double hanging light fixture, standard grade *Replace* Materials......75.00 Labor...........11.50 *Remove* .... Labor............2.75	ea	$2.75	$86.50	$89.25
	Double hanging light fixture, high grade *Replace* Materials....105.00 Labor...........11.50 *Remove* .... Labor............2.75	ea	$2.75	$116.50	$119.25
	Double hanging light fixture, deluxe grade *Replace* Materials....140.00 Labor...........11.50 *Remove* .... Labor............2.75	ea	$2.75	$151.50	$154.25
MINIMUM FIXTURE CHARGE	**Minimum charge for light fixture work** *Replace* Materials......20.00 Labor...........69.30	ea	—	$89.30	$89.30
PORCELAIN FIXTURE	**Porcelain light fixture** *Replace* Materials........4.00 Labor............8.66 *Remove* .... Labor............2.75	ea	$2.75	$12.66	$15.41
	Porcelain light fixture with pull chain *Replace* Materials........5.50 Labor............8.66 *Remove* .... Labor............2.75	ea	$2.75	$14.16	$16.91
	Remove porcelain light fixture for work, then reinstall *Replace* .... Labor...........13.90	ea	—	$13.90	$13.90

Item Description	*Unit*	*Remove*	*Replace*	*Total*
Recessed spot light fixture, economy grade ***Replace*** Materials......45.00 Labor..........31.40 ***Remove*** .... Labor..........11.00 ► 5" recessed spot.	ea	$11.00	$76.40	$87.40
Recessed spot light fixture, standard grade ***Replace*** Materials......65.00 Labor..........31.40 ***Remove*** .... Labor..........11.00 ► 7" recessed spot.	ea	$11.00	$96.40	$107.40
Recessed spot light fixture, high grade ***Replace*** Materials......80.00 Labor..........31.40 ***Remove*** .... Labor..........11.00 ► 7" recessed spot, reflector in can.	ea	$11.00	$111.40	$122.40
Recessed spot light fixture, deluxe grade ***Replace*** Materials.....110.00 Labor..........31.40 ***Remove*** .... Labor..........11.00 ► 8" recessed spot.	ea	$11.00	$141.40	$152.40
Recessed spot light fixture, custom grade ***Replace*** Materials.....145.00 Labor..........31.40 ***Remove*** .... Labor..........11.00 ► 8" recessed spot, eyeball socket.	ea	$11.00	$176.40	$187.40
Remove recessed spot light fixture for work, then reinstall ***Replace*** .... Labor..........28.80	ea	—	$28.80	$28.80
Remove recessed spot light fixture & can for work, then reinstall ***Replace*** .... Labor..........53.30	ea	—	$53.30	$53.30
Electric strip for strip lights (no fixtures) per lf ***Replace*** Materials......10.00 Labor...........9.87 ***Remove*** .... Labor...........3.03	lf	$3.03	$19.87	$22.90
Remove electric strip for strip lights for work, then reinstall ***Replace*** .... Labor..........17.30	lf	—	$17.30	$17.30
Strip light, economy grade ***Replace*** Materials......25.00 Labor..........13.90 ***Remove*** .... Labor...........4.13 ► Light gauge metal or plastic.	ea	$4.13	$38.90	$43.03
Strip light, standard grade ***Replace*** Materials......30.00 Labor..........13.90 ***Remove*** .... Labor...........4.13 ► Light gauge metal or plastic with brass or chrome trim.	ea	$4.13	$43.90	$48.03
Strip light, high grade ***Replace*** Materials......65.00 Labor..........13.90 ***Remove*** .... Labor...........4.13 ► Heavy gauge materials with brass or chrome trim.	ea	$4.13	$78.90	$83.03
Remove strip light for work, then reinstall ***Replace*** .... Labor..........24.30	ea	—	$24.30	$24.30
Exterior flood light fixture, standard grade ***Replace*** Materials......40.00 Labor..........22.30 ***Remove*** .... Labor...........8.25	ea	$8.25	$62.30	$70.55

◄ **RECESSED SPOT FIXTURE**
See quality indicators on pages 154-155.

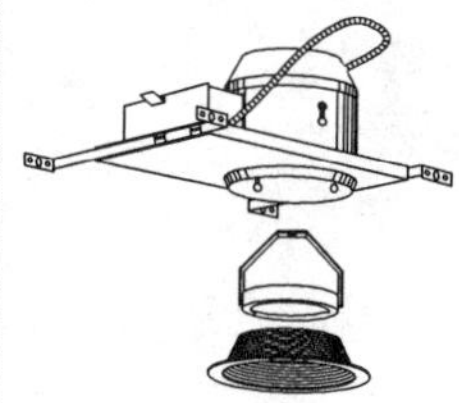

◁ **remove and reinstall**

◁ **remove and reinstall**

◄ **ELECTRIC STRIP**
Surface-mounted electric strip channel. Does not include strip-mounted spot lights. 3 lf minimum.

◄ **STRIP SPOT LIGHT**
Spot light for surface mounted electric strip channel.

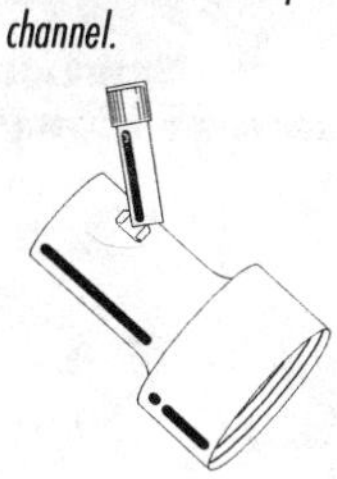

◁ **remove and reinstall**

◄ **EXTERIOR SPOT LIGHT**

RELATED ITEMS

Cleaning......................57

	Item Description	Unit	Remove	Replace	Total
Exterior ▶ spot light *continued*	**Exterior flood light fixture, high grade** ***Replace*** Materials......55.00 Labor..........22.30 ***Remove*** .... Labor............8.25	ea	$8.25	$77.30	$85.55
	Exterior double flood light fixture, standard grade ***Replace*** Materials......50.00 Labor..........22.30 ***Remove*** .... Labor............8.25	ea	$8.25	$72.30	$80.55
	Exterior double flood light fixture, high grade ***Replace*** Materials......70.00 Labor..........22.30 ***Remove*** .... Labor............8.25	ea	$8.25	$92.30	$100.55
	Exterior triple flood light fixture, standard grade ***Replace*** Materials......60.00 Labor..........22.30 ***Remove*** .... Labor............8.25	ea	$8.25	$82.30	$90.55
	Exterior triple flood light fixture, high grade ***Replace*** Materials......80.00 Labor..........22.30 ***Remove*** .... Labor............8.25	ea	$8.25	$102.30	$110.55
	Remove exterior flood light fixture for work, then reinstall ***Replace*** .... Labor..........40.70	ea	—	$40.70	$40.70
Exterior wall- ▶ mount fixture *See quality indicators on pages 154-155.*	**Exterior wall-mount light fixture, economy grade** ***Replace*** Materials......30.00 Labor...........21.60 ***Remove*** .... Labor............6.88	ea	$6.88	$51.60	$58.48
	Exterior wall-mount light fixture, standard grade ***Replace*** Materials......50.00 Labor...........21.60 ***Remove*** .... Labor............6.88	ea	$6.88	$71.60	$78.48
	Exterior wall-mount light fixture, high grade ***Replace*** Materials ....130.00 Labor...........21.60 ***Remove*** .... Labor............6.88	ea	$6.88	$151.60	$158.48
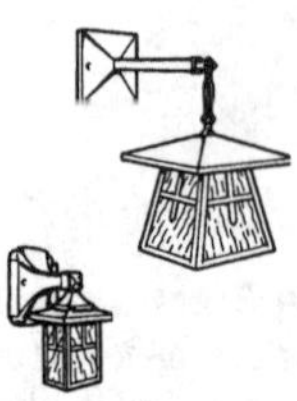 courtesy of ***Rejuvenation Lamp & Fixture Co.***	**Exterior wall-mount light fixture, deluxe grade** ***Replace*** Materials.....245.00 Labor...........21.60 ***Remove*** .... Labor............6.88	ea	$6.88	$266.60	$273.48
remove & reinstall ▷	**Remove exterior wall-mount light fixture for work, then reinstall** ***Replace*** .... Labor..........40.70	ea	—	$40.70	$40.70
Exterior ▶ recessed fixture	**Exterior recessed light fixture, economy grade** ***Replace*** Materials......55.00 Labor...........31.40 ***Remove*** .... Labor...........13.80 ▶ 5″ recessed spot.	ea	$13.80	$86.40	$100.20
	Exterior recessed light fixture, standard grade ***Replace*** Materials......75.00 Labor...........31.40 ***Remove*** .... Labor...........13.80 ▶ 7″ recessed spot.	ea	$13.80	$106.40	$120.20
	Exterior recessed light fixture, high grade ***Replace*** Materials ....140.00 Labor...........31.40 ***Remove*** .... Labor...........13.80 ▶ 7″ recessed spot, reflector in can.	ea	$13.80	$171.40	$185.20
	Exterior recessed light fixture, deluxe grade ***Replace*** Materials.....190.00 Labor...........31.40 ***Remove*** .... Labor...........13.80 ▶ 8″ recessed spot.	ea	$13.80	$221.40	$235.20

Item Description	Unit	Remove	Replace	Total	
Remove exterior recessed light fixture for work, then reinstall ***Replace*** .... Labor...........62.80	ea	—	$62.80	$62.80	◁ **remove and reinstall**
Exterior light fixture, economy grade ***Replace*** Materials......25.00 Labor..........22.30 ***Remove*** .... Labor............8.66	ea	$8.66	$47.30	$55.96	◀ **EXTERIOR LIGHT FIXTURE ALLOWANCE** *Contractor's allowance per light fixture in complete home.*
Exterior light fixture, standard grade ***Replace*** Materials......45.00 Labor..........22.30 ***Remove*** .... Labor............8.66	ea	$8.66	$67.30	$75.96	
Exterior light fixture, high grade ***Replace*** Materials......85.00 Labor..........22.30 ***Remove*** .... Labor............8.66	ea	$8.66	$107.30	$115.96	
Exterior light fixture, deluxe grade ***Replace*** Materials.....165.00 Labor..........22.30 ***Remove*** .... Labor............8.66	ea	$8.66	$187.30	$195.96	
Remove exterior light fixture for work, then reinstall ***Replace*** .... Labor..........40.70	ea	—	$40.70	$40.70	◁ **remove and reinstall**
Exterior post with light fixture, economy grade ***Replace*** Materials.....160.00 Labor........204.00 ***Remove*** .... Labor..........33.00 ► Redwood post with beveled corners or light turnings or straight metal post, up to 7′ tall. Includes post hole, concrete base and hole backfill. Does not include wiring. Plastic or light metal fixture, usually one light with polystyrene lens.	ea	$33.00	$364.00	$397.00	◀ **EXTERIOR POST WITH FIXTURE**
Exterior post with light fixture, standard grade ***Replace*** Materials....230.00 Labor........204.00 ***Remove*** .... Labor..........33.00 ► Turned redwood post to 7′ tall. Includes hole, concrete, and hole backfill. Does not include wiring. Black metal fixture, usually one light with polystyrene lens.	ea	$33.00	$434.00	$467.00	
Exterior post with light fixture, high grade ***Replace*** Materials....295.00 Labor........204.00 ***Remove*** .... Labor..........33.00 ► Turned redwood post, to 7′ tall. Includes hole, concrete, and hole backfill. Does not include wiring. Metal fixture, one to two lights clear plastic or glass lens.	ea	$33.00	$499.00	$532.00	
Exterior post with light fixture, deluxe grade ***Replace*** Materials....435.00 Labor........204.00 ***Remove*** .... Labor..........33.00 ► Aluminum post, to 7′ tall. Includes hole, concrete, J bolts, and hole backfill. Does not include wiring. Metal fixture, one to two lights clear plastic or glass lens.	ea	$33.00	$639.00	$672.00	
Exterior post with light fixture, custom grade ***Replace*** Materials.....765.00 Labor........204.00 ***Remove*** .... Labor..........33.00 ► Cast-iron post, to 7′ tall. Includes post hole, concrete base, J bolts, and hole backfill. Does not include wiring. Cast iron, brass, copper, or pewter fixture, often simulated gas light one to four lights clear plastic or glass lens.	ea	$33.00	$969.00	$1,002.00	**RELATED ITEMS** Cleaning........................57
Remove exterior post with light fixture for work, then reinstall ***Replace*** .... Labor.........385.00	ea	—	$385.00	$385.00	◁ **remove and reinstall**
Exterior post light fixture (no post), economy grade ***Replace*** Materials......55.00 Labor..........43.30 ***Remove*** .... Labor...........13.80 ► Plastic or light metal fixture. One interior light with polystyrene lens.	ea	$13.80	$98.30	$112.10	◀ **EXTERIOR POST LIGHT FIXTURE** *Fixture only, no post.*

	Item Description	Unit	Remove	Replace	Total
EXTERIOR POST ▶ LIGHT FIXTURE *continued*	**Exterior post light fixture (no post), standard grade** ***Replace*** Materials......85.00 Labor..........43.30 ***Remove*** .... Labor...........13.80 ▶ Metal fixture. Two interior lights with clear polystyrene lens.	ea	$13.80	$128.30	$142.10
	Exterior post light fixture (no post), high grade ***Replace*** Materials.....125.00 Labor..........43.30 ***Remove*** .... Labor...........13.80 ▶ Metal fixture. 2 to 4 interior lights with clear polystyrene lens.	ea	$13.80	$168.30	$182.10
	Exterior post light fixture (no post), deluxe grade ***Replace*** Materials.....195.00 Labor..........43.30 ***Remove*** .... Labor...........13.80 ▶ Copper, pewter, or antique finish. 2 to 4 interior light with clear glass lens.	ea	$13.80	$238.30	$252.10
	Exterior post light fixture (no post), custom grade ***Replace*** Materials....280.00 Labor..........43.30 ***Remove*** .... Labor...........13.80 ▶ Ornate copper, pewter, brass, or antique finish. 2 to 4 interior lights with clear glass lens.	ea	$13.80	$323.30	$337.10
remove & reinstall ▷	**Remove exterior post light fixture for work (no post), then reinstall** ***Replace*** .... Labor...........72.70	ea	—	$72.70	$72.70
POST FOR ▶ EXTERIOR FIXTURE	**Redwood post for exterior post light fixture, standard grade** ***Replace*** Materials....230.00 Labor.........161.00 ***Remove*** .... Labor..........33.00 ▶ To 7' tall. Beveled edges or light turnings. Diameter to 4".	ea	$33.00	$391.00	$424.00
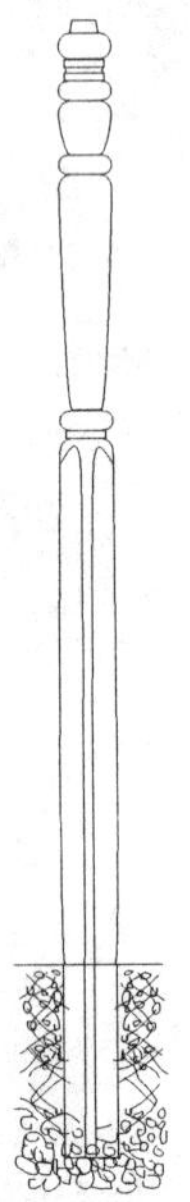	**Redwood post for exterior post light fixture, high grade** ***Replace*** Materials....320.00 Labor.........161.00 ***Remove*** .... Labor..........33.00 ▶ Turned post. to 7' tall. Diameter to 4".	ea	$33.00	$481.00	$514.00
	Metal post for exterior post light fixture, standard grade ***Replace*** Materials.....145.00 Labor.........154.00 ***Remove*** .... Labor..........33.00 ▶ Straight or tapered aluminum or steel post. Diameter to 4".	ea	$33.00	$299.00	$332.00
	Metal post for exterior post light fixture, high grade ***Replace*** Materials....230.00 Labor.........154.00 ***Remove*** .... Labor..........33.00 ▶ Straight or tapered aluminum or steel post. with flutes and/or simple turned base and cap. Diameter to 4".	ea	$33.00	$384.00	$417.00
	Metal post for exterior post light fixture, deluxe grade ***Replace*** Materials....320.00 Labor.........154.00 ***Remove*** .... Labor..........33.00 ▶ Aluminum post with elaborate turnings, diameter to 6".	ea	$33.00	$474.00	$507.00
	Metal post for exterior post light fixture, custom grade ***Replace*** Materials....405.00 Labor.........154.00 ***Remove*** .... Labor..........33.00 ▶ Aluminum post with elaborate turnings with some cast design (e.g. ivy, inlays, etc.) Diameter to 8".	ea	$33.00	$559.00	$592.00
	Metal post for exterior post light fixture, custom deluxe grade ***Replace*** Materials....635.00 Labor.........154.00 ***Remove*** .... Labor..........33.00 ▶ Cast iron with turnings and designs. Diameter to 12".	ea	$33.00	$789.00	$822.00

Item Description	Unit	Remove	Replace	Total
Add for exterior light motion sensor or infrared detector ***Replace*** Materials......65.00 ► Add to the cost of an exterior light fixture or lamp post when fixture is equipped with a motion sensor, infrared detector, or both.	ea	—	$65.00	$65.00
Replace light fixture socket and wiring ***Replace*** Materials........6.00 Labor...........18.20	ea	—	$24.20	$24.20
Replace chandelier socket and wiring, per arm ***Replace*** Materials........7.50 Labor...........19.20	ea	—	$26.70	$26.70
Bowl shade or globe for light fixture, economy grade ***Replace*** Materials.......11.00 Labor ....2.34 ► Glass bowl shade or globe only. Light glass with little or no pattern.	ea	—	$13.34	$13.34
Bowl shade or globe for light fixture, standard grade ***Replace*** Materials......18.50 Labor ....2.34 ► Glass bowl shade or globe only. Light glass with horizontal turnings.	ea	—	$20.84	$20.84
Bowl shade or globe for light fixture, high grade ***Replace*** Materials......31.50 Labor ....2.34 ► Glass bowl shade or globe only. Thick glass with vertical ridges, etched glass, angles in glass, scalloped edges.	ea	—	$33.84	$33.84
Bowl shade or globe for light fixture, deluxe grade ***Replace*** Materials......46.00 Labor ....2.34 ► Glass bowl shade or globe only. Thick glass with angles, ornate horizontal turnings, vertical ridges, patterns in glass.	ea	—	$48.34	$48.34
Bowl shade or globe for light fixture, custom grade ***Replace*** Materials......56.00 Labor ....2.34 ► Glass bowl shade or globe only. Very thick glass with angles, ornate horizontal turnings, vertical ridges, patterns in glass, specialty gradated colors, flower patterns (Entire shade looks like a flower, not just floral patterns on shade. Flower patterns may be made of thin glass.)	ea	—	$58.34	$58.34

◄ **EXTERIOR LIGHT SENSOR / DETECTOR**

◄ **FIXTURE REWIRE**

◄ **REPLACEMENT BOWL SHADE**

RELATED ITEMS

Cleaning........................57

TIME & MATERIAL CHARTS *(selected items)*

Electrical Materials

*See **Electrical** material prices with the line items and other information in the **QuickFinder** column.*

Electrical Labor

LABORER	BASE WAGE	PAID LEAVE	TRUE WAGE	FICA	FUTA	WORKER'S COMP.	UNEMPLOY. INSUR.	HEALTH INSUR.	RETIRE (401K)	LIABILITY INSUR.	COST PER HOUR
Electrician	**$26.10**	2.04	**$28.14**	2.15	.23	3.03	2.45	2.69	.84	3.80	**$43.30**
Electrician's helper	**$18.80**	1.47	**$20.27**	1.55	.16	2.19	1.76	2.69	.61	2.74	**$32.00**
Demolition laborer	**$13.90**	1.08	**$14.98**	1.15	.12	4.79	1.30	2.69	.45	2.02	**$27.50**

Paid Leave is calculated based on two weeks paid vacation, one week sick leave, and seven paid holidays. Employer's matching portion of **FICA** is 7.65 percent. **FUTA** (Federal Unemployment) is .8 percent. **Worker's compensation** for the electrical trade was calculated using a national average of 10.78 percent. **Unemployment insurance** was calculated using a national average of 8.7 percent. **Health insurance** was calculated based on a projected national average for 2002 of $535 per employee (and family when applicable) per month. Employer pays 80 percent for a per month cost of $428 per employee. **Retirement** is based on a 401(k) retirement program with employer matching of 50 percent. Employee contributions to the 401(k) plan are an average of 6 percent of the true wage. **Liability insurance** is based on a national average of 13.2 percent.

Electrical Labor Productivity

WORK DESCRIPTION	LABORER	COST PER HOUR	PRODUCTIVITY	UNIT PRICE
Demolition				
remove 240 volt switch or outlet	demolition laborer	$27.50	.200	$5.50 ea
remove 120 volt switch or outlet	demolition laborer	$27.50	.150	$4.13 ea
remove bathroom fan	demolition laborer	$27.50	.506	$13.90 ea
remove bathroom fan / light with heater	demolition laborer	$27.50	.726	$20.00 ea
remove breaker panel	electrician	$43.30	3.88	$168.00 ea
remove cable service drop	electrician	$43.30	6.68	$289.00 ea
remove conduit service drop	electrician	$43.30	8.35	$362.00 ea
remove rigid steel mast service drop	electrician	$43.30	9.82	$425.00 ea
remove circuit breaker	demolition laborer	$27.50	.200	$5.50 ea
remove door bell or chime	demolition laborer	$27.50	.100	$2.75 ea
remove kitchen exhaust fan	demolition laborer	$27.50	.539	$14.80 ea
remove whole-house exhaust fan	demolition laborer	$27.50	1.52	$41.80 ea
remove intercom system master station	demolition laborer	$27.50	.749	$20.60 ea
remove intercom system remote station	demolition laborer	$27.50	.300	$8.25 ea
remove low-voltage outlet	demolition laborer	$27.50	.150	$4.13 ea
remove detector	demolition laborer	$27.50	.200	$5.50 ea
remove thermostat	demolition laborer	$27.50	.200	$5.50 ea
remove television antenna	demolition laborer	$27.50	.835	$23.00 ea
remove recessed electric space heater	demolition laborer	$27.50	.506	$13.90 ea
remove electric baseboard heater	demolition laborer	$27.50	.165	$4.54 lf
remove light fixture	demolition laborer	$27.50	.300	$8.25 ea
remove bathroom light bar	demolition laborer	$27.50	.315	$8.66 ea
remove chandelier	demolition laborer	$27.50	.557	$15.30 ea
remove fluorescent light fixture	demolition laborer	$27.50	.500	$13.80 ea
remove fluorescent circline light fixture	demolition laborer	$27.50	.371	$10.20 ea
remove ceiling fan	demolition laborer	$27.50	.500	$13.80 ea
remove hanging light fixture	demolition laborer	$27.50	.100	$2.75 ea
remove porcelain light fixture	demolition laborer	$27.50	.100	$2.75 ea
remove recessed spot light fixture	demolition laborer	$27.50	.400	$11.00 ea
remove electric strip for electric strip lights	demolition laborer	$27.50	.110	$3.03 lf
remove electric strip light	demolition laborer	$27.50	.150	$4.13 ea
remove exterior flood light	demolition laborer	$27.50	.300	$8.25 ea
remove exterior post with light fixture	demolition laborer	$27.50	1.20	$33.00 ea
remove exterior post light fixture	demolition laborer	$27.50	.500	$13.80 ea
Electrical crew				
install wiring, boxes, and fixtures	electrician	$43.30		
install wiring, boxes, and fixtures	electrician's helper	$32.00		
install wiring, boxes, and fixtures	***electrical crew***	**$37.70**		
Install complete house electrical wiring, outlets, switches & light fixtures				
economy grade	electrical crew	$37.70	.053	$2.00 ea
deluxe grade	electrical crew	$37.70	.109	$4.11 ea
low-voltage system	electrical crew	$37.70	.100	$3.77 ea
add for wiring installation in conduit	electrical crew	$37.70	.055	$2.07 ea
Install complete house rough electrical (no light fixtures)				
standard	electrical crew	$37.70	.070	$2.64 ea
in conduit	electrical crew	$37.70	.154	$5.81 ea
low-voltage system	electrical crew	$37.70	.075	$2.83 ea
Install complete house light fixtures				
economy grade	electrical crew	$37.70	.015	$.57 ea
deluxe grade	electrical crew	$37.70	.017	$.64 ea
for low-voltage system	electrical crew	$37.70	.013	$.49 ea
Install 240 volt				
outlet or switch with wiring run & box	electrical crew	$37.70	1.34	$50.50 ea
Install 120 volt				
switch or outlet with wiring run & box	electrical crew	$37.70	.977	$36.80 ea
3-way switch with wiring run & box	electrical crew	$37.70	1.95	$73.50 ea
Install electric wiring run				
for typical 120 volt outlet	electrical crew	$37.70	.802	$30.20 ea
for 120 volt appliance	electrical crew	$37.70	1.02	$38.50 ea

. . . More ➤

Electrical Labor Productivity *continued*

WORK DESCRIPTION	LABORER	COST PER HOUR	PRODUCTIVITY	UNIT PRICE
Install conduit				
electric metallic tubing (EMT), average installation	electrical crew	$37.70	.077	**$2.90** lf
flexible metal, average installation	electrical crew	$37.70	.041	**$1.55** lf
PVC, average installation	electrical crew	$37.70	.045	**$1.70** lf
intermediate (IMC), average installation	electrical crew	$37.70	.113	**$4.26** lf
rigid metal (RMC), average installation	electrical crew	$37.70	.067	**$2.53** lf
Install wiring				
#10 2 wire with ground Romex	electrical crew	$37.70	.051	**$1.92** lf
#12 2 wire with ground Romex	electrical crew	$37.70	.047	**$1.77** lf
#14 2 wire with ground Romex	electrical crew	$37.70	.040	**$1.51** lf
Install breaker panel				
100 amp exterior breaker panel (5 breakers)	electrician	$43.30	4.89	**$212.00** ea
100 amp interior breaker panel (5 breakers)	electrician	$43.30	4.30	**$186.00** ea
150 amp exterior breaker panel (10 breakers)	electrician	$43.30	7.68	**$333.00** ea
150 amp interior breaker panel (10 breakers)	electrician	$43.30	7.17	**$310.00** ea
200 amp exterior breaker panel (15 breakers)	electrician	$43.30	10.8	**$468.00** ea
200 amp interior breaker panel (15 breakers)	electrician	$43.30	9.77	**$423.00** ea
300 amp exterior breaker panel (30 breakers)	electrician	$43.30	14.3	**$619.00** ea
300 amp interior breaker panel (30 breakers)	electrician	$43.30	13.4	**$580.00** ea
40 amp interior breaker sub-panel (5 breakers)	electrician	$43.30	2.99	**$129.00** ea
50 amp interior breaker sub-panel	electrician	$43.30	3.16	**$137.00** ea
70 amp interior breaker sub-panel	electrician	$43.30	3.47	**$150.00** ea
Install electrical service				
100 amp cable service	electrician	$43.30	11.9	**$515.00** ea
150 amp cable service	electrician	$43.30	14.3	**$619.00** ea
150 amp conduit service	electrician	$43.30	15.4	**$667.00** ea
150 amp rigid steel mast service	electrician	$43.30	15.4	**$667.00** ea
200 amp cable service	electrician	$43.30	18.5	**$801.00** ea
200 amp conduit service	electrician	$43.30	19.9	**$862.00** ea
200 amp rigid steel mast service	electrician	$43.30	19.9	**$862.00** ea
Install breaker				
single-pole (120 volt) circuit breaker	electrician	$43.30	.636	**$27.50** ea
double-pole (240 volt) circuit breaker	electrician	$43.30	.648	**$28.10** ea
ground fault circuit interrupter breaker	electrician	$43.30	.689	**$29.80** ea
main disconnect circuit breaker	electrician	$43.30	3.47	**$150.00** ea
Door bell or chime				
door bell or chime button	electrician	$43.30	.119	**$5.15** ea
door bell or chime	electrician	$43.30	1.08	**$46.80** ea
low-voltage wiring (per button)	electrician	$43.30	.489	**$21.20** ea
Install exhaust fan				
bathroom exhaust fan	electrician	$43.30	.597	**$25.90** ea
bathroom exhaust fan with heat lamp	electrician	$43.30	.768	**$33.30** ea
bathroom exhaust fan with heater	electrician	$43.30	.827	**$35.80** ea
kitchen exhaust fan	electrician	$43.30	.977	**$42.30** ea
whole-house exhaust fan	electrician	$43.30	2.69	**$116.00** ea
Install intercom				
intercom system master station	electrician	$43.30	2.15	**$93.10** ea
intercom system remote station	electrician	$43.30	.597	**$25.90** ea
120 volt wiring for intercom master station	electrician	$43.30	.779	**$33.70** ea
intercom wiring (per station)	electrician	$43.30	.538	**$23.30** ea
Install low-voltage outlet				
Install outlet	electrical crew	$37.70	.256	**$9.65** ea
wiring (per outlet)	electrical crew	$37.70	.358	**$13.50** ea
Install sound system				
speaker with grille	electrical crew	$37.70	.244	**$9.20** ea
Install detector				
battery operated	electrician	$43.30	.308	**$13.30** ea
direct-wired	electrician	$43.30	.347	**$15.00** ea

. . . More ➢

Electrical Labor Productivity *continued*

WORK DESCRIPTION	LABORER	COST PER HOUR	PRODUCTIVITY	UNIT PRICE
Check electrical circuits				
megameter test small home	electrician	$43.30	3.91	$169.00 ea
megameter test average size home	electrician	$43.30	5.66	$245.00 ea
megameter test large home	electrician	$43.30	7.79	$337.00 ea
Install thermostat				
for electric resistance heating system	electrical crew	$37.70	.183	$6.90 ea
electric heating system	electrical crew	$37.70	.326	$12.30 ea
wiring (per thermostat)	electrical crew	$37.70	.538	$20.30 ea
Install TV antenna				
television antenna	electrician	$43.30	1.08	$46.80 ea
Install recessed electric space heater				
electric space heater recessed in wall	electrician	$43.30	2.15	$93.10 ea
Install electric-resistance heating				
cable,ceiling installation	electrical crew	$37.70	.036	$1.36 ea
cable, floor installation	electrical crew	$37.70	.060	$2.26 ea
electric-resistance heating floor sensor	electrical crew	$37.70	.632	$23.80 ea
Install electric baseboard heater				
electric baseboard heater	electrical crew	$37.70	.512	$19.30 ea
remove for work, then reinstall	electrical crew	$37.70	.717	$27.00 ea
Install underground wiring for exterior post light fixture				
up to 30 feet	electrical crew	$37.70	1.22	$46.00 ea
up to 50 feet	electrical crew	$37.70	1.30	$49.00 ea
Install interior light fixture				
interior incandescent light fixture	electrician	$43.30	.499	$21.60 ea
Install bathroom bar light				
bathroom bar light	electrician	$43.30	.533	$23.10 ea
Install chandelier				
chandelier	electrician	$43.30	1.45	$62.80 ea
entrance chandelier	electrician	$43.30	2.91	$126.00 ea
grand entrance chandelier	electrician	$43.30	3.99	$173.00 ea
Install wall-mount fixture				
wall-mount light fixture	electrician	$43.30	.484	$21.00 ea
Install florescent light fixture				
surface-mounted fluorescent light fixture	electrician	$43.30	.913	$39.50 ea
drop-in fluorescent fixture in suspended ceiling	electrician	$43.30	1.84	$79.70 ea
fluorescent circline fixture	electrician	$43.30	.841	$36.40 ea
Install ceiling fan				
assemble and install ceiling fan	electrician	$43.30	2.13	$92.20 ea
remove ceiling fan for work, then reinstall	electrician	$43.30	2.38	$103.00 ea
assemble and install ceiling fan with light	electrician	$43.30	3.20	$139.00 ea
light for ceiling fan	electrician	$43.30	.457	$19.80 ea
Install hanging light fixture				
hanging light fixture	electrician	$43.30	.266	$11.50 ea
Install recessed spot fixture				
recessed spot light fixture	electrician	$43.30	.726	$31.40 ea
Install exterior flood light				
exterior flood light fixture	electrician	$43.30	.515	$22.30 ea
Install exterior post light fixture				
exterior post with light fixture	electrician	$43.30	4.70	$204.00 ea
exterior post light fixture (no post)	electrician	$43.30	.999	$43.30 ea
wood post for exterior post light fixture	electrician	$43.30	3.72	$161.00 ea
metal post for exterior post light fixture	electrician	$43.30	3.55	$154.00 ea

14 Excavation

Item Description	Unit			Total	
Excavation equipment delivery and take-home charge (mobilization) *Excavate* .... Labor 206.00	ea	—	—	$206.00	◀ **MOBILIZATION**
Excavate for slab-on-grade structure per sf of floor *Excavate* .... Labor............ .08 Equipment .... .08	sf	—	—	$.16	◀ **SLAB-ON-GRADE** *Under-slab excavation up to 1-1/2' deep. Footing excavation up to 3' deep. Does not include mobilization. See above.*
Excavate for slab-on-grade structure in medium rocky or clay soil *Excavate* .... Labor............ .13 Equipment .... .09	sf	—	—	$.22	
Excavate for slab-on-grade structure in rocky or hardpan soil *Excavate* .... Labor............ .16 Equipment .... .11	sf	—	—	$.27	
Backfill for slab-on-grade structure per sf of floor *Excavate* .... Labor............ .08 Equipment .... .05	sf	—	—	$.13	
Excavate for structure with crawl space per sf of floor *Excavate* .... Labor............ .16 Equipment .... .13	sf	—	—	$.29	◀ **CRAWL SPACE** *Crawl space excavation up to 3' deep. Footing excavation up to 4' deep. Does not include mobilization. See above.*
Excavate for structure with crawl space in medium rocky or clay soil *Excavate* .... Labor............ .21 Equipment .... .15	sf	—	—	$.36	
Excavate for structure with crawl space in rocky or hardpan soil *Excavate* .... Labor............ .21 Equipment .... .18	sf	—	—	$.39	
Backfill for structure with crawl space per sf of floor *Excavate* .... Labor............ .08 Equipment .... .08	sf	—	—	$.16	
Excavate for structure with basement per sf of floor *Excavate* .... Labor............ .46 Equipment .... .33	sf	—	—	$.79	◀ **BASEMENT** *Basement excavation up to 7' deep. Footing excavation up to 8' deep. Does not include mobilization. See above.*
Excavate for structure with basement in medium rocky or clay soil *Excavate* .... Labor............ .51 Equipment .... .38	sf	—	—	$.89	
Excavate for structure with basement in rocky or hardpan soil *Excavate* .... Labor............ .59 Equipment .... .45	sf	—	—	$1.04	
Backfill for structure with basement per sf of floor *Excavate* .... Labor............ .24 Equipment .... .15	sf	—	—	$.39	
Excavate 3' to 4' deep footings *Excavate* .... Labor............ .46 Equipment .... .32	lf	—	—	$.78	◀ **3' TO 4' DEEP FOOTINGS** *Excavation slopes to 3' width at bottom of footing trench. Does not include mobilization. See above.*
Excavate 3' to 4' deep footings in medium rocky or clay soil *Excavate* .... Labor............ .51 Equipment .... .38	lf	—	—	$.89	
Excavate 3' to 4' deep footings in rocky or hardpan soil *Excavate* .... Labor............ .59 Equipment .... .44	lf	—	—	$1.03	
Excavate 5' to 6' deep footings *Excavate* .... Labor............ .54 Equipment .... .42	lf	—	—	$.96	◀ **5' TO 6' DEEP FOOTINGS** *Excavation slopes to 3' width at bottom of footing trench. Does not include mobilization.*
Excavate 5' to 6' deep footings in medium rocky or clay soil *Excavate* .... Labor............ .62 Equipment .... .48	lf	—	—	$1.10	

RELATED ITEMS

Concrete
excavate foundation............91
drill pier hole....................86

	Item Description	Unit			Total
5′ TO 6′ DEEP FOOTINGS *continued*	**Excavate 5′ to 6′ deep footings in rocky or hardpan soil** *Excavate* .... Labor............ .76 Equipment .... .55	lf	—	—	$1.31
7′ TO 8′ DEEP FOOTINGS *Excavation slopes to 3′ width at bottom of footing trench. Does not include mobilization. See page 177.*	**Excavate 7′ to 8′ deep footings** *Excavate* .... Labor............ .67 Equipment .... .52	lf	—	—	$1.19
	Excavate 7′ to 8′ deep footings in medium rocky or clay soil *Excavate* .... Labor............ .81 Equipment .... .61	lf	—	—	$1.42
	Excavate 7′ to 8′ deep footings in rocky or hardpan soil *Excavate* .... Labor............ .92 Equipment .... .70	lf	—	—	$1.62
9′ TO 10′ DEEP FOOTINGS *Excavation slopes to 3′ width at bottom of footing trench. Does not include mobilization. See page 177.*	**Excavate 9′ to 10′ deep footings** *Excavate* .... Labor............ .84 Equipment .... .62	lf	—	—	$1.46
	Excavate 9′ to 10′ deep footings in medium rocky or clay soil *Excavate* .... Labor............ .97 Equipment .... .72	lf	—	—	$1.69
	Excavate 9′ to 10′ deep footings in rocky or hardpan soil *Excavate* .... Labor.......... 1.05 Equipment .... .82	lf	—	—	$1.87
FOUNDATION WALL BACKFILL	**Backfill foundation wall per sf of wall** *Excavate* .... Labor............ .30 Equipment .... .21 ► Typical backfill on flat lot or mild slope per sf of foundation wall. Does not include mobilization.	lf	—	—	$.51
1′ TO 2′ DEEP UTILITY TRENCH *Square trench, 2′ wide. Does not include mobilization. See page 177.*	**Excavate utility trench 1′ to 2′ deep in sandy loam soil** *Excavate* .... Labor............ .16 Equipment .... .09	lf	—	—	$.25
	Excavate utility trench 1′ to 2′ deep in typical soil *Excavate* .... Labor............ .16 Equipment .... .11	lf	—	—	$.27
	Excavate utility trench 1′ to 2′ deep in medium rocky or clay soil *Excavate* .... Labor............ .16 Equipment .... .13	lf	—	—	$.29
	Excavate utility trench 1′ to 2′ deep in rocky or hardpan soil *Excavate* .... Labor............ .21 Equipment .... .15	lf	—	—	$.36
	Backfill 1′ to 2′ utility trench per lf of trench *Excavate* .... Labor............ .10 Equipment .... .09	lf	—	—	$.19
3′ TO 4′ DEEP UTILITY TRENCH *Square trench, 2′ wide. Does not include mobilization. See page 177.*	**Excavate utility trench 3′ to 4′ deep in sandy loam soil** *Excavate* .... Labor............ .21 Equipment .... .15	lf	—	—	$.36
	Excavate utility trench 3′ to 4′ deep in typical soil *Excavate* .... Labor............ .21 Equipment .... .17	lf	—	—	$.38
	Excavate utility trench 3′ to 4′ deep in medium rocky or clay soil *Excavate* .... Labor............ .27 Equipment .... .20	lf	—	—	$.47
	Excavate utility trench 3′ to 4′ deep in rocky or hardpan soil *Excavate* .... Labor............ .27 Equipment .... .23	lf	—	—	$.50
	Backfill 3′ to 4′ utility trench per lf of trench *Excavate* .... Labor............ .15 Equipment .... .17	lf	—	—	$.32
5′ TO 6′ DEEP UTILITY TRENCH	**Excavate utility trench 5′ to 6′ deep in sandy loam soil** *Excavate* .... Labor............ .27 Equipment .... .21	lf	—	—	$.48

continued on next page

Item Description	Unit			Total
Excavate utility trench 5′ to 6′ deep in typical soil *Excavate* .... Labor............ .24 Equipment .... .27	lf	—	—	$.51
Excavate utility trench 5′ to 6′ deep in medium rocky or clay soil *Excavate* .... Labor............ .32 Equipment .... .28	lf	—	—	$.60
Excavate utility trench 5′ to 6′ deep in rocky or hardpan soil *Excavate* .... Labor............ .37 Equipment .... .33	lf	—	—	$.70
Backfill 5′ to 6′ utility trench per lf of trench *Excavate* .... Labor............ .26 Equipment .... .26	lf	—	—	$.52
Excavate water-line trench 2′ to 3′ deep, sandy loam soil *Excavate* .... Labor............ .36 Equipment .... .21	lf	—	—	$.57
Excavate water-line trench 2′ to 3′ deep, typical soil *Excavate* .... Labor............ .36 Equipment .... .24	lf	—	—	$.60
Excavate water-line trench 2′ to 3′ deep, medium rocky or clay soil *Excavate* .... Labor............ .41 Equipment .... .28	lf	—	—	$.69
Excavate water-line trench 2′ to 3′ deep, rocky or hardpan soil *Excavate* .... Labor............ .46 Equipment .... .33	lf	—	—	$.79
Backfill 2′ to 3′ water-line trench per lf of trench *Excavate* .... Labor............ .15 Equipment .... .20	lf	—	—	$.35
Excavate water-line trench 4′ to 5′ deep, sandy loam soil *Excavate* .... Labor............ .46 Equipment .... .35	lf	—	—	$.81
Excavate water-line trench 4′ to 5′ deep, typical soil *Excavate* .... Labor............ .51 Equipment .... .40	lf	—	—	$.91
Excavate water-line trench 4′ to 5′ deep, medium rocky or clay soil *Excavate* .... Labor............ .56 Equipment .... .47	lf	—	—	$1.03
Excavate water-line trench 4′ to 5′ deep, rocky or hardpan soil *Excavate* .... Labor............ .61 Equipment .... .54	lf	—	—	$1.15
Backfill 4′ to 5′ water-line trench per lf of trench *Excavate* .... Labor............ .31 Equipment .... .33	lf	—	—	$.64
Excavate water-line trench 6′ to 7′ deep, sandy loam soil *Excavate* .... Labor............ .61 Equipment .... .49	lf	—	—	$1.10
Excavate water-line trench 6′ to 7′ deep, typical soil *Excavate* .... Labor............ .67 Equipment .... .57	lf	—	—	$1.24
Excavate water-line trench 6′ to 7′ deep, medium rocky or clay soil *Excavate* .... Labor............ .72 Equipment .... .66	lf	—	—	$1.38
Excavate water-line trench 6′ to 7′ deep, rocky or hardpan soil *Excavate* .... Labor............ .82 Equipment .... .75	lf	—	—	$1.57
Backfill 6′ to 7′ water-line trench per lf of trench *Excavate* .... Labor............ .41 Equipment .... .46	lf	—	—	$.87
Excavate water-line trench 8′ to 9′ deep, sandy loam soil *Excavate* .... Labor............ .83 Equipment .... .63	lf	—	—	$1.46

◄ **5′ TO 6′ DEEP UTILITY TRENCH**
Trench slopes to 2′ width at bottom. Does not include mobilization. *See page 177.*

◄ **2′ TO 3′ DEEP WATER-LINE TRENCH**
Trench slopes to 2′ width at bottom. Does not include mobilization. *See page 177.*

◄ **4′ TO 5′ DEEP WATER-LINE TRENCH**
Trench slopes to 3′ width at bottom. Does not include mobilization. *See page 177.*

◄ **6′ TO 7′ DEEP WATER-LINE TRENCH**
Trench slopes to 3′ width at bottom. Does not include mobilization. *See page 177.*

RELATED ITEMS

Plumbing
repair underground line.....364
break-out concrete..............364
Concrete
excavate foundation.............91
backfill foundation..............92
drill pier hole.......................86

◄ **8′ TO 9′ DEEP WATER-LINE TRENCH**

	Item Description	Unit			Total
8' to 9' deep water-line trench ▶ *Trench slopes to 3' width at bottom. Does not include mobilization. .See page 177.*	**Excavate water-line trench 8' to 9' deep, typical soil** *Excavate* .... Labor........ .93 Equipment........ .73	lf	—	—	$1.66
	Excavate water-line trench 8' to 9' deep, medium rocky or clay soil *Excavate* .... Labor........ 1.03 Equipment........ .85	lf	—	—	$1.88
	Excavate water-line trench 8' to 9' deep, rocky or hardpan soil *Excavate* .... Labor........1.14 Equipment........ 1.00	lf	—	—	$2.14
	Backfill 8' to 9' water-line trench per lf of trench *Excavate* .... Labor........ .52 Equipment........ .59	lf	—	—	$1.11
3' to 4' deep sewer-line trench ▶ *Trench slopes to 3-1/2' width at bottom. Does not include mobilization. See page 177.*	**Excavate sewer-line trench 3' to 4' deep, sandy loam soil** *Excavate* .... Labor........ .461 Equipment........ .32	lf	—	—	$.78
	Excavate sewer-line trench 3' to 4' deep, typical soil *Excavate* .... Labor........ .51 Equipment........ .38	lf	—	—	$.89
	Excavate sewer-line trench 3' to 4' deep, medium rocky or clay soil *Excavate* .... Labor........ .56 Equipment........ .44	lf	—	—	$1.00
	Excavate sewer-line trench 3' to 4' deep, rocky or hardpan soil *Excavate* .... Labor........ .61 Equipment........ .51	lf	—	—	$1.12
	Backfill 3' to 4' sewer-line trench per lf of trench *Excavate* .... Labor........ .26 Equipment........ .30	lf	—	—	$.56
5' to 6' deep sewer-line trench ▶ *Trench slopes to 3-1/2' width at bottom. Does not include mobilization. See page 177.*	**Excavate sewer-line trench 5' to 6' deep, sandy loam soil** *Excavate* .... Labor........ .61 Equipment........ .49	lf	—	—	$1.10
	Excavate sewer-line trench 5' to 6' deep, typical soil *Excavate* .... Labor........ .67 Equipment........ .57	lf	—	—	$1.24
	Excavate sewer-line trench 5' to 6' deep, medium rocky or clay soil *Excavate* .... Labor........ .72 Equipment........ .66	lf	—	—	$1.38
	Excavate sewer-line trench 5' to 6' deep, rocky or hardpan soil *Excavate* .... Labor........ .82 Equipment........ .77	lf	—	—	$1.59
	Backfill 5' to 6' sewer line trench per lf of trench *Excavate* .... Labor........ .41 Equipment........ .46	lf	—	—	$.87
7' to 8' deep sewer-line trench ▶ *Trench slopes to 3-1/2' width at bottom. Does not include mobilization. See page 177.*	**Excavate sewer-line trench 7' to 8' deep, sandy loam soil** *Excavate* .... Labor........ .72 Equipment........ .65	lf	—	—	$1.37
	Excavate sewer-line trench 7' to 8' deep, typical soil *Excavate* .... Labor........ .82 Equipment........ .75	lf	—	—	$1.57
	Excavate sewer-line trench 7' to 8' deep, medium rocky or clay soil *Excavate* .... Labor........ .92 Equipment........ .87	lf	—	—	$1.79
	Excavate sewer-line trench 7' to 8' deep, rocky or hardpan soil *Excavate* .... Labor........ 1.03 Equipment........ 1.00	lf	—	—	$2.03
	Backfill 7' to 8' sewer-line trench per lf of trench *Excavate* .... Labor........ .31 Equipment........ .61	lf	—	—	$.92
Repair hole ▶ *Access hole for repairs, per lf of hole depth.*	**Excavate hole for repairs to water, sewer, or utility lines** *Excavate* .... Labor........1.81 Equipment........1.35	lf	—	—	$3.16

Item Description	Unit			Total	
General foundation, slab, & footing excavation *Excavate* .... Labor ....1.89 Equipment............1.43	cy	—	—	$3.32	◄ **GENERAL** *General excavation per cy. No mobilization included.*
Minimum charge for excavation work *Excavate* .... Labor ....206.00 Equipment........300.00	ea	—	—	$506.00	◄ **MINIMUM CHARGE**

TIME & MATERIAL CHARTS *(selected items)*

Excavation Rental Equipment

DESCRIPTION	PRICE	COVERAGE	UNIT PRICE
Backhoe / loader			
excavate slab-on-grade structure			
typical soil	$460.00 per day	5,740 per day	$.08 sf
rocky or hardpan soil	$460.00 per day	4,250 per day	$.11 sf
backfill	$460.00 per day	9,420 per day	$.05 sf
excavate for structure with crawl space			
typical soil	$460.00 per day	3,530 per day	$.13 sf
rocky or hardpan soil	$460.00 per day	2,610 per day	$.18 sf
backfill	$460.00 per day	6,123 per day	$.08 sf
excavate for structure with basement			
typical soil	$460.00 per day	1,400 per day	$.33 sf
rocky or hardpan soil	$460.00 per day	1,030 per day	$.45 sf
excavation	$460.00 per day	3,140 per day	$.15 sf
excavate for 3' to 4' deep footing			
typical soil	$460.00 per day	1,420 per day	$.32 lf
rocky or hardpan soil	$460.00 per day	1,050 per day	$.44 lf
excavate for 5' to 6' deep footing			
typical soil	$460.00 per day	1,108 per day	$.42 lf
rocky or hardpan soil	$460.00 per day	830 per day	$.55 lf
excavate for 7' to 8' deep footing			
typical soil	$460.00 per day	880 per day	$.52 lf
rocky or hardpan soil	$460.00 per day	660 per day	$.70 lf
excavate for 9' to 10' deep footing			
typical soil	$460.00 per day	738 per day	$.62 lf
rocky or hardpan soil	$460.00 per day	560 per day	$.82 lf
backfill foundation wall			
backfill	$460.00 per day	2,230 per day	$.21 lf
excavate for 1' to 2' deep utility trench			
sandy loam soil	$460.00 per day	4,930 per day	$.09 lf
rocky or hardpan soil	$460.00 per day	3,150 per day	$.15 lf
backfill	$460.00 per day	5,300 per day	$.09 lf
excavate for 3' to 4' deep utility trench			
sandy loam soil	$460.00 per day	3,057 per day	$.15 lf
rocky or hardpan soil	$460.00 per day	1,960 per day	$.23 lf
backfill	$460.00 per day	2,650 per day	$.17 lf
excavate for 5' to 6' deep utility trench			
sandy loam soil	$460.00 per day	2,219 per day	$.21 lf
rocky or hardpan soil	$460.00 per day	1,410 per day	$.33 lf
backfill	$460.00 per day	1,760 per day	$.26 lf
excavate for 2' to 3' deep water-line trench			
sandy loam soil	$460.00 per day	2,200 per day	$.21 lf
rocky or hardpan soil	$460.00 per day	1,400 per day	$.33 lf
backfill	$460.00 per day	2,350 per day	$.20 lf

. . . More ➢

Excavation Rental Equipment *continued*

DESCRIPTION	APPLICATION	PRICE	COVERAGE	UNIT PRICE
Backhoe / loader *continued*				
excavate for 4′ to 5′ deep water-line trench				
sandy loam soil		$460.00 per day	1,330 per day	$.35 lf
typical soil		$460.00 per day	1,140 per day	$.40 lf
medium rocky or clay soil		$460.00 per day	980 per day	$.47 lf
rocky or hardpan soil		$460.00 per day	850 per day	$.54 lf
backfill		$460.00 per day	1,410 per day	$.33 lf
excavate for 6′ to 7′ deep water-line trench				
sandy loam soil		$460.00 per day	940 per day	$.49 lf
typical soil		$460.00 per day	810 per day	$.57 lf
medium rocky or clay soil		$460.00 per day	700 per day	$.66 lf
rocky or hardpan soil		$460.00 per day	610 per day	$.75 lf
backfill		$460.00 per day	1,010 per day	$.46 lf
excavate for 8′ to 9′ deep water-line trench				
sandy loam soil		$460.00 per day	730 per day	$.63 lf
typical soil		$460.00 per day	630 per day	$.73 lf
medium rocky or clay soil		$460.00 per day	540 per day	$.85 lf
rocky or hardpan soil		$460.00 per day	460 per day	$1.00 lf
backfill		$460.00 per day	780 per day	$.59 lf
excavate for 3′ to 4′ deep sewer-line trench				
sandy loam soil		$460.00 per day	1,420 per day	$.32 lf
typical soil		$460.00 per day	1,220 per day	$.38 lf
medium rocky or clay soil		$460.00 per day	1,050 per day	$.44 lf
rocky or hardpan soil		$460.00 per day	900 per day	$.51 lf
backfill		$460.00 per day	1,520 per day	$.30 lf
excavate for 5′ to 6′ deep sewer-line trench				
sandy loam soil		$460.00 per day	940 per day	$.49 lf
typical soil		$460.00 per day	810 per day	$.57 lf
medium rocky or clay soil		$460.00 per day	700 per day	$.66 lf
backfill		$460.00 per day	1,010 per day	$.46 lf
excavate for 7′ to 8′ deep sewer-line trench				
sandy loam soil		$460.00 per day	710 per day	$.65 lf
typical soil		$460.00 per day	610 per day	$.75 lf
medium rocky or clay soil		$460.00 per day	530 per day	$.87 lf
rocky or hardpan soil		$460.00 per day	460 per day	$1.00 lf
backfill		$460.00 per day	750 per day	$.61 lf
excavate for repairs				
excavate hole		$460.00 per day	340 per day	$1.35 lf
general excavation				
general excavation		$460.00 per day	322 per day	$1.43 cy
minimum charge		$300.00 minimum	1 per day	$300.00 ea
Trenching				
trenching machine		$340.00 per day	1 per day	$340.00 day
minimum charge for trenching machine		$220.00 minimum	1 each	$220.00 ea
Compacting				
"jumping jack" compactor		$105.00 per day	1 per day	$105.00 day
minimum charge for compactor		$85.00 minimum	1 each	$85.00 ea

Excavation Labor

LABORER	BASE WAGE	PAID LEAVE	TRUE WAGE	FICA	FUTA	WORKER'S COMP.	UNEMPLOY. INSUR.	HEALTH INSUR.	RETIRE (401K)	LIABILITY INSUR.	COST PER HOUR
Equipment operator	$29.90	2.33	$32.23	2.47	.26	5.81	2.80	2.69	.97	4.35	$51.60
Excavation laborer	$15.10	1.18	$16.28	1.25	.13	5.37	1.42	2.69	.49	2.20	$29.80

Paid Leave is calculated based on two weeks paid vacation, one week sick leave, and seven paid holidays. Employer's matching portion of **FICA** is 7.65 percent. **FUTA** (Federal Unemployment) is .8 percent. **Worker's compensation** was calculated using a national average of 18.04 percent for the equipment operator and 33.00 percent for the excavation laborer. **Unemployment insurance** was calculated using a national average of 8.7 percent. **Health insurance** was calculated based on a projected national average for 2002 of $535 per employee (and family when applicable) per month. Employer pays 80 percent for a per month cost of $428 per employee. **Retirement** is based on a 401(k) retirement program with employer matching of 50 percent. Employee contributions to the 401(k) plan are an average of 6 percent of the true wage. **Liability insurance** is based on a national average of 13.2 percent.

Excavation Labor Productivity

WORK DESCRIPTION	LABORER	COST PER HOUR	PRODUCTIVITY	UNIT PRICE
Excavation equipment delivery and return labor charges				
backhoe mobilization	machine operator	$51.60	4.00	**$206.00** ea
Excavate slab-on-grade structure (per sf of floor)				
typical soil				
machine	machine operator	$51.60	.001	**$.05** sf
hand finish	excavation laborer	$29.80	.001	**$.03** sf
rocky or hardpan soil				
machine	machine operator	$51.60	.002	**$.10** sf
hand finish	excavation laborer	$29.80	.002	**$.06** sf
Backfill slab-on-grade structure (per sf of floor)				
all soil types				
machine	machine operator	$51.60	.001	**$.05** sf
hand labor	excavation laborer	$29.80	.001	**$.03** sf
Excavate for structure with crawl space (per sf of floor)				
typical soil				
machine	machine operator	$51.60	.002	**$.10** sf
hand finish	excavation laborer	$29.80	.002	**$.06** sf
rocky or hardpan soil				
machine	machine operator	$51.60	.003	**$.15** sf
hand finish	excavation laborer	$29.80	.002	**$.06** sf
Backfill structure with crawl space (per sf of floor)				
all soil types				
machine	machine operator	$51.60	.001	**$.05** sf
hand labor	excavation laborer	$29.80	.001	**$.03** sf
Excavate for structure with basement (per sf of floor)				
typical soil				
machine	machine operator	$51.60	.006	**$.31** sf
hand finish	excavation laborer	$29.80	.005	**$.15** sf
rocky or hardpan soil				
machine	machine operator	$51.60	.008	**$.41** sf
hand finish	excavation laborer	$29.80	.006	**$.18** sf
Backfill structure with basement (per sf of floor)				
all soil types				
machine	machine operator	$51.60	.003	**$.15** sf
hand labor	excavation laborer	$29.80	.003	**$.09** sf
Excavate for 3' to 4' deep footings				
typical soil				
machine	machine operator	$51.60	.006	**$.31** lf
hand finish	excavation laborer	$29.80	.005	**$.15** lf
rocky or hardpan soil				
machine	machine operator	$51.60	.008	**$.41** lf
hand finish	excavation laborer	$29.80	.006	**$.18** lf
Excavate for 5' to 6' deep footings				
typical soil				
machine	machine operator	$51.60	.007	**$.36** lf
hand finish	excavation laborer	$29.80	.006	**$.18** lf
rocky or hardpan soil				
machine	machine operator	$51.60	.010	**$.52** lf
hand finish	excavation laborer	$29.80	.008	**$.24** lf
Excavate for 7' to 8' deep footing				
typical soil				
machine	machine operator	$51.60	.009	**$.46** lf
hand finish	excavation laborer	$29.80	.007	**$.21** lf
hardpan or rocky soil				
machine	machine operator	$51.60	.012	**$.62** lf
hand finish	excavation laborer	$29.80	.010	**$.30** lf
Excavate for 9' to 10' deep footing				
typical soil				
machine	machine operator	$51.60	.011	**$.57** lf
hand finish	excavation laborer	$29.80	.009	**$.27** lf

. . . More ➢

Excavation Labor Productivity *continued*

WORK DESCRIPTION	LABORER	COST PER HOUR	PRODUCTIVITY	UNIT PRICE
Excavate for 9' to 10' deep footing *continued*				
hardpan or rocky soil				
machine	machine operator	$51.60	.014	$.72 lf
hand finish	excavation laborer	$29.80	.011	$.33 lf
Machine backfill foundation wall (per sf of wall)				
machine	machine operator	$51.60	.004	$.21 sf
hand labor	excavation laborer	$29.80	.003	$.09 sf
Machine excavate for 1' to 2' deep utility trench				
sandy loam soil	machine operator	$51.60	.002	$.10 lf
rocky or hardpan soil	machine operator	$51.60	.003	$.15 lf
backfill	machine operator	$51.60	.002	$.10 lf
Machine excavate for 3' to 4' deep utility trench				
sandy loam soil	machine operator	$51.60	.003	$.15 lf
rocky or hardpan soil	machine operator	$51.60	.004	$.21 lf
backfill	machine operator	$51.60	.003	$.15 lf
Machine excavate for 5' to 6' deep utility trench				
sandy loam soil	machine operator	$51.60	.004	$.21 lf
rocky or hardpan soil	machine operator	$51.60	.006	$.31 lf
backfill	machine operator	$51.60	.005	$.26 lf
Hand finish excavation for utility trench				
all soil types	excavation laborer	$29.80	.002	$.06 lf
Excavate for 2' to 3' deep water-line trench				
sandy loam soil	machine operator	$51.60	.004	$.21 lf
rocky or hardpan soil	machine operator	$51.60	.006	$.31 lf
backfill	machine operator	$51.60	.003	$.15 lf
Excavate for 4' to 5' deep water-line trench				
sandy loam soil	machine operator	$51.60	.006	$.31 lf
rocky or hardpan soil	machine operator	$51.60	.009	$.46 lf
backfill	machine operator	$51.60	.006	$.31 lf
Excavate for 6' to 7' deep water-line trench				
sandy loam soil	machine operator	$51.60	.009	$.46 lf
rocky or hardpan soil	machine operator	$51.60	.013	$.67 lf
backfill	machine operator	$51.60	.008	$.41 lf
Excavate for 8' to 9' deep water-line trench				
sandy loam soil	machine operator	$51.60	.011	$.57 lf
rocky or hardpan soil	machine operator	$51.60	.017	$.88 lf
backfill	machine operator	$51.60	.010	$.52 lf
Hand finish excavation for water-line trench				
all soil types	excavation laborer	$29.80	.005	$.15 lf
Excavate for 3' to 4' deep sewer-line trench				
sandy loam soil	machine operator	$51.60	.006	$.31 lf
rocky or hardpan soil	machine operator	$51.60	.009	$.46 lf
backfill	machine operator	$51.60	.005	$.26 lf
Excavate for 5' to 6' deep sewer-line trench				
sandy loam soil	machine operator	$51.60	.009	$.46 lf
rocky or hardpan soil	machine operator	$51.60	.013	$.67 lf
backfill	machine operator	$51.60	.008	$.41 lf
Excavate for 7' to 8' deep sewer-line trench				
sandy loam soil	machine operator	$51.60	.011	$.57 lf
rocky or hardpan soil	machine operator	$51.60	.017	$.88 lf
backfill	machine operator	$51.60	.006	$.31 lf
Hand finish excavation for sewer-line trench				
all soil types	excavation laborer	$29.80	.005	$.15 lf
Machine excavate hole for repairs to water, sewer, or utility lines				
machine excavate per lf of depth	machine operator	$51.60	.024	$1.24 lf
hand finish per lf of depth	excavation laborer	$29.80	.019	$.57 lf
General foundation, slab, & footing machine excavation				
machine excavate per cy	machine operator	$51.60	.025	$1.29 cy
hand-finish per cy	excavation laborer	$29.80	.020	$.60 cy

15 Fees

Item Description	Unit			Total
Minimum building permit fee *Fee*..........90.00	ea	—	—	$90.00
Building permit fee for job $2,001 to $5,000 *Fee*..........100.00	ea	—	—	$100.00
Building permit fee for job $5,001 to $10,000 *Fee*..........300.00	ea	—	—	$300.00
Building permit fee for job $10,001 to $20,000 *Fee*..........500.00	ea	—	—	$500.00
Building permit fee for job $20,001 to $30,000 *Fee*..........650.00	ea	—	—	$650.00
Building permit fee for job $30,001 to $40,000 *Fee*..........750.00	ea	—	—	$750.00
Building permit fee for job $40,001 to $50,000 *Fee*..........850.00	ea	—	—	$850.00
Building permit fee for job $50,001 to $60,000 *Fee*..........1100.00	ea	—	—	$1,100.00
Building permit fee for job $60,001 to $70,000 *Fee*..........1200.00	ea	—	—	$1,200.00
Building permit fee for job $70,001 to $80,000 *Fee*..........1300.00	ea	—	—	$1,300.00
Building permit fee for job $80,001 to $90,000 *Fee*..........1400.00	ea	—	—	$1,400.00
Building permit fee for job $90,001 to $100,000 *Fee*..........1500.00	ea	—	—	$1,500.00
Building permit fee for job $100,001 to $150,000 *Fee*..........1950.00	ea	—	—	$1,950.00
Building permit fee for job $150,001 to $200,000 *Fee*..........2350.00	ea	—	—	$2,350.00
Building permit fee for job $200,001 to $250,000 *Fee*..........2750.00	ea	—	—	$2,750.00
Building permit fee for job $250,001 to $300,000 *Fee*..........3150.00	ea	—	—	$3,150.00
Building permit fee for job $300,001 to $400,000 *Fee*..........4000.00	ea	—	—	$4,000.00
Building permit fee for job $400,001 to $500,000 *Fee*..........4800.00	ea	—	—	$4,800.00

◀ **BUILDING PERMIT** *Permit fees vary widely. These fees are rules of thumb for most areas of the country. Rural areas will be less and high-density areas will be more. Includes plan-check fees.*

Sidebar	Item Description	Unit			Total
Sewer connect ▶ *Rule-of-thumb charge for connecting sewer lines to city service.*	**Sewer connection fee** *Fee*..........2150.00 ▶ Typical charges for labor and materials installed by government entity. Does not include any development upcharges added to the fee. Includes connect to a city sewer line up to 50 lf from the structure, mobilization, excavation, pipe and fittings, backfill, repair to street, curb and gutter, and temporary signs.	ea	—	—	$2,150.00
Water connect ▶ *Rule-of-thumb charge for connecting water lines to city service.*	**Water connection fee** *Fee*..........2050.00 ▶ Typical charges for labor and materials installed by government entity. Does not include any development upcharges added to the fee. Includes connect to a city water line up to 50 lf from the structure, mobilization, excavation, pipe and fittings, water meter, backfill, repair to street, curb and gutter, and temporary signs.	ea	—	—	$2,050.00
Estimating ▶ *Typical rates charged to estimate insurance repair damages.*	**Estimating fees per hour** *Fee*..........45.00	hr	—	—	$45.00
	Estimating fees per day *Fee*..........425.00	dy	—	—	$425.00
	Estimating fees as percentage of estimate ▶ Rule of thumb for estimating insurance repair damages on losses under $200,000. Percentage rate drops to as low as **.75%** on large losses or multiple unit losses. This percentage is used across the country. Do not adjust with Area Modification Factor.	%	—	—	1.5%
	Minimum estimating fee *Fee*..........170.00	ea	—	—	$170.00
Soils engineer ▶	**Soils engineer fee per hour** *Fee*..........90.00	hr	—	—	$90.00
Structural engineer ▶	**Structural engineer fee per hour** *Fee*..........105.00	hr	—	—	$105.00
Plan drawing fees ▶	**Plan drawing fee, simple structure per sf of floor** *Fee*.......... .15	sf	—	—	$.15
	Plan drawing fee, typical structure per sf of floor *Fee*.......... .20	sf	—	—	$.20
	Plan drawing fee, complex structure per sf of floor *Fee*.......... .35	sf	—	—	$.35
	Plan drawing fee, ornate structure per sf of floor *Fee*.......... .50	sf	—	—	$.50
	Minimum plan drawing fee *Fee*..........190.00	ea	—	—	$190.00

✍ NOTES:

end

16 Fences

Item Description	Unit	Remove	Replace	Total
Add 11% for redwood wood fences				
Add 4% for treated-pine wood fences				
4′ high cedar post embedded in concrete *Replace* Materials.......19.90 Labor..........32.90 *Remove*......................... Labor...........10.10	ea	$10.10	$52.80	$62.90
6′ high cedar post embedded in concrete *Replace* Materials......22.90 Labor..........32.90 *Remove*......................... Labor...........10.10	ea	$10.10	$55.80	$65.90
8′ high cedar post embedded in concrete *Replace* Materials......25.90 Labor..........32.90 *Remove*......................... Labor...........10.10	ea	$10.10	$58.80	$68.90
4′ high cedar basketweave fence *Replace* Materials.......11.70 Labor...........11.50 *Remove*......................... Labor............4.43	lf	$4.43	$23.20	$27.63
6′ high cedar basketweave fence *Replace* Materials.......15.80 Labor...........12.20 *Remove*......................... Labor............4.54	lf	$4.54	$28.00	$32.54
8′ high cedar basketweave fence *Replace* Materials......20.70 Labor...........13.00 *Remove*......................... Labor............4.68	lf	$4.68	$33.70	$38.38
4′ high cedar basketweave fence gate with hardware *Replace* Materials......68.20 Labor...........97.70 *Remove*......................... Labor............8.91	ea	$8.91	$165.90	$174.81
6′ high cedar basketweave fence gate with hardware *Replace* Materials......83.60 Labor.........104.00 *Remove*......................... Labor............9.24	ea	$9.24	$187.60	$196.84
8′ high cedar basketweave fence gate with hardware *Replace* Materials......97.70 Labor.........110.00 *Remove*......................... Labor............9.52	ea	$9.52	$207.70	$217.22
4′ high cedar board fence *Replace* Materials.......11.70 Labor............9.70 *Remove*......................... Labor............4.43	lf	$4.43	$21.40	$25.83
6′ high cedar board fence *Replace* Materials.......15.80 Labor...........10.40 *Remove*......................... Labor............4.54	lf	$4.54	$26.20	$30.74
8′ high cedar board fence *Replace* Materials......20.70 Labor...........11.10 *Remove*......................... Labor............4.68	lf	$4.68	$31.80	$36.48
4′ high cedar board fence gate with hardware *Replace* Materials......68.20 Labor...........78.60 *Remove*......................... Labor............8.91	ea	$8.91	$146.80	$155.71

◄ **OTHER WOODS**

◄ **WOOD FENCE POST**
All wood fence posts include digging of 2′ deep hole and setting in concrete. Post height is above ground. For example, a 4′ high post is made from a 6′ length with 2′ underground and 4′ above ground.

◄ **BASKETWEAVE FENCE**
Posts are set in concrete and spaced up to 8′ on center with an average spacing of 7.2′ apart. Fence boards are 1″ x 6″ to 1″ x 10″. Gates are 3′ wide with a frame made from 2″ x 4″ lumber, cross braced with turnbuckle and cable. Includes heavy duty hinges, latch, and spring closer.

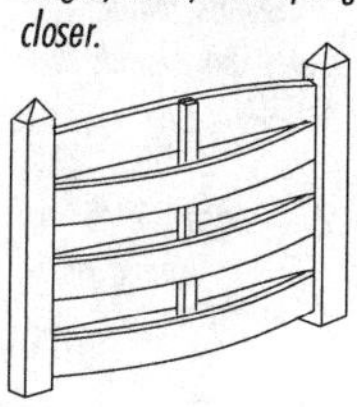

◄ **BOARD FENCE**
Fence with boards installed vertically or horizontally. Posts are set in concrete and spaced up to 8′ on center with an average spacing of 7.2′ apart. Fence boards are 1″ x 4″ to 1″ x 8″. 8′ tall fence contains three supporting rails. All other heights contain two. Gates are 3′ wide with horizontal and diagonal rails, heavy duty hinges, latch, and spring closer.

Board fence ► *continued*

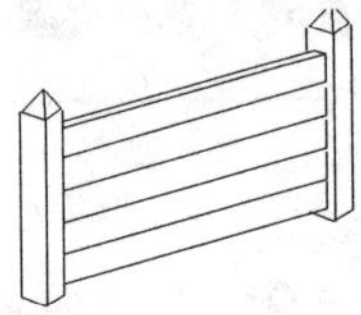

Item Description	Unit	Remove	Replace	Total
6′ high cedar board fence gate with hardware *Replace* Materials......83.60 Labor..........84.30 *Remove*......................... Labor............9.24	ea	$9.24	$167.90	$177.14
8′ high cedar board fence gate with hardware *Replace* Materials......97.70 Labor..........88.30 *Remove*......................... Labor............9.52	ea	$9.52	$186.00	$195.52

Board fence with lattice cap ►

Board fence with 12″ cap. Lattice is trimmed with 2″ x 4″ lattice rails. Posts are set in concrete and spaced up to 8′ on center with an average spacing of 7.2′. Gates are 3′ wide with a frame made from 2″ x 4″ lumber, cross braced with turn buckle and cable. Includes heavy duty hinges, latch, and spring closer.

Item Description	Unit	Remove	Replace	Total
6′ high cedar board fence with lattice cap *Replace* Materials......21.20 Labor...........12.00 *Remove*......................... Labor............4.54	lf	$4.54	$33.20	$37.74
8′ high cedar board fence with lattice cap *Replace* Materials......26.10 Labor...........13.00 *Remove*......................... Labor............4.68	lf	$4.68	$39.10	$43.78
6′ high cedar board fence gate with lattice cap *Replace* Materials......93.00 Labor.........106.00 *Remove*......................... Labor............9.20	ea	$9.20	$199.00	$208.20
8′ high cedar board fence gate with lattice cap *Replace* Materials.....107.10 Labor.........125.00 *Remove*......................... Labor............9.49	ea	$9.49	$232.10	$241.59

Board-on-board fence ►

Fence with overlapping boards installed vertically. Posts are set in concrete and spaced up to 8′ on center with an average spacing of 7.2′ apart. Fence boards are 1″ x 4″ to 1″ x 8″. 8′ tall fence contains three supporting rails. All other heights contain two. Gates are 3′ wide with horizontal and diagonal rails. Includes heavy duty hinges, latch, and spring closer.

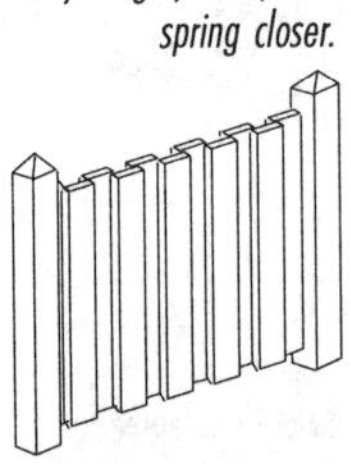

Item Description	Unit	Remove	Replace	Total
4′ high cedar board-on-board fence *Replace* Materials.......15.80 Labor...........10.70 *Remove*......................... Labor............4.43	lf	$4.43	$26.50	$30.93
6′ high cedar board-on-board fence *Replace* Materials......22.10 Labor...........11.30 *Remove*......................... Labor............4.54	lf	$4.54	$33.40	$37.94
8′ high cedar board-on-board fence *Replace* Materials......29.00 Labor...........12.00 *Remove*......................... Labor............4.68	lf	$4.68	$41.00	$45.68
4′ high cedar board-on-board fence gate with hardware *Replace* Materials......80.70 Labor..........92.70 *Remove*......................... Labor............8.91	ea	$8.91	$173.40	$182.31
6′ high cedar board-on-board fence gate with hardware *Replace* Materials....102.40 Labor...........97.70 *Remove*......................... Labor............9.24	ea	$9.24	$200.10	$209.34
8′ high cedar board-on-board fence gate with hardware *Replace* Materials.....123.00 Labor.........104.00 *Remove*......................... Labor............9.52	ea	$9.52	$227.00	$236.52

Board-and-batten fence ►

Vertically installed 1″ x 8″ to 1″ x 12″ boards with 1″ x 2″ to 1″ x 4″ battens overlapping joints. Posts are set in concrete and spaced up to 8′ on center with an average spacing of 7.2′ apart. Gates are 3′ wide with horizontal and diagonal rails. Includes heavy duty hinges, latch, and spring closer.

Item Description	Unit	Remove	Replace	Total
4′ high cedar board-and-batten fence *Replace* Materials.......13.50 Labor...........10.90 *Remove*......................... Labor............4.43	lf	$4.43	$24.40	$28.83
6′ high cedar board-and-batten fence *Replace* Materials......18.60 Labor...........11.10 *Remove*......................... Labor............4.54	lf	$4.54	$29.70	$34.24
8′ high cedar board-and-batten fence *Replace* Materials......24.40 Labor...........11.70 *Remove*......................... Labor............4.68	lf	$4.68	$36.10	$40.78

Item Description	Unit	Remove	Replace	Total
4′ high cedar board-and-batten fence gate with hardware *Replace* Materials......73.80 Labor..........95.20 *Remove*........................ Labor 8.91	ea	$8.91	$169.00	$177.91
6′ high cedar board-and-batten fence gate with hardware *Replace* Materials......92.00 Labor........101.00 *Remove*........................ Labor 9.24	ea	$9.24	$193.00	$202.24
8′ high cedar board-and-batten fence gate with hardware *Replace* Materials....108.80 Labor........106.00 *Remove*........................ Labor 9.52	ea	$9.52	$214.80	$224.32
3′ high cedar picket fence *Replace* Materials........6.85 Labor ....8.04 *Remove*........................ Labor 4.43	lf	$4.43	$14.89	$19.32
5′ high cedar picket fence *Replace* Materials......10.60 Labor ....8.62 *Remove*........................ Labor 4.54	lf	$4.54	$19.22	$23.76
3′ high cedar picket fence gate with hardware *Replace* Materials......53.40 Labor..........72.40 *Remove*........................ Labor 8.91	ea	$8.91	$125.80	$134.71
5′ high cedar picket fence gate with hardware *Replace* Materials......66.90 Labor ....86.20 *Remove*........................ Labor 9.24	ea	$9.24	$153.10	$162.34
Minimum charge for board fence work *Replace* Materials......30.00 Labor..........61.20	ea	—	$91.20	$91.20
Remove & reinstall board fence gate *Replace* .... Labor 29.10	ea	—	$29.10	$29.10
Wood gate hardware with self-closing hinges *Replace* Materials......33.30 Labor..........27.30 *Remove*........................ Labor 5.41	ea	$5.41	$60.60	$66.01
Heavy gauge wood gate hardware with self-closing hinges *Replace* Materials......51.00 Labor..........27.30 *Remove*........................ Labor 5.41	ea	$5.41	$78.30	$83.71
Wood gate closing spring *Replace* Materials......20.40 Labor..........12.00 *Remove*........................ Labor 2.76	ea	$2.76	$32.40	$35.16
3′ high chain-link fence *Replace* Materials........7.55 Labor ....4.13 *Remove*........................ Labor ....3.19 ► With 1-5/8″ line posts and 2″ terminal posts.	lf	$3.19	$11.68	$14.87
4′ high chain-link fence *Replace* Materials......10.01 Labor ....5.25 *Remove*........................ Labor ....3.33 ► With 1-7/8″ line posts and 2″ terminal posts.	lf	$3.33	$15.26	$18.59
5′ high chain-link fence *Replace* Materials ......12.50 Labor ....6.62 *Remove*........................ Labor ....3.44 ► With 1-7/8″ line posts and 2″ terminal posts.	lf	$3.44	$19.12	$22.56

RELATED ITEMS

Painting..........................337

◄ **PICKET FENCE**
Posts are set in concrete and spaced up to 8′ on center with an average spacing of 7.2′ apart. Pickets are factory pre-cut. Gates are 3′ wide with horizontal and diagonal rails. Includes heavy duty hinges, latch, and spring closer.

◄ **MINIMUM CHARGE FOR BOARD FENCE**

◄ **REMOVE & REINSTALL GATE**

◄ **WOOD GATE HARDWARE**

◄ **CHAIN-LINK FENCE**
11 gauge chain-link. Line posts and terminal posts are set 2′ deep in concrete and spaced up to 10′ on center with an average spacing of 9.2′ apart. Includes all post caps, tie wire, tension bands, nuts, bolts, and tension rods.

	Item Description	Unit	Remove	Replace	Total
CHAIN-LINK ► FENCE *continued*	**6' high chain-link fence** *Replace* Materials......14.90 Labor............8.43 *Remove*......................... Labor............3.60 ► With 1-7/8" line posts and 2" terminal posts.	lf	$3.60	$23.33	$26.93
	7' high chain-link fence *Replace* Materials.......17.40 Labor...........10.70 *Remove*......................... Labor............3.74 ► With 1-7/8" line posts and 2" terminal posts.	lf	$3.74	$28.10	$31.84
	8' high chain-link fence *Replace* Materials.......19.80 Labor...........13.60 *Remove*......................... Labor............3.93 ► With 2" line posts and 3" terminal posts.	lf	$3.93	$33.40	$37.33
	10' high chain-link fence *Replace* Materials......24.70 Labor...........17.20 *Remove*......................... Labor............4.18 ► With 2" line posts and 3" terminal posts.	lf	$4.18	$41.90	$46.08
CHAIN-LINK ► FENCE GATE *3' wide with all hardware.*	**3' high chain-link fence gate with hardware** *Replace* Materials......40.70 Labor..........92.70 *Remove*......................... Labor............5.58	ea	$5.58	$133.40	$138.98
	4' high chain-link fence gate with hardware *Replace* Materials......52.60 Labor..........92.70 *Remove*......................... Labor............5.58	ea	$5.58	$145.30	$150.88
	5' high chain-link fence gate with hardware *Replace* Materials......63.30 Labor..........92.70 *Remove*......................... Labor............5.58	ea	$5.58	$156.00	$161.58
	6' high chain-link fence gate with hardware *Replace* Materials......72.90 Labor...........95.20 *Remove*......................... Labor............5.58	ea	$5.58	$168.10	$173.68
	7' high chain-link fence gate with hardware *Replace* Materials......82.20 Labor...........95.20 *Remove*......................... Labor............5.58	ea	$5.58	$177.40	$182.98
	8' high chain-link fence gate with hardware *Replace* Materials......90.20 Labor...........95.20 *Remove*......................... Labor............5.58	ea	$5.58	$185.40	$190.98
	10' high chain-link fence gate with hardware *Replace* Materials....108.00 Labor...........95.20 *Remove*......................... Labor............5.58	ea	$5.58	$203.20	$208.78
CHAIN-LINK ► DRIVEWAY GATE *Prices per lf. Includes all hardware. Minimum of 6 lf.*	**3' high chain-link fence driveway gate with hardware** *Replace* Materials......12.00 Labor..........23.20 *Remove*......................... Labor............1.18	lf	$1.18	$35.20	$36.38
	4' high chain-link fence driveway gate with hardware *Replace* Materials......22.10 Labor..........23.20 *Remove*......................... Labor............1.18	lf	$1.18	$45.30	$46.48
	5' high chain-link fence driveway gate with hardware *Replace* Materials......35.60 Labor..........23.20 *Remove*......................... Labor............1.18	lf	$1.18	$58.80	$59.98
	6' high chain-link fence driveway gate with hardware *Replace* Materials......41.30 Labor..........23.80 *Remove*......................... Labor............1.18	lf	$1.18	$65.10	$66.28

Item Description	Unit	Remove	Replace	Total
7′ high chain-link fence driveway gate with hardware ***Replace*** Materials......46.70 Labor..........23.80 ***Remove***........................ Labor...........1.18	lf	$1.18	$70.50	$71.68
8′ high chain-link fence driveway gate with hardware ***Replace*** Materials......51.40 Labor..........23.80 ***Remove***........................ Labor...........1.18	lf	$1.18	$75.20	$76.38
Add for additional corner in chain-link fence ***Replace*** Materials......47.10 Labor..........69.90 ► The chain-link fence prices above allow for an average of 1 corner or terminal posts for every 15 lf of fence. Use this price only when estimating a fence that contains more corner or terminal posts.	ea	—	$117.00	$117.00
Add for vinyl privacy slats (per sf of fence or gate) ***Replace*** Materials........ .60 Labor............ .22	sf	—	$.82	$.82
Add for aluminum privacy slats (per sf of fence or gate) ***Replace*** Materials........ .64 Labor............ .22	sf	—	$.86	$.86
Add 3% for chain-link fence with top rail				
Add 28% for 9 gauge galvanized chain-link				
Add 25% for 9 gauge vinyl-coated chain-link and posts				
Add 41% for 6 gauge chain-link				
Remove chain-link fence gate for work, then reinstall ***Replace*** .... Labor..........10.50	ea	—	$10.50	$10.50
Remove chain-link fence (posts remain) for work, then reinstall ***Replace*** .... Labor............ .47	sf	—	$.47	$.47
Minimum charge for chain-link fence work ***Replace*** Materials......56.50 Labor..........81.50	ea	—	$138.00	$138.00
3′ high galvanized line post embedded in concrete ***Replace*** Materials......14.40 Labor..........33.20 ***Remove***........................ Labor...........11.10 ► 1-7/8″ diameter post.	ea	$11.10	$47.60	$58.70
4′ high galvanized line post embedded in concrete ***Replace*** Materials.......15.50 Labor..........33.20 ***Remove***........................ Labor...........11.10 ► 1-7/8″ diameter post.	ea	$11.10	$48.70	$59.80
5′ high galvanized line post embedded in concrete ***Replace*** Materials......16.70 Labor..........33.20 ***Remove***........................ Labor...........11.10 ► 1-7/8″ diameter post.	ea	$11.10	$49.90	$61.00
6′ high galvanized line post embedded in concrete ***Replace*** Materials.......17.80 Labor..........33.20 ***Remove***........................ Labor...........11.10 ► 1-7/8″ diameter post.	ea	$11.10	$51.00	$62.10
7′ high galvanized line post embedded in concrete ***Replace*** Materials......18.90 Labor..........33.20 ***Remove***........................ Labor...........11.10 ► 1-7/8″ diameter post.	ea	$11.10	$52.10	$63.20

◄ **ADDITIONAL CHAIN-LINK COSTS**

◄ **REMOVE CHAIN-LINK & REINSTALL**

◄ **MINIMUM FOR CHAIN-LINK**

◄ **CHAIN-LINK FENCE POST**
All chain-link fence posts include digging of 2′ deep hole and setting in concrete. Post height is above ground. For example, a 4′ high post is made from a 6′ length with 2′ underground and 4′ above ground.

	Item Description	Unit	Remove	Replace	Total
CHAIN-LINK FENCE POST *continued* ►	**8' high galvanized line post embedded in concrete** *Replace* Materials......20.40 Labor..........33.20 *Remove*......................... Labor...........11.10 ► 2" diameter post.	ea	$11.10	$53.60	$64.70
	10' high galvanized line post embedded in concrete *Replace* Materials......22.70 Labor..........33.20 *Remove*......................... Labor...........11.10 ► 2" diameter post.	ea	$11.10	$55.90	$67.00
gate or corner post ▷	**3' high galvanized gate or corner post embedded in concrete** *Replace* Materials.......13.80 Labor..........33.20 *Remove*......................... Labor...........11.10 ► 2" diameter post.	ea	$11.10	$47.00	$58.10
	4' high galvanized gate or corner post embedded in concrete *Replace* Materials ......14.70 Labor..........33.20 *Remove*......................... Labor...........11.10 ► 2" diameter post.	ea	$11.10	$47.90	$59.00
	5' high galvanized gate or corner post embedded in concrete *Replace* Materials.......15.60 Labor..........33.20 *Remove*......................... Labor...........11.10 ► 2" diameter post.	ea	$11.10	$48.80	$59.90
	6' high galvanized gate or corner post embedded in concrete *Replace* Materials ......18.00 Labor..........33.20 *Remove*......................... Labor...........11.10 ► 2-1/2" diameter post.	ea	$11.10	$51.20	$62.30
	7' high galvanized gate or corner post embedded in concrete *Replace* Materials.......19.20 Labor..........33.20 *Remove*......................... Labor...........11.10 ► 2-1/2" diameter post.	ea	$11.10	$52.40	$63.50
	8' high galvanized gate or corner post embedded in concrete *Replace* Materials ......31.70 Labor..........33.20 *Remove*......................... Labor...........11.10 ► 3" diameter post.	ea	$11.10	$64.90	$76.00
	10' high galvanized gate or corner post embedded in concrete *Replace* Materials......36.90 Labor..........33.20 *Remove*......................... Labor...........11.10 ► 3" diameter post.	ea	$11.10	$70.10	$81.20
ADD FOR ALUMINIZED ►	**Add 22% for aluminized steel fence post**				
VINYL PICKET FENCE ► *36" and 48" fences have 2 rails, 60" and 72" have three. Pickets are 7/8" x 1-1/2" spaced 3-7/8" apart. Top and bottom rails are 1-1/2" x 3-1/2". Bottom rail includes galvanized steel channel. Posts are 4" x 4" and spaced up to 8' on center with an average spacing of 7.2 feet apart. Includes picket and post caps.*	**36" high vinyl picket fence** *Replace* Materials.......13.80 Labor...........12.70 *Remove*......................... Labor 3.82	lf	$3.82	$26.50	$30.32
	48" high vinyl picket fence *Replace* Materials ......16.80 Labor...........12.90 *Remove*......................... Labor 3.82	lf	$3.82	$29.70	$33.52
	60" high vinyl picket fence *Replace* Materials.......19.90 Labor...........13.10 *Remove*......................... Labor 3.82	lf	$3.82	$33.00	$36.82
	72" high vinyl picket fence *Replace* Materials......22.90 Labor...........13.20 *Remove*......................... Labor 3.82	lf	$3.82	$36.10	$39.92

continued on next page

Item Description	Unit	Remove	Replace	Total
36″ high vinyl picket fence gate ***Replace*** Materials......40.50 Labor..........23.30 ***Remove*** .... Labor............4.18	lf	$4.18	$63.80	$67.98
48″ high vinyl picket fence gate ***Replace*** Materials......42.60 Labor..........24.00 ***Remove*** .... Labor............4.18	lf	$4.18	$66.60	$70.78
60″ high vinyl picket fence gate ***Replace*** Materials......44.70 Labor..........24.70 ***Remove*** .... Labor............4.18	lf	$4.18	$69.40	$73.58
72″ high vinyl picket fence gate ***Replace*** Materials......46.80 Labor..........25.20 ***Remove*** .... Labor............4.18	lf	$4.18	$72.00	$76.18
36″ high vinyl picket fence, large pickets ***Replace*** Materials.......15.80 Labor..........12.70 ***Remove*** .... Labor............3.82	lf	$3.82	$28.50	$32.32
48″ high vinyl picket fence, large pickets ***Replace*** Materials.......19.70 Labor..........12.90 ***Remove*** .... Labor............3.82	lf	$3.82	$32.60	$36.42
60″ high vinyl picket fence, large pickets ***Replace*** Materials......23.10 Labor..........13.10 ***Remove*** .... Labor............3.82	lf	$3.82	$36.20	$40.02
36″ high vinyl picket fence gate, large pickets ***Replace*** Materials......42.10 Labor..........23.30 ***Remove*** .... Labor............4.18	lf	$4.18	$65.40	$69.58
48″ high vinyl picket fence gate, large pickets ***Replace*** Materials......44.70 Labor..........24.00 ***Remove*** .... Labor............4.18	lf	$4.18	$68.70	$72.88
60″ high vinyl picket fence gate, large pickets ***Replace*** Materials......47.30 Labor..........24.70 ***Remove*** .... Labor............4.18	lf	$4.18	$72.00	$76.18
36″ high vinyl picket fence, scalloped pickets ***Replace*** Materials......14.80 Labor..........12.70 ***Remove*** .... Labor............3.82	lf	$3.82	$27.50	$31.32
48″ high vinyl picket fence, scalloped pickets ***Replace*** Materials......18.00 Labor..........12.90 ***Remove*** .... Labor............3.82	lf	$3.82	$30.90	$34.72
60″ high vinyl picket fence, scalloped pickets ***Replace*** Materials......21.20 Labor..........13.10 ***Remove*** .... Labor............3.82	lf	$3.82	$34.30	$38.12
36″ high vinyl picket fence gate, scalloped pickets ***Replace*** Materials......41.30 Labor..........23.30 ***Remove*** .... Labor............4.18	lf	$4.18	$64.60	$68.78
48″ high vinyl picket fence gate, scalloped pickets ***Replace*** Materials......43.40 Labor..........24.00 ***Remove*** .... Labor............4.18	lf	$4.18	$67.40	$71.58

◄ **VINYL PICKET FENCE**
continued

*Gates are priced per lf with a 3 lf minimum and a 5 lf maximum and include all hardware. For wider gates, measure the gate lf, round up to the next even number, multiply by the fence lf price, then add **$150.***

◄ **VINYL LARGE PICKET FENCE**
Same as picket fence discussed on previous page with large 7/8" x 3-1/2" pickets spaced 3-7/8" apart.

VINYL FENCES

Also called PVC fences, vinyl fences are made from a molecularly bonded blend of hi-polymer resin with UV inhibitors to prevent damage from sunlight.

All posts are filled with concrete to about 1/3 of their height and capped with decorative caps

◄ **VINYL SCALLOPED PICKET FENCE**
Same as picket fence discussed above with decorative scalloped pickets.

	Item Description	Unit	Remove	Replace	Total
VINYL SCALLOPED PICKET FENCE ► *continued*	**60" high vinyl picket fence gate, scalloped pickets** ***Replace*** Materials......45.70 Labor..........24.70 ***Remove*** .... Labor...........4.18	lf	$4.18	$70.40	$74.58
REMOVE & REINSTALL VINYL FENCE ►	**Remove vinyl fence for work, then reinstall (panels only)** ***Replace*** .... Labor..........19.50	lf	—	$19.50	$19.50
	Remove vinyl fence gate for work, then reinstall ***Replace*** .... Labor..........24.70	lf	—	$24.70	$24.70
VINYL THREE-RAIL FENCE ► *Rails are 1-1/2" x 5-1/2". Posts are 5" x 5" and spaced up to 8' apart with an average spacing of 7.2'. Gates priced per lf: 3 lf minimum, 5 lf maximum.*	**52" high vinyl three-rail fence** ***Replace*** Materials........9.20 Labor...........7.64 ***Remove*** .... Labor...........2.86	lf	$2.86	$16.84	$19.70
	52" high vinyl three-rail fence gate ***Replace*** Materials......35.30 Labor..........10.90 ***Remove*** .... Labor...........2.86 ► For gates longer than 5 lf use lf fence price, round to even number and add **$105**.	lf	$2.86	$46.20	$49.06
REMOVE & REINSTALL THREE-RAIL FENCE ►	**Remove three-rail vinyl fence for work, then reinstall (rails only)** ***Replace*** .... Labor..........13.50	lf	—	$13.50	$13.50
	Remove three-rail vinyl fence gate for work, then reinstall ***Replace*** .... Labor..........19.50	lf	—	$19.50	$19.50
VINYL SPACED SLAT FENCE ► *Contains two widths of slats. The narrow slat is 7/8" x 1-1/2" and the wide slat is 7/8" x 3-1/2". Slats are spaced 2-1/2" apart. Top and bottom rails are 1-1/2" x 3-1/2". Bottom rail includes galvanized steel channel. Posts are 4" x 4" and spaced up to 8' on center with an average spacing of 7.2 feet apart. Includes post caps. Gates are priced per lf with a 3 lf minimum and a 5 lf maximum and include all hardware. For wider gates, measure the gate lf, round up to the next even number, multiply by the fence lf price, then add **$150.***	**48" high vinyl spaced slat fence** ***Replace*** Materials......14.10 Labor..........12.90 ***Remove*** .... Labor...........3.82	lf	$3.82	$27.00	$30.82
	60" high vinyl spaced slat fence ***Replace*** Materials.......17.20 Labor..........13.10 ***Remove*** .... Labor...........3.82	lf	$3.82	$30.30	$34.12
	72" high vinyl spaced slat fence ***Replace*** Materials......20.30 Labor..........13.20 ***Remove*** .... Labor...........3.82	lf	$3.82	$33.50	$37.32
	48" high vinyl spaced slat fence gate ***Replace*** Materials......40.70 Labor..........24.00 ***Remove*** .... Labor...........4.18	lf	$4.18	$64.70	$68.88
	60" high vinyl spaced slat fence gate ***Replace*** Materials......42.90 Labor..........24.70 ***Remove*** .... Labor...........4.18	lf	$4.18	$67.60	$71.78
	72" high vinyl spaced slat fence gate ***Replace*** Materials......44.90 Labor..........25.20 ***Remove*** .... Labor...........4.18	lf	$4.18	$70.10	$74.28
VINYL SOLID SLAT FENCE ► *Slat is 7/8" x 5-1/2" with no space between slats. Top and bottom rails are 1-1/2" x 3-1/2". Bottom rail includes galvanized steel channel. Posts are 5" x 5" and spaced up to 8' on center with an average spacing of 7.2 feet.*	**48" high vinyl solid slat fence** ***Replace*** Materials......14.70 Labor..........12.90 ***Remove*** .... Labor...........3.82	lf	$3.82	$27.60	$31.42
	60" high vinyl solid slat fence ***Replace*** Materials......27.50 Labor..........13.10 ***Remove*** .... Labor...........3.82	lf	$3.82	$40.60	$44.42
	72" high vinyl solid slat fence ***Replace*** Materials......21.20 Labor..........13.20 ***Remove*** .... Labor...........3.82	lf	$3.82	$34.40	$38.22

continued on next page

Item Description	Unit	Remove	Replace	Total
48″ high vinyl solid slat fence gate **Replace** Materials......41.20 Labor..........24.00 **Remove**........................ Labor............4.18	lf	$4.18	$65.20	$69.38
60″ high vinyl solid slat fence gate **Replace** Materials......43.40 Labor..........24.70 **Remove**........................ Labor............4.18	lf	$4.18	$68.10	$72.28
72″ high vinyl solid slat fence gate **Replace** Materials......45.60 Labor..........25.20 **Remove**........................ Labor............4.18	lf	$4.18	$70.80	$74.98
60″ high vinyl solid slat fence with lattice top **Replace** Materials......24.50 Labor..........13.50 **Remove**........................ Labor............3.82	lf	$3.82	$38.00	$41.82
72″ high vinyl solid slat fence with lattice top **Replace** Materials......27.50 Labor..........13.60 **Remove**........................ Labor............3.82	lf	$3.82	$41.10	$44.92
60″ high vinyl solid slat fence with lattice top gate **Replace** Materials......47.80 Labor..........26.20 **Remove**........................ Labor............4.18	lf	$4.18	$74.00	$78.18
72″ high vinyl solid slat fence with lattice top gate **Replace** Materials......49.90 Labor..........27.40 **Remove**........................ Labor............4.18	lf	$4.18	$77.30	$81.48
60″ ornamental iron fence, straight pickets **Replace** Materials......12.30 Labor..........13.50 **Remove**........................ Labor............5.34	lf	$5.34	$25.80	$31.14
72″ ornamental iron fence, straight pickets **Replace** Materials......14.10 Labor..........13.60 **Remove**........................ Labor............5.34	lf	$5.34	$27.70	$33.04
60″ ornamental iron fence gate, straight pickets **Replace** Materials......49.00 Labor..........26.20 **Remove**........................ Labor............5.56	lf	$5.56	$75.20	$80.76
72″ ornamental iron fence gate, straight pickets **Replace** Materials......52.10 Labor..........27.40 **Remove**........................ Labor............5.56	lf	$5.56	$79.50	$85.06
60″ ornamental iron fence, twisted pickets **Replace** Materials......13.20 Labor..........13.50 **Remove**........................ Labor............5.34	lf	$5.34	$26.70	$32.04
72″ ornamental iron fence, twisted pickets **Replace** Materials......15.30 Labor..........13.60 **Remove**........................ Labor............5.34	lf	$5.34	$28.90	$34.24
60″ ornamental iron fence gate, twisted pickets **Replace** Materials......52.40 Labor..........26.20 **Remove**........................ Labor............5.56	lf	$5.56	$78.60	$84.16
72″ ornamental iron fence gate, twisted pickets **Replace** Materials......55.70 Labor..........27.40 **Remove**........................ Labor............5.56	lf	$5.56	$83.10	$88.66

◀ **VINYL SOLID SLAT FENCE** *continued*

*Includes post caps. Gates are priced per lf with a 3 lf minimum and a 5 lf maximum and include all hardware. For wider gates, measure the gate lf, round up to the next even number, multiply by the fence lf price, then add **$150.***

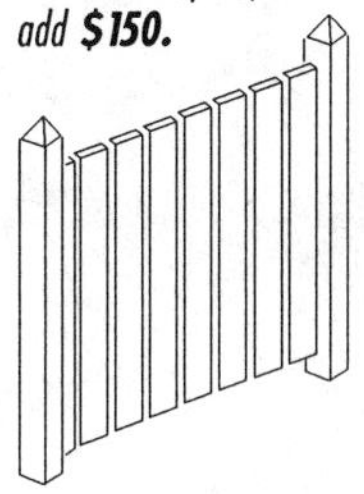

◀ **ORNAMENTAL IRON FENCE**

*On all grades except fences with ornamental casting, steel pickets are 5/8″ square 3-7/8″ apart with 1″ x 1″ top and bottom rails. Posts are 93-1/2″ apart. Pickets with decorative scrolls are straight pickets with the decorative scroll-work riveted or screwed to the pickets. Ornamental iron fences with ornamental casting have pickets that are cast in decorative scroll and plant-like patterns. Gates are priced per lf with a 3 lf minimum and a 5 lf maximum. For wider gates, measure the gate lf, round up to the next even number, multiply by the fence lf price, then add **$200.***

RELATED ITEMS

Painting..........................337

	Item Description	Unit	Remove	Replace	Total
ORNAMENTAL IRON FENCE *continued*	**60" ornamental iron fence with decorative scrolls** ***Replace*** Materials......18.70 Labor..........13.50 ***Remove***........................ Labor............5.34	lf	$5.34	$32.20	$37.54
	72" ornamental iron fence with decorative scrolls ***Replace*** Materials......21.60 Labor..........13.60 ***Remove***........................ Labor............5.34	lf	$5.34	$35.20	$40.54
	60" ornamental iron fence gate with decorative scrolls ***Replace*** Materials......74.10 Labor..........26.20 ***Remove***........................ Labor............5.56	lf	$5.56	$100.30	$105.86
	72" ornamental iron fence gate with decorative scrolls ***Replace*** Materials......78.70 Labor..........27.40 ***Remove***........................ Labor............5.56	lf	$5.56	$106.10	$111.66
	60" ornamental iron fence with ornamental casting ***Replace*** Materials......33.10 Labor..........13.50 ***Remove***........................ Labor............5.34	lf	$5.34	$46.60	$51.94
	72" ornamental iron fence with ornamental casting ***Replace*** Materials......38.30 Labor..........13.60 ***Remove***........................ Labor............5.34	lf	$5.34	$51.90	$57.24
	60" ornamental iron fence gate with ornamental casting ***Replace*** Materials.....131.00 Labor..........26.20 ***Remove***........................ Labor............5.56	lf	$5.56	$157.20	$162.76
	72" ornamental iron fence gate with ornamental casting ***Replace*** Materials.....139.00 Labor..........27.40 ***Remove***........................ Labor............5.56	lf	$5.56	$166.40	$171.96
REMOVE & REINSTALL IRON FENCE	**Remove ornamental iron fence for work, then reinstall (panels only)** ***Replace*** .... Labor..........20.20	lf	—	$20.20	$20.20
	Remove ornamental iron fence gate for work, then reinstall ***Replace*** .... Labor..........35.30	lf	—	$35.30	$35.30
ELECTRIC GATE OPENER *For swinging or roll-type gates. Includes two remote transmitters, key-pad on post by gate, all hardware and electrical wiring up to 45 lf.*	**1/2 horsepower electric gate opener** ***Replace*** Materials..2650.00 Labor.........142.00 ***Remove***........................ Labor...........21.00	ea	$21.00	$2,792.00	$2,813.00
	3/4 horsepower electric gate opener ***Replace*** Materials..3400.00 Labor.........142.00 ***Remove***........................ Labor...........21.00	ea	$21.00	$3,542.00	$3,563.00
	1 horsepower electric gate opener ***Replace*** Materials..3850.00 Labor.........142.00 ***Remove***........................ Labor...........21.00	ea	$21.00	$3,992.00	$4,013.00
	2 horsepower electric gate opener ***Replace*** Materials..4500.00 Labor.........142.00 ***Remove***........................ Labor...........21.00	ea	$21.00	$4,642.00	$4,663.00
	5 horsepower electric gate opener ***Replace*** Materials..5200.00 Labor.........142.00 ***Remove***........................ Labor...........21.00	ea	$21.00	$5,342.00	$5,363.00
	Remove electric gate opener for work, then reinstall ***Replace*** .... Labor........229.00	ea	—	$229.00	$229.00

TIME & MATERIAL CHARTS (selected items)

Fences Materials (Also see material prices with the line items and other information in the **QuickFinder** column.)

DESCRIPTION	MATERIAL PRICE	GROSS COVERAGE	WASTE	NET COVERAGE	UNIT PRICE
4" x 4" posts					
8′ cedar	$11.40 ea	1	4%	.96	**$11.90** ea
10′ cedar	$14.30 ea	1	4%	.96	**$14.90** ea
12′ cedar	$17.10 ea	2	4%	1.92	**$8.91** ea
1" x 2" x 8′ fence boards					
#2 cedar	$3.10 ea	8	4%	7.68	**$.40** lf
B grade redwood	$6.00 ea	8	4%	7.68	**$.78** lf
treated-pine	$1.90 ea	8	4%	7.68	**$.25** lf
1" x 4" x 8′ fence boards					
#2 cedar	$4.40 ea	8	4%	7.68	**$.57** lf
B grade redwood	$8.50 ea	8	4%	7.68	**$1.11** lf
treated-pine	$3.80 ea	8	4%	7.68	**$.49** lf
1" x 6" x 8′ fence boards					
#2 cedar	$6.60 ea	8	4%	7.68	**$.86** lf
B grade redwood	$12.70 ea	8	4%	7.68	**$1.65** lf
treated-pine	$4.30 ea	8	4%	7.68	**$.56** lf
1" x 8" x 8′ fence boards					
#2 cedar	$12.10 ea	8	4%	7.68	**$1.58** lf
B grade redwood	$23.30 ea	8	4%	7.68	**$3.03** lf
treated-pine	$7.70 ea	8	4%	7.68	**$1.00** lf
1" x 10" x 8′ fence boards					
#2 cedar	$14.90 ea	8	4%	7.68	**$1.94** lf
B grade redwood	$28.70 ea	8	4%	7.68	**$3.74** lf
treated-pine	$9.60 ea	8	4%	7.68	**$1.25** lf
2" x 4" x 8′ fence boards					
#2 cedar	$5.30 ea	8	4%	7.68	**$.69** lf
B grade redwood	$8.40 ea	8	4%	7.68	**$1.09** lf
treated-pine	$8.00 ea	8	4%	7.68	**$1.04** lf
1" x 3" mill-cut fence picket					
3′ cedar	$1.30 ea	1	4%	.96	**$1.35** ea
5′ cedar	$2.90 ea	1	4%	.96	**$3.02** ea
Lattice					
cedar lattice	$18.00 sh	32	4%	30.72	**$.59** sf
cedar cap mold	$6.90 ea	8	4%	7.68	**$.90** lf
Chain-link fence materials					
11 gauge chain-link	$1.79 sf	1	3%	.97	**$1.85** sf

Fences Labor

LABORER	BASE WAGE	PAID LEAVE	TRUE WAGE	FICA	FUTA	WORKER'S COMP.	UNEMPLOY. INSUR.	HEALTH INSUR.	RETIRE (401K)	LIABILITY INSUR.	COST PER HOUR
Carpenter	$23.60	1.84	$25.44	1.95	.20	4.96	2.21	2.69	.76	3.43	**$41.60**
Carpenter's helper	$17.00	1.33	$18.33	1.40	.15	3.57	1.59	2.69	.55	2.47	**$30.80**
Electrician	$26.10	2.04	$28.14	2.15	.23	3.03	2.45	2.69	.84	3.80	**$43.30**
Demolition laborer	$13.90	1.08	$14.98	1.15	.12	4.79	1.30	2.69	.45	2.02	**$27.50**

Paid Leave is calculated based on two weeks paid vacation, one week sick leave, and seven paid holidays. Employer's matching portion of **FICA** is 7.65 percent. **FUTA** (Federal Unemployment) is .8 percent. **Worker's compensation** for the fences trade was calculated using a national average of 19.50 percent. **Unemployment insurance** was calculated using a national average of 8.7 percent. **Health insurance** was calculated based on a projected national average for 2002 of $535 per employee (and family when applicable) per month. Employer pays 80 percent for a per month cost of $428 per employee. **Retirement** is based on a 401(k) retirement program with employer matching of 50 percent. Employee contributions to the 401(k) plan are an average of 6 percent of the true wage. **Liability insurance** is based on a national average of 13.2 percent.

Fences Labor Productivity

WORK DESCRIPTION	LABORER	COST PER HOUR	PRODUCTIVITY	UNIT PRICE
Demolition				
remove 4' high wood fence	demolition laborer	$27.50	.161	$4.43 lf
remove 6' high wood fence	demolition laborer	$27.50	.165	$4.54 lf
remove 8' high wood fence	demolition laborer	$27.50	.170	$4.68 lf
remove wood fence post	demolition laborer	$27.50	.367	$10.10 ea
remove 3' high chain-link fence	demolition laborer	$27.50	.116	$3.19 lf
remove 4' high chain-link fence	demolition laborer	$27.50	.121	$3.33 lf
remove 5' high chain-link fence	demolition laborer	$27.50	.125	$3.44 lf
remove 6' high chain-link fence	demolition laborer	$27.50	.131	$3.60 lf
remove 7' high chain-link fence	demolition laborer	$27.50	.136	$3.74 lf
remove 8' high chain-link fence	demolition laborer	$27.50	.143	$3.93 lf
remove 10' high chain-link fence	demolition laborer	$27.50	.152	$4.18 lf
remove chain-link fence gate	demolition laborer	$27.50	.203	$5.58 ea
remove chain-link fence driveway gate	demolition laborer	$27.50	.043	$1.18 lf
remove chain-link fence post	demolition laborer	$27.50	.402	$11.10 ea
remove vinyl fence	demolition laborer	$27.50	.139	$3.82 lf
remove vinyl rail fence	demolition laborer	$27.50	.104	$2.86 lf
remove vinyl fence gate	demolition laborer	$27.50	.152	$4.18 lf
remove ornamental iron fence	demolition laborer	$27.50	.194	$5.34 lf
remove ornamental iron fence gate	demolition laborer	$27.50	.202	$5.56 lf
remove electric gate opener	demolition laborer	$27.50	.763	$21.00 ea
Fencing crew				
fencing installation	carpenter	$41.60		
fencing installation	carpenter's helper	$30.80		
fencing installation	**fencing crew**	$36.20		
Build basketweave fence				
4' high	fencing crew	$36.20	.318	$11.50 lf
8' high	fencing crew	$36.20	.359	$13.00 lf
4' high gate	fencing crew	$36.20	2.70	$97.70 ea
8' high gate	fencing crew	$36.20	3.03	$110.00 ea
Build board fence				
4' high	fencing crew	$36.20	.268	$9.70 lf
8' high	fencing crew	$36.20	.307	$11.10 lf
4' high gate	fencing crew	$36.20	2.17	$78.60 lf
8' high gate	fencing crew	$36.20	2.44	$88.30 lf
Build board fence with lattice cap				
6' high	fencing crew	$36.20	.331	$12.00 lf
8' high	fencing crew	$36.20	.359	$13.00 lf
6' high gate	fencing crew	$36.20	2.94	$106.00 lf
8' high gate	fencing crew	$36.20	3.45	$125.00 lf
Build board-on-board fence				
4' high	fencing crew	$36.20	.296	$10.70 lf
8' high	fencing crew	$36.20	.331	$12.00 lf
4' high gate	fencing crew	$36.20	2.56	$92.70 lf
8' high gate	fencing crew	$36.20	2.86	$104.00 lf
Build board-and-batten fence				
4' high	fencing crew	$36.20	.301	$10.90 lf
8' high	fencing crew	$36.20	.324	$11.70 lf
4' high gate	fencing crew	$36.20	2.63	$95.20 lf
8' high gate	fencing crew	$36.20	2.94	$106.00 lf
Build picket fence				
3' high	fencing crew	$36.20	.222	$8.04 lf
5' high	fencing crew	$36.20	.238	$8.62 lf
3' high gate	fencing crew	$36.20	2.00	$72.40 lf
5' high gate	fencing crew	$36.20	2.38	$86.20 lf
Install chain-link fence				
3' high	fencing crew	$36.20	.114	$4.13 lf
5' high	fencing crew	$36.20	.183	$6.62 lf
7' high	fencing crew	$36.20	.295	$10.70 lf
10' high	fencing crew	$36.20	.475	$17.20 lf

17 Finish Carpentry

Item Description	Unit	Remove	Replace	Total
Minimum charge for finish carpentry work *Replace* Materials......20.00 Labor..........44.90	ea	—	$64.90	$64.90
Add 70% for walnut				
Add 563% for teak				
Add 73% for cherry				
Add 31% for hard maple				
Add 24% for cypress				
Add 17% for redwood				
Add 0% for cedar				
1-1/2" finger-joint pine clamshell base *Replace* Materials........ .74 Labor............1.58 *Remove*........................ Labor............ .72	lf	$.72	$2.32	$3.04
1-1/2" stain-grade pine clamshell base *Replace* Materials........ .86 Labor............1.58 *Remove*........................ Labor............ .72	lf	$.72	$2.44	$3.16
1-1/2" poplar clamshell base *Replace* Materials........ .91 Labor............1.58 *Remove*........................ Labor............ .72	lf	$.72	$2.49	$3.21
1-1/2" mahogany clamshell base *Replace* Materials........1.10 Labor............1.58 *Remove*........................ Labor............ .72	lf	$.72	$2.68	$3.40
1-1/2" red oak clamshell base *Replace* Materials........1.18 Labor............1.58 *Remove*........................ Labor............ .72	lf	$.72	$2.76	$3.48
2-1/2" finger-joint pine clamshell base *Replace* Materials........ .85 Labor............1.58 *Remove*........................ Labor............ .72	lf	$.72	$2.43	$3.15
2-1/2" stain-grade pine clamshell base *Replace* Materials........ .99 Labor............1.58 *Remove*........................ Labor............ .72	lf	$.72	$2.57	$3.29
2-1/2" poplar clamshell base *Replace* Materials...... 1.05 Labor............1.58 *Remove*........................ Labor............ .72	lf	$.72	$2.63	$3.35
2-1/2" mahogany clamshell base *Replace* Materials........1.26 Labor............1.58 *Remove*........................ Labor............ .72	lf	$.72	$2.84	$3.56

◄ **MINIMUM**

◄ **OTHER WOOD SPECIES**
For moldings made from these species of wood factor the cost of stain-grade pine by the percentage. All grades are kiln-dried select or better.

◄ **1-1/2" CLAMSHELL BASE**
Includes 7% waste.

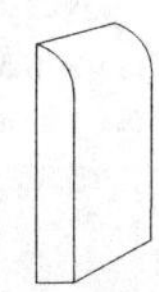

WOOD EMBOSSING

Wood moldings are often embossed to appear like they have been carved. Embossing stamps a pattern onto the wood.

Embossing is far less expensive than carving and is most successful on softer woods, such as pine.

◄ **2-1/2" CLAMSHELL BASE**
Includes 7% waste.

RELATED ITEMS

Cleaning..............................61
Painting............................337

	Item Description	Unit	Remove	Replace	Total
2-1/2" ▶ CLAMSHELL BASE *continued*	**2-1/2" red oak clamshell base** ***Replace*** Materials........1.35 Labor ....1.58 ***Remove*** .... Labor............. .72	lf	$.72	$2.93	$3.65
3-1/2" ▶ CLAMSHELL BASE *Includes 7% waste.*	**3-1/2" finger-joint pine clamshell base** ***Replace*** Materials........1.20 Labor ....1.58 ***Remove*** .... Labor............. .72	lf	$.72	$2.78	$3.50
	3-1/2" stain-grade pine clamshell base ***Replace*** Materials........1.40 Labor ....1.58 ***Remove*** .... Labor............. .72	lf	$.72	$2.98	$3.70
	3-1/2" poplar clamshell base ***Replace*** Materials........1.48 Labor ....1.58 ***Remove*** .... Labor............. .72	lf	$.72	$3.06	$3.78
	3-1/2" mahogany clamshell base ***Replace*** Materials........1.77 Labor ....1.58 ***Remove*** .... Labor............. .72	lf	$.72	$3.35	$4.07
	3-1/2" red oak clamshell base ***Replace*** Materials........1.91 Labor ....1.58 ***Remove*** .... Labor............. .72	lf	$.72	$3.49	$4.21
4-1/2" ▶ CLAMSHELL BASE	**Add 22% for 4-1/2" clamshell base** ▶ Add to the cost of 3-1/2" clamshell base.				
1-1/2" ▶ PATTERN BASE *Includes 7% waste.* 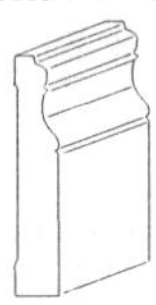	**1-1/2" finger-joint pine pattern base** ***Replace*** Materials........ .90 Labor ....1.58 ***Remove*** .... Labor............. .72	lf	$.72	$2.48	$3.20
	1-1/2" stain-grade pine pattern base ***Replace*** Materials...... 1.04 Labor ....1.58 ***Remove*** .... Labor............. .72	lf	$.72	$2.62	$3.34
	1-1/2" poplar pattern base ***Replace*** Materials........1.11 Labor ....1.58 ***Remove*** .... Labor............. .72	lf	$.72	$2.69	$3.41
	1-1/2" mahogany pattern base ***Replace*** Materials........1.33 Labor ....1.58 ***Remove*** .... Labor............. .72	lf	$.72	$2.91	$3.63
	1-1/2" red oak pattern base ***Replace*** Materials........1.44 Labor ....1.58 ***Remove*** .... Labor............. .72	lf	$.72	$3.02	$3.74
2-1/2" ▶ PATTERN BASE *Includes 7% waste.*	**2-1/2" finger-joint pine pattern base** ***Replace*** Materials........1.45 Labor ....1.58 ***Remove*** .... Labor............. .72	lf	$.72	$3.03	$3.75
	2-1/2" stain-grade pine pattern base ***Replace*** Materials........1.68 Labor ....1.58 ***Remove*** .... Labor............. .72	lf	$.72	$3.26	$3.98
	2-1/2" poplar pattern base ***Replace*** Materials........1.78 Labor ....1.58 ***Remove*** .... Labor............. .72	lf	$.72	$3.36	$4.08
	2-1/2" mahogany pattern base ***Replace*** Materials........2.15 Labor ....1.58 ***Remove*** .... Labor............. .72	lf	$.72	$3.73	$4.45

Item Description	Unit	Remove	Replace	Total	
2-1/2" red oak pattern base ***Replace*** Materials........2.32 Labor ....1.58 ***Remove***......................... Labor............ .72	lf	$.72	$3.90	$4.62	
3-1/2" finger-joint pine pattern base ***Replace*** Materials........1.91 Labor ....1.58 ***Remove***......................... Labor............ .72	lf	$.72	$3.49	$4.21	◄ **3-1/2" PATTERN BASE** *Includes 7% waste.*
3-1/2" stain-grade pine pattern base ***Replace*** Materials........2.22 Labor ....1.58 ***Remove***......................... Labor............ .72	lf	$.72	$3.80	$4.52	
3-1/2" poplar pattern base ***Replace*** Materials........2.35 Labor ....1.58 ***Remove***......................... Labor............ .72	lf	$.72	$3.93	$4.65	
3-1/2" mahogany pattern base ***Replace*** Materials........2.84 Labor ....1.58 ***Remove***......................... Labor............ .72	lf	$.72	$4.42	$5.14	
3-1/2" red oak pattern base ***Replace*** Materials........3.06 Labor ....1.58 ***Remove***......................... Labor............ .72	lf	$.72	$4.64	$5.36	
Add 10% for 5" pattern base ► Add to the cost of 3-1/2" pattern base.					◄ **5" PATTERN BASE**
Add 31% for 8" pattern base ► Add to the cost of 3-1/2" pattern base.					◄ **8" PATTERN BASE**
Remove base for work, then reinstall ***Replace*** .... Labor 2.35	lf	—	$2.35	$2.35	◄ **REMOVE BASE & REINSTALL**
3/4" finger-joint pine base shoe ***Replace*** Materials .... .45 Labor ....1.58 ***Remove***......................... Labor............ .72	lf	$.72	$2.03	$2.75	◄ **3/4" BASE SHOE** *Includes 7% waste.* 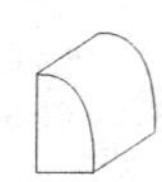
3/4" stain-grade pine base shoe ***Replace*** Materials .... .53 Labor ....1.58 ***Remove***......................... Labor............ .72	lf	$.72	$2.11	$2.83	
3/4" poplar base shoe ***Replace*** Materials .... .56 Labor ....1.58 ***Remove***......................... Labor............ .72	lf	$.72	$2.14	$2.86	
3/4" mahogany base shoe ***Replace*** Materials .... .67 Labor ....1.58 ***Remove***......................... Labor............ .72	lf	$.72	$2.25	$2.97	
3/4" red oak base shoe ***Replace*** Materials .... .72 Labor ....1.58 ***Remove***......................... Labor............ .72	lf	$.72	$2.30	$3.02	
Remove base shoe for work, then reinstall ***Replace*** .... Labor 2.35	lf	—	$2.35	$2.35	
1-1/2" paint-grade clamshell casing ***Replace*** Materials .... .76 Labor ....1.71 ***Remove***......................... Labor............ .88	lf	$.88	$2.47	$3.35	◄ **1-1/2" CLAMSHELL CASING** *Includes 7% waste.* 

RELATED ITEMS

Cleaning..............................61
Doors.................................101
Painting...........................337

	Item Description	Unit	Remove	Replace	Total
1-1/2" CLAM-SHELL CASING *continued*	**1-1/2" stain-grade pine clamshell casing** ***Replace*** Materials........ .87 Labor............1.71 ***Remove*** .... Labor............ .88	lf	$.88	$2.58	$3.46
	1-1/2" poplar clamshell casing ***Replace*** Materials........ .93 Labor............1.71 ***Remove*** .... Labor............ .88	lf	$.88	$2.64	$3.52
	1-1/2" mahogany clamshell casing ***Replace*** Materials........1.12 Labor............1.71 ***Remove*** .... Labor............ .88	lf	$.88	$2.83	$3.71
	1-1/2" red oak clamshell casing ***Replace*** Materials........1.20 Labor............1.71 ***Remove*** .... Labor............ .88	lf	$.88	$2.91	$3.79
2-1/2" CLAM-SHELL CASING *Includes 7% waste.*	**2-1/2" finger-joint pine clamshell casing** ***Replace*** Materials........ .86 Labor............1.71 ***Remove*** .... Labor............ .88	lf	$.88	$2.57	$3.45
	2-1/2" stain-grade pine clamshell casing ***Replace*** Materials...... 1.01 Labor............1.71 ***Remove*** .... Labor............ .88	lf	$.88	$2.72	$3.60
	2-1/2" poplar clamshell casing ***Replace*** Materials........1.07 Labor............1.71 ***Remove*** .... Labor............ .88	lf	$.88	$2.78	$3.66
	2-1/2" mahogany clamshell casing ***Replace*** Materials........1.28 Labor............1.71 ***Remove*** .... Labor............ .88	lf	$.88	$2.99	$3.87
	2-1/2" red oak clamshell casing ***Replace*** Materials........1.38 Labor............1.71 ***Remove*** .... Labor............ .88	lf	$.88	$3.09	$3.97
3-1/2" CLAM-SHELL CASING *Includes 7% waste.*	**3-1/2" finger-joint pine clamshell casing** ***Replace*** Materials........1.22 Labor............1.71 ***Remove*** .... Labor............ .88	lf	$.88	$2.93	$3.81
	3-1/2" stain-grade pine clamshell casing ***Replace*** Materials........1.42 Labor............1.71 ***Remove*** .... Labor............ .88	lf	$.88	$3.13	$4.01
	3-1/2" poplar clamshell casing ***Replace*** Materials........1.52 Labor............1.71 ***Remove*** .... Labor............ .88	lf	$.88	$3.23	$4.11
	3-1/2" mahogany clamshell casing ***Replace*** Materials........1.81 Labor............1.71 ***Remove*** .... Labor............ .88	lf	$.88	$3.52	$4.40
	3-1/2" red oak clamshell casing ***Replace*** Materials........1.95 Labor............1.71 ***Remove*** .... Labor............ .88	lf	$.88	$3.66	$4.54
1-1/2" PATTERN CASING *Includes 7% waste.*	**1-1/2" paint-grade pattern casing** ***Replace*** Materials........ .92 Labor............1.71 ***Remove*** .... Labor............ .88	lf	$.88	$2.63	$3.51

Item Description	Unit	Remove	Replace	Total
1-1/2" stain-grade pine pattern casing *Replace* Materials...... 1.06 Labor............1.71 *Remove*...................... Labor............ .88	lf	$.88	$2.77	$3.65
1-1/2" poplar pattern casing *Replace* Materials........1.13 Labor............1.71 *Remove*...................... Labor............ .88	lf	$.88	$2.84	$3.72
1-1/2" mahogany pattern casing *Replace* Materials........1.36 Labor............1.71 *Remove*...................... Labor............ .88	lf	$.88	$3.07	$3.95
1-1/2" red oak pattern casing *Replace* Materials........1.46 Labor............1.71 *Remove*...................... Labor............ .88	lf	$.88	$3.17	$4.05
1-1/2" curved pattern casing for half-round top window or door *Replace* Materials........6.38 Labor............5.99 *Remove*...................... Labor............ .88	lf	$.88	$12.37	$13.25
1-1/2" curved pattern casing for elliptical-top window or door *Replace* Materials........6.71 Labor............5.99 *Remove*...................... Labor............ .88	lf	$.88	$12.70	$13.58
1-1/2" curved pattern casing for round window per lf of diameter *Replace* Materials......14.90 Labor..........12.20 *Remove*...................... Labor............ .88	lf	$.88	$27.10	$27.98
2-1/2" finger-joint pine pattern casing *Replace* Materials........1.47 Labor............1.71 *Remove*...................... Labor............ .88	lf	$.88	$3.18	$4.06
2-1/2" stain-grade pine pattern casing *Replace* Materials........1.71 Labor............1.71 *Remove*...................... Labor............ .88	lf	$.88	$3.42	$4.30
2-1/2" poplar pattern casing *Replace* Materials........1.82 Labor............1.71 *Remove*...................... Labor............ .88	lf	$.88	$3.53	$4.41
2-1/2" mahogany pattern casing *Replace* Materials........2.19 Labor............1.71 *Remove*...................... Labor............ .88	lf	$.88	$3.90	$4.78
2-1/2" red oak pattern casing *Replace* Materials........2.37 Labor............1.71 *Remove*...................... Labor............ .88	lf	$.88	$4.08	$4.96
2-1/2" curved pattern casing for half-round top window or door *Replace* Materials........6.84 Labor............5.99 *Remove*...................... Labor............ .88	lf	$.88	$12.83	$13.71
2-1/2" curved pattern casing for elliptical-top window or door *Replace* Materials........7.20 Labor............5.99 *Remove*...................... Labor............ .88	lf	$.88	$13.19	$14.07
2-1/2" curved pattern casing for round window per lf of diameter *Replace* Materials......16.00 Labor..........12.20 *Remove*...................... Labor............ .88	lf	$.88	$28.20	$29.08

◀ **1-1/2" PATTERN CASING**
Includes 7% waste.

◀ **1-1/2" CURVED PATTERN CASING**
Includes 7% waste. Laminated back, factory fabricated molding. Half-round and elliptical are priced per lf of casing. Round windows are priced per diameter. If curved casing includes wood key see page 204.

◀ **2-1/2" PATTERN CASING**
Includes 7% waste.

RELATED ITEMS

Cleaning..............................61
Doors..................................101
Painting..............................337

◀ **2-1/2" CURVED PATTERN CASING**
Includes 7% waste. Laminated back, factory fabricated molding. Half-round and elliptical are priced per lf of casing. Round windows are priced per diameter. If casing includes wood key see page 204.

	Item Description	Unit	Remove	Replace	Total
3-1/2" pattern casing ▶ *Includes 7% waste.*	**3-1/2" finger-joint pine pattern casing** *Replace* Materials........1.95 Labor............1.71 *Remove*......................... Labor............. .88	lf	$.88	$3.66	$4.54
	3-1/2" stain-grade pine pattern casing *Replace* Materials........2.25 Labor............1.71 *Remove*......................... Labor............. .88	lf	$.88	$3.96	$4.84
	3-1/2" poplar pattern casing *Replace* Materials........2.40 Labor............1.71 *Remove*......................... Labor............. .88	lf	$.88	$4.11	$4.99
	3-1/2" mahogany pattern casing *Replace* Materials........2.89 Labor............1.71 *Remove*......................... Labor............. .88	lf	$.88	$4.60	$5.48
	3-1/2" red oak pattern casing *Replace* Materials........3.12 Labor............1.71 *Remove*......................... Labor............. .88	lf	$.88	$4.83	$5.71
3-1/2" curved pattern casing ▶ *Includes 7% waste. Laminated back, factory fabricated molding. Half-round and elliptical are priced per lf of casing. Round windows are priced per diameter. If casing includes wood key see below.*	**3-1/2" curved pattern casing for half-round top window or door** *Replace* Materials........6.97 Labor............5.99 *Remove*......................... Labor............. .88	lf	$.88	$12.96	$13.84
	3-1/2" curved pattern casing for elliptical-top window or door per lf *Replace* Materials........7.33 Labor............5.99 *Remove*......................... Labor............. .88	lf	$.88	$13.32	$14.20
	3-1/2" curved pattern casing for round window per lf of diameter *Replace* Materials......16.30 Labor...........12.20 *Remove*......................... Labor............. .88	lf	$.88	$28.50	$29.38
5" pattern casing ▶	**Add 10% for 5" pattern casing** ▶ Add to the cost of 3-1/2" pattern casing.				
Remove casing & reinstall ▶	**Remove casing for work, then reinstall** *Replace* .... Labor............3.00	lf	—	$3.00	$3.00
Wood key ▶	**Wood key for curved molding** *Replace* Materials.......17.50 Labor...........10.40 *Remove*......................... Labor............. .99	ea	$.99	$27.90	$28.89
 △ *with rosette*	**Wood key with light carvings for curved molding** *Replace* Materials.......27.70 Labor...........10.40 *Remove*......................... Labor............. .99	ea	$.99	$38.10	$39.09
	**Wood key with medium carvings for curved molding** *Replace* Materials......34.40 Labor...........10.40 *Remove*......................... Labor............. .99	ea	$.99	$44.80	$45.79
△ *with carvings*	**Wood key with heavy carvings for curved molding** *Replace* Materials......44.90 Labor...........10.40 *Remove*......................... Labor............. .99	ea	$.99	$55.30	$56.29
remove & reinstall ▷	**Remove wood key for work, then reinstall** *Replace* .... Labor...........11.70	ea	—	$11.70	$11.70
Base block ▶	**Pine base block** *Replace* Materials......10.90 Labor............2.62 *Remove*......................... Labor............. .99	ea	$.99	$13.52	$14.51

Item Description	Unit	Remove	Replace	Total
Poplar base block	ea	$.99	$14.12	$15.11
Replace Materials.......11.50 Labor............2.62				
Remove........................ Labor............ .99				
Mahogany base block	ea	$.99	$15.22	$16.21
Replace Materials......12.60 Labor............2.62				
Remove........................ Labor............ .99				
Red oak base block	ea	$.99	$16.82	$17.81
Replace Materials......14.20 Labor............2.62				
Remove........................ Labor............ .99				
Pine corner block with rosette	ea	$.99	$11.32	$12.31
Replace Materials........8.70 Labor............2.62				
Remove........................ Labor............ .99				
Poplar corner block with rosette	ea	$.99	$12.59	$13.58
Replace Materials........9.97 Labor............2.62				
Remove........................ Labor............ .99				
Mahogany corner block with rosette	ea	$.99	$13.82	$14.81
Replace Materials.......11.20 Labor............2.62				
Remove........................ Labor............ .99				
Red oak corner block with rosette	ea	$.99	$15.02	$16.01
Replace Materials......12.40 Labor............2.62				
Remove........................ Labor............ .99				
Add 30% for corner block with carvings				
Pine head block with rosette	ea	$.99	$13.62	$14.61
Replace Materials.......11.00 Labor............2.62				
Remove........................ Labor............ .99				
Poplar head block with rosette	ea	$.99	$15.22	$16.21
Replace Materials......12.60 Labor............2.62				
Remove........................ Labor............ .99				
Mahogany head block with rosette	ea	$.99	$16.72	$17.71
Replace Materials......14.10 Labor............2.62				
Remove........................ Labor............ .99				
Red oak head block with rosette	ea	$.99	$18.32	$19.31
Replace Materials.......15.70 Labor............2.62				
Remove........................ Labor............ .99				
Add 31% for head block with carvings				
Remove base, corner, or head block for work, then reinstall	ea	—	$2.90	$2.90
Replace........................ Labor............2.90				
Pine overdoor molding	lf	$.77	$12.01	$12.78
Replace Materials......10.30 Labor............1.71				
Remove........................ Labor............ .77				
Poplar overdoor molding	lf	$.77	$13.41	$14.18
Replace Materials.......11.70 Labor............1.71				
Remove........................ Labor............ .77				
Mahogany overdoor molding	lf	$.77	$14.71	$15.48
Replace Materials.......13.00 Labor............1.71				
Remove........................ Labor............ .77				

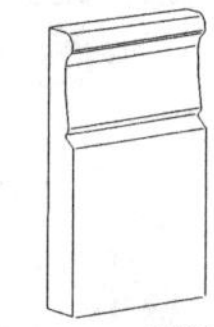

△ *with rosette*

◀ **CORNER BLOCK**

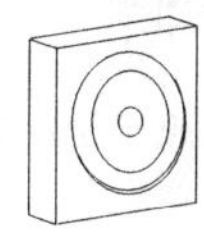

◁ **add for carvings**

◀ **HEAD BLOCK**

◁ **add for carvings**

◀ **REMOVE BLOCK & REINSTALL**

◀ **OVERDOOR MOLD**

RELATED ITEMS

Cleaning....................61
Doors....................101
Painting....................337

Overdoor mold ▶ *continued*

△ *standard*

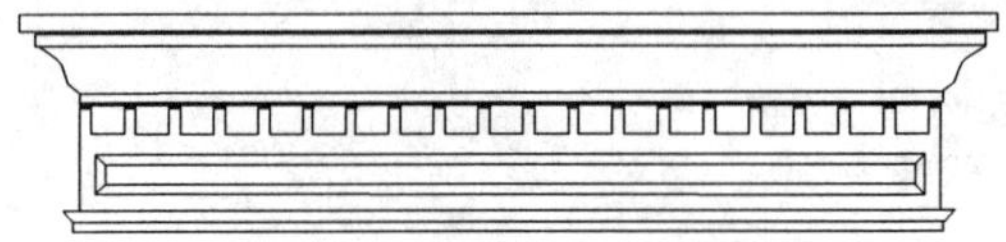

△ *with vertical milling*

△ *with hand carvings*

△ *with heavy hand carvings*

Item Description	Unit	Remove	Replace	Total
Red oak overdoor molding ***Replace*** Materials.......15.00 Labor............1.71 ***Remove***......................... Labor............ .77	lf	$.77	$16.71	$17.48
other styles ▷ **Add 72% for vertical milling in overdoor molding**				
Add 227% for hand carving in overdoor molding				
Add 411% for heavy hand carving in overdoor molding				
remove & reinstall ▷ **Remove overdoor molding for work, then reinstall** ***Replace*** .... Labor............2.06	lf	—	$2.06	$2.06
Interior architrave ▶ *Measure lf all around door: both sides and over door.* **Interior architrave, standard grade** ***Replace*** Materials........4.40 Labor............2.58 ***Remove***......................... Labor............ .88 ▶ Standard casing with rosettes in head and base blocks. Paint-grade pine or poplar or stain-grade pine.	lf	$.88	$6.98	$7.86
Interior architrave, high grade ***Replace*** Materials........5.70 Labor............2.58 ***Remove***......................... Labor............ .88 ▶ Rosettes or light embossing in base blocks. Overdoor includes horizontal moldings at top and bottom. Stain-grade pine or red oak with simple overdoor.	lf	$.88	$8.28	$9.16
Interior architrave, deluxe grade ***Replace*** Materials........7.90 Labor............2.58 ***Remove***......................... Labor............ .88 ▶ May have carvings in base blocks. Angled overdoor with horizontal moldings at top and bottom or overdoor with light carvings. Red oak, birch, or similar hardwood or paint grade with more ornate detail.	lf	$.88	$10.48	$11.36
Interior architrave, custom grade ***Replace*** Materials.......11.10 Labor............2.58 ***Remove***......................... Labor............ .88 ▶ May have carvings in base blocks. Angled or curved overdoor with horizontal moldings at top and bottom or overdoor with heavy carvings. Red oak birch or similar hardwood or paint-grade with very ornate carvings.	lf	$.88	$13.68	$14.56
Remove interior architrave for work, then reinstall ***Replace*** .... Labor............3.73	lf	—	$3.73	$3.73
Exterior architrave ▶ *Measure lf all around door: both sides and over door.* **Exterior architrave, economy grade** ***Replace*** Materials........4.30 Labor............3.33 ***Remove***......................... Labor............ .88 ▶ Standard casing with rosettes in head and base blocks. Paint-grade pine or poplar or stain-grade pine. All materials are back-primed.	lf	$.88	$7.63	$8.51

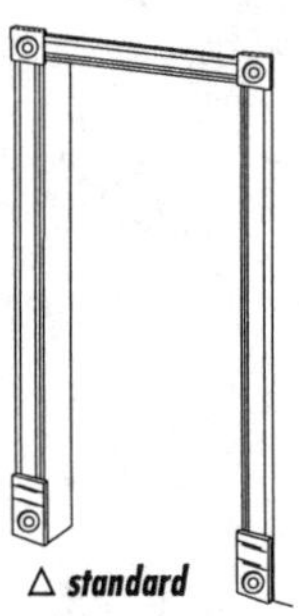

△ *standard*

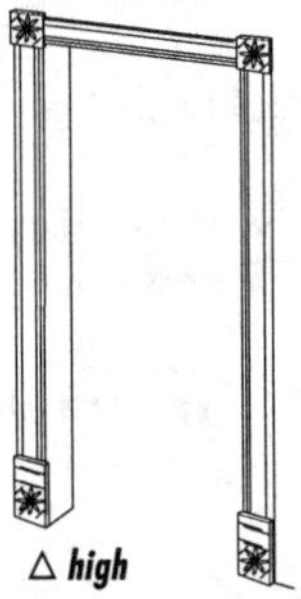

△ *high*

Item Description	Unit	Remove	Replace	Total
Exterior architrave, standard grade ***Replace*** Materials........6.20 Labor ....3.33 ***Remove***......................... Labor............. .88 ► Wide casing, may be made from two moldings. Rosettes in head and base blocks. Paint-grade pine or poplar or stain-grade pine. All materials are back-primed.	lf	$.88	$9.53	$10.41
Exterior architrave, high grade ***Replace*** Materials........8.80 Labor ....3.33 ***Remove***......................... Labor............. .88 ► Wide casing, may be made from two moldings. Rosettes or light embossing in base blocks. Overdoor includes horizontal moldings at top and bottom. Stain grade pine or red oak with simple over door. All materials are back-primed.	lf	$.88	$12.13	$13.01
Exterior architrave, deluxe grade ***Replace*** Materials ......12.30 Labor ....3.33 ***Remove***......................... Labor............. .88 ► Wide casing, may be made from two moldings. May have carvings in base blocks. Angled overdoor with horizontal moldings at top and bottom or overdoor with light carvings. Red oak, birch, or similar hardwood or paint grade with more ornate detail. All materials are back-primed.	lf	$.88	$15.63	$16.51
Exterior architrave, custom grade ***Replace*** Materials.......15.80 Labor ....3.33 ***Remove***......................... Labor............. .88 ► Wide casing, may be made from two moldings. May have carvings in base blocks. Angled or curved overdoor with horizontal moldings at top and bottom or overdoor and carvings. Red oak, birch, or similar hardwood or paint-grade with very ornate carvings. All materials are back-primed.	lf	$.88	$19.13	$20.01
Exterior architrave, custom deluxe grade ***Replace*** Materials......22.00 Labor ....3.33 ***Remove***......................... Labor............. .88 ► Wide casing, may be made from two moldings. May have carvings in base blocks. Curved overdoor with multiple carved moldings. Red oak birch or similar hardwood or paint-grade with very ornate carvings. All materials are back-primed.	lf	$.88	$25.33	$26.21
Remove exterior architrave for work, then reinstall ***Replace*** .... Labor 4.60	lf	—	$4.60	$4.60
Exterior door surround, economy grade ***Replace*** Materials......26.80 Labor ....9.73 ***Remove***......................... Labor............. .94 ► See illustration below for representative example.	lf	$.94	$36.53	$37.47

◁ **remove & reinstall**

◀ **EXTERIOR DOOR SURROUND**
Measure lf all around door: both sides and over door. All grades are for wood which is carved with intricate detail in the higher grades. Plastic or other synthetic materials should be considered economy or standard grades. Illustrations show typical complexity, actual door styling varies widely.

△ *economy* △ *standard* △ *high*

RELATED ITEMS

Cleaning.............................61
Doors.................................101
Masonry
stone architrave..............310
Painting...........................337
Plaster
stucco architrave............359

EXTERIOR DOOR ▶ SURROUND
continued

△ *deluxe*

△ *custom*

△ *custom deluxe*

	Item Description	Unit	Remove	Replace	Total
	Exterior door surround, standard grade ***Replace*** Materials......44.80 Labor...........10.70 ***Remove***......................... Labor............. .94 ▶ See illustration on previous page for representative example.	lf	$.94	$55.50	$56.44
	Exterior door surround, high grade ***Replace*** Materials......78.50 Labor...........11.40 ***Remove***......................... Labor............. .94 ▶ See illustration on previous page for representative example.	lf	$.94	$89.90	$90.84
	Exterior door surround, deluxe grade ***Replace*** Materials....150.00 Labor...........13.20 ***Remove***......................... Labor............. .94 ▶ See illustration above for representative example.	lf	$.94	$163.20	$164.14
	Exterior door surround, custom grade ***Replace*** Materials....236.00 Labor...........15.50 ***Remove***......................... Labor............. .94 ▶ See illustration above for representative example.	lf	$.94	$251.50	$252.44
	Exterior door surround, custom deluxe grade ***Replace*** Materials....394.00 Labor...........17.90 ***Remove***......................... Labor............. .94 ▶ See illustration above for representative example.	lf	$.94	$411.90	$412.84
remove & reinstall ▷	**Remove exterior door surround for work, then reinstall** ***Replace*** .... Labor..........28.00	lf	—	$28.00	$28.00
EXTERIOR ▶ WINDOW SURROUND	**Exterior window surround, economy grade** ***Replace*** Materials......21.80 Labor...........8.61 ***Remove***......................... Labor............. .94 ▶ See illustration on facing page for representative example.	lf	$.94	$30.41	$31.35
	Exterior window surround, standard grade ***Replace*** Materials......36.40 Labor...........9.44 ***Remove***......................... Labor............. .94 ▶ See illustration on facing page for representative example.	lf	$.94	$45.84	$46.78
	Exterior window surround, high grade ***Replace*** Materials......63.80 Labor...........9.94 ***Remove***......................... Labor............. .94 ▶ See illustration on facing page for representative example.	lf	$.94	$73.74	$74.68

△ economy

△ standard

△ high

△ deluxe

△ custom

△ custom deluxe

Item Description	*Unit*	*Remove*	*Replace*	*Total*
Exterior window surround, deluxe grade ***Replace*** Materials.....122.00 Labor...........11.60 ***Remove***.......................... Labor............. .94 ► See illustration below for representative example.	lf	$.94	$133.60	$134.54
Exterior window surround, custom grade ***Replace*** Materials.....192.00 Labor...........13.60 ***Remove***.......................... Labor............. .94 ► See illustration below for representative example.	lf	$.94	$205.60	$206.54
Exterior window surround, custom deluxe grade ***Replace*** Materials....320.00 Labor...........13.40 ***Remove***.......................... Labor............. .94 ► See illustration below for representative example.	lf	$.94	$333.40	$334.34
Remove exterior window surround for work, then reinstall ***Replace*** .... Labor...........24.90	lf	—	$24.90	$24.90
2-1/2" paint-grade window stool ***Replace*** Materials........1.63 Labor............2.41 ***Remove***.......................... Labor............. .72	lf	$.72	$4.04	$4.76
2-1/2" stain-grade pine window stool ***Replace*** Materials........1.89 Labor............2.41 ***Remove***.......................... Labor............. .72	lf	$.72	$4.30	$5.02

RELATED ITEMS

Cleaning..............................61
Doors..................................101
Masonry
stone architrave..............310
Painting...........................337
Plaster
stucco architrave.............359

◁ **remove & reinstall**

◀ **WINDOW STOOL**
Includes 4% waste.

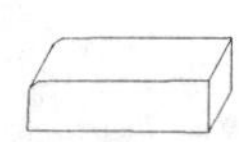

	Item Description	Unit	Remove	Replace	Total
WINDOW STOOL ▶ *continued*	**2-1/2" poplar window stool** ***Replace*** Materials........2.02 Labor............2.41 ***Remove*****.........................** Labor............ .72	lf	$.72	$4.43	$5.15
	2-1/2" mahogany window stool ***Replace*** Materials........2.40 Labor............2.41 ***Remove*****.........................** Labor............ .72	lf	$.72	$4.81	$5.53
	2-1/2" red oak window stool ***Replace*** Materials........2.58 Labor............2.41 ***Remove*****.........................** Labor............ .72	lf	$.72	$4.99	$5.71
	Remove window stool for work, then reinstall ***Replace*** .... Labor............3.91	lf	—	$3.91	$3.91
WINDOW APRON ▶ *Includes 4% waste.* 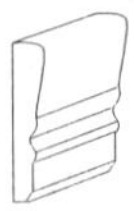	**3-1/2" paint-grade window apron** ***Replace*** Materials...... 1.05 Labor............2.04 ***Remove*****.........................** Labor............ .77	lf	$.77	$3.09	$3.86
	3-1/2" stain-grade pine window apron ***Replace*** Materials........1.23 Labor............2.04 ***Remove*****.........................** Labor............ .77	lf	$.77	$3.27	$4.04
	3-1/2" poplar window apron ***Replace*** Materials........1.31 Labor............2.04 ***Remove*****.........................** Labor............ .77	lf	$.77	$3.35	$4.12
	3-1/2" mahogany window apron ***Replace*** Materials........1.56 Labor............2.04 ***Remove*****.........................** Labor............ .77	lf	$.77	$3.60	$4.37
	3-1/2" red oak window apron ***Replace*** Materials........1.68 Labor............2.04 ***Remove*****.........................** Labor............ .77	lf	$.77	$3.72	$4.49
remove & reinstall ▷	**Remove window apron for work, then reinstall** ***Replace*** .... Labor............2.90	lf	—	$2.90	$2.90
2-1/2" CHAIR RAIL ▶ *Includes 4% waste.* 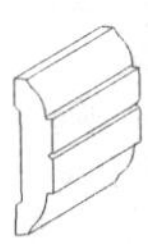	**2-1/2" paint-grade chair rail** ***Replace*** Materials........1.41 Labor............1.58 ***Remove*****.........................** Labor............ .72	lf	$.72	$2.99	$3.71
	2-1/2" stain-grade pine chair rail ***Replace*** Materials........1.63 Labor............1.58 ***Remove*****.........................** Labor............ .72	lf	$.72	$3.21	$3.93
	2-1/2" poplar chair rail ***Replace*** Materials........1.77 Labor............1.58 ***Remove*****.........................** Labor............ .72	lf	$.72	$3.35	$4.07
	2-1/2" mahogany chair rail ***Replace*** Materials........2.07 Labor............1.58 ***Remove*****.........................** Labor............ .72	lf	$.72	$3.65	$4.37
	2-1/2" red oak chair rail ***Replace*** Materials........2.24 Labor............1.58 ***Remove*****.........................** Labor............ .72	lf	$.72	$3.82	$4.54
3-1/2" CHAIR RAIL ▶ *Includes 4% waste.*	**3-1/2" paint-grade chair rail** ***Replace*** Materials........1.77 Labor............1.58 ***Remove*****.........................** Labor............ .72	lf	$.72	$3.35	$4.07

Item Description	Unit	Remove	Replace	Total	
3-1/2" stain-grade pine chair rail ***Replace*** Materials........2.05 Labor............1.58 ***Remove*** .... Labor............ .72	lf	$.72	$3.63	$4.35	
3-1/2" poplar chair rail ***Replace*** Materials........2.22 Labor............1.58 ***Remove*** .... Labor............ .72	lf	$.72	$3.80	$4.52	
3-1/2" mahogany chair rail ***Replace*** Materials........2.61 Labor............1.58 ***Remove*** .... Labor............ .72	lf	$.72	$4.19	$4.91	
3-1/2" red oak chair rail ***Replace*** Materials........2.85 Labor............1.58 ***Remove*** .... Labor............ .72	lf	$.72	$4.43	$5.15	
Remove chair rail for work, then reinstall ***Replace*** .... Labor............2.35	lf	—	$2.35	$2.35	◁ **remove & reinstall**
1-5/8" paint-grade drip cap ***Replace*** Materials........1.29 Labor............1.58 ***Remove*** .... Labor............ .88	lf	$.88	$2.87	$3.75	◀ **DRIP CAP** *Includes 4% waste.*
1-5/8" redwood drip cap ***Replace*** Materials........1.51 Labor............1.58 ***Remove*** .... Labor............ .88	lf	$.88	$3.09	$3.97	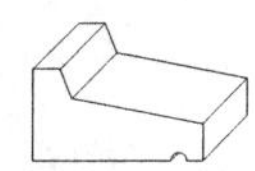
1-5/8" cedar drip cap ***Replace*** Materials........1.41 Labor............1.58 ***Remove*** .... Labor............ .88	lf	$.88	$2.99	$3.87	
2-1/4" paint-grade drip cap ***Replace*** Materials........1.45 Labor............1.58 ***Remove*** .... Labor............ .88	lf	$.88	$3.03	$3.91	
2-1/4" redwood drip cap ***Replace*** Materials........1.69 Labor............1.58 ***Remove*** .... Labor............ .88	lf	$.88	$3.27	$4.15	
2-1/4" cedar drip cap ***Replace*** Materials........1.57 Labor............1.58 ***Remove*** .... Labor............ .88	lf	$.88	$3.15	$4.03	
Remove drip cap for work, then reinstall ***Replace*** .... Labor............3.00	lf	—	$3.00	$3.00	◁ **remove & reinstall**
1-3/4" paint-grade astragal ***Replace*** Materials........2.69 Labor............1.71 ***Remove*** .... Labor............ .88	lf	$.88	$4.40	$5.28	◀ **ASTRAGAL** *Includes 4% waste.*
1-3/4" stain-grade pine astragal ***Replace*** Materials........3.11 Labor............1.71 ***Remove*** .... Labor............ .88	lf	$.88	$4.82	$5.70	
1-3/4" poplar astragal ***Replace*** Materials........3.34 Labor............1.71 ***Remove*** .... Labor............ .88	lf	$.88	$5.05	$5.93	
1-3/4" mahogany astragal ***Replace*** Materials........3.98 Labor............1.71 ***Remove*** .... Labor............ .88	lf	$.88	$5.69	$6.57	

RELATED ITEMS

Cleaning..............................61
Painting..............................337

	Item Description	Unit	Remove	Replace	Total
ASTRAGAL ▶ *continued*	**1-3/4" red oak astragal** ***Replace*** Materials........4.30 Labor............1.71 ***Remove***........................ Labor............ .88	lf	$.88	$6.01	$6.89
	2-1/4" paint-grade astragal ***Replace*** Materials........3.26 Labor............1.71 ***Remove***........................ Labor............ .88	lf	$.88	$4.97	$5.85
	2-1/4" stain-grade pine astragal ***Replace*** Materials........3.77 Labor............1.71 ***Remove***........................ Labor............ .88	lf	$.88	$5.48	$6.36
	2-1/4" poplar astragal ***Replace*** Materials........4.05 Labor............1.71 ***Remove***........................ Labor............ .88	lf	$.88	$5.76	$6.64
	2-1/4" mahogany astragal ***Replace*** Materials........4.82 Labor............1.71 ***Remove***........................ Labor............ .88	lf	$.88	$6.53	$7.41
	2-1/4" red oak astragal ***Replace*** Materials........5.22 Labor............1.71 ***Remove***........................ Labor............ .88	lf	$.88	$6.93	$7.81
remove & reinstall ▷	**Remove astragal for work, then reinstall** ***Replace*** .... Labor............3.00	lf	—	$3.00	$3.00
COVE ▶ *Includes 4% waste.* 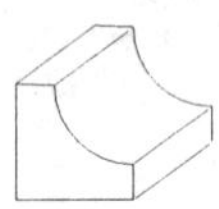	**1/2" paint-grade cove** ***Replace*** Materials........ .50 Labor............1.71 ***Remove***........................ Labor............ .88	lf	$.88	$2.21	$3.09
	1/2" stain-grade pine cove ***Replace*** Materials........ .58 Labor............1.71 ***Remove***........................ Labor............ .88	lf	$.88	$2.29	$3.17
	1/2" poplar cove ***Replace*** Materials........ .65 Labor............1.71 ***Remove***........................ Labor............ .88	lf	$.88	$2.36	$3.24
	1/2" mahogany cove ***Replace*** Materials........ .75 Labor............1.71 ***Remove***........................ Labor............ .88	lf	$.88	$2.46	$3.34
	1/2" red oak cove ***Replace*** Materials........ .79 Labor............1.71 ***Remove***........................ Labor............ .88	lf	$.88	$2.50	$3.38
	3/4" paint-grade cove ***Replace*** Materials........ .57 Labor............1.71 ***Remove***........................ Labor............ .88	lf	$.88	$2.28	$3.16
	3/4" stain-grade pine cove ***Replace*** Materials........ .67 Labor............1.71 ***Remove***........................ Labor............ .88	lf	$.88	$2.38	$3.26
	3/4" poplar cove ***Replace*** Materials........ .74 Labor............1.71 ***Remove***........................ Labor............ .88	lf	$.88	$2.45	$3.33
	3/4" mahogany cove ***Replace*** Materials........ .85 Labor............1.71 ***Remove***........................ Labor............ .88	lf	$.88	$2.56	$3.44

Item Description	Unit	Remove	Replace	Total
3/4" red oak cove *Replace* Materials........ .91 Labor ....1.71 *Remove*......................... Labor............. .88	lf	$.88	$2.62	$3.50
1" paint-grade cove *Replace* Materials........ .71 Labor ....1.71 *Remove*......................... Labor............. .88	lf	$.88	$2.42	$3.30
1" stain-grade pine cove *Replace* Materials........ .83 Labor ....1.71 *Remove*......................... Labor............. .88	lf	$.88	$2.54	$3.42
1" poplar cove *Replace* Materials........ .92 Labor ....1.71 *Remove*......................... Labor............. .88	lf	$.88	$2.63	$3.51
1" mahogany cove *Replace* Materials........1.06 Labor ....1.71 *Remove*......................... Labor............. .88	lf	$.88	$2.77	$3.65
1" red oak cove *Replace* Materials........1.13 Labor ....1.71 *Remove*......................... Labor............. .88	lf	$.88	$2.84	$3.72
Remove cove for work, then reinstall *Replace* .... Labor 2.35	lf	—	$2.35	$2.35
2-1/2" paint-grade ceiling cove *Replace* Materials........1.26 Labor ....1.91 *Remove*......................... Labor............. .88	lf	$.88	$3.17	$4.05
2-1/2" stain-grade pine ceiling cove *Replace* Materials........1.46 Labor ....1.91 *Remove*......................... Labor............. .88	lf	$.88	$3.37	$4.25
2-1/2" poplar ceiling cove *Replace* Materials........1.58 Labor ....1.91 *Remove*......................... Labor............. .88	lf	$.88	$3.49	$4.37
2-1/2" mahogany ceiling cove *Replace* Materials........1.90 Labor ....1.91 *Remove*......................... Labor............. .88	lf	$.88	$3.81	$4.69
2-1/2" red oak ceiling cove *Replace* Materials........2.06 Labor ....1.91 *Remove*......................... Labor............. .88	lf	$.88	$3.97	$4.85
3-1/2" paint-grade ceiling cove *Replace* Materials........1.64 Labor ....1.91 *Remove*......................... Labor............. .88	lf	$.88	$3.55	$4.43
3-1/2" stain-grade pine ceiling cove *Replace* Materials........1.90 Labor ....1.91 *Remove*......................... Labor............. .88	lf	$.88	$3.81	$4.69
3-1/2" poplar ceiling cove *Replace* Materials........2.05 Labor ....1.91 *Remove*......................... Labor............. .88	lf	$.88	$3.96	$4.84
3-1/2" mahogany ceiling cove *Replace* Materials........2.46 Labor ....1.91 *Remove*......................... Labor............. .88	lf	$.88	$4.37	$5.25

◁ **remove & reinstall**

◀ **CEILING COVE**
"Sprung" cove. Includes 4% waste.

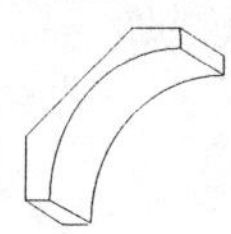

RELATED ITEMS

Cleaning..............................61
Painting..............................337

	Item Description	Unit	Remove	Replace	Total
CEILING COVE ► *continued*	**3-1/2" red oak ceiling cove** ***Replace*** Materials........2.68 Labor............1.91 ***Remove***......................... Labor............ .88	lf	$.88	$4.59	$5.47
remove & reinstall ▷	**Remove ceiling cove for work, then reinstall** ***Replace*** .... Labor............2.35	lf	—	$2.35	$2.35
HALF-ROUND ► *Includes 4% waste.* 	**1" paint-grade half-round** ***Replace*** Materials........ .57 Labor............1.71 ***Remove*** .... Labor............ .88	lf	$.88	$2.28	$3.16
	1" stain-grade pine half-round ***Replace*** Materials........ .69 Labor............1.71 ***Remove*** .... Labor............ .88	lf	$.88	$2.40	$3.28
	1" poplar half-round ***Replace*** Materials........ .74 Labor............1.71 ***Remove*** .... Labor............ .88	lf	$.88	$2.45	$3.33
	1" mahogany half-round ***Replace*** Materials........ .86 Labor............1.71 ***Remove*** .... Labor............ .88	lf	$.88	$2.57	$3.45
	1" red oak half-round ***Replace*** Materials........ .95 Labor............1.71 ***Remove*** .... Labor............ .88	lf	$.88	$2.66	$3.54
	2" paint-grade half-round ***Replace*** Materials........ .81 Labor............1.71 ***Remove*** .... Labor............ .88	lf	$.88	$2.52	$3.40
	2" stain-grade pine half-round ***Replace*** Materials........ .97 Labor............1.71 ***Remove*** .... Labor............ .88	lf	$.88	$2.68	$3.56
	2" poplar half-round ***Replace*** Materials...... 1.05 Labor............1.71 ***Remove*** .... Labor............ .88	lf	$.88	$2.76	$3.64
	2" mahogany half-round ***Replace*** Materials........1.23 Labor............1.71 ***Remove*** .... Labor............ .88	lf	$.88	$2.94	$3.82
	2" red oak half-round ***Replace*** Materials........1.34 Labor............1.71 ***Remove*** .... Labor............ .88	lf	$.88	$3.05	$3.93
	Add 19% for 3" half-round ► Add to the cost of 2" half-round.				
	Add 40% for 4" half-round ► Add to the cost of 2" half-round.				
remove & reinstall ▷	**Remove half-round for work, then reinstall** ***Replace*** .... Labor............3.00	lf	—	$3.00	$3.00
QUARTER-ROUND ► *Includes 4% waste.* 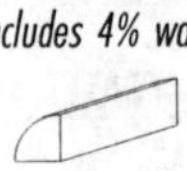	**1/2" paint-grade quarter-round** ***Replace*** Materials........ .42 Labor............1.71 ***Remove*** .... Labor............ .88	lf	$.88	$2.13	$3.01

RELATED ITEMS
Cleaning 61
Painting 337

Item Description	Unit	Remove	Replace	Total
1/2" stain-grade pine quarter-round *Replace* Materials .... .54 Labor ....1.71 *Remove* .... Labor............ .88	lf	$.88	$2.25	$3.13
1/2" poplar quarter-round *Replace* Materials .... .54 Labor ....1.71 *Remove* .... Labor............ .88	lf	$.88	$2.25	$3.13
1/2" mahogany quarter-round *Replace* Materials .... .65 Labor ....1.71 *Remove* .... Labor............ .88	lf	$.88	$2.36	$3.24
1/2" red oak quarter-round *Replace* Materials .... .73 Labor ....1.71 *Remove* .... Labor............ .88	lf	$.88	$2.44	$3.32
3/4" paint-grade quarter round *Replace* Materials .... .50 Labor ....1.71 *Remove* .... Labor............ .88	lf	$.88	$2.21	$3.09
3/4" stain-grade pine quarter-round *Replace* Materials .... .60 Labor ....1.71 *Remove* .... Labor............ .88	lf	$.88	$2.31	$3.19
3/4" poplar quarter-round *Replace* Materials .... .65 Labor ....1.71 *Remove* .... Labor............ .88	lf	$.88	$2.36	$3.24
3/4" mahogany quarter-round *Replace* Materials .... .77 Labor ....1.71 *Remove* .... Labor............ .88	lf	$.88	$2.48	$3.36
3/4" red oak quarter-round *Replace* Materials .... .86 Labor ....1.71 *Remove* .... Labor............ .88	lf	$.88	$2.57	$3.45
1" paint-grade quarter-round *Replace* Materials .... .89 Labor ....1.71 *Remove* .... Labor............ .88	lf	$.88	$2.60	$3.48
1" stain-grade pine quarter-round *Replace* Materials ...... 1.07 Labor ....1.71 *Remove* .... Labor............ .88	lf	$.88	$2.78	$3.66
1" poplar quarter-round *Replace* Materials........1.15 Labor ....1.71 *Remove* .... Labor............ .88	lf	$.88	$2.86	$3.74
1" mahogany quarter-round *Replace* Materials........1.38 Labor ....1.71 *Remove* .... Labor............ .88	lf	$.88	$3.09	$3.97
1" red oak quarter-round *Replace* Materials........1.54 Labor ....1.71 *Remove* .... Labor............ .88	lf	$.88	$3.25	$4.13
Remove quarter-round for work, then reinstall *Replace* .... Labor 3.00	lf	—	$3.00	$3.00
Paint-grade pine corner bead *Replace* Materials .... .99 Labor ....3.20 *Remove* .... Labor 1.18	lf	$1.18	$4.19	$5.37

◁ remove & reinstall

◀ **CORNER BEAD**
Standard corner bead includes 4% waste.

	Item Description	Unit	Remove	Replace	Total
CORNER BEAD ▶ *continued*	**Stain-grade pine corner bead** ***Replace*** Materials........1.17 Labor ....3.20 ***Remove***......................... Labor 1.18	lf	$1.18	$4.37	$5.55
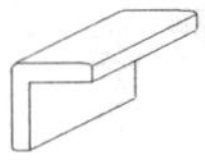 △ ***standard***	**Stain-grade pine corner bead, turned with double finials** ***Replace*** Materials ......12.90 Labor ....3.20 ***Remove***......................... Labor 1.18	lf	$1.18	$16.10	$17.28
No waste included for turned corner bead with finials.	**Mahogany corner bead** ***Replace*** Materials........2.20 Labor ....3.20 ***Remove***......................... Labor 1.18	lf	$1.18	$5.40	$6.58
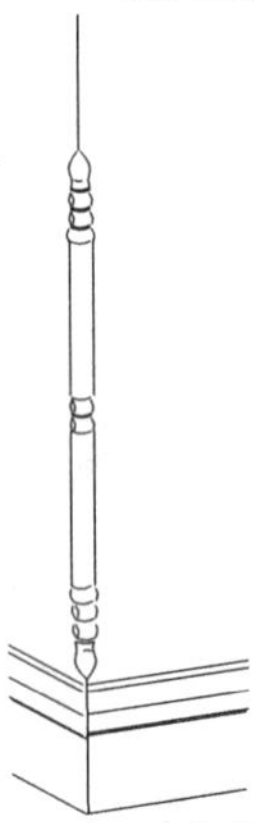	**Mahogany corner bead, turned with double finials** ***Replace*** Materials.......15.90 Labor ....3.20 ***Remove***......................... Labor 1.18	lf	$1.18	$19.10	$20.28
	Red oak corner bead ***Replace*** Materials........2.69 Labor ....3.20 ***Remove***......................... Labor 1.18	lf	$1.18	$5.89	$7.07
	Red oak corner bead, turned with double finials ***Replace*** Materials.......17.10 Labor ....3.20 ***Remove***......................... Labor 1.18	lf	$1.18	$20.30	$21.48
△ ***turned with double finials***	**Clear plastic corner bead** ***Replace*** Materials .... .92 Labor ....1.33 ***Remove***......................... Labor 1.18	lf	$1.18	$2.25	$3.43
remove & reinstall ▷	**Remove corner bead for work, then reinstall** ***Replace*** .... Labor 4.09	lf	—	$4.09	$4.09
BED MOLD ▶ *Includes 4% waste.* 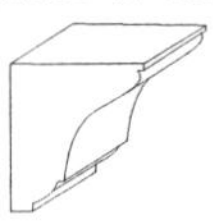	**2-1/2" paint-grade pine bed mold** ***Replace*** Materials........1.41 Labor ....1.58 ***Remove***......................... Labor............ .72	lf	$.72	$2.99	$3.71
	2-1/2" stain-grade pine bed mold ***Replace*** Materials........1.65 Labor ....1.58 ***Remove***......................... Labor............ .72	lf	$.72	$3.23	$3.95
	2-1/2" poplar bed mold ***Replace*** Materials........1.79 Labor ....1.58 ***Remove***......................... Labor............ .72	lf	$.72	$3.37	$4.09
	2-1/2" mahogany bed mold ***Replace*** Materials........2.13 Labor ....1.58 ***Remove***......................... Labor............ .72	lf	$.72	$3.71	$4.43
	2-1/2" red oak bed mold ***Replace*** Materials........2.31 Labor ....1.58 ***Remove***......................... Labor............ .72	lf	$.72	$3.89	$4.61
remove & reinstall ▷	**Remove bed mold for work, then reinstall** ***Replace*** .... Labor 2.35	lf	—	$2.35	$2.35
CROWN ▶ *Includes 4% waste.*	**3-1/2" paint-grade crown** ***Replace*** Materials........1.80 Labor ....1.91 ***Remove***......................... Labor............ .72	lf	$.72	$3.71	$4.43
	**3-1/2" stain-grade crown** ***Replace*** Materials........2.10 Labor ....1.91 ***Remove***......................... Labor............ .72	lf	$.72	$4.01	$4.73

Item Description	Unit	Remove	Replace	Total
3-1/2" poplar crown	lf	$.72	$4.20	$4.92
Replace Materials........2.29 Labor............1.91				
Remove......................... Labor............ .72				
3-1/2" mahogany crown	lf	$.72	$4.64	$5.36
Replace Materials........2.73 Labor............1.91				
Remove......................... Labor............ .72				
3-1/2" red oak crown	lf	$.72	$4.87	$5.59
Replace Materials........2.96 Labor............1.91				
Remove......................... Labor............ .72				
4-1/2" paint-grade crown	lf	$.72	$4.57	$5.29
Replace Materials........2.66 Labor............1.91				
Remove......................... Labor............ .72				
4-1/2" stain-grade crown	lf	$.72	$5.00	$5.72
Replace Materials........3.09 Labor............1.91				
Remove......................... Labor............ .72				
4-1/2" poplar crown	lf	$.72	$5.29	$6.01
Replace Materials........3.38 Labor............1.91				
Remove......................... Labor............ .72				
4-1/2" mahogany crown	lf	$.72	$6.20	$6.92
Replace Materials........4.29 Labor............1.91				
Remove......................... Labor............ .72				
4-1/2" red oak crown	lf	$.72	$6.56	$7.28
Replace Materials........4.65 Labor............1.91				
Remove......................... Labor............ .72				
Remove crown for work, then reinstall	lf	—	$2.35	$2.35
Replace .... Labor............2.35				
Paint-grade hand rail	lf	$.77	$6.36	$7.13
Replace Materials........2.28 Labor............4.08				
Remove......................... Labor............ .77				
Stain-grade pine hand rail	lf	$.77	$7.18	$7.95
Replace Materials........3.10 Labor............4.08				
Remove......................... Labor............ .77				
Mahogany hand rail	lf	$.77	$8.50	$9.27
Replace Materials........4.42 Labor............4.08				
Remove......................... Labor............ .77				
Red oak hand rail	lf	$.77	$8.80	$9.57
Replace Materials........4.72 Labor............4.08				
Remove......................... Labor............ .77				
Remove hand rail for work, then reinstall	lf	—	$5.57	$5.57
Replace .... Labor............5.57				
3/4" paint-grade molding with vertical milling	lf	$.88	$3.82	$4.70
Replace Materials........2.11 Labor............1.71				
Remove......................... Labor............ .88				
3/4" stain-grade pine molding with vertical milling	lf	$.88	$4.18	$5.06
Replace Materials........2.47 Labor............1.71				
Remove......................... Labor............ .88				

RELATED ITEMS

Cleaning..............................61
Painting............................337

◁ **remove & reinstall**

◀ **HAND RAIL**
Includes 4% waste.

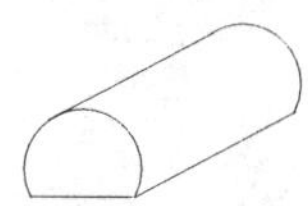

◁ **remove & reinstall**

◀ **SPECIALTY MOLDING**
General moldings for installation as crown, chair rail, panel molds, cabinet trim and so forth. Includes 4% waste.

	Item Description	Unit	Remove	Replace	Total
SPECIALTY ► MOLDING *continued*	**3/4" poplar molding with vertical milling** ***Replace*** Materials........2.67 Labor............1.71 ***Remove*** .... Labor............ .88	lf	$.88	$4.38	$5.26
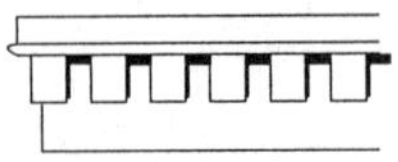 △ ***dentil*** *a vertically milled molding.*	**3/4" mahogany molding with vertical milling** ***Replace*** Materials........3.31 Labor............1.71 ***Remove*** .... Labor............ .88	lf	$.88	$5.02	$5.90
	3/4" red oak molding with vertical milling ***Replace*** Materials........3.60 Labor............1.71 ***Remove*** .... Labor............ .88	lf	$.88	$5.31	$6.19
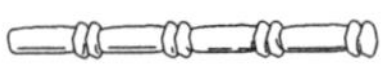 △ ***bead and reel*** *a hand-carved molding.*	**3/4" polyurethane molding with vertical patterns** ***Replace*** Materials........3.16 Labor............1.71 ***Remove*** .... Labor............ .88	lf	$.88	$4.87	$5.75
	3/4" stain-grade polyurethane molding with vertical patterns ***Replace*** Materials........3.40 Labor............1.71 ***Remove*** .... Labor............ .88	lf	$.88	$5.11	$5.99
other 3/4" styles ▷	**Deduct 41% for 3/4" molding with embossed patterns** ► For pine moldings only.				
	Add 64% for 3/4" molding with hand carvings				
	Add 198% for 3/4" molding with heavy hand carvings				
1-1/2" specialty mold ▷	**1-1/2" paint-grade molding with vertical milling** ***Replace*** Materials........2.42 Labor............1.71 ***Remove*** .... Labor............ .88	lf	$.88	$4.13	$5.01
 △ ***bead*** *a hand-carved molding.*	**1-1/2" stain-grade pine molding with vertical milling** ***Replace*** Materials........2.81 Labor............1.71 ***Remove*** .... Labor............ .88	lf	$.88	$4.52	$5.40
	1-1/2" poplar molding with vertical milling ***Replace*** Materials........3.04 Labor............1.71 ***Remove*** .... Labor............ .88	lf	$.88	$4.75	$5.63
	1-1/2" mahogany molding with vertical milling ***Replace*** Materials........3.78 Labor............1.71 ***Remove*** .... Labor............ .88	lf	$.88	$5.49	$6.37
 △ ***rope*** *a hand-carved molding.*	**1-1/2" red oak molding with vertical milling** ***Replace*** Materials........4.11 Labor............1.71 ***Remove*** .... Labor............ .88	lf	$.88	$5.82	$6.70
	1-1/2" polyurethane molding with vertical patterns ***Replace*** Materials........4.97 Labor............1.71 ***Remove*** .... Labor............ .88	lf	$.88	$6.68	$7.56
	1-1/2" stain-grade polyurethane molding with vertical patterns ***Replace*** Materials........5.33 Labor............1.71 ***Remove*** .... Labor............ .88	lf	$.88	$7.04	$7.92
other 1-1/2" styles ▷	**Deduct 37% for 1-1/2" molding with embossed patterns** ► For pine moldings only.				
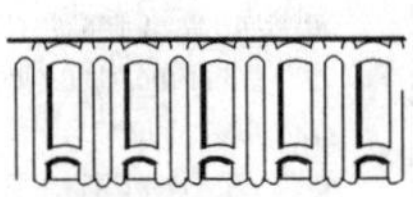	**Add 66% for 1-1/2" molding with hand carvings**				
△ ***reed*** *a molding with vertical patterns.*	**Add 205% for 1-1/2" molding with heavy hand carvings**				

Item Description	Unit	Remove	Replace	Total
2-1/2" paint-grade molding with vertical milling *Replace* Materials........2.71 Labor............1.71 *Remove*........................ Labor............ .88	lf	$.88	$4.42	$5.30
2-1/2" stain-grade pine molding with vertical milling *Replace* Materials........3.15 Labor............1.71 *Remove*........................ Labor............ .88	lf	$.88	$4.86	$5.74
2-1/2" poplar molding with vertical milling *Replace* Materials........3.41 Labor............1.71 *Remove*........................ Labor............ .88	lf	$.88	$5.12	$6.00
2-1/2" mahogany molding with vertical milling *Replace* Materials........4.24 Labor............1.71 *Remove*........................ Labor............ .88	lf	$.88	$5.95	$6.83
2-1/2" red oak molding with vertical milling *Replace* Materials........4.60 Labor............1.71 *Remove*........................ Labor............ .88	lf	$.88	$6.31	$7.19
2-1/2" polyurethane molding with vertical patterns *Replace* Materials........5.56 Labor............1.71 *Remove*........................ Labor............ .88	lf	$.88	$7.27	$8.15
2-1/2" stain-grade polyurethane molding with vertical patterns *Replace* Materials........5.97 Labor............1.71 *Remove*........................ Labor............ .88	lf	$.88	$7.68	$8.56
Deduct 37% for 2-1/2" molding with embossed patterns ► For pine moldings only.				
Add 68% for 2-1/2" molding with hand carvings				
Add 209% for 2-1/2" molding with heavy hand carvings				

◁ **2-1/2" specialty mold**

△ ***acanthus*** *a heavy hand-carved molding.*

△ ***leaf and tongue*** *a heavy hand-carved molding.*

△ ***laurel and ribbon*** *a heavy hand-carved molding.*

◁ **other 2-1/2" styles**

Item Description	Unit	Remove	Replace	Total
3-1/2" paint-grade molding with vertical milling *Replace* Materials........3.01 Labor............1.71 *Remove*........................ Labor............ .88	lf	$.88	$4.72	$5.60
3-1/2" stain-grade pine molding with vertical milling *Replace* Materials........3.50 Labor............1.71 *Remove*........................ Labor............ .88	lf	$.88	$5.21	$6.09
3-1/2" poplar molding with vertical milling *Replace* Materials........3.79 Labor............1.71 *Remove*........................ Labor............ .88	lf	$.88	$5.50	$6.38
3-1/2" mahogany molding with vertical milling *Replace* Materials........4.72 Labor............1.71 *Remove*........................ Labor............ .88	lf	$.88	$6.43	$7.31
3-1/2" red oak molding with vertical milling *Replace* Materials........5.13 Labor............1.71 *Remove*........................ Labor............ .88	lf	$.88	$6.84	$7.72
3-1/2" polyurethane molding with vertical patterns *Replace* Materials........6.19 Labor............1.71 *Remove*........................ Labor............ .88	lf	$.88	$7.90	$8.78
3-1/2" stain-grade polyurethane molding with vertical patterns *Replace* Materials........6.64 Labor............1.71 *Remove*........................ Labor............ .88	lf	$.88	$8.35	$9.23

◁ **3-1/2" specialty mold**

△ ***shell*** *a heavy hand-carved molding.*

△ ***oak leaf and ribbon*** *a heavy hand-carved molding.*

RELATED ITEMS

Cleaning..............................61
Painting..............................337
"Wood Embossing".......199

	Item Description	Unit	Remove	Replace	Total
SPECIALTY MOLDING *continued*	**Deduct 38% for 3-1/2" molding with embossed patterns** ► For pine moldings only.				
other 3-1/2" styles	**Add 69% for 3-1/2" molding with hand carvings**				
	Add 213% for 3-1/2" molding with heavy hand carvings				
5" specialty mold ▷	**5" paint-grade molding with vertical milling** ***Replace*** Materials........4.33 Labor............2.09 ***Remove***......................... Labor............. .88	lf	$.88	$6.42	$7.30
 △ ***meander*** *a molding with vertical patterns.*	**5" stain-grade pine molding with vertical milling** ***Replace*** Materials........5.04 Labor............2.09 ***Remove***......................... Labor............. .88	lf	$.88	$7.13	$8.01
	5" poplar molding with vertical milling ***Replace*** Materials........5.46 Labor............2.09 ***Remove***......................... Labor............. .88	lf	$.88	$7.55	$8.43
	**5" mahogany molding with vertical milling** ***Replace*** Materials........6.79 Labor............2.09 ***Remove***......................... Labor............. .88	lf	$.88	$8.88	$9.76
△ ***fret*** *a molding with vertical patterns.*	**5" red oak molding with vertical milling** ***Replace*** Materials........7.38 Labor............2.09 ***Remove***......................... Labor............. .88	lf	$.88	$9.47	$10.35
	5" polyurethane molding with vertical patterns ***Replace*** Materials........8.91 Labor............2.09 ***Remove***......................... Labor............. .88	lf	$.88	$11.00	$11.88
 △ ***egg and dart*** *a hand-carved molding.*	**5" stain-grade polyurethane molding with vertical patterns** ***Replace*** Materials........9.55 Labor............2.09 ***Remove***......................... Labor............. .88	lf	$.88	$11.64	$12.52
other 5" styles ▷	**Deduct 39% for 5" molding with embossed patterns** ► For pine moldings only.				
	Add 71% for 5" molding with hand carvings				
	Add 219% for 5" molding with heavy hand carvings				
8" specialty mold ▷	**8" paint-grade molding with vertical milling** ***Replace*** Materials........7.09 Labor............2.28 ***Remove***......................... Labor............. .88	lf	$.88	$9.37	$10.25
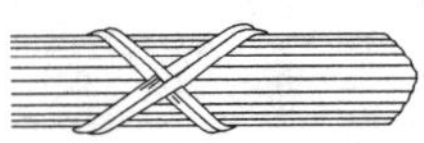 △ ***bundled reeds*** *a hand-carved molding.*	**8" stain-grade pine molding with vertical milling** ***Replace*** Materials........8.25 Labor............2.28 ***Remove***......................... Labor............. .88	lf	$.88	$10.53	$11.41
	8" poplar molding with vertical milling ***Replace*** Materials........8.94 Labor............2.28 ***Remove***......................... Labor............. .88	lf	$.88	$11.22	$12.10
	8" mahogany molding with vertical milling ***Replace*** Materials.......11.10 Labor............2.28 ***Remove***......................... Labor............. .88	lf	$.88	$13.38	$14.26
 △ ***ribbon*** *a heavy hand-carved molding.*	**8" red oak molding with vertical milling** ***Replace*** Materials......12.10 Labor............2.28 ***Remove***......................... Labor............. .88	lf	$.88	$14.38	$15.26

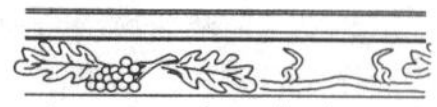

△ ***grape*** *a heavy hand-carved molding.*

Item Description	*Unit*	*Remove*	*Replace*	*Total*
8″ polyurethane molding with vertical patterns ***Replace*** Materials......14.60 Labor............2.28 ***Remove*** .... Labor............ .88	**lf**	**$.88**	**$16.88**	**$17.76**
8″ stain-grade polyurethane molding with vertical patterns ***Replace*** Materials.......15.60 Labor............2.28 ***Remove*** .... Labor............ .88	**lf**	**$.88**	**$17.88**	**$18.76**
Deduct 41% for 8″ molding with embossed patterns ► For pine moldings only.				
Add 75% for 8″ molding with hand carvings				
Add 232% for 8″ molding with heavy hand carvings				
Remove molding installed on wall for work, then reinstall ***Replace*** .... Labor............2.35	**lf**	**—**	**$2.35**	**$2.35**
Remove window or door casing for work, then reinstall ***Replace*** .... Labor............3.00	**lf**	**—**	**$3.00**	**$3.00**
Molder setup charge ***Replace*** Materials....150.00	**ea**	**—**	**$150.00**	**$150.00**
Molder custom knife charges ***Replace*** Materials....345.00	**ea**	**—**	**$345.00**	**$345.00**
1″ to 2″ pine custom-milled molding ***Replace*** Materials........1.44 Labor............1.71 ***Remove*** .... Labor............ .88	**lf**	**$.88**	**$3.15**	**$4.03**
2″ to 3″ pine custom-milled molding ***Replace*** Materials........1.61 Labor............1.71 ***Remove*** .... Labor............ .88	**lf**	**$.88**	**$3.32**	**$4.20**
3″ to 4″ pine custom-milled molding ***Replace*** Materials........2.29 Labor............2.09 ***Remove*** .... Labor............ .88	**lf**	**$.88**	**$4.38**	**$5.26**
4″ to 5″ pine custom-milled molding ***Replace*** Materials........3.65 Labor............2.09 ***Remove*** .... Labor............ .88	**lf**	**$.88**	**$5.74**	**$6.62**
6″ to 7″ pine custom-milled molding ***Replace*** Materials........5.99 Labor............2.28 ***Remove*** .... Labor............ .88	**lf**	**$.88**	**$8.27**	**$9.15**
7″ to 8″ pine custom-milled molding ***Replace*** Materials........8.46 Labor............2.28 ***Remove*** .... Labor............ .88	**lf**	**$.88**	**$10.74**	**$11.62**
Add 7% for poplar custom-milled molding				
Add 21% for mahogany custom-milled molding				
Add 30% for red oak custom-milled molding				
Add for corner radius in panel molding ***Replace*** Materials........1.60 Labor............6.20 ***Remove*** .... Labor............ .94	**ea**	**$.94**	**$7.80**	**$8.74**

◁ **other 8″ styles**

◁ **remove & reinstall**

◀ **CUSTOM-MILLED MOLDING**
Custom milled to match existing pattern or a specially designed pattern. All milling is horizontal. Includes 4% waste.

RELATED ITEMS

Cleaning..............................61
Painting............................337
"Wood Embossing".......199

◁ **other wood species**

◀ **PANEL MOLDING CORNER RADIUS**
Includes 4% waste.

	Item Description	Unit	Remove	Replace	Total
PANEL MOLDING ► CORNER RADIUS	**Add for corner radius in panel molding with vertical milling** *Replace* Materials........3.80 Labor............6.20 *Remove*........................ Labor............ .94	ea	$.94	$10.00	$10.94
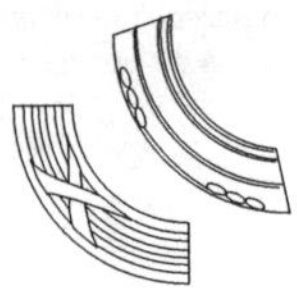	**Add for corner radius in panel molding with embossed pattern** *Replace* Materials........3.15 Labor............6.20 *Remove*........................ Labor............ .94	ea	$.94	$9.35	$10.29
	Add for corner radius in panel molding with hand carvings *Replace* Materials........5.82 Labor............6.20 *Remove*........................ Labor............ .94	ea	$.94	$12.02	$12.96
	Add for corner radius in panel molding with heavy hand carvings *Replace* Materials........8.22 Labor............6.20 *Remove*........................ Labor............ .94	ea	$.94	$14.42	$15.36
CLOSET WORK ►	**Closet shelf brackets, shelving, & rod** *Replace* Materials........9.35 Labor...........13.80 *Remove*........................ Labor............1.73	lf	$1.73	$23.15	$24.88
	Remove closet shelf brackets, shelving, & rod for work, then reinstall *Replace* .... Labor...........18.10	lf	—	$18.10	$18.10
closet organizer ▷	**Closet organizer system, standard grade** *Replace* Materials........8.70 Labor...........12.60 *Remove*........................ Labor............1.29	sf	$1.29	$21.30	$22.59
	Closet organizer system, high grade *Replace* Materials......10.60 Labor...........17.20 *Remove*........................ Labor............1.29	sf	$1.29	$27.80	$29.09
	Closet organizer system, deluxe grade *Replace* Materials.......13.30 Labor...........21.90 *Remove*........................ Labor............1.29	sf	$1.29	$35.20	$36.49
	Remove closet organizer system for work, then reinstall *Replace* .... Labor..........25.20	sf	—	$25.20	$25.20
linen closet ▷	**Linen closet shelves, standard grade** *Replace* Materials........6.95 Labor..........28.00 *Remove*........................ Labor............ .94	lf	$.94	$34.95	$35.89
	Linen closet shelves, high grade *Replace* Materials........7.60 Labor..........28.00 *Remove*........................ Labor............ .94	lf	$.94	$35.60	$36.54
	Linen closet pull-out shelves *Replace* Materials........8.77 Labor..........28.90 *Remove*........................ Labor............ .94	lf	$.94	$37.67	$38.61
	Remove linen closet shelves for work, then reinstall *Replace* .... Labor..........33.90	lf	—	$33.90	$33.90
closet rod ▷	**Closet rod, pine** *Replace* Materials........2.66 Labor............3.33 *Remove*........................ Labor............ .96	lf	$.96	$5.99	$6.95
	Closet rod, hardwood *Replace* Materials........3.33 Labor............3.33 *Remove*........................ Labor............ .96	lf	$.96	$6.66	$7.62

Item Description	Unit	Remove	Replace	Total	
Remove closet rod for work, then reinstall *Replace* .... Labor 4.34	lf	—	$4.34	$4.34	
Aromatic tongue-&-groove cedar board closet lining *Replace* Materials .... .16 Labor ....2.12 *Remove*......................... Labor............. .77	sf	$.77	$2.28	$3.05	◁ cedar closet lining
Aromatic 1/4" cedar veneer plywood closet lining *Replace* Materials........2.47 Labor ....1.54 *Remove*......................... Labor............. .61	sf	$.61	$4.01	$4.62	
8" deep built-in paint-grade bookcase *Replace* Materials........6.15 Labor ....11.20 *Remove*......................... Labor 1.40	sf	$1.40	$17.35	$18.75	◀ **BOOKCASE** *Adjustable shelves. Shelves approximately 12" on center. Measure sf of bookcase face.*
8" deep built-in stain-grade pine bookcase *Replace* Materials........7.13 Labor ....11.20 *Remove*......................... Labor 1.40	sf	$1.40	$18.33	$19.73	
8" deep built-in mahogany bookcase *Replace* Materials........7.72 Labor ....11.20 *Remove*......................... Labor 1.40	sf	$1.40	$18.92	$20.32	
8" deep built-in oak bookcase *Replace* Materials........9.09 Labor ....11.20 *Remove*......................... Labor 1.40	sf	$1.40	$20.29	$21.69	
8" deep built-in walnut bookcase *Replace* Materials ......12.50 Labor ....11.20 *Remove*......................... Labor 1.40	sf	$1.40	$23.70	$25.10	
12" deep built-in paint-grade bookcase *Replace* Materials........8.06 Labor...........12.60 *Remove*......................... Labor 1.40	sf	$1.40	$20.66	$22.06	◁ 12" deep
12" deep built-in stain-grade pine bookcase *Replace* Materials........9.34 Labor...........12.60 *Remove*......................... Labor 1.40	sf	$1.40	$21.94	$23.34	
12" deep built-in mahogany bookcase *Replace* Materials ......10.10 Labor...........12.60 *Remove*......................... Labor 1.40	sf	$1.40	$22.70	$24.10	
12" deep built-in oak bookcase *Replace* Materials ......12.00 Labor...........12.60 *Remove*......................... Labor 1.40	sf	$1.40	$24.60	$26.00	
12" deep built-in walnut bookcase *Replace* Materials ......16.40 Labor...........12.60 *Remove*......................... Labor 1.40	sf	$1.40	$29.00	$30.40	
18" deep built-in paint-grade bookcase *Replace* Materials ......10.60 Labor...........13.20 *Remove*......................... Labor 1.40	sf	$1.40	$23.80	$25.20	◁ 18" deep
18" deep built-in stain-grade pine bookcase *Replace* Materials ......12.30 Labor...........13.20 *Remove*......................... Labor 1.40	sf	$1.40	$25.50	$26.90	
18" deep built-in mahogany bookcase *Replace* Materials.......13.30 Labor...........13.20 *Remove*......................... Labor 1.40	sf	$1.40	$26.50	$27.90	

RELATED ITEMS

Cleaning..............................61
Painting...........................337

Bookcase ▶ *continued*

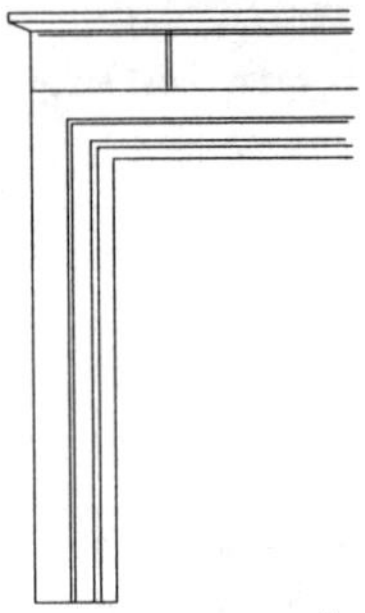

△ *economy mantel*

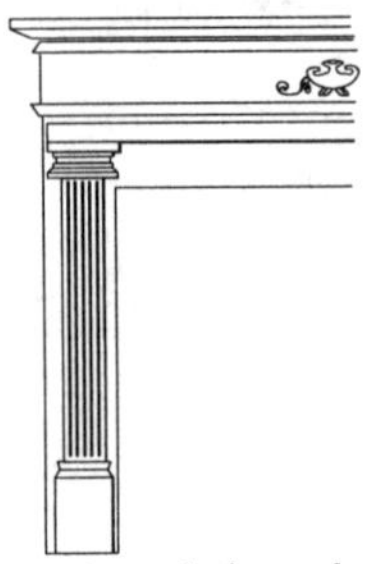

△ *standard mantel*

Item Description	Unit	Remove	Replace	Total
18" deep built-in oak bookcase *Replace* Materials.......15.70 Labor...........13.20 *Remove*......................... Labor............1.40	sf	$1.40	$28.90	$30.30
18" deep built-in walnut bookcase *Replace* Materials......21.50 Labor...........13.20 *Remove*......................... Labor............1.40	sf	$1.40	$34.70	$36.10
24" deep built-in paint-grade bookcase *Replace* Materials......14.00 Labor...........13.80 *Remove*......................... Labor............1.40	sf	$1.40	$27.80	$29.20
24" deep built-in stain-grade pine bookcase *Replace* Materials......16.10 Labor...........13.80 *Remove*......................... Labor............1.40	sf	$1.40	$29.90	$31.30
24" deep built-in mahogany bookcase *Replace* Materials.......17.50 Labor...........13.80 *Remove*......................... Labor............1.40	sf	$1.40	$31.30	$32.70
24" deep built-in oak bookcase *Replace* Materials......20.60 Labor...........13.80 *Remove*......................... Labor............1.40	sf	$1.40	$34.40	$35.80
24" deep built-in walnut bookcase *Replace* Materials......28.20 Labor...........13.80 *Remove*......................... Labor............1.40	sf	$1.40	$42.00	$43.40

Mantel beam ▶

Item Description	Unit	Remove	Replace	Total
Fireplace mantel beam, rough sawn *Replace* Materials........8.29 Labor..........22.40 *Remove*......................... Labor............2.20	lf	$2.20	$30.69	$32.89
Fireplace mantel beam, glue laminated *Replace* Materials......23.60 Labor..........22.40 *Remove*......................... Labor............2.20	lf	$2.20	$46.00	$48.20
Remove fireplace mantel beam for work, then reinstall *Replace* .... Labor..........28.90	lf	—	$28.90	$28.90

Mantel ▶ *Measure the lf of mantel width.*

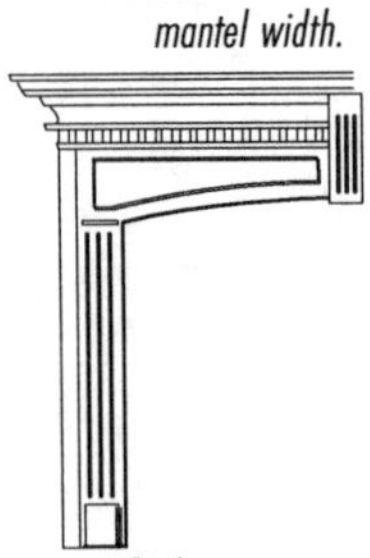

△ *high*

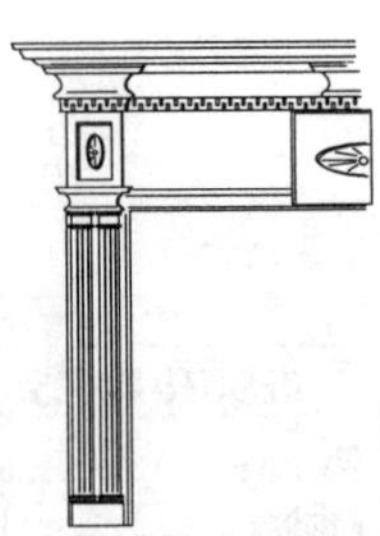

△ *deluxe*

Item Description	Unit	Remove	Replace	Total
Fireplace mantel, economy grade *Replace* Materials......45.80 Labor...........27.20 *Remove*......................... Labor............2.59 ► Paint-grade wood with simple pattern and moldings. See illustration above.	lf	$2.59	$73.00	$75.59
Fireplace mantel, standard grade *Replace* Materials......98.50 Labor...........27.20 *Remove*......................... Labor............2.59 ► Paint-grade wood or stain-grade pine, may have dentil patterns and fluted pilasters. See illustration above.	lf	$2.59	$125.70	$128.29
Fireplace mantel, high grade *Replace* Materials.....212.00 Labor...........27.20 *Remove*......................... Labor............2.59 ► Red oak, birch, stain-grade pine or more ornate paint-grade. May include a combination of some of the following: carved moldings, carved onlays, embossed patterns, fluted pilasters, face projections.	lf	$2.59	$239.20	$241.79
Fireplace mantel, deluxe grade *Replace* Materials.....475.00 Labor...........27.20 *Remove*......................... Labor............2.59 ► Cherry, walnut or more ornate red oak, birch, yellow pine, or paint-grade. May include a combination of some of the following: carved moldings, carved onlays, fluted pilasters, face projections, carved corbels, circular patterns and moldings.	lf	$2.59	$502.20	$504.79

Item Description	Unit	Remove	Replace	Total
Fireplace mantel, custom grade	lf	$2.59	$990.20	$992.79

Replace Materials....963.00 Labor...........27.20
Remove......................... Labor............2.59

► Cherry, walnut, heart pine or very ornate red oak, birch, or yellow pine. May include a combination of some of the following: carved moldings, carved onlays, fluted pilasters, round columns, capitals (Ionic, Tuscan, contemporary, etc.), face projections, ornately carved corbel (e.g. lion's head), circular openings, paneling above mantel, or mirror.

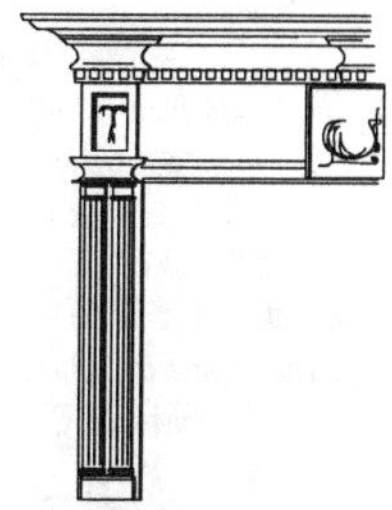

△ *custom*

Item Description	Unit	Remove	Replace	Total
Fireplace mantel, custom deluxe grade	lf	$2.59	$1,477.20	$1,479.79

Replace Materials...1450.00 Labor...........27.20
Remove......................... Labor............2.59

► Cherry, walnut or more ornate red oak, birch, or paint-grade. May include a combination of some of the following: carved moldings, ornate hand-carved patterns, fluted pilasters, round columns, ornate capitals (Scamozzi, Corinthian, etc.), face projections, circular openings, curved pilasters, paneling above mantel, or mirror.

△ *custom deluxe*

Item Description	Unit	Remove	Replace	Total
Remove fireplace mantel for work, then reinstall	lf	—	$30.00	$30.00

Replace .... Labor..........30.00

Item Description	Unit	Remove	Replace	Total
Coffered ceiling, economy grade	sf	$1.29	$19.23	$20.52

Replace Materials........8.93 Labor...........10.30
Remove......................... Labor............1.29

► Coffers are finished drywall with corner bead. Inside corners trimmed with 3-1/2" crown mold or similar.

◄ **COFFERED CEILING**
Coffers 42" to 48" on center. Unless otherwise noted, includes wood underframing, and fire-taped drywall. Does not include painting or staining and varnishing. All inside molding joints are coped.

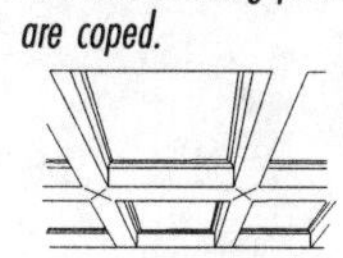

△ *economy*

Item Description	Unit	Remove	Replace	Total
Coffered ceiling, standard grade	sf	$1.29	$23.90	$25.19

Replace Materials......12.40 Labor...........11.50
Remove......................... Labor............1.29

► Coffers and beams are finished drywall. Inside corners trimmed with vertical pattern moldings. May also include wood onlays (see page 230), plaster enrichments (see page 232), or the raised beams may be cased with hardwood plywood.

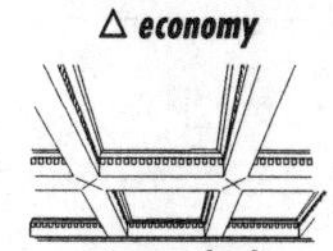

△ *standard*

Item Description	Unit	Remove	Replace	Total
Coffered ceiling, high grade	sf	$1.29	$27.30	$28.59

Replace Materials......14.50 Labor...........12.80
Remove......................... Labor............1.29

► Covered with wood paneling. Inside corners trimmed with vertical-pattern or embossed moldings. Coffers contain panel molding. May also include wood onlays (see page 230).

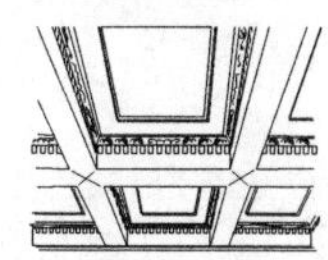

△ *high*

Item Description	Unit	Remove	Replace	Total
Coffered ceiling, deluxe grade	sf	$1.29	$36.20	$37.49

Replace Materials......21.70 Labor...........14.50
Remove......................... Labor............1.29

► Covered with hardwood plywood. Inside corners trimmed with hand-carved moldings. May also include wood onlays (see page 230).

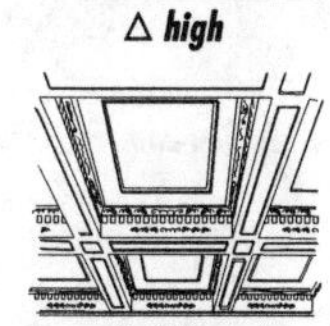

△ *deluxe*

Item Description	Unit	Remove	Replace	Total
Coffered ceiling, custom grade	sf	$1.29	$48.80	$50.09

Replace Materials......30.90 Labor...........17.90
Remove......................... Labor............1.29

► Covered with wood paneling. Inside corners trimmed with heavy hand-carved moldings. May also include wood onlays at each corner (see page 230), recessed panels on beams or in coffers, and corbels at wall corners.

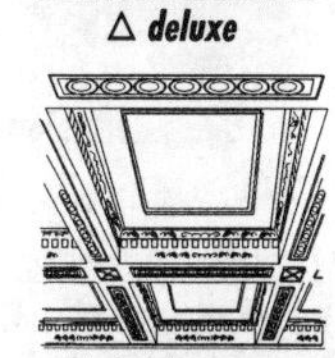

△ *custom*

Item Description	Unit	Remove	Replace	Total
Coffered ceiling, custom deluxe grade	sf	$1.29	$69.70	$70.99

Replace Materials......46.10 Labor..........23.60
Remove......................... Labor............1.29

► Covered with wood paneling. Inside corners trimmed with heavy hand-carved moldings. May also include ornate wood onlays at each corner (see page 230), recessed panels on beams or in coffers, and ornately carved corbels at wall corners (e.g. lion's head).

△ *custom deluxe*

NICHE ▶ Niches are high density polyurethane, Opaque bases allow for installation of a light beneath. Add **17%** for niches made from fiber reinforced plaster.

GINGERBREAD RUNNING TRIM ▶ Paint-grade poplar. Add **30%** for red oak.

ball-and-dowel ▷

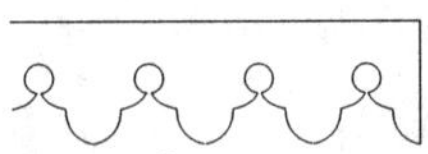

△ fleur-sawn

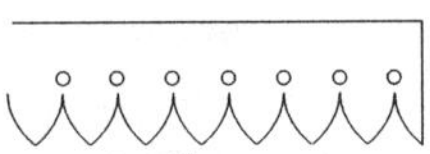

△ picket-sawn

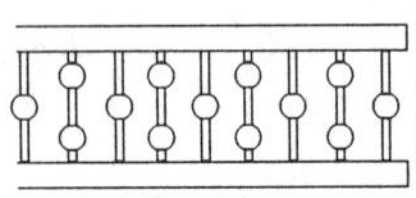

△ ball-and-dowel

spindle ▷

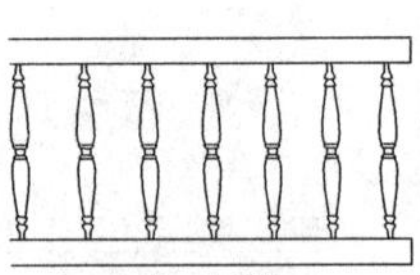

△ spindle

Item Description	Unit	Remove	Replace	Total
Niche with casing and shelf bracket *Replace* Materials.....157.00 Labor..........54.50 *Remove*......................... Labor...........8.72	ea	$8.72	$211.50	$220.22
Niche with clamshell top with casing and shelf bracket *Replace* Materials....275.00 Labor..........54.50 *Remove*......................... Labor...........8.72	ea	$8.72	$329.50	$338.22
Niche with clamshell top, casing, and clamshell shelf bracket *Replace* Materials....358.00 Labor..........54.50 *Remove*......................... Labor...........8.72	ea	$8.72	$412.50	$421.22
Remove niche for work, then reinstall *Replace*......................... Labor..........77.10	ea	—	$77.10	$77.10
Gingerbread fleur-sawn running trim *Replace* Materials......24.30 Labor............6.66 *Remove*......................... Labor............1.05	lf	$1.05	$30.96	$32.01
Gingerbread picket-sawn running trim *Replace* Materials......31.40 Labor............6.66 *Remove*......................... Labor............1.05	lf	$1.05	$38.06	$39.11
Gingerbread 2" ball-and-dowel running trim (galley rail) *Replace* Materials........7.45 Labor............6.66 *Remove*......................... Labor............1.05	lf	$1.05	$14.11	$15.16
Gingerbread 4" ball-and-dowel running trim *Replace* Materials.......11.20 Labor............6.66 *Remove*......................... Labor............1.05	lf	$1.05	$17.86	$18.91
Gingerbread 6" ball-and-dowel running trim *Replace* Materials......12.90 Labor............6.66 *Remove*......................... Labor............1.05	lf	$1.05	$19.56	$20.61
Gingerbread 8" ball-and-dowel running trim *Replace* Materials.......15.20 Labor............6.66 *Remove*......................... Labor............1.05	lf	$1.05	$21.86	$22.91
Gingerbread 10" ball-and-dowel running trim *Replace* Materials.......19.30 Labor............6.66 *Remove*......................... Labor............1.05	lf	$1.05	$25.96	$27.01
Gingerbread 12" ball-and-dowel running trim *Replace* Materials......23.00 Labor............6.66 *Remove*......................... Labor............1.05	lf	$1.05	$29.66	$30.71
Gingerbread 14" ball-and-dowel running trim *Replace* Materials......27.60 Labor............6.66 *Remove*......................... Labor............1.05	lf	$1.05	$34.26	$35.31
Gingerbread 2" spindle running trim (galley rail) *Replace* Materials........7.06 Labor............6.66 *Remove*......................... Labor............1.05	lf	$1.05	$13.72	$14.77
Gingerbread 4" spindle running trim *Replace* Materials........8.78 Labor............6.66 *Remove*......................... Labor............1.05	lf	$1.05	$15.44	$16.49
Gingerbread 6"spindle running trim *Replace* Materials.......11.20 Labor............6.66 *Remove*......................... Labor............1.05	lf	$1.05	$17.86	$18.91

Item Description	Unit	Remove	Replace	Total
Gingerbread 8" spindle running trim ***Replace*** Materials.......13.60 Labor............6.66 ***Remove***........................ Labor............1.05	lf	$1.05	$20.26	$21.31
Gingerbread 10" spindle running trim ***Replace*** Materials......18.50 Labor............6.66 ***Remove***........................ Labor............1.05	lf	$1.05	$25.16	$26.21
Gingerbread 12" spindle running trim ***Replace*** Materials......22.40 Labor............6.66 ***Remove***........................ Labor............1.05	lf	$1.05	$29.06	$30.11
Gingerbread 14" spindle running trim ***Replace*** Materials......27.10 Labor............6.66 ***Remove***........................ Labor............1.05	lf	$1.05	$33.76	$34.81
Remove gingerbread running trim for work, then reinstall ***Replace***........................ Labor............8.11	lf	—	$8.11	$8.11
Gingerbread bracket, standard grade ***Replace*** Materials......26.00 Labor...........14.50 ***Remove***........................ Labor............4.24 ► Longest leg up to 12" with simple sawn pattern.	ea	$4.24	$40.50	$44.74
Gingerbread bracket, high grade ***Replace*** Materials......31.40 Labor...........14.50 ***Remove***........................ Labor............4.24 ► Longest leg up to 23" with simple sawn pattern.	ea	$4.24	$45.90	$50.14
Gingerbread bracket, deluxe grade ***Replace*** Materials......34.60 Labor...........14.50 ***Remove***........................ Labor............4.24 ► Longest leg up to 30" with ornately sawn pattern.	ea	$4.24	$49.10	$53.34
Gingerbread bracket, custom grade ***Replace*** Materials......39.20 Labor...........14.50 ***Remove***........................ Labor............4.24 ► Longest leg up to 30" with very ornately sawn pattern.	ea	$4.24	$53.70	$57.94
Gingerbread fan bracket, standard grade ***Replace*** Materials......30.70 Labor...........14.50 ***Remove***........................ Labor............4.24 ► Longest leg up to 14" with simple pattern.	ea	$4.24	$45.20	$49.44
Gingerbread fan bracket, high grade ***Replace*** Materials......34.50 Labor...........14.50 ***Remove***........................ Labor............4.24 ► Longest leg up to 25" with simple pattern.	ea	$4.24	$49.00	$53.24
Gingerbread fan bracket, deluxe grade ***Replace*** Materials......42.70 Labor...........14.50 ***Remove***........................ Labor............4.24 ► Longest leg up to 32" with ornate pattern.	ea	$4.24	$57.20	$61.44
Gingerbread fan bracket, custom grade ***Replace*** Materials......54.70 Labor...........14.50 ***Remove***........................ Labor............4.24 ► Longest leg up to 32" with very ornate pattern.	ea	$4.24	$69.20	$73.44

standard bracket △

◄ **GINGERBREAD BRACKET**
*Paint-grade poplar corner brackets. Add **30%** for red oak.*

high △

deluxe △

◄ **GINGERBREAD FAN BRACKET**
*Brackets combining sawn elements with radiating spindles or dowel-and-ball elements. Made from paint-grade poplar. Add **30%** for red oak.*

RELATED ITEMS

Cleaning............................61
Painting..........................339

	Item Description	Unit	Remove	Replace	Total
GINGERBREAD ▶ POST BRACKET *Made from paint-grade poplar. Add **30%** for red oak.* 	**Gingerbread post bracket, standard grade** ***Replace*** Materials......39.70 Labor...........14.50 ***Remove***......................... Labor ....4.24 ► Simple pattern bracket with drop.	ea	$4.24	$54.20	$58.44
	Gingerbread post bracket, high grade ***Replace*** Materials......49.40 Labor...........14.50 ***Remove***......................... Labor ....4.24 ► Ornate pattern bracket with drop.	ea	$4.24	$63.90	$68.14
	Gingerbread post bracket, deluxe grade ***Replace*** Materials......58.10 Labor...........14.50 ***Remove***......................... Labor ....4.24 ► Very ornate pattern bracket with drop.	ea	$4.24	$72.60	$76.84
remove & reinstall ▷	**Remove gingerbread post bracket for work, then reinstall** ***Replace*** .... Labor...........15.60	ea	—	$15.60	$15.60
GINGERBREAD ▶ CORBEL *Made from paint-grade poplar. Add **30%** for red oak.* 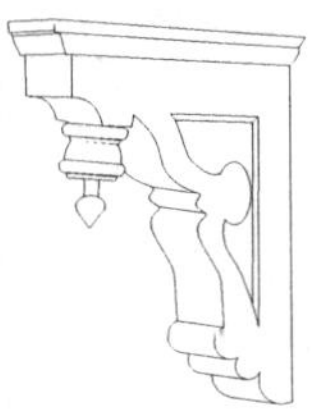	**Gingerbread corbel, standard grade** ***Replace*** Materials......28.30 Labor...........14.90 ***Remove***......................... Labor ....4.40 ► Longest leg up to 12" with simple sawn pattern.	ea	$4.40	$43.20	$47.60
	Gingerbread corbel, high grade ***Replace*** Materials......41.30 Labor...........14.90 ***Remove***......................... Labor ....4.40 ► Longest leg up to 16" with simple sawn pattern.	ea	$4.40	$56.20	$60.60
	Gingerbread corbel, deluxe grade ***Replace*** Materials......57.10 Labor...........14.90 ***Remove***......................... Labor ....4.40 ► Longest leg up to 20" with ornately sawn pattern.	ea	$4.40	$72.00	$76.40
	Gingerbread corbel, custom grade ***Replace*** Materials......81.80 Labor...........14.90 ***Remove***......................... Labor ....4.40 ► Longest leg up to 20" with very ornately sawn pattern.	ea	$4.40	$96.70	$101.10
remove & reinstall ▷	**Remove gingerbread corbel for work, then reinstall** ***Replace*** .... Labor...........15.70	ea	—	$15.70	$15.70
GINGERBREAD ▶ HEADER *Made from paint-grade poplar. Add **30%** for red oak.* 	**Gingerbread door or window header, standard grade** ***Replace*** Materials......42.40 Labor ....9.65 ***Remove***......................... Labor........... 1.02 ► Up to 14" long with sawn pattern.	lf	$1.02	$52.05	$53.07
	**Gingerbread door or window header, high grade** ***Replace*** Materials......59.00 Labor ....9.65 ***Remove***......................... Labor........... 1.02 ► Up to 25" long with sawn pattern.	lf	$1.02	$68.65	$69.67
	Gingerbread door or window header, deluxe grade ***Replace*** Materials......78.80 Labor ....9.65 ***Remove***......................... Labor........... 1.02 ► Up to 36" long with sawn pattern.	lf	$ 1.02	$88.45	$89.47
remove & reinstall ▷	**Remove gingerbread header for work, then reinstall** ***Replace*** .... Labor...........12.10	lf	—	$12.10	$12.10

Item Description	Unit	Remove	Replace	Total
10″ gingerbread post drop ***Replace*** Materials........6.29 Labor..........13.40 ***Remove***........................ Labor 4.24	ea	$4.24	$19.69	$23.93
12″ gingerbread post drop ***Replace*** Materials........7.86 Labor..........13.40 ***Remove***........................ Labor 4.24	ea	$4.24	$21.26	$25.50
18″ gingerbread post drop ***Replace*** Materials........9.43 Labor..........13.40 ***Remove***........................ Labor 4.24	ea	$4.24	$22.83	$27.07
24″ gingerbread post drop ***Replace*** Materials.......11.00 Labor..........13.40 ***Remove***........................ Labor 4.24	ea	$4.24	$24.40	$28.64
Remove gingerbread post drop for work, then reinstall ***Replace*** .... Labor..........14.80	ea	—	$14.80	$14.80
Gingerbread spandrel, standard grade ***Replace*** Materials......20.10 Labor ....9.86 ***Remove***........................ Labor ....1.05 ► Up to 6″ deep in center and 14″ deep on each side.	lf	$1.05	$29.96	$31.01
Gingerbread spandrel, high grade ***Replace*** Materials......25.50 Labor ....9.86 ***Remove***........................ Labor ....1.05 ► Up to 9″ deep in center and 17″ deep on each side.	lf	$1.05	$35.36	$36.41
Gingerbread spandrel, custom grade ***Replace*** Materials......33.20 Labor ....9.86 ***Remove***........................ Labor ....1.05 ► Up to 13″ deep in center and 21″ deep on each side.	lf	$1.05	$43.06	$44.11
Gingerbread spandrel, deluxe grade ***Replace*** Materials......45.20 Labor ....9.86 ***Remove***........................ Labor ....1.05 ► Up to 16″ deep in center and 24″ deep on each side.	lf	$1.05	$55.06	$56.11
Gingerbread spandrel, custom deluxe grade ***Replace*** Materials......56.70 Labor ....9.86 ***Remove***........................ Labor ....1.05 ► Up to 22″ deep in center and 31″ deep on each side.	lf	$1.05	$66.56	$67.61
Gingerbread arch spandrel, standard grade ***Replace*** Materials......38.50 Labor ....9.86 ***Remove***........................ Labor ....1.05 ► Leg against wall up to 12″ long.	lf	$1.05	$48.36	$49.41
Gingerbread arch spandrel, high grade ***Replace*** Materials......47.90 Labor ....9.86 ***Remove***........................ Labor ....1.05 ► Leg against wall up to 20″ long, simple pattern.	lf	$1.05	$57.76	$58.81
Gingerbread arch spandrel, custom grade ***Replace*** Materials......55.30 Labor ....9.86 ***Remove***........................ Labor ....1.05 ► Leg against wall up to 22″ long, ornate pattern, often with post drops.	lf	$1.05	$65.16	$66.21

◄ **GINGERBREAD POST DROP**
*Made from paint-grade poplar. Add **30%** for red oak.*

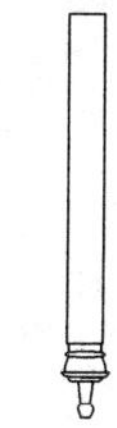

◁ **remove & reinstall**

◄ **GINGERBREAD SPANDREL**
*Spandrels are horizontal decorative elements for exterior and interior openings. Typically both corners and the center contain sawn elements. The remaining space is filled with either ball-and-dowel or spindle elements. Made from paint-grade poplar. Add **30%** for red oak.*

high △

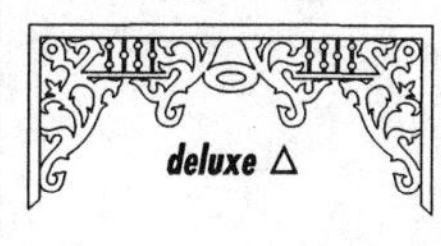

deluxe △

◄ **GINGERBREAD ARCH SPANDREL**
*Arched spandrels have arched end sections that typically contain either sawn woodwork or a spindle fan. Made from paint-grade poplar. Add **30%** for red oak.*

custom △

	Item Description	Unit	Remove	Replace	Total
GINGERBREAD ▶ ARCH SPANDREL *continued*	**Gingerbread arch spandrel, deluxe grade** ***Replace*** Materials......62.10 Labor............9.86 ***Remove*** .... Labor............1.05 ▶ Leg against wall up to 26" long, simple pattern.	lf	$1.05	$71.96	$73.01
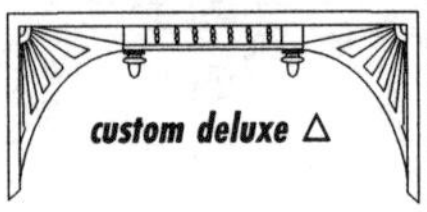 *custom deluxe* △	**Gingerbread arch spandrel, custom deluxe grade** ***Replace*** Materials......73.10 Labor............9.86 ***Remove*** .... Labor............1.05 ▶ Leg against wall up to 28" long, ornate pattern, often with post drops.	lf	$1.05	$82.96	$84.01
remove & reinstall ▷	**Remove gingerbread spandrel for work, then reinstall** ***Replace*** .... Labor...........12.40	lf	—	$12.40	$12.40
GINGERBREAD ▶ WINDOW CORNICE *Made from paint-grade poplar. Add **30%** for red oak.*	**Gingerbread window cornice, standard grade** ***Replace*** Materials......18.90 Labor...........10.10 ***Remove*** .... Labor............1.13 ▶ Cornice is 5" deep with a height of 6". Made from finish board with bed mold on top and simple panel mold on bottom.	lf	$1.13	$29.00	$30.13
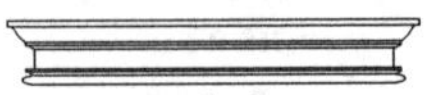 *standard* △	**Gingerbread window cornice, high grade** ***Replace*** Materials......23.60 Labor...........10.10 ***Remove*** .... Labor............1.13 ▶ Cornice is 5-1/2" deep with a height of 8-1/2". Side brackets are sawn with drop. Front of cornice is made from 2" to 4" ball and dowel running trim.	lf	$1.13	$33.70	$34.83
 *high* △	**Gingerbread window cornice, deluxe grade** ***Replace*** Materials......29.90 Labor...........10.10 ***Remove*** .... Labor............1.13 ▶ Cornice is 8" deep with a height of 9". Side brackets are sawn with drop and spindles. Front of cornice is made from 6" to 8" spindle running trim with sawn woodwork at center.	lf	$1.13	$40.00	$41.13
 *deluxe* △	**Gingerbread window cornice, custom grade** ***Replace*** Materials......30.90 Labor...........10.10 ***Remove*** .... Labor............1.13 ▶ Cornice is 8" deep with a height of 9". Side brackets are sawn with drop and spindles. Front of cornice is made from 6" to 8" spindle running trim with very ornately sawn woodwork at center.	lf	$1.13	$41.00	$42.13
 *custom deluxe* △	**Gingerbread window cornice, custom deluxe grade** ***Replace*** Materials......36.20 Labor...........10.10 ***Remove*** .... Labor............1.13 ▶ Cornice is 8" deep with a height of 9". Side brackets are sawn with drop and ball and dowels. Front of cornice is made from 6" to 8" ball-and-dowel running trim with very ornately sawn woodwork at center.	lf	$1.13	$46.30	$47.43
remove & reinstall ▷	**Remove gingerbread window cornice for work, then reinstall** ***Replace*** .... Labor...........12.80	lf	—	$12.80	$12.80
GINGERBREAD ▶ GABLE ORNAMENT *Gable ornaments can be ordered for roofs of any slope. They are typically found on roofs with a slope of 6 in 12 or more. Ornaments are placed in the gables at the peak of the roof. Made from paint-grade poplar. Add **30%** for red oak.*	**Gingerbread gable ornament, standard grade** ***Replace*** Materials....109.00 Labor...........24.20 ***Remove*** .... Labor............6.99 ▶ Fixed or adjustable ornament. Simple sawn pattern with longest leg up to 32".	ea	$6.99	$133.20	$140.19
	Gingerbread gable ornament, high grade ***Replace*** Materials.....185.00 Labor...........24.20 ***Remove*** .... Labor............6.99 ▶ Fixed ornament with legs up to 36". May contain some spindles or ball-and-dowel. Often contains drop in center.	ea	$6.99	$209.20	$216.19

Item Description	Unit	Remove	Replace	Total
Gingerbread gable ornament, deluxe grade ***Replace*** Materials....282.00 Labor..........24.20 ***Remove*** .... Labor...........6.99 ► Fixed ornament with legs up to 45". May contain some spindles or ball-and-dowel. Often contains drop in center.	ea	$6.99	$306.20	$313.19
Gingerbread gable ornament, custom grade ***Replace*** Materials....500.00 Labor..........24.20 ***Remove*** .... Labor...........6.99 ► Fixed ornament with legs up to 48". Ornate combinations of fanned spindles, ball-and-dowel and drops.	ea	$6.99	$524.20	$531.19
Gingerbread gable ornament, custom deluxe grade ***Replace*** Materials....609.00 Labor..........24.20 ***Remove*** .... Labor...........6.99 ► Fixed ornament with legs up to 60". Very ornate combinations of fanned spindles, ball-and-dowel and drops.	ea	$6.99	$633.20	$640.19
Remove gingerbread gable ornament for work, then reinstall ***Replace*** .... Labor..........39.10	ea	—	$39.10	$39.10
Gingerbread gable finial, standard grade ***Replace*** Materials......66.80 Labor..........23.30 ***Remove*** .... Labor...........6.57 ► Finial with 28" post.	ea	$6.57	$90.10	$96.67
Gingerbread gable finial, high grade ***Replace*** Materials......90.30 Labor..........23.30 ***Remove*** .... Labor...........6.57 ► Finial with 34" post.	ea	$6.57	$113.60	$120.17
Remove gingerbread gable finial for work, then reinstall ***Replace*** .... Labor..........37.30	ea	—	$37.30	$37.30
4" x 4" porch post, standard grade ***Replace*** Materials........7.75 Labor...........5.62 ***Remove*** .... Labor...........3.49 ► Turned post. Sometimes called colonist style.	lf	$3.49	$13.37	$16.86
4" x 4" porch post, high grade ***Replace*** Materials.......15.50 Labor...........5.62 ***Remove*** .... Labor...........3.49 ► Turned post with fluted columns. Or square post with flutes. Square post also trimmed with molding at base, at 1/3 shaft, and at about 12" to 16" from top.	lf	$3.49	$21.12	$24.61
4" x 4" porch post, deluxe grade ***Replace*** Materials......33.90 Labor...........5.62 ***Remove*** .... Labor...........3.49 ► Turned post with spiral pattern. Or square post with flutes. Square post also trimmed with panels to 1/3 shaft, capped at base and top of panel with moldings, and with molding trim about 12" to 16" from top.	lf	$3.49	$39.52	$43.01
6" x 6" porch post, standard grade ***Replace*** Materials.......11.40 Labor...........5.62 ***Remove*** .... Labor...........3.49 ► Turned post. Sometimes called colonist style.	lf	$3.49	$17.02	$20.51
6" x 6" porch post, high grade ***Replace*** Materials......23.10 Labor...........5.62 ***Remove*** .... Labor...........3.49 ► Turned post with fluted columns. Or square post with flutes. Square post also trimmed with molding at base, at 1/3 shaft, and at about 12" to 16" from top.	lf	$3.49	$28.72	$32.21

standard △

custom deluxe △

◁ **remove & reinstall**

◀ **GINGERBREAD GABLE FINIAL**
Finials are placed at the peak of the roof on each end. Made from cedar.

◀ **PORCH POST**
*For stain-grade add **16%**. Non-laminated posts made from clear, select Douglas fir or clear all-heart redwood. Standard grade posts may be made from cedar. Square posts are hollow and include a structural post inside.*

▽ *standard*

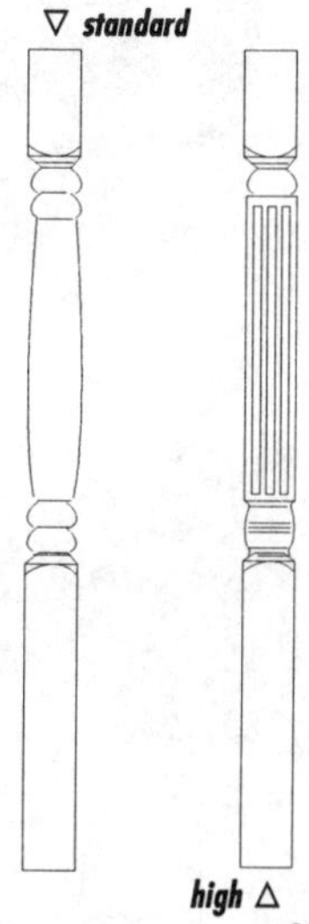

high △

Porch post ► *continued*

▽ *high*

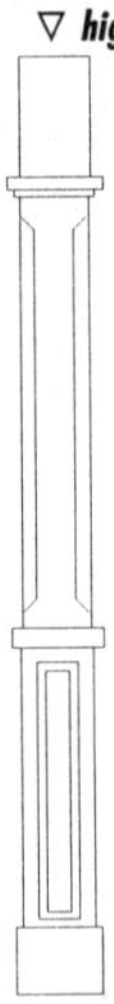

deluxe △

Item Description	Unit	Remove	Replace	Total
6" x 6" porch post, deluxe grade ***Replace*** Materials......29.10 Labor............5.62 ***Remove*****.........................** Labor............3.49 ► Turned post with spiral pattern. Or square post with flutes. Square post also trimmed with panels to 1/3 shaft, capped at base and top of panel with moldings, and with molding trim about 12" to 16" from top.	lf	$3.49	$34.72	$38.21
8" x 8" porch post, standard grade ***Replace*** Materials.......13.00 Labor............5.62 ***Remove*****.........................** Labor............3.49 ► Turned post. Sometimes called colonist style.	lf	$3.49	$18.62	$22.11
8" x 8" porch post, high grade ***Replace*** Materials......26.50 Labor............5.62 ***Remove*****.........................** Labor............3.49 ► Turned post with fluted columns. Or square post with flutes. Square post also trimmed with molding at base, at 1/3 shaft, and about at 12" to 16" from top.	lf	$3.49	$32.12	$35.61
8" x 8" porch post, deluxe grade ***Replace*** Materials......33.30 Labor............5.62 ***Remove*****.........................** Labor............3.49 ► Turned post with spiral pattern. Or square post with flutes. Square post also trimmed with panels to 1/3 shaft, capped at base and top of panel with moldings, and with molding trim about 12" to 16" from top.	lf	$3.49	$38.92	$42.41
remove & reinstall ▷ **Remove porch post for work, then reinstall** ***Replace*** .... Labor............7.82	lf	—	$7.82	$7.82

Carved onlay ►

*Onlays are available in a wide variety of styles and prices. Use these listings as indicators of complexity and price range. Made from maple. Add **25%** for red oak.*

acanthus △

ribbon △

grape △

Item Description	Unit	Remove	Replace	Total
Small carved wood onlay, acanthus ***Replace*** Materials......30.20 Labor...........21.60 ***Remove*****.........................** Labor............1.71	ea	$1.71	$51.80	$53.51
Small carved wood onlay, ribbon ***Replace*** Materials......31.60 Labor...........21.60 ***Remove*****.........................** Labor............1.71	ea	$1.71	$53.20	$54.91
Small carved wood onlay, grape ***Replace*** Materials......50.50 Labor...........21.60 ***Remove*****.........................** Labor............1.71	ea	$1.71	$72.10	$73.81
Small carved wood onlay, shell ***Replace*** Materials......44.20 Labor...........21.60 ***Remove*****.........................** Labor............1.71	ea	$1.71	$65.80	$67.51
Small carved wood onlay, floral ***Replace*** Materials......46.30 Labor...........21.60 ***Remove*****.........................** Labor............1.71	ea	$1.71	$67.90	$69.61
Medium carved wood onlay, acanthus ***Replace*** Materials......47.00 Labor...........21.60 ***Remove*****.........................** Labor............1.71	ea	$1.71	$68.60	$70.31
Medium carved wood onlay, ribbon ***Replace*** Materials......49.10 Labor...........21.60 ***Remove*****.........................** Labor............1.71	ea	$1.71	$70.70	$72.41
Medium carved wood onlay, grape ***Replace*** Materials......78.60 Labor...........21.60 ***Remove*****.........................** Labor............1.71	ea	$1.71	$100.20	$101.91

Item Description	Unit	Remove	Replace	Total
Medium carved wood onlay, shell *Replace* Materials......68.80 Labor..........21.60 *Remove*......................... Labor 1.71	ea	$1.71	$90.40	$92.11
Medium carved wood onlay, floral *Replace* Materials......71.60 Labor..........21.60 *Remove*......................... Labor 1.71	ea	$1.71	$93.20	$94.91
Large carved wood onlay, acanthus *Replace* Materials......59.70 Labor..........21.60 *Remove*......................... Labor 1.71	ea	$1.71	$81.30	$83.01
Large carved wood onlay, ribbon *Replace* Materials......63.20 Labor..........21.60 *Remove*......................... Labor 1.71	ea	$1.71	$84.80	$86.51
Large carved wood onlay, grape *Replace* Materials......98.30 Labor..........21.60 *Remove*......................... Labor 1.71	ea	$1.71	$119.90	$121.61
Large carved wood onlay, shell *Replace* Materials......88.40 Labor..........21.60 *Remove*......................... Labor 1.71	ea	$1.71	$110.00	$111.71
Large carved wood onlay, floral *Replace* Materials......91.20 Labor..........21.60 *Remove*......................... Labor 1.71	ea	$1.71	$112.80	$114.51
Remove onlay for work, then reinstall *Replace* .... Labor..........26.90	ea	—	$26.90	$26.90
1" x 2" S4S select pine *Replace* Materials........ .53 Labor ....2.04 *Remove*......................... Labor............ .72	lf	$.72	$2.57	$3.29
1" x 4" S4S select pine *Replace* Materials...... 1.05 Labor ....2.04 *Remove*......................... Labor............ .72	lf	$.72	$3.09	$3.81
1" x 6" S4S select pine *Replace* Materials........1.58 Labor ....2.04 *Remove*......................... Labor............ .72	lf	$.72	$3.62	$4.34
1" x 8" S4S select pine *Replace* Materials........2.10 Labor ....2.04 *Remove*......................... Labor............ .72	lf	$.72	$4.14	$4.86
1" x 10" S4S select pine *Replace* Materials........2.64 Labor ....2.04 *Remove*......................... Labor............ .72	lf	$.72	$4.68	$5.40
1" x 12" S4S select pine *Replace* Materials........3.16 Labor ....2.04 *Remove*......................... Labor............ .72	lf	$.72	$5.20	$5.92
Add 3% for S4S poplar				
Add 13% for S4S mahogany				
Add 17% for S4S red oak				

shell △

floral △

◁ remove & reinstall

◀ **FINISH BOARD**
Smooth four sides. Includes 4% waste.

◁ other wood species

RELATED ITEMS

Cleaning..............................61
Painting............................337

	Item Description	Unit	Remove	Replace	Total
FINISH BOARD ▶ *continued*	**Add for bull nose on 1 x boards** *Replace* Materials........ .48	lf	—	$.48	$.48
remove & reinstall ▷	**Remove finish board trim for work, then reinstall** *Replace* .... Labor 2.90	lf	—	$2.90	$2.90
FINISH PLYWOOD ▶ *Includes 4% waste.*	**1/4" aromatic cedar veneer plywood** *Replace* Materials........2.47 Labor ....1.16 *Remove*........................ Labor............ .61	sf	$.61	$3.63	$4.24
	1/4" birch veneer plywood *Replace* Materials........2.41 Labor ....1.16 *Remove*........................ Labor............ .61	sf	$.61	$3.57	$4.18
	1/4" cherry veneer plywood *Replace* Materials........2.67 Labor ....1.16 *Remove*........................ Labor............ .61	sf	$.61	$3.83	$4.44
	1/4" chestnut veneer plywood *Replace* Materials........4.23 Labor ....1.16 *Remove*........................ Labor............ .61	sf	$.61	$5.39	$6.00
	1/4" knotty pine veneer plywood *Replace* Materials........1.86 Labor ....1.16 *Remove*........................ Labor............ .61	sf	$.61	$3.02	$3.63
	1/4" lauan mahogany veneer plywood *Replace* Materials........ .94 Labor ....1.16 *Remove*........................ Labor............ .61	sf	$.61	$2.10	$2.71
	1/4" mahogany veneer plywood *Replace* Materials........2.70 Labor ....1.16 *Remove*........................ Labor............ .61	sf	$.61	$3.86	$4.47
	1/4" pecan veneer plywood *Replace* Materials........2.73 Labor ....1.16 *Remove*........................ Labor............ .61	sf	$.61	$3.89	$4.50
	1/4" red oak veneer plywood *Replace* Materials........2.44 Labor ....1.16 *Remove*........................ Labor............ .61	sf	$.61	$3.60	$4.21
	1/4" rosewood veneer plywood *Replace* Materials........3.74 Labor ....1.16 *Remove*........................ Labor............ .61	sf	$.61	$4.90	$5.51
	1/4" teak veneer plywood *Replace* Materials........4.95 Labor ....1.16 *Remove*........................ Labor............ .61	sf	$.61	$6.11	$6.72
	1/4" walnut veneer plywood *Replace* Materials........3.55 Labor ....1.16 *Remove*........................ Labor............ .61	sf	$.61	$4.71	$5.32
remove & reinstall ▷	**Remove 1/4" finish plywood for work, then reinstall** *Replace* .... Labor 1.52	sf	—	$1.52	$1.52

NOTES: ______________________________

______________________________ end

TIME & MATERIAL CHARTS *(selected items)*

Finish Carpentry Materials

DESCRIPTION	MATERIAL PRICE	GROSS COVERAGE	WASTE	NET COVERAGE	UNIT PRICE
Clamshell base					
1-1/2" stain-grade pine	$.80 lf	1	7%	.93	**$.86** lf
3-1/2" stain-grade pine	$1.30 lf	1	7%	.93	**$1.40** lf
Pattern base					
1-1/2" stain-grade pine	$.97 lf	1	7%	.93	**$1.04** lf
2-1/2" stain-grade pine	$1.56 lf	1	7%	.93	**$1.68** lf
3-1/2" stain-grade pine	$2.06 lf	1	7%	.93	**$2.22** lf
Base shoe					
3/4" stain-grade pine	$.49 lf	1	7%	.93	**$.53** lf
Clamshell casing					
1-1/2" stain-grade pine	$.83 lf	1	5%	.95	**$.87** lf
2-1/2" stain-grade pine	$.96 lf	1	5%	.95	**$1.01** lf
3-1/2" stain-grade pine	$1.35 lf	1	5%	.95	**$1.42** lf
Pattern casing					
1-1/2" stain-grade pine	$1.01 lf	1	5%	.95	**$1.06** lf
2-1/2" stain-grade pine	$1.62 lf	1	5%	.95	**$1.71** lf
3-1/2" stain-grade pine	$2.14 lf	1	5%	.95	**$2.25** lf
Window moldings					
2-1/2" stain-grade pine stool	$1.81 lf	1	4%	.96	**$1.89** lf
3-1/2" stain-grade pine apron	$1.18 lf	1	4%	.96	**$1.23** lf
Chair rail					
2-1/2" stain-grade pine	$1.56 lf	1	4%	.96	**$1.63** lf
3-1/2" stain-grade pine	$1.97 lf	1	4%	.96	**$2.05** lf
Drip cap					
1-5/8" redwood	$1.45 lf	1	4%	.96	**$1.51** lf
2-1/4" redwood	$1.62 lf	1	4%	.96	**$1.69** lf
Astragal					
1-3/4" stain-grade pine	$2.99 lf	1	4%	.96	**$3.11** lf
2-1/4" stain-grade pine	$3.62 lf	1	4%	.96	**$3.77** lf
Cove					
1/2" stain-grade pine	$.56 lf	1	4%	.96	**$.58** lf
3/4" stain-grade pine	$.64 lf	1	4%	.96	**$.67** lf
1" stain-grade pine	$.80 lf	1	4%	.96	**$.83** lf
2-1/2" stain-grade pine	$1.40 lf	1	4%	.96	**$1.46** lf
3-1/2" stain-grade pine	$1.82 lf	1	4%	.96	**$1.90** lf
Half-round					
1" stain-grade pine	$.66 lf	1	4%	.96	**$.69** lf
2" stain-grade pine	$.93 lf	1	4%	.96	**$.97** lf
Quarter-round					
1/2" stain-grade pine	$.49 lf	1	4%	.96	**$.51** lf
3/4" stain-grade pine	$.58 lf	1	4%	.96	**$.60** lf
1" stain-grade pine	$1.03 lf	1	4%	.96	**$1.07** lf
Corner bead					
stain-grade pine	$1.12 lf	1	4%	.96	**$1.17** lf
turned stain-grade pine with finials	$12.40 lf	1	4%	.96	**$12.90** lf
clear plastic	$.88 lf	1	4%	.96	**$.92** lf
Bed mold					
2-1/2" stain-grade pine	$1.58 lf	1	4%	.96	**$1.65** lf

. . . More ➢

Finish Carpentry Materials *continued*

DESCRIPTION	MATERIAL PRICE	GROSS COVERAGE	WASTE	NET COVERAGE	UNIT PRICE
Crown					
3-1/2" stain-grade pine	$2.02 lf	1	4%	.96	$2.10 lf
4-1/2" stain-grade pine	$2.97 lf	1	4%	.96	$3.09 lf
Hand rail					
stain-grade pine	$2.98 lf	1	4%	.96	$3.10 lf
Specialty moldings, 3/4"					
stain-grade pine with vertical milling	$2.37 lf	1	4%	.96	$2.47 lf
stain-grade pine embossed	$1.40 lf	1	4%	.96	$1.46 lf
stain-grade pine with hand carving	$4.38 lf	1	4%	.96	$4.56 lf
stain-grade pine with heavy hand carving	$8.59 lf	1	4%	.96	$8.95 lf
Specialty moldings, 1-1/2"					
stain-grade pine with vertical milling	$2.70 lf	1	4%	.96	$2.81 lf
stain-grade pine embossed	$1.60 lf	1	4%	.96	$1.67 lf
stain-grade pine with hand carving	$5.00 lf	1	4%	.96	$5.21 lf
stain-grade pine with heavy hand carving	$9.80 lf	1	4%	.96	$10.20 lf
Specialty moldings, 2-1/2"					
stain-grade pine with vertical milling	$3.02 lf	1	4%	.96	$3.15 lf
stain-grade pine embossed	$1.79 lf	1	4%	.96	$1.86 lf
stain-grade pine with hand carving	$5.60 lf	1	4%	.96	$5.83 lf
stain-grade pine with heavy hand carving	$11.00 lf	1	4%	.96	$11.50 lf
Specialty moldings, 3-1/2"					
stain-grade pine with vertical milling	$3.36 lf	1	4%	.96	$3.50 lf
stain-grade pine embossed	$1.99 lf	1	4%	.96	$2.07 lf
stain-grade pine with hand carving	$6.23 lf	1	4%	.96	$6.49 lf
stain-grade pine with heavy hand carving	$12.20 lf	1	4%	.96	$12.70 lf
Specialty moldings, 5"					
stain-grade pine with vertical milling	$4.84 lf	1	4%	.96	$5.04 lf
stain-grade pine embossed	$2.87 lf	1	4%	.96	$2.99 lf
stain-grade pine with hand carving	$8.97 lf	1	4%	.96	$9.34 lf
stain-grade pine with heavy hand carving	$17.60 lf	1	4%	.96	$18.30 lf
Specialty moldings, 8"					
stain-grade pine with vertical milling	$7.92 lf	1	4%	.96	$8.25 lf
stain-grade pine embossed	$4.70 lf	1	4%	.96	$4.90 lf
stain-grade pine with hand carving	$14.70 lf	1	4%	.96	$15.30 lf
stain-grade pine with heavy hand carving	$28.80 lf	1	4%	.96	$30.00 lf
Custom-milled moldings					
molder setup charge	$150.00 ea				$150.00 ea
molder custom knife charges	$345.00 ea				$345.00 ea
2" to 3" pine	$1.55 lf	1	4%	.96	$1.61 lf
2" to 3" poplar	$1.71 lf	1	4%	.96	$1.78 lf
2" to 3" mahogany	$2.05 lf	1	4%	.96	$2.14 lf
2" to 3" red oak	$2.23 lf	1	4%	.96	$2.32 lf
Inside corner radius for panel molding					
typical	$1.54 ea	1	4%	.96	$1.60 ea
with heavy carving	$7.89 ea	1	4%	.96	$8.22 ea
Closet work					
shelf brackets, shelving, & rod	$8.98 lf	1	4%	.96	$9.35 lf
organizer system, standard grade	$8.35 sf	1	4%	.96	$8.70 sf
organizer system, deluxe grade	$12.80 sf	1	4%	.96	$13.30 sf
linen closet shelves, standard grade	$6.67 lf	1	4%	.96	$6.95 lf
linen closet pull-out shelves	$8.42 ea	1	4%	.96	$8.77 ea
closet rod, pine	$2.55 lf	1	4%	.96	$2.66 lf
Built-in bookcase					
8" deep stain-grade pine	$6.84 sf	1	4%	.96	$7.13 sf
12" deep stain-grade pine	$8.97 sf	1	4%	.96	$9.34 sf
18" deep stain-grade pine	$11.80 sf	1	4%	.96	$12.30 sf
24" deep stain-grade pine	$15.50 sf	1	4%	.96	$16.10 sf

. . . More >

Finish Carpentry Materials *continued*

DESCRIPTION	MATERIAL PRICE	GROSS COVERAGE	WASTE	NET COVERAGE	UNIT PRICE
Fireplace mantel beam					
rough sawn	$7.96 lf	1	4%	.96	$8.29 lf
glue laminated	$22.70 lf	1	4%	.96	$23.60 lf
Fireplace mantel					
economy grade	$45.80 lf				$45.80 lf
custom deluxe grade	$1,450.00 lf				$1,450.00 lf
Coffered ceiling					
economy grade	$7.86 sf	1	12%	.88	$8.93 sf
custom deluxe grade	$40.60 sf	1	12%	.88	$46.10 sf
Niche with casing and shelf bracket					
typical	$157.00 ea				$157.00 ea
with clamshell top	$275.00 ea				$275.00 ea
clamshell top and clamshell shelf	$358.00 ea				$358.00 ea
Gingerbread running trim					
fleur-sawn	$23.80 lf	1	2%	.98	$24.30 lf
picket-sawn	$30.80 lf	1	2%	.98	$31.40 lf
2" ball-and-dowel	$7.30 lf	1	2%	.98	$7.45 lf
14" ball-and-dowel	$27.00 lf	1	2%	.98	$27.60 lf
2" spindle	$6.92 lf	1	2%	.98	$7.06 lf
14" spindle	$26.60 lf	1	2%	.98	$27.10 lf
Gingerbread bracket					
standard grade	$26.00 ea				$26.00 ea
custom grade	$39.20 ea				$39.20 ea
Gingerbread fan bracket					
standard grade	$30.70 ea				$30.70 ea
custom grade	$54.70 ea				$54.70 ea
Gingerbread post bracket					
standard grade	$39.70 ea				$39.70 ea
deluxe grade	$58.10 ea				$58.10 ea
Gingerbread corbel					
standard grade	$28.30 ea				$28.30 ea
custom grade	$81.80 ea				$81.80 ea
Gingerbread door or window header					
standard grade	$42.40 ea				$42.40 ea
deluxe grade	$78.80 ea				$78.80 ea
Gingerbread post drop					
10"	$6.29 ea				$6.29 ea
24"	$11.00 ea				$11.00 ea
Gingerbread spandrel					
standard grade	$20.10 lf				$20.10 lf
custom deluxe grade	$56.70 lf				$56.70 lf
Gingerbread arch spandrel					
standard grade	$38.50 lf				$38.50 lf
custom deluxe grade	$73.10 lf				$73.10 lf
Gingerbread window cornice					
standard grade	$18.90 lf				$18.90 lf
custom deluxe grade	$36.20 lf				$36.20 lf
Gingerbread gable ornament					
standard grade	$109.00 lf				$109.00 lf
custom deluxe grade	$609.00 lf				$609.00 lf
Gingerbread gable finial					
standard grade	$66.80 ea				$66.80 ea
high grade	$90.30 ea				$90.30 ea

. . . More >

Finish Carpentry Materials *continued*

DESCRIPTION	MATERIAL PRICE	GROSS COVERAGE	WASTE	NET COVERAGE	UNIT PRICE
Porch post					
4" x 4", standard grade	$62.00 8' post	8	0%	8	**$7.75** lf
4" x 4", deluxe grade	$271.00 8' post	8	0%	8	**$33.90** lf
6" x 6", standard grade	$91.00 8' post	8	0%	8	**$11.40** lf
6" x 6", deluxe grade	$233.00 8' post	8	0%	8	**$29.10** lf
8" x 8", standard grade	$104.00 8' post	8	0%	8	**$13.00** lf
8" x 8", deluxe grade	$266.00 8' post	8	0%	8	**$33.30** lf
Carved wood onlay					
medium, acanthus	$47.00 ea				**$47.00** ea
medium, ribbon	$49.10 ea				**$49.10** ea
medium, grape	$78.60 ea				**$78.60** ea
medium, shell	$68.80 ea				**$68.80** ea
medium, floral	$71.60 ea				**$71.60** ea
Finish boards					
1" x 12" S4S select pine	$3.03 lf	1	4%	.96	**$3.16** lf
Hardwood plywood					
1/4" aromatic cedar veneer	$75.80 sheet	32	4%	30.72	**$2.47** sf
1/4" birch veneer	$74.00 sheet	32	4%	30.72	**$2.41** sf
1/4" cherry veneer	$82.00 sheet	32	4%	30.72	**$2.67** sf
1/4" chestnut veneer	$130.00 sheet	32	4%	30.72	**$4.23** sf
1/4" knotty pine veneer	$57.00 sheet	32	4%	30.72	**$1.86** sf
1/4" lauan mahogany veneer	$29.00 sheet	32	4%	30.72	**$.94** sf
1/4" mahogany veneer	$83.00 sheet	32	4%	30.72	**$2.70** sf
1/4" pecan veneer	$84.00 sheet	32	4%	30.72	**$2.73** sf
1/4" red oak veneer	$75.00 sheet	32	4%	30.72	**$2.44** sf
1/4" rosewood veneer	$115.00 sheet	32	4%	30.72	**$3.74** sf
1/4" teak veneer	$152.00 sheet	32	4%	30.72	**$4.95** sf
1/4" walnut veneer	$109.00 sheet	32	4%	30.72	**$3.55** sf

Finish Carpentry Labor

LABORER	BASE WAGE	PAID LEAVE	TRUE WAGE	FICA	FUTA	WORKER'S COMP.	UNEMPLOY. INSUR.	HEALTH INSUR.	RETIRE (401K)	LIABILITY INSUR.	COST PER HOUR
Carpenter	$23.60	1.84	$25.44	1.95	.20	4.96	2.21	2.69	.76	3.43	**$41.60**
Carpenter's helper	$17.00	1.33	$18.33	1.40	.15	3.57	1.59	2.69	.55	2.47	**$30.80**
Demolition laborer	$13.90	1.08	$14.98	1.15	.12	4.79	1.30	2.69	.45	2.02	**$27.50**

Paid Leave is calculated based on two weeks paid vacation, one week sick leave, and seven paid holidays. Employer's matching portion of **FICA** is 7.65 percent. **FUTA** (Federal Unemployment) is .8 percent. **Worker's compensation** for the finish carpentry trade was calculated using a national average of 19.50 percent. **Unemployment insurance** was calculated using a national average of 8.7 percent. **Health insurance** was calculated based on a projected national average for 2002 of $535 per employee (and family when applicable) per month. Employer pays 80 percent for a per month cost of $428 per employee. **Retirement** is based on a 401(k) retirement program with employer matching of 50 percent. Employee contributions to the 401(k) plan are an average of 6 percent of the true wage. **Liability insurance** is based on a national average of 13.2 percent.

Finish Carpentry Labor Productivity

WORK DESCRIPTION	LABORER	COST PER HOUR	PRODUCTIVITY	UNIT PRICE
Demolition				
remove wall molding (base, chair rail, crown)	demolition laborer	$27.50	.026	$.72 lf
remove door and window molding	demolition laborer	$27.50	.032	$.88 lf
remove base or corner block	demolition laborer	$27.50	.036	$.99 ea
remove head block	demolition laborer	$27.50	.037	$1.02 ea
remove overdoor molding	demolition laborer	$27.50	.028	$.77 lf
remove window stool	demolition laborer	$27.50	.026	$.72 lf
remove window apron	demolition laborer	$27.50	.028	$.77 lf
remove corner bead	demolition laborer	$27.50	.043	$1.18 lf
remove hand rail	demolition laborer	$27.50	.028	$.77 lf
remove shelf brackets, shelving, and rod	demolition laborer	$27.50	.063	$1.73 lf
remove closet organizer system	demolition laborer	$27.50	.047	$1.29 sf
remove linen closet shelves	demolition laborer	$27.50	.034	$.94 lf
remove closet rod	demolition laborer	$27.50	.035	$.96 lf
remove tongue-&-groove cedar closet lining	demolition laborer	$27.50	.028	$.77 sf
remove cedar veneer plywood closet lining	demolition laborer	$27.50	.022	$.61 sf
remove built-in bookcase	demolition laborer	$27.50	.051	$1.40 sf
remove fireplace mantel beam	demolition laborer	$27.50	.080	$2.20 lf
remove fireplace mantel	demolition laborer	$27.50	.094	$2.59 lf
remove coffered ceiling	demolition laborer	$27.50	.047	$1.29 sf
remove niche	demolition laborer	$27.50	.317	$8.72 ea
remove gingerbread running trim	demolition laborer	$27.50	.038	$1.05 lf
remove gingerbread bracket	demolition laborer	$27.50	.154	$4.24 ea
remove gingerbread corbel	demolition laborer	$27.50	.160	$4.40 ea
remove gingerbread door or window header	demolition laborer	$27.50	.037	$1.02 lf
remove gingerbread post drop	demolition laborer	$27.50	.154	$4.24 ea
remove gingerbread spandrel	demolition laborer	$27.50	.038	$1.05 lf
remove gingerbread window cornice	demolition laborer	$27.50	.041	$1.13 lf
remove gingerbread gable ornament	demolition laborer	$27.50	.254	$6.99 lf
remove gingerbread gable finial	demolition laborer	$27.50	.239	$6.57 ea
remove porch post	demolition laborer	$27.50	.127	$3.49 lf
remove onlay	demolition laborer	$27.50	.062	$1.71 ea
remove finish trim board	demolition laborer	$27.50	.026	$.72 lf
remove finish plywood	demolition laborer	$27.50	.022	$.61 sf
Finish carpentry crew				
finish carpentry	finish carpenter	$41.60		
finish carpentry	finish carpenter's helper	$30.80		
finish carpentry	**finish crew**	$36.20		
Install molding				
base, chair rail	finish carpenter	$41.60	.038	$1.58 lf
window or door casing or panel moldings	finish carpenter	$41.60	.041	$1.71 lf
crown	finish carpenter	$41.60	.046	$1.91 lf
Install casing on curved window or door				
half-round top window or door per lf	finish carpenter	$41.60	.144	$5.99 lf
elliptical top window or door per lf	finish carpenter	$41.60	.144	$5.99 lf
round window per lf of diameter	finish carpenter	$41.60	.294	$12.20 lf
Install wood key in curved molding				
install	finish carpenter	$41.60	.251	$10.40 ea
Install base, corner, or head block				
install	finish carpenter	$41.60	.063	$2.62 ea
Install overdoor molding				
install	finish carpenter	$41.60	.041	$1.71 lf
Install door architrave				
interior	finish carpenter	$41.60	.062	$2.58 lf
exterior	finish carpenter	$41.60	.080	$3.33 lf
Install exterior door surround				
economy grade	finish carpenter	$41.60	.234	$9.73 lf
custom deluxe grade	finish carpenter	$41.60	.431	$17.90 lf

. . . More >

Finish Carpentry Labor Productivity *continued*

WORK DESCRIPTION	LABORER	COST PER HOUR	PRODUCTIVITY	UNIT PRICE
Install exterior window surround				
economy grade	finish carpenter	$41.60	.207	$8.61 lf
custom deluxe grade	finish carpenter	$41.60	.322	$13.40 lf
Install window trim				
stool	finish carpenter	$41.60	.058	$2.41 lf
apron	finish carpenter	$41.60	.049	$2.04 lf
Install corner bead				
wood	finish carpenter	$41.60	.077	$3.20 lf
plastic	finish carpenter	$41.60	.032	$1.33 lf
Install hand rail				
install	finish carpenter	$41.60	.098	$4.08 lf
Install panel molding inside corner radius				
install	finish carpenter	$41.60	.149	$6.20 ea
Install closet shelf brackets, shelving, & rod				
install	finish carpenter	$41.60	.332	$13.80 lf
Install closet organizer system				
standard grade	finish carpenter	$41.60	.304	$12.60 sf
deluxe grade	finish carpenter	$41.60	.526	$21.90 sf
Install linen closet shelves				
typical	finish carpenter	$41.60	.673	$28.00 lf
with pull-out shelves	finish carpenter	$41.60	.695	$28.90 lf
Install closet rod				
install	finish carpenter	$41.60	.080	$3.33 lf
Install closet lining				
tongue-&-groove cedar board	finish carpenter	$41.60	.051	$2.12 sf
1/4" cedar veneer plywood	finish carpenter	$41.60	.037	$1.54 sf
Install built-in bookcase				
8" deep	finish carpenter	$41.60	.269	$11.20 sf
12" deep	finish carpenter	$41.60	.304	$12.60 sf
18" deep	finish carpenter	$41.60	.317	$13.20 sf
24" deep	finish carpenter	$41.60	.332	$13.80 sf
Install fireplace mantel beam				
install	finish carpenter	$41.60	.539	$22.40 lf
Install fireplace mantel				
install	finish carpenter	$41.60	.653	$27.20 lf
Install coffered ceiling				
economy grade	finish carpenter	$41.60	.248	$10.30 sf
custom deluxe grade	finish carpenter	$41.60	.567	$23.60 sf
Install niche				
with casing and shelf bracket	finish carpenter	$41.60	1.31	$54.50 ea
Install gingerbread				
running trim	finish carpenter	$41.60	.160	$6.66 lf
post bracket	finish carpenter	$41.60	.348	$14.50 ea
corbel	finish carpenter	$41.60	.359	$14.90 ea
door or window header	finish carpenter	$41.60	.232	$9.65 lf
post drop	finish carpenter	$41.60	.322	$13.40 ea
spandrel	finish carpenter	$41.60	.237	$9.86 lf
window cornice	finish carpenter	$41.60	.242	$10.10 lf
gable ornament	finish carpenter	$41.60	.582	$24.20 ea
gable finial	finish carpenter	$41.60	.560	$23.30 ea
Install porch post				
install	finish carpenter	$41.60	.135	$5.62 lf
Install carved wood onlay				
install	finish carpenter	$41.60	.519	$21.60 ea
Install finish board trim				
install	finish carpenter	$41.60	.049	$2.04 lf
Install 1/4" hardwood plywood				
install	finish carpenter	$41.60	.028	$1.16 sf

18 .... Fireplaces

Item Description	Unit	Remove	Replace	Total
Fireplace, 30″ wide by 16″ deep by 29″ high, open front *Replace* Materials....386.00 Labor.........741.00 *Remove* .... Labor.........106.00	ea	$106.00	$1,127.00	$1,233.00
Fireplace, 36″ wide by 16″ deep by 29″ high, open front *Replace* Materials....463.00 Labor........777.00 *Remove* .... Labor.........106.00	ea	$106.00	$1,240.00	$1,346.00
Fireplace, 40″ wide by 16″ deep by 29″ high, open front *Replace* Materials.....515.00 Labor........805.00 *Remove* .... Labor.........106.00	ea	$106.00	$1,320.00	$1,426.00
Fireplace, 48″ wide by 18″ deep by 32″ high, open front *Replace* Materials.....618.00 Labor.........851.00 *Remove* .... Labor.........106.00	ea	$106.00	$1,469.00	$1,575.00
Fireplace, 32″ wide by 16″ deep by 26″ high, open front & one side *Replace* Materials....362.00 Labor.........768.00 *Remove* .... Labor.........106.00	ea	$106.00	$1,130.00	$1,236.00
Fireplace, 40″ wide by 16″ deep by 29″ high, open front & one side *Replace* Materials....505.00 Labor........805.00 *Remove* .... Labor.........106.00	ea	$106.00	$1,310.00	$1,416.00
Fireplace, 48″ wide by 20″ deep by 29″ high, open front & one side *Replace* Materials....604.00 Labor.........869.00 *Remove* .... Labor.........106.00	ea	$106.00	$1,473.00	$1,579.00
Fireplace, 32″ wide by 28″ deep by 29″ high, open two faces *Replace* Materials....354.00 Labor.........851.00 *Remove* .... Labor.........106.00	ea	$106.00	$1,205.00	$1,311.00
Fireplace, 36″ wide by 28″ deep by 29″ high, open two faces *Replace* Materials....398.00 Labor.........869.00 *Remove* .... Labor.........106.00	ea	$106.00	$1,267.00	$1,373.00
Fireplace, 40″ wide by 28″ deep by 29″ high, open two faces *Replace* Materials....442.00 Labor........883.00 *Remove* .... Labor.........106.00	ea	$106.00	$1,325.00	$1,431.00
Fireplace, 36″ wide by 32″ deep by 27″ high, open three sides *Replace* Materials....433.00 Labor........883.00 *Remove* .... Labor.........106.00	ea	$106.00	$1,316.00	$1,422.00
Fireplace, 36″ wide by 36″ deep by 27″ high, open three sides *Replace* Materials....487.00 Labor........920.00 *Remove* .... Labor.........106.00	ea	$106.00	$1,407.00	$1,513.00
Fireplace, 44″ wide by 40″ deep by 27″ high, open three sides *Replace* Materials....648.00 Labor........938.00 *Remove* .... Labor.........106.00	ea	$106.00	$1,586.00	$1,692.00
Prefab. fireplace, 30″ wide by 16″ deep by 29″ high, open front *Replace* Materials....437.00 Labor........209.00 *Remove* .... Labor...........67.10	ea	$67.10	$646.00	$713.10

◀ **FIREPLACE**
Includes concrete reinforced hearth, ash drop, fire brick, damper, throat, smoke shelf and smoke chamber. Does not include foundation, flue or chimney, face, or finish hearth.

◁ **open front**

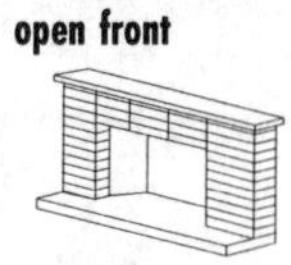

◁ **open front and side**

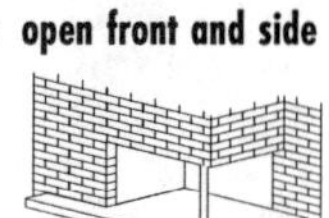

RELATED ITEMS

◁ **open both faces**
"see through"

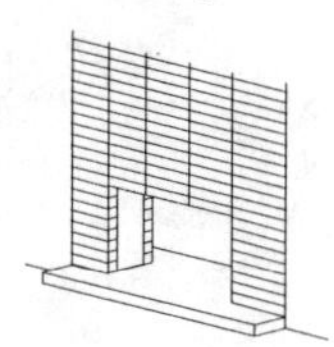

◁ **open two faces and side**

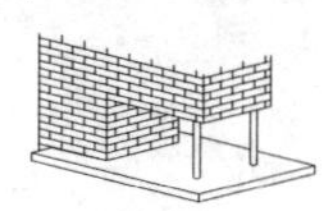

◀ **PREFABRICATED FIREPLACE**
◁ **open front**

continued on next page

PREFABRICATED FIREPLACE ▶ *continued*

Zero clearance box. Does not include flue. Actual sizes and style available vary from manufacturer to manufacturer. Choose the size and style that most closely matches.

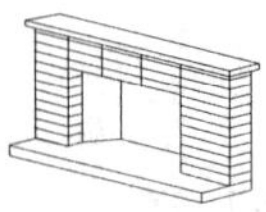

Item Description	Unit	Remove	Replace	Total
Prefab. convection fireplace, 30″ wide by 16″ deep by 29″ high, open front ***Replace*** Materials....503.00 Labor.........219.00 ***Remove*** .... Labor...........67.10	ea	$67.10	$722.00	$789.10
Prefab. forced-air fireplace, 30″ wide by 16″ deep by 29″ high, open front ***Replace*** Materials....546.00 Labor.........242.00 ***Remove*** .... Labor...........67.10	ea	$67.10	$788.00	$855.10
Prefab. fireplace, 36″ wide by 16″ deep by 29″ high, open front ***Replace*** Materials....529.00 Labor........209.00 ***Remove*** .... Labor...........67.10	ea	$67.10	$738.00	$805.10
Prefab. convection fireplace, 36″ wide by 16″ deep by 29″ high, open front ***Replace*** Materials....609.00 Labor.........219.00 ***Remove*** .... Labor...........67.10	ea	$67.10	$828.00	$895.10
Prefab. forced-air fireplace, 36″ wide by 16″ deep by 29″ high, open front ***Replace*** Materials.....661.00 Labor.........242.00 ***Remove*** .... Labor...........67.10	ea	$67.10	$903.00	$970.10
Prefab. fireplace, 40″ wide by 16″ deep by 29″ high, open front ***Replace*** Materials....797.00 Labor........209.00 ***Remove*** .... Labor...........67.10	ea	$67.10	$1,006.00	$1,073.10
Prefab. convection fireplace, 40″ wide by 16″ deep by 29″ high, open front ***Replace*** Materials....677.00 Labor.........219.00 ***Remove*** .... Labor...........67.10	ea	$67.10	$896.00	$963.10
Prefab. forced-air fireplace, 40″ wide by 16″ deep by 29″ high, open front ***Replace*** Materials....734.00 Labor.........242.00 ***Remove*** .... Labor...........67.10	ea	$67.10	$976.00	$1,043.10
Prefab. fireplace, 48″ wide by 18″ deep by 32″ high, open front ***Replace*** Materials....957.00 Labor........209.00 ***Remove*** .... Labor...........67.10	ea	$67.10	$1,166.00	$1,233.10
Prefab. convection fireplace, 48″ wide by 18″ deep by 32″ high, open front ***Replace*** Materials.....813.00 Labor.........219.00 ***Remove*** .... Labor...........67.10	ea	$67.10	$1,032.00	$1,099.10
Prefab. forced-air fireplace, 48″ wide by 18″ deep by 32″ high, open front ***Replace*** Materials....881.00 Labor.........242.00 ***Remove*** .... Labor...........67.10	ea	$67.10	$1,123.00	$1,190.10
open front and side ▷ **Prefab. fireplace, 32″ wide by 16″ deep by 26″ high, open front & side** ***Replace*** Materials....732.00 Labor........209.00 ***Remove*** .... Labor...........67.10	ea	$67.10	$941.00	$1,008.10
Prefab. fireplace, 40″ wide by 16″ deep by 29″ high, open front & side ***Replace*** Materials....879.00 Labor.........219.00 ***Remove*** .... Labor...........67.10	ea	$67.10	$1,098.00	$1,165.10
Prefab. fireplace, 48″ wide by 20″ deep by 29″ high, open front & side ***Replace*** Materials..1050.00 Labor.........242.00 ***Remove*** .... Labor...........67.10	ea	$67.10	$1,292.00	$1,359.10
open both faces ▷ *"see through"* **Prefab. fireplace, 32″ wide by 28″ deep by 29″ high, open two faces** ***Replace*** Materials....894.00 Labor........209.00 ***Remove*** .... Labor...........67.10	ea	$67.10	$1,103.00	$1,170.10

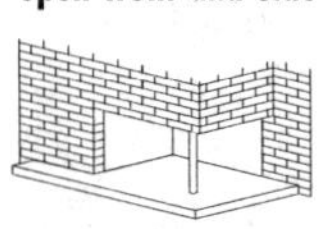

Item Description	Unit	Remove	Replace	Total
Prefab. fireplace, 36″ wide by 28″ deep by 29″ high, open two faces ***Replace*** Materials...1070.00 Labor.........219.00 ***Remove*** .... Labor...........67.10	ea	$67.10	$1,289.00	$1,356.10
Prefab. fireplace, 40″ wide by 28″ deep by 29″ high, open two faces ***Replace*** Materials ..1280.00 Labor.........242.00 ***Remove*** .... Labor...........67.10	ea	$67.10	$1,522.00	$1,589.10
Prefab. fireplace, 36″ wide by 32″ deep by 27″ high, open three sides ***Replace*** Materials ..1050.00 Labor........209.00 ***Remove*** .... Labor...........67.10	ea	$67.10	$1,259.00	$1,326.10
Prefab. fireplace, 36″ wide by 36″ deep by 27″ high, open three sides ***Replace*** Materials...1260.00 Labor.........219.00 ***Remove*** .... Labor...........67.10	ea	$67.10	$1,479.00	$1,546.10
Prefab. fireplace, 44″ wide by 40″ deep by 27″ high, open three sides ***Replace*** Materials ...1510.00 Labor.........242.00 ***Remove*** .... Labor...........67.10	ea	$67.10	$1,752.00	$1,819.10
Fireplace form, 30″ wide by 16″ deep by 29″ high, open front ***Replace*** Materials....503.00 Labor.........139.00 ***Remove*** .... Labor...........76.50	ea	$76.50	$642.00	$718.50
Fireplace form, 36″ wide by 16″ deep by 29″ high, open front ***Replace*** Materials....604.00 Labor.........139.00 ***Remove*** .... Labor...........76.50	ea	$76.50	$743.00	$819.50
Fireplace form, 40″ wide by 16″ deep by 29″ high, open front ***Replace*** Materials ....671.00 Labor.........139.00 ***Remove*** .... Labor...........76.50	ea	$76.50	$810.00	$886.50
Fireplace form, 48″ wide by 18″ deep by 32″ high, open front ***Replace*** Materials....828.00 Labor.........139.00 ***Remove*** .... Labor...........76.50	ea	$76.50	$967.00	$1,043.50
Fireplace form, 32″ wide by 16″ deep by 26″ high, open front & side ***Replace*** Materials....933.00 Labor.........139.00 ***Remove*** .... Labor...........76.50	ea	$76.50	$1,072.00	$1,148.50
Fireplace form, 40″ wide by 16″ deep by 29″ high, open front & side ***Replace*** Materials ...1120.00 Labor.........139.00 ***Remove*** .... Labor...........76.50	ea	$76.50	$1,259.00	$1,335.50
Fireplace form, 48″ wide by 20″ deep by 29″ high, open front & side ***Replace*** Materials ..1860.00 Labor.........139.00 ***Remove*** .... Labor...........76.50	ea	$76.50	$1,999.00	$2,075.50
Fireplace form, 32″ wide by 28″ deep by 29″ high, open two faces ***Replace*** Materials ...1130.00 Labor.........139.00 ***Remove*** .... Labor...........76.50	ea	$76.50	$1,269.00	$1,345.50
Fireplace form, 36″ wide by 28″ deep by 29″ high, open two faces ***Replace*** Materials...1270.00 Labor.........139.00 ***Remove*** .... Labor...........76.50	ea	$76.50	$1,409.00	$1,485.50
Fireplace form, 40″ wide by 28″ deep by 29″ high, open two faces ***Replace*** Materials ...1410.00 Labor.........139.00 ***Remove*** .... Labor...........76.50	ea	$76.50	$1,549.00	$1,625.50

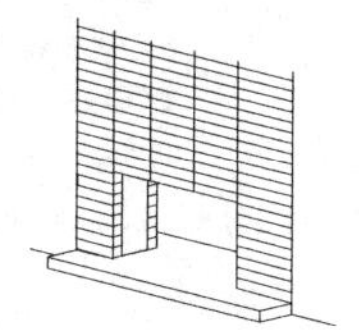

◁ **open two faces and side**

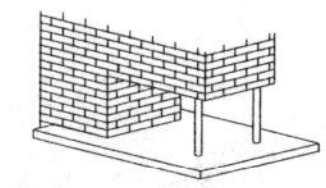

◀ **FIREPLACE FORM**
Does not include face, hearth, flue or chimney. Actual sizes and style available vary from manufacturer to manufacturer. Choose the size and style that most closely matches.

◁ **open front**

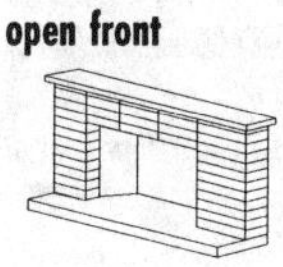

◁ **open front and side**

RELATED ITEMS

Cleaning
fireplaces........................62
masonry..........................63
Finish Carpentry
mantel beam, mantel.......224

◁ **open both faces** *"see through"*

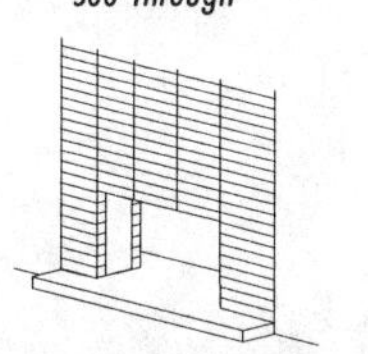

RELATED ITEMS

Masonry..........................287
Painting..........................339
Rough Carpentry
chimney cricket.............444

	Item Description	Unit	Remove	Replace	Total
Fireplace ▸ form *continued*	**Fireplace form, 36" wide by 32" deep by 27" high, open three sides** ***Replace*** Materials...1390.00 Labor.........139.00 ***Remove*** .... Labor...........76.50	ea	$76.50	$1,529.00	$1,605.50
open two faces and side ▹ 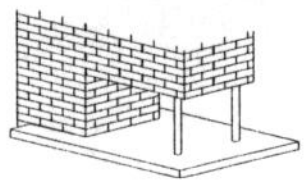	**Fireplace form, 36" wide by 36" deep by 27" high, open three sides** ***Replace*** Materials...1570.00 Labor.........139.00 ***Remove*** .... Labor...........76.50	ea	$76.50	$1,709.00	$1,785.50
	Fireplace form, 44" wide by 40" deep by 27" high, open three sides ***Replace*** Materials...1740.00 Labor.........139.00 ***Remove*** .... Labor...........76.50	ea	$76.50	$1,879.00	$1,955.50
Fireplace ▸ furnace *Also called masonry heaters.*	**Fireplace furnace** ***Replace*** Materials..4630.00 Labor.......1590.00 ***Remove*** .... Labor.........106.00 ▸ Complete fireplace furnace including two air ducts with automatic dampers, outside air supply, heat exchanger, supply and outlet ducts connected to furnace ducts.	ea	$106.00	$6,220.00	$6,326.00
Fire brick ▸ *Installation of fire brick with fire clay only, no surrounding masonry.*	**Fire brick (complete fireplace)** ***Replace*** Materials.....123.00 Labor.........139.00 ***Remove*** .... Labor...........26.20	ea	$26.20	$262.00	$288.20
	Concrete simulated fire brick (complete fireplace) ***Replace*** Materials......92.50 Labor...........85.10 ***Remove*** .... Labor...........14.50 ▸ Three-piece unit stamped and colored to look like fire brick.	ea	$14.50	$177.60	$192.10
Fireplace ▸ chimney *All brick types. Add **14%** for rubble or ashlar stone. Does not include foundation.*	**16" by 16" fireplace chimney with one 8" x 8" flue** ***Replace*** Materials......32.70 Labor...........97.50 ***Remove*** .... Labor............9.52	lf	$9.52	$130.20	$139.72
	16" by 24" fireplace chimney with two 8" x 8" flues ***Replace*** Materials......43.10 Labor.........136.00 ***Remove*** .... Labor...........13.00	lf	$13.00	$179.10	$192.10
	16" by 20" fireplace chimney with one 8" x 12" flue ***Replace*** Materials......38.90 Labor...........98.80 ***Remove*** .... Labor............9.52	lf	$9.52	$137.70	$147.22
	20" by 24" fireplace chimney with two 8" x 12" flues ***Replace*** Materials......49.80 Labor.........139.00 ***Remove*** .... Labor...........13.00	lf	$13.00	$188.80	$201.80
	20" by 20" fireplace chimney with one 12" x 12" flue ***Replace*** Materials......41.20 Labor.........100.00 ***Remove*** .... Labor............9.52	lf	$9.52	$141.20	$150.72
	20" by 32" fireplace chimney with two 12" x 12" flues ***Replace*** Materials......57.00 Labor.........143.00 ***Remove*** .... Labor...........13.00	lf	$13.00	$200.00	$213.00
	20" by 24" fireplace chimney with one 12" x 16" flue ***Replace*** Materials......43.60 Labor.........102.00 ***Remove*** .... Labor............9.52	lf	$9.52	$145.60	$155.12
	20" by 40" fireplace chimney with two 12" x 16" flues ***Replace*** Materials......72.40 Labor.........146.00 ***Remove*** .... Labor...........13.00	lf	$13.00	$218.40	$231.40
	24" by 24" fireplace chimney with one 16" x 16" flue ***Replace*** Materials......45.90 Labor.........104.00 ***Remove*** .... Labor............9.52	lf	$9.52	$149.90	$159.42

Item Description	Unit	Remove	Replace	Total	
24" by 40" fireplace chimney with two 16" x 16" flues ***Replace*** Materials......81.80 Labor.........148.00 ***Remove*** .... Labor..........13.00	lf	$13.00	$229.80	$242.80	
Add for bend in fireplace chimney with one flue ***Replace*** Materials......21.50 Labor.........147.00	ea	—	$168.50	$168.50	◁ add for chimney bend
Add for bend in fireplace chimney with two flues ***Replace*** Materials......24.20 Labor.........179.00	ea	—	$203.20	$203.20	
Add 14% for stone facing on chimney					◁ add for stone face
Reline chimney using grout and inflatable tube method ***Replace*** Materials........5.70 Labor...........26.00	lf	—	$31.70	$31.70	◀ **RELINE CHIMNEY** *With a technique designed and licensed by Ahrens Chimney Technique.* 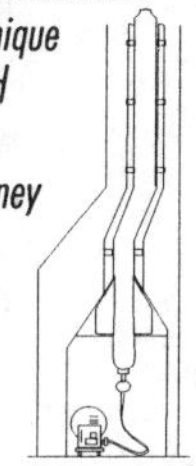
Add per bend in chimney when relining ***Replace*** Materials......16.90 Labor.........135.00	ea	—	$151.90	$151.90	
Minimum charge to reline chimney ***Replace*** Materials.....34.00 Labor........205.00	ea	—	$239.00	$239.00	
2" concrete single-flue chimney cap ***Replace*** Materials......14.90 Labor..........46.00 ***Remove*** .... Labor............8.33	ea	$8.33	$60.90	$69.23	◀ **CONCRETE CHIMNEY CAP**
2" concrete double-flue chimney cap ***Replace*** Materials......23.70 Labor..........68.50 ***Remove*** .... Labor............9.96	ea	$9.96	$92.20	$102.16	
Cast stone molded chimney cap, standard grade ***Replace*** Materials.....142.00 Labor..........58.90 ***Remove*** .... Labor............9.96 ► With simple pattern moldings on edge.	ea	$9.96	$200.90	$210.86	◀ **CAST STONE CHIMNEY CAP** *Manufactured cast stone cap with decorative patterns.*
Cast stone molded chimney cap, high grade ***Replace*** Materials.....169.00 Labor..........58.90 ***Remove*** .... Labor............9.96 ► With complex pattern moldings on edge.	ea	$9.96	$227.90	$237.86	
Cast stone molded chimney cap, deluxe grade ***Replace*** Materials....224.00 Labor..........58.90 ***Remove*** .... Labor............9.96 ► With very complex moldings on edge or with curved elements.	ea	$9.96	$282.90	$292.86	
Galvanized steel chimney cap ***Replace*** Materials......114.00 Labor...........12.50 ***Remove*** .... Labor............4.87 ► For use on metal or masonry flues, with spark arrestor.	ea	$4.87	$126.50	$131.37	◀ **STEEL CHIMNEY CAP**
Remove steel chimney cap for work, then reinstall ***Replace*** .... Labor...........21.00	ea	—	$21.00	$21.00	
Chimney pot, standard grade ***Replace*** Materials....183.00 Labor..........54.30 ***Remove*** .... Labor...........12.90 ► No designs on pot or arched design over flue.	ea	$12.90	$237.30	$250.20	◀ **CHIMNEY POT** 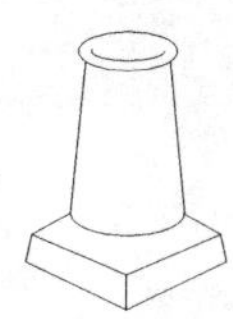
Chimney pot, high grade ***Replace*** Materials....268.00 Labor..........54.30 ***Remove*** .... Labor...........12.90 ► Simple designs on pot.	ea	$12.90	$322.30	$335.20	△ *standard*

CHIMNEY POT ▶ *continued*

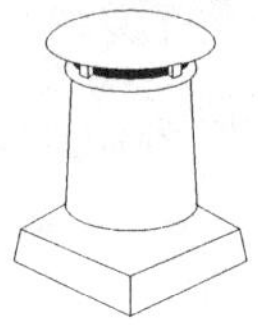

△ *high*

custom deluxe ▽

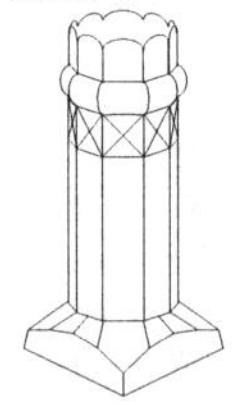

	Item Description	Unit	Remove	Replace	Total
CHIMNEY POT ▶ *continued*	**Chimney pot, deluxe grade** *Replace* Materials....335.00 Labor..........54.30 *Remove* .... Labor...........12.90 ▶ Ornate designs on pot and ornate pattern around top edge.	ea	$12.90	$389.30	$402.20
	Chimney pot, custom grade *Replace* Materials.....414.00 Labor..........54.30 *Remove* .... Labor...........12.90 ▶ Ornate designs on pot and ornate pattern around top edge with molded bands around pot.	ea	$12.90	$468.30	$481.20
	Chimney pot, custom deluxe grade *Replace* Materials....526.00 Labor..........54.30 *Remove* .... Labor...........12.90 ▶ Ornate designs on pot and ornate pattern around top edge with molded bands around pot. Octagonal or other specialty shape.	ea	$12.90	$580.30	$593.20
	Remove chimney pot for work, then reinstall *Replace* .... Labor..........93.80	ea	—	$93.80	$93.80
CHIMNEY SCREEN ▶	**Chimney bird screen for single flue chimney** *Replace* Materials......44.00 Labor...........18.40	ea	—	$62.40	$62.40
	Chimney bird screen for double flue chimney *Replace* Materials......54.00 Labor..........20.00	ea	—	$74.00	$74.00
FIREPLACE GRATE ▶	**Fireplace grate, 22″ x 16″** *Replace* Materials......45.00 Labor............5.01 *Remove* .... Labor............. .83	ea	$.83	$50.01	$50.84
	Fireplace grate, 28″ x 16″ *Replace* Materials......58.00 Labor............5.01 *Remove* .... Labor............. .83	ea	$.83	$63.01	$63.84
	Fireplace grate, 32″ x 16″ *Replace* Materials......65.00 Labor............5.01 *Remove* .... Labor............. .83	ea	$.83	$70.01	$70.84
	Fireplace grate, 38″ x 16″ *Replace* Materials......74.00 Labor............5.01 *Remove* .... Labor............. .83	ea	$.83	$79.01	$79.84
	Fireplace grate, 38″ x 20″ *Replace* Materials......79.00 Labor............5.01 *Remove* .... Labor............. .83	ea	$.83	$84.01	$84.84
	Fireplace grate, 32″ x 28″ *Replace* Materials......86.00 Labor............5.01 *Remove* .... Labor............. .83	ea	$.83	$91.01	$91.84
	Fireplace grate, 36″ x 28″ *Replace* Materials......91.00 Labor............5.01 *Remove* .... Labor............. .83	ea	$.83	$96.01	$96.84
	Fireplace grate, 40″ x 28″ *Replace* Materials......95.00 Labor............5.01 *Remove* .... Labor............. .83	ea	$.83	$100.01	$100.84
	Fireplace grate, 36″ x 32″ *Replace* Materials......99.00 Labor............5.01 *Remove* .... Labor............. .83	ea	$.83	$104.01	$104.84

Item Description	Unit	Remove	Replace	Total
Fireplace grate, 36" x 36" ***Replace*** Materials.....111.00 Labor............5.01 ***Remove*** .... Labor............ .83	ea	$.83	$116.01	$116.84
Fireplace grate, 44" x 40" ***Replace*** Materials.....151.00 Labor............5.01 ***Remove*** .... Labor............ .83	ea	$.83	$156.01	$156.84
Remove fireplace grate for work, then reinstall ***Replace*** .... Labor............6.19	ea	—	$6.19	$6.19
Fireplace screen, standard grade ***Replace*** Materials......99.00 Labor..........33.40 ***Remove*** .... Labor............5.09 ► Plain black with no trim.	ea	$5.09	$132.40	$137.49
Fireplace screen, high grade ***Replace*** Materials.....152.00 Labor..........33.40 ***Remove*** .... Labor............5.09 ► Plain black with brass or similar trim at top.	ea	$5.09	$185.40	$190.49
Fireplace screen, deluxe grade ***Replace*** Materials....207.00 Labor..........33.40 ***Remove*** .... Labor............5.09 ► Brass screen with brass or similar trim at top.	ea	$5.09	$240.40	$245.49
Remove fireplace screen for work, then reinstall ***Replace*** .... Labor..........50.10	ea	—	$50.10	$50.10
Fireplace door, standard grade ***Replace*** Materials.....169.00 Labor...........42.10 ***Remove*** .... Labor............6.96 ► Plain black.	ea	$6.96	$211.10	$218.06
Fireplace door, high grade ***Replace*** Materials....259.00 Labor...........42.10 ***Remove*** .... Labor............6.96 ► Brass face.	ea	$6.96	$301.10	$308.06
Fireplace door, deluxe grade ***Replace*** Materials....335.00 Labor...........42.10 ***Remove*** .... Labor............6.96 ► Brass face with designs.	ea	$6.96	$377.10	$384.06
Fireplace door, custom grade ***Replace*** Materials....445.00 Labor...........42.10 ***Remove*** .... Labor............6.96 ► Brass face with designs and specialty "clear view" glass.	ea	$6.96	$487.10	$494.06
Remove fireplace door for work, then reinstall ***Replace*** .... Labor...........65.70	ea	—	$65.70	$65.70
8" x 8" fireplace clean-out door ***Replace*** Materials.......19.00 Labor..........28.80 ***Remove*** .... Labor............1.90	ea	$1.90	$47.80	$49.70
12" x 12" fireplace clean-out door ***Replace*** Materials......39.00 Labor..........28.80 ***Remove*** .... Labor............1.90	ea	$1.90	$67.80	$69.70

RELATED ITEMS

◄ **FIREPLACE SCREEN**

◄ **FIREPLACE DOOR**

◄ **FIREPLACE CLEAN-OUT DOOR**
Cast iron door and jamb.

	Item Description	Unit	Remove	Replace	Total
FIREPLACE ► CLEAN-OUT DOOR *continued*	**18" x 24" fireplace clean-out door** *Replace* Materials.....117.00 Labor..........28.80 *Remove* .... Labor............1.90	ea	$1.90	$145.80	$147.70
	Salvage fireplace clean-out door, then reinstall *Replace* .... Labor..........44.70	ea	—	$44.70	$44.70
DAMPER ►	**Rotary control damper for 30" wide fireplace** *Replace* Materials......79.00 Labor...........51.10	ea	—	$130.10	$130.10
	Rotary control damper for 36" wide fireplace *Replace* Materials......85.00 Labor...........51.10	ea	—	$136.10	$136.10
	Rotary control for 40" wide fireplace *Replace* Materials....104.00 Labor...........51.10	ea	—	$155.10	$155.10
	Rotary control damper for 48" wide fireplace *Replace* Materials.....123.00 Labor...........51.10	ea	—	$174.10	$174.10
	Poker control damper for 30" wide fireplace *Replace* Materials......62.00 Labor...........41.40	ea	—	$103.40	$103.40
	Poker control damper for 36" wide fireplace *Replace* Materials......66.00 Labor...........41.40	ea	—	$107.40	$107.40
	Poker control damper for 40" wide fireplace *Replace* Materials......81.00 Labor...........41.40	ea	—	$122.40	$122.40
	Poker control damper for 48" wide fireplace *Replace* Materials......96.00 Labor...........41.40	ea	—	$137.40	$137.40
DOUBLE WALL ► CHIMNEY PIPE *stainless steel*	**8" diameter double wall chimney pipe** *Replace* Materials......26.00 Labor...........24.30 *Remove* .... Labor............. .58	lf	$.58	$50.30	$50.88
	10" diameter double wall chimney pipe *Replace* Materials......37.00 Labor...........24.30 *Remove* .... Labor............. .58	lf	$.58	$61.30	$61.88
	12" diameter double wall chimney pipe *Replace* Materials......49.00 Labor...........24.30 *Remove* .... Labor............. .58	lf	$.58	$73.30	$73.88
	14" diameter double wall chimney pipe *Replace* Materials.......61.00 Labor...........24.30 *Remove* .... Labor............. .58	lf	$.58	$85.30	$85.88
TRIPLE WALL ► CHIMNEY PIPE *stainless steel*	**8" diameter triple wall chimney pipe** *Replace* Materials......33.00 Labor...........24.30 *Remove* .... Labor............. .58	lf	$.58	$57.30	$57.88
	10" diameter triple wall chimney pipe *Replace* Materials......48.00 Labor...........24.30 *Remove* .... Labor............. .58	lf	$.58	$72.30	$72.88
	12" diameter triple wall chimney pipe *Replace* Materials......63.00 Labor...........24.30 *Remove* .... Labor............. .58	lf	$.58	$87.30	$87.88

Item Description	Unit	Remove	Replace	Total
14" diameter triple wall chimney pipe ***Replace*** Materials......78.00 Labor...........24.30 ***Remove*** .... Labor............. .58	lf	$.58	$102.30	$102.88
Add for chimney pipe through interior ceiling ***Replace*** Materials......46.00 Labor..........46.70 ► Kit to run chimney pipe through interior drywall or plaster ceiling. Includes bracket that allows for 2" clearance.	ea	—	$92.70	$92.70
Add for chimney pipe through roof ***Replace*** Materials....129.00 Labor.........124.00 ► Kit to run chimney pipe through roof. Includes bracket, boots, and so forth.	ea	—	$253.00	$253.00
Remove chimney pipe for work, then reinstall ***Replace*** .... Labor...........37.30	lf	—	$37.30	$37.30
Gas log lighter ***Replace*** Materials......88.00 Labor...........49.70 ***Remove*** .... Labor............6.24 ► Log lighter, valve, key and up to 24 lf copper gas piping.	ea	$6.24	$137.70	$143.94
Remove gas log lighter for work, then reinstall ***Replace*** .... Labor..........82.50	ea	—	$82.50	$82.50
Gas fireplace kit ***Replace*** Materials....535.00 Labor...........52.60 ***Remove*** .... Labor............6.90 ► Burners, fake logs, valve, key and up to 24 lf copper gas piping.	ea	$6.90	$587.60	$594.50
Remove gas fireplace kit for work, then reinstall ***Replace*** .... Labor..........89.70	ea	—	$89.70	$89.70
Marble fireplace face, economy grade ***Replace*** Materials......88.00 Labor.........164.00 ***Remove*** .... Labor...........45.70 ► Marble tiles laid around inside of mantel.	ea	$45.70	$252.00	$297.70
Marble fireplace face, standard grade ***Replace*** Materials....268.00 Labor.........351.00 ***Remove*** .... Labor..........83.30 ► From single or large pieces up to 5' tall and 4' wide, polished or natural finish.	ea	$83.30	$619.00	$702.30
Marble fireplace face, high grade ***Replace*** Materials....437.00 Labor.........359.00 ***Remove*** .... Labor..........83.30 ► From single pieces or large pieces up to 5' tall and 4' wide, polished or natural finish with simple designs around opening and at corner (cove or similar). Or same as standard grade up to 8' tall and 6' wide.	ea	$83.30	$796.00	$879.30
Marble fireplace face, deluxe grade ***Replace*** Materials....651.00 Labor........368.00 ***Remove*** .... Labor..........83.30 ► From single pieces or large pieces up to 5' tall and 4' wide, polished or natural finish with ornate designs around opening and at corner (crown or similar). Or same as high grade up to 8' tall and 6' wide.	ea	$83.30	$1,019.00	$1,102.30
Brick fireplace face, economy grade ***Replace*** Materials.....247.00 Labor.........741.00 ***Remove*** .... Labor..........88.80 ► Brick face in stacked or running bond, up to 5' tall and 5' wide.	ea	$88.80	$988.00	$1,076.80

◄ **ADDITIONAL CHIMNEY PIPE COSTS**

◄ **GAS LOG LIGHTER**

◄ **GAS FIREPLACE**

◄ **MARBLE FIREPLACE FACE**

◄ **BRICK FIREPLACE FACE**

RELATED ITEMS

Cleaning
fireplaces........................62
masonry.........................63
Finish Carpentry
mantel beam, mantel.......224
Masonry..........................287
Painting...........................339
Rough Carpentry
chimney cricket............444

Item Description	Unit	Remove	Replace	Total
BRICK ▶ FIREPLACE FACE *continued*				
Brick fireplace face, standard grade ***Replace*** Materials....275.00 Labor........938.00 ***Remove*** .... Labor..........88.80 ▶ Brick face in specialty bond (see *Masonry,* page 297), up to 5' tall and 5' wide. May include built-in shelf brackets, or small patterns in face. Or same as economy up to 8' tall and 6' wide.	ea	$88.80	$1,213.00	$1,301.80
Brick fireplace face, high grade ***Replace*** Materials....333.00 Labor........1150.00 ***Remove*** .... Labor..........88.80 ▶ Brick face in specialty bond (see *Masonry,* page 297), up to 5' tall and 5' wide. With arch over opening. May include built-in shelf brackets, or small patterns in face. Or same as standard up to 8' tall and 6' wide. Or same as economy up to 11' tall and 7' wide.	ea	$88.80	$1,483.00	$1,571.80
Brick fireplace face, deluxe grade ***Replace*** Materials....404.00 Labor.......1490.00 ***Remove*** .... Labor..........88.80 ▶ Brick face in specialty bond like herringbone or basket weave mixed with other patterns (see *Masonry,* page 297), up to 5' tall and 5' wide. May have arched openings or curving sides. Or same as high up to 8' tall and 6' wide. Or same as standard up to 11' tall and 7' wide. Or same as economy up to 15' tall and 10' wide.	ea	$88.80	$1,894.00	$1,982.80
RUBBLE STONE ▶ FIREPLACE FACE				
Rubble stone fireplace face, economy grade ***Replace*** Materials....421.00 Labor........805.00 ***Remove*** .... Labor...........94.90 ▶ Up to 5' tall and 5' wide, with flagstone or equivalent stone.	ea	$94.90	$1,226.00	$1,320.90
Rubble stone fireplace face, standard grade ***Replace*** Materials....468.00 Labor.......1020.00 ***Remove*** .... Labor...........94.90 ▶ Up to 5' tall and 5' wide, with sandstone, limestone, or similar stone. Or same as economy up to 8' tall and 6' wide.	ea	$94.90	$1,488.00	$1,582.90
Rubble stone fireplace face, high grade ***Replace*** Materials....567.00 Labor.......1240.00 ***Remove*** .... Labor...........94.90 ▶ Up to 5' tall and 5' wide, with specialty high priced stones or stones with high priced finishes. Or same as standard up to 8' tall and 6' wide. Or same as economy up to 10' tall and 7' wide.	ea	$94.90	$1,807.00	$1,901.90
Rubble stone fireplace face, deluxe grade ***Replace*** Materials....687.00 Labor.......1590.00 ***Remove*** .... Labor...........94.90 ▶ Up to 5' tall and 5' wide, with specialty high priced stones or stones with high priced finishes. With arch over opening or other specialty compartments or designs. Or same as high up to 8' tall and 6' wide. Or same as standard up to 11' tall and 7' wide. Or same as economy up to 14' tall and 8' wide.	ea	$94.90	$2,277.00	$2,371.90
ASHLAR STONE ▶ FIREPLACE FACE				
Ashlar stone fireplace face, economy grade ***Replace*** Materials.....491.00 Labor.........791.00 ***Remove*** .... Labor...........94.90 ▶ Up to 5' tall and 5' wide, with lowest priced stone for your area.	ea	$94.90	$1,282.00	$1,376.90
Ashlar stone fireplace face, standard grade ***Replace*** Materials....546.00 Labor.........998.00 ***Remove*** .... Labor...........94.90 ▶ Up to 5' tall and 5' wide, with sandstone, limestone, or similar stone. Or same as economy up to 8' tall and 6' wide	ea	$94.90	$1,544.00	$1,638.90

Item Description	Unit	Remove	Replace	Total
Ashlar stone fireplace face, high grade ***Replace*** Materials....662.00 Labor........1210.00 ***Remove*** .... Labor..........94.90 ► Up to 5' tall and 5' wide, with specialty high priced stones or stones with high priced finishes. Or same as standard up to 8' tall and 6' wide. Or same as economy up to 10' tall and 7' wide.	ea	$94.90	$1,872.00	$1,966.90
Ashlar stone fireplace face, deluxe grade ***Replace*** Materials....802.00 Labor.......1530.00 ***Remove*** .... Labor..........94.90 ► Up to 5' tall and 5' wide, with specialty high priced stones or stones with high priced finishes. With arch over opening or other specialty compartments or designs. Or same as high up to 8' tall and 6' wide. Or same as standard up to 11' tall and 7' wide. Or same as economy up to 14' tall and 8' wide.	ea	$94.90	$2,332.00	$2,426.90
Tile fireplace face, economy grade ***Replace*** Materials......69.00 Labor.........170.00 ***Remove*** .... Labor..........50.10 ► Standard priced tiles laid around inside of mantel.	ea	$50.10	$239.00	$289.10
Tile fireplace face, standard grade ***Replace*** Materials.....141.00 Labor.........365.00 ***Remove*** .... Labor..........80.90 ► High priced tiles laid around inside of mantel.	ea	$80.90	$506.00	$586.90
Tile fireplace face, high grade ***Replace*** Materials....184.00 Labor.........371.00 ***Remove*** .... Labor..........80.90 ► Specialty antique tiles laid around inside of mantel. Including designer hand-painted designs and raised pattern designs. May include tiles in fireback.	ea	$80.90	$555.00	$635.90
Tile fireplace face, deluxe grade ***Replace*** Materials....393.00 Labor........380.00 ***Remove*** .... Labor..........80.90 ► Same as high with specialty trim pieces and patterns that match antique Victorian styles.	ea	$80.90	$773.00	$853.90
Marble fireplace hearth, economy grade ***Replace*** Materials.....133.00 Labor..........99.40 ***Remove*** .... Labor...........21.30	ea	$21.30	$232.40	$253.70
Marble fireplace hearth, standard grade ***Replace*** Materials.....192.00 Labor.........212.00 ***Remove*** .... Labor..........39.90	ea	$39.90	$404.00	$443.90
Marble fireplace hearth, high grade ***Replace*** Materials.....314.00 Labor.........217.00 ***Remove*** .... Labor..........39.90	ea	$39.90	$531.00	$570.90
Marble fireplace hearth, deluxe grade ***Replace*** Materials....467.00 Labor........222.00 ***Remove*** .... Labor..........39.90	ea	$39.90	$689.00	$728.90
Brick fireplace hearth, economy grade ***Replace*** Materials.....165.00 Labor.........324.00 ***Remove*** .... Labor...........41.80	ea	$41.80	$489.00	$530.80
Brick fireplace hearth, standard grade ***Replace*** Materials....183.00 Labor.........407.00 ***Remove*** .... Labor...........41.80	ea	$41.80	$590.00	$631.80

RELATED ITEMS

Cleaning
fireplaces........................62
masonry..........................63
Finish Carpentry
mantel beam, mantel.......224
Masonry..........................287
Painting..........................339
Rough Carpentry
chimney cricket.............444

◄ **TILE FIREPLACE FACE**

◄ **MARBLE HEARTH**
Economy grade is flat hearth. All other grades are raised hearths. See marble fireplace face items for more information about quality.

◄ **BRICK HEARTH**
Economy grade is flat hearth. All other grades are raised hearths. See brick fireplace face items for more information about quality.

	Item Description	Unit	Remove	Replace	Total
BRICK HEARTH ▶ *continued*	**Brick fireplace hearth, high grade** *Replace* Materials....222.00 Labor........434.00 *Remove* .... Labor...........41.80	ea	$41.80	$656.00	$697.80
	Brick fireplace hearth, deluxe grade *Replace* Materials.....269.00 Labor.........511.00 *Remove* .... Labor...........41.80	ea	$41.80	$780.00	$821.80
RUBBLE STONE HEARTH ▶ *Economy grade is flat hearth. All other grades are raised hearths. See rubble stone fireplace face items for more information about quality.*	**Rubble stone fireplace hearth, economy grade** *Replace* Materials....281.00 Labor.........351.00 *Remove* .... Labor...........42.90	ea	$42.90	$632.00	$674.90
	Rubble stone fireplace hearth, standard grade *Replace* Materials.....312.00 Labor........443.00 *Remove* .... Labor...........42.90	ea	$42.90	$755.00	$797.90
	Rubble stone fireplace hearth, high grade *Replace* Materials....378.00 Labor.........469.00 *Remove* .... Labor...........42.90	ea	$42.90	$847.00	$889.90
	Rubble stone fireplace hearth, deluxe grade *Replace* Materials....458.00 Labor.........552.00 *Remove* .... Labor...........42.90	ea	$42.90	$1,010.00	$1,052.90
ASHLAR STONE HEARTH ▶ *Economy grade is flat hearth. All other grades are raised hearths. See ashlar stone fireplace face items for more information about quality.*	**Ashlar stone fireplace hearth, economy grade** *Replace* Materials....327.00 Labor........343.00 *Remove* .... Labor...........42.90	ea	$42.90	$670.00	$712.90
	Ashlar stone fireplace hearth, standard grade *Replace* Materials....364.00 Labor........434.00 *Remove* .... Labor...........42.90	ea	$42.90	$798.00	$840.90
	Ashlar stone fireplace hearth, high grade *Replace* Materials....441.00 Labor........460.00 *Remove* .... Labor...........42.90	ea	$42.90	$901.00	$943.90
	Ashlar stone fireplace hearth, deluxe grade *Replace* Materials....534.00 Labor........543.00 *Remove* .... Labor...........42.90	ea	$42.90	$1,077.00	$1,119.90
TILE HEARTH ▶ *Economy grade is flat hearth. All other grades are raised hearths. See tile fireplace face items for more information about quality.*	**Tile fireplace hearth economy grade** *Replace* Materials....104.00 Labor.........103.00 *Remove* .... Labor...........24.10	ea	$24.10	$207.00	$231.10
	Tile fireplace hearth standard grade *Replace* Materials.....141.00 Labor........220.00 *Remove* .... Labor..........39.30	ea	$39.30	$361.00	$400.30
	Tile fireplace hearth high grade *Replace* Materials....184.00 Labor.........224.00 *Remove* .... Labor..........39.30	ea	$39.30	$408.00	$447.30
	Tile fireplace hearth deluxe grade *Replace* Materials....393.00 Labor........230.00 *Remove* .... Labor..........39.30	ea	$39.30	$623.00	$662.30

NOTES:

end

TIME & MATERIAL CHARTS *(selected items)*

Fireplaces Materials *(Also see material prices with the line items and other information in the **QuickFinder** column.)*

DESCRIPTION	UNIT PRICE
Fireplace	
30″ wide by 16″ deep by 29″ high, open front	$386.00 *ea*
32″ wide by 16″ deep by 26″ high, open front and one side	$362.00 *ea*
32″ wide by 28″ deep by 29″ high, open two sides	$354.00 *ea*
36″ wide by 32″ deep by 27″ high, open two faces and one side	$433.00 *ea*
Prefabricated fireplace	
30″ wide by 16″ deep by 29″ high, open front	$437.00 *ea*
32″ wide by 16″ deep by 26″ high, open front and one side	$732.00 *ea*
32″ wide by 28″ deep by 29″ high, open two faces ("see through")	$894.00 *ea*
36″ wide by 32″ deep by 27″ high, open two faces and one side	$1,050.00 *ea*
Fireplace form	
30″ wide by 16″ deep by 29″ high, open front	$503.00 *ea*
32″ wide by 16″ deep by 26″ high, open front and one side	$933.00 *ea*
32″ wide by 28″ deep by 29″ high, open two faces ("see through")	$1,130.00 *ea*
36″ wide by 32″ deep by 27″ high, open two faces and one side	$1,390.00 *ea*
Fireplace chimney	
16″ by 16″ with one 8″ x 8″ flue	$32.70 *lf*
16″ by 24″ with two 8″ x 8″ flues	$43.10 *lf*
20″ by 32″ with two 12″ x 12″ flues	$57.00 *lf*
20″ by 40″ with two 12″ x 16″ flues	$72.40 *lf*
24″ by 40″ with two 16″ x 16″ flues	$81.80 *lf*
Fireplace face	
marble	
economy grade	$88.00 *ea*
deluxe grade	$651.00 *ea*
brick	
economy grade	$247.00 *ea*
deluxe grade	$404.00 *ea*
rubble stone	
economy grade	$421.00 *ea*
deluxe grade	$687.00 *ea*
ashlar stone	
economy grade	$491.00 *ea*
deluxe grade	$802.00 *ea*
tile	
economy grade	$69.00 *ea*
deluxe grade	$393.00 *ea*
Fireplace hearth	
marble	
economy grade	$133.00 *ea*
deluxe grade	$467.00 *ea*
brick	
economy grade	$165.00 *ea*
deluxe grade	$269.00 *ea*
rubble stone	
economy grade	$281.00 *ea*
deluxe grade	$458.00 *ea*
ashlar stone	
economy grade	$327.00 *ea*
deluxe grade	$534.00 *ea*
tile	
economy grade	$104.00 *ea*
deluxe grade	$393.00 *ea*

Fireplaces Labor

LABORER	BASE WAGE	PAID LEAVE	TRUE WAGE	FICA	FUTA	WORKER'S COMP.	UNEMPLOY. INSUR.	HEALTH INSUR.	RETIRE (401K)	LIABILITY INSUR.	COST PER HOUR
Mason	$24.40	1.90	$26.30	2.01	.21	8.15	2.29	2.69	.79	3.55	$46.00
Mason's helper	$22.20	1.73	$23.93	1.83	.19	7.42	2.08	2.69	.72	3.23	$42.10
Demolition laborer	$13.90	1.08	$14.98	1.15	.12	4.79	1.30	2.69	.45	2.02	$27.50

Paid Leave is calculated based on two weeks paid vacation, one week sick leave, and seven paid holidays. Employer's matching portion of **FICA** is 7.65 percent. **FUTA** (Federal Unemployment) is .8 percent. **Worker's compensation** for the masonry (fireplaces) trade was calculated using a national average of 30.99 percent. **Unemployment insurance** was calculated using a national average of 8.7 percent. **Health insurance** was calculated based on a projected national average for 2002 of $535 per employee (and family when applicable) per month. Employer pays 80 percent for a per month cost of $428 per employee. **Retirement** is based on a 401(k) retirement program with employer matching of 50 percent. Employee contributions to the 401(k) plan are an average of 6 percent of the true wage. **Liability insurance** is based on a national average of 13.2 percent.

Fireplaces Labor Productivity

WORK DESCRIPTION	LABORER	COST PER HOUR	PRODUCTIVITY	UNIT PRICE
Demolition				
remove fireplace	demolition laborer	$27.50	3.85	$106.00 ea
remove prefabricated fireplace	demolition laborer	$27.50	2.44	$67.10 ea
remove fire brick	demolition laborer	$27.50	.952	$26.20 ea
remove concrete simulated firebrick	demolition laborer	$27.50	.529	$14.50 ea
remove fireplace chimney with single flue	demolition laborer	$27.50	.346	$9.52 lf
remove fireplace chimney with double flue	demolition laborer	$27.50	.472	$13.00 lf
remove 2" concrete single flue chimney cap	demolition laborer	$27.50	.303	$8.33 ea
remove 2" concrete double flue chimney cap	demolition laborer	$27.50	.362	$9.96 ea
remove galvanized steel chimney cap	demolition laborer	$27.50	.177	$4.87 ea
remove chimney pot	demolition laborer	$27.50	.469	$12.90 ea
remove fireplace grate	demolition laborer	$27.50	.030	$.83 ea
remove fireplace screen	demolition laborer	$27.50	.185	$5.09 ea
remove fireplace door	demolition laborer	$27.50	.253	$6.96 ea
remove fireplace clean-out	demolition laborer	$27.50	.069	$1.90 ea
remove chimney pipe	demolition laborer	$27.50	.021	$.58 lf
remove gas log lighter	demolition laborer	$27.50	.227	$6.24 ea
remove gas fireplace kit	demolition laborer	$27.50	.251	$6.90 ea
remove marble fireplace face	demolition laborer	$27.50	3.03	$83.30 ea
remove brick fireplace face	demolition laborer	$27.50	3.23	$88.80 ea
remove stone fireplace face	demolition laborer	$27.50	3.45	$94.90 ea
remove tile fireplace face	demolition laborer	$27.50	2.94	$80.90 ea
remove marble fireplace hearth	demolition laborer	$27.50	1.45	$39.90 ea
remove brick fireplace hearth	demolition laborer	$27.50	1.52	$41.80 ea
remove stone fireplace hearth	demolition laborer	$27.50	1.56	$42.90 ea
remove tile fireplace hearth	demolition laborer	$27.50	1.43	$39.30 ea
Fireplace crew				
build fireplace	mason	$46.00		
build fireplace	mason's helper	$42.10		
build fireplace	**mason & helper**	**$44.10**		
Build fireplace				
open front				
30" wide by 16" deep by 29" high	mason	$46.00	16.1	$741.00 ea
36" wide by 16" deep by 29" high	mason	$46.00	16.9	$777.00 ea
40" wide by 16" deep by 29" high	mason	$46.00	17.5	$805.00 ea
48" wide by 18" deep by 32" high	mason	$46.00	18.5	$851.00 ea
open front and one side				
32" wide by 16" deep by 26" high	mason	$46.00	16.7	$768.00 ea
40" wide by 16" deep by 29" high	mason	$46.00	17.5	$805.00 ea
48" wide by 20" deep by 29" high	mason	$46.00	18.9	$869.00 ea

... More >

Fireplaces Labor Productivity *continued*

WORK DESCRIPTION	LABORER	COST PER HOUR	PRODUCTIVITY	UNIT PRICE
Build fireplace *continued*				
open two faces (see through)				
32" wide by 28" deep by 29" high	mason	$46.00	18.5	**$851.00** ea
36" wide by 28" deep by 29" high	mason	$46.00	18.9	**$869.00** ea
40" wide by 28" deep by 29" high	mason	$46.00	19.2	**$883.00** ea
open two faces and one side				
36" wide by 32" deep by 27" high	mason	$46.00	19.2	**$883.00** ea
36" wide by 36" deep by 27" high	mason	$46.00	20.0	**$920.00** ea
44" wide by 40" deep by 27" high	mason	$46.00	20.4	**$938.00** ea
Install prefabricated fireplace				
radiant	mason	$46.00	4.55	**$209.00** ea
convection	mason	$46.00	4.76	**$219.00** ea
forced-air	mason	$46.00	5.26	**$242.00** ea
Install fireplace form				
form	mason	$46.00	3.03	**$139.00** ea
Install fireplace furnace				
typical	mason	$46.00	34.5	**$1,590.00** ea
Install fire brick				
complete fireplace	mason	$46.00	3.03	**$139.00** ea
concrete simulated firebrick (complete fireplace)	mason	$46.00	1.85	**$85.10** ea
Build brick chimney				
16" by 16" with one 8" x 8" flue	mason & helper	$44.10	2.21	**$97.50** lf
16" by 24" with two 8" x 8" flues	mason & helper	$44.10	3.09	**$136.00** lf
16" by 20" with one 8" x 12" flue	mason & helper	$44.10	2.24	**$98.80** lf
20" by 24" with two 8" x 12" flues	mason & helper	$44.10	3.15	**$139.00** lf
20" by 20" with one 12" x 12" flue	mason & helper	$44.10	2.27	**$100.00** lf
20" by 32" with two 12" x 12" flues	mason & helper	$44.10	3.24	**$143.00** lf
20" by 24" with one 12" x 16" flue	mason & helper	$44.10	2.31	**$102.00** lf
20" by 40" with two 12" x 16" flues	mason & helper	$44.10	3.30	**$146.00** lf
24" by 24" with one 16" x 16" flue	mason & helper	$44.10	2.35	**$104.00** lf
24" by 40" with two 16" x 16" flues	mason & helper	$44.10	3.36	**$148.00** lf
add for bend in one flue	mason & helper	$44.10	3.33	**$147.00** ea
add for bend in two flues	mason & helper	$44.10	4.05	**$179.00** ea
Pour 2" thick concrete chimney cap				
single-flue	mason	$46.00	1.00	**$46.00** ea
double-flue	mason	$46.00	1.49	**$68.50** ea
Install cast stone chimney cap				
typical	mason	$46.00	1.28	**$58.90** ea
Install galvanized steel chimney cap				
with spark arrestor	mason's helper	$42.10	.298	**$12.50** ea
Install chimney pot				
typical	mason	$46.00	1.18	**$54.30** ea
Install chimney bird screen				
for single flue	mason's helper	$42.10	.437	**$18.40** ea
for double flue	mason's helper	$42.10	.476	**$20.00** ea
Install fireplace grate				
typical	mason's helper	$42.10	.119	**$5.01** ea
Install fireplace screen				
typical	mason's helper	$42.10	.794	**$33.40** ea
Install fireplace door				
typical	mason's helper	$42.10	1.00	**$42.10** ea
Install fireplace clean-out				
typical	mason	$46.00	.625	**$28.80** ea
Install fireplace damper				
rotary control	mason	$46.00	1.11	**$51.10** ea
poker control	mason	$46.00	.901	**$41.40** ea

. . . More >

Fireplaces Labor Productivity *continued*

WORK DESCRIPTION	LABORER	COST PER HOUR	PRODUCTIVITY	UNIT PRICE
Install chimney pipe				
typical	mason's helper	$42.10	.578	$24.30 lf
add through interior ceiling	mason's helper	$42.10	1.11	$46.70 ea
add through roof	mason's helper	$42.10	2.94	$124.00 ea
Install gas log lighter				
typical	mason's helper	$42.10	1.18	$49.70 ea
Install gas fireplace kit				
typical	mason's helper	$42.10	1.25	$52.60 ea
Install fireplace face				
marble				
economy grade	mason	$46.00	3.57	$164.00 ea
deluxe grade	mason	$46.00	8.00	$368.00 ea
brick				
economy grade	mason	$46.00	16.1	$741.00 ea
deluxe grade	mason	$46.00	32.3	$1,490.00 ea
rubble stone				
economy grade	mason	$46.00	17.5	$805.00 ea
deluxe grade	mason	$46.00	34.5	$1,590.00 ea
ashlar stone				
economy grade	mason	$46.00	17.2	$791.00 ea
deluxe grade	mason	$46.00	33.3	$1,530.00 ea
tile				
economy grade	mason	$46.00	3.70	$170.00 ea
deluxe grade	mason	$46.00	8.26	$380.00 ea
Install fireplace hearth				
marble				
economy grade	mason	$46.00	2.16	$99.40 ea
deluxe grade	mason	$46.00	4.83	$222.00 ea
brick				
economy grade	mason	$46.00	7.04	$324.00 ea
deluxe grade	mason	$46.00	11.1	$511.00 ea
rubble stone				
economy grade	mason	$46.00	7.63	$351.00 ea
deluxe grade	mason	$46.00	12.0	$552.00 ea
ashlar stone				
economy grade	mason	$46.00	7.46	$343.00 ea
deluxe grade	mason	$46.00	11.8	$543.00 ea
tile				
economy grade	mason	$46.00	2.24	$103.00 ea
deluxe grade	mason	$46.00	5.00	$230.00 ea

NOTES:

end

19 Flooring

Item Description	Unit	Remove	Replace	Total
Carpet, economy grade	sy	$1.71	$21.08	$22.79
Replace Materials......16.10 Labor............4.98				
Remove .... Labor............1.71				
Carpet, standard grade	sy	$1.71	$24.78	$26.49
Replace Materials.......19.80 Labor............4.98				
Remove .... Labor............1.71				
Carpet, high grade	sy	$1.71	$31.28	$32.99
Replace Materials......26.30 Labor............4.98				
Remove .... Labor............1.71				
Carpet, deluxe grade	sy	$1.71	$36.58	$38.29
Replace Materials......31.60 Labor............4.98				
Remove .... Labor............1.71				
Carpet, custom grade	sy	$1.71	$42.58	$44.29
Replace Materials......37.60 Labor............4.98				
Remove .... Labor............1.71				
Remove carpet for work, then re-lay	sy	—	$7.62	$7.62
Replace .... Labor............7.62				
Glue-down carpet, economy grade	sy	$4.26	$18.23	$22.49
Replace Materials......12.20 Labor............6.03				
Remove .... Labor............4.26				
Glue-down carpet, standard grade	sy	$4.26	$20.43	$24.69
Replace Materials......14.40 Labor............6.03				
Remove .... Labor............4.26				
Glue-down carpet, high grade	sy	$4.26	$25.03	$29.29
Replace Materials.......19.00 Labor............6.03				
Remove .... Labor............4.26				
Glue-down carpet, deluxe grade	sy	$4.26	$28.73	$32.99
Replace Materials......22.70 Labor............6.03				
Remove .... Labor............4.26				
Indoor-outdoor carpet, economy grade	sy	$4.21	$15.01	$19.22
Replace Materials........8.98 Labor............6.03				
Remove .... Labor............4.21				
Indoor-outdoor carpet, standard grade	sy	$4.21	$18.83	$23.04
Replace Materials......12.80 Labor............6.03				
Remove .... Labor............4.21				
Indoor-outdoor carpet, high grade	sy	$4.21	$25.13	$29.34
Replace Materials.......19.10 Labor............6.03				
Remove .... Labor............4.21				
Indoor-outdoor carpet, deluxe grade	sy	$4.21	$34.63	$38.84
Replace Materials......28.60 Labor............6.03				
Remove .... Labor............4.21				

◄ **CARPET**
Includes 12% waste. Carpet is available in virtually every price imaginable. These prices should be considered allowances for typical grades found in residential and light commercial structures. Top grades include wool carpets, pattern carpets, and 52 ounce cut pile carpets.

◄ **REMOVE CARPET AND RE-LAY**

◄ **GLUE-DOWN CARPET**
Includes 12% waste. These prices should be considered allowances for typical grades found in residential and light commercial structures.

◄ **INDOOR-OUTDOOR CARPET**
Includes 12% waste. These prices should be considered allowances for typical grades found in residential and light commercial structures. Economy grade is plastic grass.

RELATED ITEMS

Cleaning........................62

	Item Description	Unit	Remove	Replace	Total
WOOL CARPET ▶ *Includes 12% waste. These prices should be considered allowances for typical grades found in residential and light commercial structures. Standard and high grade may be used for simulated wool Berber style carpets.*	**Wool carpet, standard grade** ***Replace*** Materials......24.00 Labor............5.02 ***Remove*** .... Labor............1.71	sy	$1.71	$29.02	$30.73
	Wool carpet, high grade ***Replace*** Materials......30.20 Labor............5.02 ***Remove*** .... Labor............1.71	sy	$1.71	$35.22	$36.93
	Wool carpet, deluxe grade ***Replace*** Materials......39.90 Labor............5.02 ***Remove*** .... Labor............1.71	sy	$1.71	$44.92	$46.63
	Wool carpet, custom grade ***Replace*** Materials......50.20 Labor............5.02 ***Remove*** .... Labor............1.71	sy	$1.71	$55.22	$56.93
ADD FOR STAIRS ▶	**Add per step for carpet installation on stairs** ***Replace*** Materials........1.50 Labor............6.50	ea	—	$8.00	$8.00
CARPET PAD ▶	**Carpet pad, urethane rebound** ***Replace*** Materials........4.43 Labor............ .58 ***Remove*** .... Labor............ .83	sy	$.83	$5.01	$5.84
	Carpet pad, urethane ***Replace*** Materials........2.95 Labor............ .58 ***Remove*** .... Labor............ .83	sy	$.83	$3.53	$4.36
	Carpet pad, rubber waffle ***Replace*** Materials........3.41 Labor............ .58 ***Remove*** .... Labor............ .83	sy	$.83	$3.99	$4.82
	Carpet pad, jute ***Replace*** Materials........3.07 Labor............ .58 ***Remove*** .... Labor............ .83	sy	$.83	$3.65	$4.48
CARPET COVE ▶ *Carpet wrapped up the wall up to 8" high with metal cap. Grades refer to allowances for quality of carpet.*	**Add for carpet cove, economy grade** ***Replace*** Materials........1.93 Labor............4.87 ***Remove*** .... Labor............ .61	lf	$.61	$6.80	$7.41
	Add for carpet cove, standard grade ***Replace*** Materials........2.27 Labor............4.87 ***Remove*** .... Labor............ .61	lf	$.61	$7.14	$7.75
	Add for carpet cove, high grade ***Replace*** Materials........3.07 Labor............4.87 ***Remove*** .... Labor............ .61	lf	$.61	$7.94	$8.55
	Add for carpet cove, deluxe grade ***Replace*** Materials........3.75 Labor............4.87 ***Remove*** .... Labor............ .61	lf	$.61	$8.62	$9.23
	Add for carpet cove, custom grade ***Replace*** Materials........4.43 Labor............4.87 ***Remove*** .... Labor............ .61	lf	$.61	$9.30	$9.91
	Remove carpet cove for work, then re-lay ***Replace*** .... Labor............7.29	lf	—	$7.29	$7.29
CARPET TILE ▶ *Includes 12% waste. Commercial grades.*	**Carpet tile, economy grade** ***Replace*** Materials......26.40 Labor............3.86 ***Remove*** .... Labor............4.26	sy	$4.26	$30.26	$34.52

Item Description	Unit	Remove	Replace	Total
Carpet tile, standard grade ***Replace*** Materials......31.90 Labor............3.86 ***Remove*** .... Labor............4.26	sy	$4.26	$35.76	$40.02
Carpet tile, high grade ***Replace*** Materials......40.30 Labor............3.86 ***Remove*** .... Labor............4.26	sy	$4.26	$44.16	$48.42
Minimum charge for carpeting work ***Replace*** Materials......60.00 Labor..........36.10	ea	—	$96.10	$96.10
Stone floor, standard grade ***Replace*** Materials........5.94 Labor............6.90 ***Remove*** .... Labor............2.26	sf	$2.26	$12.84	$15.10
Stone floor, high grade ***Replace*** Materials........7.81 Labor............6.90 ***Remove*** .... Labor............2.26	sf	$2.26	$14.71	$16.97
Stone floor, deluxe grade ***Replace*** Materials........9.38 Labor............6.90 ***Remove*** .... Labor............2.26	sf	$2.26	$16.28	$18.54
Salvage stone floor, then reinstall ***Replace*** Materials........1.15 Labor..........18.10 ***Remove*** .... Labor............2.26 ► Usually only stone floors in grout bed built over wood framing are salvageable. Includes cost to selectively remove and re-lay.	sf	$2.26	$19.25	$21.51
Regrout stone floor ***Replace*** Materials........ .42 Labor............1.37 ► Regrouting only, for repointing see *Masonry* page 318.	sf	—	$1.79	$1.79
Minimum charge for stone floor work ***Replace*** .... Labor..........48.70	ea	—	$48.70	$48.70
Marble floor, standard grade ***Replace*** Materials........9.79 Labor............6.82 ***Remove*** .... Labor............2.20	sf	$2.20	$16.61	$18.81
Marble floor, high grade ***Replace*** Materials......20.80 Labor............6.82 ***Remove*** .... Labor............2.20	sf	$2.20	$27.62	$29.82
Marble floor, deluxe grade ***Replace*** Materials......32.20 Labor............6.82 ***Remove*** .... Labor............2.20	sf	$2.20	$39.02	$41.22
Regrout marble floor ***Replace*** Materials........ .42 Labor............1.23 ► Regrouting only, for repointing see *Masonry* page 318.	sf	—	$1.65	$1.65
Minimum charge for marble floor work ***Replace*** Materials......70.00 Labor..........48.70	ea	—	$118.70	$118.70
Slate floor, standard grade ***Replace*** Materials........7.71 Labor............6.82 ***Remove*** .... Labor............2.20	sf	$2.20	$14.53	$16.73

RELATED ITEMS

Cleaning........................62
"Stone Quality".........306

◁ **minimum carpeting**

◀ **STONE FLOOR**
Grades vary by region. Standard grade includes flagstone, Chattahoochee, and some sandstone. High grade includes better sandstone and lower to medium grade limestone. Deluxe grade includes higher grade limestone, sandstone and granite.

◁ **minimum stone floor**

◀ **MARBLE FLOOR**
Allowances for typical grades of marble used in residential and light commercial structures. See Masonry, pages 306-307 for more information about marble quality.

◁ **minimum marble floor**

◀ **SLATE FLOOR**
Allowances for typical grades of marble used in residential and light commercial structures.

	Item Description	Unit	Remove	Replace	Total
SLATE FLOOR ▸ *continued*	**Slate floor, high grade** ***Replace*** Materials.......9.58 Labor ....6.82 ***Remove*** .... Labor 2.20	sf	$2.20	$16.40	$18.60
	Slate floor, deluxe grade ***Replace*** Materials.......11.50 Labor ....6.82 ***Remove*** .... Labor 2.20	sf	$2.20	$18.32	$20.52
	Regrout slate floor ***Replace*** Materials .... .38 Labor ....1.23 ▸ Regrouting only, for repointing see *Masonry* page 318.	sf	—	$1.61	$1.61
	Salvage slate floor, then reinstall ***Replace*** Materials .... .71 Labor...........17.70 ▸ Usually only slate floors built in grout bed over wood framing are salvageable. Includes cost to selectively remove and re-lay.	sf	—	$18.41	$18.41
minimum slate floor ▹	**Minimum charge for slate floor work** ***Replace*** Materials......71.00 Labor 48.70	ea	—	$119.70	$119.70
TILE FLOOR ▸ *Allowances for typical grades of tile used in residential and light commercial structures.*	**Tile floor, standard grade** ***Replace*** Materials........5.00 Labor ....6.50 ***Remove*** .... Labor 2.20	sf	$2.20	$11.50	$13.70
	Tile floor, high grade ***Replace*** Materials........6.67 Labor ....6.50 ***Remove*** .... Labor 2.20	sf	$2.20	$13.17	$15.37
	Tile floor, deluxe grade ***Replace*** Materials........8.33 Labor ....6.50 ***Remove*** .... Labor 2.20	sf	$2.20	$14.83	$17.03
	Regrout tile floor ***Replace*** Materials .... .53 Labor ....1.26 ▸ Regrouting only, for repointing see *Masonry* page 318.	sf	—	$1.79	$1.79
minimum tile floor ▹	**Minimum charge for tile floor work** ***Replace*** Materials......60.00 Labor 48.70	ea	—	$108.70	$108.70
QUARRY ▸ TILE FLOOR *Allowances for typical grades of tile used in residential and light commercial structures.*	**Quarry tile floor, standard grade** ***Replace*** Materials........6.67 Labor ....5.16 ***Remove*** .... Labor 2.15	sf	$2.15	$11.83	$13.98
	Quarry tile floor, high grade ***Replace*** Materials........9.69 Labor ....5.16 ***Remove*** .... Labor 2.15	sf	$2.15	$14.85	$17.00
	Quarry tile floor, deluxe grade ***Replace*** Materials.......13.10 Labor ....5.16 ***Remove*** .... Labor 2.15	sf	$2.15	$18.26	$20.41
TILE BASE ▸ *Allowances for typical grades of tile used in residential and light commercial structures.*	**Tile base, standard grade** ***Replace*** Materials........4.27 Labor ....4.62 ***Remove*** .... Labor 1.68	lf	$1.68	$8.89	$10.57
	Tile base, high grade ***Replace*** Materials........5.73 Labor ....4.62 ***Remove*** .... Labor 1.68	lf	$1.68	$10.35	$12.03

Item Description	Unit	Remove	Replace	Total
Tile base, deluxe grade *Replace* Materials........7.08 Labor............4.62 *Remove* .... Labor............1.68	lf	$1.68	$11.70	$13.38
Precast terrazzo floor tiles, standard grade *Replace* Materials......12.40 Labor............4.19 *Remove* .... Labor............2.23	sf	$2.23	$16.59	$18.82
Precast terrazzo floor tiles, high grade *Replace* Materials......14.10 Labor............4.19 *Remove* .... Labor............2.23	sf	$2.23	$18.29	$20.52
Minimum charge for precast terrazzo floor work *Replace* Materials......60.00 Labor..........55.60	ea	—	$115.60	$115.60
6" high precast terrazzo base *Replace* Materials........8.44 Labor............9.24 *Remove* .... Labor............1.68	sf	$1.68	$17.68	$19.36
8" high precast terrazzo base *Replace* Materials........9.06 Labor............9.24 *Remove* .... Labor............1.68	sf	$1.68	$18.30	$19.98
Cast-in-place thinset terrazzo floor, standard grade *Replace* Materials........2.73 Labor............4.62 *Remove* .... Labor............2.26	sf	$2.26	$7.35	$9.61
Cast-in-place thinset terrazzo floor, high grade *Replace* Materials........3.98 Labor............4.62 *Remove* .... Labor............2.26	sf	$2.26	$8.60	$10.86
Minimum charge for cast-in-place terrazzo floor work *Replace* Materials......85.00 Labor........144.00	ea	—	$229.00	$229.00
Vinyl floor, economy grade *Replace* Materials......14.70 Labor............6.61 *Remove* .... Labor............4.81	sy	$4.81	$21.31	$26.12
Vinyl floor, standard grade *Replace* Materials.......19.30 Labor............6.61 *Remove* .... Labor............4.81	sy	$4.81	$25.91	$30.72
Vinyl floor, high grade *Replace* Materials......24.10 Labor............6.61 *Remove* .... Labor............4.81	sy	$4.81	$30.71	$35.52
Vinyl floor, deluxe grade *Replace* Materials......33.60 Labor............6.61 *Remove* .... Labor............4.81	sy	$4.81	$40.21	$45.02
Minimum charge for vinyl floor work *Replace* Materials......50.00 Labor..........36.10	ea	—	$86.10	$86.10
Vinyl tile floor, economy grade *Replace* Materials...... 1.02 Labor.......... 1.05 *Remove* .... Labor............ .66	sf	$.66	$2.07	$2.73
Vinyl tile floor, standard grade *Replace* Materials........1.59 Labor.......... 1.05 *Remove* .... Labor............ .66	sf	$.66	$2.64	$3.30

RELATED ITEMS

Cleaning........................62
"Stone Quality".........306

◀ **PRECAST TERRAZZO TILE**
Cast in gray cement. Add ***2%*** *for white cement. Tiles are 12" x 12". Standard grade is 1" thick, high grade is 1-1/4" thick*

◁ **minimum terrazzo floor**

◀ **PRECAST TERRAZZO BASE**
Cast in gray cement.

◀ **CAST-IN-PLACE TERRAZZO FLOOR**
Cast in gray cement with zinc divider strips. Add ***3%*** *for brass divider strips. Standard grade is 1-1/2" deep, high grade is up to 3" thick. Add* ***2%*** *for white cement.*

◀ **VINYL FLOOR**
Includes 12% waste. These prices should be considered allowances for typical grades found in residential and light commercial structures. Lower grades have smoother faces and are thinner. Higher grades are embossed, marbleized, and thicker vinyl.

◁ **minimum vinyl floor**

◀ **VINYL TILE FLOOR**
Includes 12% waste. These prices should be considered allowances for typical grades found in residential and light commercial structures. See vinyl floor above for general grade guidelines.

	Item Description	Unit	Remove	Replace	Total
VINYL TILE FLOOR ▶ *continued*	**Vinyl tile floor, high grade** ***Replace*** Materials........1.93 Labor........... 1.05 ***Remove*** .... Labor............. .66	sf	$.66	$2.98	$3.64
	Vinyl tile floor, deluxe grade ***Replace*** Materials........2.95 Labor........... 1.05 ***Remove*** .... Labor............. .66	sf	$.66	$4.00	$4.66
minimum vinyl tile floor ▷	**Minimum charge for vinyl tile floor work** ***Replace*** Materials......30.00 Labor..........36.10	ea	—	$66.10	$66.10
RESILIENT TILE FLOOR ▶ *Allowances for typical grades of resilient tile used in residential and light commercial structures.*	**Resilient tile floor, economy grade** ***Replace*** Materials........1.14 Labor........... 1.05 ***Remove*** .... Labor............. .66	sf	$.66	$2.19	$2.85
	Resilient tile floor, standard grade ***Replace*** Materials........1.36 Labor........... 1.05 ***Remove*** .... Labor............. .66	sf	$.66	$2.41	$3.07
	Resilient tile floor, high grade ***Replace*** Materials........1.70 Labor........... 1.05 ***Remove*** .... Labor............. .66	sf	$.66	$2.75	$3.41
	Resilient tile floor, deluxe grade ***Replace*** Materials........2.39 Labor........... 1.05 ***Remove*** .... Labor............. .66	sf	$.66	$3.44	$4.10
minimum resilient tile ▷	**Minimum charge for resilient tile floor work** ***Replace*** Materials......30.00 Labor..........36.10	ea	—	$66.10	$66.10
ANTIQUE STYLE LINOLEUM ▶ *Antique style linoleum is no longer made in the USA and must be imported from Europe. In recent years linoleum has become much more common in commercial and residential applications. Tiles are normally available in limited styles and colors.*	**Antique style linoleum, plain and marbleized** ***Replace*** Materials......33.60 Labor............6.82 ***Remove*** .... Labor............4.81	sy	$4.81	$40.42	$45.23
	Antique style linoleum, inlaid & molded ***Replace*** Materials......44.00 Labor............6.82 ***Remove*** .... Labor............4.81	sy	$4.81	$50.82	$55.63
	Antique style linoleum, battleship ***Replace*** Materials......30.70 Labor............6.82 ***Remove*** .... Labor............4.81	sy	$4.81	$37.52	$42.33
	Antique style linoleum tile ***Replace*** Materials........4.55 Labor............1.16 ***Remove*** .... Labor............4.81	sf	$4.81	$5.71	$10.52
minimum linoleum floor ▷	**Minimum charge for antique style linoleum floor work** ***Replace*** Materials......95.00 Labor...........55.60	ea	—	$150.60	$150.60
VINYL COVE ▶ *Vinyl wrapped up wall with metal cap. Grades refer to allowances for quality of vinyl.*	**4" high vinyl cove** ***Replace*** Materials........2.05 Labor............3.29 ***Remove*** .... Labor............. .99	lf	$.99	$5.34	$6.33
	6" high vinyl cove ***Replace*** Materials........2.16 Labor............3.29 ***Remove*** .... Labor............. .99	lf	$.99	$5.45	$6.44
	8" high vinyl cove ***Replace*** Materials........2.39 Labor............3.29 ***Remove*** .... Labor............. .99	lf	$.99	$5.68	$6.67

Item Description	Unit	Remove	Replace	Total
Minimum charge for vinyl cove work *Replace* Materials......25.00 Labor..........24.90	ea	—	$49.90	$49.90
Rubber base, economy grade *Replace* Materials........1.48 Labor............ .72 *Remove* .... Labor............ .30	lf	$.30	$2.20	$2.50
Rubber base, standard grade *Replace* Materials........1.82 Labor............ .72 *Remove* .... Labor............ .30	lf	$.30	$2.54	$2.84
Rubber base, high grade *Replace* Materials........2.50 Labor............ .72 *Remove* .... Labor............ .30	lf	$.30	$3.22	$3.52
Rubber base, deluxe grade *Replace* Materials........2.95 Labor............ .72 *Remove* .... Labor............ .30	lf	$.30	$3.67	$3.97
Minimum charge for rubber base work *Replace* Materials.......15.00 Labor..........15.70	ea	—	$30.70	$30.70
Maple strip flooring, first grade *Replace* Materials........7.34 Labor............3.18 *Remove* .... Labor............ .55 ► Face almost free of defects. (Variation in color is not a defect.)	sf	$.55	$10.52	$11.07
Maple strip flooring, second grade *Replace* Materials........5.74 Labor............3.18 *Remove* .... Labor............ .55 ► Small tight knots, slight dressing imperfections.	sf	$.55	$8.92	$9.47
Maple strip flooring, third grade *Replace* Materials........4.36 Labor............3.18 *Remove* .... Labor............ .55 ► Larger knots and imperfections that may cause waste.	sf	$.55	$7.54	$8.09
Red oak strip flooring, select & better grade *Replace* Materials........5.74 Labor............3.18 *Remove* .... Labor............ .55 ► At least 50% is clear grade. Clear grade face is practically clear, may have very small areas of bright sap. Select grade face may contain very small areas of burl, one small tight knot every 3 lf, pinworm holes and working imperfections.	sf	$.55	$8.92	$9.47
Red oak strip flooring, #1 common grade *Replace* Materials........4.79 Labor............3.18 *Remove* .... Labor............ .55 ► Same as select with larger and more common imperfections with some flags, heavy streaks, and checks.	sf	$.55	$7.97	$8.52
Red oak strip flooring, #2 common grade *Replace* Materials........3.40 Labor............3.18 *Remove* .... Labor............ .55 ► Many natural wood imperfections and milling flaws. Used in rustic or general utility applications.	sf	$.55	$6.58	$7.13
Red oak strip flooring, quartersawn, clear grade *Replace* Materials......10.10 Labor............3.18 *Remove* .... Labor............ .55 ► Face is practically clear, may have very small areas of bright sap.	sf	$.55	$13.28	$13.83

◁ **minimum vinyl cove**

◀ **RUBBER BASE**
Economy grade is black or brown 2-1/2" high. Standard grade is 4" high standard colors. High grade is 6" high. Deluxe grade is 6" high, specialty colors.

◁ **minimum rubber base**

◀ **MAPLE STRIP FLOORING**
Strip flooring is up to 3/4" thick and up to 3-1/4" wide. Grading information based on rules established by the Maple Flooring Manufacturers Association (MFMA). All wood is kiln-dried, tongue-and-groove, end-matched and hollow or scratch backed.

◀ **RED OAK STRIP FLOORING**
Strip flooring is up to 3/4" thick and up to 3-1/4" wide. Grading information based on rules established by the National Oak Flooring Manufacturers Association (NOFMA). All wood is kiln-dried, tongue-and-groove, end-matched and hollow or scratch backed.

RELATED ITEMS

Cleaning........................62
Painting......................340

◀ **QUARTERSAWN RED OAK STRIP FLOORING**
See grading information above for red oak strip flooring.

Item Description	Unit	Remove	Replace	Total
QUARTERSAWN RED OAK STRIP FLOORING *continued*				
Red oak strip flooring, quartersawn, select grade ***Replace*** Materials........8.40 Labor............3.18 ***Remove*** .... Labor............ .55 ► Face may contain very small areas of burl, one small tight knot every 3 lf, pinworm holes and working imperfections.	sf	$.55	$11.58	$12.13
PREFINISHED RED OAK STRIP FLOORING *Strip flooring is up to 3/4" thick and up to 3-1/4" wide. Grading information based on rules established by the National Oak Flooring Manufacturers Association (NOFMA). All wood is kiln-dried, tongue-and-groove, end-matched and hollow or scratch backed.*				
Prefinished red oak strip flooring, prime grade ***Replace*** Materials........6.49 Labor............3.29 ***Remove*** .... Labor............ .55 ► Almost flawless appearance with very small character marks. Sap and color variations are not flaws.	sf	$.55	$9.78	$10.33
Prefinished red oak strip flooring, standard & better grade ***Replace*** Materials........5.53 Labor............3.29 ***Remove*** .... Labor............ .55 ► Combination of standard and prime grade. See above for prime grade characteristics. Standard grade may contain filled flaws.	sf	$.55	$8.82	$9.37
Prefinished red oak strip flooring, standard grade ***Replace*** Materials........6.81 Labor............3.29 ***Remove*** .... Labor............ .55 ► May contain filled flaws.	sf	$.55	$10.10	$10.65
Prefinished red oak strip flooring, tavern & better grade ***Replace*** Materials........8.30 Labor............3.29 ***Remove*** .... Labor............ .55 ► Combination of standard and tavern grade. See above for standard grade characteristics. Tavern grade contains filled flaws and imperfections which produce rustic appearance.	sf	$.55	$11.59	$12.14
Prefinished red oak strip flooring, tavern grade ***Replace*** Materials......10.20 Labor............3.29 ***Remove*** .... Labor............ .55 ► Contains filled flaws and imperfections which produce rustic appearance.	sf	$.55	$13.49	$14.04
RED OAK PLANK FLOORING *Plank flooring is up to 3/4" thick and over 3-1/4" wide. Floors that contain a mix of plank and strip floor widths are usually considered plank floors. Grading information based on rules established by the National Oak Flooring Manufacturers Association (NOFMA). All wood is kiln-dried, tongue-and-groove, end-matched and hollow or scratch backed.*				
Red oak plank flooring, select & better grade ***Replace*** Materials........9.26 Labor............2.85 ***Remove*** .... Labor............ .52 ► At least 50% is clear grade. Clear grade face is practically clear, may have very small areas of bright sap. Select grade face may contain very small areas of burl, one small tight knot every 3 lf, pinworm holes and working imperfections.	sf	$.52	$12.11	$12.63
Red oak plank flooring, #1 common grade ***Replace*** Materials........7.66 Labor............2.85 ***Remove*** .... Labor............ .52 ► Same as select with larger and more common imperfections with some flags, heavy streaks, and checks.	sf	$.52	$10.51	$11.03
Red oak plank flooring, #2 common grade ***Replace*** Materials........5.43 Labor............2.85 ***Remove*** .... Labor............ .52 ► Same as select with larger and more common imperfections with some flags, heavy streaks, and checks.	sf	$.52	$8.28	$8.80
MAPLE PARQUET *Face pieces are practically clear, may have some small areas of bright sap. For select grade deduct **8%**. For #1 common grade deduct **15%**.*				
Maple parquet unit block flooring, clear grade ***Replace*** Materials........5.52 Labor............3.32 ***Remove*** .... Labor............ .50 ► Made from solid wood pieces glued side by side.	sf	$.50	$8.84	$9.34
Maple laminated block flooring, clear grade ***Replace*** Materials........6.56 Labor............3.32 ***Remove*** .... Labor............ .50 ► Made from at least three laminated layers (like plywood).	sf	$.50	$9.88	$10.38

Item Description	Unit	Remove	Replace	Total
Maple parquet slat block flooring, clear grade ***Replace*** Materials........6.98 Labor............3.32 ***Remove*** .... Labor............. .50 ► Made from many wood slats glued side by side with parquet pattern in block.	sf	$.50	$10.30	$10.80
Prefinished maple parquet unit block flooring, prime grade ***Replace*** Materials........6.25 Labor............3.39 ***Remove*** .... Labor............. .50 ► Made from solid wood pieces glued side by side.	sf	$.50	$9.64	$10.14
Prefinished maple laminated block flooring, prime grade ***Replace*** Materials........7.29 Labor............3.39 ***Remove*** .... Labor............. .50 ► Made from at least three laminated layers (like plywood).	sf	$.50	$10.68	$11.18
Prefinished maple parquet slat block flooring, prime grade ***Replace*** Materials........7.71 Labor............3.39 ***Remove*** .... Labor............. .50 ► Made from many wood slats glued side by side with parquet pattern in block.	sf	$.50	$11.10	$11.60
Red oak parquet unit block flooring, clear grade ***Replace*** Materials........5.52 Labor............3.32 ***Remove*** .... Labor............. .50 ► Made from solid wood pieces glued side by side.	sf	$.50	$8.84	$9.34
Red oak laminated block flooring, clear grade ***Replace*** Materials........6.46 Labor............3.32 ***Remove*** .... Labor............. .50 ► Made from at least three laminated layers (like plywood).	sf	$.50	$9.78	$10.28
Red oak parquet slat block flooring, clear grade ***Replace*** Materials........6.88 Labor............3.32 ***Remove*** .... Labor............. .50 ► Made from many wood slats glued side by side with parquet pattern in block.	sf	$.50	$10.20	$10.70
Prefinished red oak parquet unit block flooring, prime grade ***Replace*** Materials........6.25 Labor............3.39 ***Remove*** .... Labor............. .50 ► Made from solid wood pieces glued side by side.	sf	$.50	$9.64	$10.14
Prefinished red oak laminated block flooring, prime grade ***Replace*** Materials........7.19 Labor............3.39 ***Remove*** .... Labor............. .50 ► Made from at least three laminated layers (like plywood).	sf	$.50	$10.58	$11.08
Prefinished red oak parquet slat block flooring, prime grade ***Replace*** Materials........7.60 Labor............3.39 ***Remove*** .... Labor............. .50 ► Made from many wood slats glued side by side with parquet pattern in block.	sf	$.50	$10.99	$11.49
Add 8% for pickets around unit block ► Add for mitered wood trim around edges of block, called "pickets."				
Deduct 7% for beech flooring				
Deduct 7% for birch flooring				
Deduct 6% for ash flooring				
Add 46% for cherry flooring				

RELATED ITEMS

Cleaning........................62
Finish Carpentry..........199
Painting......................340

◄ **PREFINISHED MAPLE PARQUET**
Face pieces are almost flawless with very small character marks. (Sap and color variations are not flaws.) For standard grade deduct ***10%.*** *For tavern grade deduct* ***14%.***

◄ **RED OAK PARQUET**
Face pieces are practically clear, may have some small areas of bright sap. For select grade deduct ***8%.*** *For #1 common grade deduct* ***15%.***

◄ **PREFINISHED RED OAK PARQUET**
Face pieces are almost flawless with very small character marks. (Sap and color variations are not flaws.) For standard grade deduct ***10%.*** *For tavern grade deduct* ***14%.***

◄ **ADDITIONAL WOOD SPECIES**
Deduct or add these percentages to the costs listed for red oak.

	Item Description	Unit	Remove	Replace	Total
Additional wood species *continued*	**Deduct 5% for hickory flooring**				
	Add 182% for teak flooring				
	Add for 70% walnut flooring				
	Deduct 7% for white oak flooring				
Southern pine strip flooring *Strip flooring is up to 3/4" thick and up to 3-1/4" wide. Grading information based on rules established by the Southern Pine Inspection Bureau (SPIB). All wood is kiln-dried, tongue-and-groove, end-matched and hollow or scratch backed.*	**Southern pine strip flooring, B&B grade** ***Replace*** Materials........2.45 Labor............3.18 ***Remove*** .... Labor............. .55 ► Best quality, allows very small surface checks, pin knots, small closed pitch pockets, light stain and very light warp. Usually no more than one character flaw per 4 lf.	sf	$.55	$5.63	$6.18
	Southern pine strip flooring, C & better grade ***Replace*** Materials........2.23 Labor............3.18 ***Remove*** .... Labor............. .55 ► Combination of B&B and C grades. See B&B grade above. C grade is same as B&B with slightly larger and more frequent imperfections with some shakes, wane, splits, and skips.	sf	$.55	$5.41	$5.96
	Southern pine strip flooring, C grade ***Replace*** Materials........2.02 Labor............3.18 ***Remove*** .... Labor............. .55 ► C grade is same as B&B (see item above) with slightly larger and more frequent imperfections with some shakes, wane, splits, and skips.	sf	$.55	$5.20	$5.75
Southern pine plank flooring *Plank flooring is up to 3/4" thick and over 3-1/4" wide. Floors that contain a mix of plank and strip floor widths are usually considered plank floors. See southern pine strip flooring above for grading information.*	**Southern pine plank flooring, B&B grade** ***Replace*** Materials........2.98 Labor............2.85 ***Remove*** .... Labor............. .52 ► See information under same grade of southern pine strip flooring.	sf	$.52	$5.83	$6.35
	Southern pine plank flooring, C & better grade ***Replace*** Materials........2.77 Labor............2.85 ***Remove*** .... Labor............. .52 ► See information under same grade of southern pine strip flooring.	sf	$.52	$5.62	$6.14
	Southern pine plank flooring, C grade ***Replace*** Materials........2.45 Labor............2.85 ***Remove*** .... Labor............. .52 ► See information under same grade of southern pine strip flooring.	sf	$.52	$5.30	$5.82
Douglas fir strip flooring *Douglas fir or western hemlock, or white fir, or Sitka spruce. Strip flooring is up to 3/4" thick and up to 3-1/4" wide. Grading information based on rules established by the West Coast Lumbermen's Inspection Bureau (WCLIB). All wood is kiln-dried, tongue-and-groove, end-matched and hollow or scratch backed.*	**Douglas fir strip flooring, C & better grade** ***Replace*** Materials........2.66 Labor............3.18 ***Remove*** .... Labor............. .55 ► Highest quality with some pieces perfectly clear. Other pieces may contain infrequent medium stained sapwood, very small seasoning checks, small light skips, light warp, tight knots, and raised grain.	sf	$.55	$5.84	$6.39
	Douglas fir strip flooring, D grade ***Replace*** Materials........2.45 Labor............3.18 ***Remove*** .... Labor............. .55 ► Contains some stained wood, medium splits, seasoning checks, small and infrequent holes, torn or raised grain, large pitch streaks, larger and more frequent knots than are found in C grade, and some pieces with medium warp.	sf	$.55	$5.63	$6.18

Item Description	Unit	Remove	Replace	Total
Douglas fir strip flooring, E grade ***Replace*** Materials........2.23 Labor............3.18 ***Remove*** .... Labor............ .55 ► A subfloor grade that is normally not used in exposed applications. Includes larger and more frequent defects than are found in D grade, with loose knots and knot holes.	sf	$.55	$5.41	$5.96
Douglas fir plank flooring, C & better grade ***Replace*** Materials........3.19 Labor............2.85 ***Remove*** .... Labor............ .52 ► See information under same grade of Douglas fir strip flooring.	sf	$.52	$6.04	$6.56
Douglas fir plank flooring, D grade ***Replace*** Materials........2.98 Labor............2.85 ***Remove*** .... Labor............ .52 ► See information under same grade of Douglas fir strip flooring.	sf	$.52	$5.83	$6.35
Douglas fir plank flooring, E grade ***Replace*** Materials........2.66 Labor............2.85 ***Remove*** .... Labor............ .52 ► See information under same grade of Douglas fir strip flooring.	sf	$.52	$5.51	$6.03
Reclaimed antique longleaf pine flooring, crown grade ***Replace*** Materials.......11.10 Labor............3.18 ***Remove*** .... Labor............ .55 ► Best grade. 90% is free of knots with 100% dense grade heartwood face and very infrequent nail holes. Knots are tight and less than 1-1/4" in diameter.	sf	$.55	$14.28	$14.83
Reclaimed antique longleaf pine flooring, select prime grade ***Replace*** Materials........8.72 Labor............3.18 ***Remove*** .... Labor............ .55 ► 75% is free of knots with at least 97% dense grade heartwood and infrequent nail holes. Knots are tight and less than 1-1/2" in diameter.	sf	$.55	$11.90	$12.45
Reclaimed antique longleaf pine flooring, prime grade ***Replace*** Materials........8.51 Labor............3.18 ***Remove*** .... Labor............ .55 ► Varying degree of knots and nail holes with at least 85% dense grade heartwood. Knots are tight and less than 2" in diameter.	sf	$.55	$11.69	$12.24
Reclaimed antique longleaf pine flooring, naily grade ***Replace*** Materials........7.45 Labor............3.18 ***Remove*** .... Labor............ .55 ► Same as select prime grade above with many nail holes.	sf	$.55	$10.63	$11.18
Reclaimed antique longleaf pine flooring, cabin grade ***Replace*** Materials........7.55 Labor............3.18 ***Remove*** .... Labor............ .55 ► Similar to prime grade with more sapwood, larger knots, and some boards with many nail holes.	sf	$.55	$10.73	$11.28
Reclaimed antique longleaf pine flooring, distressed grade ***Replace*** Materials.......13.50 Labor............3.18 ***Remove*** .... Labor............ .55 ► Crown grade with as-is finish, including gouges, tight cracks, worm holes, worn spots, and raised grain. Boards are also machined to enhance the time-worn look. Edges and back are remilled.	sf	$.55	$16.68	$17.23

RELATED ITEMS

Cleaning........................62
Finish Carpentry..........199
Painting......................340

◄ **DOUGLAS FIR PLANK FLOORING**
Plank flooring is up to 3/4" thick and over 3-1/4" wide. Floors that contain a mix of plank and strip floor widths are usually considered plank floors. See Douglas fir strip flooring on facing page for grading information.

◄ **RECLAIMED ANTIQUE LONGLEAF PINE**
Strip or plank flooring. Although longleaf pine was once common in Southeastern America, new lumber is no longer available. Longleaf pine must be salvaged from existing structures. (Although Goodwin Heart Pine Company of Micanopy, Florida does salvage logs that sank to the bottom of rivers.) Grading is based on grades marketed by Mountain Lumber Company, Inc. of Ruckersville, Virginia.

	Item Description	Unit	Remove	Replace	Total
SAND, EDGE, & FILL WOOD FLOOR ▶	**Sand, edge, and fill new wood floor** *Replace* Materials........ .27 Labor............ .94	sf	—	$1.21	$1.21
	Light sand, edge, and fill existing wood floor *Replace* Materials........ .23 Labor.......... 1.08	sf	—	$1.31	$1.31
	Medium sand, edge, and fill old wood floor *Replace* Materials........ .31 Labor............1.19	sf	—	$1.50	$1.50
	Heavy sand, edge, and fill old wood floor *Replace* Materials........ .36 Labor............1.48	sf	—	$1.84	$1.84
WOOD FLOOR SLEEPERS ▶ *Glued and nailed with case-hardened nails to concrete floor.*	**1" x 2" sleepers on concrete floor, 24" oc** *Replace* Materials........ .19 Labor............ .29 *Remove* .... Labor............ .19	sf	$.19	$.48	$.67
	1" x 3" sleepers on concrete floor, 24" oc *Replace* Materials........ .31 Labor............ .32 *Remove* .... Labor............ .19	sf	$.19	$.63	$.82
	2" x 4" sleepers on concrete floor, 24" oc *Replace* Materials........ .72 Labor............ .43 *Remove* .... Labor............ .19	sf	$.19	$1.15	$1.34
	2" x 6" sleepers on concrete floor, 24" oc *Replace* Materials........1.14 Labor............ .47 *Remove* .... Labor............ .19	sf	$.19	$1.61	$1.80
UNDERLAYMENT ▶ *Includes 5% waste. When removing underlayment that has been heavily glued and stapled, double the removal cost.*	**3/8" particleboard floor underlayment** *Replace* Materials........3.70 Labor............6.03 *Remove* .... Labor............1.93	sy	$1.93	$9.73	$11.66
	1/2" particleboard floor underlayment *Replace* Materials........3.85 Labor............6.06 *Remove* .... Labor............1.93	sy	$1.93	$9.91	$11.84
	5/8" particleboard floor underlayment *Replace* Materials........4.23 Labor............6.06 *Remove* .... Labor............1.93	sy	$1.93	$10.29	$12.22
	3/4" particleboard floor underlayment *Replace* Materials........4.94 Labor............6.10 *Remove* .... Labor............1.93	sy	$1.93	$11.04	$12.97
	1/4" hardboard floor underlayment *Replace* Materials........4.91 Labor............6.28 *Remove* .... Labor............1.93	sy	$1.93	$11.19	$13.12
	1/2" plywood floor underlayment *Replace* Materials........6.30 Labor............6.06 *Remove* .... Labor............1.93	sy	$1.93	$12.36	$14.29
	Minimum charge for floor underlayment work *Replace* Materials......30.00 Labor..........25.80	ea	—	$55.80	$55.80

NOTES: ______________________________

____

______________________________ end

TIME & MATERIAL CHARTS *(selected items)*

Flooring Materials

DESCRIPTION	MATERIAL PRICE	GROSS COVERAGE	WASTE	NET COVERAGE	UNIT PRICE
Carpet					
economy grade	$14.20 sy	1	12%	.88	$16.10 sy
custom grade	$33.10 sy	1	12%	.88	$37.60 sy
Glue-down carpet					
economy grade	$10.70 sy	1	12%	.88	$12.20 sy
deluxe grade	$20.00 sy	1	12%	.88	$22.70 sy
Indoor-outdoor carpet					
economy grade	$7.90 sy	1	12%	.88	$8.98 sy
deluxe grade	$25.20 sy	1	12%	.88	$28.60 sy
Wool carpet					
standard grade	$21.10 sy	1	12%	.88	$24.00 sy
custom grade	$44.20 sy	1	12%	.88	$50.20 sy
Simulated wool berber carpet					
standard grade	$19.50 sy	1	12%	.88	$22.20 sy
custom grade	$31.30 sy	1	12%	.88	$35.60 sy
Carpet pad					
urethane rebound	$3.90 sy	1	12%	.88	$4.43 sy
jute	$2.70 sy	1	12%	.88	$3.07 sy
Carpet tile					
standard grade	$23.20 sy	1	12%	.88	$26.40 sy
custom grade	$35.50 sy	1	12%	.88	$40.30 sy
Stone floor					
standard grade	$5.70 sf	1	4%	.96	$5.94 sf
deluxe grade	$9.00 sf	1	4%	.96	$9.38 sf
Marble floor					
standard grade	$9.40 sf	1	4%	.96	$9.79 sf
deluxe grade	$30.90 sf	1	4%	.96	$32.20 sf
Slate floor					
standard grade	$7.40 sf	1	4%	.96	$7.71 sf
deluxe grade	$11.00 sf	1	4%	.96	$11.50 sf
Tile floor					
standard grade	$4.80 sf	1	4%	.96	$5.00 sf
deluxe grade	$8.00 sf	1	4%	.96	$8.33 sf
Quarry tile floor					
standard grade	$6.40 sf	1	4%	.96	$6.67 sf
deluxe grade	$12.60 sf	1	4%	.96	$13.10 sf
Precast terrazzo floor tiles					
standard grade	$11.90 sf	1	4%	.96	$12.40 sf
high grade	$13.50 sf	1	4%	.96	$14.10 sf
Cast-in-place thinset terrazzo floor					
standard grade	$2.40 sf	1	12%	.88	$2.73 sf
high grade	$3.50 sf	1	12%	.88	$3.98 sf
Vinyl floor					
economy grade	$12.90 sy	1	12%	.88	$14.70 sy
deluxe grade	$29.60 sy	1	12%	.88	$33.60 sy
Vinyl tile floor					
economy grade	$.90 sf	1	12%	.88	$1.02 sf
deluxe grade	$2.60 sf	1	12%	.88	$2.95 sf

. . . More ➢

Flooring Materials *continued*

DESCRIPTION	MATERIAL PRICE	GROSS COVERAGE	WASTE	NET COVERAGE	UNIT PRICE
Resilient tile floor					
economy grade	$1.00 sf	1	12%	.88	$1.14 sf
deluxe grade	$2.10 sf	1	12%	.88	$2.39 sf
Antique style linoleum					
battleship	$27.00 sy	1	12%	.88	$30.70 sy
Rubber base					
economy grade	$1.30 lf	1	12%	.88	$1.48 lf
deluxe grade	$2.60 lf	1	12%	.88	$2.95 lf
Strip flooring					
maple, first grade	$6.90 sf	1	6%	.94	$7.34 sf
red oak, select & better grade	$5.40 sf	1	6%	.94	$5.74 sf
red oak, quartersawn, clear grade	$9.50 sf	1	6%	.94	$10.10 sf
prefinished red oak, prime grade	$6.10 sf	1	6%	.94	$6.49 sf
Plank flooring					
red oak, select & better grade	$8.70 sf	1	6%	.94	$9.26 sf
Parquet or block flooring					
maple, slat block, clear grade	$6.70 sf	1	4%	.96	$6.98 sf
prefinished maple, slat block, prime grade	$6.00 sf	1	4%	.96	$6.25 sf
red oak, slat block, clear grade	$5.30 sf	1	4%	.96	$5.52 sf
prefinished red oak, slat block, prime grade	$6.00 sf	1	4%	.96	$6.25 sf
Softwood flooring					
Southern pine strip, B&B grade	$2.30 sf	1	6%	.94	$2.45 sf
Southern pine plank, B&B grade	$2.80 sf	1	6%	.94	$2.98 sf
Douglas fir strip, C & better grade	$2.50 sf	1	6%	.94	$2.66 sf
Douglas fir plank, C & better grade	$3.00 sf	1	6%	.94	$3.19 sf
reclaimed antique longleaf pine, crown grade	$10.40 sf	1	6%	.94	$11.10 sf
Sleepers on concrete floor, 24" on center					
1" x 2"					$.19 sf
2" x 4"					$.72 sf
Floor underlayment					
3/8" particleboard	$12.50 sheet	3.56	5%	3.38	$3.70 sy
1/2" particleboard	$13.00 sheet	3.56	5%	3.38	$3.85 sy
5/8" particleboard	$14.30 sheet	3.56	5%	3.38	$4.23 sy
3/4" particleboard	$16.70 sheet	3.56	5%	3.38	$4.94 sy
1/4" hardboard	$8.30 sheet	1.78	5%	1.69	$4.91 sy
1/2" plywood	$21.30 sheet	3.56	5%	3.38	$6.30 sy

Flooring Labor

LABORER	BASE WAGE	PAID LEAVE	TRUE WAGE	FICA	FUTA	WORKER'S COMP.	UNEMPLOY. INSUR.	HEALTH INSUR.	RETIRE (401K)	LIABILITY INSUR.	COST PER HOUR
Flooring installer	$23.30	1.82	$25.12	1.92	.20	5.22	2.19	2.69	.75	3.39	$41.50
Flooring installer's helper	$16.80	1.31	$18.11	1.39	.14	3.77	1.58	2.69	.54	2.44	$30.70
Demolition laborer	$13.90	1.08	$14.98	1.15	.12	4.79	1.30	2.69	.45	2.02	$27.50

Paid Leave is calculated based on two weeks paid vacation, one week sick leave, and seven paid holidays. Employer's matching portion of **FICA** is 7.65 percent. **FUTA** (Federal Unemployment) is .8 percent. **Worker's compensation** for the flooring trade was calculated using a national average of 20.79 percent. **Unemployment insurance** was calculated using a national average of 8.7 percent. **Health insurance** was calculated based on a projected national average for 2002 of $535 per employee (and family when applicable) per month. Employer pays 80 percent for a per month cost of $428 per employee. **Retirement** is based on a 401(k) retirement program with employer matching of 50 percent. Employee contributions to the 401(k) plan are an average of 6 percent of the true wage. **Liability insurance** is based on a national average of 13.2 percent.

Flooring Labor Productivity

WORK DESCRIPTION	LABORER	COST PER HOUR	PRODUCTIVITY	UNIT PRICE
Demolition				
remove carpet	demolition laborer	$27.50	.062	**$1.71** sy
remove glue-down carpet	demolition laborer	$27.50	.155	**$4.26** sy
remove indoor-outdoor carpet	demolition laborer	$27.50	.153	**$4.21** sy
remove carpet pad	demolition laborer	$27.50	.030	**$.83** sy
remove carpet cove	demolition laborer	$27.50	.022	**$.61** lf
remove carpet tile	demolition laborer	$27.50	.155	**$4.26** sy
remove stone floor	demolition laborer	$27.50	.082	**$2.26** sf
remove marble floor	demolition laborer	$27.50	.080	**$2.20** sf
remove slate floor	demolition laborer	$27.50	.080	**$2.20** sf
remove tile floor	demolition laborer	$27.50	.080	**$2.20** sf
remove quarry tile floor	demolition laborer	$27.50	.078	**$2.15** sf
remove tile base	demolition laborer	$27.50	.061	**$1.68** lf
remove precast terrazzo floor tiles	demolition laborer	$27.50	.081	**$2.23** sf
remove cast-in-place terrazzo floor	demolition laborer	$27.50	.082	**$2.26** sf
remove vinyl floor	demolition laborer	$27.50	.175	**$4.81** sy
remove vinyl tile floor	demolition laborer	$27.50	.024	**$.66** sf
remove resilient tile floor	demolition laborer	$27.50	.024	**$.66** sf
remove antique style linoleum floor	demolition laborer	$27.50	.175	**$4.81** sy
remove vinyl cove	demolition laborer	$27.50	.036	**$.99** lf
remove rubber base	demolition laborer	$27.50	.011	**$.30** lf
remove wood strip flooring	demolition laborer	$27.50	.020	**$.55** sf
remove wood plank flooring	demolition laborer	$27.50	.019	**$.52** sf
remove wood unit block flooring	demolition laborer	$27.50	.018	**$.50** sf
remove floor sleepers	demolition laborer	$27.50	.007	**$.19** sf
remove floor underlayment	demolition laborer	$27.50	.070	**$1.93** sy
Flooring crew				
install flooring	flooring installer	$41.50		
install flooring	flooring installer's helper	$30.70		
install flooring	**flooring crew**	$36.10		
Install carpet				
typical on tackless	flooring crew	$36.10	.138	**$4.98** sy
cove	flooring crew	$36.10	.135	**$4.87** lf
remove for work, then re-lay	flooring crew	$36.10	.211	**$7.62** sy
glue-down	flooring crew	$36.10	.167	**$6.03** sy
wool or simulated wool	flooring crew	$36.10	.139	**$5.02** sy
add per step for installation on stairs	flooring crew	$36.10	.180	**$6.50** ea
pad	flooring crew	$36.10	.0166	**$.58** sy
tile	flooring crew	$36.10	.107	**$3.86** sy
Install stone floor				
typical	flooring crew	$36.10	.191	**$6.90** sf
salvage, then reinstall	flooring crew	$36.10	.500	**$18.10** sf
regrout	flooring crew	$36.10	.038	**$1.37** sf
Install marble floor				
typical	flooring crew	$36.10	.189	**$6.82** sf
regrout	flooring crew	$36.10	.034	**$1.23** sf
Install slate floor				
typical	flooring crew	$36.10	.189	**$6.82** sf
regrout	flooring crew	$36.10	.034	**$1.23** sf
salvage, then reinstall	flooring crew	$36.10	.490	**$17.70** sf
Install tile floor				
typical	flooring crew	$36.10	.180	**$6.50** sf
regrout	flooring crew	$36.10	.035	**$1.26** sf
base	flooring crew	$36.10	.128	**$4.62** lf
Install quarry tile floor				
typical	flooring crew	$36.10	.143	**$5.16** sf
Install terrazzo floor				
precast tiles	flooring crew	$36.10	.116	**$4.19** sf
precast base	flooring crew	$36.10	.256	**$9.24** sf
cast-in-place thinset	flooring crew	$36.10	.128	**$4.62** sf

. . . More ➢

Flooring Labor Productivity *continued*

WORK DESCRIPTION	LABORER	COST PER HOUR	PRODUCTIVITY	UNIT PRICE
Install vinyl floor				
sheet goods	flooring crew	$36.10	.183	**$6.61** sy
cove	flooring crew	$36.10	.091	**$3.29** lf
tile	flooring crew	$36.10	.029	**$1.05** sf
resilient tile	flooring crew	$36.10	.029	**$1.05** sf
Install antique style linoleum				
typical	flooring crew	$36.10	.189	**$6.82** sy
tile	flooring crew	$36.10	.032	**$1.16** sf
Install rubber base				
typical	flooring crew	$36.10	.020	**$.72** lf
Install wood floor				
hardwood strip	flooring crew	$36.10	.088	**$3.18** sf
prefinished hardwood strip	flooring crew	$36.10	.091	**$3.29** sf
hardwood plank	flooring crew	$36.10	.079	**$2.85** sf
parquet or block	flooring crew	$36.10	.092	**$3.32** sf
prefinished hardwood block or parquet	flooring crew	$36.10	.094	**$3.39** sf
softwood strip	flooring crew	$36.10	.088	**$3.18** sf
softwood plank	flooring crew	$36.10	.079	**$2.85** sf
Sand, edge, and fill wood floor				
new	flooring crew	$36.10	.026	**$.94** sf
light sand	flooring crew	$36.10	.030	**$1.08** sf
medium	flooring crew	$36.10	.033	**$1.19** sf
heavy sand	flooring crew	$36.10	.041	**$1.48** sf
Install sleepers on concrete floor, 24" on center				
1" x 2"	flooring crew	$36.10	.008	**$.29** sf
1" x 3"	flooring crew	$36.10	.009	**$.32** sf
2" x 4"	flooring crew	$36.10	.012	**$.43** sf
2" x 6"	flooring crew	$36.10	.013	**$.47** sf
Install floor underlayment				
3/8" particleboard	flooring crew	$36.10	.167	**$6.03** sy
1/2" particleboard	flooring crew	$36.10	.168	**$6.06** sy
5/8" particleboard	flooring crew	$36.10	.168	**$6.06** sy
3/4" particleboard	flooring crew	$36.10	.169	**$6.10** sy
1/4" hardboard	flooring crew	$36.10	.174	**$6.28** sy
1/2" plywood	flooring crew	$36.10	.168	**$6.06** sy

NOTES:

end

20 Hazardous Materials

Item Description	Unit	Remove	Replace	Total	
Minimum asbestos removal charge ***Remove*** Materials....134.00 Labor.........690.00 Equipment 163.00	ea	$987.00	—	$987.00	◄ **Minimum**
Asbestos analysis ***Remove*** .... Labor.........720.00 ► Includes up to four hours, up to 12 analyzed samples, and a written report indicating severity of asbestos risk for a typical home or small commercial structure.	ea	$720.00	—	$720.00	◄ **Asbestos analysis**
Plastic cover attached to ceiling ***Remove*** Materials........1.31 Labor 1.90	sf	$3.21	—	$3.21	◄ **Seal area** *Seal area where asbestos exists. Includes tape along all seams, caulk or foam insulation in any cracks, and negative air vent system.*
Plastic cover attached to walls ***Remove*** Materials........1.33 Labor 1.81	sf	$3.14	—	$3.14	
Plastic cover and plywood over floor (2 layers) ***Remove*** Materials........2.11 Labor 4.40	sf	$6.51	—	$6.51	
Temporary containment walls with plastic cover ***Remove*** Materials........2.54 Labor ....7.71 ► 2" x 4" walls covered with 1/2" cdx plywood and plastic.	sf	$10.25	—	$10.25	
Prefabricated decontamination unit ***Remove*** .... Equipment..........70.00 ► Four day minimum. Includes decontamination equipment, shower, and clean room.	dy	$70.00	—	$70.00	◄ **Decontamination unit**
Encapsulate asbestos-based acoustical ceiling with sealant ***Remove*** Materials........ .32 Labor............. .60 Equipment .... .11 ► Penetrating sealant sprayed on ceiling with airless sprayer.	sf	$1.03	—	$1.03	◄ **Encapsulate asbestos**
Scrape asbestos-based acoustical ceiling ***Remove*** Materials........ .08 Labor ....1.47 Equipment .... .16 ► Includes disposal in glove bags and fiber drums.	sf	$1.71	—	$1.71	◄ **Remove asbestos** *Includes full Tyvek suits for workers changed four times per eight hour shift, respirators, (add* ***20%*** *for respirators with air supply) air monitoring, supervision by qualified hygiene professionals, final seal of scraped or demo'ed walls, final seal and disposal of plastic cover materials, disposal in fiber drums and hauling to dump. Does not include dump fees (typically about* ***$12*** *per drum).*
Remove asbestos-based insulation over 1/2" to 3/4" pipe ***Remove*** Materials........ .16 Labor........... 1.12 Equipment .... .08 ► Includes disposal in glove bags and fiber drums.	lf	$1.36	—	$1.36	
Remove asbestos-based insulation over 1" to 3" pipe ***Remove*** Materials........ .30 Labor ....3.45 Equipment .... .17 ► Includes disposal in glove bags and fiber drums.	lf	$3.92	—	$3.92	
Remove asbestos-based siding ***Remove*** Materials........ .88 Labor ....7.71 Equipment .... .19 ► Includes disposal in fiber drums.	sf	$8.78	—	$8.78	
Remove asbestos-based plaster ***Remove*** Materials........ .57 Labor ....5.90 Equipment .... .19 ► Includes disposal in fiber drums.	sf	$6.66	—	$6.66	

NOTES: ______________________________

______________________________ end

TIME & MATERIAL CHARTS *(selected items)*

Materials for Hazardous Materials Removal

DESCRIPTION	MATERIAL PRICE	UNIT PRICE
polyethylene (plastic)	$.19 sf	$.19 sf
Tyvek whole body suit	$16.00 ea	$16.00 ea
respirator cartridge	$4.40 ea	$4.40 ea
glove bag, 7 mil., 50″ x 64″	$8.50 ea	$8.50 ea
glove bag, 10 mil., 44″ x 60″	$9.10 ea	$9.10 ea
3 cf disposable polyethylene bags, 6 mil	$1.10 ea	$1.10 ea
3 cf disposable fiber drums	$9.30 ea	$9.30 ea
caution labels	$.22 ea	$.22 ea
encapsulation quality sealant	$80.00 gallon	$80.00 gal
vent fan filters	$7.60 ea	$7.60 ea
respirator	$23.00 ea	$23.00 ea

Hazardous Materials Rental Equipment

DESCRIPTION	PRICE	COVERAGE	UNIT PRICE
negative air vent system, two fans	$50.00 per day	1 per day	$50.00 day
HEPA vacuum cleaner, 16 gallon wet/dry	$60.00 per day	1 per day	$60.00 day
airless sprayer unit	$45.00 per day	1 per day	$45.00 day
light stand	$15.00 per day	1 per day	$15.00 day
prefabricated decontamination unit	$70.00 per day	1 per day	$70.00 day

Hazardous Materials Labor

LABORER	BASE WAGE	PAID LEAVE	TRUE WAGE	FICA	FUTA	WORKER'S COMP.	UNEMPLOY. INSUR.	HEALTH INSUR.	RETIRE (401K)	LIABILITY INSUR.	COST PER HOUR
Haz. mat. laborer	$18.40	1.44	$19.84	1.52	.16	13.84	1.73	2.69	.60	2.68	$43.10

Paid Leave is calculated based on two weeks paid vacation, one week sick leave, and seven paid holidays. Employer's matching portion of **FICA** is 7.65 percent. **FUTA** (Federal Unemployment) is .8 percent. **Worker's compensation** for the hazardous materials trade was calculated using a national average of 69.77 percent. **Unemployment insurance** was calculated using a national average of 8.7 percent. **Health insurance** was calculated based on a projected national average for 2002 of $535 per employee (and family when applicable) per month. Employer pays 80 percent for a per month cost of $428 per employee. **Retirement** is based on a 401(k) retirement program with employer matching of 50 percent. Employee contributions to the 401(k) plan are an average of 6 percent of the true wage. **Liability insurance** is based on a national average of 13.2 percent.

Hazardous Materials Labor Productivity

WORK DESCRIPTION	LABORER	COST PER HOUR	PRODUCTIVITY	UNIT PRICE
Minimum				
for asbestos removal	haz. mat. laborer	$43.10	16.0	$690.00 ea
Asbestos analysis				
typical home	haz. mat. laborer	$43.10	16.7	$720.00 ea
Seal area for work				
attach plastic cover to ceiling	haz. mat. laborer	$43.10	.044	$1.90 sf
attach plastic cover to walls	haz. mat. laborer	$43.10	.042	$1.81 sf
attach plastic cover & plywood to floor	haz. mat. laborer	$43.10	.102	$4.40 sf
build walls and attach plastic cover	haz. mat. laborer	$43.10	.179	$7.71 sf
Remove asbestos-based materials				
scrape acoustical ceiling	haz. mat. laborer	$43.10	.034	$1.47 sf
encapsulate acoustical ceiling with sealant	haz. mat. laborer	$43.10	.014	$.60 sf
insulation over 1/2″ to 3/4″ pipe	haz. mat. laborer	$43.10	.026	$1.12 lf
insulation over 1″ to 3″ pipe	haz. mat. laborer	$43.10	.080	$3.45 lf
siding	haz. mat. laborer	$43.10	.179	$7.71 sf
plaster	haz. mat. laborer	$43.10	.137	$5.90 sf

21 HVAC

Item Description	Unit	Remove	Replace	Total
Duct work per duct *Replace* Materials.....145.00 Labor.........232.00	ea	—	$377.00	$377.00
Duct work per sf of floor *Replace* Materials .... .40 Labor 1.48	sf	—	$1.88	$1.88
Forced-air ducting for home to 1,200 sf *Replace* Materials....539.00 Labor.......1660.00	ea	—	$2,199.00	$2,199.00
Forced-air ducting for home 1,200 to 1,900 sf *Replace* Materials....760.00 Labor......2030.00	ea	—	$2,790.00	$2,790.00
Forced-air ducting for home 1,900 to 2,400 sf *Replace* Materials...1190.00 Labor......2500.00	ea	—	$3,690.00	$3,690.00
Forced-air ducting for home 2,400 to 2,900 sf *Replace* Materials...1740.00 Labor 3250.00	ea	—	$4,990.00	$4,990.00
Forced-air ducting for home 2,900 to 3,400 sf *Replace* Materials..2590.00 Labor......4640.00	ea	—	$7,230.00	$7,230.00
Forced-air ducting for home 3,400 to 3,900 sf *Replace* Materials..3980.00 Labor 6030.00	ea	—	$10,010.00	$10,010.00
Forced-air ducting for home 3,900 to 4,500 sf *Replace* Materials...6210.00 Labor.......7600.00	ea	—	$13,810.00	$13,810.00
Electric forced-air furnace 10,200 btu *Replace* Materials ....375.00 Labor.........501.00 *Remove* .... Labor...........52.00	ea	$52.00	$876.00	$928.00
Electric forced-air furnace 17,100 btu *Replace* Materials....400.00 Labor.........529.00 *Remove* .... Labor...........52.00	ea	$52.00	$929.00	$981.00
Electric forced-air furnace 27,300 btu *Replace* Materials ....450.00 Labor.........585.00 *Remove* .... Labor...........52.00	ea	$52.00	$1,035.00	$1,087.00
Electric forced-air furnace 34,100 btu *Replace* Materials....500.00 Labor ....640.00 *Remove* .... Labor...........52.00	ea	$52.00	$1,140.00	$1,192.00
Remove electric forced-air furnace for work, then reinstall *Replace* .... Labor 242.00	ea	—	$242.00	$242.00
Gas forced-air furnace 45,000 btu *Replace* Materials....400.00 Labor ....524.00 *Remove* .... Labor 50.10	ea	$50.10	$924.00	$974.10
Gas forced-air furnace 60,000 btu *Replace* Materials ....450.00 Labor.........571.00 *Remove* .... Labor 50.10	ea	$50.10	$1,021.00	$1,071.10

◄ **Ducts**

◄ **Ducts per home**

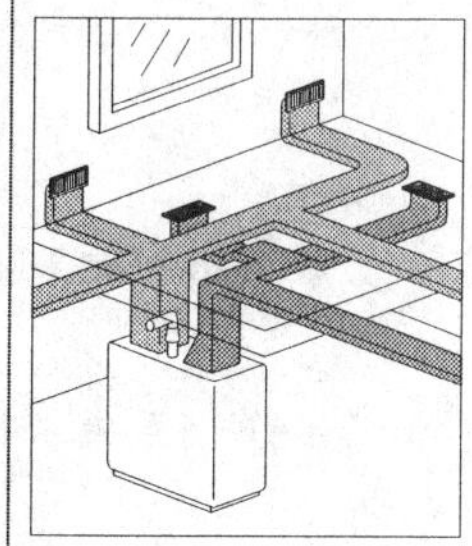

◄ **Electric furnace**
Includes connection only. Does not include wiring run, plenums, ducts, or flues.

RELATED ITEMS

Cleaning 63
Electrical
baseboard heater............... 153
baseboard heater wiring............. 142, 144
furnace wiring.................. 142
humidifier wiring............... 143
resistance wiring run......... 142
resistance cable................ 153
thermostat................ 152, 278
thermostat wiring............. 145
wall heater...................... 152

◄ **Gas furnace**
Includes connection only. Does not include wiring run, plenums, ducts, or flues.

	Item Description	Unit	Remove	Replace	Total
GAS FURNACE ▶ *continued*	**Gas forced-air furnace 75,000 btu** *Replace* Materials....500.00 Labor.........622.00 *Remove* .... Labor..........50.10	ea	$50.10	$1,122.00	$1,172.10
	Gas forced-air furnace 100,000 btu *Replace* Materials....550.00 Labor.........696.00 *Remove* .... Labor..........50.10	ea	$50.10	$1,246.00	$1,296.10
	Gas forced-air furnace, 125,000 btu *Replace* Materials....635.00 Labor.........761.00 *Remove* .... Labor..........50.10	ea	$50.10	$1,396.00	$1,446.10
	Gas forced-air furnace, 150,000 btu *Replace* Materials....785.00 Labor.........803.00 *Remove* .... Labor..........50.10	ea	$50.10	$1,588.00	$1,638.10
	Remove gas forced-air furnace for work, then reinstall *Replace* .... Labor.........236.00	ea	—	$236.00	$236.00
OIL FURNACE ▶ *Includes connection only. Does not include wiring run, plenums, ducts, or flues.*	**Oil forced-air furnace 56,000 btu** *Replace* Materials..1000.00 Labor.........575.00 *Remove* .... Labor..........56.10	ea	$56.10	$1,575.00	$1,631.10
	Oil forced-air furnace 84,000 btu *Replace* Materials...1100.00 Labor.........594.00 *Remove* .... Labor..........56.10	ea	$56.10	$1,694.00	$1,750.10
	Oil forced-air furnace 95,000 btu *Replace* Materials...1150.00 Labor.........620.00 *Remove* .... Labor..........56.10	ea	$56.10	$1,770.00	$1,826.10
	Oil forced-air furnace 134,000 btu *Replace* Materials..1500.00 Labor.........826.00 *Remove* .... Labor..........56.10	ea	$56.10	$2,326.00	$2,382.10
	Remove oil forced-air furnace for work, then reinstall *Replace* .... Labor.........253.00	ea	—	$253.00	$253.00
SERVICE FURNACE ▶	**Service furnace** *Replace* Materials........8.90 Labor..........80.00 ▶ Check, replace filters, and clean.	ea	—	$88.90	$88.90
HEAT PUMP ▶	**Heat pump, 2 ton with supplementary heat coil** *Replace* Materials..2250.00 Labor........905.00 *Remove* .... Labor..........64.10	ea	$64.10	$3,155.00	$3,219.10
	Heat pump, 4 ton with supplementary heat coil *Replace* Materials..4250.00 Labor.......1350.00 *Remove* .... Labor..........64.10	ea	$64.10	$5,600.00	$5,664.10
	Heat pump, 5 ton with supplementary heat coil *Replace* Materials..4500.00 Labor.......1620.00 *Remove* .... Labor..........64.10	ea	$64.10	$6,120.00	$6,184.10
	Remove heat pump for work, then reinstall *Replace* .... Labor.......1010.00	ea	—	$1,010.00	$1,010.00
HUMIDIFIER ▶ *Centrifugal atomizing.*	**Humidifier, 5 pounds per hour** *Replace* Materials..1250.00 Labor.........178.00 *Remove* .... Labor..........46.50	ea	$46.50	$1,428.00	$1,474.50

Item Description	Unit	Remove	Replace	Total
Humidifier, 10 pounds per hour *Replace* Materials ..1500.00 Labor ....206.00 *Remove* .... Labor 46.50	ea	$46.50	$1,706.00	$1,752.50
Remove humidifier for work, then reinstall *Replace* .... Labor 138.00	ea	—	$138.00	$138.00
3″ diameter double wall furnace vent pipe (all fuels) *Replace* Materials........3.60 Labor...........13.10 *Remove* .... Labor 1.10	lf	$1.10	$16.70	$17.80
4″ diameter double wall furnace vent pipe (all fuels) *Replace* Materials........4.50 Labor...........14.80 *Remove* .... Labor 1.10	lf	$1.10	$19.30	$20.40
5″ diameter double wall furnace vent pipe (all fuels) *Replace* Materials........5.30 Labor...........16.30 *Remove* .... Labor 1.10	lf	$1.10	$21.60	$22.70
6″ diameter double wall furnace vent pipe (all fuels) *Replace* Materials........6.20 Labor...........18.10 *Remove* .... Labor 1.10	lf	$1.10	$24.30	$25.40
7″ diameter double wall furnace vent pipe (all fuels) *Replace* Materials........9.20 Labor ....22.50 *Remove* .... Labor 1.10	lf	$1.10	$31.70	$32.80
8″ diameter double wall furnace vent pipe (all fuels) *Replace* Materials......10.20 Labor...........24.70 *Remove* .... Labor 1.10	lf	$1.10	$34.90	$36.00
Remove furnace vent pipe for work, then reinstall *Replace* .... Labor...........13.10	lf	—	$13.10	$13.10
Central air conditioning system, complete, 1 ton *Replace* Materials....720.00 Labor 284.00	ea	—	$1,004.00	$1,004.00
Central air conditioning system, complete, 1-1/2 ton *Replace* Materials.....815.00 Labor.........328.50	ea	—	$1,143.50	$1,143.50
Central air conditioning system, complete, 2 ton *Replace* Materials....900.00 Labor.........395.30	ea	—	$1,295.30	$1,295.30
Central air conditioning system, complete, 3 ton *Replace* Materials...1450.00 Labor 338.30	ea	—	$1,788.30	$1,788.30
Central air conditioning system, complete, 4 ton *Replace* Materials...1810.00 Labor.........751.70	ea	—	$2,561.70	$2,561.70
Central air conditioning system, complete, 5 ton *Replace* Materials..2230.00 Labor.......1080.00	ea	—	$3,310.00	$3,310.00
Air conditioning unit service *Replace* Materials......40.00 Labor...........81.20	ea	—	$121.20	$121.20
Recharge AC system, 5 lbs of refrigerant *Replace* Materials ....105.00 Labor...........69.60	ea	—	$174.60	$174.60
Recharge AC system, 10 lbs of refrigerant *Replace* Materials.....210.00 Labor...........76.60	ea	—	$286.60	$286.60

◄ **FURNACE VENT PIPE**

◄ **CENTRAL AC**
Includes condensing unit, coil, copper lines, and installation.

RELATED ITEMS

Cleaning 63
Electrical
baseboard heater..............153
baseboard heater wiring............142, 144
furnace wiring...................142
humidifier wiring..............143
resistance wiring run.........142
resistance cable.................153
thermostat...................152, 278
thermostat wiring.............145
wall heater........................152

◄ **AC SERVICE**

◄ **RECHARGE AC UNIT**

	Item Description	Unit	Remove	Replace	Total
RECHARGE ▶ AC UNIT *continued*	**Recharge AC system, 14 lbs of refrigerant** *Replace* Materials....295.00 Labor..........83.50	ea	—	$378.50	$378.50
THROUGH-WALL ▶ AC UNIT	**Through-wall AC unit, 5,000 btu** *Replace* Materials....750.00 Labor.........410.00 *Remove* .... Labor...........41.00	ea	$41.00	$1,160.00	$1,201.00
	Through-wall AC unit, 8,000 btu *Replace* Materials....775.00 Labor.........423.00 *Remove* .... Labor...........41.00	ea	$41.00	$1,198.00	$1,239.00
	Through-wall AC unit, 12,000 btu *Replace* Materials....925.00 Labor.........492.00 *Remove* .... Labor...........41.00	ea	$41.00	$1,417.00	$1,458.00
	Through-wall AC unit, 18,000 btu *Replace* Materials..1050.00 Labor........548.00 *Remove* .... Labor...........41.00	ea	$41.00	$1,598.00	$1,639.00
	Remove through-wall AC unit for work, then reinstall *Replace* .... Labor.........231.00	ea	—	$231.00	$231.00
THROUGH-WALL ▶ AC & HEAT UNIT	**Through-wall combination 6,000 btu AC and 4,040 btu heat unit** *Replace* Materials..1250.00 Labor.........473.00 *Remove* .... Labor...........42.90	ea	$42.90	$1,723.00	$1,765.90
	Through-wall combination 9,500 btu AC and 4,040 btu heat unit *Replace* Materials..1300.00 Labor.........487.00 *Remove* .... Labor...........42.90	ea	$42.90	$1,787.00	$1,829.90
	Through-wall combination 11,300 btu AC and 9,200 btu heat unit *Replace* Materials..1500.00 Labor........566.00 *Remove* .... Labor...........42.90	ea	$42.90	$2,066.00	$2,108.90
	Remove combination AC & heat unit for work, then reinstall *Replace* .... Labor.........249.00	ea	—	$249.00	$249.00
EVAPORATIVE ▶ COOLER *Roof mount. Includes up to 36 lf of copper water supply tubing and electrical hookup.*	**Evaporative cooler, 2,000 cfm** *Replace* Materials....700.00 Labor........348.00 *Remove* .... Labor...........45.10	ea	$45.10	$1,048.00	$1,093.10
	Evaporative cooler, 4,300 cfm *Replace* Materials....950.00 Labor........443.00 *Remove* .... Labor...........45.10	ea	$45.10	$1,393.00	$1,438.10
	Evaporative cooler, 4,700 cfm *Replace* Materials..1000.00 Labor.........469.00 *Remove* .... Labor...........45.10	ea	$45.10	$1,469.00	$1,514.10
	Evaporative cooler, 5,600 cfm *Replace* Materials...1100.00 Labor........506.00 *Remove* .... Labor...........45.10	ea	$45.10	$1,606.00	$1,651.10
grille ▷	**Evaporative cooler grille** *Replace* Materials......60.00 Labor...........31.60 *Remove* .... Labor............4.59	ea	$4.59	$91.60	$96.19
	Remove evaporative cooler for work, then reinstall *Replace* .... Labor.........437.00	ea	—	$437.00	$437.00

Item Description	Unit	Remove	Replace	Total
Cold-air return grille *Replace* Materials......30.00 Labor..........44.20 *Remove* .... Labor...........4.59	ea	$4.59	$74.20	$78.79
Remove cold-air return grille for work, then reinstall *Replace* Materials......... Labor..........11.50	ea	—	$11.50	$11.50
Heat register *Replace* Materials......20.00 Labor..........29.20 *Remove* .... Labor...........3.71	ea	$3.71	$49.20	$52.91
Remove heat register for work, then reinstall *Replace* .... Labor...........7.42	ea	—	$7.42	$7.42
Thermostat, heat only *Replace* Materials......45.00 Labor..........71.00 *Remove* .... Labor...........6.41	ea	$6.41	$116.00	$122.41
Thermostat, heat and air conditioning *Replace* Materials......70.00 Labor.........110.00 *Remove* .... Labor...........6.41	ea	$6.41	$180.00	$186.41
Thermostat, programmable *Replace* Materials......85.00 Labor.........162.00 *Remove* .... Labor...........6.41	ea	$6.41	$247.00	$253.41
Thermostat, programmable, with zone control *Replace* Materials....100.00 Labor.........199.00 *Remove* .... Labor...........6.41	ea	$6.41	$299.00	$305.41
Remove thermostat for work, then reinstall *Replace* .... Labor..........28.90	ea	—	$28.90	$28.90

◀ **COLD-AIR GRILLE**

◀ **HEAT REGISTER**

◀ **THERMOSTAT**
See Electrical on page 152 for electrical system and baseboard heater thermostats.

NOTES: ____________________

end

TIME & MATERIAL CHARTS *(selected items)*

HVAC Materials

DESCRIPTION	UNIT PRICE
Ductwork	
per sf of floor	**$.40** *sf*
Electric forced-air furnace	
10,200 btu	**$375.00** *ea*
34,100 btu	**$500.00** *ea*
Gas forced-air furnace	
45,000 btu	**$400.00** *ea*
150,000 btu	**$785.00** *ea*
Oil forced-air furnace	
56,000 btu	**$1000.00** *ea*
134,000 btu	**$1500.00** *ea*

HVAC Labor

LABORER	BASE WAGE	PAID LEAVE	TRUE WAGE	FICA	FUTA	WORKER'S COMP.	UNEMPLOY. INSUR.	HEALTH INSUR.	RETIRE (401K)	LIABILITY INSUR.	COST PER HOUR
HVAC installer	**$27.40**	2.14	**$29.54**	2.26	.24	4.25	2.57	2.69	.89	3.99	**$46.40**
Demolition laborer	**$13.90**	1.08	**$14.98**	1.15	.12	4.79	1.30	.45	2.02	27.50	**$27.50**

Paid Leave is calculated based on two weeks paid vacation, one week sick leave, and seven paid holidays. Employer's matching portion of **FICA** is 7.65 percent. **FUTA** (Federal Unemployment) is .8 percent. **Worker's compensation** for the HVAC trade was calculated using a national average of 14.37 percent. **Unemployment insurance** was calculated using a national average of 8.7 percent. **Health insurance** was calculated based on a projected national average for 2002 of $535 per employee (and family when applicable) per month. Employer pays 80 percent for a per month cost of $428 per employee. **Retirement** is based on a 401(k) retirement program with employer matching of 50 percent. Employee contributions to the 401(k) plan are an average of 6 percent of the true wage. **Liability insurance** is based on a national average of 13.2 percent.

HVAC Labor Productivity

WORK DESCRIPTION	LABORER	COST PER HOUR	PRODUCTIVITY	UNIT PRICE
Demolition				
remove electric forced-air furnace	demolition laborer	$27.50	1.89	**$52.00** ea
remove gas forced-air furnace	demolition laborer	$27.50	1.82	**$50.10** ea
remove oil forced-air furnace	demolition laborer	$27.50	2.04	**$56.10** ea
remove heat pump	demolition laborer	$27.50	2.33	**$64.10** ea
remove humidifier	demolition laborer	$27.50	1.69	**$46.50** ea
remove through-wall AC unit	demolition laborer	$27.50	1.49	**$41.00** ea
remove combination AC and heat unit	demolition laborer	$27.50	1.56	**$42.90** ea
remove evaporative cooler	demolition laborer	$27.50	1.64	**$45.10** ea
remove heat register	demolition laborer	$27.50	.135	**$3.71** ea
remove thermostat	demolition laborer	$27.50	.233	**$6.41** ea
Install electric forced air furnace				
10,200 btu	HVAC installer	$46.40	10.8	**$501.00** ea
34,100 btu	HVAC installer	$46.40	13.8	**$640.00** ea
Install gas forced-air furnace				
45,000 btu	HVAC installer	$46.40	11.3	**$524.00** ea
150,000 btu	HVAC installer	$46.40	17.3	**$803.00** ea
Install oil forced-air furnace				
56,000 btu	HVAC installer	$46.40	12.4	**$575.00** ea
134,000 btu	HVAC installer	$46.40	17.8	**$826.00** ea
Install heat pump with supplementary heat coil				
2 ton	HVAC installer	$46.40	19.5	**$905.00** ea
Install humidifier				
5 pounds	HVAC installer	$46.40	3.83	**$178.00** ea
Double wall furnace flue (all fuels)				
4" diameter	HVAC installer	$46.40	.318	**$14.80** lf
8" diameter	HVAC installer	$46.40	.533	**$24.70** lf
Through-wall AC unit				
5,000 btu	HVAC installer	$46.40	8.83	**$410.00** ea
18,000 btu	HVAC installer	$46.40	11.8	**$548.00** ea
Through-wall combination AC and heat unit				
6,000 btu AC and 4,040 btu heat unit	HVAC installer	$46.40	10.2	**$473.00** ea
11,300 btu AC and 9,200 btu heat unit	HVAC installer	$46.40	12.2	**$566.00** ea
Evaporative cooler				
2,000 cfm	HVAC installer	$46.40	7.49	**$348.00** ea
5,600 cfm	HVAC installer	$46.40	10.9	**$506.00** ea
Thermostat				
heat only	HVAC installer	$46.40	1.53	**$71.00** ea
heat and air conditioning	HVAC installer	$46.40	2.38	**$110.00** ea
programmable	HVAC installer	$46.40	3.49	**$162.00** ea
programmable, with zone control	HVAC installer	$46.40	4.29	**$199.00** ea

22 Insulation

Item Description	Unit	Remove	Replace	Total
Minimum charge for insulation work *Replace* Material ....35.00 Labor 66.00	ea	—	$101.00	$101.00
3″ deep vermiculite attic insulation *Replace* Material........ 1.04 Labor............. .24 *Remove* .... Labor............. .39	sf	$.39	$1.28	$1.67
4″ deep vermiculite attic insulation *Replace* Material ....1.39 Labor............. .27 *Remove* .... Labor............. .47	sf	$.47	$1.66	$2.13
5″ deep vermiculite attic insulation *Replace* Material ....1.73 Labor............. .27 *Remove* .... Labor............. .55	sf	$.55	$2.00	$2.55
6″ deep vermiculite attic insulation *Replace* Material ....2.08 Labor............. .30 *Remove* .... Labor............. .69	sf	$.69	$2.38	$3.07
R11 blown mineral wool attic insulation (3-1/2″ deep) *Replace* Material.......... .54 Labor............. .30 *Remove* .... Labor............. .33	sf	$.33	$.84	$1.17
R19 blown mineral wool attic insulation (6″ deep) *Replace* Material.......... .81 Labor............. .33 *Remove* .... Labor............. .36	sf	$.36	$1.14	$1.50
R30 blown mineral wool attic insulation (10″ deep) *Replace* Material ....1.32 Labor............. .40 *Remove* .... Labor............. .52	sf	$.52	$1.72	$2.24
R38 blown mineral wool attic insulation (12″ deep) *Replace* Material ....1.78 Labor............. .49 *Remove* .... Labor............. .61	sf	$.61	$2.27	$2.88
R12 blown cellulose attic insulation (3-1/2″ deep) *Replace* Material.......... .52 Labor............. .30 *Remove* .... Labor............. .39	sf	$.39	$.82	$1.21
R21 blown cellulose attic insulation (6″ deep) *Replace* Material.......... .79 Labor............. .36 *Remove* .... Labor............. .41	sf	$.41	$1.15	$1.56
R33 blown cellulose attic insulation (10″ deep) *Replace* Material ....1.28 Labor............. .40 *Remove* .... Labor............. .63	sf	$.63	$1.68	$2.31
R42 blown cellulose attic insulation (12″ deep) *Replace* Material ....1.72 Labor............. .49 *Remove* .... Labor............. .72	sf	$.72	$2.21	$2.93
R11 blown fiberglass attic insulation (5″ deep) *Replace* Material.......... .46 Labor............. .30 *Remove* .... Labor............. .33	sf	$.33	$.76	$1.09

◄ **MINIMUM**

◄ **VERMICULITE**
Poured by hand from 3 cf bags.

◄ **MINERAL WOOL**
See the next page for additional costs to blow into existing walls.

RELATED ITEMS

Masonry
Polystyrene block inserts...301
loose block insulation.......302
2″ polystyrene cavity wall insulation.....295
Rough Carpentry
factory built panels..........443
insulating sheathing..........441

◄ **CELLULOSE**
See the next page for additional costs to blow into existing walls.

◄ **BLOWN FIBERGLASS**
See the next page for additional costs to blow into existing walls.

	Item Description	Unit	Remove	Replace	Total
BLOWN ▶ FIBERGLASS *continued*	**R19 blown fiberglass attic insulation (8″ deep)** ***Replace*** Material.......... .70 Labor............. .33 ***Remove*** .... Labor............. .36	sf	$.36	$1.03	$1.39
	R30 blown fiberglass attic insulation (13″ deep) ***Replace*** Material.........1.13 Labor............. .40 ***Remove*** .... Labor............. .52	sf	$.52	$1.53	$2.05
	R38 blown fiberglass attic insulation (16″ deep) ***Replace*** Material.........1.51 Labor............. .49 ***Remove*** .... Labor............. .61	sf	$.61	$2.00	$2.61
ADD TO INSULATE ▶ EXISTING WALLS *Add to blown in costs. Includes holes drilled 16″ on center every 4′ of height, patching, and painting if necessary.*	**Add 285% to blow insulation into existing wall with stucco**				
	Add 233% to blow insulation into existing wall with siding				
	Add 318% to blow insulation into existing wall with masonry veneer				
	Add 216% to blow insulation into existing wall through drywall				
FIBERGLASS ▶ BATT IN CEILING OR FLOOR *Based on installation in framing 16″ on center. Add **5%** for 12″ oc and deduct **7%** for 24″ oc.*	**R11 batt insulation (3-1/2″ deep) attic, ceiling or floor installation** ***Replace*** Material.......... .39 Labor............. .27 ***Remove*** .... Labor............. .25	sf	$.25	$.66	$.91
	R19 batt insulation (6″ deep) attic, ceiling or floor installation ***Replace*** Material.......... .58 Labor............. .33 ***Remove*** .... Labor............. .36	sf	$.36	$.91	$1.27
	R30 batt insulation (9-1/2″ deep) attic, ceiling or floor installation ***Replace*** Material.......... .95 Labor............. .36 ***Remove*** .... Labor............. .41	sf	$.41	$1.31	$1.72
	R38 batt insulation (12″ deep) attic, ceiling or floor installation ***Replace*** Material.........1.27 Labor............. .46 ***Remove*** .... Labor............. .50	sf	$.50	$1.73	$2.23
FIBERGLASS ▶ BATT IN WALL *Based on installation in framing 16″ on center. Add **5%** for 12″ oc and deduct **7%** for 24″ oc.*	**R6 batt insulation (1-3/4″ deep) wall installation (between furring strips)** ***Replace*** Material.......... .22 Labor............. .30 ***Remove*** .... Labor............. .19	sf	$.19	$.52	$.71
	R11 batt insulation (3-1/2″ deep) wall installation ***Replace*** Material.......... .39 Labor............. .33 ***Remove*** .... Labor............. .25	sf	$.25	$.72	$.97
	R19 batt insulation (6″ deep) wall installation ***Replace*** Material.......... .58 Labor............. .40 ***Remove*** .... Labor............. .36	sf	$.36	$.98	$1.34
	R19 batt insulation (8″ deep) wall installation ***Replace*** Material.......... .77 Labor............. .46 ***Remove*** .... Labor............. .41	sf	$.41	$1.23	$1.64
ADD FOR ▶ BATT FACE	**Add 8% for Kraft face**				
	Add 10% for foil face				
	Add 14% for plastic vapor barrier				
RIGID FOAM ▶ *Glued and/or nailed in place on walls or roof.*	**1/2″ rigid foam insulation board** ***Replace*** Material.......... .48 Labor............. .43 ***Remove*** .... Labor............. .19	sf	$.19	$.91	$1.10

Item Description	Unit	Remove	Replace	Total
3/4" rigid foam insulation board *Replace* Material.......... .58 Labor............. .43 *Remove* .... Labor............. .19	sf	$.19	$1.01	$1.20
1" rigid foam insulation board *Replace* Material.......... .77 Labor............. .43 *Remove* .... Labor............. .19	sf	$.19	$1.20	$1.39
2" rigid foam insulation board *Replace* Material........ 1.01 Labor............. .43 *Remove* .... Labor............. .19	sf	$.19	$1.44	$1.63

RELATED ITEMS

Masonry
Polystyrene block inserts...301
loose block insulation.......302
2" polystyrene cavity wall insulation.....295
Rough Carpentry
factory built panels..........443
insulating sheathing..........441

NOTES: ______

______ end

TIME & MATERIAL CHARTS *(selected items)*

Insulation Materials

DESCRIPTION	MATERIAL PRICE	GROSS COVERAGE	WASTE	NET COVERAGE	UNIT PRICE
Vermiculite attic insulation					
3" deep	$1.00 sf	1	4%	.96	**$1.04** sf
4" deep	$1.33 sf	1	4%	.96	**$1.39** sf
5" deep	$1.66 sf	1	4%	.96	**$1.73** sf
6" deep	$2.00 sf	1	4%	.96	**$2.08** sf
Blown mineral wool insulation					
R11 (3-1/2" deep)	$.52 sf	1	4%	.96	**$.54** sf
R19 (6" deep)	$.78 sf	1	4%	.96	**$.81** sf
R30 (10" deep)	$1.27 sf	1	4%	.96	**$1.32** sf
R38 (12" deep)	$1.71 sf	1	4%	.96	**$1.78** sf
Blown cellulose insulation					
R12 blown (3-1/2" deep)	$.50 sf	1	4%	.96	**$.52** sf
R21 blown (6" deep)	$.76 sf	1	4%	.96	**$.79** sf
R33 blown (10" deep)	$1.23 sf	1	4%	.96	**$1.28** sf
R42 blown (12" deep)	$1.65 sf	1	4%	.96	**$1.72** sf
Blown fiberglass insulation					
R11 (5" deep)	$.44 sf	1	4%	.96	**$.46** sf
R19 (8" deep)	$.67 sf	1	4%	.96	**$.70** sf
R30 (13" deep)	$1.08 sf	1	4%	.96	**$1.13** sf
R38 (16" deep)	$1.45 sf	1	4%	.96	**$1.51** sf
Fiberglass batt insulation in ceiling or floor					
R11 (3-1/2" deep)	$.37 sf	1	4%	.96	**$.39** sf
R19 (6" deep)	$.56 sf	1	4%	.96	**$.58** sf
R30 (9-1/2" deep)	$.91 sf	1	4%	.96	**$.95** sf
R38 (12" deep)	$1.22 sf	1	4%	.96	**$1.27** sf
Fiberglass batt insulation in wall					
R6 (1-3/4" deep) (between furring strips)	$.21 sf	1	4%	.96	**$.22** sf
R11 (3-1/2" deep)	$.37 sf	1	4%	.96	**$.39** sf
R19 (6" deep)	$.56 sf	1	4%	.96	**$.58** sf
R25 (8" deep)	$.74 sf	1	4%	.96	**$.77** sf
Rigid foam insulation board					
1/2"	$.46 sf	1	4%	.96	**$.48** sf
3/4"	$.56 sf	1	4%	.96	**$.58** sf
1"	$.74 sf	1	4%	.96	**$.77** sf
2"	$.97 sf	1	4%	.96	**$1.01** sf

Insulation Labor

LABORER	BASE WAGE	PAID LEAVE	TRUE WAGE	FICA	FUTA	WORKER'S COMP.	UNEMPLOY. INSUR.	HEALTH INSUR.	RETIRE (401K)	LIABILITY INSUR.	COST PER HOUR
Insulation installer	$16.10	1.26	$17.36	1.33	.14	4.52	1.51	2.69	.52	2.34	$30.40
Demolition laborer	$13.90	1.08	$14.98	1.15	.12	4.79	1.30	2.69	.45	2.02	$27.50

Paid Leave is calculated based on two weeks paid vacation, one week sick leave, and seven paid holidays. Employer's matching portion of **FICA** is 7.65 percent. **FUTA** (Federal Unemployment) is .8 percent. **Worker's compensation** for the insulation trade was calculated using a national average of 26.03 percent. **Unemployment insurance** was calculated using a national average of 8.7 percent. **Health insurance** was calculated based on a projected national average for 2002 of $535 per employee (and family when applicable) per month. Employer pays 80 percent for a per month cost of $428 per employee. **Retirement** is based on a 401(k) retirement program with employer matching of 50 percent. Employee contributions to the 401(k) plan are an average of 6 percent of the true wage. **Liability insurance** is based on a national average of 13.2 percent.

Insulation Labor Productivity

WORK DESCRIPTION	LABORER	COST PER HOUR	PRODUCTIVITY	UNIT PRICE
Pour vermiculite attic insulation				
3" deep	*insulation installer*	$30.40	.008	**$.24** *sf*
4" deep	*insulation installer*	$30.40	.009	**$.27** *sf*
5" deep	*insulation installer*	$30.40	.009	**$.27** *sf*
6" deep	*insulation installer*	$30.40	.010	**$.30** *sf*
Blow in mineral wool insulation				
R11 (3-1/2" deep)	*insulation installer*	$30.40	.010	**$.30** *sf*
R19 (6" deep)	*insulation installer*	$30.40	.011	**$.33** *sf*
R30 (10" deep)	*insulation installer*	$30.40	.013	**$.40** *sf*
R38 (12" deep)	*insulation installer*	$30.40	.016	**$.49** *sf*
Blow in cellulose insulation				
R12 (3-1/2" deep)	*insulation installer*	$30.40	.30	**$.30** *sf*
R21 (6" deep)	*insulation installer*	$30.40	.012	**$.36** *sf*
R33 (10" deep)	*insulation installer*	$30.40	.013	**$.40** *sf*
R42 (12" deep)	*insulation installer*	$30.40	.016	**$.49** *sf*
Blow in fiberglass insulation				
R11 (5" deep)	*insulation installer*	$30.40	.010	**$.30** *sf*
R19 (8" deep)	*insulation installer*	$30.40	.011	**$.33** *sf*
R30 (13" deep)	*insulation installer*	$30.40	.013	**$.40** *sf*
R38 (16" deep)	*insulation installer*	$30.40	.016	**$.49** *sf*
Install fiberglass batt insulation in ceiling or floor				
R11 (3-1/2" deep)	*insulation installer*	$30.40	.27	**$.27** *sf*
R19 (6" deep)	*insulation installer*	$30.40	.011	**$.33** *sf*
R30 (9-1/2" deep)	*insulation installer*	$30.40	.012	**$.36** *sf*
R38 (12" deep)	*insulation installer*	$30.40	.015	**$.46** *sf*
Install fiberglass batt insulation in wall				
R6 (1-3/4" deep) (between furring strips)	*insulation installer*	$30.40	.010	**$.30** *sf*
R11 (3-1/2" deep)	*insulation installer*	$30.40	.011	**$.33** *sf*
R19 (6" deep)	*insulation installer*	$30.40	.013	**$.40** *sf*
R25 (8" deep)	*insulation installer*	$30.40	.015	**$.46** *sf*
Install rigid foam insulation board				
all thicknesses	*insulation installer*	$30.40	.014	**$.43** *sf*

NOTES:

end

23 Masking & Moving

Item Description	Unit			Total	
Minimum charge for masking or moving work *Mask* Material............16.00 Labor...........57.30	ea	—	—	$73.30	◄ MINIMUM
Mask small room *Mask* Material.............3.03 Labor..........29.30	ea	—	—	$32.33	◄ MASK ROOM
Mask average size room *Mask* Material.............3.46 Labor..........33.80	ea	—	—	$37.26	
Mask large room *Mask* Material.............4.03 Labor..........40.10	ea	—	—	$44.13	
Mask very large room *Mask* Material.............4.27 Labor..........48.80	ea	—	—	$53.07	
Mask room per lf of wall *Mask* Material............. .10 Labor............. .84	lf	—	—	$.94	◄ MASK ROOM PER LF
Mask small window *Mask* Material.............1.53 Labor............6.94	ea	—	—	$8.47	◄ MASK WINDOW
Mask average size window *Mask* Material.............1.62 Labor............8.13	ea	—	—	$9.75	
Mask large window *Mask* Material.............1.71 Labor............9.77	ea	—	—	$11.48	
Mask very large window *Mask* Material.............1.79 Labor...........12.00	ea	—	—	$13.79	
Mask door or opening per lf of opening *Mask* Material............. .06 Labor............. .79	lf	—	—	$.85	◄ MASK DOOR OR OPENING PER LF
Mask small door or opening *Mask* Material.............1.68 Labor............6.86	ea	—	—	$8.54	◄ MASK DOOR OR OPENING
Mask average size door or opening *Mask* Material.............1.77 Labor............8.00	ea	—	—	$9.77	
Mask large door or opening *Mask* Material.............1.86 Labor............9.61	ea	—	—	$11.47	
Mask very large door or opening *Mask* Material.............1.95 Labor...........11.70	ea	—	—	$13.65	
Mask woodwork per lf of woodwork *Mask* Material............. .06 Labor............. .77	lf	—	—	$.83	◄ MASK WOODWORK
Mask baseboard heater *Mask* Material.............1.29 Labor............5.86	ea	—	—	$7.15	◄ MASK HEATER
Mask light fixture *Mask* Material............. .99 Labor............4.80	ea	—	—	$5.79	◄ MASK LIGHT FIXTURE

	Item Description	Unit			Total
MASK OUTLET ▶ OR SWITCH	**Mask outlet or switch (remove cover)** *Mask* Material .23 Labor 3.01	ea	—	—	$3.24
MASK BATHROOM ▶	**Mask small bathroom** *Mask* Material 3.06 Labor 30.60	ea	—	—	$33.66
	Mask average size bathroom *Mask* Material 3.50 Labor 35.60	ea	—	—	$39.10
	Mask large bathroom *Mask* Material 4.11 Labor 42.50	ea	—	—	$46.61
	Mask very large bathroom *Mask* Material 4.37 Labor 52.80	ea	—	—	$57.17
MASK KITCHEN ▶	**Mask small kitchen** *Mask* Material 3.64 Labor 31.70	ea	—	—	$35.34
	Mask average size kitchen *Mask* Material 3.95 Labor 37.20	ea	—	—	$41.15
	Mask large kitchen *Mask* Material 4.33 Labor 44.60	ea	—	—	$48.93
	Mask very large kitchen *Mask* Material 4.51 Labor 56.20	ea	—	—	$60.71
MASK TILE, ▶ MARBLE, OR STONE	**Mask tile, marble, or stone per lf of edge** *Mask* Material .09 Labor .82	lf	—	—	$.91
MOVE & COVER ▶ ROOM CONTENTS	**Move and cover small room contents** *Move* Material 8.62 Labor 33.00	ea	—	—	$41.62
	Move and cover average room contents *Move* Material 9.79 Labor 40.10	ea	—	—	$49.89
	Move and cover heavy or above average room contents *Move* Material 11.00 Labor 50.70	ea	—	—	$61.70
	Move and cover very heavy or above average room contents *Move* Material 12.80 Labor 71.30	ea	—	—	$84.10

TIME & MATERIAL CHARTS *(selected items)*

Masking & Moving Labor

LABORER	BASE WAGE	PAID LEAVE	TRUE WAGE	FICA	FUTA	WORKER'S COMP.	UNEMPLOY. INSUR.	HEALTH INSUR.	RETIRE (401K)	LIABILITY INSUR.	COST PER HOUR
Laborer	$14.10	1.10	$15.20	1.16	.12	3.36	1.32	2.69	.46	2.05	$26.40

Paid Leave is calculated based on two weeks paid vacation, one week sick leave, and seven paid holidays. Employer's matching portion of **FICA** is 7.65 percent. **FUTA** (Federal Unemployment) is .8 percent. **Worker's compensation** for the masking & movingtrade was calculated using a national average of 22.09 percent. **Unemployment insurance** was calculated using a national average of 8.7 percent. **Health insurance** was calculated based on a projected national average for 2002 of $535 per employee (and family when applicable) per month. Employer pays 80 percent for a per month cost of $428 per employee. **Retirement** is based on a 401(k) retirement program with employer matching of 50 percent. Employee contributions to the 401(k) plan are an average of 6 percent of the true wage. **Liability insurance** is based on a national average of 13.2 percent.

24 .... Masonry

Item Description	Unit	Remove	Replace	Total
Minimum charge for masonry work ***Replace*** Materials.....125.00 Labor.........267.00	ea	—	$392.00	$392.00
Deduct 16% for common brick				
4" wide standard non-modular brick wall  ***Replace*** Materials........4.99 Labor............6.82 ***Remove*** .... Labor............2.39 ► Non-modular bricks. Actual dimensions: 3-3/4" thick by 2-1/4" high by 8" long.	sf	$2.39	$11.81	$14.20
4" wide oversize non-modular brick wall 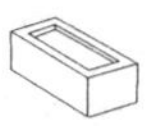 ***Replace*** Materials........4.21 Labor............6.74 ***Remove*** .... Labor............2.39 ► Non-modular bricks. Actual dimensions: 3-3/4" thick by 2-3/4" high by 8" long.	sf	$2.39	$10.95	$13.34
4" wide three-inch non-modular brick wall 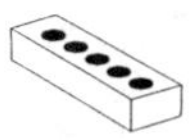 ***Replace*** Materials........4.22 Labor............6.70 ***Remove*** .... Labor............2.39 ► Non-modular bricks. Actual dimensions: 3" thick by 2-3/4" high by 9-3/4" long. Three-inch bricks also come in lengths of 9-5/8" and 8-3/4" and widths vary from 2-5/8" to 3". Normally used as a veneer unit.	sf	$2.39	$10.92	$13.31
4" wide standard brick wall  ***Replace*** Materials........3.55 Labor............6.78 ***Remove*** .... Labor............2.39 ► Modular bricks. Nominal dimensions: 4" thick by 2-2/3" high by 8" long.	sf	$2.39	$10.33	$12.72
4" wide engineer brick wall  ***Replace*** Materials........3.72 Labor............5.65 ***Remove*** .... Labor............2.39 ► Modular bricks. Nominal dimensions: 4" thick by 3-1/5" high by 8" long.	sf	$2.39	$9.37	$11.76
4" wide jumbo closure brick wall  ***Replace*** Materials........3.73 Labor............4.81 ***Remove*** .... Labor............2.39 ► Also called economy 8. Modular bricks. Nominal dimensions: 4" thick by 4" high by 8" long.	sf	$2.39	$8.54	$10.93
4" wide double brick wall  ***Replace*** Materials........3.07 Labor............4.05 ***Remove*** .... Labor............2.39 ► Modular bricks. Nominal dimensions: 4" thick by 5-1/3" high by 8" long.	sf	$2.39	$7.12	$9.51
4" wide Roman brick wall 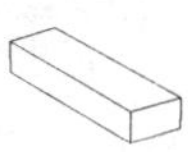 ***Replace*** Materials........4.97 Labor............6.42 ***Remove*** .... Labor............2.39 ► Modular bricks. Nominal dimensions: 4" thick by 2" high by 12" long.	sf	$2.39	$11.39	$13.78
4" wide Norman brick wall  ***Replace*** Materials........4.07 Labor............5.21 ***Remove*** .... Labor............2.39 ► Modular bricks. Nominal dimensions: 4" thick by 2-2/3" high by 12" long.	sf	$2.39	$9.28	$11.67
4" wide Norwegian brick wall  ***Replace*** Materials........3.15 Labor............4.45 ***Remove*** .... Labor............2.39 ► Modular bricks. Nominal dimensions: 4" thick by 3-1/5" high by 12" long.	sf	$2.39	$7.60	$9.99

◄ **MINIMUM**

◄ **COMMON BRICK**

◄ **4" WIDE BRICK WALL**
With 3/8" wide mortar joints. Includes 4% waste for brick and 25% waste for mortar.

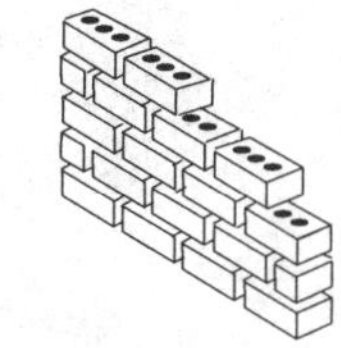

BRICK WALLS

All brick walls are made from average to high quality face brick. Standard quality bricks will be up to **15%** less and higher quality bricks will vary by as much as **45%**.

Brick sizes come in two general categories: non-modular and modular. Actual dimensions are listed for non-modular bricks.

Modular bricks are designed to fit together with a minimum of cutting which saves labor and reduces waste.

Nominal dimensions for modular bricks include the manufactured dimensions *plus* the thickness of the mortar joint for which the unit was designed (usually 1/2").

Actual brick sizes vary from manufacturer to manufacturer. The sizes in this section are typical.

RELATED ITEMS

Cleaning 63
Fireplaces 241
Painting 340

4" WIDE ▶ BRICK WALL *continued*

Item Description	Unit	Remove	Replace	Total
4" wide jumbo utility brick wall  ***Replace*** Materials........3.97 Labor............4.09 ***Remove*** .... Labor............2.39 ▶ Also called economy 12. Modular bricks. Nominal dimensions: 4" thick by 4" high by 12" long.	sf	$2.39	$8.06	$10.45
4" wide triple brick wall 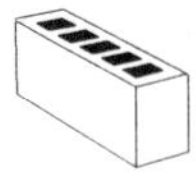 ***Replace*** Materials........3.25 Labor............3.85 ***Remove*** .... Labor............2.39 ▶ Modular bricks. Nominal dimensions: 4" thick by 5-1/3" high by 12" long.	sf	$2.39	$7.10	$9.49

6" WIDE ▶ BRICK WALL

With 3/8" wide mortar joints. Includes 4% waste for brick and 25% waste for mortar.

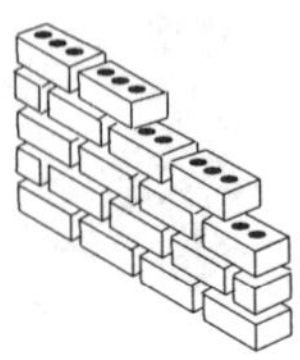

Item Description	Unit	Remove	Replace	Total
6" wide Norwegian brick wall 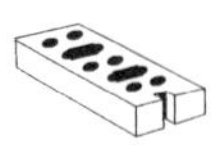 ***Replace*** Materials........4.35 Labor............4.97 ***Remove*** .... Labor............2.86 ▶ Modular bricks. Nominal dimensions: 6" thick by 3-1/5" high by 12" long.	sf	$2.86	$9.32	$12.18
6" wide Norman brick wall 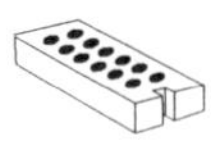 ***Replace*** Materials........5.31 Labor............5.93 ***Remove*** .... Labor............2.86 ▶ Modular bricks. Nominal dimensions: 6" thick by 2-2/3" high by 12" long.	sf	$2.86	$11.24	$14.10
6" wide jumbo brick wall 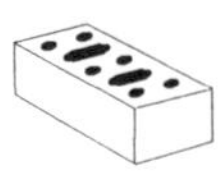 ***Replace*** Materials........4.85 Labor............4.53 ***Remove*** .... Labor............2.86 ▶ Modular bricks. Nominal dimensions: 6" thick by 4" high by 12" long.	sf	$2.86	$9.38	$12.24

8" WIDE ▶ BRICK WALL

Item Description	Unit	Remove	Replace	Total
8" wide jumbo brick wall 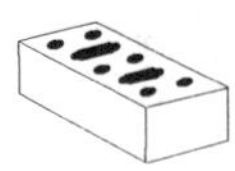 ***Replace*** Materials........5.66 Labor............5.09 ***Remove*** .... Labor............3.63 ▶ Modular bricks. Nominal dimensions: 8" thick by 4" high by 12" long. With 3/8" wide mortar joints, Includes 4% waste for brick and 25% waste for mortar.	sf	$3.63	$10.75	$14.38

8" WIDE ▶ DOUBLE WYTHE BRICK WALL

With 3/8" wide mortar joints. Includes 4% waste for brick and 25% waste for mortar.

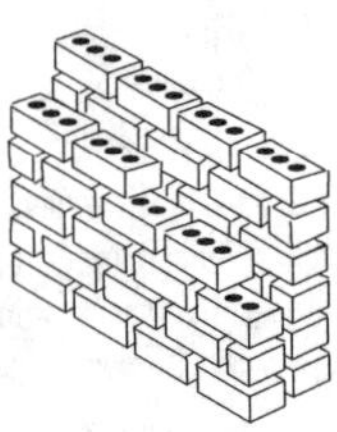

Item Description	Unit	Remove	Replace	Total
8" wide double wythe standard non-modular brick wall  ***Replace*** Materials......10.30 Labor...........12.30 ***Remove*** .... Labor............3.63 ▶ Non-modular bricks. Actual dimensions: 3-3/4" thick by 2-1/4" high by 8" long.	sf	$3.63	$22.60	$26.23
8" wide double wythe oversize non-modular brick wall 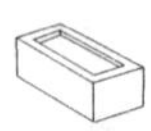 ***Replace*** Materials........8.74 Labor...........12.20 ***Remove*** .... Labor............3.63 ▶ Non-modular bricks. Actual dimensions: 3-3/4" thick by 2-3/4" high by 8" long.	sf	$3.63	$20.94	$24.57
8" wide double wythe three-inch non-modular brick wall 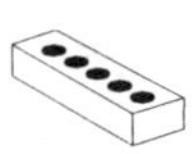 ***Replace*** Materials........8.76 Labor...........12.00 ***Remove*** .... Labor............3.63 ▶ Non-modular bricks. Actual dimensions: 3" thick by 2-3/4" high by 9-3/4" long. Three-inch bricks also come in lengths of 9-5/8" and 8-3/4" and widths vary from 2-5/8" to 3". Normally used as a veneer unit.	sf	$3.63	$20.76	$24.39
8" wide double wythe standard brick wall 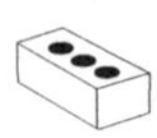 ***Replace*** Materials........7.42 Labor...........12.20 ***Remove*** .... Labor............3.63 ▶ Modular bricks. Nominal dimensions: 4" thick by 2-2/3" high by 8" long.	sf	$3.63	$19.62	$23.25
8" wide double wythe engineer brick wall  ***Replace*** Materials........7.76 Labor...........10.10 ***Remove*** .... Labor............3.63 ▶ Modular bricks. Nominal dimensions: 4" thick by 3-1/5" high by 8" long.	sf	$3.63	$17.86	$21.49
8" wide double wythe jumbo closure brick wall  ***Replace*** Materials........7.78 Labor............8.66 ***Remove*** .... Labor............3.63 ▶ Also called economy 8. Modular bricks. Nominal dimensions: 4" thick by 4" high by 8" long.	sf	$3.63	$16.44	$20.07

Item Description	Unit	Remove	Replace	Total
8″ wide double wythe double brick wall ***Replace*** Materials........6.46 Labor............7.26 ***Remove*** .... Labor............3.63 ► Modular bricks. Nominal dimensions: 4″ thick by 5-1/3″ high by 8″ long.	sf	$3.63	$13.72	$17.35
8″ wide double wythe Roman brick wall ***Replace*** Materials......10.26 Labor...........11.50 ***Remove*** .... Labor............3.63 ► Modular bricks. Nominal dimensions: 4″ thick by 2″ high by 12″ long.	sf	$3.63	$21.76	$25.39
8″ wide double wythe Norman brick wall ***Replace*** Materials........8.46 Labor............9.38 ***Remove*** .... Labor............3.63 ► Modular bricks. Nominal dimensions: 4″ thick by 2-2/3″ high by 12″ long.	sf	$3.63	$17.84	$21.47
8″ wide double wythe Norwegian brick wall ***Replace*** Materials........6.62 Labor............7.98 ***Remove*** .... Labor............3.63 ► Modular bricks. Nominal dimensions: 4″ thick by 3-1/5″ high by 12″ long.	sf	$3.63	$14.60	$18.23
8″ wide double wythe jumbo utility brick wall ***Replace*** Materials........8.26 Labor............7.38 ***Remove*** .... Labor............3.63 ► Also called economy 12. Modular bricks. Nominal dimensions: 4″ thick by 4″ high by 12″ long.	sf	$3.63	$15.64	$19.27
8″ wide double wythe triple brick wall ***Replace*** Materials........6.82 Labor............6.94 ***Remove*** .... Labor............3.63 ► Modular bricks. Nominal dimensions: 4″ thick by 5-1/3″ high by 12″ long.	sf	$3.63	$13.76	$17.39
8″ wide wall from 4″ standard non-mod. brick and 4″ block ***Replace*** Materials........7.22 Labor............9.34 ***Remove*** .... Labor............3.63 ► Modular bricks. Actual dimensions: 3-3/4″ thick by 2-1/4″ high by 8″ long. Concrete block: 4″ thick by 8″ high by 16″ long.	sf	$3.63	$16.56	$20.19
8″ wide wall from 4″ oversize non-mod. brick and 4″ block ***Replace*** Materials........6.44 Labor............9.26 ***Remove*** .... Labor............3.63 ► Modular bricks. Actual dimensions: 3-3/4″ thick by 2-3/4″ high by 8″ long. Concrete block: 4″ thick by 8″ high by 16″ long.	sf	$3.63	$15.70	$19.33
8″ wide wall from three-inch non-mod. brick and 4″ block ***Replace*** Materials........6.45 Labor............9.22 ***Remove*** .... Labor............3.63 ► Modular bricks. Actual dimensions: 3″ thick by 2-3/4″ high by 9-3/4″ long. Three-inch bricks also come in lengths of 9-5/8″ and 8-3/4″ and widths vary from 2-5/8″ to 3″. Concrete block: 4″ thick by 8″ high by 16″ long.	sf	$3.63	$15.67	$19.30
8″ wide ick wall from 4″ standard brick and 4″ concrete block ***Replace*** Materials........5.78 Labor............9.34 ***Remove*** .... Labor............3.63 ► Modular bricks. Nominal dimensions: 4″ thick by 2-2/3″ high by 8″ long. Concrete block: 4″ thick by 8″ high by 16″ long.	sf	$3.63	$15.12	$18.75
8″ wide wall from 4″ engineer brick and 4″ concrete block ***Replace*** Materials........5.95 Labor............8.26 ***Remove*** .... Labor............3.63 ► Modular bricks. Nominal dimensions: 4″ thick by 3-1/5″ high by 8″ long. Concrete block: 4″ thick by 8″ high by 16″ long.	sf	$3.63	$14.21	$17.84

◄ **8″ WIDE BRICK & BLOCK WALL**
With 3/8″ wide mortar joints. Includes 4% waste for brick and block and 25% waste for mortar.

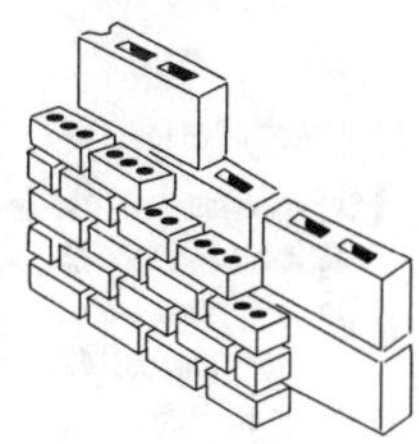

RELATED ITEMS

Cleaning 63
Fireplaces.....................241
Painting.......................340

8" WIDE BRICK & BLOCK WALL ► *continued*

Item Description	Unit	Remove	Replace	Total
8" wide wall from 4" jumbo closure brick and 4" concrete block *Replace* Materials........5.96 Labor............7.54 *Remove* .... Labor............3.63 ► Modular bricks. Nominal dimensions: 4" thick by 4" high by 8" long. Concrete block: 4" thick by 8" high by 16" long. 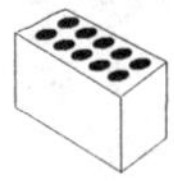	sf	$3.63	$13.50	$17.13
8" wide wall from 4" double brick and 4" concrete block *Replace* Materials........5.30 Labor............6.82 *Remove* .... Labor............3.63 ► Modular bricks. Nominal dimensions: 4" thick by 5-1/3" high by 8" long. Concrete block: 4" thick by 8" high by 16" long. 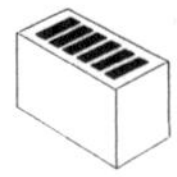	sf	$3.63	$12.12	$15.75
8" wide wall from 4" Roman brick and 4" concrete block *Replace* Materials........7.20 Labor............8.98 *Remove* .... Labor............3.63 ► Modular bricks. Nominal dimensions: 4" thick by 2" high by 12" long. Concrete block: 4" thick by 8" high by 16" long. 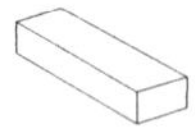	sf	$3.63	$16.18	$19.81
8" wide wall from 4" Norman and 4" concrete block *Replace* Materials........6.30 Labor............7.90 *Remove* .... Labor............3.63 ► Modular bricks. Nominal dimensions: 4" thick by 2-2/3" high by 12" long. Concrete block: 4" thick by 8" high by 16" long. 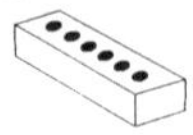	sf	$3.63	$14.20	$17.83
8" wide wall from 4" Norwegian and 4" concrete block *Replace* Materials........5.38 Labor............7.22 *Remove* .... Labor............3.63 ► Modular bricks. Nominal dimensions: 4" thick by 3-1/5" high by 12" long. Concrete block: 4" thick by 8" high by 16" long. 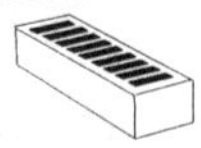	sf	$3.63	$12.60	$16.23
8" wide wall from 4" jumbo utility and 4" concrete block *Replace* Materials........6.20 Labor............6.90 *Remove* .... Labor............3.63 ► Modular bricks. Nominal dimensions: 4" thick by 4" high by 12" long. Concrete block: 4" thick by 8" high by 16" long. 	sf	$3.63	$13.10	$16.73
8" wide wall from 4" triple and 4" concrete block *Replace* Materials........5.48 Labor............6.66 *Remove* .... Labor............3.63 ► Modular bricks. Nominal dimensions: 4" thick by 5-1/3" high by 12" long. Concrete block: 4" thick by 8" high by 16" long. 	sf	$3.63	$12.14	$15.77

10" WIDE BRICK & BLOCK WALL ►

With 3/8" wide mortar joints. Includes 4% waste for brick and block and 25% waste for mortar.

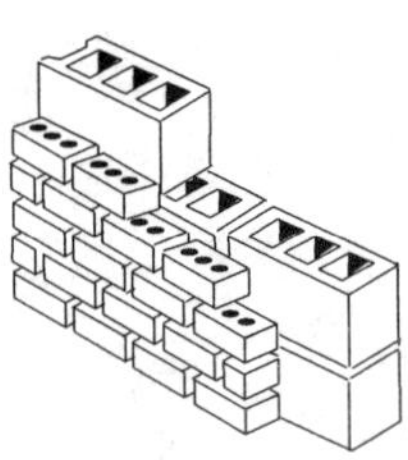

Item Description	Unit	Remove	Replace	Total
10" wide wall from 4" standard non-mod. brick and 6" block *Replace* Materials........7.54 Labor............9.46 *Remove* .... Labor............4.10 ► Modular bricks. Actual dimensions: 3-3/4" thick by 2-1/4" high by 8" long. Concrete block: 6" thick by 8" high by 16" long. 	sf	$4.10	$17.00	$21.10
10" wide wall from 4" oversize non-mod. brick and 6" block *Replace* Materials........6.76 Labor............9.38 *Remove* .... Labor............4.10 ► Modular bricks. Actual dimensions: 3-3/4" thick by 2-3/4" high by 8" long. Concrete block: 6" thick by 8" high by 16" long. 	sf	$4.10	$16.14	$20.24
10" wide wall from three-inch non-mod. brick and 6" block *Replace* Materials........6.77 Labor............9.34 *Remove* .... Labor............4.10 ► Modular bricks. Actual dimensions: 3" thick by 2-3/4" high by 9-3/4" long. Three-inch bricks also come in lengths of 9-5/8" and 8-3/4" and widths vary from 2-5/8" to 3". Concrete block: 6" thick by 8" high by 16" long. 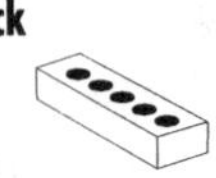	sf	$4.10	$16.11	$20.21
10" wide wall from 4" standard brick and 6" concrete block *Replace* Materials........6.10 Labor............9.42 *Remove* .... Labor............4.10 ► Modular bricks. Nominal dimensions: 4" thick by 2-2/3" high by 8" long. Concrete block: 6" thick by 8" high by 16" long. 	sf	$4.10	$15.52	$19.62

Item Description	Unit	Remove	Replace	Total
10" wide wall from 4" engineer brick and 6" concrete block ***Replace*** Materials........6.27 Labor............8.38 ***Remove*** .... Labor............4.10 ► Modular bricks. Nominal dimensions: 4" thick by 3-1/5" high by 8" long. Concrete block: 6" thick by 8" high by 16" long. 	sf	$4.10	$14.65	$18.75
10" wide wall from 4" jumbo closure and 6" concrete block ***Replace*** Materials........6.28 Labor............7.62 ***Remove*** .... Labor............4.10 ► Modular bricks. Nominal dimensions: 4" thick by 4" high by 8" long. Concrete block: 6" thick by 8" high by 16" long. 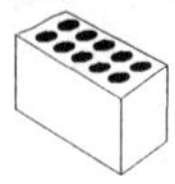	sf	$4.10	$13.90	$18.00
10" wide wall from 4" double brick and 6" concrete block ***Replace*** Materials........5.62 Labor............6.94 ***Remove*** .... Labor............4.10 ► Modular bricks. Nominal dimensions: 4" thick by 5-1/3" high by 8" long. Concrete block: 6" thick by 8" high by 16" long. 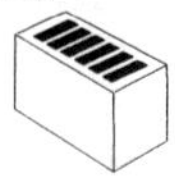	sf	$4.10	$12.56	$16.66
10" wide wall from 4" Roman brick and 6" concrete block ***Replace*** Materials........7.52 Labor............9.06 ***Remove*** .... Labor............4.10 ► Modular bricks. Nominal dimensions: 4" thick by 2" high by 12" long. Concrete block: 6" thick by 8" high by 16" long. 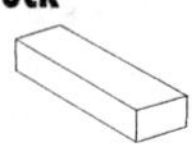	sf	$4.10	$16.58	$20.68
10" wide wall from 4" Norman and 6" concrete block ***Replace*** Materials........6.62 Labor............8.02 ***Remove*** .... Labor............4.10 ► Modular bricks. Nominal dimensions: 4" thick by 2-2/3" high by 12" long. Concrete block: 6" thick by 8" high by 16" long. 	sf	$4.10	$14.64	$18.74
10" wide wall from 4" Norwegian and 6" concrete block ***Replace*** Materials........5.70 Labor............7.30 ***Remove*** .... Labor............4.10 ► Modular bricks. Nominal dimensions: 4" thick by 3-1/5" high by 12" long. Concrete block: 6" thick by 8" high by 16" long. 	sf	$4.10	$13.00	$17.10
10" wide wall from 4" jumbo utility and 6" concrete block ***Replace*** Materials........6.52 Labor............7.02 ***Remove*** .... Labor............4.10 ► Modular bricks. Nominal dimensions: 4" thick by 4" high by 12" long. Concrete block: 6" thick by 8" high by 16" long. 	sf	$4.10	$13.54	$17.64
10" wide brick wall from 4" triple and 6" concrete block ***Replace*** Materials........5.80 Labor............6.82 ***Remove*** .... Labor............4.10 ► Modular bricks. Nominal dimensions: 4" thick by 5-1/3" high by 12" long. Concrete block: 6" thick by 8" high by 16" long. 	sf	$4.10	$12.62	$16.72
12" wide wall from 4" standard non-mod. brick and 8" concrete block ***Replace*** Materials........8.11 Labor............9.62 ***Remove*** .... Labor............4.87 ► Modular bricks. Actual dimensions: 3-3/4" thick by 2-1/4" high by 8" long. Concrete block: 8" thick by 8" high by 16" long. 	sf	$4.87	$17.73	$22.60
12" wide wall from 4" oversize non-mod. brick and 8" concrete block ***Replace*** Materials........7.33 Labor............9.58 ***Remove*** .... Labor............4.87 ► Modular bricks. Actual dimensions: 3-3/4" thick by 2-3/4" high by 8" long. Concrete block: 8" thick by 8" high by 16" long. 	sf	$4.87	$16.91	$21.78
12" wide wall from three-inch non-mod. brick and 8" concrete block ***Replace*** Materials........7.34 Labor............9.50 ***Remove*** .... Labor............4.87 ► Modular bricks. Actual dimensions: 3" thick by 2-3/4" high by 9-3/4" long. Three-inch bricks also come in lengths of 9-5/8" and 8-3/4" and widths vary from 2-5/8" to 3". Concrete block: 8" thick by 8" high by 16" long. 	sf	$4.87	$16.84	$21.71

RELATED ITEMS

Cleaning 63
Fireplaces.....................241
Painting.......................340

◄ **12" WIDE BRICK & BLOCK WALL**

With 3/8" wide mortar joints. Includes 4% waste for brick and block and 25% waste for mortar.

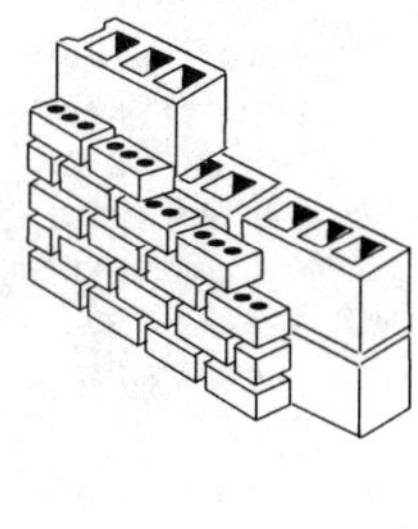

12" WIDE BRICK & BLOCK WALL *continued*

Item Description	Unit	Remove	Replace	Total
12" wide wall from 4" standard brick and 8" concrete block *Replace* Materials........6.67 Labor............9.62 *Remove* .... Labor............4.87 ► Modular bricks. Nominal dimensions: 4" thick by 2-2/3" high by 8" long. Concrete block: 8" thick by 8" high by 16" long. 	sf	$4.87	$16.29	$21.16
12" wide wall from 4" engineer brick and 8" concrete block *Replace* Materials........6.84 Labor............8.58 *Remove* .... Labor............4.87 ► Modular bricks. Nominal dimensions: 4" thick by 3-1/5" high by 8" long. Concrete block: 8" thick by 8" high by 16" long. 	sf	$4.87	$15.42	$20.29
12" wide wall from 4" jumbo closure brick and 8" concrete block *Replace* Materials........6.85 Labor............7.82 *Remove* .... Labor............4.87 ► Modular bricks. Nominal dimensions: 4" thick by 4" high by 8" long. Concrete block: 8" thick by 8" high by 16" long. 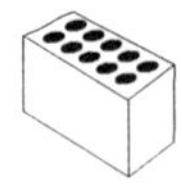	sf	$4.87	$14.67	$19.54
12" wide wall from 4" double brick and 8" concrete block *Replace* Materials........6.19 Labor............7.14 *Remove* .... Labor............4.87 ► Modular bricks. Nominal dimensions: 4" thick by 5-1/3" high by 8" long. Concrete block: 8" thick by 8" high by 16" long. 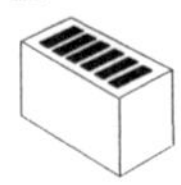	sf	$4.87	$13.33	$18.20
12" wide wall from 4" Roman brick and 8" concrete block *Replace* Materials........8.09 Labor............9.26 *Remove* .... Labor............4.87 ► Modular bricks. Nominal dimensions: 4" thick by 2" high by 12" long. Concrete block: 8" thick by 8" high by 16" long. 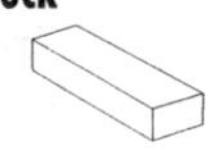	sf	$4.87	$17.35	$22.22
12" wide wall from 4" Norman brick and 8" concrete block *Replace* Materials........7.19 Labor............8.18 *Remove* .... Labor............4.87 ► Modular bricks. Nominal dimensions: 4" thick by 2-2/3" high by 12" long. Concrete block: 8" thick by 8" high by 16" long. 	sf	$4.87	$15.37	$20.24
12" wide wall from 4" Norwegian brick and 8" concrete block *Replace* Materials........6.27 Labor............7.50 *Remove* .... Labor............4.87 ► Modular bricks. Nominal dimensions: 4" thick by 3-1/5" high by 12" long. Concrete block: 8" thick by 8" high by 16" long. 	sf	$4.87	$13.77	$18.64
12" wide wall from 4" jumbo utility brick and 8" concrete block *Replace* Materials........7.09 Labor............7.22 *Remove* .... Labor............4.87 ► Modular bricks. Nominal dimensions: 4" thick by 4" high by 12" long. Concrete block: 8" thick by 8" high by 16" long. 	sf	$4.87	$14.31	$19.18
12" wide wall from 4" triple brick and 8" concrete block *Replace* Materials........6.37 Labor............6.98 *Remove* .... Labor............4.87 ► Modular bricks. Nominal dimensions: 4" thick by 5-1/3" high by 12" long. Concrete block: 8" thick by 8" high by 16" long. 	sf	$4.87	$13.35	$18.22

12" WIDE TRIPLE WYTHE BRICK WALL
With 3/8" wide mortar joints. Includes 4% waste for brick and 25% waste for mortar.

Item Description	Unit	Remove	Replace	Total
12" wide triple wythe standard non-modular brick wall *Replace* Materials.......15.30 Labor...........17.40 *Remove* .... Labor............4.87 ► Non-modular bricks. Actual dimensions: 3-3/4" thick by 2-1/4" high by 8" long. 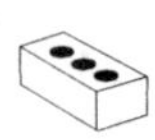	sf	$4.87	$32.70	$37.57
12" wide triple wythe oversize non-modular brick wall *Replace* Materials.......13.00 Labor...........17.10 *Remove* .... Labor............4.87 ► Non-modular bricks. Actual dimensions: 3-3/4" thick by 2-3/4" high by 8" long. 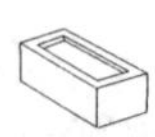	sf	$4.87	$30.10	$34.97

Item Description	Unit	Remove	Replace	Total
12″ wide triple wythe three-inch non-modular brick wall ***Replace*** Materials.......13.00 Labor...........17.00 ***Remove*** .... Labor............4.87 ► Non-modular bricks. Actual dimensions: 3″ thick by 2-3/4″ high by 9-3/4″ long. Three-inch bricks also come in lengths of 9-5/8″ and 8-3/4″ and widths vary from 2-5/8″ to 3″. 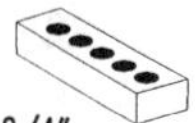	sf	$4.87	$30.00	$34.87
12″ wide triple wythe standard brick wall ***Replace*** Materials.......11.00 Labor...........17.20 ***Remove*** .... Labor............4.87 ► Modular bricks. Nominal dimensions: 4″ thick by 2-2/3″ high by 8″ long. 	sf	$4.87	$28.20	$33.07
12″ wide triple wythe engineer brick wall ***Replace*** Materials.......11.50 Labor...........14.30 ***Remove*** .... Labor............4.87 ► Modular bricks. Nominal dimensions: 4″ thick by 3-1/5″ high by 8″ long. 	sf	$4.87	$25.80	$30.67
12″ wide triple wythe jumbo closure brick wall ***Replace*** Materials.......11.50 Labor...........12.20 ***Remove*** .... Labor............4.87 ► Also called Economy 8. Modular bricks. Nominal dimensions: 4″ thick by 4″ high by 8″ long. 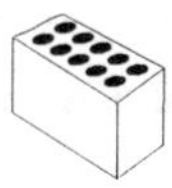	sf	$4.87	$23.70	$28.57
12″ wide triple wythe double brick wall ***Replace*** Materials........9.56 Labor...........10.20 ***Remove*** .... Labor............4.87 ► Modular bricks. Nominal dimensions: 4″ thick by 5-1/3″ high by 8″ long. 	sf	$4.87	$19.76	$24.63
12″ wide triple wythe Roman brick wall ***Replace*** Materials.......15.30 Labor...........16.30 ***Remove*** .... Labor............4.87 ► Modular bricks. Nominal dimensions: 4″ thick by 2″ high by 12″ long. 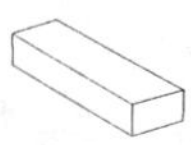	sf	$4.87	$31.60	$36.47
12″ wide triple wythe Norman brick wall ***Replace*** Materials......12.60 Labor...........13.20 ***Remove*** .... Labor............4.87 ► Modular bricks. Nominal dimensions: 4″ thick by 2-2/3″ high by 12″ long. 	sf	$4.87	$25.80	$30.67
12″ wide triple wythe Norwegian brick wall ***Replace*** Materials........9.80 Labor...........11.30 ***Remove*** .... Labor............4.87 ► Modular bricks. Nominal dimensions: 4″ thick by 3-1/5″ high by 12″ long. 	sf	$4.87	$21.10	$25.97
12″ wide triple wythe jumbo utility brick wall ***Replace*** Materials......12.30 Labor...........10.40 ***Remove*** .... Labor............4.87 ► Also called Economy 12. Modular bricks. Nominal dimensions: 4″ thick by 4″ high by 12″ long. 	sf	$4.87	$22.70	$27.57
12″ wide triple wythe triple brick wall ***Replace*** Materials......10.10 Labor............9.78 ***Remove*** .... Labor............4.87 ► Modular bricks. Nominal dimensions: 4″ thick by 5-1/3″ high by 12″ long. 	sf	$4.87	$19.88	$24.75
10″ wide cavity wall from 4″ standard non-mod. brick and 4″ block ***Replace*** Materials........7.33 Labor............9.78 ***Remove*** .... Labor............3.63 ► Modular bricks. Actual dimensions: 3-3/4″ thick by 2-1/4″ high by 8″ long. Concrete block: 4″ thick by 8″ high by 16″ long. 	sf	$3.63	$17.11	$20.74
10″ wide cavity wall from 4″ oversize non-mod. brick and 4″ block ***Replace*** Materials........6.55 Labor............9.70 ***Remove*** .... Labor............3.63 ► Modular bricks. Actual dimensions: 3-3/4″ thick by 2-3/4″ high by 8″ long. Concrete block: 4″ thick by 8″ high by 16″ long. 	sf	$3.63	$16.25	$19.88

RELATED ITEMS

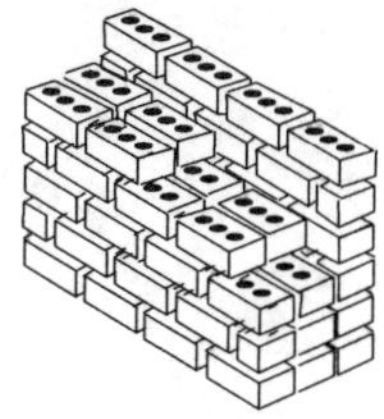

◄ **10″ WIDE BRICK & BLOCK CAVITY WALL**
With 2″ dead air space. (see page 295 for foam insulation in air space) and 3/8″ wide mortar joints. Includes 4% waste for brick and block and 25% waste for mortar.

10" WIDE BRICK & BLOCK CAVITY WALL *continued*

Item Description	Unit	Remove	Replace	Total
10" wide cavity wall from three-inch non-mod. brick and 4" block *Replace* Materials........6.56 Labor............9.66 *Remove* .... Labor............3.63 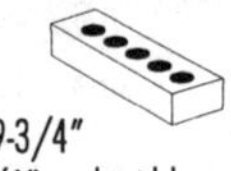 ► Modular bricks. Actual dimensions: 3" thick by 2-3/4" high by 9-3/4" long. Three-inch bricks also come in lengths of 9-5/8" and 8-3/4" and widths vary from 2-5/8" to 3". Concrete block: 4" thick by 8" high by 16" long.	sf	$3.63	$16.22	$19.85
10" wide cavity wall from 4" standard brick and 4" concrete block *Replace* Materials........5.89 Labor............9.74 *Remove* .... Labor............3.63  ► Modular bricks. Nominal dimensions: 4" thick by 2-2/3" high by 8" long. Concrete block: 4" thick by 8" high by 16" long.	sf	$3.63	$15.63	$19.26
10" wide cavity wall from 4" engineer brick and 4" concrete block *Replace* Materials........6.06 Labor............8.66 *Remove* .... Labor............3.63  ► Modular bricks. Nominal dimensions: 4" thick by 3-1/5" high by 8" long. Concrete block: 4" thick by 8" high by 16" long.	sf	$3.63	$14.72	$18.35
10" wide cavity wall from 4" jumbo closure brick and 4" concrete block *Replace* Materials........6.07 Labor............7.86 *Remove* .... Labor............3.63  ► Modular bricks. Nominal dimensions: 4" thick by 4" high by 8" long. Concrete block: 4" thick by 8" high by 16" long.	sf	$3.63	$13.93	$17.56
10" wide cavity wall from 4" double brick and 4" concrete block *Replace* Materials........5.41 Labor............7.14 *Remove* .... Labor............3.63  ► Modular bricks. Nominal dimensions: 4" thick by 5-1/3" high by 8" long. Concrete block: 4" thick by 8" high by 16" long.	sf	$3.63	$12.55	$16.18
10" wide cavity wall from 4" Roman brick and 4" concrete block *Replace* Materials........7.31 Labor............9.38 *Remove* .... Labor............3.63  ► Modular bricks. Nominal dimensions: 4" thick by 2" high by 12" long. Concrete block: 4" thick by 8" high by 16" long.	sf	$3.63	$16.69	$20.32
10" wide cavity wall from 4" Norman and 4" concrete block *Replace* Materials........6.41 Labor............8.26 *Remove* .... Labor............3.63  ► Modular bricks. Nominal dimensions: 4" thick by 2-2/3" high by 12" long. Concrete block: 4" thick by 8" high by 16" long.	sf	$3.63	$14.67	$18.30
10" wide cavity wall from 4" Norwegian brick and 4" concrete block *Replace* Materials........5.49 Labor............7.54 *Remove* .... Labor............3.63  ► Modular bricks. Nominal dimensions: 4" thick by 3-1/5" high by 12" long. Concrete block: 4" thick by 8" high by 16" long.	sf	$3.63	$13.03	$16.66
10" wide cavity wall from 4" jumbo utility brick and 4" concrete block *Replace* Materials........6.31 Labor............7.22 *Remove* .... Labor............3.63  ► Modular bricks. Nominal dimensions: 4" thick by 4" high by 12" long. Concrete block: 4" thick by 8" high by 16" long.	sf	$3.63	$13.53	$17.16
10" wide cavity wall from 4" triple brick and 4" concrete block *Replace* Materials........5.59 Labor............6.98 *Remove* .... Labor............3.63  ► Modular bricks. Nominal dimensions: 4" thick by 5-1/3" high by 12" long. Concrete block: 4" thick by 8" high by 16" long.	sf	$3.63	$12.57	$16.20

10" WIDE BRICK CAVITY WALL

Item Description	Unit	Remove	Replace	Total
10" wide cavity wall from 4" standard non-modular brick, both sides *Replace* Materials......10.41 Labor...........12.90 *Remove* .... Labor............3.63  ► Non-modular bricks. Actual dimensions: 3-3/4" thick by 2-1/4" high by 8" long.	sf	$3.63	$23.31	$26.94

continued on next page

Item Description	Unit	Remove	Replace	Total
10" wide cavity wall from 4" oversize non-modular brick, both sides ***Replace*** Materials........8.85 Labor...........12.70 ***Remove*** .... Labor............3.63 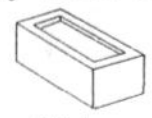 ► Non-modular bricks. Actual dimensions: 3-3/4" thick by 2-3/4" high by 8" long.	sf	$3.63	$21.55	$25.18
10" wide cavity wall from three-inch non-modular brick, both sides ***Replace*** Materials........8.87 Labor...........12.60 ***Remove*** .... Labor............3.63 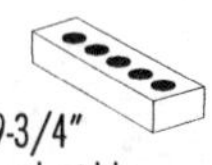 ► Non-modular bricks. Actual dimensions: 3" thick by 2-3/4" high by 9-3/4" long. Three-inch bricks also come in lengths of 9-5/8" and 8-3/4" and widths vary from 2-5/8" to 3".	sf	$3.63	$21.47	$25.10
10" wide cavity wall from 4" standard brick, both sides ***Replace*** Materials........7.53 Labor...........12.80 ***Remove*** .... Labor............3.63 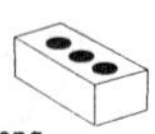 ► Modular bricks. Nominal dimensions: 4" thick by 2-2/3" high by 8" long.	sf	$3.63	$20.33	$23.96
10" wide cavity wall from 4" engineer brick, both sides ***Replace*** Materials........7.87 Labor...........10.60 ***Remove*** .... Labor............3.63  ► Modular bricks. Nominal dimensions: 4" thick by 3-1/5" high by 8" long.	sf	$3.63	$18.47	$22.10
10" wide cavity wall from 4" jumbo closure brick, both sides ***Replace*** Materials........7.89 Labor............9.06 ***Remove*** .... Labor............3.63 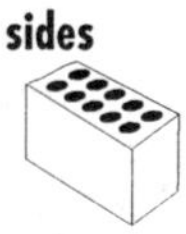 ► Also called Economy 8. Modular bricks. Nominal dimensions: 4" thick by 4" high by 8" long.	sf	$3.63	$16.95	$20.58
10" wide cavity wall from 4" double brick, both sides  ***Replace*** Materials........6.57 Labor............7.58 ***Remove*** .... Labor............3.63 ► Modular bricks. Nominal dimensions: 4" thick by 5-1/3" high by 8" long.	sf	$3.63	$14.15	$17.78
10" wide cavity wall from 4" Roman brick, both sides ***Replace*** Materials......10.37 Labor...........12.10 ***Remove*** .... Labor............3.63 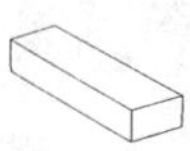 ► Modular bricks. Nominal dimensions: 4" thick by 2" high by 12" long.	sf	$3.63	$22.47	$26.10
10" wide cavity wall from 4" Norman brick, both sides ***Replace*** Materials........8.57 Labor............9.82 ***Remove*** .... Labor............3.63  ► Modular bricks. Nominal dimensions: 4" thick by 2-2/3" high by 12" long.	sf	$3.63	$18.39	$22.02
10" wide cavity wall from 4" Norwegian both sides ***Replace*** Materials........6.73 Labor............8.38 ***Remove*** .... Labor............3.63  ► Modular bricks. Nominal dimensions: 4" thick by 3-1/5" high by 12" long.	sf	$3.63	$15.11	$18.74
10" wide cavity wall from 4" jumbo utility brick, both sides ***Replace*** Materials........8.37 Labor............7.74 ***Remove*** .... Labor............3.63  ► Also called Economy 12. Modular bricks. Nominal dimensions: 4" thick by 4" high by 12" long.	sf	$3.63	$16.11	$19.74
10" wide cavity wall from 4" triple brick, both sides  ***Replace*** Materials........6.93 Labor............7.26 ***Remove*** .... Labor............3.63 ► Modular bricks. Nominal dimensions: 4" thick by 5-1/3" high by 12" long.	sf	$3.63	$14.19	$17.82
Add for 2" polystyrene insulation in cavity wall ***Replace*** Materials........ .75 Labor............. .05	sf	—	$.80	$.80

◄ **10" WIDE BRICK CAVITY WALL**
continued

With 2" dead air space. (See below for foam insulation in air space.) and 3/8" wide mortar joints. Includes 4% waste for brick and 25% waste for mortar.

RELATED ITEMS

Cleaning.......................63
Fireplaces.....................241
Painting.......................340

◄ **ADD FOR CAVITY WALL INSULATION**

BRICK VENEER ▶ *With 3/8" wide mortar joints and galvanized wall ties. Includes 4% waste for brick and block and 25% waste for mortar.*

Item Description	Unit	Remove	Replace	Total
Standard non-modular brick veneer *Replace* Materials........4.99 Labor............5.77 *Remove* .... Labor............2.26 ▶ Non-modular bricks. Actual dimensions: 3-3/4" thick by 2-1/4" high by 8" long.	sf	$2.26	$10.76	$13.02
Oversize non-modular brick veneer *Replace* Materials........4.21 Labor............5.73 *Remove* .... Labor............2.26 ▶ Non-modular bricks. Actual dimensions: 3-3/4" thick by 2-3/4" high by 8" long.	sf	$2.26	$9.94	$12.20
Three-inch non-modular brick veneer *Replace* Materials........4.22 Labor............5.65 *Remove* .... Labor............2.26 ▶ Non-modular bricks. Actual dimensions: 3" thick by 2-3/4" high by 9-3/4" long. Three-inch bricks also come in lengths of 9-5/8" and 8-3/4" and widths vary from 2-5/8" to 3". Normally used as a veneer unit.	sf	$2.26	$9.87	$12.13
Used brick veneer *Replace* Materials........7.28 Labor............5.77 *Remove* .... Labor............2.26 ▶ Modular bricks. Nominal dimensions: 4" thick by 2-2/3" high by 8" long.	sf	$2.26	$13.05	$15.31
Standard brick veneer *Replace* Materials........3.55 Labor............5.77 *Remove* .... Labor............2.26 ▶ Modular bricks. Nominal dimensions: 4" thick by 2-2/3" high by 8" long.	sf	$2.26	$9.32	$11.58
Engineer brick veneer *Replace* Materials........3.72 Labor............4.77 *Remove* .... Labor............2.26 ▶ Modular bricks. Nominal dimensions: 4" thick by 3-1/5" high by 8" long.	sf	$2.26	$8.49	$10.75
Jumbo closure brick veneer *Replace* Materials........3.73 Labor............4.09 *Remove* .... Labor............2.26 ▶ Also called Economy 8. Modular bricks. Nominal dimensions: 4" thick by 4" high by 8" long.	sf	$2.26	$7.82	$10.08
Double brick veneer *Replace* Materials........3.07 Labor............3.41 *Remove* .... Labor............2.26 ▶ Modular bricks. Nominal dimensions: 4" thick by 5-1/3" high by 8" long.	sf	$2.26	$6.48	$8.74
Roman brick veneer *Replace* Materials........4.97 Labor............5.45 *Remove* .... Labor............2.26 ▶ Modular bricks. Nominal dimensions: 4" thick by 2" high by 12" long.	sf	$2.26	$10.42	$12.68
Norman brick veneer *Replace* Materials........4.07 Labor............4.41 *Remove* .... Labor............2.26 ▶ Modular bricks. Nominal dimensions: 4" thick by 2-2/3" high by 12" long.	sf	$2.26	$8.48	$10.74
Norwegian brick veneer *Replace* Materials........3.15 Labor............3.77 *Remove* .... Labor............2.26 ▶ Modular bricks. Nominal dimensions: 4" thick by 3-1/5" high by 12" long.	sf	$2.26	$6.92	$9.18
Jumbo utility brick veneer *Replace* Materials........3.97 Labor............3.49 *Remove* .... Labor............2.26 ▶ Also called Economy 12. Modular bricks. Nominal dimensions: 4" thick by 4" high by 12" long.	sf	$2.26	$7.46	$9.72

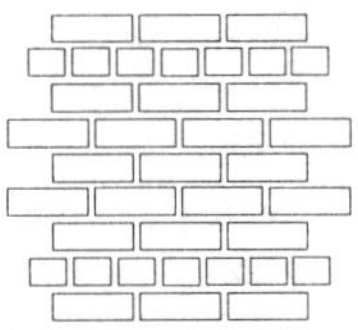
common bond △

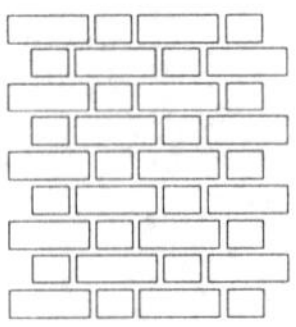
Flemish bond △

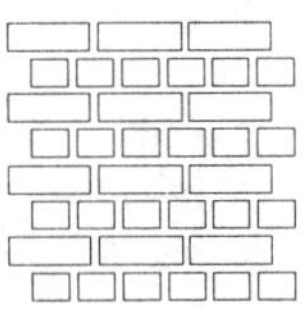
English bond △

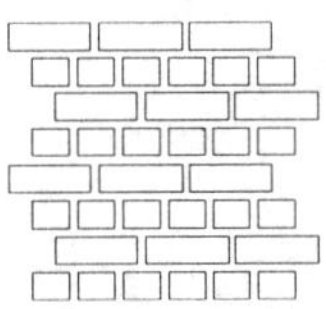
English cross bond △

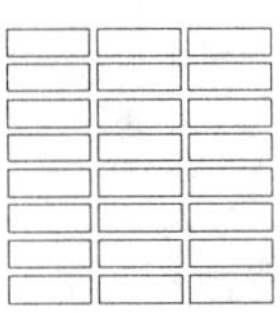
stack bond △

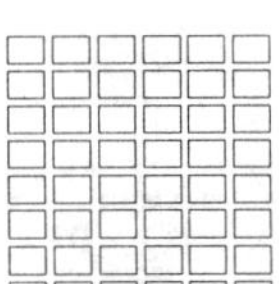
header bond △

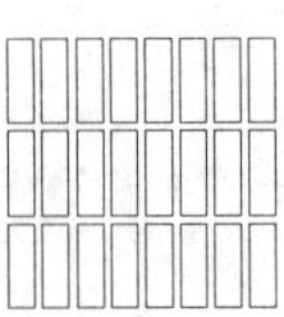
soldier course △

Item Description	Unit	Remove	Replace	Total
Triple brick veneer ***Replace*** Materials........3.25 Labor............3.29 ***Remove*** .... Labor............2.26 ► Modular bricks. Nominal dimensions: 4" thick by 5-1/3" high by 12" long.	sf	$2.26	$6.54	$8.80
Add for raked joints ***Replace*** .... Labor............ .23 ► Add for brick walls with raked joints instead of concave.	sf	—	$.23	$.23
Add 16% for common bond ► Also called American bond. Every sixth course is a full course of full-length headers.				
Add 54% for Flemish bond ► Each course is made of alternating stretchers and headers.				
Add 65% for English bond ► Alternating full courses made from stretchers and headers. The joints between stretchers in all courses align vertically.				
Add 65% for English cross bond ► Also called Dutch bond. A variation of English bond. The vertical joints between stretcher bricks, in alternate courses, align vertically with the center of the stretcher brick in the course above and below.				
Add 8% for stack bond ► All vertical and horizontal joints align.				
Add 116% for false all header bond ► All bricks are laid as headers but bricks are cut in half.				
Add 115% for all header bond ► All bricks are laid as true headers.				
Add 15% for soldier course ► All bricks are stood on end with edge showing.				
Add 5% for sailor course ► All bricks are stood on end with face showing.				
Add 122% for basketweave ► A wide variety of patterns with alternating sections of horizontal and vertical brick.				
Add 125% for herringbone weave ► Also called diagonal basketweave. Bricks are laid at an angle (usually 45 degree) in alternate sections angling up and down.				
Add 90% for diagonal bond ► All bricks laid at an angle, usually 45 degree.				
Add 70% for coursed ashlar style brick bond with two sizes of bricks ► A pattern that uses two sizes of bricks to simulate coursed ashlar stone patterns. Usually one size of brick equals two of the second size.				
Add 27% for curved brick walls				
Add for opening in 4" brick wall per lf of opening ***Replace*** Materials........4.24 Labor...........10.40 ► Includes angle iron lintel.	lf	—	$14.64	$14.64
Add for opening in 6" brick wall per lf of opening ***Replace*** Materials........7.38 Labor...........10.50 ► Includes angle iron lintel.	lf	—	$17.88	$17.88

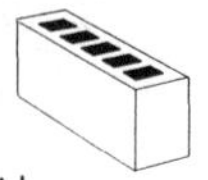

◄ **RAKED JOINTS**

◄ **ADD FOR OTHER BRICK BONDS**

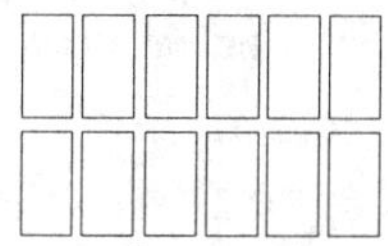

sailor course △

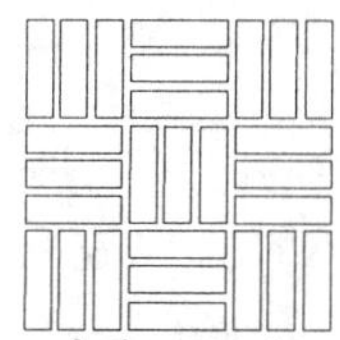

basketweave △

diagonal △

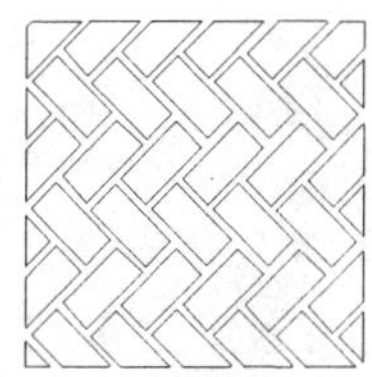

herringbone △

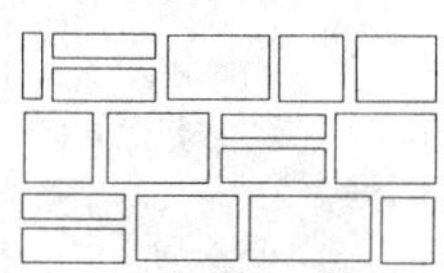

coursed ashlar style △

◄ **ADD FOR CURVED INSTALLATION**

◄ **ADD FOR OPENING IN MASONRY WALL**
Use only if sf of opening has been deducted from sf price. Includes angle iron lintel.

	Item Description	Unit	Remove	Replace	Total
ADD FOR OPENING IN MASONRY WALL *continued*	**Add for opening in 8″ brick wall per lf of opening** ***Replace*** Materials........7.38 Labor...........10.70 ► Includes angle iron lintel.	lf	—	$18.08	$18.08
	Add for opening in 10″ brick wall per lf of opening ***Replace*** Materials........8.48 Labor...........10.80 ► Includes angle iron lintel.	lf	—	$19.28	$19.28
	Add for opening in 12″ brick wall per lf of opening ***Replace*** Materials........8.48 Labor...........10.90 ► Includes angle iron lintel.	lf	—	$19.38	$19.38
ADD FOR BRICK ARCH	**Add for flat brick arch** ***Replace*** Materials.......13.30 Labor...........59.70 ► Also called a Jack arch. Do not use for standard brick wall openings that use a lintel.	lf	—	$73.00	$73.00
	Add for elliptical brick arch ***Replace*** Materials.......15.70 Labor...........74.20 ► Per lf of arch.	lf	—	$89.90	$89.90
	Add for semi-circular brick arch ***Replace*** Materials.......15.70 Labor...........78.60 ► Per lf of arch.	lf	—	$94.30	$94.30
	Add to brace existing brick arch from below for repairs ***Replace*** Materials ......12.00 Labor ....22.30 ► 2″ x 6″ or 2″ x 8″ framing members sheathed with plywood that follows curved shape of arch.	lf	—	$34.30	$34.30
	Minimum charge for arch work ***Replace*** Materials ......81.00 Labor.........401.00	ea	—	$482.00	$482.00
CONCRETE BLOCK WALL	**4″ wide concrete block wall** ***Replace*** Materials........1.93 Labor ....3.57 ***Remove*** .... Labor 2.39	sf	$2.39	$5.50	$7.89
	6″ wide concrete block wall ***Replace*** Materials........2.25 Labor ....3.69 ***Remove*** .... Labor 2.86	sf	$2.86	$5.94	$8.80
	8″ wide concrete block wall ***Replace*** Materials........2.82 Labor ....3.89 ***Remove*** .... Labor 3.63	sf	$3.63	$6.71	$10.34
	10″ wide concrete block wall ***Replace*** Materials........3.47 Labor ....4.13 ***Remove*** .... Labor 4.10	sf	$4.10	$7.60	$11.70
	12″ wide concrete block wall ***Replace*** Materials........4.45 Labor ....4.89 ***Remove*** .... Labor 4.87	sf	$4.87	$9.34	$14.21
	4″ wide lightweight concrete block wall ***Replace*** Materials........2.05 Labor ....3.33 ***Remove*** .... Labor 2.39	sf	$2.39	$5.38	$7.77
	6″ wide lightweight concrete block wall ***Replace*** Materials........2.40 Labor ....3.45 ***Remove*** .... Labor 2.86	sf	$2.86	$5.85	$8.71

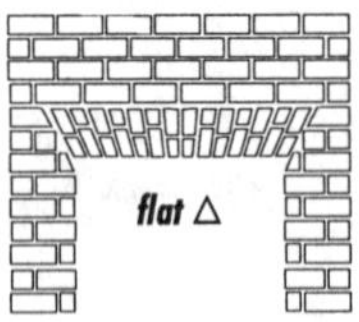

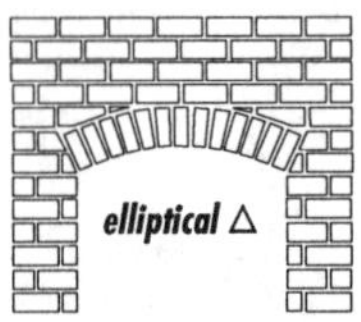

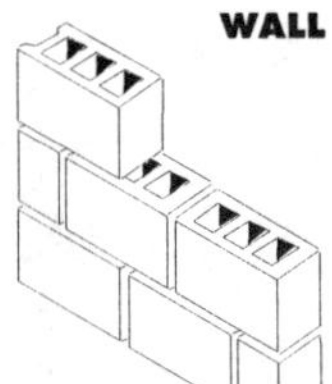

CONCRETE BLOCK WALLS

Unless otherwise noted all concrete block walls are 8″ x 16″ face block with 3/8″ wide mortar joints.

Cells are grouted 36″ on center and at each corner and include one length of #4 rebar in field cells and 2 lengths in corner cells for an average of 1.4 lengths of rebar per grouted cell.

A horizontal bond beam is also calculated for every 8′ of wall height which includes two lengths of #4 rebar.

continued on next page

Item Description	Unit	Remove	Replace	Total
8″ wide lightweight concrete block wall ***Replace*** Materials........3.00 Labor............3.65 ***Remove*** .... Labor............3.63	sf	$3.63	$6.65	$10.28
10″ wide lightweight concrete block wall ***Replace*** Materials........3.67 Labor............3.89 ***Remove*** .... Labor............4.10	sf	$4.10	$7.56	$11.66
12″ wide lightweight concrete block wall ***Replace*** Materials........4.76 Labor............4.57 ***Remove*** .... Labor............4.87	sf	$4.87	$9.33	$14.20
4″ wide slump block wall ***Replace*** Materials........3.23 Labor............3.57 ***Remove*** .... Labor............2.39	sf	$2.39	$6.80	$9.19
6″ wide slump block wall ***Replace*** Materials........3.94 Labor............3.69 ***Remove*** .... Labor............2.86	sf	$2.86	$7.63	$10.49
8″ wide slump block wall ***Replace*** Materials........4.88 Labor............3.89 ***Remove*** .... Labor............3.63	sf	$3.63	$8.77	$12.40
10″ wide slump block wall ***Replace*** Materials........5.83 Labor............4.13 ***Remove*** .... Labor............4.10	sf	$4.10	$9.96	$14.06
12″ wide slump block wall ***Replace*** Materials........7.36 Labor............4.89 ***Remove*** .... Labor............4.87	sf	$4.87	$12.25	$17.12
4″ wide fluted block wall (fluted one side) ***Replace*** Materials........2.75 Labor............3.57 ***Remove*** .... Labor............2.39	sf	$2.39	$6.32	$8.71
6″ wide fluted block wall (fluted one side) ***Replace*** Materials........3.18 Labor............3.69 ***Remove*** .... Labor............2.86	sf	$2.86	$6.87	$9.73
8″ wide fluted block wall (fluted one side) ***Replace*** Materials........3.99 Labor............3.89 ***Remove*** .... Labor............3.63	sf	$3.63	$7.88	$11.51
10″ wide fluted block wall (fluted one side) ***Replace*** Materials........4.92 Labor............4.13 ***Remove*** .... Labor............4.10	sf	$4.10	$9.05	$13.15
12″ wide fluted block wall (fluted one side) ***Replace*** Materials........6.41 Labor............4.89 ***Remove*** .... Labor............4.87	sf	$4.87	$11.30	$16.17
4″ wide fluted block wall (fluted two sides) ***Replace*** Materials........3.14 Labor............3.57 ***Remove*** .... Labor............2.39	sf	$2.39	$6.71	$9.10
6″ wide fluted block wall (fluted two sides) ***Replace*** Materials........3.60 Labor............3.69 ***Remove*** .... Labor............2.86	sf	$2.86	$7.29	$10.15

CONCRETE BLOCK WALLS

continued from prior page

Horizontal wire reinforcing appears in every other course.

Also includes 4% waste for block and 25% waste for mortar.

See page 302 for block walls with other types of reinforcing.

◄ **SLUMP BLOCK WALL**
4″ x 16″ face block.

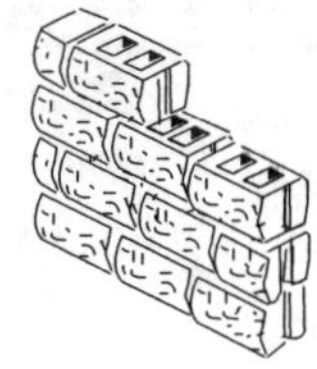

◄ **FLUTED BLOCK WALL (ONE SIDE)**

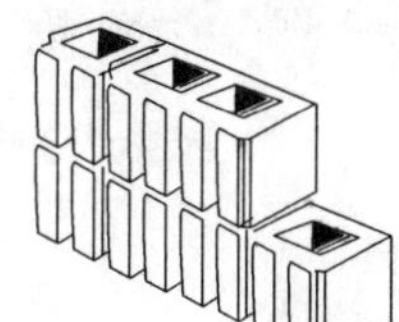

◄ **FLUTED BLOCK WALL (TWO SIDES)**

RELATED ITEMS

	Item Description	Unit	Remove	Replace	Total
FLUTED BLOCK WALL (TWO SIDES) *continued*	**8″ wide fluted block wall (fluted two sides)** *Replace* Materials........4.52 Labor............3.89 *Remove* .... Labor............3.63	sf	$3.63	$8.41	$12.04
	10″ wide fluted block wall (fluted two sides) *Replace* Materials........5.59 Labor............4.13 *Remove* .... Labor............4.10	sf	$4.10	$9.72	$13.82
	12″ wide fluted block wall (fluted two sides) *Replace* Materials........7.32 Labor............4.89 *Remove* .... Labor............4.87	sf	$4.87	$12.21	$17.08
GLAZED BLOCK WALL (ONE SIDE) See "Concrete Block Walls" on page 298.	**4″ wide glazed block wall (glazed one side)** *Replace* Materials......10.80 Labor............3.57 *Remove* .... Labor............2.39	sf	$2.39	$14.37	$16.76
	6″ wide glazed block wall (glazed one side) *Replace* Materials.......11.30 Labor............3.69 *Remove* .... Labor............2.86	sf	$2.86	$14.99	$17.85
	8″ wide glazed block wall (glazed one side) *Replace* Materials.......11.90 Labor............3.89 *Remove* .... Labor............3.63	sf	$3.63	$15.79	$19.42
	10″ wide glazed block wall (glazed one side) *Replace* Materials ......12.50 Labor............4.13 *Remove* .... Labor............4.10	sf	$4.10	$16.63	$20.73
	12″ wide glazed block wall (glazed one side) *Replace* Materials.......13.10 Labor............4.89 *Remove* .... Labor............4.87	sf	$4.87	$17.99	$22.86
GLAZED BLOCK WALL (TWO SIDES) See "Concrete Block Walls" on page 298.	**4″ wide glazed block wall (glazed two sides)** *Replace* Materials.......15.80 Labor............3.57 *Remove* .... Labor............2.39	sf	$2.39	$19.37	$21.76
	6″ wide glazed block wall (glazed two sides) *Replace* Materials ......16.80 Labor............3.69 *Remove* .... Labor............2.86	sf	$2.86	$20.49	$23.35
	8″ wide glazed block wall (glazed two sides) *Replace* Materials.......17.70 Labor............3.89 *Remove* .... Labor............3.63	sf	$3.63	$21.59	$25.22
	10″ wide glazed block wall (glazed two sides) *Replace* Materials ......18.40 Labor............4.13 *Remove* .... Labor............4.10	sf	$4.10	$22.53	$26.63
	12″ wide glazed block wall (glazed two sides) *Replace* Materials ......18.90 Labor............4.89 *Remove* .... Labor............4.87	sf	$4.87	$23.79	$28.66
SPLIT-FACE BLOCK WALL See "Concrete Block Walls" on page 298.	**4″ wide split-face block wall** *Replace* Materials........2.97 Labor............3.57 *Remove* .... Labor............2.39	sf	$2.39	$6.54	$8.93
	6″ wide split-face block wall *Replace* Materials........3.55 Labor............3.69 *Remove* .... Labor............2.86	sf	$2.86	$7.24	$10.10

RELATED ITEMS

Cleaning 63
Fireplaces 241
Painting 340

Item Description	*Unit*	*Remove*	*Replace*	*Total*
8″ wide split-face block wall	sf	$3.63	$8.56	$12.19
Replace Materials........4.67 Labor 3.89				
Remove .... Labor 3.63				
10″ wide split-face block wall	sf	$4.10	$9.36	$13.46
Replace Materials........5.23 Labor 4.13				
Remove .... Labor 4.10				
12″ wide split-face block wall	sf	$4.87	$11.69	$16.56
Replace Materials........6.80 Labor 4.89				
Remove .... Labor 4.87				
4″ wide split-rib block wall	sf	$2.39	$6.38	$8.77
Replace Materials........2.81 Labor 3.57				
Remove .... Labor 2.39				
6″ wide split-rib block wall	sf	$2.86	$6.77	$9.63
Replace Materials........3.08 Labor 3.69				
Remove .... Labor 2.86				
8″ wide split-rib block wall	sf	$3.63	$8.50	$12.13
Replace Materials........4.61 Labor 3.89				
Remove .... Labor 3.63				
10″ wide split-rib block wall	sf	$4.10	$9.40	$13.50
Replace Materials........5.27 Labor 4.13				
Remove .... Labor 4.10				
12″ wide split-rib block wall	sf	$4.87	$10.89	$15.76
Replace Materials........6.00 Labor 4.89				
Remove .... Labor 4.87				
4″ wide screen block, pattern two sides	sf	$2.39	$9.06	$11.45
Replace Materials........5.49 Labor 3.57				
Remove .... Labor 2.39				
4″ wide screen block, pattern four sides	sf	$2.39	$13.65	$16.04
Replace Materials......10.08 Labor 3.57				
Remove .... Labor 2.39				
Add 11% for light ochre colored concrete block				
► Light tans, browns, yellows, light reddish brown, and so forth.				
Add 17% darker ochre colored concrete block				
► Light red, blues, specialty grays, darker yellows, mid-tone browns.				
Add 28% for dark or bright colored concrete block				
► Black, dark blue, terra-cotta red, bright yellow, bright orange, bright red, purple, and so forth.				
Add 15% for interlocking concrete block				
► Add to the cost of *materials* only.				
Add for polystyrene inserts, 6″ block	sf	—	$.86	$.86
Replace Materials........ .86				
Add for polystyrene inserts, 8″ block	sf	—	$.93	$.93
Replace Materials........ .93				
Add for polystyrene inserts, 10″ block	sf	—	$1.04	$1.04
Replace Materials........1.04				

◄ **SPLIT-RIB BLOCK WALL** *See "Concrete Block Walls" on page 298.*

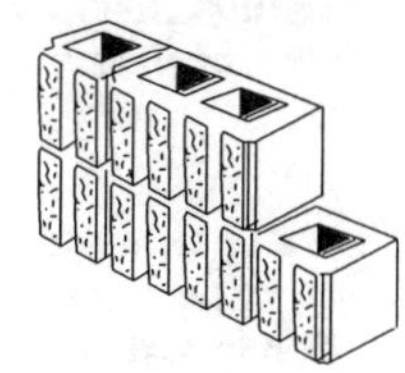

◄ **SCREEN BLOCK** *12″ x 12″ face.* *See "Concrete Block Walls" on page 298.*

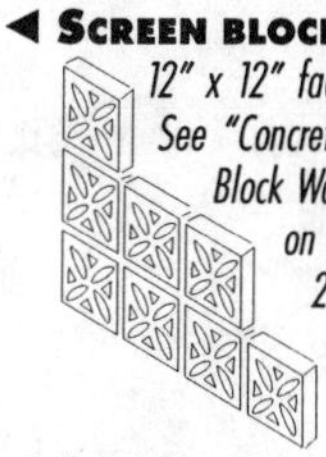

◄ **ADD FOR COLORED BLOCK**

◄ **ADD FOR INTERLOCKING BLOCK**

◄ **POLYSTYRENE BLOCK INSERTS** *Additional cost for block with polystyrene inserts already installed.*

	Item Description	Unit	Remove	Replace	Total
Polystyrene block inserts *continued*	**Add for polystyrene inserts, 12″ block** ***Replace*** Materials........1.12	sf	—	$1.12	$1.12
Loose block insulation *Includes 3% waste.*	**Add for silicone treated perlite or vermiculite loose fill, 6″ block** ***Replace*** Materials........ .341 Labor............. .16	sf	—	$.50	$.50
	Add for silicone treated perlite or vermiculite loose fill, 8″ block ***Replace*** Materials........ .49 Labor............. .18	sf	—	$.67	$.67
block pilaster ▽	**Add for silicone treated perlite or vermiculite loose fill, 10″ block** ***Replace*** Materials........ .62 Labor............. .19	sf	—	$.81	$.81
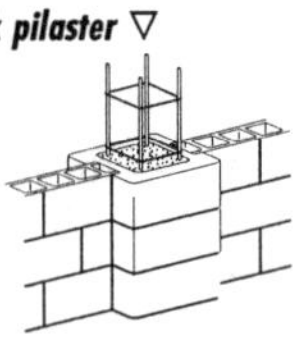	**Add for silicone treated perlite or vermiculite loose fill, 12″ block** ***Replace*** Materials........ .89 Labor............. .18	sf	—	$1.07	$1.07
Block pilaster *Includes 4% waste.*	**Add for pilaster in block wall (per vertical lf of pilaster)** ***Replace*** Materials......12.40 Labor...........11.80 ► 16″ x 16″ pilaster, single piece. For double piece 16″ x 20″ pilaster add 15%.	lf	—	$24.20	$24.20
Block wall additions & deductions *Add or deduct from the square foot price of block walls.*	**Deduct for block walls used as backing** ***Replace*** .... Labor..........- -.22 ► For walls finished on one side only.	sf	—	- $-.22	- $-.22
	Deduct for wall with no horizontal wire reinforcement ***Replace*** Materials......- -.16 Labor..........- -.04 ► Deduct when ladder or truss style wire reinforcement is not laid between every other course of block.	sf	—	- $-.20	- $-.20
	Deduct for block walls with no vertical reinforcement ***Replace*** Materials......- -.57 Labor..........- -.24 ► Deduct when block walls contain no grouted cells.	sf	—	- $-.81	- $-.81
	Deduct for block walls with vertical reinforcement every 48″ ***Replace*** Materials......- -.16 Labor..........- -.19 ► Deduct when block walls contain grouted cells with rebar every 48″ instead of 36″.	sf	—	- $-.35	- $-.35
	Add for block walls with vertical reinforcement every 24″ ***Replace*** Materials........ .20 Labor............. .20 ► Add when block walls contain grouted cells with rebar every 24″ instead of 36″.	sf	—	$.40	$.40
	Deduct for block walls with no horizontal bond beam reinforcement ***Replace*** Materials......- -.40 Labor..........- -.15 ► Deduct when block walls do not contain a bond beam per every 8′ of height.	sf	—	- $-.55	- $-.55
	Add for block walls with horizontal bond beam reinforcement 4′ ***Replace*** Materials........ .30 Labor............. .23 ► Add when block walls contain horizontal bond beams with rebar for every 4′ of wall height instead of every 8′.	sf	—	$.53	$.53
high-strength block ▷	**Add 19% for high strength concrete block, 3,000 psi** ► Add to the cost of *materials* only.				
	Add 21% for high strength concrete block, 5,000 psi ► Add to the cost of *materials* only.				
Bond beam *Includes two lengths of #4 rebar.*	**6″ wide bond beam** ***Replace*** Materials........1.30 Labor........... 1.04	lf	—	$2.34	$2.34
	**8″ wide bond beam** ***Replace*** Materials........1.52 Labor............1.14	lf	—	$2.66	$2.66

Item Description	Unit	Remove	Replace	Total
10″ wide bond beam *Replace* Materials........1.79 Labor............1.25	lf	—	$3.04	$3.04
12″ wide bond beam *Replace* Materials........2.07 Labor............1.35	lf	—	$3.42	$3.42
Parge block foundation wall *Replace* Materials........ .32 Labor............ .77 ► Up to 1/2″ thick.	sf	—	$1.09	$1.09
Add for grade beam cap on 6″ wide concrete block wall *Replace* Materials........7.40 Labor............4.25 *Remove* .... Labor............9.98	lf	$9.98	$11.65	$21.63
Add for grade beam cap on 8″ wide concrete block wall *Replace* Materials........9.52 Labor............4.41 *Remove* .... Labor............9.98	lf	$9.98	$13.93	$23.91
Add for grade beam cap on 10″ wide concrete block wall *Replace* Materials.......11.60 Labor............4.61 *Remove* .... Labor............9.98	lf	$9.98	$16.21	$26.19
Add for grade beam cap on 12″ wide concrete block wall *Replace* Materials.......13.80 Labor............4.81 *Remove* .... Labor............9.98	lf	$9.98	$18.61	$28.59
Deduct 8% for concrete block or brick wall installed as fence ► Includes wall cap (2″ block or masonry rowlock) and horizontal wire reinforcing. Does not include footing, bond beam, coping, or cell grouting.				
4″ thick clay backing tile *Replace* Materials........4.54 Labor............4.49 *Remove* .... Labor............2.39	sf	$2.39	$9.03	$11.42
6″ thick clay backing tile *Replace* Materials........4.56 Labor............5.09 *Remove* .... Labor............2.86	sf	$2.86	$9.65	$12.51
8″ thick clay backing tile *Replace* Materials........4.56 Labor............5.81 *Remove* .... Labor............3.63	sf	$3.63	$10.37	$14.00
4″ thick structural tile glazed one side *Replace* Materials........6.11 Labor............8.18 *Remove* .... Labor............2.39	sf	$2.39	$14.29	$16.68
4″ thick structural tile glazed two sides *Replace* Materials........9.31 Labor............8.56 *Remove* .... Labor............2.39	sf	$2.39	$17.87	$20.26
6″ thick structural tile glazed one side *Replace* Materials........8.12 Labor............9.78 *Remove* .... Labor............2.86	sf	$2.86	$17.90	$20.76
6″ thick structural tile glazed two sides *Replace* Materials......12.40 Labor...........10.16 *Remove* .... Labor............2.86	sf	$2.86	$22.56	$25.42
8″ thick structural tile glazed one side *Replace* Materials......10.80 Labor...........10.50 *Remove* .... Labor............3.63	sf	$3.63	$21.30	$24.93

RELATED ITEMS

Cleaning........................63
Fences..........................187
Fireplaces......................241
Painting........................340
Retaining Walls...........391

◄ **PARGETING**
Up to 1/2″ thick.

◄ **GRADE BEAM FOR BLOCK WALL**
In some states, concrete block walls are capped with a grade beam. This not only adds strength but also levels the wall top. Because the mason does not take care to maintain a level wall, deduct ***25%*** *from the labor cost for block walls capped with a grade beam. Up to 16″ tall with four lengths of #4 rebar. Rebar from grouted cells is also bent into the grade beam.*

◄ **MASONRY FENCE**

◄ **CLAY BACKING TILE WALL**
12″ x 12″ face tile with 3/8″ wide mortar joints. Includes 4% waste for tile and 25% waste for mortar.

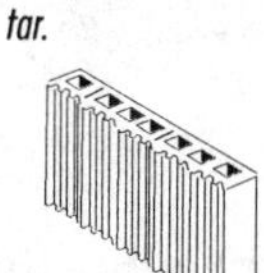

◄ **STRUCTURAL TILE WALL**
8″ x 16″ face tile with 3/8″ wide mortar joints. Includes 4% waste for tile and 25% waste for mortar.

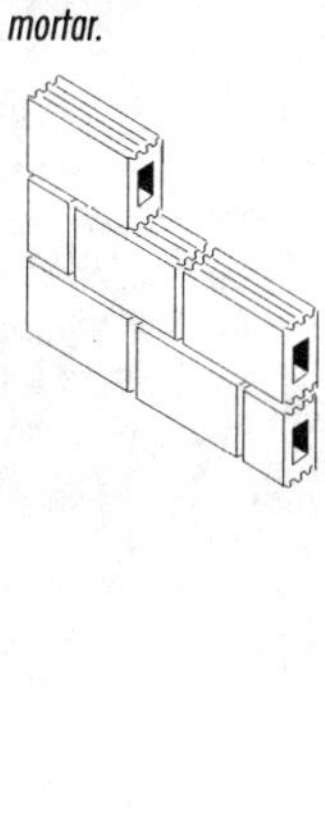

GYPSUM PARTITION TILE ▶ *12" x 30" face tile with 3/8" wide mortar joints. Includes 4% waste for tile and 25% waste for mortar. (See illustration below.)*

Item Description	Unit	Remove	Replace	Total
4" thick gypsum partition tile *Replace* Materials........1.71 Labor............2.29 *Remove* .... Labor............2.39	sf	$2.39	$4.00	$6.39
6" thick gypsum partition tile *Replace* Materials........2.47 Labor............3.33 *Remove* .... Labor............3.63	sf	$3.63	$5.80	$9.43

GLASS BLOCK WALL ▶ *White mortar with 3/8" wide joints and ladder type wire reinforcing every other course. Includes 4% waste for glass blocks and 25% waste for mortar.*

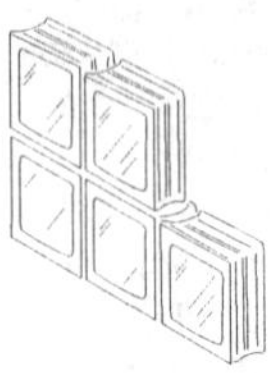

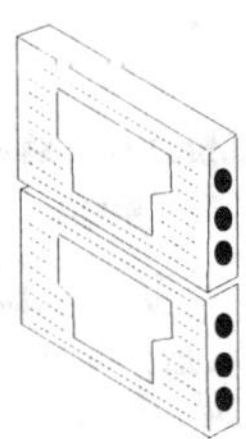

gypsum partition tile △

Item Description	Unit	Remove	Replace	Total
4" x 8" thinline smooth-face glass blocks *Replace* Materials......20.40 Labor...........13.40 *Remove* .... Labor............2.31	sf	$2.31	$33.80	$36.11
6" x 6" thinline smooth-face glass blocks *Replace* Materials......18.70 Labor...........12.50 *Remove* .... Labor............2.31	sf	$2.31	$31.20	$33.51
6" x 8" thinline smooth-face glass blocks *Replace* Materials......14.30 Labor...........10.70 *Remove* .... Labor............2.31	sf	$2.31	$25.00	$27.31
4" x 8" smooth-face glass blocks *Replace* Materials......25.60 Labor...........13.40 *Remove* .... Labor............2.31	sf	$2.31	$39.00	$41.31
6" x 6" smooth-face glass blocks *Replace* Materials......22.70 Labor...........12.50 *Remove* .... Labor............2.31	sf	$2.31	$35.20	$37.51
6" x 8" smooth-face glass blocks *Replace* Materials......20.50 Labor...........10 70 *Remove* .... Labor............2.31	sf	$2.31	$31.20	$33.51
8" x 8" smooth-face glass blocks *Replace* Materials.......15.90 Labor............8.34 *Remove* .... Labor............2.31	sf	$2.31	$24.24	$26.55
12" x 12" smooth-face glass blocks *Replace* Materials......18.60 Labor............7.02 *Remove* .... Labor............2.31	sf	$2.31	$25.62	$27.93

other glass block costs ▷

Add 80% for solar UV reflective glass block

Add 4% for patterned face on glass block

Add 12% for tinted glass block

Deduct 2% for natural gray mortar in glass block wall

Deduct 1% for colored mortar in glass block wall

PAVERS ▶ *Pavers on sand base have sand embedded in joints with vibrating compactor. Mortar base pavers have grouted joints. Includes 4% waste for pavers and 25% waste for mortar when used.*

Item Description	Unit	Remove	Replace	Total
Natural concrete pavers on sand base *Replace* Materials........3.81 Labor............5.89 *Remove* .... Labor............2.31	sf	$2.31	$9.70	$12.01
Natural concrete pavers on mortar base *Replace* Materials........3.81 Labor............7.22 *Remove* .... Labor............3.30	sf	$3.30	$11.03	$14.33
Adobe pavers on sand base *Replace* Materials........1.59 Labor............5.89 *Remove* .... Labor............2.31	sf	$2.31	$7.48	$9.79

Item Description	Unit	Remove	Replace	Total
Adobe pavers on mortar base ***Replace*** Materials........1.59 Labor ....7.22 ***Remove*** .... Labor 3.30	sf	$3.30	$8.81	$12.11
Brick paver, standard grade, on sand base ***Replace*** Materials........2.09 Labor ....5.89 ***Remove*** .... Labor 2.31	sf	$2.31	$7.98	$10.29
Brick paver, standard grade, on mortar base ***Replace*** Materials........2.16 Labor ....7.22 ***Remove*** .... Labor 3.30	sf	$3.30	$9.38	$12.68
Brick paver, high grade, on sand base ***Replace*** Materials........2.78 Labor ....5.89 ***Remove*** .... Labor 2.31	sf	$2.31	$8.67	$10.98
Brick paver, high grade, on mortar base ***Replace*** Materials........2.78 Labor ....7.22 ***Remove*** .... Labor 3.30	sf	$3.30	$10.00	$13.30
Brick paver, deluxe grade, on sand base ***Replace*** Materials........3.38 Labor ....5.89 ***Remove*** .... Labor 2.31	sf	$2.31	$9.27	$11.58
Brick paver, deluxe grade, on mortar base ***Replace*** Materials........3.45 Labor ....7.22 ***Remove*** .... Labor 3.30	sf	$3.30	$10.67	$13.97
Brick pavers made from full-size bricks, laid face up ***Replace*** Materials........3.67 Labor ....7.42 ***Remove*** .... Labor 2.48	sf	$2.48	$11.09	$13.57
Brick pavers made from full-size bricks, laid edge up ***Replace*** Materials........5.62 Labor ....8.34 ***Remove*** .... Labor 2.48	sf	$2.48	$13.96	$16.44
Add for curved edges on pavers ***Replace*** Materials........1.27 Labor 3.13	lf	—	$4.40	$4.40
Add for paver steps installed in mortar over concrete per lf of step ***Replace*** Materials........ .61 Labor...........10.80	lf	—	$11.41	$11.41
Add for paver steps installed over sand base per lf of step ***Replace*** Materials........ .57 Labor...........11.80	lf	—	$12.37	$12.37
Add for separate pattern at edges of pavers ***Replace*** Materials........1.24 Labor 3.05	lf	—	$4.29	$4.29
Add 17% for non-square pavers with interlocking patterns				
Add 8% for pavers installed in diagonal pattern				
Add 17% for pavers installed in basketweave pattern				
Add 14% for pavers installed in herringbone pattern				
Coral stone rubble wall ***Replace*** Materials......35.50 Labor..........20.80 ***Remove*** .... Labor...........12.10	cf	$12.10	$56.30	$68.40

RELATED ITEMS

Cleaning 63
Fireplaces......................241
Painting........................340

basketweave △

◁ **additional paver costs**

◀ **RUBBLE STONE WALL**

continued on next page

RUBBLE STONE WALL *continued*

Stone walls laid in a variety of rubble patterns, per cubic foot of stone. Includes an average of 1/3 cubic foot of mortar per cubic foot of wall. To estimate by the perch, multiply the cf price by 24.75. (A perch is 16-1/2' long, 1' high and 1-1/2' wide or 24-3/4 cubic feet.) See illustration below.

Item Description	Unit	Remove	Replace	Total
Field-stone rubble wall, no mortar	cf	$7.12	$45.60	$52.72
Replace Materials......26.30 Labor...........19.30				
Remove .... Labor...........7.12				
Field-stone rubble wall	cf	$12.10	$58.70	$70.80
Replace Materials......37.90 Labor..........20.80				
Remove .... Labor...........12.10				
Lava stone rubble wall	cf	$12.10	$57.30	$69.40
Replace Materials......36.50 Labor..........20.80				
Remove .... Labor...........12.10				
River stone rubble wall	cf	$12.10	$59.70	$71.80
Replace Materials......38.90 Labor..........20.80				
Remove .... Labor...........12.10				

ASHLAR STONE WALL

Stone walls laid in ashlar patterns, per cf of stone. Stone is 3-1/2" to 6" wide. Lengths and thickness vary. Includes mortar. To estimate by the perch, multiply the cf price by 24.75. (A perch is 16-1/2' long, 1' high and 1-1/2' wide or 24-3/4 cubic feet.)

Item Description	Unit	Remove	Replace	Total
Limestone ashlar wall, natural finish	cf	$12.10	$49.50	$61.60
Replace Materials......30.60 Labor...........18.90				
Remove .... Labor...........12.10				
Limestone ashlar wall, rough finish	cf	$12.10	$53.00	$65.10
Replace Materials......34.10 Labor...........18.90				
Remove .... Labor...........12.10				
Limestone ashlar wall, smooth finish	cf	$12.10	$67.50	$79.60
Replace Materials......48.60 Labor...........18.90				
Remove .... Labor...........12.10				
Marble ashlar wall, natural finish	cf	$12.10	$88.90	$101.00
Replace Materials......70.00 Labor...........18.90				
Remove .... Labor...........12.10				
Marble ashlar wall, rough finish	cf	$12.10	$94.40	$106.50
Replace Materials......75.50 Labor...........18.90				
Remove .... Labor...........12.10				
Marble ashlar wall, smooth finish	cf	$12.10	$112.00	$124.10
Replace Materials......93.10 Labor...........18.90				
Remove .... Labor...........12.10				
Sandstone ashlar wall, natural finish	cf	$12.10	$48.30	$60.40
Replace Materials......29.40 Labor...........18.90				
Remove .... Labor...........12.10				
Sandstone ashlar wall, rough finish	cf	$12.10	$51.70	$63.80
Replace Materials......32.80 Labor...........18.90				
Remove .... Labor...........12.10				
Sandstone ashlar wall, smooth finish	cf	$12.10	$65.60	$77.70
Replace Materials......46.70 Labor...........18.90				
Remove .... Labor...........12.10				
Add for flat arch in stone wall	lf	—	$186.40	$186.40
Replace Materials......71.40 Labor..........115.00				
► Also called a Jack arch. See illustration on facing page. Do not use for standard stone wall openings that use a lintel.				
Add for elliptical arch in stone wall	lf	—	$227.30	$227.30
Replace Materials......84.30 Labor.........143.00				
► Per lf of arch. See illustration on facing page.				

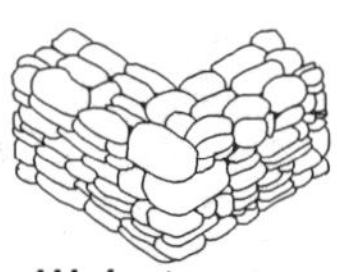

rubble lay △

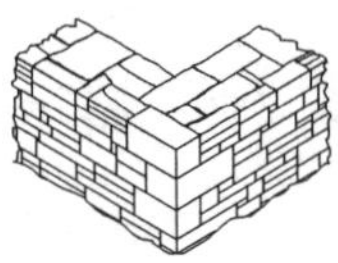

ashlar lay △

STONE QUALITY

Stones are quarried within 150 miles of job site.

Cast stone is made from a composite of crushed limestone and quartz sand.

Granite is a good quality gray stone. Add **28%** for light red (pink), light purple, and light brown. Add **88%** for deep green, red, purple, blue, black, charcoal, and brown.

Limestone is standard stock. Add **15%** for select stock and deduct **10%** for rustic stock.

continued on next page

Item Description	Unit	Remove	Replace	Total
Add for semi-circular arch in stone wall ***Replace*** Materials......84.30 Labor.........148.00 ► Per lf of arch. See illustration below.	lf	—	$232.30	$232.30
Add 27% for curved stone wall				
Coral stone rubble veneer ***Replace*** Materials.......11.90 Labor............9.74 ***Remove*** .... Labor............2.92	sf	$2.92	$21.64	$24.56
Field stone rubble veneer ***Replace*** Materials........9.62 Labor............9.74 ***Remove*** .... Labor............2.92	sf	$2.92	$19.36	$22.28
Flagstone rubble veneer ***Replace*** Materials........6.08 Labor............9.74 ***Remove*** .... Labor............2.92	sf	$2.92	$15.82	$18.74
Lava stone rubble veneer ***Replace*** Materials........9.25 Labor............9.74 ***Remove*** .... Labor............2.92	sf	$2.92	$18.99	$21.91
River stone rubble veneer ***Replace*** Materials........9.85 Labor............9.74 ***Remove*** .... Labor............2.92	sf	$2.92	$19.59	$22.51
Sandstone rubble veneer ***Replace*** Materials.......13.70 Labor............9.74 ***Remove*** .... Labor............2.92	sf	$2.92	$23.44	$26.36
Flagstone ashlar veneer ***Replace*** Materials........7.07 Labor............9.46 ***Remove*** .... Labor............2.92	sf	$2.92	$16.53	$19.45
Limestone ashlar veneer, natural finish ***Replace*** Materials........7.74 Labor............9.46 ***Remove*** .... Labor............2.92	sf	$2.92	$17.20	$20.12
Limestone ashlar veneer, rough finish ***Replace*** Materials........8.61 Labor............9.46 ***Remove*** .... Labor............2.92	sf	$2.92	$18.07	$20.99
Limestone ashlar veneer, smooth finish ***Replace*** Materials......12.20 Labor............9.46 ***Remove*** .... Labor............2.92	sf	$2.92	$21.66	$24.58
Marble ashlar veneer, natural finish ***Replace*** Materials.......17.50 Labor............9.46 ***Remove*** .... Labor............2.92	sf	$2.92	$26.96	$29.88
Marble ashlar veneer, rough finish ***Replace*** Materials......18.80 Labor............9.46 ***Remove*** .... Labor............2.92	sf	$2.92	$28.26	$31.18
Marble ashlar veneer, smooth finish ***Replace*** Materials......23.20 Labor............9.46 ***Remove*** .... Labor............2.92	sf	$2.92	$32.66	$35.58
Sandstone ashlar veneer, natural finish ***Replace*** Materials........7.44 Labor............9.46 ***Remove*** .... Labor............2.92	sf	$2.92	$16.90	$19.82

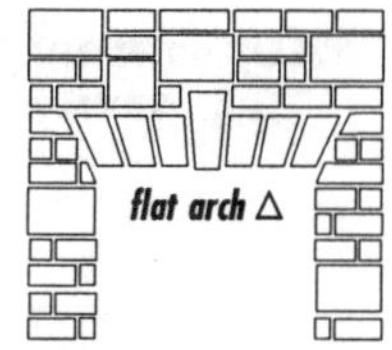

◄ **RUBBLE STONE**

STONE QUALITY

continued

Marble is grade A, average to high priced. Marble varies widely in price with little relationship to color and often even the quality of the stone. The more expensive grades are Italian.

Sandstone is standard grade. Varies from very hard rock to fairly soft. Use for Brownstone work.

Slate is standard grade, all colors.

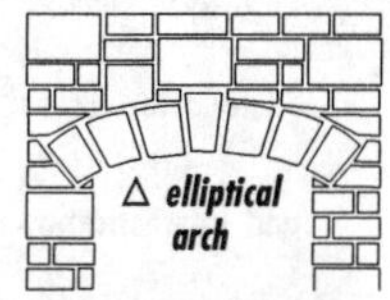

◄ **ASHLAR STONE**

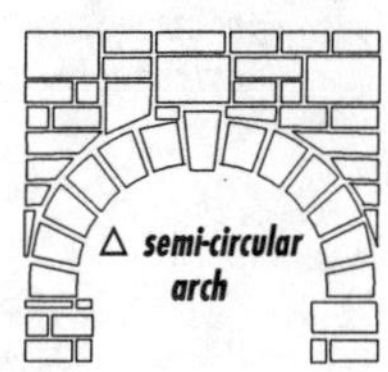

STONE FINISHES

Stone finishes are generally organized in this book as natural, rough, and smooth. In practice there are many variations of each type of finish.

Stone with **natural** finishes show the cleaving or sawing marks made in the quarry.

Rough finishes are applied after the stone is quarried to achieve a specific rough look.

Smooth finishes are achieved by polishing the stone. All molded work is finished smooth.

	Item Description	Unit	Remove	Replace	Total
ASHLAR STONE ▶ VENEER *continued*	**Sandstone ashlar veneer, rough finish** ***Replace*** Materials........8.28 Labor............9.46 ***Remove*** .... Labor............2.92	sf	$2.92	$17.74	$20.66
	Sandstone ashlar veneer, smooth finish ***Replace*** Materials.......11.70 Labor............9.46 ***Remove*** .... Labor............2.92	sf	$2.92	$21.16	$24.08
add for arch ▷	**Add for flat arch in stone veneer** ***Replace*** Materials.......17.70 Labor...........70.20 ▶ Also called a Jack arch. See illustration on previous page. Do not use for standard stone veneer openings that use a lintel.	lf	—	$87.90	$87.90
	Add for elliptical arch in stone veneer ***Replace*** Materials......20.90 Labor...........87.00 ▶ Per lf of arch. See illustration on previous page.	lf	—	$107.90	$107.90
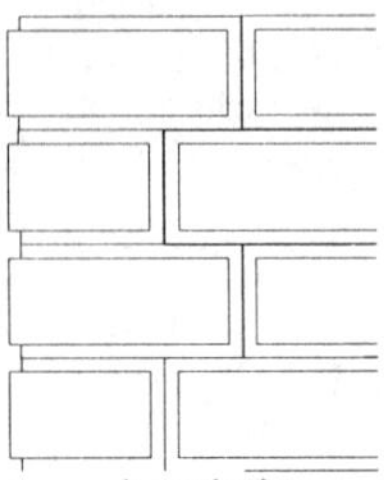 △ *rustication*	**Add for semi-circular arch in stone veneer** ***Replace*** Materials......20.90 Labor..........92.20 ▶ Per lf of arch. See illustration on previous page.	lf	—	$113.10	$113.10
	Add to support arch from below ***Replace*** Materials ......12.00 Labor..........22.30 ▶ 2" x 6" or 2" x 8" framing members sheathed with plywood that follows curved shape of arch.	lf	—	$34.30	$34.30
add for curves ▷	**Add 27% for curved stone veneer**				
add for rustication ▷	**Add 55% for rusticated stone** ▶ Edges of stone rabbeted up to 1" deep.				
KEYSTONE ▶ *For use in stone or brick arches.*	**Keystone, concrete** ***Replace*** Materials ......47.00 Labor...........24.30 ***Remove*** .... Labor............5.45 ▶ Plain key, recessed key, or winged key. See illustrations on page 322.	ea	$5.45	$71.30	$76.75
	Keystone, cast stone ***Replace*** Materials.......65.00 Labor...........24.30 ***Remove*** .... Labor............5.45 ▶ Plain key, recessed key, or winged key. See illustrations on page 322.	ea	$5.45	$89.30	$94.75
	Keystone, natural finish ***Replace*** Materials....103.00 Labor...........24.30 ***Remove*** .... Labor............5.45 ▶ Plain key, with natural or rough finish. See illustrations on page 322.	ea	$5.45	$127.30	$132.75
	Keystone, with straight patterns ***Replace*** Materials.....133.00 Labor...........24.30 ***Remove*** .... Labor............5.45 ▶ Recessed key, or winged key. See illustrations on page 322.	ea	$5.45	$157.30	$162.75
	Keystone, with complex straight patterns (Gothic) ***Replace*** Materials.....169.00 Labor...........24.30 ***Remove*** .... Labor............5.45 ▶ Key with Gothic patterns over 1" deep.	ea	$5.45	$193.30	$198.75
	Keystone, with light hand carvings ***Replace*** Materials....257.00 Labor...........24.30 ***Remove*** .... Labor............5.45 ▶ Light carvings, usually less than 3/4" deep.	ea	$5.45	$281.30	$286.75

Item Description	*Unit*	*Remove*	*Replace*	*Total*
Keystone, with medium hand carvings ***Replace*** Materials....329.00 Labor...........24.30 ***Remove*** .... Labor............5.45 ► Heavier carvings like vermiculation, Acanthus, and so forth.	ea	$5.45	$353.30	$358.75
Keystone, with heavy hand carvings ***Replace*** Materials.....461.00 Labor...........24.30 ***Remove*** .... Labor............5.45 ► Heavy and deep carvings including a lion's face, a human face, and so forth.	ea	$5.45	$485.30	$490.75
Remove keystone for work, then reinstall ***Replace*** Materials.......... Labor..........40.90	ea	—	$40.90	$40.90
Cast stone quoin ***Replace*** Materials....104.00 Labor............6.58 ***Remove*** .... Labor............5.39	ea	$5.39	$110.58	$115.97
Limestone quoin ***Replace*** Materials.....119.00 Labor............6.58 ***Remove*** .... Labor............5.39	ea	$5.39	$125.58	$130.97
Sandstone quoin ***Replace*** Materials.....112.00 Labor............6.58 ***Remove*** .... Labor............5.39	ea	$5.39	$118.58	$123.97
Remove quoin for work, then reinstall (per stone) ***Replace*** Materials.......... Labor...........17.40	ea	—	$17.40	$17.40
Cultured stone veneer panels, smooth finish ***Replace*** Materials........5.36 Labor...........10.50 ***Remove*** .... Labor............2.04	sf	$2.04	$15.86	$17.90
Cultured stone veneer panels, rough finish ***Replace*** Materials........7.20 Labor...........10.50 ***Remove*** .... Labor............2.04	sf	$2.04	$17.70	$19.74
Cultured stone veneer panels, terrazzo style finish ***Replace*** Materials......16.20 Labor...........10.50 ***Remove*** .... Labor............2.04	sf	$2.04	$26.70	$28.74
Ceramic veneer panels ***Replace*** Materials.......13.20 Labor...........10.50 ***Remove*** .... Labor............2.04	sf	$2.04	$23.70	$25.74
Granite veneer panels, natural finish ***Replace*** Materials......24.20 Labor...........11.90 ***Remove*** .... Labor............2.04	sf	$2.04	$36.10	$38.14
Granite veneer panels, rough finish ***Replace*** Materials......25.70 Labor...........11.90 ***Remove*** .... Labor............2.04	sf	$2.04	$37.60	$39.64
Granite veneer panels, smooth finish ***Replace*** Materials......29.50 Labor...........11.90 ***Remove*** .... Labor............2.04	sf	$2.04	$41.40	$43.44
Limestone veneer panels, natural finish ***Replace*** Materials.......11.10 Labor...........11.90 ***Remove*** .... Labor............2.04	sf	$2.04	$23.00	$25.04
Limestone veneer panels, rough finish ***Replace*** Materials......16.70 Labor...........11.90 ***Remove*** .... Labor............2.04	sf	$2.04	$28.60	$30.64

◄ **STONE QUOIN**
In brick, stone, or stucco walls. Made from alternate courses of headers and stretchers. Price includes one header and one stretcher (two stones). Quoins are plain, beveled, chamfered, rusticated, or rough tooled.

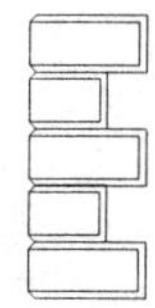

◄ **CULTURED STONE VENEER PANEL**
3/4" to 1-1/2" thick.

◄ **CERAMIC VENEER PANEL**
Precast panels.

◄ **STONE VENEER PANEL**
Granite, slate, and marble panels are 3/4" to 1-1/2" thick. Limestone and sandstone panels are 2" to 3" thick. See page 307 for more information about quality and finishes.

RELATED ITEMS

Cleaning.......................63
Fireplaces.....................241
Painting.......................340

	Item Description	Unit	Remove	Replace	Total
STONE VENEER ▶ PANELS *continued*	**Limestone veneer panels, smooth finish** ***Replace*** Materials......22.00 Labor..........11.90 ***Remove*** .... Labor...........2.04	sf	$2.04	$33.90	$35.94
	Marble veneer panels, natural finish ***Replace*** Materials......27.70 Labor..........11.90 ***Remove*** .... Labor...........2.04	sf	$2.04	$39.60	$41.64
	Marble veneer panels, rough finish ***Replace*** Materials......36.30 Labor..........11.90 ***Remove*** .... Labor...........2.04	sf	$2.04	$48.20	$50.24
	Marble veneer panels, smooth finish ***Replace*** Materials......45.40 Labor..........11.90 ***Remove*** .... Labor...........2.04	sf	$2.04	$57.30	$59.34
	Sandstone veneer panels, natural finish ***Replace*** Materials......19.90 Labor..........11.90 ***Remove*** .... Labor...........2.04	sf	$2.04	$31.80	$33.84
	Sandstone veneer panels, rough finish ***Replace*** Materials......21.70 Labor..........11.90 ***Remove*** .... Labor...........2.04	sf	$2.04	$33.60	$35.64
	Sandstone veneer panels, smooth finish ***Replace*** Materials......24.30 Labor..........11.90 ***Remove*** .... Labor...........2.04	sf	$2.04	$36.20	$38.24
	Slate veneer panels, natural finish ***Replace*** Materials......20.50 Labor..........11.90 ***Remove*** .... Labor...........2.04	sf	$2.04	$32.40	$34.44
	Slate veneer panels, rough finish ***Replace*** Materials......22.30 Labor..........11.90 ***Remove*** .... Labor...........2.04	sf	$2.04	$34.20	$36.24
	Slate veneer panels, smooth finish ***Replace*** Materials......25.00 Labor..........11.90 ***Remove*** .... Labor...........2.04	sf	$2.04	$36.90	$38.94
STONE DOOR ▶ ARCHITRAVE	**Cast stone door architrave, standard grade** ***Replace*** Materials......20.70 Labor..........39.30 ***Remove*** .... Labor...........3.60 ▶ Simple straight patterns. Cast stone is 6″ or less wide.	lf	$3.60	$60.00	$63.60
	Cast stone door architrave, high grade ***Replace*** Materials......22.60 Labor..........39.30 ***Remove*** .... Labor...........3.60 ▶ Complex straight patterns (Gothic). Cast stone is 6″ or less wide.	lf	$3.60	$61.90	$65.50
	Cast stone door architrave, deluxe grade ***Replace*** Materials......30.50 Labor..........39.30 ***Remove*** .... Labor...........3.60 ▶ Cast stone 6″ or less wide with complex straight patterns (Gothic) with arched top or flat top with decorative work around corners or center of header. Or simple straight patterns with cast stone up to 10″ wide.	lf	$3.60	$69.80	$73.40
	Cast stone door architrave, custom grade ***Replace*** Materials......37.50 Labor..........39.30 ***Remove*** .... Labor...........3.60 ▶ Cast stone 6″ or less wide with hand carvings on header or up to 10″ wide with complex straight patterns (Gothic) with arched top. Or simple straight patterns with cast stone up to 12″ wide.	lf	$3.60	$76.80	$80.40

Item Description	Unit	Remove	Replace	Total
Cast stone door architrave, custom deluxe grade ***Replace*** Materials......47.90 Labor..........39.30 ***Remove*** .... Labor............3.60 ► Cast stone 6" or less wide with heavy hand carvings on header (e.g. lion's face, human face) or lighter hand carvings throughout or up to 12" wide with complex straight patterns (Gothic). With arched top.	lf	$3.60	$87.20	$90.80
Limestone door architrave, standard grade ***Replace*** Materials......40.20 Labor..........39.30 ***Remove*** .... Labor............3.60 ► Simple straight patterns. Stone is 6" or less wide.	lf	$3.60	$79.50	$83.10
Limestone door architrave, high grade ***Replace*** Materials......73.50 Labor..........39.30 ***Remove*** .... Labor............3.60 ► Complex straight patterns (Gothic). Stone is 6" or less wide.	lf	$3.60	$112.80	$116.40
Limestone door architrave, deluxe grade ***Replace*** Materials....106.00 Labor..........39.30 ***Remove*** .... Labor............3.60 ► Stone 6" or less wide with complex straight patterns (Gothic) with arched top or flat top with decorative work around corners or center of header. Or simple straight patterns with stone up to 10" wide.	lf	$3.60	$145.30	$148.90
Limestone door architrave, custom grade ***Replace*** Materials.....131.00 Labor..........39.30 ***Remove*** .... Labor............3.60 ► Stone 6" or less wide with hand carvings on header or up to 10" wide with complex straight patterns (Gothic) with arched top. Or simple straight patterns with stone up to 12" wide.	lf	$3.60	$170.30	$173.90
Limestone door architrave, custom deluxe grade ***Replace*** Materials.....159.00 Labor..........39.30 ***Remove*** .... Labor............3.60 ► Stone 6" or less wide with heavy hand carvings on header (e.g. lion's face, human face) or lighter hand carvings throughout or up to 12" wide with complex straight patterns (Gothic). With arched top.	lf	$3.60	$198.30	$201.90
Marble door architrave, standard grade ***Replace*** Materials......60.00 Labor..........39.30 ***Remove*** .... Labor............3.60 ► Simple straight patterns. Stone is 6" or less wide.	lf	$3.60	$99.30	$102.90
Marble door architrave, high grade ***Replace*** Materials......93.80 Labor..........39.30 ***Remove*** .... Labor............3.60 ► Complex straight patterns (Gothic). Stone is 6" or less wide.	lf	$3.60	$133.10	$136.70
Marble door architrave, deluxe grade ***Replace*** Materials.....126.00 Labor..........39.30 ***Remove*** .... Labor............3.60 ► Stone 6" or less wide with complex straight patterns (Gothic) with arched top or flat top with decorative work around corners or center of header. Or simple straight patterns with stone up to 10" wide.	lf	$3.60	$165.30	$168.90
Marble door architrave, custom grade ***Replace*** Materials.....151.00 Labor..........39.30 ***Remove*** .... Labor............3.60 ► Stone 6" or less wide with hand carvings on header or up to 10" wide with complex straight patterns (Gothic) with arched top. Or simple straight patterns with stone up to 12" wide.	lf	$3.60	$190.30	$193.90

RELATED ITEMS

Cleaning........................63
Fireplaces.....................241
Painting.......................340

	Item Description	Unit	Remove	Replace	Total
STONE DOOR ▶ ARCHITRAVE *continued*	**Marble door architrave, custom deluxe grade** ***Replace*** Materials.....179.00 Labor..........39.30 ***Remove*** .... Labor............3.60 ▶ Stone 6" or less wide with heavy hand carvings on header (e.g. lion's face, human face) or lighter hand carvings throughout or up to 12" wide with complex straight patterns (Gothic). With arched top.	lf	$3.60	$218.30	$221.90
	Sandstone door architrave, standard grade ***Replace*** Materials......35.50 Labor..........39.30 ***Remove*** .... Labor............3.60 ▶ Simple straight patterns. Stone is 6" or less wide.	lf	$3.60	$74.80	$78.40
	Sandstone door architrave, high grade ***Replace*** Materials......68.90 Labor..........39.30 ***Remove*** .... Labor............3.60 ▶ Complex straight patterns (Gothic). Stone is 6" or less wide.	lf	$3.60	$108.20	$111.80
	Sandstone door architrave, deluxe grade ***Replace*** Materials....102.00 Labor..........39.30 ***Remove*** .... Labor............3.60 ▶ Stone 6" or less wide with complex straight patterns (Gothic) with arched top or flat top with decorative work around corners or center of header. Or simple straight patterns with stone up to 10" wide.	lf	$3.60	$141.30	$144.90
	Sandstone door architrave, custom grade ***Replace*** Materials.....126.00 Labor..........39.30 ***Remove*** .... Labor............3.60 ▶ Stone 6" or less wide with hand carvings on header or up to 10" wide with complex straight patterns (Gothic) with arched top. Or simple straight patterns with stone up to 12" wide.	lf	$3.60	$165.30	$168.90
	Sandstone door architrave, custom deluxe grade ***Replace*** Materials....154.00 Labor..........39.30 ***Remove*** .... Labor............3.60 ▶ Stone 6" or less wide with heavy hand carvings on header (e.g. lion's face, human face) or lighter hand carvings throughout or up to 12" wide with complex straight patterns (Gothic). With arched top.	lf	$3.60	$193.30	$196.90
STONE WINDOW ▶ ARCHITRAVE	**Cast stone window architrave, standard grade** ***Replace*** Materials......20.10 Labor..........40.10 ***Remove*** .... Labor............3.60 ▶ Simple straight patterns. Cast stone is 6" or less wide.	lf	$3.60	$60.20	$63.80
	Cast stone window architrave, high grade ***Replace*** Materials......22.00 Labor..........40.10 ***Remove*** .... Labor............3.60 ▶ Complex straight patterns (Gothic). Cast stone is 6" or less wide.	lf	$3.60	$62.10	$65.70
	Cast stone window architrave, deluxe grade ***Replace*** Materials......29.70 Labor..........40.10 ***Remove*** .... Labor............3.60 ▶ Cast stone 6" or less wide with complex straight patterns (Gothic) with arched top or flat top with decorative work around corners or center of header. Or simple straight patterns with cast stone up to 10" wide.	lf	$3.60	$69.80	$73.40
	Cast stone window architrave, custom grade ***Replace*** Materials......36.40 Labor..........40.10 ***Remove*** .... Labor............3.60 ▶ Cast stone 6" or less wide with hand carvings on header or up to 10" wide with complex straight patterns (Gothic) with arched top. Or simple straight patterns with cast stone up to 12" wide.	lf	$3.60	$76.50	$80.10

Item Description	Unit	Remove	Replace	Total
Cast stone window architrave, custom deluxe grade ***Replace*** Materials......46.50 Labor..........40.10 ***Remove*** .... Labor............3.60 ► Cast stone 6" or less wide with heavy hand carvings on header (e.g. lion's face, human face) or lighter hand carvings throughout or up to 12" wide with complex straight patterns (Gothic). With arched top.	lf	$3.60	$86.60	$90.20
Limestone window architrave, standard grade ***Replace*** Materials......39.10 Labor..........40.10 ***Remove*** .... Labor............3.60 ► Simple straight patterns. Stone is 6" or less wide.	lf	$3.60	$79.20	$82.80
Limestone window architrave, high grade ***Replace*** Materials......71.50 Labor..........40.10 ***Remove*** .... Labor............3.60 ► Complex straight patterns (Gothic). Stone is 6" or less wide.	lf	$3.60	$111.60	$115.20
Limestone window architrave, deluxe grade ***Replace*** Materials....103.00 Labor..........40.10 ***Remove*** .... Labor............3.60 ► Stone 6" or less wide with complex straight patterns (Gothic) with arched top or flat top with decorative work around corners or center of header. Or simple straight patterns with stone up to 10" wide.	lf	$3.60	$143.10	$146.70
Limestone window architrave, custom grade ***Replace*** Materials.....127.00 Labor..........40.10 ***Remove*** .... Labor............3.60 ► Stone 6" or less wide with hand carvings on header or up to 10" wide with complex straight patterns (Gothic) with arched top. Or simple straight patterns with stone up to 12" wide.	lf	$3.60	$167.10	$170.70
Limestone window architrave, custom deluxe grade ***Replace*** Materials.....155.00 Labor..........40.10 ***Remove*** .... Labor............3.60 ► Stone 6" or less wide with heavy hand carvings on header (e.g. lion's face, human face) or lighter hand carvings throughout or up to 12" wide with complex straight patterns (Gothic). With arched top.	lf	$3.60	$195.10	$198.70
Marble window architrave, standard grade ***Replace*** Materials......58.40 Labor..........40.10 ***Remove*** .... Labor............3.60 ► Simple straight patterns. Stone is 6" or less wide.	lf	$3.60	$98.50	$102.10
Marble window architrave, high grade ***Replace*** Materials......91.20 Labor..........40.10 ***Remove*** .... Labor............3.60 ► Complex straight patterns (Gothic). Stone is 6" or less wide.	lf	$3.60	$131.30	$134.90
Marble window architrave, deluxe grade ***Replace*** Materials.....123.00 Labor..........40.10 ***Remove*** .... Labor............3.60 ► Stone 6" or less wide with complex straight patterns (Gothic) with arched top or flat top with decorative work around corners or center of header. Or simple straight patterns with stone up to 10" wide.	lf	$3.60	$163.10	$166.70
Marble window architrave, custom grade ***Replace*** Materials.....147.00 Labor..........40.10 ***Remove*** .... Labor............3.60 ► Stone 6" or less wide with hand carvings on header or up to 10" wide with complex straight patterns (Gothic) with arched top. Or simple straight patterns with stone up to 12" wide.	lf	$3.60	$187.10	$190.70

RELATED ITEMS

Cleaning 63
Fireplaces......................241
Painting........................340

Item Description	Unit	Remove	Replace	Total
STONE WINDOW ARCHITRAVE *continued* ▶ **Marble window architrave, custom deluxe grade** ***Replace*** Materials.....174.00 Labor..........40.10 ***Remove*** .... Labor............3.60 ▶ Stone 6" or less wide with heavy hand carvings on header (e.g. lion's face, human face) or lighter hand carvings throughout or up to 12" wide with complex straight patterns (Gothic). With arched top.	lf	$3.60	$214.10	$217.70
Sandstone window architrave, standard grade ***Replace*** Materials......36.80 Labor..........40.10 ***Remove*** .... Labor............3.60 ▶ Simple straight patterns. Stone is 6" or less wide.	lf	$3.60	$76.90	$80.50
Sandstone window architrave, high grade ***Replace*** Materials......69.10 Labor..........40.10 ***Remove*** .... Labor............3.60 ▶ Complex straight patterns (Gothic). Stone is 6" or less wide.	lf	$3.60	$109.20	$112.80
Sandstone window architrave, deluxe grade ***Replace*** Materials.....101.00 Labor..........40.10 ***Remove*** .... Labor............3.60 ▶ Stone 6" or less wide with complex straight patterns (Gothic) with arched top or flat top with decorative work around corners or center of header. Or simple straight patterns with stone up to 10" wide.	lf	$3.60	$141.10	$144.70
Sandstone window architrave, custom grade ***Replace*** Materials.....125.00 Labor..........40.10 ***Remove*** .... Labor............3.60 ▶ Stone 6" or less wide with hand carvings on header or up to 10" wide with complex straight patterns (Gothic) with arched top. Or simple straight patterns with stone up to 12" wide.	lf	$3.60	$165.10	$168.70
Sandstone window architrave, custom deluxe grade ***Replace*** Materials.....152.00 Labor..........40.10 ***Remove*** .... Labor............3.60 ▶ Stone 6" or less wide with heavy hand carvings on header (e.g. lion's face, human face) or lighter hand carvings throughout or up to 12" wide with complex straight patterns (Gothic). With arched top.	lf	$3.60	$192.10	$195.70
add for round window ▷ **Add 65% for architrave for round or elliptical window** ▶ Measure perimeter of opening.				
replace section to match ▷ **Replace section of stone architrave cut to match** ***Replace*** Materials....525.00 Labor.........134.00 ▶ Includes plaster or clay model with work performed on site or in a shop within 150 miles of the site.	ea	—	$659.00	$659.00
CUT STONE TRIM OR CORNICE *Per 4" of width. Use for friezes, architraves, cornices, string courses, band courses, and so on.* ▶ **Cut stone trim or cornice stones, all horizontal patterns** ***Replace*** Materials......12.70 Labor...........14.80 ***Remove*** .... Labor............2.86	lf	$2.86	$27.50	$30.36
Cut stone trim or cornice stones, complex horizontal patterns (Gothic) ***Replace*** Materials.......17.80 Labor...........14.80 ***Remove*** .... Labor............2.86	lf	$2.86	$32.60	$35.46
Cut stone trim or cornice stones with vertical patterns ***Replace*** Materials.......19.70 Labor...........14.80 ***Remove*** .... Labor............2.86	lf	$2.86	$34.50	$37.36
Cut stone trim or cornice stones with light hand carvings ***Replace*** Materials......27.70 Labor...........14.80 ***Remove*** .... Labor............2.86	lf	$2.86	$42.50	$45.36

Item Description	*Unit*	*Remove*	*Replace*	*Total*
Cut stone trim or cornice stones with medium hand carvings ***Replace*** Materials......34.60 Labor...........14.80 ***Remove*** .... Labor............2.86	**lf**	**$2.86**	**$49.40**	**$52.26**
Cut stone trim or cornice stones with heavy hand carvings ***Replace*** Materials......45.00 Labor...........14.80 ***Remove*** .... Labor............2.86	**lf**	**$2.86**	**$59.80**	**$62.66**
Limestone trim or cornice stones, all horizontal patterns ***Replace*** Materials.......19.50 Labor...........14.80 ***Remove*** .... Labor............2.86	**lf**	**$2.86**	**$34.30**	**$37.16**
Limestone trim or cornice stones, complex horizontal patterns (Gothic) ***Replace*** Materials......36.90 Labor...........14.80 ***Remove*** .... Labor............2.86	**lf**	**$2.86**	**$51.70**	**$54.56**
Limestone trim or cornice stones with vertical patterns ***Replace*** Materials......70.30 Labor...........14.80 ***Remove*** .... Labor............2.86	**lf**	**$2.86**	**$85.10**	**$87.96**
Limestone trim or cornice stones with light hand carvings ***Replace*** Materials....103.00 Labor...........14.80 ***Remove*** .... Labor............2.86	**lf**	**$2.86**	**$117.80**	**$120.66**
Limestone trim or cornice stones with medium hand carvings ***Replace*** Materials.....128.00 Labor...........14.80 ***Remove*** .... Labor............2.86	**lf**	**$2.86**	**$142.80**	**$145.66**
Limestone trim or cornice stones with heavy hand carvings ***Replace*** Materials.....156.00 Labor...........14.80 ***Remove*** .... Labor............2.86	**lf**	**$2.86**	**$170.80**	**$173.66**
Marble trim or cornice stones, all horizontal patterns ***Replace*** Materials......37.10 Labor...........14.80 ***Remove*** .... Labor............2.86	**lf**	**$2.86**	**$51.90**	**$54.76**
Marble trim or cornice stones, complex horizontal patterns (Gothic) ***Replace*** Materials......54.70 Labor...........14.80 ***Remove*** .... Labor............2.86	**lf**	**$2.86**	**$69.50**	**$72.36**
Marble trim or cornice stones with vertical patterns ***Replace*** Materials......88.50 Labor...........14.80 ***Remove*** .... Labor............2.86	**lf**	**$2.86**	**$103.30**	**$106.16**
Marble trim or cornice stones with light hand carvings ***Replace*** Materials.....121.00 Labor...........14.80 ***Remove*** .... Labor............2.86	**lf**	**$2.86**	**$135.80**	**$138.66**
Marble trim or cornice stones with medium hand carvings ***Replace*** Materials ....146.00 Labor...........14.80 ***Remove*** .... Labor............2.86	**lf**	**$2.86**	**$160.80**	**$163.66**
Marble trim or cornice stones with heavy hand carvings ***Replace*** Materials.....174.00 Labor...........14.80 ***Remove*** .... Labor............2.86	**lf**	**$2.86**	**$188.80**	**$191.66**
Sandstone trim or cornice stones, all horizontal patterns ***Replace*** Materials ......14.90 Labor...........14.80 ***Remove*** .... Labor............2.86	**lf**	**$2.86**	**$29.70**	**$32.56**

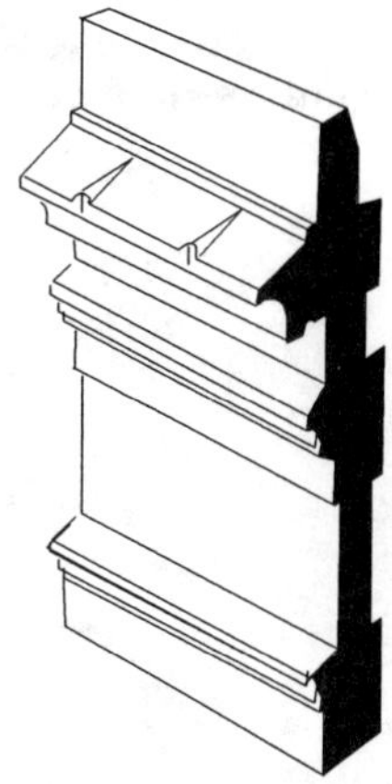

CUT STONE

All horizontal patterns are shallow. Typical depth is 3/4" or less but may be as deep as 1".

Complex horizontal patterns are deep Gothic style reliefs that require two passes through the stone planer.

Vertical patterns are straight vertical cuts like dentil, meander, or fretwork.

Light hand carvings are usually less than 3/4" deep and do not cover the entire face of the stone with detailed work.

Medium hand carvings are heavier carvings like vermiculation, Acanthus, and so forth.

Heavy hand carvings are heavy and deep carvings including a lion's face, a human face, and so forth.

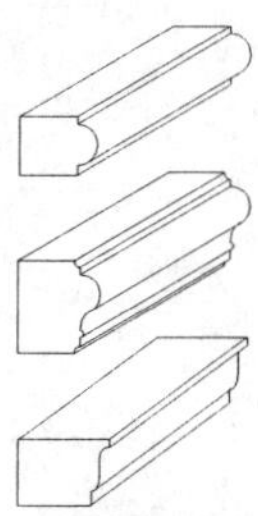

△ ***horizontal patterns***

RELATED ITEMS

Cleaning........................63
Fireplaces......................241
Painting.......................340

CUT STONE ▶ TRIM OR CORNICE *continued*

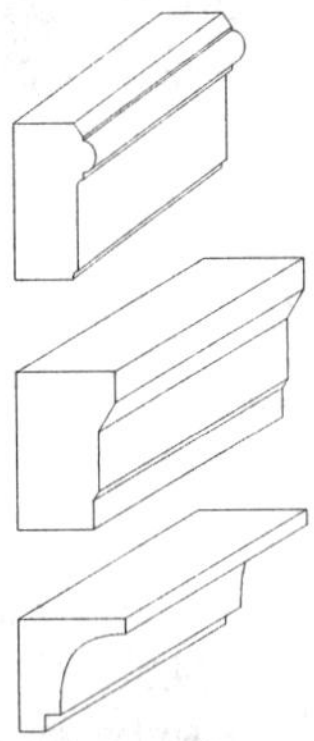

△ *horizontal patterns*

Item Description	Unit	Remove	Replace	Total
Sandstone trim or cornice stones, complex horizontal patterns (Gothic) *Replace* Materials......32.40 Labor...........14.80 *Remove* .... Labor 2.86	lf	$2.86	$47.20	$50.06
Sandstone trim or cornice stones with vertical patterns *Replace* Materials......65.70 Labor...........14.80 *Remove* .... Labor 2.86	lf	$2.86	$80.50	$83.36
Sandstone trim or cornice stones with light hand carvings *Replace* Materials......98.40 Labor...........14.80 *Remove* .... Labor 2.86	lf	$2.86	$113.20	$116.06
Sandstone trim or cornice stones with medium hand carvings *Replace* Materials.....123.00 Labor...........14.80 *Remove* .... Labor 2.86	lf	$2.86	$137.80	$140.66
Sandstone trim or cornice stones with heavy hand carvings *Replace* Materials.....151.00 Labor...........14.80 *Remove* .... Labor 2.86	lf	$2.86	$165.80	$168.66
(replace section to match ▷) **Replace section of stone trim or cornice cut to match** *Replace* Materials....431.00 Labor..........118.00 ► Includes plaster or clay model with work performed on site or in a shop within 150 miles of the site.	ea	—	$549.00	$549.00

CUT STONE SILL ▶ *Up to 10" wide.*

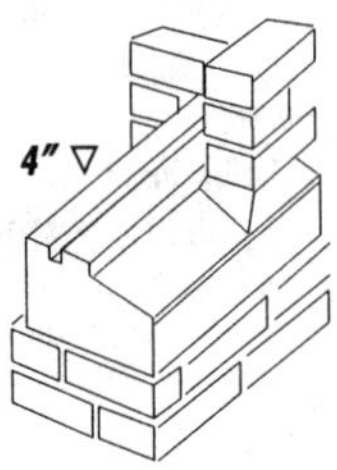

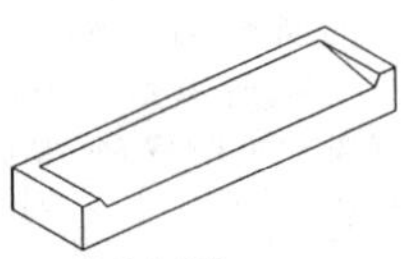

△ 1-1/2"

Item Description	Unit	Remove	Replace	Total
1-1/2" bluestone window sill or stool *Replace* Materials.......13.00 Labor...........13.40 *Remove* .... Labor 3.03	lf	$3.03	$26.40	$29.43
4" cast stone window sill *Replace* Materials........9.00 Labor...........13.40 *Remove* .... Labor ....3.03 ► 4" thick at edge. Up to 6" thick at center or end of sill.	lf	$3.03	$22.40	$25.43
1-1/2" granite window sill or stool *Replace* Materials ......14.10 Labor...........13.40 *Remove* .... Labor 3.03	lf	$3.03	$27.50	$30.53
4" granite window sill *Replace* Materials......25.50 Labor...........13.40 *Remove* .... Labor ....3.03 ► 4" thick at edge. Up to 6" thick at center or end of sill.	lf	$3.03	$38.90	$41.93
1-1/2" limestone window sill or stool *Replace* Materials ......12.70 Labor...........13.40 *Remove* .... Labor 3.03	lf	$3.03	$26.10	$29.13
4" limestone window sill *Replace* Materials......22.80 Labor...........13.40 *Remove* .... Labor ....3.03 ► 4" thick at edge. Up to 6" thick at center or end of sill.	lf	$3.03	$36.20	$39.23
1-1/2" marble window sill or stool *Replace* Materials.......15.00 Labor...........13.40 *Remove* .... Labor 3.03	lf	$3.03	$28.40	$31.43
1-1/2" sandstone window sill or stool *Replace* Materials........9.30 Labor...........13.40 *Remove* .... Labor 3.03	lf	$3.03	$22.70	$25.73

Item Description	Unit	Remove	Replace	Total
4" sandstone window sill ***Replace*** Materials......18.30 Labor..........13.40 ***Remove*** .... Labor...........3.03 ► 4" thick at edge. Up to 6" thick at center or end of sill.	lf	$3.03	$31.70	$34.73
1-1/2" slate window sill or stool ***Replace*** Materials.......15.10 Labor..........13.40 ***Remove*** .... Labor...........3.03	lf	$3.03	$28.50	$31.53
10" terra-cotta wall cap ***Replace*** Materials........6.85 Labor...........7.42 ***Remove*** .... Labor...........1.73	lf	$1.73	$14.27	$16.00
12" terra-cotta wall cap ***Replace*** Materials.......11.20 Labor...........7.42 ***Remove*** .... Labor...........1.73	lf	$1.73	$18.62	$20.35
Aluminum wall cap all wall widths ***Replace*** Materials.......13.00 Labor...........7.26 ***Remove*** .... Labor........... .52	lf	$.52	$20.26	$20.78
10" wide concrete coping ***Replace*** Materials......14.10 Labor...........6.70 ***Remove*** .... Labor...........2.86	lf	$2.86	$20.80	$23.66
12" wide concrete coping ***Replace*** Materials......14.80 Labor...........6.70 ***Remove*** .... Labor...........2.86	lf	$2.86	$21.50	$24.36
14" wide concrete coping ***Replace*** Materials......18.80 Labor...........6.70 ***Remove*** .... Labor...........2.86	lf	$2.86	$25.50	$28.36
8" wide granite coping stone ***Replace*** Materials......28.50 Labor...........7.42 ***Remove*** .... Labor...........2.86	lf	$2.86	$35.92	$38.78
10" wide granite coping stone ***Replace*** Materials......32.80 Labor...........7.42 ***Remove*** .... Labor...........2.86	lf	$2.86	$40.22	$43.08
12" wide granite coping stone ***Replace*** Materials......37.20 Labor...........7.42 ***Remove*** .... Labor...........2.86	lf	$2.86	$44.62	$47.48
8" wide limestone coping stone ***Replace*** Materials......16.90 Labor...........7.42 ***Remove*** .... Labor...........2.86	lf	$2.86	$24.32	$27.18
10" wide limestone coping stone ***Replace*** Materials.......17.30 Labor...........7.42 ***Remove*** .... Labor...........2.86	lf	$2.86	$24.72	$27.58
12" wide limestone coping stone ***Replace*** Materials......20.30 Labor...........7.42 ***Remove*** .... Labor...........2.86	lf	$2.86	$27.72	$30.58
8" wide marble coping stone ***Replace*** Materials......24.00 Labor...........7.42 ***Remove*** .... Labor...........2.86	lf	$2.86	$31.42	$34.28

◄ **WALL CAP**

◄ **WALL COPING** *From 4" to 6" thick at center with straight or curved taper to edges. Widths over 8" include drip grooves on each side as illustrated below.*

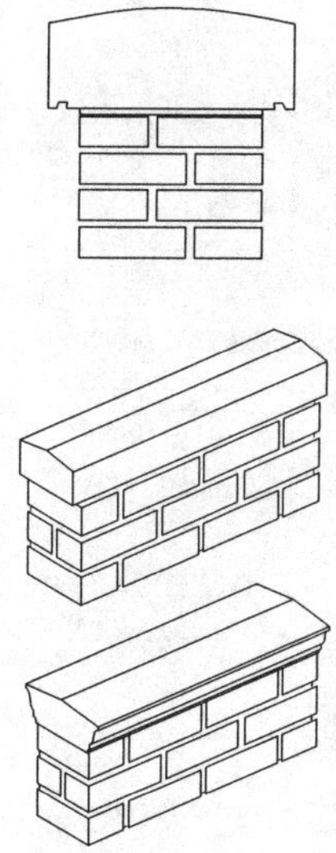

RELATED ITEMS

Cleaning........................63
Fireplaces......................241
Painting........................340

WALL COPING ► *continued*

Item Description	Unit	Remove	Replace	Total
10″ wide marble coping stone *Replace* Materials......29.70 Labor............7.42 *Remove* .... Labor............2.86	lf	$2.86	$37.12	$39.98
12″ wide marble coping stone *Replace* Materials......37.20 Labor............7.42 *Remove* .... Labor............2.86	lf	$2.86	$44.62	$47.48

REPOINT BRICK WALL ►

Tuck pointing. To mask and grout deduct ***12%.***

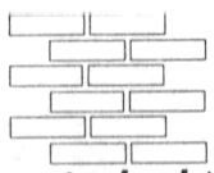

running bond △

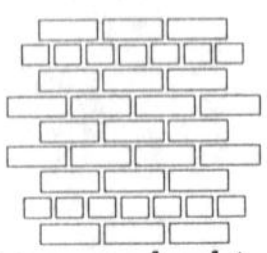

common bond △

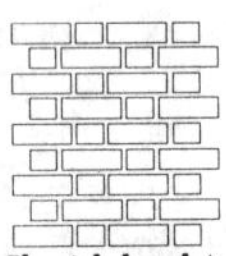

Flemish bond △

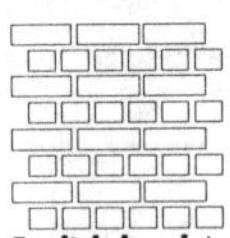

English bond △

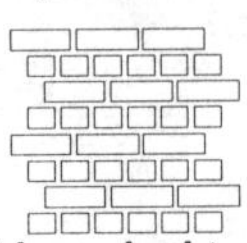

English cross bond △

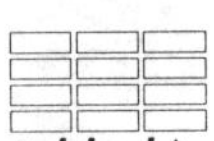

stack bond △

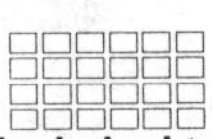

header bond △

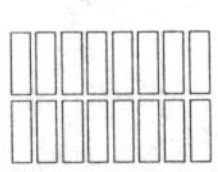

soldier course △

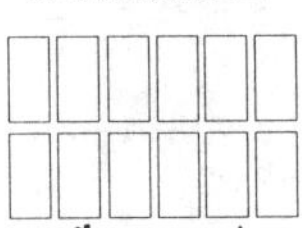

sailor course △

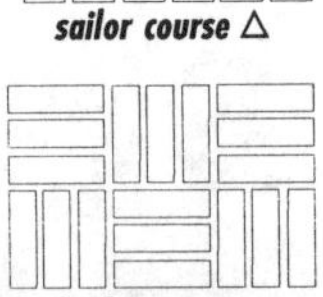

basketweave △

diagonal △

Item Description	Unit	Remove	Replace	Total
Repoint running bond brick wall *Replace* Materials........ .32 Labor............4.33	sf	—	$4.65	$4.65
Repoint common bond brick wall *Replace* Materials........ .32 Labor............4.45 ► Also called American bond. Every sixth course is a full course of full-length headers.	sf	—	$4.77	$4.77
Repoint Flemish bond brick wall *Replace* Materials........ .32 Labor............4.85 ► Each course is made of alternating stretchers and headers.	sf	—	$5.17	$5.17
Repoint English bond brick wall *Replace* Materials........ .32 Labor............5.13 ► Alternating full courses made from stretchers and headers. The joints between stretchers in all courses align vertically.	sf	—	$5.45	$5.45
Repoint English cross bond brick wall *Replace* Materials........ .32 Labor............5.13 ► Also called Dutch bond. A variation of English bond. The vertical joints between stretcher bricks, in alternate courses, align vertically with the center of the stretcher brick in the course above and below.	sf	—	$5.45	$5.45
Repoint stack bond brick wall *Replace* Materials........ .32 Labor............3.29 ► All vertical and horizontal joints align.	sf	—	$3.61	$3.61
Repoint all header bond brick wall *Replace* Materials........ .32 Labor............3.73 ► All bricks are laid as headers.	sf	—	$4.05	$4.05
Repoint soldier course brick wall *Replace* Materials........ .32 Labor............4.25 ► All bricks are stood on end with edge showing.	sf	—	$4.57	$4.57
Repoint sailor course brick wall *Replace* Materials........ .32 Labor............3.97 ► All bricks are stood on end with face showing.	sf	—	$4.29	$4.29
Repoint basketweave brick wall *Replace* Materials........ .32 Labor............6.58 ► A wide variety of patterns with alternating sections of horizontal and vertical brick.	sf	—	$6.90	$6.90
Repoint herringbone weave brick wall *Replace* Materials........ .32 Labor............6.70 ► Also called diagonal basketweave. Bricks are placed at an angle (usually 45 degree) in alternate sections angling up and down.	sf	—	$7.02	$7.02
Repoint diagonal bond brick wall *Replace* Materials........ .32 Labor............5.77 ► All bricks laid at an angle, usually 45 degree.	sf	—	$6.09	$6.09

Item Description	Unit	Remove	Replace	Total	
Repoint coursed ashlar style bond brick wall with two sizes of bricks *Replace* Materials........ .32 Labor............4.81 ► A pattern that uses two sizes of bricks to simulate coursed ashlar stone patterns. Usually one size of brick equals two of the second size.	sf	—	$5.13	$5.13	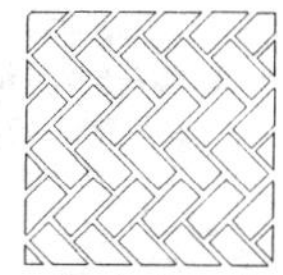 *herringbone* △
Add 12% to repoint brick wall with hard existing mortar					◁ add for hard mortar
Add 22% to repoint brick wall with very hard existing mortar					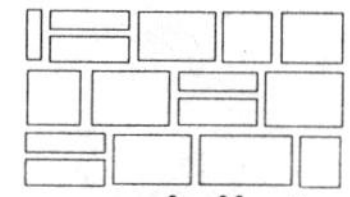
Add 18% to repoint brick wall with butter joint mortar					*coursed ashlar* △
Minimum charge to repoint brick wall *Replace* Materials......16.00 Labor.........201.00	ea	—	$217.00	$217.00	◁ minimum charge
Repoint rubble lay stone wall *Replace* Materials........1.51 Labor...........11.10	sf	—	$12.61	$12.61	◄ **REPOINT STONE WALL**
Repoint ashlar lay stone wall *Replace* Materials........1.18 Labor...........10.43	sf	—	$11.61	$11.61	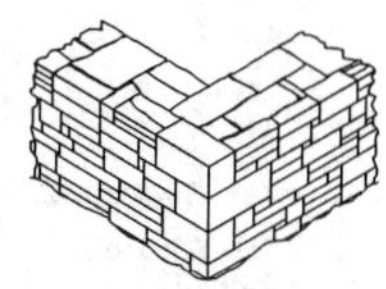
Minimum charge to repoint stone wall *Replace* Materials......16.00 Labor.........201.00	ea	—	$217.00	$217.00	*rubble lay* △
Remove brick veneer, salvage bricks, and re-lay *Replace* Materials........1.72 Labor...........35.20 ► Existing bricks are removed and old mortar chipped away. An average of 75% of the bricks are salvaged. To replace the missing bricks, 25% of the salvaged bricks are sawn in half length wise and back filled with mortar to fit. Finish wall includes 50% full bricks and 50% backfilled half bricks. Normally not used for large walls, but on sections of damaged wall where bricks cannot be matched.	sf	—	$36.92	$36.92	◄ **SALVAGE BRICK**
Replace single brick *Replace* Materials........2.02 Labor...........17.30 ► A single damaged brick is broken out and replaced.	sf	—	$19.32	$19.32	◄ **BRICK WALL REPAIR**
Tooth in brick patch up to 4 sf *Replace* Materials......37.00 Labor..........20.20 ► A small section of brick (less than 4 sf) is broken out and replaced.	sf	—	$57.20	$57.20	
Tooth in brick patch, 4 to 20 sf *Replace* Materials........9.30 Labor...........16.40 ► A small section over 4 sf but less than 20 sf is replaced Existing bricks remain either above, below, or both. (Does not include demolition.)	sf	—	$25.70	$25.70	
Minimum charge to repair brick wall *Replace* Materials.......61.00 Labor........460.00	ea	—	$521.00	$521.00	◁ minimum charge
Replace single stone *Replace* Materials........3.90 Labor...........18.10 ► A single damaged stone is broken out and replaced.	ea	—	$22.00	$22.00	◄ **STONE WALL REPAIR**
Tooth in stone patch up to 4 sf *Replace* Materials......71.50 Labor..........22.70 ► A small section of stone (less than 4 sf) is broken out and replaced.	ea	—	$94.20	$94.20	
Tooth in stone patch, 4 to 20 sf *Replace* Materials.......17.90 Labor..........23.50 ► A section of stone veneer is replaced in an area over 4 sf but less than 20 sf. Existing stones remain either above, below, or both. (Does not include demolition.)	ea	—	$41.40	$41.40	

RELATED ITEMS

Cleaning........................63
Fireplaces.....................241
Painting.......................340

	Item Description	Unit	Remove	Replace	Total
STONE WALL ▶ REPAIR *continued*	**Remove segment of rubble stone wall and re-lay** ***Replace*** Materials........4.30 Labor.........176.00 ▶ Existing stones are removed, old mortar is chipped away and wall is re-laid.	cf	—	$180.30	$180.30
	Remove segment of rubble stone veneer and re-lay ***Replace*** Materials........1.45 Labor..........84.70 ▶ Existing stones are removed, old mortar is chipped away and veneer is re-laid.	sf	—	$86.15	$86.15
	Remove segment of ashlar stone wall and re-lay ***Replace*** Materials........3.13 Labor.........170.00 ▶ Existing stones are removed, old mortar is chipped away and wall is re-laid.	cf	—	$173.13	$173.13
	Remove segment of ashlar stone veneer and re-lay ***Replace*** Materials...... 1.04 Labor..........83.30 ▶ Existing stones are removed, old mortar is chipped away and veneer is re-laid.	sf	—	$84.34	$84.34
	Minimum charge to repair stone wall ***Replace*** Materials.....117.00 Labor.........511.00	ea	—	$628.00	$628.00
STONE CARVING ▶ *Work performed on site or in a shop within 150 miles of the site. Does not include clay or plaster model.*	**Carve stone with light hand carvings** ***Replace*** .... Labor............1.62 ▶ Light carvings usually less than 3/4" deep and do not cover the entire face of the stone with detailed work.	si	—	$1.62	$1.62
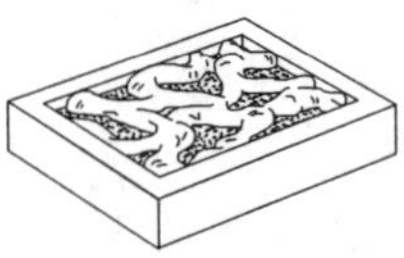	**Carve stone with medium hand carvings** ***Replace*** .... Labor............2.38 ▶ Heavier carvings like vermiculation, Acanthus, and so forth.	si	—	$2.38	$2.38
△ ***vermiculation***	**Carve stone with heavy hand carvings** ***Replace*** .... Labor............3.35 ▶ Heavy and deep carvings including a lion's face, a human face, and so forth.	si	—	$3.35	$3.35
	Add 120% for carving stone to match existing work				
clay or plaster model ▷	**Clay or plaster model for stone carvings** ***Replace*** Materials........1.43 ▶ Models for light carvings may run 15% less and models for heavy carvings like faces may run 20% to 45% more. It is not unusual for models to cost as much or more as the actual carving.	si	—	$1.43	$1.43
	Minimum charge for clay or plaster model for stone carvings ***Replace*** Materials 148.00	si	—	$148.00	$148.00
CARVED STONE ▶ REPAIR	**Repair carved stone with epoxy** ***Replace*** Materials .... .23 Labor........... 1.10 ▶ Reattach broken piece of carved stone using epoxy and, when necessary, non-ferrous pins.	si	—	$1.33	$1.33
	Repair carved stone with stucco ***Replace*** Materials .... .03 Labor........... 1.01 ▶ Reface damaged or weathered stone with stucco and shape stucco to match carving.	si	—	$1.04	$1.04
minimum charge ▷	**Minimum charge to repair carved stone** ***Replace*** Materials......34.00 Labor.........184.00	ea	—	$218.00	$218.00
STONE REPAIR ▶	**Epoxy repair and pin broken stone** ***Replace*** Materials........8.75 Labor...........61.20 ▶ Reattach broken piece of stone using epoxy and, when necessary, non-ferrous pins.	ea	—	$69.95	$69.95

Item Description	Unit	Remove	Replace	Total
Reconstitute delaminating stone with epoxy and reinforcing pins *Replace* Materials........ .26 Labor............ .60 ► Drill holes and inject epoxy in between layers of delaminating stone. Non-ferrous reinforcing pins are also added for strength.	si	—	$.86	$.86
Reface damaged stone with grout mixed to match *Replace* Materials........ .03 Labor............6.85 ► Grout or plaster colored to match stone is applied over the face of damaged or weathered stone and shaped to match.	si	—	$6.88	$6.88
Minimum charge for stone epoxy repair work *Replace* Materials......34.00 Labor.........128.00	ea	—	$162.00	$162.00
Hand clean brick wall *Replace* Materials........ .07 Labor............1.35 ► With bristle brush and muriatic acid (or similar).	sf	—	$1.42	$1.42
Hand clean stone wall *Replace* Materials........ .07 Labor............1.45 ► With bristle brush and muriatic acid (or similar).	sf	—	$1.52	$1.52
Pressure spray brick wall *Replace* Materials........ .09 Labor............ .35 ► With water only or with cleaning chemicals.	sf	—	$.44	$.44
Pressure spray stone wall *Replace* Materials........ .09 Labor............ .35 ► With water only or with cleaning chemicals.	sf	—	$.44	$.44
Steam clean brick wall *Replace* .... Labor............ .48	sf	—	$.48	$.48
Steam clean stone wall *Replace* .... Labor............ .52	sf	—	$.52	$.52
Wet sandblast brick wall *Replace* Materials........ .30 Labor............1.46	sf	—	$1.76	$1.76
Wet sandblast stone wall *Replace* Materials........ .30 Labor............1.54	sf	—	$1.84	$1.84
Cut opening in brick wall to 6" thick *Replace* .... Labor............7.89	lf	—	$7.89	$7.89
Cut opening in brick wall 7" to 12" thick *Replace* .... Labor............8.82	lf	—	$8.82	$8.82
Cut opening in brick veneer wall *Replace* .... Labor............7.59	lf	—	$7.59	$7.59
Cut opening in stone wall to 6" thick *Replace* .... Labor............8.82	lf	—	$8.82	$8.82
Cut opening in stone wall 7" to 12" thick *Replace* .... Labor..........10.00	lf	—	$10.00	$10.00
Cut opening in stone veneer wall *Replace* .... Labor............8.47	lf	—	$8.47	$8.47

◁ minimum charge

◀ **CLEAN MASONRY**

◀ **CUT OPENING IN MASONRY WALL**
Cut masonry wall with concrete saw. See next page for prices to insert lintels into opening.

RELATED ITEMS

Cleaning........................63
Fireplaces....................241
Painting.......................340

	Item Description	Unit	Remove	Replace	Total
Shore masonry opening ▶	**Shore masonry opening for work per lf of header** ***Replace*** Materials.......11.40 Labor...........17.00 ▶ 2" x 6" or 2" x 8" framing members sheathed with plywood.	lf	—	$28.40	$28.40
	Shore arched masonry opening for work ***Replace*** Materials......12.00 Labor..........22.30 ▶ 2" x 6" or 2" x 8" framing members sheathed with plywood that follows curved shape of arch.	lf	—	$34.30	$34.30
Concrete lintel ▶	**Concrete lintel for opening in 4" thick brick or stone** ***Replace*** Materials........9.20 Labor............3.44	lf	—	$12.64	$12.64
	Concrete lintel for opening in 6" thick brick or stone ***Replace*** Materials......12.30 Labor............4.41	lf	—	$16.71	$16.71
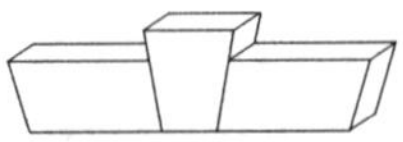 *lintel with plain key* △	**Concrete lintel for opening in 8" thick brick or stone** ***Replace*** Materials.......13.30 Labor............4.94	lf	—	$18.24	$18.24
	Concrete lintel for opening in 10" thick brick or stone ***Replace*** Materials......22.80 Labor............5.95	lf	—	$28.75	$28.75
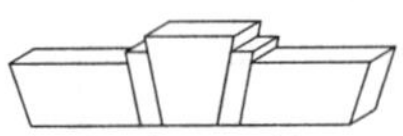 *lintel with winged key* △	**Concrete lintel for opening in 12" thick brick or stone** ***Replace*** Materials......30.40 Labor............6.57	lf	—	$36.97	$36.97
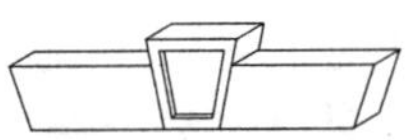 *lintel with recessed key* △	**Add for key cast into lintel** ***Replace*** Materials......47.00	ea	—	$47.00	$47.00
Angle-iron lintel ▶	**Angle iron lintel for opening in 4" thick brick or stone** ***Replace*** Materials........3.69 Labor............2.69	lf	—	$6.38	$6.38
	Angle iron lintel for opening in 6" thick brick or stone ***Replace*** Materials........7.38 Labor............2.69	lf	—	$10.07	$10.07
	Angle iron lintel for opening in 8" thick brick or stone ***Replace*** Materials........7.84 Labor............2.91	lf	—	$10.75	$10.75
	Angle iron lintel for opening in 10" thick brick or stone ***Replace*** Materials........8.80 Labor............2.95	lf	—	$11.75	$11.75
	Angle iron lintel for opening in 12" thick brick or stone ***Replace*** Materials......12.70 Labor............3.00	lf	—	$15.70	$15.70

NOTES:

end

TIME & MATERIAL CHARTS *(selected items)*

Masonry Materials

DESCRIPTION	MATERIAL PRICE	GROSS COVERAGE	WASTE	NET COVERAGE	UNIT PRICE
Rebar					
#3 (3/8" .376 pound per lf)	$3.44 per 20' bar	20	4%	19.2	$.18 lf
#4 (1/2" .668 pounds per lf)	$4.39 per 20' bar	20	4%	19.2	$.23 lf
#5 (5/8" 1.043 pounds per lf)	$6.82 per 20' bar	20	4%	19.2	$.36 lf
#6 (3/4" 1.502 pounds per lf)	$10.30 per 20' bar	20	4%	19.2	$.54 lf
Mortar and grout supplies					
gypsum cement	$15.70 per bag	80	12%	70.4	$.22 lb
masonry cement	$6.70 per bag	70	12%	61.6	$.11 lb
white masonry cement	$20.30 per bag	70	12%	61.6	$.33 lb
hydrated lime	$6.89 per bag	50	12%	44	$.16 lb
double hydrated lime	$9.40 per bag	50	12%	44	$.21 lb
screened and washed sand, delivered	$23.20 per ton	1	0%	1	$23.20 ton
Reinforcing wire strip					
4" ladder style	$.13 lf	1	2%	.98	$.13 lf
12" ladder style	$.19 lf	1	2%	.98	$.19 lf
4" truss style	$.18 lf	1	2%	.98	$.18 lf
12" truss style	$.23 lf	1	2%	.98	$.23 lf
*add **30%** for galvanized*					
Masonry ties					
galvanized 22 gauge corrugated veneer wall tie	$.18 ea	1	2%	.98	$.18 ea
galvanized 16 gauge corrugated veneer wall tie	$.19 ea	1	2%	.98	$.19 ea
rectangular galvanized wall tie	$.22 ea	1	2%	.98	$.22 ea
galvanized "Z" style cavity wall tie	$.20 ea	1	2%	.98	$.20 ea
Grout					
for 6" wide bond beam	$.75 lf	1	11%	.89	$.84 lf
for 8" wide bond beam	$.94 lf	1	11%	.89	$1.06 lf
for 10" wide bond beam	$1.18 lf	1	11%	.89	$1.33 lf
for 12" wide bond beam	$1.43 lf	1	11%	.89	$1.61 lf
for cells in 6" wide concrete block	$.90 lf	1	11%	.89	$1.01 lf
for cells in 8" wide concrete block	$1.32 lf	1	11%	.89	$1.48 lf
for cells in 10" wide concrete block	$1.68 lf	1	11%	.89	$1.89 lf
for cells in 12" wide concrete block	$2.13 lf	1	11%	.89	$2.39 lf
3/8" brick mortar					
for 4" wide standard non-modular or three-inch	$7.59 cf	25	25%	18.75	$.40 sf
for 4" wide oversize non-modular	$7.59 cf	26	25%	19.5	$.39 sf
for 4" wide engineer	$7.59 cf	27	25%	20.25	$.37 sf
for 4" wide jumbo closure	$7.59 cf	31	25%	23.25	$.33 sf
for 4" wide double	$7.59 cf	37	25%	27.75	$.27 sf
for 4" wide Roman	$7.59 cf	21	25%	15.75	$.48 sf
for 4" wide Norman	$7.59 cf	26	25%	19.5	$.39 sf
for 4" wide Norwegian	$7.59 cf	30	25%	22.5	$.34 sf
for 4" wide jumbo utility	$7.59 cf	36	25%	27	$.28 sf
for 4" wide triple	$7.59 cf	44	25%	33	$.23 sf
for 6" wide Norwegian	$7.59 cf	20	25%	15	$.51 sf
for 6" wide Norman	$7.59 cf	16.8	25%	12.6	$.60 sf
for 6" wide jumbo	$7.59 cf	24	25%	18	$.42 sf
for 8" wide jumbo	$7.59 cf	18	25%	13.5	$.56 sf
3/8" concrete block mortar (8" x 16" face)					
for 4" wide	$7.59 cf	40	25%	30	$.25 sf
for 6" wide	$7.59 cf	30	25%	22.5	$.34 sf
for 8" wide	$7.59 cf	25	25%	18.75	$.40 sf
for 10" wide	$7.59 cf	20.5	25%	15.38	$.49 sf
for 12" wide	$7.59 cf	16.6	25%	12.45	$.61 sf

. . . More ➤

Masonry Materials *continued*

DESCRIPTION	MATERIAL PRICE	GROSS COVERAGE	WASTE	NET COVERAGE	UNIT PRICE
3/8" concrete slump block mortar (4" x 16" face)					
for 4" wide	$7.59 cf	34	25%	25.5	$.30 sf
for 6" wide	$7.59 cf	24	25%	18	$.42 sf
for 8" wide	$7.59 cf	21	25%	15.75	$.48 sf
for 10" wide	$7.59 cf	16.5	25%	12.38	$.61 sf
for 12" wide	$7.59 cf	12.6	25%	9.45	$.80 sf
3/8" concrete screen block mortar (12" x 12" face)					
for 4" wide	$7.59 cf	35.6	25%	26.7	$.28 sf
3/8" backing tile mortar (12" x 12" face)					
for 4" thick	$7.59 cf	35.6	25%	26.7	$.28 sf
for 6" thick	$7.59 cf	26.5	25%	19.88	$.38 sf
for 8" thick	$7.59 cf	22.5	25%	16.88	$.45 sf
3/8" structural tile mortar (8" x 16" face)					
for 4" thick	$7.59 cf	40	25%	30	$.25 sf
for 6" thick	$7.59 cf	30	25%	22.5	$.34 sf
for 8" thick	$7.59 cf	25	25%	18.75	$.40 sf
3/8" gypsum partition tile mortar (12" x 30" face)					
for 4" thick	$7.59 cf	78	25%	58.5	$.13 sf
for 6" thick	$7.59 cf	66	25%	49.5	$.15 sf
3/8" white mortar for glass blocks					
for block with 4" x 8" face	$9.63 cf	26	25%	19.5	$.49 sf
for block with 6" x 6" face	$9.63 cf	29	25%	21.75	$.44 sf
for block with 6" x 8" face	$9.63 cf	36	25%	27	$.36 sf
for block with 8" x 8" face	$9.63 cf	44	25%	33	$.29 sf
for block with 12" x 12" face	$9.63 cf	35.6	25%	26.7	$.36 sf
*deduct **22%** for natural gray mortar in glass block wall*					
*deduct **8%** for colored mortar in glass block wall*					
Mortar for stone walls					
mortar for rubble stone wall	$7.59 cf	4.41	32%	3	$2.53 cf
mortar for ashlar stone wall	$7.59 cf	5.5	25%	4.13	$1.84 cf
mortar for rubble stone veneer	$7.59 cf	13.2	32%	8.98	$.85 sf
mortar for ashlar stone veneer	$7.59 cf	16.5	25%	12.38	$.61 sf
Brick					
*deduct **16%** for common brick*					
*add **$565.00** per thousand for glazed brick*					
4" wide standard non-modular	$657.00 per thousand	1,000	4%	960	$.68 ea
4" wide oversize non-modular	$654.00 per thousand	1,000	4%	960	$.68 ea
4" wide three-inch non-modular	$648.00 per thousand	1,000	4%	960	$.68 ea
4" wide standard	$522.00 per thousand	1,000	4%	960	$.54 ea
4" wide used	$1,130.00 per thousand	1,000	4%	960	$1.18 ea
4" wide engineer	$642.00 per thousand	1,000	4%	960	$.67 ea
4" wide jumbo closure	$798.00 per thousand	1,000	4%	960	$.83 ea
4" wide double	$845.00 per thousand	1,000	4%	960	$.88 ea
4" wide Roman	$905.00 per thousand	1,000	4%	960	$.94 ea
4" wide Norman	$884.00 per thousand	1,000	4%	960	$.92 ea
4" wide Norwegian	$798.00 per thousand	1,000	4%	960	$.83 ea
4" wide jumbo utility	$1,290.00 per thousand	1,000	4%	960	$1.34 ea
4" wide triple	$1,370.00 per thousand	1,000	4%	960	$1.43 ea
6" wide Norwegian	$1,260.00 per thousand	1,000	4%	960	$1.31 ea
6" wide Norman	$1,180.00 per thousand	1,000	4%	960	$1.23 ea
6" wide jumbo	$1,510.00 per thousand	1,000	4%	960	$1.57 ea
8" wide jumbo	$2,010.00 per thousand	1,000	4%	960	$2.09 ea
Concrete block					
4" wide	$902.00 per thousand	1,000	4%	960	$.94 ea
6" wide	$1,010.00 per thousand	1,000	4%	960	$1.05 ea
8" wide	$1,270.00 per thousand	1,000	4%	960	$1.32 ea
10" wide	$1,580.00 per thousand	1,000	4%	960	$1.65 ea
12" wide	$2,140.00 per thousand	1,000	4%	960	$2.23 ea

. . . More ➢

Masonry Materials *continued*

DESCRIPTION	MATERIAL PRICE	GROSS COVERAGE	WASTE	NET COVERAGE	UNIT PRICE
Lightweight concrete block					
4″ wide	$1,020.00 per thousand	1,000	4%	960	**$1.06** ea
6″ wide	$1,140.00 per thousand	1,000	4%	960	**$1.19** ea
8″ wide	$1,430.00 per thousand	1,000	4%	960	**$1.49** ea
10″ wide	$1,770.00 per thousand	1,000	4%	960	**$1.84** ea
12″ wide	$2,420.00 per thousand	1,000	4%	960	**$2.52** ea
Slump block					
4″ wide	$957.00 per thousand	1,000	4%	960	**$1.00** ea
6″ wide	$1,160.00 per thousand	1,000	4%	960	**$1.21** ea
8″ wide	$1,440.00 per thousand	1,000	4%	960	**$1.50** ea
10″ wide	$1,700.00 per thousand	1,000	4%	960	**$1.77** ea
12″ wide	$2,170.00 per thousand	1,000	4%	960	**$2.26** ea
Fluted block (fluted one side)					
4″ wide	$1,650.00 per thousand	1,000	4%	960	**$1.72** ea
6″ wide	$1,850.00 per thousand	1,000	4%	960	**$1.93** ea
8″ wide	$2,320.00 per thousand	1,000	4%	960	**$2.42** ea
10″ wide	$2,900.00 per thousand	1,000	4%	960	**$3.02** ea
12″ wide	$3,920.00 per thousand	1,000	4%	960	**$4.08** ea
Fluted block (fluted two sides)					
4″ wide	$2,000.00 per thousand	1,000	4%	960	**$2.08** ea
6″ wide	$2,230.00 per thousand	1,000	4%	960	**$2.32** ea
8″ wide	$2,800.00 per thousand	1,000	4%	960	**$2.92** ea
10″ wide	$3,500.00 per thousand	1,000	4%	960	**$3.65** ea
12″ wide	$4,740.00 per thousand	1,000	4%	960	**$4.94** ea
Glazed block (glazed one side)					
4″ wide	$8,980.00 per thousand	1,000	4%	960	**$9.35** ea
6″ wide	$9,220.00 per thousand	1,000	4%	960	**$9.60** ea
8″ wide	$9,520.00 per thousand	1,000	4%	960	**$9.92** ea
10″ wide	$9,760.00 per thousand	1,000	4%	960	**$10.20** ea
12″ wide	$10,000.00 per thousand	1,000	4%	960	**$10.40** ea
Glazed block (glazed two sides)					
4″ wide	$13,400.00 per thousand	1,000	4%	960	**$14.00** ea
6″ wide	$14,200.00 per thousand	1,000	4%	960	**$14.80** ea
8″ wide	$14,800.00 per thousand	1,000	4%	960	**$15.40** ea
10″ wide	$15,100.00 per thousand	1,000	4%	960	**$15.70** ea
12″ wide	$15,300.00 per thousand	1,000	4%	960	**$15.90** ea
Split-face block					
4″ wide	$1,840.00 per thousand	1,000	4%	960	**$1.92** ea
6″ wide	$2,190.00 per thousand	1,000	4%	960	**$2.28** ea
8″ wide	$2,950.00 per thousand	1,000	4%	960	**$3.07** ea
10″ wide	$3,180.00 per thousand	1,000	4%	960	**$3.31** ea
12″ wide	$4,270.00 per thousand	1,000	4%	960	**$4.45** ea
Split-rib block					
4″ wide	$1,700.00 per thousand	1,000	4%	960	**$1.77** ea
6″ wide	$1,760.00 per thousand	1,000	4%	960	**$1.83** ea
8″ wide	$2,890.00 per thousand	1,000	4%	960	**$3.01** ea
10″ wide	$3,220.00 per thousand	1,000	4%	960	**$3.35** ea
12″ wide	$3,540.00 per thousand	1,000	4%	960	**$3.69** ea
Screen block					
4″ wide, pattern two sides	$4,920.00 per thousand	1,000	4%	960	**$5.13** ea
4″ wide, pattern four sides	$9,330.00 per thousand	1,000	4%	960	**$9.72** ea
Silicone treated perlite or vermiculite loose fill insulation					
in 6″ wide block	$6.89 4 cf bag	21	3%	20.37	**$.34** sf
in 8″ wide block	$6.89 4 cf bag	14.5	3%	14.07	**$.49** sf
in 10″ wide block	$6.89 4 cf bag	11.5	3%	11.16	**$.62** sf
in 12″ wide block	$6.89 4 cf bag	8	3%	7.76	**$.89** sf

. . . More ➢

Masonry Materials *continued*

DESCRIPTION	MATERIAL PRICE	GROSS COVERAGE	WASTE	NET COVERAGE	UNIT PRICE
Glass block					
4" x 8" thinline smooth-face	$19.10 sf	1	4%	.96	**$19.90** sf
6" x 6" thinline smooth-face	$17.60 sf	1	4%	.96	**$18.30** sf
4" x 8" smooth-face	$24.10 sf	1	4%	.96	**$25.10** sf
6" x 6" smooth-face	$21.40 sf	1	4%	.96	**$22.30** sf
8" x 8" smooth-face	$15.00 sf	1	4%	.96	**$15.60** sf
*add **83%** for solar UV reflective*					
*add **11%** for patterned face*					
*add **55%** for tinted*					
Rubble stone					
coral-stone rubble	$31.70 cf	1	4%	.96	**$33.00** cf
field-stone rubble	$25.20 cf	1	4%	.96	**$26.30** cf
flagstone rubble	$14.50 cf	1	4%	.96	**$15.10** cf
river stone rubble	$25.90 cf	1	4%	.96	**$27.00** cf
lava stone rubble	$24.20 cf	1	4%	.96	**$25.20** cf
sandstone rubble	$37.00 cf	1	4%	.96	**$38.50** cf
Ashlar stone					
flagstone	$15.10 cf	1	4%	.96	**$15.70** cf
limestone, natural finish	$20.50 cf	1	4%	.96	**$21.40** cf
limestone, rough finish	$23.00 cf	1	4%	.96	**$24.00** cf
limestone, smooth finish	$33.30 cf	1	4%	.96	**$34.70** cf
marble, natural finish	$48.60 cf	1	4%	.96	**$50.60** cf
marble, rough finish	$52.50 cf	1	4%	.96	**$54.70** cf
marble, smooth finish	$65.10 cf	1	4%	.96	**$67.80** cf
sandstone, natural finish	$19.70 cf	1	4%	.96	**$20.50** cf
sandstone, rough finish	$22.10 cf	1	4%	.96	**$23.00** cf
sandstone, smooth finish	$32.00 cf	1	4%	.96	**$33.30** cf
Wall coping					
aluminum, all wall widths	$12.50 lf	1	4%	.96	**$13.00** lf
10" wide concrete	$13.20 lf	1	2%	.98	**$13.50** lf
14" wide concrete	$17.80 lf	1	2%	.98	**$18.20** lf
8" wide granite	$27.30 lf	1	2%	.98	**$27.90** lf
12" wide granite	$35.90 lf	1	2%	.98	**$36.60** lf
8" wide limestone	$16.00 lf	1	2%	.98	**$16.30** lf
12" wide limestone	$19.30 lf	1	2%	.98	**$19.70** lf
8" wide marble	$23.50 lf	1	2%	.98	**$24.00** lf
12" wide marble	$36.50 lf	1	2%	.98	**$37.20** lf

Masonry Labor

LABORER	BASE WAGE	PAID LEAVE	TRUE WAGE	FICA	FUTA	WORKER'S COMP.	UNEMPLOY. INSUR.	HEALTH INSUR.	RETIRE (401K)	LIABILITY INSUR.	COST PER HOUR
Mason	$24.40	1.90	$26.30	2.01	.21	8.15	2.29	2.69	.79	3.55	**$46.00**
Mason's helper	$22.20	1.73	$23.93	1.83	.19	7.42	2.08	2.69	.72	3.23	**$42.10**
Hod carrier	$16.60	1.29	$17.89	1.37	.14	5.54	1.56	2.69	.54	2.42	**$32.20**
Plasterer	$22.90	1.79	$24.69	1.89	.20	7.10	2.15	2.69	.74	3.33	**$42.80**
Stone carver	$59.20	4.62	$63.82	4.88	.51	19.78	5.55	2.69	1.91	8.62	**$108.00**
Demolition laborer	$13.90	1.08	$14.98	1.15	.121	4.79	1.30	2.69	.45	2.02	**$27.50**

Paid Leave is calculated based on two weeks paid vacation, one week sick leave, and seven paid holidays. Employer's matching portion of **FICA** is 7.65 percent. **FUTA** (Federal Unemployment) is .8 percent. **Worker's Compensation** was calculated using a national average of 30.99 percent for masonry workers and .28.74 percent for plastering workers. **Unemployment insurance** was calculated using a national average of 8.7 percent. **Health insurance** was calculated based on a projected national average for 2002 of $535 per employee (and family when applicable) per month. Employer pays 80 percent for a per month cost of $428 per employee. **Retirement** is based on a 401(k) retirement program with employer matching of 50 percent. Employee contributions to the 401(k) plan are an average of 6 percent of the true wage. **Liability insurance** is based on a national average of 13.2 percent.

Masonry Labor Productivity

WORK DESCRIPTION	LABORER	COST PER HOUR	PRODUCTIVITY	UNIT PRICE
Demolition				
remove 4″ masonry wall	demolition laborer	$27.50	.087	**$2.39** sf
remove 12″ masonry wall	demolition laborer	$27.50	.177	**$4.87** sf
remove brick veneer	demolition laborer	$27.50	.082	**$2.26** sf
remove block wall pilaster	demolition laborer	$27.50	.121	**$3.33** lf
remove block wall grade beam cap	demolition laborer	$27.50	.363	**$9.98** lf
remove terra-cotta wall cap	demolition laborer	$27.50	.063	**$1.73** lf
remove coping stone	demolition laborer	$27.50	.104	**$2.86** lf
remove glass block wall	demolition laborer	$27.50	.084	**$2.31** sf
remove pavers on mortar base	demolition laborer	$27.50	.120	**$3.30** sf
remove pavers on sand base	demolition laborer	$27.50	.084	**$2.31** sf
remove stone rubble wall with no mortar	demolition laborer	$27.50	.259	**$7.12** cf
remove stone rubble wall with mortar	demolition laborer	$27.50	.439	**$12.10** cf
remove ashlar wall	demolition laborer	$27.50	.439	**$12.10** cf
remove stone veneer	demolition laborer	$27.50	.106	**$2.92** sf
remove keystone	demolition laborer	$27.50	.198	**$5.45** ea
remove quoin	demolition laborer	$27.50	.196	**$5.39** ea
remove veneer panels	demolition laborer	$27.50	.074	**$2.04** sf
remove door or window architrave	demolition laborer	$27.50	.131	**$3.60** lf
remove trim or cornice stones	demolition laborer	$27.50	.104	**$2.86** ea
remove stone window sill	demolition laborer	$27.50	.110	**$3.03** lf
remove precast concrete lintel	demolition laborer	$27.50	.120	**$3.30** lf
Masonry crew				
install masonry	mason	$46.00		
install masonry	mason's helper	$42.10		
install masonry	hod carrier / laborer	$32.20		
install masonry	**masonry crew**	$40.10		
Mason & helper				
install masonry	mason	$46.00		
install masonry	mason's helper	$42.10		
install masonry	**mason & helper**	$44.10		
Install brick wall				
4″ wide standard non-modular	masonry crew	$40.10	.170	**$6.82** sf
4″ wide oversize non-modular	masonry crew	$40.10	.168	**$6.74** sf
4″ wide three-inch non-modular	masonry crew	$40.10	.167	**$6.70** sf
4″ wide standard	masonry crew	$40.10	.169	**$6.78** sf
4″ wide engineer	masonry crew	$40.10	.141	**$5.65** sf
4″ wide jumbo closure	masonry crew	$40.10	.120	**$4.81** sf
4″ wide double	masonry crew	$40.10	.101	**$4.05** sf
4″ wide Roman	masonry crew	$40.10	.160	**$6.42** sf
4″ wide Norman	masonry crew	$40.10	.130	**$5.21** sf
4″ wide Norwegian	masonry crew	$40.10	.111	**$4.45** sf
4″ wide jumbo utility	masonry crew	$40.10	.102	**$4.09** sf
4″ wide triple	masonry crew	$40.10	.096	**$3.85** sf
6″ wide Norwegian	masonry crew	$40.10	.124	**$4.97** sf
6″ wide Norman	masonry crew	$40.10	.148	**$5.93** sf
6″ wide jumbo	masonry crew	$40.10	.113	**$4.53** sf
8″ wide jumbo	masonry crew	$40.10	.127	**$5.09** sf
Install 8″ wide double wythe brick wall				
with standard non-modular brick	masonry crew	$40.10	.307	**$12.30** sf
with oversize non-modular brick	masonry crew	$40.10	.303	**$12.20** sf
with three-inch non-modular brick	masonry crew	$40.10	.300	**$12.00** sf
with standard brick	masonry crew	$40.10	.305	**$12.20** sf
with engineer brick	masonry crew	$40.10	.253	**$10.10** sf
with jumbo closure brick	masonry crew	$40.10	.216	**$8.66** sf
with double brick	masonry crew	$40.10	.181	**$7.26** sf
with Roman brick	masonry crew	$40.10	.287	**$11.50** sf
with Norman brick	masonry crew	$40.10	.234	**$9.38** sf
with Norwegian brick brick	masonry crew	$40.10	.199	**$7.98** sf
with jumbo utility	masonry crew	$40.10	.184	**$7.38** sf
with triple brick	masonry crew	$40.10	.173	**$6.94** sf

. . . More ➢

Masonry Labor Productivity *continued*

WORK DESCRIPTION	LABORER	COST PER HOUR	PRODUCTIVITY	UNIT PRICE
Install 8" wide wall with 4" wide brick and 4" wide concrete block				
with standard non-modular brick	masonry crew	$40.10	.233	$9.34 sf
with standard brick	masonry crew	$40.10	.233	$9.34 sf
with engineer brick	masonry crew	$40.10	.206	$8.26 sf
with jumbo closure brick	masonry crew	$40.10	.188	$7.54 sf
with double brick	masonry crew	$40.10	.170	$6.82 sf
with Roman brick	masonry crew	$40.10	.224	$8.98 sf
with Norman brick	masonry crew	$40.10	.197	$7.90 sf
with Norwegian brick	masonry crew	$40.10	.180	$7.22 sf
with jumbo utility brick	masonry crew	$40.10	.172	$6.90 sf
with triple brick	masonry crew	$40.10	.166	$6.66 sf
Install 10" wide wall with 4" wide brick and 6" wide concrete block				
with standard non-modular brick	masonry crew	$40.10	.236	$9.46 sf
with standard brick	masonry crew	$40.10	.235	$9.42 sf
with engineer brick	masonry crew	$40.10	.209	$8.38 sf
with jumbo brick	masonry crew	$40.10	.190	$7.62 sf
with double brick	masonry crew	$40.10	.173	$6.94 sf
with Roman brick	masonry crew	$40.10	.226	$9.06 sf
with Norman brick	masonry crew	$40.10	.200	$8.02 sf
with Norwegian brick	masonry crew	$40.10	.182	$7.30 sf
with jumbo utility brick	masonry crew	$40.10	.175	$7.02 sf
with triple brick	masonry crew	$40.10	.170	$6.82 sf
Install 12" wide wall with 4" wide brick and 8" wide concrete block				
with standard non-modular brick	masonry crew	$40.10	.240	$9.62 sf
with standard brick	masonry crew	$40.10	.240	$9.62 sf
with engineer brick	masonry crew	$40.10	.214	$8.58 sf
with jumbo closure brick	masonry crew	$40.10	.195	$7.82 sf
with double brick	masonry crew	$40.10	.178	$7.14 sf
with Roman brick	masonry crew	$40.10	.231	$9.26 sf
with Norman brick	masonry crew	$40.10	.204	$8.18 sf
with Norwegian brick	masonry crew	$40.10	.187	$7.50 sf
with jumbo utility brick	masonry crew	$40.10	.180	$7.22 sf
with triple brick	masonry crew	$40.10	.174	$6.98 sf
Install 12" wide triple wythe wall				
with standard non-modular brick	masonry crew	$40.10	.433	$17.40 sf
with oversize non-modular brick	masonry crew	$40.10	.427	$17.10 sf
with three-inch non-modular brick	masonry crew	$40.10	.424	$17.00 sf
with standard brick	masonry crew	$40.10	.429	$17.20 sf
with engineer brick	masonry crew	$40.10	.357	$14.30 sf
with jumbo closure brick	masonry crew	$40.10	.305	$12.20 sf
with double brick	masonry crew	$40.10	.255	$10.20 sf
with Roman brick	masonry crew	$40.10	.407	$16.30 sf
with Norman brick	masonry crew	$40.10	.330	$13.20 sf
with Norwegian brick	masonry crew	$40.10	.282	$11.30 sf
with jumbo utility brick	masonry crew	$40.10	.260	$10.40 sf
with triple brick	masonry crew	$40.10	.244	$9.78 sf
Install 10" wide cavity wall with 4" brick and 4" concrete block				
with standard non-modular brick	masonry crew	$40.10	.244	$9.78 sf
with standard brick	masonry crew	$40.10	.243	$9.74 sf
with engineer brick	masonry crew	$40.10	.216	$8.66 sf
with jumbo closure brick	masonry crew	$40.10	.196	$7.86 sf
with double brick	masonry crew	$40.10	.178	$7.14 sf
with Roman brick	masonry crew	$40.10	.234	$9.38 sf
with Norman brick	masonry crew	$40.10	.206	$8.26 sf
with Norwegian brick	masonry crew	$40.10	.188	$7.54 sf
with jumbo utility brick	masonry crew	$40.10	.180	$7.22 sf
with triple brick	masonry crew	$40.10	.174	$6.98 sf
Install 10" wide cavity wall with 4" brick on both sides				
with standard non-modular brick	masonry crew	$40.10	.321	$12.90 sf
with oversize non-modular brick	masonry crew	$40.10	.317	$12.70 sf
with three-inch non-modular brick	masonry crew	$40.10	.314	$12.60 sf
with standard brick	masonry crew	$40.10	.319	$12.80 sf

. . . More ➤

Masonry Labor Productivity *continued*

WORK DESCRIPTION	LABORER	COST PER HOUR	PRODUCTIVITY	UNIT PRICE
Install 10" wide cavity wall with 4" brick on both sides *continued*				
with engineer brick	masonry crew	$40.10	.265	**$10.60** sf
with jumbo closure brick	masonry crew	$40.10	.226	**$9.06** sf
with double brick	masonry crew	$40.10	.189	**$7.58** sf
with Roman brick	masonry crew	$40.10	.301	**$12.10** sf
with Norman brick	masonry crew	$40.10	.245	**$9.82** sf
with Norwegian brick	masonry crew	$40.10	.209	**$8.38** sf
with jumbo utility brick	masonry crew	$40.10	.193	**$7.74** sf
with triple brick	masonry crew	$40.10	.181	**$7.26** sf
Install brick veneer				
with standard brick	masonry crew	$40.10	.144	**$5.77** sf
with oversize non-modular brick	masonry crew	$40.10	.143	**$5.73** sf
with three-inch non-modular brick	masonry crew	$40.10	.141	**$5.65** sf
with standard brick	masonry crew	$40.10	.144	**$5.77** sf
with engineer brick	masonry crew	$40.10	.119	**$4.77** sf
with jumbo closure brick	masonry crew	$40.10	.102	**$4.09** sf
with double brick	masonry crew	$40.10	.085	**$3.41** sf
with Roman brick	masonry crew	$40.10	.136	**$5.45** sf
with Norman brick	masonry crew	$40.10	.110	**$4.41** sf
with Norwegian brick	masonry crew	$40.10	.094	**$3.77** sf
with jumbo utility brick	masonry crew	$40.10	.087	**$3.49** sf
with triple brick	masonry crew	$40.10	.082	**$3.29** sf
Install brick arch				
flat brick arch	masonry crew	$40.10	1.49	**$59.70** lf
elliptical brick arch	masonry crew	$40.10	1.85	**$74.20** lf
semi-circular brick arch	masonry crew	$40.10	1.96	**$78.60** lf
Install block wall with 8" x 16" face				
4" wide	masonry crew	$40.10	.089	**$3.57** sf
6" wide	masonry crew	$40.10	.092	**$3.69** sf
8" wide	masonry crew	$40.10	.097	**$3.89** sf
10" wide	masonry crew	$40.10	.103	**$4.13** sf
12" wide	masonry crew	$40.10	.122	**$4.89** sf
Install block wall with 4" x 16" face				
4" wide	masonry crew	$40.10	.102	**$4.09** sf
6" wide	masonry crew	$40.10	.106	**$4.25** sf
8" wide	masonry crew	$40.10	.112	**$4.49** sf
10" wide	masonry crew	$40.10	.119	**$4.77** sf
12" wide	masonry crew	$40.10	.140	**$5.61** sf
Install lightweight block wall with 8" x 16" face				
4" wide	masonry crew	$40.10	.083	**$3.33** sf
6" wide	masonry crew	$40.10	.086	**$3.45** sf
8" wide	masonry crew	$40.10	.091	**$3.65** sf
10" wide	masonry crew	$40.10	.097	**$3.89** sf
12" wide	masonry crew	$40.10	.114	**$4.57** sf
Form and pour grade-beam cap on block wall				
6" wide	masonry crew	$40.10	.106	**$4.25** lf
12" wide	masonry crew	$40.10	.120	**$4.81** lf
Install glass block				
4" x 8"	masonry crew	$40.10	.333	**$13.40** sf
6" x 8"	masonry crew	$40.10	.267	**$10.70** sf
8" x 8"	masonry crew	$40.10	.208	**$8.34** sf
12" x 12"	masonry crew	$40.10	.175	**$7.02** sf
Install pavers				
on sand base	masonry crew	$40.10	.147	**$5.89** sf
on mortar base	masonry crew	$40.10	.180	**$7.22** sf
full-size bricks, laid face up	masonry crew	$40.10	.185	**$7.42** sf
full-size bricks, laid edge up	masonry crew	$40.10	.208	**$8.34** sf
add for paver steps installed in mortar over concrete	masonry crew	$40.10	.270	**$10.80** lf
add for paver steps installed over sand base	masonry crew	$40.10	.294	**$11.80** lf
add for separate pattern at edges of pavers	masonry crew	$40.10	.076	**$3.05** lf

. . . More ➢

Masonry Labor Productivity *continued*

WORK DESCRIPTION	LABORER	COST PER HOUR	PRODUCTIVITY	UNIT PRICE
Lay stone wall				
field stone rubble with no mortar	masonry crew	$40.10	.481	$19.30 cf
rubble wall	masonry crew	$40.10	.518	$20.80 cf
ashlar wall	masonry crew	$40.10	.472	$18.90 cf
add to install flat arch	masonry crew	$40.10	2.86	$115.00 lf
add to install elliptical arch	masonry crew	$40.10	3.57	$143.00 lf
add to install semi-circular arch	masonry crew	$40.10	3.70	$148.00 lf
Lay stone veneer				
rubble	masonry crew	$40.10	.243	$9.74 sf
ashlar	masonry crew	$40.10	.236	$9.46 sf
add to install flat arch	masonry crew	$40.10	1.75	$70.20 lf
add to install elliptical arch	masonry crew	$40.10	2.17	$87.00 lf
add to install semi-circular arch	masonry crew	$40.10	2.30	$92.20 lf
Install veneer panels				
cultured stone	masonry crew	$40.10	.263	$10.50 sf
natural stone	masonry crew	$40.10	.298	$11.90 sf
Install stone architrave				
door	masonry crew	$40.10	.980	$39.30 lf
window	masonry crew	$40.10	1.00	$40.10 lf
Install trim or cornice stones				
all stone types	masonry crew	$40.10	.370	$14.80 lf
Install wall cap or coping				
terra-cotta cap	masonry crew	$40.10	.185	$7.42 lf
aluminum cap	masonry crew	$40.10	.181	$7.26 lf
concrete coping	masonry crew	$40.10	.167	$6.70 lf
stone coping	masonry crew	$40.10	.185	$7.42 lf
Salvage brick veneer				
remove, salvage bricks, and re-lay	masonry crew	$40.10	.877	$35.20 sf
Repoint brick wall				
running bond	masonry crew	$40.10	.108	$4.33 sf
common bond (also called American bond)	masonry crew	$40.10	.111	$4.45 sf
Flemish bond	masonry crew	$40.10	.121	$4.85 sf
English bond	masonry crew	$40.10	.128	$5.13 sf
English cross bond (also called Dutch bond)	masonry crew	$40.10	.128	$5.13 sf
stack bond	masonry crew	$40.10	.082	$3.29 sf
all header bond	masonry crew	$40.10	.093	$3.73 sf
soldier course	masonry crew	$40.10	.106	$4.25 sf
sailor course	masonry crew	$40.10	.099	$3.97 sf
basketweave	masonry crew	$40.10	.164	$6.58 sf
herringbone weave	masonry crew	$40.10	.167	$6.70 sf
diagonal bond	masonry crew	$40.10	.144	$5.77 sf
coursed ashlar style bond	masonry crew	$40.10	.120	$4.81 sf
Repoint stone wall				
rubble	masonry crew	$40.10	.278	$11.10 sf
ashlar	masonry crew	$40.10	.260	$10.43 sf
Stone wall repair				
repair carved stone with epoxy	mason	$46.00	.024	$1.10 si
repair carved stone with stucco or grout	mason	$46.00	.022	$1.01 si
epoxy repair and pin broken stone	mason	$46.00	1.33	$61.20 ea
reconstitute delaminating stone with epoxy	mason	$46.00	.013	$.60 si
reface stone with grout mixed to match	mason	$46.00	.149	$6.85 sf
remove segment of rubble wall and re-lay	mason & helper	$44.10	4.00	$176.00 cf
remove segment of rubble veneer and re-lay	mason & helper	$44.10	1.92	$84.70 sf
remove segment of ashlar wall and re-lay	mason & helper	$44.10	3.85	$170.00 cf
remove segment of ashlar veneer and re-lay	mason & helper	$44.10	1.89	$83.30 sf
Carve stone				
with light hand carvings	stone carver	$108.00	.015	$1.62 si
with medium hand carvings	stone carver	$108.00	.022	$2.38 si
with heavy hand carvings	stone carver	$108.00	.031	$3.35 si

25 Outbuildings

Item Description	Unit	Remove	Replace	Total
8′ x 6′ metal storage shed ***Replace*** Material .....238.00 Labor ....200.00 ***Remove*** .... Labor 68.80	ea	$68.80	$438.00	$506.80
8′ x 10′ metal storage shed ***Replace*** Material ......319.00 Labor ....216.00 ***Remove*** .... Labor...........75.40	ea	$75.40	$535.00	$610.40
9′ x 10′ metal storage shed ***Replace*** Material .....333.00 Labor.........231.00 ***Remove*** .... Labor...........78.70	ea	$78.70	$564.00	$642.70
10′ x 12′ metal storage shed ***Replace*** Material ......519.00 Labor.........246.00 ***Remove*** .... Labor 83.60	ea	$83.60	$765.00	$848.60
8′ x 6′ wood storage shed ***Replace*** Material .....550.00 Labor ....216.00 ***Remove*** .... Labor 90.20	ea	$90.20	$766.00	$856.20
8′ x 10′ wood storage shed ***Replace*** Material....1290.00 Labor.........231.00 ***Remove*** .... Labor.........106.00	ea	$106.00	$1,521.00	$1,627.00
9′ x 10′ wood storage shed ***Replace*** Material ....1470.00 Labor.........246.00 ***Remove*** .... Labor..........117.00	ea	$117.00	$1,716.00	$1,833.00
10′ x 12′ wood storage shed ***Replace*** Material ....1730.00 Labor.........262.00 ***Remove*** .... Labor.........128.00	ea	$128.00	$1,992.00	$2,120.00
9′ gazebo, standard grade ***Replace*** Material ...5800.00 Labor.........545.00 ***Remove*** .... Labor.........122.00 ► With cupola, simple fretwork and rails with cross-grain detailing.	ea	$122.00	$6,345.00	$6,467.00
9′ gazebo, high grade ***Replace*** Material....7060.00 Labor ....624.00 ***Remove*** .... Labor.........122.00 ► With cupola, fretwork, raised-panel rails.	ea	$122.00	$7,684.00	$7,806.00
9′ gazebo, deluxe grade ***Replace*** Material....8010.00 Labor.........728.00 ***Remove*** .... Labor.........122.00 ► With cupola, Queen Anne fretwork, and rails.	ea	$122.00	$8,738.00	$8,860.00
12′ gazebo, standard grade ***Replace*** Material ...8250.00 Labor.........728.00 ***Remove*** .... Labor.........153.00 ► With cupola, simple fretwork and rails with cross-grain detailing.	ea	$153.00	$8,978.00	$9,131.00
12′ gazebo, high grade ***Replace*** Material ...9340.00 Labor.........728.00 ***Remove*** .... Labor.........153.00 ► With cupola, fretwork, raised-panel rails.	ea	$153.00	$10,068.00	$10,221.00

◄ **Metal shed**
*Prefabricated metal storage shed with baked enamel finish and gable roof. Includes assembly. Does not include concrete slab or footings. Add **16%** for gambrel roof. Add **30%** for vinyl covered metal.*

◄ **Wood shed**
*Pre-built and delivered to site. Painted with trim, truss gambrel roof, panel siding, 1/2″ roof sheathing, 3/4″ tongue and groove floor sheathing with floor skids. Does not include footings or pier blocks. Deduct **12%** for gable roof. Deduct **15%** for gambrel roof on top of walls that are 5′ tall or less.*

◄ **Gazebo**
*High quality octagonal gazebos priced by diameter. Made from D grade or better kiln-dried western red cedar surfaced four sides. Wood cedar shingles. Prefabricated parts assembled on site. Add **116%** to 15' diameter price for 21' diameter triple roof gazebo. Add **$175** for bench in 9' and 12' diameter gazebos. Add **$200** for bench in 15' diameter gazebo. Add **$500** for bow roof (all sizes). Add **$300** for steps with balustrades. Deduct **25%** for no floor deck. Deduct **17%** if made from select #1 grade western red cedar.*

Gazebo ► *continued*

single roof △

double roof △

triple roof △

Item Description	Unit	Remove	Replace	Total
12′ gazebo, deluxe grade *Replace* Material..10900.00 Labor.........728.00 *Remove*......................... Labor.........153.00 ► With cupola, Queen Anne fretwork, and rails.	ea	$153.00	$11,628.00	$11,781.00
15′ gazebo, standard grade *Replace* Material ..11600.00 Labor.........874.00 *Remove*......................... Labor.........196.00 ► Double roof with cupola, simple fretwork and rails with cross-grain detailing.	ea	$196.00	$12,474.00	$12,670.00
15′ gazebo, high grade *Replace* Material ..13700.00 Labor.......1090.00 *Remove*......................... Labor.........196.00 ► Double roof with cupola, fretwork, raised-panel rails.	ea	$196.00	$14,790.00	$14,986.00
15′ gazebo, deluxe grade *Replace* Material ..15100.00 Labor.......1090.00 *Remove*......................... Labor.........196.00 ► Double roof with cupola, Queen Anne fretwork, and rails.	ea	$196.00	$16,190.00	$16,386.00

Free-standing greenhouse ► *Residential style, aluminum frame. Automatic electric roof vent.*

Item Description	Unit	Remove	Replace	Total
8′ x 9′ free-standing greenhouse *Replace* Material.....4170.00 Labor........543.00 *Remove*......................... Labor..........83.60	ea	$83.60	$4,713.00	$4,796.60
8′ x 11′ free-standing greenhouse *Replace* Material....4550.00 Labor........543.00 *Remove*......................... Labor..........94.60	ea	$94.60	$5,093.00	$5,187.60
8′ x 14′ free-standing greenhouse *Replace* Material....4730.00 Labor........634.00 *Remove*......................... Labor.........110.00	ea	$110.00	$5,364.00	$5,474.00
8′ x 17′ free-standing greenhouse *Replace* Material....5670.00 Labor........634.00 *Remove*......................... Labor.........119.00	ea	$119.00	$6,304.00	$6,423.00

Lean-to greenhouse ► *Residential style, aluminum frame. Manually controlled vents.*

Item Description	Unit	Remove	Replace	Total
4′ x 8′ lean-to greenhouse *Replace* Material ....1770.00 Labor.........317.00 *Remove*......................... Labor...........78.70	ea	$78.70	$2,087.00	$2,165.70
7′ x 14′ lean-to greenhouse *Replace* Material....4520.00 Labor.........474.00 *Remove*......................... Labor..........90.20	ea	$90.20	$4,994.00	$5,084.20
8′ x 16′ lean-to greenhouse *Replace* Material ...5530.00 Labor........543.00 *Remove*......................... Labor...........96.30	ea	$96.30	$6,073.00	$6,169.30

Screened swimming pool enclosure ►

Item Description	Unit	Remove	Replace	Total
Screened swimming pool enclosure *Replace* Material ....5.40 Labor............. .65 *Remove*......................... Labor............. .25 ► Aluminum frame, vinyl screen.	sf	$.25	$6.05	$6.30

Chickhee hut ► *Per sf of floor. Typically found in the southern United States.*

Item Description	Unit	Remove	Replace	Total
Chickhee hut *Replace* Material........21.70 Labor...........37.80 *Remove*......................... Labor............2.75	sf	$2.75	$59.50	$62.25
Thatched roof for chickhee hut *Replace* Material ....4.30 Labor ....23.10 *Remove*......................... Labor........... 1.05 ► Per sf of roof area.	sf	$1.05	$27.40	$28.45

26 Painting

Item Description	Unit	prime/stain	1 Coat	2 Coats	3 Coats
Minimum charge for painting work ***Materials*** Minimum..32.00 ***Labor*** Minimum.........29.70	ea	—	—	—	$61.70
Paint acoustic ceiling texture ***Materials*** Prime .... .26 1 Coat........ .29 2 Coats........ .40 3 Coats........ .53 ***Labor*** Prime .... .47 1 Coat........ .47 2 Coats........ .73 3 Coats........ .98	sf	$.73	$.76	$1.13	$1.51
Paint acoustical ceiling tile ***Materials*** Prime .... .26 1 Coat........ .29 2 Coats........ .40 3 Coats........ .53 ***Labor*** Prime .... .47 1 Coat........ .47 2 Coats........ .73 3 Coats........ .98	sf	$.73	$.76	$1.13	$1.51
Paint aluminum carport or awning ***Materials*** Prime .... .18 1 Coat........ .20 2 Coats........ .28 3 Coats........ .37 ***Labor*** Prime .... .26 1 Coat........ .26 2 Coats........ .43 3 Coats........ .56	sf	$.44	$.46	$.71	$.93
Paint plaster or drywall ***Materials*** Prime .... .12 1 Coat........ .13 2 Coats........ .18 3 Coats........ .24 ***Labor*** Prime .... .26 1 Coat........ .26 2 Coats........ .43 3 Coats........ .56	sf	$.38	$.39	$.61	$.80
Paint stucco ***Materials*** Prime .... .21 1 Coat........ .23 2 Coats........ .32 3 Coats........ .43 ***Labor*** Prime .... .60 1 Coat........ .64 2 Coats........ .98 3 Coats.......1.28	sf	$.81	$.87	$1.30	$1.71
Paint column ***Materials*** Prime .... .32 1 Coat........ .36 2 Coats........ .50 3 Coats........ .66 ***Labor*** Prime .... .73 1 Coat........ .73 2 Coats.......1.16 3 Coats.......1.54	lf	$1.05	$1.09	$1.66	$2.20
Stain & varnish column ***Materials*** Stain........... .34 1 Coat........ .38 2 Coats........ .53 3 Coats........ .70 ***Labor*** Stain.................. .68 1 Coat........ .68 2 Coats...... 1.07 3 Coats.......1.41	lf	$1.02	$1.06	$1.60	$2.11
Paint capital, simple design ***Materials*** Prime ....17.50 1 Coat......19.40 2 Coats......26.90 3 Coats......35.70 ***Labor*** Prime...............27.90 1 Coat.....28.70 2 Coats.....44.10 3 Coats......59.90	ea	$45.40	$48.10	$71.00	$95.60
Paint capital complex design ***Materials*** Prime........22.60 1 Coat.....25.10 2 Coats.....34.90 3 Coats.....46.40 ***Labor*** Prime...............35.90 1 Coat.....36.90 2 Coats.....56.90 3 Coats.....77.00	ea	$58.50	$62.00	$91.80	$123.40
Stain & varnish capital, simple design ***Materials*** Stain.........19.30 1 Coat.....21.40 2 Coats.....29.70 3 Coats......39.50 ***Labor*** Stain...............28.70 1 Coat.....29.50 2 Coats......45.40 3 Coats......61.60	ea	$48.00	$50.90	$75.10	$101.10
Stain & varnish capital complex design ***Materials*** Stain.........24.90 1 Coat.....27.70 2 Coats.....38.50 3 Coats......51.20 ***Labor*** Stain...............39.80 1 Coat.....41.00 2 Coats......62.90 3 Coats......85.60	ea	$64.70	$68.70	$101.40	$136.80
Paint column pedestal ***Materials*** Prime ....14.40 1 Coat......16.00 2 Coats.....22.20 3 Coats.....29.50 ***Labor*** Prime...............22.90 1 Coat.....23.60 2 Coats.....36.30 3 Coats......49.20	ea	$37.30	$39.60	$58.50	$78.70
Stain & varnish column pedestal ***Materials*** Stain.........16.00 1 Coat......17.80 2 Coats......24.70 3 Coats......32.80 ***Labor*** Stain...............25.30 1 Coat.....26.00 2 Coats.....40.00 3 Coats.....54.40	ea	$41.30	$43.80	$64.70	$87.20
Paint concrete floor ***Materials*** Prime .... .17 1 Coat........ .19 2 Coats........ .26 3 Coats........ .35 ***Labor*** Prime .... .34 1 Coat........ .34 2 Coats........ .51 3 Coats........ .68	sf	$.51	$.53	$.77	$1.03

◄ **MINIMUM**

◄ **ACOUSTIC CEILINGS**

◄ **AWNINGS AND CARPORTS**

◄ **DRYWALL, PLASTER AND STUCCO**

◄ **COLUMNS**
*Deduct **26%** for pilasters, pilaster capitals, pilaster pedestals, and so on.*

PAINTING COATS

Prices for one coat, two coats and three coats do *not* include: the primer coat, sealer coat, or stain.

To estimate painting, add the cost of the primer coat to the number of paint coats.

For example, to estimate the cost to prime a wall then paint with two coats, add the prime price to the two coats price.

To estimate the cost to stain an item then cover with two coats of varnish, add the stain cost to the two coats price (unless otherwise noted).

◄ **CONCRETE**

	Item Description	Unit	prime/stain	1 Coat	2 Coats	3 Coats
CONCRETE ► *continued*	**Paint concrete wall** ***Materials*** Prime .... .17 1 Coat........ .19 2 Coats........ .26 3 Coats........ .35 ***Labor*** Prime .... .34 1 Coat........ .34 2 Coats........ .56 3 Coats........ .73	sf	$.51	$.53	$.82	$1.08
	Paint concrete step (per step) ***Materials*** Prime .... .53 1 Coat........ .59 2 Coats........ .82 3 Coats...... 1.09 ***Labor*** Prime .... .98 1 Coat ..... 1.03 2 Coats.......1.58 3 Coats 2.14	ea	$1.51	$1.62	$2.40	$3.23
DOORS ► *Unless otherwise noted, does not include jamb and casing. Includes painting both sides of door. Folding and bypassing doors are for both sides of each section. Add **20%** for half-round or elliptical top door.*	**Paint folding door** ***Materials*** Prime.........10.02 1 Coat......11.10 2 Coats......15.40 3 Coats .....20.50 ***Labor*** Prime................17.20 1 Coat......17.70 2 Coats......27.20 3 Coats 36.90	ea	$27.22	$28.80	$42.60	$57.40
	Stain & varnish folding door ***Materials*** Stain.........14.70 1 Coat......16.30 2 Coats .....22.60 3 Coats .....30.00 ***Labor*** Stain................26.30 1 Coat .....27.00 2 Coats......41.60 3 Coats 56.50	ea	$41.00	$43.30	$64.20	$86.50
folding door ▷	**Paint half-louvered folding door** ***Materials*** Prime ....11.10 1 Coat......12.30 2 Coats......17.10 3 Coats .....22.70 ***Labor*** Prime ....19.30 1 Coat......19.90 2 Coats .....30.60 3 Coats......41.40	ea	$30.40	$32.20	$47.70	$64.10
	Stain & varnish half-louvered folding door ***Materials*** Stain.........16.30 1 Coat .....18.10 2 Coats......25.10 3 Coats .....33.40 ***Labor*** Stain................29.50 1 Coat .....30.30 2 Coats .....46.70 3 Coats 63.30	ea	$45.80	$48.40	$71.80	$96.70
	Paint full-louvered folding door ***Materials*** Prime ....12.30 1 Coat......13.70 2 Coats......19.00 3 Coats......25.20 ***Labor*** Prime ....21.70 1 Coat .....22.30 2 Coats .....34.30 3 Coats 46.70	ea	$34.00	$36.00	$53.30	$71.90
	Stain & varnish full-louvered folding door ***Materials*** Stain.........18.10 1 Coat .....20.10 2 Coats......27.90 3 Coats......37.10 ***Labor*** Stain................33.10 1 Coat .....34.10 2 Coats......52.20 3 Coats......71.00	ea	$51.20	$54.20	$80.10	$108.10
	Paint folding panel door ***Materials*** Prime ....11.00 1 Coat......12.20 2 Coats......16.90 3 Coats .....22.50 ***Labor*** Prime ....18.80 1 Coat......19.40 2 Coats .....29.80 3 Coats 40.40	ea	$29.80	$31.60	$46.70	$62.90
	Stain & varnish folding panel door ***Materials*** Stain.........16.10 1 Coat......17.90 2 Coats......24.90 3 Coats .....33.10 ***Labor*** Stain................28.80 1 Coat .....29.60 2 Coats......45.80 3 Coats......61.60	ea	$44.90	$47.50	$70.70	$94.70
bypassing door ▷	**Paint bypassing door** ***Materials*** Prime ....12.70 1 Coat......14.10 2 Coats......19.60 3 Coats......26.00 ***Labor*** Prime ....35.50 1 Coat .....36.60 2 Coats .....56.50 3 Coats......76.20	ea	$48.20	$50.70	$76.10	$102.20
	Stain & varnish bypassing door ***Materials*** Stain.........18.60 1 Coat .....20.70 2 Coats......28.70 3 Coats .....38.10 ***Labor*** Stain................54.40 1 Coat .....56.10 2 Coats .....86.00 3 Coats.....116.00	ea	$73.00	$76.80	$114.70	$154.10
	Paint half-louvered bypassing door ***Materials*** Prime ....14.10 1 Coat......15.70 2 Coats......21.80 3 Coats .....29.00 ***Labor*** Prime ....39.90 1 Coat .....41.00 2 Coats .....63.30 3 Coats......85.60	ea	$54.00	$56.70	$85.10	$114.60
	Stain & varnish half-louvered bypassing door ***Materials*** Stain ....20.70 1 Coat .....23.00 2 Coats......31.90 3 Coats......42.40 ***Labor*** Stain ....61.20 1 Coat .....62.90 2 Coats......96.70 3 Coats 131.00	ea	$81.90	$85.90	$128.60	$173.40
	Paint full-louvered bypassing door ***Materials*** Prime ....15.70 1 Coat......17.40 2 Coats......24.20 3 Coats......32.20 ***Labor*** Prime...............44.90 1 Coat .....46.20 2 Coats......71.00 3 Coats......95.90	ea	$60.60	$63.60	$95.20	$128.10
	Stain & varnish full-louvered bypassing door ***Materials*** Stain ....23.00 1 Coat .....25.60 2 Coats......35.60 3 Coats......47.30 ***Labor*** Stain...............68.50 1 Coat .....70.60 2 Coats....108.00 3 Coats 147.00	ea	$91.50	$96.20	$143.60	$194.30
	Paint bypassing panel door ***Materials*** Prime ....14.10 1 Coat......15.70 2 Coats......21.80 3 Coats .....29.00 ***Labor*** Prime...............38.50 1 Coat .....39.60 2 Coats .....60.80 3 Coats 82.60	ea	$52.60	$55.30	$82.60	$111.60

Item Description	Unit	prime/stain	1 Coat	2 Coats	3 Coats	
Stain & varnish bypassing panel door	ea	$79.80	$83.80	$125.20	$168.40	
Materials Stain........20.70 1 Coat.....23.00 2 Coats......31.90 3 Coats......42.40						
Labor Stain...............59.10 1 Coat.....60.80 2 Coats.....93.30 3 Coats....126.00						
Paint interior door	ea	$22.17	$23.31	$34.70	$47.00	◁ interior door
Materials Prime..........7.57 1 Coat.......8.41 2 Coats......11.70 3 Coats.......15.80						
Labor Prime ....14.60 1 Coat......14.90 2 Coats.....23.00 3 Coats......31.20						
Stain & varnish interior door	ea	$33.60	$35.70	$52.90	$70.80	
Materials Stain ....11.40 1 Coat......12.80 2 Coats......17.70 3 Coats 23.30						
Labor Stain...............22.20 1 Coat.....22.90 2 Coats......35.20 3 Coats......47.50						
Paint half-louvered door	ea	$24.72	$26.15	$38.90	$52.30	
Materials Prime..........8.42 1 Coat.......9.35 2 Coats......13.00 3 Coats......17.30						
Labor Prime ....16.30 1 Coat......16.80 2 Coats......25.90 3 Coats......35.00						
Stain & varnish half-louvered door	ea	$37.70	$39.80	$59.10	$79.50	
Materials Stain ....12.70 1 Coat......14.10 2 Coats......19.60 3 Coats......26.00						
Labor Stain...............25.00 1 Coat.....25.70 2 Coats......39.50 3 Coats 53.50						
Paint full-louvered door	ea	$27.67	$29.21	$43.50	$58.60	
Materials Prime..........9.37 1 Coat .....10.41 2 Coats......14.50 3 Coats......19.30						
Labor Prime ....18.30 1 Coat .....18.80 2 Coats .....29.00 3 Coats......39.30						
Stain & varnish full-louvered door	ea	$42.10	$44.50	$66.30	$88.90	
Materials Stain ....14.10 1 Coat......15.70 2 Coats......21.80 3 Coats 29.00						
Labor Stain...............28.00 1 Coat.....28.80 2 Coats .....44.50 3 Coats......59.90						
Paint door jamb & casing	lf	$.62	$.64	$.97	$1.30	◁ door jamb and casing
Materials Prime .... .15 1 Coat........ .17 2 Coats........ .24 3 Coats........ .32						
Labor Prime .... .47 1 Coat........ .47 2 Coats........ .73 3 Coats........ .98						
Stain & varnish door jamb & casing	lf	$.95	$.97	$1.44	$1.94	
Materials Stain........... .22 1 Coat........ .24 2 Coats........ .33 3 Coats........ .44						
Labor Stain .... .73 1 Coat........ .73 2 Coats.......1.11 3 Coats.......1.50						
Paint French door	ea	$48.00	$50.40	$75.60	$101.50	◁ French door
Materials Prime ....13.00 1 Coat......14.40 2 Coats .....20.00 3 Coats......26.60						
Labor Prime ....35.00 1 Coat.....36.00 2 Coats......55.60 3 Coats......74.90						
Stain & varnish French door	ea	$72.60	$76.40	$114.10	$154.10	
Materials Stain ....19.10 1 Coat .....21.20 2 Coats .....29.40 3 Coats......39.10						
Labor Stain...............53.50 1 Coat .....55.20 2 Coats .....84.70 3 Coats.....115.00						
Paint full-lite door	ea	$37.80	$39.90	$59.20	$79.70	◁ full-lite door
Materials Prime ....12.60 1 Coat......14.00 2 Coats......19.40 3 Coats......25.80						
Labor Prime ....25.20 1 Coat.....25.90 2 Coats......39.80 3 Coats 53.90						
Stain & varnish full-lite door	ea	$57.00	$60.20	$89.40	$120.60	
Materials Stain.........18.50 1 Coat.....20.60 2 Coats......28.60 3 Coats 38.00						
Labor Stain...............38.50 1 Coat.....39.60 2 Coats .....60.80 3 Coats 82.60						
Paint panel door	ea	$43.90	$46.30	$68.70	$92.80	◁ panel door
Materials Prime ....13.80 1 Coat......15.30 2 Coats......21.20 3 Coats......28.20						
Labor Prime..............30.10 1 Coat .....31.00 2 Coats......47.50 3 Coats 64.60						
Stain & varnish panel door	ea	$66.50	$70.10	$104.20	$140.60	
Materials Stain ....20.30 1 Coat.....22.60 2 Coats......31.40 3 Coats......41.70						
Labor Stain...............46.20 1 Coat .....47.50 2 Coats......72.80 3 Coats......98.90						
Paint transom	ea	$22.07	$23.27	$34.78	$46.90	◁ transom
Materials Prime..........6.27 1 Coat.......6.97 2 Coats ....9.68 3 Coats......12.90						
Labor Prime...............15.80 1 Coat......16.30 2 Coats......25.10 3 Coats 34.00						
Stain & varnish transom	ea	$33.40	$35.22	$52.50	$70.70	
Materials Stain ....9.20 1 Coat .....10.22 2 Coats......14.20 3 Coats......18.90						
Labor Stain ....24.20 1 Coat .....25.00 2 Coats .....38.30 3 Coats......51.80						

RELATED ITEMS

Concrete........................83
Doors...............................101

	Item Description	Unit	prime/stain	1 Coat	2 Coats	3 Coats
storm door ▷	**Paint storm door** ***Materials*** Prime..........6.52 1 Coat.......7.24 2 Coats......10.05 3 Coats......13.40 ***Labor*** Prime ....16.30 1 Coat......16.70 2 Coats......25.70 3 Coats 34.90	ea	$22.82	$23.94	$35.75	$48.30
	Stain & varnish storm door ***Materials*** Stain ....9.57 1 Coat .....10.63 2 Coats......14.80 3 Coats......19.70 ***Labor*** Stain................24.90 1 Coat .....25.60 2 Coats......39.40 3 Coats 53.50	ea	$34.47	$36.23	$54.20	$73.20
Dutch door ▷ *both sections both sides*	**Paint Dutch door** ***Materials*** Prime ....13.70 1 Coat......15.20 2 Coats......21.10 3 Coats......28.00 ***Labor*** Prime...............28.50 1 Coat .....29.40 2 Coats......45.40 3 Coats......61.20	ea	$42.20	$44.60	$66.50	$89.20
	Stain & varnish Dutch door ***Materials*** Stain ....20.10 1 Coat .....22.30 2 Coats......31.00 3 Coats......41.20 ***Labor*** Stain...............43.70 1 Coat .....44.90 2 Coats .....68.90 3 Coats 93.70	ea	$63.80	$67.20	$99.90	$134.90
entry door ▷	**Paint steel entry door** ***Materials*** Prime ....12.30 1 Coat......13.70 2 Coats......19.00 3 Coats......25.20 ***Labor*** Prime ....26.60 1 Coat .....27.30 2 Coats......42.10 3 Coats 56.90	ea	$38.90	$41.00	$61.10	$82.10
	Paint wood entry door ***Materials*** Prime ....13.30 1 Coat......14.20 2 Coats......19.20 3 Coats......26.90 ***Labor*** Prime ....31.80 1 Coat .....32.70 2 Coats .....50.50 3 Coats 68.10	ea	$45.10	$46.90	$69.70	$95.00
	Stain & varnish wood entry door ***Materials*** Stain.........19.10 1 Coat .....20.70 2 Coats......26.60 3 Coats......37.20 ***Labor*** Stain...............48.40 1 Coat .....50.10 2 Coats .....77.00 3 Coats....104.00	ea	$67.50	$70.80	$103.60	$141.20
entry door side lite ▷	**Paint entry door side lite** ***Materials*** Prime........10.50 1 Coat......11.70 2 Coats......16.20 3 Coats......21.50 ***Labor*** Prime ....28.80 1 Coat .....29.60 2 Coats.....45.40 3 Coats......61.60	ea	$39.30	$41.30	$61.60	$83.10
	Stain & varnish entry door side lite ***Materials*** Stain ....15.40 1 Coat......17.10 2 Coats .....23.70 3 Coats......31.50 ***Labor*** Stain...............44.10 1 Coat .....45.40 2 Coats......69.80 3 Coats......94.20	ea	$59.50	$62.50	$93.50	$125.70
entry door fan lite ▷	**Paint fan lite** ***Materials*** Prime..........9.31 1 Coat .....10.34 2 Coats......14.40 3 Coats......19.10 ***Labor*** Prime ....27.20 1 Coat .....28.00 2 Coats .....43.20 3 Coats 58.20	ea	$36.51	$38.34	$57.60	$77.30
	Stain & varnish fan lite ***Materials*** Stain ....13.70 1 Coat......15.20 2 Coats......21.10 3 Coats......28.00 ***Labor*** Stain ....41.60 1 Coat .....42.80 2 Coats......65.90 3 Coats 89.00	ea	$55.30	$58.00	$87.00	$117.00
cafe doors ▷	**Paint cafe doors** ***Materials*** Prime ....10.40 1 Coat......11.60 2 Coats......16.10 3 Coats......21.40 ***Labor*** Prime...............25.30 1 Coat .....26.10 2 Coats .....40.10 3 Coats 54.40	ea	$35.70	$37.70	$56.20	$75.80
	Stain & varnish cafe doors ***Materials*** Stain ....15.30 1 Coat......17.00 2 Coats .....23.60 3 Coats......31.40 ***Labor*** Stain...............38.70 1 Coat .....39.90 2 Coats......61.20 3 Coats 83.00	ea	$54.00	$56.90	$84.80	$114.40
sliding patio door ▷	**Paint wood sliding patio door** ***Materials*** Prime..........4.41 1 Coat.......4.90 2 Coats ....6.80 3 Coats ....9.04 ***Labor*** Prime ....27.60 1 Coat .....28.50 2 Coats .....43.70 3 Coats......59.50	ea	$32.01	$33.40	$50.50	$68.54
	Stain & varnish wood sliding patio door ***Materials*** Stain ....6.47 1 Coat.......7.19 2 Coats ....9.98 3 Coats......13.30 ***Labor*** Stain...............42.30 1 Coat .....43.70 2 Coats .....66.80 3 Coats 90.70	ea	$48.77	$50.89	$76.78	$104.00
garage door ▷	**Paint garage door** ***Materials*** Prime.......... .18 1 Coat........ .20 2 Coats........ .28 3 Coats........ .37 ***Labor*** Prime .... .26 1 Coat........ .26 2 Coats........ .39 3 Coats........ .56	sf	$.44	$.46	$.67	$.93
	Stain & varnish garage door ***Materials*** Stain........... .26 1 Coat........ .29 2 Coats........ .40 3 Coats........ .53 ***Labor*** Stain .... .39 1 Coat........ .39 2 Coats........ .60 3 Coats........ .81	sf	$.65	$.68	$1.00	$1.34

Item Description	Unit	prime/stain	1 Coat	2 Coats	3 Coats
Paint medicine cabinet	ea	$20.32	$21.16	$32.07	$43.31
Materials Prime..........3.02 1 Coat.......3.36 2 Coats.......4.67 3 Coats.......6.21					
Labor Prime................17.30 1 Coat......17.80 2 Coats......27.40 3 Coats......37.10					
Stain & varnish medicine cabinet	ea	$30.93	$32.12	$48.73	$65.58
Materials Stain..........4.43 1 Coat.......4.92 2 Coats.......6.83 3 Coats.......9.08					
Labor Stain................26.50 1 Coat.....27.20 2 Coats......41.90 3 Coats.....56.50					
Paint exterior light-fixture post	ea	$7.06	$7.56	$11.03	$14.83
Materials Prime..........3.68 1 Coat.......4.09 2 Coats.......5.68 3 Coats.......7.55					
Labor Prime.................3.38 1 Coat.......3.47 2 Coats.......5.35 3 Coats.......7.28					
Paint 4' high wood fence	lf	$3.00	$3.18	$4.73	$6.34
Materials Prime.......... .82 1 Coat........ .91 2 Coats.......1.26 3 Coats.......1.67					
Labor Prime.................2.18 1 Coat.......2.27 2 Coats.......3.47 3 Coats.......4.67					
Seal or stain 4' high wood fence	lf	$4.54	$4.75	$7.11	$9.61
Materials Seal/stain..1.20 1 Coat.......1.33 2 Coats.......1.85 3 Coats.......2.46					
Labor Seal/stain.........3.34 1 Coat.......3.42 2 Coats.......5.26 3 Coats.......7.15					
Paint 6' high wood fence	lf	$4.51	$4.72	$7.08	$9.53
Materials Prime..........1.21 1 Coat.......1.34 2 Coats.......1.86 3 Coats.......2.47					
Labor Prime.................3.30 1 Coat.......3.38 2 Coats.......5.22 3 Coats.......7.06					
Seal or stain 6' high wood fence	lf	$6.79	$7.16	$10.71	$14.45
Materials Seal/stain..1.78 1 Coat.......1.98 2 Coats.......2.75 3 Coats.......3.65					
Labor Seal/stain.........5.01 1 Coat.......5.18 2 Coats.......7.96 3 Coats......10.80					
Paint 8' high wood fence	lf	$5.95	$6.25	$9.37	$12.61
Materials Prime..........1.58 1 Coat.......1.76 2 Coats.......2.44 3 Coats.......3.24					
Labor Prime.................4.37 1 Coat.......4.49 2 Coats.......6.93 3 Coats.......9.37					
Seal or stain 8' high wood fence	lf	$9.00	$9.47	$14.18	$19.06
Materials Seal/stain..2.32 1 Coat.......2.58 2 Coats.......3.58 3 Coats.......4.76					
Labor Seal/stain.........6.68 1 Coat.......6.89 2 Coats......10.60 3 Coats......14.30					
Paint 3' high picket fence	lf	$2.38	$2.50	$3.71	$5.01
Materials Prime.......... .63 1 Coat........ .70 2 Coats........ .97 3 Coats.......1.29					
Labor Prime.................1.75 1 Coat.......1.80 2 Coats.......2.74 3 Coats.......3.72					
Paint 5' high picket fence	lf	$3.81	$4.01	$5.99	$8.09
Materials Prime........ 1.03 1 Coat.......1.14 2 Coats.......1.58 3 Coats.......2.10					
Labor Prime.................2.78 1 Coat.......2.87 2 Coats.......4.41 3 Coats.......5.99					
Paint 48" high ornamental iron fence	lf	$4.45	$4.66	$6.96	$9.39
Materials Prime..........1.15 1 Coat.......1.28 2 Coats.......1.78 3 Coats.......2.37					
Labor Prime.................3.30 1 Coat.......3.38 2 Coats.......5.18 3 Coats.......7.02					
Paint 60" high ornamental iron fence	lf	$5.65	$5.90	$8.83	$11.92
Materials Prime..........1.54 1 Coat.......1.71 2 Coats.......2.37 3 Coats.......3.15					
Labor Prime.................4.11 1 Coat.......4.19 2 Coats.......6.46 3 Coats.......8.77					
Paint 72" high ornamental iron fence	lf	$7.08	$7.45	$11.12	$15.03
Materials Prime..........2.16 1 Coat.......2.40 2 Coats.......3.33 3 Coats.......4.43					
Labor Prime.................4.92 1 Coat.......5.05 2 Coats.......7.79 3 Coats......10.60					
Paint wood trim, simple design	lf	$.59	$.60	$.91	$1.22
Materials Prime.......... .12 1 Coat........ .13 2 Coats........ .18 3 Coats........ .24					
Labor Prime................. .47 1 Coat........ .47 2 Coats........ .73 3 Coats........ .98					
Stain & varnish wood trim, simple design	lf	$.86	$.86	$1.29	$1.74
Materials Stain........... .18 1 Coat........ .13 2 Coats........ .18 3 Coats........ .24					
Labor Stain.................. .68 1 Coat........ .73 2 Coats.......1.11 3 Coats.......1.50					
Paint wood trim, ornate design	lf	$.71	$.77	$1.14	$1.52
Materials Prime.......... .15 1 Coat........ .17 2 Coats........ .24 3 Coats........ .32					
Labor Prime................ .56 1 Coat........ .60 2 Coats........ .90 3 Coats.......1.20					

◄ **MEDICINE CABINET**

◄ **EXTERIOR LIGHT-FIXTURE POST**

◄ **FENCES**
Wood fence prices are for one side only. Ornamental iron fence prices are for both sides.

◁ **ornamental iron**

◄ **FINISH CARPENTRY**

◁ **wood trim**

RELATED ITEMS

Bathroom Hardware......41
Doors............................101
Electrical.......................139
Fences...........................187
Finish Carpentry..........199

	Item Description	Unit	prime/stain	1 Coat	2 Coats	3 Coats
FINISH ▶ CARPENTRY *continued*	**Stain & varnish wood trim, ornate design** ***Materials*** Stain .22 1 Coat .24 2 Coats .33 3 Coats .44 ***Labor*** Stain .86 1 Coat .90 2 Coats 1.37 3 Coats 1.88	lf	$1.08	$1.14	$1.70	$2.32
	Paint wood trim, very ornate design ***Materials*** Prime .18 1 Coat .20 2 Coats .28 3 Coats .37 ***Labor*** Prime .73 1 Coat .73 2 Coats 1.11 3 Coats 1.50	lf	$.91	$.93	$1.39	$1.87
	Stain & varnish wood trim, very ornate design ***Materials*** Stain .26 1 Coat .29 2 Coats .40 3 Coats .53 ***Labor*** Stain 1.07 1 Coat 1.11 2 Coats 1.71 3 Coats 2.31	lf	$1.33	$1.40	$2.11	$2.84
interior architrave ▷	**Paint interior architrave, simple design** ***Materials*** Prime .18 1 Coat .20 2 Coats .28 3 Coats .37 ***Labor*** Prime .64 1 Coat .64 2 Coats .98 3 Coats 1.37	lf	$.82	$.84	$1.26	$1.74
	Stain & varnish interior architrave, simple design ***Materials*** Stain .26 1 Coat .29 2 Coats .40 3 Coats .53 ***Labor*** Stain .98 1 Coat .98 2 Coats 1.54 3 Coats 2.05	lf	$1.24	$1.27	$1.94	$2.58
	Paint interior architrave, complex design ***Materials*** Prime .26 1 Coat .29 2 Coats .40 3 Coats .53 ***Labor*** Prime 1.28 1 Coat 1.28 2 Coats 2.01 3 Coats 2.70	lf	$1.54	$1.57	$2.41	$3.23
	Stain & varnish interior architrave, complex design ***Materials*** Stain .38 1 Coat .42 2 Coats .58 3 Coats .77 ***Labor*** Stain 1.93 1 Coat 2.01 2 Coats 3.08 3 Coats 4.15	lf	$2.31	$2.43	$3.66	$4.92
exterior architrave ▷	**Paint exterior architrave, simple design** ***Materials*** Prime .35 1 Coat .39 2 Coats .54 3 Coats .72 ***Labor*** Prime 1.41 1 Coat 1.50 2 Coats 2.27 3 Coats 3.08	lf	$1.76	$1.89	$2.81	$3.80
	Paint exterior architrave, complex design ***Materials*** Prime .71 1 Coat .79 2 Coats 1.10 3 Coats 1.46 ***Labor*** Prime 2.87 1 Coat 2.95 2 Coats 4.54 3 Coats 6.12	lf	$3.58	$3.74	$5.64	$7.58
exterior door surround ▷	**Paint exterior door surround, simple design** ***Materials*** Prime 1.41 1 Coat 1.57 2 Coats 2.18 3 Coats 2.90 ***Labor*** Prime 5.01 1 Coat 5.14 2 Coats 7.92 3 Coats 10.70	lf	$6.42	$6.71	$10.10	$13.60
	Paint exterior door surround, complex design ***Materials*** Prime 2.99 1 Coat 3.32 2 Coats 4.61 3 Coats 6.13 ***Labor*** Prime 12.30 1 Coat 12.60 2 Coats 19.50 3 Coats 26.40	lf	$15.29	$15.92	$24.11	$32.53
exterior window surround ▷	**Paint exterior window surround, simple design** ***Materials*** Prime 1.41 1 Coat 1.57 2 Coats 2.18 3 Coats 2.90 ***Labor*** Prime 5.01 1 Coat 5.14 2 Coats 7.92 3 Coats 10.70	lf	$6.42	$6.71	$10.10	$13.60
	Paint exterior window surround, complex design ***Materials*** Prime 2.99 1 Coat 3.32 2 Coats 4.61 3 Coats 6.13 ***Labor*** Prime 12.30 1 Coat 12.60 2 Coats 19.50 3 Coats 26.40	lf	$15.29	$15.92	$24.11	$32.53
closets ▷	**Paint closet rod, shelf, and brackets** ***Materials*** Prime .22 1 Coat .24 2 Coats .33 3 Coats .44 ***Labor*** Prime 5.44 1 Coat 5.61 2 Coats 8.60 3 Coats 11.70	lf	$5.66	$5.85	$8.93	$12.14
	Paint closet organizer system ***Materials*** Prime .24 1 Coat .27 2 Coats .37 3 Coats .49 ***Labor*** Prime .47 1 Coat .47 2 Coats .73 3 Coats .98	sf	$.71	$.74	$1.10	$1.47
bookcase ▷	**Paint bookcase** ***Materials*** Prime .55 1 Coat .61 2 Coats .85 3 Coats 1.13 ***Labor*** Prime .60 1 Coat .64 2 Coats .98 3 Coats 1.28	sf	$1.15	$1.25	$1.83	$2.41
	Stain & varnish bookcase ***Materials*** Stain .81 1 Coat .90 2 Coats 1.25 3 Coats 1.66 ***Labor*** Stain .94 1 Coat .98 2 Coats 1.50 3 Coats 2.01	sf	$1.75	$1.88	$2.75	$3.67

Item Description	Unit	prime/stain	1 Coat	2 Coats	3 Coats	
Paint fireplace mantel beam	lf	$1.05	$1.08	$1.63	$2.20	◁ mantel beams and mantels
Materials Prime .... .28 1 Coat........ .31 2 Coats........ .43 3 Coats........ .57						
Labor Prime .... .77 1 Coat........ .77 2 Coats.......1.20 3 Coats.......1.63						
Stain & varnish mantel beam	lf	$1.57	$1.66	$2.48	$3.38	
Materials Stain........... .41 1 Coat........ .46 2 Coats........ .64 3 Coats........ .85						
Labor Stain..................1.16 1 Coat.......1.20 2 Coats.......1.84 3 Coats.......2.53						
Paint fireplace mantel	lf	$1.44	$1.52	$2.28	$3.07	
Materials Prime .... .37 1 Coat........ .41 2 Coats........ .57 3 Coats........ .76						
Labor Prime .... 1.07 1 Coat.......1.11 2 Coats.......1.71 3 Coats.......2.31						
Stain & varnish mantel	lf	$2.17	$2.27	$3.44	$4.61	
Materials Stain........... .54 1 Coat........ .60 2 Coats........ .83 3 Coats.......1.10						
Labor Stain..................1.63 1 Coat.......1.67 2 Coats.......2.61 3 Coats.......3.51						
Paint coffered ceiling, simple design	sf	$1.17	$1.26	$1.84	$2.48	◁ coffered ceiling
Materials Prime .... .44 1 Coat........ .49 2 Coats........ .68 3 Coats........ .90						
Labor Prime .... .73 1 Coat........ .77 2 Coats.......1.16 3 Coats.......1.58						
Stain & varnish coffered ceiling, simple design	sf	$1.76	$1.88	$2.80	$3.73	
Materials Stain........... .65 1 Coat........ .72 2 Coats...... 1.00 3 Coats.......1.33						
Labor Stain..................1.11 1 Coat.......1.16 2 Coats.......1.80 3 Coats.......2.40						
Paint coffered ceiling, complex design	sf	$2.53	$2.67	$3.99	$5.42	
Materials Prime .... .78 1 Coat........ .87 2 Coats.......1.21 3 Coats.......1.61						
Labor Prime.................1.75 1 Coat.......1.80 2 Coats.......2.78 3 Coats.......3.81						
Stain & varnish coffered ceiling, complex design	sf	$3.84	$4.05	$6.04	$8.12	
Materials Stain ....1.14 1 Coat.......1.27 2 Coats.......1.76 3 Coats.......2.34						
Labor Stain..................2.70 1 Coat.......2.78 2 Coats.......4.28 3 Coats.......5.78						
Paint niche	ea	$30.19	$31.69	$47.50	$64.00	◁ niche
Materials Prime..........7.19 1 Coat.......7.99 2 Coats......11.10 3 Coats......14.80						
Labor Prime...............23.00 1 Coat.....23.70 2 Coats.....36.40 3 Coats......49.20						
Stain & varnish niche	ea	$45.75	$47.90	$71.80	$96.80	
Materials Stain.........10.55 1 Coat......11.70 2 Coats......16.20 3 Coats......21.50						
Labor Stain................35.20 1 Coat.....36.20 2 Coats......55.60 3 Coats......75.30						
Paint gingerbread running trim	lf	$3.05	$3.25	$4.80	$6.44	◁ running trim
Materials Prime..........1.12 1 Coat.......1.24 2 Coats.......1.72 3 Coats.......2.29						
Labor Prime.................1.93 1 Coat.......2.01 2 Coats.......3.08 3 Coats.......4.15						
Stain & varnish gingerbread running trim	lf	$4.59	$4.86	$7.24	$9.69	
Materials Stain ....1.64 1 Coat.......1.82 2 Coats.......2.53 3 Coats.......3.36						
Labor Stain..................2.95 1 Coat.......3.04 2 Coats.......4.71 3 Coats.......6.33						
Paint gingerbread bracket	ea	$16.09	$16.68	$25.41	$34.37	◁ bracket
Materials Prime..........1.69 1 Coat.......1.88 2 Coats.......2.61 3 Coats.......3.47						
Labor Prime ....14.40 1 Coat......14.80 2 Coats.....22.80 3 Coats.....30.90						
Stain & varnish gingerbread bracket	ea	$24.48	$25.46	$38.73	$52.19	
Materials Stain ....2.48 1 Coat.......2.76 2 Coats.......3.83 3 Coats.......5.09						
Labor Stain................22.00 1 Coat.....22.70 2 Coats.....34.90 3 Coats......47.10						
Paint gingerbread corbel	ea	$15.76	$16.44	$24.96	$33.70	◁ corbel
Materials Prime..........1.66 1 Coat.......1.84 2 Coats.......2.56 3 Coats.......3.40						
Labor Prime ....14.10 1 Coat......14.60 2 Coats.....22.40 3 Coats.....30.30						
Stain & varnish gingerbread corbel	ea	$24.04	$25.01	$37.96	$51.20	
Materials Stain ....2.44 1 Coat.......2.71 2 Coats.......3.76 3 Coats.......5.00						
Labor Stain................21.60 1 Coat.....22.30 2 Coats.....34.20 3 Coats.....46.20						
Paint gingerbread door or window header	lf	$2.86	$2.96	$4.49	$6.05	◁ door or window header
Materials Prime .... .55 1 Coat........ .61 2 Coats........ .85 3 Coats.......1.13						
Labor Prime.................2.31 1 Coat.......2.35 2 Coats.......3.64 3 Coats.......4.92						

RELATED ITEMS

Finish Carpentry..........199

	Item Description	Unit	prime/stain	1 Coat	2 Coats	3 Coats
FINISH CARPENTRY *continued*	**Stain & varnish gingerbread door or window header** ***Materials*** Stain........... .81 1 Coat........ .90 2 Coats.......1.25 3 Coats.......1.66 ***Labor*** Stain..................3.51 1 Coat.......3.60 2 Coats.......5.56 3 Coats.......7.53	lf	$4.32	$4.50	$6.81	$9.19
spandrel	**Paint gingerbread spandrel** ***Materials*** Prime.......... .58 1 Coat........ .64 2 Coats........ .89 3 Coats.......1.18 ***Labor*** Prime.................3.21 1 Coat.......3.30 2 Coats.......5.09 3 Coats.......6.89	lf	$3.79	$3.94	$5.98	$8.07
	Stain & varnish gingerbread spandrel ***Materials*** Stain........... .85 1 Coat........ .94 2 Coats.......1.31 3 Coats.......1.74 ***Labor*** Stain..................4.92 1 Coat.......5.05 2 Coats.......7.79 3 Coats......10.60	lf	$5.77	$5.99	$9.10	$12.34
gable ornament *add **51%** to stain & varnish.*	**Paint gingerbread gable ornament** ***Materials*** Prime........12.10 1 Coat......13.40 2 Coats......18.60 3 Coats......24.70 ***Labor*** Prime...............31.90 1 Coat.....32.80 2 Coats.....50.50 3 Coats.....68.50	ea	$44.00	$46.20	$69.10	$93.20
gable finial *add **51%** to stain & varnish.*	**Paint gingerbread gable finial** ***Materials*** Prime..........2.40 1 Coat.......2.67 2 Coats.......3.71 3 Coats.......4.93 ***Labor*** Prime...............10.80 1 Coat......11.20 2 Coats......17.20 3 Coats.....23.20	ea	$13.20	$13.87	$20.91	$28.13
porch post	**Paint porch post** ***Materials*** Prime..........3.82 1 Coat.......4.24 2 Coats.......5.89 3 Coats.......7.83 ***Labor*** Prime.................5.05 1 Coat.......5.22 2 Coats.......8.00 3 Coats......10.90	ea	$8.87	$9.46	$13.89	$18.73
	Stain & varnish porch post ***Materials*** Stain..........5.61 1 Coat.......6.23 2 Coats.......8.65 3 Coats......11.50 ***Labor*** Stain..................7.75 1 Coat.......7.96 2 Coats......12.20 3 Coats......16.60	ea	$13.36	$14.19	$20.85	$28.10
FLOORING *See Flooring for costs to prep wood floors for finish*	**Seal stone floor** ***Materials*** Seal........... .15 1 Coat........ .17 2 Coats........ .24 3 Coats........ .32 ***Labor*** Seal................... .47 1 Coat........ .47 2 Coats........ .73 3 Coats........ .98	sf	$.62	$.64	$.97	$1.30
	Paint wood floor ***Materials*** Prime.......... .19 1 Coat........ .21 2 Coats........ .29 3 Coats........ .39 ***Labor*** Prime................. .51 1 Coat........ .51 2 Coats........ .81 3 Coats.......1.11	sf	$.70	$.72	$1.10	$1.50
	Stain & varnish wood floor ***Materials*** Stain........... .28 1 Coat........ .31 2 Coats........ .43 3 Coats........ .57 ***Labor*** Stain.................. .77 1 Coat........ .81 2 Coats.......1.24 3 Coats.......1.67	sf	$1.05	$1.12	$1.67	$2.24
PANELING	**Paint wall paneling, simple pattern** ***Materials*** Prime.......... .30 1 Coat........ .33 2 Coats........ .46 3 Coats........ .61 ***Labor*** Prime................. .51 1 Coat........ .51 2 Coats........ .81 3 Coats.......1.11	sf	$.81	$.84	$1.27	$1.72
	Stain & varnish wall paneling, simple pattern ***Materials*** Stain........... .44 1 Coat........ .49 2 Coats........ .68 3 Coats........ .90 ***Labor*** Stain.................. .77 1 Coat........ .81 2 Coats.......1.24 3 Coats.......1.67	sf	$1.21	$1.30	$1.92	$2.57
	Paint wall paneling, ornate pattern ***Materials*** Prime.......... .40 1 Coat........ .44 2 Coats........ .61 3 Coats........ .81 ***Labor*** Prime................. .73 1 Coat........ .73 2 Coats.......1.16 3 Coats.......1.54	sf	$1.13	$1.17	$1.77	$2.35
	Stain & varnish wall paneling, ornate pattern ***Materials*** Stain........... .59 1 Coat........ .66 2 Coats........ .92 3 Coats.......1.22 ***Labor*** Stain..................1.11 1 Coat.......1.16 2 Coats.......1.75 3 Coats.......2.40	sf	$1.70	$1.82	$2.67	$3.62
	Paint wall paneling, very ornate pattern ***Materials*** Prime.......... .47 1 Coat........ .52 2 Coats........ .72 3 Coats........ .96 ***Labor*** Prime.................1.20 1 Coat.......1.24 2 Coats.......1.88 3 Coats.......2.57	sf	$1.67	$1.76	$2.60	$3.53
	Stain & varnish wall paneling, very ornate pattern ***Materials*** Stain........... .69 1 Coat........ .77 2 Coats.......1.07 3 Coats.......1.42 ***Labor*** Stain..................1.84 1 Coat.......1.88 2 Coats.......2.91 3 Coats.......3.98	sf	$2.53	$2.65	$3.98	$5.40
MASONRY *Deduct **26%** for previously painted block or brick.*	**Paint concrete block** ***Materials*** Prime.......... .30 1 Coat........ .33 2 Coats........ .46 3 Coats........ .61 ***Labor*** Prime................. .60 1 Coat........ .64 2 Coats........ .98 3 Coats.......1.28	sf	$.90	$.97	$1.44	$1.89

Item Description	Unit	prime/stain	1 Coat	2 Coats	3 Coats
Paint brick	sf	$1.04	$1.07	$1.58	$2.12
Materials Prime .31 · 1 Coat .34 · 2 Coats .47 · 3 Coats .62					
Labor Prime .73 · 1 Coat .73 · 2 Coats 1.11 · 3 Coats 1.50					
Paint stone wall	sf	$.66	$.69	$1.04	$1.38
Materials Prime .23 · 1 Coat .26 · 2 Coats .36 · 3 Coats .48					
Labor Prime .43 · 1 Coat .43 · 2 Coats .68 · 3 Coats .90					
Seal stone wall	sf	$.65	$.73	$1.03	$1.39
Materials Seal .31 · 1 Coat .34 · 2 Coats .47 · 3 Coats .62					
Labor Seal .34 · 1 Coat .39 · 2 Coats .56 · 3 Coats .77					
Paint metal roofing	sf	$1.06	$1.14	$1.67	$2.26
Materials Prime .33 · 1 Coat .37 · 2 Coats .51 · 3 Coats .68					
Labor Prime .73 · 1 Coat .77 · 2 Coats 1.16 · 3 Coats 1.58					
Treat wood shingles or shakes with shingle oil	sf	$.78	$.84	$1.23	$1.64
Materials Treat .22 · 1 Coat .24 · 2 Coats .33 · 3 Coats .44					
Labor Treat .56 · 1 Coat .60 · 2 Coats .90 · 3 Coats 1.20					
Seal wall framing	sf	$.92	$.94	$1.44	$1.95
Materials Seal .15 · 1 Coat .17 · 2 Coats .24 · 3 Coats .32					
Labor Seal .77 · 1 Coat .77 · 2 Coats 1.20 · 3 Coats 1.63					
Seal floor framing	sf	$1.15	$1.21	$1.82	$2.44
Materials Seal .21 · 1 Coat .23 · 2 Coats .32 · 3 Coats .43					
Labor Seal .94 · 1 Coat .98 · 2 Coats 1.50 · 3 Coats 2.01					
Seal roof framing	sf	$1.46	$1.53	$2.28	$3.06
Materials Seal .26 · 1 Coat .29 · 2 Coats .40 · 3 Coats .53					
Labor Seal 1.20 · 1 Coat 1.24 · 2 Coats 1.88 · 3 Coats 2.53					
Paint exterior siding	sf	$.91	$.93	$1.41	$1.87
Materials Prime .23 · 1 Coat .25 · 2 Coats .34 · 3 Coats .46					
Labor Prime .68 · 1 Coat .68 · 2 Coats 1.07 · 3 Coats 1.41					
Stain exterior siding	sf	$1.01	$1.05	$1.55	$2.13
Materials Stain .37 · 1 Coat .41 · 2 Coats .57 · 3 Coats .76					
Labor Stain .64 · 1 Coat .64 · 2 Coats .98 · 3 Coats 1.37					
Paint window shutter (per shutter, per side)	ea	$21.19	$22.24	$33.39	$45.02
Materials Prime 4.99 · 1 Coat 5.54 · 2 Coats 7.69 · 3 Coats 10.22					
Labor Prime 16.20 · 1 Coat 16.70 · 2 Coats 25.70 · 3 Coats 34.80					
Stain window shutter (per shutter, per side)	ea	$32.12	$33.63	$50.60	$68.10
Materials Stain 7.32 · 1 Coat 8.13 · 2 Coats 11.30 · 3 Coats 15.00					
Labor Stain 24.80 · 1 Coat 25.50 · 2 Coats 39.30 · 3 Coats 53.10					
Paint exterior fascia	lf	$.57	$.58	$.88	$1.18
Materials Prime .10 · 1 Coat .11 · 2 Coats .15 · 3 Coats .20					
Labor Prime .47 · 1 Coat .47 · 2 Coats .73 · 3 Coats .98					
Stain exterior wood fascia	lf	$.57	$.59	$.90	$1.19
Materials Stain .14 · 1 Coat .16 · 2 Coats .22 · 3 Coats .29					
Labor Stain .43 · 1 Coat .43 · 2 Coats .68 · 3 Coats .90					
Paint exterior soffit	sf	$.70	$.77	$1.13	$1.51
Materials Prime .23 · 1 Coat .26 · 2 Coats .36 · 3 Coats .48					
Labor Prime .47 · 1 Coat .51 · 2 Coats .77 · 3 Coats 1.03					
Stain exterior wood soffit	sf	$.81	$.84	$1.27	$1.72
Materials Stain .30 · 1 Coat .33 · 2 Coats .46 · 3 Coats .61					
Labor Stain .51 · 1 Coat .51 · 2 Coats .81 · 3 Coats 1.11					
Paint rain gutter or downspout	lf	$.96	$1.02	$1.53	$2.06
Materials Prime .19 · 1 Coat .21 · 2 Coats .29 · 3 Coats .39					
Labor Prime .77 · 1 Coat .81 · 2 Coats 1.24 · 3 Coats 1.67					

RELATED ITEMS

Finish Carpentry 199
Flooring 257
sand, edge & fill wood floor 268
Paneling 347
Masonry 287
Roofing 393
Rough Carpentry 409
Siding 455

◀ ROOFING

◀ ROUGH CARPENTRY

◁ **seal framing**
seal smoke-stained framing for odor control

◀ SIDING

◁ **shutters**

◁ **fascia**

◁ **soffit**

◁ **gutter or downspout**

	Item Description	Unit	prime/stain	1 Coat	2 Coats	3 Coats
STAIRS ▶	**Paint stair balustrade** *Materials* Prime..........2.72 1 Coat.......3.02 2 Coats.......4.20 3 Coats.......5.60 *Labor* Prime.................8.13 1 Coat.......8.35 2 Coats......12.80 3 Coats......17.40	lf	$10.85	$11.37	$17.00	$23.00
	Stain & varnish stair balustrade *Materials* Stain ....4.03 1 Coat.......4.43 2 Coats.......6.20 3 Coats.......8.27 *Labor* Stain ....12.40 1 Coat......12.80 2 Coats......19.60 3 Coats......26.60	lf	$16.43	$17.23	$25.80	$34.87
	Paint stair riser *Materials* Prime..........2.28 1 Coat.......2.53 2 Coats.......3.51 3 Coats.......4.66 *Labor* Prime.................4.79 1 Coat.......4.92 2 Coats.......7.58 3 Coats......10.30	ea	$7.07	$7.45	$11.09	$14.96
	Stain & varnish stair riser *Materials* Stain ....3.35 1 Coat.......3.72 2 Coats.......5.17 3 Coats.......6.87 *Labor* Stain..................7.32 1 Coat.......7.53 2 Coats......11.60 3 Coats......15.70	ea	$10.67	$11.25	$16.77	$22.57
	Paint stair tread *Materials* Prime..........2.54 1 Coat.......2.82 2 Coats.......3.92 3 Coats.......5.21 *Labor* Prime.................5.18 1 Coat.......5.35 2 Coats.......8.22 3 Coats......11.10	ea	$7.72	$8.17	$12.14	$16.31
	Stain & finish stair tread *Materials* Stain ....3.73 1 Coat.......4.14 2 Coats.......5.75 3 Coats.......7.64 *Labor* Stain..................7.92 1 Coat.......8.17 2 Coats......12.60 3 Coats......17.00	ea	$11.65	$12.31	$18.35	$24.64
	Paint stair bracket *Materials* Prime..........2.10 1 Coat.......2.33 2 Coats.......3.24 3 Coats.......4.31 *Labor* Prime.................3.94 1 Coat.......4.02 2 Coats.......6.21 3 Coats.......8.39	ea	$6.04	$6.35	$9.45	$12.70
	Stain & finish stair bracket *Materials* Stain ....3.08 1 Coat.......3.42 2 Coats.......4.75 3 Coats.......6.31 *Labor* Stain..................5.99 1 Coat.......6.16 2 Coats.......9.50 3 Coats......12.80	ea	$9.07	$9.58	$14.25	$19.11
WINDOW ▶	**Paint small window (per side)** *Materials* Prime..........7.25 1 Coat.......8.05 2 Coats......11.20 3 Coats......14.90 *Labor* Prime ....12.60 1 Coat......13.00 2 Coats.....20.00 3 Coats.....27.10	ea	$19.85	$21.05	$31.20	$42.00
	Paint average size window (per side) *Materials* Prime ....11.00 1 Coat......12.20 2 Coats......16.90 3 Coats .....22.50 *Labor* Prime ....18.00 1 Coat ......18.50 2 Coats......28.50 3 Coats 38.60	ea	$29.00	$30.70	$45.40	$61.10
	Paint large window (per side) *Materials* Prime ....14.00 1 Coat.......15.60 2 Coats.......21.70 3 Coats......28.80 *Labor* Prime...............22.90 1 Coat .....23.50 2 Coats .....36.20 3 Coats......49.20	ea	$36.90	$39.10	$57.90	$78.00
	Paint very large window (per side) *Materials* Prime........20.10 1 Coat.....22.30 2 Coats......31.00 3 Coats.....41.20 *Labor* Prime...............28.60 1 Coat .....29.40 2 Coats......45.40 3 Coats......61.20	ea	$48.70	$51.70	$76.40	$102.40
WALLPAPER ▶	**Paint wallpaper** *Materials* Prime .... .18 1 Coat........ .20 2 Coats........ .28 3 Coats........ .37 *Labor* Prime .... .47 1 Coat........ .47 2 Coats........ .73 3 Coats........ .98	sf	$.65	$.67	$1.01	$1.35
STRIP PAINT ▶ *Costs to strip paint that does not contain lead.*	**Strip paint or varnish from trim, simple design** *Materials* Strip ....1.33 1 Coat.......1.57 2 Coats.......2.12 3 Coats.......2.78 *Labor* Strip ....3.47 1 Coat.......3.55 2 Coats.......5.39 3 Coats.......7.36	lf	$4.80	$5.12	$7.51	$10.14
	Strip paint or varnish from trim, complex design *Materials* Strip ....1.62 1 Coat.......1.81 2 Coats.......2.86 3 Coats.......4.35 *Labor* Strip ....6.55 1 Coat.......6.76 2 Coats......12.50 3 Coats.....22.00	lf	$8.17	$8.57	$15.36	$26.35
	Strip paint or varnish from door (slab only) *Materials* Strip..........14.40 1 Coat......17.20 2 Coats......24.30 3 Coats .....36.20 *Labor* Strip ....22.70 1 Coat ......23.30 2 Coats .....36.20 3 Coats 54.40	ea	$37.10	$40.50	$60.50	$90.60
	Strip paint or varnish from door jamb and casing *Materials* Strip ....2.28 1 Coat.......2.69 2 Coats.......3.63 3 Coats.......4.76 *Labor* Strip ....3.94 1 Coat.......4.07 2 Coats.......6.25 3 Coats.......8.47	lf	$6.22	$6.76	$9.88	$13.23

RELATED ITEMS

Stairs..........................465
Wall Coverings...........495
Windows......................501

TIME & MATERIAL CHARTS (selected items)

Painting Materials

DESCRIPTION	APPLIED TO	MATERIAL PRICE	COVERAGE	UNIT PRICE
Prime or seal				
primer or sealer	plaster or drywall	$21.20 gallon	178	$.12 sf
primer or sealer	interior door	$21.20 gallon	2.8	$7.57 ea
primer or sealer	entry door	$21.20 gallon	1.6	$13.30 ea
primer or sealer	wood trim, simple design	$21.20 gallon	178	$.12 lf
primer or sealer	exterior siding	$21.20 gallon	94	$.23 sf
primer or sealer	stair balustrade	$21.20 gallon	7.8	$2.72 lf
Paint, one coat				
oil or latex paint	plaster or drywall	$26.90 gallon	205	$.13 sf
oil or latex paint	interior door	$26.90 gallon	3.2	$8.41 ea
oil or latex paint	entry door	$26.90 gallon	1.9	$14.20 ea
oil or latex paint	wood trim, simple design	$26.90 gallon	205	$.13 lf
oil or latex paint	exterior siding	$26.90 gallon	108	$.25 sf
oil or latex paint	stair balustrade	$26.90 gallon	8.9	$3.02 lf
Paint, two coats				
oil or latex paint	plaster or drywall	$26.90 gallon	151	$.18 sf
oil or latex paint	interior door	$26.90 gallon	2.3	$11.70 ea
oil or latex paint	entry door	$26.90 gallon	1.4	$19.20 ea
oil or latex paint	wood trim, simple design	$26.90 gallon	151	$.18 lf
oil or latex paint	exterior siding	$26.90 gallon	78	$.34 sf
oil or latex paint	stair balustrade	$26.90 gallon	6.4	$4.20 lf
Paint, three coats				
oil or latex paint	plaster or drywall	$26.90 gallon	113	$.24 sf
oil or latex paint	interior door	$26.90 gallon	1.7	$15.80 ea
oil or latex paint	entry door	$26.90 gallon	1	$26.90 ea
oil or latex paint	wood trim, simple design	$26.90 gallon	113	$.24 lf
oil or latex paint	exterior siding	$26.90 gallon	58	$.46 sf
oil or latex paint	stair balustrade	$26.90 gallon	4.8	$5.60 lf
Stain				
stain	interior door	$28.60 gallon	2.5	$11.40 ea
stain	entry door	$28.60 gallon	1.5	$19.10 ea
stain	wood trim, simple design	$28.60 gallon	159	$.18 lf
stain	exterior siding, one coat	$28.60 gallon	77	$.37 sf
stain	stair balustrade	$28.60 gallon	7.1	$4.03 lf
Varnish, one coat				
varnish, clear	interior door	$37.20 gallon	2.9	$12.80 ea
varnish, clear	entry door	$37.20 gallon	1.8	$20.70 ea
varnish, clear	wood trim, simple design	$37.20 gallon	284	$.13 lf
varnish, clear	stair balustrade	$37.20 gallon	8.4	$4.43 lf
Varnish, two coats				
varnish, clear	interior door	$37.20 gallon	2.1	$17.70 ea
varnish, clear	entry door	$37.20 gallon	1.4	$26.60 ea
varnish, clear	wood trim, simple design	$37.20 gallon	208	$.18 lf
varnish, clear	stair balustrade	$37.20 gallon	6	$6.20 lf
Varnish, three coats				
varnish, clear	interior door	$37.20 gallon	1.6	$23.30 ea
varnish, clear	entry door	$37.20 gallon	1	$37.20 ea
varnish, clear	wood trim, simple design	$37.20 gallon	156	$.24 lf
varnish, clear	stair balustrade	$37.20 gallon	4.5	$8.27 lf

Painting Labor

Laborer	Base Wage	Paid Leave	True Wage	FICA	FUTA	Worker's Comp.	Unemploy. Insur.	Health Insur.	Retire (401k)	Liability Insur.	Cost per Hour
Painter	$23.20	1.81	$25.01	1.91	.20	6.65	2.18	2.69	.75	3.38	$42.80

Paid Leave is calculated based on two weeks paid vacation, one week sick leave, and seven paid holidays. Employer's matching portion of **FICA** is 7.65 percent. **FUTA** (Federal Unemployment) is .8 percent. **Worker's compensation** for the painting trade was calculated using a national average of 26.59 percent. **Unemployment insurance** was calculated using a national average of 8.7 percent. **Health insurance** was calculated based on a projected national average for 2002 of $535 per employee (and family when applicable) per month. Employer pays 80 percent for a per month cost of $428 per employee. **Retirement** is based on a 401(k) retirement program with employer matching of 50 percent. Employee contributions to the 401(k) plan are an average of 6 percent of the true wage. **Liability insurance** is based on a national average of 13.2 percent.

Painting Labor Productivity

Work Description	Laborer	Cost per Hour	Productivity	Unit Price
Prime or seal				
acoustic ceiling texture	painter	$42.80	.011	$.47 sf
plaster or drywall	painter	$42.80	.006	$.26 sf
masonry, block	painter	$42.80	.014	$.60 sf
concrete floor	painter	$42.80	.008	$.34 sf
wood floor	painter	$42.80	.012	$.51 sf
folding door	painter	$42.80	.402	$17.20 ea
bypassing door	painter	$42.80	.830	$35.50 ea
interior door	painter	$42.80	.340	$14.60 ea
door jamb & casing	painter	$42.80	.011	$.47 lf
wood entry door	painter	$42.80	.742	$31.80 ea
wood sliding patio door	painter	$42.80	.646	$27.60 ea
garage door	painter	$42.80	.006	$.26 sf
4' high wood fence (per side)	painter	$42.80	.051	$2.18 lf
48" high ornamental iron fence (both sides)	painter	$42.80	.077	$3.30 lf
wood trim, simple design	painter	$42.80	.011	$.47 lf
wood trim, very ornate design	painter	$42.80	.025	$.73 lf
seal smoke-stained frame walls	painter	$42.80	.018	$.77 sf
seal smoke-stained joists	painter	$42.80	.022	$.94 sf
seal smoke-stained rafters or trusses	painter	$42.80	.028	$1.20 sf
siding	painter	$42.80	.016	$.68 sf
stucco	painter	$42.80	.014	$.60 sf
stair balustrade	painter	$42.80	.190	$8.13 lf
small window	painter	$42.80	.295	$12.60 ea
very large window	painter	$42.80	.668	$28.60 ea
Paint, one coat				
acoustic ceiling texture	painter	$42.80	.011	$.47 sf
plaster or drywall	painter	$42.80	.006	$.26 sf
masonry, block	painter	$42.80	.015	$.64 sf
concrete floor	painter	$42.80	.008	$.34 sf
wood floor	painter	$42.80	.012	$.51 sf
folding door	painter	$42.80	.413	$17.70 ea
bypassing door	painter	$42.80	.854	$36.60 ea
interior door	painter	$42.80	.349	$14.90 ea
door jamb & casing	painter	$42.80	.011	$.47 lf
wood entry door	painter	$42.80	.763	$32.70 ea
wood sliding patio door	painter	$42.80	.665	$28.50 sf
garage door	painter	$42.80	.006	$.26 sf
4' high wood fence (per side)	painter	$42.80	.053	$2.27 lf
48" high ornamental iron fence (both sides)	painter	$42.80	.079	$3.38 lf
wood trim, simple design	painter	$42.80	.011	$.47 lf
wood trim, very ornate design	painter	$42.80	.017	$.73 lf
siding	painter	$42.80	.016	$.68 sf
stucco	painter	$42.80	.015	$.64 sf
stair balustrade	painter	$42.80	.195	$8.35 sf
small window	painter	$42.80	.304	$13.00 ea
very large window	painter	$42.80	.687	$29.40 ea

. . . More ➢

Painting Labor Productivity *continued*

WORK DESCRIPTION	LABORER	COST PER HOUR	PRODUCTIVITY	UNIT PRICE
Paint, two coats				
acoustic ceiling texture	painter	$42.80	.017	**$.73** sf
plaster or drywall	painter	$42.80	.010	**$.43** sf
masonry, block	painter	$42.80	.023	**$.98** sf
concrete floor	painter	$42.80	.012	**$.51** sf
wood floor	painter	$42.80	.019	**$.81** sf
folding door	painter	$42.80	.636	**$27.20** ea
bypassing door	painter	$42.80	1.32	**$56.50** ea
interior door	painter	$42.80	.538	**$23.00** ea
door jamb & casing	painter	$42.80	.017	**$.73** lf
wood entry door	painter	$42.80	1.18	**$50.50** ea
wood sliding patio door	painter	$42.80	1.02	**$43.70** sf
garage door	painter	$42.80	.009	**$.39** sf
4' high wood fence (per side)	painter	$42.80	.081	**$3.47** lf
48" high ornamental iron fence (both sides)	painter	$42.80	.121	**$5.18** lf
wood trim, simple design	painter	$42.80	.017	**$.73** lf
wood trim, very ornate design	painter	$42.80	.026	**$1.11** lf
siding	painter	$42.80	.025	**$1.07** sf
stucco	painter	$42.80	.023	**$.98** sf
stair balustrade	painter	$42.80	.300	**$12.80** lf
small window	painter	$42.80	.467	**$20.00** ea
very large window	painter	$42.80	1.06	**$45.40** ea
Paint, three coats				
acoustic ceiling texture	painter	$42.80	.023	**$.98** sf
plaster or drywall	painter	$42.80	.013	**$.56** sf
masonry, block	painter	$42.80	.030	**$1.28** sf
concrete floor	painter	$42.80	.016	**$.68** sf
wood floor	painter	$42.80	.026	**$1.11** sf
folding door	painter	$42.80	.861	**$36.90** ea
bypassing door	painter	$42.80	1.78	**$76.20** ea
interior door	painter	$42.80	.729	**$31.20** ea
door jamb & casing	painter	$42.80	.023	**$.98** lf
wood entry door	painter	$42.80	1.59	**$68.10** ea
wood sliding patio door	painter	$42.80	1.39	**$59.50** sf
garage door	painter	$42.80	.013	**$.56** sf
4' high wood fence (per side)	painter	$42.80	.109	**$4.67** lf
48" high ornamental iron fence (both sides)	painter	$42.80	.164	**$7.02** lf
wood trim, simple design	painter	$42.80	.023	**$.98** lf
wood trim, very ornate design	painter	$42.80	.035	**$1.50** lf
siding	painter	$42.80	.033	**$1.41** sf
stucco	painter	$42.80	.030	**$1.28** sf
stair balustrade	painter	$42.80	.407	**$17.40** lf
small window	painter	$42.80	.633	**$27.10** ea
very large window	painter	$42.80	1.43	**$61.20** ea
Stain				
wood floor	painter	$42.80	.018	**$.77** sf
folding door	painter	$42.80	.614	**$26.30** ea
bypassing door	painter	$42.80	1.27	**$54.40** ea
interior door	painter	$42.80	.519	**$22.20** ea
French door	painter	$42.80	1.25	**$53.50** ea
panel door	painter	$42.80	1.08	**$46.20** ea
door jamb & casing	painter	$42.80	.017	**$.73** lf
wood entry door	painter	$42.80	1.13	**$48.40** ea
wood sliding patio door	painter	$42.80	.988	**$42.30** ea
garage door	painter	$42.80	.009	**$.39** sf
4' high wood fence (per side)	painter	$42.80	.078	**$3.34** lf
wood trim, simple design	painter	$42.80	.016	**$.68** lf
wood trim, very ornate design	painter	$42.80	.025	**$1.07** lf
wood paneling, simple pattern	painter	$42.80	.018	**$.77** sf
wood paneling, very ornate pattern	painter	$42.80	.043	**$1.84** sf
siding	painter	$42.80	.015	**$.64** sf
stair balustrade	painter	$42.80	.290	**$12.40** lf

. . . More ➢

Painting Labor Productivity *continued*

WORK DESCRIPTION	LABORER	COST PER HOUR	PRODUCTIVITY	UNIT PRICE
Varnish, one coat				
wood floor	painter	$42.80	.019	**$.81** sf
folding door	painter	$42.80	.632	**$27.00** ea
bypassing door	painter	$42.80	1.31	**$56.10** ea
interior door	painter	$42.80	.534	**$22.90** ea
French door	painter	$42.80	1.29	**$55.20** ea
panel door	painter	$42.80	1.11	**$47.50** ea
door jamb & casing	painter	$42.80	.017	**$.73** lf
wood entry door	painter	$42.80	1.17	**$50.10** ea
wood sliding patio door	painter	$42.80	1.02	**$43.70** ea
garage door	painter	$42.80	.009	**$.39** sf
4' high wood fence (per side)	painter	$42.80	.080	**$3.42** lf
wood trim, simple design	painter	$42.80	.017	**$.73** lf
wood trim, very ornate design	painter	$42.80	.026	**$1.11** lf
wood paneling, simple pattern	painter	$42.80	.019	**$.81** sf
wood paneling, very ornate pattern	painter	$42.80	.044	**$1.88** sf
siding	painter	$42.80	.015	**$.64** sf
stair balustrade	painter	$42.80	.298	**$12.80** lf
Varnish, two coats				
wood floor	painter	$42.80	.029	**$1.24** sf
folding door	painter	$42.80	.972	**$41.60** ea
bypassing door	painter	$42.80	2.01	**$86.00** ea
interior door	painter	$42.80	.822	**$35.20** ea
French door	painter	$42.80	1.98	**$84.70** ea
panel door	painter	$42.80	1.70	**$72.80** ea
door jamb & casing	painter	$42.80	.026	**$1.11** lf
wood entry door	painter	$26.00	1.80	**$77.00** ea
wood sliding patio door	painter	$42.80	1.56	**$66.80** ea
garage door	painter	$42.80	.014	**$.60** sf
4' high wood fence (per side)	painter	$42.80	.123	**$5.26** lf
wood trim, simple design	painter	$42.80	.026	**$1.11** lf
wood trim, very ornate design	painter	$42.80	.040	**$1.71** lf
wood paneling, simple pattern	painter	$42.80	.029	**$1.24** sf
wood paneling, very ornate pattern	painter	$42.80	.068	**$2.91** sf
siding	painter	$42.80	.023	**$.98** sf
stair balustrade	painter	$42.80	.459	**$19.60** lf
Varnish, three coats				
wood floor	painter	$42.80	.039	**$1.67** sf
folding door	painter	$42.80	1.32	**$56.50** ea
bypassing door	painter	$42.80	2.72	**$116.00** ea
interior door	painter	$42.80	1.11	**$47.50** ea
French door	painter	$42.80	2.68	**$115.00** ea
panel door	painter	$42.80	2.31	**$98.90** ea
door jamb & casing	painter	$42.80	.035	**$1.50** lf
wood entry door	painter	$42.80	2.43	**$104.00** ea
wood sliding patio door	painter	$42.80	2.12	**$90.70** ea
garage door	painter	$42.80	.019	**$.81** sf
4' high wood fence (per side)	painter	$42.80	.167	**$7.15** lf
wood trim, simple design	painter	$42.80	.035	**$1.50** lf
wood trim, very ornate design	painter	$42.80	.054	**$2.31** lf
wood paneling, simple pattern	painter	$42.80	.039	**$1.67** sf
wood paneling, very ornate pattern	painter	$42.80	.093	**$3.98** sf
siding	painter	$42.80	.032	**$1.37** sf
stair balustrade	painter	$42.80	.621	**$26.60** lf

NOTES:

end

27 Paneling

Item Description	Unit	Remove	Replace	Total
Minimum charge for paneling work *Replace* Materials......25.00 Labor..........30.10	ea	—	$55.10	$55.10
Minimum charge for frame-and-panel wall work *Replace* Materials......75.00 Labor.........144.00	ea	—	$219.00	$219.00
Hardboard paneling, economy grade *Replace* Materials........ .71 Labor...........1.19 *Remove* .... Labor............ .19 ► 1/8" thick.	sf	$.19	$1.90	$2.09
Hardboard paneling, standard grade *Replace* Materials........ .86 Labor...........1.19 *Remove* .... Labor............ .19 ► 1/4" thick, little or no texture.	sf	$.19	$2.05	$2.24
Hardboard paneling, high grade *Replace* Materials........1.30 Labor...........1.19 *Remove* .... Labor............ .19 ► 1/4" thick, heavy texture or special finish.	sf	$.19	$2.49	$2.68
Hardboard wall paneling, with simulated brick face *Replace* Materials........ .90 Labor...........1.19 *Remove* .... Labor............ .19 ► 1/4" thick.	sf	$.19	$2.09	$2.28
Hardboard wall paneling, with simulated stone face *Replace* Materials........ .97 Labor...........1.19 *Remove* .... Labor............ .19 ► 1/4" thick.	sf	$.19	$2.16	$2.35
Pegboard *Replace* Materials........ .67 Labor...........1.08 *Remove* .... Labor............ .19	sf	$.19	$1.75	$1.94
1/4" ash plywood paneling *Replace* Materials........2.98 Labor...........1.30 *Remove* .... Labor............ .22	sf	$.22	$4.28	$4.50
1/4" birch plywood paneling *Replace* Materials........1.49 Labor...........1.30 *Remove* .... Labor............ .22	sf	$.22	$2.79	$3.01
1/4" cherry plywood paneling *Replace* Materials........3.36 Labor...........1.30 *Remove* .... Labor............ .22	sf	$.22	$4.66	$4.88
1/4" hickory plywood paneling *Replace* Materials........3.16 Labor...........1.30 *Remove* .... Labor............ .22	sf	$.22	$4.46	$4.68
1/4" knotty pine plywood paneling *Replace* Materials........2.55 Labor...........1.30 *Remove* .... Labor............ .22	sf	$.22	$3.85	$4.07

◄ **MINIMUM**

◄ **HARDBOARD PANELING**
Prefinished. Installed with adhesive and nails. Includes 5% waste.

◄ **PEGBOARD**
Tempered. Includes 5% waste.

◄ **PLYWOOD PANELING**
Includes 5% waste. Unfinished with top grade veneer.

RELATED ITEMS

Cleaning........................64
Painting........................340
Siding........................455

	Item Description	Unit	Remove	Replace	Total
PLYWOOD PANELING *continued.* ►	**1/4" mahogany plywood paneling** *Replace* Materials........2.74 Labor............1.30 *Remove* .... Labor............ .22	sf	$.22	$4.04	$4.26
	1/4" white maple plywood paneling *Replace* Materials........2.22 Labor............1.30 *Remove* .... Labor............ .22	sf	$.22	$3.52	$3.74
	1/4" red or white oak plywood paneling *Replace* Materials........1.52 Labor............1.30 *Remove* .... Labor............ .22	sf	$.22	$2.82	$3.04
	1/4" quartersawn red or white oak plywood paneling *Replace* Materials........2.44 Labor............1.30 *Remove* .... Labor............ .22	sf	$.22	$3.74	$3.96
	1/4" walnut plywood paneling *Replace* Materials........4.34 Labor............1.30 *Remove* .... Labor............ .22	sf	$.22	$5.64	$5.86
	1/4" rough-sawn cedar plywood paneling *Replace* Materials........2.07 Labor............1.30 *Remove* .... Labor............ .22	sf	$.22	$3.37	$3.59
ADD FOR WALL MOLDING ► *Includes 6% waste. Add to plywood paneling prices above for moldings that form repeating squares on wall with radius corners. Add* ***11%*** *for slope-matched wall molding along stairways.*	**Add 44% for wall molding, standard grade** ► Simple horizontal pattern moldings.				
	Add 53% for wall molding, high grade ► Vertical or embossed pattern moldings.				
	Add 70% for wall molding, deluxe grade ► Simple hand-carved moldings.				
	Add 84% for wall molding, custom grade ► Ornate hand carved moldings.				
PLYWOOD PANELING WITH GROOVES ► *Prefinished. Includes 5% waste.*	**1/4" ash plywood paneling with grooves** *Replace* Materials........2.91 Labor............1.30 *Remove* .... Labor............ .22	sf	$.22	$4.21	$4.43
	1/4" birch plywood paneling with grooves *Replace* Materials........1.45 Labor............1.30 *Remove* .... Labor............ .22	sf	$.22	$2.75	$2.97
	1/4" cherry plywood paneling with grooves *Replace* Materials........3.28 Labor............1.30 *Remove* .... Labor............ .22	sf	$.22	$4.58	$4.80
	1/4" hickory plywood paneling with grooves *Replace* Materials........3.09 Labor............1.30 *Remove* .... Labor............ .22	sf	$.22	$4.39	$4.61
	1/4" knotty pine plywood paneling with grooves *Replace* Materials........2.49 Labor............1.30 *Remove* .... Labor............ .22	sf	$.22	$3.79	$4.01
	1/4" mahogany plywood paneling with grooves *Replace* Materials........2.68 Labor............1.30 *Remove* .... Labor............ .22	sf	$.22	$3.98	$4.20

Item Description	Unit	Remove	Replace	Total
1/4" white maple plywood paneling with grooves ***Replace*** Materials........2.17 Labor............1.30 ***Remove*** .... Labor............ .22	sf	$.22	$3.47	$3.69
1/4" red or white oak plywood paneling with grooves ***Replace*** Materials........1.49 Labor............1.30 ***Remove*** .... Labor............ .22	sf	$.22	$2.79	$3.01
1/4" quartersawn red or white oak plywood paneling with grooves ***Replace*** Materials........2.38 Labor............1.30 ***Remove*** .... Labor............ .22	sf	$.22	$3.68	$3.90
1/4" walnut plywood paneling with grooves ***Replace*** Materials........4.24 Labor............1.30 ***Remove*** .... Labor............ .22	sf	$.22	$5.54	$5.76
1/4" rough-sawn cedar plywood paneling with grooves ***Replace*** Materials........2.02 Labor............1.30 ***Remove*** .... Labor............ .22	sf	$.22	$3.32	$3.54
Pine board-on-board paneling ***Replace*** Materials........3.63 Labor............1.37 ***Remove*** .... Labor............ .30	sf	$.30	$5.00	$5.30
Pine board-and-batten paneling ***Replace*** Materials........3.55 Labor............1.52 ***Remove*** .... Labor............ .30	sf	$.30	$5.07	$5.37
Add 10% for chevron installation				
Add 18% for herringbone installation				
Pine tongue-&-groove paneling, simple pattern ***Replace*** Materials........3.76 Labor............1.70 ***Remove*** .... Labor............ .30 ► V or bull nose pattern at joints.	sf	$.30	$5.46	$5.76
Pine tongue-&-groove paneling, fancy pattern ***Replace*** Materials........4.02 Labor............1.70 ***Remove*** .... Labor............ .30 ► V or bull nose pattern at joints with beaded V, nose, or cove in field.	sf	$.30	$5.72	$6.02
Pine tongue-&-groove paneling, ornate pattern ***Replace*** Materials........4.69 Labor............1.70 ***Remove*** .... Labor............ .30 ► V or bull nose pattern at joints with double beaded V, noses, or coves in field.	sf	$.30	$6.39	$6.69
Cedar tongue-&-groove closet lining ***Replace*** Materials........2.14 Labor............1.70 ***Remove*** .... Labor............ .30	sf	$.30	$3.84	$4.14
Add 14% for paneling installed as wainscoting				
Pine frame-and-panel wall, standard grade ***Replace*** Materials......18.40 Labor...........26.20 ***Remove*** .... Labor............ .52 ► Simple crown and base if included, panels are 1/4" plywood with no onlays.	sf	$.52	$44.60	$45.12
Pine frame-and-panel wall, high grade ***Replace*** Materials......25.10 Labor...........31.40 ***Remove*** .... Labor............ .52 ► Simple crown and base if included, panels are solid wood, may be raised.	sf	$.52	$56.50	$57.02

RELATED ITEMS

Cleaning........................64
Painting........................340
Siding..........................455

▽ *board-on-board*

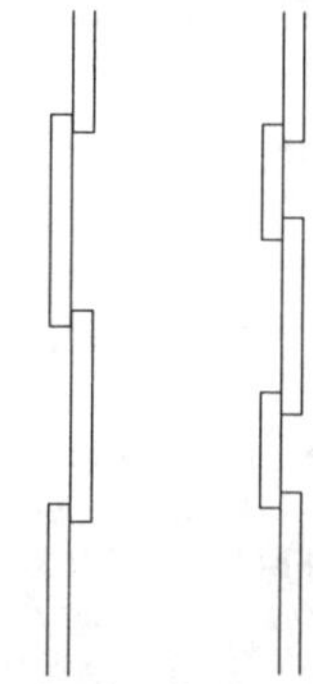

board-and-batten △

◄ **BOARD-ON-BOARD OR BOARD-AND-BATTEN PANELING**
Includes 5% waste. Prices for paneling are slightly higher than those for siding because there are more angles indoors.

◁ **add for angled installations**

◄ **TONGUE-&-GROOVE PANELING**
Includes 5% waste.

◁ **add for wainscot installation**

◄ **PINE FRAME-AND-PANEL WALL**
Includes 5% waste. Complete wall systems with furring strips and other backing, moldings between panels, crown and base.

	Item Description	Unit	Remove	Replace	Total
PINE FRAME-AND-PANEL WALL *continued* ►	**Pine frame-and-panel wall, deluxe grade**	sf	$.52	$67.50	$68.02
	Replace Materials......29.60 Labor..........37.90				
	Remove .... Labor............ .52				
	► Crown and base with vertical patterns if included, panels are solid wood, may be raised, and may have cathedral top. May have bolection molding around panels.				
	Pine frame-and-panel wall, custom grade	sf	$.52	$89.20	$89.72
	Replace Materials......44.10 Labor..........45.10				
	Remove .... Labor............ .52				
	► Crown and base with vertical patterns if included, panels are solid wood, may be raised, and may have cathedral top. Panels may be linenfold or wall may contain other components that are hand carved. May also include corbels and pilasters with capitals.				
OAK FRAME-AND-PANEL WALL ► *See pine frame-and-panel items above and on the previous page for explanation of grades. Includes 5% waste. Complete wall systems with furring strips and other backing, moldings between panels, crown and base.*	**Oak frame-and-panel wall, standard grade**	sf	$.52	$48.80	$49.32
	Replace Materials......22.60 Labor..........26.20				
	Remove .... Labor............ .52				
	Oak frame-and-panel wall, high grade	sf	$.52	$62.10	$62.62
	Replace Materials......30.70 Labor..........31.40				
	Remove .... Labor............ .52				
	Oak frame-and-panel wall, deluxe grade	sf	$.52	$74.20	$74.72
	Replace Materials......36.30 Labor..........37.90				
	Remove .... Labor............ .52				
	Oak frame-and-panel wall, custom grade	sf	$.52	$99.20	$99.72
	Replace Materials......54.10 Labor..........45.10				
	Remove .... Labor............ .52				
WALNUT FRAME-AND-PANEL WALL ► *See pine frame-and-panel items above and on the previous page for explanation of grades. Includes 5% waste. Complete wall systems with furring strips and other backing, moldings between panels, crown and base.*	**Walnut frame-and-panel wall, standard grade**	sf	$.52	$63.30	$63.82
	Replace Materials......37.10 Labor..........26.20				
	Remove .... Labor............ .52				
	Walnut frame-and-panel wall, high grade	sf	$.52	$81.90	$82.42
	Replace Materials......50.50 Labor..........31.40				
	Remove .... Labor............ .52				
	Walnut frame-and-panel wall, deluxe grade	sf	$.52	$97.60	$98.12
	Replace Materials......59.70 Labor..........37.90				
	Remove .... Labor............ .52				
	Walnut frame-and-panel wall, custom grade	sf	$.52	$134.10	$134.62
	Replace Materials......89.00 Labor..........45.10				
	Remove .... Labor............ .52				
ADD FOR OTHER WOOD SPECIES ► *Add to the costs of oak frame-and-panel walls for these wood species.*	**Add 12% for quartersawn oak frame-and-panel wall**				
	Add 17% for cherry frame-and-panel wall				
	Add 65% for teak frame-and-panel wall				
	Add 10% for mahogany frame-and-panel wall				
	Add 14% for hickory frame-and-panel wall				

NOTES: ____

end

TIME & MATERIAL CHARTS *(selected items)*

Paneling Materials

DESCRIPTION	MATERIAL PRICE	GROSS COVERAGE	WASTE	NET COVERAGE	UNIT PRICE
Hardboard paneling					
economy grade	$21.50 sheet	32	5%	30.4	**$.71** sf
high grade	$39.60 sheet	32	5%	30.4	**$1.30** sf
1/4" plywood paneling					
rough-sawn cedar	$63.00 sheet	32	5%	30.4	**$2.07** sf
ash	$90.60 sheet	32	5%	30.4	**$2.98** sf
birch	$45.20 sheet	32	5%	30.4	**$1.49** sf
cherry	$102.00 sheet	32	5%	30.4	**$3.36** sf
hickory	$96.00 sheet	32	5%	30.4	**$3.16** sf
knotty pine	$77.40 sheet	32	5%	30.4	**$2.55** sf
mahogany	$83.40 sheet	32	5%	30.4	**$2.74** sf
white maple	$67.60 sheet	32	5%	30.4	**$2.22** sf
red or white oak	$46.30 sheet	32	5%	30.4	**$1.52** sf
quartersawn red or white oak	$74.20 sheet	32	5%	30.4	**$2.44** sf
walnut	$132.00 sheet	32	5%	30.4	**$4.34** sf
1/4" plywood paneling with grooves					
rough-sawn cedar	$61.50 sheet	32	5%	30.4	**$2.02** sf
ash	$88.50 sheet	32	5%	30.4	**$2.91** sf
birch	$44.10 sheet	32	5%	30.4	**$1.45** sf
cherry	$99.60 sheet	32	5%	30.4	**$3.28** sf
hickory	$93.80 sheet	32	5%	30.4	**$3.09** sf
knotty pine	$75.60 sheet	32	5%	30.4	**$2.49** sf
mahogany	$81.50 sheet	32	5%	30.4	**$2.68** sf
white maple	$66.00 sheet	32	5%	30.4	**$2.17** sf
red or white oak	$45.20 sheet	32	5%	30.4	**$1.49** sf
quartersawn red or white oak	$72.50 sheet	32	5%	30.4	**$2.38** sf
walnut	$129.00 sheet	32	5%	30.4	**$4.24** sf
Pine board paneling					
board-on-board	$3.48 sf	1	4%	.96	**$3.63** sf
board-and-batten	$3.41 sf	1	4%	.96	**$3.55** sf
tongue-&-groove, simple pattern	$3.61 sf	1	4%	.96	**$3.76** sf
tongue-&-groove, ornate pattern	$4.50 sf	1	4%	.96	**$4.69** sf
Frame and panel wall					
pine, standard grade	$17.30 sf	1	6%	.94	**$18.40** sf
pine, custom grade	$41.50 sf	1	6%	.94	**$44.10** sf
oak, standard grade	$21.20 sf	1	6%	.94	**$22.60** sf
oak, custom grade	$50.90 sf	1	6%	.94	**$54.10** sf
walnut, standard grade	$34.90 sf	1	6%	.94	**$37.10** sf
walnut, custom grade	$83.70 sf	1	6%	.94	**$89.00** sf

Paneling Labor

LABORER	BASE WAGE	PAID LEAVE	TRUE WAGE	FICA	FUTA	WORKER'S COMP.	UNEMPLOY. INSUR.	HEALTH INSUR.	RETIRE (401K)	LIABILITY INSUR.	COST PER HOUR
Paneling installer	$23.50	1.83	$25.33	1.94	.20	4.94	2.20	2.69	.76	3.42	**$41.50**
Paneling installer's helper	$16.90	1.32	$18.22	1.39	.15	3.55	1.59	2.69	.55	2.46	**$30.60**
Demolition laborer	$13.90	1.08	$14.98	1.15	.12	4.79	1.30	2.69	.45	2.02	**$27.50**

Paid Leave is calculated based on two weeks paid vacation, one week sick leave, and seven paid holidays. Employer's matching portion of **FICA** is 7.65 percent. **FUTA** (Federal Unemployment) is .8 percent. **Worker's compensation** for the paneling trade was calculated using a national average of 19.50 percent. **Unemployment insurance** was calculated using a national average of 8.7 percent. **Health insurance** was calculated based on a projected national average for 2002 of $535 per employee (and family when applicable) per month. Employer pays 80 percent for a per month cost of $428 per employee. **Retirement** is based on a 401(k) retirement program with employer matching of 50 percent. Employee contributions to the 401(k) plan are an average of 6 percent of the true wage. **Liability insurance** is based on a national average of 13.2 percent.

Paneling Labor Productivity

WORK DESCRIPTION	LABORER	COST PER HOUR	PRODUCTIVITY	UNIT PRICE
Demolition				
remove hardboard paneling	demolition laborer	$27.50	.007	$.19 sf
remove pegboard	demolition laborer	$27.50	.007	$.19 sf
remove plywood paneling	demolition laborer	$27.50	.008	$.22 sf
remove board paneling	demolition laborer	$27.50	.011	$.30 sf
remove tongue-and-groove paneling	demolition laborer	$27.50	.011	$.30 sf
remove frame-and-panel wall	demolition laborer	$27.50	.019	$.52 sf
Paneling installation crew				
install paneling	paneling installer	$41.50		
install paneling	paneling installer's helper	$30.60		
install paneling	paneling crew	$36.10		
Minimum charge				
for paneling work	paneling crew	$36.10	.833	$30.10 ea
for frame-and-panel wall work	paneling crew	$36.10	4.00	$144.00 ea
Install paneling				
hardboard	paneling crew	$36.10	.033	$1.19 sf
pegboard	paneling crew	$36.10	.030	$1.08 sf
plywood	paneling crew	$36.10	.036	$1.30 sf
board on board	paneling crew	$36.10	.038	$1.37 sf
board and batten	paneling crew	$36.10	.042	$1.52 sf
tongue-&-groove	paneling crew	$36.10	.047	$1.70 sf
Install frame-and-panel wall				
standard grade	paneling crew	$36.10	.725	$26.20 sf
high grade	paneling crew	$36.10	.870	$31.40 sf
deluxe grade	paneling crew	$36.10	1.05	$37.90 sf
custom grade	paneling crew	$36.10	1.25	$45.10 sf

NOTES:

end

28 Plaster & Stucco

Item Description	Unit	Remove	Replace	Total
Minimum charge to repair plaster wall or ceiling *Replace* Materials......50.00 Labor..........84.80	ea	—	$134.80	$134.80
Repair hair-line plaster crack *Replace* Materials........ .29 Labor............2.59	lf	—	$2.88	$2.88
Repair plaster crack less than 1″ wide *Replace* Materials........ .44 Labor............3.22	lf	—	$3.66	$3.66
Patch small plaster hole less than 2″ square *Replace* Materials........1.32 Labor..........33.40	ea	—	$34.72	$34.72
Patch plaster hole 2″ to 10″ square *Replace* Materials........5.93 Labor...........42.20	ea	—	$48.13	$48.13
Patch plaster hole 10″ to 20″ square *Replace* Materials......10.30 Labor...........52.50	ea	—	$62.80	$62.80
Patch plaster section *Replace* Materials........2.18 Labor............6.21 ► For plaster repair of an area no greater than 20 sf in size.	sf	—	$8.39	$8.39
Repair plaster wall outside corner damage *Replace* Materials........2.80 Labor...........11.50	lf	—	$14.30	$14.30
Repair plaster wall inside corner damage *Replace* Materials........2.29 Labor............8.12	lf	—	$10.41	$10.41
Repair section of plaster pilaster or column *Replace* Materials.......19.00 Labor..........36.20	lf	—	$55.20	$55.20
Repair crack in plaster molding less than 1/4″ wide *Replace* Materials........ .29 Labor............2.83	lf	—	$3.12	$3.12
Take flexible mold of plaster molding or decorative plaster *Replace* Materials......37.50 Labor..........23.40	ea	—	$60.90	$60.90
Create running mold for plaster molding *Replace* Materials......49.50 Labor.........159.00	ea	—	$208.50	$208.50
Repair section of plaster molding or decorative plaster *Replace* Materials........5.80 Labor..........50.90 ► Repair section no greater than 3 lf.	ea	—	$56.70	$56.70
Minimum charge to repair plaster molding or decorative plaster *Replace* Materials......24.40 Labor.........142.00	ea	—	$166.40	$166.40
Two coat acoustical plaster on 3/8″ gypsum lath on wall *Replace* Materials........1.16 Labor............2.03 *Remove* .... Labor............ .63	sf	$.63	$3.19	$3.82
Two coat acoustical plaster on 3/8″ gypsum lath on ceiling *Replace* Materials........1.16 Labor............2.43 *Remove* .... Labor............ .63	sf	$.63	$3.59	$4.22

◄ **REPAIR PLASTER**

FLEXIBLE MOLDS

Cracks to decorative plaster that are larger than a hairline are often repaired using flexible molds.

Flexible molds are made by constructing a wood box to fit around the area where the mold will be taken.

A release agent is sprayed on the box and the original plaster to help the mold release when dried.

Cold-cure silicone is usually used to make the mold, although many professionals use hot-melt mold-making compounds.

◄ **REPAIR DECORATIVE PLASTER**
Repairs to enrichments, moldings, ceiling rose, ceiling medallion, and so on.

RELATED ITEMS

Acoustic Ceiling.............15
Drywall.......................133
Painting......................333
Suspended Ceilings.....483

◄ **ACOUSTICAL PLASTER**
Includes lathing and plastering with trowel finish.

	Item Description	Unit	Remove	Replace	Total
ACOUSTICAL PLASTER *continued*	**Three coat acoustical plaster on painted metal lath on wall** *Replace* Materials...... 1.01 Labor............2.27 *Remove* .... Labor............. .66	sf	$.66	$3.28	$3.94
	Three coat acoustical plaster on painted metal lath on ceiling *Replace* Materials...... 1.01 Labor............2.71 *Remove* .... Labor............. .66	sf	$.66	$3.72	$4.38
GYPSUM PLASTER *Includes lathing and plastering with trowel finish.*	**Two coat gypsum plaster on 3/8" gypsum lath on wall** *Replace* Materials...... 1.01 Labor............2.07 *Remove* .... Labor............. .63	sf	$.63	$3.08	$3.71
	Two coat gypsum plaster on 3/8" gypsum lath on ceiling *Replace* Materials...... 1.01 Labor............2.47 *Remove* .... Labor............. .63	sf	$.63	$3.48	$4.11
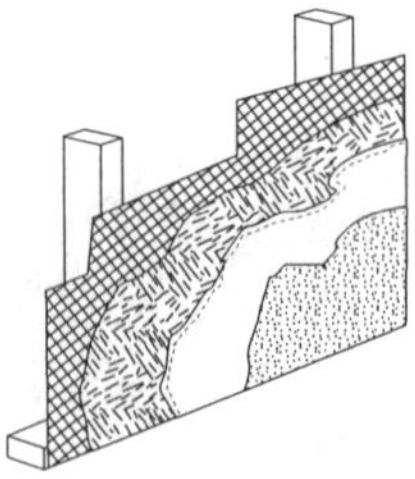	**Three coat gypsum plaster on painted metal lath on wall** *Replace* Materials........ .86 Labor............2.31 *Remove* .... Labor............. .66	sf	$.66	$3.17	$3.83
	Three coat gypsum plaster on painted metal lath on ceiling *Replace* Materials........ .86 Labor............2.75 *Remove* .... Labor............. .66	sf	$.66	$3.61	$4.27
PERLITE OR VERMICULITE PLASTER *Includes lathing and plastering with trowel finish*	**Two coat perlite or vermiculite plaster on 3/8" gypsum lath on wall** *Replace* Materials...... 1.06 Labor............2.35 *Remove* .... Labor............. .63	sf	$.63	$3.41	$4.04
	Two coat perlite or vermiculite plaster on 3/8" gypsum lath on ceiling *Replace* Materials...... 1.06 Labor............2.83 *Remove* .... Labor............. .63	sf	$.63	$3.89	$4.52
	Three coat perlite or vermiculite plaster on painted metal lath on wall *Replace* Materials........1.72 Labor............2.75 *Remove* .... Labor............. .66	sf	$.66	$4.47	$5.13
	Three coat perlite or vermiculite plaster on painted metal lath on ceiling *Replace* Materials........1.72 Labor............3.30 *Remove* .... Labor............. .66	sf	$.66	$5.02	$5.68
KEENE'S CEMENT PLASTER *Includes lathing and plastering with trowel finish.*	**Two coat Keene's cement plaster on 3/8" gypsum lath on wall** *Replace* Materials........1.26 Labor............2.99 *Remove* .... Labor............. .63	sf	$.63	$4.25	$4.88
	Two coat Keene's cement plaster on 3/8" gypsum lath on ceiling *Replace* Materials........1.26 Labor............3.58 *Remove* .... Labor............. .63	sf	$.63	$4.84	$5.47
	Three coat Keene's cement plaster on painted metal lath on wall *Replace* Materials........1.11 Labor............3.26 *Remove* .... Labor............. .66	sf	$.66	$4.37	$5.03
	Three coat Keene's cement plaster on painted metal lath on ceiling *Replace* Materials........1.11 Labor............3.70 *Remove* .... Labor............. .66	sf	$.66	$4.81	$5.47
THIN-COAT PLASTER	**Thin-coat plaster on 3/8" thick gypsum lath** *Replace* Materials........ .37 Labor............1.75 *Remove* .... Labor............. .58	sf	$.58	$2.12	$2.70
	Thin-coat plaster on 1/2" thick gypsum lath *Replace* Materials........ .26 Labor............1.75 *Remove* .... Labor............. .58	sf	$.58	$2.01	$2.59

Item Description	Unit	Remove	Replace	Total
Add 28% for curved wall				
Add 60% for plaster installed on old-style wood lath				
Square plaster pilaster, plain ***Replace*** Materials........3.27 Labor............7.52 ***Remove*** .... Labor............1.18	lf	$1.18	$10.79	$11.97
Square plaster pilaster, rusticated ***Replace*** Materials........3.29 Labor............9.03 ***Remove*** .... Labor............1.18	lf	$1.18	$12.32	$13.50
Square plaster column, plain ***Replace*** Materials........6.54 Labor...........13.70 ***Remove*** .... Labor............2.12	lf	$2.12	$20.24	$22.36
Square plaster column, rusticated ***Replace*** Materials........6.57 Labor...........17.30 ***Remove*** .... Labor............2.12	lf	$2.12	$23.87	$25.99
Add 30% for round pilaster or column				
Cast-in-place plaster molding to 3" wide ***Replace*** Materials........5.87 Labor...........62.10	lf	—	$67.97	$67.97
Cast-in-place plaster molding 3" to 6" wide ***Replace*** Materials.......11.70 Labor...........67.30	lf	—	$79.00	$79.00
Cast-in-place plaster molding 6" to 14" wide ***Replace*** Materials......21.80 Labor...........75.20	lf	—	$97.00	$97.00
Add for inside corner in cast-in-place plaster molding ***Replace*** Materials........5.93 Labor.........129.00	ea	—	$134.93	$134.93
Add for outside corner in cast-in-place plaster molding ***Replace*** Materials........1.58 Labor...........61.30	ea	—	$62.88	$62.88
Production plaster molding to 3" wide ***Replace*** Materials......24.40 Labor...........10.47	lf	—	$34.87	$34.87
Production plaster molding 3" to 6" wide ***Replace*** Materials......36.30 Labor...........10.70	lf	—	$47.00	$47.00
Production plaster molding to 6" to 14" wide ***Replace*** Materials......58.40 Labor...........11.40	lf	—	$69.80	$69.80
Add for inside corner in production plaster molding ***Replace*** Materials........1.29 Labor...........13.30	ea	—	$14.59	$14.59
Add for outside corner in production plaster molding ***Replace*** Materials........1.48 Labor...........13.30	ea	—	$14.78	$14.78
Plaster enrichment, straight patterns ***Replace*** Materials......22.30 Labor...........10.50 ► All straight work like scotia, coves, rounds, etc.	lf	—	$32.80	$32.80
Plaster enrichment, ornate patterns ***Replace*** Materials......33.60 Labor...........10.70 ► Includes fretwork, meander, fluting, Greek key, bead and reel, and simple egg and dart designs.	lf	—	$44.30	$44.30

◄ **ADDITIONAL PLASTER COSTS**

◄ **PLASTER PILASTER OR COLUMN**
Additional costs for plaster pilasters and columns.

UNITS OF MEASURE

In some areas, plaster and stucco are estimated by the square yard.

However, computer estimating systems usually calculate plaster and stucco by the square foot. The square foot method is used in this section.

◄ **CAST-IN-PLACE PLASTER MOLD**
For straight-pattern moldings cast in place on walls and/or ceilings using a running mold. Inside corners require a great deal of handwork by a skilled specialist. Outside corners are less complex.

◄ **PRODUCTION PLASTER MOLD**
For moldings available from specialized suppliers in a wide variety of patterns.

◄ **PLASTER ENRICHMENT**
Enrichments are placed on walls or ceilings to further accent friezes, cornices, ceiling medallions and so forth.

PLASTER ENRICHMENT *continued*

Item Description	Unit	Remove	Replace	Total
Plaster enrichment, very ornate patterns ***Replace*** Materials......48.40 Labor...........11.40 ► Very elaborate designs including figures, harps, Acanthus, swags, festoons, leaf and dart, Anthemion patterns and so forth.	lf	—	$59.80	$59.80

PLASTER FRIEZE *Usually flat with ornate patterns, plaster friezes can be up to 14" wide.*

Item Description	Unit	Remove	Replace	Total
Plaster frieze, straight patterns ***Replace*** Materials......37.10 Labor...........10.50 ► All straight work like scotia, coves, rounds, etc.	lf	—	$47.60	$47.60
Plaster frieze, ornate patterns ***Replace*** Materials......55.90 Labor...........10.70 ► Includes fretwork, meander, fluting, Greek key, bead and reel, and simple egg and dart style designs.	lf	—	$66.60	$66.60
Plaster frieze, very ornate patterns ***Replace*** Materials......80.60 Labor...........11.40 ► Very elaborate designs including figures, harps, Acanthus, swags, festoons, leaf and dart, Anthemion patterns and so forth.	lf	—	$92.00	$92.00

PLASTER ARCHITRAVE *Most complex plaster architraves are production units built by a specialty supplier. See Finish Carpentry, page 206 for more information about architraves.*

Item Description	Unit	Remove	Replace	Total
Plaster architrave, plain ***Replace*** Materials........2.61 Labor............6.13 ► Square raised design. Usually raised 1" to 2" and about 4" to 6" wide.	lf	—	$8.74	$8.74
Plaster architrave, rusticated ***Replace*** Materials........2.80 Labor............7.36 ► Same as above with rusticated "stones" shaped into the raised section. Rusticated architrave may also be much wider and show simulated Jack arch "stone" pattern.	lf	—	$10.16	$10.16
Plaster architrave, straight patterns ***Replace*** Materials........3.20 Labor...........18.90 ► Molded straight work like scotia, coves, rounds, etc.	lf	—	$22.10	$22.10
Plaster architrave, ornate patterns ***Replace*** Materials........3.30 Labor...........27.80 ► Includes fretwork, fluting, Greek key, bead & reel, egg and dart, Acanthus, urns, pediments, etc. All or most of the elaborate work will appear on the header.	lf	—	$31.10	$31.10

PLASTER CEILING MEDALLION *Usually round or oval in shape designed for the center of the ceiling.*

Item Description	Unit	Remove	Replace	Total
Plaster ceiling medallion, simple pattern ***Replace*** Materials.....130.00 Labor..........36.20 ► Round or oval with some simple raised patterns.	ea	—	$166.20	$166.20
Plaster ceiling medallion, ornate pattern ***Replace*** Materials.....249.00 Labor...........37.90 ► Round or oval with elaborate patterns, like scalloped edges, some simple leaf patterns, ridges, fluting, fretwork, and so forth.	ea	—	$286.90	$286.90
Plaster ceiling medallion, very ornate pattern ***Replace*** Materials....454.00 Labor..........39.80 ► Very elaborate designs including figures, harps, Acanthus, swags, festoons, leaf and dart, Anthemion patterns and so forth.	ea	—	$493.80	$493.80

PLASTER CEILING ROSE *Very ornate ceiling medallion common to Victorian homes.*

Item Description	Unit	Remove	Replace	Total
Plaster small ceiling rose ***Replace*** Materials.....221.00 Labor..........36.20	ea	—	$257.20	$257.20
Plaster average size ceiling rose ***Replace*** Materials....338.00 Labor...........37.90	ea	—	$375.90	$375.90
Plaster large ceiling rose ***Replace*** Materials....641.00 Labor..........39.80	ea	—	$680.80	$680.80

Item Description	Unit	Remove	Replace	Total
Three coat Portland cement stucco, sand float finish *Replace* Materials .... .90 Labor ....3.82 *Remove* .... Labor............. .74	sf	$.74	$4.72	$5.46
Three coat Portland cement stucco, sand float finish, on masonry *Replace* Materials .... .34 Labor ....2.99 *Remove* .... Labor............. .74	sf	$.74	$3.33	$4.07
Three coat Portland cement stucco, trowel float finish *Replace* Materials .... .91 Labor ....5.65 *Remove* .... Labor............. .74	sf	$.74	$6.56	$7.30
Three coat Portland cement stucco, trowel float finish, on masonry *Replace* Materials .... .36 Labor ....4.82 *Remove* .... Labor............. .74	sf	$.74	$5.18	$5.92
Add 26% for stucco application on soffits				
Add 10% for colors				
Add 19% for white cement				
Add 32% for pebble dash (rough cast) stucco finish ► Colorful aggregate that is "thrown" into the stucco.				
Add 88% for vermiculated stucco finish ► Snake-like pattern found on some historical structures, especially around entries.				
Patch single "stone" section in stucco rustication *Replace* Materials........4.58 Labor 30.60	ea	—	$35.18	$35.18
Add for stucco quoin *Replace* Materials........7.12 Labor...........24.90	ea	—	$32.02	$32.02
Add for stucco key *Replace* Materials.......11.00 Labor 43.00	ea	—	$54.00	$54.00
Add for stucco raised trim *Replace* Materials........2.78 Labor ....5.93 ► For raised trim around doors see architraves on page 357.	lf	—	$8.71	$8.71
Add for stucco raised curved trim *Replace* Materials........3.22 Labor ....9.95 ► Raised, curved trim over doors, windows, and so forth.	lf	—	$13.17	$13.17
Add for stucco color change *Replace* Materials .... .18 Labor ....2.15 ► Use when stucco changes colors on a wall. For example, each layer of raised trim may be of a different color.	ea	—	$2.33	$2.33
Synthetic stucco over 1/2" cement board *Replace* Materials .... .84 Labor ....2.95 *Remove* .... Labor............. .74	sf	$.74	$3.79	$4.53
Synthetic stucco over 1" insulating foam board *Replace* Materials .... .69 Labor ....2.95 *Remove* .... Labor............. .74	sf	$.74	$3.64	$4.38
Synthetic stucco over 2" insulating foam board *Replace* Materials .... .73 Labor ....2.95 *Remove* .... Labor............. .74	sf	$.74	$3.68	$4.42

◄ **STUCCO**
Includes felt or building paper, metal lath, and control joint and corner metal.

◄ **ADDITIONAL STUCCO COSTS**

RELATED ITEMS

Acoustic Ceiling.............15
Drywall........................133
Finish Carpentry..........199
architrave.....................206
Masonry.......................287
stone architrave..............310
cut stone trim................314
Painting.......................333
Suspended Ceilings.....483

◄ **SYNTHETIC STUCCO**
Includes cement board or polystyrene foam insulation board, adhesive primer, color coat stucco, and corner mesh.

	Item Description	Unit	Remove	Replace	Total
Additional synthetic stucco costs ▶	**Add for synthetic stucco quoin** *Replace* Materials........4.02 Labor...........37.20	ea	—	$41.22	$41.22
	Add for synthetic stucco key *Replace* Materials........6.21 Labor..........64.10	ea	—	$70.31	$70.31
	Add for synthetic stucco raised trim *Replace* Materials........1.57 Labor............8.88 ▶ For raised trim around doors see architraves on facing page.	lf	—	$10.45	$10.45
	Add for synthetic stucco raised curved trim *Replace* Materials........1.82 Labor...........14.80 ▶ Raised, curved trim over doors, windows, and so forth.	lf	—	$16.62	$16.62
	Add for synthetic stucco color change *Replace* Materials........ .10 Labor............3.22 ▶ Use when stucco changes colors on a wall. For example, each layer of raised trim may be of a different color.	lf	—	$3.32	$3.32
Stucco repair ▶ For repair of standard or synthetic stucco.	**Minimum charge to repair stucco** *Replace* Materials......51.00 Labor..........86.40	ea	—	$137.40	$137.40
	Repair hair-line stucco crack *Replace* Materials........ .30 Labor............2.63	lf	—	$2.93	$2.93
	Repair stucco crack less than 1" wide *Replace* Materials........ .45 Labor............3.30	lf	—	$3.75	$3.75
	Patch small stucco hole less than 2" square *Replace* Materials........1.35 Labor..........34.00	ea	—	$35.35	$35.35
	Patch stucco hole 2" to 10" square *Replace* Materials........6.06 Labor..........43.40	ea	—	$49.46	$49.46
	Patch stucco hole 10" to 20" square *Replace* Materials......10.50 Labor...........52.90	ea	—	$63.40	$63.40
	Patch stucco section *Replace* Materials........2.23 Labor............6.33 ▶ For stucco repair of an area no greater than 20 sf in size.	sf	—	$8.56	$8.56
	Repair stucco wall outside corner damage per lf of damage *Replace* Materials........2.86 Labor...........11.80	lf	—	$14.66	$14.66
	Repair stucco wall inside corner damage per lf of damage *Replace* Materials........2.34 Labor............8.28	lf	—	$10.62	$10.62
Stucco pilaster or column ▶ Additional costs for stucco pilasters and columns. For use with standard or synthetic stucco.	**Square stucco pilaster, plain** *Replace* Materials........3.40 Labor............7.64 *Remove* .... Labor............1.32	lf	$1.32	$11.04	$12.36
	Square stucco pilaster, rusticated *Replace* Materials........3.42 Labor............9.15 *Remove* .... Labor............1.32	lf	$1.32	$12.57	$13.89
	Square stucco column, plain *Replace* Materials........6.79 Labor...........13.90 *Remove* .... Labor............2.28	lf	$2.28	$20.69	$22.97

Item Description	Unit	Remove	Replace	Total
Square stucco column, rusticated *Replace* Materials........6.83 Labor...........17.60 *Remove* .... Labor............2.28	lf	$2.28	$24.43	$26.71
Add 30% for round stucco pilaster or column				
Repair section of stucco pilaster or column *Replace* Materials......20.00 Labor..........36.90 ► Repair section by hand or by pouring into mold then patching into architrave.	ea	—	$56.90	$56.90
Minimum charge to repair stucco pilaster or column *Replace* Materials......34.00 Labor..........40.20	ea	—	$74.20	$74.20
Stucco architrave, plain *Replace* Materials........2.72 Labor............6.21 ► Square raised design. Usually raised 1" to 2" and about 4" to 6" wide.	lf	—	$8.93	$8.93
Stucco architrave, rusticated *Replace* Materials........2.74 Labor............7.48 ► Same as above with rusticated "stones" shaped into the raised section. Rusticated architrave may also be much wider and show simulated Jack arch "stone" pattern.	lf	—	$10.22	$10.22
Stucco architrave, straight patterns *Replace* Materials........2.92 Labor...........19.20 ► Molded straight work like scotia, coves, rounds, etc.	lf	—	$22.12	$22.12
Stucco architrave, ornate patterns *Replace* Materials........3.34 Labor..........28.20 ► Includes fretwork, fluting, Greek key, bead & reel, egg and dart, Acanthus, urns, pediments, etc. All or most of the elaborate work will appear on the header.	lf	—	$31.54	$31.54
Take flexible mold of existing stucco architrave *Replace* Materials......37.50 Labor..........23.70	ea	—	$61.20	$61.20
Create mold for stucco architrave *Replace* Materials......49.50 Labor.........159.00	ea	—	$208.50	$208.50
Repair section of stucco architrave *Replace* Materials........6.07 Labor..........53.70 ► Repair section by hand or by pouring into mold then patching into architrave.	ea	—	$59.77	$59.77
Minimum charge to repair stucco architrave *Replace* Materials......24.40 Labor.........147.00	ea	—	$171.40	$171.40

◄ **STUCCO ARCHITRAVE**
Most complex stucco architraves are production units built by a specialty supplier.

RELATED ITEMS

TIME & MATERIAL CHARTS *(selected items)*

Plaster & Stucco Materials

DESCRIPTION	MATERIAL PRICE		GROSS COVERAGE	WASTE	NET COVERAGE	UNIT PRICE
Plaster and stucco materials						
gauging plaster	$20.90	*100 lb. bag*	1	21%	.79	**$26.50** *ea*
gypsum plaster	$16.40	*80 lb. bag*	1	21%	.79	**$20.80** *ea*
thin-coat plaster	$11.40	*50 lb. bag*	1	21%	.79	**$14.40** *ea*
Keene's cement	$23.90	*100 lb. bag*	1	21%	.79	**$30.30** *ea*
perlite or vermiculite plaster	$16.00	*100 lb. bag*	1	21%	.79	**$20.30** *ea*
3/8" perforated gypsum lath	$15.90	*sheet*	32	4%	30.72	**$.52** *sf*
1/2" perforated gypsum lath	$16.80	*sheet*	32	4%	30.72	**$.55** *sf*
painted metal lath	$.26	*sf*	1	4%	.96	**$.27** *sf*
painted stucco mesh	$.40	*sf*	1	4%	.96	**$.42** *sf*

Plaster & Stucco Labor

Laborer	Base Wage	Paid Leave	True Wage	FICA	FUTA	Worker's Comp.	Unemploy. Insur.	Health Insur.	Retire (401k)	Liability Insur.	Cost per Hour
Plasterer	$22.90	1.79	$24.69	1.89	.20	7.10	2.15	2.69	.74	3.33	$42.80
Plasterer's helper	$19.40	1.51	$20.91	1.60	.17	6.01	1.82	2.69	.63	2.82	$36.70
Demolition laborer	$13.90	1.08	$14.98	1.15	.12	4.79	1.30	2.69	.45	2.02	$27.50

Paid Leave is calculated based on two weeks paid vacation, one week sick leave, and seven paid holidays. Employer's matching portion of **FICA** is 7.65 percent. **FUTA** (Federal Unemployment) is .8 percent. **Worker's compensation** for the plaster and stucco trade was calculated using a national average of 28.74 percent. **Unemployment insurance** was calculated using a national average of 8.7 percent. **Health insurance** was calculated based on a projected national average for 2002 of $535 per employee (and family when applicable) per month. Employer pays 80 percent for a per month cost of $428 per employee. **Retirement** is based on a 401(k) retirement program with employer matching of 50 percent. Employee contributions to the 401(k) plan are an average of 6 percent of the true wage. **Liability insurance** is based on a national average of 13.2 percent.

Plaster & Stucco Labor Productivity

Work Description	Laborer	Cost per Hour	Productivity	Unit Price
Demolition				
remove plaster on gypsum lath	demolition laborer	$27.50	.023	**$.63** sf
remove plaster on metal lath	demolition laborer	$27.50	.024	**$.66** sf
remove thin-coat plaster on gypsum	demolition laborer	$27.50	.021	**$.58** sf
remove plaster pilaster	demolition laborer	$27.50	.043	**$1.18** lf
remove plaster column	demolition laborer	$27.50	.077	**$2.12** lf
remove stucco	demolition laborer	$27.50	.027	**$.74** sf
remove synthetic stucco on cement board	demolition laborer	$27.50	.027	**$.74** sf
remove stucco pilaster	demolition laborer	$27.50	.048	**$1.32** lf
remove stucco column	demolition laborer	$27.50	.083	**$2.28** lf
Plaster installation crew				
install plaster	plasterer	$42.80		
install plaster	plasterer's helper	$36.70		
install plaster	**plastering crew**	$39.80		
Install acoustical plaster				
two coat on 3/8" gypsum lath on wall	plastering crew	$39.80	.051	**$2.03** sf
two coat on 3/8" gypsum lath on ceiling	plastering crew	$39.80	.061	**$2.43** sf
three coat on painted metal lath on wall	plastering crew	$39.80	.057	**$2.27** sf
three coat on painted metal lath on ceiling	plastering crew	$39.80	.068	**$2.71** sf
Install gypsum plaster				
two coat on 3/8" gypsum lath on wall	plastering crew	$39.80	.052	**$2.07** sf
two coat on 3/8" gypsum lath on ceiling	plastering crew	$39.80	.062	**$2.47** sf
three coat on painted metal lath on wall	plastering crew	$39.80	.058	**$2.31** sf
three coat on painted metal lath on ceiling	plastering crew	$39.80	.069	**$2.75** sf
Install perlite or vermiculite plaster				
two coat on 3/8" gypsum lath on wall	plastering crew	$39.80	.059	**$2.35** sf
two coat on 3/8" gypsum lath on ceiling	plastering crew	$39.80	.071	**$2.83** sf
three coat on painted metal lath on wall	plastering crew	$39.80	.069	**$2.75** sf
three coat on painted metal lath on ceiling	plastering crew	$39.80	.083	**$3.30** sf
Install Keene's cement plaster				
two coat on 3/8" gypsum lath on wall	plastering crew	$39.80	.075	**$2.99** sf
two coat on 3/8" gypsum lath on ceiling	plastering crew	$39.80	.090	**$3.58** sf
three coat on painted metal lath on wall	plastering crew	$39.80	.082	**$3.26** sf
three coat on painted metal lath on ceiling	plastering crew	$39.80	.093	**$3.70** sf
Install thin-coat plaster				
on 3/8" thick gypsum lath	plastering crew	$39.80	.044	**$1.75** sf
on 1/2" thick gypsum lath	plastering crew	$39.80	.044	**$1.75** sf
Install three-coat Portland cement stucco				
sand float finish	plastering crew	$39.80	.096	**$3.82** sf
sand float finish, on masonry	plastering crew	$39.80	.075	**$2.99** sf
trowel float finish	plastering crew	$39.80	.142	**$5.65** sf
trowel float finish, on masonry	plastering crew	$39.80	.121	**$4.82** sf
Install synthetic stucco				
all applications	plastering crew	$39.80	.074	**$2.95** sf

29 Plumbing

Item Description	Unit	Remove	Replace	Total	
Minimum charge for plumbing work *Replace* Materials......40.00 Labor...........59.50	ea	—	$99.50	$99.50	◀ **MINIMUM**
1/2" diameter black steel supply pipe *Replace* Materials........2.15 Labor............5.68	lf	—	$7.83	$7.83	◀ **BLACK STEEL PIPE** *Field threaded with fitting or coupling every 8.5 lf and hanger every 10 lf.*
3/4" diameter black steel supply pipe *Replace* Materials........2.31 Labor............6.08	lf	—	$8.39	$8.39	
1" diameter black steel supply pipe *Replace* Materials........3.08 Labor............7.06	lf	—	$10.14	$10.14	
2" diameter black steel supply pipe *Replace* Materials........5.97 Labor...........10.30	lf	—	$16.27	$16.27	
Replace section of black steel supply pipe *Replace* Materials......25.40 Labor...........45.60 ► Includes cut-out in typical drywall wall, replacement section and couplings. Does not include wall repair (see *Drywall* page 136)	ea	—	$71.00	$71.00	
1/2" diameter brass water supply pipe *Replace* Materials........6.39 Labor............7.69	lf	—	$14.08	$14.08	◀ **BRASS WATER SUPPLY PIPE** *Field threaded with fitting or coupling every 8.5 lf and hanger every 10 lf.*
3/4" diameter brass water supply pipe *Replace* Materials........8.47 Labor............8.05	lf	—	$16.52	$16.52	
1" diameter brass water supply pipe *Replace* Materials.......11.20 Labor............8.58	lf	—	$19.78	$19.78	
2" diameter brass water supply pipe *Replace* Materials......28.00 Labor............9.39	lf	—	$37.39	$37.39	
Replace section of brass water supply pipe *Replace* Materials......51.60 Labor...........62.10 ► Includes cut-out in typical drywall wall, replacement section and couplings. Does not include wall repair.	ea	—	$113.70	$113.70	◁ **replace section**
1/2" diameter type K copper water supply pipe *Replace* Materials........2.21 Labor............4.65	lf	—	$6.86	$6.86	◀ **COPPER WATER SUPPLY PIPE TYPE K** *With sweated fitting or coupling every 8.5 lf and hanger every 10 lf.*
3/4" diameter type K copper water supply pipe *Replace* Materials........2.27 Labor............4.87	lf	—	$7.14	$7.14	
1" diameter type K copper water supply pipe *Replace* Materials........4.24 Labor............5.45	lf	—	$9.69	$9.69	
2" diameter type K copper water supply pipe *Replace* Materials........9.96 Labor............9.03	lf	—	$18.99	$18.99	
1/2" diameter type L copper water supply pipe *Replace* Materials........1.92 Labor............4.65	lf	—	$6.57	$6.57	◀ **COPPER WATER SUPPLY PIPE TYPE L** *With sweated fitting or coupling every 8.5 lf and hanger every 10 lf.*
3/4" diameter type L copper water supply pipe *Replace* Materials........2.08 Labor............4.87	lf	—	$6.95	$6.95	

RELATED ITEMS

Bathroom Hardware......41
Cleaning........................64

	Item Description	Unit	Remove	Replace	Total
COPPER WATER SUPPLY PIPE TYPE L *continued* ▶	**1" diameter type L copper water supply pipe** *Replace* Materials........3.66 Labor............5.45	lf	—	$9.11	$9.11
	2" diameter type L copper water supply pipe *Replace* Materials........9.00 Labor............9.03	lf	—	$18.03	$18.03
COPPER WATER SUPPLY PIPE TYPE M ▶ *With sweated fitting or coupling every 8.5 lf and hanger every 10 lf.*	**1/2" diameter type M copper water supply pipe** *Replace* Materials........1.58 Labor............4.65	lf	—	$6.23	$6.23
	3/4" diameter type M copper water supply pipe *Replace* Materials........2.08 Labor............4.87	lf	—	$6.95	$6.95
	1" diameter type M copper water supply pipe *Replace* Materials........2.88 Labor............5.45	lf	—	$8.33	$8.33
replace section ▷	**Replace section of copper water supply pipe** *Replace* Materials......18.20 Labor..........36.90 ▶ Includes cut-out in typical drywall wall, replacement section and couplings. Does not include wall repair (see *Drywall* page 136).	ea	—	$55.10	$55.10
GALVANIZED STEEL WATER SUPPLY PIPE ▶ *Field threaded with fitting or coupling every 8.5 lf and hanger every 10 lf.*	**1/2" diameter galvanized steel water supply pipe** *Replace* Materials........2.60 Labor............5.77	lf	—	$8.37	$8.37
	3/4" diameter galvanized steel water supply pipe *Replace* Materials........2.82 Labor............6.08	lf	—	$8.90	$8.90
	1" diameter galvanized steel water supply pipe *Replace* Materials........4.04 Labor............6.93	lf	—	$10.97	$10.97
	2" diameter galvanized steel water supply pipe *Replace* Materials........7.42 Labor..........10.30	lf	—	$17.72	$17.72
replace section ▷	**Replace section of galvanized steel water supply pipe** *Replace* Materials......31.20 Labor..........46.50 ▶ Includes cut-out in typical drywall wall, replacement section and couplings. Does not include wall repair (see *Drywall* page 136).	ea	—	$77.70	$77.70
CPVC WATER SUPPLY PIPE ▶ *With fitting or coupling every 8.5 lf and hanger every 3.5 lf.*	**1/2" diameter CPVC schedule 40 water supply pipe** *Replace* Materials........3.37 Labor............6.84	lf	—	$10.21	$10.21
	3/4" diameter CPVC schedule 40 water supply pipe *Replace* Materials........4.10 Labor............7.24	lf	—	$11.34	$11.34
	1" diameter CPVC schedule 40 water supply pipe *Replace* Materials........5.00 Labor............8.45	lf	—	$13.45	$13.45
PVC WATER SUPPLY PIPE ▶ *With fitting or coupling every 8.5 lf and hanger every 3.5 lf.*	**1/2" diameter PVC schedule 40 cold water supply pipe** *Replace* Materials........1.95 Labor............6.84	lf	—	$8.79	$8.79
	3/4" diameter PVC schedule 40 cold water supply pipe *Replace* Materials........2.00 Labor............7.24	lf	—	$9.24	$9.24
	1" diameter PVC schedule 40 cold water supply pipe *Replace* Materials........2.34 Labor............8.45	lf	—	$10.79	$10.79
REPLACE SECTION OF PVC OR CPVC SUPPLY PIPE ▶	**Replace section of PVC or CPVC water supply pipe** *Replace* Materials.......15.20 Labor...........55.00 ▶ Includes cut-out in typical drywall wall, replacement section and couplings. Does not include wall repair (see *Drywall* page 136).	ea	—	$70.20	$70.20

Item Description	Unit	Remove	Replace	Total	
Minimum charge for supply pipe work *Replace* Materials......60.00 Labor..........81.40	ea	—	$141.40	$141.40	◀ **MINIMUM SUPPLY PIPE**
2" cast-iron DWV pipe *Replace* Materials........5.52 Labor..........10.50	lf	—	$16.02	$16.02	◀ **CAST-IRON DWV PIPE** *Lead and oakum joints with fitting every 9.5 lf.*
3" cast-iron DWV pipe *Replace* Materials........7.57 Labor..........11.10	lf	—	$18.67	$18.67	
4" cast-iron DWV pipe *Replace* Materials......10.06 Labor..........12.10	lf	—	$22.16	$22.16	
5" cast-iron DWV pipe *Replace* Materials.......13.20 Labor..........13.60	lf	—	$26.80	$26.80	
6" cast-iron DWV pipe *Replace* Materials......16.10 Labor..........14.20	lf	—	$30.30	$30.30	
Replace section of cast-iron DWV pipe *Replace* Materials......94.00 Labor..........74.60 ► Includes cut-out in typical drywall wall, replacement section and couplings. Does not include wall repair (see *Drywall* page 136).	ea	—	$168.60	$168.60	◁ **replace section**
Repack cast-iron DWV pipe joint with oakum and caulk *Replace* Materials.......11.30 Labor............8.09	ea	—	$19.39	$19.39	◁ **repack**
2" cast-iron no-hub DWV pipe *Replace* Materials........6.54 Labor............9.39	lf	—	$15.93	$15.93	◀ **CAST-IRON NO-HUB DWV PIPE** *With fitting or coupling every 9.5 lf.*
3" cast-iron no-hub DWV pipe *Replace* Materials........8.79 Labor............9.92	lf	—	$18.71	$18.71	
4" cast-iron no-hub DWV pipe *Replace* Materials.......11.00 Labor..........10.80	lf	—	$21.80	$21.80	
5" cast-iron no-hub DWV pipe *Replace* Materials.......15.80 Labor..........12.20	lf	—	$28.00	$28.00	
6" cast-iron no-hub DWV pipe *Replace* Materials......18.50 Labor..........12.70	lf	—	$31.20	$31.20	
Replace section of cast-iron no-hub DWV pipe *Replace* Materials......72.60 Labor..........66.60 ► Includes cut-out in typical drywall wall, replacement section and couplings. Does not include wall repair (see *Drywall* page 136).	ea	—	$139.20	$139.20	◁ **replace section**
Repair pin-hole leak in cast-iron DWV pipe with epoxy *Replace* Materials........7.99 Labor..........24.30	ea	—	$32.29	$32.29	◁ **repair pin-hole leak**
1-1/4" PVC DWV pipe *Replace* Materials........2.59 Labor............8.85	lf	—	$11.44	$11.44	◀ **PVC DWV PIPE** *With fitting or coupling every 8.5 lf and hanger every 10 lf.*
1-1/2" PVC DWV pipe *Replace* Materials........2.88 Labor..........10.30	lf	—	$13.18	$13.18	
2" PVC DWV pipe *Replace* Materials........3.06 Labor..........11.20	lf	—	$14.26	$14.26	
3" PVC DWV pipe *Replace* Materials........4.50 Labor..........12.60	lf	—	$17.10	$17.10	

RELATED ITEMS

	Item Description	Unit	Remove	Replace	Total
PVC DWV PIPE ▸ *continued*	**4″ PVC DWV pipe** ***Replace*** Materials........5.75 Labor...........13.90	lf	—	$19.65	$19.65
	5″ PVC DWV pipe ***Replace*** Materials........7.89 Labor...........15.50	lf	—	$23.39	$23.39
	6″ PVC DWV pipe ***Replace*** Materials.......11.10 Labor...........17.00	lf	—	$28.10	$28.10
replace section ▹	**Replace section of PVC DWV pipe** ***Replace*** Materials......35.60 Labor..........64.80 ▸ Includes cut-out in typical drywall wall, replacement section and couplings. Does not include wall repair (see *Drywall* page 136).	ea	—	$100.40	$100.40
MINIMUM DWV PIPE ▸	**Minimum charge for DWV line work** ***Replace*** Materials......58.00 Labor..........68.80	ea	—	$126.80	$126.80
EXTERIOR LINES ▸ *Includes excavation up to 8′ deep, backfill, laying pipe, pipe, and fittings. Does not include mobilization or shoring. Also see Excavation, page 178.*	**4″ diameter exterior sewer lines** ***Replace*** Materials......23.50 Labor...........73.30	lf	—	$96.80	$96.80
	6″ diameter exterior sewer lines ***Replace*** Materials......33.70 Labor...........75.50	lf	—	$109.20	$109.20
	1″ diameter exterior water supply line ***Replace*** Materials.......15.90 Labor...........73.30	lf	—	$89.20	$89.20
	1-1/2″ diameter exterior water supply line ***Replace*** Materials......18.70 Labor...........75.50	lf	—	$94.20	$94.20
minimum ▹	**Minimum charge for exterior line work** ***Replace*** Materials......94.00 Labor.........447.00	ea	—	$541.00	$541.00
SHUT-OFF AND PRESSURE VALVES ▸	**Interior water supply shut-off valve with pressure valve,1-1/2″ line** ***Replace*** Materials....372.00 Labor...........49.20	ea	—	$421.20	$421.20
	Interior water supply shut-off valve with pressure valve, 2″ line ***Replace*** Materials....479.00 Labor...........49.20	ea	—	$528.20	$528.20
REPAIR UNDER-GROUND LINE ▸ *Includes excavation to specified depth, backfill, laying pipe, pipe, and fittings. Does not include mobilization or shoring. Also see Excavation, page 178.*	**Excavate and repair underground line 4′ deep or less** ***Replace*** Materials.......50.10 Labor...........74.60	lf	—	$124.70	$124.70
	Excavate and repair underground line 4′ to 8′ deep ***Replace*** Materials......50.10 Labor...........97.00	lf	—	$147.10	$147.10
	Excavate and repair underground line 8′ to 12′ deep ***Replace*** Materials......50.10 Labor.........135.00	lf	—	$185.10	$185.10
	Excavate and repair underground line 12′ to 16′ deep ***Replace*** Materials......50.10 Labor.........194.00	lf	—	$244.10	$244.10
BREAK-OUT CONCRETE & INSTALL PIPE ▸	**Install pipe underneath existing concrete slab** ***Replace*** Materials......16.30 Labor..........99.20 ▸ Saw concrete slab and break-out, hand excavate, lay pipe, hand back fill, and patch concrete. Includes sand bed for pipe as necessary.	lf	—	$115.50	$115.50
minimum ▹	**Minimum charge to install pipe underneath existing concrete slab** ***Replace*** Materials....102.00 Labor.........559.00	ea	—	$661.00	$661.00

Item Description	Unit	Remove	Replace	Total
Complete supply lines, waste lines & finish fixtures, economy grade *Replace* Materials........2.07 Labor............3.62 ► With PVC drain, waste, and vent lines, CPVC hot water lines, PVC cold water lines.	sf	—	$5.69	$5.69
Complete supply lines, waste lines, & finish fixtures, standard grade *Replace* Materials........3.31 Labor............3.80 ► With PVC drain, waste, and vent lines, copper water supply lines.	sf	—	$7.11	$7.11
Complete supply lines, waste lines, & finish fixtures, high grade *Replace* Materials........3.59 Labor............3.84 ► With PVC drain, waste, and vent lines, copper water supply lines.	sf	—	$7.43	$7.43
Complete supply lines, waste lines, & finish fixtures, deluxe grade *Replace* Materials........4.13 Labor............4.07 ► With cast-iron drain, waste, and vent lines, copper water supply lines.	sf	—	$8.20	$8.20
Complete supply lines, waste lines, & finish fixtures, custom deluxe grade *Replace* Materials........4.55 Labor............4.11 ► With cast-iron drain, waste, and vent lines, copper water supply lines.	sf	—	$8.66	$8.66
Complete house rough plumbing (no fixtures), economy grade *Replace* Materials........ .55 Labor............1.70 ► PVC drain, waste, and vent lines, CPVC hot water lines, PVC cold water lines.	sf	—	$2.25	$2.25
Complete house rough plumbing (no fixtures) standard grade *Replace* Materials........ .80 Labor............1.88 ► PVC drain, waste, and vent lines, copper water supply lines.	sf	—	$2.68	$2.68
Complete house rough plumbing (no fixtures) high grade *Replace* Materials........1.15 Labor............2.01 ► Cast-iron drain, waste, and vent lines, copper water supply lines.	sf	—	$3.16	$3.16
Complete house plumbing fixtures, economy grade *Replace* Materials........1.52 Labor............1.92	sf	—	$3.44	$3.44
Complete house plumbing fixtures, standard grade *Replace* Materials........2.51 Labor............1.97	sf	—	$4.48	$4.48
Complete house plumbing fixtures, high grade *Replace* Materials........2.79 Labor............1.97	sf	—	$4.76	$4.76
Complete house plumbing fixtures, deluxe grade *Replace* Materials........2.98 Labor............2.01	sf	—	$4.99	$4.99
Complete house plumbing fixtures, custom deluxe grade *Replace* Materials........3.40 Labor............2.06	sf	—	$5.46	$5.46
Rough plumbing, two fixture bathroom, plastic supply, plastic DWV *Replace* Materials.....310.00 Labor.........876.00	ea	—	$1,186.00	$1,186.00
Rough plumbing, two fixture bathroom, copper supply, plastic DWV *Replace* Materials....375.00 Labor.........912.00	ea	—	$1,287.00	$1,287.00
Rough plumbing, two fixture bathroom, copper supply, cast-iron DWV *Replace* Materials....425.00 Labor.........952.00	ea	—	$1,377.00	$1,377.00

◄ **COMPLETE HOUSE ROUGH & FINISH PLUMBING**
Grades refer to quality of plumbing fixtures. For residential structures only. See page 369 for information about plumbing fixture quality.

◄ **COMPLETE HOUSE ROUGH PLUMBING**

◄ **COMPLETE HOUSE FINISH PLUMBING (FIXTURES)**
See page 369 for information about plumbing fixture quality.

◄ **ROUGH PLUMBING TWO FIXTURE BATHROOM**
Typically rough plumbing for one toilet and one sink. Does not include fixtures.

RELATED ITEMS

Bathroom Hardware.....39
Cleaning........................62

	Item Description	Unit	Remove	Replace	Total
ROUGH PLUMBING ▶ THREE FIXTURE BATHROOM *Typically rough plumbing for one toilet, one sink and a shower or bathtub. Does not include fixtures.*	**Rough plumbing, three fixture bathroom, plastic supply, plastic DWV** *Replace* Materials....400.00 Labor........1120.00	ea	—	$1,520.00	$1,520.00
	Rough plumbing, three fixture bathroom, copper supply, plastic DWV *Replace* Materials....480.00 Labor.......1180.00	ea	—	$1,660.00	$1,660.00
	Rough plumbing, three fixture bathroom, copper supply, cast-iron DWV *Replace* Materials....550.00 Labor.......1280.00	ea	—	$1,830.00	$1,830.00
ROUGH PLUMBING ▶ FOUR FIXTURE BATHROOM *Typically rough plumbing for one toilet, one sink one shower and a bathtub. Does not include fixtures.*	**Rough plumbing, four fixture bathroom, plastic supply, plastic DWV** *Replace* Materials....495.00 Labor.......1490.00	ea	—	$1,985.00	$1,985.00
	Rough plumbing, four fixture bathroom, copper supply, plastic DWV *Replace* Materials....600.00 Labor.......1600.00	ea	—	$2,200.00	$2,200.00
	Rough plumbing, four fixture bathroom, copper supply, cast-iron DWV *Replace* Materials....685.00 Labor.......1720.00	ea	—	$2,405.00	$2,405.00
ROUGH PLUMBING ▶ FIVE FIXTURE BATHROOM *Typically rough plumbing for one toilet, two sinks one shower and a bathtub. Does not include fixtures.*	**Rough plumbing, five fixture bathroom, plastic supply, plastic DWV** *Replace* Materials....600.00 Labor.......1860.00	ea	—	$2,460.00	$2,460.00
	Rough plumbing, five fixture bathroom, copper supply, plastic DWV *Replace* Materials....720.00 Labor.......1940.00	ea	—	$2,660.00	$2,660.00
	Rough plumbing, five fixture bathroom, copper supply, cast-iron DWV *Replace* Materials....820.00 Labor......2030.00	ea	—	$2,850.00	$2,850.00
ROUGH PLUMBING ▶ LAUNDRY ROOM *Includes supply valves and recessed wall box.*	**Rough plumbing, laundry room, plastic supply, plastic DWV** *Replace* Materials.....135.00 Labor........290.00	ea	—	$425.00	$425.00
	Rough plumbing, laundry room, copper supply, plastic DWV *Replace* Materials.....160.00 Labor........304.00	ea	—	$464.00	$464.00
	Rough plumbing, laundry room, copper supply, cast-iron DWV *Replace* Materials.....185.00 Labor.........321.00	ea	—	$506.00	$506.00
ROUGH PLUMBING ▶ LAUNDRY ROOM WITH SINK *Includes supply valves, recessed wall box, and plumbing for one or two hole laundry sink.*	**Rough plumbing, laundry room with sink, plastic supply, plastic DWV** *Replace* Materials.....315.00 Labor........568.00	ea	—	$883.00	$883.00
	Rough plumbing, laundry room with sink, copper supply, plastic DWV *Replace* Materials....380.00 Labor.........581.00	ea	—	$961.00	$961.00
	Rough plumbing, laundry room with sink, copper supply, cast-iron DWV *Replace* Materials....430.00 Labor.........595.00	ea	—	$1,025.00	$1,025.00
ROUGH PLUMBING ▶ KITCHEN *Rough plumbing for one, two or three hole kitchen sink. With ice maker includes line from sink to refrigerator ice maker or water dispenser.*	**Rough plumbing, kitchen, plastic supply, plastic DWV** *Replace* Materials....230.00 Labor.........367.00	ea	—	$597.00	$597.00
	Rough plumbing, kitchen, copper supply, plastic DWV *Replace* Materials....255.00 Labor........382.00	ea	—	$637.00	$637.00
	Rough plumbing, kitchen, copper supply, cast-iron DWV *Replace* Materials....280.00 Labor.........392.00	ea	—	$672.00	$672.00
	Rough plumbing, kitchen with ice maker, plastic supply, plastic DWV *Replace* Materials....265.00 Labor........438.00	ea	—	$703.00	$703.00
	Rough plumbing, kitchen with ice maker, copper supply, plastic DWV *Replace* Materials....290.00 Labor.........451.00	ea	—	$741.00	$741.00

Item Description	Unit	Remove	Replace	Total
Rough plumbing, kitchen with icemaker, copper supply, cast-iron DWV ***Replace*** Materials.....315.00 Labor.........465.00	ea	—	$780.00	$780.00
Rough plumbing, wet bar sink, plastic supply, plastic DWV ***Replace*** Materials .....115.00 Labor.........331.00	ea	—	$446.00	$446.00
Rough plumbing, wet bar sink, copper supply, plastic DWV ***Replace*** Materials.....135.00 Labor 344.00	ea	—	$479.00	$479.00
Rough plumbing, wet bar sink, copper supply, cast-iron DWV ***Replace*** Materials.....160.00 Labor.........355.00	ea	—	$515.00	$515.00
Rough plumbing, bathroom sink, plastic supply, plastic DWV ***Replace*** Materials .....115.00 Labor.........331.00	ea	—	$446.00	$446.00
Rough plumbing, bathroom sink, copper supply, plastic DWV ***Replace*** Materials ....140.00 Labor 344.00	ea	—	$484.00	$484.00
Rough plumbing, bathroom sink, copper supply, cast-iron DWV ***Replace*** Materials.....165.00 Labor.........355.00	ea	—	$520.00	$520.00
Rough plumbing, kitchen sink, plastic supply, plastic DWV ***Replace*** Materials....200.00 Labor.........367.00	ea	—	$567.00	$567.00
Rough plumbing, kitchen sink, copper supply, plastic DWV ***Replace*** Materials....225.00 Labor 382.00	ea	—	$607.00	$607.00
Rough plumbing, kitchen sink, copper supply, cast-iron DWV ***Replace*** Materials....250.00 Labor.........392.00	ea	—	$642.00	$642.00
Rough plumbing, laundry sink, plastic supply, plastic DWV ***Replace*** Materials.....115.00 Labor 290.00	ea	—	$405.00	$405.00
Rough plumbing, laundry sink, copper supply, plastic DWV ***Replace*** Materials.....135.00 Labor 304.00	ea	—	$439.00	$439.00
Rough plumbing, laundry sink, copper supply, cast-iron DWV ***Replace*** Materials.....160.00 Labor.........321.00	ea	—	$481.00	$481.00
Rough plumbing, bathtub or shower, plastic supply, plastic DWV ***Replace*** Materials.....165.00 Labor 308.00	ea	—	$473.00	$473.00
Rough plumbing, bathtub or shower, copper supply, plastic DWV ***Replace*** Materials....205.00 Labor.........324.00	ea	—	$529.00	$529.00
Rough plumbing, bathtub or shower, copper supply, cast-iron DWV ***Replace*** Materials ....240.00 Labor 339.00	ea	—	$579.00	$579.00
Rough plumbing, toilet, plastic supply & plastic DWV ***Replace*** Materials.....145.00 Labor.........261.00	ea	—	$406.00	$406.00
Rough plumbing, toilet, copper supply & plastic DWV ***Replace*** Materials ....180.00 Labor.........278.00	ea	—	$458.00	$458.00
Rough plumbing, toilet, copper supply & cast-iron DWV ***Replace*** Materials.....210.00 Labor 288.00	ea	—	$498.00	$498.00
Rough plumbing, bidet, plastic supply & plastic DWV ***Replace*** Materials.....160.00 Labor 290.00	ea	—	$450.00	$450.00

◀ **ROUGH PLUMBING WET BAR SINK**
Rough plumbing for one hole bar sink. For feeds only see page 375. For wet bar sink faucets see page 370 and 384. For wet bar sinks see page 374.

◀ **ROUGH PLUMBING BATHROOM SINK**
Rough plumbing for one hole bathroom sink. For feeds only see page 375. For bathroom sink faucets see page 368 and 384. For bathroom sinks see page 371 and 385.

◀ **ROUGH PLUMBING KITCHEN SINK**
Rough plumbing for one, two or three hole kitchen sink. For feeds only see page 375. For kitchen sink faucets see page 369 and 384. For kitchen sinks see page 373.

◀ **ROUGH PLUMBING LAUNDRY SINK**
For one or two hole laundry sink. For feeds only see page 375. For laundry sink faucets see page 369. For laundry sinks see page 374.

◀ **ROUGH PLUMBING BATHTUB OR SHOWER**
For bathtub and shower faucets see page 370 and 384-385. For bathtubs see page 377 and 387. For showers see page 387.

◀ **ROUGH PLUMBING TOILET**
For toilets see page 376 and 386.

RELATED ITEMS

◀ **ROUGH PLUMBING BIDET**
For bidets see page 376.

	Item Description	Unit	Remove	Replace	Total
ROUGH PLUMBING ▶ BIDET *continued*	**Rough plumbing, bidet, copper supply & plastic DWV** *Replace* Materials....200.00 Labor........308.00	ea	—	$508.00	$508.00
	Rough plumbing, bidet, copper supply & cast iron DWV *Replace* Materials....235.00 Labor........319.00	ea	—	$554.00	$554.00
ROUGH PLUMBING ▶ CLOTHES WASHER *Includes supply valves and recessed wall box. For clothes washers see page 31.*	**Rough plumbing, clothes washer, plastic supply & plastic DWV** *Replace* Materials.....120.00 Labor........324.00	ea	—	$444.00	$444.00
	Rough plumbing, clothes washer, copper supply & plastic DWV *Replace* Materials....140.00 Labor........336.00	ea	—	$476.00	$476.00
	Rough plumbing, clothes washer, copper supply & cast iron DWV *Replace* Materials.....165.00 Labor........346.00	ea	—	$511.00	$511.00
ROUGH PLUMBING ▶ DISHWASHER *Connection from kitchen sink (see previous page) to dishwasher. For dishwashers see page 26.*	**Rough plumbing, dishwasher, plastic supply & plastic DWV** *Replace* Materials......20.00 Labor..........62.10	ea	—	$82.10	$82.10
	Rough plumbing, dishwasher, copper supply & plastic DWV *Replace* Materials......26.00 Labor..........66.60	ea	—	$92.60	$92.60
	Rough plumbing, dishwasher, copper supply & cast iron DWV *Replace* Materials......31.00 Labor..........71.10	ea	—	$102.10	$102.10
ROUGH PLUMBING ▶ HOSE BIBB *Freeze-proof hose bibb.*	**Cold water plastic supply line for exterior hose bibb** *Replace* Materials......69.00 Labor........159.00	ea	—	$228.00	$228.00
	Cold water copper supply line for exterior hose bibb *Replace* Materials......94.00 Labor........157.00	ea	—	$251.00	$251.00
ROUGH PLUMBING ▶ EVAP. COOLER	**Cold water copper supply line for evaporative cooler** *Replace* Materials......49.00 Labor........120.00	ea	—	$169.00	$169.00
ROUGH PLUMBING ▶ ICE MAKER *Supply lines only. For supply line installation including hookup see Appliances on page 31.*	**Cold water plastic supply line for refrigerator ice maker** *Replace* Materials.......13.00 Labor..........93.90	ea	—	$106.90	$106.90
	Cold water copper supply line for refrigerator ice maker *Replace* Materials......33.00 Labor..........98.80	ea	—	$131.80	$131.80
ROUGH PLUMBING ▶ FLOOR DRAIN	**Drain lines for in-floor French drain** *Replace* Materials....100.00 Labor........144.00 ▶ Includes drain, up to 12 lf drain pipe, and two cubic yard gravel drain field. Does not include excavation or backfill.	ea	—	$244.00	$244.00
	Drain lines for in-floor drain connected to sewer *Replace* Materials....240.00 Labor........235.00 ▶ Includes drain, up to 32 lf drain pipe. Does not include excavation or backfill.	ea	—	$475.00	$475.00
BATHROOM SINK ▶ FAUCET *For antique style faucets see page 384. For bathroom sink rough plumbing see page 367. For bathroom sinks see page 371 and 385.*	**Bathroom sink faucet, economy grade** *Replace* Materials......90.00 Labor..........24.90 *Remove* .... Labor...........9.82	ea	$9.82	$114.90	$124.72
	Bathroom sink faucet, standard grade *Replace* Materials.....165.00 Labor..........24.90 *Remove* .... Labor...........9.82	ea	$9.82	$189.90	$199.72
	Bathroom sink faucet, high grade *Replace* Materials.....310.00 Labor..........24.90 *Remove* .... Labor...........9.82	ea	$9.82	$334.90	$344.72

Item Description	Unit	Remove	Replace	Total
Bathroom sink faucet, deluxe grade *Replace* Materials....535.00 Labor...........24.90 *Remove* .... Labor 9.82	ea	$9.82	$559.90	$569.72
Remove bathroom sink faucet for work, then reinstall *Replace* .... Labor..........37.20	ea	—	$37.20	$37.20
Bidet faucet, standard grade *Replace* Materials ....270.00 Labor...........26.60 *Remove* .... Labor 9.82	ea	$9.82	$296.60	$306.42
Bidet faucet, high grade *Replace* Materials....430.00 Labor...........26.60 *Remove* .... Labor 9.82	ea	$9.82	$456.60	$466.42
Bidet faucet, deluxe grade *Replace* Materials ....705.00 Labor...........26.60 *Remove* .... Labor 9.82	ea	$9.82	$731.60	$741.42
Remove bidet faucet for work, then reinstall *Replace* .... Labor 38.90	ea	—	$38.90	$38.90
Kitchen sink faucet, economy grade *Replace* Materials ....100.00 Labor ....25.10 *Remove* .... Labor 9.82	ea	$9.82	$125.10	$134.92
Kitchen sink faucet, standard grade *Replace* Materials ....180.00 Labor ....25.10 *Remove* .... Labor 9.82	ea	$9.82	$205.10	$214.92
Kitchen sink faucet, high grade *Replace* Materials ....350.00 Labor ....25.10 *Remove* .... Labor 9.82	ea	$9.82	$375.10	$384.92
Kitchen sink faucet, deluxe grade *Replace* Materials....600.00 Labor ....25.10 *Remove* .... Labor 9.82	ea	$9.82	$625.10	$634.92
Remove kitchen sink faucet for work, then reinstall *Replace* .... Labor..........37.90	ea	—	$37.90	$37.90
Laundry sink faucet, economy grade *Replace* Materials ......55.00 Labor...........24.40 *Remove* .... Labor 9.82	ea	$9.82	$79.40	$89.22
Laundry sink faucet, standard grade *Replace* Materials ....100.00 Labor...........24.40 *Remove* .... Labor 9.82	ea	$9.82	$124.40	$134.22
Laundry sink faucet, high grade *Replace* Materials ....140.00 Labor...........24.40 *Remove* .... Labor 9.82	ea	$9.82	$164.40	$174.22
Laundry sink faucet, deluxe grade *Replace* Materials.....245.00 Labor...........24.40 *Remove* .... Labor 9.82	ea	$9.82	$269.40	$279.22
Remove laundry sink faucet for work, then reinstall *Replace* .... Labor 36.70	ea	—	$36.70	$36.70

RELATED ITEMS

◁ **remove & reinstall** (bathroom sink faucet)

◀ **BIDET FAUCET**
For rough plumbing see page 367. For bidets see page 376.

◁ **remove & reinstall** (bidet faucet)

◀ **KITCHEN SINK FAUCET**
For antique style faucets see page 384. For rough plumbing see page 367. For kitchen sinks see page 373.

◁ **remove & reinstall** (kitchen sink faucet)

◀ **LAUNDRY SINK FAUCET**
For rough plumbing see page 367. For laundry sinks see page 374.

FAUCET QUALITY

Some faucet quality rules of thumb:

Economy: Light gauge metal, chrome plated. May have some plastic components. Little or no pattern.

Standard: Heavier gauge metal, chrome or brass plated with little or no pattern or with wood handles made of ash or oak.

continued on next page

SHOWER FAUCET ► *For rough plumbing see page 367. For shower stalls and bathtub surrounds see page 378 and page 491.*

FAUCET QUALITY

continued

High: Brass, chrome over brass, or nickel over brass with minimal detail or plated hardware with ornate detail, or with European style plastic or porcelain components.

Deluxe: Brass, chrome over brass, or nickel over brass with ornate detail.

BATHTUB FAUCET ► *For antique style faucets see page 384. For rough plumbing see page 367. For bathtubs see page 377 and page 386.*

BATHUB WITH SHOWER FAUCET ► *For antique style faucets see page 384. For rough plumbing see page 367. For bathtubs see page 377 and page 386.*

WET BAR SINK FAUCET ► *For rough plumbing see page 367. For wet bar sink see page 374.*

Item Description	Unit	Remove	Replace	Total
Shower faucet, economy grade	ea	$9.82	$145.70	$155.52
Replace Materials.....120.00 Labor..........25.70				
Remove .... Labor............9.82				
Shower faucet, standard grade	ea	$9.82	$245.70	$255.52
Replace Materials....220.00 Labor..........25.70				
Remove .... Labor............9.82				
Shower faucet, high grade	ea	$9.82	$400.70	$410.52
Replace Materials....375.00 Labor..........25.70				
Remove .... Labor............9.82				
Shower faucet, deluxe grade	ea	$9.82	$580.70	$590.52
Replace Materials....555.00 Labor..........25.70				
Remove .... Labor............9.82				
Remove shower faucet for work, then reinstall	ea	—	$39.60	$39.60
Replace .... Labor..........39.60				
Bathtub faucet, economy grade	ea	$9.82	$160.40	$170.22
Replace Materials.....135.00 Labor..........25.40				
Remove .... Labor............9.82				
Bathtub faucet, standard grade	ea	$9.82	$270.40	$280.22
Replace Materials.....245.00 Labor..........25.40				
Remove .... Labor............9.82				
Bathtub faucet, high grade	ea	$9.82	$445.40	$455.22
Replace Materials....420.00 Labor..........25.40				
Remove .... Labor............9.82				
Bathtub faucet, deluxe grade	ea	$9.82	$645.40	$655.22
Replace Materials....620.00 Labor..........25.40				
Remove .... Labor............9.82				
remove & reinstall ▷ **Remove bathtub faucet for work, then reinstall**	ea	—	$39.20	$39.20
Replace .... Labor..........39.20				
Bathtub with shower faucet, economy grade	ea	$11.00	$177.10	$188.10
Replace Materials....150.00 Labor...........27.10				
Remove .... Labor...........11.00				
Bathtub with shower faucet, standard grade	ea	$11.00	$297.10	$308.10
Replace Materials....270.00 Labor...........27.10				
Remove .... Labor...........11.00				
Bathtub with shower faucet, high grade	ea	$11.00	$487.10	$498.10
Replace Materials....460.00 Labor...........27.10				
Remove .... Labor...........11.00				
Bathub with shower faucet, deluxe grade	ea	$11.00	$707.10	$718.10
Replace Materials....680.00 Labor...........27.10				
Remove .... Labor...........11.00				
remove & reinstall ▷ **Remove bathtub with shower faucet for work, then reinstall**	ea	—	$40.30	$40.30
Replace .... Labor..........40.30				
Wet bar sink faucet, economy grade	ea	$9.82	$104.20	$114.02
Replace Materials......80.00 Labor...........24.20				
Remove .... Labor............9.82				

Item Description	Unit	Remove	Replace	Total
Wet bar sink faucet, standard grade ***Replace*** Materials.....145.00 Labor...........24.20 ***Remove*** .... Labor............9.82	ea	$9.82	$169.20	$179.02
Wet bar sink faucet, high grade ***Replace*** Materials....275.00 Labor...........24.20 ***Remove*** .... Labor............9.82	ea	$9.82	$299.20	$309.02
Wet bar sink faucet, deluxe grade ***Replace*** Materials.....475.00 Labor...........24.20 ***Remove*** .... Labor............9.82	ea	$9.82	$499.20	$509.02
Remove wet bar sink faucet for work, then reinstall ***Replace*** .... Labor...........35.80	ea	—	$35.80	$35.80
Refurbish and repack faucet ***Replace*** Materials.......15.00 Labor..........20.30	ea	—	$35.30	$35.30
Bathroom oval sink, wall-hung porcelain-enamel cast iron ***Replace*** Materials....395.00 Labor..........39.20 ***Remove*** .... Labor...........10.10	ea	$10.10	$434.20	$444.30
Bathroom round sink, wall-hung porcelain-enamel cast iron ***Replace*** Materials....390.00 Labor..........39.20 ***Remove*** .... Labor...........10.10	ea	$10.10	$429.20	$439.30
Bathroom hexagonal sink, wall-hung porcelain-enamel cast iron ***Replace*** Materials....425.00 Labor..........39.20 ***Remove*** .... Labor...........10.10	ea	$10.10	$464.20	$474.30
Bathroom oval sink, wall-hung porcelain-enamel steel ***Replace*** Materials....330.00 Labor..........39.20 ***Remove*** .... Labor...........10.10	ea	$10.10	$369.20	$379.30
Bathroom round sink, wall-hung porcelain-enamel steel ***Replace*** Materials....325.00 Labor..........39.20 ***Remove*** .... Labor...........10.10	ea	$10.10	$364.20	$374.30
Bathroom hexagonal sink, wall-hung porcelain-enamel steel ***Replace*** Materials....355.00 Labor..........39.20 ***Remove*** .... Labor...........10.10	ea	$10.10	$394.20	$404.30
Bathroom oval sink, wall-hung vitreous china ***Replace*** Materials....320.00 Labor..........39.20 ***Remove*** .... Labor...........10.10	ea	$10.10	$359.20	$369.30
Bathroom oval sink, wall-hung vitreous china with pattern ***Replace*** Materials....420.00 Labor..........39.20 ***Remove*** .... Labor...........10.10	ea	$10.10	$459.20	$469.30
Bathroom round sink, wall-hung vitreous china ***Replace*** Materials.....310.00 Labor..........39.20 ***Remove*** .... Labor...........10.10	ea	$10.10	$349.20	$359.30
Bathroom round sink, wall-hung vitreous china with pattern ***Replace*** Materials.....410.00 Labor..........39.20 ***Remove*** .... Labor...........10.10	ea	$10.10	$449.20	$459.30
Bathroom hexagonal sink, wall-hung vitreous china ***Replace*** Materials....330.00 Labor..........39.20 ***Remove*** .... Labor...........10.10	ea	$10.10	$369.20	$379.30

◁ **remove & reinstall**

◀ **REPACK FAUCET**

◀ **BATHROOM SINK**
With visible plumbing including water feeds, P trap, escutcheons, and so forth, to wall or floor. Does not include faucet. *For rough plumbing see page 367. For bathroom sink faucets see page 368.*

◁ **wall-hung**

RELATED ITEMS

Bathroom Hardware......41
Cleaning.......................64

	Item Description	Unit	Remove	Replace	Total
BATHROOM SINK ▶ *continued*	**Remove wall-hung bathroom sink for work, then reinstall** *Replace* .... Labor..........48.70	ea	—	$48.70	$48.70
self-rimming ▷	**Bathroom oval sink, self-rimming vitreous china** *Replace* Materials....285.00 Labor..........40.60 *Remove* .... Labor...........10.10	ea	$10.10	$325.60	$335.70
	Bathroom oval sink, self-rimming vitreous china with pattern *Replace* Materials....380.00 Labor..........40.60 *Remove* .... Labor...........10.10	ea	$10.10	$420.60	$430.70
	Bathroom round sink, self-rimming vitreous china *Replace* Materials....280.00 Labor..........40.60 *Remove* .... Labor...........10.10	ea	$10.10	$320.60	$330.70
	Bathroom round sink, self-rimming vitreous china with pattern *Replace* Materials....370.00 Labor..........40.60 *Remove* .... Labor...........10.10	ea	$10.10	$410.60	$420.70
	Bathroom hexagonal sink, self-rimming vitreous china *Replace* Materials....295.00 Labor..........40.60 *Remove* .... Labor...........10.10	ea	$10.10	$335.60	$345.70
	Bathroom oval sink, self-rimming stainless steel *Replace* Materials.....310.00 Labor..........40.60 *Remove* .... Labor...........10.10	ea	$10.10	$350.60	$360.70
	Bathroom oval sink, self-rimming scalloped stainless steel *Replace* Materials....355.00 Labor..........40.60 *Remove* .... Labor...........10.10	ea	$10.10	$395.60	$405.70
	Bathroom oval sink, self-rimming polished brass *Replace* Materials....345.00 Labor..........40.60 *Remove* .... Labor...........10.10	ea	$10.10	$385.60	$395.70
	Bathroom oval sink, self-rimming hammered finish brass *Replace* Materials....390.00 Labor..........40.60 *Remove* .... Labor............9.04	ea	$10.10	$430.60	$440.70
	Bathroom oval sink, self-rimming scalloped polished brass *Replace* Materials....425.00 Labor..........40.60 *Remove* .... Labor...........10.10	ea	$10.10	$465.60	$475.70
	Remove self-rimming bathroom sink for work, then reinstall *Replace* .... Labor...........51.00	ea	—	$51.00	$51.00
under-counter ▷	**Bathroom oval sink, under-counter vitreous china** *Replace* Materials....300.00 Labor...........42.60 *Remove* .... Labor...........10.10	ea	$10.10	$342.60	$352.70
	Bathroom oval sink, under-counter vitreous china with pattern *Replace* Materials....395.00 Labor...........42.60 *Remove* .... Labor...........10.10	ea	$10.10	$437.60	$447.70
	Bathroom round sink, under-counter vitreous china *Replace* Materials....290.00 Labor...........42.60 *Remove* .... Labor...........10.10	ea	$10.10	$332.60	$342.70
	Bathroom round sink, under-counter vitreous china with pattern *Replace* Materials....385.00 Labor...........42.60 *Remove* .... Labor...........10.10	ea	$10.10	$427.60	$437.70

Item Description	Unit	Remove	Replace	Total
Bathroom hexagonal sink, under-counter vitreous china *Replace* Materials.....310.00 Labor..........42.60 *Remove* .... Labor..........10.10	ea	$10.10	$352.60	$362.70
Remove under-counter bathroom sink for work, then reinstall *Replace* .... Labor..........52.70	ea	—	$52.70	$52.70
24" by 21" single-bowl porcelain-enamel, cast-iron kitchen sink *Replace* Materials.....315.00 Labor..........41.40 *Remove* .... Labor..........10.10	ea	$10.10	$356.40	$366.50
30" by 21" single-bowl porcelain-enamel, cast-iron kitchen sink *Replace* Materials....390.00 Labor..........41.40 *Remove* .... Labor..........10.10	ea	$10.10	$431.40	$441.50
32" by 21" double-bowl porcelain-enamel, cast-iron kitchen sink *Replace* Materials....465.00 Labor..........41.40 *Remove* .... Labor..........10.10	ea	$10.10	$506.40	$516.50
42" by 21" triple-bowl porcelain-enamel, cast-iron kitchen sink *Replace* Materials...1015.00 Labor..........41.40 *Remove* .... Labor..........10.10	ea	$10.10	$1,056.40	$1,066.50
24" by 21" single-bowl porcelain-enamel, steel kitchen sink *Replace* Materials.....160.00 Labor..........41.40 *Remove* .... Labor..........10.10	ea	$10.10	$201.40	$211.50
30" by 21" single-bowl porcelain-enamel, steel kitchen sink *Replace* Materials.....185.00 Labor..........41.40 *Remove* .... Labor..........10.10	ea	$10.10	$226.40	$236.50
32" by 21" double-bowl porcelain-enamel, steel kitchen sink *Replace* Materials.....195.00 Labor..........41.40 *Remove* .... Labor..........10.10	ea	$10.10	$236.40	$246.50
42" by 21" triple-bowl porcelain-enamel, steel kitchen sink *Replace* Materials....860.00 Labor..........41.40 *Remove* .... Labor..........10.10	ea	$10.10	$901.40	$911.50
19" by 18" single-bowl stainless steel kitchen sink *Replace* Materials....240.00 Labor..........41.40 *Remove* .... Labor..........10.10	ea	$10.10	$281.40	$291.50
25" by 22" single-bowl stainless steel kitchen sink *Replace* Materials....255.00 Labor..........41.40 *Remove* .... Labor..........10.10	ea	$10.10	$296.40	$306.50
33" by 22" double-bowl stainless steel kitchen sink *Replace* Materials....345.00 Labor..........41.40 *Remove* .... Labor..........10.10	ea	$10.10	$386.40	$396.50
43" by 22" double-bowl stainless steel kitchen sink *Replace* Materials....365.00 Labor..........41.40 *Remove* .... Labor..........10.10	ea	$10.10	$406.40	$416.50
43" by 22" triple-bowl stainless steel kitchen sink *Replace* Materials....490.00 Labor..........41.40 *Remove* .... Labor..........10.10	ea	$10.10	$531.40	$541.50
Remove kitchen sink for work, then reinstall *Replace* .... Labor..........49.60	ea	—	$49.60	$49.60

RELATED ITEMS

Bathroom Hardware......41
Cleaning 64

◀ **KITCHEN SINK**
With visible plumbing including water feeds, P trap, escutcheons, and so forth, to wall or floor. Does not include faucet. For rough plumbing see page 367. For kitchen sink faucets see page 369.

◁ **remove & reinstall**

	Item Description	Unit	Remove	Replace	Total
Laundry sink ▶ *With visible plumbing including water feeds, P trap, escutcheons, and so forth, to wall or floor. Does not include faucet. For rough plumbing see page 367. For laundry sink faucet see page 369.*	**22" x 17" single-bowl stainless steel laundry sink in countertop** *Replace* Materials....340.00 Labor..........40.30 *Remove* .... Labor...........10.10	ea	$10.10	$380.30	$390.40
	19" x 22" single-bowl stainless steel laundry sink in countertop *Replace* Materials....360.00 Labor..........40.30 *Remove* .... Labor...........10.10	ea	$10.10	$400.30	$410.40
	33" x 22" double-bowl stainless steel laundry sink in countertop *Replace* Materials....390.00 Labor..........40.30 *Remove* .... Labor...........10.10	ea	$10.10	$430.30	$440.40
porcelain-enamel ▷	**24" x 20" single-bowl porcelain-enamel, cast-iron laundry sink on iron frame** *Replace* Materials.....475.00 Labor...........37.20 *Remove* .... Labor...........10.10	ea	$10.10	$512.20	$522.30
	24" x 23" single-bowl porcelain-enamel, cast-iron laundry sink on iron frame *Replace* Materials.....515.00 Labor...........37.20 *Remove* .... Labor...........10.10	ea	$10.10	$552.20	$562.30
plastic ▷	**18" x 23" single-bowl plastic laundry sink on plastic legs** *Replace* Materials.....125.00 Labor...........37.20 *Remove* .... Labor...........10.10	ea	$10.10	$162.20	$172.30
	20" x 24" single-bowl plastic laundry sink on plastic legs *Replace* Materials.....165.00 Labor...........37.20 *Remove* .... Labor...........10.10	ea	$10.10	$202.20	$212.30
	36" x 23" double-bowl plastic laundry sink on plastic legs *Replace* Materials.....195.00 Labor...........37.20 *Remove* .... Labor...........10.10	ea	$10.10	$232.20	$242.30
	40" x 24" double-bowl plastic laundry sink on plastic legs *Replace* Materials....270.00 Labor...........37.20 *Remove* .... Labor...........10.10	ea	$10.10	$307.20	$317.30
remove & reinstall ▷	**Remove laundry sink for work, then reinstall** *Replace* .... Labor..........50.10	ea	—	$50.10	$50.10
Wet bar sink ▶ *With visible plumbing including water feeds, P trap, escutcheons, and so forth to wall or floor. Does not include faucet. For rough plumbing see page 367. For wet bar sink faucet see page 370.*	**Wet bar sink, self-rimming vitreous china** *Replace* Materials.....475.00 Labor..........40.60 *Remove* .... Labor............9.85	ea	$9.85	$515.60	$525.45
	Wet bar sink, self-rimming vitreous china with pattern *Replace* Materials....570.00 Labor..........40.60 *Remove* .... Labor............9.85	ea	$9.85	$610.60	$620.45
self-rimming ▷	**Wet bar sink, self-rimming porcelain-enamel cast iron** *Replace* Materials....405.00 Labor..........40.60 *Remove* .... Labor............9.85	ea	$9.85	$445.60	$455.45
	Wet bar sink, self-rimming porcelain-enamel steel *Replace* Materials....230.00 Labor..........40.60 *Remove* .... Labor............9.85	ea	$9.85	$270.60	$280.45
	Wet bar sink, self-rimming stainless steel *Replace* Materials.....175.00 Labor..........40.60 *Remove* .... Labor............9.85	ea	$9.85	$215.60	$225.45
	Wet bar sink, self-rimming scalloped stainless steel *Replace* Materials....255.00 Labor..........40.60 *Remove* .... Labor............9.85	ea	$9.85	$295.60	$305.45

Item Description	Unit	Remove	Replace	Total
Wet bar sink, self-rimming polished brass ***Replace*** Materials....350.00 Labor..........40.60 ***Remove*** .... Labor............9.85	ea	$9.85	$390.60	$400.45
Wet bar sink, self-rimming hammered finish brass ***Replace*** Materials....400.00 Labor..........40.60 ***Remove*** .... Labor............9.85	ea	$9.85	$440.60	$450.45
Wet bar sink, self-rimming scalloped polished brass ***Replace*** Materials....450.00 Labor..........40.60 ***Remove*** .... Labor............9.85	ea	$9.85	$490.60	$500.45
Remove self-rimming wet bar sink for work, then reinstall ***Replace*** .... Labor..........51.00	ea	—	$51.00	$51.00
Wet bar sink, under-counter vitreous china ***Replace*** Materials....320.00 Labor..........42.60 ***Remove*** .... Labor............9.85	ea	$9.85	$362.60	$372.45
Wet bar sink, under-counter vitreous china with pattern ***Replace*** Materials.....415.00 Labor..........42.60 ***Remove*** .... Labor............9.85	ea	$9.85	$457.60	$467.45
Wet bar sink, under-counter porcelain enamel cast iron ***Replace*** Materials....395.00 Labor..........42.60 ***Remove*** .... Labor............9.85	ea	$9.85	$437.60	$447.45
Wet bar sink, under-counter porcelain enamel steel ***Replace*** Materials....225.00 Labor..........42.60 ***Remove*** .... Labor............9.85	ea	$9.85	$267.60	$277.45
Wet bar sink, under-counter stainless steel ***Replace*** Materials.....170.00 Labor..........42.60 ***Remove*** .... Labor............9.85	ea	$9.85	$212.60	$222.45
Wet bar sink, under-counter scalloped stainless steel ***Replace*** Materials....250.00 Labor..........42.60 ***Remove*** .... Labor............8.84	ea	$9.85	$292.60	$302.45
Wet bar sink, under-counter polished brass ***Replace*** Materials....340.00 Labor..........42.60 ***Remove*** .... Labor............9.85	ea	$9.85	$382.60	$392.45
Wet bar sink, under-counter hammered finish brass ***Replace*** Materials....390.00 Labor..........42.60 ***Remove*** .... Labor............9.85	ea	$9.85	$432.60	$442.45
Wet bar sink, under-counter scalloped polished brass ***Replace*** Materials....440.00 Labor..........42.60 ***Remove*** .... Labor............9.85	ea	$9.85	$482.60	$492.45
Remove under-counter wet bar sink for work, then reinstall ***Replace*** .... Labor..........52.70	ea	—	$52.70	$52.70
Add for brass supply and waste lines	ea	—	$125.00	$125.00
Add 33% for almond colored porcelain enamel				
Add 65% for colored porcelain enamel				
Sink plumbing, chrome ***Replace*** Materials.....110.00 Labor..........21.30	ea	—	$131.30	$131.30

RELATED ITEMS

Bathroom Hardware......41
Cleaning......................64

◁ under-counter

◀ **ADDITIONAL SINK COSTS**

◀ **SINK PLUMBING**

continued on next page

	Item Description	Unit	Remove	Replace	Total
SINK PLUMBING ▶ With visible plumbing including water feeds, P trap, escutcheons, and so forth, to wall or floor. Does not include faucet.	**Sink plumbing, brass** *Replace* Materials....180.00 Labor..........21.30	ea	—	$201.30	$201.30
	Sink plumbing, chrome-plated brass *Replace* Materials....230.00 Labor..........21.30	ea	—	$251.30	$251.30
TOILET PLUMBING ▶ Includes cold water supply, shut-off valve, wax ring, and toilet bolts.	**Toilet plumbing, chrome** *Replace* Materials......75.00 Labor..........15.40	ea	—	$90.40	$90.40
	Toilet plumbing, brass *Replace* Materials.....120.00 Labor..........15.40	ea	—	$135.40	$135.40
BIDET ▶ Includes water supply lines with shut-off valves. For rough plumbing see page 367. For bidet faucet see page 369.	**Bidet, standard grade** *Replace* Materials....370.00 Labor..........65.70 *Remove* .... Labor...........9.93	ea	$9.93	$435.70	$445.63
	Bidet, deluxe grade *Replace* Materials....545.00 Labor..........65.70 *Remove* .... Labor...........9.93	ea	$9.93	$610.70	$620.63
remove & reinstall ▷	**Remove bidet for work, then reinstall** *Replace* Materials........1.80 Labor.........106.00	ea	—	$107.80	$107.80
TOILET ▶ Economy grade toilets are typically white with round bowls. Standard grade toilets are typically white with elongated bowls. High and deluxe grades are typically low-tank toilets, in a variety of colors, with elongated bowls. Deluxe grade may also be "jet" toilets which combine low-water consumption with a direct-fed jet, siphon-assisted blow out action. For rough plumbing see page 367. For antique styles see page 386.	**Toilet, economy grade** *Replace* Materials....140.00 Labor..........59.50 *Remove* .... Labor...........9.52	ea	$9.52	$199.50	$209.02
	Toilet, standard grade *Replace* Materials.....170.00 Labor..........59.50 *Remove* .... Labor...........9.52	ea	$9.52	$229.50	$239.02
	Toilet, high grade *Replace* Materials....255.00 Labor..........59.50 *Remove* .... Labor...........9.52	ea	$9.52	$314.50	$324.02
	Toilet, deluxe grade *Replace* Materials....435.00 Labor..........59.50 *Remove* .... Labor...........9.52	ea	$9.52	$494.50	$504.02
	Remove toilet for work, then reinstall *Replace* Materials........1.80 Labor..........97.00	ea	—	$98.80	$98.80
TOILET SEAT ▶	**Toilet seat, plain round** *Replace* Materials......25.00 Labor...........9.92 *Remove* .... Labor...........3.82	ea	$3.82	$34.92	$38.74
	Toilet seat, hardwood *Replace* Materials......25.00 Labor...........9.92 *Remove* .... Labor...........3.82	ea	$3.82	$34.92	$38.74
	Toilet seat, with pattern *Replace* Materials......35.00 Labor...........9.92 *Remove* .... Labor...........3.82	ea	$3.82	$44.92	$48.74
	Toilet seat, elongated *Replace* Materials......50.00 Labor...........9.92 *Remove* .... Labor...........3.82	ea	$3.82	$59.92	$63.74
	Toilet seat, padded *Replace* Materials......40.00 Labor...........9.92 *Remove* .... Labor...........3.82	ea	$3.82	$49.92	$53.74

Item Description	Unit	Remove	Replace	Total
Remove toilet seat for work, then reinstall *Replace* .... Labor...........14.40	ea	—	$14.40	$14.40
48″ long by 44″ deep cast-iron corner bathtub *Replace* Materials...1650.00 Labor.........131.00 *Remove* .... Labor..........44.30	ea	$44.30	$1,781.00	$1,825.30
48″ long by 44″ deep acrylic fiberglass corner bathtub *Replace* Materials.....675.00 Labor..........80.00 *Remove* .... Labor..........28.10	ea	$28.10	$755.00	$783.10
60″ long by 32″ deep acrylic fiberglass bathtub *Replace* Materials.....310.00 Labor..........80.00 *Remove* .... Labor..........28.10	ea	$28.10	$390.00	$418.10
60″ long by 32″ deep porcelain-enamel, cast-iron bathtub *Replace* Materials....755.00 Labor.........131.00 *Remove* .... Labor..........44.30	ea	$44.30	$886.00	$930.30
60″ long by 32″ deep porcelain-enamel, steel bathtub *Replace* Materials....305.00 Labor.........131.00 *Remove* .... Labor..........44.30	ea	$44.30	$436.00	$480.30
72″ long by 36″ deep acrylic fiberglass bathtub *Replace* Materials....630.00 Labor..........80.00 *Remove* .... Labor..........28.10	ea	$28.10	$710.00	$738.10
72″ long by 36″ deep porcelain-enamel, cast-iron bathtub *Replace* Materials...1550.00 Labor.........131.00 *Remove* .... Labor..........44.30	ea	$44.30	$1,681.00	$1,725.30
72″ long by 36″ deep porcelain-enamel, steel bathtub *Replace* Materials.....470.00 Labor.........131.00 *Remove* .... Labor..........44.30	ea	$44.30	$601.00	$645.30
Remove fiberglass bathtub for work, then reinstall *Replace* .... Labor.........154.00	ea	—	$154.00	$154.00
Remove cast-iron or steel bathtub for work, then reinstall *Replace* .... Labor.........235.00	ea	—	$235.00	$235.00
60″ long by 32″ deep acrylic fiberglass bathtub with whirlpool jets *Replace* Materials..1600.00 Labor.........154.00 *Remove* .... Labor..........39.90	ea	$39.90	$1,754.00	$1,793.90
60″ long by 32″ deep porcelain-enamel, cast-iron bathtub with whirlpool jets *Replace* Materials..3800.00 Labor.........179.00 *Remove* .... Labor..........58.60	ea	$58.60	$3,979.00	$4,037.60
72″ long by 36″ deep acrylic fiberglass bathtub with whirlpool jets *Replace* Materials..3300.00 Labor.........154.00 *Remove* .... Labor..........39.90	ea	$39.90	$3,454.00	$3,493.90
72″ long by 36″ deep porcelain-enamel, cast-iron bathtub with whirlpool jets *Replace* Materials..7900.00 Labor.........179.00 *Remove* .... Labor..........58.60	ea	$58.60	$8,079.00	$8,137.60
66″ long by 48″ deep fiberglass bathtub with whirlpool jets *Replace* Materials..2900.00 Labor.........154.00 *Remove* .... Labor..........39.90	ea	$39.90	$3,054.00	$3,093.90

◀ **BATHTUB**
Includes standard chrome drain and overflow assembly. Does not include faucet. For rough plumbing see page 367. For bathtub faucets see page 370. For antique style bathtubs see page 386. For antique style faucets see page 384.

◁ **remove & reinstall**

◀ **BATHTUB WITH WHIRLPOOL JETS**
Includes standard chrome drain and overflow assembly and jets and electrical pump hookup. Does not include faucet or electrical rough wiring. For rough plumbing see page 367. For bathtub faucets see page 370. For antique style bathtubs see page 386. For antique style faucets see page 384.

RELATED ITEMS

Bathroom Hardware......41
Cleaning........................64

	Item Description	Unit	Remove	Replace	Total
BATHTUB WITH WHIRLPOOL JETS *continued*	**72" long by 36" deep fiberglass bathtub with whirlpool jets** *Replace* Materials..2800.00 Labor.........154.00 *Remove* .... Labor..........39.90	ea	$39.90	$2,954.00	$2,993.90
	60" long by 30" deep fiberglass bathtub with whirlpool jets *Replace* Materials..2200.00 Labor.........154.00 *Remove* .... Labor..........39.90	ea	$39.90	$2,354.00	$2,393.90
	72" long by 42" deep fiberglass bathtub with whirlpool jets *Replace* Materials..3500.00 Labor.........154.00 *Remove* .... Labor..........39.90	ea	$39.90	$3,654.00	$3,693.90
	83" long by 65" deep fiberglass bathtub with whirlpool jets *Replace* Materials..6050.00 Labor.........154.00 *Remove* .... Labor..........39.90	ea	$39.90	$6,204.00	$6,243.90
remove & reinstall ▷	**Remove fiberglass bathtub with whirlpool jets for work, then reinstall** *Replace* .... Labor.........298.00	ea	—	$298.00	$298.00
	Remove cast iron bathtub with whirlpool jets for work, then reinstall *Replace* .... Labor........406.00	ea	—	$406.00	$406.00
BATHTUB & SHOWER *Does not include faucet. High and deluxe quality usually indicates thicker fiberglass with glossier finishes and more ornate soap and wash cloth compartments. For rough plumbing see page 367. For bathtub faucets see page 370. For antique style bathtubs see page 386. For antique style faucets see page 384.*	**Acrylic fiberglass bathtub & shower combination, standard grade** *Replace* Materials....425.00 Labor.........144.00 *Remove* .... Labor..........46.50	ea	$46.50	$569.00	$615.50
	Acrylic fiberglass bathtub & shower combination, high grade *Replace* Materials.....670.00 Labor.........144.00 *Remove* .... Labor..........46.50	ea	$46.50	$814.00	$860.50
	Acrylic fiberglass bathtub & shower combination, deluxe grade *Replace* Materials....850.00 Labor.........144.00 *Remove* .... Labor..........46.50	ea	$46.50	$994.00	$1,040.50
	Remove fiberglass bathtub & shower combination for work, then reinstall *Replace* .... Labor.........249.00	ea	—	$249.00	$249.00
SHOWER STALL *Includes concrete reinforcement under base. Does not include faucet.*	**32" wide by 32" deep acrylic fiberglass shower stall** *Replace* Materials....355.00 Labor.........121.00 *Remove* .... Labor..........33.60	ea	$33.60	$476.00	$509.60
	32" wide by 32" deep acrylic fiberglass shower stall with terrazzo base *Replace* Materials....425.00 Labor.........121.00 *Remove* .... Labor..........33.60	ea	$33.60	$546.00	$579.60
	32" wide by 32" deep metal shower stall *Replace* Materials.....165.00 Labor.........121.00 *Remove* .... Labor..........33.60	ea	$33.60	$286.00	$319.60
	48" wide by 35" deep acrylic fiberglass shower stall *Replace* Materials....400.00 Labor.........121.00 *Remove* .... Labor..........33.60	ea	$33.60	$521.00	$554.60
	60" wide by 35" deep acrylic fiberglass shower stall *Replace* Materials....445.00 Labor.........121.00 *Remove* .... Labor..........33.60	ea	$33.60	$566.00	$599.60
remove & reinstall ▷	**Remove fiberglass shower stall for work, then reinstall** *Replace* .... Labor.........194.00	ea	—	$194.00	$194.00
SHOWER PAN *Pan and drain for tile shower.*	**Shower pan, typical size** *Replace* Materials......50.00 Labor...........45.60	ea	—	$95.60	$95.60

Item Description	Unit	Remove	Replace	Total
Shower pan, large size *Replace* Materials......75.00 Labor..........45.60	ea	—	$120.60	$120.60
Shower base, fiberglass *Replace* Materials.....115.00 Labor..........46.90	ea	—	$161.90	$161.90
Shower base, terrazzo style *Replace* Materials.....410.00 Labor..........46.90	ea	—	$456.90	$456.90
Corner entry shower base, fiberglass *Replace* Materials.....135.00 Labor..........46.90	ea	—	$181.90	$181.90
Corner entry shower base, terrazzo style *Replace* Materials.....455.00 Labor..........46.90	ea	—	$501.90	$501.90
Cultured stone bathtub surround *Replace* Materials....550.00 Labor..........89.40 *Remove* .... Labor..........24.60	ea	$24.60	$639.40	$664.00
Fiberglass bathtub surround, standard grade *Replace* Materials....320.00 Labor..........68.80 *Remove* .... Labor..........24.60	ea	$24.60	$388.80	$413.40
Fiberglass bathtub surround, high grade *Replace* Materials....500.00 Labor..........68.80 *Remove* .... Labor..........24.60	ea	$24.60	$568.80	$593.40
Fiberglass bathtub surround, deluxe grade *Replace* Materials.....715.00 Labor..........68.80 *Remove* .... Labor..........24.60	ea	$24.60	$783.80	$808.40
Remove bathtub surround for work, then reinstall *Replace* .... Labor.........118.00	ea	—	$118.00	$118.00
Glass shower, with cultured stone slabs on walls, standard grade *Replace* Materials.....715.00 Labor.........104.00 *Remove* .... Labor..........33.60	ea	$33.60	$819.00	$852.60
Glass shower, with cultured stone slabs on walls, high grade *Replace* Materials....790.00 Labor.........104.00 *Remove* .... Labor..........33.60	ea	$33.60	$894.00	$927.60
Corner entry glass shower, cultured stone slabs on walls, standard grade *Replace* Materials....930.00 Labor.........121.00 *Remove* .... Labor..........33.60	ea	$33.60	$1,051.00	$1,084.60
Corner entry glass shower, cultured slabs on walls, high grade *Replace* Materials..1025.00 Labor.........121.00 *Remove* .... Labor..........33.60	ea	$33.60	$1,146.00	$1,179.60
Glass shower, fiberglass panels on walls, standard grade *Replace* Materials....650.00 Labor..........93.00 *Remove* .... Labor..........33.60	ea	$33.60	$743.00	$776.60
Glass shower, fiberglass panels on walls, high grade *Replace* Materials....720.00 Labor..........93.00 *Remove* .... Labor..........33.60	ea	$33.60	$813.00	$846.60
Corner entry glass shower, fiberglass panels on walls, standard grade *Replace* Materials....845.00 Labor.........109.00 *Remove* .... Labor..........33.60	ea	$33.60	$954.00	$987.60

◀ **SHOWER BASE**
Prefabricated

◀ **BATHTUB SURROUND**
Three walls surrounding bathtub: two widths and one length. See bathtubs on page 377. For bathtub rough plumbing see page 367. For bathtub faucets see page 370. For antique style bathtubs see page 386. For antique style faucets see page 384.

◁ **remove & reinstall**

◀ **GLASS SHOWER**
Cultured stone slabs or fiberglass panels on two walls, glass on one wall, and a glass door on one wall. Corner entry showers have two glass walls and a corner entry door.

RELATED ITEMS

Bathroom Hardware......41
Cleaning.......................64

	Item Description	Unit	Remove	Replace	Total
GLASS SHOWER ▶ *continued*	**Corner entry glass shower, fiberglass panels on walls, high grade** ***Replace*** Materials....935.00 Labor.........109.00 ***Remove*** .... Labor.........33.60	ea	$33.60	$1,044.00	$1,077.60
remove & reinstall ▷	**Remove glass shower for work, then reinstall** ***Replace*** .... Labor.........140.00	ea	—	$140.00	$140.00
SLIDING BATHTUB DOOR ▶ *See tubs on page 377.*	**Sliding glass bathtub door, mill finish trim** ***Replace*** Materials....205.00 Labor...........61.20 ***Remove*** .... Labor...........14.20	ea	$14.20	$266.20	$280.40
	Sliding glass bathtub door, mill finish trim with fancy glass ***Replace*** Materials....260.00 Labor...........61.20 ***Remove*** .... Labor...........14.20	ea	$14.20	$321.20	$335.40
	Sliding glass bathtub door, gold finish trim ***Replace*** Materials....250.00 Labor...........61.20 ***Remove*** .... Labor...........14.20	ea	$14.20	$311.20	$325.40
	Sliding glass bathtub door, gold finish trim with fancy glass ***Replace*** Materials....320.00 Labor...........61.20 ***Remove*** .... Labor...........14.20	ea	$14.20	$381.20	$395.40
	Sliding glass bathtub door, brass trim ***Replace*** Materials.....470.00 Labor...........61.20 ***Remove*** .... Labor...........14.20	ea	$14.20	$531.20	$545.40
	Sliding glass bathtub door, brass trim with etched glass ***Replace*** Materials ....595.00 Labor...........61.20 ***Remove*** .... Labor...........14.20	ea	$14.20	$656.20	$670.40
remove & reinstall ▷	**Remove sliding glass bathtub door for work, then reinstall** ***Replace*** .... Labor.........101.90	ea	—	$101.90	$101.90
FOLDING BATHTUB DOOR ▶ *See tubs on page 377.*	**Folding plastic bathtub doors** ***Replace*** Materials....200.00 Labor...........55.90 ***Remove*** .... Labor...........13.80	ea	$13.80	$255.90	$269.70
remove & reinstall ▷	**Remove folding plastic bathtub door for work, then reinstall** ***Replace*** .... Labor...........75.50	ea	—	$75.50	$75.50
SHOWER DOOR ▶ *See showers on page 378 and below.*	**Shower door, solid glass** ***Replace*** Materials.....245.00 Labor ....53.60 ***Remove*** .... Labor...........13.30	ea	$13.30	$298.60	$311.90
	Shower door, mill finish trim with fancy glass ***Replace*** Materials ....275.00 Labor ....53.60 ***Remove*** .... Labor...........13.30	ea	$13.30	$328.60	$341.90
	Shower door, gold finish trim ***Replace*** Materials ....275.00 Labor ....53.60 ***Remove*** .... Labor...........13.30	ea	$13.30	$328.60	$341.90
	Shower door, gold finish trim with fancy glass ***Replace*** Materials.....310.00 Labor ....53.60 ***Remove*** .... Labor...........13.30	ea	$13.30	$363.60	$376.90
	Shower door, brass finish trim ***Replace*** Materials....460.00 Labor ....53.60 ***Remove*** .... Labor...........13.30	ea	$13.30	$513.60	$526.90

RELATED ITEMS
Bathroom Hardware......41
Cleaning 64

Item Description	Unit	Remove	Replace	Total	
Shower doors, brass trim with etched glass *Replace* Materials.....515.00 Labor..........53.60 *Remove* .... Labor..........13.30	ea	$13.30	$568.60	$581.90	
Remove shower door for work, then reinstall *Replace* .... Labor..........73.30	ea	—	$73.30	$73.30	◁ remove & reinstall
10 gallon gas water heater *Replace* Materials....290.00 Labor.........149.00 *Remove* .... Labor..........30.50	ea	$30.50	$439.00	$469.50	◀ **GAS WATER HEATER**
20 gallon gas water heater *Replace* Materials.....315.00 Labor.........149.00 *Remove* .... Labor..........30.50	ea	$30.50	$464.00	$494.50	
30 gallon gas water heater *Replace* Materials....355.00 Labor.........149.00 *Remove* .... Labor..........30.50	ea	$30.50	$504.00	$534.50	
40 gallon gas water heater *Replace* Materials....370.00 Labor.........149.00 *Remove* .... Labor..........30.50	ea	$30.50	$519.00	$549.50	
50 gallon gas water heater *Replace* Materials....430.00 Labor.........149.00 *Remove* .... Labor..........30.50	ea	$30.50	$579.00	$609.50	
75 gallon gas water heater *Replace* Materials....760.00 Labor.........149.00 *Remove* .... Labor..........30.50	ea	$30.50	$909.00	$939.50	
Remove gas water heater for work, then reinstall *Replace* .... Labor.........224.00	ea	—	$224.00	$224.00	◁ remove & reinstall
10 gallon electric water heater *Replace* Materials....230.00 Labor.........140.00 *Remove* .... Labor..........29.20	ea	$29.20	$370.00	$399.20	◀ **ELECTRIC WATER HEATER**
20 gallon electric water heater *Replace* Materials....290.00 Labor.........140.00 *Remove* .... Labor..........29.20	ea	$29.20	$430.00	$459.20	
30 gallon electric water heater *Replace* Materials....330.00 Labor.........140.00 *Remove* .... Labor..........29.20	ea	$29.20	$470.00	$499.20	
40 gallon electric water heater *Replace* Materials....350.00 Labor.........140.00 *Remove* .... Labor..........29.20	ea	$29.20	$490.00	$519.20	
50 gallon electric water heater *Replace* Materials....420.00 Labor.........140.00 *Remove* .... Labor..........29.20	ea	$29.20	$560.00	$589.20	
75 gallon electric water heater *Replace* Materials....775.00 Labor.........140.00 *Remove* .... Labor..........29.20	ea	$29.20	$915.00	$944.20	
Replace element in electric water heater *Replace* Materials......85.00 Labor..........57.20	ea	—	$142.20	$142.20	◁ replace element
Remove electric water heater for work, then reinstall *Replace* .... Labor.........213.00	ea	—	$213.00	$213.00	

	Item Description	Unit	Remove	Replace	Total
WATER SOFTENER ▶	**Water softener, automatic two tank up to 30 grains per gallon** *Replace* Materials.....515.00 Labor.........149.00 *Remove* .... Labor...........11.20	ea	$11.20	$664.00	$675.20
	Water softener, automatic two tank up to 100 grains per gallon *Replace* Materials...1100.00 Labor.........149.00 *Remove* .... Labor...........11.20	ea	$11.20	$1,249.00	$1,260.20
remove & reinstall ▷	**Remove water softener for work, then reinstall** *Replace* .... Labor.........235.00	ea	—	$235.00	$235.00
SEPTIC TANK ▶ WITH LEACH FIELD *Includes mobilization, excavation, backfill, gravel, crushed stone, pipe, couplings, connectors, building paper, tank, and distribution box.*	**1,000 gallon concrete septic tank with 1,000 sf leach field** *Replace* Materials..2400.00 Labor......3480.00	ea	—	$5,880.00	$5,880.00
	1,000 gallon concrete septic tank with 2,000 sf leach field *Replace* Materials..3450.00 Labor.......5010.00	ea	—	$8,460.00	$8,460.00
	1,250 gallon concrete septic tank with 1,000 sf leach field *Replace* Materials..2550.00 Labor.......3560.00	ea	—	$6,110.00	$6,110.00
	1,250 gallon concrete septic tank with 2,000 sf leach field *Replace* Materials..3600.00 Labor.......5100.00	ea	—	$8,700.00	$8,700.00
	1,500 gallon concrete septic tank with 1,000 sf leach field *Replace* Materials..2700.00 Labor.......3610.00	ea	—	$6,310.00	$6,310.00
	1,500 gallon concrete septic tank with 2,000 sf leach field *Replace* Materials..3750.00 Labor.......5140.00	ea	—	$8,890.00	$8,890.00
	1,000 gallon fiberglass septic tank with 1,000 sf leach field *Replace* Materials..2350.00 Labor......3460.00	ea	—	$5,810.00	$5,810.00
	1,000 gallon fiberglass septic tank with 2,000 sf leach field *Replace* Materials..3350.00 Labor.......5010.00	ea	—	$8,360.00	$8,360.00
	1,250 gallon fiberglass septic tank with 1,000 sf leach field *Replace* Materials..2500.00 Labor......3540.00	ea	—	$6,040.00	$6,040.00
	1,250 gallon fiberglass septic tank with 2,000 sf leach field *Replace* Materials..3500.00 Labor.......5100.00	ea	—	$8,600.00	$8,600.00
	1,500 gallon fiberglass septic tank with 1,000 sf leach field *Replace* Materials..2650.00 Labor.......3590.00	ea	—	$6,240.00	$6,240.00
	1,500 gallon fiberglass septic tank with 2,000 sf leach field *Replace* Materials..3650.00 Labor.......5140.00	ea	—	$8,790.00	$8,790.00
	1,000 gallon polyethylene septic tank with 1,000 sf leach field *Replace* Materials...2150.00 Labor......3460.00	ea	—	$5,610.00	$5,610.00
	1,000 gallon polyethylene septic tank with 2,000 sf leach field *Replace* Materials..3200.00 Labor.......5010.00	ea	—	$8,210.00	$8,210.00
	1,250 gallon polyethylene septic tank with 1,000 sf leach field *Replace* Materials..2300.00 Labor......3540.00	ea	—	$5,840.00	$5,840.00
	1,250 gallon polyethylene septic tank with 2,000 sf leach field *Replace* Materials..3350.00 Labor.......5100.00	ea	—	$8,450.00	$8,450.00

Item Description	Unit	Remove	Replace	Total
1,500 gallon polyethylene septic tank with 1,000 sf leach field *Replace* Materials...2450.00 Labor.......3590.00	ea	—	$6,040.00	$6,040.00
1,500 gallon polyethylene septic tank with 2,000 sf leach field *Replace* Materials..3500.00 Labor.......5140.00	ea	—	$8,640.00	$8,640.00
Submersible 1/2 hp water pump *Replace* Materials....500.00 Labor.........247.00 *Remove* .... Labor..........48.10	ea	$48.10	$747.00	$795.10
Submersible 3/4 hp water pump *Replace* Materials....550.00 Labor.........247.00 *Remove* .... Labor..........48.10	ea	$48.10	$797.00	$845.10
Submersible 1 hp water pump *Replace* Materials....555.00 Labor.........247.00 *Remove* .... Labor..........48.10	ea	$48.10	$802.00	$850.10
Submersible 1-1/2 hp water pump *Replace* Materials.....695.00 Labor.........247.00 *Remove* .... Labor..........48.10	ea	$48.10	$942.00	$990.10
Submersible 2 hp water pump *Replace* Materials....760.00 Labor.........247.00 *Remove* .... Labor..........48.10	ea	$48.10	$1,007.00	$1,055.10
Submersible 3 hp water pump *Replace* Materials....990.00 Labor.........247.00 *Remove* .... Labor..........48.10	ea	$48.10	$1,237.00	$1,285.10
Submersible 5 hp water pump *Replace* Materials...1150.00 Labor.........247.00 *Remove* .... Labor..........48.10	ea	$48.10	$1,397.00	$1,445.10
Remove submersible pump for work then reinstall *Replace* .... Labor........344.00	ea	—	$344.00	$344.00
1/4 hp automatic plastic sump pump *Replace* Materials.....185.00 Labor...........62.10 *Remove* .... Labor...........15.50	ea	$15.50	$247.10	$262.60
1/3 hp automatic plastic sump pump *Replace* Materials....225.00 Labor...........62.10 *Remove* .... Labor...........15.50	ea	$15.50	$287.10	$302.60
1/2 hp automatic plastic sump pump *Replace* Materials....295.00 Labor...........62.10 *Remove* .... Labor...........15.50	ea	$15.50	$357.10	$372.60
1/4 hp automatic cast-iron sump pump *Replace* Materials....230.00 Labor...........62.10 *Remove* .... Labor...........15.50	ea	$15.50	$292.10	$307.60
1/3 hp automatic cast-iron sump pump *Replace* Materials....255.00 Labor...........62.10 *Remove* .... Labor...........15.50	ea	$15.50	$317.10	$332.60
1/2 hp automatic cast-iron sump pump *Replace* Materials....335.00 Labor...........62.10 *Remove* .... Labor...........15.50	ea	$15.50	$397.10	$412.60
Remove sump pump for work, then reinstall *Replace* .... Labor.........109.00	ea	—	$109.00	$109.00

RELATED ITEMS

Bathroom Hardware......41
Cleaning......................64

◀ **SUBMERSIBLE WATER PUMP**
Includes wiring and placement for well up to 100' deep.

◁ **remove & reinstall**

◀ **SUMP PUMP**
Basement style installation, includes up to 45 lf 1-1/2" PVC pipe and wiring hookup. Does not include rough electrical.

◁ **remove & reinstall**

	Item Description	Unit	Remove	Replace	Total
ANTIQUE STYLE ▶ SINK FAUCET See page 369 for information about faucet quality. Antique style faucets are usually brass, chrome over brass, or nickel over brass with ornate detail. Often used in homes that are not historical. For standard faucets see page 368 and 369.	**Antique style sink faucet, standard grade** *Replace* Materials.....165.00 Labor..........24.90 *Remove* Labor..........9.82	ea	$9.82	$189.90	$199.72
	Antique style sink faucet, high grade *Replace* Materials....280.00 Labor..........24.90 *Remove* Labor..........9.82	ea	$9.82	$304.90	$314.72
	Antique style sink faucet, deluxe grade *Replace* Materials....375.00 Labor..........24.90 *Remove* Labor..........9.82	ea	$9.82	$399.90	$409.72
	Antique style sink faucet, custom grade *Replace* Materials....550.00 Labor..........24.90 *Remove* Labor..........9.82	ea	$9.82	$574.90	$584.72
	Antique style sink faucet, custom deluxe grade *Replace* Materials....785.00 Labor..........24.90 *Remove* Labor..........9.82	ea	$9.82	$809.90	$819.72
remove & reinstall ▷	**Remove antique style sink faucet for work, then reinstall** *Replace* Labor..........37.20	ea	—	$37.20	$37.20
ANTIQUE STYLE ▶ BATHTUB FAUCET See page 369 for information about faucet quality. Antique style are usually brass, chrome over brass, or nickel over brass with ornate detail. Often used in homes that are not historical. For standard faucets see page 370.	**Claw-foot bathtub faucet, economy grade** *Replace* Materials.....210.00 Labor..........39.90 *Remove* Labor..........9.93	ea	$9.93	$249.90	$259.83
	Claw-foot bathtub faucet, standard grade *Replace* Materials....360.00 Labor..........39.90 *Remove* Labor..........9.93	ea	$9.93	$399.90	$409.83
	Claw-foot bathtub faucet, high grade *Replace* Materials....485.00 Labor..........39.90 *Remove* Labor..........9.93	ea	$9.93	$524.90	$534.83
	Claw-foot bathtub faucet, deluxe grade *Replace* Materials....710.00 Labor..........39.90 *Remove* Labor..........9.93	ea	$9.93	$749.90	$759.83
	Claw-foot bathtub faucet, custom grade *Replace* Materials...1010.00 Labor..........39.90 *Remove* Labor..........9.93	ea	$9.93	$1,049.90	$1,059.83
remove & reinstall ▷	**Remove claw-foot bathtub faucet for work, then reinstall** *Replace* Labor..........51.00	ea	—	$51.00	$51.00
ANTIQUE STYLE ▶ BATHTUB FAUCET WITH HAND-HELD SHOWER See page 369 for information about faucet quality. Antique style faucets are usually brass, chrome over brass, or nickel over brass with ornate detail. Often used in homes that are not historical. For standard faucets see page 370.	**Claw-foot bathtub faucet with hand-held shower, standard grade** *Replace* Materials....325.00 Labor..........44.30 *Remove* Labor..........9.96	ea	$9.96	$369.30	$379.26
	Claw-foot bathtub faucet with hand-held shower, high grade *Replace* Materials....560.00 Labor..........44.30 *Remove* Labor..........9.96	ea	$9.96	$604.30	$614.26
	Claw-foot bathtub faucet with hand-held shower, deluxe grade *Replace* Materials....755.00 Labor..........44.30 *Remove* Labor..........9.96	ea	$9.96	$799.30	$809.26
	Claw-foot bathtub faucet with hand-held shower, custom grade *Replace* Materials...1100.00 Labor..........44.30 *Remove* Labor..........9.96	ea	$9.96	$1,144.30	$1,154.26

Item Description	Unit	Remove	Replace	Total
Remove claw-foot bathtub faucet with hand-held shower for work, then reinstall	ea	—	$53.20	$53.20
Replace .... Labor..........53.20				
Claw-foot bathtub faucet with shower conversion, standard grade	ea	$13.90	$517.00	$530.90
Replace Materials....420.00 Labor...........97.00				
Remove .... Labor...........13.90				
Claw-foot bathtub faucet with shower conversion, high grade	ea	$13.90	$707.00	$720.90
Replace Materials.....610.00 Labor...........97.00				
Remove .... Labor...........13.90				
Claw-foot bathtub faucet with shower conversion, deluxe grade	ea	$13.90	$842.00	$855.90
Replace Materials.....745.00 Labor...........97.00				
Remove .... Labor...........13.90				
Claw-foot bathtub faucet with shower conversion, custom grade	ea	$13.90	$1,152.00	$1,165.90
Replace Materials...1055.00 Labor...........97.00				
Remove .... Labor...........13.90				
Remove claw-foot bathtub faucet with shower conversion, for work, then reinstall	ea	—	$140.00	$140.00
Replace .... Labor.........140.00				
Claw-foot bathtub supply lines, chrome-plated brass	ea	$11.80	$215.10	$226.90
Replace Materials.....165.00 Labor..........50.10				
Remove .... Labor...........11.80				
Claw-foot bathtub supply lines, brass	ea	$11.80	$195.10	$206.90
Replace Materials.....145.00 Labor..........50.10				
Remove .... Labor...........11.80				
Claw-foot bathtub drain, chrome-plated brass	ea	$11.10	$206.40	$217.50
Replace Materials.....155.00 Labor...........51.40				
Remove .... Labor...........11.10				
Claw-foot bathtub drain, brass	ea	$11.10	$176.40	$187.50
Replace Materials.....125.00 Labor...........51.40				
Remove .... Labor...........11.10				
Free-standing water feeds for claw-foot or slipper bathtub, chrome-plated brass	ea	$12.00	$294.50	$306.50
Replace Materials....240.00 Labor..........54.50				
Remove .... Labor...........12.00				
Free-standing water feeds for claw-foot or slipper bathtub, brass	ea	$12.00	$339.50	$351.50
Replace Materials....285.00 Labor..........54.50				
Remove .... Labor...........12.00				
Pedestal sink, economy grade	ea	$13.30	$424.50	$437.80
Replace Materials....370.00 Labor..........54.50				
Remove .... Labor...........13.30				
Pedestal sink, standard grade	ea	$13.30	$489.50	$502.80
Replace Materials....435.00 Labor..........54.50				
Remove .... Labor...........13.30				
Pedestal sink, high grade	ea	$13.30	$634.50	$647.80
Replace Materials....580.00 Labor..........54.50				
Remove .... Labor...........13.30				
Pedestal sink, deluxe grade	ea	$13.30	$1,054.50	$1,067.80
Replace Materials..1000.00 Labor..........54.50				
Remove .... Labor...........13.30				

◁ remove & reinstall

◀ **ANTIQUE STYLE BATHTUB FAUCET WITH SHOWER CONVERSION**
With exposed shower supply pipe and circular shower curtain rod. *See standard faucets on page 370.*

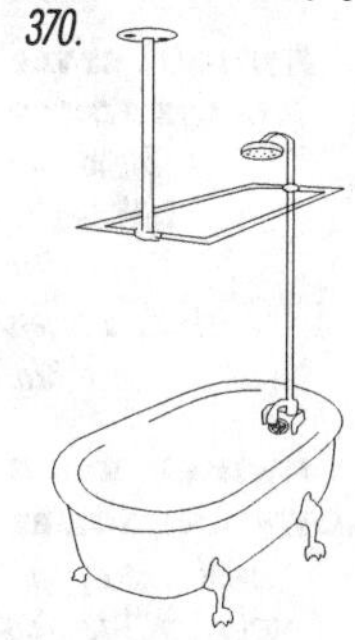

◀ **ANTIQUE STYLE TUB SUPPLY LINES**
Exposed lines used on antique style bathtubs.

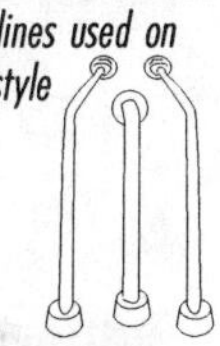

◀ **ANTIQUE STYLE BATHTUB DRAIN**

◀ **ANTIQUE STYLE FREE-STANDING SUPPLY LINES**
Exposed lines used on antique style bathtubs that do not rely on the bathtub for support.

◀ **PEDESTAL SINK**
Antique or contemporary style. *See standard sinks on page 371.*

RELATED ITEMS

Bathroom Hardware......41
Cleaning.......................64

	Item Description	Unit	Remove	Replace	Total
Pedestal sink ► *continued*	**Pedestal sink, custom grade** ***Replace*** Materials...1450.00 Labor..........54.50 ***Remove*** .... Labor...........13.30	ea	$13.30	$1,504.50	$1,517.80
	Pedestal sink, custom deluxe grade ***Replace*** Materials ..1850.00 Labor..........54.50 ***Remove*** .... Labor...........13.30	ea	$13.30	$1,904.50	$1,917.80
remove & reinstall ▷	**Remove pedestal sink for work, then reinstall** ***Replace*** .... Labor...........95.20	ea	—	$95.20	$95.20
Antique style ► pillbox toilet  *Round tank with beaded rim. See standard toilets on page 376.*	**Antique style pillbox toilet** ***Replace*** Materials ..1800.00 Labor..........99.20 ***Remove*** .... Labor...........11.80	ea	$11.80	$1,899.20	$1,911.00
	Remove antique style pillbox toilet for work, then reinstall ***Replace*** .... Labor.........154.00	ea	—	$154.00	$154.00
Antique style ► low-tank toilet *Identifiable by pipe (usually brass) running from tank to bowl. See standard toilets on page 376.* 	**Antique style low-tank toilet with porcelain tank** ***Replace*** Materials ....960.00 Labor..........99.20 ***Remove*** .... Labor...........11.80	ea	$11.80	$1,059.20	$1,071.00
	Antique style low-tank toilet with oak tank ***Replace*** Materials ....795.00 Labor..........99.20 ***Remove*** .... Labor...........11.80	ea	$11.80	$894.20	$906.00
	Remove antique style low-tank toilet for work, then reinstall ***Replace*** Materials........1.80 Labor.........154.00	ea	—	$155.80	$155.80
Antique style ► high-tank toilet 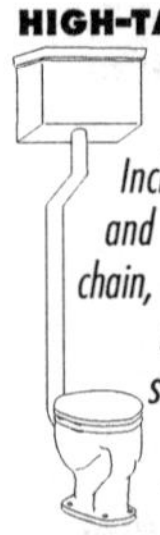 *Tank mounted high on wall. Includes brass pipe and connectors, pull chain, hardwood toilet seat, brass tank support brackets. Wood tanks include plastic liner.*	**Antique style high-tank toilet with porcelain tank** ***Replace*** Materials ..1200.00 Labor..........118.00 ***Remove*** .... Labor...........16.60	ea	$16.60	$1,318.00	$1,334.60
	Antique style high-tank toilet with oak tank ***Replace*** Materials ..1030.00 Labor..........118.00 ***Remove*** .... Labor...........16.60	ea	$16.60	$1,148.00	$1,164.60
	Remove antique style high-tank toilet for work, then reinstall ***Replace*** Materials........1.68 Labor.........165.00	ea	—	$166.80	$166.80
Antique bathtub ► *Claw-foot or ball-foot. Does not include supply lines or faucet. Includes **$90** for crating and **$270** for shipping. See standard bathtubs on page 377.*	**60" antique claw-foot or ball-foot cast-iron bathtub (as is condition)** ***Replace*** Materials ....690.00 Labor.........235.00 ***Remove*** .... Labor..........50.10	ea	$50.10	$925.00	$975.10
	66" antique claw-foot or ball-foot cast-iron bathtub (as is condition) ***Replace*** Materials ....760.00 Labor.........249.00 ***Remove*** .... Labor..........50.10	ea	$50.10	$1,009.00	$1,059.10
Refinished ► antique bathtub *Claw-foot or ball-foot. Interior and lip refinished exterior surfaces painted. Does not include visible supply lines or faucet. Includes **$90** for crating and **$270** for shipping. See standard bathtubs on page 377.* 	**48" refinished antique claw-foot or ball-foot cast-iron bathtub** ***Replace*** Materials ..2100.00 Labor.........213.00 ***Remove*** .... Labor..........50.10	ea	$50.10	$2,313.00	$2,363.10
	52" refinished antique claw-foot or ball-foot cast-iron bathtub ***Replace*** Materials..2050.00 Labor.........224.00 ***Remove*** .... Labor..........50.10	ea	$50.10	$2,274.00	$2,324.10
	60" refinished antique claw-foot or ball-foot cast-iron bathtub ***Replace*** Materials ..1800.00 Labor.........235.00 ***Remove*** .... Labor..........50.10	ea	$50.10	$2,035.00	$2,085.10

Item Description	Unit	Remove	Replace	Total
66″ refinished antique claw-foot or ball-foot cast-iron bathtub ***Replace*** Materials..1850.00 Labor.........249.00 ***Remove*** .... Labor..........50.10	ea	$50.10	$2,099.00	$2,149.10
60″ antique reproduction claw-foot or ball-foot cast-iron bathtub ***Replace*** Materials...1450.00 Labor.........235.00 ***Remove*** .... Labor..........50.10	ea	$50.10	$1,685.00	$1,735.10
66″ antique reproduction claw-foot or ball-foot cast-iron bathtub ***Replace*** Materials..1800.00 Labor.........249.00 ***Remove*** .... Labor..........50.10	ea	$50.10	$2,049.00	$2,099.10
60″ antique reproduction fiberglass claw-foot or ball-foot bathtub ***Replace*** Materials..2000.00 Labor.........140.00 ***Remove*** .... Labor..........39.90	ea	$39.90	$2,140.00	$2,179.90
66″ antique reproduction fiberglass claw-foot or ball-foot bathtub ***Replace*** Materials..2700.00 Labor.........149.00 ***Remove*** .... Labor..........39.90	ea	$39.90	$2,849.00	$2,888.90
Remove antique (or antique style) bathtub for work, then reinstall ***Replace*** .... Labor.........249.00	ea	—	$249.00	$249.00
60″ antique cast-iron slipper bathtub ***Replace*** Materials..2550.00 Labor.........235.00 ***Remove*** .... Labor..........50.10	ea	$50.10	$2,785.00	$2,835.10
66″ antique reproduction fiberglass slipper bathtub ***Replace*** Materials..4700.00 Labor.........249.00 ***Remove*** .... Labor..........39.90	ea	$39.90	$4,949.00	$4,988.90
Add for solid brass legs ***Replace*** Materials......80.00	ea	—	$80.00	$80.00
Add for brass-plated legs ***Replace*** Materials......50.00	ea	—	$50.00	$50.00
Add for oak trim around lip of antique bathtub ***Replace*** Materials...1450.00	ea	—	$1,450.00	$1,450.00

RELATED ITEMS

Bathroom Hardware......41
Cleaning......................64

◄ **REPRODUCTION ANTIQUE BATHTUB**
*Claw-foot or ball-foot. New tubs built in the antique style. Does not include supply lines or faucet. Includes **$90** for crating and **$270** for shipping. (**$160** shipping for fiberglass tubs.) See standard tubs on page 377.*

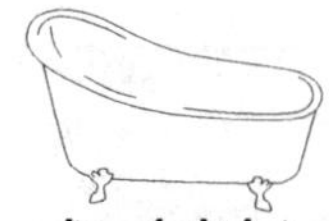

slipper bathtub △

◄ **REMOVE ANTIQUE BATHTUB & REINSTALL**

◄ **REPRODUCTION SLIPPER BATHTUB**
*Claw-foot or ball-foot. Does not include supply lines or faucet. Includes **$90** for crating and **$270** for shipping. (**$160** shipping for fiberglass tubs.) See standard tubs on page 377.*

◄ **ADDITIONAL ANTIQUE BATHTUB COSTS**

TIME & MATERIAL CHARTS *(selected items)*

Plumbing Materials

DESCRIPTION	UNIT PRICE
Black steel pipe	
1/2″ pipe	**$1.10** *lf*
3/4″ pipe	**$1.31** *lf*
1″ pipe	**$1.85** *lf*
2″ pipe	**$5.90** *lf*
Brass pipe	
1/2″ pipe	**$3.76** *lf*
3/4″ pipe	**$5.00** *lf*
1″ pipe	**$8.17** *lf*
2″ pipe	**$12.80** *lf*
Type K copper pipe	
1/2″ pipe	**$2.05** *lf*
3/4″ pipe	**$2.72** *lf*
1″ pipe	**$3.53** *lf*
2″ pipe	**$8.55** *lf*

. . . More ➢

Plumbing Materials *continued*

DESCRIPTION	UNIT PRICE
Type L copper pipe	
1/2" pipe	**$1.21** lf
3/4" pipe	**$1.99** lf
1" pipe	**$2.72** lf
2" pipe	**$6.58** lf
Type M copper pipe	
1/2" pipe	**$.93** lf
3/4" pipe	**$1.52** lf
1" pipe	**$2.06** lf
Galvanized steel pipe	
1/2" pipe	**$1.34** lf
3/4" pipe	**$1.60** lf
1" pipe	**$2.26** lf
2" pipe	**$7.20** lf
CPVC pipe	
1/2" pipe	**$.76** lf
3/4" pipe	**$.93** lf
1" pipe	**$1.12** lf
PVC pipe	
1/2" pipe	**$.48** lf
3/4" pipe	**$.51** lf
1" pipe	**$.57** lf
1-1/2" pipe	**$.76** lf
2" pipe	**$.91** lf
3" pipe	**$1.32** lf
4" pipe	**$1.73** lf
5" pipe	**$2.48** lf
6" pipe	**$2.96** lf
Cast-iron pipe	
2" pipe	**$4.87** lf
3" pipe	**$6.68** lf
4" pipe	**$9.43** lf
5" pipe	**$27.00** lf
6" pipe	**$34.60** lf
No-hub cast-iron pipe	
2" pipe	**$6.74** lf
3" pipe	**$8.63** lf
4" pipe	**$11.20** lf
5" pipe	**$16.30** lf

Plumbing Labor

LABORER	BASE WAGE	PAID LEAVE	TRUE WAGE	FICA	FUTA	WORKER'S COMP.	UNEMPLOY. INSUR.	HEALTH INSUR.	RETIRE (401K)	LIABILITY INSUR.	COST PER HOUR
Plumber	**$25.90**	2.02	**$27.92**	2.14	.22	4.66	2.43	2.69	.84	3.77	**$44.70**
Plumber's helper	**$21.80**	1.70	**$23.50**	1.80	.19	3.92	2.04	2.69	.71	3.17	**$38.00**
Demolition laborer	**$13.90**	1.08	**$14.98**	1.15	.12	4.79	1.30	2.69	.45	2.02	**$27.50**

Paid Leave is calculated based on two weeks paid vacation, one week sick leave, and seven paid holidays. Employer's matching portion of **FICA** is 7.65 percent. **FUTA** (Federal Unemployment) is .8 percent. **Worker's compensation** for the plumbing trade was calculated using a national average of 16.69 percent. **Unemployment insurance** was calculated using a national average of 8.7 percent. **Health insurance** was calculated based on a projected national average for 2002 of $535 per employee (and family when applicable) per month. Employer pays 80 percent for a per month cost of $428 per employee. **Retirement** is based on a 401(k) retirement program with employer matching of 50 percent. Employee contributions to the 401(k) plan are an average of 6 percent of the true wage. **Liability insurance** is based on a national average of 13.2 percent.

Plumbing Labor Productivity

WORK DESCRIPTION	LABORER	COST PER HOUR	PRODUCTIVITY	UNIT PRICE
Demolition				
remove faucet	demolition laborer	$27.50	.357	$9.82 ea
remove bathroom sink	demolition laborer	$27.50	.366	$10.10 ea
remove kitchen or laundry sink	demolition laborer	$27.50	.369	$10.10 ea
remove wet bar sink	demolition laborer	$27.50	.358	$9.85 ea
remove toilet	demolition laborer	$27.50	.346	$9.52 ea
remove fiberglass bathtub	demolition laborer	$27.50	1.02	$28.10 ea
remove cast-iron or steel bathtub	demolition laborer	$27.50	1.61	$44.30 ea
remove fiberglass bathtub with whirlpool jets	demolition laborer	$27.50	1.45	$39.90 ea
remove cast-iron or steel tub with whirlpool jets	demolition laborer	$27.50	2.13	$58.60 ea
remove glass shower	demolition laborer	$27.50	1.22	$33.60 ea
remove bathtub and shower combination	demolition laborer	$27.50	1.69	$46.50 ea
remove shower stall	demolition laborer	$27.50	1.22	$33.60 ea
remove bathtub surround	demolition laborer	$27.50	.893	$24.60 ea
remove sliding glass bathtub door	demolition laborer	$27.50	.515	$14.20 ea
remove shower door	demolition laborer	$27.50	.485	$13.30 ea
remove gas water heater	demolition laborer	$27.50	1.11	$30.50 ea
remove electric water heater	demolition laborer	$27.50	1.06	$29.20 ea
remove water softener	demolition laborer	$27.50	.408	$11.20 ea
remove submersible pump	demolition laborer	$27.50	1.75	$48.10 ea
remove sump pump	demolition laborer	$27.50	.562	$15.50 ea
remove antique style sink faucet	demolition laborer	$27.50	.357	$9.82 ea
remove antique style bathtub faucet	demolition laborer	$27.50	.361	$9.93 ea
remove claw-foot bathtub supply lines	demolition laborer	$27.50	.429	$11.80 ea
remove claw-foot bathtub drain	demolition laborer	$27.50	.403	$11.10 ea
remove free-standing water feeds	demolition laborer	$27.50	.437	$12.00 ea
remove pedestal sink	demolition laborer	$27.50	.483	$13.30 ea
remove antique style pillbox toilet	demolition laborer	$27.50	.429	$11.80 ea
remove antique style low-tank toilet	demolition laborer	$27.50	.429	$11.80 ea
remove antique style high-tank toilet	demolition laborer	$27.50	.602	$16.60 ea
remove cast-iron claw-foot bathtub	demolition laborer	$27.50	1.82	$50.10 ea
remove fiberglass claw-foot bathtub	demolition laborer	$27.50	1.45	$39.90 ea
Install field threaded pipe				
1/2"	plumber	$44.70	.127	$5.68 lf
3/4"	plumber	$44.70	.136	$6.08 lf
1"	plumber	$44.70	.158	$7.06 lf
2"	plumber	$44.70	.231	$10.30 lf
Install copper pipe				
1/2"	plumber	$44.70	.104	$4.65 lf
3/4"	plumber	$44.70	.109	$4.87 lf
1"	plumber	$44.70	.122	$5.45 lf
2"	plumber	$44.70	.202	$9.03 lf
Install plastic pipe				
1/2"	plumber	$44.70	.153	$6.84 lf
3/4"	plumber	$44.70	.162	$7.24 lf
1"	plumber	$44.70	.189	$8.45 lf
2"	plumber	$44.70	.251	$11.20 lf
3"	plumber	$44.70	.281	$12.60 lf
4"	plumber	$44.70	.311	$13.90 lf
5"	plumber	$44.70	.346	$15.50 lf
6"	plumber	$44.70	.380	$17.00 lf
Install cast-iron pipe				
2"	plumber	$44.70	.235	$10.50 lf
3"	plumber	$44.70	.248	$11.10 lf
4"	plumber	$44.70	.270	$12.10 lf
5"	plumber	$44.70	.305	$13.60 lf
6"	plumber	$44.70	.317	$14.20 lf
Install no-hub cast-iron pipe				
2"	plumber	$44.70	.210	$9.39 lf
3"	plumber	$44.70	.222	$9.92 lf
4"	plumber	$44.70	.242	$10.80 lf
6"	plumber	$44.70	.283	$12.70 lf

. . . More ➢

Plumbing Labor Productivity *continued*

WORK DESCRIPTION	LABORER	COST PER HOUR	PRODUCTIVITY	UNIT PRICE
Install faucet				
bathroom sink	plumber	$44.70	.556	$24.90 ea
kitchen sink	plumber	$44.70	.562	$25.10 ea
laundry sink	plumber	$44.70	.546	$24.40 ea
shower	plumber	$44.70	.575	$25.70 ea
bathtub	plumber	$44.70	.568	$25.40 ea
bathtub with shower	plumber	$44.70	.606	$27.10 ea
Install bathroom sink				
wall-hung	plumber	$44.70	.877	$39.20 ea
self-rimming	plumber	$44.70	.909	$40.60 ea
under-counter	plumber	$44.70	.952	$42.60 ea
Install kitchen sink				
install	plumber	$44.70	.926	$41.40 ea
Install laundry sink				
in countertop	plumber	$44.70	.901	$40.30 ea
on legs or frame	plumber	$44.70	.833	$37.20 ea
Install wet bar sink				
self-rimming	plumber	$44.70	.909	$40.60 ea
under-counter	plumber	$44.70	1.14	$51.00 ea
Install fixtures				
toilet	plumber	$44.70	1.33	$59.50 ea
cast-iron or steel bathtub	plumber	$44.70	2.94	$131.00 ea
fiberglass bathtub	plumber	$44.70	1.79	$80.00 ea
cast-iron or steel bathtub with whirlpool jets	plumber	$44.70	4.00	$179.00 ea
fiberglass bathtub with whirlpool jets	plumber	$44.70	3.45	$154.00 ea
fiberglass bathtub & shower combination	plumber	$44.70	3.23	$144.00 ea
shower stall	plumber	$44.70	2.70	$121.00 ea
Install shower / bathtub door				
sliding bathtub door	plumber	$44.70	1.37	$61.20 ea
shower door	plumber	$44.70	1.20	$53.60 ea
Install water heater				
gas	plumber	$44.70	3.33	$149.00 ea
electric	plumber	$44.70	3.13	$140.00 ea
Install water softener				
install	plumber	$44.70	3.33	$149.00 ea
Install septic system				
with concrete tank				
1,000 gallon with 1,000 sf leach field	plumber	$44.70	77.8	$3,480.00 ea
1,000 gallon with 2,000 sf leach field	plumber	$44.70	112	$5,010.00 ea
with fiberglass tank				
1,000 gallon with 1,000 sf leach field	plumber	$44.70	77.5	$3,460.00 ea
1,000 gallon with 2,000 sf leach field	plumber	$44.70	112	$5,010.00 ea
with polyethylene tank				
1,000 gallon with 1,000 sf leach field	plumber	$44.70	77.5	$3,460.00 ea
1,000 gallon with 2,000 sf leach field	plumber	$44.70	112	$5,010.00 ea
Install water pump				
submersible	plumber	$44.70	5.52	$247.00 ea
automatic sump	plumber	$44.70	1.39	$62.10 ea
Install claw-foot bathtub faucet				
faucet	plumber	$44.70	.893	$39.90 ea
faucet with shower conversion	plumber	$44.70	2.17	$97.00 ea
Install pedestal sink				
install	plumber	$44.70	1.22	$54.50 ea
Install antique style toilet				
pillbox or low tank	plumber	$44.70	2.22	$99.20 ea
high-tank	plumber	$44.70	2.63	$118.00 ea
Install antique style bathtub				
52" cast-iron	plumber	$44.70	5.00	$224.00 ea
60" cast-iron	plumber	$44.70	5.26	$235.00 ea
66" cast-iron	plumber	$44.70	5.56	$249.00 ea
60" reproduction fiberglass	plumber	$44.70	3.13	$140.00 ea
66" reproduction fiberglass	plumber	$44.70	3.33	$149.00 ea

30 Retaining Walls

Item Description	Unit	Remove	Replace	Total	
Minimum charge for retaining wall work *Replace* Materials....150.00 Labor.........101.30 Equipment........100.10	ea	—	$351.40	$351.40	◄ **MINIMUM**
Concrete retaining wall *Replace* Materials........7.09 Labor............9.19 Equipment............2.55 *Remove* .... Labor............9.49 ► Includes 4" perforated pipe drain line at inside base that is set in gravel.	sf	$9.49	$18.83	$28.32	◄ **CONCRETE** *See Masonry, page 296 for brick veneer and page 317 for wall caps and wall coping.*
Wood pile retaining wall with wood lagging *Replace* Materials........5.47 Labor............3.85 Equipment............1.49 *Remove* .... Labor............5.09	sf	$5.09	$10.81	$15.90	◄ **PILE WITH LAGGING**
Steel pile retaining wall with wood lagging *Replace* Materials........5.68 Labor............4.21 Equipment............1.49 *Remove* .... Labor............5.61	sf	$5.61	$11.38	$16.99	
Add for anchored tieback *Replace* Materials....109.00 Labor..........98.80 Equipment..........29.50 *Remove* .... Labor..........50.10	ea	$50.10	$237.30	$287.40	◄ **ANCHORED TIEBACK** *For all retaining wall types.*
Railroad tie retaining wall with tie tiebacks *Replace* Materials........5.58 Labor............9.88 Equipment............1.44 *Remove* .... Labor............5.50	sf	$5.50	$16.90	$22.40	◄ **RAILROAD TIE**
Railroad tie retaining wall without tie tiebacks *Replace* Materials........5.05 Labor............6.76 Equipment............1.28 *Remove* .... Labor............5.20	sf	$5.20	$13.09	$18.29	
Cedar tie retaining wall with tie tiebacks *Replace* Materials........7.09 Labor..........10.13 Equipment............1.33 *Remove* .... Labor............5.17	sf	$5.17	$18.55	$23.72	◄ **CEDAR TIE**
Cedar tie retaining wall without tie tiebacks *Replace* Materials........6.79 Labor............6.84 Equipment............1.24 *Remove* .... Labor............4.90	sf	$4.90	$14.87	$19.77	
Random stone retaining wall, dry set *Replace* Materials......16.00 Labor..........17.70 Equipment............1.49 *Remove* .... Labor..........10.60	sf	$10.60	$35.19	$45.79	◄ **STONE** *Includes 4" perforated pipe drain line at inside base set in gravel.*
Random stone retaining wall, mortar set *Replace* Materials......16.60 Labor..........15.30 Equipment............1.49 *Remove* .... Labor..........10.60	sf	$10.60	$33.39	$43.99	
Cut stone retaining wall, dry set *Replace* Materials......20.20 Labor..........15.10 Equipment............1.49 *Remove* .... Labor..........10.60	sf	$10.60	$36.79	$47.39	
Cut stone retaining wall, mortar set *Replace* Materials......20.80 Labor..........14.90 Equipment............1.49 *Remove* .... Labor..........10.60	sf	$10.60	$37.19	$47.79	
Interlocking masonry block retaining wall *Replace* Materials........9.79 Labor..........12.70 Equipment............1.49 *Remove* .... Labor............9.16	sf	$9.16	$23.98	$33.14	◄ **INTERLOCKING BLOCK**

RETAINING WALLS

Retaining walls include excavation and backfill. Measure sf of surface area. Includes sand and/or gravel base and 2' to 3' of walls buried beneath exposed surface.

	Item Description	Unit	Remove	Replace	Total
Interlocking ▶ block *continued*	**Add for solid cap on interlocking masonry block retaining wall** ***Replace*** Materials........4.77 Labor............1.94 ▶ 4" high by 16" wide by 10" deep. Per lf of wall.	lf	—	$6.71	$6.71
	Add for knock-out cap on interlocking masonry block retaining wall ***Replace*** Materials........5.53 Labor............1.94 ▶ Same as above except 3" to 4" back the cap is cut out to about half its thickness to allow soil and vegetation to overlap the top of the wall. Per lf of wall.	lf	—	$7.47	$7.47
Add for fabric ▶ reinforcement *One common brand name is called GeoGrid. Fabric ties retaining walls into hillside.*	**Add for 4-1/2' deep reinforced fabric, one row every 2' of wall height** ***Replace*** Materials........3.58 Labor............ .28	sf	—	$3.86	$3.86
	Add for 4-1/2' deep reinforced fabric, one row every 3' of wall height ***Replace*** Materials........2.39 Labor............ .20	sf	—	$2.59	$2.59
	Add for 6' deep reinforced fabric, one row every 2' of wall height ***Replace*** Materials........4.32 Labor............ .28	sf	—	$4.60	$4.60
	Add for 6' deep reinforced fabric, one row every 3' of wall height ***Replace*** Materials........2.88 Labor............ .20	sf	—	$3.08	$3.08
Shotcrete ▶	**Shotcrete slope stabilization with wire mesh (per inch deep)** ***Replace*** Materials........1.64 Labor............4.21 Equipment............ .24	sf	—	$6.09	$6.09

Time & Material Charts *(selected items)*

Retaining Walls Materials

*See **Retaining Walls** material prices with the line items and other information in the **QuickFinder** column.*

Retaining Walls Labor

LABORER	BASE WAGE	PAID LEAVE	TRUE WAGE	FICA	FUTA	WORKER'S COMP.	UNEMPLOY. INSUR.	HEALTH INSUR.	RETIRE (401K)	LIABILITY INSUR.	COST PER HOUR
Retaining wall installer	**$23.20**	1.81	**$25.01**	1.91	.20	4.34	2.18	2.69	.75	3.38	**$40.50**
Mason	**$24.40**	1.90	**$26.30**	2.01	.21	8.15	2.29	2.69	.79	3.55	**$46.00**
Equipment operator	**$29.90**	2.33	**$32.23**	2.47	.26	5.81	2.80	2.69	.97	4.35	**$51.60**
Demolition laborer	**$13.90**	1.08	**$14.98**	1.15	.12	4.79	1.30	2.69	.45	2.02	**$27.50**

Paid Leave is calculated based on two weeks paid vacation, one week sick leave, and seven paid holidays. Employer's matching portion of **FICA** is 7.65 percent. **FUTA** (Federal Unemployment) is .8 percent. **Worker's Compensation** was calculated using a national average of 17.36 percent for the retaining wall installer; 30.99 percent for the mason, and 18.04 percent for the equipment operator. **Unemployment insurance** was calculated using a national average of 8.7 percent. **Health insurance** was calculated based on a projected national average for 2002 of $535 per employee (and family when applicable) per month. Employer pays 80 percent for a per month cost of $428 per employee. **Retirement** is based on a 401(k) retirement program with employer matching of 50 percent. Employee contributions to the 401(k) plan are an average of 6 percent of the true wage. **Liability insurance** is based on a national average of 13.2 percent.

Retaining Walls Labor Productivity

WORK DESCRIPTION	LABORER	COST PER HOUR	PRODUCTIVITY	UNIT PRICE
Install retaining wall				
concrete	*retaining wall installer*	**$40.50**	**.227**	**$9.19** *sf*
railroad tie with tie tiebacks	*retaining wall installer*	**$40.50**	**.244**	**$9.88** *sf*
railroad tie, no tie tiebacks	*retaining wall installer*	**$40.50**	**.167**	**6.76** *sf*
cedar tie with tie tiebacks	*retaining wall installer*	**$40.50**	**.250**	**$10.13** *sf*
cedar tie, no tie tiebacks	*retaining wall installer*	**$40.50**	**.169**	**$6.84** *sf*
interlocking masonry block	*retaining wall installer*	**$40.50**	**.313**	**$12.70** *sf*

31 Roofing

Item Description	Unit	Remove	Replace	Total	
Minimum charge for roofing work *Replace* Materials......60.00 Labor..........55.00	ea	—	$115.00	$115.00	◄ **MINIMUM**
Add 35% for steep roofs 6-12 to 8-12 slope					◄ **ADD FOR STEEP & COMPLEX ROOFS** *Cut-up roofs contain four to six intersecting roof lines. Very cut-up roofs contain seven or more.*
Add 50% for steep roofs greater than 8-12 slope					
Add 30% for cut-up roof					
Add 50% for very cut-up roof					
Aluminum shingles, .02″ thick, natural finish *Replace* Materials....253.00 Labor..........48.90 *Remove* .... Labor..........28.60	sq	$28.60	$301.90	$330.50	◄ **ALUMINUM SHINGLES** *See **Roofing** box on page 394.*
Aluminum shingles, .03″ thick, natural finish *Replace* Materials....263.00 Labor..........48.90 *Remove* .... Labor..........28.60	sq	$28.60	$311.90	$340.50	
Add 20% for colored aluminum shingles (all colors)					◁ add for colored finish
Galvanized steel shingles, 26 gauge, natural finish *Replace* Materials....189.00 Labor..........51.20 *Remove* .... Labor..........28.60	sq	$28.60	$240.20	$268.80	◄ **GALVANIZED STEEL SHINGLES** *See **Roofing** box on page 394.*
Galvanized steel shingles, 24 gauge, natural finish *Replace* Materials....200.00 Labor..........51.20 *Remove* .... Labor..........28.60	sq	$28.60	$251.20	$279.80	
Galvanized steel shingles, 22 gauge, natural finish *Replace* Materials.....211.00 Labor..........51.20 *Remove* .... Labor..........28.60	sq	$28.60	$262.20	$290.80	
Add 21% for galvanized steel shingles with baked enamel factory finish					◁ add for colored finish
Add 10% for metal shingles with 1″ polystyrene insulation					◁ add for insulation
Minimum charge for metal shingle roof repair *Replace* Materials......40.00 Labor..........92.20	ea	—	$132.20	$132.20	◄ **MINIMUM METAL SHINGLES**
20 year asphalt shingles (210 to 230 lb) *Replace* Materials......39.40 Labor..........57.20 *Remove* .... Labor..........28.10	sq	$28.10	$96.60	$124.70	◄ **ASPHALT SHINGLES** *See **Roofing** box on page 394. Prices are for standard three tab shingles. Add **14%** for 4 to 6 tab. Add **16%** for thatch style edge. Add **15%** for shingles with cut-outs. Add **10%** for textured shingles.*
25 year asphalt shingles (220 to 240 lb) *Replace* Materials......52.80 Labor..........57.20 *Remove* .... Labor..........28.10	sq	$28.10	$110.00	$138.10	
30 year asphalt shingles (240 to 260 lb) *Replace* Materials......71.70 Labor..........58.50 *Remove* .... Labor..........28.10	sq	$28.10	$130.20	$158.30	
40 year asphalt shingles (260 to 300 lb) *Replace* Materials......86.70 Labor..........58.50 *Remove* .... Labor..........28.10	sq	$28.10	$145.20	$173.30	

RELATED ITEMS

Rough Carpentry

chimney cricket..............444

	Item Description	Unit	Remove	Replace	Total
LAMINATED ASPHALT SHINGLES ▶ *See **Roofing** box below.*	**Laminated asphalt shingles, standard grade (250 to 300 lb)** *Replace* Materials......75.20 Labor..........95.00 *Remove* .... Labor..........28.10	sq	$28.10	$170.20	$198.30
	Laminated asphalt shingles, standard grade (300 to 390 lb) *Replace* Materials......92.10 Labor..........95.00 *Remove* .... Labor..........28.10	sq	$28.10	$187.10	$215.20
	Laminated asphalt shingles, high grade (260 to 300 lb) *Replace* Materials......89.30 Labor..........113.00 *Remove* .... Labor..........28.10	sq	$28.10	$202.30	$230.40
	Laminated asphalt shingles, high grade (300 to 400 lb) *Replace* Materials....105.00 Labor..........113.00 *Remove* .... Labor..........28.10	sq	$28.10	$218.00	$246.10
T-LOCK, DIAMOND & HEXAGONAL ▶ *See **Roofing** box below.*	**T-lock asphalt shingles (210 to 230 lb)** *Replace* Materials......37.60 Labor..........58.50 *Remove* .... Labor..........28.10	sq	$28.10	$96.10	$124.20
	Diamond asphalt shingles (210 to 230 lb) *Replace* Materials......38.60 Labor..........58.50 *Remove* .... Labor..........28.10	sq	$28.10	$97.10	$125.20
	Hexagonal asphalt shingles (210 to 230 lb) *Replace* Materials......39.40 Labor..........58.50 *Remove* .... Labor..........28.10	sq	$28.10	$97.90	$126.00
MINIMUM ASPHALT SHINGLES ▶	**Minimum charge for asphalt shingle roof repair** *Replace* Materials......30.00 Labor..........92.20	ea	—	$122.20	$122.20
ROLL ROOFING ▶ *Add **82%** for double selvage lay.*	**90 lb roll roofing** *Replace* Materials......27.20 Labor..........29.70 *Remove* .... Labor..........20.20	sq	$20.20	$56.90	$77.10
	110 lb roll roofing *Replace* Materials......47.00 Labor..........29.70 *Remove* .... Labor..........20.20	sq	$20.20	$76.70	$96.90
	140 lb roll roofing *Replace* Materials......71.30 Labor..........29.70 *Remove* .... Labor..........20.20	sq	$20.20	$101.00	$121.20
SLATE ▶ *See **Roofing** box below.* **unfading** ▷	**Vermont unfading green slate, clear** *Replace* Materials....671.00 Labor.........184.00 *Remove* .... Labor.........102.00	sq	$102.00	$855.00	$957.00
	Vermont unfading purple slate, clear *Replace* Materials....684.00 Labor.........184.00 *Remove* .... Labor.........102.00	sq	$102.00	$868.00	$970.00
	Vermont unfading variegated purple slate, clear *Replace* Materials....770.00 Labor.........184.00 *Remove* .... Labor.........102.00	sq	$102.00	$954.00	$1,056.00
	Vermont unfading dark gray or black slate, clear *Replace* Materials....706.00 Labor.........184.00 *Remove* .... Labor.........102.00	sq	$102.00	$890.00	$992.00
	Vermont unfading red slate, clear *Replace* Materials...1700.00 Labor.........184.00 *Remove* .... Labor.........102.00	sq	$102.00	$1,884.00	$1,986.00

ROOFING

Roofing costs are based on a typical 2,550 sf house with a 6 in 12 slope roof or less. Roof height is less than 16′ so ropes and other safety equipment are not required.

Includes costs for ridges and rakes. Typical roof has an intersecting or L-shaped roof and two dormers. Also includes boots and flashing.

Item Description	Unit	Remove	Replace	Total	
Pennsylvania black weathering slate, clear ***Replace*** Materials....657.00 Labor.........184.00 ***Remove*** .... Labor.........102.00	sq	$102.00	$841.00	$943.00	◁ weathering slate
Vermont weathering green slate, clear ***Replace*** Materials....635.00 Labor.........184.00 ***Remove*** .... Labor.........102.00	sq	$102.00	$819.00	$921.00	**RELATED ITEMS** **Rough Carpentry** *chimney cricket*.............444
Deduct 15% for slate with ribbons of foreign color					◁ deduct for lower grade
Minimum charge for slate roof repair ***Replace*** Materials....225.00 Labor.........184.00	ea	—	$409.00	$409.00	◁ minimum
Replace single slate ***Replace*** Materials......20.00 Labor...........17.70	ea	—	$37.70	$37.70	◁ replace single slate
16" blue label cedar shingles (Royals) ***Replace*** Materials....250.00 Labor.........132.00 ***Remove*** .... Labor..........33.00	sq	$33.00	$382.00	$415.00	◀ **WOOD SHINGLES** *See **Roofing** box on facing page.*
18" blue label cedar shingles (Perfections) ***Replace*** Materials....266.00 Labor..........118.00 ***Remove*** .... Labor..........33.00	sq	$33.00	$384.00	$417.00	
16" red label cedar shingles (Royals) ***Replace*** Materials....243.00 Labor.........132.00 ***Remove*** .... Labor..........33.00	sq	$33.00	$375.00	$408.00	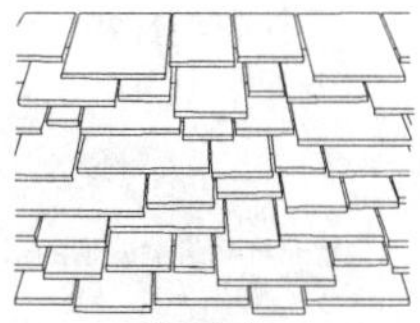
18" red label cedar shingles (Perfections) ***Replace*** Materials....256.00 Labor..........118.00 ***Remove*** .... Labor..........33.00	sq	$33.00	$374.00	$407.00	*thatch* △
Minimum charge for wood shingle repair ***Replace*** Materials......60.00 Labor..........92.20	ea	—	$152.20	$152.20	◁ minimum
Replace single wood shingle ***Replace*** Materials.......15.00 Labor............9.59	ea	—	$24.59	$24.59	◁ replace single shingle
Deduct 6% for black label shingles					◁ additional costs
Add 20% for 16" wood shingles with 4" exposure					
Deduct 17% for 16" wood shingles with 5-1/2" exposure					
Deduct 20% for 16" wood shingles with 6" exposure					*serrated* △
Add 18% for wood shingles treated with fire retardant					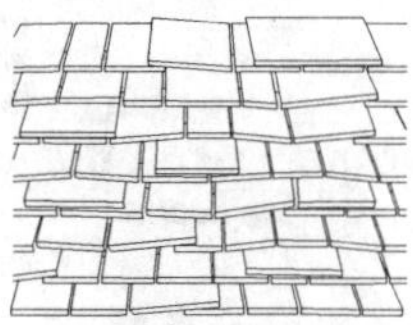
Add 16% for wood shingles treated with mildew retardant					
Add 16% for wood shingle staggered installation					
Add 26% for wood shingle thatch installation					*Dutch weave* △
Add 24% for wood shingle serrated installation					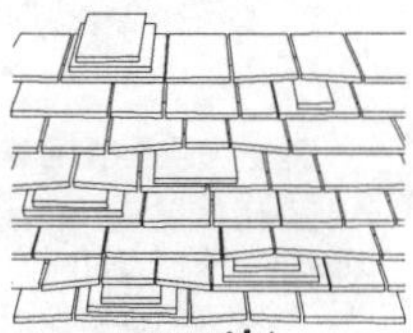
Add 38% for wood shingle Dutch weave installation					
Add 45% for wood shingle pyramid installation					*pyramid* △
18" medium handsplit and resawn shakes ***Replace*** Materials ....164.00 Labor.........154.00 ***Remove*** .... Labor..........33.00	sq	$33.00	$318.00	$351.00	◀ **WOOD SHAKES** *See **Roofing** box on facing page.*

	Item Description	Unit	Remove	Replace	Total
WOOD SHAKES ▶ *continued* **handsplit and resawn** ▷	**18" heavy handsplit and resawn shakes** *Replace* Materials....180.00 Labor.........154.00 *Remove* .... Labor..........33.00	sq	$33.00	$334.00	$367.00
	24" medium handsplit and resawn shakes *Replace* Materials.....219.00 Labor.........132.00 *Remove* .... Labor..........33.00	sq	$33.00	$351.00	$384.00
	24" heavy handsplit and resawn shakes *Replace* Materials....243.00 Labor.........132.00 *Remove* .... Labor..........33.00	sq	$33.00	$375.00	$408.00
taper split ▷	**24" tapersplit shakes** *Replace* Materials.....172.00 Labor.........132.00 *Remove* .... Labor..........33.00	sq	$33.00	$304.00	$337.00
straight split ▷	**18" straight split shakes** *Replace* Materials.....147.00 Labor.........154.00 *Remove* .... Labor..........33.00	sq	$33.00	$301.00	$334.00
	24" straight split shakes *Replace* Materials.....156.00 Labor.........132.00 *Remove* .... Labor..........33.00	sq	$33.00	$288.00	$321.00
other exposures ▷	**Add 20% for 8" shake exposure**				
	Deduct 20% for 12" shake exposure				
staggered installation ▷	**Add 16% for staggered shake installation**				
minimum charge ▷	**Minimum charge for shake roof repair** *Replace* Materials......60.00 Labor..........92.20	ea	—	$152.20	$152.20
replace single shake ▷	**Replace single shake** *Replace* Materials......10.00 Labor............9.59	ea	—	$19.59	$19.59
FIBER AND CEMENT SHINGLES ▶ *Older style shingles may contain asbestos. This is a hazardous material which requires special techniques and equipment to remove.*	**Fiber and cement shingles, weathering shake** *Replace* Materials......83.10 Labor.........110.00 *Remove* .... Labor..........30.50	sq	$30.50	$193.10	$223.60
	Fiber and cement shingles, Spanish tile *Replace* Materials....104.00 Labor..........115.00 *Remove* .... Labor..........30.50	sq	$30.50	$219.00	$249.50
minimum ▷	**Minimum charge for fiber and cement shingle roof repair** *Replace* Materials......31.30 Labor...........71.00	sq	—	$102.30	$102.30
GRANULAR COATED METAL TILE ▶ *See **Roofing** box on page 394.*	**Granular coated metal tile, simple pattern** *Replace* Materials.....276.00 Labor.........193.00 *Remove* .... Labor..........28.60	sq	$28.60	$469.00	$497.60
	Granular coated metal tile, complex pattern *Replace* Materials....334.00 Labor.........193.00 *Remove* .... Labor..........28.60	sq	$28.60	$527.00	$555.60
FLAT CLAY TILE ▶ *See **Roofing** box on page 394. Old style clay tile shingles.*	**Flat clay tile shingle, terra-cotta red** *Replace* Materials......97.00 Labor.........149.00 *Remove* .... Labor...........94.90	sq	$94.90	$246.00	$340.90
	Flat clay tile shingle, glazed red *Replace* Materials.....198.00 Labor.........149.00 *Remove* .... Labor...........94.90	sq	$94.90	$347.00	$441.90

Item Description	Unit	Remove	Replace	Total
Mission tile, terra-cotta red ***Replace*** Materials....189.00 Labor........256.00 ***Remove*** .... Labor..........94.90	sq	$94.90	$445.00	$539.90
Mission tile, peach ***Replace*** Materials.....216.00 Labor........256.00 ***Remove*** .... Labor..........94.90	sq	$94.90	$472.00	$566.90
Mission tile, white ***Replace*** Materials....251.00 Labor........256.00 ***Remove*** .... Labor..........94.90	sq	$94.90	$507.00	$601.90
Mission tile, color blends ***Replace*** Materials....236.00 Labor........256.00 ***Remove*** .... Labor..........94.90	sq	$94.90	$492.00	$586.90
Mission tile, glazed white ***Replace*** Materials.....513.00 Labor........256.00 ***Remove*** .... Labor..........94.90	sq	$94.90	$769.00	$863.90
Mission tile, glazed gray ***Replace*** Materials.....519.00 Labor........256.00 ***Remove*** .... Labor..........94.90	sq	$94.90	$775.00	$869.90
Mission tile, glazed burgundy ***Replace*** Materials....521.00 Labor........256.00 ***Remove*** .... Labor..........94.90	sq	$94.90	$777.00	$871.90
Mission tile, glazed terra-cotta red ***Replace*** Materials....520.00 Labor........256.00 ***Remove*** .... Labor..........94.90	sq	$94.90	$776.00	$870.90
Mission tile, glazed teal ***Replace*** Materials....652.00 Labor........256.00 ***Remove*** .... Labor..........94.90	sq	$94.90	$908.00	$1,002.90
Mission tile, glazed blue ***Replace*** Materials....669.00 Labor........256.00 ***Remove*** .... Labor..........94.90	sq	$94.90	$925.00	$1,019.90
Add for vertical furring strips under all cap tiles ***Replace*** Materials....100.10 Labor.........150.00	sq	—	$250.10	$250.10
Add for Mission tiles attached with wire ***Replace*** Materials......16.90 Labor.........102.00	sq	—	$118.90	$118.90
Add for Mission tiles attached with stainless steel nails ***Replace*** Materials......23.30	sq	—	$23.30	$23.30
Add for Mission tiles attached with brass or copper nails ***Replace*** Materials......31.20	sq	—	$31.20	$31.20
Add for Mission tiles with wire attached to braided wire runners ***Replace*** Materials......30.20 Labor.........100.00	sq	—	$130.20	$130.20
Add for Mission tiles attached with hurricane clips or wind locks ***Replace*** Materials......20.40 Labor.........140.00	sq	—	$160.40	$160.40
Add for adhesive between Mission tiles ***Replace*** Materials......16.20 Labor...........6.80	sq	—	$23.00	$23.00

◄ **MISSION TILE**
*See **Roofing** box on page 394. Includes 30 lb felt underlayment, doubled felt on rakes and eaves, bird stop, booster tiles, ridge and rake tiles.*

◁ **add for vertical strips**

◁ **add for other attachment**

RELATED ITEMS

Spanish tile ▶ See **Roofing** box on page 394. Includes 30 lb felt underlayment, doubled felt on rakes and eaves, bird stop, ridge and rake tiles.

Item Description	Unit	Remove	Replace	Total
Spanish tile, terra-cotta red ***Replace*** Materials.....119.00 Labor.........154.00 ***Remove*** .... Labor...........94.90	sq	$94.90	$273.00	$367.90
Spanish tile, peach ***Replace*** Materials....146.00 Labor.........154.00 ***Remove*** .... Labor...........94.90	sq	$94.90	$300.00	$394.90
Spanish tile, white ***Replace*** Materials.....181.00 Labor.........154.00 ***Remove*** .... Labor...........94.90	sq	$94.90	$335.00	$429.90
Spanish tile, color blends ***Replace*** Materials.....168.00 Labor.........154.00 ***Remove*** .... Labor...........94.90	sq	$94.90	$322.00	$416.90
Spanish tile, glazed white ***Replace*** Materials....466.00 Labor.........154.00 ***Remove*** .... Labor...........94.90	sq	$94.90	$620.00	$714.90
Spanish tile, glazed gray ***Replace*** Materials....468.00 Labor.........154.00 ***Remove*** .... Labor...........94.90	sq	$94.90	$622.00	$716.90
Spanish tile, glazed burgundy ***Replace*** Materials....588.00 Labor.........154.00 ***Remove*** .... Labor...........94.90	sq	$94.90	$742.00	$836.90
Spanish tile, glazed terra-cotta red ***Replace*** Materials.....470.00 Labor.........154.00 ***Remove*** .... Labor...........94.90	sq	$94.90	$624.00	$718.90
Spanish tile, glazed teal ***Replace*** Materials ....594.00 Labor.........154.00 ***Remove*** .... Labor...........94.90	sq	$94.90	$748.00	$842.90
Spanish tile, glazed blue ***Replace*** Materials.....614.00 Labor.........154.00 ***Remove*** .... Labor...........94.90	sq	$94.90	$768.00	$862.90

add for other attachment ▷

Item Description	Unit	Remove	Replace	Total
Add for Spanish tiles attached with wire ***Replace*** Materials ......14.10 Labor 80.70	sq	—	$94.80	$94.80
Add for Spanish tiles attached with stainless steel nails ***Replace*** Materials.......19.70	sq	—	$19.70	$19.70
Add for Spanish tiles attached with brass or copper nails ***Replace*** Materials......26.20	sq	—	$26.20	$26.20
Add for Spanish tiles with wire attached to braided wire runners ***Replace*** Materials ......24.90 Labor...........67.80	sq	—	$92.70	$92.70
Add for Spanish tiles attached with hurricane clips or wind locks ***Replace*** Materials.......15.60 Labor 83.90	sq	—	$99.50	$99.50
Add for Spanish tiles attached using mortar set method ***Replace*** Materials......46.00 Labor 121.00	sq	—	$167.00	$167.00
Add for adhesive between Spanish tiles ***Replace*** Materials ......16.20 Labor 6.10	sq	—	$22.30	$22.30

Item Description	Unit	Remove	Replace	Total
Deduct 5% for ASTM grade 2 moderate weathering tiles				
Deduct 11% for ASTM grade 3 negligible weathering tiles				
Deduct 12% for low profile Spanish or Mission tiles				
Furring strips for roofing tiles, vertically laid only *Replace* Materials.......19.10 Labor...........27.90 *Remove* .... Labor...........13.10	sq	$13.10	$47.00	$60.10
Furring strips for roofing tiles, vertically and horizontally laid *Replace* Materials......31.30 Labor..........40.40 *Remove* .... Labor..........23.10	sq	$23.10	$71.70	$94.80
Corrugated concrete tile, natural gray *Replace* Materials......97.20 Labor.........144.00 *Remove* .... Labor.........106.00	sq	$106.00	$241.20	$347.20
Corrugated concrete tile, black *Replace* Materials....109.00 Labor.........144.00 *Remove* .... Labor.........106.00	sq	$106.00	$253.00	$359.00
Corrugated concrete tile, browns and terra-cotta reds *Replace* Materials.....118.00 Labor.........144.00 *Remove* .... Labor.........106.00	sq	$106.00	$262.00	$368.00
Corrugated concrete tile, bright reds *Replace* Materials.....125.00 Labor.........144.00 *Remove* .... Labor.........106.00	sq	$106.00	$269.00	$375.00
Corrugated concrete tile, greens *Replace* Materials.....135.00 Labor.........144.00 *Remove* .... Labor.........106.00	sq	$106.00	$279.00	$385.00
Corrugated concrete tile, blues *Replace* Materials.....142.00 Labor.........144.00 *Remove* .... Labor.........106.00	sq	$106.00	$286.00	$392.00
Flat concrete tile, natural gray *Replace* Materials......89.00 Labor.........140.00 *Remove* .... Labor.........106.00	sq	$106.00	$229.00	$335.00
Flat concrete tile, black *Replace* Materials.....101.00 Labor.........140.00 *Remove* .... Labor.........106.00	sq	$106.00	$241.00	$347.00
Flat concrete tile, browns and terra-cotta reds *Replace* Materials....108.00 Labor.........140.00 *Remove* .... Labor.........106.00	sq	$106.00	$248.00	$354.00
Flat concrete tile, bright reds *Replace* Materials.....115.00 Labor.........140.00 *Remove* .... Labor.........106.00	sq	$106.00	$255.00	$361.00
Flat concrete tile, greens *Replace* Materials.....125.00 Labor.........140.00 *Remove* .... Labor.........106.00	sq	$106.00	$265.00	$371.00
Flat concrete tile, blues *Replace* Materials....130.00 Labor.........140.00 *Remove* .... Labor.........106.00	sq	$106.00	$270.00	$376.00

◄ **OTHER CLAY TILE GRADES**
Deduct from the cost of Spanish or mission tiles.

◄ **FURRING STRIPS**
*See **Roofing** box on page 394.*

◄ **CONCRETE TILE**
*See **Roofing** box on page 394.*

◁ **flat**

RELATED ITEMS

Rough Carpentry
chimney cricket.............444

	Item Description	Unit	Remove	Replace	Total
CONCRETE TILE ▶ *continued*	**Add 2% for glazed concrete tiles**				
additional costs ▷	**Add 5% for painted concrete tiles**				
ALUMINUM SHEET ▶ **CORRUGATED** See **Roofing** box on page 394.	**.016″ thick corrugated aluminum roofing, natural finish** *Replace* Materials........ .87 Labor........... 1.11 *Remove* Labor............ .28	sf	$.28	$1.98	$2.26
	.019″ thick corrugated aluminum roofing, natural finish *Replace* Materials........ .95 Labor........... 1.11 *Remove* Labor............ .28	sf	$.28	$2.06	$2.34
colored finish ▷	**.016″ thick corrugated aluminum roofing, colored finish** *Replace* Materials........1.07 Labor............1.11 *Remove* Labor............ .28	sf	$.28	$2.18	$2.46
	.019″ thick corrugated aluminum roofing, colored finish *Replace* Materials........1.19 Labor............1.11 *Remove* Labor............ .28	sf	$.28	$2.30	$2.58
ALUMINUM SHEET ▶ **RIBBED** See **Roofing** box on page 394.	**.016″ thick ribbed aluminum roofing, natural finish** *Replace* Materials........ .91 Labor............1.20 *Remove* Labor............ .28	sf	$.28	$2.11	$2.39
	.019″ thick ribbed aluminum roofing, natural finish *Replace* Materials........1.23 Labor............1.20 *Remove* Labor............ .28	sf	$.28	$2.43	$2.71
	.032″ thick ribbed aluminum roofing, natural finish *Replace* Materials........1.77 Labor............1.20 *Remove* Labor............ .28	sf	$.28	$2.97	$3.25
	.04″ thick ribbed aluminum roofing, natural finish *Replace* Materials........2.32 Labor............1.20 *Remove* Labor............ .28	sf	$.28	$3.52	$3.80
	.05″ thick ribbed aluminum roofing, natural finish *Replace* Materials........2.72 Labor............1.20 *Remove* Labor............ .28	sf	$.28	$3.92	$4.20
colored finish ▷	**.016″ thick ribbed aluminum roofing, colored finish** *Replace* Materials........1.07 Labor............1.20 *Remove* Labor............ .28	sf	$.28	$2.27	$2.55
	.019″ thick ribbed aluminum roofing, colored finish *Replace* Materials........1.20 Labor............1.20 *Remove* Labor............ .28	sf	$.28	$2.40	$2.68
	.032″ thick ribbed aluminum roofing, colored finish *Replace* Materials........1.81 Labor............1.20 *Remove* Labor............ .28	sf	$.28	$3.01	$3.29
	.04″ thick ribbed aluminum roofing, colored finish *Replace* Materials........3.07 Labor............1.20 *Remove* Labor............ .28	sf	$.28	$4.27	$4.55
	.05″ thick ribbed aluminum roofing, colored finish *Replace* Materials........3.52 Labor............1.20 *Remove* Labor............ .28	sf	$.28	$4.72	$5.00
FIBERGLASS ▶ **CORRUGATED** See **Roofing** page 394.	**8 ounce corrugated fiberglass roofing** *Replace* Materials........2.33 Labor............1.11 *Remove* Labor............ .25	sf	$.25	$3.44	$3.69

Item Description	Unit	Remove	Replace	Total
12 ounce corrugated fiberglass roofing ***Replace*** Materials........3.09 Labor............1.11 ***Remove*** .... Labor............ .25	sf	$.25	$4.20	$4.45
30 gauge galvanized steel corrugated roofing ***Replace*** Materials........ .87 Labor............1.15 ***Remove*** .... Labor............ .28	sf	$.28	$2.02	$2.30
28 gauge galvanized steel corrugated roofing ***Replace*** Materials........ .91 Labor............1.15 ***Remove*** .... Labor............ .28	sf	$.28	$2.06	$2.34
26 gauge galvanized steel corrugated roofing ***Replace*** Materials........ .96 Labor............1.15 ***Remove*** .... Labor............ .28	sf	$.28	$2.11	$2.39
24 gauge galvanized steel corrugated roofing ***Replace*** Materials........1.07 Labor............1.15 ***Remove*** .... Labor............ .28	sf	$.28	$2.22	$2.50
30 gauge galvanized steel ribbed roofing ***Replace*** Materials........ .91 Labor............1.20 ***Remove*** .... Labor............ .28	sf	$.28	$2.11	$2.39
28 gauge galvanized steel ribbed roofing ***Replace*** Materials........ .95 Labor............1.20 ***Remove*** .... Labor............ .28	sf	$.28	$2.15	$2.43
26 gauge galvanized steel ribbed roofing ***Replace*** Materials...... 1.00 Labor............1.20 ***Remove*** .... Labor............ .28	sf	$.28	$2.20	$2.48
24 gauge galvanized steel ribbed roofing ***Replace*** Materials........1.11 Labor............1.20 ***Remove*** .... Labor............ .28	sf	$.28	$2.31	$2.59
30 gauge galvanized steel ribbed roofing with colored finish ***Replace*** Materials........1.24 Labor............1.20 ***Remove*** .... Labor............ .28	sf	$.28	$2.44	$2.72
28 gauge galvanized steel ribbed roofing with colored finish ***Replace*** Materials........1.31 Labor............1.20 ***Remove*** .... Labor............ .28	sf	$.28	$2.51	$2.79
26 gauge galvanized steel ribbed roofing with colored finish ***Replace*** Materials........1.39 Labor............1.20 ***Remove*** .... Labor............ .28	sf	$.28	$2.59	$2.87
24 gauge galvanized steel ribbed roofing with colored finish ***Replace*** Materials........1.53 Labor............1.20 ***Remove*** .... Labor............ .28	sf	$.28	$2.73	$3.01
16 ounce copper standing seam roofing ***Replace*** Materials....545.00 Labor.........307.00 ***Remove*** .... Labor..........28.30	sq	$28.30	$852.00	$880.30
18 ounce copper standing seam roofing ***Replace*** Materials....606.00 Labor.........329.00 ***Remove*** .... Labor..........28.30	sq	$28.30	$935.00	$963.30
20 ounce copper standing seam roofing ***Replace*** Materials....693.00 Labor.........355.00 ***Remove*** .... Labor..........28.30	sq	$28.30	$1,048.00	$1,076.30

◄ **GALVANIZED STEEL CORRUGATED**
*See **Roofing** box on page 394.*

◄ **GALVANIZED STEEL RIBBED**
*See **Roofing** box on page 394.*

◁ **colored finish**

◄ **COPPER**
*See **Roofing** box on page 394.*

◁ **standing seam**

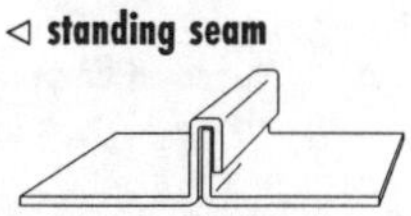

RELATED ITEMS

Rough Carpentry

	Item Description	Unit	Remove	Replace	Total
Copper ▶ *continued* **batten seam ▷**	**16 ounce copper batten seam roofing** ***Replace*** Materials....558.00 Labor.........355.00 ***Remove*** .... Labor..........28.30	sq	$28.30	$913.00	$941.30
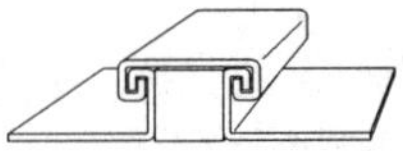	**18 ounce copper batten seam roofing** ***Replace*** Materials....620.00 Labor........384.00 ***Remove*** .... Labor..........28.30	sq	$28.30	$1,004.00	$1,032.30
	20 ounce copper batten seam roofing ***Replace*** Materials....710.00 Labor.........419.00 ***Remove*** .... Labor..........28.30	sq	$28.30	$1,129.00	$1,157.30
flat seam ▷ 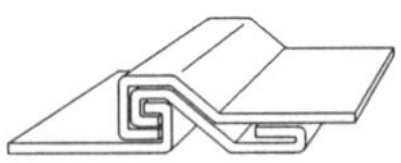	**16 ounce copper flat seam roofing** ***Replace*** Materials....500.00 Labor........329.00 ***Remove*** .... Labor..........28.30	sq	$28.30	$829.00	$857.30
	18 ounce copper flat seam roofing ***Replace*** Materials....558.00 Labor.........355.00 ***Remove*** .... Labor..........28.30	sq	$28.30	$913.00	$941.30
	20 ounce copper flat seam roofing ***Replace*** Materials....625.00 Labor........384.00 ***Remove*** .... Labor..........28.30	sq	$28.30	$1,009.00	$1,037.30
Lead ▶ *See **Roofing** box on page 394.*	**3 lb batten seam lead roof** ***Replace*** Materials....644.00 Labor........329.00 ***Remove*** .... Labor..........28.30	sq	$28.30	$973.00	$1,001.30
	3 lb flat seam lead roof ***Replace*** Materials....581.00 Labor.........355.00 ***Remove*** .... Labor..........28.30	sq	$28.30	$936.00	$964.30
Stainless steel ▶ *See **Roofing** box on page 394.* **standing seam ▷**	**28 gauge stainless steel standing seam roof** ***Replace*** Materials.....418.00 Labor........329.00 ***Remove*** .... Labor..........28.30	sq	$28.30	$747.00	$775.30
	26 gauge stainless steel standing seam roof ***Replace*** Materials....465.00 Labor.........307.00 ***Remove*** .... Labor..........28.30	sq	$28.30	$772.00	$800.30
batten seam ▷	**28 gauge stainless steel batten seam roof** ***Replace*** Materials....429.00 Labor.........355.00 ***Remove*** .... Labor..........28.30	sq	$28.30	$784.00	$812.30
	26 gauge stainless steel batten seam roof ***Replace*** Materials....479.00 Labor........329.00 ***Remove*** .... Labor..........28.30	sq	$28.30	$808.00	$836.30
flat seam ▷	**28 gauge stainless steel flat seam roof** ***Replace*** Materials....398.00 Labor........329.00 ***Remove*** .... Labor..........28.30	sq	$28.30	$727.00	$755.30
	26 gauge stainless steel flat seam roof ***Replace*** Materials....443.00 Labor.........307.00 ***Remove*** .... Labor..........28.30	sq	$28.30	$750.00	$778.30
coated finish ▷	**Add 13% for terne coated stainless steel**				
	Add 14% for lead coated stainless steel				
Terne ▶ *See **Roofing** box on page 394.*	**40 lb terne standing seam roof** ***Replace*** Materials....948.00 Labor........384.00 ***Remove*** .... Labor..........28.30	sq	$28.30	$1,332.00	$1,360.30

Item Description	Unit	Remove	Replace	Total
40 lb terne batten seam roof *Replace* Materials....966.00 Labor.........355.00 *Remove* .... Labor..........28.30	sq	$28.30	$1,321.00	$1,349.30
40 lb terne flat seam roof *Replace* Materials....905.00 Labor.........419.00 *Remove* .... Labor..........28.30	sq	$28.30	$1,324.00	$1,352.30
Solder patch into metal roof (less than 1' square) *Replace* Materials......40.00 Labor..........50.10	ea	—	$90.10	$90.10
Minimum charge for seamed metal roof repair *Replace* Materials....100.00 Labor.........125.00	ea	—	$225.00	$225.00
Built-up 3 ply roofing *Replace* Materials......51.50 Labor.........154.00 Equipment............9.62 *Remove* .... Labor...........67.10	sq	$67.10	$215.12	$282.22
Built-up 4 ply roofing *Replace* Materials......72.00 Labor.........184.00 Equipment..........10.72 *Remove* .... Labor..........83.30	sq	$83.30	$266.72	$350.02
Built-up 5 ply roofing *Replace* Materials.....107.00 Labor.........219.00 Equipment...........11.80 *Remove* .... Labor.........106.00	sq	$106.00	$337.80	$443.80
Minimum charge for roofing work requiring hot asphalt *Replace* Materials.....160.00 Labor........229.00	ea	—	$389.00	$389.00
Add for built-up roofing gravel surface embedded in flood coat *Replace* Materials......12.90 Labor...........18.40 Equipment............1.48 *Remove* .... Labor..........23.30	sq	$23.30	$32.78	$56.08
Add for flood coat *Replace* Materials......16.20 Labor..........32.90 Equipment............3.95	sq	—	$53.05	$53.05
Add to paint built-up roof with aluminum UV coating *Replace* Materials.......15.50 Labor..........38.40	sq	—	$53.90	$53.90
Add to paint built-up roof with aluminum UV coating with fiber *Replace* Materials.......19.30 Labor..........38.40	sq	—	$57.70	$57.70
Add for mineral faced cap sheet *Replace* Materials......16.20	sq	—	$16.20	$16.20
Remove gravel, flood coat, then replace gravel *Replace* Materials......34.50 Labor..........111.60 Equipment..........15.90	sq	—	$162.00	$162.00
Add per lf of parapet wall on built-up roof *Replace* Materials........9.20 Labor...........10.50 Equipment........... .71	lf	—	$20.41	$20.41
45 mil SCPE elastomeric roofing, loose laid and ballasted with stone *Replace* Materials.....157.00 Labor..........46.10 Equipment...........2.82 *Remove* .... Labor..........56.10	sq	$56.10	$205.92	$262.02
45 mil SCPE elastomeric roofing, attached at seams with batten strips *Replace* Materials.....166.00 Labor..........38.40 Equipment............4.51 *Remove* .... Labor...........27.00	sq	$27.00	$208.91	$235.91
45 mil SCPE elastomeric roofing, fully attached to deck *Replace* Materials.....173.00 Labor...........47.90 Equipment...........8.60 *Remove* .... Labor...........42.90	sq	$42.90	$229.50	$272.40

◀ **TERNE**
Terne is short for Terneplate. Terneplate is sheet iron or steel that is plated with an alloy that is one part tin and three to four parts lead.

◀ **SEAMED METAL ROOF REPAIR**
For repairs to standing seam, batten seam, or flat seam metal roofs.

◀ **BUILT-UP**
Does not include finish coat or wrap up parapet wall (see below).

◁ **minimum**

◁ **surface finish**

RELATED ITEMS

Rough Carpentry
chimney cricket.............444

◁ **replace gravel**

◁ **add for parapet wall**
Includes cant strip and roofing wrap up wall.

◀ **SCPE ELASTOMERIC**
Chlorosulfonated polyethylene-hypalon roofing is abbreviated SCPE. Ballasted roofs contain 1/2 ton of stone per square.

	Item Description	Unit	Remove	Replace	Total
EPDM ► **ELASTOMERIC** *Ethylene propylene diene monomer roofing is abbreviated EPDM. Ballasted roofs contain 1/2 ton of stone per square.*	**45 mil EPDM elastomeric roofing, loose laid & ballasted with stone** ***Replace*** Materials......88.00 Labor..........112.00 Equipment............2.82 ***Remove*** Labor..........56.10	sq	$56.10	$202.82	$258.92
	45 mil EPDM elastomeric roofing, attached to deck at seams ***Replace*** Materials......75.70 Labor..........92.20 Equipment............4.51 ***Remove*** Labor..........27.00	sq	$27.00	$172.41	$199.41
	45 mil EPDM elastomeric roofing, fully attached to deck ***Replace*** Materials....106.00 Labor.........132.00 Equipment............8.60 ***Remove*** Labor..........42.90	sq	$42.90	$246.60	$289.50
55 mil ▷	**55 mil EPDM elastomeric roofing, loose laid & ballasted with stone** ***Replace*** Materials....102.00 Labor..........115.00 Equipment............2.82 ***Remove*** Labor..........56.10	sq	$56.10	$219.82	$275.92
	55 mil EPDM elastomeric roofing, attached to deck at seams ***Replace*** Materials......89.40 Labor..........94.00 Equipment............4.51 ***Remove*** Labor..........27.00	sq	$27.00	$187.91	$214.91
	55 mil EPDM elastomeric roofing, fully attached to deck ***Replace*** Materials.....121.00 Labor.........136.00 Equipment............8.60 ***Remove*** Labor..........42.90	sq	$42.90	$265.60	$308.50
60 mil ▷	**60 mil EPDM elastomeric roofing, loose laid & ballasted with stone** ***Replace*** Materials....108.00 Labor..........118.00 Equipment............2.82 ***Remove*** Labor..........56.10	sq	$56.10	$228.82	$284.92
	60 mil EPDM elastomeric roofing, attached to deck at seams ***Replace*** Materials......92.20 Labor..........95.90 Equipment............4.51 ***Remove*** Labor..........27.00	sq	$27.00	$192.61	$219.61
	60 mil EPDM elastomeric roofing, fully attached to deck ***Replace*** Materials.....123.00 Labor.........140.00 Equipment............8.60 ***Remove*** Labor..........42.90	sq	$42.90	$271.60	$314.50
PVC ► *Polyvinyl chloride roofing is abbreviated PVC. Ballasted roofs contain 1/2 ton of stone per square.*	**45 mil PVC elastomeric roofing, loose laid & ballasted with stone** ***Replace*** Materials....106.00 Labor..........27.10 Equipment............2.82 ***Remove*** Labor..........56.10	sq	$56.10	$135.92	$192.02
45 mil ▷	**45 mil PVC elastomeric roofing, attached to deck at seams** ***Replace*** Materials.....132.00 Labor..........41.90 Equipment............4.51 ***Remove*** Labor..........27.00	sq	$27.00	$178.41	$205.41
	45 mil PVC elastomeric roofing, fully attached to deck ***Replace*** Materials....143.00 Labor..........61.30 Equipment............8.60 ***Remove*** Labor..........42.90	sq	$42.90	$212.90	$255.80
add for reinforced ▷	**Add 22% for 45 mil reinforced PVC elastomeric roofing**				
48 mil ▷	**48 mil PVC elastomeric roofing, loose laid & ballasted with stone** ***Replace*** Materials.....114.00 Labor..........28.80 Equipment............2.82 ***Remove*** Labor..........56.10	sq	$56.10	$145.62	$201.72
	48 mil PVC elastomeric roofing, attached to deck at seams ***Replace*** Materials.....137.00 Labor..........46.10 Equipment............4.51 ***Remove*** Labor..........27.00	sq	$27.00	$187.61	$214.61
	48 mil PVC elastomeric roofing, fully attached to deck ***Replace*** Materials.....149.00 Labor..........62.20 Equipment............8.60 ***Remove*** Labor..........42.90	sq	$42.90	$219.80	$262.70

Item Description	Unit	Remove	Replace	Total	
60 mil PVC elastomeric roofing, loose laid & ballasted with stone ***Replace*** Materials.....157.00 Labor..........30.70 Equipment............2.82 ***Remove*** .... Labor..........56.10	sq	$56.10	$190.52	$246.62	◁ **60 mil**
60 mil PVC elastomeric roofing, attached to deck at seams ***Replace*** Materials.....168.00 Labor...........47.00 Equipment............4.51 ***Remove*** .... Labor...........27.00	sq	$27.00	$219.51	$246.51	
60 mil PVC elastomeric roofing, fully attached to deck ***Replace*** Materials.....190.00 Labor..........64.10 Equipment............8.60 ***Remove*** .... Labor..........42.90	sq	$42.90	$262.70	$305.60	
120 mil modified bitumen roofing, loose laid & ballasted with stone ***Replace*** Materials......79.80 Labor...........45.60 Equipment............7.05 ***Remove*** .... Labor..........56.10	sq	$56.10	$132.45	$188.55	◀ **MODIFIED BITUMEN** *Comes in hot-mop or torch-down styles.*
120 mil modified bitumen roofing, attached to deck at seams ***Replace*** Materials......75.70 Labor..........53.00 Equipment............7.05 ***Remove*** .... Labor...........27.00	sq	$27.00	$135.75	$162.75	◁ **120 mil**
120 mil modified bitumen roofing, fully attached to deck with torch ***Replace*** Materials......74.20 Labor..........68.70 Equipment............8.46 ***Remove*** .... Labor...........42.90	sq	$42.90	$151.36	$194.26	
120 mil modified bitumen roofing, fully attached with hot asphalt ***Replace*** Materials......82.50 Labor..........68.70 Equipment...........11.30 ***Remove*** .... Labor...........42.90	sq	$42.90	$162.50	$205.40	
150 mil modified bitumen roofing, loose laid & ballasted with stone ***Replace*** Materials......85.30 Labor..........46.10 Equipment............7.05 ***Remove*** .... Labor..........56.10	sq	$56.10	$138.45	$194.55	◁ **150 mil**
150 mil modified bitumen roofing, attached to deck at seams ***Replace*** Materials......79.80 Labor..........54.40 Equipment............7.05 ***Remove*** .... Labor...........27.00	sq	$27.00	$141.25	$168.25	
150 mil modified bitumen roofing, fully attached to deck ***Replace*** Materials......78.40 Labor...........70.10 Equipment............8.46 ***Remove*** .... Labor...........42.90	sq	$42.90	$156.96	$199.86	
150 mil modified bitumen roofing, fully attached with hot asphalt ***Replace*** Materials......86.60 Labor...........71.90 Equipment...........11.30 ***Remove*** .... Labor...........42.90	sq	$42.90	$169.80	$212.70	
160 mil modified bitumen roofing, loose laid & ballasted with stone ***Replace*** Materials......86.60 Labor...........47.00 Equipment............7.05 ***Remove*** .... Labor..........56.10	sq	$56.10	$140.65	$196.75	◁ **160 mil**
160 mil modified bitumen roofing, attached to deck at seams ***Replace*** Materials......82.50 Labor...........55.30 Equipment............7.05 ***Remove*** .... Labor...........27.00	sq	$27.00	$144.85	$171.85	
160 mil modified bitumen roofing, fully attached to deck ***Replace*** Materials......81.10 Labor...........71.00 Equipment............8.46 ***Remove*** .... Labor...........42.90	sq	$42.90	$160.56	$203.46	
160 mil modified bitumen roofing, fully attached with hot asphalt ***Replace*** Materials......94.80 Labor...........73.30 Equipment...........11.30 ***Remove*** .... Labor...........42.90	sq	$42.90	$179.40	$222.30	
15-pound roofing felt ***Replace*** Materials........4.12 Labor............3.92 ***Remove*** .... Labor............4.10	sq	$4.10	$8.04	$12.14	◀ **ROOFING FELT**

RELATED ITEMS

Rough Carpentry
chimney cricket.............444

	Item Description	Unit	Remove	Replace	Total
ROOFING FELT ▶ *continued*	**30-pound roofing felt** *Replace* Materials........7.42 Labor............3.92 *Remove* .... Labor............4.10	sq	$4.10	$11.34	$15.44
ICE AND WATER SHIELD ▶	**Ice and water shield** *Replace* Materials .... .48 Labor............ .37	sf	—	$.85	$.85
DRIP EDGE ▶	**Drip edge** *Replace* Materials .... .45 Labor............ .28 *Remove* .... Labor............ .14	lf	$.14	$.73	$.87
GRAVEL STOP ▶	**Gravel stop** *Replace* Materials .... .78 Labor............ .28 *Remove* .... Labor............ .14	lf	$.14	$1.06	$1.20
STEP FLASHING ▶	**Step flashing** *Replace* Materials........1.28 Labor............1.84	lf	—	$3.12	$3.12
CHIMNEY SAW-KERF FLASHING ▶	**Chimney saw-kerf flashing** *Replace* Materials........6.30 Labor............7.28	lf	—	$13.58	$13.58
	Minimum charge for chimney saw-kerf flashing *Replace* Materials......37.70 Labor..........46.10	ea	—	$83.80	$83.80
VALLEY METAL ▶	**Valley metal (galvanized or aluminum)** *Replace* Materials........1.69 Labor............ .78 *Remove* .... Labor............ .28	lf	$.28	$2.47	$2.75
	Copper valley metal *Replace* Materials........6.80 Labor............ .80 *Remove* .... Labor............ .28	lf	$.28	$7.60	$7.88
PIPE JACK ▶	**Pipe jack** *Replace* Materials........8.25 Labor............8.07 *Remove* .... Labor............9.45	ea	$9.45	$16.32	$25.77
ROOF VENT ▶	**Roof vent, turbine** *Replace* Materials......31.60 Labor..........13.60 *Remove* .... Labor..........11.70	ea	$11.70	$45.20	$56.90
	Roof vent, turtle *Replace* Materials.......15.20 Labor..........11.70 *Remove* .... Labor..........11.70	ea	$11.70	$26.90	$38.60
	Roof vent, gable *Replace* Materials.......19.30 Labor..........11.80 *Remove* .... Labor..........11.70	ea	$11.70	$31.10	$42.80
	Remove roof vent for work, then reinstall *Replace* .... Labor..........22.50	ea	—	$22.50	$22.50
FURNACE VENT ▶	**Furnace vent cap** *Replace* Materials.......11.00 Labor............9.45 *Remove* .... Labor..........11.80	ea	$11.80	$20.45	$32.25
	Remove vent cap for work, then reinstall *Replace* .... Labor..........16.40	ea	—	$16.40	$16.40
REPAIR LEAK WITH MASTIC ▶	**Repair roof leak with mastic** *Replace* Materials........2.99 Labor..........20.80	ea	—	$23.79	$23.79
	Repair flashing leak with mastic *Replace* Materials........2.99 Labor..........20.10	ea	—	$23.09	$23.09

Time & Material Charts *(selected items)*

Roofing Materials

See **Roofing** material prices with the line items and other information in the **QuickFinder** column.

Roofing Labor

Laborer	Base Wage	Paid Leave	True Wage	FICA	FUTA	Worker's Comp.	Unemploy. Insur.	Health Insur.	Retire (401k)	Liability Insur.	Cost per Hour
Roofer / slater	$23.00	1.79	$24.79	1.90	.20	14.31	2.16	2.69	.74	3.35	$50.10
Roofer's helper	$19.10	1.49	$20.59	1.58	.16	11.88	1.79	2.69	.62	2.78	$42.10
Demolition laborer	$13.90	1.08	$14.98	1.15	.12	4.79	1.30	2.69	.45	2.02	$27.50

Paid Leave is calculated based on two weeks paid vacation, one week sick leave, and seven paid holidays. Employer's matching portion of **FICA** is 7.65 percent. **FUTA** (Federal Unemployment) is .8 percent. **Worker's compensation** for the roofing trade was calculated using a national average of 57.71 percent. **Unemployment insurance** was calculated using a national average of 8.7 percent. **Health insurance** was calculated based on a projected national average for 2002 of $535 per employee (and family when applicable) per month. Employer pays 80 percent for a per month cost of $428 per employee. **Retirement** is based on a 401(k) retirement program with employer matching of 50 percent. Employee contributions to the 401(k) plan are an average of 6 percent of the true wage. **Liability insurance** is based on a national average of 13.2 percent.

Roofing Labor Productivity

Work Description	Laborer	Cost per Hour	Productivity	Unit Price
Demolition				
remove metal shingles	demolition laborer	$27.50	1.04	$28.60 sq
remove asphalt shingles	demolition laborer	$27.50	1.02	$28.10 sq
remove roll roofing	demolition laborer	$27.50	.735	$20.20 sq
remove slate shingles	demolition laborer	$27.50	3.70	$102.00 sq
remove wood shingles or shakes	demolition laborer	$27.50	1.20	$33.00 sq
remove fiber and cement shingles	demolition laborer	$27.50	1.11	$30.50 sq
remove mission or Spanish tile shingles	demolition laborer	$27.50	3.45	$94.90 sq
remove vertically laid furring strips	demolition laborer	$27.50	.478	$13.10 sq
remove vertically & horizontally laid furring strips	demolition laborer	$27.50	.840	$23.10 sq
remove concrete shingles	demolition laborer	$27.50	3.85	$106.00 sq
remove preformed metal roofing	demolition laborer	$27.50	.010	$.28 sf
remove preformed fiberglass roofing	demolition laborer	$27.50	.009	$.25 sf
remove seamed metal roofing	demolition laborer	$27.50	1.03	$28.30 sq
remove built-up 3 ply roofing	demolition laborer	$27.50	2.44	$67.10 sq
remove built-up 4 ply roofing	demolition laborer	$27.50	3.03	$83.30 sq
remove built-up 5 ply roofing	demolition laborer	$27.50	3.85	$106.00 sq
add to remove built-up roof with ballast	demolition laborer	$27.50	.847	$23.30 sq
remove single ply roof partially adhered	demolition laborer	$27.50	.980	$27.00 sq
remove single ply roof fully adhered	demolition laborer	$27.50	1.56	$42.90 sq
remove single ply roof with ballast	demolition laborer	$27.50	2.04	$56.10 sq
Roofing crew				
install roofing	roofer	$50.10		
install roofing	roofer's helper	$42.10		
install roofing	***roofing crew***	$46.10		
Install shingles				
aluminum shingles	roofing crew	$46.10	1.06	$48.90 sq
galvanized steel shingles	roofing crew	$46.10	1.11	$51.20 sq
20 year to 25 year asphalt	roofing crew	$46.10	1.24	$57.20 sq
30 year to 40 year asphalt	roofing crew	$46.10	1.27	$58.50 sq
standard grade laminated asphalt	roofing crew	$46.10	2.06	$95.00 sq
high grade laminated asphalt	roofing crew	$46.10	2.45	$113.00 sq
T-lock asphalt	roofing crew	$46.10	1.27	$58.50 sq
hexagonal asphalt	roofing crew	$46.10	1.27	$58.50 sq
diamond asphalt	roofing crew	$46.10	1.27	$58.50 sq

. . . More ➢

Roofing Labor Productivity *continued*

WORK DESCRIPTION	LABORER	COST PER HOUR	PRODUCTIVITY	UNIT PRICE
Install roll roofing				
all weights	roofing crew	$46.10	.645	$29.70 sq
Install slate				
typical	roofing crew	$46.10	4.00	$184.00 sq
replace single slate shingle	roofing crew	$46.10	.385	$17.70 ea
Install wood shingles				
16"	roofing crew	$46.10	2.86	$132.00 sq
24"	roofing crew	$46.10	2.00	$92.20 sq
replace single wood shingle	roofing crew	$46.10	.208	$9.59 ea
Install wood shakes				
18"	roofing crew	$46.10	3.33	$154.00 sq
24"	roofing crew	$46.10	2.86	$132.00 sq
replace single shake	roofing crew	$46.10	.208	$9.59 ea
Install fiber and cement shingles				
weathering shake style	roofing crew	$46.10	2.38	$110.00 sq
Spanish tile style	roofing crew	$46.10	2.50	$115.00 sq
Install clay tile				
flat	roofing crew	$46.10	3.23	$149.00 sq
Mission tile	roofing crew	$46.10	5.56	$256.00 sq
Spanish tile	roofing crew	$46.10	3.33	$154.00 sq
Install tile furring strips				
vertically laid only	roofing crew	$46.10	.606	$27.90 sq
vertically and horizontally laid	roofing crew	$46.10	.877	$40.40 sq
Install concrete tile				
corrugated	roofing crew	$46.10	3.13	$144.00 sq
flat	roofing crew	$46.10	3.03	$140.00 sq
Install pre-formed roofing				
corrugated aluminum or fiberglass	roofing crew	$46.10	.024	$1.11 sf
corrugated galvanized steel	roofing crew	$46.10	.025	$1.15 sf
ribbed (all types)	roofing crew	$46.10	.026	$1.20 sf
Install standing seam metal roofing				
16 ounce copper	roofing crew	$46.10	6.67	$307.00 sq
20 ounce copper	roofing crew	$46.10	7.69	$355.00 sq
28 gauge stainless steel	roofing crew	$46.10	7.14	$329.00 sq
40 lb terne	roofing crew	$46.10	8.33	$384.00 sq
Install batten seam metal roofing				
16 ounce copper	roofing crew	$46.10	7.69	$355.00 sq
20 ounce copper	roofing crew	$46.10	9.09	$419.00 sq
28 gauge stainless steel	roofing crew	$46.10	7.69	$355.00 sq
26 gauge stainless steel	roofing crew	$46.10	7.14	$329.00 sq
3 lb lead	roofing crew	$46.10	7.14	$329.00 sq
40 lb terne	roofing crew	$46.10	7.69	$355.00 sq
Install flat seam metal roofing				
16 ounce copper	roofing crew	$46.10	7.14	$329.00 sq
20 ounce copper	roofing crew	$46.10	8.33	$384.00 sq
28 gauge stainless steel	roofing crew	$46.10	7.14	$329.00 sq
26 gauge stainless steel	roofing crew	$46.10	6.67	$307.00 sq
3 lb lead	roofing crew	$46.10	7.69	$355.00 sq
40 lb terne	roofing crew	$46.10	9.09	$419.00 sq
Seamed metal roofing repair				
solder patch (less than 1' square)	roofer	$50.10	1.00	$50.10 ea
Install built-up roof				
3 ply	roofing crew	$46.10	3.33	$154.00 sq
4 ply	roofing crew	$46.10	4.00	$184.00 sq
5 ply	roofing crew	$46.10	4.76	$219.00 sq

NOTES:

end

32 .... Rough Carpentry

Item Description	Unit	Remove	Replace	Total
Minimum charge for rough carpentry work *Replace* Materials......50.00 Labor..........48.10	ea	—	$98.10	$98.10
2″ x 4″ interior partition wall 8′ tall 16″ on center *Replace* Materials........7.71 Labor............8.72 *Remove*........................ Labor............1.24	lf	$1.24	$16.43	$17.67
2″ x 4″ interior partition wall 8′ tall 24″ on center *Replace* Materials........6.45 Labor............7.42 *Remove*........................ Labor............1.24	lf	$1.24	$13.87	$15.11
2″ x 4″ interior partition wall 10′ tall 16″ on center *Replace* Materials........9.19 Labor............8.83 *Remove*........................ Labor............1.57	lf	$1.57	$18.02	$19.59
2″ x 4″ interior partition wall 10′ tall 24″ on center *Replace* Materials........7.59 Labor............7.49 *Remove*........................ Labor............1.57	lf	$1.57	$15.08	$16.65
2″ x 6″ interior partition wall 8′ tall 16″ on center *Replace* Materials.......11.10 Labor............8.83 *Remove*........................ Labor............1.32	lf	$1.32	$19.93	$21.25
2″ x 6″ interior partition wall 8′ tall 24″ on center *Replace* Materials........9.29 Labor............7.49 *Remove*........................ Labor............1.32	lf	$1.32	$16.78	$18.10
2″ x 6″ interior partition wall 10′ tall 16″ on center *Replace* Materials.......13.20 Labor............8.94 *Remove*........................ Labor............1.65	lf	$1.65	$22.14	$23.79
2″ x 6″ interior partition wall 10′ tall 24″ on center *Replace* Materials......10.90 Labor............7.57 *Remove*........................ Labor............1.65	lf	$1.65	$18.47	$20.12
2″ x 8″ interior partition wall 8′ tall 16″ on center *Replace* Materials......14.50 Labor............8.94 *Remove*........................ Labor............1.35	lf	$1.35	$23.44	$24.79
2″ x 8″ interior partition wall 8′ tall 24″ on center *Replace* Materials......12.20 Labor............7.57 *Remove*........................ Labor............1.35	lf	$1.35	$19.77	$21.12
2″ x 8″ interior partition wall 10′ tall 16″ on center *Replace* Materials.......17.10 Labor............9.05 *Remove*........................ Labor............1.68	lf	$1.68	$26.15	$27.83
2″ x 8″ interior partition wall 10′ tall 24″ on center *Replace* Materials......14.30 Labor............7.64 *Remove*........................ Labor............1.68	lf	$1.68	$21.94	$23.62
2″ x 4″ interior bearing wall 8′ tall 12″ on center *Replace* Materials.......11.20 Labor...........11.10 *Remove*........................ Labor............1.24	lf	$1.24	$22.30	$23.54
2″ x 4″ interior bearing wall 8′ tall 16″ on center *Replace* Materials........9.93 Labor............9.45 *Remove*........................ Labor............1.24	lf	$1.24	$19.38	$20.62

◄ **MINIMUM**

◄ **PER LF**
INTERIOR PARTITION WALL
Includes 5% waste. Based on an average wall with 4 openings and 5 corners per 56 lf of wall. A net of 2.2 studs is added for each corner and opening. All walls have two top plates and a single bottom plate.

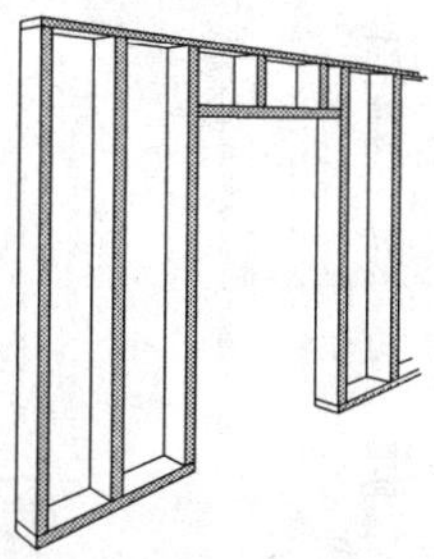

LUMBER PRICES

Some lumber prices, such as oak timbers, vary by as much as 60% depending on the region. These prices will be 15% to 30% lower in the Northeast, South, and most Great Lake states and provinces. In many areas of the western mid-west and mountain states and provinces, oak timbers are not available unless specially shipped for a particular job.

For the most accurate results, compare your local prices with the prices found in the material charts for this section starting on page 445 and create a materials factor.

◄ **PER LF**
INTERIOR BEARING WALL

continued on next page

PER LF ▶ INTERIOR BEARING WALL *continued*

Includes 5% waste. Based on an average wall with 4 openings and 5 corners per 56 lf of wall. A net of 2.2 studs is added for each corner and opening. (Four openings are, two 3′ wide, one 4′ wide, and one 5′ wide for a total of 15 lf.) Headers in openings are made from sandwiched 2″ x 10″ boards with 1/2″ CDX plywood stiffeners between. All walls have two top plates and a single bottom plate.

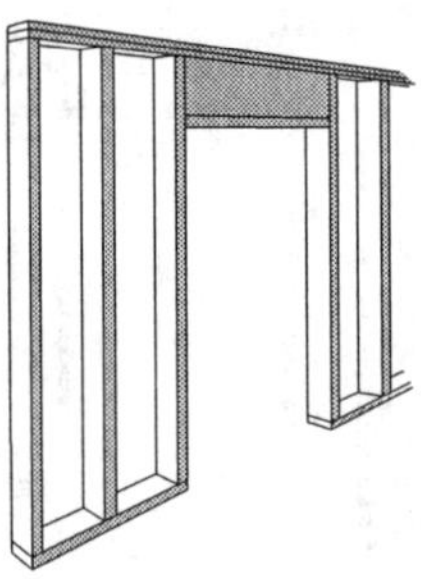

Item Description	Unit	Remove	Replace	Total
2″ x 4″ interior bearing wall 10′ tall 12″ on center ***Replace*** Materials.......13.00 Labor...........11.30 ***Remove*** .... Labor............1.57	lf	$1.57	$24.30	$25.87
2″ x 4″ interior bearing wall 10′ tall 16″ on center ***Replace*** Materials.......11.40 Labor............9.59 ***Remove*** .... Labor............1.57	lf	$1.57	$20.99	$22.56
2″ x 6″ interior bearing wall 8′ tall 12″ on center ***Replace*** Materials.......19.00 Labor...........11.20 ***Remove*** .... Labor............1.32	lf	$1.32	$30.20	$31.52
2″ x 6″ interior bearing wall 8′ tall 16″ on center ***Replace*** Materials.......17.10 Labor............9.52 ***Remove*** .... Labor............1.32	lf	$1.32	$26.62	$27.94
2″ x 6″ interior bearing wall 10′ tall 12″ on center ***Replace*** Materials......21.50 Labor...........11.40 ***Remove*** .... Labor............1.65	lf	$1.65	$32.90	$34.55
2″ x 6″ interior bearing wall 10′ tall 16″ on center ***Replace*** Materials.......19.20 Labor............9.67 ***Remove*** .... Labor............1.65	lf	$1.65	$28.87	$30.52
2″ x 8″ interior bearing wall 8′ tall 12″ on center ***Replace*** Materials......24.80 Labor...........11.30 ***Remove*** .... Labor............1.35	lf	$1.35	$36.10	$37.45
2″ x 8″ interior bearing wall 8′ tall 16″ on center ***Replace*** Materials......22.50 Labor............9.63 ***Remove*** .... Labor............1.35	lf	$1.35	$32.13	$33.48
2″ x 8″ interior bearing wall 10′ tall 12″ on center ***Replace*** Materials......28.00 Labor...........11.50 ***Remove*** .... Labor............1.68	lf	$1.68	$39.50	$41.18
2″ x 8″ interior bearing wall 10′ tall 16″ on center ***Replace*** Materials......25.20 Labor............9.77 ***Remove*** .... Labor............1.68	lf	$1.68	$34.97	$36.65

PER LF ▶ EXTERIOR WALL

Includes 5% waste. Based on an average wall with 4 openings and 5 corners per 56 lf of wall. A net of 2.2 studs is added for each corner and opening. (Four openings are, two 3′ wide, one 4′ wide, and one 5′ wide for a total of 15 lf.) Headers in openings are made from sandwiched 2″ x 10″ boards with 1/2″ CDX plywood stiffeners between boards. Includes 4 metal let-in braces for every 56 lf of wall. All walls have two top plates and a single bottom plate. Does not include exterior sheathing.

Item Description	Unit	Remove	Replace	Total
2″ x 4″ exterior wall 8′ tall 12″ on center ***Replace*** Materials.......11.43 Labor...........11.30 ***Remove*** .... Labor............1.24	lf	$1.24	$22.73	$23.97
2″ x 4″ exterior wall 8′ tall 16″ on center ***Replace*** Materials......10.17 Labor............9.67 ***Remove*** .... Labor............1.24	lf	$1.24	$19.84	$21.08
2″ x 4″ exterior wall 8′ tall 24″ on center ***Replace*** Materials........8.90 Labor............7.82 ***Remove*** .... Labor............1.24	lf	$1.24	$16.72	$17.96
2″ x 4″ exterior wall 10′ tall 12″ on center ***Replace*** Materials.......13.20 Labor...........11.50 ***Remove*** .... Labor............1.57	lf	$1.57	$24.70	$26.27
2″ x 4″ exterior wall 10′ tall 16″ on center ***Replace*** Materials.......11.60 Labor............9.77 ***Remove*** .... Labor............1.57	lf	$1.57	$21.37	$22.94
2″ x 4″ exterior wall 10′ tall 24″ on center ***Replace*** Materials......10.04 Labor............7.89 ***Remove*** .... Labor............1.57	lf	$1.57	$17.93	$19.50

Item Description	Unit	Remove	Replace	Total
2" x 6" exterior wall 8' tall 12" on center *Replace* Materials.......19.20 Labor...........11.40 *Remove* .... Labor............1.24	lf	$1.24	$30.60	$31.84
2" x 6" exterior wall 8' tall 16" on center *Replace* Materials.......17.40 Labor............9.77 *Remove*........................ Labor............1.24	lf	$1.24	$27.17	$28.41
2" x 6" exterior wall 8' tall 24" on center *Replace* Materials.......15.50 Labor............7.89 *Remove*........................ Labor............1.24	lf	$1.24	$23.39	$24.63
2" x 6" exterior wall 10' tall 12" on center *Replace* Materials......21.70 Labor...........11.60 *Remove*........................ Labor............1.57	lf	$1.57	$33.30	$34.87
2" x 6" exterior wall 10' tall 16" on center *Replace* Materials.......19.40 Labor............9.88 *Remove*........................ Labor............1.57	lf	$1.57	$29.28	$30.85
2" x 6" exterior wall 10' tall 24" on center *Replace* Materials........17.10 Labor............8.00 *Remove*........................ Labor............1.57	lf	$1.57	$25.10	$26.67
2" x 8" exterior wall 8' tall 12" on center *Replace* Materials......25.00 Labor...........11.50 *Remove* .... Labor............1.24	lf	$1.24	$36.50	$37.74
2" x 8" exterior wall 8' tall 16" on center *Replace* Materials......22.80 Labor............9.85 *Remove* .... Labor............1.24	lf	$1.24	$32.65	$33.89
2" x 8" exterior wall 8' tall 24" on center *Replace* Materials......20.50 Labor............7.96 *Remove* .... Labor............1.24	lf	$1.24	$28.46	$29.70
2" x 8" exterior wall 10' tall 12" on center *Replace* Materials......28.30 Labor...........11.70 *Remove* .... Labor............1.57	lf	$1.57	$40.00	$41.57
2" x 8" exterior wall 10' tall 16" on center *Replace* Materials......25.40 Labor............9.96 *Remove* .... Labor............1.57	lf	$1.57	$35.36	$36.93
2" x 8" exterior wall 10' tall 24" on center *Replace* Materials......22.50 Labor............8.07 *Remove* .... Labor............1.57	lf	$1.57	$30.57	$32.14
2" x 4" interior partition wall 16" on center *Replace* Materials .... .96 Labor........... 1.09 *Remove*........................ Labor............ .17	sf	$.17	$2.05	$2.22
2" x 4" interior partition wall 24" on center *Replace* Materials .... .81 Labor............ .94 *Remove*........................ Labor............ .17	sf	$.17	$1.75	$1.92
2" x 6" interior partition wall 16" on center *Replace* Materials........1.39 Labor........... 1.09 *Remove* .... Labor............ .17	sf	$.17	$2.48	$2.65
2" x 6" interior partition wall 24" on center *Replace* Materials........1.16 Labor............ .94 *Remove* .... Labor............ .17	sf	$.17	$2.10	$2.27

◁ 2" x 6"

◁ 2" x 8"

RELATED ITEMS

Columns........................71
Fences..........................187
Finish Carpentry..........199
Outbuildings................331
Painting.......................341
Paneling......................347
Siding..........................455
Stairs..........................465

◀ **PER SF INTERIOR PARTITION WALL**
Includes 5% waste. Based on an average wall with 4 openings and 5 corners per 448 sf of wall. A net of 2.2 studs is added for each corner and opening. All walls have two top plates and a single bottom plate.

PER SF ▶ INTERIOR PARTITION WALL *continued*

Item Description	Unit	Remove	Replace	Total
2" x 8" interior partition wall 16" on center *Replace* Materials........3.50 Labor............1.12 *Remove* .... Labor............ .17	sf	$.17	$4.62	$4.79
2" x 8" interior partition wall 24" on center *Replace* Materials........3.15 Labor............ .94 *Remove* .... Labor............ .17	sf	$.17	$4.09	$4.26

PER SF ▶ SLOPING INTERIOR PARTITION WALL

Includes 5% waste. Based on an average wall with one 3' wide opening, two 4'6" wide openings, and 2 corners per 24 lf of wall. A net of 2.4 studs is added per corner or opening. All walls have two top plates and a single bottom plate.

Item Description	Unit	Remove	Replace	Total
2" x 4" sloping interior partition wall 16" on center *Replace* Materials........ .76 Labor............1.48 *Remove*........................ Labor............ .17	sf	$.17	$2.24	$2.41
2" x 4" sloping interior partition wall 24" on center *Replace* Materials........ .64 Labor............1.27 *Remove*........................ Labor............ .17	sf	$.17	$1.91	$2.08
2" x 6" sloping interior partition wall 16" on center *Replace* Materials........1.09 Labor............1.52 *Remove* .... Labor............ .17	sf	$.17	$2.61	$2.78
2" x 6" sloping interior partition wall 24" on center *Replace* Materials........ .92 Labor............1.30 *Remove* .... Labor............ .17	sf	$.17	$2.22	$2.39
2" x 8" sloping interior partition wall 16" on center *Replace* Materials........1.40 Labor............1.52 *Remove* .... Labor............ .17	sf	$.17	$2.92	$3.09
2" x 8" sloping interior partition wall 24" on center *Replace* Materials........1.19 Labor............1.30 *Remove* .... Labor............ .17	sf	$.17	$2.49	$2.66

PER SF ▶ SLOPING INTERIOR BEARING WALL

Includes 5% waste. Based on an average wall with one 3' wide opening, two 4'6" wide openings, and 2 corners per 24 lf of wall. A net of 2.4 studs is added per corner or opening. Headers in openings are made from sandwiched 2" x 10" boards with 1/2" CDX plywood stiffeners between boards. All walls have two top plates and a single bottom plate.

Item Description	Unit	Remove	Replace	Total
2" x 4" sloping interior bearing wall 12" on center *Replace* Materials........1.11 Labor............2.14 *Remove*........................ Labor............ .17	sf	$.17	$3.25	$3.42
2" x 4" sloping interior bearing wall 16" on center *Replace* Materials........ .99 Labor............1.81 *Remove*........................ Labor............ .17	sf	$.17	$2.80	$2.97
2" x 6" sloping interior bearing wall 12" on center *Replace* Materials........1.50 Labor............2.14 *Remove* .... Labor............ .17	sf	$.17	$3.64	$3.81
2" x 6" sloping interior bearing wall 16" on center *Replace* Materials........1.33 Labor............1.81 *Remove* .... Labor............ .17	sf	$.17	$3.14	$3.31
2" x 8" sloping interior bearing wall 12" on center *Replace* Materials........1.85 Labor............2.17 *Remove* .... Labor............ .17	sf	$.17	$4.02	$4.19
2" x 8" sloping interior bearing wall 16" on center *Replace* Materials........1.64 Labor............1.85 *Remove* .... Labor............ .17	sf	$.17	$3.49	$3.66

PER SF ▶ INTERIOR BEARING WALL

Includes 5% waste. Based on an average wall with 4 openings and 5 corners per 56 lf.

Item Description	Unit	Remove	Replace	Total
2" x 4" interior bearing wall 12" on center *Replace* Materials........1.40 Labor............1.38 *Remove*........................ Labor............ .17	sf	$.17	$2.78	$2.95
2" x 4" interior bearing wall 16" on center *Replace* Materials........1.24 Labor............1.19 *Remove*........................ Labor............ .17	sf	$.17	$2.43	$2.60

continued on next page

Item Description	Unit	Remove	Replace	Total
2" x 6" interior bearing wall 12" on center *Replace* Materials........2.38 Labor............1.41 *Remove* .... Labor............ .17	sf	$.17	$3.79	$3.96
2" x 6" interior bearing wall 16" on center *Replace* Materials........2.14 Labor............1.19 *Remove* .... Labor............ .17	sf	$.17	$3.33	$3.50
2" x 8" interior bearing wall 12" on center *Replace* Materials........3.10 Labor............1.41 *Remove* .... Labor............ .17	sf	$.17	$4.51	$4.68
2" x 8" interior bearing wall 16" on center *Replace* Materials........2.81 Labor............1.19 *Remove* .... Labor............ .17	sf	$.17	$4.00	$4.17
2" x 4" exterior wall 12" on center *Replace* Materials........1.43 Labor............1.45 *Remove*........................ Labor............ .17	sf	$.17	$2.88	$3.05
2" x 4" exterior wall 16" on center *Replace* Materials........1.27 Labor............1.23 *Remove*........................ Labor............ .17	sf	$.17	$2.50	$2.67
2" x 4" exterior wall 24" on center *Replace* Materials........1.11 Labor............ .98 *Remove*........................ Labor............ .17	sf	$.17	$2.09	$2.26
2" x 6" exterior wall 12" on center *Replace* Materials........2.40 Labor............1.45 *Remove* .... Labor............ .17	sf	$.17	$3.85	$4.02
2" x 6" exterior wall 16" on center *Replace* Materials........2.18 Labor............1.23 *Remove* .... Labor............ .17	sf	$.17	$3.41	$3.58
2" x 6" exterior wall 24" on center *Replace* Materials........1.94 Labor............ .98 *Remove* .... Labor............ .17	sf	$.17	$2.92	$3.09
2" x 8" exterior wall 12" on center *Replace* Materials........3.13 Labor............1.45 *Remove* .... Labor............ .17	sf	$.17	$4.58	$4.75
2" x 8" exterior wall 16" on center *Replace* Materials........2.85 Labor............1.23 *Remove* .... Labor............ .17	sf	$.17	$4.08	$4.25
2" x 8" exterior wall 24" on center *Replace* Materials........2.56 Labor.......... 1.01 *Remove* .... Labor............ .17	sf	$.17	$3.57	$3.74
2" x 4" sloping exterior wall 12" on center *Replace* Materials........1.29 Labor............1.95 *Remove*........................ Labor............ .17	sf	$.17	$3.24	$3.41
2" x 4" sloping exterior wall 16" on center *Replace* Materials........1.16 Labor............1.67 *Remove*........................ Labor............ .17	sf	$.17	$2.83	$3.00
2" x 4" sloping exterior wall 24" on center *Replace* Materials...... 1.03 Labor............1.38 *Remove*........................ Labor............ .17	sf	$.17	$2.41	$2.58

◄ **PER SF**
INTERIOR BEARING WALL
continued
A net of 2.2 studs is added for each corner and opening. Openings are two 3′ wide, one 4′ wide, and one 5′ wide for a total of 15 lf. Headers are made from sandwiched 2″ x 10″ boards with 1/2″ CDX plywood stiffeners. All walls have two top plates and a single bottom plate.

◄ **PER SF**
EXTERIOR WALL
Includes 5% waste. Based on an average wall with 4 openings and 5 corners per 56 lf of wall. A net of 2.2 studs is added for each corner and opening. Openings are two 3′ wide, one 4′ wide, and one 5′ wide for a total of 15 lf. Headers in openings are made from sandwiched 2″ x 10″ boards with 1/2″ CDX plywood stiffeners between boards. Includes 4 metal let-in braces for every 56 lf of wall. All walls have two top plates and a single bottom plate. Does not include exterior sheathing.

◁ **2″ x 8″**

RELATED ITEMS

◄ **PER SF**
SLOPING EXTERIOR WALL
Includes 5% waste. Based on an average wall with one 3′ wide opening, two 4′6″ openings, and 2 corners per 24 lf. A net of 2.4 studs is added per corner or opening.

continued on next page

	Item Description	Unit	Remove	Replace	Total
PER SF ▶ SLOPING EXTERIOR WALL *continued*	**2" x 6" sloping exterior wall 12" on center** *Replace* Materials........1.71 Labor............1.95 *Remove* .... Labor............ .17	sf	$.17	$3.66	$3.83
Headers in openings are made from sandwiched 2" x 10" boards with 1/2" CDX plywood stiffeners between boards. Includes 3 metal let-in braces for every 24 lf of wall. All walls have two top plates and a single bottom plate.	**2" x 6" sloping exterior wall 16" on center** *Replace* Materials........1.52 Labor............1.67 *Remove* .... Labor............ .17	sf	$.17	$3.19	$3.36
	2" x 6" sloping exterior wall 24" on center *Replace* Materials........1.33 Labor............1.38 *Remove* .... Labor............ .17	sf	$.17	$2.71	$2.88
	2" x 8" sloping exterior wall 12" on center *Replace* Materials........2.10 Labor............1.99 *Remove* .... Labor............ .17	sf	$.17	$4.09	$4.26
	2" x 8" sloping exterior wall 16" on center *Replace* Materials........1.87 Labor............1.70 *Remove* .... Labor............ .17	sf	$.17	$3.57	$3.74
	2" x 8" sloping exterior wall 24" on center *Replace* Materials........1.63 Labor............1.38 *Remove* .... Labor............ .17	sf	$.17	$3.01	$3.18
ADDITIONAL ▶ WALL FRAMING COSTS	**Add for beam pocket in exterior or bearing wall** *Replace* Materials......38.30 Labor..........40.20	ea	—	$78.50	$78.50
	Add to frame round- or elliptical-top door or window per lf of opening *Replace* Materials........3.09 Labor...........21.30	lf	—	$24.39	$24.39
	Add to frame round window per diameter of opening *Replace* Materials........3.58 Labor..........23.10	lf	—	$26.68	$26.68
	Add to frame bay window per lf of wall *Replace* Materials........3.58 Labor...........21.00	lf	—	$24.58	$24.58
	Add to frame bow window per lf of wall *Replace* Materials........3.58 Labor..........23.50	lf	—	$27.08	$27.08
ADDITIONAL ▶ COST FOR CEC BRACING *Additional cost to nail, brace, and shear panel to California Earthquake Code standards. Per sf of wall.*	**Add for CEC bracing and shear paneling of interior bearing wall** *Replace* Materials........ .26 Labor............ .40	sf	—	$.66	$.66
	Add for CEC bracing and shear paneling of sloping interior wall *Replace* Materials........ .29 Labor............ .51	sf	—	$.80	$.80
	Add for CEC bracing and shear paneling of exterior wall *Replace* Materials........ .32 Labor............ .40	sf	—	$.72	$.72
	Add for CEC bracing and shear paneling of sloping exterior wall *Replace* Materials........ .36 Labor............ .54	sf	—	$.90	$.90
PER BF ▶ WALL FRAMING *Includes 7% waste.*	**Interior wall per bf** *Replace* Materials...... 1.02 Labor............1.23 *Remove* .... Labor............ .19	bf	$.19	$2.25	$2.44
	Sloping interior wall per bf *Replace* Materials........1.09 Labor............1.70 *Remove* .... Labor............ .19	bf	$.19	$2.79	$2.98
	Exterior wall per bf *Replace* Materials........1.25 Labor............1.34 *Remove* .... Labor............ .19	bf	$.19	$2.59	$2.78

CEC = California Earthquake Code.

Item Description	Unit	Remove	Replace	Total
Sloping exterior wall per bf ***Replace*** Materials........1.33 Labor............1.85 ***Remove*** .... Labor............ .19	bf	$.19	$3.18	$3.37
2″ x 4″ top plate ***Replace*** Materials........ .67 Labor............ .62 ***Remove*** .... Labor............ .36	lf	$.36	$1.29	$1.65
2″ x 6″ top plate ***Replace*** Materials........ .96 Labor............ .65 ***Remove*** .... Labor............ .36	lf	$.36	$1.61	$1.97
2″ x 8″ top plate ***Replace*** Materials........1.40 Labor............ .65 ***Remove*** .... Labor............ .36	lf	$.36	$2.05	$2.41
2″ x 4″ treated-wood foundation sill plate ***Replace*** Materials........1.11 Labor............2.43 ***Remove*** .... Labor............1.24	lf	$1.24	$3.54	$4.78
2″ x 6″ treated-wood foundation sill plate ***Replace*** Materials........1.64 Labor............2.43 ***Remove*** .... Labor............1.24	lf	$1.24	$4.07	$5.31
2″ x 8″ treated-wood foundation sill plate ***Replace*** Materials........2.18 Labor............2.46 ***Remove*** .... Labor............1.24	lf	$1.24	$4.64	$5.88
2″ x 4″ con common redwood foundation sill plate ***Replace*** Materials........1.29 Labor............2.35 ***Remove*** .... Labor............1.24	lf	$1.24	$3.64	$4.88
2″ x 6″ con common redwood foundation sill plate ***Replace*** Materials........1.64 Labor............2.35 ***Remove*** .... Labor............1.24	lf	$1.24	$3.99	$5.23
2″ x 8″ con common redwood foundation sill plate ***Replace*** Materials........2.28 Labor............2.39 ***Remove*** .... Labor............1.24	lf	$1.24	$4.67	$5.91
4″ x 6″ header beam ***Replace*** Materials........4.73 Labor............1.45 ***Remove*** .... Labor............1.10 ► For 2″ x 4″. Doubled 2″ x 6″ with 1/2″ CDX plywood stiffener.	lf	$1.10	$6.18	$7.28
4″ x 8″ header beam ***Replace*** Materials........5.35 Labor............1.52 ***Remove*** .... Labor............1.10 ► For 2″ x 4″ wall. Doubled 2″ x 8″ with 1/2″ CDX plywood stiffener.	lf	$1.10	$6.87	$7.97
4″ x 10″ header beam ***Replace*** Materials........7.49 Labor............1.56 ***Remove*** .... Labor............1.10 ► For 2″ x 4″ wall. Doubled 2″ x 10″ with 1/2″ CDX plywood stiffener.	lf	$1.10	$9.05	$10.15
4″ x 12″ header beam ***Replace*** Materials........9.07 Labor............1.63 ***Remove*** .... Labor............1.10 ► For 2″ x 4″ wall. Doubled 2″ x 12″ with 1/2″ CDX plywood stiffener.	lf	$1.10	$10.70	$11.80
6″ x 6″ header beam ***Replace*** Materials........8.50 Labor............2.21 ***Remove*** .... Labor............1.10 ► For 2″ x 6″ wall. Three 2″ x 6″ with two 1/2″ CDX plywood stiffeners.	lf	$1.10	$10.71	$11.81

◄ **TOP PLATE**
Includes 5% waste. Cost to remove and replace a damaged top plate on an existing wall.

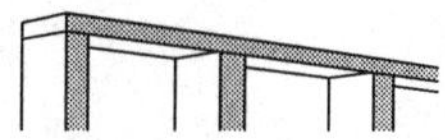

◄ **FOUNDATION SILL PLATE**
Includes foam sealer strip, hole drilling for anchor bolts, and fastening.

CALIFORNIA EARTHQUAKE CODE

Items that include "CEC" in the description are priced according to California earthquake code requirements.

Although these *Universal Building Code* standards are also required in other areas, they are most commonly associated with efforts initiated in California to improve the construction and engineering of structures in quake zones.

◄ **WALL HEADER**
Includes 5% waste.

◁ **for 2″ x 4″ wall**

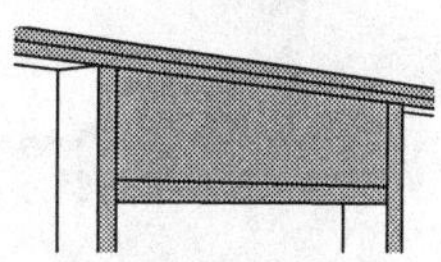

RELATED ITEMS

Columns........................71
Fences...........................187
Finish Carpentry..........199
Outbuildings................331
Painting.......................341
Paneling......................347
Siding..........................455
Stairs...........................465

◁ **for 2″ x 6″ wall**

	Item Description	Unit	Remove	Replace	Total
Wall header ► *continued*	**6" x 8" header beam** ***Replace*** Materials........9.50 Labor............2.35 ***Remove*** .... Labor............1.10 ► For 2" x 6" wall. Three 2" x 8" with two 1/2" CDX plywood stiffeners.	lf	$1.10	$11.85	$12.95
	6" x 10" header beam ***Replace*** Materials.......13.10 Labor............2.50 ***Remove*** .... Labor............1.10 ► For 2" x 6" wall. Three 2" x 10" with two 1/2" CDX plywood stiffeners.	lf	$1.10	$15.60	$16.70
	6" x 12" header beam ***Replace*** Materials......16.00 Labor............2.68 ***Remove*** .... Labor............1.10 ► For 2" x 6" wall. Three 2" x 12" with two 1/2" CDX plywood stiffeners.	lf	$1.10	$18.68	$19.78
for 2" x 8" wall ▷	**8" x 6" header beam** ***Replace*** Materials......12.30 Labor............2.64 ***Remove*** .... Labor............1.10 ► For 2" x 8" wall. Four 2" x 6" with three 1/2" CDX plywood stiffeners.	lf	$1.10	$14.94	$16.04
	8" x 8" header beam ***Replace*** Materials.......13.70 Labor............2.82 ***Remove*** .... Labor............1.10 ► For 2" x 8" wall. Four 2" x 8" with three 1/2" CDX plywood stiffeners.	lf	$1.10	$16.52	$17.62
	8" x 10" header beam ***Replace*** Materials.......15.00 Labor............3.08 ***Remove*** .... Labor............1.10 ► For 2" x 8" wall. Four 2" x 10" with three 1/2" CDX plywood stiffeners.	lf	$1.10	$18.08	$19.18
	8" x 12" header beam ***Replace*** Materials......22.90 Labor............3.37 ***Remove*** .... Labor............1.10 ► For 2" x 8" wall. Four 2" x 12" with three 1/2" CDX plywood stiffeners.	lf	$1.10	$26.27	$27.37
Posts ► *Includes 4% waste.* 4" x 4" ▷	**4" x 4" pine post** ***Replace*** Materials........2.68 Labor............1.52 ***Remove*** .... Labor............1.62	lf	$1.62	$4.20	$5.82
	4" x 4" con common redwood post ***Replace*** Materials........3.24 Labor............1.52 ***Remove*** .... Labor............1.62	lf	$1.62	$4.76	$6.38
	4" x 4" treated pine post ***Replace*** Materials........3.49 Labor............1.52 ***Remove*** .... Labor............1.62	lf	$1.62	$5.01	$6.63
4" x 6" ▷	**4" x 6" pine post** ***Replace*** Materials........3.11 Labor............1.56 ***Remove*** .... Labor............1.62	lf	$1.62	$4.67	$6.29
	4" x 6" con common redwood post ***Replace*** Materials........3.46 Labor............1.56 ***Remove*** .... Labor............1.62	lf	$1.62	$5.02	$6.64
	4" x 6" treated pine post ***Replace*** Materials........4.05 Labor............1.56 ***Remove*** .... Labor............1.62	lf	$1.62	$5.61	$7.23
4" x 8" ▷	**4" x 8" pine post** ***Replace*** Materials.......4.97 Labor............1.56 ***Remove*** .... Labor............1.62	lf	$1.62	$6.53	$8.15

RELATED ITEMS

Item Description	Unit	Remove	Replace	Total	
4" x 8" con common redwood post *Replace* Materials........4.99 Labor............1.56 *Remove* .... Labor............1.62	lf	$1.62	$6.55	$8.17	
4" x 8" treated pine post *Replace* Materials........6.47 Labor............1.56 *Remove* .... Labor............1.62	lf	$1.62	$8.03	$9.65	
6" x 6" pine post *Replace* Materials........6.52 Labor............1.59 *Remove* .... Labor............1.62	lf	$1.62	$8.11	$9.73	◁ 6" x 6"
6" x 6" con common redwood post *Replace* Materials........5.61 Labor............1.59 *Remove* .... Labor............1.62	lf	$1.62	$7.20	$8.82	
6" x 6" treated pine post *Replace* Materials........8.48 Labor............1.59 *Remove* .... Labor............1.62	lf	$1.62	$10.07	$11.69	
6" x 8" pine post *Replace* Materials........8.71 Labor............1.63 *Remove* .... Labor............1.62	lf	$1.62	$10.34	$11.96	◁ 6" x 8"
6" x 8" con common redwood post *Replace* Materials........7.49 Labor............1.63 *Remove* .... Labor............1.62	lf	$1.62	$9.12	$10.74	
6" x 8" treated pine post *Replace* Materials.......11.30 Labor............1.63 *Remove* .... Labor............1.62	lf	$1.62	$12.93	$14.55	
6" x 10" pine post *Replace* Materials......10.90 Labor............1.70 *Remove* .... Labor............1.62	lf	$1.62	$12.60	$14.22	◁ 6" x 10"
6" x 10" con common redwood post *Replace* Materials........9.35 Labor............1.70 *Remove* .... Labor............1.62	lf	$1.62	$11.05	$12.67	
6" x 10" treated pine post *Replace* Materials......14.20 Labor............1.70 *Remove* .... Labor............1.62	lf	$1.62	$15.90	$17.52	
8" x 8" pine post *Replace* Materials.......11.60 Labor............1.74 *Remove* .... Labor............1.62	lf	$1.62	$13.34	$14.96	◁ 8" x 8"
8" x 8" con common redwood post *Replace* Materials........9.97 Labor............1.74 *Remove* .... Labor............1.62	lf	$1.62	$11.71	$13.33	
8" x 8" treated pine post *Replace* Materials.......15.10 Labor............1.74 *Remove* .... Labor............1.62	lf	$1.62	$16.84	$18.46	
Pre-cast concrete pier *Replace* Materials......18.10 Labor............9.45 *Remove* .... Labor............7.43	ea	$7.43	$27.55	$34.98	◀ **Precast pier** 
51" to 90" adjustable steel jackpost to 13,000 pound load *Replace* Materials......48.90 Labor...........12.90 *Remove* .... Labor............8.61	ea	$8.61	$61.80	$70.41	◀ **Jackpost**

	Item Description	Unit	Remove	Replace	Total
Jackpost ▶ *continued*	**20″ to 36″ adjustable steel jackpost to 16,000 pound load** ***Replace*** Materials......32.00 Labor............8.80 ***Remove*** .... Labor............8.61	ea	$8.61	$40.80	$49.41
	48″ to 100″ adjustable steel jackpost to 16,000 pound load ***Replace*** Materials......55.20 Labor...........13.90 ***Remove*** .... Labor............8.61	ea	$8.61	$69.10	$77.71
	37″ to 60″ adjustable steel jackpost to 17,500 pound load ***Replace*** Materials......40.30 Labor............9.85 ***Remove*** .... Labor............8.61	ea	$8.61	$50.15	$58.76
	56″ to 96″ adjustable steel jackpost to 25,000 pound load ***Replace*** Materials......63.00 Labor...........12.70 ***Remove*** .... Labor............8.61	ea	$8.61	$75.70	$84.31
Lally column ▶ 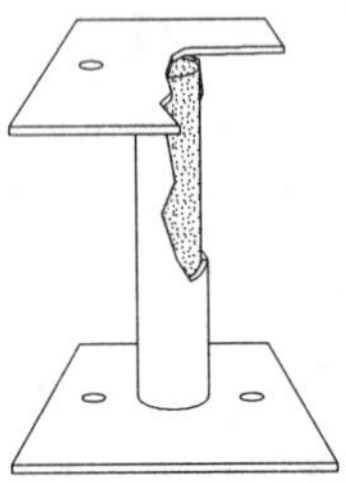	**3-1/2″ diameter concrete-filled lally column, 6′ to 8′** ***Replace*** Materials......77.30 Labor...........19.00 ***Remove*** .... Labor............9.82	ea	$9.82	$96.30	$106.12
	3-1/2″ diameter concrete-filled lally column, 8′ to 10′ ***Replace*** Materials......86.40 Labor...........20.10 ***Remove*** .... Labor............9.82	ea	$9.82	$106.50	$116.32
	3-1/2″ diameter concrete-filled lally column, 10′ to 12′ ***Replace*** Materials....106.90 Labor...........21.30 ***Remove*** .... Labor............9.82	ea	$9.82	$128.20	$138.02
Glue-laminated ▶ beam per bf *Includes 3% waste.*	**Glue-laminated beam per bf** ***Replace*** Materials........4.39 Labor............2.17 Equipment............ .33 ***Remove*** .... Labor............ .69	bf	$.69	$6.89	$7.58
Glue-laminated ▶ beam per lf *Includes 3% waste.* **3-1/8″ wide ▷**	**3-1/8″ x 7-1/2″ glue-laminated beam** ***Replace*** Materials........8.57 Labor............5.25 Equipment............ .62 ***Remove*** .... Labor............6.11	lf	$6.11	$14.44	$20.55
	3-1/8″ x 9″ glue-laminated beam ***Replace*** Materials......10.30 Labor............5.29 Equipment............ .62 ***Remove*** .... Labor............6.11	lf	$6.11	$16.21	$22.32
	3-1/8″ x 10-1/2″ glue-laminated beam ***Replace*** Materials......12.00 Labor............6.23 Equipment............ .62 ***Remove*** .... Labor............6.11	lf	$6.11	$18.85	$24.96
	3-1/8″ x 12″ glue-laminated beam ***Replace*** Materials.......13.70 Labor............6.84 Equipment............ .62 ***Remove*** .... Labor............6.11	lf	$6.11	$21.16	$27.27
	3-1/8″ x 13-1/2″ glue-laminated beam ***Replace*** Materials.......15.50 Labor............7.64 Equipment............ .62 ***Remove*** .... Labor............6.11	lf	$6.11	$23.76	$29.87
	3-1/8″ x 15″ glue-laminated beam ***Replace*** Materials.......17.10 Labor............7.67 Equipment............ .62 ***Remove*** .... Labor............6.11	lf	$6.11	$25.39	$31.50
	3-1/8″ x 16-1/2″ glue-laminated beam ***Replace*** Materials......18.90 Labor............7.75 Equipment............ .62 ***Remove*** .... Labor............6.11	lf	$6.11	$27.27	$33.38
	3-1/8″ x 18″ glue-laminated beam ***Replace*** Materials......20.60 Labor............7.82 Equipment............ .62 ***Remove*** .... Labor............6.11	lf	$6.11	$29.04	$35.15

Item Description			Unit	Remove	Replace	Total	
3-1/2" x 9" glue-laminated beam			lf	$6.11	$17.41	$23.52	◁ 3-1/2" wide
Replace Materials.......11.50	Labor 5.29	Equipment .... .62					
Remove	Labor 6.11						
3-1/2" x 12" glue-laminated beam			lf	$6.11	$22.32	$28.43	
Replace Materials.......15.40	Labor 6.30	Equipment .... .62					
Remove	Labor 6.11						
3-1/2" x 15" glue-laminated beam			lf	$6.11	$26.84	$32.95	
Replace Materials.......19.20	Labor 7.02	Equipment .... .62					
Remove	Labor 6.11						
3-1/2" x 19-1/2" glue-laminated beam			lf	$6.11	$33.52	$39.63	
Replace Materials 24.90	Labor 8.00	Equipment .... .62					
Remove	Labor 6.11						
3-1/2" x 21" glue-laminated beam			lf	$6.11	$35.59	$41.70	
Replace Materials 26.90	Labor 8.07	Equipment .... .62					
Remove	Labor 6.11						
5-1/8" x 7-1/2" glue-laminated beam			lf	$6.11	$20.88	$26.99	◁ 5-1/8" wide
Replace Materials 14.00	Labor 6.26	Equipment .... .62					
Remove	Labor 6.11						
5-1/8" x 9" glue-laminated beam			lf	$6.11	$23.86	$29.97	
Replace Materials 16.90	Labor 6.34	Equipment .... .62					
Remove	Labor 6.11						
5-1/8" x 10-1/2" glue-laminated beam			lf	$6.11	$27.34	$33.45	
Replace Materials.......19.70	Labor 7.02	Equipment .... .62					
Remove	Labor 6.11						
5-1/8" x 12" glue-laminated beam			lf	$6.11	$31.51	$37.62	
Replace Materials......23.00	Labor 7.89	Equipment .... .62					
Remove	Labor 6.11						
5-1/8" x 13-1/2" glue-laminated beam			lf	$6.11	$34.02	$40.13	
Replace Materials......25.40	Labor 8.00	Equipment .... .62					
Remove	Labor 6.11						
5-1/8" x 15" glue-laminated beam			lf	$6.11	$36.83	$42.94	
Replace Materials......28.10	Labor 8.11	Equipment .... .62					
Remove	Labor 6.11						
5-1/8" x 16-1/2" glue-laminated beam			lf	$6.11	$39.74	$45.85	
Replace Materials......30.90	Labor 8.22	Equipment .... .62					
Remove	Labor 6.11						
5-1/8" x 18" glue-laminated beam			lf	$6.11	$42.78	$48.89	
Replace Materials......33.80	Labor 8.36	Equipment .... .62					
Remove	Labor 6.11						
5-1/8" x 19-1/2" glue-laminated beam			lf	$6.11	$45.69	$51.80	
Replace Materials......36.60	Labor 8.47	Equipment .... .62					
Remove	Labor 6.11						
5-1/8" x 21" glue-laminated beam			lf	$6.11	$48.64	$54.75	
Replace Materials......39.40	Labor 8.62	Equipment .... .62					
Remove	Labor 6.11						
5-1/8" x 22-1/2" glue-laminated beam			lf	$6.11	$51.58	$57.69	
Replace Materials......42.20	Labor 8.76	Equipment .... .62					
Remove	Labor 6.11						

RELATED ITEMS

	Item Description	Unit	Remove	Replace	Total
Glue-laminated beam ▶ continued	**5-1/8" x 24" glue-laminated beam**	lf	$6.11	$54.59	$60.70
	Replace Materials......45.10 Labor............8.87 Equipment............ .62				
	Remove .... Labor............6.11				
6-3/4" wide ▷	**6-3/4" x 18" glue-laminated beam**	lf	$6.11	$53.85	$59.96
	Replace Materials......44.40 Labor............8.83 Equipment............ .62				
	Remove .... Labor............6.11				
	6-3/4" x 19-1/2" glue-laminated beam	lf	$6.11	$57.77	$63.88
	Replace Materials......48.10 Labor............9.05 Equipment............ .62				
	Remove .... Labor............6.11				
	6-3/4" x 24" glue-laminated beam	lf	$6.11	$69.59	$75.70
	Replace Materials......59.30 Labor............9.67 Equipment............ .62				
	Remove .... Labor............6.11				
Micro-laminated beam ▶ Includes 4% waste.	**1-3/4" x 7-1/4" micro-laminated beam**	lf	$2.92	$6.77	$9.69
	Replace Materials........5.03 Labor............1.74				
	Remove .... Labor............2.92				
	1-3/4" x 9-1/2" micro-laminated beam	lf	$2.92	$8.39	$11.31
	Replace Materials........6.58 Labor............1.81				
	Remove .... Labor............2.92				
	1-3/4" x 11-7/8" micro-laminated beam	lf	$2.92	$10.16	$13.08
	Replace Materials........8.24 Labor............1.92				
	Remove .... Labor............2.92				
	1-3/4" x 14" micro-laminated beam	lf	$2.92	$11.74	$14.66
	Replace Materials........9.71 Labor............2.03				
	Remove .... Labor............2.92				
	1-3/4" x 16" micro-laminated beam	lf	$2.92	$13.24	$16.16
	Replace Materials.......11.10 Labor............2.14				
	Remove .... Labor............2.92				
	1-3/4" x 18" micro-laminated beam	lf	$2.92	$14.78	$17.70
	Replace Materials......12.50 Labor............2.28				
	Remove .... Labor............2.92				
Pine beam ▶ Includes 4% waste. Deduct **12%** for #1 and better grade pine. Rough sawn. Installed as posts, beams, joists, and purlins. Pine species vary by region. Western coastal areas: Douglas fir, hemlock fir; Mountain states and provinces: spruce, pine, Douglas fir, South: southern yellow pine; Midwest: spruce, pine, Douglas fir, southern yellow pine; Southwest: southern yellow pine; Northeast: spruce, pine, Douglas fir, and hemlock fir.	**4" x 6" pine beam, select structural grade**	lf	$6.11	$7.09	$13.20
	Replace Materials........3.65 Labor............2.82 Equipment............ .62				
	Remove .... Labor............6.11				
	4" x 8" pine beam, select structural grade	lf	$6.11	$8.81	$14.92
	Replace Materials........4.86 Labor............3.33 Equipment............ .62				
	Remove .... Labor............6.11				
	4" x 10" pine beam, select structural grade	lf	$6.11	$10.82	$16.93
	Replace Materials........6.07 Labor............4.13 Equipment............ .62				
	Remove .... Labor............6.11				
	4" x 12" pine beam, select structural grade	lf	$6.11	$13.30	$19.41
	Replace Materials........7.29 Labor............5.39 Equipment............ .62				
	Remove .... Labor............6.11				
	4" x 14" pine beam, select structural grade	lf	$6.11	$15.57	$21.68
	Replace Materials........8.51 Labor............6.44 Equipment............ .62				
	Remove .... Labor............6.11				
	4" x 16" pine beam, select structural grade	lf	$6.11	$16.86	$22.97
	Replace Materials........9.72 Labor............6.52 Equipment............ .62				
	Remove .... Labor............6.11				

Item Description			Unit	Remove	Replace	Total	
6" x 6" pine beam, select structural grade			lf	$6.11	$9.78	$15.89	◁ 6" wide
Replace Materials........5.47	Labor 3.69	Equipment .... .62					
Remove	Labor 6.11						
6" x 8" pine beam, select structural grade			lf	$6.11	$12.07	$18.18	
Replace Materials........7.29	Labor 4.16	Equipment .... .62					
Remove	Labor 6.11						
6" x 10" pine beam, select structural grade			lf	$6.11	$14.51	$20.62	
Replace Materials........9.11	Labor 4.78	Equipment .... .62					
Remove	Labor 6.11						
6" x 12" pine beam, select structural grade			lf	$6.11	$17.09	$23.20	
Replace Materials 10.90	Labor 5.57	Equipment .... .62					
Remove	Labor 6.11						
6" x 14" pine beam, select structural grade			lf	$6.11	$19.54	$25.65	
Replace Materials 12.80	Labor 6.12	Equipment .... .62					
Remove	Labor 6.11						
6" x 16" pine beam, select structural grade			lf	$6.11	$22.06	$28.17	
Replace Materials 14.60	Labor 6.84	Equipment .... .62					
Remove	Labor 6.11						
8" x 8" pine beam, select structural grade			lf	$6.11	$15.37	$21.48	◁ 8" wide
Replace Materials........9.72	Labor 5.03	Equipment .... .62					
Remove	Labor 6.11						
8" x 10" pine beam, select structural grade			lf	$6.11	$18.47	$24.58	
Replace Materials 12.20	Labor 5.65	Equipment .... .62					
Remove	Labor 6.11						
8" x 12" pine beam, select structural grade			lf	$6.11	$21.81	$27.92	
Replace Materials 14.60	Labor 6.59	Equipment .... .62					
Remove	Labor 6.11						
8" x 14" pine beam, select structural grade			lf	$6.11	$24.61	$30.72	
Replace Materials.......17.00	Labor 6.99	Equipment .... .62					
Remove	Labor 6.11						
8" x 16" pine beam, select structural grade			lf	$6.11	$27.32	$33.43	
Replace Materials.......19.50	Labor 7.20	Equipment .... .62					
Remove	Labor 6.11						
10" x 10" pine beam, select structural grade			lf	$6.11	$22.19	$28.30	◁ 10" wide
Replace Materials.......15.20	Labor 6.37	Equipment .... .62					
Remove	Labor 6.11						
10" x 12" pine beam, select structural grade			lf	$6.11	$25.92	$32.03	
Replace Materials 18.20	Labor 7.10	Equipment .... .62					
Remove	Labor 6.11						
10" x 14" pine beam, select structural grade			lf	$6.11	$29.27	$35.38	
Replace Materials 21.30	Labor 7.35	Equipment .... .62					
Remove	Labor 6.11						
10" x 16" pine beam, select structural grade			lf	$6.11	$32.52	$38.63	
Replace Materials 24.30	Labor 7.60	Equipment .... .62					
Remove	Labor 6.11						
12" x 12" pine beam, select structural grade			lf	$6.11	$29.90	$36.01	◁ 12" wide
Replace Materials 21.90	Labor 7.38	Equipment .... .62					
Remove	Labor 6.11						

RELATED ITEMS

Columns 71
Fences..........................187
Finish Carpentry..........199
Outbuildings................331
Painting.......................341
Paneling......................347
Siding..........................455
Stairs 465

	Item Description	Unit	Remove	Replace	Total
PINE BEAM ▶ *continued*	**12″ x 14″ pine beam, select structural grade** *Replace* Materials......25.50 Labor............7.71 Equipment............ .62 *Remove* .... Labor............6.11	lf	$6.11	$33.83	$39.94
	12″ x 16″ pine beam, select structural grade *Replace* Materials......29.20 Labor............8.04 Equipment............ .62 *Remove* .... Labor............6.11	lf	$6.11	$37.86	$43.97
OAK BEAM ▶ *Includes 4% waste. Installed as posts, beams, joists, and purlins.*	**4″ x 6″ oak beam, select structural grade** *Replace* Materials........8.00 Labor............2.82 Equipment............ .62 *Remove* .... Labor............6.11	lf	$6.11	$11.44	$17.55
	4″ x 8″ oak beam, select structural grade *Replace* Materials......10.60 Labor............3.33 Equipment............ .62 *Remove* .... Labor............6.11	lf	$6.11	$14.55	$20.66
	4″ x 10″ oak beam, select structural grade *Replace* Materials.......13.30 Labor............4.13 Equipment............ .62 *Remove* .... Labor............6.11	lf	$6.11	$18.05	$24.16
	4″ x 12″ oak beam, select structural grade *Replace* Materials......16.00 Labor............5.39 Equipment............ .62 *Remove* .... Labor............6.11	lf	$6.11	$22.01	$28.12
	4″ x 14″ oak beam, select structural grade *Replace* Materials......18.60 Labor............6.44 Equipment............ .62 *Remove* .... Labor............6.11	lf	$6.11	$25.66	$31.77
	4″ x 16″ oak beam, select structural grade *Replace* Materials......21.40 Labor............6.52 Equipment............ .62 *Remove* .... Labor............6.11	lf	$6.11	$28.54	$34.65
6″ wide ▷	**6″ x 6″ oak beam, select structural grade** *Replace* Materials......12.00 Labor............3.69 Equipment............ .62 *Remove* .... Labor............6.11	lf	$6.11	$16.31	$22.42
	6″ x 8″ oak beam, select structural grade *Replace* Materials......16.70 Labor............4.16 Equipment............ .62 *Remove* .... Labor............6.11	lf	$6.11	$21.48	$27.59
	6″ x 10″ oak beam, select structural grade *Replace* Materials......20.00 Labor............4.78 Equipment............ .62 *Remove* .... Labor............6.11	lf	$6.11	$25.40	$31.51
	6″ x 12″ oak beam, select structural grade *Replace* Materials......24.00 Labor............5.57 Equipment............ .62 *Remove* .... Labor............6.11	lf	$6.11	$30.19	$36.30
	6″ x 14″ oak beam, select structural grade *Replace* Materials......28.00 Labor............6.12 Equipment............ .62 *Remove* .... Labor............6.11	lf	$6.11	$34.74	$40.85
	6″ x 16″ oak beam, select structural grade *Replace* Materials......32.00 Labor............6.84 Equipment............ .62 *Remove* .... Labor............6.11	lf	$6.11	$39.46	$45.57
8″ wide ▷	**8″ x 8″ oak beam, select structural grade** *Replace* Materials......21.40 Labor............5.03 Equipment............ .62 *Remove* .... Labor............6.11	lf	$6.11	$27.05	$33.16
	8″ x 10″ oak beam, select structural grade *Replace* Materials......26.70 Labor............5.65 Equipment............ .62 *Remove* .... Labor............6.11	lf	$6.11	$32.97	$39.08

Item Description	Unit	Remove	Replace	Total
8″ x 12″ oak beam, select structural grade	lf	$6.11	$39.21	$45.32
Replace Materials......32.00 Labor............6.59 Equipment............ .62				
Remove .... Labor............6.11				
8″ x 14″ oak beam, select structural grade	lf	$6.11	$44.91	$51.02
Replace Materials......37.30 Labor............6.99 Equipment............ .62				
Remove .... Labor............6.11				
8″ x 16″ oak beam, select structural grade	lf	$6.11	$50.52	$56.63
Replace Materials......42.70 Labor............7.20 Equipment............ .62				
Remove .... Labor............6.11				
10″ x 10″ oak beam, select structural grade	lf	$6.11	$40.29	$46.40
Replace Materials......33.30 Labor............6.37 Equipment............ .62				
Remove .... Labor............6.11				
10″ x 12″ oak beam, select structural grade	lf	$6.11	$47.72	$53.83
Replace Materials......40.00 Labor............7.10 Equipment............ .62				
Remove .... Labor............6.11				
10″ x 14″ oak beam, select structural grade	lf	$6.11	$54.67	$60.78
Replace Materials......46.70 Labor............7.35 Equipment............ .62				
Remove .... Labor............6.11				
10″ x 16″ oak beam, select structural grade	lf	$6.11	$61.52	$67.63
Replace Materials......53.30 Labor............7.60 Equipment............ .62				
Remove .... Labor............6.11				
12″ x 12″ oak beam, select structural grade	lf	$6.11	$56.00	$62.11
Replace Materials......48.00 Labor............7.38 Equipment............ .62				
Remove .... Labor............6.11				
12″ x 14″ oak beam, select structural grade	lf	$6.11	$64.33	$70.44
Replace Materials......56.00 Labor............7.71 Equipment............ .62				
Remove .... Labor............6.11				
12″ x 16″ oak beam, select structural grade	lf	$6.11	$72.66	$78.77
Replace Materials......64.00 Labor............8.04 Equipment............ .62				
Remove .... Labor............6.11				
Add for hand-hewn pine beam per square inch of surface	si	—	$.02	$.02
Replace Materials........ .02				
Add for curved pine framing member in post & beam framing	lf	—	$41.00	$41.00
Replace .... Labor..........41.00				
Add for hand-hewn oak beam per square inch of surface	si	—	$.04	$.04
Replace Materials........ .04				
Add for curved oak framing member in post & beam framing	lf	—	$54.10	$54.10
Replace .... Labor..........54.10				
Pine post & beam single-story bent with simple truss	sf	$1.95	$27.17	$29.12
Replace Materials........3.09 Labor.........23.70 Equipment............ .38				
Remove .... Labor...........1.95				
Pine post & beam single-story bent with king post truss	sf	$1.95	$29.43	$31.38
Replace Materials........3.45 Labor.........25.60 Equipment............ .38				
Remove .... Labor...........1.95				
Pine post & beam single-story bent with king post & struts truss	sf	$1.95	$32.04	$33.99
Replace Materials........3.86 Labor..........27.80 Equipment............ .38				
Remove .... Labor...........1.95				

RELATED ITEMS

◁ 10″ wide

◁ 12″ wide

◀ **ADDITIONAL BEAM COSTS**

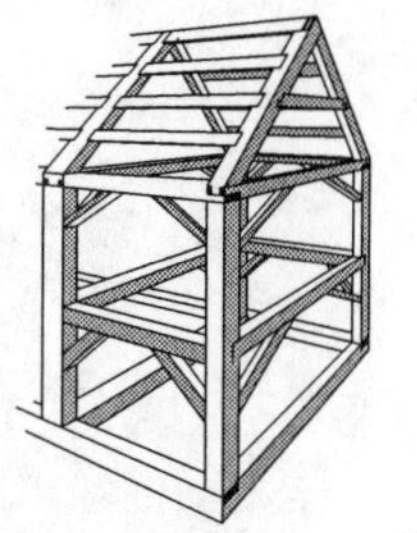

◀ **PINE POST & BEAM BENT WITH TRUSS**
With pine posts and beams, per sf of bent. Post & beam framing styles are nearly unlimited. The following styles are representative.

PINE POST & ▶ BEAM BENT WITH TRUSS
continued

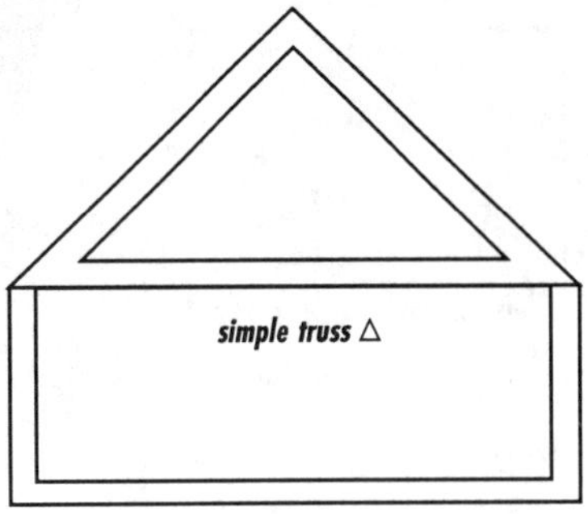

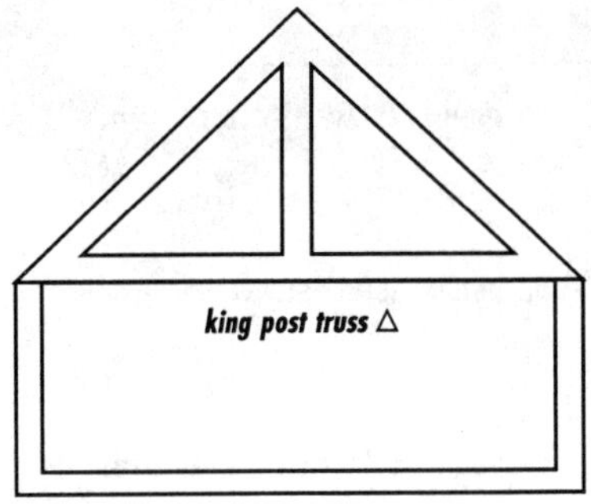

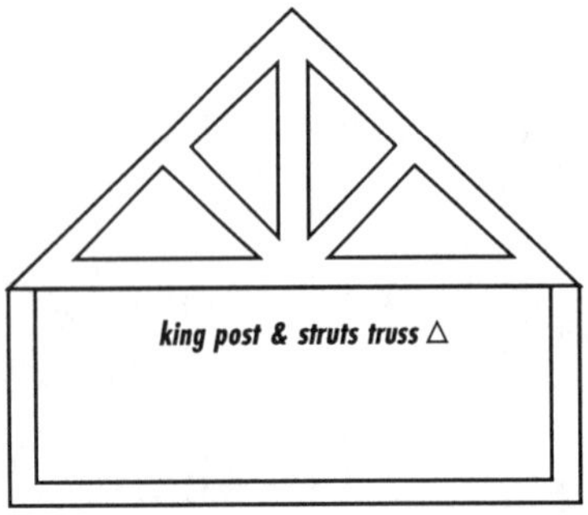

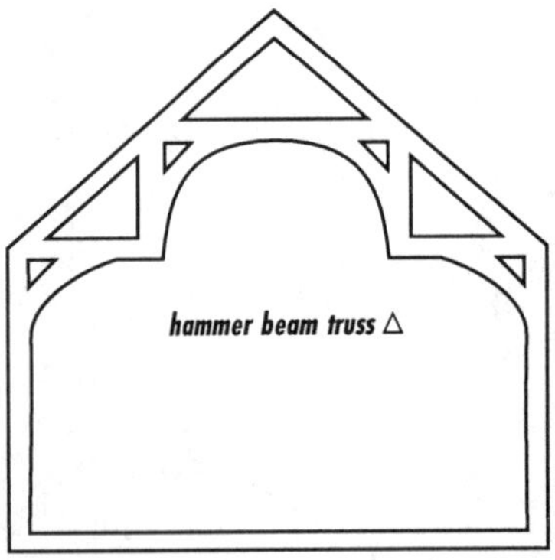

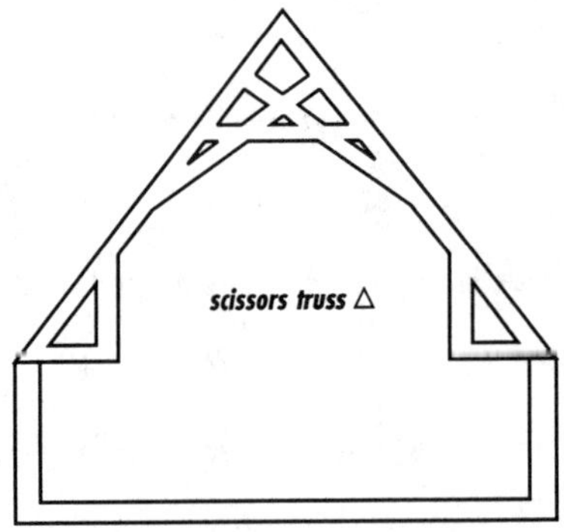

Item Description	Unit	Remove	Replace	Total
Pine post & beam single-story bent with queen post truss ***Replace*** Materials........3.61 Labor...........27.50 Equipment .... .38 ***Remove*** .... Labor 1.95	sf	$1.95	$31.49	$33.44
Pine post & beam single-story bent with hammer beam truss ***Replace*** Materials........3.82 Labor...........47.40 Equipment .... .38 ***Remove*** .... Labor 1.95	sf	$1.95	$51.60	$53.55
Pine post & beam single-story bent with scissors truss ***Replace*** Materials........4.01 Labor ....44.60 Equipment .... .38 ***Remove*** .... Labor 1.95	sf	$1.95	$48.99	$50.94
Pine post & beam two-story bent with simple truss ***Replace*** Materials........2.86 Labor ....25.80 Equipment .... .38 ***Remove*** .... Labor 1.95	sf	$1.95	$29.04	$30.99
Pine post & beam two-story bent with king post truss ***Replace*** Materials........3.08 Labor ....28.00 Equipment .... .38 ***Remove*** .... Labor 1.95	sf	$1.95	$31.46	$33.41
Pine post & beam two-story bent with king post & struts truss ***Replace*** Materials........3.33 Labor ....30.70 Equipment .... .38 ***Remove*** .... Labor 1.95	sf	$1.95	$34.41	$36.36
Pine post & beam two-story bent with queen post truss ***Replace*** Materials........3.17 Labor ....30.30 Equipment .... .38 ***Remove*** .... Labor 1.95	sf	$1.95	$33.85	$35.80

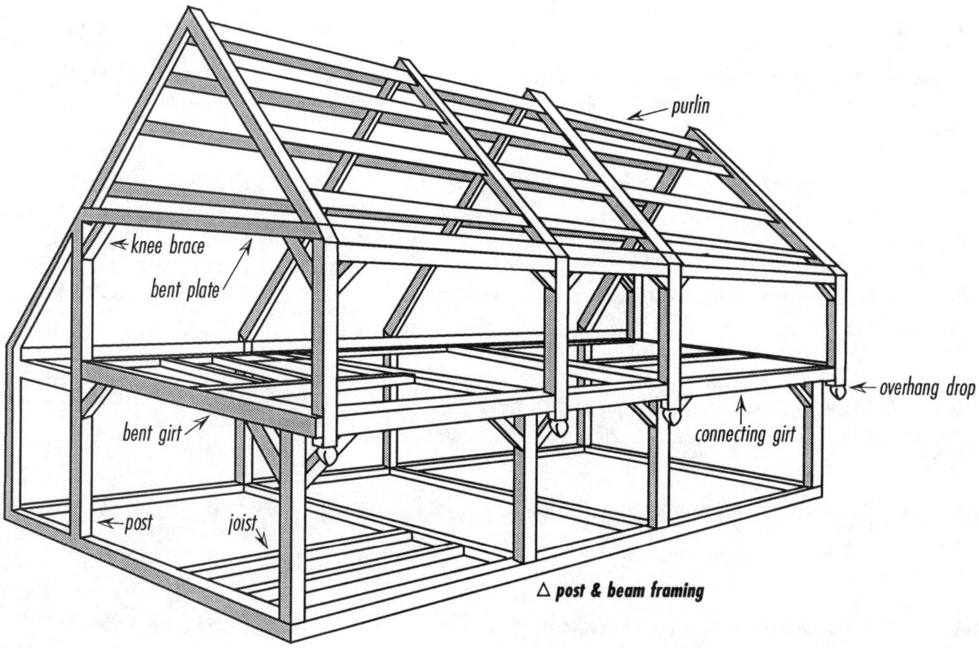

△ post & beam framing

Item Description	Unit	Remove	Replace	Total
Pine post & beam two-story bent with hammer beam truss *Replace* Materials........3.31 Labor..........56.40 Equipment............ .38 *Remove* .... Labor............1.95	sf	$1.95	$60.09	$62.04
Pine post & beam two-story bent with scissors truss *Replace* Materials........3.42 Labor..........46.90 Equipment............ .38 *Remove* .... Labor............1.95	sf	$1.95	$50.70	$52.65
Add for overhang drop in pine two-story bent *Replace* Materials.....173.00 Labor........902.00 Equipment............ .38	ea	—	$1,075.38	$1,075.38
Pine connecting members between single-story bents and trusses *Replace* Materials........5.45 Labor..........50.10 *Remove* .... Labor............5.89	sf	$5.89	$55.55	$61.44
Pine connecting members between two-story bents and trusses *Replace* Materials........8.14 Labor..........83.40 *Remove* .... Labor............7.87	sf	$7.87	$91.54	$99.41
Oak post & beam single-story bent with simple truss *Replace* Materials........6.77 Labor..........23.70 Equipment............ .38 *Remove* .... Labor............1.95	sf	$1.95	$30.85	$32.80
Oak post & beam single-story bent with king post truss *Replace* Materials........7.55 Labor..........25.60 Equipment............ .38 *Remove* .... Labor............1.95	sf	$1.95	$33.53	$35.48
Oak post & beam single-story bent with king post & struts truss *Replace* Materials........8.46 Labor...........27.80 Equipment............ .38 *Remove* .... Labor............1.75	sf	$1.95	$36.64	$38.59
Oak post & beam single-story bent with queen post truss *Replace* Materials........7.90 Labor...........27.50 Equipment............ .38 *Remove* .... Labor............1.95	sf	$1.95	$35.78	$37.73
Oak post & beam single-story bent with hammer beam truss *Replace* Materials........8.34 Labor...........47.40 Equipment............ .38 *Remove* .... Labor............1.95	sf	$1.95	$56.12	$58.07
Oak post & beam single-story bent with scissors truss *Replace* Materials........8.81 Labor..........44.60 Equipment............ .38 *Remove* .... Labor............1.95	sf	$1.95	$53.79	$55.74

◁ **add for overhang**

◀ **PINE CONNECTING MEMBERS BETWEEN BENTS**
Pine. Includes floor joists, roof purlins, diagonal braces, and beams. Per sf of area beneath roof. Measure only one floor.

◀ **OAK POST & BEAM BENT WITH TRUSS**
With oak posts and beams, per sf of bent. Post & beam framing styles are nearly unlimited. The following styles are representative.

RELATED ITEMS

Columns........................71
Fences........................187
Finish Carpentry..........199
Outbuildings.................331
Painting........................341
Paneling.......................347
Siding..........................455
Stairs..........................465

OAK POST & BEAM BENT WITH TRUSS ► *continued*

Item Description	Unit	Remove	Replace	Total
Oak post & beam two-story bent with simple truss *Replace* Materials........6.27 Labor..........25.80 Equipment............ .38 *Remove* .... Labor............1.95	sf	$1.95	$32.45	$34.40
Oak post & beam two-story bent with king post truss *Replace* Materials........6.73 Labor..........28.00 Equipment............ .38 *Remove* .... Labor............1.95	sf	$1.95	$35.11	$37.06
Oak post & beam two-story bent with king post & struts truss *Replace* Materials........7.29 Labor..........30.70 Equipment............ .38 *Remove* .... Labor............1.95	sf	$1.95	$38.37	$40.32
Oak post & beam two-story bent with queen post truss *Replace* Materials........6.94 Labor..........30.30 Equipment............ .38 *Remove* .... Labor............1.95	sf	$1.95	$37.62	$39.57
Oak post & beam two-story bent with hammer beam truss *Replace* Materials........7.21 Labor..........56.40 Equipment............ .38 *Remove* .... Labor............1.95	sf	$1.95	$63.99	$65.94
Oak post & beam two-story bent with scissors truss *Replace* Materials........7.50 Labor..........46.90 Equipment............ .38 *Remove* .... Labor............1.95	sf	$1.95	$54.78	$56.73

△ sill corner half-lap

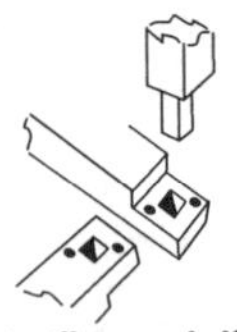

△ sill corner half-lap with through tenon

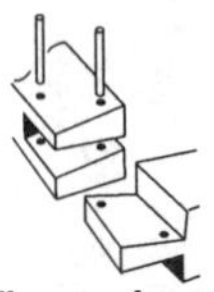

sill corner dovetail △

add for overhang ▷ *see framed overhang illustration on facing page*

Item Description	Unit	Remove	Replace	Total
Add for overhang drop in oak two-story bent *Replace* Materials....340.00 Labor........902.00 Equipment............ .38	ea	—	$1,242.38	$1,242.38

OAK CONNECTING MEMBERS BETWEEN BENTS ► *Includes floor joists, roof purlins, diagonal braces, and beams. Per sf of area beneath roof. Measure only one floor.*

Item Description	Unit	Remove	Replace	Total
Oak connecting members between single-story bents and trusses *Replace* Materials.......11.90 Labor..........50.10 *Remove* .... Labor............5.89	sf	$5.89	$62.00	$67.89
Oak connecting members between two-story bents and trusses *Replace* Materials.......17.70 Labor..........83.40 *Remove* .... Labor............7.87	sf	$7.87	$101.10	$108.97

minimum p & b ▷

Item Description	Unit	Remove	Replace	Total
Minimum charge for post & beam framing work *Replace* Materials....354.00 Labor........902.00 Equipment........500.00	ea	—	$1,756.00	$1,756.00

P & B JOINTS ► *Includes cutting, drilling, and joining with pegs.*

Item Description	Unit	Remove	Replace	Total
Sill corner half-lap joint *Replace* .... Labor..........58.20 ► Joint connects two timbers that form the sill and intersect at a 90 degree angle.	ea	—	$58.20	$58.20
Sill corner half-lap joint with through tenon *Replace* .... Labor.........147.00 ► Joint connects three timbers. Two level timbers form the sill and intersect at a 90 degree angle. A mortise is also cut at the corner. The third member is the plumb corner post with a tenon on the bottom.	ea	—	$147.00	$147.00
Sill corner dovetail joint *Replace* .... Labor.........106.00 ► Joint connects two timbers that form the sill and intersect at a 90 degree angle.	ea	—	$106.00	$106.00
Sill corner dovetail joint with through tenon *Replace* .... Labor........204.00 ► Joint connects three timbers. Two level timbers form the sill and intersect at a 90 degree angle. A mortise is also cut at the corner. The third member is the plumb corner post with a tenon on the bottom.	ea	—	$204.00	$204.00
Sill corner tongue & fork joint *Replace* .... Labor...........94.70 ► Joint connects two timbers that form the sill and intersect at a 90 degree angle.	ea	—	$94.70	$94.70

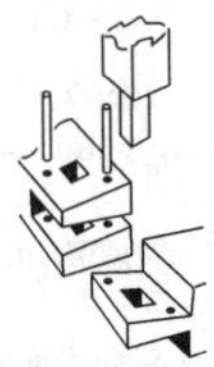

sill corner dovetail △ with through tenon

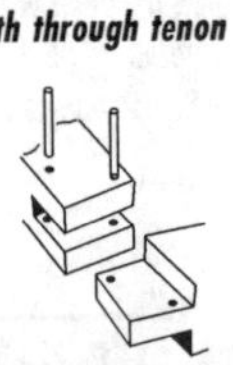

sill corner tongue & fork △

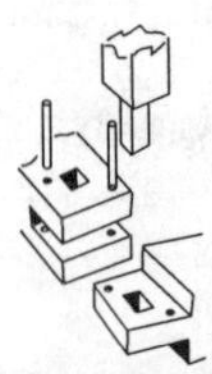

sill corner tongue & fork △ with through tenon

Item Description	Unit	Remove	Replace	Total
Sill corner tongue & fork joint with through tenon *Replace* .... Labor.........183.00 ► Joint connects three timbers. Two level timbers form the sill and intersect at a 90 degree angle. A mortise is also cut at the corner. The third member is the plumb corner post with a tenon on the bottom.	ea	—	$183.00	$183.00
Lapped dovetail joint *Replace* .... Labor.........108.00 ► Joint connects two timbers that intersect at a 90 degree angle. Usually the connection between a purlin and a rafter or a joist and a summer beam.	ea	—	$108.00	$108.00
Housed lapped dovetail joint *Replace* .... Labor.........135.00 ► Joint connects two timbers that intersect at a 90 degree angle. Usually the connection between a purlin and a rafter or a joist and a summer beam.	ea	—	$135.00	$135.00
Tusk tenon joint *Replace* .... Labor.........147.00 ► Joint connects two timbers that intersect at a 90 degree angle. Usually the connection between a purlin and a rafter or a joist and a summer beam.	ea	—	$147.00	$147.00
Half-lap joint *Replace* .... Labor...........57.10 ► Joint connects two timbers that intersect at a 90 degree angle. Usually the connection between a purlin and a rafter or a joist and a summer beam.	ea	—	$57.10	$57.10
Through mortise & tenon with shoulders joint *Replace* .... Labor.........120.00 ► Joint connects two timbers that intersect at a 90 degree angle. Usually the connection between beam and a post. The level shouldered beam connects into a mortise in the plumb post.	ea	—	$120.00	$120.00
Housed mortise & tenon joint *Replace* .... Labor.........126.00 ► Joint connects two timbers that intersect at a 90 degree angle. Usually the connection between beam and a post. The level beam connects into a mortise in the plumb post.	ea	—	$126.00	$126.00
Shouldered mortise & tenon joint *Replace* .... Labor.........123.00 ► Joint connects two timbers that intersect at a 90 degree angle. Usually the connection between beam and a post. The level beam connects into a mortise in the plumb post.	ea	—	$123.00	$123.00
Wedged dovetail mortise & tenon joint *Replace* .... Labor.........126.00 ► Joint connects two timbers that intersect at a 90 degree angle. Usually the connection between beam and a post. The level beam connects into a mortise in the plumb post.	ea	—	$126.00	$126.00
Mortise & tenon joint (90 degree intersection) *Replace* .... Labor..........66.10 ► Joint connects two timbers that intersect at a 90 degree angle. A beam or post connects into a mortise in the second beam or post.	ea	—	$66.10	$66.10
Anchor-beam joint *Replace* .... Labor.........156.00 ► Joint connects two level beams to opposite sides of a post. The post and beams intersect at 90 degree angles. Each level shouldered beam connects into a mortise in the plumb post.	ea	—	$156.00	$156.00
Framed overhang joint *Replace* .... Labor.........529.00 ► Includes decorative cutting of the "acorn" on the free-hanging post. Three mortises are cut into the post. One for the cantilevered level beam and two for connecting beams on each side of the post. All three beams are cut with shouldered tenons.	ea	—	$529.00	$529.00

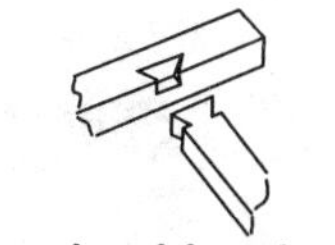
lapped dovetail △

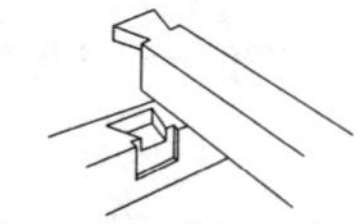
housed lapped dovetail △

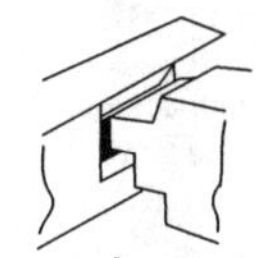
tusk tenon △

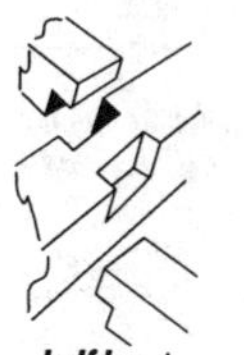
half-lap △

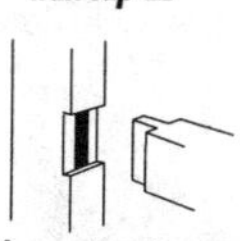
through mortise & tenon △

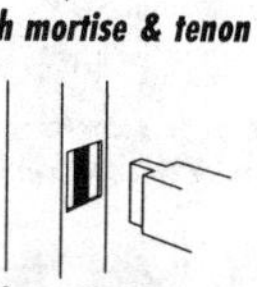
housed mortise & tenon △

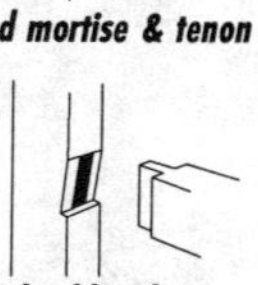
shouldered △ *mortise & tenon*

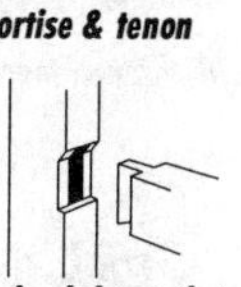
wedged dovetail △ *mortise & tenon*

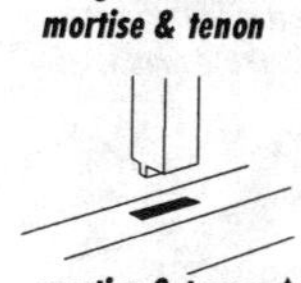
mortise & tenon △

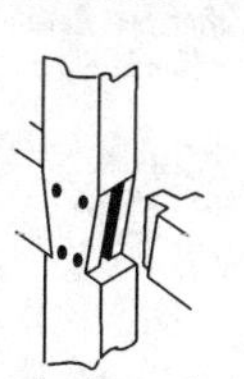
anchor beam △

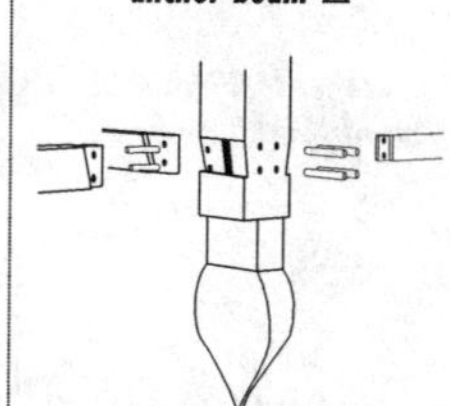
framed overhang △

P&B JOINTS ▶ *continued*

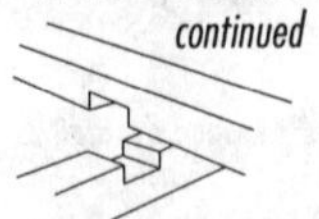
through half-lap △

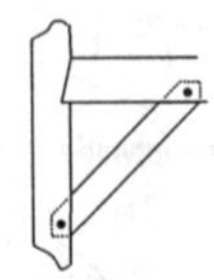
mortise & tenon △ knee brace

collar tie lapped △ half dovetail

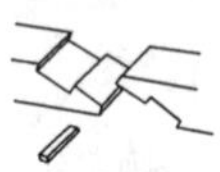
stopped splayed scarf △

stopped splayed scarf △ with through tenon

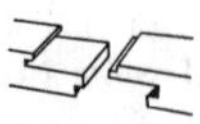
bladed scarf △

bladed scarf △ with through tenon

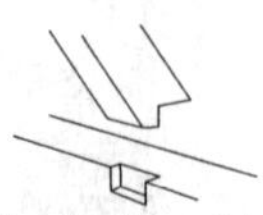
rafter foot housed △ bird's mouth

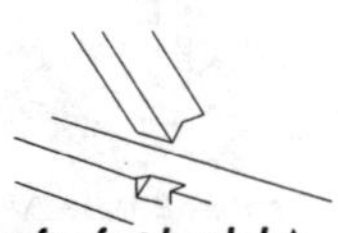
rafter foot beveled △ shoulder bird's mouth

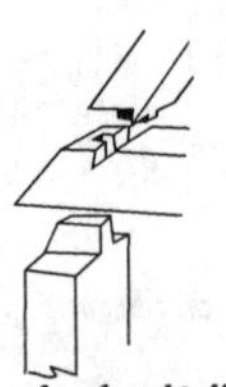
rafter foot bird's △ mouth, purlin, and post

rafter foot bird's mouth △

Item Description	Unit	Remove	Replace	Total
Through half-lap joint *Replace* .... Labor..........63.50 ► Used when two members cross and neither member terminates at the joint. Both members overlap and continue.	ea	—	$63.50	$63.50
Mortise & tenon knee brace joint (45 degree intersection) *Replace* .... Labor..........82.50 ► Used for diagonal corner braces. Knee brace connects into a post on the bottom and a beam on the top. A mortise is cut into both the post and beam. Tenons are cut at a 45 degree angle in the knee brace. Price is for mortise and tenon on one end only. For a complete knee brace installation use this price twice.	ea	—	$82.50	$82.50
Collar tie lapped half dovetail joint *Replace* .... Labor.........104.00 ► Used for connecting collar ties to rafters. Collar tie is plumb and intersects with rafters at an angle dictated by the slope of the roof. Price is for joint on one side of the collar tie only. For a complete collar tie use this price twice.	ea	—	$104.00	$104.00
Stopped splayed scarf joint *Replace* .... Labor.........171.00 ► Used to splice two level beams together.	ea	—	$171.00	$171.00
Stopped splayed scarf joint with through tenon *Replace* .... Labor.........265.00 ► Used to splice two level beams together. A mortise is cut through the center of the joint. A tenon is cut at the top of the plumb post that supports the beam.	ea	—	$265.00	$265.00
Bladed scarf joint *Replace* .... Labor.........129.00 ► Used to splice two level beams together.	ea	—	$129.00	$129.00
Bladed scarf joint with through tenon *Replace* .... Labor........230.00 ► Used to splice two level beams together. A mortise is cut through the center of the joint. A tenon is cut at the top of the plumb post that supports the beam.	ea	—	$230.00	$230.00
Rafter foot housed bird's mouth joint *Replace* .... Labor...........73.50 ► Bird's mouth is cut at foot of rafter. Top plate is cut to receive inside of bird's mouth.	ea	—	$73.50	$73.50
Rafter foot beveled shoulder bird's mouth joint *Replace* .... Labor ....68.80 ► Bird's mouth is cut at foot of rafter. Top plate is bevel-cut to receive inside of bird's mouth.	ea	—	$68.80	$68.80
Rafter foot bird's mouth, purlin, and post joint *Replace* .... Labor.........166.00 ► Bird's mouth is cut at foot of rafter. The rafter connects to the timber that is the bottom chord of the truss. A relief for the bird's mouth is cut into the bottom chord. Price also includes the mortise and tenon joint between the bottom chord and the post.	ea	—	$166.00	$166.00
Rafter foot bird's mouth joint *Replace* .... Labor...........52.90 ► Bird's mouth is cut at foot of rafter. Rafter connects to beam that forms wall plate. No cut is made in the beam.	ea	—	$52.90	$52.90
Rafter foot bird's mouth with tenon joint *Replace* .... Labor ....151.00 ► Direct connection between rafter and a post. (Does not connect with a beam.) Bird's mouth with a tenon is cut at foot of rafter. A mortise is cut in the post. (See illustration on top of facing page.)	ea	—	$151.00	$151.00

Item Description	Unit	Remove	Replace	Total
Rafter peak tongue & fork joint *Replace* .... Labor...........94.70 ► The connection between rafters at the peak. One rafter end is cut with a tongue and the other is cut with a fork. The angle of the joint varies with the slope of the roof. (See illustration lower right.)	ea	—	$94.70	$94.70
2" x 6" joist system for a deck with support beam & posts *Replace* Materials........2.11 Labor............2.43 *Remove* .... Labor............ .36	sf	$.36	$4.54	$4.90
2" x 8" joist system for a deck with support beam & posts *Replace* Materials........2.33 Labor............2.57 *Remove* .... Labor............ .36	sf	$.36	$4.90	$5.26
2" x 10" joist system for a deck with support beam & posts *Replace* Materials........2.98 Labor............2.79 *Remove* .... Labor............ .36	sf	$.36	$5.77	$6.13
2" x 12" joist system for a deck with support beam & posts *Replace* Materials........3.26 Labor............3.00 *Remove* .... Labor............ .36	sf	$.36	$6.26	$6.62
2" x 4" redwood decking, con common *Replace* Materials........4.13 Labor............1.45 *Remove* .... Labor............ .72	sf	$.72	$5.58	$6.30
2" x 4" redwood decking, con heart *Replace* Materials........4.77 Labor............1.45 *Remove* .... Labor............ .72	sf	$.72	$6.22	$6.94
2" x 6" redwood deck, con common *Replace* Materials........3.30 Labor............1.34 *Remove* .... Labor............ .72	sf	$.72	$4.64	$5.36
2" x 6" redwood deck, con heart *Replace* Materials........3.82 Labor............1.34 *Remove* .... Labor............ .72	sf	$.72	$5.16	$5.88
2" x 8" redwood deck, con common *Replace* Materials........3.53 Labor............1.19 *Remove* .... Labor............ .72	sf	$.72	$4.72	$5.44
2" x 8" redwood deck, con heart *Replace* Materials........4.09 Labor............1.19 *Remove* .... Labor............ .72	sf	$.72	$5.28	$6.00
2" x 4" treated wood deck *Replace* Materials........3.55 Labor............1.45 *Remove* .... Labor............ .72	sf	$.72	$5.00	$5.72
2" x 6" treated wood deck *Replace* Materials........3.43 Labor............1.34 *Remove* .... Labor............ .72	sf	$.72	$4.77	$5.49
2" x 8" treated wood deck *Replace* Materials........3.38 Labor............1.19 *Remove* .... Labor............ .72	sf	$.72	$4.57	$5.29
Redwood deck railing, con common *Replace* Materials........7.39 Labor............9.92 *Remove* .... Labor............ .94	lf	$.94	$17.31	$18.25
Redwood deck railing, con heart *Replace* Materials........8.61 Labor............9.92 *Remove* .... Labor............ .94	lf	$.94	$18.53	$19.47

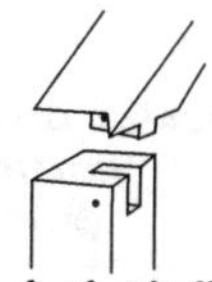

rafter foot bird's △ mouth with tenon

◄ **EXTERIOR DECK JOIST SYSTEM**
Includes 5% waste. Complete joist system. Does not include decking, railing, or stairs. Includes footings, excavation for footings, column stirrups and connectors, posts, and beams on outside edge of deck, connection with joist hangers against house, and joists.

◄ **EXTERIOR DECKING**
*Includes 5% waste. Deduct **14%** for 5/4 treated wood decking (decking that is 1-1/4" thick instead of 1-1/2" thick).*

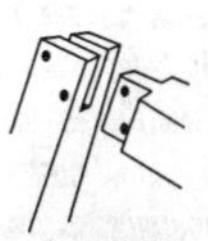

rafter peak △ tongue & fork

RELATED ITEMS

Columns........................71
Fences........................187
Finish Carpentry..........199
Outbuildings...............331
Painting........................341
Paneling......................347
Siding..........................455
Stairs..........................465

◄ **EXTERIOR DECK RAILING**
Includes 5% waste. With 2" x 2" balusters placed approximately 4" on center.

	Item Description	Unit	Remove	Replace	Total
Exterior deck railing *continued* ▶	**Treated wood deck railing** *Replace* Materials........7.26 Labor............9.92 *Remove* .... Labor............ .94	lf	$.94	$17.18	$18.12
Exterior deck stairs ▶ *Per step. Includes 5% waste. With three stringers made from 2" x 12" lumber. Each step has up to three 2" x 4" treads. Balusters are approximately 4" on center.*	**2' 6" wide con common redwood deck stairs with railing** *Replace* Materials......31.00 Labor...........19.60 *Remove* .... Labor...........1.68	ea	$1.68	$50.60	$52.28
	2' 6" wide con heart redwood deck stairs with railing *Replace* Materials......33.40 Labor...........19.60 *Remove* .... Labor...........1.68	ea	$1.68	$53.00	$54.68
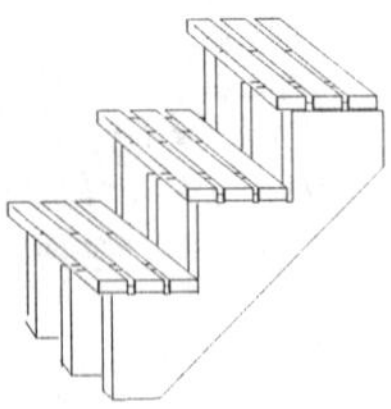	**2' 6" wide treated wood deck stairs with railing** *Replace* Materials......30.70 Labor...........19.60 *Remove* .... Labor...........1.68	ea	$1.68	$50.30	$51.98
	3' wide con common redwood deck stairs with railing *Replace* Materials......32.90 Labor...........21.30 *Remove* .... Labor...........1.68	ea	$1.68	$54.20	$55.88
	3' wide con heart redwood deck stairs with railing *Replace* Materials......35.40 Labor...........21.30 *Remove* .... Labor...........1.68	ea	$1.68	$56.70	$58.38
	3' wide treated wood deck stairs with railing *Replace* Materials......32.70 Labor...........21.30 *Remove* .... Labor...........1.68	ea	$1.68	$54.00	$55.68
Exterior deck landing ▶ *Includes 5% waste. 2" x 10" joist system with beams, posts, stirrups, footings, excavation for footings, and all fasteners.*	**Redwood deck stairway landing, con common decking** *Replace* Materials.......11.00 Labor............2.68 *Remove* .... Labor............ .41	sf	$.41	$13.68	$14.09
	Redwood deck stairway landing, con heart decking *Replace* Materials......12.20 Labor............2.68 *Remove* .... Labor............ .41	sf	$.41	$14.88	$15.29
	Treated wood deck stairway landing *Replace* Materials......10.80 Labor............2.68 *Remove* .... Labor............ .41	sf	$.41	$13.48	$13.89
Furring strips ▶ *Includes 5% waste.* **1" x 2"** ▷	**1" x 2" furring strips applied to wood 12" on center** *Replace* Materials........ .19 Labor............ .54 *Remove* .... Labor............ .30	sf	$.30	$.73	$1.03
	1" x 2" furring strips applied to wood 16" on center *Replace* Materials........ .16 Labor............ .47 *Remove* .... Labor............ .30	sf	$.30	$.63	$.93
	1" x 2" furring strips applied to wood 24" on center *Replace* Materials........ .12 Labor............ .40 *Remove* .... Labor............ .30	sf	$.30	$.52	$.82
	1" x 2" furring strips applied to masonry or concrete 12" on center *Replace* Materials........ .19 Labor............ .72 *Remove* .... Labor............ .33	sf	$.33	$.91	$1.24
	1" x 2" furring strips applied to masonry or concrete 16" on center *Replace* Materials........ .16 Labor............ .58 *Remove* .... Labor............ .33	sf	$.33	$.74	$1.07
	1" x 2" furring strips applied to masonry or concrete 24" on center *Replace* Materials........ .12 Labor............ .51 *Remove* .... Labor............ .33	sf	$.33	$.63	$.96

Item Description	Unit	Remove	Replace	Total
2" x 2" furring strips applied to wood 12" on center *Replace* Materials........ .45 Labor............. .54 *Remove* .... Labor............. .30	sf	$.30	$.99	$1.29
2" x 2" furring strips applied to wood 16" on center *Replace* Materials........ .36 Labor............. .47 *Remove* .... Labor............. .30	sf	$.30	$.83	$1.13
2" x 2" furring strips applied to wood 24" on center *Replace* Materials........ .28 Labor............. .40 *Remove* .... Labor............. .30	sf	$.30	$.68	$.98
2" x 2" furring strips applied to masonry or concrete 12" on center *Replace* Materials........ .45 Labor............. .72 *Remove* .... Labor............. .33	sf	$.33	$1.17	$1.50
2" x 2" furring strips applied to masonry or concrete 16" on center *Replace* Materials........ .36 Labor............. .58 *Remove* .... Labor............. .33	sf	$.33	$.94	$1.27
2" x 2" furring strips applied to masonry or concrete 24" on center *Replace* Materials........ .28 Labor............. .51 *Remove* .... Labor............. .33	sf	$.33	$.79	$1.12
2" x 4" joist system 12" on center with blocking *Replace* Materials........ .83 Labor............. .65 *Remove* .... Labor............. .39	sf	$.39	$1.48	$1.87
2" x 4" joist system 16" on center with blocking *Replace* Materials........ .66 Labor............. .51 *Remove* .... Labor............. .39	sf	$.39	$1.17	$1.56
2" x 4" joist system 24" on center with blocking *Replace* Materials........ .47 Labor............. .40 *Remove* .... Labor............. .39	sf	$.39	$.87	$1.26
2" x 6" joist system 12" on center with blocking and cross bracing *Replace* Materials........1.22 Labor............. .91 *Remove* .... Labor............. .39	sf	$.39	$2.13	$2.52
2" x 6" joist system 16" on center with blocking and cross bracing *Replace* Materials........ .97 Labor............. .69 *Remove* .... Labor............. .39	sf	$.39	$1.66	$2.05
2" x 6" joist system 24" on center with blocking and cross bracing *Replace* Materials........ .70 Labor............. .47 *Remove* .... Labor............. .39	sf	$.39	$1.17	$1.56
2" x 8" joist system 12" on center with blocking and cross bracing *Replace* Materials........1.50 Labor.......... 1.05 *Remove* .... Labor............. .39	sf	$.39	$2.55	$2.94
2" x 8" joist system 16" on center with blocking and cross bracing *Replace* Materials........1.19 Labor............. .87 *Remove* .... Labor............. .39	sf	$.39	$2.06	$2.45
2" x 8" joist system 24" on center with blocking and cross bracing *Replace* Materials........ .84 Labor............. .65 *Remove* .... Labor............. .39	sf	$.39	$1.49	$1.88
2" x 10" joist system 12" on center with blocking and cross bracing *Replace* Materials........2.25 Labor............1.30 *Remove* .... Labor............. .39	sf	$.39	$3.55	$3.94

◁ 2"x 2"

RELATED ITEMS

◀ **JOIST SYSTEM PER SF**

Includes 5% waste. All joist systems include joists, rim joists, blocking, and steel X braces at center span. (Except 2" x 4" joists which include solid blocking at center of span.)

◁ 2"x 6"

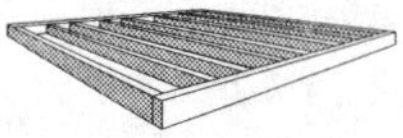

◁ 2"x 8"

◁ 2"x 10"

	Item Description	Unit	Remove	Replace	Total
JOIST SYSTEM ▶ *continued*	**2" x 10" joist system 16" on center with blocking and cross bracing** ***Replace*** Materials........1.77 Labor.......... 1.05 ***Remove*** .... Labor............ .39	sf	$.39	$2.82	$3.21
	2" x 10" joist system 24" on center with blocking and cross bracing ***Replace*** Materials........1.23 Labor............ .80 ***Remove*** .... Labor............ .39	sf	$.39	$2.03	$2.42
2" x 12" ▷	**2" x 12" joist system 12" on center with blocking and cross bracing** ***Replace*** Materials........2.57 Labor ....1.63 ***Remove*** .... Labor............ .39	sf	$.39	$4.20	$4.59
	2" x 12" joist system 16" on center with blocking and cross bracing ***Replace*** Materials........2.02 Labor ....1.19 ***Remove*** .... Labor............ .39	sf	$.39	$3.21	$3.60
	2" x 12" joist system 24" on center with blocking and cross bracing ***Replace*** Materials........1.40 Labor.......... 1.05 ***Remove*** .... Labor............ .39	sf	$.39	$2.45	$2.84
joists per bf ▷	**Joist system per bf** ***Replace*** Materials........1.21 Labor............ .76 ***Remove*** .... Labor............ .17	bf	$.17	$1.97	$2.14
LAMINATED I JOIST ▶ *Includes 3% waste. The lf price includes I joist, rim joists, blocking, and steel X braces at center span.*	**Laminated lumber I joist with 1-3/4" flange, 9-1/2" deep** ***Replace*** Materials........2.27 Labor ....1.23 ***Remove*** .... Labor............ .39	lf	$.39	$3.50	$3.89
	Laminated lumber I joist with 1-3/4" flange, 11-7/8" deep ***Replace*** Materials........2.76 Labor ....1.30 ***Remove*** .... Labor............ .39	lf	$.39	$4.06	$4.45
	Laminated lumber I joist with 1-3/4" flange, 14" deep ***Replace*** Materials........3.38 Labor ....1.34 ***Remove*** .... Labor............ .39	lf	$.39	$4.72	$5.11
2-5/16" wide ▷	**Laminated lumber I joist with 2-5/16" flange, 11-7/8" deep** ***Replace*** Materials........3.92 Labor ....1.30 ***Remove*** .... Labor............ .39	lf	$.39	$5.22	$5.61
	Laminated lumber I joist with 2-5/16" flange, 14" deep ***Replace*** Materials........4.78 Labor ....1.38 ***Remove*** .... Labor............ .39	lf	$.39	$6.16	$6.55
	Laminated lumber I joist with 2-5/16" flange, 16" deep ***Replace*** Materials........5.66 Labor ....1.41 ***Remove*** .... Labor............ .39	lf	$.39	$7.07	$7.46
FLOOR TRUSS ▶ *The lf price includes cat walks, diagonal braces, fasteners and rim materials.*	**Floor truss** ***Replace*** Materials........3.98 Labor ....3.29 ***Remove*** .... Labor............ .39	lf	$.39	$7.27	$7.66
	Floor truss designed for heavy loading ***Replace*** Materials........4.32 Labor ....3.40 ***Remove*** .... Labor............ .39	lf	$.39	$7.72	$8.11
HAND-FRAMED ROOF ▶ *Gable roof. Includes 5% waste. Measure the sf of area beneath roof.*	**Hand-framed roof 4 in 12 slope with 2" x 4" rafters** ***Replace*** Materials........ .59 Labor ....1.23 ***Remove*** .... Labor............ .44	sf	$.44	$1.82	$2.26
continued on next page	**Hand-framed roof 6 in 12 slope with 2" x 4" rafters** ***Replace*** Materials........ .62 Labor ....1.30 ***Remove*** .... Labor............ .47	sf	$.47	$1.92	$2.39

Item Description	Unit	Remove	Replace	Total
Hand-framed roof 8 in 12 slope with 2" x 4" rafters *Replace* Materials .... .65 Labor ....1.45 *Remove* .... Labor............ .52	sf	$.52	$2.10	$2.62
Hand-framed roof 10 in 12 slope with 2" x 4" rafters *Replace* Materials .... .69 Labor ....1.59 *Remove* .... Labor............ .66	sf	$.66	$2.28	$2.94
Hand-framed roof 12 in 12 slope with 2" x 4" rafters *Replace* Materials .... .74 Labor ....1.77 *Remove* .... Labor............ .88	sf	$.88	$2.51	$3.39
Hand-framed roof 14 in 12 slope with 2" x 4" rafters *Replace* Materials .... .78 Labor ....1.95 *Remove* .... Labor.......... 1.05	sf	$1.05	$2.73	$3.78
Hand-framed roof 16 in 12 slope with 2" x 4" rafters *Replace* Materials .... .84 Labor ....2.17 *Remove* .... Labor 1.38	sf	$1.38	$3.01	$4.39
Hand-framed roof 18 in 12 slope with 2" x 4" rafters *Replace* Materials .... .91 Labor ....2.43 *Remove* .... Labor 2.12	sf	$2.12	$3.34	$5.46
Hand-framed roof 4 in 12 slope with 2" x 6" rafters *Replace* Materials .... .84 Labor ....1.27 *Remove* .... Labor............ .44	sf	$.44	$2.11	$2.55
Hand-framed roof 6 in 12 slope with 2" x 6" rafters *Replace* Materials .... .88 Labor ....1.38 *Remove* .... Labor............ .47	sf	$.47	$2.26	$2.73
Hand-framed roof 8 in 12 slope with 2" x 6" rafters *Replace* Materials .... .94 Labor ....1.52 *Remove* .... Labor............ .52	sf	$.52	$2.46	$2.98
Hand-framed roof 10 in 12 slope with 2" x 6" rafters *Replace* Materials .... .99 Labor ....1.67 *Remove* .... Labor............ .66	sf	$.66	$2.66	$3.32
Hand-framed roof 12 in 12 slope with 2" x 6" rafters *Replace* Materials ...... 1.06 Labor ....1.85 *Remove* .... Labor............ .88	sf	$.88	$2.91	$3.79
Hand-framed roof 14 in 12 slope with 2" x 6" rafters *Replace* Materials........1.13 Labor ....2.03 *Remove* .... Labor.......... 1.05	sf	$1.05	$3.16	$4.21
Hand-framed roof 16 in 12 slope with 2" x 6" rafters *Replace* Materials........1.21 Labor ....2.24 *Remove* .... Labor 1.38	sf	$1.38	$3.45	$4.83
Hand-framed roof 18 in 12 slope with 2" x 6" rafters *Replace* Materials........1.29 Labor ....2.53 *Remove* .... Labor 2.12	sf	$2.12	$3.82	$5.94
Hand-framed roof 4 in 12 slope with 2" x 8" rafters *Replace* Materials........1.21 Labor ....1.30 *Remove* .... Labor............ .44	sf	$.44	$2.51	$2.95
Hand-framed roof 6 in 12 slope with 2" x 8" rafters *Replace* Materials........1.27 Labor ....1.41 *Remove* .... Labor............ .47	sf	$.47	$2.68	$3.15

◄ **HAND-FRAMED ROOF**
continued

(The sf of bottom floor plus sf under overhangs.) Do not measure the sf of roof. Includes rafters, collar ties, a ridge board that is 2" wider than the rafter (except for 2" x 12" rafters which have a ridge made from a 1-1/2" x 11-7/8" micro-laminated beam), rough fascia board, blocking, and wall fasteners. If roof has a hip or a Dutch hip see page 435. There is no additional charge for a Dutch gable. (see illustrations on page 435.)

◁ **2"x 6"**

◁ **2"x 8"**

RELATED ITEMS

	Item Description	Unit	Remove	Replace	Total
Hand-framed roof *continued*	**Hand-framed roof 8 in 12 slope with 2" x 8" rafters** ***Replace*** Materials........1.33 Labor............1.56 ***Remove*** .... Labor............ .52	sf	$.52	$2.89	$3.41
	Hand-framed roof 10 in 12 slope with 2" x 8" rafters ***Replace*** Materials........1.42 Labor............1.70 ***Remove*** .... Labor............ .66	sf	$.66	$3.12	$3.78
	Hand-framed roof 12 in 12 slope with 2" x 8" rafters ***Replace*** Materials........1.53 Labor............1.88 ***Remove*** .... Labor............ .88	sf	$.88	$3.41	$4.29
	Hand-framed roof 14 in 12 slope with 2" x 8" rafters ***Replace*** Materials........1.62 Labor............2.10 ***Remove*** .... Labor........... 1.05	sf	$1.05	$3.72	$4.77
	Hand-framed roof 16 in 12 slope with 2" x 8" rafters ***Replace*** Materials........1.73 Labor............2.32 ***Remove*** .... Labor............1.38	sf	$1.38	$4.05	$5.43
	Hand-framed roof 18 in 12 slope with 2" x 8" rafters ***Replace*** Materials........1.86 Labor............2.61 ***Remove*** .... Labor............2.12	sf	$2.12	$4.47	$6.59
2" x 10" ▷	**Hand-framed roof 4 in 12 slope with 2" x 10" rafters** ***Replace*** Materials........1.57 Labor............1.34 ***Remove*** .... Labor............ .44	sf	$.44	$2.91	$3.35
	Hand-framed roof 6 in 12 slope with 2" x 10" rafters ***Replace*** Materials........1.64 Labor............1.45 ***Remove*** .... Labor............ .47	sf	$.47	$3.09	$3.56
	Hand-framed roof 8 in 12 slope with 2" x 10" rafters ***Replace*** Materials........1.73 Labor............1.59 ***Remove*** .... Labor............ .52	sf	$.52	$3.32	$3.84
	Hand-framed roof 10 in 12 slope with 2" x 10" rafters ***Replace*** Materials........1.86 Labor............1.77 ***Remove*** .... Labor............ .66	sf	$.66	$3.63	$4.29
	Hand-framed roof 12 in 12 slope with 2" x 10" rafters ***Replace*** Materials........1.99 Labor............1.95 ***Remove*** .... Labor............ .88	sf	$.88	$3.94	$4.82
	Hand-framed roof 14 in 12 slope with 2" x 10" rafters ***Replace*** Materials........2.13 Labor............2.14 ***Remove*** .... Labor............1.05	sf	$1.05	$4.27	$5.32
	Hand-framed roof 16 in 12 slope with 2" x 10" rafters ***Replace*** Materials........2.28 Labor............2.39 ***Remove*** .... Labor............1.38	sf	$1.38	$4.67	$6.05
	Hand-framed roof 18 in 12 slope with 2" x 10" rafters ***Replace*** Materials........2.45 Labor............2.72 ***Remove*** .... Labor............2.12	sf	$2.12	$5.17	$7.29
2" x 12" ▷	**Hand-framed roof 4 in 12 slope with 2" x 12" rafters** ***Replace*** Materials........2.13 Labor............1.38 ***Remove*** .... Labor............ .44	sf	$.44	$3.51	$3.95
	Hand-framed roof 6 in 12 slope with 2" x 12" rafters ***Replace*** Materials........2.21 Labor............1.52 ***Remove*** .... Labor............ .47	sf	$.47	$3.73	$4.20

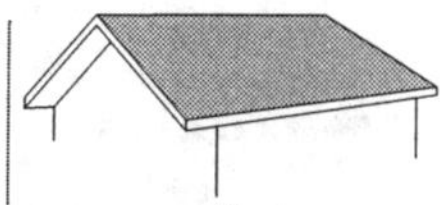
gable △

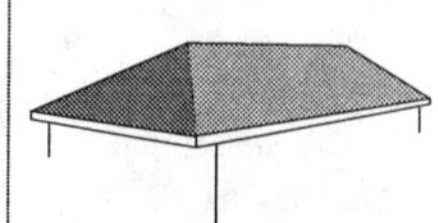
hip △

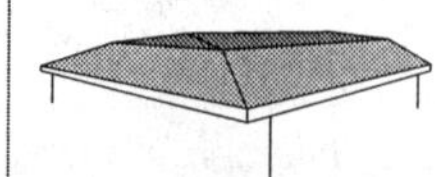
mansard △

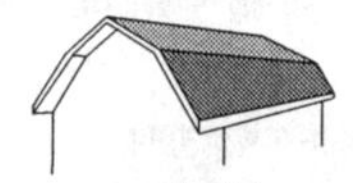
gambrel △

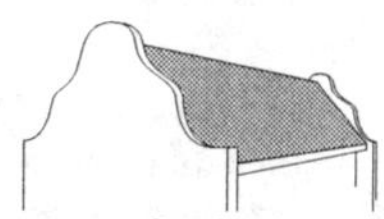
Dutch gable △

Item Description	Unit	Remove	Replace	Total
Hand-framed roof 8 in 12 slope with 2″ x 12″ rafters ***Replace*** Materials........2.32 Labor............1.67 ***Remove*** .... Labor............. .52	sf	$.52	$3.99	$4.51
Hand-framed roof 10 in 12 slope with 2″ x 12″ rafters ***Replace*** Materials........2.46 Labor............1.81 ***Remove*** .... Labor............. .66	sf	$.66	$4.27	$4.93
Hand-framed roof 12 in 12 slope with 2″ x 12″ rafters ***Replace*** Materials........2.61 Labor............2.03 ***Remove*** .... Labor............. .88	sf	$.88	$4.64	$5.52
Hand-framed roof 14 in 12 slope with 2″ x 12″ rafters ***Replace*** Materials........2.78 Labor............2.21 ***Remove*** .... Labor........... 1.05	sf	$1.05	$4.99	$6.04
Hand-framed roof 16 in 12 slope with 2″ x 12″ rafters ***Replace*** Materials........2.96 Labor............2.46 ***Remove*** .... Labor............1.38	sf	$1.38	$5.42	$6.80
Hand-framed roof 18 in 12 slope with 2″ x 12″ rafters ***Replace*** Materials........3.15 Labor............2.79 ***Remove*** .... Labor............2.12	sf	$2.12	$5.94	$8.06

◄ **ADDITIONAL COSTS FOR HAND-FRAMED ROOFS**

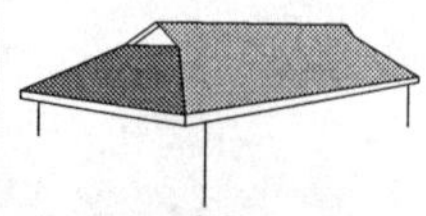
Dutch hip △

Item Description	Unit	Remove	Replace	Total
Add for each lf of valley in hand-framed roof ***Replace*** Materials......12.60 Labor..........28.50 ► Includes additional labor, materials, and waste to frame a valley.	lf	—	$41.10	$41.10
For a hand-framed hip roof add for each lf of width ***Replace*** Materials........1.99 Labor............7.60 ► Includes additional labor, materials, and waste to frame a hip. Per lf of hip. (For a hip on both ends of a roof measure the lf of both sides.)	lf	—	$9.59	$9.59
For a hand-framed Dutch hip roof add for each lf of width ***Replace*** Materials........2.20 Labor............8.29 ► Includes additional labor, materials, and waste to frame a Dutch hip. Per lf of hip. (For a Dutch hip on both ends of a roof measure the lf of both sides.)	lf	—	$10.49	$10.49

◄ **HAND-FRAMED MANSARD ROOF**
Includes 7% waste. Roof area equals roof system width times height times length. Includes rafters, collar ties, ridge boards, hip rafters, rough fascia board, blocking, and wall fasteners.

Item Description	Unit	Remove	Replace	Total
Hand-framed mansard roof with 2″ x 4″ rafters ***Replace*** Materials........ .10 Labor............. .18 ***Remove*** .... Labor............. .06	cf	$.06	$.28	$.34
Hand-framed mansard roof with 2″ x 6″ rafters ***Replace*** Materials........ .14 Labor............. .18 ***Remove*** .... Labor............. .06	cf	$.06	$.32	$.38
Hand-framed mansard roof with 2″ x 8″ rafters ***Replace*** Materials........ .20 Labor............. .18 ***Remove*** .... Labor............. .06	cf	$.06	$.38	$.44
Hand-framed mansard roof with 2″ x 10″ rafters ***Replace*** Materials........ .25 Labor............. .18 ***Remove*** .... Labor............. .06	cf	$.06	$.43	$.49
Hand-framed mansard roof with 2″ x 12″ rafters ***Replace*** Materials........ .29 Labor............. .22 ***Remove*** .... Labor............. .06	cf	$.06	$.51	$.57
Add for each lf of valley in hand-framed mansard roof ***Replace*** Materials.......15.10 Labor..........39.10 ► Includes additional labor, materials, and waste to frame a valley.	lf	—	$54.20	$54.20

◁ **mansard roof valley**

◄ **HAND FRAMED GAMBREL ROOF**
continued on next page

Item Description	Unit	Remove	Replace	Total
Hand-framed gambrel roof with 2″ x 4″ rafters ***Replace*** Materials........ .13 Labor............. .14 ***Remove*** .... Labor............. .06	cf	$.06	$.27	$.33

	Item Description	Unit	Remove	Replace	Total
HAND-FRAMED GAMBREL ROOF *continued* ▶	**Hand-framed gambrel roof with 2" x 6" rafters** ***Replace*** Materials .... .18 Labor............. .18 ***Remove*** .... Labor............. .06	cf	$.06	$.36	$.42
Includes 7% waste. Roof area equals roof system width times height times length. Includes rafters, collar ties, ridge boards, valley rafters, rough fascia board, blocking, and wall fasteners. Does not include wall that must be built at the intersection of the top and bottom sloping roof sections.	**Hand-framed gambrel roof with 2" x 8" rafters** ***Replace*** Materials .... .26 Labor............. .18 ***Remove*** .... Labor............. .06	cf	$.06	$.44	$.50
	Hand-framed gambrel roof with 2" x 10" rafters ***Replace*** Materials .... .33 Labor............. .18 ***Remove*** .... Labor............. .06	cf	$.06	$.51	$.57
	Hand-framed gambrel roof with 2" x 12" rafters ***Replace*** Materials .... .38 Labor............. .22 ***Remove*** .... Labor............. .06	cf	$.06	$.60	$.66
gambrel roof valley ▷	**Add for each lf of valley in hand-framed gambrel roof** ***Replace*** Materials.......15.70 Labor...........41.30 ▶ Includes additional labor, materials, and waste to frame a valley in a gambrel roof.	lf	—	$57.00	$57.00
HAND-FRAMED ROOF PER BF ▶ *Includes 5% waste.*	**Hand-framed gable roof per bf** ***Replace*** Materials ...... 1.00 Labor............. .83 ***Remove*** .... Labor............. .19	bf	$.19	$1.83	$2.02
	Hand-framed hip roof per bf ***Replace*** Materials........1.11 Labor............. .83 ***Remove*** .... Labor............. .19	bf	$.19	$1.94	$2.13
	Hand-framed Dutch hip roof per bf ***Replace*** Materials........1.12 Labor............. .87 ***Remove*** .... Labor............. .19	bf	$.19	$1.99	$2.18
	Hand-framed mansard roof per bf ***Replace*** Materials........1.22 Labor............. .94 ***Remove*** .... Labor............. .19	bf	$.19	$2.16	$2.35
	Hand-framed gambrel roof per bf ***Replace*** Materials........1.29 Labor............. .91 ***Remove*** .... Labor............. .19	bf	$.19	$2.20	$2.39
MINIMUM FOR ROOF FRAMING ▶	**Minimum charge for roof framing** ***Replace*** Materials......50.00 Labor...........45.30	ea	—	$95.30	$95.30
HAND-FRAMED SHED DORMER ▶ *Includes 7% waste. Complete dormer including all side walls and roof framing.*	**Shed dormer 4 in 12 slope (length x width of dormer)** ***Replace*** Materials .... .99 Labor ....1.63 ***Remove*** .... Labor............. .47	sf	$.47	$2.62	$3.09
	Shed dormer 6 in 12 slope (length x width of dormer) ***Replace*** Materials ...... 1.04 Labor ....1.70 ***Remove*** .... Labor............. .50	sf	$.50	$2.74	$3.24
	Shed dormer 8 in 12 slope (length x width of dormer) ***Replace*** Materials........1.11 Labor ....1.77 ***Remove*** .... Labor............. .55	sf	$.55	$2.88	$3.43
	Shed dormer 10 in 12 slope (length x width of dormer) ***Replace*** Materials........1.17 Labor ....1.95 ***Remove*** .... Labor............. .69	sf	$.69	$3.12	$3.81
	Shed dormer 12 in 12 slope (length x width of dormer) ***Replace*** Materials........1.25 Labor ....2.17 ***Remove*** .... Labor............. .91	sf	$.91	$3.42	$4.33

Item Description	Unit	Remove	Replace	Total
Shed dormer 14 in 12 slope (length x width of dormer) ***Replace*** Materials........1.33 Labor............2.24 ***Remove*** .... Labor............1.10	sf	$1.10	$3.57	$4.67
Shed dormer 16 in 12 slope (length x width of dormer) ***Replace*** Materials........1.43 Labor............2.32 ***Remove*** .... Labor............1.46	sf	$1.46	$3.75	$5.21
Shed dormer 18 in 12 slope (length x width of dormer) ***Replace*** Materials........1.52 Labor............2.43 ***Remove*** .... Labor............2.23	sf	$2.23	$3.95	$6.18
Gable dormer 4 in 12 slope (length of ridge x width of dormer) ***Replace*** Materials........1.11 Labor............1.70 ***Remove*** .... Labor............ .47	sf	$.47	$2.81	$3.28
Gable dormer 6 in 12 slope (length of ridge x width of dormer) ***Replace*** Materials........1.16 Labor............1.77 ***Remove*** .... Labor............ .50	sf	$.50	$2.93	$3.43
Gable dormer 8 in 12 slope (length of ridge x width of dormer) ***Replace*** Materials........1.24 Labor............1.85 ***Remove*** .... Labor............ .55	sf	$.55	$3.09	$3.64
Gable dormer 10 in 12 slope (length of ridge x width of dormer) ***Replace*** Materials........1.31 Labor............2.03 ***Remove*** .... Labor............ .69	sf	$.69	$3.34	$4.03
Gable dormer 12 in 12 slope (length of ridge x width of dormer) ***Replace*** Materials........1.40 Labor............2.24 ***Remove*** .... Labor............ .91	sf	$.91	$3.64	$4.55
Gable dormer 14 in 12 slope (length of ridge x width of dormer) ***Replace*** Materials........1.49 Labor............2.35 ***Remove*** .... Labor............1.10	sf	$1.10	$3.84	$4.94
Gable dormer 16 in 12 slope (length of ridge x width of dormer) ***Replace*** Materials........1.60 Labor............2.43 ***Remove*** .... Labor............1.46	sf	$1.46	$4.03	$5.49
Gable dormer 18 in 12 slope (length of ridge x width of dormer) ***Replace*** Materials........1.70 Labor............2.53 ***Remove*** .... Labor............2.23	sf	$2.23	$4.23	$6.46
Hip dormer 4 in 12 slope (length x width of dormer) ***Replace*** Materials........1.14 Labor............1.77 ***Remove*** .... Labor............ .47	sf	$.47	$2.91	$3.38
Hip dormer 6 in 12 slope (length x width of dormer) ***Replace*** Materials........1.20 Labor............1.85 ***Remove*** .... Labor............ .50	sf	$.50	$3.05	$3.55
Hip dormer 8 in 12 slope (length x width of dormer) ***Replace*** Materials........1.28 Labor............1.92 ***Remove*** .... Labor............ .55	sf	$.55	$3.20	$3.75
Hip dormer 10 in 12 slope (length x width of dormer) ***Replace*** Materials........1.35 Labor............2.10 ***Remove*** .... Labor............ .69	sf	$.69	$3.45	$4.14
Hip dormer 12 in 12 slope (length x width of dormer) ***Replace*** Materials........1.44 Labor............2.35 ***Remove*** .... Labor............ .91	sf	$.91	$3.79	$4.70

◄ **HAND-FRAMED GABLE DORMER** *Includes 7% waste. Complete dormer including all side walls and roof framing.*

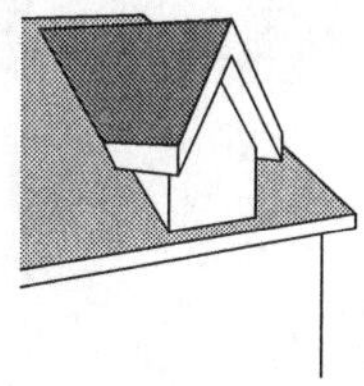

◄ **HAND-FRAMED HIP DORMER** *Includes 7% waste. Complete dormer including all side walls and roof framing.*

RELATED ITEMS

	Item Description	Unit	Remove	Replace	Total
HAND-FRAMED ► HIP DORMER *continued*	**Hip dormer 14 in 12 slope (length x width of dormer)** *Replace* Materials........1.54 Labor............2.43 *Remove* .... Labor............1.10	sf	$1.10	$3.97	$5.07
	Hip dormer 16 in 12 slope (length x width of dormer) *Replace* Materials........1.65 Labor............2.53 *Remove* .... Labor............1.46	sf	$1.46	$4.18	$5.64
	Hip dormer 18 in 12 slope (length x width of dormer) *Replace* Materials........1.75 Labor............2.64 *Remove* .... Labor............2.23	sf	$2.23	$4.39	$6.62
HAND-FRAMED ► DUTCH-HIP DORMER *Includes 7% waste. Complete dormer including all side walls and roof framing.*	**Dutch-hip dormer 4 in 12 slope (length x width of dormer)** *Replace* Materials........1.18 Labor............1.85 *Remove* .... Labor............ .47	sf	$.47	$3.03	$3.50
	Dutch-hip dormer 6 in 12 slope (length x width of dormer) *Replace* Materials........1.23 Labor............1.88 *Remove* .... Labor............ .50	sf	$.50	$3.11	$3.61
	Dutch-hip dormer 8 in 12 slope (length x width of dormer) *Replace* Materials........1.32 Labor............1.95 *Remove* .... Labor............ .55	sf	$.55	$3.27	$3.82
	Dutch-hip dormer 10 in 12 slope (length x width of dormer) *Replace* Materials........1.39 Labor............2.17 *Remove* .... Labor............ .69	sf	$.69	$3.56	$4.25
	Dutch-hip dormer 12 in 12 slope (length x width of dormer) *Replace* Materials........1.48 Labor............2.43 *Remove* .... Labor............ .91	sf	$.91	$3.91	$4.82
	Dutch-hip dormer 14 in 12 slope (length x width of dormer) *Replace* Materials........1.58 Labor............2.50 *Remove* .... Labor............1.10	sf	$1.10	$4.08	$5.18
	Dutch-hip dormer 16 in 12 slope (length x width of dormer) *Replace* Materials........1.69 Labor............2.61 *Remove* .... Labor............1.46	sf	$1.46	$4.30	$5.76
	Dutch-hip dormer 18 in 12 slope (length x width of dormer) *Replace* Materials........1.81 Labor............2.68 *Remove* .... Labor............2.23	sf	$2.23	$4.49	$6.72
HAND-FRAMED ► GAMBREL DORMER *Includes 7% waste.*	**Gambrel dormer (length x width of dormer)** *Replace* Materials........1.21 Labor............2.14 *Remove* .... Labor............ .47	sf	$.47	$3.35	$3.82
HAND-FRAMED ► ROOF DORMER PER BF	**Shed dormer per bf** *Replace* Materials........1.62 Labor............1.23 *Remove* .... Labor............ .28	bf	$.28	$2.85	$3.13
	Gable dormer per bf *Replace* Materials........1.72 Labor............1.27 *Remove* .... Labor............ .47	bf	$.47	$2.99	$3.46
	Hip dormer per bf *Replace* Materials........1.77 Labor............1.30 *Remove* .... Labor............ .50	bf	$.50	$3.07	$3.57
	Dutch-hip dormer per bf *Replace* Materials........1.83 Labor............1.38 *Remove* .... Labor............ .52	bf	$.52	$3.21	$3.73

Item Description	Unit	Remove	Replace	Total
Gambrel dormer per bf ***Replace*** Materials........1.87 Labor............1.34 ***Remove*** .... Labor............ .63	bf	$.63	$3.21	$3.84
Flat roof truss ***Replace*** Materials........3.98 Labor............ .83 Equipment .... .16 ***Remove*** .... Labor...........1.16	lf	$1.16	$4.97	$6.13
4 in 12 slope truss ***Replace*** Materials........4.19 Labor............ .83 Equipment .... .16 ***Remove*** .... Labor...........1.16	lf	$1.16	$5.18	$6.34
6 in 12 slope truss ***Replace*** Materials........4.52 Labor............ .83 Equipment .... .16 ***Remove*** .... Labor...........1.16	lf	$1.16	$5.51	$6.67
8 in 12 slope truss ***Replace*** Materials........6.11 Labor............ .87 Equipment .... .16 ***Remove*** .... Labor...........1.16	lf	$1.16	$7.14	$8.30
10 in 12 slope truss ***Replace*** Materials........7.02 Labor............ .87 Equipment .... .16 ***Remove*** .... Labor...........1.16	lf	$1.16	$8.05	$9.21
12 in 12 slope truss ***Replace*** Materials........8.17 Labor............ .87 Equipment .... .16 ***Remove*** .... Labor...........1.16	lf	$1.16	$9.20	$10.36
14 in 12 slope truss ***Replace*** Materials........8.66 Labor............ .91 Equipment .... .16 ***Remove*** .... Labor...........1.16	lf	$1.16	$9.73	$10.89
16 in 12 slope truss ***Replace*** Materials........9.32 Labor............ .94 Equipment .... .16 ***Remove*** .... Labor...........1.16	lf	$1.16	$10.42	$11.58
17 in 12 slope truss ***Replace*** Materials......10.10 Labor........... 1.011 Equipment .... .16 ***Remove*** .... Labor...........1.16	lf	$1.16	$11.27	$12.43
Flat roof truss designed for slate or tile roofing ***Replace*** Materials........4.23 Labor............ .83 Equipment .... .16 ***Remove*** .... Labor...........1.16	lf	$1.16	$5.22	$6.38
4 in 12 slope truss designed for slate or tile roofing ***Replace*** Materials........4.52 Labor............ .83 Equipment .... .16 ***Remove*** .... Labor...........1.16	lf	$1.16	$5.51	$6.67
6 in 12 slope truss designed for slate or tile roofing ***Replace*** Materials........4.80 Labor............ .83 Equipment .... .16 ***Remove*** .... Labor...........1.16	lf	$1.16	$5.79	$6.95
8 in 12 slope truss designed for slate or tile roofing ***Replace*** Materials........6.42 Labor............ .87 Equipment .... .16 ***Remove*** .... Labor...........1.16	lf	$1.16	$7.45	$8.61
10 in 12 slope truss designed for slate or tile roofing ***Replace*** Materials........7.35 Labor............ .87 Equipment .... .16 ***Remove*** .... Labor...........1.16	lf	$1.16	$8.38	$9.54
12 in 12 slope truss designed for slate or tile roofing ***Replace*** Materials........8.48 Labor............ .87 Equipment .... .16 ***Remove*** .... Labor...........1.16	lf	$1.16	$9.51	$10.67

◄ **ROOF TRUSS PER LF**
*Add **10%** for treated trusses. Per lf of truss bottom chord. The lf price includes cat walks, diagonal braces, fasteners and rough fascia.*

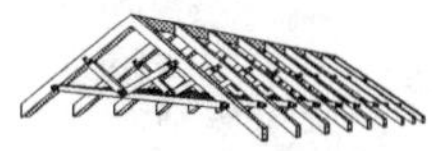

◄ **ROOF TRUSS FOR HEAVY LOAD PER LF**
*Add **10%** for treated trusses. Per lf of truss bottom chord. The lf price includes cat walks, diagonal braces, fasteners and rough fascia.*

RELATED ITEMS

Columns........................71
Fences........................187
Finish Carpentry..........199
Outbuildings................331
Painting........................341
Paneling.......................347
Siding..........................455
Stairs..........................465

	Item Description	Unit	Remove	Replace	Total
ROOF TRUSS FOR HEAVY LOAD PER LF *continued*	**14 in 12 slope truss designed for slate or tile roofing** *Replace* Materials........8.99 Labor............. .91 Equipment .... .16 *Remove* .... Labor............1.16	lf	$1.16	$10.06	$11.22
	16 in 12 slope truss designed for slate or tile roofing *Replace* Materials........9.67 Labor............. .94 Equipment .... .16 *Remove* .... Labor............1.16	lf	$1.16	$10.77	$11.93
	17 in 12 slope truss designed for slate or tile roofing *Replace* Materials......10.40 Labor.......... 1.01 Equipment .... .16 *Remove* .... Labor............1.16	lf	$1.16	$11.57	$12.73
ROOF TRUSS PER SF Add **10%** for treated trusses. Per sf of area underneath the roof. For roofs with asphalt, metal, or wood roofing. Includes cat walks, diagonal braces, fasteners and rough fascia.	**Truss roof system 4 in 12 slope** *Replace* Materials........2.43 Labor............. .43 Equipment .... .09 *Remove* .... Labor............. .47	sf	$.47	$2.95	$3.42
	Truss roof system 6 in 12 slope *Replace* Materials........2.62 Labor............. .43 Equipment .... .09 *Remove* .... Labor............. .50	sf	$.50	$3.14	$3.64
	Truss roof system 8 in 12 slope *Replace* Materials........3.54 Labor............. .43 Equipment .... .09 *Remove* .... Labor............. .58	sf	$.58	$4.06	$4.64
	Truss roof system 10 in 12 slope *Replace* Materials........4.07 Labor............. .47 Equipment .... .09 *Remove* .... Labor............. .69	sf	$.69	$4.63	$5.32
	Truss roof system 12 in 12 slope *Replace* Materials........4.74 Labor............. .47 Equipment .... .09 *Remove* .... Labor............. .94	sf	$.94	$5.30	$6.24
	Truss roof system 14 in 12 slope *Replace* Materials........5.02 Labor............. .47 Equipment .... .09 *Remove* .... Labor............1.10	sf	$1.10	$5.58	$6.68
	Truss roof system 16 in 12 slope *Replace* Materials........5.41 Labor............. .47 Equipment .... .09 *Remove* .... Labor............1.46	sf	$1.46	$5.97	$7.43
	Truss roof system 17 in 12 slope *Replace* Materials........5.86 Labor............. .47 Equipment .... .09 *Remove* .... Labor............2.26	sf	$2.26	$6.42	$8.68
ROOF TRUSS FOR HEAVY LOAD PER SF Add **10%** for treated trusses. Per sf of area underneath the roof. For roofs with slate, tile, or other heavy roofing. Includes cat walks, diagonal braces, fasteners and rough fascia.	**Truss roof system 4 in 12 slope designed for slate or tile roofing** *Replace* Materials........2.62 Labor............. .43 Equipment .... .09 *Remove* .... Labor............. .47	sf	$.47	$3.14	$3.61
	Truss roof system 6 in 12 slope designed for slate or tile roofing *Replace* Materials........2.78 Labor............. .43 Equipment .... .09 *Remove* .... Labor............. .50	sf	$.50	$3.30	$3.80
	Truss roof system 8 in 12 slope designed for slate or tile roofing *Replace* Materials........3.72 Labor............. .43 Equipment .... .09 *Remove* .... Labor............. .58	sf	$.58	$4.24	$4.82
	Truss roof system 10 in 12 slope designed for slate or tile roofing *Replace* Materials........4.26 Labor............. .47 Equipment .... .09 *Remove* .... Labor............. .69	sf	$.69	$4.82	$5.51
	Truss roof system 12 in 12 slope designed for slate or tile roofing *Replace* Materials........4.92 Labor............. .47 Equipment .... .09 *Remove* .... Labor............. .94	sf	$.94	$5.48	$6.42

Item Description	Unit	Remove	Replace	Total
Truss roof system 14 in 12 slope designed for slate or tile roofing *Replace* Materials........5.21 Labor............ .47 Equipment............ .09 *Remove* .... Labor.......... 1.10	sf	$1.10	$5.77	$6.87
Truss roof system 16 in 12 slope designed for slate or tile roofing *Replace* Materials........5.61 Labor............ .47 Equipment............ .09 *Remove* .... Labor...........1.46	sf	$1.46	$6.17	$7.63
Truss roof system 17 in 12 slope designed for slate or tile roofing *Replace* Materials........6.03 Labor............ .47 Equipment............ .09 *Remove* .... Labor...........2.26	sf	$2.26	$6.59	$8.85
Add for each lf of valley in truss roof *Replace* Materials......25.10 Labor..........29.40 ► Includes materials and labor for "California" fill between truss roofs with ridge board and jack rafters. Does not include sheathing.	lf	—	$54.50	$54.50
Add for each lf of width in a hip truss roof *Replace* Materials......22.60 Labor...........13.00 ► Includes additional cost for trusses designed to create a hip. Add per lf of hip.	lf	—	$35.60	$35.60
Add for each lf of width in a Dutch hip truss roof *Replace* Materials......24.60 Labor...........14.80 ► Includes additional cost for trusses designed to create a hip. The Dutch hip is stacked and hand framed. Add per lf of Dutch hip.	lf	—	$39.40	$39.40
Truss mansard roof system *Replace* Materials........ .38 Labor............ .11 *Remove* .... Labor............ .17	cf	$.17	$.49	$.66
Truss mansard roof system designed for slate or tile roofing *Replace* Materials........ .43 Labor............ .11 *Remove* .... Labor............ .17	cf	$.17	$.54	$.71
Add for each lf of valley in trussed mansard roof *Replace* Materials......24.80 Labor..........34.50 ► Includes materials and labor to fill between truss roofs with ridge boards and jack rafters. Does not include sheathing.	lf	—	$59.30	$59.30
Truss gambrel roof system *Replace* Materials........ .47 Labor............ .11 *Remove* .... Labor............ .17	cf	$.17	$.58	$.75
Truss gambrel roof system designed for slate or tile roofing *Replace* Materials........ .54 Labor............ .11 *Remove* .... Labor............ .17	cf	$.17	$.65	$.82
Add for each lf of valley in trussed gambrel roof *Replace* Materials......25.00 Labor...........42.00 ► Includes materials and labor to fill between truss roofs with ridge boards and jack rafters. Does not include sheathing.	lf	—	$67.00	$67.00
Remove truss for work, then reinstall *Replace* .... Labor...........3.29	lf	—	$3.29	$3.29
1/2" fiberboard sheathing *Replace* Materials........ .43 Labor............ .54 *Remove* .... Labor............ .36	sf	$.36	$.97	$1.33
3/4" fiberboard sheathing *Replace* Materials........ .59 Labor............ .54 *Remove* .... Labor............ .36	sf	$.36	$1.13	$1.49

RELATED ITEMS

◄ **ADDITIONAL TRUSS ROOF COSTS**

◄ **TRUSS MANSARD ROOF**
*Add **10%** for treated trusses. Roof area equals the roof system width times height times length. Includes cat walks, diagonal braces, fasteners and rough fascia.*

◄ **TRUSS GAMBREL ROOF**
*Add **10%** for treated trusses. Roof area equals the roof system width times height times length. Includes cat walks, diagonal braces, fasteners and rough fascia.*

◄ **REMOVE TRUSS THEN REINSTALL**

◄ **WALL OR ROOF SHEATHING**
Includes 4% waste.

WALL OR ROOF SHEATHING *continued*

Item Description	Unit	Remove	Replace	Total
1/2" sound-deadening fiberboard *Replace* Materials .42 Labor .54 *Remove* Labor .36	sf	$.36	$.96	$1.32
1/2" foil-faced foam sheathing *Replace* Materials .49 Labor .54 *Remove* Labor .36	sf	$.36	$1.03	$1.39
3/4" foil-faced foam sheathing *Replace* Materials .66 Labor .54 *Remove* Labor .36	sf	$.36	$1.20	$1.56
1" foil-faced foam sheathing *Replace* Materials .85 Labor .58 *Remove* Labor .36	sf	$.36	$1.43	$1.79
3/8" CDX plywood sheathing *Replace* Materials .63 Labor .58 *Remove* Labor .36	sf	$.36	$1.21	$1.57
1/2" CDX plywood sheathing *Replace* Materials .59 Labor .58 *Remove* Labor .36	sf	$.36	$1.17	$1.53
1/2" treated plywood sheathing *Replace* Materials .68 Labor .58 *Remove* Labor .36	sf	$.36	$1.26	$1.62
1/2" waferboard sheathing *Replace* Materials .55 Labor .58 *Remove* Labor .36	sf	$.36	$1.13	$1.49
1/2" oriented strand board (OSB) sheathing *Replace* Materials .62 Labor .58 *Remove* Labor .36	sf	$.36	$1.20	$1.56
5/8" CDX plywood sheathing *Replace* Materials .87 Labor .58 *Remove* Labor .36	sf	$.36	$1.45	$1.81
5/8" treated plywood sheathing *Replace* Materials 1.01 Labor .58 *Remove* Labor .36	sf	$.36	$1.59	$1.95
5/8" waferboard sheathing *Replace* Materials .96 Labor .58 *Remove* Labor .36	sf	$.36	$1.54	$1.90
5/8" oriented strand board (OSB) sheathing *Replace* Materials .96 Labor .58 *Remove* Labor .36	sf	$.36	$1.54	$1.90
3/4" CDX plywood sheathing *Replace* Materials 1.06 Labor .58 *Remove* Labor .36	sf	$.36	$1.64	$2.00
3/4" tongue-&-groove plywood sheathing *Replace* Materials 1.07 Labor .58 *Remove* Labor .36	sf	$.36	$1.65	$2.01
3/4" treated plywood sheathing *Replace* Materials 1.25 Labor .58 *Remove* Labor .36	sf	$.36	$1.83	$2.19

Item Description	Unit	Remove	Replace	Total
3/4" tongue-&-groove waferboard sheathing ***Replace*** Materials........1.13 Labor............ .58 ***Remove*** .... Labor............ .36	sf	$.36	$1.71	$2.07
3/4" tongue-&-groove oriented strand board (OSB) sheathing ***Replace*** Materials........1.14 Labor............ .58 ***Remove*** .... Labor............ .36	sf	$.36	$1.72	$2.08
1" x 6" sheathing ***Replace*** Materials........2.08 Labor............ .62 ***Remove*** .... Labor............ .39	sf	$.39	$2.70	$3.09
1" x 6" tongue-&-groove sheathing ***Replace*** Materials........3.25 Labor............ .62 ***Remove*** .... Labor............ .39	sf	$.39	$3.87	$4.26
2" x 6" tongue-&-groove sheathing ***Replace*** Materials........7.65 Labor............ .62 ***Remove*** .... Labor............ .44	sf	$.44	$8.27	$8.71
2" x 8" tongue-&-groove sheathing ***Replace*** Materials........4.98 Labor............ .62 ***Remove*** .... Labor............ .41	sf	$.41	$5.60	$6.01
Add for shear-panel sheathing installation ***Replace*** .... Labor............ .11 ► Includes shear paneling installed with nailing patterns and splicing according to code specifications for a shear panel.	sf	—	$.11	$.11
Frame interior soffit (two sides) ***Replace*** Materials........5.09 Labor...........2.14 ***Remove*** .... Labor...........1.24	lf	$1.24	$7.23	$8.47
Frame interior soffit with recess for indirect lighting (two sides) ***Replace*** Materials........7.43 Labor...........3.62 ***Remove*** .... Labor...........1.24	lf	$1.24	$11.05	$12.29
Frame interior soffit (three sides) ***Replace*** Materials........6.76 Labor...........2.90 ***Remove*** .... Labor...........1.24	lf	$1.24	$9.66	$10.90
Frame interior soffit with recess for indirect lighting (three sides) ***Replace*** Materials........8.10 Labor...........4.67 ***Remove*** .... Labor...........1.24	lf	$1.24	$12.77	$14.01
6" thick factory designed & fabricated structural wall panel ***Replace*** Materials........5.19 Labor...........1.85 Equipment............ .31 ***Remove*** .... Labor............ .19	sf	$.19	$7.35	$7.54
8" thick factory designed & fabricated structural wall panel ***Replace*** Materials........5.84 Labor...........1.88 Equipment............ .31 ***Remove*** .... Labor............ .19	sf	$.19	$8.03	$8.22
10" thick factory designed & fabricated structural wall panel ***Replace*** Materials........6.36 Labor...........1.95 Equipment............ .31 ***Remove*** .... Labor............ .19	sf	$.19	$8.62	$8.81
12" thick factory designed & fabricated structural wall panel ***Replace*** Materials........7.06 Labor...........1.95 Equipment............ .31 ***Remove*** .... Labor............ .19	sf	$.19	$9.32	$9.51
6" thick factory designed & fabricated structural floor panel ***Replace*** Materials........5.58 Labor...........1.85 Equipment............ .31 ***Remove*** .... Labor............ .22	sf	$.22	$7.74	$7.96

RELATED ITEMS

◁ **shear-panel install**

◀ **INTERIOR SOFFIT FRAMING**

◀ **FACTORY BUILT PANELS**
Often called stress-skin panels. Wall panels are installed with dimensional lumber top and bottom plates. Roof and floor panels must be installed between structural members. Does not include the cost for these structural members.

Section	Item Description	Unit	Remove	Replace	Total
Factory built ▶ panels *continued*	**8" thick factory designed & fabricated structural floor panel** *Replace* Materials........6.23 Labor............1.85 Equipment............ .31 *Remove* .... Labor............ .22	sf	$.22	$8.39	$8.61
	10" thick factory designed & fabricated structural floor panel *Replace* Materials........6.85 Labor............1.92 Equipment............ .31 *Remove* .... Labor............ .22	sf	$.22	$9.08	$9.30
	12" thick factory designed & fabricated structural floor panel *Replace* Materials........7.54 Labor............1.95 Equipment............ .31 *Remove* .... Labor............ .22	sf	$.22	$9.80	$10.02
	6" thick factory designed & fabricated structural roof panel *Replace* Materials........6.19 Labor............2.10 Equipment............ .30 *Remove* .... Labor............ .39	sf	$.41	$8.59	$8.98
	8" thick factory designed & fabricated structural roof panel *Replace* Materials........7.01 Labor............2.13 Equipment............ .30 *Remove* .... Labor............ .39	sf	$.41	$9.44	$9.83
	10" thick factory designed & fabricated structural roof panel *Replace* Materials........7.89 Labor............2.28 Equipment............ .31 *Remove* .... Labor............ .41	sf	$.41	$10.48	$10.89
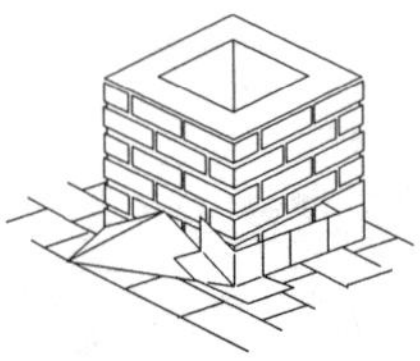	**12" thick factory designed & fabricated structural roof panel** *Replace* Materials........8.72 Labor............2.39 Equipment............ .31 *Remove* .... Labor............ .41	sf	$.41	$11.42	$11.83
Chimney cricket ▶ *Includes 5% waste.*	**Wood-frame chimney cricket (length x width)** *Replace* Materials........1.51 Labor............3.00 *Remove* .... Labor............ .52	sf	$.52	$4.51	$5.03
Mail box ▶ *Mail box is standard rural style. Black, white, or gray.*	**Mail box** *Replace* Materials.......11.70 Labor............6.70 *Remove* .... Labor............2.20	sf	$2.20	$18.40	$20.60
	Mail-box post *Replace* Materials......28.50 Labor..........23.60 *Remove* .... Labor...........12.40	sf	$12.40	$52.10	$64.50
	Mail box with post *Replace* Materials......40.20 Labor..........30.30 *Remove* .... Labor...........15.90	sf	$15.90	$70.50	$86.40
	Remove mail box for work, then reinstall *Replace* Materials........ .32 Labor...........10.40	sf	—	$10.72	$10.72

NOTES:

end

TIME & MATERIAL CHARTS *(selected items)*

Rough Carpentry Materials

DESCRIPTION	MATERIAL PRICE		GROSS COVERAGE	WASTE	NET COVERAGE	UNIT PRICE
Lumber, random lengths per 1,000 bf						
#2 pine or better 2" wide framing lumber	$960.00	per mbf	1,000	7%	930	**$1.03** bf
#2 pine or better 1" wide framing lumber	$1,170.00	per mbf	1,000	7%	930	**$1.26** bf
#2 treated pine or better 2" wide framing lumber	$1,200.00	per mbf	1,000	7%	930	**$1.29** bf
redwood con common 2" wide framing lumber	$1,940.00	per mbf	1,000	7%	930	**$2.09** bf
redwood con heart 2" wide framing lumber	$2,250.00	per mbf	1,000	7%	930	**$2.42** bf
heavy oak timber	$3,840.00	per mbf	1,000	7%	930	**$4.13** bf
heavy pine timber	$1,750.00	per mbf	1,000	7%	930	**$1.88** bf
Fasteners and metal braces						
16d gun nails	$65.00	per box	2,500	5%	2375	**$.03** ea
12d gun nails	$61.00	per box	2,500	5%	2375	**$.05** ea
2" gun staples	$102.00	per box	10,000	5%	9500	**$.01** ea
construction adhesive per 29 ounce tube	$6.80	per tube	75	5%	71.25	**$.10** lf
metal let-in brace with V-shape for saw kerf	$6.70	per 11.5' stick				**$6.70** ea
metal X bracing for between joists	$1.83	per 24" oc				**$1.83** ea
Furring strips						
1" x 2" x 8' #2 or better pine	$1.36	ea	8	5%	7.6	**$.18** lf
2" x 2" x 8' #2 or better pine	$3.16	ea	8	5%	7.6	**$.42** lf
2" x 2" x 8' con heart redwood	$4.69	ea	8	5%	7.6	**$.62** lf
2" x 2" x 8' con common redwood	$4.05	ea	8	5%	7.6	**$.53** lf
#2 or better pine framing lumber						
2" x 4", random lengths	$5.07	ea	8	5%	7.6	**$.67** lf
2" x 6", random lengths	$7.32	ea	8	5%	7.6	**$.96** lf
2" x 8", random lengths	$9.15	ea	8	5%	7.6	**$1.20** lf
2" x 10", random lengths	$14.30	ea	8	5%	7.6	**$1.88** lf
2" x 12", random lengths	$16.60	ea	8	5%	7.6	**$2.18** lf
Redwood framing lumber						
2" x 4" con heart, random lengths	$11.40	ea	8	5%	7.6	**$1.50** lf
2" x 6" con heart, random lengths	$13.20	ea	8	5%	7.6	**$1.74** lf
2" x 8" con heart, random lengths	$20.00	ea	8	5%	7.6	**$2.63** lf
2" x 4" con common, random lengths	$9.80	ea	8	5%	7.6	**$1.29** lf
2" x 6" con common, random lengths	$11.40	ea	8	5%	7.6	**$1.50** lf
2" x 8" con common, random lengths	$17.20	ea	8	5%	7.6	**$2.26** lf
Treated framing lumber						
2" x 4", random lengths	$8.30	ea	8	5%	7.6	**$1.09** lf
2" x 6" random lengths	$12.50	ea	8	5%	7.6	**$1.64** lf
2" x 8", random lengths	$20.70	ea	8	5%	7.6	**$2.72** lf
Posts						
4" x 4"						
#2 or better pine	$20.60	8' post	8	4%	7.68	**$2.68** lf
con common redwood	$24.90	8' post	8	4%	7.68	**$3.24** lf
treated pine	$26.80	8' post	8	4%	7.68	**$3.49** lf
4" x 6"						
#2 or better pine	$23.90	8' post	8	4%	7.68	**$3.11** lf
con common redwood	$26.60	8' post	8	4%	7.68	**$3.46** lf
treated pine	$31.10	8' post	8	4%	7.68	**$4.05** lf
6" x 6"						
#2 or better pine	$50.10	8' post	8	4%	7.68	**$6.52** lf
con common redwood	$43.10	8' post	8	4%	7.68	**$5.61** lf
treated pine	$65.10	8' post	8	4%	7.68	**$8.48** lf
8" x 8"						
#2 or better pine	$89.20	8' post	8	4%	7.68	**$11.60** lf
con common redwood	$76.60	8' post	8	4%	7.68	**$9.97** lf
treated pine	$116.00	8' post	8	4%	7.68	**$15.10** lf

... More ➢

Rough Carpentry Materials *continued*

DESCRIPTION	MATERIAL PRICE	GROSS COVERAGE	WASTE	NET COVERAGE	UNIT PRICE
Adjustable steel jack post					
51" to 90" to 13,000 pound load	$48.90 ea				**$48.90** ea
20" to 36" to 16,000 pound load	$32.00 ea				**$32.00** ea
37" to 60" to 17,500 pound load	$40.30 ea				**$40.30** ea
56" to 96" to 25,000 pound load	$63.00 ea				**$63.00** ea
Lally column					
3 1/2" diameter, 6' to 8'	$71.40 ea				**$71.40** ea
3 1/2" diameter, 8' to 10'	$80.50 ea				**$80.50** ea
3 1/2" diameter, 10' to 12'	$101.00 ea				**$101.00** ea
Glue-laminated beam					
per bf	4.26 bf	1	3%	.97	**$4.39** bf
Micro-laminated beam					
1-3/4" x 9-1/2"	$6.32 lf	1	4%	.96	**$6.58** lf
1-3/4" x 11-7/8"	$7.91 lf	1	4%	.96	**$8.24** lf
1-3/4" x 14"	$9.32 lf	1	4%	.96	**$9.71** lf
1-3/4" x 18"	$12.00 lf	1	4%	.96	**$12.50** lf
Beams, select structural grade, per bf					
pine	$1.75 bf	1	4%	.96	**$1.82** bf
oak	$3.84 bf	1	4%	.96	**$4.00** bf
Laminated lumber I joist					
1-3/4" flange, 9-1/2" deep	$2.20 lf	1	3%	.97	**$2.27** lf
1-3/4" flange, 11-7/8" deep	$2.68 lf	1	3%	.97	**$2.76** lf
1-3/4" flange, 14" deep	$3.28 lf	1	3%	.97	**$3.38** lf
2-5/16" flange, 11-7/8" deep	$3.80 lf	1	3%	.97	**$3.92** lf
Floor truss					
typical loading	$3.98 lf				**$3.98** lf
heavy loading	$4.32 lf				**$4.32** lf
Roof truss					
flat	$3.98 lf				**$3.98** lf
4 in 12 slope	$4.19 lf				**$4.19** lf
8 in 12 slope	$6.11 lf				**$6.11** lf
12 in 12 slope	$8.17 lf				**$8.17** lf
17 in 12 slope	$10.10 lf				**$10.10** lf
Roof or wall sheathing					
1/2" fiberboard	$13.20 8' sheet	32	4%	30.72	**$.43** sf
3/4" fiberboard	$18.00 8' sheet	32	4%	30.72	**$.59** sf
1/2" foil-faced foam	$15.20 8' sheet	32	4%	30.72	**$.49** sf
3/4" foil-faced foam	$20.30 8' sheet	32	4%	30.72	**$.66** sf
1" foil-faced foam	$26.20 8' sheet	32	4%	30.72	**$.85** sf
1/2" cdx plywood	$18.10 8' sheet	32	4%	30.72	**$.59** sf
1/2" waferboard	$16.80 8' sheet	32	4%	30.72	**$.55** sf
1/2" oriented strand board (OSB)	$19.10 8' sheet	32	4%	30.72	**$.62** sf
5/8" cdx plywood	$26.60 8' sheet	32	4%	30.72	**$.87** sf
5/8" waferboard	$29.40 8' sheet	32	4%	30.72	**$.96** sf
5/8" oriented strand board (OSB)	$29.60 8' sheet	32	4%	30.72	**$.96** sf
3/4" cdx plywood	$32.60 8' sheet	32	4%	30.72	**$1.06** sf
3/4" tongue-&-groove plywood	$32.90 8' sheet	32	4%	30.72	**$1.07** sf
3/4" tongue-&-groove waferboard	$34.70 8' sheet	32	4%	30.72	**$1.13** sf
3/4" tongue-&-groove oriented strand board (OSB)	$35.00 8' sheet	32	4%	30.72	**$1.14** sf
1" x 6" tongue-&-groove sheathing	$1.56 lf	.50	4%	.48	**$3.25** sf
2" x 6" tongue-&-groove sheathing	$3.67 lf	.50	4%	.48	**$7.65** sf
Factory designed and fabricated building panel					
6" thick wall panel	$5.19 sf				**$5.19** sf
8" thick wall panel	$5.84 sf				**$5.84** sf
10" thick floor panel	$6.85 sf				**$6.85** sf
12" thick floor panel	$7.54 sf				**$7.54** sf
6" thick roof panel	$6.41 sf				**$6.41** sf
8" thick roof panel	$7.25 sf				**$7.25** sf

Rough Carpentry Labor

LABORER	BASE WAGE	PAID LEAVE	TRUE WAGE	FICA	FUTA	WORKER'S COMP.	UNEMPLOY. INSUR.	HEALTH INSUR.	RETIRE (401K)	LIABILITY INSUR.	COST PER HOUR
Carpenter	$23.60	1.84	$25.44	1.95	.20	4.96	2.21	2.69	.76	3.43	$41.60
Carpenter's helper	$17.00	1.33	$18.33	1.40	.15	3.57	1.59	2.69	.55	2.47	$30.80
Post & beam carpenter	$30.40	2.37	$32.77	2.51	.26	6.39	2.85	2.69	.98	4.42	$52.90
P & B carpenter's helper	$20.90	1.63	$22.53	1.72	.18	4.39	1.96	2.69	.68	3.04	$37.20
Equipment operator	$29.90	2.33	$32.23	2.47	.26	5.81	2.80	2.69	.97	4.35	$51.60
Demolition laborer	$13.90	1.08	$14.98	1.15	.12	4.79	1.30	2.69	.45	2.02	$27.50

Paid Leave is calculated based on two weeks paid vacation, one week sick leave, and seven paid holidays. Employer's matching portion of **FICA** is 7.65 percent. **FUTA** (Federal Unemployment) is .8 percent. **Worker's Compensation** for the rough carpentry trade was calculated using a national average of 19.50 percent. **Unemployment insurance** was calculated using a national average of 8.7 percent. **Health insurance** was calculated based on a projected national average for 2002 of $535 per employee (and family when applicable) per month. Employer pays 80 percent for a per month cost of $428 per employee. **Retirement** is based on a 401(k) retirement program with employer matching of 50 percent. Employee contributions to the 401(k) plan are an average of 6 percent of the true wage. **Liability insurance** is based on a national average of 13.2 percent.

Rough Carpentry Labor Productivity

WORK DESCRIPTION	LABORER	COST PER HOUR	PRODUCTIVITY	UNIT PRICE
Demolition				
remove 2" x 4" wall 8' tall	demolition laborer	$27.50	.045	**$1.24** lf
remove 2" x 6" wall 8' tall	demolition laborer	$27.50	.048	**$1.32** lf
remove 2" x 8" wall 8' tall	demolition laborer	$27.50	.049	**$1.35** lf
remove wood post	demolition laborer	$27.50	.059	**$1.62** lf
remove glue-laminated beam	demolition laborer	$27.50	.222	**$6.11** lf
remove micro-laminated beam	demolition laborer	$27.50	.106	**$2.92** lf
remove sheathing	demolition laborer	$27.50	.012	**$.33** sf
remove beam	demolition laborer	$27.50	.222	**$6.11** lf
remove deck planking	demolition laborer	$27.50	.026	**$.72** sf
remove deck railing	demolition laborer	$27.50	.034	**$.94** lf
remove deck stairway per step	demolition laborer	$27.50	.061	**$1.68** ea
remove furring strips applied to wood	demolition laborer	$27.50	.011	**$.30** sf
remove joist system	demolition laborer	$27.50	.014	**$.39** sf
remove floor truss system	demolition laborer	$27.50	.014	**$.39** lf
remove hand-framed roof 4 in 12 slope	demolition laborer	$27.50	.016	**$.44** sf
remove hand-framed roof 8 in 12 slope	demolition laborer	$27.50	.019	**$.52** sf
remove hand-framed roof 12 in 12 slope	demolition laborer	$27.50	.032	**$.88** sf
remove hand-framed roof 16 in 12 slope	demolition laborer	$27.50	.050	**$1.38** sf
remove hand-framed roof 18 in 12 slope	demolition laborer	$27.50	.077	**$2.12** sf
remove flat roof truss	demolition laborer	$27.50	.016	**$.44** sf
remove truss roof 4 in 12 slope	demolition laborer	$27.50	.017	**$.47** sf
remove truss roof 8 in 12 slope	demolition laborer	$27.50	.021	**$.58** sf
remove truss roof 12 in 12 slope	demolition laborer	$27.50	.034	**$.94** sf
remove truss roof 16 in 12 slope	demolition laborer	$27.50	.053	**$1.46** sf
remove truss roof 17 in 12 slope	demolition laborer	$27.50	.082	**$2.26** sf
remove hand-framed dormer, 4 in 12 slope	demolition laborer	$27.50	.017	**$.47** sf
remove hand-framed dormer, 10 in 12 slope	demolition laborer	$27.50	.025	**$.69** sf
remove hand-framed dormer, 18 in 12 slope	demolition laborer	$27.50	.081	**$2.23** sf
remove pre-fabricated structural wall panel	demolition laborer	$27.50	.007	**$.19** sf
remove pre-fabricated structural floor panel	demolition laborer	$27.50	.008	**$.22** sf
remove pre-fabricated structural roof panel	demolition laborer	$ 27.50	.015	**$.41** sf
Framing crew				
rough carpentry	carpenter	$41.60		
rough carpentry	carpenter's helper	$30.80		
rough carpentry	**framing crew**	$36.20		
Post & beam framing crew				
post & beam framing	post & beam carpenter	$52.90		
post & beam framing	post & beam carpenter's helper	$37.20		
post & beam framing	**post & beam crew**	$45.10		

. . . More ➢

Rough Carpentry Labor Productivity *continued*

WORK DESCRIPTION	LABORER	COST PER HOUR	PRODUCTIVITY	UNIT PRICE
Build interior partition wall				
2″ x 4″ 8′ tall 16″ on center	framing crew	$36.20	.241	**$8.72** lf
2″ x 4″ 10′ tall 16″ on center	framing crew	$36.20	.244	**$8.83** lf
2″ x 6″ 8′ tall 16″ on center	framing crew	$36.20	.244	**$8.83** lf
2″ x 6″ 10′ tall 16″ on center	framing crew	$36.20	.247	**$8.94** lf
2″ x 8″ 8′ tall 16″ on center	framing crew	$36.20	.247	**$8.94** lf
2″ x 8″ 10′ tall 16″ on center	framing crew	$36.20	.250	**$9.05** lf
Build interior bearing wall				
2″ x 4″ 8′ tall 16″ on center	framing crew	$36.20	.261	**$9.45** lf
2″ x 4″ 10′ tall 16″ on center	framing crew	$36.20	.265	**$9.59** lf
2″ x 6″ 8′ tall 16″ on center	framing crew	$36.20	.263	**$9.52** lf
2″ x 6″ 10′ tall 16″ on center	framing crew	$36.20	.267	**$9.67** lf
2″ x 8″ 8′ tall 16″ on center	framing crew	$36.20	.266	**$9.63** lf
2″ x 8″ 10′ tall 16″ on center	framing crew	$36.20	.270	**$9.77** lf
Build exterior wall				
2″ x 4″ 8′ tall 16″ on center	framing crew	$36.20	9.67	**$9.67** lf
2″ x 4″ 10′ tall 16″ on center	framing crew	$36.20	.270	**$9.77** lf
2″ x 6″ 8′ tall 16″ on center	framing crew	$36.20	.270	**$9.77** lf
2″ x 6″ 10′ tall 16″ on center	framing crew	$36.20	.273	**$9.88** lf
2″ x 8″ 8′ tall 16″ on center	framing crew	$36.20	.272	**$9.85** lf
2″ x 8″ 10′ tall 16″ on center	framing crew	$36.20	.275	**$9.96** lf
Build interior partition wall per sf				
2″ x 4″ 16″ on center	framing crew	$36.20	.030	**$1.09** sf
2″ x 6″ 16″ on center	framing crew	$36.20	.030	**$1.09** sf
2″ x 8″ 16″ on center	framing crew	$36.20	.031	**$1.12** sf
Build sloping interior partition wall per sf				
2″ x 4″ 16″ on center	framing crew	$36.20	.041	**$1.48** sf
2″ x 6″ 16″ on center	framing crew	$36.20	.042	**$1.52** sf
2″ x 8″ 16″ on center	framing crew	$36.20	.042	**$1.52** sf
Build sloping interior bearing wall per sf				
2″ x 4″ 16″ on center	framing crew	$36.20	.050	**$1.81** sf
2″ x 6″ 16″ on center	framing crew	$36.20	.050	**$1.81** sf
2″ x 8″ 16″ on center	framing crew	$36.20	.051	**$1.85** sf
Build interior bearing wall per sf				
2″ x 4″ 16″ on center	framing crew	$36.20	.033	**$1.19** sf
2″ x 6″ 16″ on center	framing crew	$36.20	.033	**$1.19** sf
2″ x 8″ 16″ on center	framing crew	$36.20	.033	**$1.19** sf
Build exterior wall per sf				
2″ x 4″ 16″ on center	framing crew	$36.20	.034	**$1.23** sf
2″ x 6″ 16″ on center	framing crew	$36.20	.034	**$1.23** sf
2″ x 8″ 16″ on center	framing crew	$36.20	.034	**$1.23** sf
Build sloping exterior wall per sf				
2″ x 4″ 16″ on center	framing crew	$36.20	.046	**$1.67** sf
2″ x 6″ 16″ on center	framing crew	$36.20	.046	**$1.67** sf
2″ x 8″ 16″ on center	framing crew	$36.20	.047	**$1.70** sf
Build walls per bf				
interior wall	framing crew	$36.20	.034	**$1.23** bf
sloping interior wall	framing crew	$36.20	.047	**$1.70** bf
exterior wall	framing crew	$36.20	.037	**$1.34** bf
sloping exterior wall	framing crew	$36.20	.051	**$1.85** bf
Build and install wall header *Made from 2″ x dimension lumber and 1/2″ cdx plywood*				
4″ x 10″ header	framing crew	$36.20	.043	**$1.56** lf
4″ x 12″ header	framing crew	$36.20	.045	**$1.63** lf
6″ x 10″ header	framing crew	$36.20	.069	**$2.50** lf
6″ x 12″ header	framing crew	$36.20	.074	**$2.68** lf
Install posts				
4″ x 4″ post	framing crew	$36.20	.042	**$1.52** lf
6″ x 6″ post	framing crew	$36.20	.044	**$1.59** lf
8″ x 8″ post	framing crew	$36.20	.048	**$1.74** lf

. . . More ➢

Rough Carpentry Labor Productivity *continued*

WORK DESCRIPTION	LABORER	COST PER HOUR	PRODUCTIVITY	UNIT PRICE
Install adjustable steel jackpost				
20" to 36" adjustable	framing crew	$36.20	.243	**$8.80** ea
37" to 60" adjustable	framing crew	$36.20	.272	**$9.85** ea
48" to 100" adjustable	framing crew	$36.20	.385	**$13.90** ea
56" to 96" adjustable	framing crew	$36.20	.351	**$12.70** ea
Install lally column				
3-1/2" diameter, 6' to 8'	framing crew	$36.20	.526	**$19.00** ea
3-1/2" diameter, 8' to 10'	framing crew	$36.20	.556	**$20.10** ea
3-1/2" diameter, 10' to 12'	framing crew	$36.20	.588	**$21.30** ea
Install glue-laminated beam				
per bf	framing crew	$36.20	.060	**$2.17** bf
Install micro-laminated beam				
1-3/4" x 7-1/4"	framing crew	$36.20	.048	**$1.74** lf
1-3/4" x 9-1/2"	framing crew	$36.20	.050	**$1.81** lf
1-3/4" x 11-7/8"	framing crew	$36.20	.053	**$1.92** lf
1-3/4" x 14"	framing crew	$36.20	.056	**$2.03** lf
1-3/4" x 18"	framing crew	$36.20	.063	**$2.28** lf
Install beam				
4" x 10"	framing crew	$36.20	.114	**$4.13** lf
4" x 12"	framing crew	$36.20	.149	**$5.39** lf
6" x 10"	framing crew	$36.20	.132	**$4.78** lf
6" x 12"	framing crew	$36.20	.154	**$5.57** lf
8" x 10"	framing crew	$36.20	.156	**$5.65** lf
8" x 12"	framing crew	$36.20	.182	**$6.59** lf
10" x 10"	framing crew	$36.20	.176	**$6.37** lf
10" x 12"	framing crew	$36.20	.196	**$7.10** lf
12" x 12"	framing crew	$36.20	.204	**$7.38** lf
12" x 16"	framing crew	$36.20	.222	**$8.04** lf
Post & beam framing				
Cut and assemble bent with truss				
single-story with simple truss	post & beam crew	$45.10	.526	**$23.70** sf
two-story with simple truss	post & beam crew	$45.10	.571	**$25.80** sf
single-story with king post truss	post & beam crew	$45.10	.568	**$25.60** sf
two-story with king post truss	post & beam crew	$45.10	.621	**$28.00** sf
single-story with king post & struts truss	post & beam crew	$45.10	.617	**$27.80** sf
two-story with king post & struts truss	post & beam crew	$45.10	.680	**$30.70** sf
single-story with queen post truss	post & beam crew	$45.10	.610	**$27.50** sf
two-story with queen post truss	post & beam crew	$45.10	.671	**$30.30** sf
single-story with hammer beam truss	post & beam crew	$45.10	1.05	**$47.40** sf
two-story with hammer beam truss	post & beam crew	$45.10	1.25	**$56.40** sf
single-story with scissors truss	post & beam crew	$45.10	.990	**$44.60** sf
two-story with scissors truss	post & beam crew	$45.10	1.04	**$46.90** sf
add for overhang drop in two-story bent	post & beam crew	$45.10	20.0	**$902.00** ea
Cut and assemble connecting members between bents *per sf of area beneath*				
between single-story bents	post & beam crew	$45.10	1.11	**$50.10** sf
Cut post & beam framing joint and join timbers				
sill corner half-lap	p & b carpenter	$52.90	1.10	**$58.20** ea
sill corner half-lap with through tenon	p & b carpenter	$52.90	2.78	**$147.00** ea
sill corner dovetail	p & b carpenter	$52.90	2.00	**$106.00** ea
sill corner dovetail with through tenon	p & b carpenter	$52.90	3.85	**$204.00** ea
sill corner tongue & fork	p & b carpenter	$52.90	1.79	**$94.70** ea
sill corner tongue & fork with through tenon	p & b carpenter	$52.90	3.45	**$183.00** ea
lapped dovetail	p & b carpenter	$52.90	2.04	**$108.00** ea
housed lapped dovetail	p & b carpenter	$52.90	2.56	**$135.00** ea
tusk tenon	p & b carpenter	$52.90	2.78	**$147.00** ea
half-lap	p & b carpenter	$52.90	1.08	**$57.10** ea
through mortise & tenon with shoulders	p & b carpenter	$52.90	2.27	**$120.00** ea
housed mortise & tenon	p & b carpenter	$52.90	2.38	**$126.00** ea
shouldered mortise & tenon	p & b carpenter	$52.90	2.33	**$123.00** ea
wedged dovetail mortise & tenon	p & b carpenter	$52.90	2.38	**$126.00** ea
mortise & tenon (90 degree)	p & b carpenter	$52.90	1.25	**$66.10** ea

. . . More >

Rough Carpentry Labor Productivity *continued*

WORK DESCRIPTION	LABORER	COST PER HOUR	PRODUCTIVITY	UNIT PRICE
Post & beam framing *continued*				
Cut post & beam framing joint and join timbers *continued*				
anchor-beam	p & b carpenter	$52.90	2.94	**$156.00** ea
framed overhang	p & b carpenter	$52.90	10.0	**$529.00** ea
through half-lap	p & b carpenter	$52.90	1.20	**$63.50** ea
mortise & tenon knee brace (45 degree)	p & b carpenter	$52.90	1.56	**$82.50** ea
collar tie lapped half dovetail	p & b carpenter	$52.90	1.96	**$104.00** ea
stopped splayed scarf	p & b carpenter	$52.90	3.23	**$171.00** ea
stopped splayed scarf with through tenon	p & b carpenter	$52.90	5.00	**$265.00** ea
bladed scarf	p & b carpenter	$52.90	2.44	**$129.00** ea
bladed scarf with through tenon	p & b carpenter	$52.90	4.35	**$230.00** ea
rafter foot housed bird's mouth	p & b carpenter	$52.90	1.39	**$73.50** ea
rafter foot beveled shoulder bird's mouth	p & b carpenter	$52.90	1.30	**$68.80** ea
rafter foot bird's mouth, purlin, & post joint	p & b carpenter	$52.90	3.13	**$166.00** ea
rafter foot bird's mouth joint	p & b carpenter	$52.90	1.00	**$52.90** ea
rafter foot bird's mouth with tenon	p & b carpenter	$52.90	2.86	**$151.00** ea
rafter peak tongue & fork	p & b carpenter	$52.90	1.79	**$94.70** ea
Build joist system for outdoor deck *with support beams, posts and concrete footing*				
2" x 8" joists	framing crew	$36.20	.071	**$2.57** sf
2" x 10" joists	framing crew	$36.20	.077	**$2.79** sf
2" x 12" joists	framing crew	$36.20	.083	**$3.00** sf
Install outdoor deck planking per sf				
2" x 4"	framing crew	$36.20	.040	**$1.45** sf
2" x 6"	framing crew	$36.20	.037	**$1.34** sf
2" x 8"	framing crew	$36.20	.033	**$1.19** sf
Install deck railing and stairs				
deck railing	framing crew	$36.20	.274	**$9.92** lf
3' wide deck stairs with balustrades	framing crew	$36.20	.588	**$21.30** ea
deck stairway landing per sf	framing crew	$36.20	.074	**$2.68** sf
Install furring strips				
on wood 16" on center	framing crew	$36.20	.013	**$.47** sf
on wood 24" on center	framing crew	$36.20	.011	**$.40** sf
on masonry or concrete 16" on center	framing crew	$36.20	.016	**$.58** sf
on masonry or concrete 24" on center	framing crew	$36.20	.014	**$.51** sf
Build joist systems with blocking and cross bracing				
per bf	framing crew	$36.20	.021	**$.76** bf
Install laminated lumber I truss				
1-3/4" flange, 11-7/8" deep	framing crew	$36.20	.036	**$1.30** lf
1-3/4" flange, 14" deep	framing crew	$36.20	.037	**$1.34** lf
2-5/16" flange, 11-7/8" deep	framing crew	$36.20	.036	**$1.30** lf
2-5/16" flange, 14" deep	framing crew	$36.20	.038	**$1.38** lf
2-5/16" flange, 16" deep	framing crew	$36.20	.039	**$1.41** lf
Install floor truss				
typical	framing crew	$36.20	.091	**$3.29** lf
Hand-frame roof, 24" on center				
with 2" x 4" rafters				
4 in 12 slope	framing crew	$36.20	.034	**$1.23** sf
8 in 12 slope	framing crew	$36.20	.040	**$1.45** sf
12 in 12 slope	framing crew	$36.20	.049	**$1.77** sf
16 in 12 slope	framing crew	$36.20	.060	**$2.17** sf
with 2" x 6" rafters				
4 in 12 slope	framing crew	$36.20	.035	**$1.27** sf
8 in 12 slope	framing crew	$36.20	.042	**$1.52** sf
12 in 12 slope	framing crew	$36.20	.051	**$1.85** sf
16 in 12 slope	framing crew	$36.20	.062	**$2.24** sf
with 2" x 8" rafters				
4 in 12 slope	framing crew	$36.20	.036	**$1.30** sf
8 in 12 slope	framing crew	$36.20	.043	**$1.56** sf
12 in 12 slope	framing crew	$36.20	.052	**$1.88** sf
16 in 12 slope	framing crew	$36.20	.064	**$2.32** sf

. . . More ➢

Rough Carpentry Labor Productivity *continued*

WORK DESCRIPTION	LABORER	COST PER HOUR	PRODUCTIVITY	UNIT PRICE
Hand-frame roof, 24" on center *continued*				
with 2" x 10" rafters				
4 in 12 slope	framing crew	$36.20	.037	**$1.34** sf
8 in 12 slope	framing crew	$36.20	.044	**$1.59** sf
12 in 12 slope	framing crew	$36.20	.054	**$1.95** sf
16 in 12 slope	framing crew	$36.20	.066	**$2.39** sf
with 2" x 12" rafters				
4 in 12 slope	framing crew	$36.20	.038	**$1.38** sf
8 in 12 slope	framing crew	$36.20	.046	**$1.67** sf
12 in 12 slope	framing crew	$36.20	.056	**$2.03** sf
16 in 12 slope	framing crew	$36.20	.068	**$2.46** sf
additional hand-framed roof labor costs				
add for each lf of valley	framing crew	$36.20	.787	**$28.50** lf
add for each lf of hip width	framing crew	$36.20	.211	**$7.60** lf
add for each lf of Dutch hip width	framing crew	$36.20	.229	**$8.29** lf
Hand-frame mansard roof, 24" on center *per cf of roof*				
2" x 4" rafters	framing crew	$36.20	.005	**$.18** cf
2" x 8" rafters	framing crew	$36.20	.005	**$.18** cf
2" x 12" rafters	framing crew	$36.20	.006	**$.22** cf
add for each lf of valley	framing crew	$36.20	1.08	**$39.10** lf
Hand-frame gambrel roof, 24" on center *per cf of roof*				
2" x 4" rafters	framing crew	$36.20	.004	**$.14** cf
2" x 8" rafters	framing crew	$36.20	.005	**$.18** cf
2" x 12" rafters	framing crew	$36.20	.006	**$.22** cf
add for each lf of valley	framing crew	$36.20	1.14	**$41.30** lf
Hand-frame roof per bf				
gable roof	framing crew	$36.20	.023	**$.83** bf
hip roof	framing crew	$36.20	.023	**$.83** bf
Dutch hip roof	framing crew	$36.20	.024	**$.87** bf
mansard roof	framing crew	$36.20	.026	**$.94** bf
gambrel roof	framing crew	$36.20	.025	**$.91** bf
Hand-frame dormer, 24" on center				
shed dormer				
4 in 12 slope	framing crew	$36.20	.045	**$1.63** sf
8 in 12 slope	framing crew	$36.20	.049	**$1.77** sf
12 in 12 slope	framing crew	$36.20	.060	**$2.17** sf
16 in 12 slope	framing crew	$36.20	.064	**$2.32** sf
gable dormer				
4 in 12 slope	framing crew	$36.20	.047	**$1.70** sf
8 in 12 slope	framing crew	$36.20	.051	**$1.85** sf
12 in 12 slope	framing crew	$36.20	.062	**$2.24** sf
16 in 12 slope	framing crew	$36.20	.067	**$2.43** sf
hip dormer				
4 in 12 slope	framing crew	$36.20	1.77	**$1.77** sf
8 in 12 slope	framing crew	$36.20	.053	**$1.92** sf
12 in 12 slope	framing crew	$36.20	.065	**$2.35** sf
16 in 12 slope	framing crew	$36.20	.070	**$2.53** sf
Dutch hip dormer				
4 in 12 slope	framing crew	$36.20	.051	**$1.85** sf
8 in 12 slope	framing crew	$36.20	.054	**$1.95** sf
12 in 12 slope	framing crew	$36.20	.067	**$2.43** sf
16 in 12 slope	framing crew	$36.20	.072	**$2.61** sf
gambrel dormer				
per length of ridge x width of dormer	framing crew	$36.20	.059	**$2.14** sf
Hand-frame dormer, per bf				
shed dormer	framing crew	$36.20	.034	**$1.23** bf
gable dormer	framing crew	$36.20	.035	**$1.27** bf
hip dormer	framing crew	$36.20	.036	**$1.30** bf
Dutch-hip dormer	framing crew	$36.20	.038	**$1.38** bf
gambrel dormer	framing crew	$36.20	.037	**$1.34** bf

. . . More ➢

Rough Carpentry Labor Productivity *continued*

WORK DESCRIPTION	LABORER	COST PER HOUR	PRODUCTIVITY	UNIT PRICE
Install roof truss				
flat roof	framing crew	$36.20	.023	$.83 lf
4 in 12 slope	framing crew	$36.20	.023	$.83 lf
8 in 12 slope	framing crew	$36.20	.024	$.87 lf
12 in 12 slope	framing crew	$36.20	.024	$.87 lf
16 in 12 slope	framing crew	$36.20	.026	$.94 lf
Install truss system, 24" on center, per sf				
4 in 12 slope	framing crew	$36.20	.012	$.43 sf
8 in 12 slope	framing crew	$36.20	.012	$.43 sf
12 in 12 slope	framing crew	$36.20	.013	$.47 sf
16 in 12 slope	framing crew	$36.20	.013	$.47 sf
Additional truss roof costs				
add labor for each lf of valley	framing crew	$36.20	.813	$29.40 lf
add labor for each lf of width in a hip	framing crew	$36.20	.360	$13.00 lf
add labor for each lf of width in a Dutch hip	framing crew	$36.20	.408	$14.80 lf
Install mansard truss system, 24" on center, per cf				
per width x height x length	framing crew	$36.20	.003	$.11 cf
add labor for each lf of valley	framing crew	$36.20	.952	$34.50 lf
Install gambrel truss system, 24" on center, per cf				
per width x height x length	framing crew	$36.20	.003	$.11 cf
add labor for each lf of valley	framing crew	$36.20	1.16	$42.00 lf
Install wall or floor sheathing				
builder board	framing crew	$36.20	.015	$.54 lf
plywood, waferboard, or OSB	framing crew	$36.20	.016	$.58 sf
1" x 6" sheathing	framing crew	$36.20	.017	$.62 sf
1" x 6" tongue-&-groove	framing crew	$36.20	.017	$.62 sf
2" x 6" tongue-&-groove	framing crew	$36.20	.017	$.62 sf
2" x 8" tongue-&-groove	framing crew	$36.20	.017	$.62 sf
add labor for shear-panel installation	framing crew	$36.20	.003	$.11 sf
Build interior soffit				
two sides	framing crew	$36.20	.059	$2.14 lf
two sides with recess for indirect lighting	framing crew	$36.20	.100	$3.62 lf
three sides	framing crew	$36.20	.080	$2.90 lf
three sides with recess for indirect lighting	framing crew	$36.20	.129	$4.67 lf
Install factory designed and fabricated structural panel				
6" thick wall panel	framing crew	$36.20	.051	$1.85 sf
8" thick wall panel	framing crew	$36.20	.052	$1.88 sf
10" thick wall panel	framing crew	$36.20	.054	$1.95 sf
12" thick wall panel	framing crew	$36.20	.054	$1.95 sf
6" thick floor panel	framing crew	$36.20	.051	$1.85 sf
8" thick floor panel	framing crew	$36.20	.051	$1.85 sf
10" thick floor panel	framing crew	$36.20	.053	$1.92 sf
12" thick floor panel	framing crew	$36.20	.054	$1.95 sf
6" thick roof panel	framing crew	$36.20	.061	$2.21 sf
8" thick roof panel	framing crew	$36.20	.062	$2.24 sf
10" thick roof panel	framing crew	$36.20	.063	$2.28 sf
12" thick roof panel	framing crew	$36.20	.066	$2.39 sf
Wood-frame chimney cricket				
length of ridge x width	framing crew	$36.20	.083	$3.00 sf

NOTES:

end

33 Security Systems

Item Description	Unit	Remove	Replace	Total	
Minimum charge for security system work ***Replace*** Materials......25.00 Labor..........38.90	ea	—	$63.90	$63.90	◄ **MINIMUM**
Add 37% for security system installed in finished structure					◄ **IN EXISTING BUILDING**
Security system control panel, standard grade ***Replace*** Materials....320.00 Labor.........191.00 ***Remove*** .... Labor............6.88 ► Controls audio alarms and lights.	ea	$6.88	$511.00	$517.88	◄ **CONTROL PANEL** *Includes up to 50 lf of wiring.*
Security system control panel, high grade ***Replace*** Materials.....410.00 Labor........254.00 ***Remove*** .... Labor............6.88 ► Controls audio alarms and lights. Digital read-out reports location of security breach and automatically calls security center.	ea	$6.88	$664.00	$670.88	
Security system key pad ***Replace*** Materials.....160.00 Labor..........48.40 ***Remove*** .... Labor............5.50 ► Shows armed / unarmed status with lights, usually red and green.	ea	$5.50	$208.40	$213.90	◄ **KEY PAD** *Includes up to 50 lf of wiring.*
Security system key pad with LED read-out ***Replace*** Materials.....210.00 Labor..........48.40 ***Remove*** .... Labor............5.50 ► Shows armed / unarmed status with LED read-out that also reports location of security breach.	ea	$5.50	$258.40	$263.90	
Security system outside key control ***Replace*** Materials......95.00 Labor..........43.40 ***Remove*** .... Labor............3.93 ► Shows armed / unarmed status with lights, usually red and green.	ea	$3.93	$138.40	$142.33	◄ **KEY CONTROL** *Includes up to 50 lf of wiring.*
Security system mechanical contact per opening ***Replace*** Materials......54.50 Labor..........36.30 ***Remove*** .... Labor............3.93	ea	$3.93	$90.80	$94.73	◄ **CONTACT** *Includes up to 50 lf of wiring.*
Security system magnetic contact per opening ***Replace*** Materials......65.00 Labor...........52.20 ***Remove*** .... Labor............4.59	ea	$4.59	$117.20	$121.79	
Security system sound detector ***Replace*** Materials ....150.00 Labor...........59.40 ***Remove*** .... Labor............4.59	ea	$4.59	$209.40	$213.99	◄ **SOUND DETECTOR** *Includes up to 50 lf of wiring.*
Security system motion detector ***Replace*** Materials....285.00 Labor..........56.80 ***Remove*** .... Labor............4.59	ea	$4.59	$341.80	$346.39	◄ **MOTION DETECTOR** *Includes up to 50 lf of wiring.*
Security system pressure mat detector ***Replace*** Materials......50.00 Labor...........57.90 ***Remove*** .... Labor............5.09	lf	$5.09	$107.90	$112.99	◄ **PRESSURE MAT** *Includes up to 50 lf of wiring.*

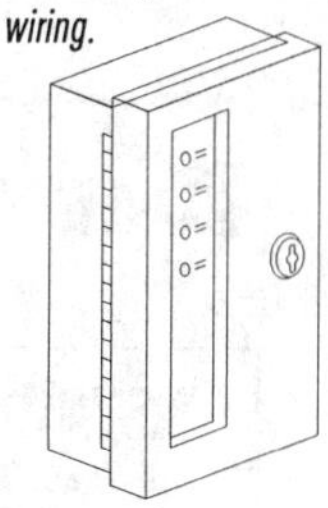

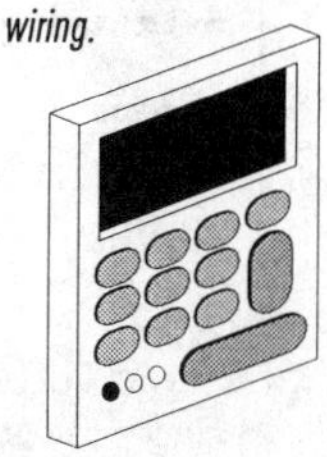

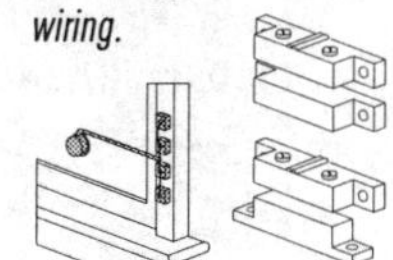

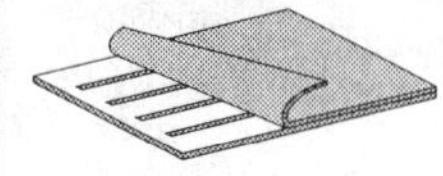

	Item Description	Unit	Remove	Replace	Total
SMOKE DETECTOR ► *Includes up to 50 lf of wiring.*	**Security system smoke detector** ***Replace*** Materials....180.00 Labor...........56.80 ***Remove*** .... Labor............4.59 ► For smoke detectors that are not connected to an alarm system see *Electrical* on page 149. For wiring see page 140.	ea	$4.59	$236.80	$241.39
HORN OR SIREN ► *Includes up to 50 lf of wiring.* 	**Security system horn or siren** ***Replace*** Materials......60.00 Labor...........48.80 ***Remove*** .... Labor............3.93 ► Exterior or interior.	ea	$3.93	$108.80	$112.73
PANIC BUTTON ► *Includes up to 50 lf of wiring.*	**Security system panic button** ***Replace*** Materials......50.00 Labor...........24.60 ***Remove*** .... Labor............3.44	ea	$3.44	$74.60	$78.04

TIME & MATERIAL CHARTS *(selected items)*

Security Systems Materials

See **Security Systems** material prices with the line items and other information in the **QuickFinder** column.

Security Systems Labor

LABORER	BASE WAGE	PAID LEAVE	TRUE WAGE	FICA	FUTA	WORKER'S COMP.	UNEMPLOY. INSUR.	HEALTH INSUR.	RETIRE (401K)	LIABILITY INSUR.	COST PER HOUR
Security system installer	**$22.60**	1.76	**$24.36**	1.86	.19	2.88	2.12	2.69	.73	3.29	**$38.10**
Demolition laborer	**$13.90**	1.08	**$14.98**	1.15	.12	4.79	1.30	2.69	.45	2.02	**$27.50**

Paid Leave is calculated based on two weeks paid vacation, one week sick leave, and seven paid holidays. Employer's matching portion of **FICA** is 7.65 percent. **FUTA** (Federal Unemployment) is .8 percent. **Worker's compensation** for the security systems trade was calculated using a national average of 11.84 percent. **Unemployment insurance** was calculated using a national average of 8.7 percent. **Health insurance** was calculated based on a projected national average for 2002 of $535 per employee (and family when applicable) per month. Employer pays 80 percent for a per month cost of $428 per employee. **Retirement** is based on a 401(k) retirement program with employer matching of 50 percent. Employee contributions to the 401(k) plan are an average of 6 percent of the true wage. **Liability insurance** is based on a national average of 13.2 percent.

Security Systems Labor Productivity

WORK DESCRIPTION	LABORER	COST PER HOUR	PRODUCTIVITY	UNIT PRICE
Demolition				
remove control panel	*demolition laborer*	**$27.50**	**.250**	**$6.88** *ea*
remove exterior key pad	*demolition laborer*	**$27.50**	**.200**	**$5.50** *ea*
remove contact	*demolition laborer*	**$27.50**	**.143**	**$3.93** *ea*
remove detector (all types)	*demolition laborer*	**$27.50**	**.167**	**$4.59** *ea*
remove pressure mat detector	*demolition laborer*	**$27.50**	**.185**	**$5.09** *ea*
remove horn or siren	*demolition laborer*	**$27.50**	**.143**	**$3.93** *ea*
remove panic button	*demolition laborer*	**$27.50**	**.125**	**$3.44** *ea*
Install security system				
control panel, standard grade	*security system installer*	**$38.10**	5.00	**$191.00** *ea*
control panel, high grade	*security system installer*	**$38.10**	6.67	**$254.00** *ea*
key pad	*security system installer*	**$38.10**	1.27	**$48.40** *ea*
outside key control	*security system installer*	**$38.10**	1.14	**$43.40** *ea*
mechanical contact per opening	*security system installer*	**$38.10**	.952	**$36.30** *ea*
magnetic contact per opening	*security system installer*	**$38.10**	1.37	**$52.20** *ea*
sound detector	*security system installer*	**$38.10**	1.56	**$59.40** *ea*
motion detector	*security system installer*	**$38.10**	1.49	**$56.80** *ea*
pressure mat detector	*security system installer*	**$38.10**	1.52	**$57.90** *lf*
smoke detector	*security system installer*	**$38.10**	1.49	**$56.80** *ea*
horn or siren	*security system installer*	**$38.10**	1.28	**$48.80** *ea*
panic button	*security system installer*	**$38.10**	.645	**$24.60** *ea*

34 Siding

Item Description	Unit	Remove	Replace	Total
Minimum charge for siding work *Replace* Materials......46.00 Labor..........35.80	ea	—	$81.80	$81.80
Fiberglass corrugated siding, 6 ounce *Replace* Materials........1.90 Labor.......... 1.00 *Remove* .... Labor............ .19	sf	$.19	$2.90	$3.09
Fiberglass corrugated siding, 8 ounce *Replace* Materials........2.04 Labor.......... 1.00 *Remove* .... Labor............ .19	sf	$.19	$3.04	$3.23
Fiberglass corrugated siding, 12 ounce *Replace* Materials........2.82 Labor.......... 1.00 *Remove* .... Labor............ .19	sf	$.19	$3.82	$4.01
Aluminum siding, standard grade *Replace* Materials........1.42 Labor............1.22 *Remove* .... Labor............ .22 ► .019" to .021" thick. Lightly embossed wood patterns.	sf	$.22	$2.64	$2.86
Aluminum siding, high grade *Replace* Materials........1.66 Labor............1.22 *Remove* .... Labor............ .22 ► .024" thick. Embossed patterns with fancy detail work around openings, porches, or in gables.	sf	$.22	$2.88	$3.10
Aluminum siding, deluxe grade *Replace* Materials........1.97 Labor............1.22 *Remove* .... Labor............ .22 ► .024" thick. Board-and-batten, board-on-board, or similar embossed patterns.	sf	$.22	$3.19	$3.41
Aluminum siding, custom grade *Replace* Materials........2.85 Labor............1.22 *Remove* .... Labor............ .22 ► .024" thick. Shake shingle, or similar embossed patterns.	sf	$.22	$4.07	$4.29
Add for insulated aluminum siding *Replace* Materials........ .39 ► Add for R-3 to R-4 insulation integrated into siding.	sf	—	$.39	$.39
Cement fiber shingle siding, standard grade *Replace* Materials........1.24 Labor............1.61 *Remove* .... Labor............ .36 ► 1/8" to 1/4" thick, lightly embossed shingles with square edges.	sf	$.36	$2.85	$3.21
Cement fiber shingle siding, high grade *Replace* Materials........1.55 Labor............1.61 *Remove* .... Labor............ .36 ► 1/8" to 1/4" thick, heavily embossed shingles with patterned edges.	sf	$.36	$3.16	$3.52
Replace single cement fiber shingle *Replace* Materials........2.59 Labor..........17.00	sf	—	$19.59	$19.59
Minimum charge to repair cement fiber siding *Replace* Materials......37.00 Labor..........35.80	ea	—	$72.80	$72.80

◄ **MINIMUM**

◄ **FIBERGLASS CORRUGATED SIDING**
Greenhouse style. Includes purlins with corrugated pattern and 4% waste. Weights are per sf.

◄ **ALUMINUM SIDING**
Includes 4% waste.

RELATED ITEMS

Finish Carpentry..........199
Paneling..........347
Rough Carpentry..........409

◁ **add for insulation**

◄ **CEMENT FIBER SHINGLE SIDING**
Includes 4% waste. Also called asbestos cement. Some older styles contain dangerous asbestos which must be removed using hazardous material removal techniques.

◁ **single shingle**

◁ **minimum**

	Item Description	Unit	Remove	Replace	Total
SHAKE OR WOOD SHINGLE SIDING ▶ *Includes 4% waste.*	**Shake or wood shingle siding, standard grade** ***Replace*** Materials...... 1.01 Labor............1.61 ***Remove*** .... Labor............. .39 ▶ #2 red label wood shingles, straight overlap installation.	sf	$.39	$2.62	$3.01
	Shake or wood shingle siding, high grade ***Replace*** Materials........1.16 Labor............1.61 ***Remove*** .... Labor............. .39 ▶ #1 shakes or #1 blue label wood shingles, straight overlap installation; or #2 red label wood shingles staggered installation.	sf	$.39	$2.77	$3.16
	Shake or wood shingle siding, deluxe grade ***Replace*** Materials........1.39 Labor............1.61 ***Remove*** .... Labor............. .39 ▶ #1 shakes or #1 blue wood shingles, staggered installation; or #2 red label wood shingles double coursed installation.	sf	$.39	$3.00	$3.39
	Shake or wood shingle siding, custom grade (fancy cut) ***Replace*** Materials........1.86 Labor............1.61 ***Remove*** .... Labor............. .39 ▶ #1 shakes or #1 blue fancy cut wood shingle.	sf	$.39	$3.47	$3.86
single shake or shingle ▷	**Replace single shake or wood shingle** ***Replace*** Materials........2.98 Labor...........14.60	ea	—	$17.58	$17.58
minimum ▷	**Minimum charge to repair shake or wood shingle siding** ***Replace*** Materials......41.00 Labor...........35.80	ea	—	$76.80	$76.80
VINYL SIDING ▶ *Includes 4% waste.*	**Vinyl siding, standard grade** ***Replace*** Materials........1.76 Labor............1.22 ***Remove*** .... Labor............. .19 ▶ Lightly embossed wood patterns.	sf	$.19	$2.98	$3.17
	Vinyl siding, high grade ***Replace*** Materials........2.01 Labor............1.22 ***Remove*** .... Labor............. .19 ▶ Heavy embossed patterns such as board-and-batten, board-on-board or similar patterns, with fancy detail work around openings, porches, or in gables.	sf	$.19	$3.23	$3.42
	Vinyl siding, deluxe grade ***Replace*** Materials........3.03 Labor............1.22 ***Remove*** .... Labor............. .19 ▶ Shake shingle, gable fans, or similar embossed patterns.	sf	$.19	$4.25	$4.44
add for insulation ▷	**Add for insulated vinyl siding** ***Replace*** Materials........ .48 ▶ Add for R-3 to R-4 insulation integrated into siding.	sf	—	$.48	$.48
HARDBOARD SIDING ▶ *Includes 4% waste.*	**7/16" thick hardboard siding, standard grade** ***Replace*** Materials........ .66 Labor............. .86 ***Remove*** .... Labor............. .25	sf	$.25	$1.52	$1.77
	7/16" thick hardboard siding, painted-board finish ***Replace*** Materials........ .74 Labor............. .86 ***Remove*** .... Labor............. .25	sf	$.25	$1.60	$1.85
	7/16" thick hardboard siding, stained-board finish ***Replace*** Materials...... 1.02 Labor............. .86 ***Remove*** .... Labor............. .25	sf	$.25	$1.88	$2.13

Item Description	Unit	Remove	Replace	Total
7/16" thick hardboard siding, simulated stucco finish *Replace* Materials........ .80 Labor............ .86 *Remove* .... Labor............ .25	sf	$.25	$1.66	$1.91
Hardboard lap siding *Replace* Materials........ .76 Labor............ .93 *Remove* .... Labor............ .28	sf	$.28	$1.69	$1.97
5/8" thick plywood siding, texture 1-11, cedar face *Replace* Materials........1.27 Labor............ .90 *Remove* .... Labor............ .28	sf	$.28	$2.17	$2.45
5/8" thick plywood siding, texture 1-11, rough-sawn cedar face *Replace* Materials........1.56 Labor............ .90 *Remove* .... Labor............ .28	sf	$.28	$2.46	$2.74
5/8" thick plywood siding, texture 1-11, fir face *Replace* Materials........1.13 Labor............ .90 *Remove* .... Labor............ .28	sf	$.28	$2.03	$2.31
5/8" thick plywood siding, texture 1-11, rough-sawn fir face *Replace* Materials........1.28 Labor............ .90 *Remove* .... Labor............ .28	sf	$.28	$2.18	$2.46
5/8" thick plywood siding, texture 1-11, Southern yellow pine face *Replace* Materials........ .93 Labor............ .90 *Remove* .... Labor............ .28	sf	$.28	$1.83	$2.11
5/8" thick plywood siding, texture 1-11, redwood face *Replace* Materials........2.13 Labor............ .90 *Remove* .... Labor............ .28	sf	$.28	$3.03	$3.31
Add for factory stained plywood siding *Replace* Materials........ .17	sf	—	$.17	$.17
1/2" plywood with 1" x 4" stained cedar boards *Replace* Materials........3.23 Labor...........2.04 *Remove* .... Labor............ .50	sf	$.50	$5.27	$5.77
5/8" plywood with 1" x 4" stained cedar boards *Replace* Materials........3.30 Labor...........2.04 *Remove* .... Labor............ .50	sf	$.50	$5.34	$5.84
Pine board-and-batten siding, select grade *Replace* Materials........3.34 Labor...........1.32 *Remove* .... Labor............ .30	sf	$.30	$4.66	$4.96
Cedar board-and-batten siding, A grade *Replace* Materials........3.50 Labor...........1.32 *Remove* .... Labor............ .30	sf	$.30	$4.82	$5.12
Pine board-on-board siding, select grade *Replace* Materials........3.41 Labor...........1.22 *Remove* .... Labor............ .30	sf	$.30	$4.63	$4.93
Cedar board-on-board siding, A grade *Replace* Materials........3.57 Labor...........1.22 *Remove* .... Labor............ .30	sf	$.30	$4.79	$5.09
Pine channel rustic siding, select grade *Replace* Materials........3.43 Labor...........1.40 *Remove* .... Labor............ .30	sf	$.30	$4.83	$5.13

◁ **lap**

◀ **PLYWOOD T1-11 SIDING**
Includes 5% waste.

RELATED ITEMS

◁ **add for factory stain**

◀ **BOARD OVER PLYWOOD SIDING**
Includes 4% waste.

◀ **BOARD-AND-BATTEN SIDING**
*Includes 4% waste. Deduct **9%** for next lower grade, deduct **14%** for third grade.*

◀ **BOARD-ON-BOARD SIDING**
*Includes 4% waste. Deduct **9%** for next lower grade, deduct **14%** for third grade.*

◀ **CHANNEL RUSTIC SIDING**
Includes 4% waste.

CHANNEL RUSTIC SIDING *continued*

Deduct 9% for next lower grade, deduct 14% for third grade.

Item Description	Unit	Remove	Replace	Total
Cedar channel rustic siding, A grade *Replace* Materials........4.30 Labor............1.40 *Remove* .... Labor............ .30	sf	$.30	$5.70	$6.00
Redwood channel rustic siding, clear all heart grade *Replace* Materials........9.23 Labor............1.40 *Remove* .... Labor............ .30	sf	$.30	$10.63	$10.93

SHIPLAP SIDING *Includes 4% waste. Deduct 9% for next lower grade, deduct 14% for third grade.*

Item Description	Unit	Remove	Replace	Total
Pine shiplap siding, select grade *Replace* Materials........3.47 Labor............1.40 *Remove* .... Labor............ .30	sf	$.30	$4.87	$5.17
Cedar shiplap siding, A grade *Replace* Materials........4.35 Labor............1.40 *Remove* .... Labor............ .30	sf	$.30	$5.75	$6.05
Redwood shiplap siding, clear all heart grade *Replace* Materials........9.34 Labor............1.40 *Remove* .... Labor............ .30	sf	$.30	$10.74	$11.04

TONGUE-&-GROOVE SIDING *Includes 4% waste. Deduct 9% for next lower grade, deduct 14% for third grade.*

▽ *simple pattern*

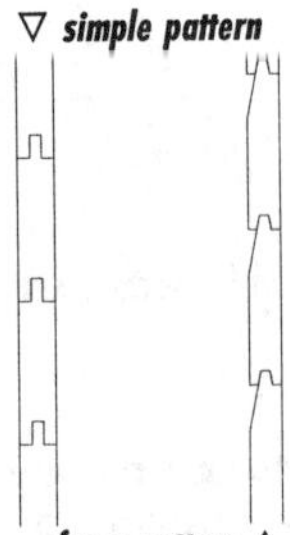

fancy pattern △

Item Description	Unit	Remove	Replace	Total
Pine tongue-&-groove siding, simple pattern, select grade *Replace* Materials........3.54 Labor............1.40 *Remove* .... Labor............ .30	sf	$.30	$4.94	$5.24
Pine tongue-&-groove siding, fancy pattern, select grade *Replace* Materials........3.78 Labor............1.40 *Remove* .... Labor............ .30	sf	$.30	$5.18	$5.48
Cedar tongue-&-groove siding, simple pattern, A grade *Replace* Materials........4.45 Labor............1.40 *Remove* .... Labor............ .30	sf	$.30	$5.85	$6.15
Cedar tongue-&-groove siding, fancy pattern, A grade *Replace* Materials........4.74 Labor............1.40 *Remove* .... Labor............ .30	sf	$.30	$6.14	$6.44
Redwood tongue-&-groove siding, simple pattern, clear all heart grade *Replace* Materials........9.54 Labor............1.40 *Remove* .... Labor............ .30	sf	$.30	$10.94	$11.24
Redwood tongue-&-groove siding, fancy pattern, clear all heart grade *Replace* Materials......10.20 Labor............1.40 *Remove* .... Labor............ .30	sf	$.30	$11.60	$11.90

CLAPBOARD SIDING *True clapboard. Based on grades marketed by Donnell's Clapboard Mill of Sedgwick, Maine.*

Item Description	Unit	Remove	Replace	Total
Radially sawn clapboard siding, eastern pine, #1 premium clear *Replace* Materials........5.02 Labor............1.97 *Remove* .... Labor............ .30	sf	$.30	$6.99	$7.29
Radially sawn clapboard siding, eastern pine, #1 New England Cape *Replace* Materials........4.39 Labor............1.97 *Remove* .... Labor............ .30	sf	$.30	$6.36	$6.66

BEVELED SIDING *Siding that looks like clapboard but is not radially sawn. (The grain in radially sawn board runs at a consistent 90 degree angle to the board face. In resawn boards grain orientation is inconsistent.)*

Item Description	Unit	Remove	Replace	Total
Pine resawn beveled siding, select grade *Replace* Materials........1.85 Labor............1.47 *Remove* .... Labor............ .30	sf	$.30	$3.32	$3.62
Cedar resawn beveled siding, select grade *Replace* Materials........2.32 Labor............1.47 *Remove* .... Labor............ .30	sf	$.30	$3.79	$4.09

Item Description	Unit	Remove	Replace	Total
Redwood resawn beveled siding, clear all heart grade ***Replace*** Materials........4.98 Labor ....1.47 ***Remove*** .... Labor............ .30	sf	$.30	$6.45	$6.75
Pine bungalow siding, select grade ***Replace*** Materials........2.50 Labor ....1.40 ***Remove*** .... Labor............ .30	sf	$.30	$3.90	$4.20
Cedar bungalow siding, select grade ***Replace*** Materials........3.14 Labor ....1.40 ***Remove*** .... Labor............ .30	sf	$.30	$4.54	$4.84
Redwood bungalow siding, clear all heart grade ***Replace*** Materials........6.73 Labor ....1.40 ***Remove*** .... Labor............ .30	sf	$.30	$8.13	$8.43
Pine Dolly Varden siding, select grade ***Replace*** Materials........2.69 Labor ....1.40 ***Remove*** .... Labor............ .30	sf	$.30	$4.09	$4.39
Cedar Dolly Varden siding, select grade ***Replace*** Materials........3.38 Labor ....1.40 ***Remove*** .... Labor............ .30	sf	$.30	$4.78	$5.08
Redwood Dolly Varden siding, clear all heart grade ***Replace*** Materials........7.24 Labor ....1.40 ***Remove*** .... Labor............ .30	sf	$.30	$8.64	$8.94
Pine log cabin siding, select grade ***Replace*** Materials........2.51 Labor ....1.40 ***Remove*** .... Labor............ .30	sf	$.30	$3.91	$4.21
Cedar log cabin siding, select grade ***Replace*** Materials........3.15 Labor ....1.40 ***Remove*** .... Labor............ .30	sf	$.30	$4.55	$4.85
Add for one coat factory stain ***Replace*** Materials........ .38	sf	—	$.38	$.38
Add for two coat factory stain ***Replace*** Materials........ .56	sf	—	$.56	$.56
Replace section of wood siding ***Replace*** Materials......20.00 Labor 29.60	ea	—	$49.60	$49.60
Minimum charge to repair wood siding ***Replace*** Materials......55.00 Labor..........35.80	ea	—	$90.80	$90.80
Aluminum fascia to 6" wide ***Replace*** Materials........1.56 Labor ....1.22 ***Remove*** .... Labor............ .17	lf	$.17	$2.78	$2.95
Aluminum fascia 6" to 12" wide ***Replace*** Materials........2.10 Labor ....1.22 ***Remove*** .... Labor............ .17	lf	$.17	$3.32	$3.49
Vinyl fascia to 6" wide ***Replace*** Materials........2.26 Labor ....1.22 ***Remove*** .... Labor............ .17	lf	$.17	$3.48	$3.65

◀ **BUNGALOW SIDING**
*Tapered siding that is thicker and wider than beveled siding. Includes 4% waste. Deduct **9%** for next lower grade, deduct **14%** for third grade.*

◀ **DOLLY VARDEN SIDING**
*Includes 4% waste. Deduct **9%** for next lower grade, deduct **14%** for third grade.*

◀ **LOG CABIN SIDING**
*Includes 4% waste. Deduct **9%** for next lower grade, deduct **14%** for third grade.*

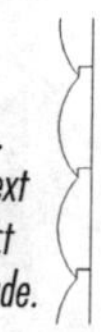

◀ **ADD FOR FACTORY STAINED SIDING**

◀ **SIDING REPAIR**

◁ **minimum**

◀ **FASCIA**
Includes 4% waste.

RELATED ITEMS

Finish Carpentry..........199
Paneling........................347
Rough Carpentry........409

	Item Description	Unit	Remove	Replace	Total
FASCIA ▶ *continued*	**Vinyl fascia 6" to 12" wide** *Replace* Materials........3.14 Labor............1.22 *Remove* .... Labor............ .17	lf	$.17	$4.36	$4.53
	Cedar fascia to 6" wide *Replace* Materials........1.93 Labor............1.32 *Remove* .... Labor............ .19	lf	$.19	$3.25	$3.44
	Cedar fascia 6" to 12" wide *Replace* Materials........2.57 Labor............1.32 *Remove* .... Labor............ .19	lf	$.19	$3.89	$4.08
	Redwood fascia to 6" wide *Replace* Materials........3.86 Labor............1.32 *Remove* .... Labor............ .19	lf	$.19	$5.18	$5.37
	Redwood fascia 6" to 12" wide *Replace* Materials........5.16 Labor............1.32 *Remove* .... Labor............ .19	lf	$.19	$6.48	$6.67
minimum ▷	**Minimum charge for soffit & fascia work** *Replace* Materials......59.00 Labor..........35.80	ea	—	$94.80	$94.80
SOFFIT ▶ *Includes 4% waste.*	**Aluminum soffit** *Replace* Materials........2.64 Labor............1.75 *Remove* .... Labor............ .25	sf	$.25	$4.39	$4.64
	Vinyl soffit *Replace* Materials........3.88 Labor............1.75 *Remove* .... Labor............ .25	sf	$.25	$5.63	$5.88
	Cedar plywood soffit *Replace* Materials........1.82 Labor............1.86 *Remove* .... Labor............ .28	sf	$.28	$3.68	$3.96
	Cedar rough-sawn plywood soffit *Replace* Materials........1.85 Labor............1.86 *Remove* .... Labor............ .28	sf	$.28	$3.71	$3.99
	Fir plywood soffit *Replace* Materials........1.61 Labor............1.86 *Remove* .... Labor............ .28	sf	$.28	$3.47	$3.75
	Fir rough-sawn plywood soffit *Replace* Materials........1.66 Labor............1.86 *Remove* .... Labor............ .28	sf	$.28	$3.52	$3.80
	Redwood plywood soffit *Replace* Materials........3.94 Labor............1.86 *Remove* .... Labor............ .28	sf	$.28	$5.80	$6.08
	Redwood rough-sawn plywood soffit *Replace* Materials........4.00 Labor............1.86 *Remove* .... Labor............ .28	sf	$.28	$5.86	$6.14
tongue-&-groove soffit ▷	**Cedar tongue-&-groove soffit, simple pattern** *Replace* Materials........3.50 Labor............2.18 *Remove* .... Labor............ .33	sf	$.33	$5.68	$6.01
	Cedar tongue-&-groove soffit, fancy pattern *Replace* Materials........4.20 Labor............2.18 *Remove* .... Labor............ .33	sf	$.33	$6.38	$6.71

Item Description	Unit	Remove	Replace	Total
Fir tongue-&-groove soffit, simple pattern ***Replace*** Materials........3.25 Labor............2.18 ***Remove*** .... Labor............ .33	sf	$.33	$5.43	$5.76
Fir tongue-&-groove soffit, fancy pattern ***Replace*** Materials........3.43 Labor............2.18 ***Remove*** .... Labor............ .33	sf	$.33	$5.61	$5.94
Redwood tongue-&-groove soffit, simple pattern ***Replace*** Materials........5.94 Labor............2.18 ***Remove*** .... Labor............ .33	sf	$.33	$8.12	$8.45
Redwood tongue-&-groove soffit, fancy pattern ***Replace*** Materials........6.46 Labor............2.18 ***Remove*** .... Labor............ .33	sf	$.33	$8.64	$8.97
Aluminum rain gutter ***Replace*** Materials........3.74 Labor............1.47 ***Remove*** .... Labor............ .30	lf	$.30	$5.21	$5.51
Copper built-in box rain gutter ***Replace*** Materials......34.40 Labor..........60.50 ***Remove*** .... Labor............ .72 ► Includes additional framing material and labor costs for a typical rain gutter integrated into the roof system and flashed with copper. Removal costs include only copper flashing.	lf	$.72	$94.90	$95.62
Copper rain gutter ***Replace*** Materials.......19.00 Labor............1.47 ***Remove*** .... Labor............ .30	lf	$.30	$20.47	$20.77
Galvanized steel rain gutter ***Replace*** Materials........9.44 Labor............1.47 ***Remove*** .... Labor............ .30	lf	$.30	$10.91	$11.21
Plastic rain gutter ***Replace*** Materials........3.03 Labor............1.47 ***Remove*** .... Labor............ .30	lf	$.30	$4.50	$4.80
Redwood rain gutter ***Replace*** Materials......34.30 Labor............1.47 ***Remove*** .... Labor............ .30	lf	$.30	$35.77	$36.07
Tin built-in box rain gutter ***Replace*** Materials......24.20 Labor..........60.50 ***Remove*** .... Labor............ .72 ► Includes additional framing material and labor costs for a typical rain gutter integrated into the roof system and flashed with 40 pound terne tin. Removal costs include only copper flashing.	lf	$.72	$84.70	$85.42
Tin rain gutter ***Replace*** Materials......16.80 Labor............1.47 ***Remove*** .... Labor............ .30	lf	$.30	$18.27	$18.57
Aluminum rain gutter downspout ***Replace*** Materials........4.58 Labor............1.36 ***Remove*** .... Labor............ .25	lf	$.25	$5.94	$6.19
Copper built-in box rain gutter downspout ***Replace*** Materials......21.60 Labor..........20.10 ***Remove*** .... Labor............ .25 ► Includes additional framing material and labor costs for an enclosed, concealed downspout. Also includes PVC pipe and excavation to drain field.	lf	$.25	$41.70	$41.95

RELATED ITEMS

Finish Carpentry..........199
Paneling......................347
Rough Carpentry........409

◄ **RAIN GUTTER**
Includes 3% waste.

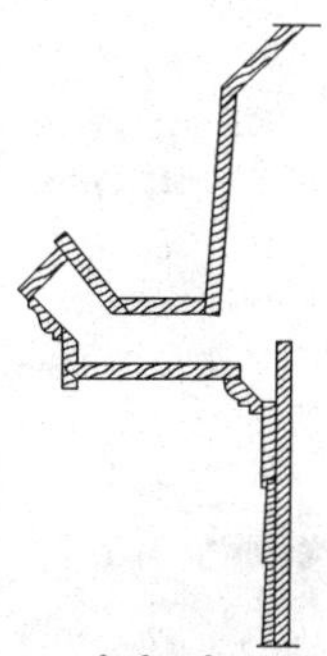

built-in box △

◄ **RAIN GUTTER DOWNSPOUT**
Includes 3% waste.

	Item Description	Unit	Remove	Replace	Total
Rain gutter downspout *continued*	**Copper rain gutter downspout** ***Replace*** Materials......23.20 Labor............1.36 ***Remove*** .... Labor............ .25	lf	$.25	$24.56	$24.81
	Galvanized steel rain gutter downspout ***Replace*** Materials.......11.50 Labor............1.36 ***Remove*** .... Labor............ .25	lf	$.25	$12.86	$13.11
	Plastic rain gutter downspout ***Replace*** Materials........3.70 Labor............1.36 ***Remove*** .... Labor............ .25	lf	$.25	$5.06	$5.31
	Tin built-in box rain gutter downspout ***Replace*** Materials......16.50 Labor............1.36 ***Remove*** .... Labor............ .25 ► Includes additional framing material and labor costs for an enclosed, concealed downspout. Also includes PVC pipe and excavation to drain field.	lf	$.25	$17.86	$18.11
	Tin rain gutter downspout ***Replace*** Materials......20.50 Labor..........20.10 ***Remove*** .... Labor............ .25	lf	$.25	$40.60	$40.85
Downspout conductor	**Copper downspout conductor, standard grade** ***Replace*** Materials......47.00 Labor...........15.40 ► Simple or clear decorative work.	ea	—	$62.40	$62.40
 *high grade* △	**Copper downspout conductor, high grade** ***Replace*** Materials......89.50 Labor...........15.40 ► Decorative embossed design.	ea	—	$104.90	$104.90
	Galvanized steel downspout conductor, standard grade ***Replace*** Materials......37.70 Labor...........15.40 ► Simple or clear decorative work.	ea	—	$53.10	$53.10
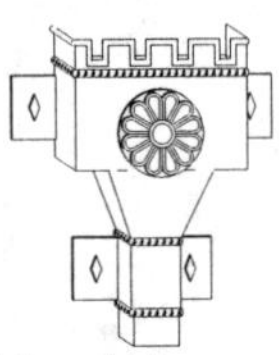 *high grade* △	**Galvanized steel downspout conductor, high grade** ***Replace*** Materials......71.90 Labor...........15.40 ► Decorative embossed design.	ea	—	$87.30	$87.30
Polypropylene shutter *Per 16" wide pair. For 12" wide deduct **42%**; for 18" wide add **8%**; for 20" wide add **14%**; for 24" wide add **26%**.*	**24" tall polypropylene fixed shutter** ***Replace*** Materials......34.00 Labor...........11.60 ***Remove*** .... Labor............4.29	ea	$4.29	$45.60	$49.89
	48" tall polypropylene fixed shutter ***Replace*** Materials......52.90 Labor...........11.60 ***Remove*** .... Labor............4.29	ea	$4.29	$64.50	$68.79
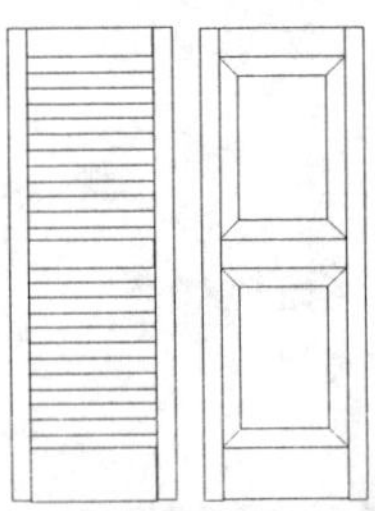	**60" tall polypropylene fixed shutter** ***Replace*** Materials.......61.30 Labor...........11.60 ***Remove*** .... Labor............4.29	ea	$4.29	$72.90	$77.19
	66" tall polypropylene fixed shutter ***Replace*** Materials......70.90 Labor...........11.60 ***Remove*** .... Labor............4.29	ea	$4.29	$82.50	$86.79
Wood shutter *Per 16" wide pair. For 12" wide deduct **6%**; for 18" wide add **10%**; for 20" wide add **52%**; for 24" wide add **78%**.*	**36" tall wood fixed shutter** ***Replace*** Materials .....111.00 Labor...........11.60 ***Remove*** .... Labor............4.29	ea	$4.29	$122.60	$126.89
	48" tall wood fixed shutter ***Replace*** Materials.....125.00 Labor...........11.60 ***Remove*** .... Labor............4.29	ea	$4.29	$136.60	$140.89

Item Description	Unit	Remove	Replace	Total
60" tall wood fixed shutter *Replace* Materials.....141.00 Labor..........11.60 *Remove* .... Labor..........4.29	ea	$4.29	$152.60	$156.89
72" tall wood fixed shutter *Replace* Materials.....155.00 Labor..........11.60 *Remove* .... Labor..........4.29	ea	$4.29	$166.60	$170.89
36" tall wood moveable shutter *Replace* Materials.....175.00 Labor..........11.90 *Remove* .... Labor..........4.35	ea	$4.35	$186.90	$191.25
48" tall wood moveable shutter *Replace* Materials....204.00 Labor..........11.90 *Remove* .... Labor..........4.35	ea	$4.35	$215.90	$220.25
60" tall wood moveable shutter *Replace* Materials....237.00 Labor..........11.90 *Remove* .... Labor..........4.35	ea	$4.35	$248.90	$253.25
72" tall wood moveable shutter *Replace* Materials....293.00 Labor..........11.90 *Remove* .... Labor..........4.35	ea	$4.35	$304.90	$309.25
Remove shutter for work, then reinstall *Replace* .... Labor..........16.10	ea	—	$16.10	$16.10

RELATED ITEMS

Finish Carpentry..........199
Paneling......................347
Rough Carpentry........409

◄ **WOOD MOVEABLE SHUTTER**
*Per 16" wide pair including hardware. For 12" wide deduct **15%**; for 18" wide add **7%**; for 20" wide add **14%**; for 24" wide add **27%**. For fixed half circle top add **$120** per pair. For moveable louvers with half-circle top add **$210** per pair. For raised panel shutter with half-circle top add **$140** per pair. For Gothic peaked top (Gothic arch) add **$220** per pair.*

NOTES: ______________________________

end

TIME & MATERIAL CHARTS *(selected items)*

Siding Materials

*See **Siding** material prices with the line items and waste information in the **QuickFinder** column.*

Siding Labor

LABORER	BASE WAGE	PAID LEAVE	TRUE WAGE	FICA	FUTA	WORKER'S COMP.	UNEMPLOY. INSUR.	HEALTH INSUR.	RETIRE (401K)	LIABILITY INSUR.	COST PER HOUR
Siding installer	$23.30	1.82	$25.12	1.92	.20	4.81	2.19	2.69	.75	3.39	$41.10
Siding installer's helper	$16.80	1.31	$18.11	1.39	.14	3.47	1.58	2.69	.54	2.45	$30.40
Demolition laborer	$13.90	1.08	$14.98	1.15	.12	4.79	1.30	2.69	.45	2.02	$27.50

Paid Leave is calculated based on two weeks paid vacation, one week sick leave, and seven paid holidays. Employer's matching portion of **FICA** is 7.65 percent. **FUTA** (Federal Unemployment) is .8 percent. **Worker's compensation** for the siding trade was calculated using a national average of 19.16 percent. **Unemployment insurance** was calculated using a national average of 8.7 percent. **Health insurance** was calculated based on a projected national average for 2002 of $535 per employee (and family when applicable) per month. Employer pays 80 percent for a per month cost of $428 per employee. **Retirement** is based on a 401(k) retirement program with employer matching of 50 percent. Employee contributions to the 401(k) plan are an average of 6 percent of the true wage. **Liability insurance** is based on a national average of 13.2 percent.

Siding Labor Productivity

WORK DESCRIPTION	LABORER	COST PER HOUR	PRODUCTIVITY	UNIT PRICE
Demolition				
remove fiberglass corrugated siding	demolition laborer	$27.50	.007	**$.19** sf
remove aluminum siding	demolition laborer	$27.50	.008	**$.22** sf
remove cement fiber shingle siding	demolition laborer	$27.50	.013	**$.36** sf
remove shake or wood shingle siding	demolition laborer	$27.50	.014	**$.39** sf
remove vinyl siding	demolition laborer	$27.50	.007	**$.19** sf
remove hardboard siding	demolition laborer	$27.50	.009	**$.25** sf
remove hardboard beveled siding	demolition laborer	$27.50	.010	**$.28** sf
remove plywood siding	demolition laborer	$27.50	.010	**$.28** sf
remove wood siding	demolition laborer	$27.50	.011	**$.30** sf
remove aluminum or vinyl fascia	demolition laborer	$27.50	.006	**$.17** lf
remove wood fascia	demolition laborer	$27.50	.007	**$.19** lf
remove aluminum or vinyl soffit	demolition laborer	$27.50	.009	**$.25** sf
remove plywood soffit	demolition laborer	$27.50	.010	**$.28** sf
remove tongue-&-groove soffit	demolition laborer	$27.50	.012	**$.33** lf
remove rain gutter	demolition laborer	$27.50	.011	**$.30** lf
remove built-in box rain gutter	demolition laborer	$27.50	.026	**$.72** lf
remove downspout	demolition laborer	$27.50	.009	**$.25** lf
remove fixed shutter	demolition laborer	$27.50	.156	**$4.29** ea
remove moveable shutter	demolition laborer	$27.50	.158	**$4.35** ea
Siding installation crew				
install siding	siding installer	$41.10		
install siding	siding installer's helper	$30.40		
install siding	**siding crew**	$35.80		
Install siding				
fiberglass corrugated	siding crew	$35.80	.028	**$1.00** sf
aluminum	siding crew	$35.80	.034	**$1.22** sf
cement fiber shingle	siding crew	$35.80	.045	**$1.61** sf
shake or wood shingle	siding crew	$35.80	.045	**$1.61** sf
vinyl	siding crew	$35.80	.034	**$1.22** sf
7/16" thick hardboard	siding crew	$35.80	.024	**$.86** sf
hardboard lap	siding crew	$35.80	.026	**$.93** sf
5/8" thick plywood	siding crew	$35.80	.025	**$.90** sf
plywood with 1" x 4" boards	siding crew	$35.80	.057	**$2.04** sf
board-and-batten	siding crew	$35.80	.037	**$1.32** sf
board-on-board	siding crew	$35.80	.034	**$1.22** sf
drop siding	siding crew	$35.80	.039	**$1.40** sf
clapboard	siding crew	$35.80	.055	**$1.97** sf
bevel	siding crew	$35.80	.041	**$1.47** sf
Install fascia				
aluminum or vinyl	siding crew	$35.80	.034	**$1.22** lf
wood fascia	siding crew	$35.80	.037	**$1.32** lf
Install soffit				
aluminum or vinyl	siding crew	$35.80	.049	**$1.75** sf
plywood	siding crew	$35.80	.052	**$1.86** sf
tongue-&-groove	siding crew	$35.80	.061	**$2.18** sf
Install rain gutter				
typical	siding crew	$35.80	.041	**$1.47** lf
built-in box	siding crew	$35.80	1.69	**$60.50** lf
Install rain gutter downspout				
typical	siding crew	$35.80	.038	**$1.36** lf
built-in box	siding crew	$35.80	.562	**$20.10** lf
Install downspout conductor				
typical	siding crew	$35.80	.431	**$15.40** ea
Install shutter				
fixed	siding crew	$35.80	.323	**$11.60** ea
moveable	siding crew	$35.80	.333	**$11.90** ea

NOTES:

end

35 .... Stairs

Item Description	Unit	Remove	Replace	Total
3′ wide utility stairs ***Replace*** Materials......16.80 Labor...........15.00 ***Remove***........................ Labor............2.78 ► Includes three 2″ x 12″ stringers and 2″ dimensional lumber treads.	st	$2.78	$31.80	$34.58
3′ wide enclosed stairs for covered treads & risers ***Replace*** Materials......30.50 Labor...........19.70 ***Remove***........................ Labor............3.36 ► Treads and risers are plywood or particleboard with pine risers. Treads and risers will be completely covered by carpeting or other flooring.	st	$3.36	$50.20	$53.56
3′ wide enclosed stairs with false oak tread & riser ***Replace*** Materials......64.30 Labor..........23.10 ***Remove***........................ Labor............3.36 ► Particleboard treads with pine risers covered with two wall end false red oak tread and riser assemblies. (Carpet runs between false treads.)	st	$3.36	$87.40	$90.76
3′ wide enclosed stairs with oak treads & paint-grade risers ***Replace*** Materials......65.00 Labor...........19.70 ***Remove***........................ Labor............3.36 ► Treads are red oak and risers are paint-grade pine.	st	$3.36	$84.70	$88.06
3′ wide enclosed stairs with oak treads & oak risers ***Replace*** Materials......69.50 Labor...........19.70 ***Remove***........................ Labor............3.36 ► Treads and risers are red oak.	st	$3.36	$89.20	$92.56
3′ wide stairs, one side open, for covered treads & risers ***Replace*** Materials......30.50 Labor..........20.20 ***Remove***........................ Labor............3.36 ► Particleboard treads and pine risers. Treads and risers will be completely covered by carpeting or other flooring.	st	$3.36	$50.70	$54.06
3′ wide stairs, one side open, with false oak tread & riser ***Replace*** Materials......78.70 Labor..........23.60 ***Remove***........................ Labor............3.36 ► Particleboard treads with pine risers covered with one open end and one wall end false red oak tread and riser assemblies. (Carpet runs between false treads.)	st	$3.36	$102.30	$105.66
3′ wide stairs, one side open, with oak treads & paint-grade risers ***Replace*** Materials......65.00 Labor..........20.20 ***Remove***........................ Labor............3.36 ► Treads are red oak with easing on open side and 1/2″ red oak cove trim beneath tread. Risers are paint-grade pine.	st	$3.36	$85.20	$88.56
3′ wide stairs, one side open, with oak treads & oak risers ***Replace*** Materials......69.50 Labor..........20.20 ***Remove***........................ Labor............3.36 ► Treads are red oak with easing on open side and 1/2″ red oak cove trim beneath tread. Risers are red oak.	st	$3.36	$89.70	$93.06
3′ wide stairs, two sides open, for covered treads & risers ***Replace*** Materials......30.50 Labor...........21.50 ***Remove***........................ Labor............3.36 ► Particleboard tread and pine risers. Treads and risers will be completely covered by carpeting or other flooring.	st	$3.36	$52.00	$55.36

◄ **UTILITY STAIRS**
Per step. Does not include railing.

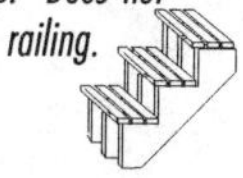

◄ **STRAIGHT STAIRS**
Per step. Each stair system includes four 2″ x 12″ stringers reinforced with plywood or waferboard. Does not include balustrade.

◁ **enclosed**

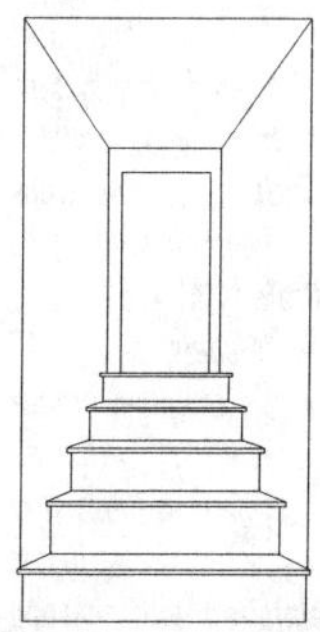

◁ **one side open**

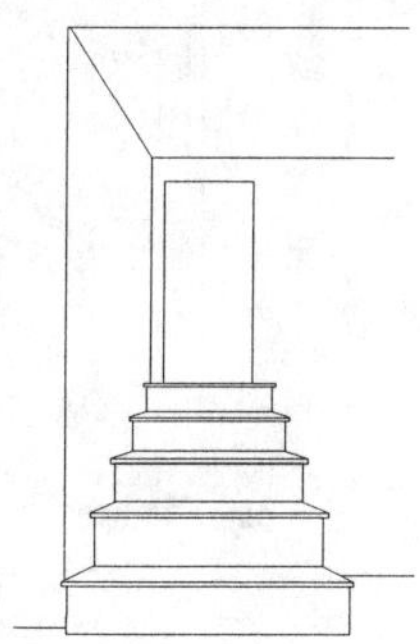

RELATED ITEMS

Columns........................71
Finish Carpentry..........199
porch posts...................231
Rough Carpentry........409
exterior deck stairs.........430

◁ **two sides open**

Straight stairs ► *continued*

Item Description	Unit	Remove	Replace	Total
3' wide stairs, two sides open, with false oak tread & riser ***Replace*** Materials......93.10 Labor..........24.90 ***Remove***........................ Labor ....3.36 ► Particleboard treads with pine risers covered with two open end false red oak tread and riser assemblies. (Carpet runs between false treads.)	st	$3.36	$118.00	$121.36
3' wide stairs, two sides open, with oak treads & paint-grade risers ***Replace*** Materials......65.00 Labor..........21.50 ***Remove***........................ Labor ....3.36 ► Treads are red oak with easing on both sides and 1/2" red oak cove trim beneath tread. Risers are paint-grade pine.	st	$3.36	$86.50	$89.86
3' wide stairs, two sides open, with oak treads & oak risers ***Replace*** Materials......69.50 Labor..........21.50 ***Remove***........................ Labor ....3.36 ► Treads are red oak with easing on both sides and 1/2" red oak cove trim beneath tread. Risers are red oak.	st	$3.36	$91.00	$94.36

1/4 turn stairs ► *Per step. Ten step minimum. L-shaped stair system with 3' by 3' landing. Includes bearing walls beneath landing as indicated, 2" x 8" joists, headers, and 3/4" tongue-&-groove sheathing. Each stair system includes four 2" x 12" stringers reinforced with plywood or waferboard. Does not include balustrade.*

enclosed ▷

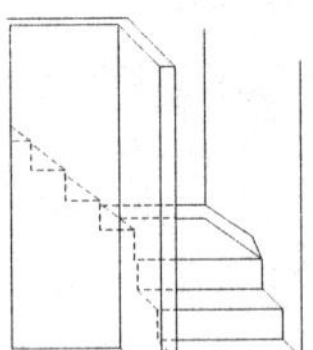

Item Description	Unit	Remove	Replace	Total
3' wide enclosed 1/4 turn stairs for covered treads & risers ***Replace*** Materials......39.30 Labor..........34.40 ***Remove***........................ Labor ....3.71 ► 6 lf of landing bearing wall. Particleboard treads and pine risers or plywood treads and risers. Treads, risers, and landing will be covered by the flooring.	st	$3.71	$73.70	$77.41
3' wide enclosed 1/4 turn stairs with false oak tread & riser ***Replace*** Materials......77.00 Labor..........48.20 ***Remove***........................ Labor ....3.71 ► 6 lf of landing bearing wall. Particleboard treads with pine risers covered with two wall end false red oak tread and riser assemblies. (Carpet runs between false treads.) Landing covered with oak flooring with stair edged trimmed with landing nose.	st	$3.71	$125.20	$128.91
3' wide enclosed 1/4 turn stairs with oak treads & paint-grade risers ***Replace*** Materials......81.60 Labor..........42.40 ***Remove***........................ Labor ....3.71 ► 6 lf of landing bearing wall. Treads are red oak and risers are paint-grade pine. Landing covered with oak flooring with stair edge trimmed with landing nose.	st	$3.71	$124.00	$127.71
3' wide enclosed 1/4 turn stairs with oak treads & oak risers ***Replace*** Materials......86.10 Labor..........42.40 ***Remove***........................ Labor ....3.71 ► 6 lf of landing bearing wall. Treads and risers are red oak. Landing covered with oak flooring with stair edge trimmed with landing nose.	st	$3.71	$128.50	$132.21

one side open ▷

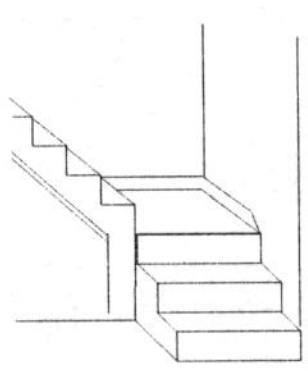

Item Description	Unit	Remove	Replace	Total
3' wide 1/4 turn stairs, one side open, for covered treads & risers ***Replace*** Materials......39.30 Labor..........35.60 ***Remove***........................ Labor ....3.71 ► 6 lf of landing bearing wall. Particleboard treads and pine risers. Treads, risers, and landing will be completely covered by carpeting or other flooring.	st	$3.71	$74.90	$78.61
3' wide 1/4 turn stairs, one side open, with false oak tread & riser ***Replace*** Materials......91.40 Labor..........50.00 ***Remove***........................ Labor ....3.71 ► 6 lf of landing bearing wall. Particleboard treads with pine risers covered with one open end and one wall end false red oak tread and riser assemblies. (Carpet runs between false treads.) Landing covered with oak flooring with stair edge trimmed with landing nose.	st	$3.71	$141.40	$145.11
3' wide 1/4 turn stairs, one side open, with oak treads & paint-grade risers ***Replace*** Materials......81.60 Labor..........43.30 ***Remove***........................ Labor ....3.71 ► 6 lf of landing bearing wall. Treads are red oak with easing on open side and 1/2" red oak cove trim beneath tread. Risers are paint-grade pine. Landing covered with oak flooring with stair edge trimmed with landing nose.	st	$3.71	$124.90	$128.61

Item Description	Unit	Remove	Replace	Total
3′ wide 1/4 turn stairs, one side open, with oak treads & oak risers *Replace* Materials......86.10 Labor..........43.30 *Remove*........................ Labor............3.71 ► 6 lf of landing bearing wall. Treads are red oak with easing on open side and 1/2″ red oak cove trim beneath tread. Risers are red oak. Landing covered with oak flooring with stair edge trimmed with landing nose.	st	$3.71	$129.40	$133.11
3′ wide 1/4 turn stairs, two sides open, for covered treads & risers *Replace* Materials......39.30 Labor..........36.80 *Remove*........................ Labor............3.71 ► 12 lf of landing bearing wall. Particleboard treads and pine risers or plywood treads and risers. Treads, risers, and landing will be completely covered by flooring.	st	$3.71	$76.10	$79.81
3′ wide 1/4 turn stairs, two sides open, with false oak tread & riser *Replace* Materials....105.80 Labor...........51.20 *Remove*........................ Labor............3.71 ► 12 lf of landing bearing wall. Particleboard treads with pine risers covered with two open end false red oak tread and riser assemblies. (Space is left for carpet to run between treads.) Landing covered with oak flooring with stair edge trimmed with landing nose.	st	$3.71	$157.00	$160.71
3′ wide 1/4 turn stairs, two sides open, with oak treads & paint-grade risers *Replace* Materials......81.60 Labor..........43.70 *Remove*........................ Labor............3.71 ► 12 lf of landing bearing wall. Treads are red oak with easing on both sides and 1/2″ red oak cove trim beneath tread. Risers are paint-grade pine. Landing covered with oak flooring with stair edge trimmed with landing nose.	st	$3.71	$125.30	$129.01
3′ wide 1/4 turn stairs, two sides open, with oak treads & oak risers *Replace* Materials......86.10 Labor..........43.70 *Remove*........................ Labor............3.71 ► 12 lf of landing bearing wall. Treads are red oak with easing on both sides and 1/2″ red oak cove trim beneath tread, Risers are red oak. Landing covered with oak flooring with stair edge trimmed with landing nose.	st	$3.71	$129.80	$133.51
3′ wide enclosed 1/2 turn stairs for covered treads and risers *Replace* Materials......48.00 Labor...........37.80 *Remove*........................ Labor............4.13 ► 9 lf of landing bearing wall. Particleboard treads and pine risers or plywood treads and risers. Treads, risers, and landing will be completely covered by flooring.	st	$4.13	$85.80	$89.93
3′ wide enclosed 1/2 turn stairs with false oak tread and riser *Replace* Materials......89.70 Labor...........52.40 *Remove*........................ Labor............4.13 ► 9 lf of landing bearing wall. Particleboard treads with pine risers covered with two wall end false red oak tread and riser assemblies. (Carpet runs between false treads.) Landing covered with oak flooring with stair edged trimmed with landing nose.	st	$4.13	$142.10	$146.23
3′ wide enclosed 1/2 turn stairs with oak treads & paint-grade risers *Replace* Materials......94.30 Labor..........46.60 *Remove*........................ Labor............4.13 ► 9 lf of landing bearing wall. Treads are red oak and risers are paint-grade pine. Landing covered with oak flooring with stair edge trimmed with landing nose.	st	$4.13	$140.90	$145.03
3′ wide enclosed 1/2 turn stairs with oak treads & oak risers *Replace* Materials......98.80 Labor..........46.60 *Remove*........................ Labor............4.13 ► 9 lf of landing bearing wall. Treads and risers are red oak. Landing covered with oak flooring with stair edge trimmed with landing nose.	st	$4.13	$145.40	$149.53

RELATED ITEMS

◁ **two sides open**

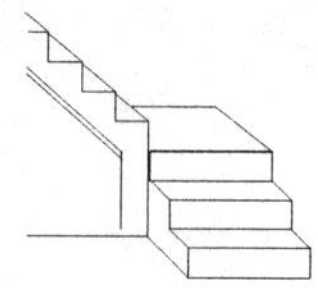

◀ **1/2 TURN STAIRS**
Per step. Ten step minimum. U shaped stair system with 6′ by 3′ landing. Includes bearing walls beneath landing as indicated, 2″ x 8″ joists, headers, and 3/4″ tongue-&-groove sheathing. Each stair system includes four 2″ x 12″ stringers reinforced with plywood or waferboard.

◁ **enclosed**

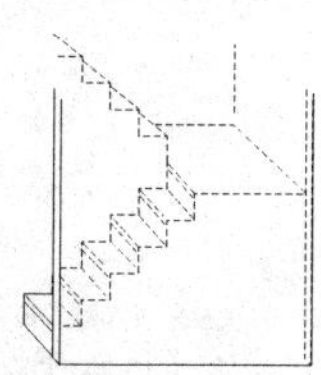

Item Description	Unit	Remove	Replace	Total

1/2 TURN STAIRS ► *continued*

one side open ▷

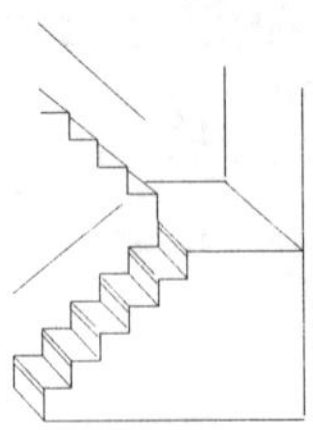

Item Description	Unit	Remove	Replace	Total
3′ wide 1/2 turn stairs, one side open, for covered treads & risers ***Replace*** Materials......48.00 Labor..........39.20 ***Remove***........................ Labor............4.13 ► 9 lf of landing bearing wall. Particleboard treads and pine risers. Treads and risers will be completely covered by carpeting or other flooring.	st	$4.13	$87.20	$91.33
3′ wide 1/2 turn stairs, one side open, with false oak tread & riser ***Replace*** Materials.....118.00 Labor..........54.50 ***Remove***........................ Labor............4.13 ► 9 lf of landing bearing wall. Particleboard treads with pine risers covered with one open end and one wall end false red oak tread and riser assemblies. (Space is left for carpet to run between treads.) Landing covered with oak flooring with stair edge trimmed with landing nose.	st	$4.13	$172.50	$176.63
3′ wide 1/2 turn stairs, one side open, with oak treads & paint-grade risers ***Replace*** Materials......94.30 Labor..........47.80 ***Remove***........................ Labor............4.13 ► 9 lf of landing bearing wall. Treads are red oak with easing on open side and 1/2″ red oak cove trim beneath tread. Risers are paint-grade pine. Landing covered with oak flooring with stair edge trimmed with landing nose.	st	$4.13	$142.10	$146.23
3′ wide 1/2 turn stairs, one side open, with oak treads & oak risers ***Replace*** Materials......98.80 Labor..........47.80 ***Remove***........................ Labor............4.13 ► 9 lf of landing bearing wall. Treads are red oak with easing on open side and 1/2″ red oak cove trim beneath tread. Risers are red oak. Landing covered with oak flooring with stair edge trimmed with landing nose.	st	$4.13	$146.60	$150.73

two sides open ▷

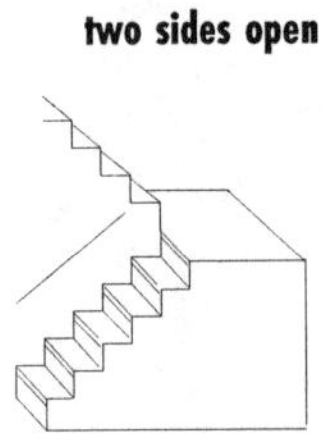

Item Description	Unit	Remove	Replace	Total
3′ wide 1/2 turn stairs, two sides open, for covered treads & risers ***Replace*** Materials......48.00 Labor..........40.40 ***Remove***........................ Labor............4.13 ► 18 lf of landing bearing wall. Particleboard treads and pine risers or plywood treads and risers. Treads, risers, and landing will be completely covered by flooring.	st	$4.13	$88.40	$92.53
3′ wide 1/2 turn stairs, two sides open, with false oak tread & riser ***Replace*** Materials.....118.00 Labor..........55.80 ***Remove***........................ Labor............4.13 ► 18 lf of landing bearing wall. Particleboard treads with pine risers covered with two open end false red oak tread and riser assemblies. (Space is left for carpet to run between treads.) Landing covered with oak flooring with stair edge trimmed with landing nose.	st	$4.13	$173.80	$177.93
3′ wide 1/2 turn stairs, two sides open, with oak treads & paint-grade risers ***Replace*** Materials......94.30 Labor..........48.30 ***Remove***........................ Labor............4.13 ► 18 lf of landing bearing wall. Treads are red oak with easing on both sides and 1/2″ red oak cove trim beneath tread. Risers are paint-grade pine. Landing covered with oak flooring with stair edge trimmed with landing nose.	st	$4.13	$142.60	$146.73
3′ wide 1/2 turn stairs, two sides open, with oak treads & oak risers ***Replace*** Materials......98.80 Labor..........48.30 ***Remove***........................ Labor............4.13 ► 18 lf of landing bearing wall. Treads and risers are red oak with easing on both sides and 1/2″ red oak cove trim beneath tread. Landing covered with oak flooring with stair edge trimmed with landing nose.	st	$4.13	$147.10	$151.23

CIRCULAR STAIRS ►

Circular stairs usually form half of a circle or less. Based on 9′ radius.

Item Description	Unit	Remove	Replace	Total
3′ wide enclosed circular stairs for covered treads and risers ***Replace*** Materials.....194.00 Labor........483.00 ***Remove***........................ Labor............4.35 ► Treads and risers are plywood or particleboard treads with pine risers. Treads and risers will be completely covered by carpeting or other flooring.	st	$4.35	$677.00	$681.35

continued on next page

Item Description	Unit	Remove	Replace	Total
3′ wide enclosed circular stairs with false oak tread and riser ***Replace*** Materials....227.00 Labor.........490.00 ***Remove*** .... Labor ....4.35 ► Particleboard treads with pine risers covered with two wall end false red oak tread and riser assemblies. (Carpet runs between false treads.)	st	$4.35	$717.00	$721.35
3′ wide enclosed circular stairs with oak treads and paint-grade risers ***Replace*** Materials....228.00 Labor........483.00 ***Remove*** .... Labor ....4.35 ► Treads are red oak and risers are paint-grade pine.	st	$4.35	$711.00	$715.35
3′ wide enclosed circular stairs with oak treads and oak risers ***Replace*** Materials....233.00 Labor........483.00 ***Remove*** .... Labor ....4.35 ► Treads and risers are red oak.	st	$4.35	$716.00	$720.35
3′ wide circular stairs, one side open, for covered treads and risers ***Replace*** Materials.....194.00 Labor.........491.00 ***Remove*** .... Labor ....4.35 ► Particleboard treads and pine risers. Treads and risers will be completely covered by carpeting or other flooring.	st	$4.35	$685.00	$689.35
3′ wide circular stairs, one side open, with false oak tread and riser ***Replace*** Materials.....242.00 Labor.........498.00 ***Remove*** .... Labor ....4.35 ► Particleboard treads with pine risers covered with one open end and one wall end false red oak tread and riser assemblies. (Carpet runs between treads.)	st	$4.35	$740.00	$744.35
3′ wide circular stairs, one side open, with oak treads and paint-grade risers ***Replace*** Materials....228.00 Labor.........491.00 ***Remove*** .... Labor ....4.35 ► Treads are red oak with easing on open side and 1/2″ red oak cove trim beneath tread. Risers are paint-grade pine.	st	$4.35	$719.00	$723.35
3′ wide circular stairs, one side open, with oak treads and oak risers ***Replace*** Materials....233.00 Labor.........491.00 ***Remove*** .... Labor ....4.35 ► Treads are red oak with easing on open side and 1/2″ red oak cove trim beneath tread. Risers are paint-grade pine.	st	$4.35	$724.00	$728.35
3′ wide circular stairs, two sides open, for covered treads and risers ***Replace*** Materials.....194.00 Labor.........495.00 ***Remove*** .... Labor ....4.35 ► Particleboard tread and pine risers. Treads and risers will be completely covered by carpeting or other flooring.	st	$4.35	$689.00	$693.35
3′ wide circular stairs, two sides open, with false oak tread and riser ***Replace*** Materials....256.00 Labor........502.00 ***Remove*** .... Labor ....4.35 ► Particleboard treads with pine risers covered with two open end false red oak tread and riser assemblies. (Carpet runs between false treads.)	st	$4.35	$758.00	$762.35
3′ wide circular stairs, two sides open, with oak treads and paint-grade risers ***Replace*** Materials....228.00 Labor.........495.00 ***Remove*** .... Labor ....4.35 ► Treads are red oak with easing on both sides and 1/2″ red oak cove trim beneath tread. Risers are paint-grade pine.	st	$4.35	$723.00	$727.35
3′ wide circular stairs, two sides open, with oak treads and oak risers ***Replace*** Materials....233.00 Labor.........495.00 ***Remove*** .... Labor ....4.35 ► Treads are red oak with easing on both sides and 1/2″ red oak cove trim beneath tread, Risers are red oak.	st	$4.35	$728.00	$732.35

◄ **CIRCULAR STAIRS**
Labor prices are for hand-framed open or closed stringer stairs. Overall these prices also apply to purchase and installation of prefabricated circular stairs. Does not include balustrade.

◁ **one side open**

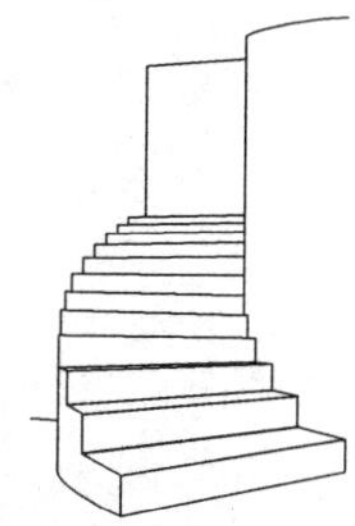

◁ **two sides open**

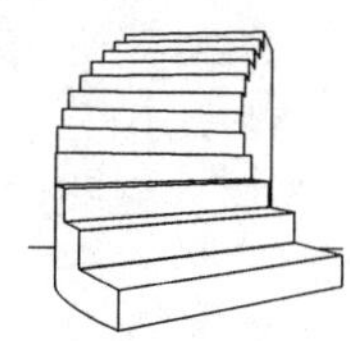

RELATED ITEMS

	Item Description	Unit	Remove	Replace	Total
Add for 4' wide stairs ▶	**Add 12% for 4' wide stairs** ▶ For 4' wide straight, 1/4 turn, or 1/2 turn stairs containing the same number of stringers as 3' wide stairs (4) with wider treads and risers. 1/4 turn stair landing is 4' x 4' and 1/2 turn stair landing is 8' x 4'. Add **16%** for 4' wide circular stairs.				
Add for stair winders ▶ 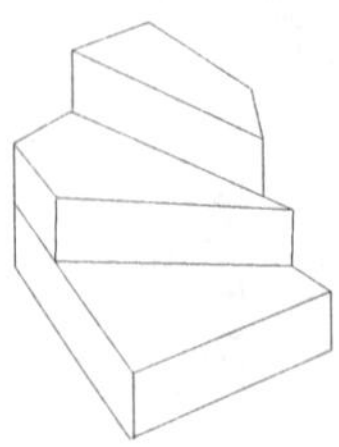	**Add for winder with particleboard tread, paint-grade riser** *Replace* Materials......44.80 Labor...........16.60 ▶ For use with 1/4 turn and 1/2 turn stairs. Winders are pie-shaped stair treads, usually placed on top of the landing. Each winder is a box made from 2" x 8" boards ripped to the height of the riser. Additional ripped 2" x 8" boards are placed 12" on center inside the box for reinforcement. (Add **3%** for risers over 7-3/8" made from ripped 2" x 10" boards.) Winders are stacked on top of each other.	ea	—	$61.40	$61.40
	Add for winder with oak tread, paint-grade riser *Replace* Materials......79.30 Labor...........16.60 ▶ For details see above.	ea	—	$95.90	$95.90
	Add for winder with oak tread, oak riser *Replace* Materials......83.80 Labor...........16.60 ▶ For details see above.	ea	—	$100.40	$100.40
Add for mitered steps ▶ 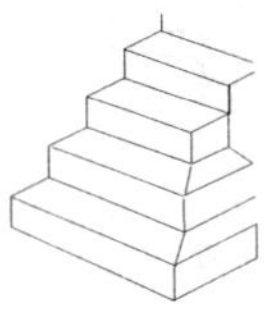	**Add for mitered corners on bottom three treads** *Replace* Materials.....121.00 Labor...........96.90 ▶ For stairs where the bottom three steps turn at a 45 degree angle (or less) making three steps from the side and front. The three steps on the side are made from stacked boxes made from 2" x 8" boards ripped to the riser height, sheathed with 3/4" plywood then capped with the tread and riser material. Cost per side. (For example, for stairs with mitered corners on both sides, use this price twice.)	ea	—	$217.90	$217.90
Add for bull nose on starting step ▶ 	**Add for starting step with bull nose one side, standard grade** *Replace* Materials....221.00 Labor ....20.50 ▶ Red oak up to 4' wide.	ea	—	$241.50	$241.50
	Add for starting step with bull nose one side, high grade *Replace* Materials....268.00 Labor ....20.50 ▶ Red oak up to 5' wide.	ea	—	$288.50	$288.50
	Add for starting step with bull nose two sides, standard grade *Replace* Materials....305.00 Labor ....20.50 ▶ Red oak up to 4' wide.	ea	—	$325.50	$325.50
	Add for starting step with bull nose two sides, high grade *Replace* Materials ....369.00 Labor ....20.50 ▶ Red oak up to 5' wide.	ea	—	$389.50	$389.50
Spiral stairs ▶ *Per step. Prefabricated spiral stairs assembled and installed by carpenter on site. Includes balustrade.*	**Prefabricated spiral stairs, economy grade** *Replace* Materials.....179.00 Labor...........35.60 *Remove*........................ Labor ....3.38 ▶ 48" to 54" diameter. Balusters are made from straight wood, steel, or aluminum with matching hand rail. One baluster per tread. Treads are made from aluminum, steel, or waferboard (for carpet). Add **$50** per lf for landing or balcony railing to match.	st	$3.38	$214.60	$217.98
	Prefabricated spiral stairs, standard grade *Replace* Materials.....316.00 Labor...........35.60 *Remove*........................ Labor ....3.38 ▶ 48" to 54" diameter. Balusters are made from turned wood, twisted steel, or aluminum with steel or laminated wood hand rail. One baluster per tread. Treads are made from aluminum, steel, or waferboard (for carpet). Add **$70** per lf for landing or balcony railing to match.	st	$3.38	$351.60	$354.98

Item Description	Unit	Remove	Replace	Total
Prefabricated spiral stairs, high grade ***Replace*** Materials....347.00 Labor...........35.60 ***Remove*** .... Labor ....3.38 ► 55" to 66" diameter. Balusters made from ornate wood or octagonal wood, twisted steel with decorative wrought iron work, or aluminum with matching hand rail. Two balusters per tread. Treads are made from aluminum, steel, or waferboard (for carpet). Add **$80** per lf for landing or balcony railing to match.	st	$3.38	$382.60	$385.98
Prefabricated spiral stairs, custom grade ***Replace*** Materials....379.00 Labor...........35.60 ***Remove*** .... Labor ....3.38 ► 55" to 66" diameter. Balusters made from spiral wood or octagonal wood, steel or cast iron with decorative wrought iron work including brass elements with matching hand rail. Two balusters per tread. Treads are made from aluminum, steel, decorative cast iron, or waferboard (for carpet). Add **$90** per lf for landing or balcony railing to match.	st	$3.38	$414.60	$417.98
Prefabricated spiral stairs, deluxe grade ***Replace*** Materials....458.00 Labor...........35.60 ***Remove*** .... Labor ....3.38 ► 67" to 72" diameter. Balusters made from ornate wood or octagonal wood, twisted steel with decorative wrought iron work with matching hand rail. Two balusters per tread. Treads are made from aluminum, steel, decorative cast iron or waferboard (for carpet). Add **$100** per lf for landing or balcony railing to match.	st	$3.38	$493.60	$496.98
Prefabricated spiral stairs, custom deluxe grade ***Replace*** Materials....500.00 Labor...........35.60 ***Remove*** .... Labor ....3.38 ► 67" to 72" diameter. Balusters made from spiral wood or octagonal wood, steel or cast iron with decorative wrought iron work including brass elements with matching hand rail. Two balusters per tread. Treads are made from aluminum, steel, decorative cast iron, or waferboard (for carpet). Add **$120** per lf for landing or balcony railing to match.	st	$3.38	$535.60	$538.98
Disappearing attic stairs, standard grade ***Replace*** Materials....332.00 Labor..........99.00 ***Remove*** .... Labor ....7.43 ► Pine components with stain-grade panel door.	ea	$7.43	$431.00	$438.43
Disappearing attic stairs, high grade ***Replace*** Materials....557.00 Labor..........99.00 ***Remove*** .... Labor ....7.43 ► Pine components with stain-grade panel door, spring loaded, heavier quality side rails and treads.	ea	$7.43	$656.00	$663.43
Disappearing attic stairs, deluxe grade ***Replace*** Materials....942.00 Labor..........99.00 ***Remove*** .... Labor ....7.43 ► Pine components with stain-grade panel door, spring loaded, heavy duty side rails and treads.	ea	$7.43	$1,041.00	$1,048.43
Remove disappearing attic stairs for work, then reinstall ***Replace*** .... Labor.........139.00	ea	—	$139.00	$139.00
Pine stair balustrade with 1-1/2" balusters ***Replace*** Materials......25.90 Labor..........54.90 ***Remove*** .... Labor 1.46	lf	$1.46	$80.80	$82.26
Pine stair balustrade with 1-1/2" fluted balusters ***Replace*** Materials......31.00 Labor..........54.90 ***Remove*** .... Labor 1.46	lf	$1.46	$85.90	$87.36

RELATED ITEMS

Columns........................71
Finish Carpentry..........199
porch posts...................231
Rough Carpentry........409
exterior deck stairs.........430

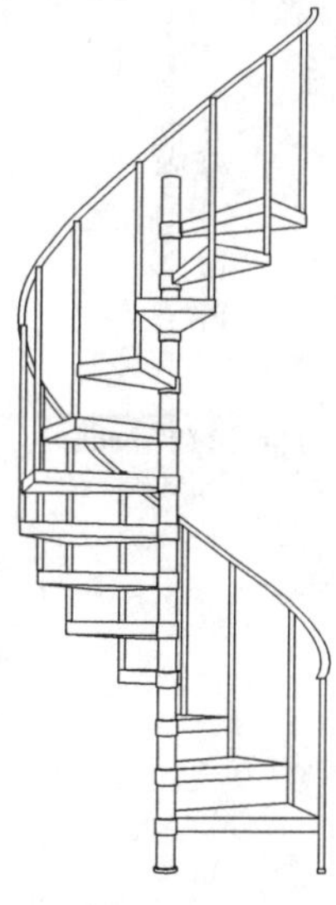

◄ **DISAPPEARING ATTIC STAIRS**
Fold-up attic access stairs with side rails.

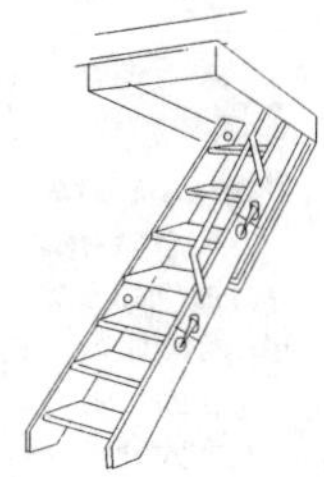

◁ **remove & reinstall**

◄ **PINE STAIR BALUSTRADE**
*Includes newel post. Add **9%** for red oak rail and newel in pine balustrade. Add **85%** for installation on curved stair. Deduct **10%** for balustrade installed on porch or other level application.*

	Item Description	Unit	Remove	Replace	Total
PINE STAIR ▶ BALUSTRADE *continued*	**Pine stair balustrade with 1-1/2" spiral balusters** ***Replace*** Materials......48.20 Labor..........54.90 ***Remove*** .... Labor............1.46	lf	$1.46	$103.10	$104.56
with 2-1/2" balusters ▷ 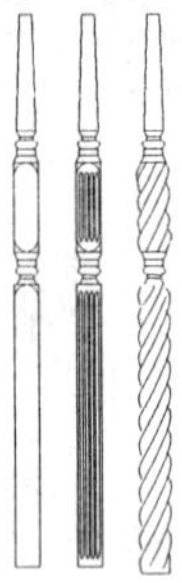	**Pine stair balustrade with 2-1/2" balusters** ***Replace*** Materials......29.20 Labor..........55.30 ***Remove*** .... Labor............1.46	lf	$1.46	$84.50	$85.96
	Pine stair balustrade with 2-1/2" fluted balusters ***Replace*** Materials......35.00 Labor..........55.30 ***Remove*** .... Labor............1.46	lf	$1.46	$90.30	$91.76
	Pine stair balustrade with 2-1/2" spiral balusters ***Replace*** Materials......54.30 Labor..........55.30 ***Remove*** .... Labor............1.46	lf	$1.46	$109.60	$111.06
with 3-1/2" balusters ▷	**Pine stair balustrade with 3-1/2" balusters** ***Replace*** Materials......35.60 Labor..........56.20 ***Remove*** .... Labor............1.46	lf	$1.46	$91.80	$93.26
	Pine stair balustrade with 3-1/2" fluted balusters ***Replace*** Materials......42.70 Labor..........56.20 ***Remove*** .... Labor............1.46	lf	$1.46	$98.90	$100.36
	Pine stair balustrade with 3-1/2" spiral balusters ***Replace*** Materials......66.30 Labor..........56.20 ***Remove*** .... Labor............1.46	lf	$1.46	$122.50	$123.96
with 5-1/2" balusters ▷	**Pine stair balustrade with 5-1/2" balusters** ***Replace*** Materials......56.60 Labor..........58.70 ***Remove*** .... Labor............1.46	lf	$1.46	$115.30	$116.76
	Pine stair balustrade with 5-1/2" fluted balusters ***Replace*** Materials......66.90 Labor..........58.70 ***Remove*** .... Labor............1.46	lf	$1.46	$125.60	$127.06
	Pine stair balustrade with 5-1/2" spiral balusters ***Replace*** Materials....100.10 Labor..........58.70 ***Remove*** .... Labor............1.46	lf	$1.46	$158.80	$160.26
POPLAR STAIR ▶ BALUSTRADE *Includes newel post. Add **9%** for red oak rail and newel in poplar balustrade. Add **85%** for installation on curved stair. Deduct **10%** for balustrade installed on porch or other level application.*	**Poplar stair balustrade with 1-1/2" balusters** ***Replace*** Materials......42.90 Labor..........54.90 ***Remove*** .... Labor............1.46	lf	$1.46	$97.80	$99.26
	Poplar stair balustrade with 1-1/2" fluted balusters ***Replace*** Materials......52.00 Labor..........54.90 ***Remove*** .... Labor............1.46	lf	$1.46	$106.90	$108.36
	Poplar stair balustrade with 1-1/2" spiral balusters ***Replace*** Materials......82.40 Labor..........54.90 ***Remove*** .... Labor............1.46	lf	$1.46	$137.30	$138.76
with 2-1/2" balusters ▷	**Poplar stair balustrade with 2-1/2" balusters** ***Replace*** Materials......48.50 Labor..........55.30 ***Remove*** .... Labor............1.46	lf	$1.46	$103.80	$105.26
	Poplar stair balustrade with 2-1/2" fluted balusters ***Replace*** Materials......58.80 Labor..........55.30 ***Remove*** .... Labor............1.46	lf	$1.46	$114.10	$115.56
	Poplar stair balustrade with 2-1/2" spiral balusters ***Replace*** Materials......92.80 Labor..........55.30 ***Remove*** .... Labor............1.46	lf	$1.46	$148.10	$149.56

Item Description	Unit	Remove	Replace	Total	
Poplar stair balustrade with 3-1/2" balusters ***Replace*** Materials......59.00 Labor..........56.20 ***Remove***........................ Labor............1.46	lf	$1.46	$115.20	$116.66	◁ **with 3-1/2" balusters**
Poplar stair balustrade with 3-1/2" fluted balusters ***Replace*** Materials......71.50 Labor..........56.20 ***Remove***........................ Labor............1.46	lf	$1.46	$127.70	$129.16	
Poplar stair balustrade with 3-1/2" spiral balusters ***Replace*** Materials.....113.00 Labor..........56.20 ***Remove***........................ Labor............1.46	lf	$1.46	$169.20	$170.66	
Poplar stair balustrade with 5-1/2" balusters ***Replace*** Materials......92.40 Labor..........58.70 ***Remove***........................ Labor............1.46	lf	$1.46	$151.10	$152.56	◁ **with 5-1/2" balusters**
Poplar stair balustrade with 5-1/2" fluted balusters ***Replace*** Materials.....110.00 Labor..........58.70 ***Remove***........................ Labor............1.46	lf	$1.46	$168.70	$170.16	
Poplar stair balustrade with 5-1/2" spiral balusters ***Replace*** Materials.....169.00 Labor..........58.70 ***Remove***........................ Labor............1.46	lf	$1.46	$227.70	$229.16	
Redwood stair balustrade with 1-1/2" balusters ***Replace*** Materials......47.90 Labor..........54.90 ***Remove***........................ Labor............1.46	lf	$1.46	$102.80	$104.26	◀ **REDWOOD STAIR BALUSTRADE** *Includes newel post. Add **85%** for installation on curved stair. Deduct **10%** for balustrade installed on porch or other level application.*
Redwood stair balustrade with 1-1/2" fluted balusters ***Replace*** Materials......57.90 Labor..........54.90 ***Remove***........................ Labor............1.46	lf	$1.46	$112.80	$114.26	
Redwood stair balustrade with 1-1/2" spiral balusters ***Replace*** Materials......91.70 Labor..........54.90 ***Remove***........................ Labor............1.46	lf	$1.46	$146.60	$148.06	
Redwood stair balustrade with 2-1/2" balusters ***Replace*** Materials......54.00 Labor..........55.30 ***Remove***........................ Labor............1.46	lf	$1.46	$109.30	$110.76	◁ **with 2-1/2" balusters**
Redwood stair balustrade with 2-1/2" fluted balusters ***Replace*** Materials......65.50 Labor..........55.30 ***Remove***........................ Labor............1.46	lf	$1.46	$120.80	$122.26	
Redwood stair balustrade with 2-1/2" spiral balusters ***Replace*** Materials....103.40 Labor..........55.30 ***Remove***........................ Labor............1.46	lf	$1.46	$158.70	$160.16	
Redwood stair balustrade with 3-1/2" balusters ***Replace*** Materials......65.70 Labor..........56.20 ***Remove***........................ Labor............1.46	lf	$1.46	$121.90	$123.36	◁ **with 3-1/2" balusters**
Redwood stair balustrade with 3-1/2" fluted balusters ***Replace*** Materials......79.80 Labor..........56.20 ***Remove***........................ Labor............1.46	lf	$1.46	$136.00	$137.46	
Redwood stair balustrade with 3-1/2" spiral balusters ***Replace*** Materials.....126.00 Labor..........56.20 ***Remove***........................ Labor............1.46	lf	$1.46	$182.20	$183.66	
Redwood stair balustrade with 5-1/2" balusters ***Replace*** Materials....103.20 Labor..........58.70 ***Remove***........................ Labor............1.46	lf	$1.46	$161.90	$163.36	◁ **with 5-1/2" balusters**

RELATED ITEMS

Columns........................71
Finish Carpentry..........199
porch posts....................231
Rough Carpentry........409
exterior deck stairs.........430

	Item Description	Unit	Remove	Replace	Total
Redwood stair balustrade *continued* ▶	**Redwood stair balustrade with 5-1/2" fluted balusters** *Replace* Materials.....123.00 Labor..........58.70 *Remove*......................... Labor............1.46	lf	$1.46	$181.70	$183.16
	Redwood stair balustrade with 5-1/2" spiral balusters *Replace* Materials....188.00 Labor..........58.70 *Remove*......................... Labor............1.46	lf	$1.46	$246.70	$248.16
Red oak stair balustrade ▶ *Includes newel post. Add **85%** for installation on curved stair. Deduct **10%** for balustrade installed on porch or other level application.*	**Red oak stair balustrade with 1-1/2" balusters** *Replace* Materials......60.50 Labor..........54.90 *Remove*......................... Labor............1.46	lf	$1.46	$115.40	$116.86
	Red oak stair balustrade with 1-1/2" fluted balusters *Replace* Materials......73.10 Labor..........54.90 *Remove*......................... Labor............1.46	lf	$1.46	$128.00	$129.46
	Red oak stair balustrade with 1-1/2" spiral balusters *Replace* Materials.....114.00 Labor..........54.90 *Remove*......................... Labor............1.46	lf	$1.46	$168.90	$170.36
	Red oak stair balustrade with 1-1/2" hand-carved balusters *Replace* Materials....231.00 Labor..........54.90 *Remove*......................... Labor............1.46	lf	$1.46	$285.90	$287.36
	Red oak stair balustrade with 1-1/2" heavy hand-carved balusters *Replace* Materials.....249.00 Labor..........54.90 *Remove*......................... Labor............1.46	lf	$1.46	$303.90	$305.36
with 2-1/2" balusters ▷	**Red oak stair balustrade with 2-1/2" balusters** *Replace* Materials......68.10 Labor...........55.30 *Remove*......................... Labor............1.46	lf	$1.46	$123.40	$124.86
	Red oak stair balustrade with 2-1/2" fluted balusters *Replace* Materials......81.90 Labor...........55.30 *Remove*......................... Labor............1.46	lf	$1.46	$137.20	$138.66
	Red oak stair balustrade with 2-1/2" spiral balusters *Replace* Materials.....128.00 Labor...........55.30 *Remove*......................... Labor............1.46	lf	$1.46	$183.30	$184.76
	Red oak stair balustrade with 2-1/2" hand-carved balusters *Replace* Materials....235.00 Labor...........55.30 *Remove*......................... Labor............1.46	lf	$1.46	$290.30	$291.76
	Red oak stair balustrade with 2-1/2" heavy hand-carved balusters *Replace* Materials....253.00 Labor...........55.30 *Remove*......................... Labor............1.46	lf	$1.46	$308.30	$309.76
with 3-1/2" balusters ▷	**Red oak stair balustrade with 3-1/2" balusters** *Replace* Materials......83.00 Labor..........56.20 *Remove*......................... Labor............1.46	lf	$1.46	$139.20	$140.66
	Red oak stair balustrade with 3-1/2" fluted balusters *Replace* Materials......99.80 Labor..........56.20 *Remove*......................... Labor............1.46	lf	$1.46	$156.00	$157.46
	Red oak stair balustrade with 3-1/2" spiral balusters *Replace* Materials.....155.00 Labor..........56.20 *Remove*......................... Labor............1.46	lf	$1.46	$211.20	$212.66
	Red oak stair balustrade with 3-1/2" hand-carved balusters *Replace* Materials....287.00 Labor..........56.20 *Remove*......................... Labor............1.46	lf	$1.46	$343.20	$344.66

Item Description	Unit	Remove	Replace	Total
Red oak stair balustrade with 3-1/2" heavy hand-carved balusters ***Replace*** Materials.....312.00 Labor..........56.20 ***Remove*** .... Labor............1.46	lf	$1.46	$368.20	$369.66
Red oak stair balustrade with 5-1/2" balusters ***Replace*** Materials.....131.00 Labor..........58.70 ***Remove*** .... Labor............1.46	lf	$1.46	$189.70	$191.16
Red oak stair balustrade with 5-1/2" fluted balusters ***Replace*** Materials.....156.00 Labor..........58.70 ***Remove*** .... Labor............1.46	lf	$1.46	$214.70	$216.16
Red oak stair balustrade with 5-1/2" spiral balusters ***Replace*** Materials....235.00 Labor..........58.70 ***Remove*** .... Labor............1.46	lf	$1.46	$293.70	$295.16
Red oak stair balustrade with 5-1/2" hand-carved balusters ***Replace*** Materials....281.00 Labor..........58.70 ***Remove*** .... Labor............1.46	lf	$1.46	$339.70	$341.16
Red oak stair balustrade with 5-1/2" heavy hand-carved balusters ***Replace*** Materials.....310.00 Labor..........58.70 ***Remove*** .... Labor............1.46	lf	$1.46	$368.70	$370.16
Pine stair balustrade with sawn balusters ***Replace*** Materials......43.20 Labor..........54.90 ***Remove*** .... Labor............1.46	lf	$1.46	$98.10	$99.56
Pine stair balustrade with sawn baluster panels ***Replace*** Materials......73.20 Labor..........54.90 ***Remove*** .... Labor............1.46	lf	$1.46	$128.10	$129.56
Poplar stair balustrade with sawn balusters ***Replace*** Materials......59.00 Labor..........54.90 ***Remove*** .... Labor............1.46	lf	$1.46	$113.90	$115.36
Poplar stair balustrade with sawn baluster panels ***Replace*** Materials......89.60 Labor..........54.90 ***Remove*** .... Labor............1.46	lf	$1.46	$144.50	$145.96
Add for red oak rail & newel in paint-grade sawn stair balustrade ***Replace*** Materials......12.00	lf	—	$12.00	$12.00
Redwood stair balustrade with sawn balusters ***Replace*** Materials......90.40 Labor..........54.90 ***Remove*** .... Labor............1.46	lf	$1.46	$145.30	$146.76
Redwood stair balustrade with sawn baluster panels ***Replace*** Materials....143.00 Labor..........54.90 ***Remove*** .... Labor............1.46	lf	$1.46	$197.90	$199.36
Red oak stair balustrade with sawn balusters ***Replace*** Materials......80.20 Labor..........54.90 ***Remove*** .... Labor............1.46	lf	$1.46	$135.10	$136.56
Red oak stair balustrade with sawn baluster panels ***Replace*** Materials.....120.00 Labor..........54.90 ***Remove*** .... Labor............1.46	lf	$1.46	$174.90	$176.36
Remove stair balustrade for work, then reinstall ***Replace*** .... Labor..........99.00	lf	—	$99.00	$99.00

◁ **with 5-1/2" balusters**

◀ **SAWN STAIR BALUSTRADE**
Includes newel post
*Deduct **10%** for balustrade installed on porch or other level application.*

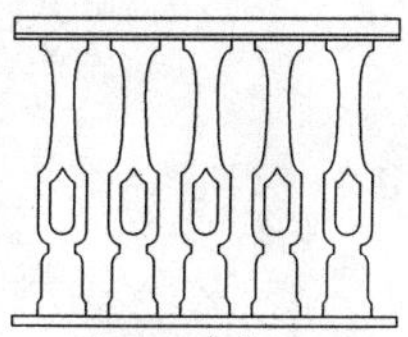

△ *sawn balusters*

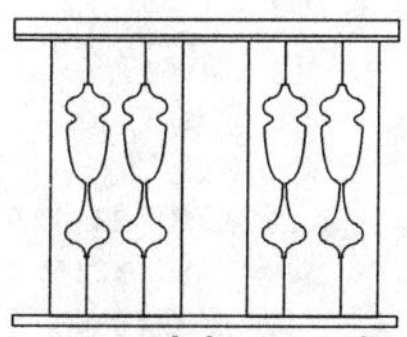

△ *sawn baluster panels*

RELATED ITEMS

Columns.........................71
Finish Carpentry..........199
porch posts....................231
Rough Carpentry........409
exterior deck stairs.........430

◀ **REMOVE & REINSTALL BALUSTRADE**

	Item Description		Unit	Remove	Replace	Total
Additional balustrade costs ▶	**Add for volute end** *Replace* Materials.....245.00 Labor.........126.00 ▶ Oak, poplar, or pine. Includes additional balusters and labor to install volute end with circled balusters and newel. Usually not used on stairs with balusters larger than 2-1/2".		ea	—	$371.00	$371.00
	Add for goose neck *Replace* Materials....280.00 Labor.........102.00 ▶ Oak, poplar, or pine.	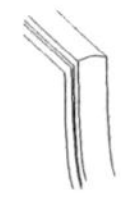	ea	—	$382.00	$382.00
	Add for 1/4 turn in stair rail *Replace* Materials......86.60 Labor...........94.40 ▶ Oak, poplar, or pine. 90 degree turn slopes up on one side and down on the other.		ea	—	$181.00	$181.00
	Add for 1/2 turn in stair rail *Replace* Materials.....198.00 Labor.........102.00 ▶ Oak, poplar, or pine. 180 degree turn slopes up on one side and down on the other.		ea	—	$300.00	$300.00
Stair bracket ▶ *Brackets installed beneath open end of tread.*	**Stair bracket, standard grade** *Replace* Materials........9.66 Labor............3.79 *Remove*......................... Labor............1.49 ▶ Paint-grade. No inside pattern.	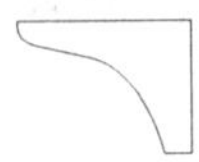	ea	$1.49	$13.45	$14.94
	Stair bracket, high grade *Replace* Materials.......11.30 Labor............3.79 *Remove*......................... Labor............1.49 ▶ Poplar or red oak. Simple inside pattern.		ea	$1.49	$15.09	$16.58
	Stair bracket, deluxe grade *Replace* Materials.......13.50 Labor............3.79 *Remove*......................... Labor............1.49 ▶ Poplar or red oak. Ornate inside pattern.		ea	$1.49	$17.29	$18.78
	Stair bracket, custom grade *Replace* Materials.......15.10 Labor............3.79 *Remove*......................... Labor............1.49 ▶ Poplar or red oak. Very ornate inside pattern.	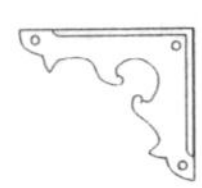	ea	$1.49	$18.89	$20.38
	Remove stair bracket for work, then reinstall *Replace* .... Labor............6.20		ea	—	$6.20	$6.20
Stair tread trim ▶ *Up to 3/4" cove, quarter-round, cove, or similar installed beneath the open end of the tread.*	**Pine molding trim beneath tread** *Replace* Materials .... .56 Labor............4.49 *Remove*......................... Labor............ .52		ea	$.52	$5.05	$5.57
	Red oak molding trim beneath tread *Replace* Materials .... .88 Labor............4.49 *Remove*......................... Labor............ .52		ea	$.52	$5.37	$5.89
Pine newel ▶ **for 1-1/2" balusters** ▷ *newel is 3-1/2" to 4" wide*	**Pine newel post for 1-1/2" balusters** *Replace* Materials......44.20 Labor..........40.00 *Remove*......................... Labor............5.17		ea	$5.17	$84.20	$89.37
	Pine fluted newel post for 1-1/2" balusters *Replace* Materials......58.60 Labor..........40.00 *Remove*......................... Labor............5.17		ea	$5.17	$98.60	$103.77
	Pine spiral newel post for 1-1/2" balusters *Replace* Materials......60.00 Labor..........40.00 *Remove*......................... Labor............5.17		ea	$5.17	$100.00	$105.17

Item Description	Unit	Remove	Replace	Total	
Pine newel post for 2-1/2″ balusters *Replace* Materials......53.00 Labor..........40.00 *Remove*........................ Labor............5.17	ea	$5.17	$93.00	$98.17	◁ **for 2-1/2″ balusters** *newel is 4″ to 4-1/2″ wide.*
Pine fluted newel post for 2-1/2″ balusters *Replace* Materials......70.30 Labor..........40.00 *Remove*........................ Labor............5.17	ea	$5.17	$110.30	$115.47	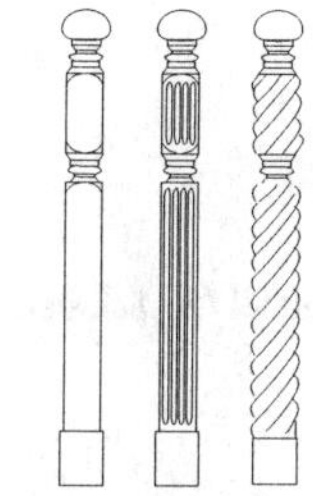
Pine spiral newel post for 2-1/2″ balusters *Replace* Materials......72.10 Labor..........40.00 *Remove*........................ Labor............5.17	ea	$5.17	$112.10	$117.27	
Pine newel post for 3-1/2″ balusters *Replace* Materials......63.60 Labor..........40.00 *Remove*........................ Labor............5.17	ea	$5.17	$103.60	$108.77	◁ **for 3-1/2″ balusters** *newel is 4-1/2″ to 5″ wide.*
Pine fluted newel post for 3-1/2″ balusters *Replace* Materials......84.40 Labor..........40.00 *Remove*........................ Labor............5.17	ea	$5.17	$124.40	$129.57	
Pine spiral newel post for 3-1/2″ balusters *Replace* Materials......86.60 Labor..........40.00 *Remove*........................ Labor............5.17	ea	$5.17	$126.60	$131.77	
Pine newel post for 5-1/2″ balusters *Replace* Materials....100.80 Labor..........40.00 *Remove*........................ Labor............5.17	ea	$5.17	$140.80	$145.97	◁ **for 5-1/2″ balusters** *newel is 6″ to 7″ wide.*
Pine fluted newel post for 5-1/2″ balusters *Replace* Materials....134.00 Labor..........40.00 *Remove*........................ Labor............5.17	ea	$5.17	$174.00	$179.17	
Pine spiral newel post for 5-1/2″ balusters *Replace* Materials.....137.00 Labor..........40.00 *Remove*........................ Labor............5.17	ea	$5.17	$177.00	$182.17	
Poplar newel post for 1-1/2″ balusters *Replace* Materials......73.60 Labor..........40.00 *Remove*........................ Labor............5.17	ea	$5.17	$113.60	$118.77	◀ **POPLAR NEWEL** ◁ **for 1-1/2″ balusters** *newel is 3-1/2″ to 4″ wide.*
Poplar fluted newel post for 1-1/2″ balusters *Replace* Materials......97.70 Labor..........40.00 *Remove*........................ Labor............5.17	ea	$5.17	$137.70	$142.87	
Poplar spiral newel post for 1-1/2″ balusters *Replace* Materials....100.00 Labor..........40.00 *Remove*........................ Labor............5.17	ea	$5.17	$140.00	$145.17	
Poplar newel post for 2-1/2″ balusters *Replace* Materials......88.30 Labor..........40.00 *Remove*........................ Labor............5.17	ea	$5.17	$128.30	$133.47	◁ **for 2-1/2″ balusters** *newel is 4″ to 4-1/2″ wide.*
Poplar fluted newel post for 2-1/2″ balusters *Replace* Materials.....117.00 Labor..........40.00 *Remove*........................ Labor............5.17	ea	$5.17	$157.00	$162.17	
Poplar spiral newel post for 2-1/2″ balusters *Replace* Materials.....120.00 Labor..........40.00 *Remove*........................ Labor............5.17	ea	$5.17	$160.00	$165.17	
Poplar newel post for 3-1/2″ balusters *Replace* Materials....106.00 Labor..........40.00 *Remove*........................ Labor............5.17	ea	$5.17	$146.00	$151.17	◁ **for 3-1/2″ balusters** *newel is 4-1/2″ to 5″ wide.*

RELATED ITEMS

Columns............................71
Finish Carpentry..........199
porch posts...................231
Rough Carpentry........409
exterior deck stairs.........430

	Item Description	Unit	Remove	Replace	Total
POPLAR NEWEL ► *continued*	**Poplar fluted newel post for 3-1/2" balusters** ***Replace*** Materials.....141.00 Labor..........40.00 ***Remove***.......................... Labor............5.17	ea	$5.17	$181.00	$186.17
	Poplar spiral newel post for 3-1/2" balusters ***Replace*** Materials....144.00 Labor..........40.00 ***Remove***.......................... Labor............5.17	ea	$5.17	$184.00	$189.17
for 5-1/2" balusters ▷ *newel is 6" to 8" wide*	**Poplar newel post for 5-1/2" balusters** ***Replace*** Materials.....168.00 Labor..........40.00 ***Remove***.......................... Labor............5.17	ea	$5.17	$208.00	$213.17
	Poplar fluted newel post for 5-1/2" balusters ***Replace*** Materials....223.00 Labor..........40.00 ***Remove***.......................... Labor............5.17	ea	$5.17	$263.00	$268.17
	Poplar spiral newel post for 5-1/2" balusters ***Replace*** Materials....229.00 Labor..........40.00 ***Remove***.......................... Labor............5.17	ea	$5.17	$269.00	$274.17
REDWOOD NEWEL ► **for 1-1/2" balusters ▷** *newel is 3-1/2" to 4" wide*	**Redwood newel post for 1-1/2" balusters** ***Replace*** Materials......83.00 Labor..........40.00 ***Remove***.......................... Labor............5.17	ea	$5.17	$123.00	$128.17
	Redwood fluted newel post for 1-1/2" balusters ***Replace*** Materials.....110.00 Labor..........40.00 ***Remove***.......................... Labor............5.17	ea	$5.17	$150.00	$155.17
	Redwood spiral newel post for 1-1/2" balusters ***Replace*** Materials.....113.00 Labor..........40.00 ***Remove***.......................... Labor............5.17	ea	$5.17	$153.00	$158.17
for 2-1/2" balusters ▷ *newel is 4" to 4-1/2" wide*	**Redwood newel post for 2-1/2" balusters** ***Replace*** Materials......99.50 Labor..........40.00 ***Remove***.......................... Labor............5.17	ea	$5.17	$139.50	$144.67
	Redwood fluted newel post for 2-1/2" balusters ***Replace*** Materials.....132.00 Labor..........40.00 ***Remove***.......................... Labor............5.17	ea	$5.17	$172.00	$177.17
	Redwood spiral newel post for 2-1/2" balusters ***Replace*** Materials.....136.00 Labor..........40.00 ***Remove***.......................... Labor............5.17	ea	$5.17	$176.00	$181.17
for 3-1/2" balusters ▷ *newel is 4-1/2" to 5" wide.*	**Redwood newel post for 3-1/2" balusters** ***Replace*** Materials.....119.00 Labor..........40.00 ***Remove***.......................... Labor............5.17	ea	$5.17	$159.00	$164.17
	Redwood fluted newel post for 3-1/2" balusters ***Replace*** Materials.....159.00 Labor..........40.00 ***Remove***.......................... Labor............5.17	ea	$5.17	$199.00	$204.17
	Redwood spiral newel post for 3-1/2" balusters ***Replace*** Materials.....163.00 Labor..........40.00 ***Remove***.......................... Labor............5.17	ea	$5.17	$203.00	$208.17
for 5-1/2" balusters ▷ *newel is 6" to 8" wide*	**Redwood newel post for 5-1/2" balusters** ***Replace*** Materials.....190.00 Labor..........40.00 ***Remove***.......................... Labor............5.17	ea	$5.17	$230.00	$235.17
	Redwood fluted newel post for 5-1/2" balusters ***Replace*** Materials....252.00 Labor..........40.00 ***Remove***.......................... Labor............5.17	ea	$5.17	$292.00	$297.17

Item Description	Unit	Remove	Replace	Total
Redwood spiral newel post for 5-1/2" balusters ***Replace*** Materials....258.00 Labor..........40.00 ***Remove***......................... Labor............5.17	ea	$5.17	$298.00	$303.17
Red oak newel post for 1-1/2" balusters ***Replace*** Materials....108.00 Labor..........40.00 ***Remove***......................... Labor............5.17	ea	$5.17	$148.00	$153.17
Red oak fluted newel post for 1-1/2" balusters ***Replace*** Materials....144.00 Labor..........40.00 ***Remove***......................... Labor............5.17	ea	$5.17	$184.00	$189.17
Red oak spiral newel post for 1-1/2" balusters ***Replace*** Materials.....147.00 Labor..........40.00 ***Remove***......................... Labor............5.17	ea	$5.17	$187.00	$192.17
Red oak hand-carved newel post for 1-1/2" balusters ***Replace*** Materials.....198.00 Labor..........40.00 ***Remove***......................... Labor............5.17	ea	$5.17	$238.00	$243.17
Red oak heavy hand-carved newel post for 1-1/2" balusters ***Replace*** Materials.....213.00 Labor..........40.00 ***Remove***......................... Labor............5.17	ea	$5.17	$253.00	$258.17
Red oak newel post for 2-1/2" balusters ***Replace*** Materials.....123.00 Labor..........40.00 ***Remove***......................... Labor............5.17	ea	$5.17	$163.00	$168.17
Red oak fluted newel post for 2-1/2" balusters ***Replace*** Materials.....163.00 Labor..........40.00 ***Remove***......................... Labor............5.17	ea	$5.17	$203.00	$208.17
Red oak spiral newel post for 2-1/2" balusters ***Replace*** Materials.....167.00 Labor..........40.00 ***Remove***......................... Labor............5.17	ea	$5.17	$207.00	$212.17
Red oak hand-carved newel post for 2-1/2" balusters ***Replace*** Materials....225.00 Labor..........40.00 ***Remove***......................... Labor............5.17	ea	$5.17	$265.00	$270.17
Red oak heavy hand-carved newel post for 2-1/2" balusters ***Replace*** Materials.....242.00 Labor..........40.00 ***Remove***......................... Labor............5.17	ea	$5.17	$282.00	$287.17
Red oak newel post for 3-1/2" balusters ***Replace*** Materials ....148.00 Labor..........40.00 ***Remove***......................... Labor............5.17	ea	$5.17	$188.00	$193.17
Red oak fluted newel post for 3-1/2" balusters ***Replace*** Materials.....196.00 Labor..........40.00 ***Remove***......................... Labor............5.17	ea	$5.17	$236.00	$241.17
Red oak spiral newel post for 3-1/2" balusters ***Replace*** Materials....200.00 Labor..........40.00 ***Remove***......................... Labor............5.17	ea	$5.17	$240.00	$245.17
Red oak hand-carved newel post for 3-1/2" balusters ***Replace*** Materials.....245.00 Labor..........40.00 ***Remove***......................... Labor............5.17	ea	$5.17	$285.00	$290.17
Red oak heavy hand-carved newel post for 3-1/2" balusters ***Replace*** Materials ....262.00 Labor..........40.00 ***Remove***......................... Labor............5.17	ea	$5.17	$302.00	$307.17

◄ **RED OAK NEWEL**

◁ **for 1-1/2" balusters** *newel is 3-1/2" to 4" wide.*

◁ **for 2-1/2" balusters** *newel is 4" to 4-1/2" wide.*

◁ **for 3-1/2" balusters** *newel is 4-1/2" to 5" wide.*

RELATED ITEMS

Red oak newel ► *continued*

for 5-1/2" balusters ▷ *newel is 6" to 8" wide*

Item Description	Unit	Remove	Replace	Total
Red oak newel post for 5-1/2" balusters *Replace* Materials....235.00 Labor..........40.00 *Remove*........................ Labor............5.17	ea	$5.17	$275.00	$280.17
Red oak fluted newel post for 5-1/2" balusters *Replace* Materials.....311.00 Labor..........40.00 *Remove*........................ Labor............5.17	ea	$5.17	$351.00	$356.17
Red oak spiral newel post for 5-1/2" balusters *Replace* Materials.....318.00 Labor..........40.00 *Remove*........................ Labor............5.17	ea	$5.17	$358.00	$363.17
Red oak hand-carved newel post for 5-1/2" balusters *Replace* Materials....437.00 Labor..........40.00 *Remove*........................ Labor............5.17	ea	$5.17	$477.00	$482.17
Red oak heavy hand-carved newel post for 5-1/2" balusters *Replace* Materials....469.00 Labor..........40.00 *Remove*........................ Labor............5.17	ea	$5.17	$509.00	$514.17
Remove newel post for work, then reinstall *Replace* .... Labor..........58.70	ea	—	$58.70	$58.70

Add for other wood species ► *Add to the cost of poplar stair components.*

Item Description	Unit	Remove	Replace	Total
Add 24% for mahogany				
Add 43% for cherry				
Add 11% for maple				
Add 2% for birch				

Time & Material Charts *(selected items)*

Stairs Materials

*See **Stairs** material prices with the line items and waste information in the **QuickFinder** column.*

Stairs Labor

Laborer	Base Wage	Paid Leave	True Wage	FICA	FUTA	Worker's Comp.	Unemploy. Insur.	Health Insur.	Retire (401k)	Liability Insur.	Cost per Hour
Carpenter	$23.60	1.84	$25.44	1.95	.20	4.96	2.21	2.69	.76	3.43	$41.60
Demolition laborer	$13.90	1.08	$14.98	1.15	.12	4.79	1.30	2.69	.45	2.02	$27.50

Paid Leave is calculated based on two weeks paid vacation, one week sick leave, and seven paid holidays. Employer's matching portion of **FICA** is 7.65 percent. **FUTA** (Federal Unemployment) is .8 percent. **Worker's compensation** for the stairs trade was calculated using a national average of 19.50 percent. **Unemployment insurance** was calculated using a national average of 8.7 percent. **Health insurance** was calculated based on a projected national average for 2002 of $535 per employee (and family when applicable) per month. Employer pays 80 percent for a per month cost of $428 per employee. **Retirement** is based on a 401(k) retirement program with employer matching of 50 percent. Employee contributions to the 401(k) plan are an average of 6 percent of the true wage. **Liability insurance** is based on a national average of 13.2 percent.

Stairs Labor Productivity

WORK DESCRIPTION	LABORER	COST PER HOUR	PRODUCTIVITY	UNIT PRICE
Demolition				
remove utility stairs	demolition laborer	$27.50	.101	**$2.78** st
remove stairs	demolition laborer	$27.50	.122	**$3.36** st
remove 1/4 turn stairs	demolition laborer	$27.50	.135	**$3.71** st
remove 1/2 turn stairs	demolition laborer	$27.50	.150	**$4.13** st
remove circular stairs	demolition laborer	$27.50	.158	**$4.35** st
remove spiral stairs	demolition laborer	$27.50	.123	**$3.38** st
remove disappearing attic stairs	demolition laborer	$27.50	.270	**$7.43** ea
remove stair balustrade	demolition laborer	$27.50	.053	**$1.46** lf
remove stair bracket	demolition laborer	$27.50	.054	**$1.49** ea
remove newel post	demolition laborer	$27.50	.188	**$5.17** ea
Build 3' wide stairs with three stringers				
utility stairs	finish carpenter	$41.60	.361	**$15.00** st
Build 3' wide straight stairs with four stringers				
3' wide enclosed	finish carpenter	$41.60	.474	**$19.70** st
3' wide, one side open	finish carpenter	$41.60	.485	**$20.20** st
3' wide , two sides open	finish carpenter	$41.60	.518	**$21.50** st
Build 3' wide 1/4 turn stairs with four stringers, 3' x 3' landing				
3' wide enclosed	finish carpenter	$41.60	.826	**$34.40** st
3' wide enclosed & oak plank on landing	finish carpenter	$41.60	1.02	**$42.40** st
3' wide, one side open	finish carpenter	$41.60	.855	**$35.60** st
3' wide, one side open & oak plank on landing	finish carpenter	$41.60	1.04	**$43.30** st
3' wide, two sides open	finish carpenter	$41.60	.885	**$36.80** st
3' wide, two sides open & oak plank on landing	finish carpenter	$41.60	1.05	**$43.70** st
Build 3' wide 1/2 turn stairs with four stringers, 6' x 3' landing				
3' wide enclosed	finish carpenter	$41.60	.909	**$37.80** st
3' wide enclosed with oak plank on landing	finish carpenter	$41.60	1.12	**$46.60** st
3' wide, one side open	finish carpenter	$41.60	.943	**$39.20** st
3' wide, one side open & oak plank on landing	finish carpenter	$41.60	1.15	**$47.80** st
3' wide, two sides open	finish carpenter	$41.60	.971	**$40.40** st
3' wide, two sides open & oak plank on landing	finish carpenter	$41.60	1.16	**$48.30** st
Additional stair costs				
add to build platform winders	finish carpenter	$41.60	.400	**$16.60** st
add to build mitered corner on bottom step	finish carpenter	$41.60	2.33	**$96.90** ea
add to install bull-nose starting step	finish carpenter	$41.60	.493	**$20.50** ea
Install false treads and risers				
closed end	finish carpenter	$41.60	.070	**$2.91** ea
open end	finish carpenter	$41.60	.090	**$3.74** ea
Build 3' wide circular stairs				
enclosed	finish carpenter	$41.60	11.6	**$483.00** st
one side open	finish carpenter	$41.60	11.8	**$491.00** st
two sides open	finish carpenter	$41.60	11.9	**$495.00** st
Install prefabricated spiral stairs				
all grades	finish carpenter	$41.60	.855	**$35.60** st
Install disappearing attic stairs				
all grades	finish carpenter	$41.60	2.38	**$99.00** ea
remove for work, then reinstall	finish carpenter	$41.60	3.33	**$139.00** ea
Install wood stair balustrade				
with 1-1/2" balusters	finish carpenter	$41.60	1.32	**$54.90** lf
with 2-1/2" balusters	finish carpenter	$41.60	1.33	**$55.30** lf
with 3-1/2" balusters	finish carpenter	$41.60	1.35	**$56.20** lf
with 5-1/2" balusters	finish carpenter	$41.60	1.41	**$58.70** lf
remove for work, then reinstall	finish carpenter	$41.60	2.38	**$99.00** lf
Install newel post				
install	finish carpenter	$41.60	.962	**$40.00** ea
remove for work, then reinstall	finish carpenter	$41.60	1.41	**$58.70** ea

✍ NOTES:

end

36 .... Suspended Ceilings

Item Description	Unit	Remove	Replace	Total	
12″ x 12″ concealed grid suspended ceiling tile, smooth face *Replace* Materials........1.14 Labor............ .64 *Remove* .... Labor............ .17	sf	$.17	$1.78	$1.95	◀ **12″ x 12″ TILE** *Prices are for tile and installation only. For concealed grid systems, see below.*
12″ x 12″ concealed grid suspended ceiling tile, fissured face *Replace* Materials........1.34 Labor............ .64 *Remove* .... Labor............ .17	sf	$.17	$1.98	$2.15	
12″ x 12″ concealed grid suspended ceiling tile, textured face *Replace* Materials........1.53 Labor............ .64 *Remove* .... Labor............ .17	sf	$.17	$2.17	$2.34	
12″ x 12″ concealed grid suspended ceiling tile, patterned face *Replace* Materials........1.65 Labor............ .64 *Remove* .... Labor............ .17	sf	$.17	$2.29	$2.46	
Grid for 12″ x 12″ concealed grid system *Replace* Materials........1.22 Labor............ .68 *Remove* .... Labor............ .17 ► Includes main runners, cross tees, wires, and eyelet screws. Does not include tiles.	sf	$.17	$1.90	$2.07	◀ **12″ x 12″ GRID**
Access panel in 12″ x 12″ concealed grid system *Replace* Materials......55.00 Labor...........24.10 *Remove* .... Labor...........2.60	ea	$2.60	$79.10	$81.70	
Re-level sagging 12″ x 12″ concealed suspended grid *Replace* Materials......... Labor............ .66	sf	—	$.66	$.66	◁ re-level
2′ x 4′ suspended ceiling tile, smooth face *Replace* Materials........ .49 Labor............ .32 *Remove* .... Labor............ .14	sf	$.14	$.81	$.95	◀ **2′ x 4′ TILES**
2′ x 4′ suspended ceiling tile, fissured face *Replace* Materials........ .65 Labor............ .32 *Remove* .... Labor............ .14	sf	$.14	$.97	$1.11	
2′ x 4′ suspended ceiling tile, textured face *Replace* Materials........ .86 Labor............ .32 *Remove* .... Labor............ .14	sf	$.14	$1.18	$1.32	
2′ x 4′ suspended ceiling tile, patterned face *Replace* Materials........1.10 Labor............ .32 *Remove* .... Labor............ .14	sf	$.14	$1.42	$1.56	
Add for fire-rated 2′ x 4′ suspended ceiling tile installed with clips *Replace* Materials........ .36 Labor............ .29	sf	—	$.65	$.65	◁ add for fire-rated tile
2′ x 4′ polystyrene cracked-ice or mist-white luminous panel *Replace* Materials........1.20 Labor............ .29 *Remove* .... Labor............ .14	sf	$.14	$1.49	$1.63	◀ **2′ x 4′ LUMINOUS PANEL**
2′ x 4′ acrylic cracked-ice or mist-white luminous panel *Replace* Materials........2.30 Labor............ .29 *Remove* .... Labor............ .14	sf	$.14	$2.59	$2.73	

RELATED ITEMS

Acoustic Ceilings............15
Drywall......................133
Electrical
drop-in fixtures..............166

	Item Description	Unit	Remove	Replace	Total
2' x 4' ▶ LUMINOUS PANEL *continued*	**2' x 4' polystyrene egg crate luminous panel** ***Replace*** Materials........1.17 Labor............ .29 ***Remove*** .... Labor............ .14	sf	$.14	$1.46	$1.60
	2' x 4' acrylic egg crate luminous panel ***Replace*** Materials........4.30 Labor............ .29 ***Remove*** .... Labor............ .14	sf	$.14	$4.59	$4.73
	2' x 4' acrylic egg crate luminous panel with stainless-steel finish ***Replace*** Materials........4.69 Labor............ .29 ***Remove*** .... Labor............ .14	sf	$.14	$4.98	$5.12
	2' x 4' acrylic egg crate luminous panel with brass finish ***Replace*** Materials........4.73 Labor............ .29 ***Remove*** .... Labor............ .14	sf	$.14	$5.02	$5.16
	2' x 4' square crate polystyrene luminous panel ***Replace*** Materials........1.15 Labor............ .29 ***Remove*** .... Labor............ .14	sf	$.14	$1.44	$1.58
	2' x 4' square crate acrylic luminous panel ***Replace*** Materials........4.04 Labor............ .29 ***Remove*** .... Labor............ .14	sf	$.14	$4.33	$4.47
	2' x 4' square crate acrylic luminous panel with stainless-steel finish ***Replace*** Materials........4.57 Labor............ .29 ***Remove*** .... Labor............ .14	sf	$.14	$4.86	$5.00
	2' x 4' square crate acrylic luminous panel with brass finish ***Replace*** Materials........4.62 Labor............ .29 ***Remove*** .... Labor............ .14	sf	$.14	$4.91	$5.05
2' x 4' GRID ▶ *Includes main runners 4' on center. Cross tees, wire, and eyelet screws. Does not include tiles or luminous panels.*	**2' x 4' suspended grid** ***Replace*** Materials........ .45 Labor............ .44 ***Remove*** .... Labor............ .11	sf	$.11	$.89	$1.00
	2' x 4' colored suspended grid ***Replace*** Materials........ .52 Labor............ .44 ***Remove*** .... Labor............ .11	sf	$.11	$.96	$1.07
	2' x 4' brass finish suspended grid ***Replace*** Materials........ .70 Labor............ .44 ***Remove*** .... Labor............ .11	sf	$.11	$1.14	$1.25
	2' x 4' stainless steel finish suspended grid ***Replace*** Materials........ .88 Labor............ .44 ***Remove*** .... Labor............ .11	sf	$.11	$1.32	$1.43
add for fire-rated grid ▷	**Add for fire-rated 2' x 4' suspended grid** ***Replace*** Materials........ .30	sf	—	$.30	$.30
2' x 4' ▶ NARROW GRID *Includes main runners 4' on center. Cross tees, wire, and eyelet screws. Does not include tiles or luminous panels.*	**2' x 4' narrow suspended grid** ***Replace*** Materials........ .49 Labor............ .44 ***Remove*** .... Labor............ .11	sf	$.11	$.93	$1.04
	2' x 4' colored narrow suspended grid ***Replace*** Materials........ .49 Labor............ .44 ***Remove*** .... Labor............ .11	sf	$.11	$.93	$1.04
	2' x 4' brass finish narrow suspended grid ***Replace*** Materials........ .86 Labor............ .44 ***Remove*** .... Labor............ .11	sf	$.11	$1.30	$1.41

Item Description	Unit	Remove	Replace	Total	
2′ x 4′ stainless steel finish narrow suspended grid *Replace* Materials........ .88 Labor............ .44 *Remove* .... Labor............ .11	sf	$.11	$1.32	$1.43	
Add for fire-rated 2′ x 4′ narrow suspended grid *Replace* Materials........ .34 Labor............ .44	sf	—	$.78	$.78	◁ add for fire-rated grid
Re-level sagging 2′ x 4′ suspended grid *Replace* .... Labor............ .47	sf	—	$.47	$.47	◀ RE-LEVEL 2′ x 4′ GRID
Remove 2′ x 4′ tiles for work, then reinstall *Replace* .... Labor............ .36	sf	—	$.36	$.36	◀ REMOVE 2′ x 4′ TILES & REINSTALL
Remove 2′ x 4′ tiles & blanket or insulation for work, then reinstall *Replace* .... Labor............ .44	sf	—	$.44	$.44	
2′ x 2′ suspended ceiling tile, smooth face *Replace* Materials........ .59 Labor............ .32 *Remove* .... Labor............ .11	sf	$.11	$.91	$1.02	◀ 2′ x 2′ TILES
2′ x 2′ suspended ceiling tile, fissured face *Replace* Materials...... 1.01 Labor............ .32 *Remove* .... Labor............ .11	sf	$.11	$1.33	$1.44	
2′ x 2′ suspended ceiling tile, textured face *Replace* Materials...... 1.03 Labor............ .32 *Remove* .... Labor............ .11	sf	$.11	$1.35	$1.46	
2′ x 2′ suspended ceiling tile, patterned face *Replace* Materials........1.32 Labor............ .32 *Remove* .... Labor............ .11	sf	$.11	$1.64	$1.75	
Add for fire-rated 2′ x 2′ suspended ceiling tile installed with clips *Replace* Materials........ .42 Labor............ .32	sf	—	$.74	$.74	◁ add for fire-rated tile
2′ x 2′ recessed edge suspended ceiling tile, smooth face *Replace* Materials........ .68 Labor............ .32 *Remove* .... Labor............ .11	sf	$.11	$1.00	$1.11	◀ RECESSED 2′ x 2′ TILES
2′ x 2′ recessed edge suspended ceiling tile, fissured face *Replace* Materials........ .89 Labor............ .32 *Remove* .... Labor............ .11	sf	$.11	$1.21	$1.32	
2′ x 2′ recessed edge suspended ceiling tile, textured face *Replace* Materials........1.18 Labor............ .32 *Remove* .... Labor............ .11	sf	$.11	$1.50	$1.61	
2′ x 2′ recessed edge suspended ceiling tile, patterned face *Replace* Materials........1.52 Labor............ .32 *Remove* .... Labor............ .11	sf	$.11	$1.84	$1.95	
Add for fire-rated 2′ x 2′ recessed edge tile installed with clips *Replace* Materials........ .03 Labor............ .32	sf	—	$.35	$.35	◁ add for fire-rated tile
2′ x 2′ polystyrene cracked-ice or mist-white luminous panel *Replace* Materials........1.43 Labor............ .17 *Remove* .... Labor............ .11	sf	$.11	$1.60	$1.71	◀ 2′ x 2′ LUMINOUS PANEL
2′ x 2′ acrylic cracked-ice or mist-white luminous panel *Replace* Materials........2.76 Labor............ .17 *Remove* .... Labor............ .11	sf	$.11	$2.93	$3.04	

RELATED ITEMS

Acoustic Ceilings............15
Drywall........................133
Electrical
drop in fixtures..............166

	Item Description	Unit	Remove	Replace	Total
2′ x 2′ ▶ LUMINOUS PANEL *continued*	**2′ x 2′ polystyrene egg crate luminous panel** *Replace* Materials........1.41 Labor............ .17 *Remove* .... Labor............ .11	sf	$.11	$1.58	$1.69
	2′ x 2′ acrylic egg crate luminous panel *Replace* Materials........5.16 Labor............ .17 *Remove* .... Labor............ .11	sf	$.11	$5.33	$5.44
	2′ x 2′ acrylic egg crate luminous panel with stainless steel finish *Replace* Materials........5.63 Labor............ .17 *Remove* .... Labor............ .11	sf	$.11	$5.80	$5.91
	2′ x 2′ acrylic egg crate luminous panel with brass finish *Replace* Materials........5.68 Labor............ .17 *Remove* .... Labor............ .11	sf	$.11	$5.85	$5.96
	2′ x 2′ square crate polystyrene luminous panel *Replace* Materials........1.38 Labor............ .17 *Remove* .... Labor............ .11	sf	$.11	$1.55	$1.66
	2′ x 2′ square crate acrylic luminous panel *Replace* Materials........4.84 Labor............ .17 *Remove* .... Labor............ .11	sf	$.11	$5.01	$5.12
	2′ x 2′ square crate acrylic luminous panel with stainless-steel finish *Replace* Materials........5.49 Labor............ .17 *Remove* .... Labor............ .11	sf	$.11	$5.66	$5.77
	2′ x 2′ square crate acrylic luminous panel with brass finish *Replace* Materials........5.55 Labor............ .17 *Remove* .... Labor............ .11	sf	$.11	$5.72	$5.83
2′ x 2′ GRID ▶ *Includes main runners 4′ on center. Cross tees, wire, and eyelet screws. Does not include tiles or luminous panels.*	**2′ x 2′ suspended grid** *Replace* Materials........ .73 Labor............ .44 *Remove* .... Labor............ .11	sf	$.11	$1.17	$1.28
	2′ x 2′ colored suspended grid *Replace* Materials........ .84 Labor............ .44 *Remove* .... Labor............ .11	sf	$.11	$1.28	$1.39
	2′ x 2′ brass finish suspended grid *Replace* Materials........1.05 Labor............ .44 *Remove* .... Labor............ .11	sf	$.11	$1.49	$1.60
	2′ x 2′ stainless steel finish suspended grid *Replace* Materials........1.11 Labor............ .44 *Remove* .... Labor............ .11	sf	$.11	$1.55	$1.66
add for fire-rated grid ▷	**Add for fire-rated 2′ x 2′ suspended grid** *Replace* Materials........ .61	sf	—	$.61	$.61
2′ x 2′ ▶ NARROW GRID *Includes main runners 4′ on center. Cross tees, wire, and eyelet screws. Does not include tiles or luminous panels.*	**2′ x 2′ narrow suspended grid** *Replace* Materials........ .77 Labor............ .44 *Remove* .... Labor............ .11	sf	$.11	$1.21	$1.32
	2′ x 2′ colored narrow suspended grid *Replace* Materials........ .78 Labor............ .44 *Remove* .... Labor............ .11	sf	$.11	$1.22	$1.33
	2′ x 2′ brass finish narrow suspended grid *Replace* Materials........1.05 Labor............ .44 *Remove* .... Labor............ .11	sf	$.11	$1.49	$1.60

Item Description	Unit	Remove	Replace	Total	
2′ x 2′ stainless steel finish suspended grid *Replace* Materials........1.36 Labor............ .44 *Remove* .... Labor............ .11	sf	$.11	$1.80	$1.91	
Add for fire-rated 2′ x 2′ narrow suspended grid *Replace* Materials........ .61	sf	—	$.61	$.61	◁ add for fire-rated grid
Re-level sagging 2′ x 2′ suspended grid *Replace* Materials......... Labor............ .54	sf	—	$.54	$.54	◀ **RE-LEVEL 2′ X 2′ GRID**
Remove 2′ x 2′ tiles for work, then reinstall *Replace* Materials......... Labor............ .39	sf	—	$.39	$.39	◀ **REMOVE 2′ X 2′ TILES & REINSTALL**
Remove 2′ x 2′ tiles & blanket for work, then reinstall *Replace* Materials......... Labor............ .47	sf	—	$.47	$.47	
Minimum charge for suspended ceiling work *Replace* Materials......52.00 Labor..........58.50	ea	—	$110.50	$110.50	◀ **MINIMUM CHARGE**
Suspended ceiling cold-air return panel *Replace* Materials......50.00 Labor..........20.20 *Remove* .... Labor...........3.71	ea	3.71	$70.20	$73.91	◀ **DROP-IN HVAC PANELS**
Suspended ceiling air diffuser panel *Replace* Materials......50.00 Labor..........20.20 *Remove* .... Labor...........3.71	ea	3.71	$70.20	$73.91	
2″ sound absorbing blanket above suspended grid system *Replace* Materials........ .41 labor............ .31 *Remove* .... Labor............ .22	sf	$.22	$.72	$.94	◀ **SOUND BLANKET** *Sound absorbing blanket installed above grid.*
3″ sound absorbing blanket above suspended grid system *Replace* Materials........ .64 labor............ .31 *Remove* .... Labor............ .25	sf	$.25	$.95	$1.20	

RELATED ITEMS

Acoustic Ceilings............15
Drywall..........................133
Electrical
drop in fixtures.............166

NOTES: ________________________________

________________________________ end

TIME & MATERIAL CHARTS *(selected items)*

Suspended Ceilings Materials

DESCRIPTION	PRICE	GROSS COVERAGE	WASTE	NET COVERAGE	UNIT PRICE
Suspended ceiling with concealed grid					
wall angle	$5.70 per 12′ stick	83	4%	79.68	**$.07** sf
main tee	$7.30 per 12′ stick	15.00	4%	14.40	**$.51** sf
cross tee (12″ x 12″ installation)	$.70 per 1′ stick	1.14	4%	1.09	**$.64** sf
Suspended ceiling grid baked enamel finish					
wall angle	$4.50 per 12′ stick	43.20	4%	41.47	**$.11** sf
main tee	$7.30 per 12′ stick	27.48	4%	26.38	**$.28** sf
cross tee in 2′ x 4′ installation	$2.40 per 4′ stick	41.60	4%	39.94	**$.06** sf
cross tee in 2′ x 2′ installation	$1.50 per 2′ stick	4.58	4%	4.40	**$.34** sf

. . . More ➢

Suspended Ceilings Materials *continued*

DESCRIPTION	MATERIAL PRICE	GROSS COVERAGE	WASTE	NET COVERAGE	UNIT PRICE
12" x 12" suspended tile for concealed grid system					
smooth face	**$1.08** per tile	1	5%	.95	**$1.14** sf
patterned face	**$1.57** per tile	1	5%	.95	**$1.65** sf
add for fire rating	**$.39** per tile	1	5%	.95	**$.41** sf
2' x 4' suspended tile					
smooth face	**$3.73** per tile	8	5%	7.6	**$.49** sf
patterned face	**$8.38** per tile	8	5%	7.6	**$1.10** sf
add for 2' x 4' tile with fire rating	**$2.44** per tile	8	5%	7.6	**$.32** sf
2' x 4' luminous panel					
polystyrene cracked-ice or mist-white	**$9.20** per panel	8	4%	7.68	**$1.20** sf
acrylic mist-white	**$17.70** per panel	8	4%	7.68	**$2.30** sf
polystyrene egg crate	**$9.00** per panel	8	4%	7.68	**$1.17** sf
acrylic egg crate	**$33.00** per panel	8	4%	7.68	**$4.30** sf
acrylic egg crate with stainless-steel finish	**$36.00** per panel	8	4%	7.68	**$4.69** sf
acrylic egg crate with brass finish	**$36.30** per panel	8	4%	7.68	**$4.73** sf

Suspended Ceiling Labor

LABORER	BASE WAGE	PAID LEAVE	TRUE WAGE	FICA	FUTA	WORKER'S COMP.	UNEMPLOY. INSUR.	HEALTH INSUR.	RETIRE (401K)	LIABILITY INSUR.	COST PER HOUR
Installer	$23.00	1.79	$24.79	1.90	.20	3.07	2.16	2.69	.74	3.35	**$38.90**
Installer's helper	$16.60	1.29	$17.89	1.37	.14	2.22	1.56	2.69	.54	2.42	**$28.80**
Demolition laborer	$13.90	1.08	$14.98	1.15	.12	4.79	1.30	2.69	.45	2.02	**$27.50**

Paid Leave is calculated based on two weeks paid vacation, one week sick leave, and seven paid holidays. Employer's matching portion of **FICA** is 7.65 percent. **FUTA** (Federal Unemployment) is .8 percent. **Worker's compensation** for the suspended ceilings trade was calculated using a national average of 12.40 percent. **Unemployment insurance** was calculated using a national average of 8.7 percent. **Health insurance** was calculated based on a projected national average for 2002 of $535 per employee (and family when applicable) per month. Employer pays 80 percent for a per month cost of $428 per employee. **Retirement** is based on a 401(k) retirement program with employer matching of 50 percent. Employee contributions to the 401(k) plan are an average of 6 percent of the true wage. **Liability insurance** is based on a national average of 13.2 percent.

Suspended Ceiling Labor Productivity

WORK DESCRIPTION	LABORER	COST PER HOUR	PRODUCTIVITY	UNIT PRICE
Demolition				
remove 2' x 4' ceiling tiles	demolition laborer	$27.50	.005	**$.14** sf
remove 2' x 4' suspended grid only	demolition laborer	$27.50	.004	**$.11** sf
remove 2' x 4' suspended tiles & grid	demolition laborer	$27.50	.009	**$.25** sf
remove 2' x 2' suspended tiles only	demolition laborer	$27.50	.004	**$.11** sf
remove 2' x 2' grid only	demolition laborer	$27.50	.004	**$.11** sf
remove 2' x 2' tiles & grid	demolition laborer	$27.50	.010	**$.28** sf
remove 12" x 12" ceiling tiles only	demolition laborer	$27.50	.006	**$.17** sf
remove 12" x 12" grid only	demolition laborer	$27.50	.006	**$.17** sf
remove 12" x 12" tiles & grid	demolition laborer	$27.50	.011	**$.30** sf
Suspended ceiling installation crew				
install suspended ceiling	installer	$38.90		
install suspended ceiling	installer's helper	$28.80		
install suspended ceiling	**installation crew**	$33.90		
Install 2' x 4' suspended ceiling				
grid only	installation crew	$33.90	.013	**$.44** sf
grid and tiles	installation crew	$33.90	.025	**$.85** sf
ceiling tiles only	installer's helper	$28.80	.011	**$.32** sf
luminous panels	installer's helper	$28.80	.010	**$.29** sf
Install 12" x 12" concealed suspended ceiling				
grid only	installation crew	$33.90	.020	**$.68** sf
grid and tiles	installation crew	$33.90	.038	**$1.29** sf
tiles only	installation crew	$33.90	.019	**$.64** sf

37 Swimming Pools

Item Description	Unit	Remove	Replace	Total	
Minimum charge for swimming pool work *Replace* Materials......36.60 Labor...........51.00	ea	—	$87.60	$87.60	◄ **Minimum**
Gunite swimming pool with plaster *Replace* Materials......27.20 Labor...........10.30 *Remove* .... Labor............6.74	sf	$6.74	$37.50	$44.24	◄ **Swimming pools** *Per square feet of walls and bottom of pool. Includes all equipment (average to high quality) and 6" x 6" tile border. Does not includes coping or deck.*
Concrete swimming pool with vinyl liner *Replace* Materials......18.80 Labor............8.43 *Remove* .... Labor............5.83	sf	$5.83	$27.23	$33.06	
Galvanized steel swimming pool with vinyl liner *Replace* Materials......16.20 Labor............6.86 *Remove* .... Labor............3.91	sf	$3.91	$23.06	$26.97	
Aluminum swimming pool with vinyl liner *Replace* Materials......16.30 Labor............7.16 *Remove* .... Labor............3.91	sf	$3.91	$23.46	$27.37	
Fiberglass swimming pool *Replace* Materials......25.20 Labor............8.84 *Remove* .... Labor............3.33	sf	$3.33	$34.04	$37.37	
Brick coping *Replace* Materials......14.60 Labor...........11.60 *Remove* .... Labor............1.38	lf	$1.38	$26.20	$27.58	◄ **Coping**
Precast concrete coping *Replace* Materials.......13.10 Labor...........10.00 *Remove* .... Labor............1.38	lf	$1.38	$23.10	$24.48	
Flagstone coping *Replace* Materials.......15.90 Labor...........12.90 *Remove* .... Labor............1.38	lf	$1.38	$28.80	$30.18	
Remove coping for work, then reinstall *Replace* Materials........ .75 Labor...........15.70	lf	—	$16.45	$16.45	
Swimming pool deck, concrete with epoxy aggregate surface *Replace* Materials........2.34 Labor............2.29 *Remove* .... Labor............1.35	sf	$1.35	$4.63	$5.98	◄ **Deck**
Swimming pool deck, stamped and dyed conrete *Replace* Materials........2.13 Labor............2.03 *Remove* .... Labor............1.35	sf	$1.35	$4.16	$5.51	
Bond beam repair *Replace* Materials........8.79 Labor..........54.40	lf	—	$63.19	$63.19	◄ **Bond beam repair**
Regrout tile swimming pool *Replace* Materials........ .15 Labor........... 1.22	sf	—	$1.37	$1.37	◄ **Regrout tile**
Leak detection *Replace* Materials........2.76 Labor........208.00	ea	—	$210.76	$210.76	◄ **Leak detection**

	Item Description	Unit	Remove	Replace	Total
REPAIR LEAK ▶	**Repair pool leak in vinyl lining, underwater** *Replace* Materials.......11.50 Labor.........183.00	ea	—	$194.50	$194.50
	Repair pool leak with hydraulic cement, underwater *Replace* Materials......18.80 Labor........228.00	ea	—	$246.80	$246.80
	Remove rusted rebar & stain, patch with plaster, underwater *Replace* Materials......33.40 Labor.........356.00	ea	—	$389.40	$389.40
	Repair plaster popoff, underwater *Replace* Materials......14.60 Labor.........214.00	ea	—	$228.60	$228.60
REPLASTER ▶	**Replaster swimming pool** *Replace* Materials........1.44 Labor............1.93	sf	—	$3.37	$3.37
PAINT ▶	**Paint pool with rubber base paint** *Replace* Materials........ .70 Labor............1.37	sf	—	$2.07	$2.07
	Paint pool with epoxy paint *Replace* Materials........ .77 Labor............1.78	sf	—	$2.55	$2.55
VINYL LINER ▶	**Replace vinyl liner** *Replace* Materials........2.35 Labor............1.12 *Remove* .... Labor............ .25	sf	$.25	$3.47	$3.72
TILE BORDER ▶	**Tile border, 6" x 6"** *Replace* Materials........7.14 Labor...........11.70 *Remove* .... Labor............1.71	lf	$1.71	$18.84	$20.55
	Tile border, 12" x 12" *Replace* Materials........9.30 Labor...........16.10 *Remove* .... Labor............1.71	lf	$1.71	$25.40	$27.11
	Remove tiles for work, then reinstall *Replace* Materials........ .77 Labor..........32.10	lf	—	$32.87	$32.87
ACID WASH ▶	**Acid wash swimming pool plaster** *Replace* Materials........ .13 Labor............ .20	sf	—	$.33	$.33
	Minimum charge to acid wash swimming pool *Replace* Materials......18.20 Labor........203.00	ea	—	$221.20	$221.20
DRAIN ▶	**Drain pool** *Replace* .... Labor.........213.00	ea	—	$213.00	$213.00
	Drain and clean pool *Replace* Materials.......15.70 Labor.........478.00	ea	—	$493.70	$493.70
SHOCK TREATMENT ▶	**Swimming pool chemical shock treatment** *Replace* Materials......31.30 Labor..........63.50	ea	—	$94.80	$94.80
OPEN POOL ▶	**Open swimming pool for the summer (cold climates)** *Replace* Materials......47.00 Labor.........165.00	ea	—	$212.00	$212.00
CLOSE POOL ▶	**Close swimming pool for the winter (cold climates)** *Replace* Materials......62.70 Labor........254.00	ea	—	$316.70	$316.70
CAULK ▶	**Caulk expansion joint** *Replace* Materials........2.09 Labor............1.47	lf	—	$3.56	$3.56

38 Temporary

Item Description	Unit			Total	
Cover opening with single sheet of plywood Materials....18.60 Labor....29.70	ea	—	—	$48.30	◀ **Emergency board up** *Prices are for work done between 7:00 a.m. and 6:00 p.m. Monday through Friday. Add **25%** for emergency work between 6:00 p.m. and 10:00 p.m. Monday through Friday. Add **65%** for emergency work between 10:00 p.m. and 7:00 a.m. Monday through Friday, on weekends, or on holidays.*
Cover opening with two sheets of plywood Materials....37.20 Labor....37.80	ea	—	—	$75.00	
Install temporary framing and cover opening Materials.... .83 Labor.... .92	sf	—	—	$1.75	
Cover roof or wall with tarp Materials.... .56 Labor.... .37	sf	—	—	$.93	
Cover roof or wall with plastic Materials.... .28 Labor.... .37	sf	—	—	$.65	
Minimum charge for emergency board up Materials....100.00 Labor....83.20	ea	—	—	$183.20	◁ minimum
Temporary electrical hookup Materials....100.00 Labor....57.80	ea	—	—	$157.80	◀ **Temporary power**
Temporary electrical, per week Materials....87.00	wk	—	—	$87.00	
Temporary heating, per week Materials....170.00	wk	—	—	$170.00	◀ **Temporary heating**
Scaffolding .... Equipment.... .19	sf	—	—	$.19	◀ **Scaffolding** *Per week. Per sf of wall that scaffolding covers. 60" wide scaffolding attached with scissor braces.*
Add for hook-end cat walk .... Equipment.... .98	ea	—	—	$.98	
Add for tented scaffolding .... Labor.... .21 Equipment.... .24	sf	—	—	$.45	◁ tented scaffolding
Scaffolding delivery, setup, and take down .... Labor.... .21	sf	—	—	$.21	◁ setup and take down
Minimum charge for scaffolding .... Labor....41.60 Equipment....50.00	ea	—	—	$91.60	◁ minimum
Temporary 5' tall chain-link fence .... Labor....4.91 Equipment....2.50	lf	—	—	$7.41	◀ **Temporary chain-link fence** *Per job. Up to 12 months.*
Temporary 6' tall chain-link fence .... Labor....5.12 Equipment....2.70	lf	—	—	$7.82	
Minimum charge for chain-link fence .... Labor....83.20 Equipment....130.00	ea	—	—	$213.20	◁ minimum
Security guard .... Labor....14.00	hr	—	—	$14.00	◀ **Security guard** *Per hour.*

	Item Description	Unit			Total
SECURITY GUARD ▶ *continued*	**Security guard with dog** Labor.........19.30	hr	—	—	$19.30
minimum ▷	**Minimum charge for security guard** Labor........280.00	ea	—	—	$280.00
OFFICE TRAILER ▶ *Per week.*	**8′ x 32′ office trailer** Equipment..........50.00	ea	—	—	$50.00
STORAGE TRAILER ▶ *Per week.*	**Storage trailer** Equipment..........29.00	ea	—	—	$29.00
PORTABLE TOILET ▶ *Chemical. Per week.*	**Portable toilet** Equipment..........25.00	ea	—	—	$25.00
BARRICADES ▶ *Per week.*	**Folding reflective barricades** Equipment............4.10	ea	—	—	$4.10
	Folding reflective barricade with flashing light Equipment............5.10	ea	—	—	$5.10
TRAFFIC CONE ▶ *Per week.*	**28″ traffic cone** Equipment .... .40	ea	—	—	$.40
SAFETY FENCE ▶	**4′ tall orange plastic safety fence** Materials........................ .43 Labor............. .17	lf	—	—	$.60
	5′ tall orange plastic safety fence Materials........................ .64 Labor............. .17	lf	—	—	$.81
SAFETY TAPE ▶	**Plastic "do not cross" barricade tape** Materials........................ .03 Labor............. .08	lf	—	—	$.11

TIME & MATERIAL CHARTS *(selected items)*

Temporary Items Labor

LABORER	BASE WAGE	PAID LEAVE	TRUE WAGE	FICA	FUTA	WORKER'S COMP.	UNEMPLOY. INSUR.	HEALTH INSUR.	RETIRE (401K)	LIABILITY INSUR.	COST PER HOUR
Carpenter	$23.60	1.84	$25.44	1.95	.20	4.96	2.21	2.69	.76	3.43	$41.60

Paid Leave is calculated based on two weeks paid vacation, one week sick leave, and seven paid holidays. Employer's matching portion of **FICA** is 7.65 percent. **FUTA** (Federal Unemployment) is .8 percent. **Worker's compensation** for carpentry work in the temporary trade was calculated using a national average of 19.50 percent. **Unemployment insurance** was calculated using a national average of 8.7 percent. **Health insurance** was calculated based on a projected national average for 2002 of $535 per employee (and family when applicable) per month. Employer pays 80 percent for a per month cost of $428 per employee. **Retirement** is based on a 401(k) retirement program with employer matching of 50 percent. Employee contributions to the 401(k) plan are an average of 6 percent of the true wage. **Liability insurance** is based on a national average of 13.2 percent.

Temporary Items Labor Productivity

WORK DESCRIPTION	LABORER	COST PER HOUR	PRODUCTIVITY	UNIT PRICE
Temporary board up / fencing				
cover opening with single sheet of plywood	*carpenter*	$41.60	.714	**$29.70** *ea*
over opening with two sheets of plywood	*carpenter*	$41.60	.909	**$37.80** *ea*
install temporary framing and cover opening	*carpenter*	$41.60	.022	**$.92** *sf*
cover roof or wall with tarp	*carpenter*	$41.60	.009	**$.37** *sf*
cover roof or wall with plastic	*carpenter*	$41.60	.009	**$.37** *sf*
install temporary 5′ tall chain link fence	*carpenter*	$41.60	.118	**$4.91** *lf*
install temporary 6′ tall chain link fence	*carpenter*	$41.60	.123	**$5.12** *lf*

39 Tile

with cultured marble

Item Description	Unit	Remove	Replace	Total
Minimum charge for tile work *Replace* Materials......50.00 Labor..........86.40	ea	—	$136.40	$136.40
6′ tall tile bathtub surround, adhesive set on moisture-resistant drywall *Replace* Materials....270.00 Labor........205.00 *Remove* .... Labor...........78.70	ea	$78.70	$475.00	$553.70
6′ tall tile bathtub surround, adhesive set on tile backer board *Replace* Materials....300.00 Labor........205.00 *Remove* .... Labor...........78.70	ea	$78.70	$505.00	$583.70
6′ tall tile bathtub surround, mortar set *Replace* Materials....320.00 Labor........299.00 *Remove* .... Labor...........98.20	ea	$98.20	$619.00	$717.20
7′ tall tile bathtub surround, adhesive set on moisture-resistant drywall *Replace* Materials.....315.00 Labor.........243.00 *Remove* .... Labor..........80.90	ea	$80.90	$558.00	$638.90
7′ tall tile bathtub surround, adhesive set on tile backer board *Replace* Materials....350.00 Labor.........243.00 *Remove* .... Labor..........80.90	ea	$80.90	$593.00	$673.90
7′ tall tile bathtub surround, mortar set *Replace* Materials....370.00 Labor.........324.00 *Remove* .... Labor.........102.00	ea	$102.00	$694.00	$796.00
8′ tall tile bathtub surround, adhesive set on moisture-resistant drywall *Replace* Materials....360.00 Labor.........278.00 *Remove* .... Labor..........83.30	ea	$83.30	$638.00	$721.30
8′ tall tile bathtub surround, adhesive set on tile backer board *Replace* Materials....400.00 Labor.........278.00 *Remove* .... Labor..........83.30	ea	$83.30	$678.00	$761.30
8′ tall tile bathtub surround, mortar set *Replace* Materials....425.00 Labor.........354.00 *Remove* .... Labor.........106.00	ea	$106.00	$779.00	$885.00
36″ x 36″ tile shower, adhesive set on tile backer board *Replace* Materials....445.00 Labor........299.00 *Remove* .... Labor...........91.60	ea	$91.60	$744.00	$835.60
36″ x 36″ tile shower, mortar set *Replace* Materials.....470.00 Labor.........354.00 *Remove* .... Labor.........102.00	ea	$102.00	$824.00	$926.00
Add for tile ceiling on 36″ x 36″ tile shower *Replace* Materials......70.00 Labor..........33.80	ea	—	$103.80	$103.80
36″ x 48″ tile shower, adhesive set on tile backer board *Replace* Materials....495.00 Labor.........354.00 *Remove* .... Labor..........94.90	ea	$94.90	$849.00	$943.90

◄ **MINIMUM**

◄ **TILE TUB SURROUND**
Both sides and one length of tub including trim tile and one tile soap dish.

◁ **6′**

◁ **7′**

◁ **8′**

◄ **TILE SHOWER**
Includes walls, floor, all trim pieces, and one tile soap dish. Does not include shower pan, fixtures, door or any plumbing.

RELATED ITEMS

Cabinets
tile countertop.................52
Cleaning.........................67
Plumbing
rough plumbing.............365
tub & shower combo.......378
shower stall, pan...........378
tub surround.................379
glass shower..................379

	Item Description	Unit	Remove	Replace	Total
TILE SHOWER ▶ *continued*	**36″ x 48″ tile shower, mortar set** *Replace* Materials....520.00 Labor........389.00 *Remove* .... Labor...........94.90	ea	$94.90	$909.00	$1,003.90
	Add for tile ceiling on 36″ x 48″ tile shower *Replace* Materials......80.00 Labor..........44.30	ea	—	$124.30	$124.30
TILE ACCESSORY ▶ *Add to above prices for each additional accessory.*	**Add for tile soap holder or other accessory** *Replace* Materials......30.00 Labor...........16.20	ea	—	$46.20	$46.20
CULTURED MARBLE TUB SURROUND ▶ *Three-pieces, one length and two widths of tub.*	**Cultured marble tub surround** *Replace* Materials....330.00 Labor.........150.00 *Remove* .... Labor...........35.20	ea	$35.20	$480.00	$515.20
TILE WINDOW SILL ▶	**Tile window sill 4″ thick wall** *Replace* Materials........5.45 Labor............2.45 *Remove* .... Labor............1.62	lf	$1.62	$7.90	$9.52
	Tile window sill 6″ thick wall *Replace* Materials........5.84 Labor............2.45 *Remove* .... Labor............1.62	lf	$1.62	$8.29	$9.91
	Tile window sill 8″ thick wall *Replace* Materials........6.36 Labor............2.53 *Remove* .... Labor............1.62	lf	$1.62	$8.89	$10.51
CULTURED MARBLE WINDOW SILL ▶	**Cultured marble window sill 4″ thick wall** *Replace* Materials........5.63 Labor............2.06 *Romovo* .... Labor............ .50	lf	$.50	$7.69	$8.19
	Cultured marble window sill 6″ thick wall *Replace* Materials........7.18 Labor............2.06 *Remove* .... Labor............ .50	lf	$.50	$9.24	$9.74
	Cultured marble window sill 8″ thick wall *Replace* Materials........9.70 Labor............2.10 *Remove* .... Labor............ .50	lf	$.50	$11.80	$12.30
REGROUT TILE ▶	**Regrout tile** *Replace* Materials........ .26 Labor............1.56	sf	—	$1.82	$1.82
REPLACE TILE ▶ *With an original tile furnished by owner.*	**Replace single tile** *Replace* .... Labor..........36.00	ea	—	$36.00	$36.00

TIME & MATERIAL CHARTS *(selected items)*

Tile Labor

LABORER	BASE WAGE	PAID LEAVE	TRUE WAGE	FICA	FUTA	WORKER'S COMP.	UNEMPLOY. INSUR.	HEALTH INSUR.	RETIRE (401K)	LIABILITY INSUR.	COST PER HOUR
Tile layer	$22.10	1.72	$23.82	1.82	.19	4.32	2.07	2.69	.72	3.22	$38.90
Demolition laborer	$13.90	1.08	$14.98	1.15	.12	4.79	1.30	2.69	.45	2.02	$27.50

Paid Leave is calculated based on two weeks paid vacation, one week sick leave, and seven paid holidays. Employer's matching portion of **FICA** is 7.65 percent. **FUTA** (Federal Unemployment) is .8 percent. **Worker's compensation** for the tile trade was calculated using a national average of 18.14 percent. **Unemployment insurance** was calculated using a national average of 8.7 percent. **Health insurance** was calculated based on a projected national average for 2002 of $535 per employee (and family when applicable) per month. Employer pays 80 percent for a per month cost of $428 per employee. **Retirement** is based on a 401(k) retirement program with employer matching of 50 percent. Employee contributions to the 401(k) plan are an average of 6 percent of the true wage. **Liability insurance** is based on a national average of 13.2 percent.

40 Wall Coverings

Item Description	Unit	Remove	Replace	Total	
Remove wallpaper, strippable ***Remove*** .... Labor............ .46	sf	$.46	—	$.46	◄ **Strip wallpaper** *Add **25%** for two layers, **36%** for three layers and **42%** for four layers.*
Remove wallpaper, non-strippable ***Remove*** .... Labor............ .74	sf	$.74	—	$.74	
Minimum charge for wall covering work ***Replace*** Material.......32.00 Labor..........35.30	sf	—	$67.30	$67.30	◄ **Minimum**
Wallpaper underliner ***Replace*** Material.......... .51 Labor............ .46 ***Remove*** .... Labor............ .46	sf	$.46	$.97	$1.43	◄ **Underliner** *Blank stock used to cover flaws in walls or over paneling.*
Grass cloth wallpaper, standard grade ***Replace*** Material.........1.60 Labor...........1.20 ***Remove*** .... Labor............ .46	sf	$.46	$2.80	$3.26	◄ **Grass cloth** *Includes wall sizing and 21% waste. Add **$.30** per sf to patch small holes, gouges, and cracks.*
Grass cloth wallpaper, high grade ***Replace*** Material.........2.58 Labor...........1.20 ***Remove*** .... Labor............ .46	sf	$.46	$3.78	$4.24	
Wallpaper, standard grade ***Replace*** Material.......... .85 Labor............ .92 ***Remove*** .... Labor............ .46	sf	$.46	$1.77	$2.23	◄ **Paper** *From flat to high gloss papers. Includes wall sizing and 21% waste. Add **$.30** per sf to patch small holes, gouges, and cracks.*
Wallpaper, high grade ***Replace*** Material.........1.17 Labor............ .92 ***Remove*** .... Labor............ .46	sf	$.46	$2.09	$2.55	
Vinyl-coated wallpaper, standard grade ***Replace*** Material.........1.08 Labor............ .99 ***Remove*** .... Labor............ .46	sf	$.46	$2.07	$2.53	◄ **Vinyl-coated** *Vinyl with paper back. Includes wall sizing and 21% waste. Add **$.30** per sf to patch small holes, gouges, and cracks.*
Vinyl-coated wallpaper, high grade ***Replace*** Material.........1.43 Labor............ .99 ***Remove*** .... Labor............ .46	sf	$.46	$2.42	$2.88	
Vinyl wallpaper, standard grade ***Replace*** Material.........1.15 Labor............ .99 ***Remove*** .... Labor............ .46	sf	$.46	$2.14	$2.60	◄ **Vinyl** *Seams overlapped, then cut. Includes wall sizing and 21% waste. Add **$.30** per sf to patch small holes, gouges, and cracks.*
Vinyl wallpaper, high grade ***Replace*** Material.........1.51 Labor............ .99 ***Remove*** .... Labor............ .46	sf	$.46	$2.50	$2.96	
Foil wallpaper, standard grade ***Replace*** Material.........1.39 Labor............ .95 ***Remove*** .... Labor............ .46	sf	$.46	$2.34	$2.80	◄ **Foil** *Includes wall sizing and 21% waste. Add **$.30** per sf to patch small holes, gouges, and cracks.*
Foil wallpaper, high grade ***Replace*** Material.........1.75 Labor............ .95 ***Remove*** .... Labor............ .46	sf	$.46	$2.70	$3.16	
Wallpaper border, standard grade ***Replace*** Material.........1.52 Labor............ .81 ***Remove*** .... Labor............ .35	lf	$.35	$2.33	$2.68	◄ **Border** *All styles. Includes 21% waste.*

	Item Description	Unit	Remove	Replace	Total
BORDER ► *continued* *Use remove price when removing border only.*	**Wallpaper border, high grade** ***Replace*** Material.........2.13 Labor............. .81 ***Remove*** .... Labor............. .35	lf	$.35	$2.94	$3.29
ANAGLYPTA ► *Brand name for a highly embossed wall or ceiling covering made from material similar to linoleum. Must be painted. Higher grades contain cotton fibers for extra strength and durability. Includes 21% waste.*	**Anaglypta embossed wall or ceiling covering, standard grade** ***Replace*** Material.........1.23 Labor............1.59 ***Remove*** .... Labor............. .64	sf	$.64	$2.82	$3.46
	Anaglypta embossed wall or ceiling covering, high grade ***Replace*** Material.........1.76 Labor............1.59 ***Remove*** .... Labor............. .64	sf	$.64	$3.35	$3.99
	Anaglypta embossed wall or ceiling covering, deluxe grade ***Replace*** Material.........1.95 Labor............1.59 ***Remove*** .... Labor............. .64	sf	$.64	$3.54	$4.18
LINCRUSTA ► *Brand name for a highly embossed wall or ceiling covering made from material similar to linoleum. Lincrusta is typically much heavier than Anaglypta. Must be painted. Includes 21% waste.*	**Lincrusta embossed wall or ceiling covering, standard grade** ***Replace*** Material.........3.55 Labor............1.98 ***Remove*** .... Labor............. .92	sf	$.92	$5.53	$6.45
	Lincrusta embossed wall or ceiling covering, high grade ***Replace*** Material.........4.79 Labor............1.98 ***Remove*** .... Labor............. .92	sf	$.92	$6.77	$7.69
	Lincrusta embossed wall or ceiling covering, deluxe grade ***Replace*** Material.........5.92 Labor............1.98 ***Remove*** .... Labor............. .92	sf	$.92	$7.90	$8.82
ANAGLYPTA FRIEZE ► *See Anaglypta above. Friezes are 12" to 21" wide. Includes 13% waste.*	**Anaglypta embossed frieze, standard grade** ***Replace*** Material.........3.80 Labor............1.52 ***Remove*** .... Labor............. .53	lf	$.53	$5.32	$5.85
	Anaglypta embossed frieze, high grade ***Replace*** Material.........4.28 Labor............1.52 ***Remove*** .... Labor............. .53	lf	$.53	$5.80	$6.33
LINCRUSTA FRIEZE ► *See Lincrusta above. Friezes are approximately 21" wide. Includes 13% waste.*	**Lincrusta embossed frieze, standard grade** ***Replace*** Material.........4.41 Labor............1.87 ***Remove*** .... Labor............. .74	lf	$.74	$6.28	$7.02
	Lincrusta embossed frieze, high grade ***Replace*** Material.........5.51 Labor............1.87 ***Remove*** .... Labor............. .74	lf	$.74	$7.38	$8.12
ANAGLYPTA PELMET ► *See Anaglypta above. Pelmets are narrower and often less ornate than friezes. Pelmets are from 4" to 7" wide. Includes 13% waste.*	**Anaglypta embossed pelmet, standard grade** ***Replace*** Material.........2.37 Labor............1.41 ***Remove*** .... Labor............. .53	lf	$.53	$3.78	$4.31
	Anaglypta embossed pelmet, high grade ***Replace*** Material.........3.38 Labor............1.41 ***Remove*** .... Labor............. .53	lf	$.53	$4.79	$5.32
ANAGLYPTA DADO ► *See Anaglypta above. Dados are heavy, highly embossed wall panels installed as a wainscot. Includes 13% waste.*	**Anaglypta embossed dado, standard grade** ***Replace*** Material........18.20 Labor............3.92 ***Remove*** .... Labor............3.57 ► Typical panels are about 22" wide and 36" tall. Five panels per box.	lf	$3.57	$22.12	$25.69
	Anaglypta embossed dado, high grade ***Replace*** Material.......22.60 Labor............3.92 ***Remove*** .... Labor............3.57 ► Typical panels are about 24" wide and 40" tall. Five panels per box.	lf	$3.57	$26.52	$30.09

TIME & MATERIAL CHARTS *(selected items)*

Wall Coverings Materials

Wallpaper materials were calculated based on double European size rolls with approximately 28 sf per single roll and 56 sf in a double roll. (Most manufacturers no longer make American size rolls which contained approximately 36 sf per single roll and 72 sf in a double roll.) Prices include sizing and glue application, even on pre-pasted rolls.

DESCRIPTION	PRICE	GROSS COVERAGE	WASTE	NET COVERAGE	UNIT PRICE
Minimum					
for wall covering work	**$32.00** *ea*	**1**	0%	**1**	**$32.00** *ea*
Wallpaper underliner					
blank stock	**$22.60** *double roll*	**56**	21%	**44.24**	**$.51** *sf*
Grass cloth wallpaper					
standard grade	**$70.90** *double roll*	**56**	21%	**44.24**	**$1.60** *sf*
high grade	**$114.00** *double roll*	**56**	21%	**44.24**	**$2.58** *sf*
Paper wallpaper					
standard grade	**$37.50** *double roll*	**56**	21%	**44.24**	**$.85** *sf*
high grade	**$51.70** *double roll*	**56**	21%	**44.24**	**$1.17** *sf*
Vinyl-coated wallpaper					
standard grade	**$47.80** *double roll*	**56**	21%	**44.24**	**$1.08** *sf*
high grade	**$63.40** *double roll*	**56**	21%	**44.24**	**$1.43** *sf*
Vinyl wallpaper					
standard grade	**$50.70** *double roll*	**56**	21%	**44.24**	**$1.15** *sf*
high grade	**$66.70** *double roll*	**56**	21%	**44.24**	**$1.51** *sf*
Foil wallpaper					
standard grade	**$61.50** *double roll*	**56**	21%	**44.24**	**$1.39** *sf*
high grade	**$77.60** *double roll*	**56**	21%	**44.24**	**$1.75** *sf*
Wallpaper border					
standard grade	**$36.00** *bolt*	**30**	21%	**23.70**	**$1.52** *lf*
high grade	**$50.40** *bolt*	**30**	21%	**23.70**	**$2.13** *lf*
Anaglypta embossed wall or ceiling covering					
standard grade	**$54.30** *double roll*	**56**	21%	**44.24**	**$1.23** *sf*
high grade	**$77.90** *double roll*	**56**	21%	**44.24**	**$1.76** *sf*
deluxe grade	**$86.40** *double roll*	**56**	21%	**44.24**	**$1.95** *sf*
Lincrusta embossed wall or ceiling covering					
standard grade	**$157.00** *double roll*	**56**	21%	**44.24**	**$3.55** *sf*
high grade	**$212.00** *double roll*	**56**	21%	**44.24**	**$4.79** *sf*
deluxe grade	**$262.00** *double roll*	**56**	21%	**44.24**	**$5.92** *sf*
Anaglypta embossed frieze					
standard grade	**$109.00** *bolt*	**33**	13%	**28.71**	**$3.80** *lf*
high grade	**$123.00** *bolt*	**33**	13%	**28.71**	**$4.28** *lf*
Lincrusta embossed frieze					
standard grade	**$128.00** *bolt*	**33**	12%	**29.04**	**$4.41** *lf*
high grade	**$160.00** *bolt*	**33**	12%	**29.04**	**$5.51** *lf*
Anaglypta embossed pelmet					
standard grade	**$68.10** *bolt*	**33**	13%	**28.71**	**$2.37** *lf*
high grade	**$96.90** *bolt*	**33**	13%	**28.71**	**$3.38** *lf*
Anaglypta embossed dado *(five panels per box)*					
standard grade	**$262.00** *box*	**16**	10%	**14.40**	**$18.20** *lf*
high grade	**$325.00** *box*	**16**	10%	**14.40**	**$22.60** *lf*

Wall Coverings Labor

LABORER	BASE WAGE	PAID LEAVE	TRUE WAGE	FICA	FUTA	WORKER'S COMP.	UNEMPLOY. INSUR.	HEALTH INSUR.	RETIRE (401K)	LIABILITY INSUR.	COST PER HOUR
Wallpaper hanger	$19.40	1.51	$20.91	1.60	.17	4.62	1.82	2.69	.63	2.82	$35.30

Paid Leave is calculated based on two weeks paid vacation, one week sick leave, and seven paid holidays. Employer's matching portion of **FICA** is 7.65 percent. **FUTA** (Federal Unemployment) is .8 percent. **Worker's compensation** for the wall coverings trade was calculated using a national average of 22.09 percent. **Unemployment insurance** was calculated using a national average of 8.7 percent. **Health insurance** was calculated based on a projected national average for 2002 of $535 per employee (and family when applicable) per month. Employer pays 80 percent for a per month cost of $428 per employee. **Retirement** is based on a 401(k) retirement program with employer matching of 50 percent. Employee contributions to the 401(k) plan are an average of 6 percent of the true wage. **Liability insurance** is based on a national average of 13.2 percent.

Wall Coverings Labor Productivity

WORK DESCRIPTION	LABORER	COST PER HOUR	PRODUCTIVITY	UNIT PRICE
Remove wallpaper				
strippable	wallpaper hanger	$35.30	.013	$.46 sf
non-strippable	wallpaper hanger	$35.30	.021	$.74 sf
Minimum				
for wall covering work	wallpaper hanger	$35.30	1.00	$35.30 ea
Install wallpaper				
underliner	wallpaper hanger	$35.30	.013	$.46 sf
grass cloth wallpaper	wallpaper hanger	$35.30	.034	$1.20 sf
paper wallpaper	wallpaper hanger	$35.30	.026	$.92 sf
vinyl-coated	wallpaper hanger	$35.30	.028	$.99 sf
vinyl	wallpaper hanger	$35.30	.028	$.99 sf
foil	wallpaper hanger	$35.30	.027	$.95 sf
Install border				
all styles	wallpaper hanger	$35.30	.023	$.81 lf
Install Anaglypta embossed wall or ceiling covering				
wall or ceiling	wallpaper hanger	$35.30	.045	$1.59 sf
Install Lincrusta embossed wall or ceiling covering				
wall or ceiling	wallpaper hanger	$35.30	.056	$1.98 sf
Install embossed frieze				
Anaglypta	wallpaper hanger	$35.30	.043	$1.52 lf
Lincrusta	wallpaper hanger	$35.30	.053	$1.87 lf
Install Anaglypta embossed pelmet				
all grades	wallpaper hanger	$35.30	.040	$1.41 lf
Install Anaglypta embossed dado				
all grades	wallpaper hanger	$35.30	.111	$3.92 lf

NOTES:

end

41 Water Extraction

Item Description	Unit			Total
Minimum charge for water extraction work *Replace* .... Labor ......53.30 Equipment 90.00	ea	—	—	$143.30
Equipment delivery, setup, and take-home charge *Replace* .... Equipment ......30.00 ► Per loss charge to deliver water extraction equipment, set the equipment up, and take the equipment home once the water is extracted and drying is complete.	ea	—	—	$30.00
Extract water from lightly soaked carpet *Replace* .... Labor ...... .18 Equipment ...... .07 ► Carpet and pad are wet but water does not rise around feet as carpet is stepped on.	sf	—	—	$.25
Extract water from typically wet carpet *Replace* .... Labor ...... .25 Equipment ...... .07 ► Water in carpet and pad rises around feet as carpet is stepped on.	sf	—	—	$.32
Extract water from heavily soaked carpet *Replace* .... Labor ...... .36 Equipment ...... .08 ► Water is visible over the surface of the carpet mat.	sf	—	—	$.44
Extract water from very heavily soaked carpet *Replace* .... Labor ...... .50 Equipment ...... .11 ► Standing water over the surface of the carpet.	sf	—	—	$.61
Treat carpet with germicide *Replace* Material ...... .02 Labor ...... .11	sf	—	—	$.13
Treat carpet with mildewcide *Replace* Material ...... .03 Labor ...... .11	sf	—	—	$.14
Detach carpet, lift, and block for drying *Replace* .... Labor ...... .14	sf	—	—	$.14
Remove wet carpet *Remove* .... Labor 2.84	sy	—	—	$2.84
Remove wet carpet pad *Remove* .... Labor ...... .18	sf	—	—	$.18
Dehumidifier unit, 10 gallon daily capacity *Replace* .... Labor ......14.60 Equipment 30.00	day	—	—	$44.60
Dehumidifier unit, 19 gallon daily capacity *Replace* .... Labor ......14.60 Equipment 50.00	day	—	—	$64.60
Dehumidifier unit, 24 gallon daily capacity *Replace* .... Labor ......14.60 Equipment 65.00	day	—	—	$79.60
Drying fan *Replace* .... Labor ......3.69 Equipment 25.00	day	—	—	$28.69

◄ **MINIMUM**

◄ **SETUP AND TAKE-HOME CHARGES**

◄ **EXTRACT WATER**

EMERGENCY SERVUCE

All prices are for work done between 7:00 a.m. and 6:00 p.m. Monday through Friday.

Add **25%** for emergency work between 6:00 p.m. and 10:00 p.m. Monday through Friday.

Add **65%** for emergency work between 10:00 p.m. and 7:00 a.m. Monday through Friday, on weekends, or on holidays.

◄ **GERMICIDE AND MILDEWCIDE TREATMENT**
Treatments to kill germs and mildew in wet carpet.

◄ **DETACH, LIFT & BLOCK CARPET FOR DRYING**

◄ **REMOVE WET CARPET AND PAD**
See Flooring chapter, pages 257-258 for prices to tear-out dry carpet and pad.

◄ **DEHUMIDIFIERS**
Does not include delivery, setup and take-home (see above). Does include daily monitoring and adjustment.

◄ **DRYING FAN**
Does not include delivery, setup and take-home (see above). Does include daily monitoring and adjustment.

HANG & DRY CARPET IN PLANT ► *Square foot price to haul carpet to plant, hang, and dry. Includes transport to and from plant. Does not include carpet removal (see page 257-258) or reinstallation (see page 257).*

PAD AND BLOCK FURNITURE ►

Item Description	Unit			Total
Hang and dry carpet in plant *Replace* .... Labor........ .18 Equipment .... .09	sf	—	—	**$.27**
Hang and dry oriental rug in plant *Replace* .... Labor........ .28 Equipment .... .14	sf	—	—	**$.42**
Minimum charge to hang and dry carpet in plant *Replace* .... Labor........72.10 Equipment........40.00	sf	—	—	**$112.10**
Pad and block furniture, small room *Replace* .... Labor........14.20	ea	—	—	**$14.20**
Pad and block furniture, average room *Replace* .... Labor........19.80	ea	—	—	**$19.80**
Pad and block furniture, large room *Replace* .... Labor........25.50	ea	—	—	**$25.50**
Pad and block furniture, very large room *Replace* .... Labor........35.40	ea	—	—	**$35.40**

TIME & MATERIAL CHARTS *(selected items)*

Water Extraction Materials

*See **Water Extraction** material prices with the line items and other information in the **QuickFinder** column.*

Water Extraction Rental Equipment

DESCRIPTION	UNIT PRICE
Dehumidifier	
10 gallon capacity	**$30.00** *per day*
19 gallon capacity	**$50.00** *per day*
24 gallon capacity	**$65.00** *per day*
Drying fan	
typical	**$25.00** *per day*

Water Extraction Labor

LABORER	BASE WAGE	PAID LEAVE	TRUE WAGE	FICA	FUTA	WORKER'S COMP.	UNEMPLOY. INSUR.	HEALTH INSUR.	RETIRE (401K)	LIABILITY INSUR.	COST PER HOUR
Water extractor	**$20.20**	1.58	**$21.78**	1.67	.17	3.71	1.90	2.69	.65	2.94	**$35.50**

Paid Leave is calculated based on two weeks paid vacation, one week sick leave, and seven paid holidays. Employer's matching portion of **FICA** is 7.65 percent. **FUTA** (Federal Unemployment) is .8 percent. **Worker's compensation** for the water extraction trade was calculated using a national average of 17.02 percent. **Unemployment insurance** was calculated using a national average of 8.7 percent. **Health insurance** was calculated based on a projected national average for 2002 of $535 per employee (and family when applicable) per month. Employer pays 80 percent for a per month cost of $428 per employee. **Retirement** is based on a 401(k) retirement program with employer matching of 50 percent. Employee contributions to the 401(k) plan are an average of 6 percent of the true wage. **Liability insurance** is based on a national average of 13.2 percent.

Water Extraction Labor Productivity

WORK DESCRIPTION	LABORER	COST PER HOUR	PRODUCTIVITY	UNIT PRICE
Extract water				
from lightly soaked carpet	*water extractor*	**$35.50**	**.005**	**$.18** *sf*
from very heavily soaked carpet	*water extractor*	**$35.50**	**.014**	**$.50** *sf*
Pad and block furniture				
small room	*water extractor*	**$35.50**	**.400**	**$14.20** *ea*
very large room	*water extractor*	**$35.50**	**.998**	**$35.40** *ea*

42 .... Windows

Item Description	Unit	small	average	large	very large	
Remove window ***Materials*** Small..........1.30 Average.......1.30 Large.......1.30 Very Large.......1.30 ***Labor*** Small................10.90 Average......11.20 Large......11.60 Very Large......11.90	ea	$12.20	$12.50	$12.90	$13.20	◀ **DEMOLITION**
Remove window for work then reinstall ***Materials*** Small..........1.30 Average.......1.30 Large.......1.30 Very Large.......1.30 ***Labor*** Small................51.20 Average.....71.60 Large....104.00 Very Large....154.00	ea	$52.50	$72.90	$105.30	$155.30	◀ **REMOVE & REINSTALL**

Item Description		all types			
Deduct for single-glazed window (all types) ***Materials*** All types..- -4.30	sf	- $-4.30			
Add for gray or bronze tinted glass (all window types) ***Materials*** All types......2.80	sf	$2.80			
Add 8% for Low-E between panes (all window types)					
Add 5% for argon fill between panes (all window types)					
Add 11% for thermal break (aluminum windows only)					

◀ **OTHER OPTIONS**
All windows in this chapter are double-glazed (insulated) units with clear glass. Use for all window types except skylights and roof windows. For information on Low-E and argon see page 501.

RELATED ITEMS
Doors
sliding patio..................119

Item Description		tempered	laminated	obscure	polished wire	
Add for alternative glazing (all window types) ***Materials*** Tempered .....7.50 Laminated.......4.90 Obscure........ .96 Polished wire....22.90	sf	$7.50	$4.90	$.96	$22.90	◁ **other glass types**

◀ **ALUMINUM**

Item Description		24" x 12"	36" x 18"	48" x 24"	72" x 36"	
Half-round aluminum window top ***Materials*** 24" x 12" ..279.00 36" x 18"...346.00 48" x 24".....411.00 72" x 36" ...608.00 ***Labor*** 24" x 12"...........41.20 36" x 18" .....41.20 48" x 24"......57.80 72" x 36" 83.20	ea	$320.20	$387.20	$468.80	$691.20	◁ **half-round** 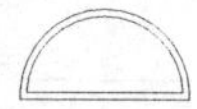

Item Description		36" x 15"	48" x 16"	60" x 19"	90" x 20"	
Half-elliptical aluminum window top ***Materials*** 36" x 15" ..531.00 48" x 16"...588.00 60" x 19"....645.00 90" x 20"....938.00 ***Labor*** 36" x 15" ....41.20 48" x 16" .....41.20 60" x 19"......57.80 90" x 20" 83.20	ea	$572.20	$629.20	$702.80	$1,021.20	◁ **half-elliptical** 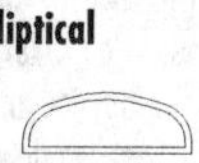

Item Description		20" x 20"	30" x 30"	40" x 40"	48" x 48"	
Round aluminum window ***Materials*** 20" x 20"..561.00 30" x 30"...686.00 40" x 40"....791.00 48" x 48"....871.00 ***Labor*** 20" x 20"..........41.20 30" x 30" .....41.20 40" x 40"......57.80 48" x 48" 83.20	ea	$602.20	$727.20	$848.80	$954.20	◁ **round** 

Item Description		15" x 24"	24" x 36"	25" x 40"	30" x 48"	
Elliptical aluminum window ***Materials*** 15" X 24..1060.00 24" x 36"...1170.00 25" x 40" ..1240.00 30" x 48" ..1340.00 ***Labor*** 15" X 24"...........41.20 24" x 36" .....41.20 25" x 40"......57.80 30" x 48" 83.20	ea	$1,101.20	$1,211.20	$1,297.80	$1,423.20	◁ **elliptical** 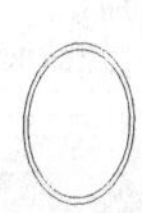

Item Description		24" x 24"	36" x 36"			
Quarter round aluminum window ***Materials*** 24" x 24" ..456.00 36" x 36" ...655.00 ***Labor*** 24" x 24"...........41.20 36" x 36" 41.20	ea	$497.20	$696.20	—	—	◁ **quarter-round** 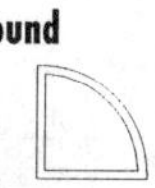

ALUMINUM ▶ *continued*

casement ▷

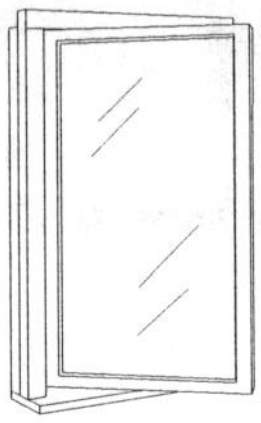

Item Description	Unit	36″ tall	48″ tall	60″ tall
18″ wide aluminum casement window ***Materials*** 36″ tall...332.00 48″ tall...359.00 60″ tall....412.00 ***Labor*** 36″ tall.............41.20 48″ tall.....41.20 60″ tall......41.20	ea	$373.20	$400.20	$453.20
24″ wide aluminum casement window ***Materials*** 36″ tall...357.00 48″ tall...387.00 60″ tall....437.00 ***Labor*** 36″ tall.............41.20 48″ tall.....41.20 60″ tall......57.80	ea	$398.20	$428.20	$494.80
30″ wide aluminum casement window ***Materials*** .... 48″ tall....418.00 60″ tall...468.00 ***Labor*** .... 48″ tall.....57.80 60″ tall......57.80	ea	—	$475.80	$525.80
36″ wide aluminum casement window ***Materials*** .... 48″ tall....497.00 60″ tall....571.00 ***Labor*** .... 48″ tall.....57.80 60″ tall......57.80	ea	—	$554.80	$628.80

awning ▷

Item Description	Unit	20″ tall	24″ tall	30″ tall
24″ wide aluminum awning window ***Materials*** 20″ tall...306.00 24″ tall...345.00 30″ tall....376.00 ***Labor*** 20″ tall.............41.20 24″ tall.....41.20 30″ tall......41.20	ea	$347.20	$386.20	$417.20
30″ wide aluminum awning window ***Materials*** 20″ tall...355.00 24″ tall...389.00 30″ tall....425.00 ***Labor*** 20″ tall.............41.20 24″ tall.....41.20 30″ tall......41.20	ea	$396.20	$430.20	$466.20
36″ wide aluminum awning window ***Materials*** .... 24″ tall....421.00 30″ tall....473.00 ***Labor*** .... 24″ tall.....41.20 30″ tall......41.20	ea	—	$462.20	$514.20
40″ wide aluminum awning window ***Materials*** .... 24″ tall...467.00 30″ tall....526.00 ***Labor*** .... 24″ tall.....41.20 30″ tall......41.20	ea	—	$508.20	$567.20

ALUMINUM

All aluminum windows are double-glazed, clear glass with white or bronze finish frames.

For mill-finish windows deduct **13%**.

All costs are for standard windows. Manufacturers' window sizes vary. For standard units round measurements to the nearest size. For custom sizes add **80%**.

double-hung ▷

Item Description	Unit	36″ tall	48″ tall	60″ tall	72″ tall
24″ wide aluminum double-hung window ***Materials*** 36″ tall...180.00 48″ tall...201.00 60″ tall....227.00 72″ tall...254.00 ***Labor*** 36″ tall.............41.20 48″ tall.....41.20 60″ tall......41.20 72″ tall......41.20	ea	$221.20	$242.20	$268.20	$295.20
36″ wide aluminum double-hung window ***Materials*** 36″ tall...222.00 48″ tall...247.00 60″ tall....265.00 72″ tall...290.00 ***Labor*** 36″ tall.............41.20 48″ tall.....41.20 60″ tall......41.20 72″ tall......57.80	ea	$263.20	$288.20	$306.20	$347.80
42″ wide aluminum double-hung window ***Materials*** 36″ tall...243.00 48″ tall...266.00 60″ tall...290.00 72″ tall....316.00 ***Labor*** 36″ tall.............41.20 48″ tall.....41.20 60″ tall......57.80 72″ tall......57.80	ea	$284.20	$307.20	$347.80	$373.80
24″ wide aluminum single-hung window ***Materials*** 36″ tall....149.00 48″ tall....170.00 60″ tall....196.00 72″ tall...223.00 ***Labor*** 36″ tall.............41.20 48″ tall.....41.20 60″ tall......41.20 72″ tall......41.20	ea	$190.20	$211.20	$237.20	$264.20
36″ wide aluminum single-hung window ***Materials*** 36″ tall....191.00 48″ tall....216.00 60″ tall...234.00 72″ tall....259.00 ***Labor*** 36″ tall.............41.20 48″ tall.....41.20 60″ tall......41.20 72″ tall......57.80	ea	$232.20	$257.20	$275.20	$316.80
42″ wide aluminum single-hung window ***Materials*** 36″ tall....212.00 48″ tall....235.00 60″ tall....259.00 72″ tall....285.00 ***Labor*** 36″ tall.............41.20 48″ tall.....41.20 60″ tall......57.80 72″ tall......57.80	ea	$253.20	$276.20	$316.80	$342.80

GRILLES AND GRID

For aluminum grid between panes of glass or removable grilles outside of window add (per window):

Half-round **$20**
Half-elliptical **$31**
Round **$20**
Elliptical **$25**
Quarter-round **$20**
Casement **$25**
Awning **$25**
Single-hung **$20**
Sliding **$21**
Fixed (picture) **$24**

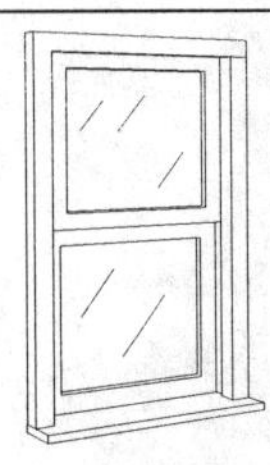

Item Description	Unit	24" tall	36" tall	48" tall	60" tall
36" wide aluminum sliding window	ea	$105.80	$113.20	$141.20	$174.20
Materials 24" tall.....64.60 36" tall.....72.00 48" tall....100.00 60" tall....133.00					
Labor 24" tall............41.20 36" tall.....41.20 48" tall......41.20 60" tall......41.20					
48" wide aluminum sliding window	ea	$113.50	$121.20	$152.20	$205.80
Materials 24" tall.....72.30 36" tall.....80.00 48" tall.....111.00 60" tall....148.00					
Labor 24" tall............41.20 36" tall.....41.20 48" tall......41.20 60" tall......57.80					
60" wide aluminum sliding window	ea	$120.30	$129.20	$179.80	$219.80
Materials 24" tall.....79.10 36" tall.....88.00 48" tall....122.00 60" tall....162.00					
Labor 24" tall............41.20 36" tall.....41.20 48" tall......57.80 60" tall......57.80					
72" wide aluminum sliding window	ea	$134.70	$161.80	$201.80	$274.20
Materials 24" tall.....93.50 36" tall...104.00 48" tall....144.00 60" tall....191.00					
Labor 24" tall............41.20 36" tall.....57.80 48" tall......57.80 60" tall.....83.20					

◁ **sliding**

THERMAL BREAK

Aluminum is an excellent conductor, which means heat and cold easily flow through it, reducing efficiency.

To cure this, a plastic or rubber spacer is introduced into the jamb to break the flow of hot or cold.

Add **11%** for each aluminum window with a thermal break.

Item Description	Unit	36" tall	48" tall	60" tall	72" tall
24" wide aluminum fixed (picture) window	ea	$133.20	$173.20	$199.20	$211.20
Materials 36" tall.....92.00 48" tall....132.00 60" tall....158.00 72" tall....170.00					
Labor 36" tall............41.20 48" tall.....41.20 60" tall......41.20 72" tall......41.20					
30" wide aluminum fixed (picture) window	ea	$152.20	$180.20	$194.20	$237.20
Materials 36" tall....111.00 48" tall....139.00 60" tall....153.00 72" tall....196.00					
Labor 36" tall............41.20 48" tall.....41.20 60" tall......41.20 72" tall......41.20					
36" wide aluminum fixed (picture) window	ea	$161.20	$200.20	$202.20	$285.80
Materials 36" tall...120.00 48" tall....159.00 60" tall.....161.00 72" tall....228.00					
Labor 36" tall............41.20 48" tall.....41.20 60" tall......41.20 72" tall......57.80					
42" wide aluminum fixed (picture) window	ea	$173.20	$230.20	$286.80	$320.80
Materials 36" tall....132.00 48" tall...189.00 60" tall...229.00 72" tall....263.00					
Labor 36" tall............41.20 48" tall.....41.20 60" tall......57.80 72" tall......57.80					
48" wide aluminum fixed (picture) window	ea	$200.20	$237.20	$307.80	$343.80
Materials 36" tall....159.00 48" tall....196.00 60" tall...250.00 72" tall....286.00					
Labor 36" tall............41.20 48" tall.....41.20 60" tall......57.80 72" tall......57.80					
60" wide aluminum fixed (picture) window	ea	$202.20	$260.80	$292.80	$396.20
Materials 36" tall....161.00 48" tall...203.00 60" tall....235.00 72" tall....313.00					
Labor 36" tall............41.20 48" tall.....57.80 60" tall......57.80 72" tall.....83.20					
72" wide aluminum fixed (picture) window	ea	$311.20	$370.20	$435.00	$496.00
Materials 36" tall...228.00 48" tall....287.00 60" tall....313.00 72" tall....374.00					
Labor 36" tall............83.20 48" tall.....83.20 60" tall....122.00 72" tall....122.00					

◁ **fixed (picture)**

LOW-E AND ARGON

Higher quality windows may have Low-E or argon gas or both.

Low-E A coating that increases heat retention in winter and reduces ultraviolet rays that fade carpet and upholstery. Also called high-performance glass and other brand names.

Argon gas An odorless gas that improves the window's energy efficiency when injected between panes of glass.

Argon is usually not available for windows with true divided lights.

See page 499 to add Low-E or argon to windows and page 506 to add to skylights and roof windows.

◀ **VINYL**

Item Description	Unit	24" x 12"	36" x 18"	48" x 24"	72" x 36"
Half-round vinyl window top	ea	$235.20	$279.20	$343.80	$507.20
Materials 24" x 12"...194.00 36" x 18"...238.00 48" x 24"....286.00 72" x 36"....424.00					
Labor 24" x 12"...........41.20 36" x 18"....41.20 48" x 24"......57.80 72" x 36".....83.20					

◁ **half-round**

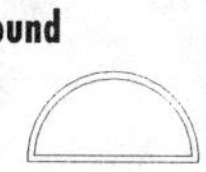

Item Description	Unit	36" x 15"	48" x 16"	60" x 19"	90" x 20"
Half-elliptical vinyl window top	ea	$410.20	$446.20	$508.80	$736.20
Materials 36" x 15"..369.00 48" x 16"...405.00 60" x 19"....451.00 90" x 20"....653.00					
Labor 36" x 15............41.20 48" x 16"....41.20 60" x 19"......57.80 90" x 20".....83.20					

◁ **half-elliptical**

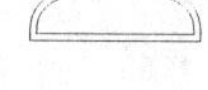

Item Description	Unit	20" x 20"	30" x 30"	40" x 40"	48" x 48"
Round vinyl window	ea	$432.20	$513.20	$609.80	$689.20
Materials 20" x 20"..391.00 30" x 30"....472.00 40" x 40"....552.00 48" x 48"...606.00					
Labor 20" x 20"...........41.20 30" x 30"....41.20 40" x 40"......57.80 48" x 48".....83.20					

◁ **round**

VINYL ▶ *continued*

elliptical ▷

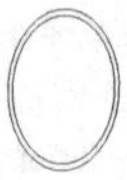

Item Description	Unit	15″ x 24″	24″ x 36″	25″ x 40″	30″ x 48″
Elliptical vinyl window ***Materials*** 15″ x 24″ ..740.00 24″ x 36″...802.00 25″ x 40″....867.00 30″ x 48″....933.00 ***Labor*** 15″ x 24″............41.20 24″ x 36″ .....41.20 25″ x 40″......57.80 30″ x 48″ 83.20	ea	$781.20	$843.20	$924.80	$1,016.20

quarter-round ▷

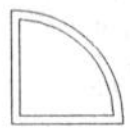

Item Description	Unit	24″ x 24″	36″ x 36″
Quarter-round vinyl window ***Materials*** 24″ x 24″ ...317.00 36″ x 36″....452.00 ***Labor*** 24″ x 24″............41.20 36″ x 36″ 41.20	ea	$358.20	$493.20

casement ▷

Item Description	Unit	36″ tall	48″ tall	60″ tall
18″ wide vinyl casement window ***Materials*** 36″ tall ...230.00 48″ tall ...250.00 60″ tall....287.00 ***Labor*** 36″ tall............41.20 48″ tall .....41.20 60″ tall......41.20	ea	$271.20	$291.20	$328.20
24″ wide vinyl casement window ***Materials*** 36″ tall ...248.00 48″ tall....269.00 60″ tall ...305.00 ***Labor*** 36″ tall............41.20 48″ tall .....41.20 60″ tall......57.80	ea	$289.20	$310.20	$362.80
30″ wide vinyl casement window ***Materials***...................... 48″ tall ...292.00 60″ tall....326.00 ***Labor***............................ 48″ tall .....57.80 60″ tall......57.80	ea	—	$349.80	$383.80
36″ wide vinyl casement window (double) ***Materials***...................... 48″ tall ...346.00 60″ tall....398.00 ***Labor***............................ 48″ tall .....57.80 60″ tall......57.80	ea	—	$403.80	$455.80

VINYL

All vinyl windows are double-glazed with clear glass.

All costs are for standard windows. Manufacturers' window sizes vary. For standard units round measurements to the nearest size. Add approximately **80%** for custom sizes.

Some manufacturers provide a less rigid, lower grade of windows for **15%** less.

awning ▷

Item Description	Unit	20″ tall	24″ tall	30″ tall
24″ wide vinyl awning window ***Materials*** 20″ tall....214.00 24″ tall ...239.00 30″ tall....263.00 ***Labor*** 20″ tall............41.20 24″ tall .....41.20 30″ tall......41.20	ea	$255.20	$280.20	$304.20
30″ wide vinyl awning window ***Materials*** 20″ tall....247.00 24″ tall ...270.00 30″ tall....296.00 ***Labor*** 20″ tall............41.20 24″ tall .....41.20 30″ tall......41.20	ea	$288.20	$311.20	$337.20
36″ wide vinyl awning window ***Materials***...................... 24″ tall ...294.00 30″ tall ...330.00 ***Labor***............................ 24″ tall .....41.20 30″ tall......41.20	ea	—	$335.20	$371.20
40″ wide vinyl awning window ***Materials***...................... 24″ tall ...326.00 30″ tall....367.00 ***Labor***............................ 24″ tall .....41.20 30″ tall......41.20	ea	—	$367.20	$408.20

GRILLES AND GRID

For aluminum grid between panes or removable grilles outside of window add:

Half-round..............**$20**
Half-elliptical **$31**
Round.....................**$20**
Elliptical..................**$25**
Quarter-round..........**$20**
Casement................**$25**
Awning **$25**
Single-hung.............**$20**
Sliding **$21**
Fixed (picture)........**$24**

single-hung ▷

Item Description	Unit	36″ tall	48″ tall	60″ tall	72″ tall
24″ wide vinyl single-hung window ***Materials*** 36″ tall ...104.00 48″ tall ....118.00 60″ tall ....136.00 72″ tall ....156.00 ***Labor*** 36″ tall............41.20 48″ tall .....41.20 60″ tall......41.20 72″ tall......41.20	ea	$145.20	$159.20	$177.20	$197.20
36″ wide vinyl single-hung window ***Materials*** 36″ tall ...134.00 48″ tall....151.00 60″ tall....164.00 72″ tall....180.00 ***Labor*** 36″ tall............41.20 48″ tall .....41.20 60″ tall......41.20 72″ tall......57.80	ea	$175.20	$192.20	$205.20	$237.80
42″ wide vinyl single-hung window ***Materials*** 36″ tall ...148.00 48″ tall....165.00 60″ tall....180.00 72″ tall ....198.00 ***Labor*** 36″ tall............41.20 48″ tall .....41.20 60″ tall......57.80 72″ tall......57.80	ea	$189.20	$206.20	$237.80	$255.80

Item Description	Unit	24″ tall	36″ tall	48″ tall	60″ tall
48″ wide vinyl sliding window ***Materials*** 24″ tall....109.00 36″ tall....134.00 48″ tall ....152.00 60″ tall....180.00 ***Labor*** 24″ tall............41.20 36″ tall .....41.20 48″ tall......41.20 60″ tall......41.20	ea	$150.20	$175.20	$193.20	$221.20
60″ wide vinyl sliding window ***Materials*** .... 36″ tall....151.00 48″ tall ....175.00 60″ tall....215.00 ***Labor*** .... 36″ tall .....41.20 48″ tall......41.20 60″ tall......57.80	ea	—	$192.20	$216.20	$272.80
72″ wide vinyl sliding window ***Materials*** .... 48″ tall ...200.00 60″ tall ...233.00 ***Labor*** .... 48″ tall......57.80 60″ tall......57.80	ea	—	—	$257.80	$290.80

◁ **sliding**

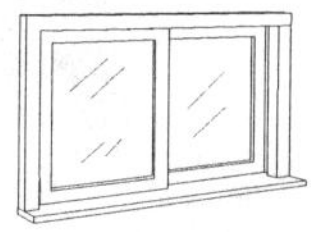

Item Description	Unit	36″ tall	48″ tall	60″ tall	72″ tall
24″ wide vinyl fixed (picture) window ***Materials*** 36″ tall.....64.40 48″ tall .....91.00 60″ tall....109.00 72″ tall.....118.00 ***Labor*** 36″ tall............41.20 48″ tall .....41.20 60″ tall......41.20 72″ tall......41.20	ea	$105.60	$132.20	$150.20	$159.20
30″ wide vinyl fixed (picture) window ***Materials*** 36″ tall.....77.30 48″ tall .....97.00 60″ tall....107.00 72″ tall....136.00 ***Labor*** 36″ tall............41.20 48″ tall .....41.20 60″ tall......41.20 72″ tall......41.20	ea	$118.50	$138.20	$148.20	$177.20
36″ wide vinyl fixed (picture) window ***Materials*** 36″ tall.....82.40 48″ tall.....111.00 60″ tall.....112.00 72″ tall....158.00 ***Labor*** 36″ tall............41.20 48″ tall .....41.20 60″ tall......41.20 72″ tall......57.80	ea	$123.60	$152.20	$153.20	$215.80
42″ wide vinyl fixed (picture) window ***Materials*** 36″ tall ...106.00 48″ tall....151.00 60″ tall....184.00 72″ tall ....211.00 ***Labor*** 36″ tall............41.20 48″ tall .....41.20 60″ tall......57.80 72″ tall......57.80	ea	$147.20	$192.20	$241.80	$268.80
48″ wide vinyl fixed (picture) window ***Materials*** 36″ tall ....111.00 48″ tall....136.00 60″ tall ....175.00 72″ tall ...200.00 ***Labor*** 36″ tall............41.20 48″ tall .....41.20 60″ tall......57.80 72″ tall......57.80	ea	$152.20	$177.20	$232.80	$257.80
60″ wide vinyl fixed (picture) window ***Materials*** 36″ tall ....112.00 48″ tall....142.00 60″ tall ....165.00 72″ tall ....218.00 ***Labor*** 36″ tall............41.20 48″ tall .....57.80 60″ tall......57.80 72″ tall 83.20	ea	$153.20	$199.80	$222.80	$301.20
72″ wide vinyl fixed (picture) window ***Materials*** 36″ tall....158.00 48″ tall...200.00 60″ tall....218.00 72″ tall....260.00 ***Labor*** 36″ tall............83.20 48″ tall.....83.20 60″ tall....122.00 72″ tall....122.00	ea	$241.20	$283.20	$340.00	$382.00

◁ **fixed (picture)**

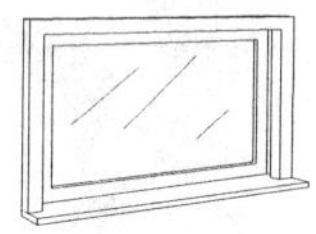

RELATED ITEMS

Doors

sliding patio 119

Item Description	Unit	24″ x 12″	36″ x 18″	48″ x 24″	60″ x 30″
Half-round wood window top ***Materials*** 24″ x 12″ ..594.00 36″ x 18″....767.00 48″ x 24″....756.00 60″ x 30″..1040.00 ***Labor*** 24″ x 12″...........41.20 36″ x 18″ .....41.20 48″ x 24″......57.80 60″ x 30″ 83.20	ea	$635.20	$808.20	$813.80	$1,123.20

◀ **WOOD**

◁ **half-round**

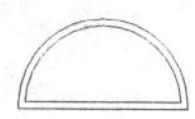

Item Description	Unit	36″ x 15″	48″ x 16″	60″ x 17″	72″ x 19″
Half-elliptical wood window top ***Materials*** 36″ x 15″ ..930.00 48″ x 16″ .1020.00 60″ x 17″ ..1100.00 72″ x 19″ ..1320.00 ***Labor*** 36″ x 15″ ....41.20 48″ x 16″ .....41.20 60″ x 17″......57.80 72″ x 19″ 83.20	ea	$971.20	$1,061.20	$1,157.80	$1,403.20
Add 114% for true divided light, spoke pattern (half-round or half-elliptical)					
Add $20 for 3 spoke hub grille (half-round window)					

◁ **half-elliptical**

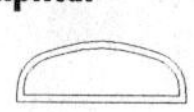

Item Description	Unit	30″ x 30″	48″ x 48″		
Round wood window ***Materials*** 30″ x 30″1300.00 48″ x 48″ .1500.00 ***Labor*** 30″ x 30″...........41.20 48″ x 48″ 41.20	ea	$1,341.20	$1,541.20		

◁ **round**

WOOD ▶ *continued*

elliptical ▷

Item Description	Unit	25" x 30"	30" x 36"		
Elliptical (oval) wood window ***Materials*** 25" x 30" 1500.00 30" x 36"..1690.00 ***Labor*** 25" x 30"..........41.20 30" x 36" 41.20	ea	$1,541.20	$1,731.20		
Add $18 for 4-lite grille in round or elliptical window					
Add $23 for 9-lite grille in round or elliptical window					
Add $28 for sunburst grille in round or elliptical window					

quarter-round ▷

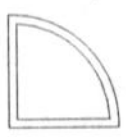

Item Description		24" x 24"	36" x 36"		
Quarter-round wood window ***Materials*** 24" x 24" ..731.00 36" x 36"....861.00 ***Labor*** 24" x 24"..........41.20 36" x 36" 41.20	ea	$772.20	$902.20		

Item Description		all sizes			
Add for single spoke grille in quarter-round window ***Materials*** All sizes.....22.00	ea	$22.00			
Add for double spoke grille in quarter-round window ***Materials*** All sizes.....26.00	ea	$26.00			
Add for single radial bar grille in quarter-round window ***Materials*** All sizes.....30.00	ea	$30.00			
Add for double radial bar grille in quarter-round window ***Materials*** All sizes.....34.00	ea	$34.00			

casement ▷

Item Description		36" tall	48" tall	60" tall	72" tall
18" wide wood casement window ***Materials*** 36" tall....197.00 48" tall ...263.00 60" tall ....315.00 72" tall....369.00 ***Labor*** 36" tall............41.20 48" tall .....41.20 60" tall......41.20 72" tall......41.20	ea	$238.20	$304.20	$356.20	$410.20
24" wide wood casement window ***Materials*** 36" tall....249.00 48" tall ...284.00 60" tall....326.00 72" tall ...386.00 ***Labor*** 36" tall............41.20 48" tall .....41.20 60" tall......57.80 72" tall......41.20	ea	$290.20	$325.20	$383.80	$427.20
30" wide wood casement window ***Materials*** 36" tall......... 48" tall....319.00 60" tall....375.00 72" tall....407.00 ***Labor*** 36" tall .... 48" tall .....57.80 60" tall......57.80 72" tall......41.20	ea	—	$376.80	$432.80	$448.20
36" wide wood casement window ***Materials*** 36" tall......... 48" tall....360.00 60" tall ....424.00 72" tall....462.00 ***Labor*** 36" tall .... 48" tall .....57.80 60" tall......57.80 72" tall......57.80	ea	—	$417.80	$481.80	$519.80
Add 87% for authentic divided lites in casement window					
Add $13 for removable wood grille in casement window					
Add $12 for aluminum grille between panes in casement window					

WOOD

All wood windows are double-glazed with clear glass. Interiors are natural wood and exteriors are primed wood or aluminum clad or vinyl clad.

Hardware on wood windows is bright brass, brushed brass, antique brass, or white.

All costs are for standard windows. Manufacturers' window sizes vary. For standard units, round to the nearest size. Add approximately **80%** for custom sizes.

awning ▷

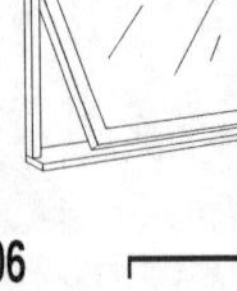

Item Description		20" tall	24" tall	30" tall	
24" wide wood awning window ***Materials*** 20" tall....210.00 24" tall ...227.00 30" tall....243.00 ***Labor*** 20" tall............41.20 24" tall .....41.20 30" tall......41.20	ea	$251.20	$268.20	$284.20	
30" wide wood awning window ***Materials*** 20" tall ...221.00 24" tall ...236.00 30" tall....252.00 ***Labor*** 20" tall............41.20 24" tall .....41.20 30" tall......57.80	ea	$262.20	$277.20	$309.80	

Item Description	Unit	20″ tall	24″ tall	30″ tall
36″ wide wood awning window ***Materials*** 20″ tall...235.00 24″ tall...252.00 30″ tall....266.00 ***Labor*** 20″ tall............41.20 24″ tall.....57.80 30″ tall......57.80	ea	$276.20	$309.80	$323.80
48″ wide wood awning window ***Materials*** 20″ tall...281.00 24″ tall...289.00 30″ tall....322.00 ***Labor*** 20″ tall............41.20 24″ tall.....57.80 30″ tall......57.80	ea	$322.20	$346.80	$379.80
Add 80% for authentic divided lites in awning window				
Add $14 for removable wood grille in awning window				
Add $13 for aluminum grille between panes in awning window				

Item Description	Unit	36″ tall	48″ tall	60″ tall	72″ tall
24″ wide wood double-hung window ***Materials*** 36″ tall....213.00 48″ tall....247.00 60″ tall....278.00 72″ tall....314.00 ***Labor*** 36″ tall............41.20 48″ tall.....41.20 60″ tall......41.20 72″ tall......41.20	ea	$254.20	$288.20	$319.20	$355.20
36″ wide wood double-hung window ***Materials*** 36″ tall...259.00 48″ tall...297.00 60″ tall....337.00 72″ tall...382.00 ***Labor*** 36″ tall............41.20 48″ tall.....41.20 60″ tall......41.20 72″ tall......57.80	ea	$300.20	$338.20	$378.20	$439.80
48″ wide wood double-hung window ***Materials*** 36″ tall...329.00 48″ tall...329.00 60″ tall....381.00 72″ tall...440.00 ***Labor*** 36″ tall............41.20 48″ tall.....41.20 60″ tall......57.80 72″ tall......57.80	ea	$370.20	$370.20	$438.80	$497.80
Add 105% for authentic divided lites in double-hung window					
Add $14 for removable wood grille in double-hung window					
Add $13 for aluminum grille between panes in double-hung window					
24″ wide wood single-hung window ***Materials*** 36″ tall....158.00 48″ tall....192.00 60″ tall...223.00 72″ tall....259.00 ***Labor*** 36″ tall............41.20 48″ tall.....41.20 60″ tall......41.20 72″ tall......41.20	ea	$199.20	$233.20	$264.20	$300.20
36″ wide wood single-hung window ***Materials*** 36″ tall....204.00 48″ tall....242.00 60″ tall....282.00 72″ tall....327.00 ***Labor*** 36″ tall............41.20 48″ tall.....41.20 60″ tall......41.20 72″ tall......57.80	ea	$245.20	$283.20	$323.20	$384.80
40″ wide wood single-hung window ***Materials*** 36″ tall...274.00 48″ tall....274.00 60″ tall....326.00 72″ tall....385.00 ***Labor*** 36″ tall............41.20 48″ tall.....41.20 60″ tall......57.80 72″ tall......57.80	ea	$315.20	$315.20	$383.80	$442.80
Add 105% for authentic divided lites in single-hung window					
Add $14 for removable wood grille in single-hung window					
Add $13 for aluminum grille between panes in single-hung window					
Add 97% for segmented top in single-hung window					

◁ **double-hung**

◁ **single-hung**

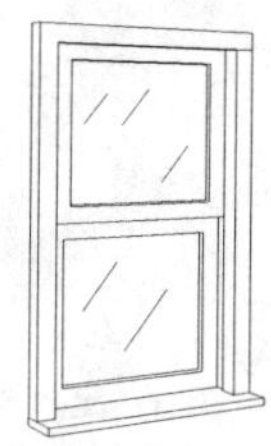

RELATED ITEMS

Doors

sliding patio 119

Item Description	Unit	24″ tall	36″ tall	48″ tall	60″ tall
48″ wide wood sliding window ***Materials*** 24″ tall....310.00 36″ tall...333.00 48″ tall....392.00 60″ tall....449.00 ***Labor*** 24″ tall............41.20 36″ tall.....41.20 48″ tall......41.20 60″ tall......41.20	ea	$351.20	$374.20	$433.20	$490.20
60″ wide wood sliding window ***Materials***...................... 36″ tall...398.00 48″ tall....450.00 60″ tall....516.00 ***Labor*** .... 36″ tall.....41.20 48″ tall......41.20 60″ tall......57.80	ea	—	$439.20	$491.20	$573.80

◁ **sliding**

Wood ▶ *continued*

sliding ▷ *continued*

Item Description	Unit			48" tall	60" tall
72" wide wood sliding window ***Materials*** .... 48" tall ...508.00 60" tall....572.00 ***Labor*** .... 48" tall......57.80 60" tall.........	ea			$565.80	$629.80
Add 90% for authentic divided lites in sliding window					
Add $14 for removable wood grille in sliding window					
Add $13 for aluminum grille between panes in sliding window					

fixed (picture) ▷

Item Description	Unit	36" tall	48" tall	60" tall	72" tall
24" wide wood fixed (picture) window ***Materials*** 36" tall...180.00 48" tall....214.00 60" tall ...245.00 72" tall....281.00 ***Labor*** 36" tall............41.20 48" tall .....41.20 60" tall......41.20 72" tall......41.20	ea	$221.20	$255.20	$286.20	$322.20
36" wide wood fixed (picture) window ***Materials*** 36" tall...226.00 48" tall ...264.00 60" tall ...304.00 72" tall....349.00 ***Labor*** 36" tall............41.20 48" tall .....41.20 60" tall......41.20 72" tall......57.80	ea	$267.20	$305.20	$345.20	$406.80
48" wide wood fixed (picture) window ***Materials*** 36" tall...296.00 48" tall ...296.00 60" tall ...348.00 72" tall....407.00 ***Labor*** 36" tall............41.20 48" tall .....41.20 60" tall......57.80 72" tall......57.80	ea	$337.20	$337.20	$405.80	$464.80
60" wide wood fixed (picture) window ***Materials*** .... 48" tall ...352.00 60" tall ...404.00 72" tall....470.00 ***Labor*** .... 48" tall .....57.80 60" tall......57.80 72" tall 83.20	ea	—	$409.80	$461.80	$553.20
72" wide wood fixed (picture) window ***Materials*** .... 60" tull....462.00 72" tall....526.00 ***Labor*** .... 60" tall .....83.20 72" tall 83.20	ea	—	—	$545.20	$609.20
Add 80% for authentic divided lites in fixed window					
Add $15 for removable wood grille in fixed window					
Add $14 for aluminum grille between panes in fixed window					
Add 97% for segmented top in fixed window					

Skylight ▶

additional costs ▷

See "Low-E and Argon" on page 501. Skylight prices include flashing for roof with low-profile roofing such as asphalt shingles. For tile shingles, or ribbed metal roofing add for high-profile roof. Low-slope roof includes a curb and flat roof includes a special sloped curb.

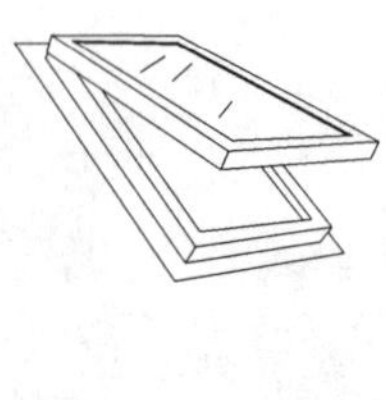

Item Description	Unit	all types			
Add for laminated glass over tempered glass in skylight or roof window ***Materials*** All types....32.00	ea	$32.00			
Add for Low-E in skylight or roof window ***Materials*** All types......8.00	ea	$8.00			
Add for argon gas filled skylight or roof window ***Materials*** All types......7.00	ea	$7.00			
Add or bronze or gray tint (all sizes) ***Materials*** All types.....13.00	ea	$13.00			
Add for skylight or roof window installed on high-profile roof ***Materials*** All types 21.00	ea	$21.00			
Add for skylight or roof window installed on low-slope roof (less than 4-12) ***Materials*** All types...267.00	ea	$267.00			
Add for skylight or roof window installed on flat roof (less than 2-12) ***Materials*** All types...276.00	ea	$276.00			

Item Description	Unit	24" x 24"	24" x 48"	30" x 30"	48" x 48"	
Single dome skylight ***Materials*** 24" x 24"....58.00 24" x 48"....114.00 30" x 30"......91.30 48" x 48"....289.00 ***Labor*** 24" x 24".........109.00 24" x 48"...109.00 30" x 30"....109.00 48" x 48"....109.00	ea	$167.00	$223.00	$200.30	$398.00	◁ dome
Double dome skylight ***Materials*** 24" x 24"....77.00 24" x 48"....159.00 30" x 30"....148.00 48" x 48"....341.00 ***Labor*** 24" x 24".........109.00 24" x 48"...109.00 30" x 30"....109.00 48" x 48"....109.00	ea	$186.00	$268.00	$257.00	$450.00	
Triple dome skylight ***Materials*** 24" x 24"....99.00 24" x 48"...229.00 30" x 30"....181.00 48" x 48"....437.00 ***Labor*** 24" x 24".........109.00 24" x 48"...109.00 30" x 30"....109.00 48" x 48"....109.00	ea	$208.00	$338.00	$290.00	$546.00	
Single dome ventilating skylight ***Materials*** 24" x 24"...121.00 24" x 48"...238.00 30" x 30"....190.00 48" x 48"...602.00 ***Labor*** 24" x 24".........116.00 24" x 48"....116.00 30" x 30".....116.00 48" x 48".....116.00	ea	$237.00	$354.00	$306.00	$718.00	◁ ventilating
Double dome ventilating skylight ***Materials*** 24" x 24"...161.00 24" x 48"...332.00 30" x 30"...309.00 48" x 48"....707.00 ***Labor*** 24" x 24".........116.00 24" x 48"....116.00 30" x 30".....116.00 48" x 48".....116.00	ea	$277.00	$448.00	$425.00	$823.00	
Triple dome ventilating skylight ***Materials*** 24" x 24"..206.00 24" x 48"....476.00 30" x 30"....378.00 48" x 48"....910.00 ***Labor*** 24" x 24".........116.00 24" x 48"....116.00 30" x 30".....116.00 48" x 48".....116.00	ea	$322.00	$592.00	$494.00	$1,026.00	

Item Description	Unit	28" long	38" long	48" long	55" long	
22" wide fixed skylight ***Materials*** 28" long..210.00 38" long...244.00 48" long....273.00 55" long....297.00 ***Labor*** 28" long..........112.00 38" long....112.00 48" long.....112.00 55" long.....112.00	ea	$322.00	$356.00	$385.00	$409.00	◁ fixed
30" wide fixed skylight ***Materials*** .... 38" long....283.00 55" long....345.00 ***Labor*** .... 38" long....112.00 55" long.....112.00	ea	—	$395.00	—	$457.00	
44" wide fixed skylight ***Materials*** 28" long..307.00 48" long....391.00 ***Labor*** 28" long..........112.00 48" long.....112.00	ea	$419.00	—	$503.00	—	
22" wide fixed skylight with ventilation flap ***Materials*** 28" long..237.00 38" long...273.00 48" long...302.00 55" long....320.00 ***Labor*** 28" long..........112.00 38" long....112.00 48" long.....112.00 55" long.....112.00	ea	$349.00	$385.00	$414.00	$432.00	◁ fixed with vent flap
30" wide fixed skylight with ventilation flap ***Materials*** .... 38" long....318.00 55" long....373.00 ***Labor*** .... 38" long....112.00 55" long.....112.00	ea	—	$430.00	—	$485.00	
44" wide fixed skylight with ventilation flap ***Materials*** 28" long..357.00 48" long....428.00 ***Labor*** 28" long..........112.00 48" long.....112.00	ea	$469.00	—	$540.00	—	
22" wide ventilating skylight ***Materials*** 28" long..393.00 38" long...428.00 48" long...468.00 55" long....487.00 ***Labor*** 28" long.........122.00 38" long....122.00 48" long....122.00 55" long....122.00	ea	$515.00	$550.00	$590.00	$609.00	◁ ventilating
30" wide ventilating skylight ***Materials*** .... 38" long....476.00 55" long....550.00 ***Labor*** .... 38" long....122.00 55" long....122.00	ea	—	$598.00	—	$672.00	
44" wide ventilating skylight ***Materials*** 28" long..501.00 48" long.....611.00 ***Labor*** 28" long.........122.00 48" long....122.00	ea	$623.00	—	$733.00	—	

RELATED ITEMS

Doors

sliding patio 119

SKYLIGHTS ▶ *continued*

roof window ▷

Item Description	Unit	28" long	38" long	48" long	55" long
22" wide roof window *Materials* 28" long..539.00 48" long....594.00 *Labor* 28" long.........122.00 48" long....122.00	ea	$661.00	—	$716.00	—
30" wide roof window *Materials* .... 38" long ...598.00 55" long ...683.00 *Labor* .... 38" long....122.00 55" long....122.00	ea	—	$720.00	—	$805.00
44" wide roof window *Materials* .... 55" long....746.00 *Labor* .... 55" long....122.00	ea	—	—	—	$868.00

accessories ▷

Item Description	Unit	28" long	38" long	48" long	55" long
Add for cord-operated roller shades *Materials* 28" long....57.00 38" long.....57.00 48" long......57.00 55" long......57.00 *Labor* 28" long..........34.70 38" long.....34.70 48" long.....34.70 55" long.....34.70	ea	$91.70	$91.70	$91.70	$91.70
Add for motorized rod cord control for roller shades *Materials*28" long....176.00 38" long....176.00 48" long....176.00 55" long....176.00	ea	$176.00	$176.00	$176.00	$176.00
Add for manually controlled Venetian blinds *Materials* 28" long...80.00 38" long.....94.00 48" long.....99.00 55" long....126.00	ea	$80.00	$94.00	$99.00	$126.00
Add for electrically controlled skylight system *Materials* 28" long..130.00 38" long....130.00 48" long....130.00 55" long....130.00 *Labor* 28" long..........83.20 38" long.....83.20 48" long.....83.20 55" long.....83.20	ea	$213.20	$213.20	$213.20	$213.20
Add for electrically controlled window or skylight opener *Materials* 28" long..130.00 38" long....130.00 48" long....130.00 55" long....130.00 *Labor* 28" long..........57.80 38" long.....57.80 48" long......57.80 55" long......57.80	ea	$187.80	$187.80	$187.80	$187.80
Add for infrared remote control system for opener *Materials* 28" long..287.00 38" long...287.00 48" long....287.00 55" long....287.00 *Labor* 28" long..........46.20 38" long.....46.20 48" long.....46.20 55" long.....46.20	ea	$333.20	$333.20	$333.20	$333.20

STORM WINDOW ▶

Item Description	Unit	24" tall	36" tall	48" tall	60" tall
aluminum ▷ **24" wide aluminum storm window** *Materials* 24" tall......61.00 36" tall.....89.00 48" tall.....111.00 60" tall....125.00 *Labor* 24" tall............41.60 36" tall.....41.60 48" tall......41.60 60" tall......41.60	ea	$102.60	$130.60	$152.60	$166.60
36" wide aluminum storm window *Materials* 24" tall.....89.00 36" tall....117.00 48" tall....136.00 60" tall....156.00 *Labor* 24" tall............41.60 36" tall.....41.60 48" tall......41.60 60" tall.....44.90	ea	$130.60	$158.60	$177.60	$200.90
48" wide aluminum storm window *Materials* 24" tall.....111.00 36" tall....136.00 48" tall....163.00 60" tall....189.00 *Labor* 24" tall............41.60 36" tall.....41.60 48" tall.....44.90 60" tall.....44.90	ea	$152.60	$177.60	$207.90	$233.90
60" wide aluminum storm window *Materials* 24" tall....125.00 36" tall....156.00 48" tall....189.00 60" tall....221.00 *Labor* 24" tall............41.60 36" tall.....44.90 48" tall.....44.90 60" tall.....44.90	ea	$166.60	$200.90	$233.90	$265.90
72" wide aluminum storm window *Materials* 24" tall....136.00 36" tall....175.00 48" tall....215.00 60" tall...254.00 *Labor* 24" tall............41.60 36" tall.....44.90 48" tall.....44.90 60" tall.....50.80	ea	$177.60	$219.90	$259.90	$304.80
wood ▷ **24" wide wood storm window** *Materials* 24" tall......74.80 36" tall...106.30 48" tall....123.00 60" tall....139.00 *Labor* 24" tall............41.60 36" tall.....41.60 48" tall......41.60 60" tall......41.60	ea	$116.40	$147.90	$164.60	$180.60

Item Description	Unit	24" tall	36" tall	48" tall	60" tall
36" wide wood storm window ***Materials*** 24" tall....106.30 36" tall....130.00 48" tall....152.00 60" tall....175.00 ***Labor*** 24" tall............41.60 36" tall.....41.60 48" tall......41.60 60" tall.....44.90	ea	$147.90	$171.60	$193.60	$219.90
48" wide wood storm window ***Materials*** 24" tall....123.00 36" tall....152.00 48" tall....181.00 60" tall....211.00 ***Labor*** 24" tall............41.60 36" tall.....41.60 48" tall.....44.90 60" tall.....44.90	ea	$164.60	$193.60	$225.90	$255.90
60" wide wood storm window ***Materials*** 24" tall....139.00 36" tall....175.00 48" tall....211.00 60" tall....247.00 ***Labor*** 24" tall............41.60 36" tall.....44.90 48" tall.....44.90 60" tall.....44.90	ea	$180.60	$219.90	$255.90	$291.90
72" wide wood storm window ***Materials*** 24" tall....152.00 36" tall....197.00 48" tall....240.00 60" tall...284.00 ***Labor*** 24" tall............41.60 36" tall.....44.90 48" tall.....44.90 60" tall.....50.80	ea	$193.60	$241.90	$284.90	$334.80
24" wide window screen ***Materials*** 24" tall......10.20 36" tall......12.50 48" tall......14.10 60" tall......17.00 ***Labor*** 24" tall.............5.20 36" tall.......5.20 48" tall.......5.20 60" tall.......5.20	ea	$15.40	$17.70	$19.30	$22.20
36" wide window screen ***Materials*** 24" tall......12.20 36" tall......13.10 48" tall......17.90 60" tall.....20.00 ***Labor*** 24" tall.............5.20 36" tall.......5.20 48" tall.......5.20 60" tall.......5.20	ea	$17.40	$18.30	$23.10	$25.20

◄ **SCREEN**

Item Description		1/8" thick	3/16" thick	1/4" thick	3/8" thick
Reglaze window with clear glass ***Materials*** 1/8"..........3.80 3/16".......5.10 1/4".......4.20 3/8"......13.40 ***Labor*** 1/8"..................2.62 3/16".......2.62 1/4".......2.62 3/8".......2.62	sf	$6.42	$7.72	$6.82	$16.02
Reglaze window with tempered glass ***Materials*** 1/8"..........6.30 3/16".......7.50 1/4".......7.90 ***Labor*** 1/8"..................2.62 3/16".......2.62 1/4".......2.62	sf	$8.92	$10.12	$10.52	—
Reglaze window with laminated glass ***Materials*** .... 1/4".......9.40 3/8"......13.10 ***Labor*** .... 1/4".......2.62 3/8".......2.62	sf	—	—	$12.02	$15.72
Reglaze window with polished wire glass ***Materials*** .... 1/4"......24.90 ***Labor*** .... 1/4".......2.62	sf	—	—	$27.52	—
Minimum charge for reglazing work ***Materials*****..................32.00 ***Labor***.........................41.60	ea	$73.60	—	—	—

◄ **REGLAZE**

◁ minimum

Item Description		all sizes			
Rehang sash weight in antique double-hung window ***Materials*** All sizes .....16.00 ***Labor*** All sizes...........94.40	ea	$110.40			
Refurbish antique double-hung window ***Materials*** All sizes.....29.00 ***Labor*** All sizes..........130.00	ea	$159.00			
Recondition antique wood window sash ***Materials*** All sizes .....14.00 ***Labor*** All sizes...........86.50	ea	$100.50			

◄ **REPAIR**

RELATED ITEMS

Doors

sliding patio.................119

NOTES: ______

______ end

TIME & MATERIAL CHARTS *(selected items)*

Windows Materials

See **Windows** *material prices with the line items and other information in the* **QuickFinder** *column.*

Windows Labor

LABORER	BASE WAGE	PAID LEAVE	TRUE WAGE	FICA	FUTA	WORKER'S COMP.	UNEMPLOY. INSUR.	HEALTH INSUR.	RETIRE (401K)	LIABILITY INSUR.	COST PER HOUR
Installer	$23.60	1.84	$25.44	1.95	.20	4.96	2.21	2.69	.76	3.43	$41.60
Demolition laborer	$13.90	1.08	$14.98	1.15	.12	4.79	1.30	2.69	.45	2.02	$27.50

Paid Leave is calculated based on two weeks paid vacation, one week sick leave, and seven paid holidays. Employer's matching portion of **FICA** is 7.65 percent. **FUTA** (Federal Unemployment) is .8 percent. **Worker's compensation** for the windows trade was calculated using a national average of 19.50 percent. **Unemployment insurance** was calculated using a national average of 8.7 percent. **Health insurance** was calculated based on a projected national average for 2002 of $535 per employee (and family when applicable) per month. Employer pays 80 percent for a per month cost of $428 per employee. **Retirement** is based on a 401(k) retirement program with employer matching of 50 percent. Employee contributions to the 401(k) plan are an average of 6 percent of the true wage. **Liability insurance** is based on a national average of 13.2 percent.

Windows Labor Productivity

WORK DESCRIPTION	LABORER	COST PER HOUR	PRODUCTIVITY	UNIT PRICE
Remove window				
small (4 to 10 sf)	carpenter	$41.60	.263	$10.90 ea
average size (11 to 16 sf)	carpenter	$41.60	.270	$11.20 ea
large (17 to 29 sf)	carpenter	$41.60	.278	$11.60 ea
very large (30 sf and larger)	carpenter	$41.60	.286	$11.90 ea
Remove window for work & reinstall				
small (4 to 10 sf)	carpenter	$41.60	1.23	$51.20 ea
average size (11 to 16 sf)	carpenter	$41.60	1.72	$71.60 ea
large (17 to 28 sf)	carpenter	$41.60	2.50	$104.00 ea
very large (30 sf and larger)	carpenter	$41.60	3.70	$154.00 ea
Install window				
small (4 to 10 sf)	carpenter	$41.60	.990	$41.20 ea
average size (11 to 16 sf)	carpenter	$41.60	1.39	$57.80 ea
large (17 to 28 sf)	carpenter	$41.60	2.00	$83.20 ea
very large (30 sf and larger)	carpenter	$41.60	2.94	$122.00 ea
Install skylight or roof window				
dome ventilating	carpenter	$41.60	2.78	$116.00 ea
fixed	carpenter	$41.60	2.70	$112.00 ea
ventilating	carpenter	$41.60	2.94	$122.00 ea
cord-operated roller shades	carpenter	$41.60	.833	$34.70 ea
electrically controlled system	carpenter	$41.60	2.00	$83.20 ea
electrically controlled opener	carpenter	$41.60	1.39	$57.80 ea
infrared remote control system for opener	carpenter	$41.60	1.11	$46.20 ea
Install storm window				
small (4 to 14 sf)	carpenter	$41.60	1.00	$41.60 ea
average size (15 to 25 sf)	carpenter	$41.60	1.08	$44.90 ea
large storm (26 sf and larger)	carpenter	$41.60	1.22	$50.80 ea
Reglaze window				
remove and replace glass	carpenter	$41.60	.063	$2.62 sf
Repair antique double-hung window				
rehang sash weight	carpenter	$41.60	2.27	$94.40 ea
refurbish	carpenter	$41.60	3.13	$130.00 ea
recondition	carpenter	$41.60	2.08	$86.50 ea

mini price list .... Manufactured Housing

SELECTED PRICES FROM THE *NATIONAL MANUFACTURED HOUSING ESTIMATOR*

This chapter contains some of the most common items found in manufactured housing. ***It is not a complete price list.*** A comprehensive costbook of manufactured housing costs is in the planning stages at *Craftsman Book Company*.

Item Description	Unit	Remove	Replace	Total
APPLIANCES				
Clothes line				
30-line, exterior	ea	$7.01	$157.80	$164.81
Replace Mat. ....126.00 Lab. 31.80				
Remove .... Lab. 7.01				
7-line, exterior	ea	$6.65	$105.80	$112.45
Replace Mat. ....75.30 Lab. 30.50				
Remove .... Lab. 6.65				
remove for work, then reinstall	ea	—	$9.18	$9.18
Replace .... Lab. 9.18				
Sidewall exhaust ventilator				
for 2" to 3" thick walls	ea	$9.87	$110.00	$119.87
Replace Mat. ....51.60 Lab. 58.40				
Remove .... Lab. 9.87				
for 2-3/4" to 4" thick walls	ea	$9.87	$109.80	$119.67
Replace Mat. ....52.00 Lab. 57.80				
Remove .... Lab. 9.70				
remove for work, then reinstall	ea	—	$93.00	$93.00
Replace Mat. ....2.10 Lab. 90.90				
CABINETS				
Mobile-home type cabinets, average grade				
lower units	lf	$3.07	$54.62	$57.69
Replace Mat. ....48.50 Lab. 6.12				
Remove .... Lab. 3.07				
upper units	lf	$3.07	$38.05	$41.12
Replace Mat. ....33.00 Lab. 5.05				
Remove .... Lab. 3.07				
lower island units	lf	$3.07	$75.75	$78.82
Replace Mat. ....68.10 Lab. 7.65				
Remove .... Lab. 3.07				

◄ **CLOTHES LINE**
Steel posts, umbrella-style supports with vinyl-coated rayon lines.

◄ **VENTILATOR**
Louvered inside grille, insulated outside door, approximately 9" x 9".

◄ **CABINETS**
Mobile-home style

	Item Description	Unit	Remove	Replace	Total
CABINETS ▶ *continued*	**upper island units**	lf	$3.07	$64.31	$67.38
	Replace Mat. 58.80 Lab. 5.51				
	Remove Lab. 3.07				
	remove for work, then reinstall	lf	—	$7.04	$7.04
	Replace Lab. 7.04				
	DOORS				
ACCESS DOOR ▶	**access door**				
	for water heater or furnace	ea	$14.70	$70.50	$85.20
	Replace Mat. 46.00 Lab. 24.50				
	Remove Lab. 14.70				
	remove for work, then reinstall	ea	—	$30.60	$30.60
	Replace Lab. 30.60				
ENTRY DOOR ▶	**mobile-home type entry door, fiberglass**				
	flush	ea	$15.40	$121.10	$136.50
	Replace Mat. 98.10 Lab. 23.00				
	Remove Lab. 15.40				
	flush with fixed lite	ea	$15.40	$135.00	$150.40
	Replace Mat. 112.00 Lab. 23.00				
	Remove Lab. 15.40				
	flush with sliding window	ea	$15.40	$147.00	$162.40
	Replace Mat. 124.00 Lab. 23.00				
	Remove Lab. 15.40				
	remove for work, then reinstall	ea	—	$32.10	$32.10
	Replace Lab. 32.10				
COMBINATION DOOR ▶	**mobile-home type combination entry door (with storm door)**				
	flush	ea	$18.40	$154.10	$172.50
	Replace Mat. 128.00 Lab. 26.10				
	Remove Lab. 18.40				
	flush with fixed lite	ea	$18.40	$173.10	$191.50
	Replace Mat. 147.00 Lab. 26.10				
	Remove Lab. 18.40				
	flush with sliding window	ea	$18.40	$188.10	$206.50
	Replace Mat. 162.00 Lab. 26.10				
	Remove Lab. 18.40				
	remove for work, then reinstall	ea	—	$32.70	$32.70
	Replace Lab. 32.70				
	DOOR HARDWARE				
LOCKSET ▶	**mobile-home type lockset**				
	interior passage	ea	$6.38	$24.30	$30.68
	Replace Mat. 12.50 Lab. 11.80				
	Remove Lab. 6.38				
	interior privacy	ea	$6.38	$26.20	$32.58
	Replace Mat. 14.40 Lab. 11.80				
	Remove Lab. 6.38				
	remove for work, then reinstall	ea	—	$13.80	$13.80
	Replace Lab. 13.80				

Item Description	Unit	Remove	Replace	Total	
mobile-home type entrance lockset					◀ **ENTRANCE LOCKSET**
standard quality	ea	$7.87	$45.50	$53.37	
Replace Mat. ....28.50 Lab. 17.00					
Remove .... Lab. 7.87					
remove for work, then reinstall	ea	—	$22.60	$22.60	
Replace .... Lab. 22.60					
mobile-home type deadbolt					◀ **DEADBOLT**
standard quality	ea	$5.48	$38.10	$43.58	
Replace Mat. ....18.60 Lab. 19.50					
Remove .... Lab. 5.48					
remove for work, then reinstall	ea	—	$23.00	$23.00	
Replace .... Lab...........23.00					
ELECTRICAL					
Light fixture, mobile-home style					◀ **LIGHT FIXTURE**
average quality	ea	$11.31	$30.00	$41.31	
Replace Mat. ....12.40 Lab. 17.60					
Remove .... Lab. 11.31					
high quality	ea	$11.31	$37.40	$48.71	
Replace Mat. ....19.80 Lab. 17.60					
Remove .... Lab. 11.31					
remove for work, then reinstall	ea	—	$18.90	$18.90	
Replace .... Lab...........18.90					
FINISH CARPENTRY					
Casing (door or window)					◀ **CASING**
2-1/2" prefinished plastic	lf	$.45	$1.43	$1.88	
Replace Mat. .... .30 Lab. 1.13					
Remove .... Lab. .... .45					
Ceiling cove					◀ **COVE**
3/4" prefinished plastic	lf	$.45	$1.42	$1.87	
Replace Mat. .... .29 Lab. 1.13					
Remove .... Lab. .... .45					
Gimp molding					◀ **GIMP MOLDING**
3/4" prefinished plastic	lf	$.45	$1.43	$1.88	
Replace Mat. .... .30 Lab. 1.13					
Remove .... Lab. .... .45					
1" prefinished plastic	lf	$.45	$1.43	$1.88	
Replace Mat. .... .30 Lab. 1.13					
Remove .... Lab. .... .45					
Outside corner trim					◀ **OUTSIDE CORNER**
1" prefinished plastic	lf	$.45	$1.43	$1.88	
Replace Mat. .... .30 Lab. 1.13					
Remove .... Lab. .... .45					

	Item Description	Unit	Remove	Replace	Total
SHOE ▶	**Shoe molding**				
	3/4" prefinished plastic	lf	$.45	$1.43	$1.88
	Replace Mat. .... .30 Lab. 1.13				
	Remove .... Lab. .... .45				
	FOUNDATIONS, SETUP, & SITE PREP				
ANCHOR ▶ *Galvanized*	**Anchor**				
	30" auger type	ea	$3.67	$22.60	$26.27
	Replace Mat. ....10.30 Lab. 12.30				
	Remove .... Lab. 3.67				
	48" auger type	ea	$3.67	$25.00	$28.67
	Replace Mat. ....12.70 Lab. 12.30				
	Remove .... Lab. 3.67				
	Slab type (includes concrete slab)	ea	$5.54	$32.60	$38.14
	Replace Mat............17.30 Lab. 15.30				
	Remove .... Lab. 5.54				
JACK ▶	**Jack, adjustable**				
	from 1'8" to 3'	ea	$3.07	$42.18	$45.25
	Replace Mat...........33.00 Lab. 9.18				
	Remove .... Lab. 3.07				
	from 3'1" to 5'	ea	$3.07	$50.48	$53.55
	Replace Mat. ....41.30 Lab. 9.18				
	Remove .... Lab. 3.07				
	from 4'6" to 7'9"	ea	$3.07	$62.88	$65.95
	Replace Mat............53.70 Lab. 9.18				
	Remove .... Lab. 3.07				
	remove for work, then reinstall	ea	—	$13.80	$13.80
	Replace .... Lab. 13.80				
SETUP ▶ *All materials furnished by manufacturer.*	**Raise, setup, block, & level**				
	single wide	ea	—	$551.00	$551.00
	Replace Mat. .... Lab. 551.00				
	double wide	ea	—	$734.00	$734.00
	Replace Mat. .... Lab...........734.00				
	triple wide	ea	—	$1,040.00	$1,040.00
	Replace Mat. .... Lab. 1,040.00				
RELEVEL ▶	**Relevel**				
	single wide	ea	—	$188.10	$188.10
	Replace Mat. ....35.10 Lab. 153.00				
	double wide	ea	—	$437.20	$437.20
	Replace Mat. ....70.20 Lab. 367.00				
	triple wide	ea	—	$686.00	$686.00
	Replace Mat. ....105.00 Lab...........581.00				
SITE PREP ▶	**Site prep**				
	standard conditions	ea	—	$1,620.00	$1,620.00
	Replace .... Lab........1,620.00				

Item Description		Unit	Remove	Replace	Total
Tie-down strap					
frame type		ea	$4.46	$15.62	$20.08
Replace Mat. 9.50	Lab. 6.12				
Remove	Lab. 4.46				
roof type		ea	$6.76	$30.35	$37.11
Replace Mat. 22.70	Lab. 7.65				
Remove	Lab. 6.76				
Utility hookup					
sewer & water		ea	—	$702.00	$702.00
Replace 702.00					
electrical		ea	—	$743.00	$743.00
Replace Mat. 743.00					
HVAC					
Baseboard heater, mobile-home type, electric					
1,500 watt		lf	$3.07	$15.52	$18.59
Replace Mat. 9.40	Lab. 6.12				
Remove	Lab. 3.07				
2,000 watt		lf	$3.07	$18.92	$21.99
Replace Mat. 12.80	Lab. 6.12				
Remove	Lab. 3.07				
2,500 watt		lf	$3.07	$20.52	$23.59
Replace Mat. 14.40	Lab. 6.12				
Remove	Lab. 3.07				
remove for work, then reinstall		lf	—	$9.18	$9.18
Replace	Lab. 9.18				
Furnace, mobile-home type, gas or electric					
35,000 btu		ea	$38.60	$650.00	$688.60
Replace Mat. 497.00	Lab. 153.00				
Remove	Lab. 38.60				
55,000 btu		ea	$38.60	$936.00	$974.60
Replace Mat. 768.00	Lab. 168.00				
Remove	Lab. 38.60				
70,000 btu		ea	$38.60	$1,049.00	$1,087.60
Replace Mat. 866.00	Lab. 183.00				
Remove	Lab. 38.60				
80,000 btu		ea	$38.60	$1,109.00	$1,147.60
Replace Mat. 926.00	Lab. 183.00				
Remove	Lab. 38.60				
100,000 btu		ea	$38.60	$1,140.00	$1,178.60
Replace Mat. 1,040.00	Lab. 100.00				
Remove	Lab. 38.60				
125,000 btu		ea	$38.60	$1,323.00	$1,361.60
Replace Mat. 1,140.00	Lab. 183.00				
Remove	Lab. 38.60				
remove for work, then reinstall		ea	—	$260.00	$260.00
Replace	Lab. 260.00				

◀ **TIE-DOWN STRAP**
Galvanized. Frame type includes adapter and is 6′ long. Roof type is 37′ long.

◀ **UTILITY HOOKUP**

◀ **BASEBOARD HEATER**

◀ **FURNACE**

	Item Description	Unit	Remove	Replace	Total
	MOVING & TOWING				
TRANSPORT ▶	**Transport fees**				
	average, per section, per mile	ea	—	$2.36	$2.36
	Replace .... Lab. 2.36				
	average, pilot car, per mile	ea	—	$.70	$.70
	Replace .... Lab. .... .70				
	PLUMBING				
ELECTRIC WATER HEATER ▶	**Water heater, mobile-home style, electric**				
	10 gallon	ea	$23.00	$145.90	$168.90
	Replace Mat. ....100.00 Lab. 45.90				
	Remove .... Lab. 23.00				
	20 gallon	ea	$23.00	$156.90	$179.90
	Replace Mat. ....111.00 Lab. 45.90				
	Remove .... Lab. 23.00				
	30 gallon	ea	$23.00	$186.90	$209.90
	Replace Mat. ....141.00 Lab. 45.90				
	Remove .... Lab. 23.00				
	40 gallon	ea	$23.00	$200.90	$223.90
	Replace Mat. ....155.00 Lab. 45.90				
	Remove .... Lab. 23.00				
	50 gallon	ea	$23.00	$245.90	$268.90
	Replace Mat. ....200.00 Lab. 45.90				
	Remove .... Lab. 23.00				
	remove for work. then reinstall	ea	—	$58.10	$58.10
	Replace Mat. .... Lab. 58.10				
GAS WATER HEATER ▶	**Water heater, mobile-home style, gas**				
	20 gallon	ea	$23.00	$167.60	$190.60
	Replace Mat. ....111.00 Lab. 56.60				
	Remove .... Lab. 23.00				
	30 gallon	ea	$23.00	$192.60	$215.60
	Replace Mat. ....136.00 Lab. 56.60				
	Remove .... Lab. 23.00				
	40 gallon	ea	$23.00	$216.60	$239.60
	Replace Mat. ....160.00 Lab. 56.60				
	Remove .... Lab. 23.00				
	50 gallon	ea	$23.00	$251.60	$274.60
	Replace Mat. ....195.00 Lab. 56.60				
	Remove .... Lab. 23.00				
	remove for work. then reinstall	ea	—	$58.10	$58.10
	Replace Mat. .... Lab. 58.10				
	ROOFING				
DRIP EDGE ▶	**Drip edge**				
	aluminum	lf	$.12	$1.22	$1.34
	Replace Mat. .... .30 Lab. .... .92				
	Remove .... Lab. .... .12				

Item Description	Unit	Remove	Replace	Total	
galvanized	lf	$.12	$1.22	$1.34	
Replace Mat. .30 Lab. .92					
Remove Lab. .12					
Flashing					◄ FLASHING
aluminum, flexible	lf	$.12	$2.02	$2.14	
Replace Mat. 1.10 Lab. .92					
Remove Lab. .12					
galvanized	lf	$.12	$1.92	$2.04	
Replace Mat. 1.00 Lab. .92					
Remove Lab. .12					
J-rail					◄ J-RAIL
aluminum	lf	$.12	$1.32	$1.44	
Replace Mat. .40 Lab. .92					
Remove Lab. .12					
Roof coating					◄ ROOF COATING
complete roof (all types)	sf	—	$.38	$.38	
Replace Mat. .20 Lab. .18					
seams and edges only	lf	—	$.48	$.48	
Replace Mat. .20 Lab. .28					
Roof repair					
patch	ea	—	$27.40	$27.40	
Replace Mat. 4.40 Lab. 23.00					
replace section (per lf of 4′ wide section)	lf	$.62	$7.06	$7.68	
Replace Mat. 4.00 Lab. 3.06					
Remove Lab. .62					
ROUGH CARPENTRY					
Belt rail					◄ BELT RAIL
1″ x 2″	lf	$.30	$.81	$1.11	
Replace Mat. .20 Lab. .61					
Remove Lab. .30					
1″ x 4″	lf	$.30	$1.07	$1.37	
Replace Mat. .30 Lab. .77					
Remove Lab. 1.07					
Belt rail including dado cut					◄ BELT RAIL WITH DADO
1″ x 2″	lf	$.45	$1.42	$1.87	
Replace Mat. .20 Lab. 1.22					
Remove Lab. .45					
1″ x 4″	lf	$.45	$1.68	$2.13	
Replace Mat. .30 Lab. 1.38					
Remove Lab. .45					
Exterior wall, mobile home, with belt rail					◄ EXTERIOR WALL
2″ x 2″	lf	$1.24	$15.18	$16.42	
Replace Mat. 6.00 Lab. 9.18					
Remove Lab. 1.24					
2″ x 4″	lf	$1.24	$19.10	$20.34	
Replace Mat. 8.40 Lab. 10.70					
Remove Lab. 1.24					

	Item Description	Unit	Remove	Replace	Total
EXTERIOR WALLS ▶ *continued*	**2″ x 6″**	lf	$1.24	$24.50	$25.74
	Replace Mat. ....12.20 Lab. 12.30				
	Remove .... Lab. 1.24				
INTERIOR WALL ▶	**Interior wall, mobile home**				
	2″ x 2″	lf	$1.09	$11.52	$12.61
	Replace Mat. ....5.40 Lab. 6.12				
	Remove .... Lab. 1.09				
	2″ x 4″	lf	$1.09	$13.52	$14.61
	Replace Mat. ....7.40 Lab. 6.12				
	Remove .... Lab. 1.09				
	2″ x 6″	lf	$1.09	$19.37	$20.46
	Replace Mat. ....10.80 Lab. 8.57				
	Remove .... Lab. 1.09				
JOIST SYSTEM ▶ 2″ x 6″ PER JOIST	**Joist system, mobile home, per joist, 2″ x 6″**				
	10′	ea	$3.69	$15.76	$19.45
	Replace Mat. ....9.30 Lab. 6.46				
	Remove .... Lab. 3.69				
	12′	ea	$3.84	$18.84	$22.68
	Replace Mat. ....11.10 Lab. 7.74				
	Remove .... Lab. 3.84				
	14′	ea	$4.01	$22.03	$26.04
	Replace Mat. ....13.00 Lab. 9.03				
	Remove .... Lab. 4.01				
	16′	ea	$4.16	$25.20	$29.36
	Replace Mat. ....14.90 Lab. 10.30				
	Remove .... Lab. 4.16				
JOIST SYSTEM ▶ 2″ x 8″ PER JOIST	**Joist system, mobile home, per joist, 2″ x 8″**				
	10′	ea	$3.84	$16.88	$20.72
	Replace Mat. ....10.30 Lab. 6.58				
	Remove .... Lab. 3.84				
	12′	ea	$4.01	$20.20	$24.21
	Replace Mat. ....12.40 Lab. 7.80				
	Remove .... Lab. 4.01				
	14′	ea	$4.16	$23.58	$27.74
	Replace Mat. ....14.40 Lab. 9.18				
	Remove .... Lab. 4.16				
	16′	ea	$4.31	$27.10	$31.41
	Replace Mat. ....16.60 Lab. 10.50				
	Remove .... Lab. 4.31				
JOIST SYSTEM ▶ PER SF	**Joist system, mobile home, per sf**				
	2″ x 6″, 16″ on center	sf	$.37	$1.64	$2.01
	Replace Mat. .... 1.00 Lab. .... .64				
	Remove .... Lab. .... .37				
	2″ x 8″, 16″ on center	sf	$.37	$1.93	$2.30
	Replace Mat. ....1.20 Lab. .... .73				
	Remove .... Lab. .... .37				
	2″ x 6″, 24″ on center	sf	$.30	$1.25	$1.55
	Replace Mat. .... .70 Lab. .... .55				
	Remove .... Lab. .... .30				

Item Description	Unit	Remove	Replace	Total
2" x 8", 24" on center	sf	$.30	$1.29	$1.59
Replace Mat. .80 Lab. .49				
Remove Lab. .30				
Rafter, mobile home, 2" x 8"				
10'	lf	$3.37	$18.68	$22.05
Replace Mat. 9.50 Lab. 9.18				
Remove Lab. 3.37				
12'	lf	$3.37	$21.19	$24.56
Replace Mat. 11.40 Lab. 9.79				
Remove Lab. 3.37				
14'	lf	$3.37	$23.70	$27.07
Replace Mat. 13.30 Lab. 10.40				
Remove Lab. 3.37				
16'	lf	$3.37	$26.90	$30.27
Replace Mat. 15.20 Lab. 11.70				
Remove Lab. 3.37				
Truss, mobile home, bow roof				
10'	lf	$4.01	$33.50	$37.51
Replace Mat. 22.80 Lab. 10.70				
Remove Lab. 4.01				
12'	lf	$4.01	$38.90	$42.91
Replace Mat. 27.20 Lab. 11.70				
Remove Lab. 4.01				
14'	lf	$4.01	$44.50	$48.51
Replace Mat. 31.90 Lab. 12.60				
Remove Lab. 4.01				
16'	lf	$4.01	$49.40	$53.41
Replace Mat. 35.60 Lab. 13.80				
Remove Lab. 4.01				
Truss, mobile home, gable roof				
10'	ea	$4.01	$36.00	$40.01
Replace Mat. 23.70 Lab. 12.30				
Remove Lab. 4.01				
12'	ea	$4.01	$41.40	$45.41
Replace Mat. 28.50 Lab. 12.90				
Remove Lab. 4.01				
14'	ea	$4.01	$46.70	$50.71
Replace Mat. 33.20 Lab. 13.50				
Remove Lab. 4.01				
16'	ea	$4.01	$51.80	$55.81
Replace Mat. 38.00 Lab. 13.80				
Remove Lab. 4.01				
SIDING				
Horizontal lap siding, mobile home, all styles				
aluminum	sf	$.30	$.83	$1.13
Replace Mat. .40 Lab. .43				
Remove Lab. .30				

◄ RAFTER, 2" X 8" PER RAFTER

◄ TRUSS, BOW PER TRUSS

◄ TRUSS, GABLE ROOF PER TRUSS

◄ LAP SIDING

	Item Description	Unit	Remove	Replace	Total
LAP SIDING ► *continued*	**vinyl**	sf	$.30	$.83	$1.13
	Replace Mat. .40 Lab. .43				
	Remove Lab. .30				
VERTICAL SIDING ►	**Vertical siding, mobile-home style, all patterns**				
	aluminum	sf	$.30	$1.03	$1.33
	Replace Mat. .60 Lab. .43				
	Remove Lab. .30				
SHUTTERS, 9″ ►	**Shutters, mobile-home style, per pair, 9″ wide**				
	24″ tall	ea	$2.15	$31.92	$34.07
	Replace Mat. 25.80 Lab. 6.12				
	Remove Lab. 2.15				
	28″ tall	ea	$2.15	$32.92	$35.07
	Replace Mat. 26.80 Lab. 6.12				
	Remove Lab. 2.15				
	35″ tall	ea	$2.15	$34.52	$36.67
	Replace Mat. 28.40 Lab. 6.12				
	Remove Lab. 2.15				
	39″ tall	ea	$2.15	$35.52	$37.67
	Replace Mat. 29.40 Lab. 6.12				
	Remove Lab. 2.15				
	41″ tall	ea	$2.15	$36.52	$38.67
	Replace Mat. 30.40 Lab. 6.12				
	Remove Lab. 2.15				
	53″ tall	ea	$2.15	$39.12	$41.27
	Replace Mat. 33.00 Lab. 6.12				
	Remove Lab. 2.15				
	71″ tall	ea	$2.15	$45.32	$47.47
	Replace Mat. 39.20 Lab. 6.12				
	Remove Lab. 2.15				
	remove for work, then reinstall	ea	—	$9.18	$9.18
	Replace Lab. 9.18				
SHUTTERS, 12″ ►	**Shutters, mobile-home style, per pair, 12″ wide**				
	24″ tall	ea	$2.15	$35.55	$37.70
	Replace Mat. 27.90 Lab. 7.65				
	Remove Lab. 2.15				
	28″ tall	ea	$2.15	$37.55	$39.70
	Replace Mat. 29.90 Lab. 7.65				
	Remove Lab. 2.15				
	35″ tall	ea	$2.15	$39.65	$41.80
	Replace Mat. 32.00 Lab. 7.65				
	Remove Lab. 2.15				
	39″ tall	ea	$2.15	$40.65	$42.80
	Replace Mat. 33.00 Lab. 7.65				
	Remove Lab. 2.15				
	47″ tall	ea	$2.15	$42.75	$44.90
	Replace Mat. 35.10 Lab. 7.65				
	Remove Lab. 2.15				
	55″ tall	ea	$2.15	$40.65	$42.80
	Replace Mat. 33.00 Lab. 7.65				
	Remove Lab. 2.15				

Item Description	Unit	Remove	Replace	Total
63″ tall	ea	$2.15	$47.95	$50.10
Replace Mat. 40.30 Lab. 7.65				
Remove Lab. 2.15				
71″ tall	ea	$2.15	$49.95	$52.10
Replace Mat. 42.30 Lab. 7.65				
Remove Lab. 2.15				
80″ tall	ea	$2.15	$50.95	$53.10
Replace Mat. 43.30 Lab. 7.65				
Remove Lab. 2.15				
remove for work, then reinstall	ea	—	$10.70	$10.70
Replace Lab. 10.70				

STEPS

◄ **REDWOOD STEPS**

Item Description	Unit	Remove	Replace	Total
Redwood frame, steps, and side handrails (no landing)				
24″ high x 48″ wide, 3 steps	ea	$11.40	$282.80	$294.20
Replace Mat. 90.80 Lab. 192.00				
Remove Lab. 11.40				
28″ high x 48″ wide, 4 steps	ea	$11.40	$299.00	$310.40
Replace Mat. 103.00 Lab. 196.00				
Remove Lab. 11.40				
32″ high x 48″ wide, 4 steps	ea	$11.40	$327.00	$338.40
Replace Mat. 122.00 Lab. 205.00				
Remove Lab. 11.40				
Redwood frame, steps, and railing, 48″ x 48″ landing				
24″ high x 48″ wide, 3 steps	ea	$13.80	$341.00	$354.80
Replace Mat. 116.00 Lab. 225.00				
Remove Lab. 13.80				
28″ high x 48″ wide, 4 steps	ea	$13.80	$360.00	$373.80
Replace Mat. 130.00 Lab. 230.00				
Remove Lab. 13.80				
32″ high x 48″ wide, 4 steps	ea	$13.80	$394.00	$407.80
Replace Mat. 151.00 Lab. 243.00				
Remove Lab. 13.80				

◄ **STEEL STEPS** *Steel frame and balustrade. Steps are made from 2″ dimensional lumber.*

Item Description	Unit	Remove	Replace	Total
Steel frame, steps, and side handrails (no landing)				
24″ high x 48″ wide, 3 steps	ea	$9.84	$154.60	$164.44
Replace Mat. 124.00 Lab. 30.60				
Remove Lab. 9.84				
28″ high x 48″ wide, 4 steps	ea	$9.84	$174.60	$184.44
Replace Mat. 144.00 Lab. 30.60				
Remove Lab. 9.84				
32″ high x 48″ wide, 4 steps	ea	$9.84	$185.60	$195.44
Replace Mat. 155.00 Lab. 30.60				
Remove Lab. 9.84				
Steel frame and railing, wood steps with 27″ x 36″ landing				
24″ high x 36″ wide, 2 steps	ea	$9.84	$201.70	$211.54
Replace Mat. 165.00 Lab. 36.70				
Remove Lab. 9.84				

	Item Description	Unit	Remove	Replace	Total
STEEL STEPS ▶ *continued*	**28″ high x 36″ wide, 3 steps**	ea	$9.84	$227.70	$237.54
	Replace Mat. 191.00 Lab. 36.70				
	Remove Lab. 9.84				
	32″ high x 36″ wide, 3 steps	ea	$9.84	$232.70	$242.54
	Replace Mat. 196.00 Lab. 36.70				
	Remove Lab. 9.84				
	Steel frame, steps, and railing, 27″ x 72″ landing				
	24″ high x 72″ wide, 3 steps	ea	$9.84	$280.30	$290.14
	Replace Mat. 243.00 Lab. 37.30				
	Remove Lab. 9.84				
	28″ high x 72″ wide, 4 steps	ea	$9.84	$311.30	$321.14
	Replace Mat. 274.00 Lab. 37.30				
	Remove Lab. 9.84				
	32″ high x 72″ wide, 4 steps	ea	$9.84	$321.30	$331.14
	Replace Mat. 284.00 Lab. 37.30				
	Remove Lab. 9.84				
	Steel frame and railing, wood steps with 4′ x 5-1/2′ landing				
	24″ high x 48″ wide, 2 steps	ea	$13.80	$498.70	$512.50
	Replace Mat. 439.00 Lab. 59.70				
	Remove Lab. 13.80				
	28″ high x 48″ wide, 3 steps	ea	$13.80	$523.70	$537.50
	Replace Mat. 464.00 Lab. 59.70				
	Remove Lab. 13.80				
	32″ high x 48″ wide, 3 steps	ea	$13.80	$575.70	$589.50
	Replace Mat. 516.00 Lab. 59.70				
	Remove Lab. 13.80				
	Steel frame and railing, wood steps with 9′ x 5′ landing				
	24″ high x 36″ wide, 2 steps	ea	$13.80	$861.20	$875.00
	Replace Mat. 800.00 Lab. 61.20				
	Remove Lab. 13.80				
	28″ high x 36″ wide, 3 steps	ea	$13.80	$912.20	$926.00
	Replace Mat. 851.00 Lab. 61.20				
	Remove Lab. 13.80				
	32″ high x 36″ wide, 3 steps	ea	$13.80	$938.20	$952.00
	Replace Mat. 877.00 Lab. 61.20				
	Remove Lab. 13.80				
	SKIRTING				
ALUMINUM SKIRTING ▶	**Aluminum skirting, solid with vented panels**				
	24″ tall	lf	$.62	$5.18	$5.80
	Replace Mat. 3.50 Lab. 1.68				
	Remove Lab. .62				
	28″ tall	lf	$.62	$5.98	$6.60
	Replace Mat. 4.30 Lab. 1.68				
	Remove Lab. .62				
	30″ tall	lf	$.62	$6.08	$6.70
	Replace Mat. 4.40 Lab. 1.68				
	Remove Lab. .62				

Item Description		Unit	Remove	Replace	Total
36" tall		lf	$.62	$7.08	$7.70
Replace Mat.............5.40	Lab. 1.68				
Remove	Lab.............. .62				
42" tall		lf	$.62	$8.78	$9.40
Replace Mat.............7.10	Lab. 1.68				
Remove	Lab.............. .62				
add for access door		ea	$3.07	$65.30	$68.37
Replace Mat...........45.40	Lab............19.90				
Remove	Lab.............3.07				
Vinyl skirting, simulated rock					
30" tall		lf	$.62	$10.08	$10.70
Replace Mat.............8.40	Lab. 1.68				
Remove	Lab.............. .62				
36" tall		lf	$.62	$12.18	$12.80
Replace Mat...........10.50	Lab. 1.68				
Remove	Lab.............. .62				
48" tall		lf	$.62	$16.28	$16.90
Replace Mat...........14.60	Lab. 1.68				
Remove	Lab.............. .62				
add for access door		ea	$3.07	$67.40	$70.47
Replace Mat...........47.50	Lab............19.90				
Remove	Lab.............3.07				
Vinyl skirting, solid with vented panels					
24" tall		lf	$.62	$4.88	$5.50
Replace Mat.............3.20	Lab. 1.68				
Remove	Lab.............. .62				
28" tall		lf	$.62	$5.58	$6.20
Replace Mat.............3.90	Lab. 1.68				
Remove	Lab.............. .62				
30" tall		lf	$.62	$5.58	$6.20
Replace Mat.............3.90	Lab. 1.68				
Remove	Lab.............. .62				
36" tall		lf	$.62	$6.48	$7.10
Replace Mat.............4.80	Lab. 1.68				
Remove	Lab.............. .62				
42" tall		lf	$.62	$7.98	$8.60
Replace Mat.............6.30	Lab. 1.68				
Remove	Lab.............. .62				
add for access door		ea	$3.07	$60.90	$63.97
Replace Mat...........41.00	Lab............19.90				
Remove	Lab.............3.07				
Wood skirting, rough-sawn plywood					
24" tall		lf	$.62	$3.98	$4.60
Replace Mat.............2.30	Lab. 1.68				
Remove	Lab.............. .62				
28" tall		lf	$.62	$4.38	$5.00
Replace Mat.............2.70	Lab. 1.68				
Remove	Lab.............. .62				

◄ VINYL SIMULATED ROCK SKIRTING

◄ VINYL SKIRTING

◄ WOOD SKIRTING

	Item Description		Unit	Remove	Replace	Total
WOOD SKIRTING ► *continued*	**30″ tall**		lf	$.62	$4.48	$5.10
	Replace Mat. 2.80	Lab. 1.68				
	Remove	Lab. .62				
	36″ tall		lf	$.62	$5.08	$5.70
	Replace Mat. 3.40	Lab. 1.68				
	Remove	Lab. .62				
	42″ tall		lf	$.62	$6.08	$6.70
	Replace Mat. 4.40	Lab. 1.68				
	Remove	Lab. .62				
	add for access door		ea	$3.07	$48.90	$51.97
	Replace Mat. 29.00	Lab. 19.90				
	Remove	Lab. 3.07				
	Wood skirting, T1-11 or hardboard					
	24″ tall		lf	$.62	$3.78	$4.40
	Replace Mat. 2.10	Lab. 1.68				
	Remove	Lab. .62				
	28″ tall		lf	$.62	$4.28	$4.90
	Replace Mat. 2.60	Lab. 1.68				
	Remove	Lab. .62				
	30″ tall		lf	$.62	$4.28	$4.90
	Replace Mat. 2.60	Lab. 1.68				
	Remove	Lab. .62				
	36″ tall		lf	$.62	$4.88	$5.50
	Replace Mat. 3.20	Lab. 1.68				
	Remove	Lab. .62				
	42″ tall		lf	$.62	$5.88	$6.50
	Replace Mat. 4.20	Lab. 1.68				
	Remove	Lab. .62				
	add for access door		ea	$3.07	$46.90	$49.97
	Replace Mat. 27.00	Lab. 19.90				
	Remove	Lab. 3.07				
	WALL & CEILING PANELS					
CEILING PANEL ►	**Ceiling panel, drywall with textured finish**					
	3/8″, no battens		sf	$.18	$1.31	$1.49
	Replace Mat. .54	Lab. .77				
	Remove	Lab. .18				
	3/8″ with battens		sf	$.18	$1.48	$1.66
	Replace Mat. .62	Lab. .86				
	Remove	Lab. .18				
WALL PANEL ►	**Wall panel, drywall**					
	1/2″ with vinyl		sf	$.18	$1.74	$1.92
	Replace Mat. .91	Lab. .83				
	Remove	Lab. ..18				
	1/2″ with wallpaper		sf	$.18	$1.55	$1.73
	Replace Mat. .72	Lab. .83				
	Remove	Lab. .18				

Item Description	Unit	Remove	Replace	Total	
Ceiling and wall panel attachment					◀ PANEL ATTACHMENT
batten	lf	$.12	$.64	$.76	
Replace Mat. .15 Lab. .49					
Remove Lab. .12					
screw with rosette	ea	$.07	$.37	$.44	
Replace Mat. .22 Lab. .15					
Remove Lab. .07					
screw with wing clips	ea	$.07	$.46	$.53	
Replace Mat. .31 Lab. .15					
Remove Lab. .07					
WINDOWS					
Awning window, mobile home					◀ AWNING WINDOW
14" x 27" with 2 lites	ea	$9.22	$85.80	$95.02	
Replace Mat. 61.90 Lab. 23.90					
Remove Lab. 9.22					
14" x 39" with 3 lites	ea	$9.22	$101.30	$110.52	
Replace Mat. 77.40 Lab. 23.90					
Remove Lab. 9.22					
24" x 27" with 2 lites	ea	$9.22	$101.30	$110.52	
Replace Mat. 77.40 Lab. 23.90					
Remove Lab. 9.22					
30" x 27" with 2 lites	ea	$9.22	$106.50	$115.72	
Replace Mat. 82.60 Lab. 23.90					
Remove Lab. 9.22					
30" x 39" with 3 lites	ea	$9.22	$122.00	$131.22	
Replace Mat. 98.10 Lab. 23.90					
Remove Lab. 9.22					
30" x 53" with 4 lites	ea	$9.22	$147.90	$157.12	
Replace Mat. 124.00 Lab. 23.90					
Remove Lab. 9.22					
36" x 39" with 3 lites	ea	$9.22	$137.90	$147.12	
Replace Mat. 114.00 Lab. 23.90					
Remove Lab. 9.22					
36" x 53" with 4 lites	ea	$9.22	$157.90	$167.12	
Replace Mat. 134.00 Lab. 23.90					
Remove Lab. 9.22					
46" x 27" with 2 lites	ea	$9.22	$126.90	$136.12	
Replace Mat. 103.00 Lab. 23.90					
Remove Lab. 9.22					
46" x 39" with 3 lites	ea	$9.22	$147.90	$157.12	
Replace Mat. 124.00 Lab. 23.90					
Remove Lab. 9.22					
remove for work, then reinstall	ea	—	$30.60	$30.60	
Replace Lab. 30.60					
Skylight, fixed, mobile home					◀ SKYLIGHT
14" x 22"	ea	$15.40	$114.90	$130.30	
Replace Mat. 61.30 Lab. 53.60					
Remove Lab. 15.40					

	Item Description	Unit	Remove	Replace	Total
SKYLIGHT ▶ *continued*	**14" x 46"**	ea	$15.40	$160.60	$176.00
	Replace Mat. ....107.00 Lab. 53.60				
	Remove .... Lab. 15.40				
	22" x 22"	ea	$15.40	$124.20	$139.60
	Replace Mat. ....70.60 Lab. 53.60				
	Remove .... Lab. 15.40				
	22" x 34"	ea	$15.40	$303.60	$319.00
	Replace Mat. ....250.00 Lab. 53.60				
	Remove .... Lab. 15.40				
	remove for work, then reinstall	ea	—	$67.30	$67.30
	Replace .... Lab. 67.30				
	Skylight, ventilating, mobile home				
	14" x 22"	ea	$15.40	$143.70	$159.10
	Replace Mat. ....76.40 Lab. 67.30				
	Remove .... Lab. 15.40				
	14" x 46"	ea	$15.40	$190.30	$205.70
	Replace Mat. ....123.00 Lab. 67.30				
	Remove .... Lab. 15.40				
	22" x 22"	ea	$15.40	$149.90	$165.30
	Replace Mat. ....82.60 Lab. 67.30				
	Remove .... Lab. 15.40				
	22" x 34"	ea	$15.40	$353.30	$368.70
	Replace Mat. ....286.00 Lab. 67.30				
	Remove .... Lab. 15.40				
	remove for work, then reinstall	ea	—	$76.50	$76.50
	Replace .... Lab. 76.50				

TIME & MATERIAL CHARTS *(selected items)*

Manufactured Housing Labor

LABORER	BASE WAGE	PAID LEAVE	TRUE WAGE	FICA	FUTA	WORKER'S COMP.	UNEMPLOY. INSUR.	HEALTH INSUR.	RETIRE (401K)	LIABILITY INSUR.	COST PER HOUR
MH repair specialist	**$16.70**	1.33	**$18.33**	1.40	.15	3.44	1.59	2.69	.55	2.47	**$30.60**
MH repair specialist's helper	**$8.50**	.66	**$9.16**	.70	.07	1.72	.80	2.69	.27	1.24	**$16.70**

Paid Leave is calculated based on two weeks paid vacation, one week sick leave, and seven paid holidays. Employer's matching portion of **FICA** is 7.65 percent. **FUTA** (Federal Unemployment) is .80 percent. **Worker's compensation** was calculated using a national average of 18.75 percent for a manufactured housing repair professional. **Unemployment insurance** was calculated using a national average of 8.70 percent. **Health insurance** was calculated based on a projected national average for 2002 of $428.00 per employee (and family when applicable) per month. Employer pays 80 percent for a per month cost of $428.00 per employee. **Retirement** is based on a 401(k) retirement program with employer matching of 50 percent. Employee contributions to the 401(k) plan are an average of 6 percent of the true wage. **Liability insurance** is based on a national average of 13.2 percent.

QuickCalculators

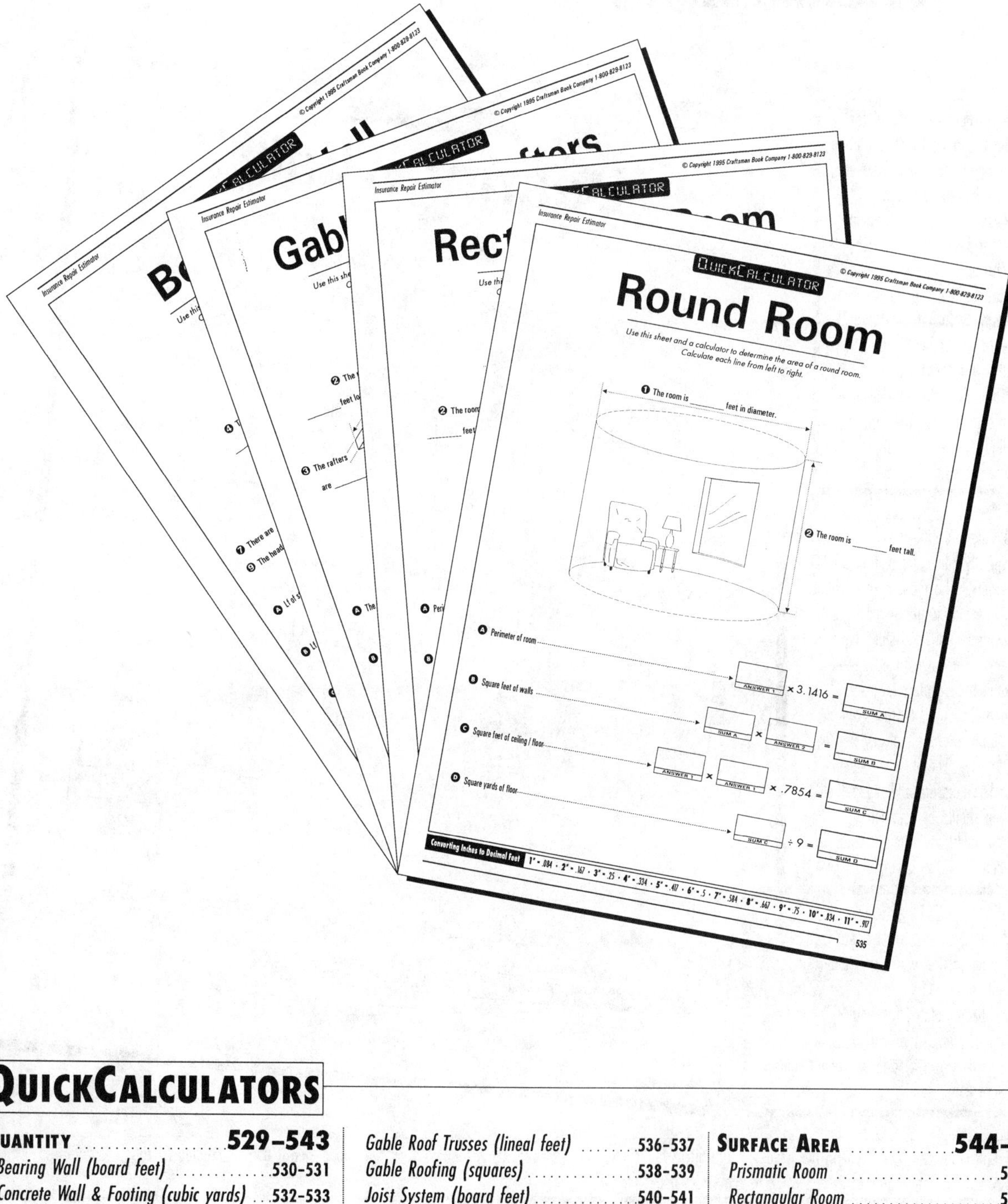

QuickCalculators

QuickCalculators are designed to help you quickly calculate quantities and the surface areas of some basic room shapes. Pages 529-543 contain *QuickCalculators* that are designed to calculate quantities, and pages 544-549 contain *QuickCalculators* that are designed to calculate the surface area of rooms.

Instruction for each *QuickCalculator* sheet are contained on the left facing page.

The person who purchased this book or the person for whom this book was purchased may photo-copy or otherwise reproduce *QuickCalculator* pages so long as:

❶ the sheets are reproduced for that person's use only.
❷ the sheets are not reproduced for resale or as part of a package that is produced for resale.
❸ the sheets are not used in any promotional or advertising materials.

USING THE BEARING WALL QUICKCALCULATOR

A Calculates the lineal feet of studs in a wall *before* adding for openings and corners. The length of the wall (Answer 1) is converted into inches by multiplying it by 12. The number of studs is calculated by dividing the wall length in inches by the stud centers (Answer 8), then adding 1 for the first stud. The calculation should now be rounded *up*, then multiplied by the wall height (Answer 4).

B Calculates the lineal feet of studs typically added for openings and corners. The number of openings (Answer 6) is multiplied by 2.4 (the *average* additional studs typically needed for an opening). The number of corners (Answer 7) is multiplied by 2.6 (the *average* additional studs typically needed at corners). The studs for openings and corners are added together, then should be rounded *up*. The total additional studs is then multiplied by the wall height (Answer 1).

C Calculates the total lineal feet of lumber in the wall. The length of the wall (Answer 1) is multiplied by the number of plates (Answer 3). The lineal feet of plates is added to the lineal feet of studs (Sum A) and additional studs (Sum B).

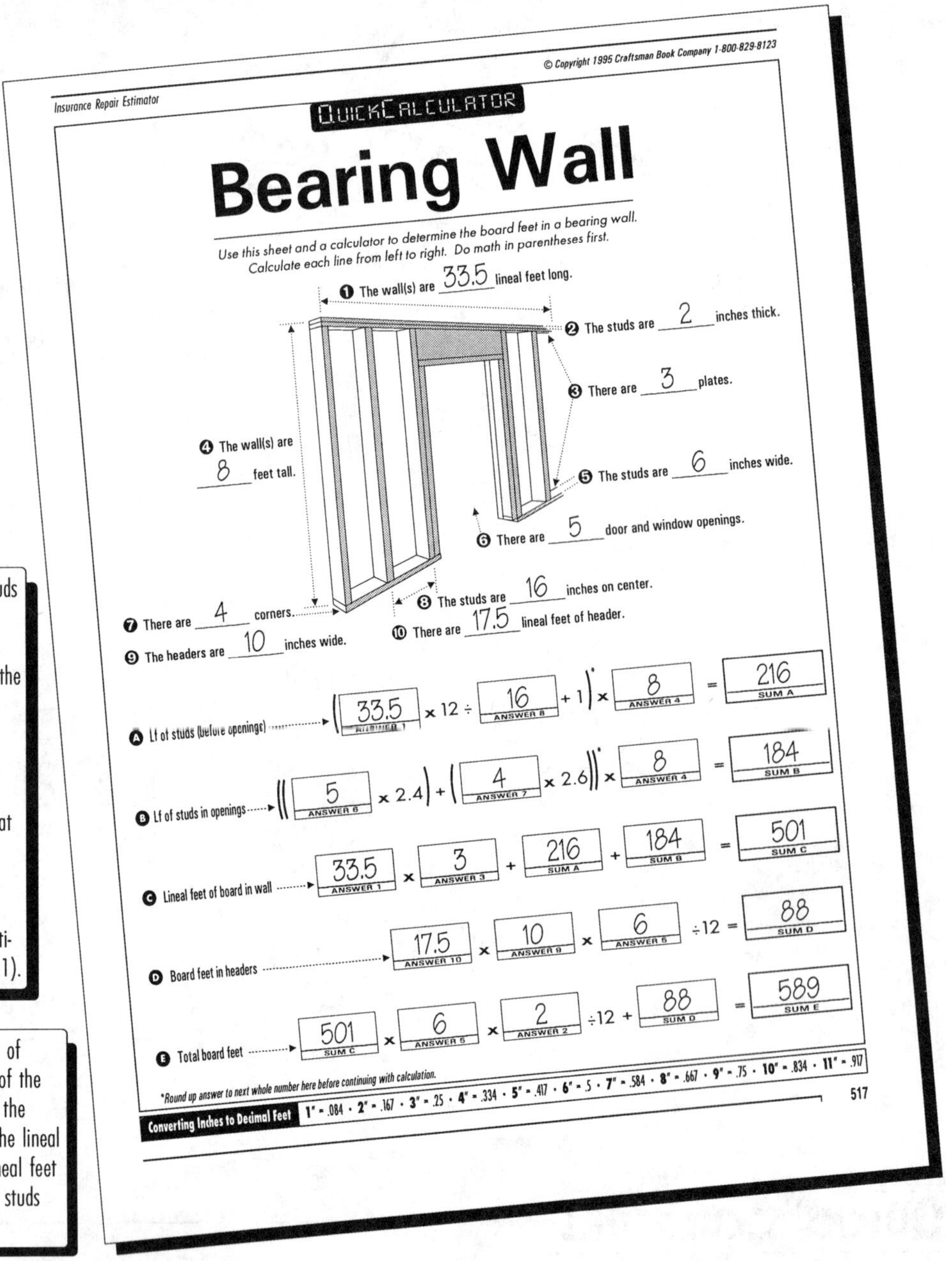

D Calculates the board feet in the headers. The lineal feet of headers (Answer 10) is multiplied by the header width then multiplied by the wall thickness (Answer 5). This total is divided by 12 to convert to board feet.

E Calculates the total board feet in the wall. The lineal feet of board in the wall (Sum C) is multiplied by the wall width (Answer 5) then by the stud thickness (Answer 2). The total is divided by twelve to convert to board feet then added to the board feet in the headers (Sum D).

QUICK FACTS

☞ See page 550 for more information about the geometric formulas used in this *QuickCalculator*. See page 414-415 for wall framing priced per board foot.

QUICKCALCULATOR

Bearing Wall

Use this sheet and a calculator to determine the board feet in a bearing wall. Calculate each line from left to right. Do math in parentheses first.

❶ The wall(s) are ________ lineal feet long.

❷ The studs are ________ inches thick.

❸ There are ________ plates.

❹ The wall(s) are ________ feet tall.

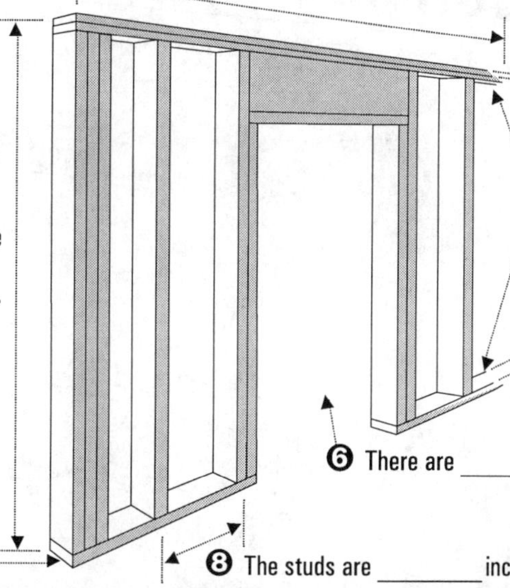

❺ The studs are ________ inches wide.

❻ There are ________ door and window openings.

❼ There are ________ corners.

❽ The studs are ________ inches on center.

❾ The headers are ________ inches wide.

❿ There are ________ lineal feet of header.

Ⓐ Lf of studs (before openings) .... ▸ ([ANSWER 1] × 12 ÷ [ANSWER 8] + 1)* × [ANSWER 4] = [SUM A]

Ⓑ Lf of studs in openings ...... ▸ (([ANSWER 6] × 2.4) + ([ANSWER 7] × 2.6))* × [ANSWER 4] = [SUM B]

Ⓒ Lineal feet of board in wall .... ▸ [ANSWER 1] × [ANSWER 3] + [SUM A] + [SUM B] = [SUM C]

Ⓓ Board feet in headers .... ▸ [ANSWER 10] × [ANSWER 9] × [ANSWER 5] ÷12 = [SUM D]

Ⓔ Total board feet .... ▸ [SUM C] × [ANSWER 5] × [ANSWER 2] ÷12 + [SUM D] = [SUM E]

**Round up answer to next whole number here before continuing with calculation.*

Converting Inches to Decimal Feet **1″** = .084 · **2″** = .167 · **3″** = .25 · **4″** = .334 · **5″** = .417 · **6″** = .5 · **7″** = .584 · **8″** = .667 · **9″** = .75 · **10″** = .834 · **11″** = .917

USING THE CONCRETE WALL & FOOTING QUICKCALCULATOR

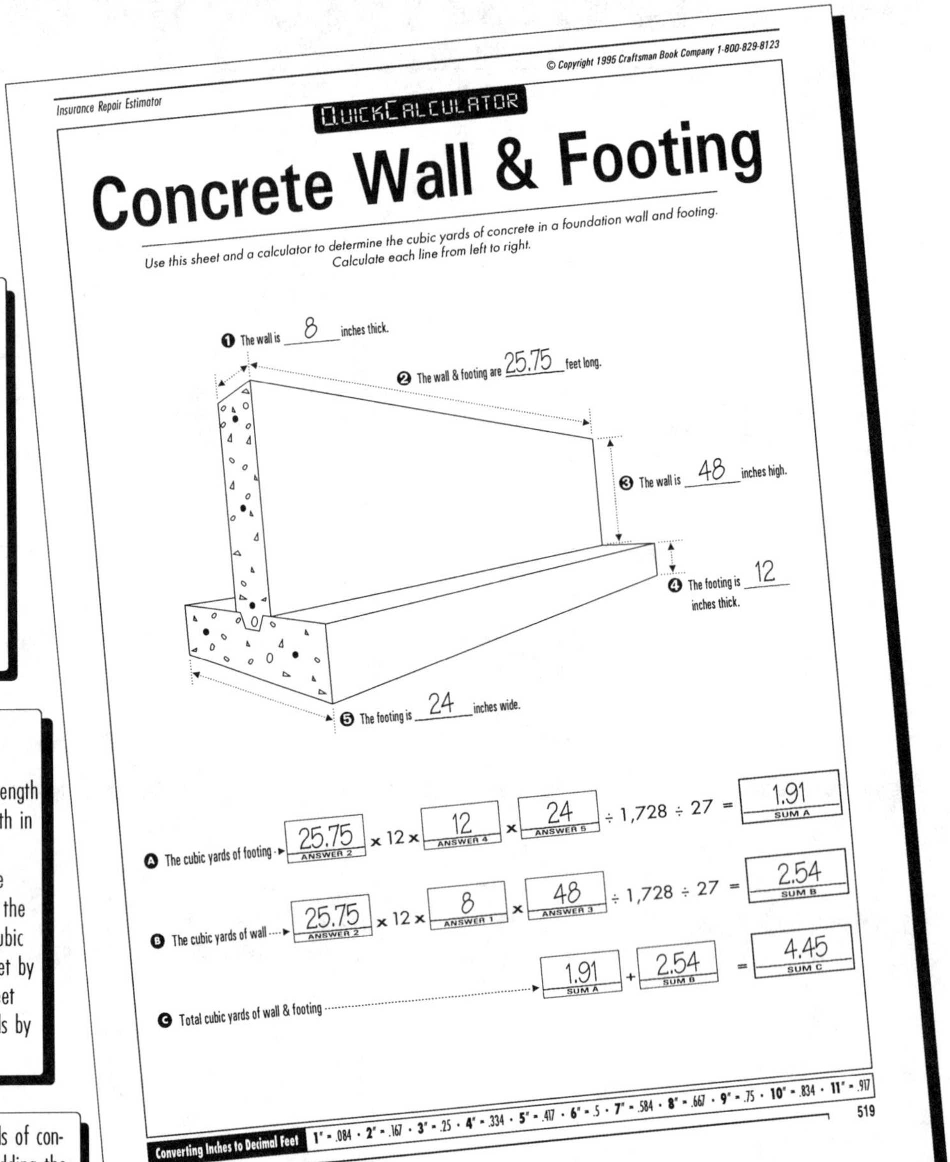
Insurance Repair Estimator

© Copyright 1995 Craftsman Book Company 1-800-829-8123

QUICKCALCULATOR

Concrete Wall & Footing

Use this sheet and a calculator to determine the cubic yards of concrete in a foundation wall and footing. Calculate each line from left to right.

1 The wall is 8 inches thick.

2 The wall & footing are 25.75 feet long.

3 The wall is 48 inches high.

4 The footing is 12 inches thick.

5 The footing is 24 inches wide.

A The cubic yards of footing → 25.75 (ANSWER 2) x 12 x 12 (ANSWER 4) x 24 (ANSWER 5) ÷ 1,728 ÷ 27 = 1.91 (SUM A)

B The cubic yards of wall → 25.75 (ANSWER 2) x 12 x 8 (ANSWER 1) x 48 (ANSWER 3) ÷ 1,728 ÷ 27 = 2.54 (SUM B)

C Total cubic yards of wall & footing → 1.91 (SUM A) + 2.54 (SUM B) = 4.45 (SUM C)

Converting Inches to Decimal Feet 1" = .084 · 2" = .167 · 3" = .25 · 4" = .334 · 5" = .417 · 6" = .5 · 7" = .584 · 8" = .667 · 9" = .75 · 10" = .834 · 11" = .917

519

A Calculates the cubic yards of footing by multiplying Answer 1 by 12 to convert the length of the footing to inches. The length in inches is then multiplied by the thickness (Answer 4) and by the width (Answer 5) to determine the cubic inches in the footing. The cubic inches are converted to cubic feet by dividing by 1,728. The cubic feet are then converted to cubic yards by dividing by 27.

B Calculates the cubic yards of foundation wall by multiplying Answer 2 by 12 to convert the length of the wall to inches. The length in inches is then multiplied by the thickness (Answer 1) and by the height (Answer 3) to determine the cubic inches in the wall. The cubic inches are converted to cubic feet by dividing by 1,728. The cubic feet are then converted to cubic yards by dividing by 27.

C Calculates the total cubic yards of concrete in the wall & footing by adding the cubic yards of footing (Sum A) to the cubic yards of foundation wall (Sum B).

QUICK FACTS

☞ The sample *QuickCalculator* sheet shown above contains quantities that have been rounded. We suggest rounding to two decimal places. We also suggest rounding the final total (Sum C) *up* to the next 1/4 yards since this how concrete must usually be ordered. (In the example above the Sum C total of 4.45 should be rounded up to 4.5 cubic yards.) See pages 83-85 for concrete walls and footings per cubic yard.

☞ See page 550 for more information about the geometric formulas used in this *QuickCalculator*.

QUICKCALCULATOR

Concrete Wall & Footing

Use this sheet and a calculator to determine the cubic yards of concrete in a foundation wall and footing. Calculate each line from left to right.

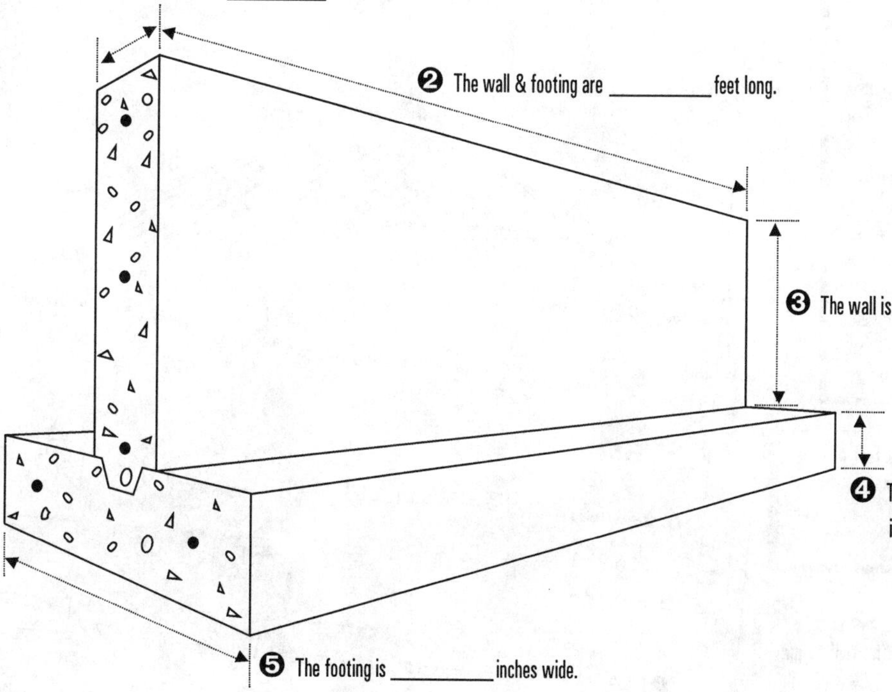

❶ The wall is ________ inches thick.

❷ The wall & footing are ________ feet long.

❸ The wall is ________ inches high.

❹ The footing is ________ inches thick.

❺ The footing is ________ inches wide.

Ⓐ The cubic yards of footing ▸ [ANSWER 2] × 12 × [ANSWER 4] × [ANSWER 5] ÷ 1,728 ÷ 27 = [SUM A]

Ⓑ The cubic yards of wall ▸ [ANSWER 2] × 12 × [ANSWER 1] × [ANSWER 3] ÷ 1,728 ÷ 27 = [SUM B]

Ⓒ Total cubic yards of wall & footing ▸ [SUM A] + [SUM B] = [SUM C]

Converting Inches to Decimal Feet **1"** = .084 • **2"** = .167 • **3"** = .25 • **4"** = .334 • **5"** = .417 • **6"** = .5 • **7"** = .584 • **8"** = .667 • **9"** = .75 • **10"** = .834 • **11"** = .917

USING THE GABLE ROOF RAFTERS QUICKCALCULATOR

A Calculates the total number of rafters in the roof. The length of the roof (Answer 1) is converted into inches by multiplying it by 12.

The number of rafters in the roof is calculated by taking the length in inches and dividing by the rafter centers (Answer 4) then adding 1 for the first rafter.

Because you can never have a fraction of a rafter, the final answer should always be rounded *up* to the next *even* number.

This calculates the total for one side of the roof only so the total is multiplied by 2.

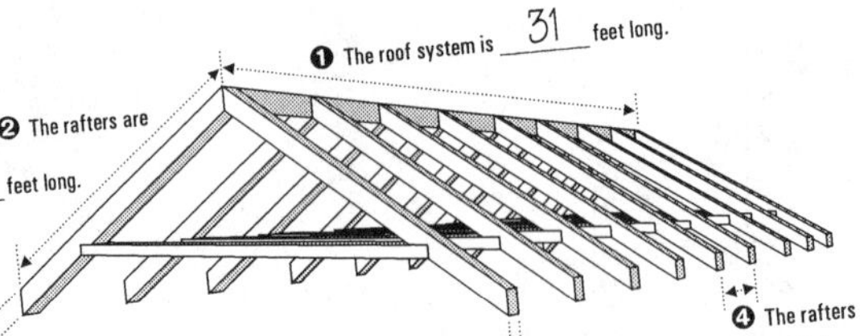

Insurance Repair Estimator

© Copyright 1995 Craftsman Book Company 1-800-829-8123

QUICKCALCULATOR

Gable Roof Rafters

Use this sheet and a calculator to determine the board feet of rafters in a gable roof. Calculate each line from left to right. Do math in parentheses first.

Round up to next even number

A The number of rafters (31 [ANSWER 1] x 12 ÷ 24 [ANSWER 4] + 1) x 2 = 34 [SUM A]

B Lineal feet of rafters 34 [SUM A] x 12.5 [ANSWER 2] = 425 [SUM B]

C Bf in ridge & sub-fascia* 31 [ANSWER 1] x 3 x 2 [ANSWER 5] x (8 [ANSWER 3] + 2) ÷ 12 = 155 [SUM C]

D Total board feet in roof** 425 [SUM B] x 2 [ANSWER 5] x 8 [ANSWER 3] ÷ 12 + 155 [SUM C] = 722 [SUM D]

*The ridge and sub-fascia boards are calculated to be 2 inches wider than the rafters. **Does not include ceiling joists for the room below (as illustrated) or collar ties.

Converting Inches to Decimal Feet 1" = .084 · 2" = .167 · 3" = .25 · 4" = .334 · 5" = .417 · 6" = .5 · 7" = .584 · 8" = .667 · 9" = .75 · 10" = .834 · 11" = .917

521

B Calculates the lineal feet of rafters in the roof by multiplying the number of rafters (Sum A) by the rafter length (Answer 2).

C Calculates the board feet in the ridge and sub-fascia. The roof length (Answer 1) is multiplied by 3 (2 sub-fascia boards and 1 ridge) to get the total lineal feet of sub-fascia and ridge. This total is multiplied by the rafter thickness (Answer 5), then by the rafter width (Answer 3) plus 2″ (e.g. a roof with 2″ x 8″ rafters will have 10″ wide ridge and sub-fascia boards). This total is divided by 12 to get the total board feet in the ridge and sub-fascia boards.

D Calculates the total board feet in the roof system. The total lineal feet of rafters (Sum B) is multiplied by the rafter thickness (Answer 5) then by the rafter width (Answer 3). This total is divided by 12 to get the total board feet in the rafters. The total board feet of rafters is then added to the total board feet in the ridge and sub-fascia boards (Sum C) for the total board feet in the entire roof system.

QUICK FACTS

☞ The sample *QuickCalculator* sheet shown above contains quantities that have been rounded. The total number of rafters should always be rounded up to the next even number. We also suggest rounding lineal feet and board feet to the nearest whole number.

☞ See page 550 for more information about the geometric formulas used in this *QuickCalculator*. See page 436 for rafter systems priced per board foot.

QUICKCALCULATOR

Gable Roof Rafters

Use this sheet and a calculator to determine the board feet of rafters in a gable roof. Calculate each line from left to right. Do math in parentheses first.

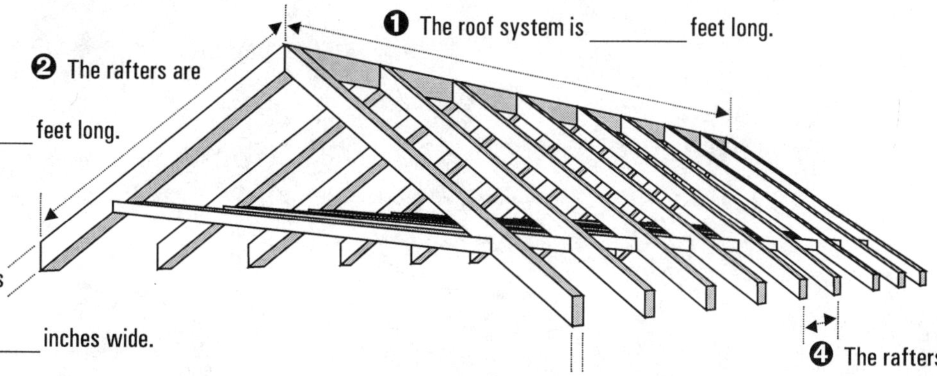

❶ The roof system is ________ feet long.

❷ The rafters are ________ feet long.

❸ The rafters are ________ inches wide.

❹ The rafters are ________ inches on center.

❺ The rafters are ________ inches thick.

Ⓐ The number of rafters ········► ([ANSWER 1] x 12 ÷ [ANSWER 4] + 1) x 2 = [SUM A] *(Round up to next even number)*

Ⓑ Lineal feet of rafters ········► [SUM A] x [ANSWER 2] = [SUM B]

Ⓒ Bf in ridge & sub-fascia*········► [ANSWER 1] x 3 x [ANSWER 5] x ([ANSWER 3] + 2) ÷12 = [SUM C]

Ⓓ Total board feet in roof**··► [SUM B] x [ANSWER 5] x [ANSWER 3] ÷12 + [SUM C] = [SUM D]

*The ridge and sub-fascia boards are calculated to be 2 inches wider than the rafters. **Does not include ceiling joists for the room below (as illustrated) or collar ties.*

Converting Inches to Decimal Feet **1″** = .084 · **2″** = .167 · **3″** = .25 · **4″** = .334 · **5″** = .417 · **6″** = .5 · **7″** = .584 · **8″** = .667 · **9″** = .75 · **10″** = .834 · **11″** = .917

USING THE GABLE ROOF TRUSSES QUICKCALCULATOR

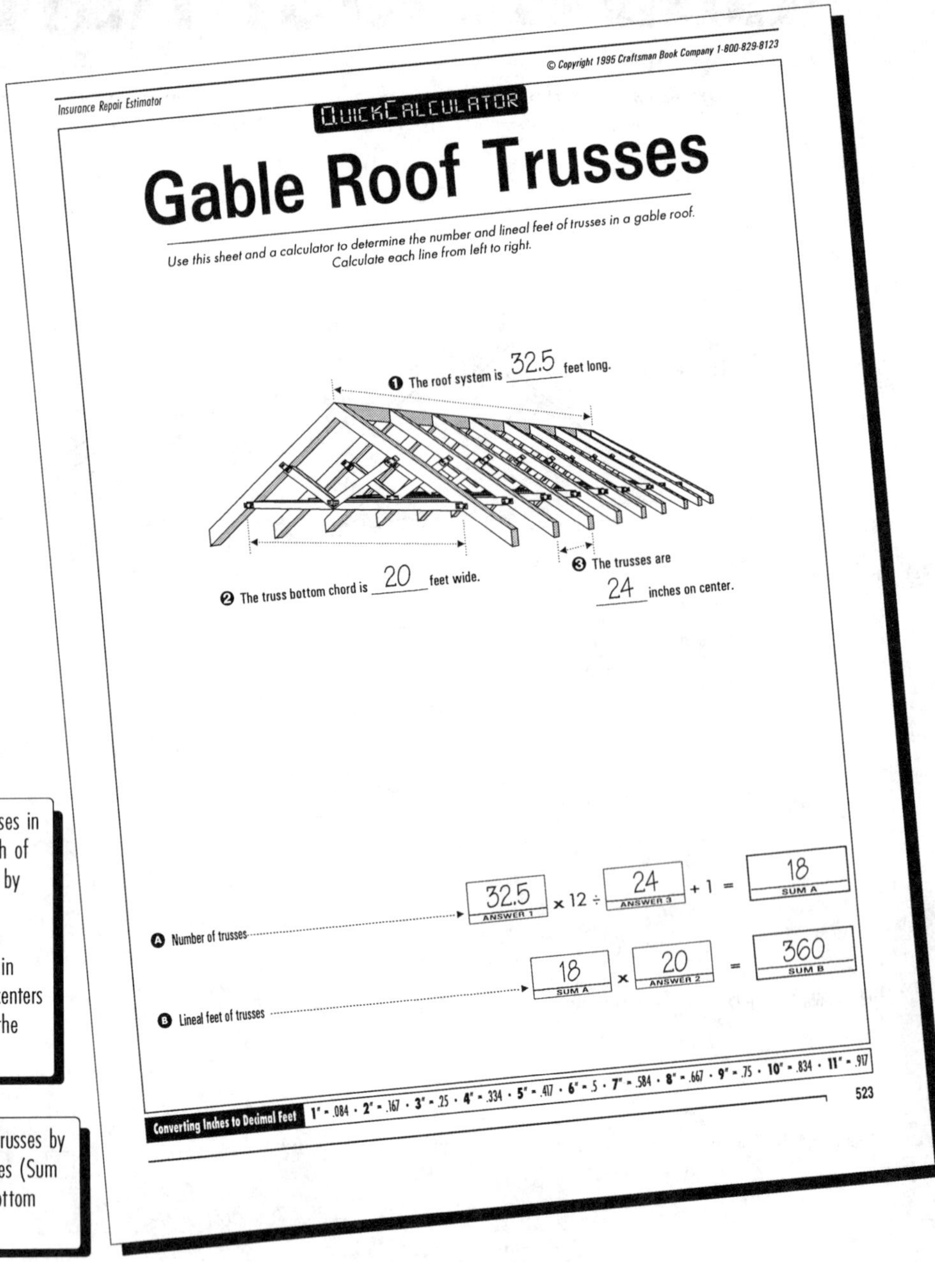

Insurance Repair Estimator

© Copyright 1995 Craftsman Book Company 1-800-829-8123

QUICKCALCULATOR

Gable Roof Trusses

Use this sheet and a calculator to determine the number and lineal feet of trusses in a gable roof. Calculate each line from left to right.

1. The roof system is 32.5 feet long.
2. The truss bottom chord is 20 feet wide.
3. The trusses are 24 inches on center.

A. Number of trusses .... 32.5 (ANSWER 1) × 12 ÷ 24 (ANSWER 3) + 1 = 18 (SUM A)

B. Lineal feet of trusses .... 18 (SUM A) × 20 (ANSWER 2) = 360 (SUM B)

Converting Inches to Decimal Feet: 1" = .084 · 2" = .167 · 3" = .25 · 4" = .334 · 5" = .417 · 6" = .5 · 7" = .584 · 8" = .667 · 9" = .75 · 10" = .834 · 11" = .917

523

A Calculates the number of trusses in the roof by converting the length of the roof (Answer 1) into inches by multiplying it by 12.
The number of trusses is then calculated by taking this length in inches, dividing it by the truss centers (Answer 3), then adding 1 for the first truss.

B Calculates the lineal feet of trusses by multiplying the number of trusses (Sum A) by the length of the truss bottom chord (Answer 2).

QUICK FACTS

- The sample *QuickCalculator* sheet shown above contains quantities that have been rounded. The total number of trusses should always be rounded up to the next whole number. We also suggest rounding lineal feet lineal feet to the nearest whole number.
- See page 550 for more information about the geometric formulas used in this *QuickCalculator*. See page 439 for truss systems priced per lineal foot.

QUICKCALCULATOR

Gable Roof Trusses

Use this sheet and a calculator to determine the number and lineal feet of trusses in a gable roof. Calculate each line from left to right.

❶ The roof system is ________ feet long.

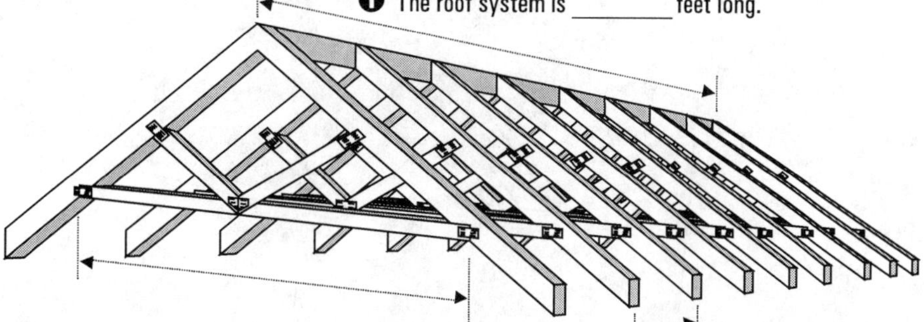

❷ The truss bottom chord is ________ feet wide.

❸ The trusses are ________ inches on center.

Round up to next whole number

Ⓐ Number of trusses → [ANSWER 1] × 12 ÷ [ANSWER 3] + 1 = [SUM A]

Ⓑ Lineal feet of trusses → [SUM A] × [ANSWER 2] = [SUM B]

Converting Inches to Decimal Feet **1″** = .084 · **2″** = .167 · **3″** = .25 · **4″** = .334 · **5″** = .417 · **6″** = .5 · **7″** = .584 · **8″** = .667 · **9″** = .75 · **10″** = .834 · **11″** = .917

USING THE GABLE ROOFING QUICKCALCULATOR

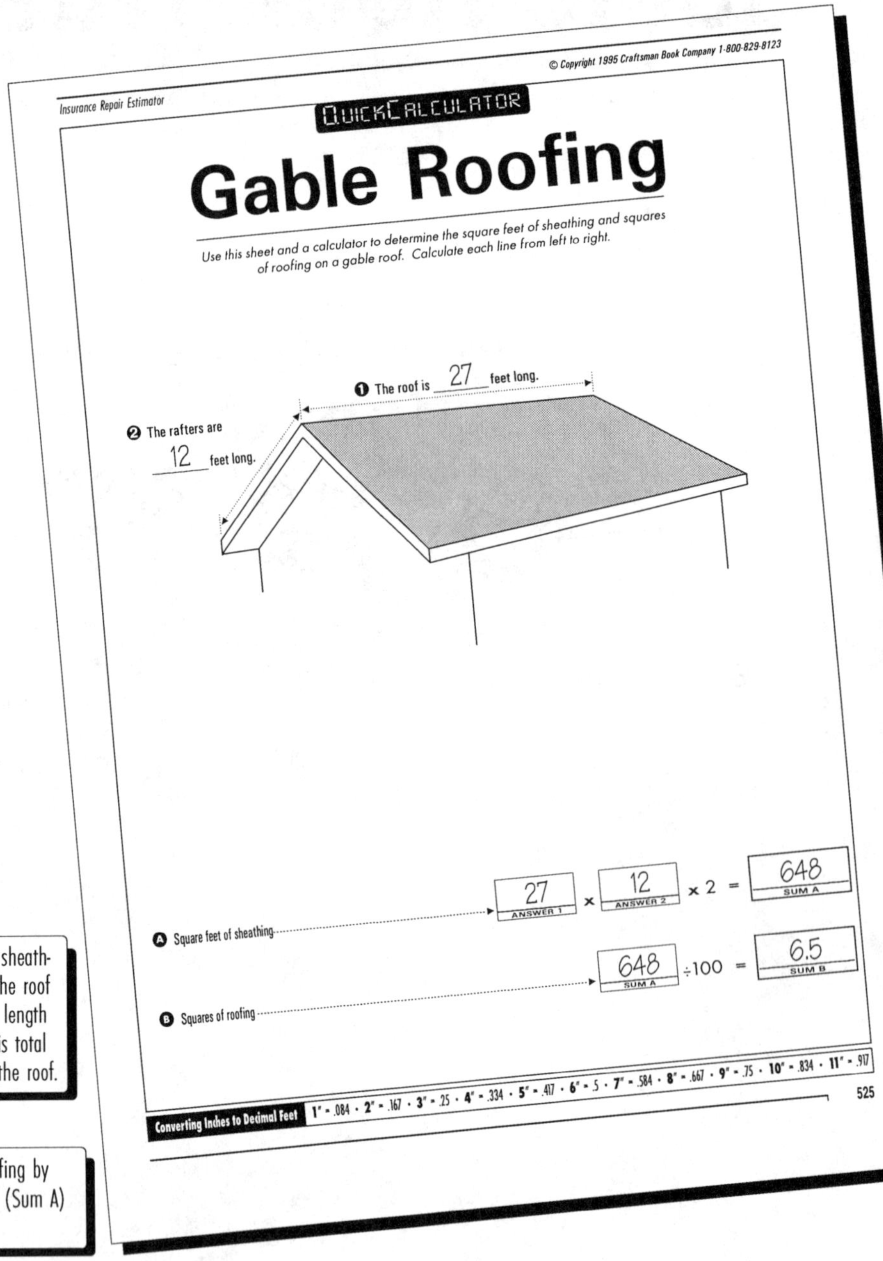

© Copyright 1995 Craftsman Book Company 1-800-829-8123

Insurance Repair Estimator

QUICKCALCULATOR

Gable Roofing

Use this sheet and a calculator to determine the square feet of sheathing and squares of roofing on a gable roof. Calculate each line from left to right.

❶ The roof is 27 feet long.

❷ The rafters are 12 feet long.

Ⓐ Square feet of sheathing .... 27 (ANSWER 1) × 12 (ANSWER 2) × 2 = 648 (SUM A)

Ⓑ Squares of roofing .... 648 (SUM A) ÷100 = 6.5 (SUM B)

Converting Inches to Decimal Feet 1" = .084 · 2" = .167 · 3" = .25 · 4" = .334 · 5" = .417 · 6" = .5 · 7" = .584 · 8" = .667 · 9" = .75 · 10" = .834 · 11" = .917

525

Ⓐ Calculates the square feet of sheathing on the roof by multiplying the roof length (Answer 1) by the rafter length (Answer 2), then multiplying this total by 2 to calculate both sides of the roof.

Ⓑ Calculates the squares of roofing by dividing the square feet of roof (Sum A) by 100.

QUICK FACTS

☞ The sample *QuickCalculator* sheet shown above contains quantities that have been rounded. We suggest rounding sheathing to the nearest square foot and rounding squares *up* to the next 1/5 square for shakes, the next 1/4 square for wood shingles and clay tile, and the next 1/3 square for asphalt shingles.

☞ See page 550 for more information about the geometric formulas used in this *QuickCalculator*. Also see *Roofing* beginning on page 393.

QUICKCALCULATOR

Gable Roofing

Use this sheet and a calculator to determine the square feet of sheathing and squares of roofing on a gable roof. Calculate each line from left to right.

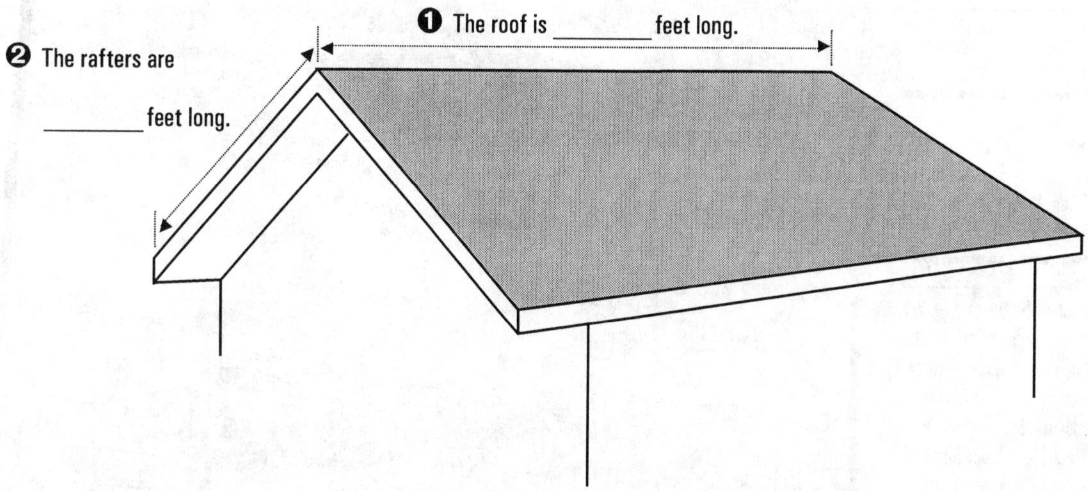

Ⓐ Square feet of sheathing .... [ANSWER 1] x [ANSWER 2] x 2 = [SUM A]

Ⓑ Squares of roofing .... [SUM A] ÷100 = [SUM B]

Converting Inches to Decimal Feet **1″** = .084 · **2″** = .167 · **3″** = .25 · **4″** = .334 · **5″** = .417 · **6″** = .5 · **7″** = .584 · **8″** = .667 · **9″** = .75 · **10″** = .834 · **11″** = .917

USING THE JOIST SYSTEM QUICKCALCULATOR

A Calculates the total number of joists. The length of the joist system (Answer 1) is converted into inches by multiplying it by 12.
The number of joists is calculated by taking the joist system length in inches and dividing it by the joist centers (Answer 4) then adding 1 for the first joist.

B Calculates the lineal feet of joists by multiplying the number of joists (Sum A) by the joist length (Answer 2).

C Calculates the lineal feet in rim joists and in solid blocking. The length of the rim joist (Answer 1) is multiplied by 2 for rim joists on both sides of the joist system. The total lineal feet of rim joists are then added to the lineal feet of solid blocking (Answer 6).

D Calculates total lineal feet of lumber in the joist system by adding the lineal feet of joists (Sum B) to the lineal feet of rim joists and solid blocking (Sum C).

E Calculates the board feet in the joist system by multiplying the total lineal feet of joists (Sum D) by the joist thickness (Answer 5), then by the joist width (Answer 3). This total is then divided by 12.

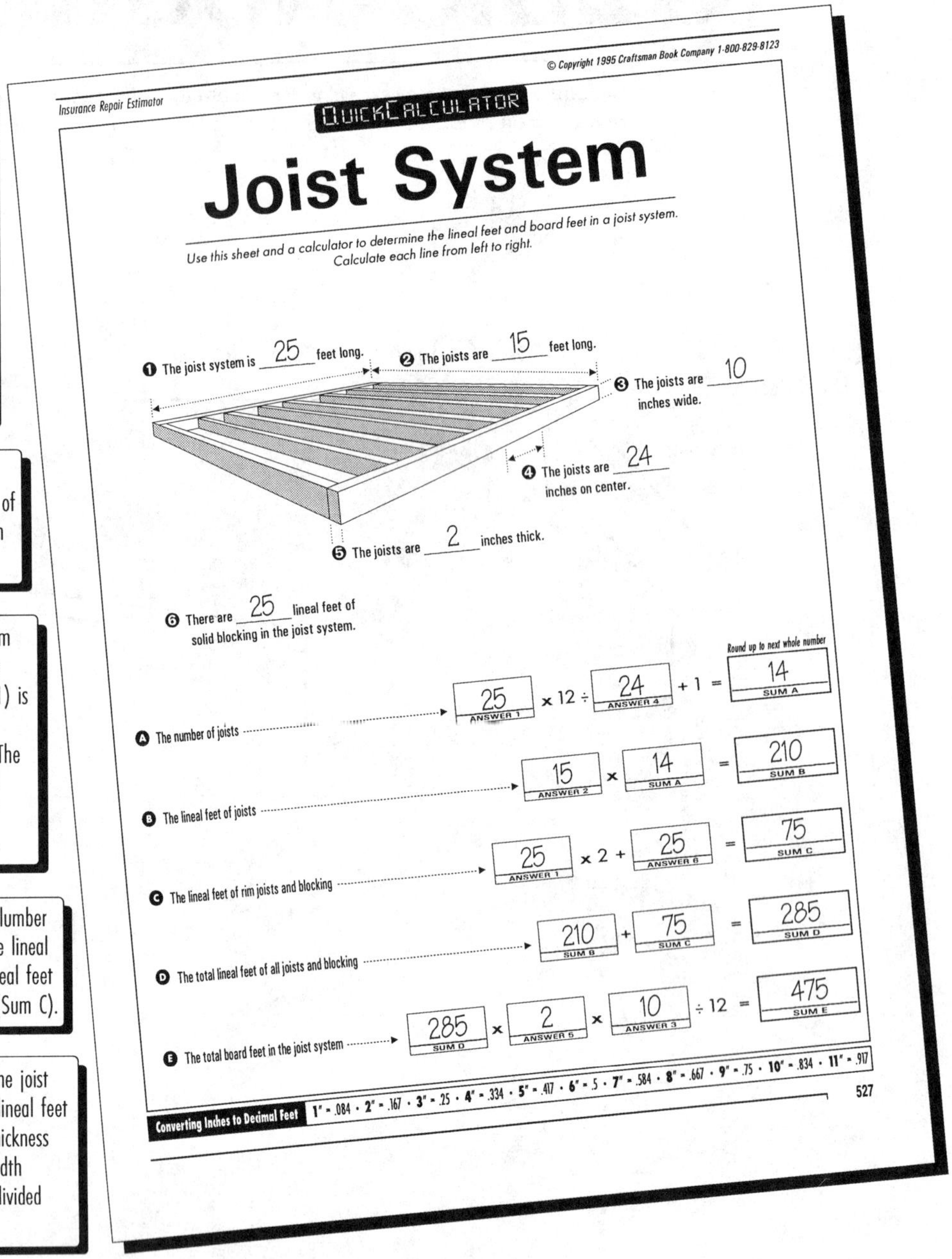

© Copyright 1995 Craftsman Book Company 1-800-829-8123

Insurance Repair Estimator

QUICKCALCULATOR

Joist System

Use this sheet and a calculator to determine the lineal feet and board feet in a joist system. Calculate each line from left to right.

6 There are 25 lineal feet of solid blocking in the joist system.

A The number of joists: 25 (ANSWER 1) × 12 ÷ 24 (ANSWER 4) + 1 = 14 (SUM A) — Round up to next whole number

B The lineal feet of joists: 15 (ANSWER 2) × 14 (SUM A) = 210 (SUM B)

C The lineal feet of rim joists and blocking: 25 (ANSWER 1) × 2 + 25 (ANSWER 6) = 75 (SUM C)

D The total lineal feet of all joists and blocking: 210 (SUM B) + 75 (SUM C) = 285 (SUM D)

E The total board feet in the joist system: 285 (SUM D) × 2 (ANSWER 5) × 10 (ANSWER 3) ÷ 12 = 475 (SUM E)

Converting Inches to Decimal Feet: 1" = .084 · 2" = .167 · 3" = .25 · 4" = .334 · 5" = .417 · 6" = .5 · 7" = .584 · 8" = .667 · 9" = .75 · 10" = .834 · 11" = .917

527

QUICK FACTS

☞ The sample *QuickCalculator* sheet shown above contains quantities that have been rounded. The total number of joists should always be rounded *up* to the next whole number. We also suggest rounding lineal feet and board feet to the nearest whole number.

☞ See page 550 for more information about the geometric formulas used in this *QuickCalculator*. See page 432 for joist systems priced per board foot.

QUICKCALCULATOR

Joist System

Use this sheet and a calculator to determine the lineal feet and board feet in a joist system. Calculate each line from left to right.

❶ The joist system is ________ feet long.

❷ The joists are ________ feet long.

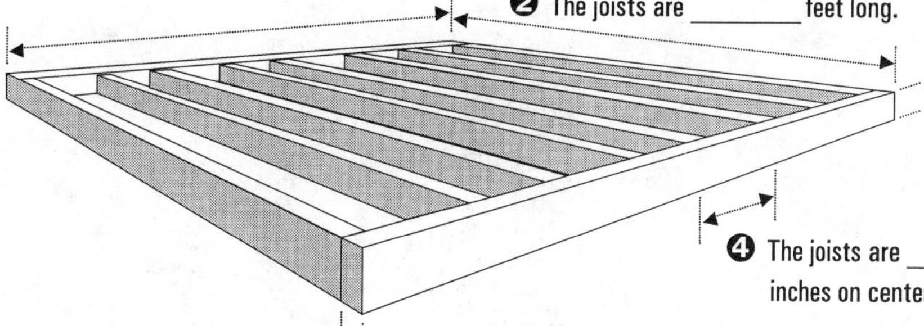

❸ The joists are ________ inches wide.

❹ The joists are ________ inches on center.

❺ The joists are ________ inches thick.

❻ There are ________ lineal feet of solid blocking in the joist system.

Ⓐ The number of joists → [ANSWER 1] × 12 ÷ [ANSWER 4] + 1 = [SUM A] *(Round up to next whole number)*

Ⓑ The lineal feet of joists → [ANSWER 2] × [SUM A] = [SUM B]

Ⓒ The lineal feet of rim joists and blocking → [ANSWER 1] × 2 + [ANSWER 6] = [SUM C]

Ⓓ The total lineal feet of all joists and blocking → [SUM B] + [SUM C] = [SUM D]

Ⓔ The total board feet in the joist system → [SUM D] × [ANSWER 5] × [ANSWER 3] ÷ 12 = [SUM E]

Converting Inches to Decimal Feet **1″** = .084 • **2″** = .167 • **3″** = .25 • **4″** = .334 • **5″** = .417 • **6″** = .5 • **7″** = .584 • **8″** = .667 • **9″** = .75 • **10″** = .834 • **11″** = .917

USING THE NON-BEARING WALL QUICKCALCULATOR

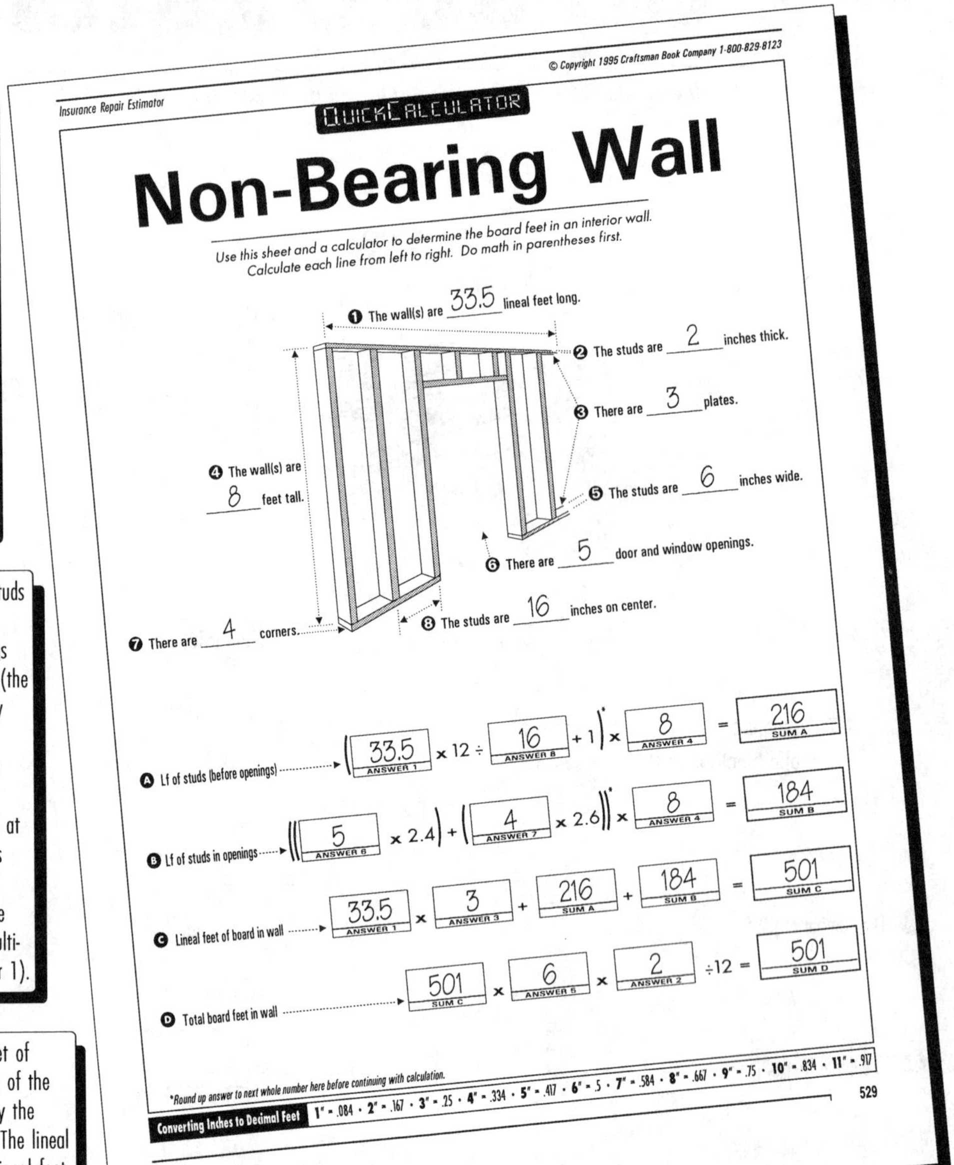

© Copyright 1995 Craftsman Book Company 1-800-829-8123

Insurance Repair Estimator

QUICKCALCULATOR

Non-Bearing Wall

Use this sheet and a calculator to determine the board feet in an interior wall. Calculate each line from left to right. Do math in parentheses first.

❶ The wall(s) are 33.5 lineal feet long.

❷ The studs are 2 inches thick.

❸ There are 3 plates.

❹ The wall(s) are 8 feet tall.

❺ The studs are 6 inches wide.

❻ There are 5 door and window openings.

❼ There are 4 corners.

❽ The studs are 16 inches on center.

Ⓐ Lf of studs (before openings) → (33.5 [ANSWER 1] × 12 ÷ 16 [ANSWER 8] + 1)* × 8 [ANSWER 4] = 216 [SUM A]

Ⓑ Lf of studs in openings → ((5 [ANSWER 6] × 2.4) + (4 [ANSWER 7] × 2.6))* × 8 [ANSWER 4] = 184 [SUM B]

Ⓒ Lineal feet of board in wall → 33.5 [ANSWER 1] × 3 [ANSWER 3] + 216 [SUM A] + 184 [SUM B] = 501 [SUM C]

Ⓓ Total board feet in wall → 501 [SUM C] × 6 [ANSWER 5] × 2 [ANSWER 2] ÷ 12 = 501 [SUM D]

*Round up answer to next whole number here before continuing with calculation.

Converting Inches to Decimal Feet 1" = .084 · 2" = .167 · 3" = .25 · 4" = .334 · 5" = .417 · 6" = .5 · 7" = .584 · 8" = .667 · 9" = .75 · 10" = .834 · 11" = .917

529

Ⓐ Calculates the lineal feet of studs in a wall *before* adding for openings and corners. The length of the wall (Answer 1) is converted into inches by multiplying it by 12. The number of studs is calculated by dividing the wall length in inches by the stud centers (Answer 8), then adding 1 for the first stud. The calculation should now be rounded *up*, then multiplied by the wall height (Answer 4).

Ⓑ Calculates the lineal feet of studs typically added for openings and corners. The number of openings (Answer 6) is multiplied by 2.4 (the *average* additional studs typically needed for an opening). The number of corners (Answer 7) is multiplied by 2.6 (the *average* additional studs typically needed at corners). The studs for openings and corners are added together, then should be rounded *up*. The total additional studs is then multiplied by the wall height (Answer 1).

Ⓒ Calculates the total lineal feet of lumber in the wall. The length of the wall (Answer 1) is multiplied by the number of plates (Answer 3). The lineal feet of plates is added to the lineal feet of studs (Sum A) and additional studs (Sum B).

Ⓓ Calculates the total board feet in the wall. The lineal feet of board in the wall (Sum C) is multiplied by the wall width (Answer 5) then by the stud thickness (Answer 2). The total is divided by twelve to convert to board feet.

QUICK FACTS

☞ The sample *QuickCalculator* sheet shown above contains quantities that have been rounded. When calculating Sum A and Sum B we suggest rounding the calculation *up* to the next whole number at the asterisk. Board feet and lineal feet should be rounded.

☞ See page 550 for more information about the geometric formulas used in this *QuickCalculator*. See page 414-415 for walls priced per board foot.

QUICKCALCULATOR

Non-Bearing Wall

Use this sheet and a calculator to determine the board feet in an interior wall. Calculate each line from left to right. Do math in parentheses first.

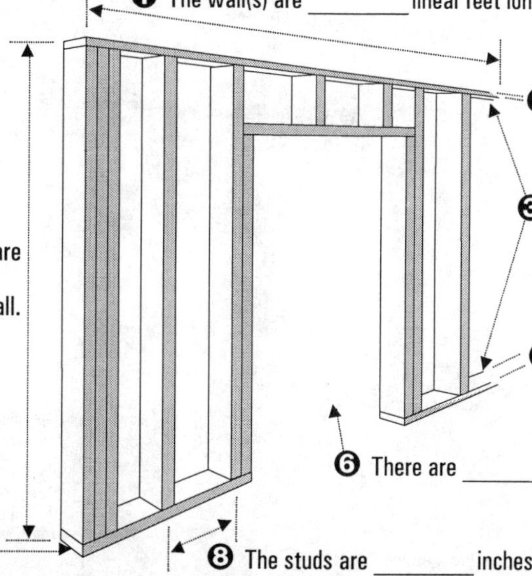

❶ The wall(s) are ________ lineal feet long.

❷ The studs are ________ inches thick.

❸ There are ________ plates.

❹ The wall(s) are ________ feet tall.

❺ The studs are ________ inches wide.

❻ There are ________ door and window openings.

❼ There are ________ corners.

❽ The studs are ________ inches on center.

Ⓐ Lf of studs (before openings) ········► ([ANSWER 1] x 12 ÷ [ANSWER 8] + 1)* x [ANSWER 4] = [SUM A]

Ⓑ Lf of studs in openings ······► (([ANSWER 6] x 2.4) + ([ANSWER 7] x 2.6))* x [ANSWER 4] = [SUM B]

Ⓒ Lineal feet of board in wall ········► [ANSWER 1] x [ANSWER 3] + [SUM A] + [SUM B] = [SUM C]

Ⓓ Total board feet in wall ········► [SUM C] x [ANSWER 5] x [ANSWER 2] ÷12 = [SUM D]

***Round up answer to next whole number here before continuing with calculation.*

Converting Inches to Decimal Feet **1"** = .084 · **2"** = .167 · **3"** = .25 · **4"** = .334 · **5"** = .417 · **6"** = .5 · **7"** = .584 · **8"** = .667 · **9"** = .75 · **10"** = .834 · **11"** = .917

USING THE PRISMATIC ROOM QUICKCALCULATOR

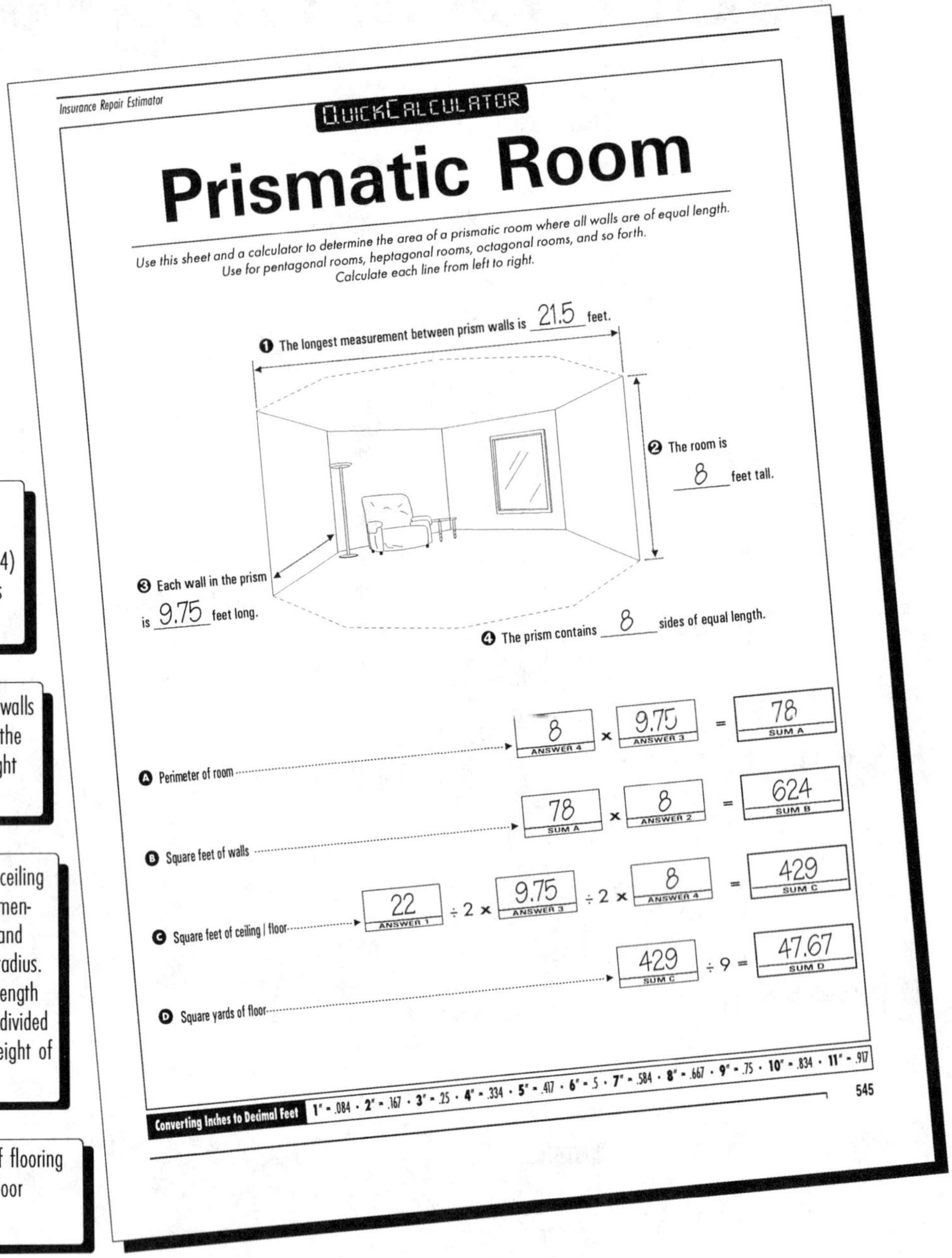
Insurance Repair Estimator

QUICKCALCULATOR

Prismatic Room

Use this sheet and a calculator to determine the area of a prismatic room where all walls are of equal length. Use for pentagonal rooms, heptagonal rooms, octagonal rooms, and so forth. Calculate each line from left to right.

1. The longest measurement between prism walls is 21.5 feet.
2. The room is 8 feet tall.
3. Each wall in the prism is 9.75 feet long.
4. The prism contains 8 sides of equal length.

A Perimeter of room: 8 (ANSWER 4) × 9.75 (ANSWER 3) = 78 (SUM A)

B Square feet of walls: 78 (SUM A) × 8 (ANSWER 2) = 624 (SUM B)

C Square feet of ceiling / floor: 22 (ANSWER 1) ÷ 2 × 9.75 (ANSWER 3) ÷ 2 × 8 (ANSWER 4) = 429 (SUM C)

D Square yards of floor: 429 (SUM C) ÷ 9 = 47.67 (SUM D)

Converting Inches to Decimal Feet 1" = .084 · 2" = .167 · 3" = .25 · 4" = .334 · 5" = .417 · 6" = .5 · 7" = .584 · 8" = .667 · 9" = .75 · 10" = .834 · 11" = .917

545

A Calculates the perimeter of the prism by multiplying the number of prism walls (Answer 4) by the length of the prism walls (Answer 3).

B Calculates the square feet of walls by multiplying the perimeter of the room (Sum A) by the room height (Answer 2).

C Calculates the square feet of ceiling / floor by taking the longest dimension between walls (Answer 1) and dividing by 2 to determine the radius. The radius is multiplied by the length of each prism wall (Answer 3), divided by two and multiplied by the height of the walls (Answer 2).

D Calculates the square yards of flooring by dividing the square feet of floor (Sum C) by 9.

QUICK FACTS

- The sample *QuickCalculator* sheet shown above contains quantities that have been rounded. We suggest rounding lineal feet to two decimal places then to the nearest inch when converting to inches. Square feet should probably be rounded to the nearest square foot and square yards should be rounded up to the nearest 1/3 or 1/4 yard.
- See page 550 for more information about the geometric formulas used in this *QuickCalculator*.

QUICKCALCULATOR

Prismatic Room

Use this sheet and a calculator to determine the area of a prismatic room where all walls are of equal length. Use for pentagonal rooms, heptagonal rooms, octagonal rooms, and so forth. Calculate each line from left to right.

❶ The longest measurement between prism walls is ________ feet.

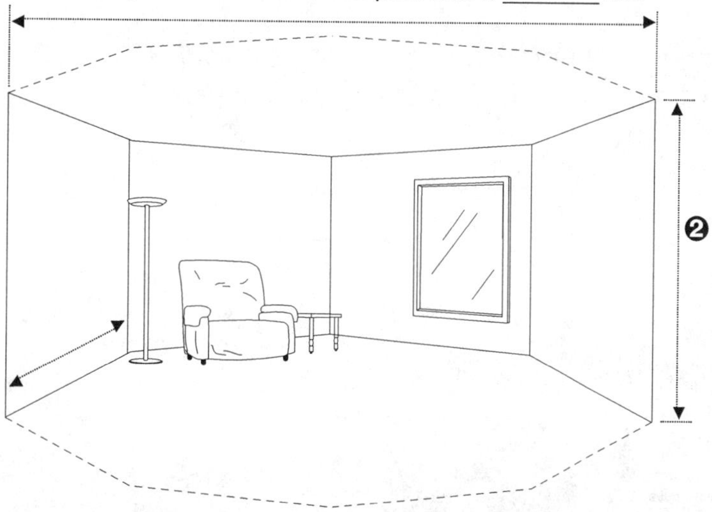

❷ The room is ________ feet tall.

❸ Each wall in the prism is ________ feet long.

❹ The prism contains ________ sides of equal length.

Ⓐ Perimeter of room .... ▶ [ANSWER 4] × [ANSWER 3] = [SUM A]

Ⓑ Square feet of walls .... ▶ [SUM A] × [ANSWER 2] = [SUM B]

Ⓒ Square feet of ceiling / floor .... ▶ [ANSWER 1] ÷ 2 × [ANSWER 3] ÷ 2 × [ANSWER 4] = [SUM C]

Ⓓ Square yards of floor .... ▶ [SUM C] ÷ 9 = [SUM D]

Converting Inches to Decimal Feet **1″** = .084 · **2″** = .167 · **3″** = .25 · **4″** = .334 · **5″** = .417 · **6″** = .5 · **7″** = .584 · **8″** = .667 · **9″** = .75 · **10″** = .834 · **11″** = .917

USING THE RECTANGULAR ROOM QUICKCALCULATOR

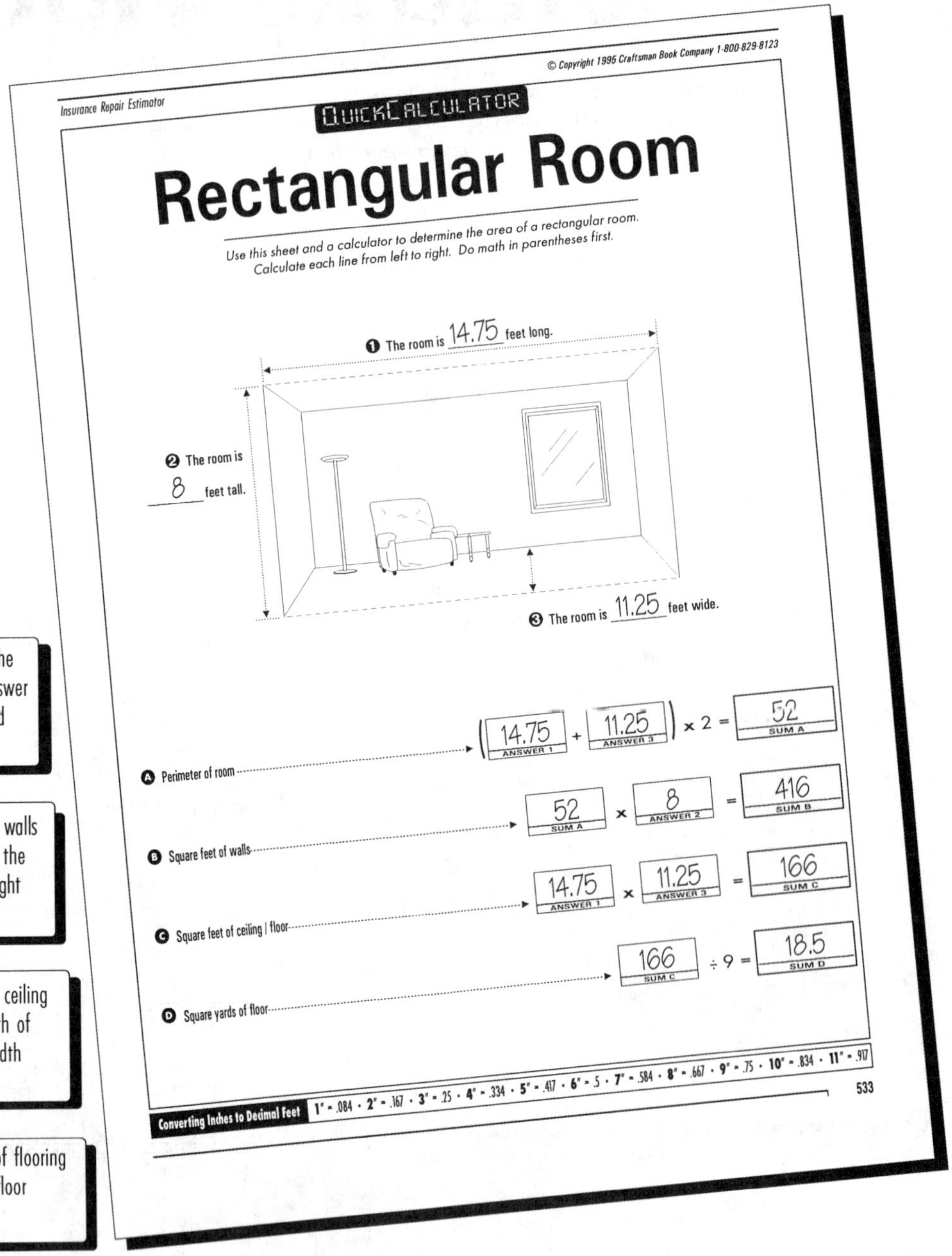
© Copyright 1995 Craftsman Book Company 1-800-829-8123

Insurance Repair Estimator

QUICKCALCULATOR

Rectangular Room

Use this sheet and a calculator to determine the area of a rectangular room. Calculate each line from left to right. Do math in parentheses first.

❶ The room is 14.75 feet long.

❷ The room is 8 feet tall.

❸ The room is 11.25 feet wide.

Ⓐ Perimeter of room (14.75 [ANSWER 1] + 11.25 [ANSWER 3]) × 2 = 52 [SUM A]

Ⓑ Square feet of walls 52 [SUM A] × 8 [ANSWER 2] = 416 [SUM B]

Ⓒ Square feet of ceiling / floor 14.75 [ANSWER 1] × 11.25 [ANSWER 3] = 166 [SUM C]

Ⓓ Square yards of floor 166 [SUM C] ÷ 9 = 18.5 [SUM D]

533

Converting Inches to Decimal Feet 1" = .084 · 2" = .167 · 3" = .25 · 4" = .334 · 5" = .417 · 6" = .5 · 7" = .584 · 8" = .667 · 9" = .75 · 10" = .834 · 11" = .917

Ⓐ Calculates the perimeter of the room by adding the length (Answer 1) to the width (Answer 3) and multiplying by two.

Ⓑ Calculates the square feet of walls by multiplying the perimeter of the room (Sum A) by the room height (Answer 2).

Ⓒ Calculates the square feet of ceiling / floor by multiplying the length of the room (Answer 1) by the width (Answer 3).

Ⓓ Calculates the square yards of flooring by dividing the square feet of floor (Sum C) by 9.

QUICK FACTS

☞ The sample *QuickCalculator* sheet shown above contains quantities that have been rounded. We suggest rounding lineal feet to two decimal places then to the nearest inch when converting to inches. Square feet should probably be rounded to the nearest square foot and square yards should be rounded to the nearest 1/3 or 1/4 yard.

☞ See page 550 for more information about the geometric formulas used in this *QuickCalculator*.

QUICKCALCULATOR

Rectangular Room

Use this sheet and a calculator to determine the area of a rectangular room. Calculate each line from left to right. Do math in parentheses first.

❶ The room is ________ feet long.

❷ The room is ________ feet tall.

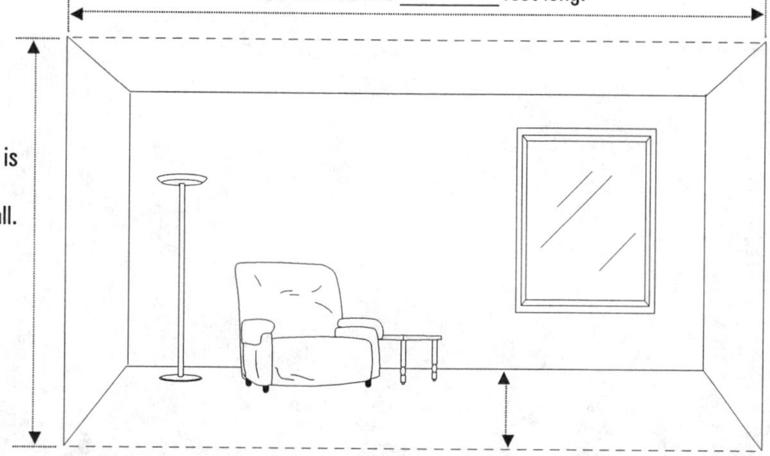

❸ The room is ________ feet wide.

Ⓐ Perimeter of room .... ([ANSWER 1] + [ANSWER 3]) × 2 = [SUM A]

Ⓑ Square feet of walls .... [SUM A] × [ANSWER 2] = [SUM B]

Ⓒ Square feet of ceiling / floor .... [ANSWER 1] × [ANSWER 3] = [SUM C]

Ⓓ Square yards of floor .... [SUM C] ÷ 9 = [SUM D]

Converting Inches to Decimal Feet **1″** = .084 • **2″** = .167 • **3″** = .25 • **4″** = .334 • **5″** = .417 • **6″** = .5 • **7″** = .584 • **8″** = .667 • **9″** = .75 • **10″** = .834 • **11″** = .917

USING THE ROUND ROOM QUICKCALCULATOR

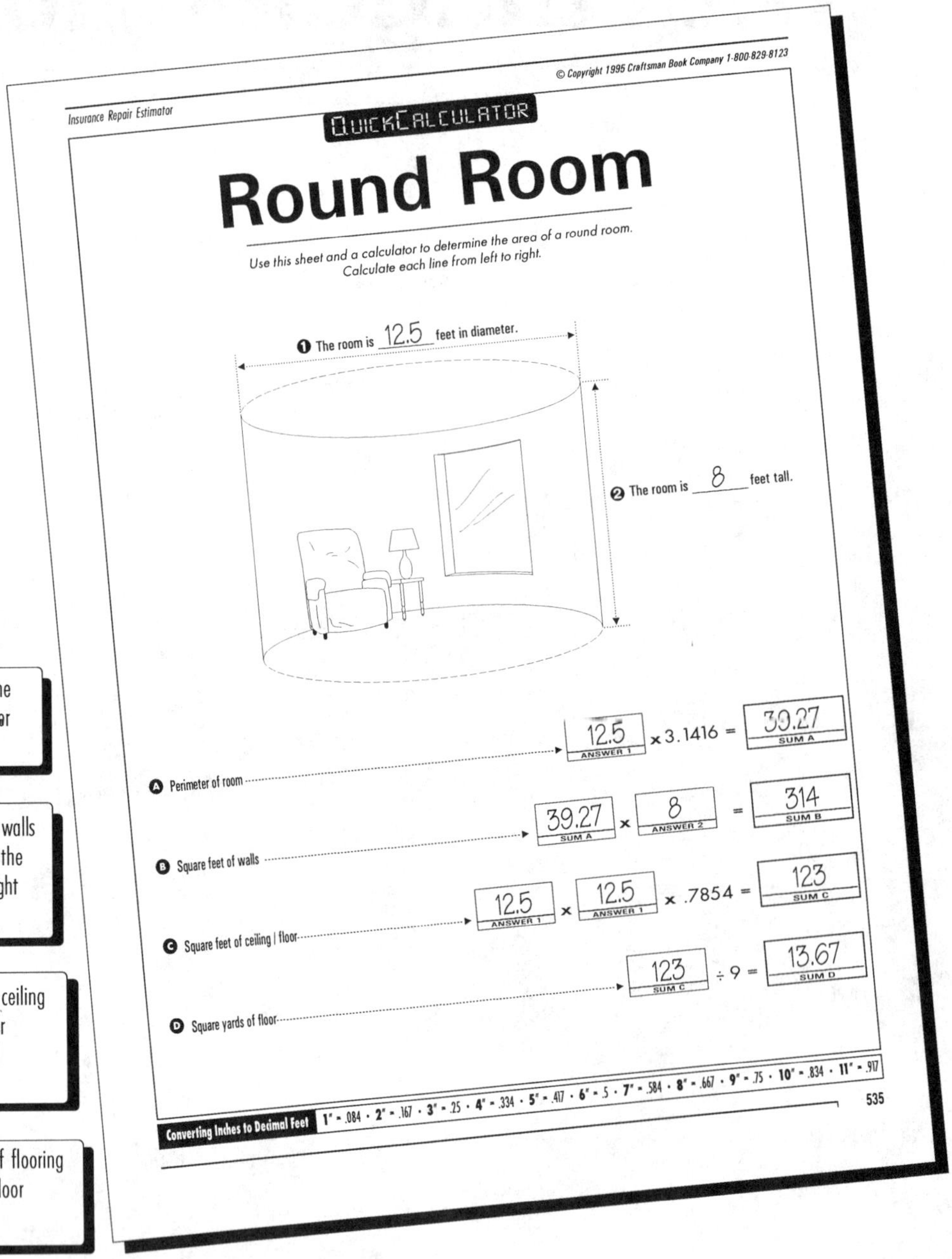

Ⓐ Calculates the perimeter of the circle by multiplying the diameter (Answer 1) by Pi (3.1416).

Ⓑ Calculates the square feet of walls by multiplying the perimeter of the room (Sum A) by the room height (Answer 2).

Ⓒ Calculates the square feet of ceiling / floor by squaring the diameter (Answer 1 times Answer 1) and multiplying by .7854.

Ⓓ Calculates the square yards of flooring by dividing the square feet of floor (Sum C) by 9.

QUICK FACTS

☞ The sample *QuickCalculator* sheet shown above contains quantities that have been rounded. We suggest rounding lineal feet to two decimal places then to the nearest inch when converting to inches. Square feet should probably be rounded to the nearest square foot and square yards should be rounded to the nearest 1/3 or 1/4 yard.

☞ See page 550 for more information about the geometric formulas used in this *QuickCalculator*.

QUICKCALCULATOR

Round Room

Use this sheet and a calculator to determine the area of a round room.
Calculate each line from left to right.

❶ The room is ________ feet in diameter.

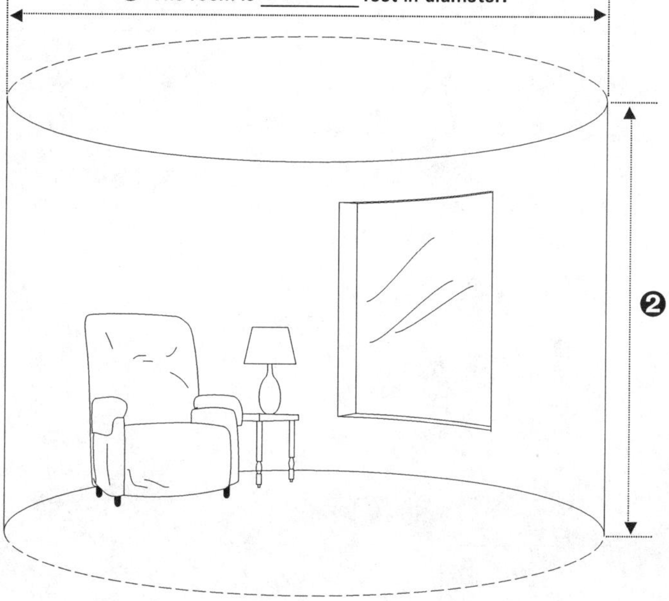

❷ The room is ________ feet tall.

Ⓐ Perimeter of room .... [ANSWER 1] × 3.1416 = [SUM A]

Ⓑ Square feet of walls .... [SUM A] × [ANSWER 2] = [SUM B]

Ⓒ Square feet of ceiling / floor .... [ANSWER 1] × [ANSWER 1] × .7854 = [SUM C]

Ⓓ Square yards of floor .... [SUM C] ÷ 9 = [SUM D]

Converting Inches to Decimal Feet **1″** = .084 • **2″** = .167 • **3″** = .25 • **4″** = .334 • **5″** = .417 • **6″** = .5 • **7″** = .584 • **8″** = .667 • **9″** = .75 • **10″** = .834 • **11″** = .917

QuickCalculator mathematics

CIRCLE

Area

❶ = Pi x radius^2

❷ = .7854 x diameter^2

❸ = .0796 x perimeter^2

Perimeter

❶ = Pi x diameter

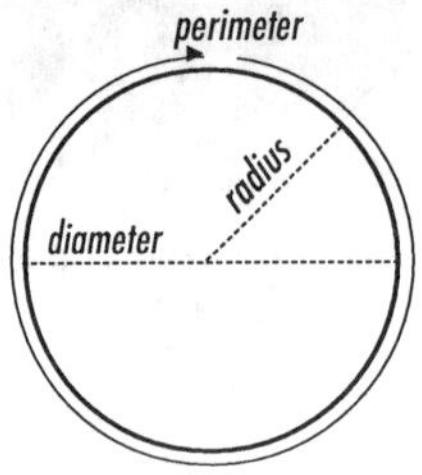

PARALLELOGRAM

Area

❶ = base x height

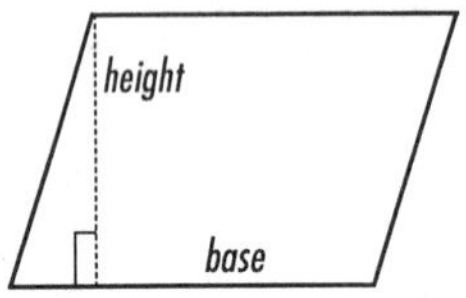

PRISM

Area

❶ = sum of sides ÷ 2 x radius

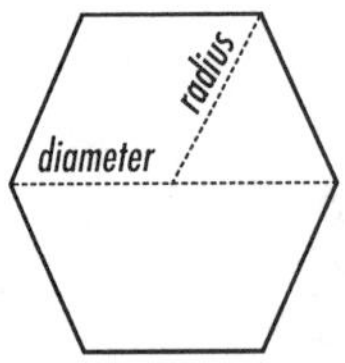

RECTANGLE

Area

❶ = length x width

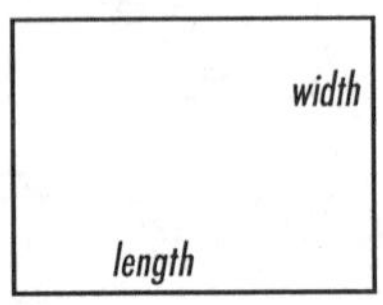

TRAPEZOID

Area

❶ = base + top ÷ 2 x height

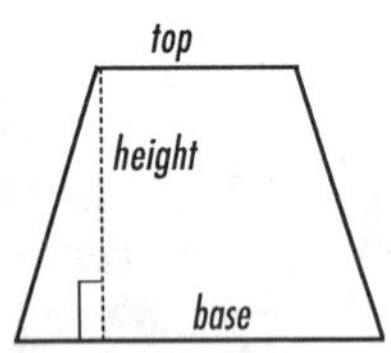

TRIANGLE

Area

❶ = base x height ÷ 2

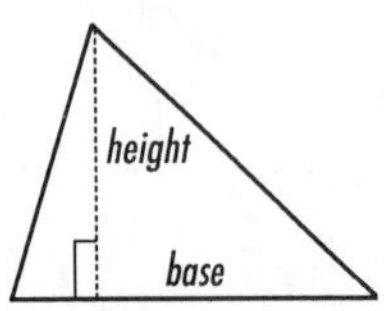

PYTHAGOREAN THEORM

Rafter length

❶ rafter length^2 = rise^2 + run^2

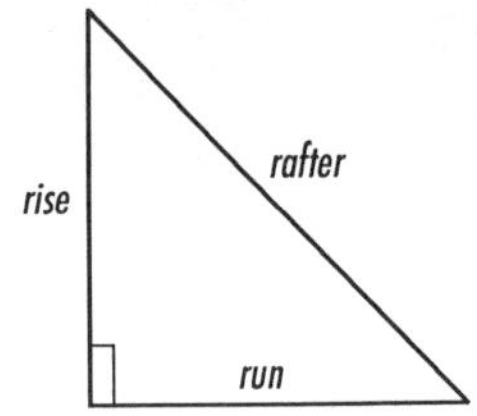

CONVERSION FACTORS

DIVIDE	BY	TO CONVERT TO
square inches	144	square feet
square inches	144	board feet
cubic inches	1,728	cubic feet
cubic inches	46,656	cubic yards
square feet	9	square yards
square feet	100	squares
cubic feet	27	cubic yards
feet	16.5	rods
rods	40	furlongs
feet	5,280	miles
meters	1,609	miles
yards	1,760	miles

MULTIPLY	BY	TO CONVERT TO
inches	2.54	centimeters
square inches	6.4516	square centimeters
square inches	.0069	square feet
square feet	9.29	square centimeters
square feet	.0929	square meters
square yards	.8361	square meters
square meters	1.1959	square yards
centimeters	.3937	inches
feet	.3048	meters
meters	3.281	feet
yards	91.44	centimeters
yards	.9144	meters
cubic feet	.0283	cubic meters
cubic meters	35.3145	cubic feet
cubic meters	1.3079	cubic yards
cubic yards	.7646	cubic meters
cubic inches	16.3872	cubic centimeters
cubic centimeters	.0610	cubic inches
cubic meters	1,000	cubic liters

index

A

B

D

E

F

G

S

T

U

V

Practical References for Builders

Construction Forms & Contracts

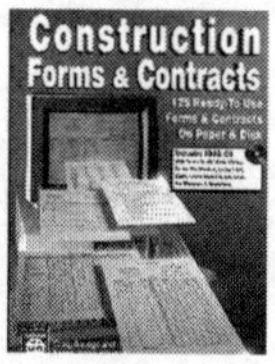

125 forms you can copy and use — or load into your computer (from the FREE disk enclosed). Then you can customize the forms to fit your company, fill them out, and print. Loads into *Word* for *Windows*™, *Lotus 1-2-3*, *WordPerfect*, *Works*, or *Excel* programs. You'll find forms covering accounting, estimating, fieldwork, contracts, and general office. Each form comes with complete instructions on when to use it and how to fill it out. These forms were designed, tested and used by contractors, and will help keep your business organized, profitable and out of legal, accounting and collection troubles. Includes a CD-ROM for *Windows*™ and Mac.
400 pages, 8½ x 11, $41.75

CD Estimator

If your computer has *Windows*™ and a CD-ROM drive, *CD Estimator* puts at your fingertips 85,000 construction costs for new construction, remodeling, renovation & insurance repair, electrical, plumbing, HVAC and painting. You'll also have the *National Estimator* program — a stand-alone estimating program for *Windows*™ that *Remodeling* magazine called a "computer wiz." Quarterly cost updates are available at no charge on the Internet. To help you create professional-looking estimates, the disk includes over 40 construction estimating and bidding forms in a format that's perfect for nearly any word processing or spreadsheet program for *Windows*™. And to top it off, a 70-minute interactive video teaches you how to use this CD-ROM to estimate construction costs. **CD Estimator is $68.50**

Contractor's Guide to QuickBooks Pro 2001

This user-friendly manual walks you through QuickBooks Pro's detailed setup procedure and explains step-by-step how to create a first-rate accounting system. You'll learn in days, rather than weeks, how to use QuickBooks Pro to get your contracting business organized, with simple, fast accounting procedures. On the CD included with the book you'll find a QuickBooks Pro file preconfigured for a construction company (you drag it over onto your computer and plug in your own company's data). You'll also get a complete estimating program, including a database, and a job costing program that lets you export your estimates to QuickBooks Pro. It even includes many useful construction forms to use in your business.
328 pages, 8½ x 11, $45.25

Basic Engineering for Builders

If you've ever been stumped by an engineering problem on the job, yet wanted to avoid the expense of hiring a qualified engineer, you should have this book. Here you'll find engineering principles explained in non-technical language and practical methods for applying them on the job. With the help of this book you'll be able to understand engineering functions in the plans and how to meet the requirements, how to get permits issued without the help of an engineer, and anticipate requirements for concrete, steel, wood and masonry. See why you sometimes have to hire an engineer and what you can undertake yourself: surveying, concrete, lumber loads and stresses, steel, masonry, plumbing, and HVAC systems. This book is designed to help the builder save money by understanding engineering principles that you can incorporate into the jobs you bid.
400 pages, 8½ x 11, $36.50

National Painting Cost Estimator

A complete guide to estimating painting costs for just about any type of residential, commercial, or industrial painting, whether by brush, spray, or roller. Shows typical costs and bid prices for fast, medium, and slow work, including material costs per gallon; square feet covered per gallon; square feet covered per manhour; labor, material, overhead, and taxes per 100 square feet; and how much to add for profit. Includes a CD-ROM with an electronic version of the book with *National Estimator*, a stand-alone *Windows*™ estimating program, plus an interactive multimedia video that shows how to use the disk to compile construction cost estimates.
440 pages, 8½ x 11, $48.00. Revised annually

National Construction Estimator

Current building costs for residential, commercial, and industrial construction. Estimated prices for every common building material. Provides man-hours, recommended crew, and gives the labor cost for installation. Includes a CD-ROM with an electronic version of the book with *National Estimator*, a stand-alone *Windows*™ estimating program, plus an interactive multimedia video that shows how to use the disk to compile construction cost estimates. **616 pages, 8½ x 11, $47.50. Revised annually**

Contracting in All 50 States

Every state has its own licensing requirements that you must meet to do business there. These are usually written exams, financial requirements, and letters of reference. This book shows how to get a building, mechanical or specialty contractor's license, qualify for DOT work, and register as an out-of-state corporation, for every state in the U.S. It lists addresses, phone numbers, application fees, requirements, where an exam is required, what's covered on the exam and how much weight each area of construction is given on the exam. You'll find just about everything you need to know in order to apply for your out-of-state license.
416 pages, 8½ x 11, $36.00

Contractor's Guide to the Building Code Revised

This new edition was written in collaboration with the International Conference of Building Officials, writers of the code. It explains in plain English exactly what the latest edition of the *Uniform Building Code* requires. Based on the 1997 code, it explains the changes and what they mean for the builder. Also covers the *Uniform Mechanical Code* and the *Uniform Plumbing Code.* Shows how to design and construct residential and light commercial buildings that'll pass inspection the first time. Suggests how to work with an inspector to minimize construction costs, what common building shortcuts are likely to be cited, and where exceptions may be granted. **320 pages, 8½ x 11, $39.00**

Finish Carpenter's Manual

Everything you need to know to be a finish carpenter: assessing a job before you begin, and tricks of the trade from a master finish carpenter. Easy-to-follow instructions for installing doors and windows, ceiling treatments (including fancy beams, corbels, cornices and moldings), wall treatments (including wainscoting and sheet paneling), and the finishing touches of chair, picture, and plate rails. Specialized interior work includes cabinetry and built-ins, stair finish work, and closets. Also covers exterior trims and porches. Includes manhour tables for finish work, and hundreds of illustrations and photos. **208 pages, 8½ x 11, $22.50**

Troubleshooting Guide to Residential Construction

How to solve practically every construction problem — before it happens to you! With this book you'll learn from the mistakes other builders made as they faced 63 typical residential construction problems. Filled with clear photos and drawings that explain how to enhance your reputation as well as your bottom line by avoiding problems that plague most builders. Shows how to avoid, or fix, problems ranging from defective slabs, walls and ceilings, through roofing, plumbing & HVAC, to paint.
304 pages, 8½ x 11, $32.50

Roofing Construction & Estimating

Installation, repair and estimating for nearly every type of roof covering available today in residential and commercial structures: asphalt shingles, roll roofing, wood shingles and shakes, clay tile, slate, metal, built-up, and elastomeric. Covers sheathing and underlayment techniques, as well as secrets for installing leakproof valleys. Many estimating tips help you minimize waste, as well as insure a profit on every job. Troubleshooting techniques help you identify the true source of most leaks. Over 300 large, clear illustrations help you find the answer to just about all your roofing questions.
432 pages, 8½ x 11, $38.00

How to Succeed With Your Own Construction Business

Everything you need to start your own construction business: setting up the paperwork, finding the work, advertising, using contracts, dealing with lenders, estimating, scheduling, finding and keeping good employees, keeping the books, and coping with success. If you're considering starting your own construction business, all the knowledge, tips, and blank forms you need are here. **336 pages, 8½ x 11, $28.50**

Estimating With Microsoft *Excel*

Most builders estimate with *Excel* because it's easy to learn, quick to use, and can be customized to your style of estimating. Here you'll find step-by-step instructions on how to create your own customized automated spreadsheet estimating program for use with *Excel*. You'll learn how to use the magic of *Excel* to create detail sheets, cost breakdown summaries, and links. You'll put this all to use in estimating concrete, rebar, permit fees, and roofing. You can even create your own macros. Includes a CD-ROM that illustrates examples in the book and provides you with templates you can use to set up your own estimating system. **150 pages, 7 x 9, $49.95**

Construction Estimating Reference Data

Provides the 300 most useful manhour tables for practically every item of construction. Labor requirements are listed for sitework, concrete work, masonry, steel, carpentry, thermal and moisture protection, doors and windows, finishes, mechanical and electrical. Each section details the work being estimated and gives appropriate crew size and equipment needed. Includes a CD-ROM with an electronic version of the book with *National Estimator*, a stand-alone *Windows*™ estimating program, plus an interactive multimedia video that shows how to use the disk to compile construction cost estimates. **432 pages, 11 x 8½ , $39.50**

Basic Lumber Engineering for Builders

Beam and lumber requirements for many jobs aren't always clear, especially with changing building codes and lumber products. Most of the time you rely on your own "rules of thumb" when figuring spans or lumber engineering. This book can help you fill the gap between what you can find in the building code span tables and what you need to pay a certified engineer to do. With its large, clear illustrations and examples, this book shows you how to figure stresses for pre-engineered wood or wood structural members, how to calculate loads, and how to design your own girders, joists and beams. Included FREE with the book — an easy-to-use limited version of NorthBridge Software's *Wood Beam Sizing* program.
272 pages, 8½ x 11, $38.00

Cost Records for Construction Estimating

How to organize and use cost information from jobs just completed to make more accurate estimates in the future. Explains how to keep the records you need to track costs for sitework, footings, foundations, framing, interior finish, siding and trim, masonry, and subcontract expense. Provides sample forms. **208 pages, 8½ x 11, $15.75**

Concrete Construction & Estimating

Explains how to estimate the quantity of labor and materials needed, plan the job, erect fiberglass, steel, or prefabricated forms, install shores and scaffolding, handle the concrete into place, set joints, finish and cure the concrete. Full of practical reference data, cost estimates, and examples.
571 pages, 5½ x 8½, $25.00

Building Contractor's Exam Preparation Guide

Passing today's contractor's exams can be a major task. This book shows you how to study, how questions are likely to be worded, and the kinds of choices usually given for answers. Includes sample questions from actual state, county, and city examinations, plus a sample exam to practice on. This book isn't a substitute for the study material that your testing board recommends, but it will help prepare you for the types of questions — and their correct answers — that are likely to appear on the actual exam. Knowing how to answer these questions, as well as what to expect from the exam, can greatly increase your chances of passing. **320 pages, 8½ x 11, $35.00**

Contractor's Survival Manual

How to survive hard times and succeed during the up cycles. Shows what to do when the bills can't be paid, finding money and buying time, transferring debt, and all the alternatives to bankruptcy. Explains how to build profits, avoid problems in zoning and permits, taxes, time-keeping, and payroll. Unconventional advice on how to invest in inflation, get high appraisals, trade and postpone income, and stay hip-deep in profitable work.
160 pages, 8½ x 11, $22.25

Estimating Electrical Construction

Like taking a class in how to estimate materials and labor for residential and commercial electrical construction. Written by an A.S.P.E. National Estimator of the Year, it teaches you how to use labor units, the plan take-off, and the bid summary to make an accurate estimate, how to deal with suppliers, use pricing sheets, and modify labor units. Provides extensive labor unit tables and blank forms for your next electrical job.
272 pages, 8½ x 11, $19.00

Electrician's Exam Preparation Guide

Need help in passing the apprentice, journeyman, or master electrician's exam? This is a book of questions and answers based on actual electrician's exams over the last few years. Almost a thousand multiple-choice questions — exactly the type you'll find on the exam — cover every area of electrical installation: electrical drawings, services and systems, transformers, capacitors, distribution equipment, branch circuits, feeders, calculations, measuring and testing, and more. It gives you the correct answer, an explanation, and where to find it in the latest *NEC*. Also tells how to apply for the test, how best to study, and what to expect on examination day.
352 pages, 8½ x 11, $32.00

Moving to Commercial Construction

In commercial work, a single job can keep you and your crews busy for a year or more. The profit percentages are higher, but so is the risk involved. This book takes you step-by-step through the process of setting up a successful commercial business; finding work, estimating and bidding, value engineering, getting through the submittal and shop drawing process, keeping a stable work force, controlling costs, and promoting your business. Explains the design/build and partnering business concepts and their advantage over the competitive bid process. Includes sample letters, contracts, checklists and forms that you can use in your business, plus a CD-ROM with blank copies in several word-processing formats for both Mac and PC computers. **256 pages, 8½ x 11, $42.00**

National Electrical Estimator

This year's prices for installation of all common electrical work: conduit, wire, boxes, fixtures, switches, outlets, loadcenters, panelboards, raceway, duct, signal systems, and more. Provides material costs, manhours per unit, and total installed cost. Explains what you should know to estimate each part of an electrical system. Includes a CD-ROM with an electronic version of the book with *National Estimator*, a stand-alone *Windows*™ estimating program, plus an interactive multimedia video that shows how to use the disk to compile construction cost estimates.
520 pages, 8½ x 11, $47.75. Revised annually

National Repair & Remodeling Estimator

The complete pricing guide for dwelling reconstruction costs. Reliable, specific data you can apply on every repair and remodeling job. Up-to-date material costs and labor figures based on thousands of jobs across the country. Provides recommended crew sizes; average production rates; exact material, equipment, and labor costs; a total unit cost and a total price including overhead and profit. Separate listings for high- and low-volume builders, so prices shown are specific for any size business. Estimating tips specific to repair and remodeling work to make your bids complete, realistic, and profitable. Includes a CD-ROM with an electronic version of the book with *National Estimator*, a stand-alone *Windows*™ estimating program, plus an interactive multimedia video that shows how to use the disk to compile construction cost estimates.
296 pages, 8½ x 11, $48.50. Revised annually

Steel-Frame House Construction

Framing with steel has obvious advantages over wood, yet building with steel requires new skills that can present challenges to the wood builder. This new book explains the secrets of steel framing techniques for building homes, whether pre-engineered or built stick by stick. It shows you the techniques, the tools, the materials, and how you can make it happen. Includes hundreds of photos and illustrations, plus a CD-ROM with steel framing details, a database of steel materials and manhours, with an estimating program. **320 pages, 8½ x 11, $39.75**

Home Inspection Handbook

Every area you need to check in a home inspection — especially in older homes. Twenty complete inspection checklists: building site, foundation and basement, structural, bathrooms, chimneys and flues, ceilings, interior & exterior finishes, electrical, plumbing, HVAC, insects, vermin and decay, and more. Also includes information on starting and running your own home inspection business. **324 pages, 5½ x 8½, $24.95**

National Building Cost Manual

Square foot costs for residential, commercial, industrial, and farm buildings. Quickly work up a reliable budget estimate based on actual materials and design features, area, shape, wall height, number of floors, and support requirements. Includes all the important variables that can make any building unique from a cost standpoint.
240 pages, 8½ x 11, $23.00. Revised annually

Markup & Profit: A Contractor's Guide

In order to succeed in a construction business, you have to be able to price your jobs to cover all labor, material and overhead expenses, and make a decent profit. The problem is knowing what markup to use. You don't want to lose jobs because you charge too much, and you don't want to work for free because you've charged too little. If you know how to calculate markup, you can apply it to your job costs to find the right sales price for your work. This book gives you tried and tested formulas, with step-by-step instructions and easy-to-follow examples, so you can easily figure the markup that's right for your business. Includes a CD-ROM with forms and checklists for your use. **320 pages, 8½ x 11, $32.50**

Inspecting A House

Here you'll find a rational sequence of home inspection so that you won't miss anything in heating, electrical, plumbing, and drainage systems. Whether it's an overloaded electrical panel, a driveway that sends water into the basement when it rains, or a gas furnace that's improperly vented, you'll be shown how to spot and evaluate problem areas.
266 pages, 8 x 10, $24.95

National Building Assembly Costs

Complete assembly costs for all construction across the 16 CSI divisions. These prices include all the individual line items included in a typical construction assembly, added together to generate an assembly "unit" price. With unit price estimates from the assemblies section, and subcontractor unit prices from the line item cost information, you can put together an estimate for just about any project in minutes. It's far more accurate than a square foot cost estimate, yet takes a fraction of the time a stick-by-stick estimate takes. Includes a CD-ROM with estimating data you can use, and a demo version of WinEst LT, a powerful estimating program for light construction that includes the cost data from Craftsman's *National Construction Estimator*. **320 pages, 8½ x 11, $44.75**

Plumbing & HVAC Manhour Estimates

Hundreds of tested and proven manhours for installing just about any plumbing and HVAC component you're likely to use in residential, commercial, and industrial work. You'll find manhours for installing piping systems, specialties, fixtures and accessories, ducting systems, and HVAC equipment. If you estimate the price of plumbing, you shouldn't be without the reliable, proven manhours in this unique book.
224 pages, 5½ x 8½, $28.25

Rough Framing Carpentry

If you'd like to make good money working outdoors as a framer, this is the book for you. Here you'll find shortcuts to laying out studs; speed cutting blocks, trimmers and plates by eye; quickly building and blocking rake walls; installing ceiling backing, ceiling joists, and truss joists; cutting and assembling hip trusses and California fills; arches and drop ceilings — all with production line procedures that save you time and help you make more money. Over 100 on-the-job photos of how to do it right and what can go wrong. **304 pages, 8½ x 11, $26.50**

Residential Electrical Estimating

A fast, accurate pricing system proven on over 1000 residential jobs. Using the manhours provided, combined with material prices from your wholesaler, you quickly work up estimates based on degree of difficulty. These manhours come from a working electrical contractor's records — not some pricing agency. You'll find prices for every type of electrical job you're likely to estimate — from service entrances to ceiling fans.
320 pages, 8½ x 11, $29.00

Residential Structure & Framing

With this easy-to-understand guide you'll learn how to calculate loads, size joists and beams, and tackle many common structural problems facing residential contractors. It covers cantilevered floors, complex roof structures, tall window walls, and seismic and wind bracing. Plus, you'll learn field-proven production techniques for advanced wall, floor, and roof framing with both dimensional and engineered lumber. You'll find information on sizing joists and beams, framing with wood I-joists, supporting oversized dormers, unequal-pitched roofs, coffered ceilings, and more. Fully illustrated with lots of photos. **272 pages, 8½ x 11, $34.95**

Carpentry Estimating

Simple, clear instructions to help you take off quantities and figure costs for all rough and finish carpentry. Provides checklists, manhour tables, and worksheets with calculation factors built in. Take the guesswork out of estimating carpentry so you get accurate labor and material costs every time. Includes FREE *National Estimator* software, with all the manhours in the book, plus the carpentry estimating worksheets in formats that work with *Word, Excel, WordPerfect*, and *MS Works* for *Windows*™.
336 pages, 8½ x 11, $35.50

Constructionary

A unique pocket-sized dictionary of up-to-date construction words and phrases in English-Spanish and Spanish-English. Here you'll find over 1000 construction terms and 70 commonly used on-the-job phrases. This dictionary includes phonetic pronunciation, tool section, commonly used sentences, and conversion tables. **170 pages, 4 x 7, $14.95**

Builder's Guide to Accounting Revised

Step-by-step, easy-to-follow guidelines for setting up and maintaining records for your building business. This practical, newly-revised guide to all accounting methods shows how to meet state and federal accounting requirements, explains the new depreciation rules, and describes how the Tax Reform Act can affect the way you keep records. Full of charts, diagrams, simple directions and examples, to help you keep track of where your money is going. Recommended reading for many state contractor's exams. Includes test questions for every chapter.
356 pages, 8½ x 11, $30.50

Simplified Guide to Construction Law

Here you'll find easy-to-read, paragraphed-sized samples of how the courts have viewed common areas of disagreement — and litigation — in the building industry. You'll read about legal problems that real builders have faced, and how the court ruled. This book will tell you what you need to know about contracts, torts, fraud, misrepresentation, warranty and strict liability, construction defects, indemnity, insurance, mechanics liens, bonds and bonding, statutes of limitation, arbitration, and more. These are simplified examples that illustrate not necessarily who is right and who is wrong — but who the law has sided with. **298 pages, 5½ x 8½, $29.95**

Contractor's Year-Round Tax Guide Revised

How to set up and run your construction business to minimize taxes: corporate tax strategy and how to use it to your advantage, and what you should be aware of in contracts with others. Covers tax shelters for builders, write-offs and investments that will reduce your taxes, accounting methods that are best for contractors, and what the I.R.S. allows and what it often questions. **192 pages, 8½ x 11, $26.50**

Kitchens & Baths

Practical, detailed solutions to every problem you're likely to approach when constructing or remodeling kitchens and baths. Over 50 articles from the *Journal of Light Construction* plus up-to-date reference material on codes, safety, space planning and construction methods for kitchens and bathrooms. Includes over 400 photos and illustrations. If you're looking for a complete reference on designing, remodeling, or constructing kitchens and baths, you should have this book. **256 pages, 8 x 11, $34.95**

Roof Framing

Shows how to frame any type of roof in common use today, even if you've never framed a roof before. Includes using a pocket calculator to figure any common, hip, valley, or jack rafter length in seconds. Over 400 illustrations cover every measurement and every cut on each type of roof: gable, hip, Dutch, Tudor, gambrel, shed, gazebo, and more.
480 pages, 5½ x 8½, $22.00

How to Make Money In Insurance Repair

Here you'll find what insurance companies require of contractors, how to work with agents and adjusters, and how they'll affect your business. You'll learn how to use an "assignment sheet" and what it means in the insurance repair industry. You'll read about the different types of insurance losses that typically require the repair services that you can offer, and how to estimate damages and write an insurance loss estimate. Suggests typical overhead and profit to add to insurance estimates, as well as instructions for nailing down the scope and agreed price, and submitting that price to the adjuster. **103 pages, 8½ x 11, $49.95**

Professional Kitchen Design

Remodeling kitchens requires a "special" touch — one that blends artistic flair with function to create a kitchen with charm and personality as well as one that is easy to work in. Here you'll find how to make the best use of the space available in any kitchen design job, as well as tips and lessons on how to design one-wall, two-wall, L-shaped, U-shaped, peninsula and island kitchens. Also includes what you need to know to run a profitable kitchen design business. **176 pages, 8½ x 11, $24.50**

Vest Pocket Guide to HVAC Electricity

This handy guide will be a constant source of useful information for anyone working with electrical systems for heating, ventilating, refrigeration, and air conditioning. Includes essential tables and diagrams for calculating and installing electrical systems for powering and controlling motors, fans, heating elements, compressors, transformers and every electrical part of an HVAC system. **304 pages, 3½ x 5½, $18.00**

Wood-Frame House Construction

Step-by-step construction details, from the layout of the outer walls, excavation and formwork, to finish carpentry and painting. Contains all new, clear illustrations and explanations updated for construction in the '90s. Everything you need to know about framing, roofing, siding, interior finishings, floor covering and stairs — your complete book of wood-frame homebuilding. **320 pages, 8½ x 11, $25.50. Revised edition**

Profits in Buying & Renovating Homes

Step-by-step instructions for selecting, repairing, improving, and selling highly profitable "fixer-uppers." Shows which price ranges offer the highest profit-to-investment ratios, which neighborhoods offer the best return, practical directions for repairs, and tips on dealing with buyers, sellers, and real estate agents. Shows you how to determine your profit before you buy, what "bargains" to avoid, and how to make simple, profitable, inexpensive upgrades. **304 pages, 8½ x 11, $19.75**

Craftsman Book Company
6058 Corte del Cedro
P.O. Box 6500
Carlsbad, CA 92018

☎ 24 hour order line
1-800-829-8123
Fax (760) 438-0398

Name

e-mail address (for order tracking and special offers)

Company

Address

City/State/Zip

❍ This is a residence

Total enclosed________________(In California add 7% tax)
We pay shipping when your check covers your order in full.

In A Hurry?

We accept phone orders charged to your
❍ Visa, ❍ MasterCard, ❍ Discover or ❍ American Express

Card#________________

Exp. date__________Initials__________

Tax Deductible: Treasury regulations make these references tax deductible when used in your work. Save the canceled check or charge card statement as your receipt.

Order online http://www.craftsman-book.com
Free on the Internet! Download any of Craftsman's estimating costbooks for a 30-day free trial! http://costbook.com

10-Day Money Back Guarantee

❍ 36.50 Basic Engineering for Builders
❍ 38.00 Basic Lumber Engineering for Builders
❍ 30.50 Builder's Guide to Accounting Revised
❍ 35.00 Building Contractor's Exam Preparation Guide
❍ 35.50 Carpentry Estimating with FREE *National Estimator* carpentry estimating program on a CD-ROM.
❍ 68.50 CD Estimator
❍ 25.00 Concrete Construction & Estimating
❍ 14.95 Constructionary
❍ 39.50 Construction Estimating Reference Data with FREE *National Estimator* on a CD-ROM.
❍ 41.75 Construction Forms & Contracts with a CD-ROM for *Windows*TM and Macintosh.
❍ 36.00 Contracting in All 50 States
❍ 45.25 Contractor's Guide to QuickBooks Pro 2001
❍ 39.00 Contractor's Guide to the Building Code Revised
❍ 22.25 Contractor's Survival Manual
❍ 26.50 Contractor's Year-Round Tax Guide Revised
❍ 15.75 Cost Records for Construction Estimating
❍ 32.00 Electrician's Exam Preparation Guide
❍ 19.00 Estimating Electrical Construction
❍ 49.95 Estimating with Microsoft *Excel*
❍ 22.50 Finish Carpenter's Manual
❍ 24.95 Home Inspection Handbook
❍ 49.95 How to Make Money in Insurance Repair
❍ 28.50 How to Succeed w/Your Own Construction Business
❍ 24.95 Inspecting a House
❍ 34.95 Kitchens & Baths
❍ 32.50 Markup & Profit: A Contractor's Guide
❍ 42.00 Moving to Commercial Construction
❍ 44.75 National Building Assembly Costs
❍ 23.00 National Building Cost Manual
❍ 47.50 National Construction Estimator with FREE *National Estimator* on a CD-ROM.
❍ 47.75 National Electrical Estimator with FREE *National Estimator* on a CD-ROM.
❍ 48.00 National Painting Cost Estimator with FREE *National Estimator* on a CD-ROM.
❍ 48.50 National Repair & Remodeling Estimator with FREE *National Estimator* on a CD-ROM.
❍ 28.25 Plumbing & HVAC Manhour Estimates
❍ 24.50 Professional Kitchen Design
❍ 19.75 Profits in Buying & Renovating Homes
❍ 29.00 Residential Electrical Estimating
❍ 34.95 Residential Structure & Framing
❍ 22.00 Roof Framing
❍ 38.00 Roofing Construction & Estimating
❍ 26.50 Rough Framing Carpentry
❍ 29.95 A Simplified Guide to Construction Law
❍ 39.75 Steel-Frame House Construction
❍ 32.50 Troubleshooting Guide to Residential Construction
❍ 18.00 Vest Pocket Guide to HVAC Electricity
❍ 25.50 Wood-Frame House Construction
❍ 49.50 National Renovation & Insurance Repair Estimator with FREE *National Estimator* on a CD-ROM.
❍ FREE Full Color Catalog

Prices subject to change without notice